D0161502

# The Foundations of Computer Architecture and Organization

## OTHER TITLES OF INTEREST

**Miron Abramovici, Melvin A. Breuer, and Arthur D. Friedman**
*Digital Systems Testing and Testable Design*

**Jean-Loup Baer**
*Computer Systems Architecture*

**Ruth E. Davis**
*Truth, Deduction, and Computation: Logic and Semantics for Computer Science*

**Vladimir Drobot**
*Formal Languages and Automata Theory*

**Eitan M. Gurari**
*An Introduction to the Theory of Computation*

**Richard A. Haddad and Thomas W. Parsons**
*Digital Signal Processing: Theory, Applications, and Hardware*

**Ellis Horowitz and Sartaj Sahni**
*Fundamentals of Data Structures in Pascal, Third Edition*

**Steven Tanimoto**
*The Elements of Artificial Intelligence: An Introduction using Common Lisp*

**Jeffrey D. Ullman**
*Principles of Database and Knowledge-Base Systems I*

**Jeffrey D. Ullman**
*Principles of Database and Knowledge-Base Systems II: The New Technologies*

# The Foundations of Computer Architecture and Organization

**Ivan Tomek**

Acadia University
Wolfville, Nova Scotia

COMPUTER SCIENCE PRESS
An imprint of W. H. Freeman and Company • New York

**Library of Congress Cataloging-in-Publication Data**

Tomek, Ivan.
The foundations of computer architecture and organization / Ivan Tomek.
p. cm. — (Digital systems design series)
Includes bibliographical references.
ISBN 0-7167-8161-1
1. Computer architecture. 2. Computer organization. I. Title. II. Series.
QA76.9.A73T649 1990
004.2′2 — dc20 89-23916
CIP

Copyright © 1990 by W. H. Freeman and Company

Formerly published as "Introduction to Computer Organization," Copyright © 1981 Computer Science Press, Inc.

No part of this book may be reproduced by any mechanical, photographic, or electronic process, or in the form of a phonographic recording, nor may it be stored in a retrieval system, transmitted, or otherwise copied for public or private use, without written permission from the publisher.

Printed in the United States of America

Computer Science Press

An imprint of W. H. Freeman and Company
41 Madison Avenue, New York, NY 10010
20 Beaumont Street, Oxford OX1 2NQ, England

1 2 3 4 5 6 7 8 9 0 RRD 9 9 8 7 6 5 4 3 2 1 0

*To my wife, Jana,*
*my sons, Ivan and Ondrej,*
*my daughter, Dominika,*
*and my parents, Olga and Pavel Tomek.*

# CONTENTS

# PREFACE

*Never, never will the gray cells function unless you stimulate them.*
—AGATHA CHRISTIE, *Poirot's Early Cases*

The study of computers has two complementary aspects: their use (programming) and their internal operation. This text deals with the second aspect, focusing on the principles that make computers work.

We begin with gates, the basic physical components that generate and process internal computer signals, and proceed through all of the intermediate stages of computer operation—arithmetic, CPU design and programming, peripheral devices and interfacing, and operating systems—up to the level of compilers that translate computer programs written in high-level languages.

Because the scope of the book is so wide, we cannot cover every detail or present all the latest computers; presumably, the student will later take more advanced and more specialized courses dealing with the individual subjects. However, nothing that is essential is omitted. Indeed, the depth of our coverage is sufficient to explain not only how computers work but also how computer hardware is designed and integrated with software.

**Importance of Studying All Aspects of Computer Operation**

Not very long ago almost all computers were located in air-conditioned rooms, operated and maintained by specially trained people, and visible only through a window from the user area. At that time, it was reasonable to study selected general aspects of computer architecture and organization in a rather abstract way with paper and pencil.

Today's situation is very different. Many of us have computers on our desks or within easy reach, and it is thus much more tempting and easier to explore the mysteries of their hardware and software. Moreover, one can, and sometimes must, modify the hardware or the software, and this makes an understanding of their principles essential. A more concrete and integrated approach to the study of computer architecture and organization is thus possible and necessary.

## Scope and Philosophy of Presentation

The book covers the requirements of courses *CS 3* and *CS 4* of the *ACM '78* curriculum. I have also considered the undergraduate curriculum of Carnegie-Mellon University to modernize the perspective of the *ACM '78*.

Curricula that present the individual aspects of computer architecture and organization in different texts and courses often obscure the connections between them. As an example, a typical book on digital design does not show how the presented concepts and methods are used in the design of a computer. Similarly, an introductory book on computer architecture usually does not explain how architecture relates to the principles of digital design on one side and to the principles of operating systems or the functions of a compiler on the other. Finally, books on operating systems often lack a background on peripherals and similar architectural topics, and this often makes it difficult to understand the reasons for certain solutions and to visualize their concrete implementation.

To remedy this problem, I have introduced all aspects of computer operation in an integrated fashion. To make the subject manageable, I have presented the computer as a machine consisting of several interdependent layers of hardware and software. After briefly defining the layers and their relations, the book explains each of them in detail. To keep the amount of material within reasonable limits and within the realm of hardware and software directly accessible to the typical student, the presentation centers around a personal computer model.

A major goal of the book is to give concrete, realistic, and up-to-date examples of all important concepts, and this sometimes presents problems because modern devices are often too complex for the beginner. The most difficult decision in this respect was choosing a CPU to present, and I will now briefly explain my choice. For the chapters dealing with elementary principles of computer operation and CPU design, I have chosen to formulate my own specification. TOY, as the CPU is called, is quite primitive but contains all essential CPU features and its simplicity makes it well-suited for a detailed presentation of principles of both hardwired and microprogrammed design.

For the rest of the book, I have chosen to illustrate the principles of assembly language programming, input/output programming and interfacing, operating systems, and compilers using the 6800 CPU family by Motorola. The 6800 family contains the main features of a typical CPU, is easy to understand, and is available in several lab kits, allowing many interesting hands-on experiments. Although the first member of the 6800 family was designed a rather long time ago, it continues to be widely used, mainly in industrial applications. It has also been used in several recent texts on topics such as microcomputer interfacing that can serve as a continuation of certain passages of this book.

For those who do not have access to the 6800, a simulator program that not only implements all 6800 functions but also demonstrates their internal operation is available from the publisher.

Although the 6800 contains most of the important features of modern computers, it is not used by machines that one finds in a typical computer environment. For this reason, I have complemented the detailed treatment of the 6800 by a shorter outline of the 8086 Intel CPU family, which is very popular in personal computers—particularly the IBM PC family—and which continues to be the basis for the development of new machines. Standard PC peripherals are also used as examples in the chapter on input/output, and MS-DOS is used as a model in the chapter on operating systems.

Given the rate at which technology is developing, even the 8086 is outdated and a text restricted to the 6800 and 8086 families would yield an incomplete view of computer architecture. To correct this, I have included a chapter outlining the basics of additional aspects of computer architectures such as instruction sets, memory hierarchies, and parallel computing.

Another goal of this text is to allow the student to experiment with the presented material. For this reason, I have included a list of lab experiments covering all of the major topics presented in the book, a sample lab report, suggestions for debugging, and pinout diagrams. I have also included the specification of a larger lab project.

## A Brief Outline of the Book

The introduction explains the partitioning of computer architecture and organization into layers and outlines their relation.

Chapter 1 introduces the basic concepts of logic (truth tables and manipulation of logic expressions), as well as certain engineering aspects of their implementation (gates, integrated circuits, and their main parameters).

Chapter 2 presents the classical methods of designing memoryless (combinational) logic circuits based on Karnaugh maps.

Chapter 3 introduces more complicated combinational building blocks, such as multiplexers and programmable logic devices, and shows how they can be used in digital design.

Chapter 4 explains the concepts and building blocks of circuits with memory (sequential circuits).

Chapter 5 deals with the design of sequential circuits using flip-flops, counters, and programmable logic devices.

Chapter 6 moves from the processing of individual signals to the processing of codes. It presents coding conventions for text and numbers, explains arithmetic operations on them, and shows how they can be implemented in hardware.

Chapter 7 introduces digital systems, which are circuits operating on codes. It presents building blocks such as buses, memories, and control units as well as procedures for the design of hardwired and microprogrammed control units.

Chapter 8 describes a simple fictitious central processing unit (CPU) and demonstrates its programming.

Chapter 9 presents two styles of CPU design and illustrates them on two versions of the CPU from Chapter 8.

Chapter 10 deals with the programming aspects of a real CPU, the Motorola 6800, and introduces principles of assembly language programming. The chapter briefly outlines the 8086 by Intel as an example of a more recent and more powerful CPU.

Chapter 11 discusses the principles of the main peripheral devices used by computers. It presents keyboards, displays, printers, disk drives, and principles of communication.

Chapter 12 shows how the CPU and the peripherals are interfaced, both in the physical and in the programming sense. It presents a detailed analysis of a simple commercial computer, the Heathkit 6800-based microcomputer trainer, to show how the principles of interfacing are used in a real machine.

Chapter 13 presents some architectural alternatives to the simple view of a computer introduced in the previous chapters. It deals with essential aspects of instruction sets, memory hierarchies, input and output on large computers, and similar topics.

Chapter 14 moves beyond computer hardware and presents the principles of operating systems, the software interface between the programmer and the computer. The first part of this chapter concentrates on an outline of the structure and operation of MS-DOS, the operating system used by IBM PC computers. The second part introduces OS68, a simulated 6800 CPU-based operating system resembling MS-DOS, and shows how its functions can be used in programming.

Chapter 15 concludes the text with an introduction to translation. Following a discussion of assemblers, a simple high-level language is designed as well as a complete OS68-based recursive descent compiler for it.

The main text is complemented by six appendices. The first deals with the principles of electricity and integrated circuits; the remaining ones contain a list of lab experiments and integrated circuits, explain data sheets of two typical integrated circuits and the operation of three important chips (the 6800 CPU and the ACIA and PIA support chips), and demonstrate the new logic symbols introduced by the IEEE/ANSI standard.

A large glossary and an annotated list of references complete the text.

### Available Study Aids

A collection of tools to help the instructor and the student build a complete teaching environment for the course are available from the publisher. Included are:

- A large set of transparency masters covering the whole text.
- Solutions of selected exercises.
- Detailed descriptions of the solution of the project and most experiments.
- A collection of computer programs designed to complement the book is also available. Its purpose is to let students experiment with all the presented topics and gain deeper insight into their internal operation. The programs can be divided into two categories.

  The first category includes programs that allow the student to explore various concepts and methods presented in the book, such as Karnaugh maps, the analysis and design of sequential circuits, number conversion, and the operation of a compiler. These tools allow the student to explore the selected topic by creating examples and observing their solution by the program. They can also be used for demonstration during the lecture.

  The second category includes three simulation programs. The first is a package for the simulation of logic circuits at the gate level.The second is a simulator of the 6800 CPU with a display of memory, step-by-step execution, display of stack, and a number of other features that can be selected by the student. The third program simulates a fictitious 6800 CPU-based operating system implementing some of the most important functions of MS-DOS and allowing the student to experiment with the basic uses of an operating system, compilation, and related topics. The package also includes an assembler and an editor.

## How to Use this Book

This book is intended for use in an introductory or intermediate course on computer architecture and organization for computer science or engineering students. At Acadia University we use it in a two-semester first-year computer science course taught in parallel with programming and discrete mathematics. Whereas the programming course gives the students a foundation in the use of computers, discrete mathematics provides a theoretical basis, and the course on basic computer organization and architecture taught from this book gives an introduction to the internal operation of computer hardware and software. After taking these three courses, the students have a good understanding of the principles and relationships of various aspects of computer science and are ready to study them in more advanced courses with much greater insight.

In our program, we cover Chapters 1 – 7 in the first semester and the rest of the book in the second semester. This is a large amount of material, but it can be mastered with the help of transparencies, tutorials, the supporting software, and a hardware lab. If pressed for time the instructor may choose to omit or restrict certain sections such as testing and fault detection, and the sections dealing with the 8088 CPU, MS-DOS, and communication. One can also omit Chapter 13 as the rest of the text does not depend on it. Alternatively, the material may be spread over three semesters.

We consider the experiments listed in Appendix 2 an important part of the course and our students perform most of them in weekly one and half hour lab sessions. Most experiments could, in principle, be replaced by simulations but the lab equipment is inexpensive, the experiments simple, and the insight obtained from them worth the cost.

**Acknowledgments**

I am very grateful to Dr. Vaclav Dvorak, who used a draft of the text to teach the course and helped me remove several embarrassing mistakes. He also suggested several interesting problems for exercises and labs, supervised the lab experiments, and built the project. I learned a lot from him. Professor George Novak and Drs. Mostaffa Nassar, and Dore Subrao read several chapters and appendices and provided useful comments.

I also want to thank Bill Gruener and particularly Rita Gold from W. H. Freeman and Company for their understanding and patience.

In spite of the help that I received and although I did my best to get everything right, some errors may have crept into a few of the many illustrations, program listings, and examples. I would be grateful if the reader would communicate them to me via the publisher.

Several students contributed to the development of the software but Dave Astels and Tony Wong deserve special mention.

Several companies allowed me to test the usefulness of their products in teaching this course. Among them, I would like to especially mention Douglas CAD/CAM Systems for giving me the opportunity to evaluate their CAD package (we used it to test one version of the CPU described in Chapter 9, and an example of a diagram produced with it is given in Chapter 1), and Wintek Corporation who let me test their PCB design program. I thank them all.

I am deeply grateful to my family for tolerating my frequent absences during the work on this book. I hope that my children will still recognize their aged, balding and limping father when he finally returns home after correcting the last illustration.

**Ivan Tomek**
*Wolfville, December 1, 1989.*

# INTRODUCTION

# THE LAYERED COMPUTER

## AN OVERVIEW

Computers are very complex machines but their study and design can be considerably simplified if one stratifies them into several layers. In this introduction, I will outline the layers of computer operation and show how they fit together. The reader may not fully understand all of the terms and concepts used here; their detailed discussion is the purpose of the following chapters. The immediate goal is to put everything into perspective and to justify the organization of the remaining chapters of the book.

## THE LAYERED COMPUTER

Students of medicine commonly explore the human body in stages, beginning with chemical and microscopic components and proceeding to bones, organs, and mind processes. Computers, too, must be studied in stages, successively taking a more and more global perspective. This book is based on that approach. The reader will see that the individual layers are not complicated and that the logical relations of these layers make it easier to understand the operation of computers.

The layering of computer operation depicted in Figure I.1 is analogous to that suggested above for the students of the human body. It starts at the microscopic level and ends at the highest level of abstraction. The following is an outline of the individual layers illustrated with simple examples.

1. The *electronic level* (Figure I.2). The lowest level of the computer hierarchy relies on the concepts of electricity and deals with transistors: their fabrication, how they function, and how they can be connected to form basic computer components. Information processed at this level has the form of electric current and voltage. I will leave the basics of the electronic level for

| Translator |
|---|
| Operating system |
| Interface |
| I/O Devices |
| CPU |
| Register transfer |
| Logic |
| Electronic |

**Figure I.1.** Hierarchy of layers of a computer system.

Appendix 1 because they are not always included in computer science courses. The book can be studied without this background.

2. The *logic level* (Figure I.3). The next level of computer operation relies on the electronic level and deals with abstractions of the physical signals—units of information called bits that can assume the values 0 or 1. The transition from electric signals to bits allows one to ignore many nonessential details with the result that most of the design of computers can be understood and performed at or above the level of abstract logic.

3. The *register transfer level* (Figure I.4). The unit of information processed by a computer is not a bit but a code, a group of bits. Thus, after mastering the bit level one must make another abstraction and deal with codes, their storage in memories and registers, their transformation by arithmetic operations, and their transfer between storage locations. This is called the register transfer level.

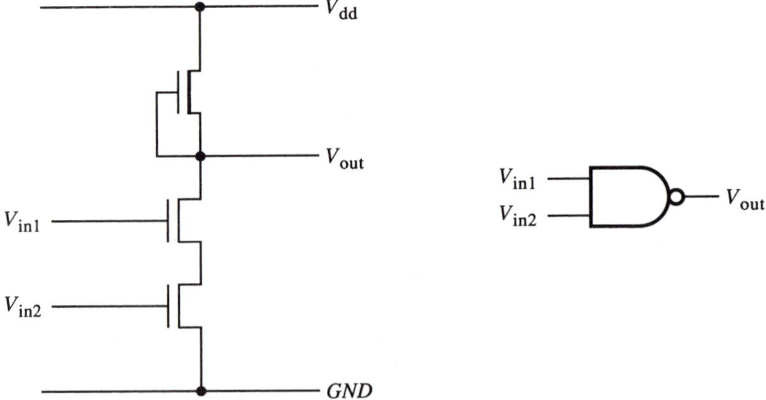


**Figure I.2.** Electronic level. Example: an N-MOS NAND gate circuit and its logic symbol.

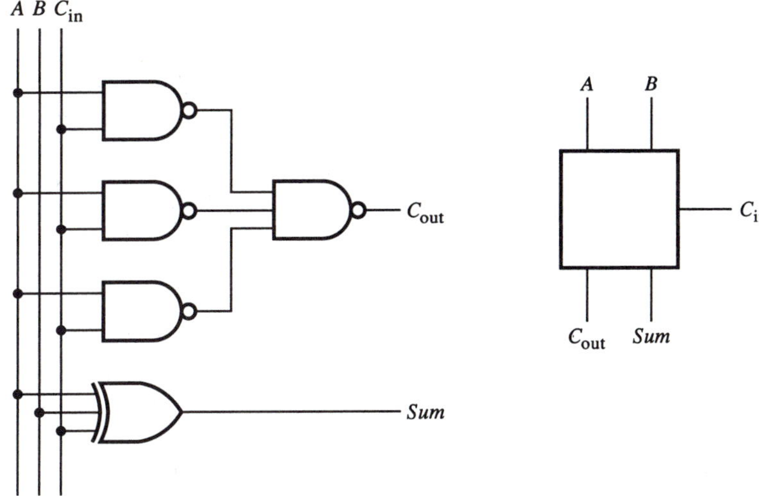


**Figure I.3.** Logic level. Example: the full adder and its symbol. Note the use of the NAND gate from Figure I.2.

4. The *CPU level* (Figure I.5). Register level devices are the building blocks of the central processing unit (CPU), which is the essential component of each computer. The CPU can be viewed from two different perspectives, as a structure to be used or as a structure to be built. To use the analogy of a building, the former is the perspective of an architect, who designs the building's external appearance, the layout of its rooms and staircases, their intended uses, and so on. The latter view is that of a structural engineer, who designs the building's foundation and supporting walls, and the internal

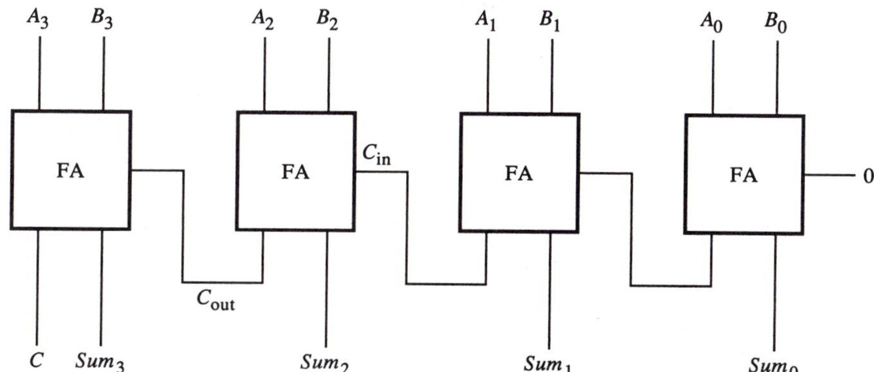


**Figure I.4.** Four-bit adder as an example of a register transfer level component. Note the use of the full adder from Figure I.3.

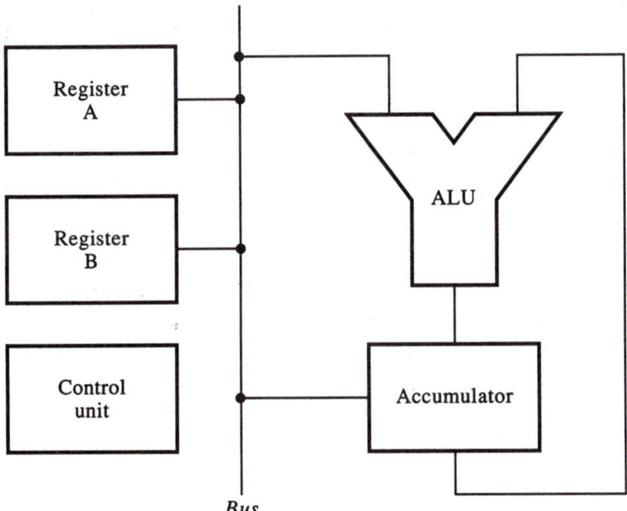


**Figure I.5.** Diagram of a CPU using the four-bit adder from Figure I.4 as a part of its Arithmetic Logic Unit.

placement of pipes and wires. A similar division is useful for our purpose as well. Thus, computer architecture concentrates on how the computer appears to the user, the instructions it executes and the signals it generates. Computer organization is concerned with the internal implementation of this architecture.

Architecture and organization are very closely related. It is impossible to design the supporting structure of a building if its internal layout and appearance are unknown. It is also meaningless to plan an architecture without knowing which materials and building blocks are available. This creates a dilemma: Should one study computer architecture first and discuss uses before learning which building blocks are available? Or should one begin with computer organization and discuss components and their connections before learning their intended use? I will alternate between the two views. Essential architectural concepts will be presented as needed to justify basic organization, and details of implementation will prove that the architectural decisions presented are sound.

5. The *I/O and interface levels* (Figure I.6). After covering the CPU level, the reader must learn how the other parts of the computer, the peripherals, work and how they are connected to the CPU. The main subjects here are the fundamentals of peripherals, and the hardware and programming principles required for computer input and output.

6. The *operating system* (Figure I.7). Up to this point, the text has revolved largely around hardware. However, a usable computer is more than a mere

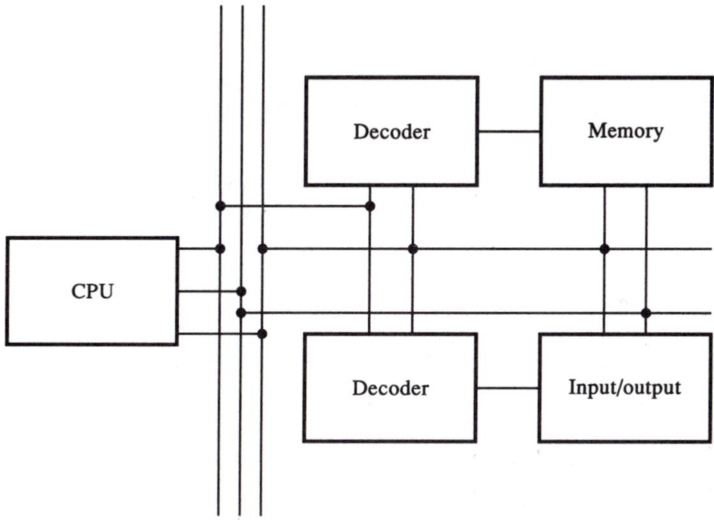


**Figure I.6.** Interface and I/O level. Note the use of the CPU from Figure I.5.

collection of properly connected parts. Although a "bare machine" could be programmed, it would be very difficult to do so. As an example, to use the computer to retrieve data from a floppy disk and display it on a screen requires hundreds of elementary operations that must be performed in a specified order and with proper timing. The design of such a program requires special expertise, and even those capable of doing it would not want to communicate with the machine only at such an elementary level. This is why even the simplest computers are supplied with an operating system, a core of programs that facilitate essential and useful I/O functions and that manage I/O, memory, and other resources of the computer.

7. The *translation level* (Figure I.8). A computer with an operating system is still a primitive machine that is difficult to use. The operating system increases the apparent power of the hardware but does little to improve the level

```
            ...
SIN:        LDA     IN_STAT     ; LOAD INPUT STATES
            RTS                 ; RETURN TO CALLER
CON_IN:     JSR     SIN         ; GET INPUT STATUS
            BNE     CON_IN      ; REPEAT IF NOT READY
            LDA     INPUT       ; LOAD DATA
            RTS                 ; RETURN TO CALLER
            ...
```

**Figure I.7.** Part of a fictitious operating system, a section of a program that accesses a computer terminal via an interface such as in Figure I.6.

```
...
JSR        CON_IN     ; GET DATA x
PUSHA                 ; PUSH ON STACK
JSR        CON_IN     ; GET DATA y
PUSHA                 ; PUSH ON STACK
...
```

**Figure I.8.** Fragment of machine code that could be generated by translating the Pascal statement READ (*x*,*y*). Note the use of the operating system function from Figure I.7.

of abstraction at which humans can communicate with it. Even with the operating system, most programs are long sequences of elementary "machine instructions."

Machine level programming is complicated and expensive. Another analogy with the construction of a building suggests how it can be minimized: The time required to nail together a frame is not much different from the time needed to join two prefabricated half-frames or to tighten a screw between two halves of a prefabricated house. Similarly, the time and effort required to write and test just three of the hundreds of machine instructions needed to read and display a block of text is about the same as the time needed to write three high level Pascal or BASIC statements that perform the same operation. The productivity of programming in Pascal or another high-level language is thus much greater than that of programming in machine language, and programming in high-level languages is thus preferable.

Because computers cannot directly execute programs written in Pascal or BASIC, the use of high-level languages requires special programs that translate higher level languages into machine code. This forms the translation level that resides on top of the operating system.

Translation is the highest level of computer architecture and organization presented in this book. Beyond it lie questions of the design of programming languages, algorithms, and other topics.

## CONCLUSION

I have already explained that presenting the computer as a layered machine defines an organizing principle that divides a large body of knowledge into smaller parts that are logically related to one another. This makes computers easier to understand.

The student, however, is not the only one who gains from this approach; the computer designer benefits too. The structured view makes it possible to distribute design among several groups of engineers having specialized knowledge and more narrowly defined responsibilities. The logic designer, for example, does not need to be an expert in electronics and CPUs. His or her task can be limited to designing a logic system according to the specifications formulated by a CPU architect and using the building blocks constructed by an electronics specialist. Similar observations apply to other layers of design as well.

With this general framework the reader is now ready to study the individual layers of computer operation. However, in studying the detail, one must not lose sight of the whole. In reading the following chapters, take time to note how the layers depend on one another, how the structure of a computer emerges and how the picture assumes a more familiar shape. Study the individual "trees" but do not forget that the ultimate goal is to understand the forest.

# CHAPTER 1

# SIGNALS, CIRCUITS, FUNCTIONS, AND COMPONENTS

## AN OVERVIEW

Computer systems are based on circuits that process logic signals: zeros and ones. Because signals can only be combined or stored in memory, the computer's logic components can be divided into combinational and storage devices. This classification is the foundation of logic design and is the main principle of our presentation. Chapters 1 through 3 deal with combinational circuits; Chapters 4 and 5 deal with memory-based, or sequential, circuits.

The study of logic circuits requires a convention to represent their behavior and structure. We will therefore introduce the truth table to describe a circuit's behavior, use it to define a set of basic logic functions, and present symbols used in logic diagrams.

Logic circuits can be simplified by using certain formal properties of logic functions. We will examine the most important of these properties and will prove them by a method known as perfect induction.

Most logic design can be done at the abstract level but physical realities cannot be ignored. We will discuss the physical nature of logic signals, and introduce a model of the behavior of a logic device that can be used to verify whether an engineering implementation of a logic design works as desired.

## IMPORTANT WORDS

Analysis, BCD (Binary Coded Decimal), binary, bit, circuit (combinational, digital, sequential), duality, fan-in, fan-out, gate (AND, XOR, NAND, NOR, NOT, OR), inverter, logic (positive, negative), perfect induction, positional representation, propagation delay, timing diagram, truth table.

## 1.1 LOGIC CIRCUITS AND SIGNALS—ABSTRACTION AND REALITY

The study and design of logic circuits used in computers are considerably simplified if one replaces continuous physical signals with idealized discrete signals. A discrete signal can assume only a few allowed values and can make instantaneous transitions between them (Figure 1.1). Most logic devices are based on binary discrete signals, which can assume only two values. Multi-valued logic, the theory of devices working with discrete signals that can assume more than two values, is important and interesting but we will not consider it here because its current practical use is very limited.

The real signals behind our binary abstraction can use any physical principle. Light, hydraulic pressure, mechanical position, chemical reactions, and other phenomena have been used but most logic circuits are electronic. At least five different electronic technologies are now in commercial use. If the different technologies and physical principles required different design methods, logic design would be very difficult to learn. Fortunately, replacing the physical signal with a logic abstraction makes it possible to formulate strategies that apply to all technologies in the same way.

Before we can start logic design, we must have a convention to represent and name signals and devices. In binary systems we need symbols to represent

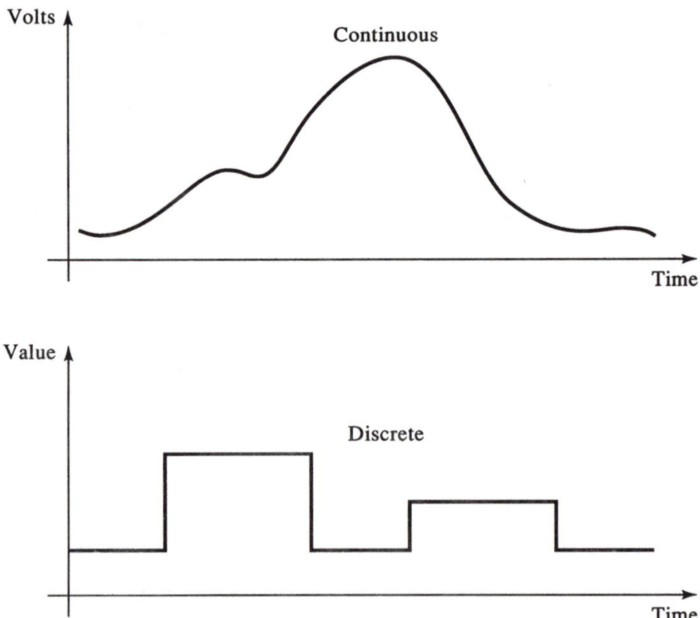


**Figure 1.1.** A continuous and a discrete signal. The two signals are unrelated.

two-valued signals. It does not matter which symbols we use because they are only symbols, but the following four conventions have been generally accepted and are used for one purpose or another:

| 0 | Off | Low | False |
|---|---|---|---|
| 1 | On | High | True |

In most contexts, the following equivalence is implied

$$0 = \text{Off} = \text{Low} = \text{False} \qquad \text{and} \qquad 1 = \text{On} = \text{High} = \text{True}$$

The 0/1 notation was introduced by mathematicians and is very common; we will use it most of the time. It is important to note that logic 0 and 1 do not have numeric meaning and must be treated as mere symbols. However, because logic signals are often used to encode digits, a numeric connotation exists and logic 0 and 1 are thus called binary digits or bits.

The notations Off/On and Low/High (or L/H) have their origin in engineering and are related to switches and voltage levels. They are not used as much as 0/1. The False/True system has been used by philosophers for two thousand years and is common in computer programming.

As we have already mentioned, the view that logic devices work only with two values is a simplification. Real signals do not have narrowly defined values such as exactly 0 volts or exactly 1 volt because the tolerance (inaccuracy) of device parameters, fluctuations in voltages, and other phenomena cause signals to deviate from ideal values. Moreover, physical signals pass through intermediate values during transitions between the levels that represent logic 0 and 1. The physical reality behind a logic value is thus a continuous (analog) signal and only its handling by logic components enforces its binary character.

Because the physical signal is continuous and its value fluctuates, logic components interpret a certain range of values as logic 0, rather than one exact value, and another range as logic 1. As an example, TTL (transistor-transistor-logic) circuits used in our experiments (Appendix 2) treat any voltage in the range 0.0–0.8 volts as logic 0 and any voltage in the range 2.0–5.0 volts as logic 1. Signals with voltages between the two ranges have no logic value.

Figure 1.2 illustrates the concepts presented so far. It shows a continuous physical signal and its logic interpretation with 0 and 1 values. Note that although it is natural to associate the High voltage level with 1 and the Low level with 0, the opposite convention is also possible. After all, logic 0 and 1 are not numbers and logic 0 is not "smaller" than logic 1. However, engineers normally use 0 for Low and 1 for High and call this convention positive logic. Negative logic, 0 for High and 1 for Low, is less popular and we will not use it.

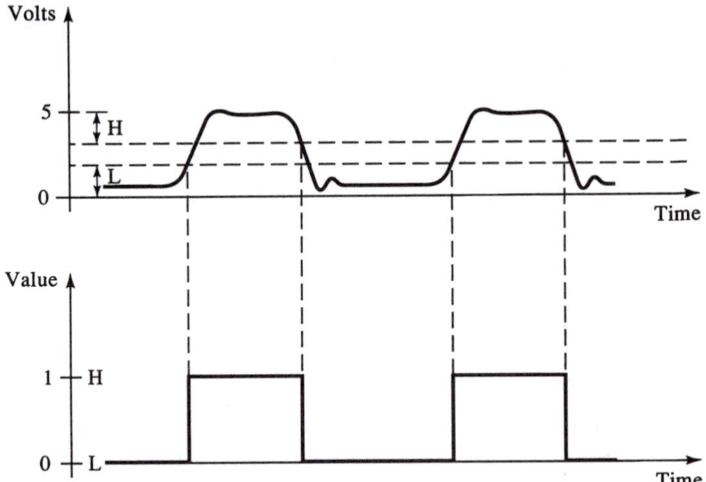


**Figure 1.2.** Timing diagram of a physicial (upper) and logic (lower) signal and its H/L and 0/1 representation.

### Exercise

1. The continuous signals processed by logic circuits can be observed by an instrument called the oscilloscope. Their logic interpretation can be displayed on an instrument called the logic analyzer. Draw a signal such as in Figure 1.2 that could be observed on an oscilloscope and show its corresponding representation on a logic analyzer.

## 1.2 COMBINATIONAL AND SEQUENTIAL CIRCUITS

Logic signals can be combined to calculate new signals and can be stored in memory. No other operations are possible and all logic circuits are thus based on combination and storage.

The simplest digital circuits, which can only combine and have no memory, are called combinational. Most logic circuits, however, combine and store results in memory. They are usually called sequential because their operation depends not only on current inputs but also on the stored sequence of past inputs and results. A general sequential circuit thus contains a combinational part and memory. In the model shown in Figure 1.3, the lines representing the flow of signals indicate that the combinational part combines new inputs with stored values to obtain new outputs and new values to be stored.

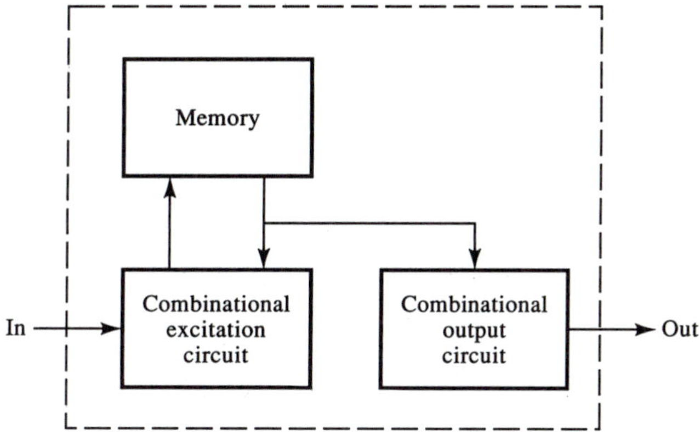


**Figure 1.3.** General model of a digital circuit.

Our model of a general logic circuit completely separates calculation from storage, the combinational part has no memory and the memory has no combinational power. This is a very useful division because it allows one to study digital circuits in two independent steps and to design them more systematically. We will study combinational circuits in Chapters 1 through 3, and memory elements and sequential circuits in Chapters 4 and 5.

## 1.3 REPRESENTATION OF THE BEHAVIOR OF COMBINATIONAL CIRCUITS

Because a combinational circuit has no memory, its response to a given combination of inputs is always the same, unless the circuit is faulty. If, for example, we observe that a one-input combinational circuit outputs 1 when its input is 0, we assume that it always produces 1 for input 0. Because of its predictability, such "deterministic" behavior can be described by listing the circuit's outputs for all possible input combinations. Historically such records were written with True/False values; for this reason they are called truth tables.

If we know the truth table of a circuit we can predict its output for any combination of inputs. The truth table thus fully describes the operation of the circuit. It can be obtained from the specification of the desired behavior, as a record of an experiment or a simulation of an existing circuit, or by analyzing an engineering diagram of the circuit.

**Example.** Let us derive the truth table of a three-input circuit whose specification says that its output is 1 if and only if (written "iff") the majority of its inputs is 1. We will call it a three-input majority voter.

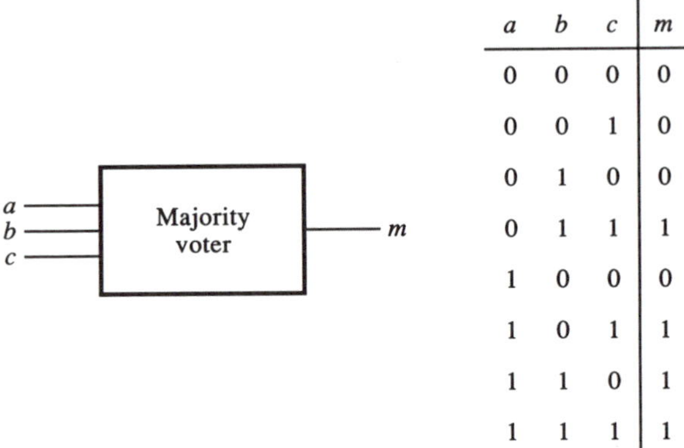


| $a$ | $b$ | $c$ | $m$ |
|---|---|---|---|
| 0 | 0 | 0 | 0 |
| 0 | 0 | 1 | 0 |
| 0 | 1 | 0 | 0 |
| 0 | 1 | 1 | 1 |
| 1 | 0 | 0 | 0 |
| 1 | 0 | 1 | 1 |
| 1 | 1 | 0 | 1 |
| 1 | 1 | 1 | 1 |

**Figure 1.4.** Majority voter and its truth table.

To construct the truth table, we list all possible input combinations and find outputs from the specification (Figure 1.4). As an example, if the input combination $(a,b,c)$ is (0,1,1), the majority of inputs is 1 and the output is thus 1. For $(a,b,c) = (0,1,0)$ the majority of inputs is 0 and the output is 0. Other outputs are obtained similarly. Note that the truth table tells us nothing about the structure of the circuit, and our majority voter is thus a "black box" with an unknown internal structure but controllable inputs and an observable output.

### Exercise

1. Construct truth tables of the following functions:
   a. A detector of equality: a circuit with two inputs whose output is 1 iff both inputs have the same value.
   b. A four-input equality detector with inputs $a_1,a_2,b_1,b_2$ whose output is 1 iff $(a_1,a_2)$ is the same as $(b_1,b_2)$: $a_1 = b_1$ and $a_2 = b_2$.
   c. A (0,1,1) detector whose output is 1 iff its three inputs are (0,1,1).
   d. A three-bit detector of even parity: a circuit whose output is 1 iff the three-bit input has even parity (even number of ls).
   e. A three-bit odd-parity detector: a circuit whose output is 1 iff the three-bit input has odd parity (odd number of ls).
   f. A five-input majority voter.

## 1.4 LOGIC FUNCTIONS

A truth table defines a function by specifying circuit outputs for all input combinations. Functions whose values and arguments are binary logic values are called logic or Boolean functions in memory of George Boole, the British mathematician who made major contributions to their study.

It is useful to classify logic functions and to derive relations between them because they provide a compact representation and a basis for design. We will start by organizing logic functions according to the number of inputs.

## Functions of One-Input Variable

A one-input combinational device can only work in one of the following ways (Figure 1.5):

The output is always 0.

The output is always 1.

The output is always equal to the input.

The output is always the inverse of the input.

The first three functions are trivial and no "device" is needed to implement them. The last function is called NOT, the inverse, negation, or complement, and is very important. The physical device that implements it is called the *inverter.*

An example of a commercially available inverter is the 7404 *integrated circuit* (IC or chip) shown in Figure 1.6. It has fourteen pins for connections to other devices and to the power supply, and contains six independent inverters, hence its name "hex inverter." It should be noted that the electronic circuit implementing the six inverters occupies only a small fraction of the area taken by the IC package; the package is large only to accommodate connections between chips. For more information on the TTL family, refer to Appendix 1.

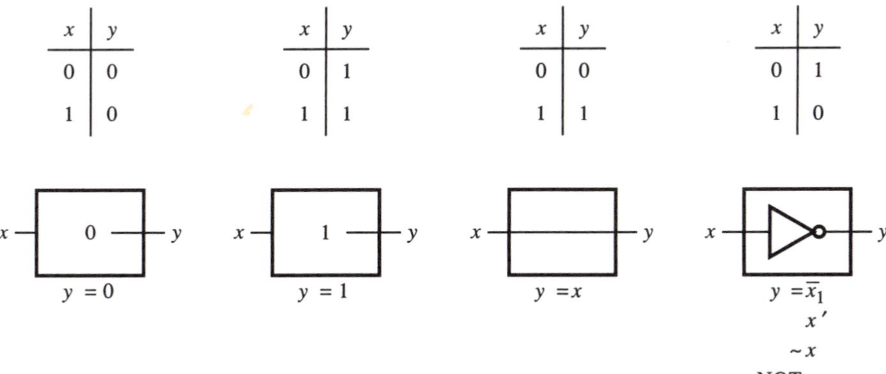


**Figure 1.5.** All possible logic functions of one variable, their implementation, and the conventional symbol for an inverter. The "bubble" on the output of the inverter indicates negation. See Appendix 7 for an alternative set of symbols.

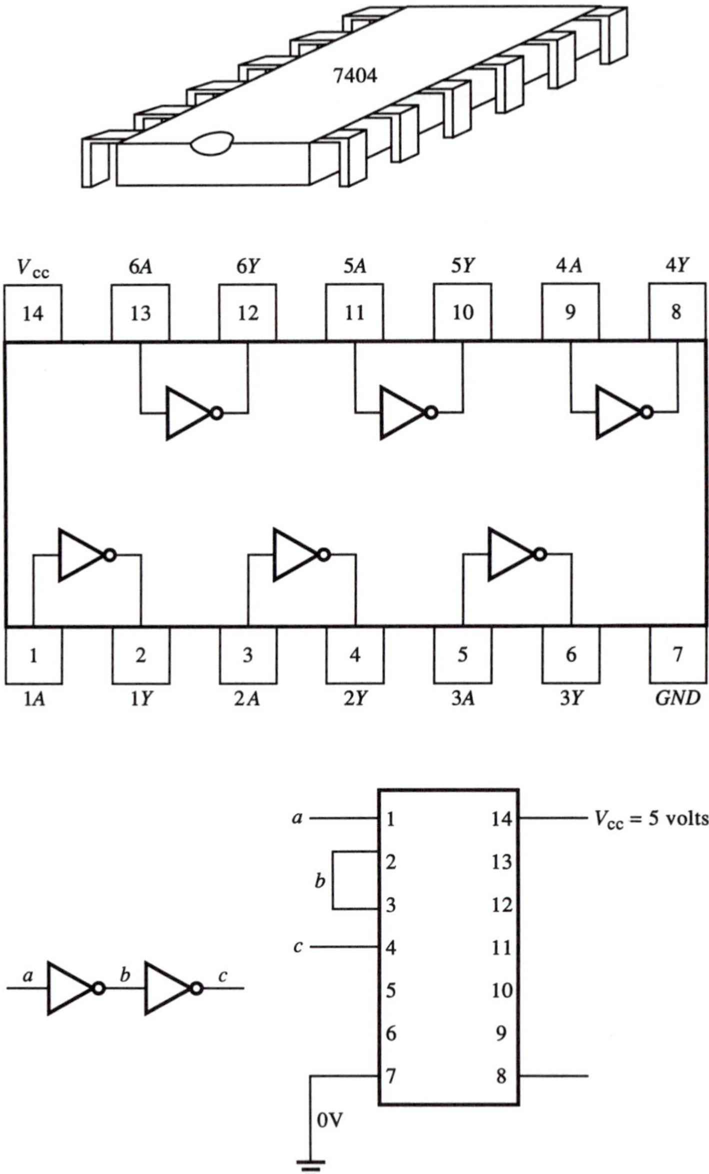


**Figure 1.6.** The 7404 hex inverter and its pinout (*top*), an example of a symbolic logic diagram with inverters, and the corresponding wiring diagram that shows the connections of pins to implement the function (*bottom*).

The 74 prefix of the code "7404" means that the chip belongs to the "regular TTL family" of devices; "04" identifies its function. One of the characteristics of all TTL devices is that they require a 5-volt power supply; each TTL chip thus has pins for connections to 0 V and 5 V. The "pinout" (assignment of functions to pins) of the 7404 and some other TTL chips is also given in Appendix 4. It is useful to know that most 74 family chips cost less than one dollar and can be bought from mailorder companies.

**Functions of Two-Input Variables**

Although there are sixteen different truth tables of two variables, only those in Figure 1.7 are important for logic design. The remaining ones can be obtained by connecting inverters and these six basic devices (gates) in ways explained in Chapter 2.

The names of the basic logic functions are derived from English and this makes it easier to remember their truth tables. As an example, the truth table of NOT can be interpreted as follows: If a statement is True (logic value 1), its inverse is False (logic value 0). As an example,

"2 is smaller than 3"

is a True statement and so its inverse

"2 is NOT smaller than 3"

is a False statement. If a statement is False, then its inverse is True:

"2 is greater than 3"

is a False statement and so

"2 is NOT greater than 3"

is a True statement.

The truth table of AND can be explained similarly, but OR requires more care. For example, suppose a student has $10,000 and wants to buy a car. Cars A and B cost $10,000 each. If the student says, "I will buy car A or car B," he means that he will buy one but not the other. This variety of OR is called the "exclusive OR" (XOR).

The English word "or" also has another meaning illustrated by the following example: If someone says, "I eat meals that taste good or are healthy," they don't mean that they don't eat meals that are both tasty and healthy. This is "inclusive OR" or simply, OR. Compare these two examples with the truth tables of OR and XOR.

| $a$ $b$ | AND | OR | NAND | NOR | XOR | NEXOR |
|---|---|---|---|---|---|---|
| 0 0 | 0 | 0 | 1 | 1 | 0 | 1 |
| 0 1 | 0 | 1 | 1 | 0 | 1 | 0 |
| 1 0 | 0 | 1 | 1 | 0 | 1 | 0 |
| 1 1 | 1 | 1 | 0 | 0 | 0 | 1 |

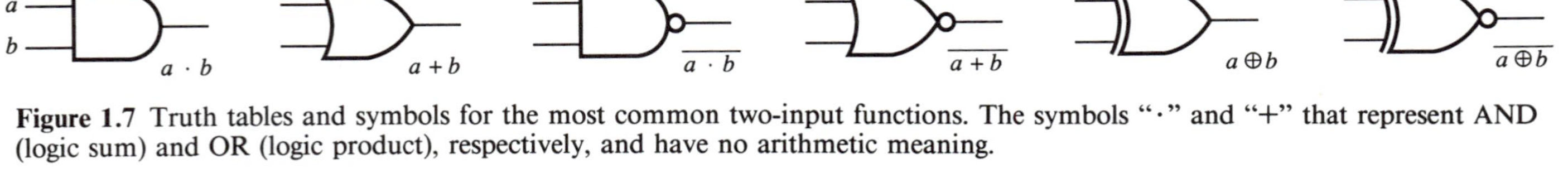


**Figure 1.7** Truth tables and symbols for the most common two-input functions. The symbols "·" and "+" that represent AND (logic sum) and OR (logic product), respectively, and have no arithmetic meaning.

NAND is an abbreviation of NOT AND, and its table is the inverse of the AND truth table. Similarly, NOR is NOT OR, and NEXOR is the inverse of XOR. Note that NEXOR indicates identity: Its value is 1 when both inputs have the same value. NEXOR is also called XNOR or "exclusive product."

The 74 family contains several hundred chips that include all of the functions given in Figure 1.7. The pinout of one of them, the 7400 "quad 2-input NAND," is shown in Figure 1.8 with an example of its use in a simple logic circuit.

## Functions of More Than Two Input Variables

The number of different truth tables increases rapidly with the number of inputs. This is because the number of ways of combining inputs grows very quickly and each input can assume the values 0 or 1. There are four different logic functions of one variable, 16 functions of two variables, 256 functions of three variables, 65,536 functions of four variables, and so on. In general, the number $N$ of different logic functions of $n$ variables is

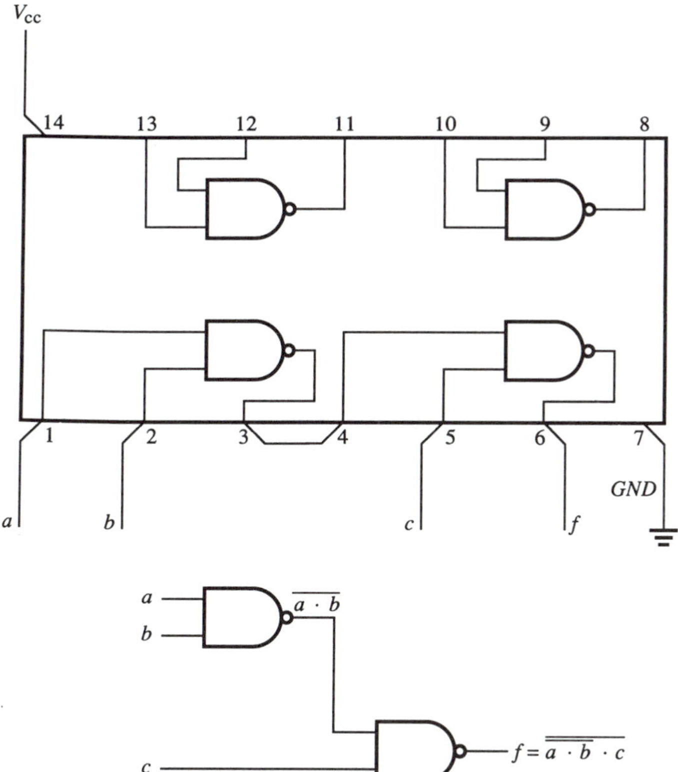


**Figure 1.8.** The 7400 quad two-input NAND contains four two-input NANDs.

$$N = 2^{2^n}$$

This is frightening when one considers that circuits with 16 or more logic signals are common even in simple microcomputers. Does this mean that we need thousands of different chips to implement all necessary functions? Fortunately, we do not. We will show in Chapter 2 that all logic functions can be obtained by combining NOT and the basic two-input functions generalized to any number of inputs:

AND: The output is 1 iff all inputs are 1.

OR: The output is 0 iff all inputs are 0.

XOR: The output is 1 iff an odd number of inputs are 1.

NAND is AND inverted.

NOR is OR inverted.

NEXOR is XOR inverted.

As an illustration, Figure 1.9 shows the AND and OR truth tables of three-input variables derived from these definitions.

### Exercises

1. Prove the formula given in the text for the number of different binary functions of $n$ variables.
2. Calculate the number of different logic functions of 20 variables. How many of them are NOT, AND, OR, and XOR gates?
3. Draw the truth tables of all logic functions of two variables.
4. Check that the verbal definitions of AND and other multi-input functions are consistent with the original two-input definitions.

| $a$ | $b$ | $c$ | AND | OR |
|---|---|---|---|---|
| 0 | 0 | 0 | 0 | 0 |
| 0 | 0 | 1 | 0 | 1 |
| 0 | 1 | 0 | 0 | 1 |
| 0 | 1 | 1 | 0 | 1 |
| 1 | 0 | 0 | 0 | 1 |
| 1 | 0 | 1 | 0 | 1 |
| 1 | 1 | 0 | 0 | 1 |
| 1 | 1 | 1 | 1 | 1 |

**Figure 1.9.** Truth tables for three-input AND, and OR.

5. We said that a two-input NEXOR implements identity. Does this hold for multi-input NEXOR?
6. Convert the truth tables of AND, OR, NAND, NOR, and NOT from 0/1 to L/H and determine their interpretation in negative logic (0/H, 1/L). Use these findings to explain why data sheets for integrated circuits use L/H rather than the 0/1 notation.

### Analysis of Logic Diagrams

To analyze a circuit means to determine its function from a diagram and to express that function in the form of a truth table or logic formula. To obtain the result, one starts at the circuit inputs and follows each wire to the device to which it is connected. The output of the device is then labeled according to its function and its inputs. This process is repeated until the output wire is reached.

For the circuit in Figure 1.8, this procedure gives

$$f = \overline{(\overline{a \cdot b}) \cdot c}$$

For the circuit in Figure 1.10 we get

$$f = ab + \bar{c} + bcd$$

To make logic diagrams more readable, engineers usually place inputs on the left and outputs on the right.

If the truth table of or the value of the output are required, one can use the following methods:

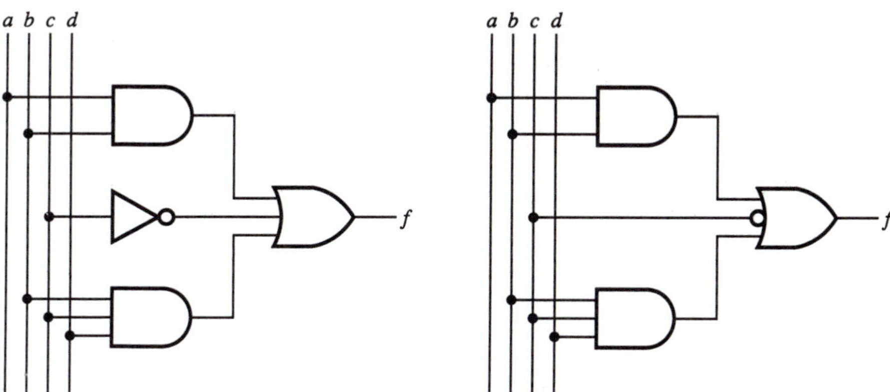


**Figure 1.10.** Multi-input gates and their use. The diagram on the right is a shorthand representation of the circuit on the left with negation indicated by a bubble instead of an inverter. Note the standard convention that two crossing wires are connected only if their intersection is marked with a filled circle.

Find the formula and calculate its outputs by directly substituting input values into it. This method is useful to calculate many outputs.

Find the formula and derive its truth table by taking advantage of some special properties of the logic functions. This method is useful when the formula is not too complicated.

Label each input wire by its value and calculate intermediate values by proceeding towards outputs. This approach is useful if one needs only a few outputs.

We will now consider two examples of the first two methods.

**Example 1.** We are to construct the truth table of the following formula derived from a logic diagram

$$f(a,b,c) = ab + \bar{a}c$$

If we use the first method, we obtain the truth table by substituting individual input combinations. For $a = b = c = 0$, we get $ab = 0 \cdot 0 = 0$, $\bar{a}c = \bar{0} \cdot 0 = 1 \cdot 0 = 0$, and finally $ab + \bar{a}c = 0 + 0 = 0$. The first entry in the truth table is thus 0. The remaining lines are obtained similarly.

Using the second method, we can reason as follows: Because $f$ is an OR function, its value is 1 iff $ab$ is 1 (this requires that $a = b = 1$, $c$ is irrelevant) or $\bar{a}c$ is 1 ($a = 0$ and $c = 1$, $b$ is irrelevant). We write 1 into the output column of the corresponding lines and 0 into the remaining lines. The resulting truth table is given below.

**Example 2.** To construct the truth table of

$$g(a,b,c) = a \oplus bc$$

using the second method, we first note that $g$ is an XOR function and its value is thus 1 iff the two operands are different. This means that if $a = 0$, then $g = 1$ if $bc = 1$, which corresponds to $(a,b,c) = (0,1,1)$. If $a = 1$ then $bc$ must be zero, and consequently $g = 1$ for $(a,b,c) = (1,0,0)$, $(1,0,1)$, and $(1,1,0)$. For all other combinations, $g$ is zero. The whole truth table of $g$ is given below.

| ***abc*** | ***f g*** |
|---|---|
| 000 | 0 0 |
| 001 | 1 0 |
| 010 | 0 0 |
| 011 | 1 1 |
| 100 | 0 1 |
| 101 | 0 1 |
| 110 | 1 1 |
| 111 | 1 0 |

In Example 2, one might prefer to use the first method (line-by-line calculation) because the formula is a bit too complicated. In this case, the truth table could be found by constructing truth tables of individual parts of the expression and combining them together as follows:

| ***abc*** | ***bc*** $g = a \oplus bc$ |
|---|---|
| 000 | 0 0 |
| 001 | 0 0 |
| 010 | 0 0 |
| 011 | 1 1 |
| 100 | 0 1 |
| 101 | 0 1 |
| 110 | 0 1 |
| 111 | 1 0 |

To obtain $g$, we combined columns $a$ and $bc$.

**Exercises**

1. Find the formula for the *sum* and *carry-out* outputs of the adder in Figure 1.11 and construct their truth tables. Use both methods suggested in this section. Study the truth table and explain why the circuit is called an adder, and its outputs *sum* and *carry-out*.
2. Draw an arbitrary logic diagram and find the formula for it.
3. Draw the logic diagram and the truth table of $(a \cdot b) \oplus a \cdot c$
4. Draw the wiring diagram of the adder using the pinouts in Appendix 4.

**Truth Tables and Binary Representation of Numbers**

One of the most common uses of binary codes is to represent numbers. Binary codes are covered in detail in Chapter 6 but we will introduce them now to help us understand truth tables and to provide material for interesting problems.

The most common number systems are positional, which means that each digit in the code has a fixed weight and the value of a code is the sum of individual digits multiplied by their weights. In the ordinary decimal system, the weights are (from right to left) 1, 10, 100, 1000, and so on. In binary positional representation, weights are 1, 2, 4, 8, etc. We see that decimal weights are powers of ten and binary weights are powers of two. If we number the bits in a binary code from right to left, the value of the code $\ldots b_3 b_2 b_1 b_0$ is

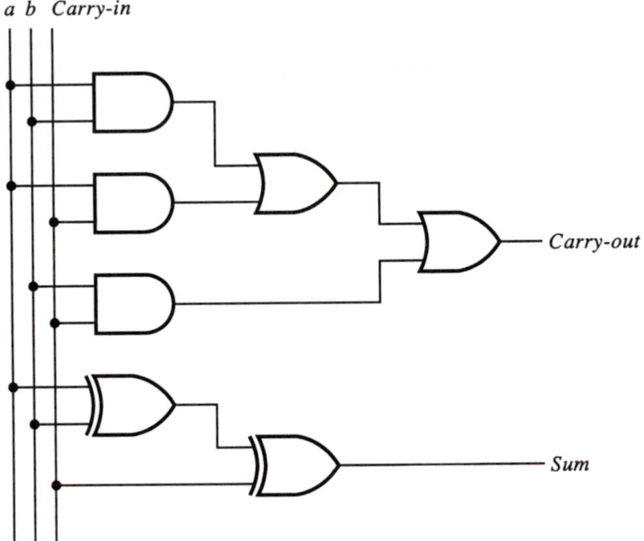


**Figure 1.11.** Logic diagram of an adder.

$$value = \ldots + b_3*8 + b_2*4 + b_1*2 + b_0*1$$
$$= \ldots + b_3*2^3 + b_2*2^2 + b_1*2^1 + b_0*2^0$$

Note that the values of the exponents of individual weights are the same as the values of the subscripts, and the contribution of bit $b_i$ is

$$b_i*2^i$$

The following are a few examples of positional binary codes and their decimal values:

| binary code | 000 | 111 | 01 | 00001 | 1010 | 101 |
|---|---|---|---|---|---|---|
| decimal value | 0 | 7 | 1 | 1 | 10 | 5 |

Note the relation of binary codes and the labels in a truth table: One usually writes the input combinations in the left column of a truth table in order of increasing numerical value. As an example, the input combinations of a three-input table are

| binary code | 000 | 001 | 010 | 011 | 100 | 101 | 110 | 111 |
|---|---|---|---|---|---|---|---|---|
| decimal value | 0 | 1 | 2 | 3 | 4 | 5 | 6 | 7 |

A useful variation on positional binary notation is the *binary coded decimal*, or BCD convention. Binary coded decimal codes consist of four-bit groups representing the decimal digits 0 to 9:

| BCD code | 0000 | 0001 | 0010 | 0011 | 0100 | 0101 | 0110 | 0111 | 1000 | 1001 |
|---|---|---|---|---|---|---|---|---|---|---|
| decimal value | 0 | 1 | 2 | 3 | 4 | 5 | 6 | 7 | 8 | 9 |

and the BCD code of an arbitrary decimal value is obtained by concatenating BCD codes of individual digits as in the following examples:

| Decimal | BCD |
|---|---|
| 13 | 0001 0011 |
| 495 | 0100 1001 0101 |
| 7 | 0111 |

Note again that in a BCD code, each decimal digit is represented by four bits.

Binary coded decimal notation is very important because input and output of devices such as computers, calculators, watches, and many instruments is decimal and BCD representation simplifies their design.

## Exercises

1. What are the decimal values of the binary codes 011, 0111, 1000, and 1010? Which of them are BCD codes?
2. What are the binary codes of 6, 4, 16, 15, and 17?
3. What are the BCD codes of the numbers in the preceding exercise?
4. Does each bit in a multidigit BCD code have a fixed weight? In other words, are BCD codes positional?
5. What is the minimum number of bits needed for the binary code of 200, 300? How many are needed in BCD notation?
6. What is the largest value that can be represented with 4 bits in binary notation? What are the largest values that can be represented by 8 bits, 10 bits, and $N$ bits.
7. Repeat the previous exercise with BCD notation.
8. Truth tables can be described by listing the numbers of lines with 1 output. As an example, the OR table is (1,2,3) and the AND table is (3). Give similar descriptions for the functions NOT, NAND, NOR, XOR, and NEXOR.
9. Explain why the rightmost bit of a code is often called the least significant bit and the leftmost bit the most significant bit.

## 1.5 FORMAL PROPERTIES OF LOGIC FUNCTIONS

Most mathematical functions can be expressed in many ways. As an example, the values of algebraic expressions

$$(x + 1)(y - 1) \qquad \text{and} \qquad xy - x + y - 1$$

are the same for all values of $x$ and $y$. This is due to certain properties of multiplication, addition, and subtraction. Logic functions can also be written in various forms, with the simpler formulas corresponding to simpler circuits. To determine whether a modification of a formula preserves its meaning, we must know how to decide whether two logic functions are equivalent or not. The most natural way to define logic equivalence is with reference to physical circuits (Figure 1.12).

Two circuits that produce the same outputs for all input combinations are indistinguishable, or functionally equivalent, and their truth tables are identical. Because logic functions are abstractions of logic circuits, two logic functions are equivalent if their truth tables are identical. The process of determining logic equivalence by comparing truth tables is called *proof by perfect induction.*

**Example 1** To decide whether $x = \overline{\overline{x}}$ we construct the truth table of $\overline{\overline{x}}$ and compare it with $x$. The tables are identical (Figure 1.13), and therefore the identity holds.

**Example 2** Decide whether $\overline{a \cdot b} = \overline{a} \cdot \overline{b}$. The two tables (Figure 1.13) are different and the identity thus does not hold.

Several interesting and important equalities that can be proved by perfect induction are listed on the following page:

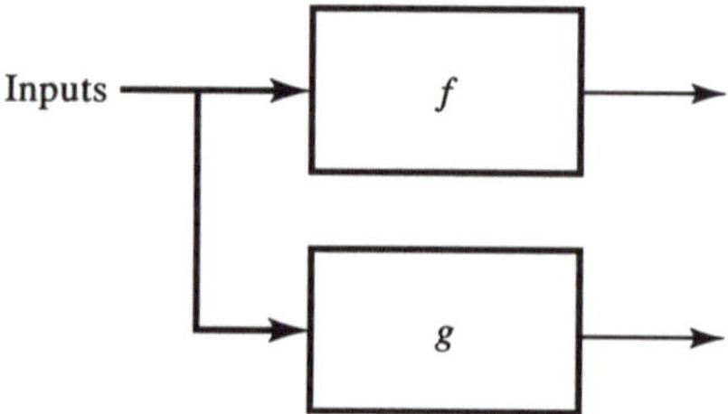


**Figure 1.12.** To decide whether two combinational circuits are equivalent, connect their inputs to the same signals and test if they produce the same outputs for all input combinations.

| $x$ | $\bar{x}$ | $\bar{\bar{x}}$ |
|---|---|---|
| 0 | 1 | 0 |
| 1 | 0 | 1 |

| $a$ | $b$ | $\overline{a \cdot b}$ | $a$ | $b$ | $\bar{a} \cdot \bar{b}$ |
|---|---|---|---|---|---|
| 0 | 0 | 1 | 1 | 1 | 1 |
| 0 | 1 | 1 | 1 | 0 | 0 |
| 1 | 0 | 1 | 0 | 1 | 0 |
| 1 | 1 | 0 | 0 | 0 | 0 |

**Figure 1.13.** Proving that $x = \bar{\bar{x}}$ and $\overline{a \cdot b} \neq \bar{a} \cdot \bar{b}$ by perfect induction.

1. $x = \bar{\bar{x}}$
2. $x \cdot x = x$ $\qquad x + x = x$
3. $x \cdot \bar{x} = 0$ $\qquad x + \bar{x} = 1$
4. $x \cdot 0 = 0$ $\qquad x + 1 = 1$
5. $x \cdot 1 = x$ $\qquad x + 0 = x$
6. $x \cdot y = y \cdot x$ $\qquad x + y = y + x$
7. $\overline{x \cdot y} = \bar{x} + \bar{y}$ $\qquad \overline{x + y} = \bar{x} \cdot \bar{y}$
8. $x \cdot (y + z) = (x \cdot y) + (x \cdot z)$ $\qquad x + (y \cdot z) = (x + y) \cdot (x + z)$
9. $x \cdot (y \cdot z) = (x \cdot y) \cdot z$ $\qquad x + (y + z) = (x + y) + z$

## Notes

1. Property 6 is called commutativity, equalities 7 are DeMorgan's laws, property 8 is distributivity, and property 9 is associativity.
2. The left and right columns are very similar and can be obtained from one another by exchanging ANDs with ORs and zeros with ones. The two formulas in such pairs are called dual. As an example, rules

$$x \cdot 0 = 0 \qquad \text{and} \qquad x + 1 = 1$$

are dual.

Duality is very useful because it implies that any design method that depends on a subset of the above rules can be automatically converted to a dual method by exchanging zeros with ones and ANDs with ORs. For any given design method, another design method, which may in some cases produce simpler results than the original one, is thus obtained with no additional effort.

3. Rules 1–9 can be extended to more variables. As an example, the commutativity of AND holds also for three inputs:

$$\begin{aligned} x \cdot y \cdot z &= x \cdot (y \cdot z) = x \cdot (z \cdot y) = x \cdot z \cdot y \\ &= (x \cdot z) \cdot y = (z \cdot x) \cdot y = z \cdot x \cdot y \\ &= z \cdot (x \cdot y) = z \cdot (y \cdot x) = z \cdot y \cdot x \end{aligned}$$

and so forth.

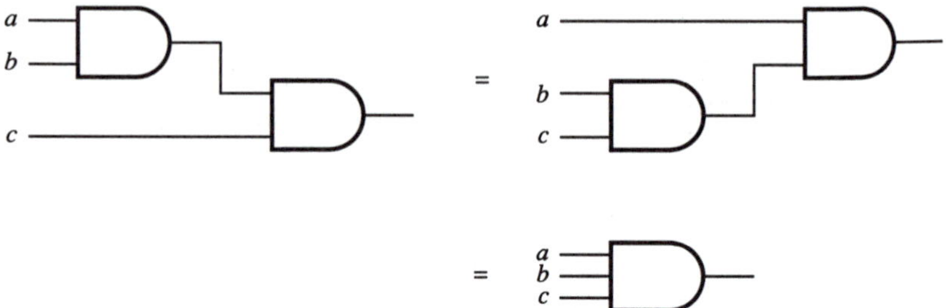


**Figure 1.14.** Associativity forms the basis of the definition of a multiple-input AND gate.

4. The associativity of AND implies that if we want to implement a 3-input AND with 2 input gates, it does not matter how we connect the inputs to the AND gates (Figure 1.14). This argument holds for any number of inputs and for the OR function as well. It is the basis of the multi-input definitions of AND and OR given in the previous section.
5. DeMorgan's laws can be used to transform diagrams in ways that preserve the function and produce structures that may convey more meaning. An example of a meaning-preserving transformation is given in Figure 1.15.

### Boolean Algebra

Formal manipulation of logic functions is one of the subjects of Boolean algebra. It can be used to simplify functions or to convert one formula into another. As an example,

$$x + x\cdot y = x\cdot 1 + x\cdot y = x\cdot(1+y) = x\cdot(y+1) = x\cdot 1 = x$$

This result, which is known as the principle of subsumption, can be used to simplify complex circuits. We suggest that you justify the individual steps of the transformation by finding the identities on which they are based.

The following is a more involved example:

$$\begin{aligned}&\overline{a}\,\overline{b}\,\overline{c}\,\overline{d} + \overline{a}\,\overline{b}\,\overline{c}\,d + \overline{a}b\overline{c}\,\overline{d} + \overline{a}b\overline{c}d \\ &= \overline{a}\,\overline{b}\,\overline{c}(\overline{d} + d) + \overline{a}b\overline{c}(\overline{d} + d) = \overline{a}\,\overline{b}\,\overline{c}(d + \overline{d}) + \overline{a}b\overline{c}(d + \overline{d}) \\ &= \overline{a}\,\overline{b}\,\overline{c}\cdot 1 + \overline{a}b\overline{c}\cdot 1 = \overline{a}\,\overline{b}\,\overline{c} + \overline{a}b\overline{c} = \overline{a}\,\overline{c}\,\overline{b} + \overline{a}\,\overline{c}b\end{aligned}$$

**Figure 1.15.** Function NAND can be drawn as OR with inverted inputs because $\overline{a\cdot b} = \overline{a} + \overline{b}$. A similar, dual rule applies to NOR.

$$= \bar{a}\bar{c}(\bar{b} + b) = \bar{a}\bar{c}(b + \bar{b}) = \bar{a}\bar{c}\cdot 1 = \bar{a}\bar{c}$$

The reader should draw the logic diagrams implementing the initial and the simplified formulas to see how many gates and connections have been saved.

Algebraic manipulation can also be used to derive certain identities from others. As an example, the identity

$$x + x = x$$

can be proved as follows:

$$x + x = (x + x)\cdot 1 = (x + x)(x + \bar{x})$$
$$= xx + xx + x\bar{x} + x\bar{x}$$
$$= xx + x\bar{x} = x + 0 = x$$

A useful principle of algebraic manipulation is substitution. It states that if we take a valid rule and rename some or all of its variables, or even replace them with other expressions, we get another valid rule. Take, as an example, $\overline{uv}\cdot\overline{xy}$. If we replace $\overline{uv}$ by $a$ and $\overline{xy}$ with $b$, we get

$$f = \overline{\overline{uv}\cdot\overline{xy}} = \overline{ab} = \bar{a} + \bar{b} = \overline{\overline{uv}} + \overline{\overline{xy}}$$

If we now replace $uv$ by $c$ and $xy$ by $d$, we get

$$f = \bar{\bar{c}} + \bar{\bar{d}} = c + d = uv + xy$$

Intuitive algebraic manipulation as demonstrated above is very useful because it often allows us to simplify circuits. Fortunately, most logic design does not depend on intuition but rather on systematic mechanical procedures. We will introduce two such methods in Chapter 2.

## Exercises

1. Equivalence forms the basis for testing a circuit's operation by comparing it with a circuit that is known to be good. Tests can be automated by using a comparator, a two-input combinational circuit that outputs 1 when its inputs are identical and 0 otherwise. Draw the truth table of a comparator. Which basic logic function is it? Draw the circuit that implements it.
2. What is the formula for $f$ in Figure 1.16 when $d = 0$? What is the formula when $d = 1$? What are these two functions? Circuits in which certain inputs are intended to control the effect of the remaining inputs are sometimes called programmable. Our circuit is a simple example of a

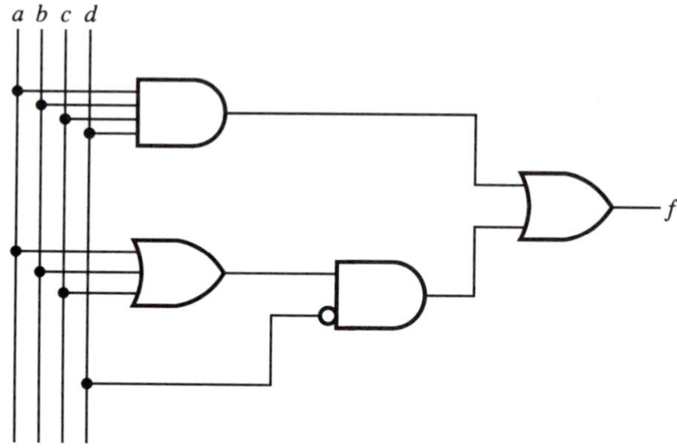


**Figure 1.16.** A circuit that can be programmed to perform one of two useful functions.

programmable circuit and $d$ is its "control input." Analyzing a circuit by keeping one of its inputs constant is useful with complex circuits, especially when they are programmable.

3. Prove or disprove the following by perfect induction or by formal simplification:

$$x \cdot \overline{y} + \overline{x} \cdot y = x \oplus y$$

$$x \cdot y + x \cdot \overline{y} = x$$

$$x + \overline{y} = xyz + x\overline{yz}$$

$$\overline{x \oplus y} = \overline{x} \oplus y = x \oplus \overline{y}$$

4. Show that each dual rule can be proved by using negation, applying DeMorgan's rules, and substituting into the original rule.
5. Find the dual of $x + (y + \overline{z})$.
6. Write a program to convert a logic formula into a truth table.
7. Simplify the following formulas: $xyz + x\overline{y}z$, $\overline{a}b\overline{c} + \overline{ac}$, $a(a + b)$, $a + abc\overline{d}$.
8. Show that the definition of three-input AND derived from associativity is consistent with our previous definition of three-input AND.
9. Use mathematical induction to extend associativity of AND and OR to any number of inputs.
10. Is NAND associative? In other words, is $\overline{\overline{ab}c} = \overline{a\overline{bc}}$?

## 1.6 PHYSICAL CONSIDERATIONS

Logic circuits are not abstract devices and to understand them we must be aware of the differences between the abstraction and the reality. The two simplifications we have been making so far are to replace the continuous physical signals by discrete ones and to assume that the 0→1 and 1→0 transitions are instantaneous. Both simplifications are reasonable unless we have to measure time or voltage in very small units. For instance, if the circuit must perform fast calculations, or if the voltages are distorted, or if the internal events depend on exact timing, then our assumptions must be reexamined. To prepare for such situations we will now discuss some aspects of the operation of real gates and the nature of logic signals in more detail.

The proper operation of a physical implementation of a logic gate is guaranteed only if the voltage of the power supply and the operating temperature are within certain limits. Moreover, the input signal must have the correct magnitude, its shape must be clean, and the transitions must be fast. Most gate inputs arrive from other gates and it is thus important to know how a gate changes the shape and timing of the input signal. In other words, one must consider the relation between the magnitude and the time of arrival of input and the magnitude and timing of the output. The truth table does not answer this question. It shows, for example, that an inverter changes a High input into a Low output, but it does not let us predict the exact shape and timing of the physical waveform.

An exact analysis of the signals passing through a chip is complex and requires good knowledge of electronics. It is, however, possible to define gate models that let us predict signal behavior with various degrees of accuracy and without recourse to electronics. We will present the simplest of such models sufficient for our needs and for the understanding of chip specifications in component data books. It is based on the separation of signal shape from timing and represents the effect of the gate as a time-independent change of the magnitude followed by a delay (Figure 1.17).

### Part 1 of the Model—the Magnitude

Our model of the effect of the gate on the magnitude of the signal is based on the voltage levels that a device recognizes as logic 0/1 input, and the levels that it produces as 0/1 logic output. For TTL chips the rules are as in Figure 1.18. Note the following:

Input voltages between 0.0 and 0.8 V are interpreted as logic Low and voltages between 2.0 and 5.0 V are interpreted as logic High.

Logic Low outputs produce voltages of at most 0.4 V, a logic High output is at least 2.4 V.

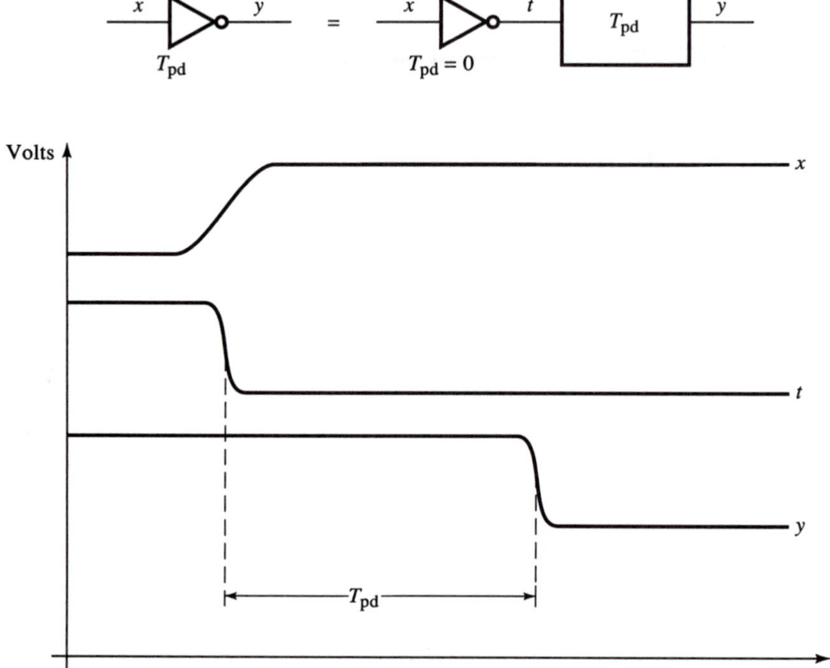


**Figure 1.17.** Effect of a gate on its input represented as a change of shape and delay.

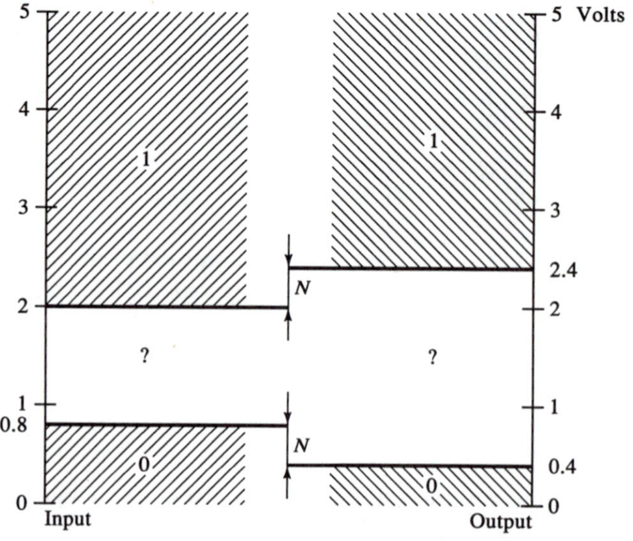


**Figure 1.18.** Input and output voltage levels and their logic interpretation. Noise margin $N = 0.4$ V.

Our input/output description raises two questions: What is the meaning of signals whose value is between logic Low and logic High? Why are input and output limits different?

The logic value of a signal whose amplitude is between logic Low and High is indeterminate. As an example, the output produced by an inverter with input voltage between 0.8 and 2.0 V is not logically valid and its value will probably not be above 2.4 V (logic 1) or below 0.8 V (logic 0).

Because transitions between Low and High are unavoidable, logic circuits must be designed to produce outputs with sharp transitions to minimize the duration of the intermediate values.

The difference between input and output voltage levels (0.4–0.8 V for logic 0, 2.0–2.8 V for logic 1) makes it possible to interpret the output signal correctly even if it is somewhat corrupted by noise or attenuated when it reaches the input of the next gate (Figure 1.19). The larger the difference

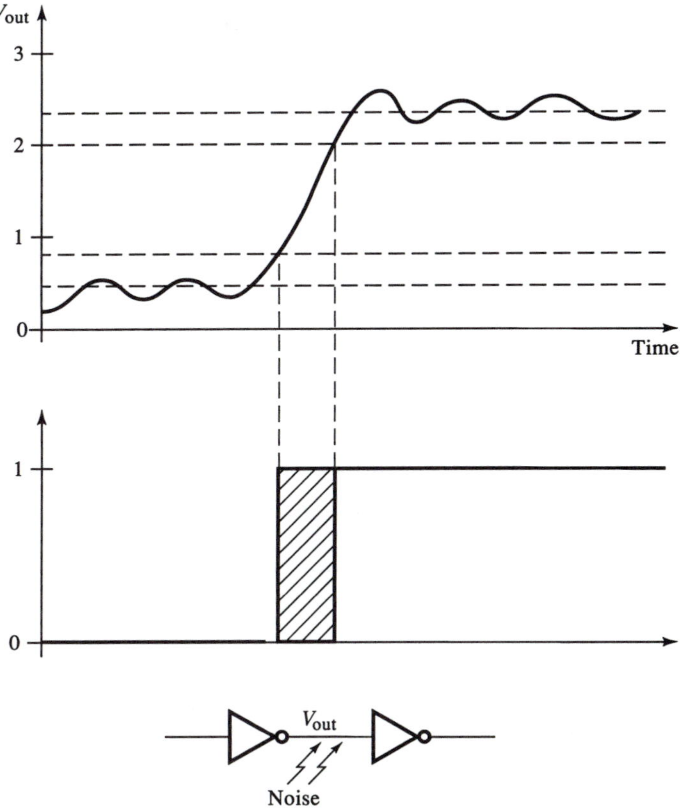


**Figure 1.19.** Input and output levels. If the distortion of a signal is within the noise margin limits, the value is still correctly recognized.

between input and output levels (the "noise margin"), the larger the noise immunity of the chip; that is, the more noise it can withstand before the logic interpretation of the signal becomes incorrect.

### Part 2 of the Model—Timing

The second part of our model is the delay imposed on the signal by the gate. The delay is the time that it takes for an input change to propagate through the gate and to produce a corresponding output change. Data books refer to this as the *propagation delay* and denote it as $T_{pd}$ (Figures 1.17 and 1.20).

Whereas voltage levels are a purely electronic problem, signal delay is a parameter that must be considered even at the level of abstract logic. The reason is that if the output of a gate is used before it has had time to complete a transition, its value may be incorrect. Circuits must thus be given enough time to complete all transitions, and the propagation delays therefore determine the maximum operating speed of the circuit.

To provide some feeling for timing parameters of logic components, the table below lists several propagation delays for TTL devices obtained from data sheets.

| Type Number and Name | Typical $T_{pdLH}$ | Maximum $T_{pdLH}$ | Typical $T_{pdHL}$ | Maximum $T_{pdHL}$ |
|---|---|---|---|---|
| 7400 quad NAND | 11 | 22 | 7 | 15 |
| 7404 hex inverter | 12 | 22 | 8 | 15 |
| 7408 quad AND | 17 | 27 | 12 | 19 |
| 7432 quad OR | 10 | 15 | 14 | 22 |

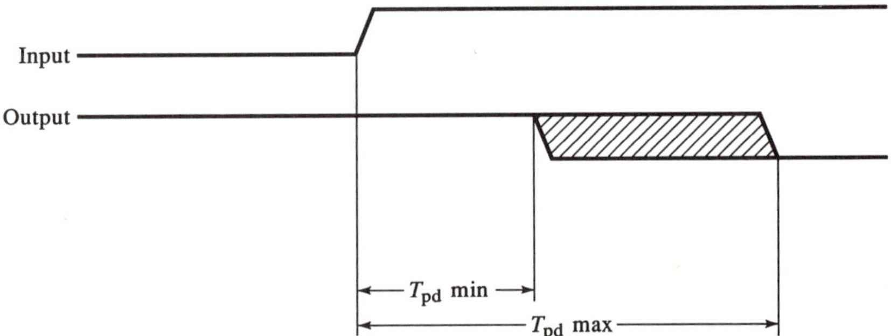


**Figure 1.20.** Output of a logic device is known to reach its valid output value within some time after the change of input.

Note the following:

Propagation delays are given in nanoseconds (billionths of a second). The reader may be interested to learn that light travels about 30 centimeters in one nanosecond and that a voltage change such as a signal transition travels through a wire at about one-half to two-thirds of this speed. The fact that the speed of ordinary gates and the speed of a signal propagating through a wire are comparable explains why the length of connections between chips becomes a critical parameter in designing ultrafast systems like supercomputers.

$T_{pdLH}$ delays (propagation delays of Low-to-High transitions) are different from $T_{pdHL}$ delays (High-to-Low transitions).

Individual batches of chips, different chips within one batch, and different gates on the same chip may have different delays. Moreover, the propagation delay of each gate depends on the temperature, the electric loading, and the age of the component. The times given by the manufacturer are thus obtained by evaluating a large number of chips under well defined "typical" operating conditions. The typical values are satisfied by most components, whereas the maximum values represent the typical behavior under the worst operating conditions within specifications. Operation is not guaranteed outside the operating range.

In addition to typical and maximum delays, data sheets sometimes also specify the minimum delay (Figure 1.20).

Different types of gates have different delays because their internal electronic circuits or number of inputs are different.

As we mentioned, output levels and propagation delays are guaranteed only if the component works under proper operating conditions. These are determined by the voltage and current levels of the power supply, the operating temperature, and limits on the external loads of individual gates. To illustrate these parameters, we now briefly summarize the requirements of TTL chips.

TTL chips are divided into two large categories, the 74 "regular" chips and the 54 "military" family. The difference between the two is mainly in the range of operating temperatures: 0–70°C for the 74 family and −55–125°C for the 54 family. For most chips, regular and military devices with the same type code have the same function and pinout but slightly different current requirements and delays.

Parameters relevant to the power supply are the voltage and current. Voltage must be within 10% of 5 volts (4.5–5.5 V) for the 54 family and within 5% of 5 volts for the 74 family. The current required by a circuit can be calculated by adding together the currents required by individual chips in the circuit.

The maximum load on a given output pin is called the "fan-out." (The term is also sometimes used to denote the number of inputs connected to an output.) The fan-out determines the maximum number of "standard" inputs that may be connected to one output. It can be calculated from the amount of electric current required by the gate and varies somewhat from chip to chip. (The calculation is explained in the following exercises.) The fan-out of most TTL devices is 10, which means that up to 10 standard inputs (inputs with a fan-in equal to 1) may be connected to one output without unacceptable signal deterioration. If it is necessary to connect the output to more inputs, we must provide components that amplify the signal without changing its logic value. These can be ordinary gates, drivers, or buffers; the latter two are devices having an especially large fan-out (Figure 1.21). Drivers and buffers are very common in computers because many computer chips use technologies having much smaller fan-outs than TTL and because computer signals often must be fed to many destinations, thus requiring a large fan-out.

This completes our introduction to the physical aspects of logic circuits. Sample data sheets and explanatory comments appear in Appendix 3.

For the simple circuits found in this book, we can neglect fan-in, fan-out, and signal shape considerations. For most of the circuits considered, we can ignore delays as well. For fast circuits, however, timing analysis is critical and we will return to that topic.

**Exercises**

1. Assume that a chip treats a voltage value of 0.5 V as the only boundary between logic 0 and logic 1 and has no safety region. Show how this chip interprets a 0.55-V signal corrupted by a 0.2-V peak-to-peak noise.
2. Repeat the previous exercise with a signal making a slow transition from 0 to 1 corrupted by a 0.1-V noise.

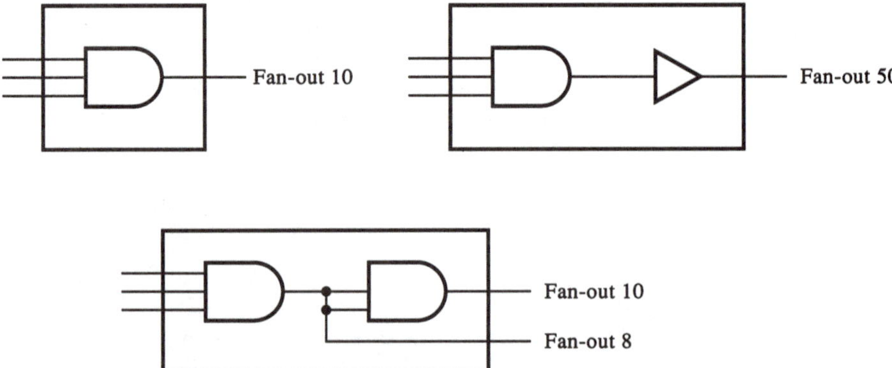


**Figure 1.21.** To increase the fan-out, use a driver or an extra gate that does not change the logic value of the signal.

3. Assume that input and output voltage levels are identical ($V_{iL} = V_{oL}$ and $V_{iH} = V_{oH}$). Draw a graph showing what happens when an output value close to the limits travels along a wire and is affected by small attenuation and noise.
4. Use a data book to compare the delays of two-, three-, four-, and eight-input TTL NAND gates. (Look for "totem pole" circuits.)
5. Give a model of the circuit in Figure 1.8 neglecting the shape of the signal and considering only delays. Is the behavior symmetric with respect to the direction of the transition?
6. Compare the times and power consumption of standard 74 gates and gates in the S and LS series. The S, or Schottky, series and the LS, or low-power Schottky, are the modern versions of TTL.
7. The fan-in $f_i$ is the number of "standard" loads represented by the input current of a given gate. For TTL chips, the standard is the NAND gate in the 7400 chip whose low-level input $I_{iL}$ is 1.6 mA. Use a TTL data book to calculate the fan-in of several gates from $f_i = I_{iL}/1.6$.
8. The fan-out of a gate is the maximum number of standard loads that can be connected to its output without causing its operation to deteriorate. Inasmuch as the standard load is $I_{iL}$=1.6 mA, the fan-out is $I_{oL}/1.6$. Its value is usually 10. Calculate the fan-out of several commercial gates. (More accurate calculation requires finding the minimum of $I_{oL}/I_{iL}$ and $I_{oH}/I_{iH}$.)
9. How many inputs of components with fan-in $f_i$=1 can be connected to the output of a gate with fan-out 10? Repeat with fan-in 2, and for fan-in 0.5 and fan-out 30.
10. How much current must be supplied by a power supply that drives a TTL circuit consisting of five NOR chips requiring 45 mA each, three AND-OR-invert chips requiring 16 mA each, and two OR gates on the four-gate 7432 chip for which the average one-gate consumption is estimated at 5 mA. The voltage of the power supply is assumed to be within 10% of 5 V. Note that power supply and logic signal currents are different.
11. Draw a simple logic circuit, use a TTL data book to select suitable chips to implement it, calculate the required current of the power supply, and check that all fan-out requirements are satisfied. If fan-out requirements are exceeded, find suitable gates or driver chips to amplify the signal.
12. We stated that if a logic circuit is used at a speed exceeding the delays of its components, the signals may be incorrectly interpreted. Explain this statement and demonstrate it in an example.

## 1.7 SIMULATION OF LOGIC CIRCUITS

Building and testing logic circuits is time consuming and expensive. Moreover, certain conditions of the working circuit cannot be physically observed or depend on the parameters of the chips used in the prototype. For these reasons it is important to use computer simulation, particularly in the initial stages of design when different alternatives have to be evaluated and compared. Simulation is also an excellent study aid that helps one to understand logic components, circuits, and design methods, and that can be used to test circuits before they are laboriously implemented in hardware for a lab experiment. The student is strongly encouraged to simulate the devices, problems, examples, and experiments given in this book using a suitable simulation program.

With the growing complexity of digital circuits, the use, number, and sophistication of logic simulators and related computer-aided design (CAD) tools is quickly growing. Many simulation packages with a broad range of prices, sophistication, and hardware requirements are now available. Some of the programs go beyond circuit design and simulation, and generate files that can be used to help automate production as well. This is referred to as computer-aided manufacturing or CAM.

In preparing this book, several such programs were tested and we will now briefly consider two of them: the CAD/CAM commercial package developed by Douglas Electronics, and the HARD simulator designed by the author.

The Douglas Electronics program runs on the Macintosh computer. It is intended for professional use and includes facilities for drawing diagrams, running simulations, and creating files for the automated manufacture of circuit boards. It was used to simulate the TOY CPU in Chapter 9. Figure 1.22 shows an example of a Macintosh screen with a circuit diagram and a simulation.

HARD is an IBM PC-based simulation package developed for teaching. It consists of a language with which the user describes the structure of the circuit, and a simulator that allows the user to test the circuit's response to different input combinations. The following HARD description of the circuit in Figure 1.23 illustrates the language:

```
CIRCUIT:  Sample                  – Heading—gives the circuit a name
PARTS:    INPUT:    a,b           – List of components
          AND:      And
          OUTPUT:   x
CONNECT:  a,b TO:   And           – List of connections
          And TO:   x
END
```

When a circuit description such as the one above is completed, the HARD compiler translates it into a form that can be used for simulation with the HARD simulator. Any number of simulations may then be performed, using inputs entered manually or from a file created by the user.

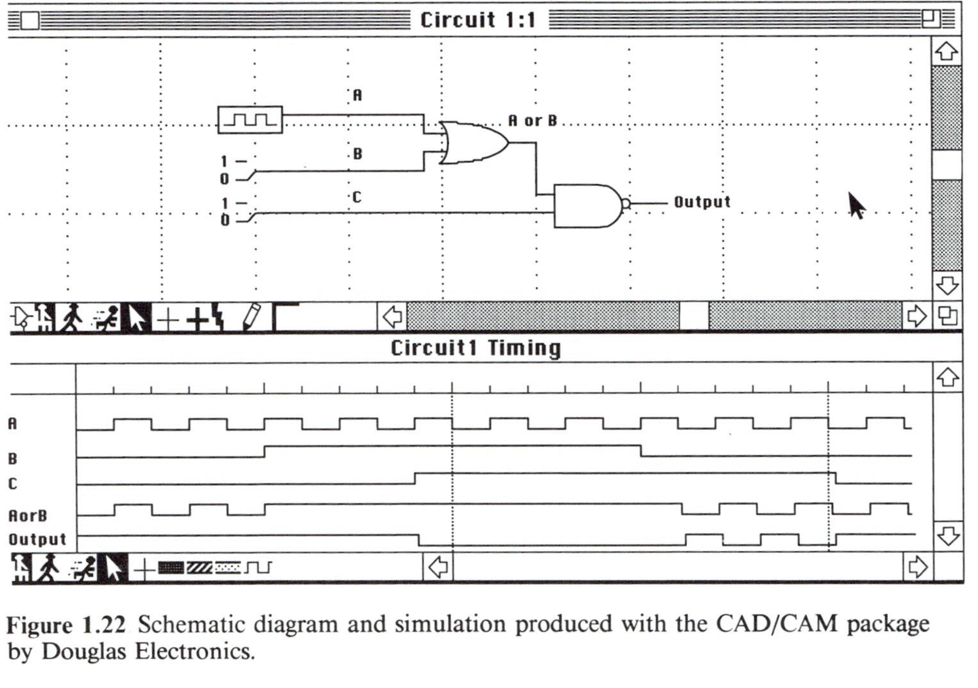


**Figure 1.22** Schematic diagram and simulation produced with the CAD/CAM package by Douglas Electronics.

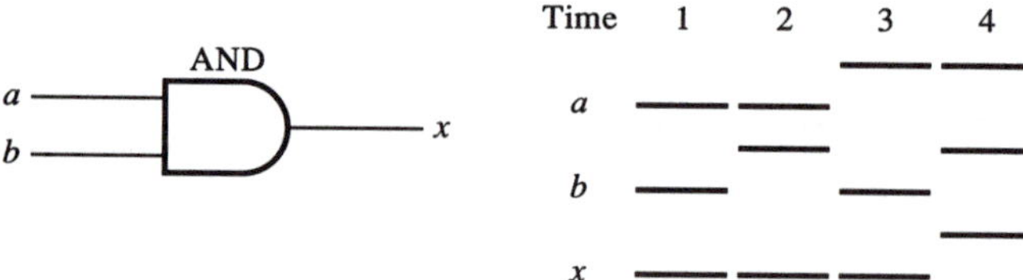


**Figure 1.23.** A simple circuit and its simulation by HARD.

## Exercises

1. Simulate all of the one- and two-input components introduced in this chapter. It is instructive to simulate several of them simultaneously and to compare their behavior.
2. Simulate both sides of several identifies from Section 1.5 to show that they hold. Note that an exhaustive simulation constitutes a proof by perfect induction.
3. Mechanize the comparisons in the preceding exercise by connecting the outputs of both sides to an XOR gate.
4. Repeat the preceding exercises using components with delays. When do identities hold for components with delays?

## SUMMARY

Logic circuits can only combine and store logic signals and it is useful to study and design them on the basis of a model separating the combinational and memory parts. This chapter begins our examination of combinational circuits that have no memory; sequential circuits with memory will be studied later.

To make it possible to describe logic behavior and express it concisely, we first defined the discrete binary signal and presented the notations used to represent it (1/0, On/Off, High/Low, True/False). We then introduced the concepts of a truth table (the list of output values for all input combinations) and a Boolean function. We related the equivalence of functions to the equivalence of their physical implementation and truth tables. We presented several important identities and proved some of them by perfect induction; that is, by comparing their truth tables. We defined basic logic functions—NOT, AND, OR, NAND, NOR, and XOR—and their engineering symbols. We introduced the representation of numbers by positional binary codes along with one of its popular variants, Binary Coded Decimal (BCD).

Binary logic deals with two-valued signals with sharp step-like transitions between the two possible values. This is an abstraction of real physical signals, which have continuous transitions and fluctuating levels. The principle of logic circuits is that their components respond differently to two regions of values—below and above certain characteristic values—and convert them into outputs whose levels fall into similar disjoint regions. This makes the logic abstraction functionally equivalent to the physical reality and allows us to design logic circuits using abstract 0/1 logic while disregarding physical behavior in most circumstances. The major part of logic design then becomes independent of the underlying technology.

The 0/1 model is usually adequate because most circuits work at speeds far below the speed of their components. For fast circuits, however, the model fails and could result in incorrect operation. Fortunately, extending the 0/1 model by adding signal propagation delays is usually sufficient to get a good picture of real operation. For more detailed analysis, we have to consider input and output voltage levels corresponding to 0 and 1 values and compliance with prescribed operating conditions, particularly the limits on the loading of gate outputs. Engineers use the concepts of fan-in (the number of standard loads represented by a given input) and fan-out (the maximum number of standard loads that may be connected to a given output) to simplify loading calculations. If even more accurate results are needed, for example in the design of integrated circuits themselves, an electronic model of the circuit becomes necessary.

In the final section, we introduced the simulation of logic circuits by computer programs. We noted that the growing complexity of logic circuits makes use of CAD essential in modern design. CAD programs can also be very useful for learning and much insight may be gained by simulating the hardware-related exercises, examples, and experiments.

## REVIEW QUESTION

1. Define the following terms: Digital/analog signal, binary, bit, combinational/sequential circuit, positive/negative logic, truth table, parity, NOT, AND, OR, OR, NAND, NOR, integrated circuit, pinout, gate, analysis, positional representation, BCD code, perfect induction, duality, DeMorgan's laws, Boolean algebra, propagation delay, nanosecond, fan-out, fan-in.

## REFERENCES

The following titles listed in the references at the end of the book are relevant to this chapter:

A.D. Friedman. *Fundamentals of Logic Design and Switching Theory.*

D. Lancaster. *TTL Cookbook.*

Texas Instruments. *The TTL Data Book.*

# CHAPTER 2

# DESIGN OF COMBINATIONAL CIRCUITS

## AN OVERVIEW

In this chapter we will design combinational circuits by converting truth tables to AND/OR formulas. Section 2.1 describes the basic procedure; and Section 2.2 presents its modification. The modified method uses a representation called the Karnaugh map and yields better results. Both approaches can be formalized as computer programs that perform conversion automatically.

In many practical problems, the value of a function is not prescribed for all input combinations and these "don't-care" conditions usually allow one to simplify the circuit. We will develop a systematic procedure for handling these situations.

Logic functions are usually specified in words rather than by truth tables or formulas. We will show how to interpret verbal specifications and design circuits directly from them.

The closing section deals with engineering aspects of design: The effects of propagation delays, faulty circuits, and testing.

## IMPORTANT WORDS

Canonic formula, cascading, don't-care, essential test, fault, function table, glitch, hazard, Karnaugh map, minimization, prime implicant (essential, nonessential), product of sums, product term, sum of products, stuck-at fault, test set.

## 2.1 CANONIC REPRESENTATION OF TRUTH TABLES

The truth table in Figure 2.1 has only one line whose output is 1. If all the inputs of that line were ls, the table would represent the AND function. Although our table is not of this kind, we can transform it into an AND function by inverting all values in the $b$ column; in other words, by replacing $b$ with $\bar{b}$. Because this new table is AND of its variables $a$ and $\bar{b}$, we find that

$$f = a \cdot \bar{b} = a\bar{b}$$

Similar reasoning applies to any truth table that has a single 1 output, and we can thus formulate the following rule:

If a truth table contains only one line with a 1 output, it can be represented by an AND formula (a *product* term) whose structure is given by combining the input values on the corresponding line. This product term contains all of the input variables in their true or inverted form such that any variable whose value is 1 is left in its "true" form, while any variable whose value is 0 is inverted. A product term containing all input variables is called *canonic*.

The following examples show how to convert input combinations to their corresponding product terms for a three-input truth table of variables $a$, $b$, $c$:

| **Input Combination** | **Corresponding Product Term** |
|---|---|
| 010 | $\bar{a}b\bar{c}$ |
| 110 | $ab\bar{c}$ |

| $a$ | $b$ | $f$ |
|---|---|---|
| 0 | 0 | 0 |
| 0 | 1 | 0 |
| 1 | 0 | 1 |
| 1 | 1 | 0 |

→

| $a$ | $\bar{b}$ | $f$ |
|---|---|---|
| 0 | 1 | 0 |
| 0 | 0 | 0 |
| 1 | 1 | 1 |
| 1 | 0 | 0 |

**Figure 2.1.** Derivation of a product formula.

To make our finding more useful, we must extend it to truth tables that have more than one 1 output. Consider the truth table of function $g$ in Figure 2.2. If we separate the table into functions $u$ and $v$ each having a single 1 output, we can apply our procedure to $u$ and $v$ to obtain

$$u = a\bar{b} \qquad \text{and} \qquad v = ab$$

Because $g$ is 0 iff both $u$ and $v$ are 0, we find that

$$g = u + v = a\bar{b} + ab$$

This result can be generalized to any truth table: A truth table having $n$ 1 outputs would yield a sum of $n$ canonic product terms. Thus we can express any function as a *canonic sum of products*; that is, as an OR function of canonic product terms. Note this implies that every logic function can be implemented using only AND, OR, and NOT gates.

The procedure for constructing the canonic sum of products for a function $f$ can be summarized as follows:

1. Find all lines with $f = 1$.
2. Express each line found in Step 1 as a product term containing all of the input variables such that those whose value on the line is 1 remain in their true form while all others are inverted.
3. Apply OR to all obtained product terms.

Several examples are shown in Figure 2.3.

| $a$ | $b$ | $u$ | $v$ | $g$ |
|---|---|---|---|---|
| 0 | 0 | 0 | 0 | 0 |
| 0 | 1 | 0 | 0 | 0 |
| 1 | 0 | 1 | 0 | 1 |
| 1 | 1 | 0 | 1 | 1 |

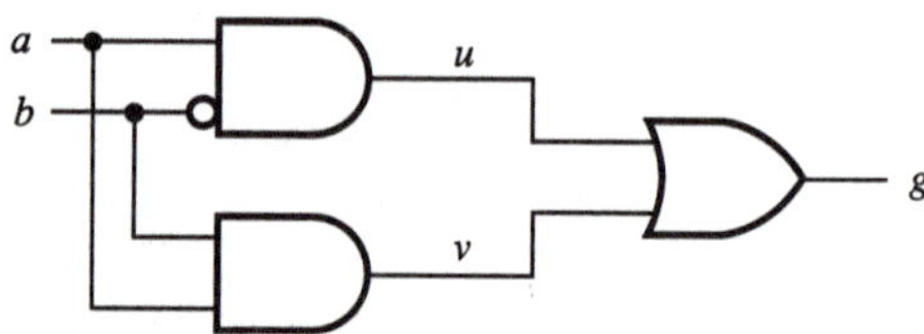


**Figure 2.2.** Derivation of the canonic sum of products.

| $a$ | $b$ | $c$ | $f$ | $g$ |
|---|---|---|---|---|
| 0 | 0 | 0 | 1 | 0 |
| 0 | 0 | 1 | 0 | 0 |
| 0 | 1 | 0 | 0 | 1 |
| 0 | 1 | 1 | 1 | 0 |
| 1 | 0 | 0 | 0 | 0 |
| 1 | 0 | 1 | 0 | 1 |
| 1 | 1 | 0 | 0 | 1 |
| 1 | 1 | 1 | 1 | 1 |

**Figure 2.3.** Examples of the canonic sum of products: $f = \bar{a}\bar{b}\bar{c} + \bar{a}bc + abc$; $g = \bar{a}b\bar{c} + a\bar{b}c + ab\bar{c} + abc$.

Circuits corresponding to canonic sum-of-product (CSP) formulas have one level of AND gates connected to a single OR gate and are thus often called two-level AND/OR circuits. The name neglects the fact that the circuit may also contain inverters.

Because our method is stated in terms of ANDs, ORs, 0s, and 1s, we may apply the principle of duality to obtain an alternative procedure for constructing the *canonic product of sums* (CPS):

1. Find all lines with $f = 0$.
2. Express each line found in Step 1 as a sum term containing all of the input variables such that variables whose value on the line is 0 remain in their true form while all others are inverted.
3. Apply AND to all obtained sum terms.

Note that in this procedure OR and AND, as well as 0 and 1 are interchanged.

Applying this procedure to the tables in Figure 2.3 yields

$$f = (a + b + \bar{c})(a + \bar{b} + c)(\bar{a} + b + c)(\bar{a} + b + \bar{c})(\bar{a} + \bar{b} + c)$$
$$g = (a + b + c)(a + b + \bar{c})(a + \bar{b} + \bar{c})(\bar{a} + b + c)$$

We now have systematic methods for finding two formulas that are formally different but logically equivalent. (Their truth tables are identical.) For a given truth table, one of the two forms may have fewer terms than the other, requiring fewer gates and connections. In that case the two results would not be equivalent from the engineering point of view because circuits with fewer gates usually require fewer chips and are thus cheaper and more reliable. As

| | $a$ | $b$ | $f$ | $g$ | $h$ |
|---|---|---|---|---|---|
| $a+b$ | 0 | 0 | 0 | 0 | 0 |
| $a+\bar{b}$ | 0 | 1 | 1 | 0 | 1 |
| $\bar{a}+b$ | 1 | 0 | 1 | 0 | 1 |
| $\bar{a}+\bar{b}$ | 1 | 1 | 1 | 1 | 0 |

**Figure 2.4.** Canonic sum of products may be less, equally, or more complicated than the canonic product of sums.

an example, for the tables shown in Figure 2.4 we obtain the following equivalent results:

| Function | Evaluation |
|---|---|
| $f = ab + a\bar{b} + \bar{a}b = a + b$ | Product of sums is better |
| $g = ab = (a + b)(\bar{a} + b)(a + \bar{b})$ | Sum of products is better |
| $h = \bar{a}b + a\bar{b} = (a + b)(\bar{a} + \bar{b})$ | Equal number of terms but |
| $= a \oplus b$ | only one XOR gate! |

The results for the function $h$ show that intuition and experience sometimes yield a better formula than either of the CSP or CPS methods. However, although *ad hoc* design procedures such as these may occasionally lead to substantial improvements, they are not a good engineering strategy—engineers prefer well-defined nonambiguous procedures. We will see in Section 2.3 that there exists a modification of canonic sums of products and products of sums that gives the best possible (minimal) two-level AND/OR circuits and thus provides an ideal design tool.

## Exercises

1. Verify the formula for Figure 2.2 by perfect induction.
2. Functions of more variables may require gates with many inputs, and such gates are not commercially available. Fortunately, a large AND can be obtained by cascading several ANDs with fewer inputs, as shown in Figure 2.5. A similar method applies to OR gates. Use this principle to implement the following truth table assuming that only inverters and two-input AND and OR gates are available.

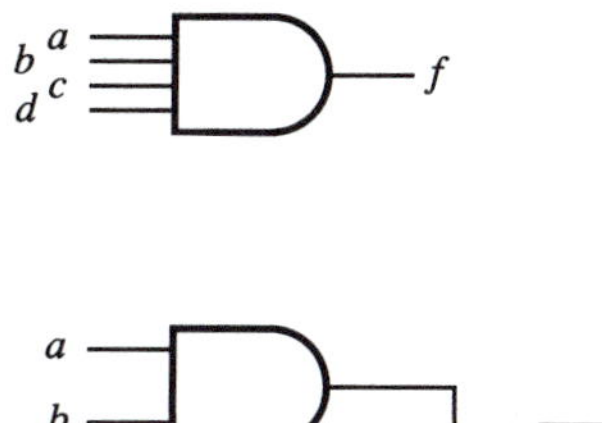


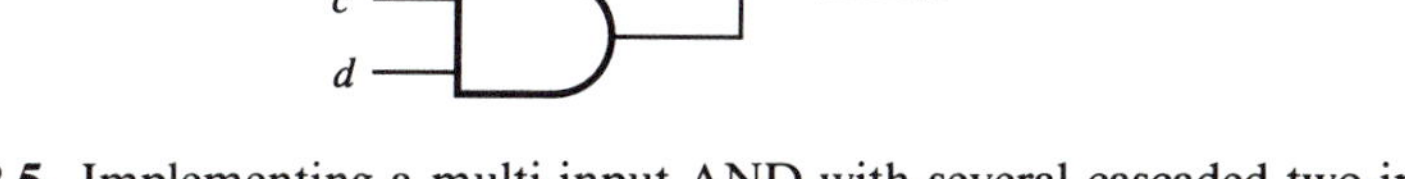

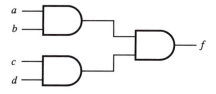

**Figure 2.5.** Implementing a multi-input AND with several cascaded two-input ANDs: $a \cdot b \cdot c \cdot d = (a \cdot b) \cdot (c \cdot d)$.

| ***a b c*** | ***f*** |
|---|---|
| 0 0 0 | 0 |
| 0 0 1 | 1 |
| 0 1 0 | 1 |
| 0 1 1 | 0 |
| 1 0 0 | 0 |
| 1 0 1 | 1 |
| 1 1 0 | 0 |
| 1 1 1 | 0 |

3. Show that NAND and NOR gates cannot be cascaded. As an example,

$$\overline{a \cdot b \cdot c} \neq \overline{\overline{a \cdot b} \cdot c}$$

4. Show that any function of one variable can be expressed as

$$f(x) = \overline{x} \cdot f(0) + x \cdot f(1)$$

where $f(0)$ and $f(1)$ are the values of $f$ for $x = 0$ and $x = 1$, respectively. This and related expressions are called Shannon's formulas.

5. Prove the following version of Shannon's formula for functions of two variables:

$$\begin{aligned} f(x_2,x_1) &= \overline{x_2} \cdot f(0,x_1) + x_2 \cdot f(1,x_1) \\ &= \overline{x_2} \cdot \overline{x_1} \cdot f(0,0) + \overline{x_2} \cdot x_1 \cdot f(0,1) \\ &\quad + x_2 \cdot \overline{x_1} \cdot f(1,0) + x_2 \cdot x_1 \cdot f(1,1) \end{aligned}$$

6. Generalize Shannon's formula to any number of variables and show how it can be used to derive the canonic sum-of-products procedure.
7. Use Shannon's formula from Exercise 5 to derive the canonic sum of products for XOR, NAND, NOR, and OR and compare the results with canonic formulas obtained from their truth tables.
8. Derive Shannon's formula for products of sums.

## 2.2 CIRCUITS USING ONLY NAND GATES

Canonic sum-of-product and product-of-sum procedures prove that any logic function can be converted to a combination of AND, OR, and NOT. We will now show that the NAND function is even more powerful in that any truth table can be expressed using only NANDs. We leave as an exercise for the reader the proof that this also holds for NOR.

As we know, we can write any function as a combination of NOT, AND, and OR; therefore it is sufficient to show that NAND can express AND, OR, and NOT (Figure 2.6). For any given function we can then find the canonic formula and replace all ANDs, ORs, and NOTs with NANDs.

To express NOT with NAND we use

$$a = a \cdot a$$

which gives

$$\overline{a} = \overline{a \cdot a} = \text{NAND}(a,a)$$

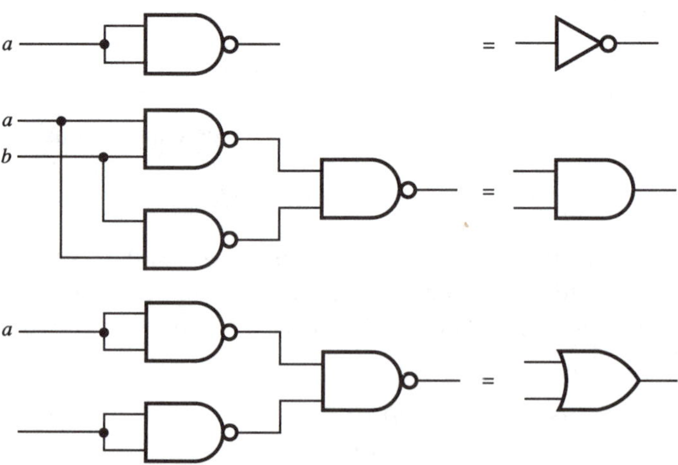


**Figure 2.6.** Implementing the inverter, AND, and OR with NAND gates.

To obtain the NAND replacement for AND and OR we use

$$x = \overline{\overline{x}}$$

We can now proceed as follows:

$$\begin{aligned} a \cdot b &= \overline{\overline{a \cdot b}} \\ &= \overline{\text{NAND}(a,b)} \\ &= \text{NAND}(\text{NAND}(a,b),\text{NAND}(a,b)) \end{aligned}$$

where we have used our NAND replacement for NOT. Similarly OR becomes

$$\begin{aligned} a + b &= \overline{\overline{a + b}} \\ &= \overline{\overline{a} \cdot \overline{b}} \\ &= \text{NAND}(\text{NAND}(a,a),\text{NAND}(b,b)) \end{aligned}$$

This completes our proof.

In addition to gate-by-gate conversion on the basis of the above formulas, there is another, simpler way to replace AND and OR gates with NAND. However, it applies only to sum-of-products formulas (canonic or not). We will demonstrate it on the following example:

$$\begin{aligned} f &= abc + \overline{b}c \\ &= \overline{\overline{f}} \\ &= \overline{\overline{abc + \overline{b}c}} \\ &= \overline{\overline{abc} \cdot \overline{\overline{b}c}} \\ &= \text{NAND}(\text{NAND}(abc),\text{NAND}(\overline{b}c)) \end{aligned}$$

The derivation of this expression seems complicated until one notices that the initial and the resulting logic diagrams (Figure 2.7) have identical structures. The only difference is that the second circuit uses NAND gates for all of the AND and OR gates in the first circuit. This replacement holds for all sum-of-product circuits and can be expressed as follows: To convert a sum-of-products circuit to NAND gates, replace all AND and OR gates with NAND gates.

We note, however, that:

The procedure applies to AND/OR circuits, but not to OR/AND circuits.

The procedure is applicable only to "pure" AND/OR functions. As an example, the procedure is invalid for the function

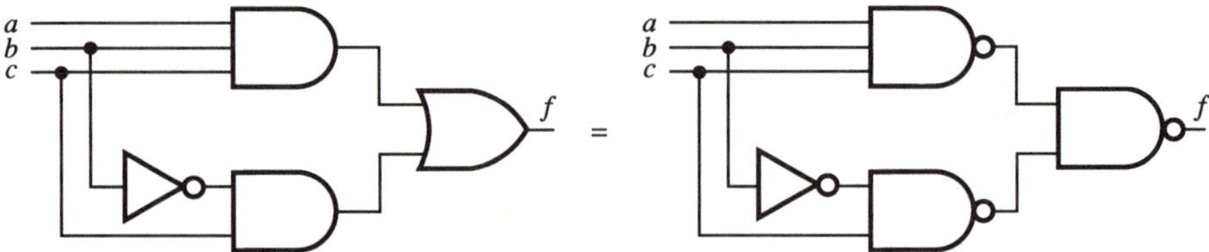


**Figure 2.7.** Two-level AND-OR circuits can be directly converted to NAND-NAND circuits. The structure remains the same.

$$f = ab + c$$

because one "leg" of this circuit comes directly from input $c$ without passing through an AND gate.

The procedure replaces ANDs and ORs, but we can also remove inverters because

$$a = \text{NAND}(a,a)$$

In practice, inputs are often available in both their true and negated forms, and inverters are therefore unnecessary. (Double-rail systems have one "rail" for the true signal and one for its inverse.)

Because any function can be expressed as a sum of products, our finding confirms that any function can be implemented using only NAND gates.

## Exercises

1. Derive the NOR formula for NOT, AND, and OR.
2. Derive a rule for converting OR/AND circuits to NOR circuits.
3. Prove the circuit conversion rules formally. Start from

$$f = \text{sum(product terms)}$$

   and proceed as in our example.
4. We stated that NAND replacement is invalid for functions that are not sums of complete products. Illustrate this by proving that

$$f = ab + c \neq NAND(NAND(a,b),c)$$

5. Is it possible to modify functions such as $f$ in the previous exercise so that the NAND replacement *can* be used? (Hint: Convert $f$ to a "pure" sum of products.)
6. Show that $\overline{a} = \text{NAND}(a,1) = \text{NOR}(a,0)$.

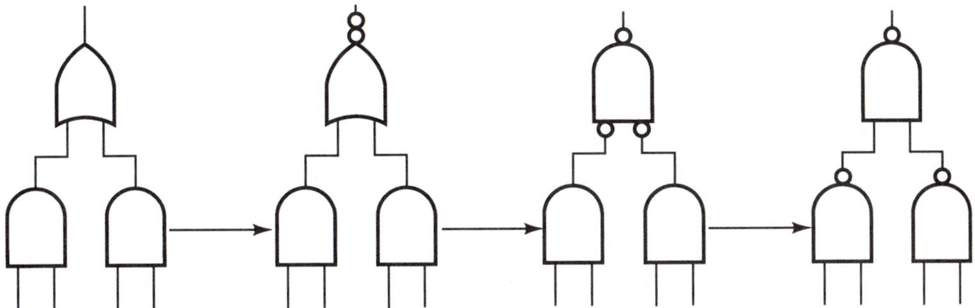

**Figure 2.8.** Symbolic proof of the conversion of AND/OR to NAND/NAND.

7. Figure 2.8 shows that AND/OR circuits can be converted to NAND/NAND circuits graphically, by moving bubbles. This technique, which is based on DeMorgan's rules, can be used even if the circuit is not AND/OR. Try it on a more complicated circuit.
8. Implement NAND($a,b,c,d,e,f$) with the 7430 eight-input NAND gate. Make sure to connect all input pins; otherwise, the gate might not work properly.
9. Is it possible to implement $abc + ad + bd$ using only two-input NAND gates?
10. Converting AND/OR circuits to NAND-only circuits often reduces the number of chips used because only one type of gate is needed. Test this claim by counting the number of chips needed to implement several sum-of-products functions using both methods.

## 2.3 KARNAUGH MAPS AND MINIMIZATION

The canonic sum of products of the truth table in Figure 2.9 can be simplified as follows:

$$\begin{aligned} f = a \cdot b + a \cdot \overline{b} &= a \cdot (b + \overline{b}) \\ &= a \cdot 1 \\ &= a \end{aligned}$$

This is a very useful result, but it seems to require a certain experience with Boolean algebra. Could we obtain the simplified formula directly from the table without algebraic manipulation? Is there some recognizable pattern that indicates when two product terms can be merged? We will now show that the answer to both these questions is yes.

Our transformation shows that two product terms can be merged if they differ in the value of exactly one symbol, in this case, in the value of $b$. When

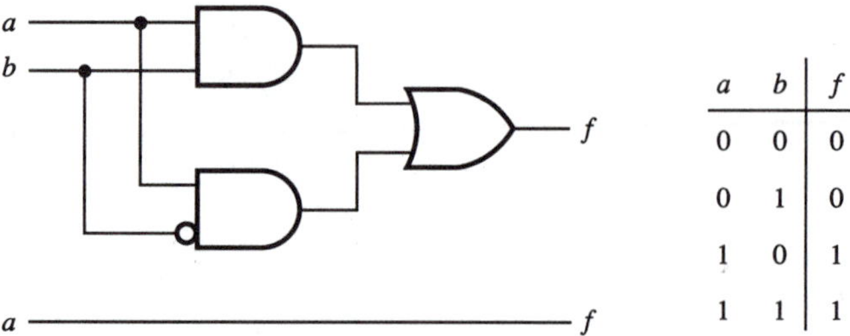


| a | b | f |
|---|---|---|
| 0 | 0 | 0 |
| 0 | 1 | 0 |
| 1 | 0 | 1 |
| 1 | 1 | 1 |

**Figure 2.9.** Truth table whose canonic formula can be simplified so that no gates are required.

we relate the product terms to their input combinations, we see that two input combinations can be merged if they differ in the value of exactly one input. Consequently, to spot a pair of terms that can be merged we must find lines having output 1 that differ in the value of exactly one input variable. Each such pair of lines can be reduced to a single product term containing only those symbols that have the same value in both input combinations; the "different" variable cancels out. In our example, we must look at lines 10 and 11; the different variable is $b$ and can be dropped.

One may easily apply this procedure to functions of two variables, however, it becomes awkward for larger truth tables. As an example, it is not immediately obvious that one can use the procedure to simplify the functions $f$ and $g$ in Figure 2.10 to

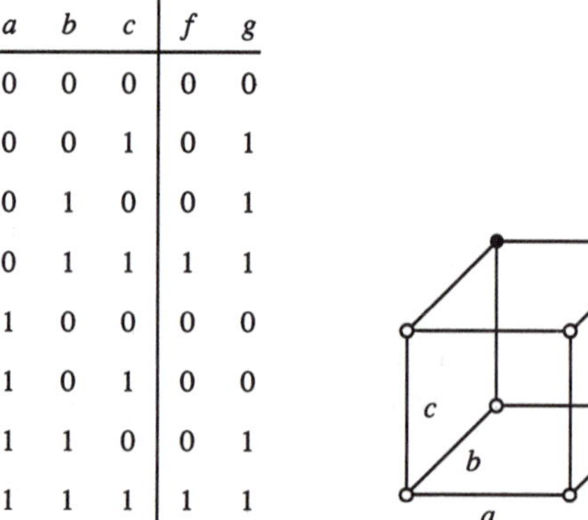

| a | b | c | f | g |
|---|---|---|---|---|
| 0 | 0 | 0 | 0 | 0 |
| 0 | 0 | 1 | 0 | 1 |
| 0 | 1 | 0 | 0 | 1 |
| 0 | 1 | 1 | 1 | 1 |
| 1 | 0 | 0 | 0 | 0 |
| 1 | 0 | 1 | 0 | 0 |
| 1 | 1 | 0 | 0 | 1 |
| 1 | 1 | 1 | 1 | 1 |



**Figure 2.10.** Functions whose canonic formulas can be simplified; a three-dimensional representation of $f$, with $f = 1$ vertices filled.

$$f = bc \qquad \text{and} \qquad g = b + \bar{a}c$$

To simplify the following presentation we will now introduce another definition: Two terms or input combinations are (logically) adjacent if they differ in the value of exactly one input variable. The term "adjacent" comes from geometric representations of input combinations in a binary-valued multidimensional space; Figure 2.10 shows an example. Note that logical adjacency is exactly what we are looking for when we want to determine if two AND terms can be merged.

If we could draw truth tables as cubes in a multidimensional binary space, logical adjacency would be easy to spot because logically adjacent combinations would be spatially adjacent. This would make merging very easy. Multidimensional drawing is impractical but representations called *Karnaugh maps* provide a similar geometric insight and make adjacencies very visible.

Unlike truth tables, which are one-dimensional columns, Karnaugh maps are two-dimensional grids of intersecting rows and columns (Figure 2.11) with function values written into the cells. Their distinguishing feature is the special labeling of rows and columns: Labels of geometrically adjacent rows differ in exactly one value and the rows are thus logically adjacent. Consequently, any two cells that are vertically adjacent correspond to logically adjacent terms. The same holds for columns and horizontally adjacent cells.

Our findings about simplification and the concept of a Karnaugh map allow us to conclude that a simplified AND/OR formula can be obtained as follows:

1. Construct a Karnaugh map.
2. Find all pairs of horizontally or vertically adjacent cells containing 1 and express them as product terms. Only variables having the same value in both cells appear in the final expression; any variable whose value changes from cell to cell drops out.

   As an example, the function in Figure 2.11 can be expressed as $f = bc$ because $a$ drops out.
3. If the Karnaugh map contains several terms, the formula for the complete function is their logic sum. This is because cells with 1s correspond to truth

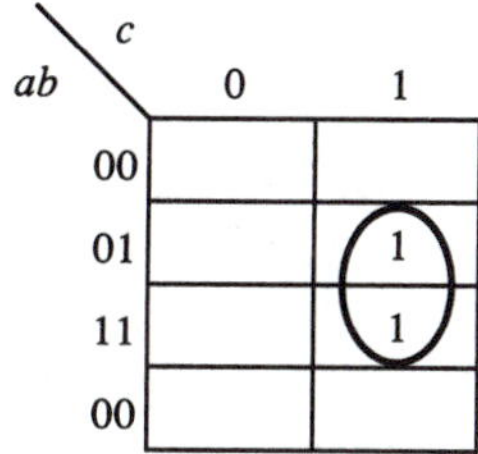


**Figure 2.11.** Karnaugh map of function $f$ from Figure 2.10.

table lines with 1s, and all such lines must be covered, as in the CSP method.

Figure 2.11 produces only one term and this step does not apply.

When one examines this method more closely, one finds that it can be further generalized. Applying our rules to the map in Figure 2.12, we get

$$\begin{aligned} f &= \bar{a}b + ab = (\bar{a} + a)\cdot b \\ &= 1\cdot b \\ &= b \end{aligned}$$

The geometric meaning of this simplification is that we have merged two pairs of previously merged cells. Note that the final expression again includes only those symbols that have the same value in all four cells. Merging can thus be continued with patterns that have the same shape and are adjacent. Note that adjacency applies also across the horizontal borders because border rows are logically adjacent. The same holds for border columns.

The pattern and the product term obtained when further merging is impossible is called a *prime implicant*, or PI. Our goal, to find a simple set of terms that covers all ls, is thus achieved by finding a set of PIs that covers all ls. The smallest set of PIs that covers a given Karnaugh map is the minimal sum of products for that function. Because we equate "minimal" (that is, having the least number of terms) and "best," we conclude that the above procedure produces the optimal circuit for the given function. Note that this view of circuit optimization is merely one of convenience because the true goal of design is to minimize the number of chips rather than the number of gates. However, converting minimized AND/OR circuits to NAND gates usually yields very good results, even in terms of the number of chips.

We will now formulate a preliminary set of rules for constructing the minimal sum of products and illustrate it on Figure 2.13.

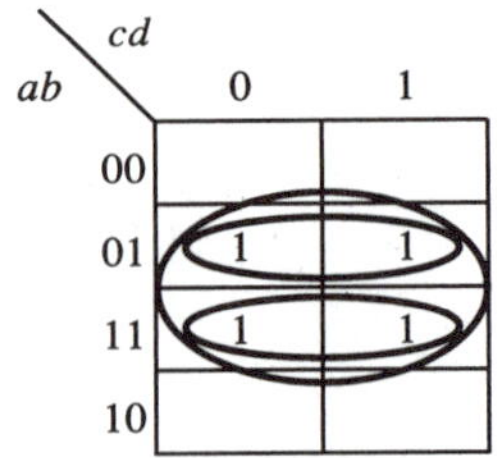


**Figure 2.12.** Karnaugh map that can be simplified twice.

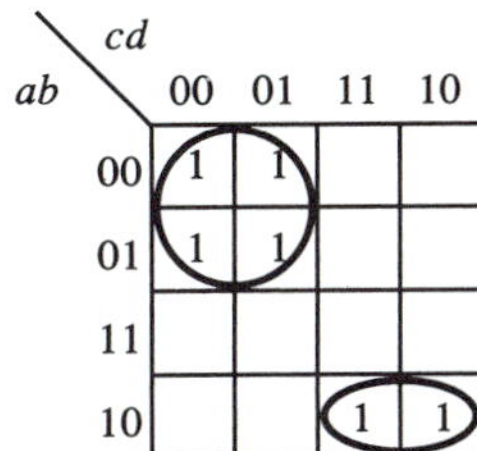

**Figure 2.13.** Karnaugh map and its PIs, $f = \bar{a}\bar{c} + a\bar{b}c$.

To obtain a minimal sum of products,

1. Draw the Karnaugh map.
2. Find all PIs.
3. Apply OR to the PIs.

The upper left map in Figure 2.14 shows that there are situations in which applying OR to all PIs gives a formula with too many terms. In this case, applying OR to all PIs produces

$$f = \bar{a}\bar{b}c + \bar{a}bd + a\bar{b}\bar{c} + \bar{a}cd$$

which is correct but not minimal because the last term is unnecessary. To prevent such redundancy, we must apply OR only to the smallest number of PIs that covers all of the ls. This is best done by dividing PIs into two groups:

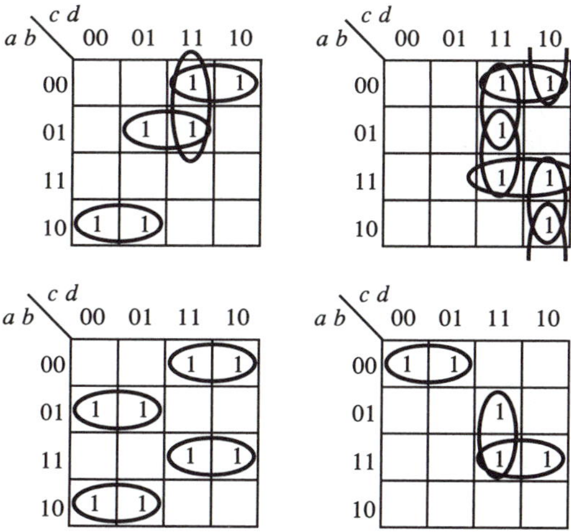

**Figure 2.14.** Karnaugh maps having essential and nonessential PIs, no essential PIs, and only essential PIs. The minimal expressions are (clockwise from top left) $\bar{a}\bar{b}c + \bar{a}bd + a\bar{b}\bar{c}$, $\bar{a}\bar{b}c + bcd + ac\bar{d}$ (one of two expressions possible), $\bar{a}\bar{b}\bar{c} + bcd + abc$, and $\bar{a}\bar{b}c + \bar{a}b\bar{c} + abc + a\bar{b}\bar{c}$.

Those that cannot be omitted because they cover a 1 not covered by any other PI; such PIs are called *essential.*

All others.

We can now precisely state the minimization procedure as follows:

1. Draw the Karnaugh map.
2. Find all PIs.
3. Identify essential PIs and include them in the formula.
4. Add the smallest possible number of PIs to cover the ls not included in the essential PIs.

The leftmost Karnaugh map in Figure 2.14 contains three essential PIs—$\bar{a}\bar{b}c$, $\bar{a}bd$, and $a\bar{b}\bar{c}$—that completely cover all 1s. The fourth PI is thus unnecessary, and the minimal sum of products is

$$f = \bar{a}\bar{b}c + \bar{a}bd + a\bar{b}\bar{c}$$

In closing, note the following:

1. One can formally state the procedure for constructing the minimal covering and use it to write a computer program. However, functions that can be represented by Karnaugh maps can be minimized by visual inspection without following formal rules.

2. One must practice to become proficient at using Karnaugh maps. After solving a few problems, one develops the ability to recognize PIs visually—they form rectangular or square patterns and may extend across borders. The number of cells in a PI must be a power of 2. With practice, even finding minimal covering becomes easy.

3. Some Karnaugh maps have no essential prime implicants and others consist entirely of essential PIs (Figure 2.14).

4. One normally uses Karnaugh maps only for functions of two, three, or four variables; extensions to five and six variables are possible but awkward. Beyond this, there is no way to draw truth tables so that logical adjacency can be easily recognized by visual inspection. The minimization process must then be performed by executing the corresponding algorithm, either manually or by using a computer program.

5. The number of calculations required to minimize a function increases very rapidly with the number of variables. For functions having twenty or more variables, even computer programs take too long to find the optimal solution. In such cases one must settle for using simpler algorithms that find suboptimal solutions giving good but not necessarily the best results.

6. One may also apply the method of Karnaugh maps to the dual task of finding the minimal product of sums.

7. Karnaugh maps and related methods were very important when only primitive circuit components, such as gates, were available. Modern complex chips contain circuits with tens or hundreds of thousands of gates, and the minimization of small circuits has lost some of its importance. The emphasis of minimization has therefore shifted toward the design of chips themselves because simplifying the internal logic allows us to put more functions on one chip.

8. As we have already stated, formulas obtained with a Karnaugh map or a computer program are optimal only in a limited sense:

For a given Karnaugh map there may be several different optimal AND/OR formulas, all requiring the same number of gates.

The minimal product-of-sums formula may be simpler than the sum-of-products formula. Both expressions should be constructed and compared.

There may be a simpler solution using different gates. As an example, the XOR function requires two inverters, two AND gates, and one OR gate, but only one XOR gate. Unfortunately, there is no systematic method for finding the simplest possible formula with restrictions other than those implied by AND/OR circuits.

In some cases special structures (multilevel, cellular, and so forth) give much better results than AND/OR circuits.

When we apply minimization to individual functions in circuits with multiple outputs we may obtain good but not optimal results because a simpler circuit may often be found by enlarging individual expressions and sharing some terms (Figure 2.15). It is possible to extend sum-of-products optimization to multiple output functions but the algorithm is considerably more complicated than the minimization of individual functions and we will not present it.

## Exercises

1. Prove that Karnaugh maps give the minimal sum of products.
2. Describe how one could use Karnaugh maps to find the minimal product of sums.
3. Find the minimal sum of products and the minimal product of sums for the Karnaugh maps in Figure 2.16 and compare the results.
4. Prove that a PI is a rectangular or square pattern having $2^n$ cells that satisfies certain restrictions. (Hint: Use mathematical induction.)
5. Design a four-input comparator that outputs 1 when $(a,b) = (c,d)$. Obtain a solution with commercial chips and convert it to NAND gates and inverters.

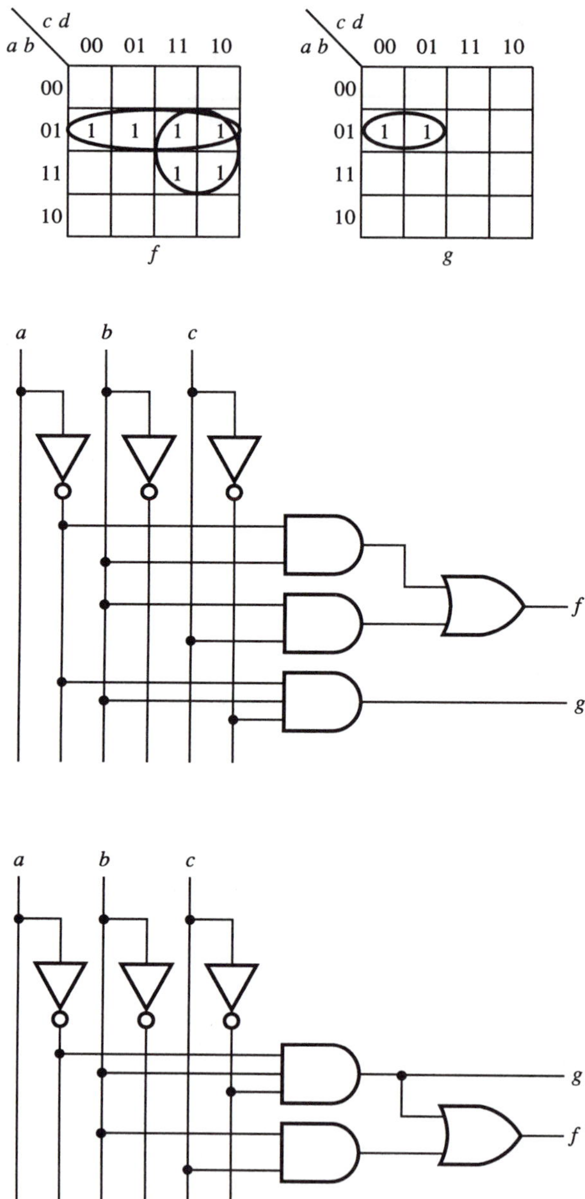


**Figure 2.15.** Optimization of individual outputs does not always give the optimal overall result: top, Karnaugh maps; middle, a circuit obtained by separate optimization; bottom, a simpler AND–OR implementation using a shared gate.

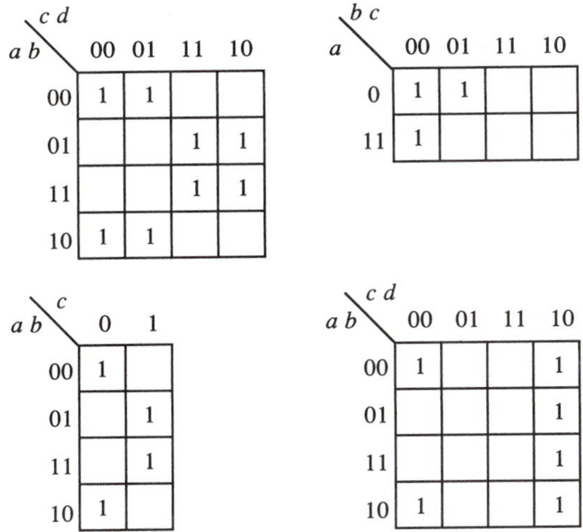


**Figure 2.16.** Examples of Karnaugh maps.

6. Consider a function of four variables. How many cells does its Karnaugh map have? How many variables would be included in a prime implicant containing 1, 2, 4, 8, or 16 cells? What is the relation between the size of a PI and the complexity of its product term?
7. Explain why the circled cells in Figure 2.17 are not prime implicants. Find the correct prime implicants.

## 2.4 DON'T-CARE CONDITIONS

In many problems, certain input combinations can never occur and the corresponding outputs are thus irrelevant. These entries are called *don't-cares* and are usually denoted $X$.

To construct a circuit we must, of course, start from a complete truth table and the missing values must be filled in but the choice has no effect on the correct operation. This gives us an extra degree of freedom and an opportunity to simplify the circuit. We will now give two examples of circuits with

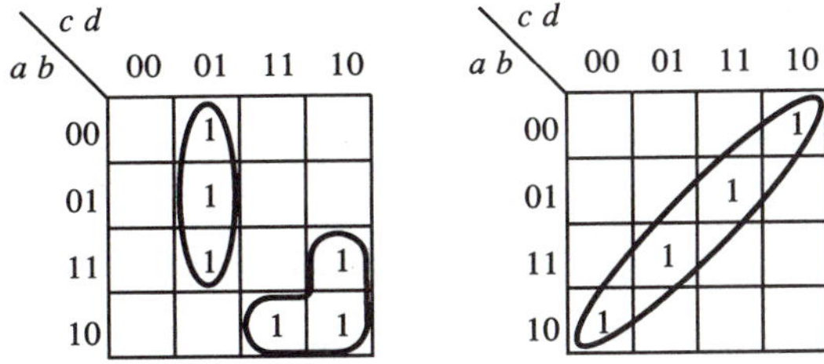


**Figure 2.17.** Marked cells are not PIs.

don't-cares to show that the intelligent replacement of $X$s with 0s and 1s can simplify the circuit. Note that a don't-care is not a new logic value, it is just a placeholder for a 0 or a 1.

**Example 1.** To design a circuit that satisfies the specification in Figure 2.18, we must replace all $X$s with 0s or 1s, choosing the values so as to make the solution as simple as possible. We can achieve this goal by maximizing the size of PIs because the larger a prime implicant, the simpler its product term. The best result can be obtained by the following procedure:

Mark the don't-care cells and replace $X$s with 1s.

Find the optimal solution that covers all original 1s. Take advantage of cells originally containing $X$s if this enlarges the PIs:

Find all prime implicants.

Identify essential PIs and include them in the formula.

Add the smallest possible number of PIs to cover the original 1s not yet covered. (Don't-care cells that are not part of any selected PIs are effectively replaced with 0s.)

The procedure is a simple extension of the minimization of ordinary Karnaugh maps. The important point is that we only need to cover those 1s that were in the map before we replaced $X$s with 1s. For the function in Figure 2.18 we find

$$f = \overline{a}b$$

With practice, one learns how to select the best replacements for $X$s by visual inspection of the original map and without drawing the intermediate table.

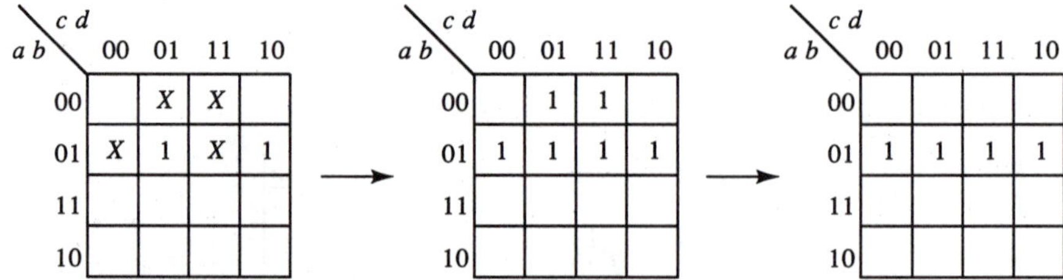


**Figure 2.18.** Minimization with don't-cares. From left to right: The original specification, the intermediate map, and the implied assignment of 0s and 1s to $X$s implied by the final solution.

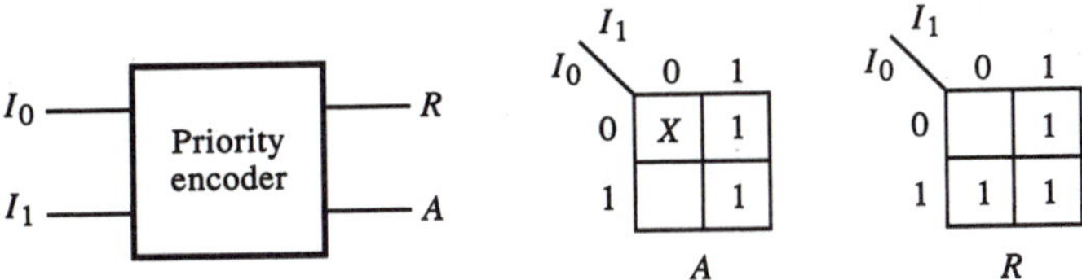


**Figure 2.19.** Two-input priority decoder.

**Example 2.** Consider the "priority decoder" in Figure 2.19. Its outputs $A$ and $R$ are assumed to be connected to a computer and its inputs are controlled by two devices that occasionally request some operation from the computer. The two devices have different priorities. The higher priority device uses line $I_1$; line $I_0$ is for the lower priority device. We define the term "priority" as follows: If both devices request service simultaneously, only request $I_1$ is granted because at most one request can be satisfied at a time.

The function of outputs $R$ and $A$ is as follows: $R$ (Request pending) is 1 iff there is a service request; in other words, when at least one of the $I$ inputs is active. The value of $A$ is the code (address) of the highest priority request; its value is 0 when only $I_0$ is On and 1 whenever $I_1$ is On. (Recall that $I_1$ has higher priority.) What should the value of $A$ be when neither $I_0$ nor $I_1$ are On? Because the computer does not care about $A$ when $R$ is Off, the value of $A$ for $(I_1,I_0) = (0,0)$ is "don't-care."

Figure 2.19 shows the maps of $R$ and $A$ obtained from this specification; the solutions are

$$R = I_0 + I_1 \qquad \text{and} \qquad A = I_1$$

The don't-care notation is used not only in Karnaugh maps but also in a shorthand representation of truth tables called *function tables*. Figure 2.20 shows the function table of a four-input priority decoder, an extension of our priority decoder. Note that it uses $X$s for both output and input values. The advantage of function tables is that they are much more compact than truth tables. Function tables are frequently used in component data books.

### Exercises

1. Design the $a$ and $c$ circuits of a BCD-to-seven-segment decoder that controls the individual segments of a seven-segment display (Figure 2.21). The circuit has four inputs that represent the BCD code of the digit to be displayed and seven outputs that determine whether individual segments are On or Off.
2. Design the four-input priority decoder from Figure 2.20.

| $I_0$ | $I_1$ | $I_2$ | $I_3$ | $R$ | $A_1$ | $A_0$ |
|---|---|---|---|---|---|---|
| 0 | 0 | 0 | 0 | 0 | $X$ | $X$ |
| 1 | 0 | 0 | 0 | 1 | 0 | 0 |
| $X$ | 1 | 0 | 0 | 1 | 0 | 1 |
| $X$ | $X$ | 1 | 0 | 1 | 1 | 0 |
| $X$ | $X$ | $X$ | 1 | 1 | 1 | 1 |

**Figure 2.20.** Function table of a four-input priority encoder.

3. Convert the function table in Figure 2.20 to a truth table. Compare the size and readability of both.
4. Prove that our algorithm for don't-cares gives the minimal result.

## 2.5 DIRECT DESIGN FROM VERBAL SPECIFICATION

It is often advantageous to design a circuit directly from its verbal specification without first constructing a Karnaugh map. We will now give several examples of such situations and show how to handle them.

**Example 1.** We are to design a circuit that recognizes BCD codes. Its output should be 1 when input $(k,l,m,n)$ is a valid BCD code and 0 otherwise. The solution can be derived from a Karnaugh map or by the following series of transformations:

$$\begin{aligned}
f &= (k,l,m,n) \text{ is a BCD code} \\
&= (k,l,m,n) \text{ is the code of one of } 0,\ldots,9 \\
&= ((k,l,m,n) = 8) + ((k,l,m,n) = 9) + ((k,l,m,n) = 0,\ldots,7) \\
&= ((k,l,m,n) = 1000) + ((k,l,m,n) = 1001) + (k = 0) \\
&= k\bar{l}\bar{m}\bar{n} + k\bar{l}\bar{m}n + \bar{k} \\
&= k\bar{l}\bar{m} + \bar{k}
\end{aligned}$$

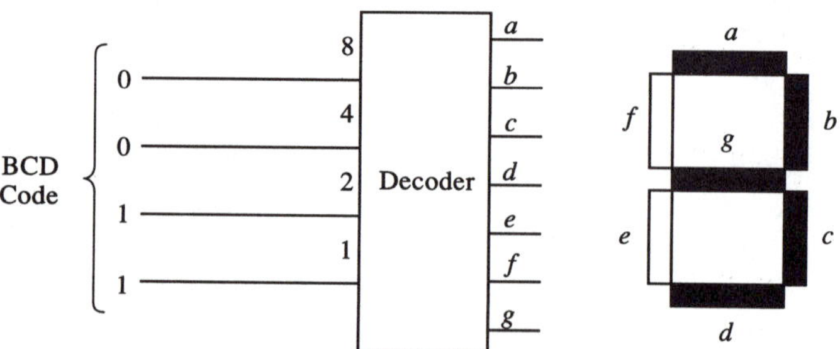


**Figure 2.21.** Seven-segment display and its control.

We have used the fact that $(k,l,m,n) = 1000$ defines the product $k\overline{l}\overline{m}\overline{n}$, and 1001 corresponds to $k\overline{l}\overline{m}n$. The result is the same as if we had used a Karnaugh map.

**Example 2.** Assume that a certain computer circuit uses signals $C_2$, $C_1$, and $C_0$ as the operation code (*opcode*) that determines the operation to be executed, and that signal $S$ represents the current state of execution. Let the opcodes be as follows:

| | | | |
|---|---|---|---|
| 000 ADD | 001 SUB | 010 MULT | 011 DIV |
| 100 NOT | 101 AND | 110 OR | 111 XOR |

We are to design a circuit that outputs 1 whenever

The opcode represents an arithmetic operation and the state is 1

The opcode represents a two-input logic operation and the state is 0

The opcode represents NOT.

***Solution*** Arithmetic opcodes and no others start with 0. The first condition is thus satisfied when $C_2$ is Off and S is On:

$$\overline{C_2}\cdot S$$

The two-input logic operations are AND, OR, and XOR. They all start with 1 and their second or third bits are 1. This is equivalent to

$$C_2(C_1 + C_0)$$

To satisfy the state requirement, $S$ must be 0. The complete second condition is thus

$$C_2(C_1 + C_0)\overline{S}$$

To satisfy the third condition, $C_2C_1C_0$ must be 100, which gives

$$C_2\overline{C_1}\,\overline{C_0}$$

Our function $f$ is On if any of the three conditions holds and so

$$f = \overline{C_2}\cdot S + C_2(C_1 + C_0)\overline{S} + C_2\cdot\overline{C_1}\cdot\overline{C_0}$$

**Example 3** We need a formula to describe the following conditions:

$$a\oplus b = 0 \qquad \text{or} \qquad a = 1$$

***Solution*** If we denote the first condition by $C_1$ and the second by $C_2$, the desired formula is

$$f = C_1 + C_2$$

Condition $C_1$ is True when $a \oplus b = 0$; in other words, when $\overline{a \oplus b} = 1$. This means that

$$C_1 = \overline{a \oplus b}$$

Condition $C_2$ is True when $a = 1$ and so

$$C_2 = a$$

The combined conditions can thus be expressed as

$$f = \overline{a \oplus b} + a$$

**Example 4** We are to design a circuit that examines a twenty-bit address code $(A_{19}, A_{18}, \ldots, A_0)$ and outputs a 1 when the code starts with 1101.

If we wanted to use truth tables, we would either have to construct a truth table with twenty variables (over a million lines) or run a very time-consuming computer program. Yet the answer is obvious: The device is On when $A_{19}$, $A_{18}$, $\overline{A_{17}}$, and $A_{16}$ are all On:

$$f = A_{19} \cdot A_{18} \cdot \overline{A_{17}} \cdot A_{16}$$

**Example 5** We want to derive a formula describing the condition

$$(C_1\colon a \oplus b = 0) \qquad \text{AND} \qquad (C_2\colon (b \oplus 0) + bc \neq a \oplus b)$$

If $C_1$ holds, $C_2$ can be simplified to

$$C_2\colon b \oplus 0 + bc \neq 0$$

or

$$C_2\colon b \oplus 0 + bc = 1$$

Perfect induction shows that

$$b \oplus 0 = b$$

and $C_2$ can be thus reduced to

$$C_2\colon b + bc = 1 \qquad \text{or} \qquad b = 1$$

The complete condition is thus

$$C_1 \cdot C_2 = (\overline{a \oplus b}) \cdot b = 1$$

After these rather unambiguously stated problems, let us now examine several less formal verbal specifications.

**BUT**

The meaning of

*f* is On if *a* and *b* are On but *c* is Off

is

*f* is On if *a* and *b* are On and *c* is Off

which gives

$$f = a \cdot b \cdot \bar{c}$$

**IF-THEN**

In English, the statement

IF $a = b$
THEN $f = 1$

is somewhat ambiguous, but the most likely meaning is "if $a = b$ then $f = 1$" or "ELSE $f = 0$."

**IF-THEN-ELSE**

This is an explicit statement of the preceding:

IF $a = b$
THEN $f = 1$
ELSE $f = 0$

An interesting way to solve problems involving conditions is to use a *flowchart* as in Figure 2.22. To determine the value of *f*, we must first decide whether $a = b$. If $a = b$ is True then $f = 1$, otherwise $f = 0$. The oval in the flowchart represents condition $a = b$ and its value (True or False) selects cells in the Karnaugh map. Rectangles determine function values in the selected

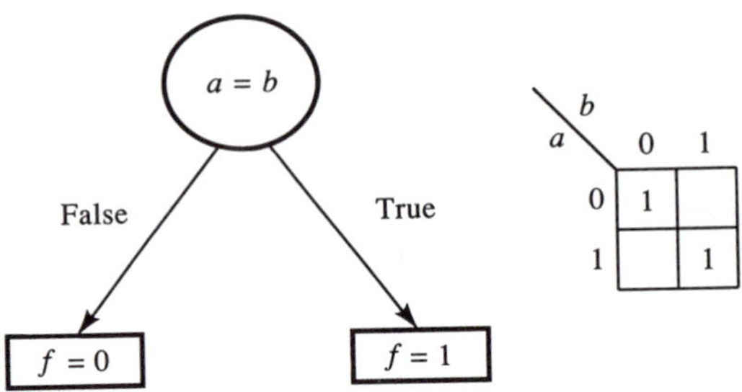


**Figure 2.22.** Flowchart representation of an IF specification, and its conversion to a Karnaugh map.

cells. One can then use the flowchart to derive the Karnaugh map; map variables are those that appear in the ovals.

The True path corresponds to cells for which $a = b$; these are the combinations (0,0) and (1,1). The rectangle to which this path leads shows that in these cells $f = 1$. The False path corresponds to cells for which $a \neq b$ and requires that $f = 0$. The map obtained from this analysis gives

$$f = \overline{ab} + ab$$

## Several Functions in One Specification

The following example involves two functions:

IF $a$ AND $b$ are 1
THEN $f = 1$
ELSE $g = 1$

or simply

IF $a$ AND $b$
THEN $f$
ELSE $g$

Assuming that the unspecified values are 0, we get the flowchart and Karnaugh maps in Figure 2.23 and the result is

$$f = a \cdot b \qquad \text{and} \qquad g = \overline{a \cdot b} = \overline{a} + \overline{b}$$

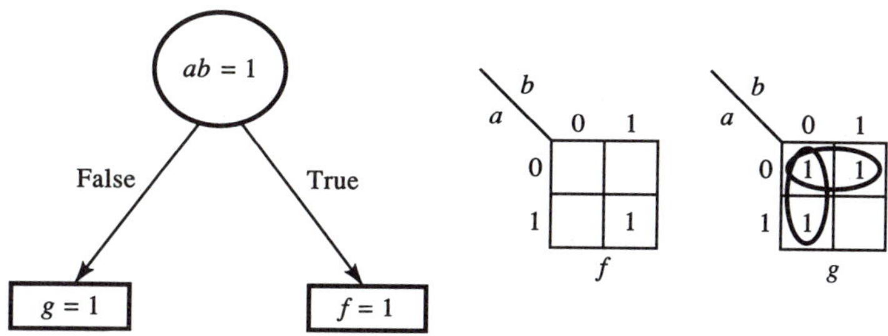


**Figure 2.23.** Flowchart and Karnaugh maps for the functions $f = ab$, $g = \bar{a} + \bar{b}$.

## NESTED IF

IF $a$ AND $b$
THEN
IF $c$
THEN $f$
ELSE $g$

Assuming that unstated alternatives mean zero value, we get the diagram and the Karnaugh map in Figure 2.24 and the result is

$$f = a \cdot b \cdot c \qquad \text{and} \qquad g = a \cdot b \cdot \bar{c}$$

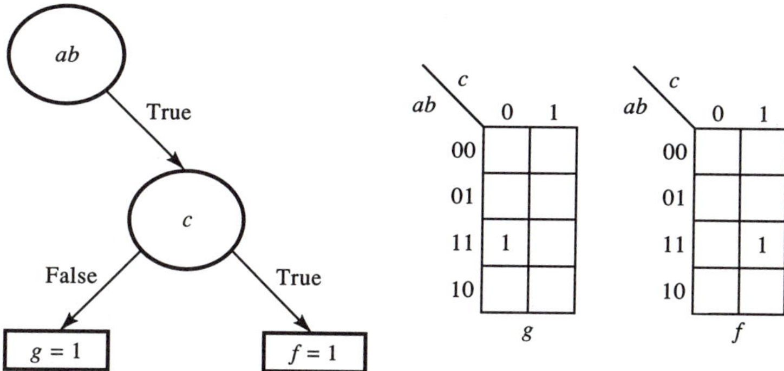


**Figure 2.24.** Flowchart and Karnaugh maps for the functions $f = a \cdot b \cdot c$, $g = a \cdot b \cdot \bar{c}$.

### Function Values Involving Other Signals

The function

$$f \text{ is } 0 \text{ if } a = b, \text{ otherwise } f = z$$

is best evaluated using the generalized Karnaugh map in Figure 2.25. This map contains not only 0s and 1s but variables as well. In general, such a map can contain even logic expressions. It is used as follows:

Get PIs for cells containing identical expressions.

Multiply each prime implicant by the contents of the cell.

Cover nonzero cells in the usual way.

Note that if the map contains only 0s and 1s, the procedure gives the same result as the standard method. The ordinary map is thus a special case of a generalized Karnaugh map.

The following example is a bit more complicated:

$$\begin{aligned} f &= a \text{ if } x \text{ is not equal to } y \\ &\text{otherwise } f = b \cdot c \text{ if } z \text{ is } 1 \end{aligned}$$

With the usual assumption that $f = 0$ for the unspecified combinations, we can construct the flowchart and map in Figure 2.26 and the solution is

$$f = a \cdot (x \cdot \overline{y} + \overline{x} \cdot y) + b \cdot c \cdot (\overline{x}\overline{y} + xy) \cdot z$$

### Unless

The statement

$$f \text{ is } 1 \text{ unless } c \text{ or } d \text{ are } 1$$

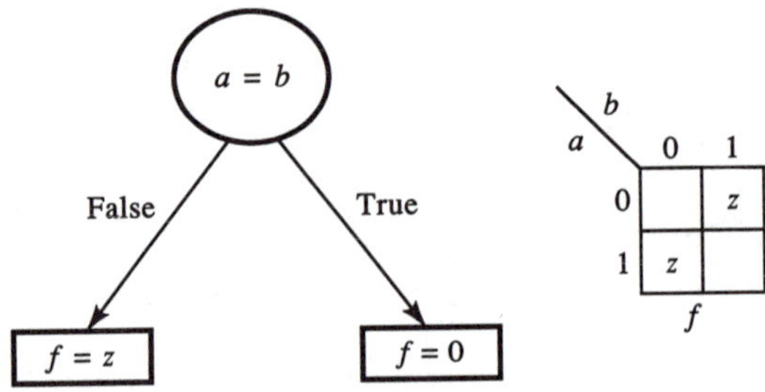


**Figure 2.25.** Generalized Karnaugh maps with PIs. The result is $f = (a\overline{b} + \overline{a}b) \cdot z$.

means

$$\text{IF } c \text{ OR } d \text{ are } 1$$
$$\text{THEN } f \text{ is } 0$$
$$\text{ELSE } f \text{ is } 1$$

It is left to the reader to show that the result is

$$f = \overline{c + d} = \bar{c} \cdot \bar{d}$$

**Exercises**

1. Find formulas describing the following conditions:
   a. $x \oplus y = 0$ AND $z = 1$.
   b. $x \oplus y = 1$ AND $x = 0$.
   c. ($x = 0$ AND $y = 1$) OR ($x \neq y$), but only if $z = 1$.
2. Construct a circuit that recognizes all additive codes (OR, ADD) in Example 2.
3. Construct a circuit that recognizes all multiplicative codes (AND, MULT) in state 1 and all additive codes in state 0.
4. Formalize the meaning of

   "$f$ is 1 if either $a$ or $b$ are 1"

5. Formalize the meaning of

   "$f$ is 1 only if $a$ and $b$ are the same"

6. Prove the validity of generalized Karnaugh maps.
7. Can generalized Karnaugh maps be used to calculate product-of-sums expressions?
8. Extend generalized Karnaugh maps to don't-cares.
9. Convert the problems and exercises from this section to Karnaugh maps to see if the solutions can be simplified.

## 2.6 WHAT CAN GO WRONG

Malfunctions can develop in digital circuits at any stage—during their design and testing, in production, or in the field. Malfunctions may have various causes: The specification may have been wrong or ambiguous, the design method may not have been used properly, an important physical parameter may not have been considered, the manufacturing process or materials may

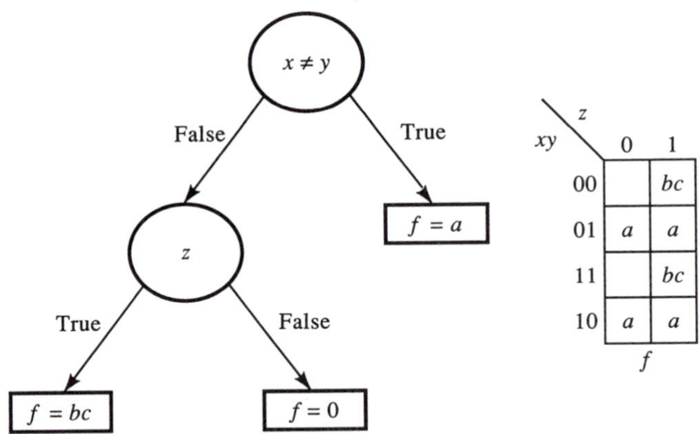


**Figure 2.26.** Problem solved with a generalized Karnaugh map.

have been imperfect, the environment in which the product was used may have been too harsh, and so on. To design circuits correctly and to guarantee their proper operation, one must understand all of the parameters that affect their operation and test the completed products. We will now deal with two physical aspects of circuits that fall in this area: the effect of component delays on circuit operation and the principles of testing.

## The Effect of Delays on Combinational Circuits

The Karnaugh map in Figure 2.27 can be described by

$$f = \overline{a}b + ac$$

Let us assume that the inverter has a non-negligible delay but that the delays of other gates are zero. (The latter assumption is made to simplify our analysis.) The timing diagram in Figure 2.27 shows the output of the circuit when $a$ makes transitions $0 \rightarrow 1 \rightarrow 0$ and $b = c = 1$. According to the Karnaugh map, this input sequence should not have any effect on the output. In reality, the a transition and the inverter delay cause a brief $1 \rightarrow 0 \rightarrow 1$ output change. This spurious signal is called a *glitch* and the situation that caused it is called a *hazard.* Hazards are caused by unbalanced delays in two signal paths that meet at some point in the circuit.

How serious are hazards? The answer depends on the function of the signal. A 10-nsec glitch in a signal that drives a traffic light is irrelevant because nobody can see a 10-nsec signal and the light cannot produce such a short flash anyway. A hazard is also irrelevant if the system that depends on the signal is designed to ignore the glitch or if the event that causes the glitch never occurs in real operation.

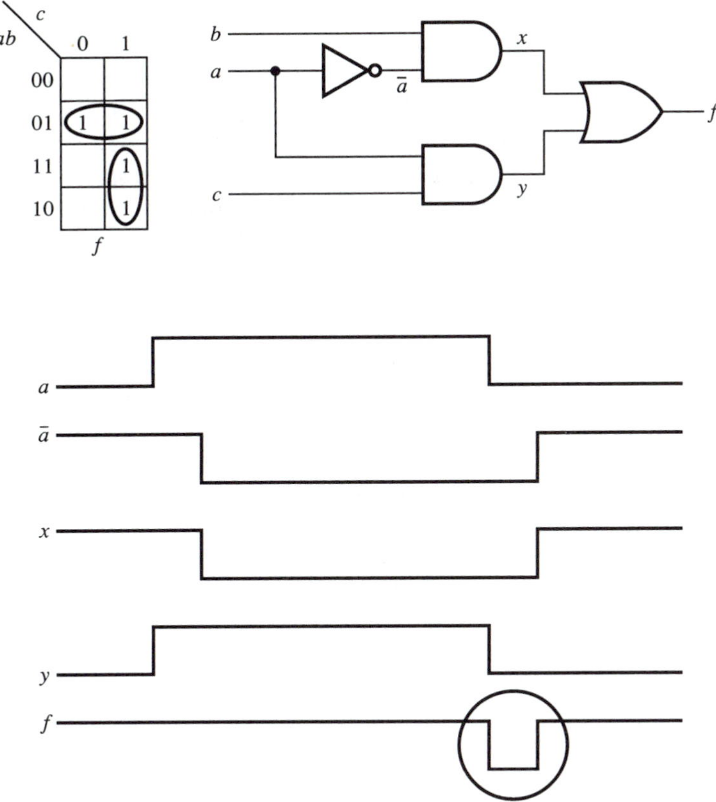


**Figure 2.27.** Effect of delays; assume $b = c = 1$.

In some situations, hazards may be catastrophic. When the signal steers a complex sequential circuit, an unanticipated glitch could drive it off the predicted course. We will return to this problem in Chapter 4.

To analyze our example and find a remedy, it is useful to reexamine the Karnaugh map. Figure 2.27 shows that the glitch occurs during the transition between two adjacent nonoverlapping PIs. The output of the circuit is the OR of two PIs; if there were no delays in the circuit the transition would replace the 1 produced by the first AND gate by the 1 from the second AND gate and no change of output would occur. In the presence of delays, however, the second 1 appears some time after the first 1 changes to 0, and this causes the glitch.

If a transition between two PIs may cause a glitch, what about transitions within PIs? Each PI corresponds to an AND gate and it is easy to see that a transition within the PI involves a change in a signal not connected to its AND gate whereas none of the inputs of this AND gate change. Consequently, the outputs of the gate and the circuit do not change and a transition within a PI thus does not cause a glitch.

Our analysis implies that hazards can be removed: A hazard is due to a transition between adjacent PIs, and for every two adjacent PIs there is a PI that contains both adjacent cells—the PI that was eliminated during minimization. If we add this PI to the circuit the hazard disappears because the transition is now within the added PI and consequently does not cause a glitch. In our example, the hazard is removed by changing

$$f = \bar{a}b + ac \qquad \text{and} \qquad f = \bar{a}b + ac + bc$$

This modification increases the complexity of the circuit and to some extent defeats minimization. However, the circuit is still simpler than a canonic sum of products and thus all the benefits of minimization are not lost.

Because hazards are due to unequal path delays, they can also be removed by carefully controlling the timing of individual signal paths or by using special delay-producing devices; this approach is, however, unsafe and it is not recommended. The best defense against hazards is to design the circuit so that if a hazard occurs, it has no effect. This is not as difficult as it may seem because most circuits are sequential and are controlled by timing signals that activate them only at predetermined intervals. Timing can be designed to let signals stabilize and to let glitches disappear before signal values are used as inputs. The disadvantage of this approach is that it may slow down the operation of the system.

## Exercises

1. Explain why the glitch in our example occurs on the 1→0 transition but not on the 0→1 transition. Formulate a rule to identify the dangerous transitions by inspection of the circuit or the map?
2. Analyze hazards in product-of-sums circuits and show how they can be removed.
3. Can a minimal sum of products contain a hazard if the corresponding minimal product of sums does not?
4. Analyze the effect of delays in other gates in Figure 2.27.
5. Propagation delays are sometimes useful. Figure 2.28 shows how they can be used to detect 0→1 and 1→0 transitions. Explain why the propagation delay in the inverter causes the circuit on the left to recognize a 0→1 transition (the positive edge) and why the second circuit recognizes a 1→0 transition. How can two circuits be logically equivalent and yet perform different functions?
6. Hazards that can be eliminated by redesigning the circuit are sometimes called logic hazards and those that cannot are called function hazards.

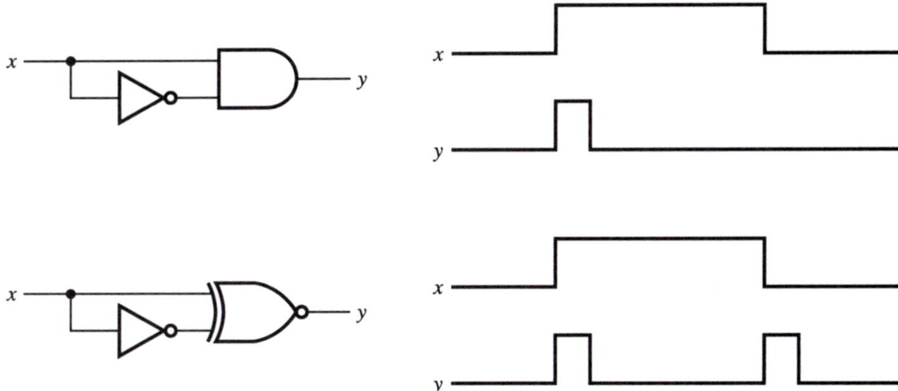


**Figure 2.28.** Two edge recognizers.

Explain why hazards due to the change in a single variable are logic hazards but those that are caused by the change of more than one variable are function hazards.

**Testing and Test Generation**

Digital systems must be tested during design, production, and in the field. Because testing is very important and because different situations require different approaches, many test methods have been developed.

When the number of products (boards or chips) to be tested is large, testing is performed automatically by computer-driven automatic test equipment (ATE). An ATE applies predetermined inputs to the unit under test (UUT), monitors outputs, and compares them with the outputs of a simultaneously tested "known good" unit or with previously calculated values. Testing restricted to logic values is called logic testing; testing of voltages, currents, and timing is called parametric. We will deal only with logic testing based on precalculated values and will restrict our interest to calculating the test set, which is the collection of input combinations and expected outputs.

The guiding criteria for the calculation of a test set are:

1. Testing should give a high assurance that a passing component is faultless. Note that this does not mean that the testing must be exhaustive. As an example, testing that is restricted to observing circuit outputs that are controlled via circuit inputs cannot guarantee that the circuit's internal operation is faultless or that all its internal parts are good, however, it is usually sufficient.
2. The test set should be small, otherwise testing will take too long and will cost too much. Because complex circuits cannot be tested fully in a reason-

able amount of time, their testing must be based on some simplifying assumptions and on a measure of test completeness (such as a percentage of selected possible faults that must be tested). The constructed tests must guarantee that some prescribed minimal value of this measure is attained.

3. Calculation of the test set should not be too complicated, otherwise it could be more expensive than the testing itself.

How can test patterns be calculated? For combinational circuits, the obvious approach is exhaustive testing with all input combinations of the truth table. This is reasonable if the circuit has only a few inputs but it is unrealistic for multi-input circuits. For sequential circuits, exhaustive testing is out of the question. To simplify test generation of more complex circuits, we must devise a model of how a component can fail and assume that only these types of faults occur. The price of this simplification is that it makes certain types of faults undetectable. To be useful, a fault model must not only decrease the number of input patterns to be tested but must also uncover a large proportion of faulty products.

The most common fault model is the single stuck-at permanent fault, which assumes that

If a circuit is faulty, it contains exactly one fault.

The fault is equivalent to a short between a logic signal and the ground (the logic value is then stuck at 0) or between the signal and the power (the logic value is then stuck at 1). In reality signal lines may also be shorted to one another (a "bridge" fault) and other more complex fault patterns may be present.

If the fault is present it is permanent ("hard") and does not go away. In reality, faults are often intermittent ("soft") and come and go with changes in temperature, humidity, vibrations, electrical loading, and so on. Intermittent faults are very difficult to deal with.

The single stuck-at permanent fault model is very popular because it leads to manageable test generation algorithms, substantially reduces the size of the test set, and catches most faulty circuits.

To generate tests for a given circuit, we first examine the logic diagram and select faults that we consider critical or likely to occur. A test generation program then finds an initial test set to detect at least a certain percentage of the selected faults, and reduces this set by eliminating redundant tests. An input combination detects a fault if it forces the faulty circuit to produce an output that is different from the output of the faultless circuit. Initial test generation is performed either by simulation or by a special test-generating algorithm.

The most common test generation method is to simulate the correct circuit and the faulty circuit and to find combinations that produce the different outputs. This is repeated until tests that detect, for example, 90% of the selected faults are obtained.

Sophisticated test generation procedures are beyond the scope of this book and we will instead demonstrate a very simple approach on the example in Figure 2.29.

The most obvious way to find test inputs is to draw truth tables for the correct circuit and the faulty circuit and compare them to uncover all tests that detect the faults. This initial test set can then be minimized by selecting the smallest number of test patterns that will detect all faults. The circuit and faults marked in Figure 2.29 have the following truth tables:

| *abc* | correct | 1-s-a-0 | 2-s-a-1 | 3-s-a-0 | 4-s-a-1 | 5-s-a-1 |
|---|---|---|---|---|---|---|
| 000 | | | 1 | | | |
| 001 | | | 1 | | | 1 |
| 010 | | | 1 | | 1 | |
| 011 | 1 | 1 | 1 | | 1 | 1 |
| 100 | | | 1 | | | 1 |
| 101 | | | 1 | | | 1 |
| 110 | 1 | | 1 | 1 | 1 | 1 |
| 111 | 1 | 1 | 1 | 1 | 1 | 1 |

Because we are interested not in circuit outputs but rather in the differences between correct and faulty outputs, we will convert the truth tables into the following form, in which intersections of faults and the inputs that detect them are marked with an *x*:

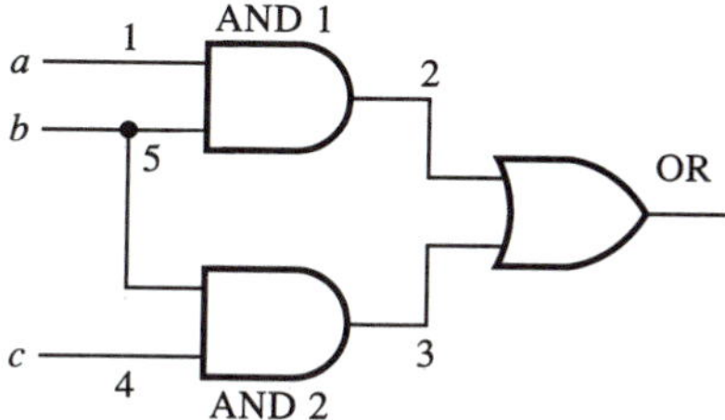


**Figure 2.29.** Circuit with several randomly selected stuck-at faults: 1-s-a-0, (point 1 stuck at 0), 2-s-a-1, 3-s-a-0, 4-s-a-1, 5-s-a-1.

| abc | 1-s-a-0 | 2-s-a-1 | 3-s-a-0 | 4-s-a-1 | 5-s-a-1 |
|---|---|---|---|---|---|
| 000 | | $x$ | | | |
| 001 | | $x$ | | | $x$ |
| 010 | | $x$ | | $x$ | |
| 011 | | | $x$ | | |
| 100 | | $x$ | | | $x$ |
| 101 | | $x$ | | | $x$ |
| 110 | $x$ | | | | |
| 111 | | | | | |

This table shows that

The output of the 1-s-a-0 circuit is different from the correct output only when $(abc) = (110)$. The only input pattern that detects this fault is thus (110).

The output of the 2-s-a-0 circuit is different from the correct output for inputs (000), (001), (010), (100), and (101). Any of these combinations can be used to detect the fault.

3-s-a-0 can only be detected by $(abc) = (011)$.

4-s-a-1 can only be detected by (010).

5-s-a-1 can be detected by (001), (100), and (101).

In summary, the set (000, 001, 010, 011, 100, 101, 110) detects all the selected faults. To minimize the time required to test the circuit, we will now select the smallest subset that covers all the faults. This minimization problem resembles covering a Karnaugh map, and its solution is similar. We start by identifying essential tests that must be included because they detect a fault that cannot be detected by any other test in the set. In our example, (110) is essential because no other test detects 1-s-a-0. On the other hand (000), which detects fault 2, is not essential because fault 2 can also be detected by any of (001, 010, 100, 101). Clearly, essential tests are those that detect faults with a single $x$ in their column. Examination of the table shows that the following tests are essential:

(010) (011) (110)

The next step is to check whether the essential tests detect all faults. In our case we find that 5-s-a-1 is not covered and we must thus add one of the tests that cover the 5-s-a-1 column. This gives three equivalent minimal test sets:

(010), (011), (110), (001)

(010), (011), (110), (100)

(010), (011), (110), (101)

Each of these test sets detects all selected faults and requires only one-half of the tests that would be needed to test the whole truth table.

The procedure that we have just described requires constructing the complete truth table for each fault, and this is very time-consuming. More efficient methods are available but they are much more difficult to understand and their coverage is beyond the scope of this book.

Progress in technology results in increasingly complex digital circuits, and this makes testing ever more important and difficult. Consequently, testing and design for testability have become two of the most important problems of modern digital systems and the subject of much research.

## Exercises

1. Explain in detail how simulation could be used to find the initial test set.
2. Some faults cannot be detected. Give an example. (Hint: Consider redundant circuits in which the same signal is produced by two different paths.)
3. Which of tests (00), (11) detects fault 1 in Figure 2.30? Repeat for faults 2 and 3.
4. Find the minimal test set for the faults in Figure 2.30 using:
   a. simulation.
   b. truth table comparison.
5. Analyze the circuit in Figure 2.30 assuming that two simultaneous stuck-at faults are possible.

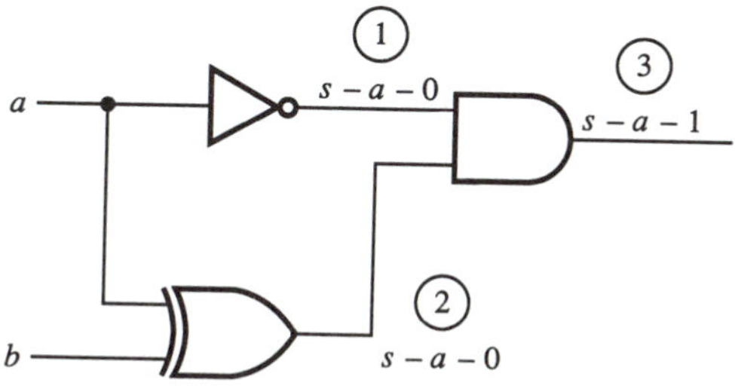


**Figure 2.30.** A circuit to be tested.

6. Can a single test detect s-a-0 and s-a-1 at the same location?
7. Name one advantage and one disadvantage of testing by comparison with a known-good circuit.

## SUMMARY

This chapter introduced several methods of abstract design of combinational circuits and pointed to certain physical realities that affect the behavior of digital systems and must be considered.

We began by developing the canonic approach that lets us express any truth table as a sum of products or as a product of sums. The method is mechanical and applies to any truth table but results in unnecessarily complex circuits. Its importance lies in the fact that it is the basis of more powerful methods.

The fact that all logic functions can be expressed with NOT, AND, and OR is interesting, but we showed that NAND is even more powerful because all functions can be obtained using NAND gates only. The same applies to NOR. Moreover, all two-level sum-of-product circuits can be mechanically converted to NAND gates, and NOR gates can similarly replace product-of-sums circuits. Conversion to NAND gates is very useful because it usually reduces the number of chips needed for the circuit.

We introduced Karnaugh maps as one of several related methods that produce minimal sums of products and minimal products of sums. In modern design, Karnaugh maps have lost some of their importance, but the use of computerized minimization by other methods keep growing because it is needed to reduce the size of internal circuits in chips.

In many situations, circuit outputs for certain input combinations are irrelevant. Such outputs are called don't-cares, and we showed that they usually allow further circuit simplification.

Verbal specification of combinational functions can usually be directly converted into a formula without the use of the truth table. We gave several examples to show how to proceed in such cases and derived the concept of a generalized Karnaugh map.

The chapter ends with a discussion of hazards and tests—topics related to faulty behavior. Hazards are undesirable signal transitions caused by signal delays and can cause faulty outputs even in circuits designed correctly on the abstract level. We saw that hazards can be removed. The existence of hazards draws attention to the need for careful timing analysis of logic circuits.

All circuits must be tested during design, production, and in the field. Testing must be systematically planned, particularly if the circuits are produced in large quantities. Test patterns can be generated automatically either by simulation or by using a test generation procedure. We presented test generation from truth tables, assuming the stuck-at fault model. Testing and test generation are among the most pressing problems of modern digital design and fabrication.

## REVIEW QUESTIONS

1. Define the following: Product term, canonic formula, sum of products, product of sums, AND/OR circuit, Karnaugh map, minimization, prime implicant, essential prime implicant, don't-care, function table, hazard, glitch, stuck-at fault, essential test, and test set.
2. Describe the following procedures: Finding canonic formula, using Karnaugh maps to minimize a function, minimization with don't-cares, and finding a minimal test set using the truth table.

## REFERENCES

The following titles further described in the references at the end of the book are relevant to this chapter:

A. D. Friedman. *Fundamentals of Logic Design and Switching Theory.*

T. W. Williams, and K. P. Parker. *Design for Testability.*

R. E. Gasperini. *Digital Troubleshooting.*

Z. Kohavi. *Switching and Finite Automata Theory.*

D. Lancaster. *TTL Cookbook.*

J. F. Passafiume, and M. Douglas. *Digital Logic Design Tutorials and Lab Exercises.*

K. D. Wagner, and E. J. McCluskey. *Pseudorandom Testing.*

# CHAPTER 3

# DESIGN WITH MORE POWERFUL COMPONENTS

## AN OVERVIEW

Modern digital design increasingly relies on components much more powerful than individual gates. Most of these components are sequential but some are combinational and are well-suited as gate replacement. The combinational devices can be divided into two groups. The first group (multiplexers, programmable logic devices, and read-only memories) contains chips that can be used for general logic design, somewhat like gates but more easily and more efficiently. The second group (encoders, decoders, arithmetic functions, and comparators, and others) includes devices that implement specialized but frequently needed functions.

## IMPORTANT WORDS

Active High/Low, address, data selector/distributor, decoder, demultiplexer, EEPROM, enable, encoder, EPROM, HAL, LSI, MSI, multiplexer, PAL, PLA, PLD, PROM, RAM, ROM, RWM, SSI, VLSI, UVPROM.

## 3.1 INTRODUCTION

Although gates form the basis of all logic circuits, design using only individual gates is now obsolete. Currently available integrated circuits implement functions equivalent to hundreds or thousands of gates, which enables one to design better circuits more quickly: to reduce the number of components they require as well as their size, power consumption, and cost, and to improve their speed and reliability.

We will divide the building blocks presented in this chapter into two major categories: those that can be used to build arbitrary logic circuits and those that perform specialized tasks. Devices of the second type implement universally required functions such as encoding and decoding, and their main contribution to circuit design is that they eliminate the need to build commonly needed functions from scratch.

General purpose combinational devices include multiplexers, read-only memories, and programmable logic devices (Figure 3.1).

1. Multiplexer (MUXs) can implement functions described by truth tables. To realize a function with a multiplexer, we connect input variables to control inputs and use them to select one of several data lines. Data lines are connected directly to function values obtained from the truth table and when the select signal selects a data line the function value appears on the output pin. Because each line of the truth table requires a data pin, multiplexers cannot be used for large truth tables.
2. *Read-only memory* (ROM) chips store values in memory cells inside the chip and their control inputs select the desired cell. If we use the cells to store truth table values, a ROM implements a combinational circuit. Because ROMs do not require data input pins, they can realize very large tables.
3. *Programmable logic devices* (PLDs) do not store a copy of a truth table but rather a sum-of-products formula. To make this possible, a PLD contains an array of partially connected AND and OR gates and final connections are made ("programmed") by the manufacturer or the user. Because a minimized formula is usually much more compact than a truth table,

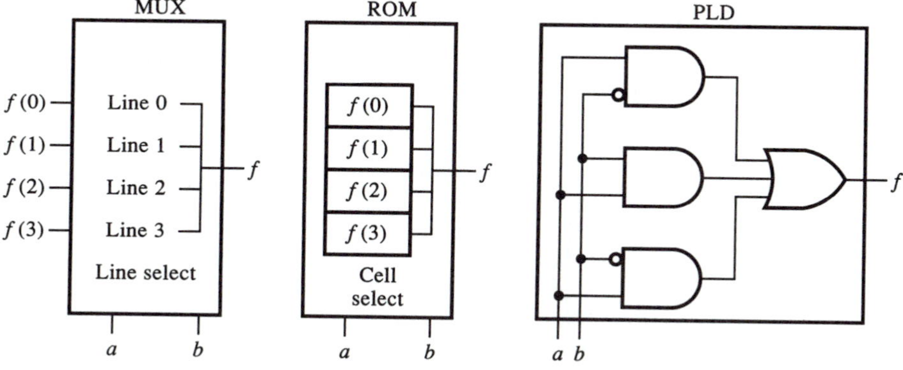


**Figure 3.1.** Three types of devices suited for logic design: multiplexers, read-only memories, and programmable logic devices.

PLD-based circuits normally require chips that are simpler than ROMs for the same function. The size of the implemented function that can be implemented with a PLD is limited more by the number of internal AND and OR gates than by the number of inputs.

In spite of their advantages, MUXs, ROMs, PLDs, and similar devices do not make individual gates obsolete. Gates remain necessary as "logic glue" to connect more complicated chips (Figure 3.2) and to implement simple functions for which complex chips are unnecessarily powerful.

The devices introduced above cover a broad range of circuit complexities and design styles. Depending on their complexity, Gates, MUXs, ROMs, and PLDs can be classified as follows: Gates are small-scale integration (SSI) components, MUXs are medium-scale integration (MSI) components, and most ROMs and PLDs are large-scale (LSI) or very-large-scale (VLSI) integration devices. (SSI devices have up to 10 gates per chip; MSI devices have 10–100 gates per chip; LSI devices have 100–1000 gates per chip; and VLSI devices have over 1000 gates per chip. The boundaries between LSI and VLSI devices are not well defined.) Multiplexers are very simple to use and do not require any special design or production tools. ROMs and PLDs, on the other hand, must be tailored for a specific use by the chip manufacturer or by special but inexpensive "programming" equipment.

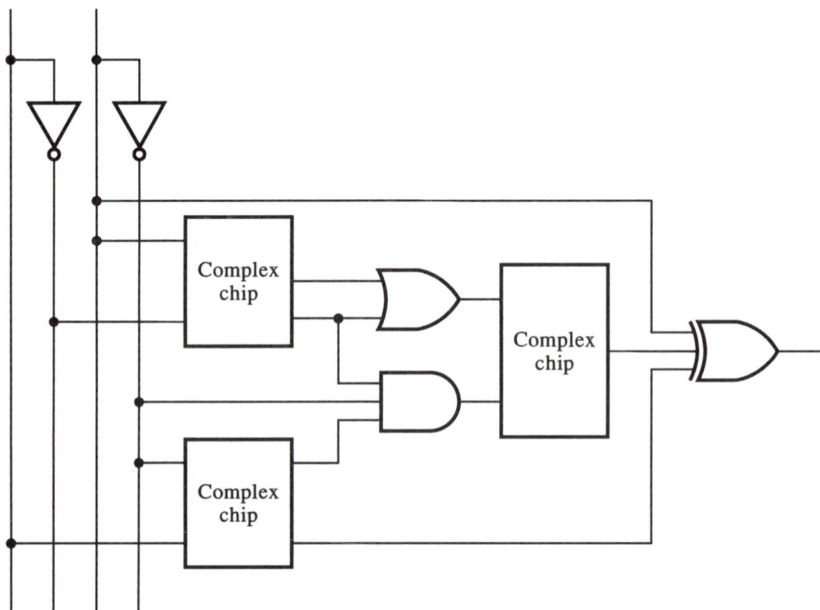


**Figure 3.2.** Elementary functions are necessary to "glue" more complicated chips together.

PLDs and ROMs in logic applications are usually found in more complicated circuits that are produced in larger quantities whereas MUXs are used to reduce the number of chips needed for simple logic functions. It is interesting to note that only PLDs were originally designed for logic design. Multiplexers are used primarily to select one of several streams of data while ROMs are used to store computer programs, and the use of these devices in logic design remains of secondary importance.

The increasing sophistication of devices has had a direct effect on design procedures. This is most obvious in the growing reliance on computer-assisted design tools that incorporate minimization and other functions. Even the role of minimization has changed. Instead of using minimization to simplify functions of a few variables, it is now used mainly to reduce large expressions to make them fit on PLDs and to simplify the internal structure of chips.

After this brief introduction we will now explore MUXs, ROMs, and PLDs in more detail.

## 3.2 MULTIPLEXERS

An MUX is essentially a switch that is controlled by "select" lines. When activated, the MUX connects the data line identified by the code on the select lines to the output. In the example in Figure 3.3, "select" combination 101

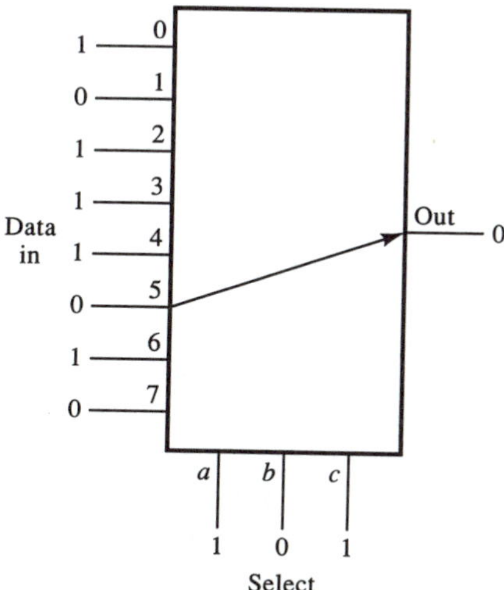


**Figure 3.3.** Principle of a MUX.

connects data line 101 (decimal 5) to the output, and the output thus becomes 0. Because the MUX selects one of $n$ values, it is also called a data selector.

Figure 3.4 shows the pinout of a commercially available multiplexer, the 74151 one-of-eight data selector, which has one output, eight data inputs, and three select pins. The chip is activated or deactivated (enabled or disabled) by the strobe signal $S$. When $S$ is active, the values $a,b,c$ select a data line to be connected to the output. When inactive, $S$ disables the chip, which means that values on the select lines and the data lines have no effect, and the output remains Low. Note that the strobe signal is denoted $\overline{\text{S}}$ and that its input is shown with an inverting bubble. These conventions indicate that this signal is active Low, activated by a Low voltage level.

As an example of the use of an MUX in logic design, the circuit in Figure 3.4 implements our familiar majority voter using only one 74151 chip. One can design a combinational function with an MUX as follows:

1. Draw the truth table.
2. Connect function variables to select pins.
3. Connect function values to appropriately labeled data pins.

If the desired function is too large, MUXs can be cascaded into trees as in Figure 3.5. The principle is simple: The select input of the second-level MUX chooses one of the first-level MUXs, and its select inputs choose a line of the truth table. Second-level selection corresponds to choosing one of two halves of the truth table.

One can design a two-level MUX tree as follows:

1. Divide the truth table into equal sections. The number of sections is given by the type of the second-level MUX.
2. Connect the outputs corresponding to individual sections of the truth table to the data lines of the individual first-level MUXs.
3. Connect the outputs of the first-level MUXs to the data lines of the second-level MUX following the order of the sections.
4. Connect the least significant variables, those which are rightmost in the truth table, to first-level select lines.
5. Connect the remaining variables to the select lines of the second level of the tree.

In principle, MUX trees can be used for any number of variables and may be any number of levels deep. In practice, however, MUXs are practical only for functions of a few variables because each input connection requires one data line and large truth tables would require too many connections and chips. We will now show that one may use MUXs more efficiently by using an alternative design method called *folding*. With folding, one can double the size of the truth table that a given MUX can handle.

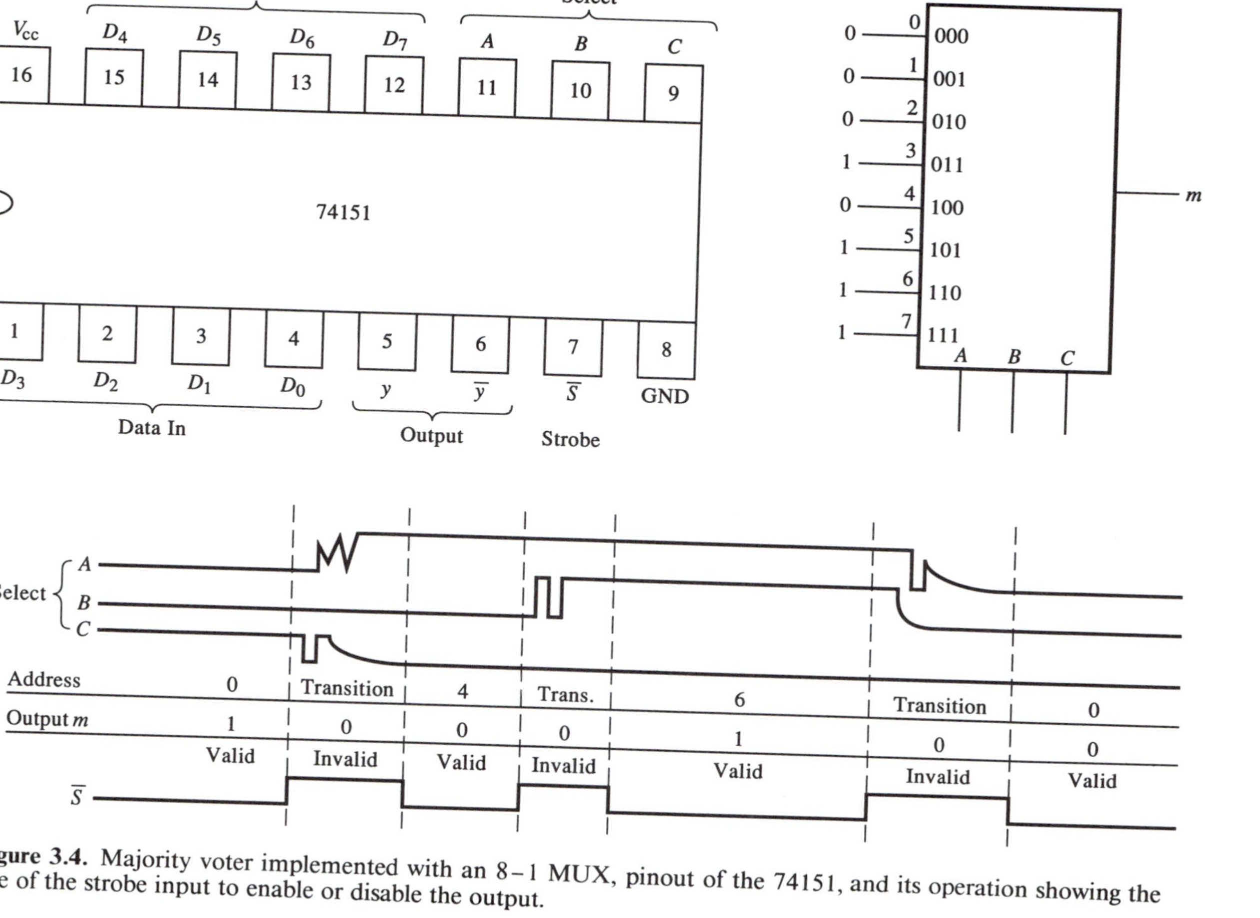


**Figure 3.4.** Majority voter implemented with an 8–1 MUX, pinout of the 74151, and its operation showing the use of the strobe input to enable or disable the output.

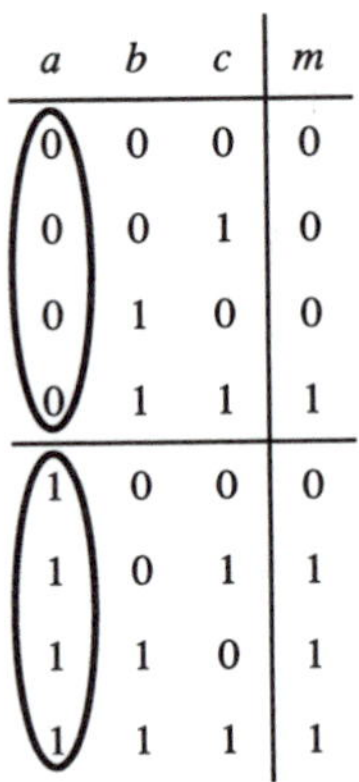

| $a$ | $b$ | $c$ | $m$ |
|---|---|---|---|
| 0 | 0 | 0 | 0 |
| 0 | 0 | 1 | 0 |
| 0 | 1 | 0 | 0 |
| 0 | 1 | 1 | 1 |
| 1 | 0 | 0 | 0 |
| 1 | 0 | 1 | 1 |
| 1 | 1 | 0 | 1 |
| 1 | 1 | 1 | 1 |

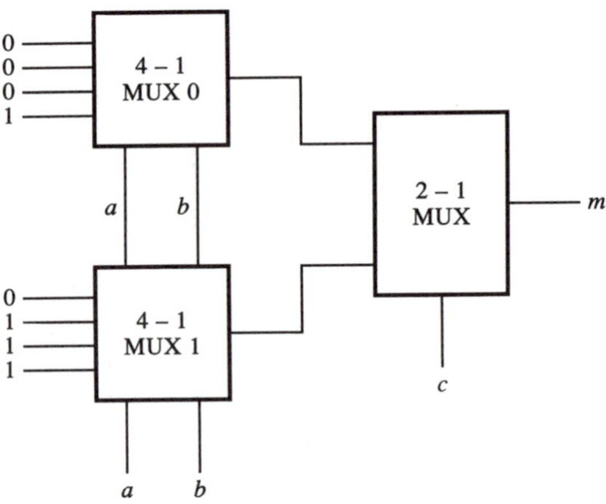


**Figure 3.5.** Majority voter implemented with an MUX tree of 4–1 MUXs. Note the labeling of input lines and their relation to the truth table.

Consider as an example the function in Figure 3.6. If we connect variables $a$ and $b$ to the select lines of a 4–1 MUX (read "four-to-one"), each data pin will correspond to two lines of the truth table. As an example, line 0 corresponds to lines 000 and 001 in the truth table because it is selected by $a = b = 0$. The value that should be connected to data line 0 thus depends on the free variable $c$. As we know, the only functions of one variable are

$$f = 0, \quad f = 1, \quad f = c, \quad \text{and} \quad f = \bar{c}$$

and each data line must therefore be connected to one of these four functions. If we divide the table into two-line sections corresponding to all of the possible

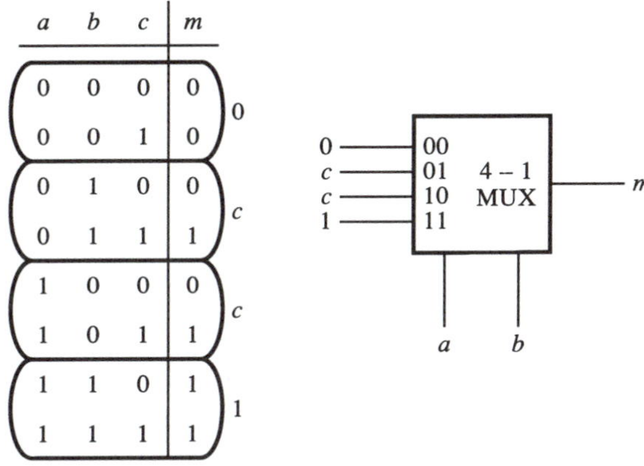


**Figure 3.6.** Majority voter implemented with folding.

combinations of $a$ and $b$, we can easily determine which of the four possibilities applies.

The whole procedure is as follows:

1. For a function of $n$ variables, connect the leftmost $n-1$ inputs $x_{n-1},\dots,x_1$ to the select lines.
2. Divide the table into two-line sections and express $f$ for each section as a function of the rightmost variable $x_0$. Connect this value to the data input labeled with the combination $x_n,\dots,x_1$ for this section of the table.

One can use folding to double the size of the truth table that a given MUX can handle or to halve the size of the MUX that is needed to implement a given table. Its disadvantage is that some inputs may require the negation of an input variable (in our example $\overline{c}$), which requires an extra inverter.

One can combine folding and MUX trees as in Figure 3.7. Note that in this example we saved one MUX because two sections of the truth table are identical. The function could also have been implemented using a 16 – 1 MUX or an 8 – 1 MUX and folding.

The internal structure of a 4 – 1 MUX is easily obtained from its generalized Karnaugh map (Figure 3.8), which gives

$$f = \overline{s_1} \cdot \overline{s_0} \cdot f(0) + \overline{s_1} \cdot s_0 \cdot f(1) + s_1 \cdot \overline{s_0} \cdot f(2) + s_1 \cdot s_0 \cdot f(3)$$

To close this section let us briefly return to the original purpose of MUXs —communication, which we will study in detail in Chapter 11. If we wish to transmit $n$-bit codes between locations A and B, we have two choices: We can use $n$ wires to send all $n$ bits simultaneously or we can multiplex the signals; that is, we can use only one wire to sample and send the individual bits of the

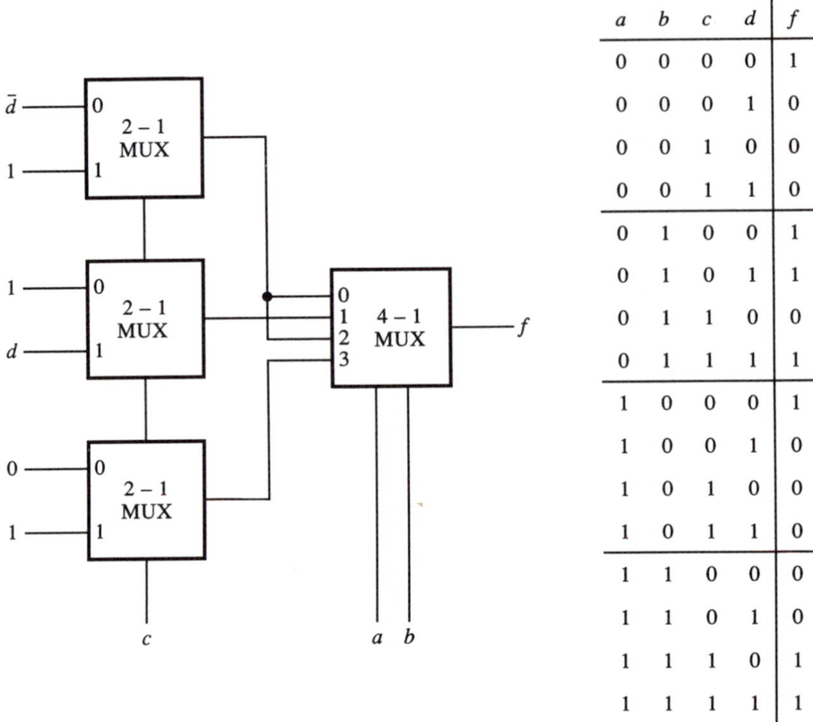


| a | b | c | d | f |
|---|---|---|---|---|
| 0 | 0 | 0 | 0 | 1 |
| 0 | 0 | 0 | 1 | 0 |
| 0 | 0 | 1 | 0 | 0 |
| 0 | 0 | 1 | 1 | 0 |
| 0 | 1 | 0 | 0 | 1 |
| 0 | 1 | 0 | 1 | 1 |
| 0 | 1 | 1 | 0 | 0 |
| 0 | 1 | 1 | 1 | 1 |
| 1 | 0 | 0 | 0 | 1 |
| 1 | 0 | 0 | 1 | 0 |
| 1 | 0 | 1 | 0 | 0 |
| 1 | 0 | 1 | 1 | 0 |
| 1 | 1 | 0 | 0 | 0 |
| 1 | 1 | 0 | 1 | 0 |
| 1 | 1 | 1 | 0 | 1 |
| 1 | 1 | 1 | 1 | 1 |

**Figure 3.7.** An MUX tree with folding.

code one at a time. The first method is called parallel transmission; the second is called serial transmission. The tradeoff between serial and parallel communication is speed and cost: If each signal must remain on the line for $t$ units of time, parallel transmission of $n$-bits requires $t$ units of time and $n$ wires whereas serial transmission of the same information requires $n*t$ units of time but only one wire.

Serial communication is very popular because the decrease in transmission speed that it entails is often unimportant in comparison to the saving of wires. Also, telephone lines can be used for single-bit transmission.

The principle of serial communication using MUXs is shown in Figure 3.9: We connect $n$ sources of data to the data inputs of a MUX whose output is connected to the communication line. Selector bits cycle through the successive bit combinations (0, 1, 2,...) and the values on the selected input lines appear on the communication line one after another. At the receiving end, data is distributed (demultiplexed) to $n$ output lines by a *demultiplexer* (DEMUX or distributor). The cycling values of the select inputs of the

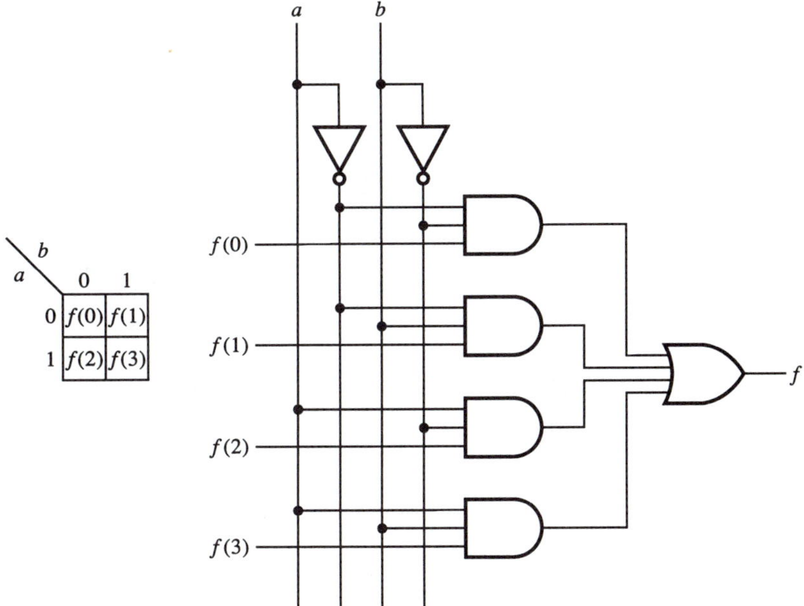


**Figure 3.8.** Formal specification of a 4 – 1 MUX and the corresponding logic diagram.

DEMUX cause it to cycle through the $n$ output lines in the same order that the MUX cycles through its data inputs.

In modern communication of digital data, multiplexing is used to maximize the use of communication lines. Very often, a line can transmit 100 or more times the number of bits that a device such as a keyboard can produce in the same amount of time. Several such devices can be connected to an MUX on a single line, and a DEMUX at the other end makes it possible to reconstruct the individual messages in the same way as in the previous example.

The principle of time-domain multiplexing, as it is called, is also often used to save pins on complicated chips. As an example, some popular computer chips operate with sixteen-bit data but use only eight data pins by sending the sixteen-bit code as two eight-bit groups. This reduces the number of pins but slows down transmission.

### Exercises

1. Add a strobe input that enables and disables select lines to the MUX in Figure 3.4.
2. Draw an arbitrary truth table of four variables and implement it with an MUX using the ordinary method, and the method of folding.

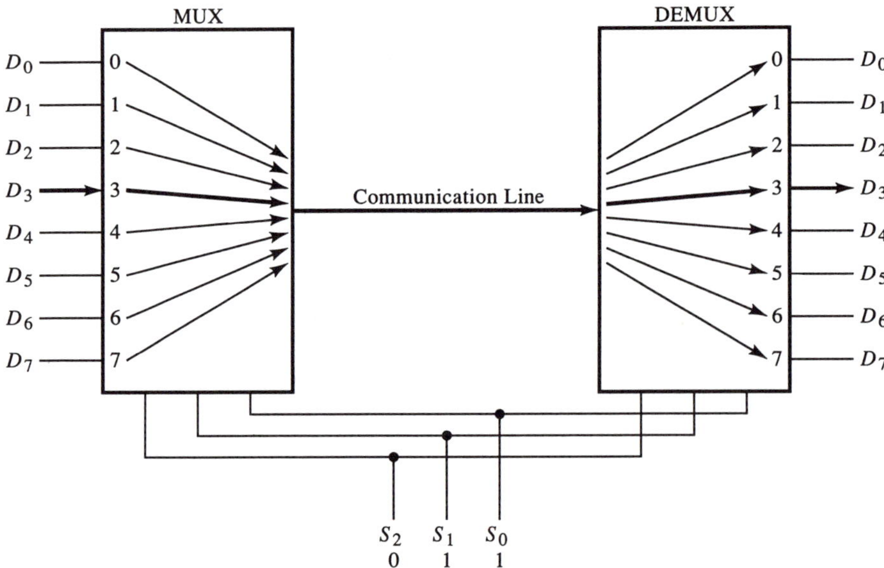


**Figure 3.9.** Use of MUXs and DEMUXs for serial communication. The indicated combination (011) transmits bit $D_3$.

3. Show how to implement a function of five variables using only 2–1 and 4–1 MUXs with and without folding.
4. Repeat the previous exercise using a multilevel tree consisting of 2–1 MUXs.
5. Relate folding to Shannon's formula:

$$f(x_3,x_2,x_1) = \overline{x}_3\overline{x}_2 f(0,0,x_1) + \overline{x}_3 x_2 f(0,1,x_1) + x_3\overline{x}_2 f(1,0,x_1) + x_3 x_2 f(1,1,x_1)$$

6. Relate design with MUX trees to Shannon's formula.
7. Draw a timing diagram illustrating serial communication with MUXs and DEMUXs.
8. Derive the internal structure of a DEMUX.
9. What is the nature of the "switch" in a MUX?

## 3.3 READ-ONLY MEMORIES

A ROM is a storage device. It is referred to as "read-only" because normally data is written into it only once and is thereafter read without being altered. Memories intended for equally frequent reading and rewriting are called *random access memories* (RAMs) or *read/write memories* (RWM). We will deal with these in Chapter 6.

A ROM stores data in an array of *memory cells* each of which has a unique address. In a given ROM each cell has the same size, the same number of bits stored in it, but different ROM chips may have different cell sizes. Many ROMs have eight-bit cells and can thus store up to eight truth tables but some ROMs have one-bit cells.

To read a value from a ROM, one must place the address code of the desired cell on the address pins of the ROM. (Most ROMs have additional control inputs that enable the chip in a way similar to the strobe input of a MUX but we will not consider them here.) The number of cells in a single ROM chip may be very large, up to a million, but the ROM shown in Figure 3.10 is an 8 $\times$ 1 ROM; that is, it has eight cells with one bit each. This ROM has three address lines because the address of each of the eight internal cells can be represented by a three-bit code. Finally, there it has one output for reading the data stored at the selected address. The following examples show the output that would appear if we placed the indicated values on the address inputs given in the table on the following page.

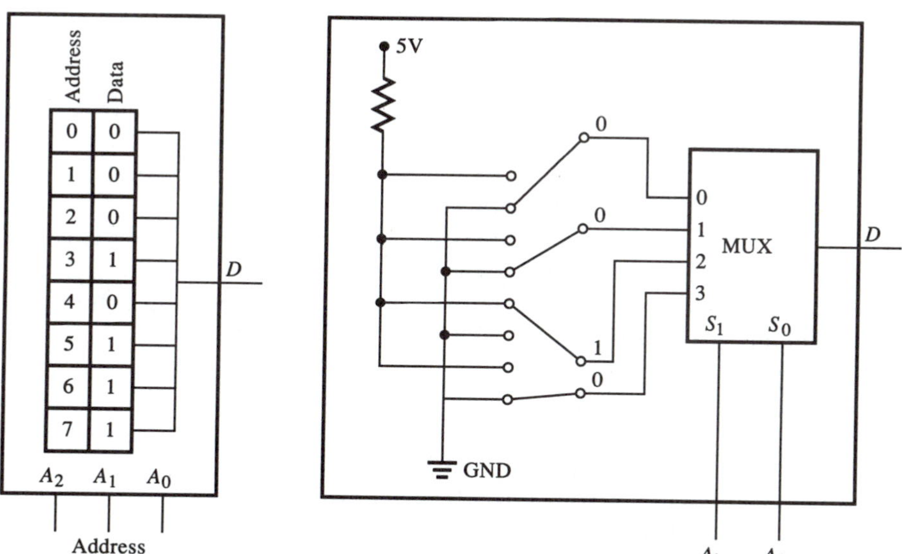


**Figure 3.10.** Principle of a ROM: left, an 8 $\times$ 1 ROM with its inputs, outputs, and stored values; right, a possible implementation of a 4 $\times$ 1 ROM using switches.

| Address Input | Decimal Address | Data Output |
|---|---|---|
| 001 | 1 | 0 |
| 011 | 3 | 1 |
| 110 | 6 | 1 |

Internally, a ROM consists of an array of storage cells and a circuit that selects the addressed cell. Figure 3.10 shows that the storage of a $4 \times 1$ ROM could be implemented by four switches and the selection circuit could be a 4-1 MUX. Real ROMs are, of course, implemented differently.

Depending on their use, ROMs can be divided into true ROMs, programmable ROMs (PROMs), and erasable-programmable ROMs (EPROMs). True ROMs are programmed by the manufacturer during fabrication. PROMs can be programmed by the user but only once; however, EPROMs can be programmed, erased, and reprogrammed many times. Each type has its advantages and disadvantages.

True ROMs, also called mask-programmed ROMs, are programmed and fabricated by the manufacturer according to the customer's detailed specification. To produce a ROM, the manufacturer takes a ROM blueprint ("mask"), which is complete except for the contents of individual cells, and modifies it to store the desired values. The chip is then fabricated. Because the mask is largely complete, designing ROMs is less costly than designing chips from scratch. Although the initial ROM cost is still high, once the customization is completed production is relatively inexpensive. Mask-programmed ROMs are thus economical when used in large quantities where inexpensive fabrication offsets the design cost (Figure 3.11).

Programmable ROMs (PROMs) are ready-to-use chips that do not require any further processing by the manufacturer. An example is the 2764 8kx8 PROM, which has eight-bit cells and 13 address lines ($1k = 2^{10}$), costs around $5, and is initialized with 1s stored in all its cells. Each bit is a fuse, a conductor that can be melted by larger than normal current, connected as in Figure 3.12; blowing a fuse changes the stored value to 0. One can program, or "personalize," PROMs using commercially available PROM programmers either manually (by using switches to select cells and data) or under computer control. A programming error can render a PROM useless, however, because blown fuses cannot be restored.

Figure 3.11 shows that for smaller quantities, PROMs are cheaper than ROMs because they do not require customized fabrication. In larger quantities, however, PROMs are more expensive because they are more complicated and their unit price is thus higher. Consequently, PROMs are used when the anticipated quantity is small.

Erasable PROMs can also be programmed by the user. However, the data is stored as electric charges rather than as blown fuses and can be erased by

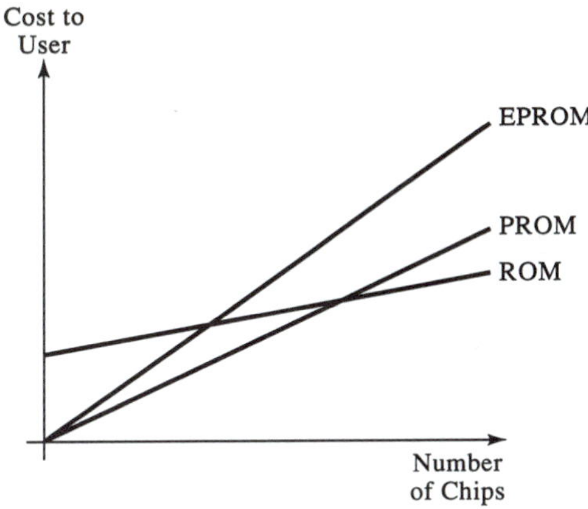


**Figure 3.11.** Cost of ROMs, PROMs, and EPROMs as a function of the number of chips needed. Note the high initial cost of ROMs. The slope of the lines is the unit price of fabrication of a chip.

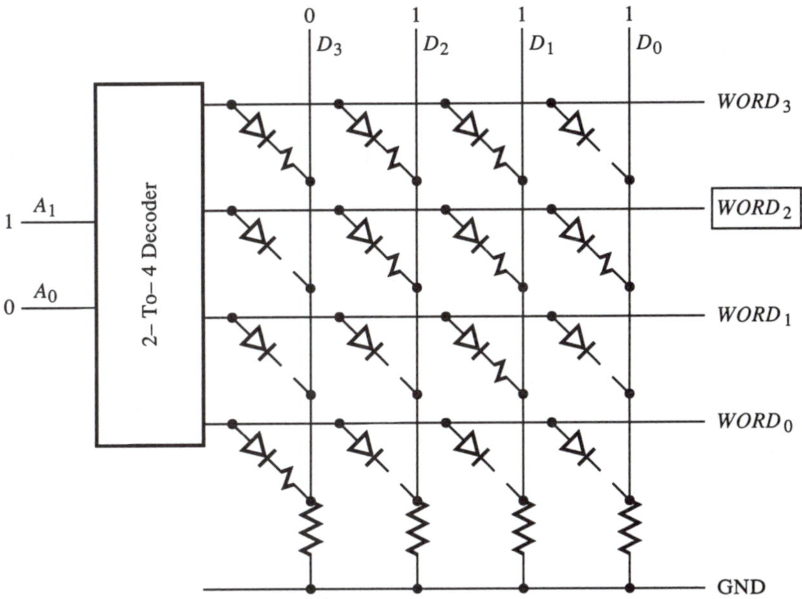


**Figure 3.12.** Internal structure of a 4 × 4 PROM storing (1000), (0010), (0111), and (1110). As an example of its operation, address $(A_1,A_0) = (1,0)$ selects $WORD_2$ and line $WORD_2$ goes High. Data lines $D_i$ that are connected to it go High while the other data lines remain at the ground voltage level (Low). The result is output (0111).

ultraviolet light (UVPROMs) or electric impulses (EEPROMs) and rewritten. Ultraviolet PROMs are conspicuous by the quartz window that makes the circuit accessible to ultraviolet light.

Because EPROMs are reusable they are suitable for developing and debugging new circuits and for experiments. Writing and rewriting an EPROM until the design is debugged is cheaper than wasting a PROM for each correction. An EPROM can be reprogrammed thousands of times before it deteriorates to the point that it cannot be used any more. Once programmed, it can hold the stored data for ten years or so, depending on the chip and environmental factors. (Exposure to light having ultraviolet components causes a faster loss of data.) True ROMs and PROMs hold data indefinitely unless an internal physical breakdown occurs.

Erasable PROMs are more complex, and thus more expensive, than PROMs. For this reason, when debugged circuits are to be produced in larger quantities EPROMs are usually replaced with PROMs or ROMs. To make this easier, manufacturers fabricate pin compatible (same pin, same function) PROMs and EPROMs that are physically and functionally interchangeable. As an example, the 27 × X series of 1k-, 2k-, 4k-, 8k-, 16k-, and 32kx8 chips is available in all three varieties.

In the rest of this section, we will use the term ROM for all types of read-only memories because they are logically equivalent.

### Using ROMs in Combinational Circuits

As we have already stated, ROMs are storage components and their use for memoryless combinational functions is thus something of a paradox. However, the value of a logic function need not be obtained by "calculating" it with gates; we can also store its truth table in memory and read the value using the input combination as the address.

**Example 1.** We shall see in Chapter 6 that addition and subtraction can be implemented easily in hardware. Multiplication and division are not conceptually difficult either but the necessary circuits are relatively complex. Until recently, only the more expensive computers did multiplication and division in hardware whereas smaller computers used a program to perform these operations. The alternative to fast-but-expensive hardware (physical circuits) and cheap-but-slow software (computer programs) is "firmware," the storage of programs and data in a ROM. We will use this approach to implement multiplication.

Assume that we want to store products of two-bit codes $(a,d)$ and $(x,y)$ in a ROM. What size should the ROM and its cells be? There are four different two-bit codes, which means there are 16 possible combinations of two operands and therefore 16 results, so our ROM must have 16 cells. The largest result is obtained by multiplying binary 11 (decimal 3) by itself. The result is 1001 ($3 \times 3 = 9$). Our products therefore require four bits and we need a

16 × 4 ROM. Individual cells will store values from the multiplication table as shown in Figure 3.13.

The variables $(ab)$ and $(xy)$ select the product $(P_3P_2P_1P_0)$; they are also addresses into the table stored in the ROM. We will use the labeling shown in Figure 3.13, with the most significant bit of the address connected to $a$ and the least significant bit connected to $y$.

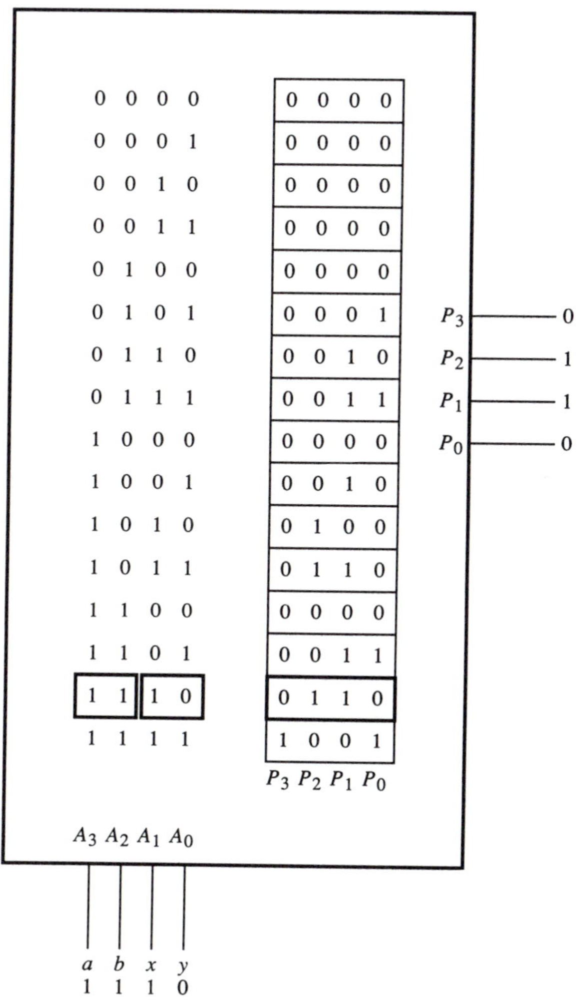


**Figure 3.13.** The 2 × 2 multiplication table implemented with a ROM. Each cell is marked with its address and the four-bit binary code of the product. The indicated inputs and outputs show how 3 × 2 produces the correct result 6.

Multiplication realized in this fashion would be quite fast because the access time of a small ROM is less than 100 nsec. It would also require only one chip. However, multiplication of operands having more bits would require several very large ROMs to store the entire multiplication table. As an example, multiplication of two sixteen-bit operands (the usual size of integer codes in personal computers) would require $2^{32}$ thirty-two-bit cells. This is impractical and fast computer multiplication is thus better implemented with combinational circuits.

**Example 2.** We will now outline how ROMs are used to produce text on computer displays. (The reader should see Chapter 11 for additional detail.)

Most computer displays use cathode ray tube (CRT) screens that work on the same principle as ordinary television. A CRT produces an image by sweeping an electron beam of controlled energy across a glass surface coated with phosphorus. When an intensive beam hits a phosphorus particle, it emits a burst of light. By turning the beam's intensity on and off, we can make dots on the screen visible or invisible.

The manner in which the beam moves distinguishes two kinds of CRTs. Vector graphics systems display images by moving the beam directly from one end of a line to the other, and are used mainly for graphics. In the much more common raster scan CRT monitors (used also in TVs), the image is created by writing horizontal rows of dots in a fixed raster pattern (grid) across the screen. Symbols are created as combinations of dots inscribed into rectangles of a fixed size, for example 7 × 9 dots. Text display on these monitors thus requires the conversion of coded text into a pattern of dots and this is usually done with a ROM. (Figure 3.14).

Each line of text consists of several rows of dots. To write a line, the CRT controller logic reads the code of a symbol to be displayed and generates a

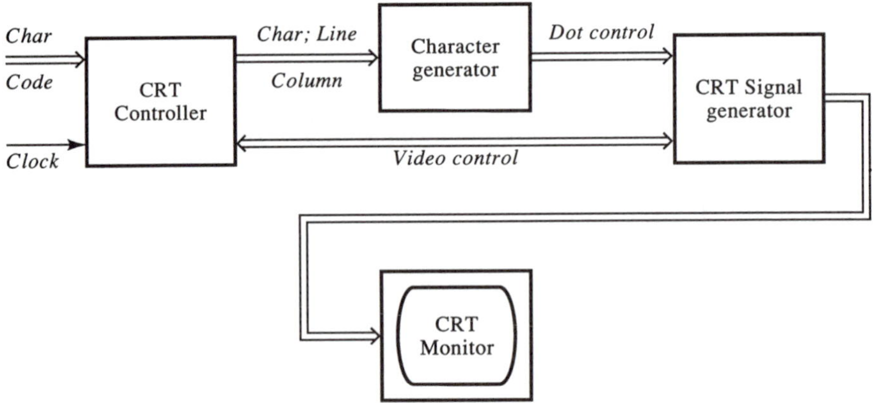


**Figure 3.14.** Principle of text display on a CRT screen.

series of On/Off signals whose dot pattern corresponds to the symbol and the row that is being written. First the line of text and then the whole screen are displayed in this manner. To create the appearance of stability (the visibility of the light dot is very short) dots are rewritten at least 30 times per second.

The basis of this operation is the conversion of symbol codes to dot patterns and this is done by reading the patterns from a ROM. Codes and row numbers are used as addresses. The code-row-symbol information is, in fact, an index into a large truth table whose outputs are 0s and 1s corresponding to the desired pattern. An example of the detail of a CRT display and the possible contents of the character generator ROM are shown in Figure 3.15.

It should be mentioned that the specifications of ROM-like devices for data storage are slightly different from those for logic applications. Special varieties of PROM chips for logic design are available from some manufacturers.

The need for computer memories and applications like character generators makes ROM and RAM chips the most popular integrated circuits. They are also the densest integrated circuits (containing the largest number of transistors) because their internal structure is very regular and allows very close packing of transistors. At the time of this writing, the maximum size of commercially available ROMs was two-Mbit ($2^{20}$ bits) chips organized as 256kx8 cells. In RAMs, the maximum available capacity is 4 Mbits.

Our examples show that a logic function can be read from memory and suggest that digital functions can also be implemented by computer programs rather than by "hardwired logic." This approach is often used in industrial applications where special purpose computers called controllers produce logic functions by reading their values from memory while executing other tasks in the remaining time.

## Exercises

1. Draw the diagram of a 4 × 4 ROM using switches for storage.
2. How many address lines and data outputs does a 32kx8 ROM have? Repeat for a 256kx8 chip.
3. Write the part of the ROM character generator code that corresponds to the first two rows of letter *B*.
4. What is the maximum number of variables of a truth table that can be stored in the ROM in Exercise 2? How many such truth tables can be stored in it?
5. Label the inputs and outputs of a 32kx8 ROM storing five tables of seven variables. How are the five values stored in the eight-bit cells?
6. Explain why ROMs and PROMs can hold data indefinitely but EPROMs hold data only for a limited length of time. What are some possible consequences of the limited length of storage for microcomputers and appliances that use EPROMs?

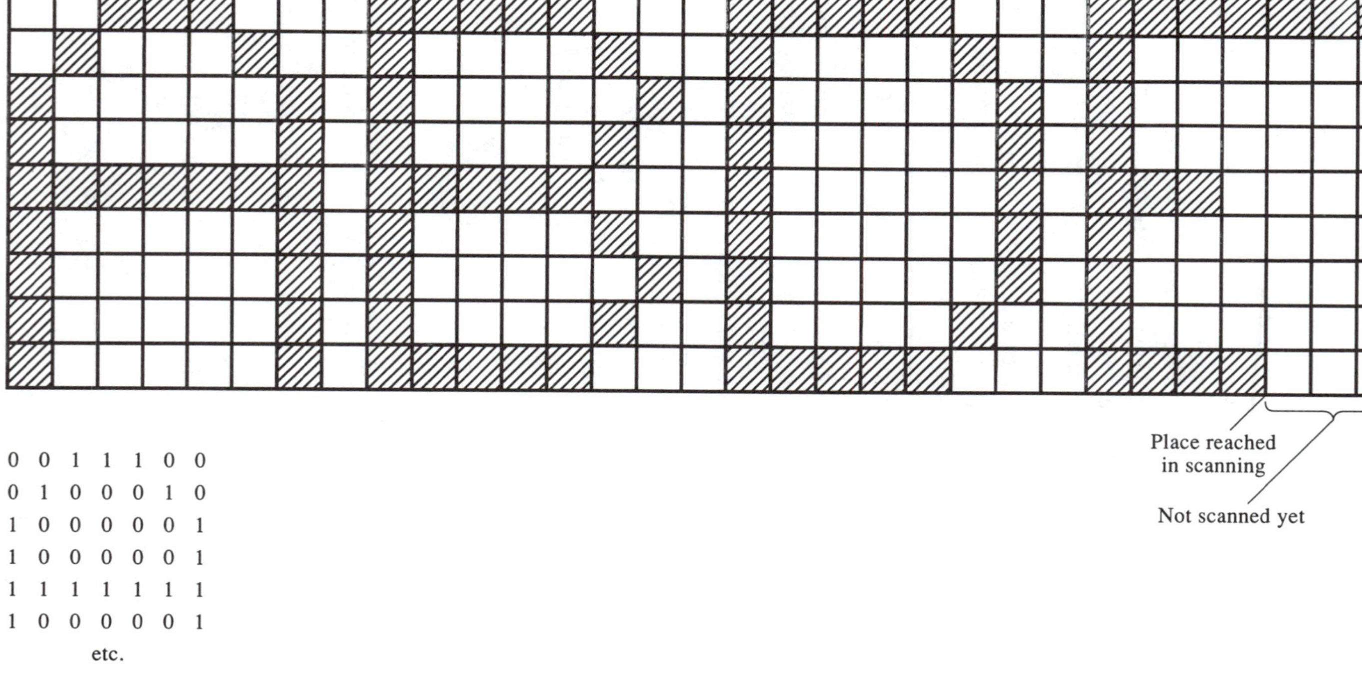


**Figure 3.15.** Incomplete display of the letters *A B D E*, and the partial contents of the character generator showing the bit patterns that produce the first six rows of the letter *A*.

## 3.4 PROGRAMMABLE LOGIC DEVICES

Programmable logic devices can be categorized as purely combinational or sequential devices. They all share the same basic circuit: a large two-level array of gates, usually an AND/OR sum of products with incomplete connections.

The first commercial PLD chips were *programmable logic arrays* (PLAs). All input lines of a PLA (Figure 3.16) are double-railed: This means that all inputs are connected to inverters to provide both true and inverted inputs to all AND gates. Any input rail can be connected to any AND gate and any AND gate can be connected to any OR gate. Connections are established by the manufacturer, or for field-programmable logic arrays (FPLA), by a PLA programmer. Because the principles of FPLA and PROM programming are identical, some PROM programmers can also handle FPLAs.

To implement a function with a PLA (Figure 3.17), the specification is first converted to an AND/OR formula and then usually reduced to fit in the smallest possible PLA. Some PLAs allow internally generated products to be

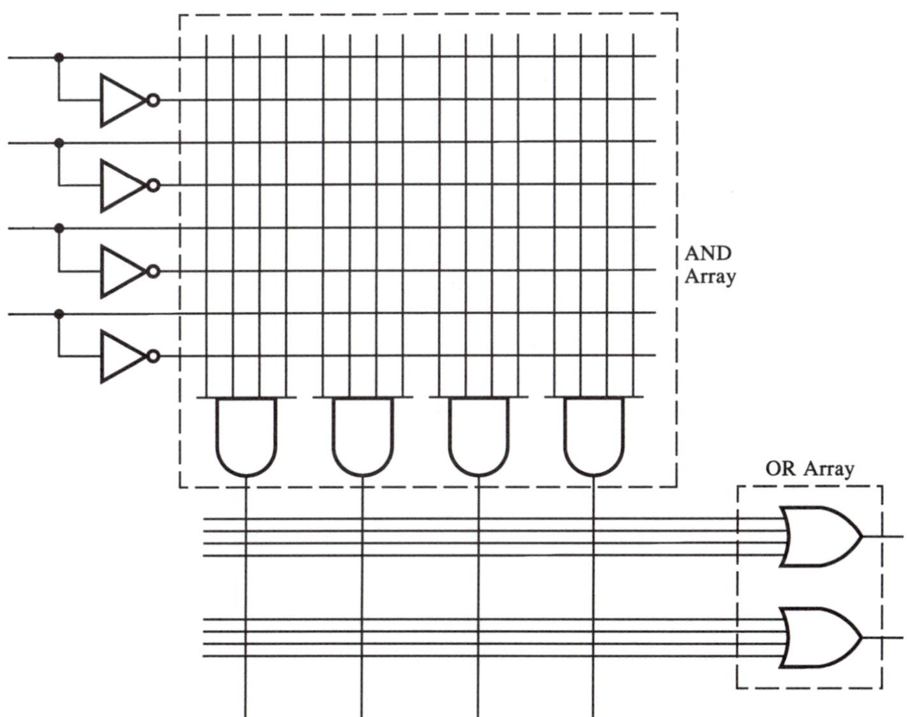


**Figure 3.16.** "Uncommitted" PLA with unfinished connections.

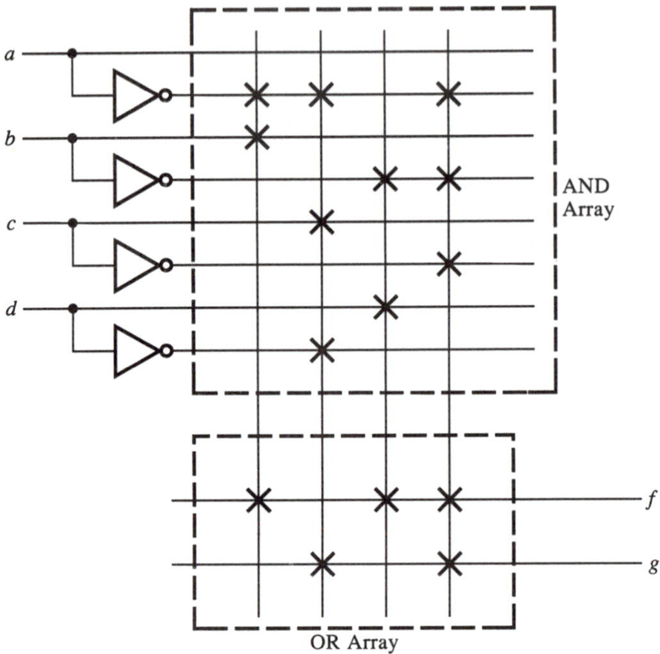


**Figure 3.17.** Conventional representation of a combinational PLA and its use to implement $f = \bar{a}b + \bar{b}d + \bar{a}\bar{b}\bar{c}$ and $g = \bar{a}c\bar{d} = \bar{a}\bar{b}\bar{c}$.

fed back to inputs and this feature can be used to share product terms and to use the PLA more efficiently. Computer programs and special purpose languages are available that simplify the conversion from functions or truth tables to minimal PLA specifications ("fuse maps"). They often allow simulation of the generated circuit.

At present, PLAs are less popular than another form of PLDs, which are called programmable array logic devices (PAL). PALs have the same structure as PLAs but only AND inputs may be programmed. PALs evolved from PLAs when it was realized that only a limited number of AND/OR connections are usually needed in a circuit and that the circuit can be greatly simplified by eliminating programmability of the AND/OR connections. This change yields the following benefits:

Programmable array logic (PAL) chips have more room for inputs, outputs, gates, and other elements than PLAs using the same area and technology because programmable connections require extra space.

The simpler PAL structure is easier to program and faster in operation.

**Example.** To illustrate the use of PALs, we will now implement a circuit similar to the 74147 ten-to-four priority encoder with a commercial PAL chip. The desired circuit has nine input lines $I_i$, where $i$=1,...,9, and four active Low outputs for the BCD code $O_3O_2O_1O_0$ of the highest priority input. The output is 1111 when none of the nine inputs is active. Input $I_9$ has the highest priority and all inputs are active Low. The following are a few examples of the desired operation:

| **Input $I$,...,$I_q$** | **Active Low Output** | **Comment** |
|---|---|---|
| 111111111 | 1111 | No input active, BCD code 0 |
| 011111111 | 1110 | Only input 1 active, BCD = 1 |
| 110100111 | 1001 | 6 is highest priority active |
| 000000000 | 0110 | All inputs active, BCD = 9 |

Because the circuit has nine inputs, we cannot use Karnaugh maps to derive the formula. Fortunately, the problem is relatively simple and, moreover, we need not be too concerned about minimization because the PAL chip has enough gates. We will obtain the solution by analyzing the BCD codes and the desired priority system.

Output $O_3$ is active (Low) iff inputs $I_8$ or $I_9$ are active (Low):

$$\overline{O_3} = \overline{I_8} + \overline{I_9}$$

Output $O_2$, whose weight is 4, is active iff inputs $I_4$,$I_5$,$I_6$, or $I_7$ (whose codes include weight 4) are active (Off) but inputs $I_8$ and $I_9$ (whose codes do not include weight 4) are not:

$$\begin{aligned}\overline{O_2} &= (\overline{I_4} + \overline{I_5} + \overline{I_6} + \overline{I_7})I_8I_9 \\ &= \overline{I_4}I_8I_9 + \overline{I_5}I_8I_9 + \overline{I_6}I_8I_9 + \overline{I_7}I_8I_9\end{aligned}$$

Note that we have had to convert the formula to a sum of products to match the structure of the PAL.

Output $O_1$ is active when $I_2$ or $I_3$ are Off and all higher priority inputs are On (inactive), or when $I_6$ or $I_7$ are Off and all higher priority inputs are On (inactive):

$$\begin{aligned}\overline{O_1} &= (\overline{I_7} + \overline{I_6})I_8I_9 + (\overline{I_3} + \overline{I_2})I_4I_5I_8I_9 \\ &= \overline{I_7}I_8I_9 + \overline{I_6}I_8I_9 + \overline{I_3}I_4I_5I_8I_9 + \overline{I_2}I_4I_5I_8I_9\end{aligned}$$

Note that an AND gate with so many inputs is not normally available but that this connection is possible on a PAL. The reader can derive the formula for $O_0$ and complete the diagram.

These functions can be comfortably implemented with the 24-pin 18L4 PAL from Monolithic Memories, a major PLD producer, or with similar chips available from other manufacturers. As its code indicates, the 18L4 is a logic PAL with 18 inputs and four active Low outputs. Its fuse map for our circuit is shown in Figure 3.18. Line crossings marked $x$ represent connections; unmarked crossings are fuses that must be blown. The numbers on vertical and horizontal lines define the geometry of the map and can be used to specify the connections.

As an exercise, the student should show that if we wanted to implement our function with inverters and NAND gates, we would need more than 10 chips. This would require much more space, power, and interchip connections than the single 18L4 chip that implements the same function. The multichip circuit would also be slower.

One can see that PLDs reduce the number of chips, eliminate interchip connections, and save space on the circuit board. According to Monolithic Memories, the saving in chip count is at least four to one. PLDs also increase speed because functions integrated inside a chip are faster than those obtained by connecting separate chips. Internal connections are also more durable and PLD-based circuits are thus more reliable as well.

PALs can be divided in two groups. Some are programmed during fabrication; these devices are also called HALs for "Hard Array Logic." Other PALs can be programmed by the customer using equipment similar to PROM programmers. In addition to HALs and PALS, erasable and reprogrammable PLDs are also available. These include EPLDs, which are erasable by ultraviolet light, and EEPLDs, which are erasable by electric current. ELPDs are structurally simpler but must be removed from the circuit for reprogramming, which is inconvenient and dangerous. EELPDs can be reprogrammed in the circuit without removal.

PLAs, PALs, and PROMs are related in that they are all essentially programmable AND/OR arrays. The main difference between them is the number of connections they provide and whether these connections are fixed or programmable (Figure 3.19). Because of their similarity they can be used in related applications. We have already seen how PROMs can replace combinational logic, which normally is the domain of PLAs and PALs, and PLAs and PALs can similarly be employed in applications usually reserved for memories.

The use of PLDs, MUXs, ROMs, and similar useful structures is not limited to prefabricated ready-to-use chips. The principle of using a library of blocks that only need to be assembled and connected forms the basis for *application specific integrated circuits* (ASICs). The internal logic of these chips consists of predesigned and tested blocks, which can be custom con-

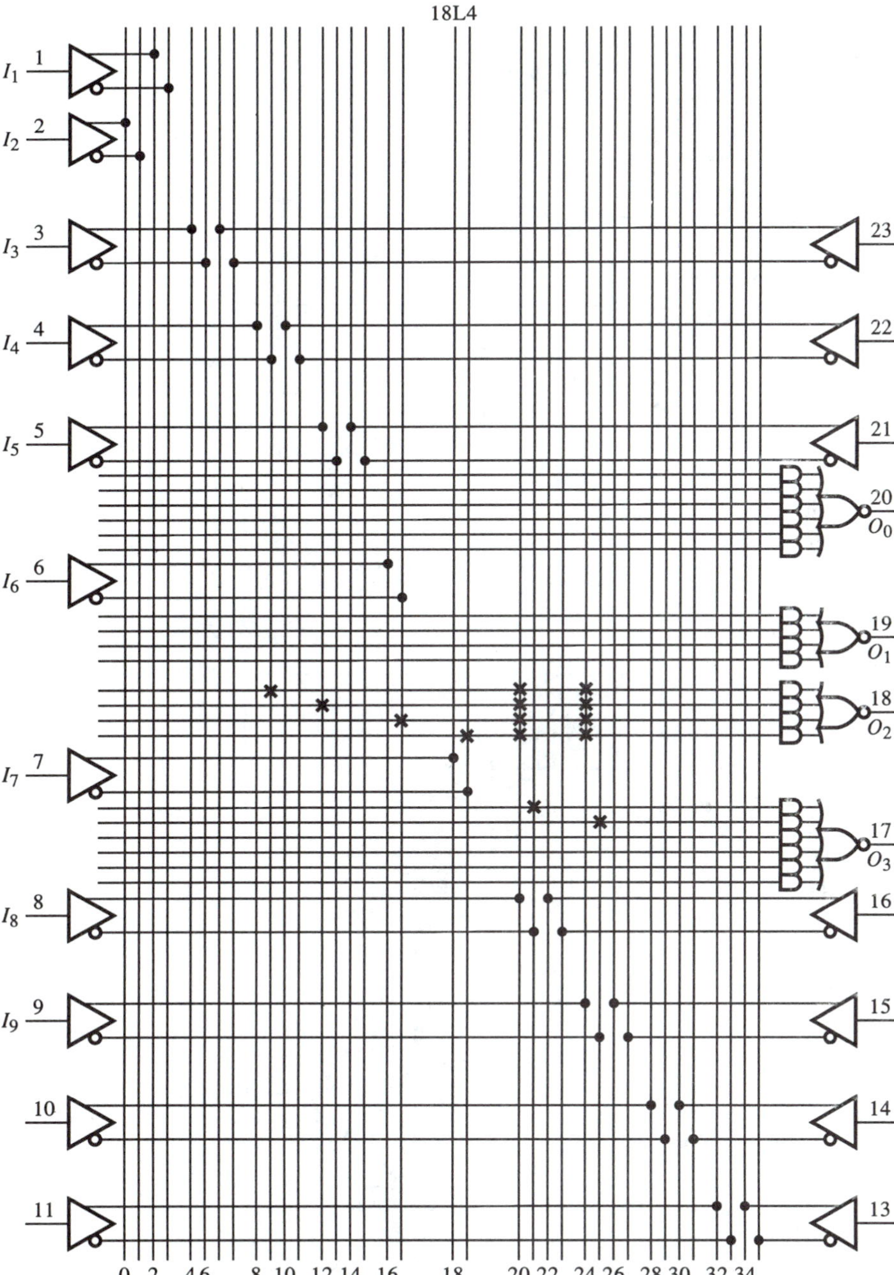


**Figure 3.18.** Part of a ten-to-four priority encoder implemented with the 18L4 PAL.

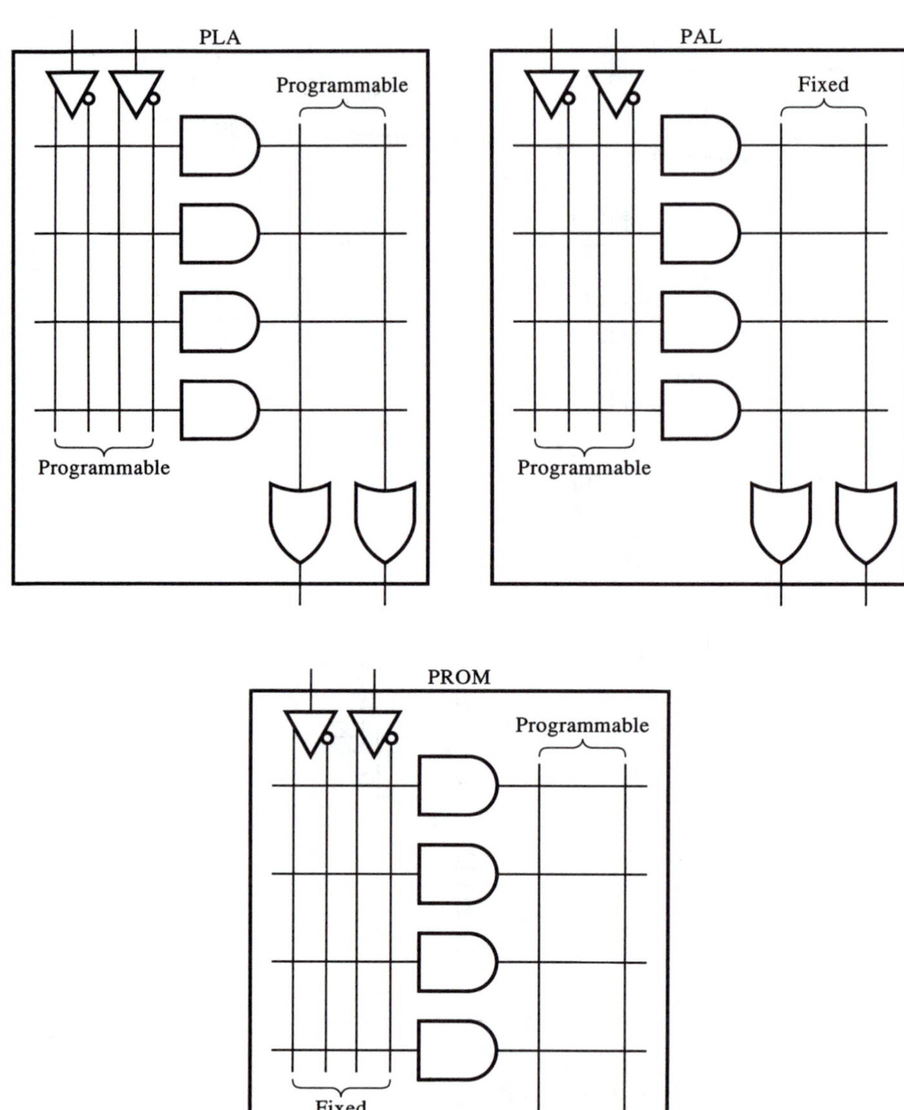


**Figure 3.19.** Schematic representation of the internal structure of PLA, PAL, and PROM chips.

nected to implement the desired function. These circuits are routinely used on complex special purpose chips that are usually manufactured in small volumes and needed on very short notice. The disadvantage of fast ASIC design and fabrication is that chips produced in this way are not optimized for the given application and do not attain the highest possible speed and density.

**Exercises**

Try to implement the following functions with the 18L4 PAL and compare the solution with circuits obtained with ordinary gates.

1. Draw the fuse map of a quad 4 – 1 MUX (four 4 – 1 MUXs in one chip).
2. Draw the fuse map of a sixteen-to-four converter that translates a signal connected to lines 0, ...,15 into a four-bit code of the line number. Only one input line is active at any time.
3. Draw the fuse map of a two-word comparator that outputs the larger of two four-bit input codes.

## 3.5 OTHER COMBINATIONAL STRUCTURES

Medium- and large-scale integration technology makes it possible to provide many frequently needed functions as "off-the-shelf" chips. TTL data books contains hundreds of such devices that are produced in large quantities and are available from distributors, dealers, and mail order outlets. We will restrict our attention in this section to encoders and decoders because they are essential for our ultimate purpose: the design of computers.

Encoders and decoders are combinational circuits used in the following applications:

To recognize which of several input combinations is being processed. This is essential for interfacing memory chips, input and output devices, as well as for the proper operation of ROM, RAM, and other chips.

To convert one representation of information into another, for example, BCD to seven-segment codes.

We will only deal with the first application because it is very important in computer systems; the second is used mainly in special purpose digital circuits and instruments.

What is the difference between decoders and encoders? Unfortunately, the distinction is sometimes vague and the terminology is ambiguous. The same chip may be called a decoder by one author and an encoder by another. In principle, however, a decoder accepts a binary code and activates an output line that identifies it; it recognizes a code. Encoders provide the inverse function.

An example of a three-to-eight decoder (Figure 3.20) is the 74138. It has three active High data inputs and eight active Low outputs. When it is enabled, the input combination activates the output line whose number corresponds to the input code; all other output lines remain inactive. Outputs are active Low. As an example, the input combination (0,1,1) activates output line 3 and its voltage goes Low. When the chip is disabled, all outputs are High. Enable control is by pins $G_1$, $G_{2A}$, and $G_{2B}$, which must satisfy

$$G_1 \cdot \overline{(G_{2A} + G_{2B})} = 1$$

for the circuit to decode. We will see later that the enable function is important for interfacing.

The 74148 is an eight-to-three priority encoder with eight prioritized inputs and three active Low outputs that produce the code of the highest currently active input line. As an example, when the highest priority active input is line number 5, output becomes (010), the active Low code of 5.

What is inside a basic three-to-eight decoder? The answer can be obtained from the map in Figure 3.20 in which ($C_2$, $C_1$, $C_0$) denotes the input code, and 7, 6,...,1, 0 denote the output lines. Output $i$ is active iff the input combination ($C_2$,$C_1$,$C_0$) is the code of $i$ and so

$$0 = \overline{C_2} \cdot \overline{C_1} \cdot \overline{C_0}$$

$$1 = \overline{C_2} \cdot \overline{C_1} \cdot C_0$$

.

.

.

$$7 = C_2 \cdot C_1 \cdot C_0$$

Note that the map represents eight Karnaugh maps merged into one.

## Exercises

1. Add an enable circuit to our three-to-eight decoder.
2. Design the following encoders and decoders:

   Decimal-to-BCD (ten input lines, four outputs).

   Decimal-to-seven segment (ten input lines, seven outputs to control segments $a$ to $g$.

3. List the similarities and differences between decoders and demultiplexers.

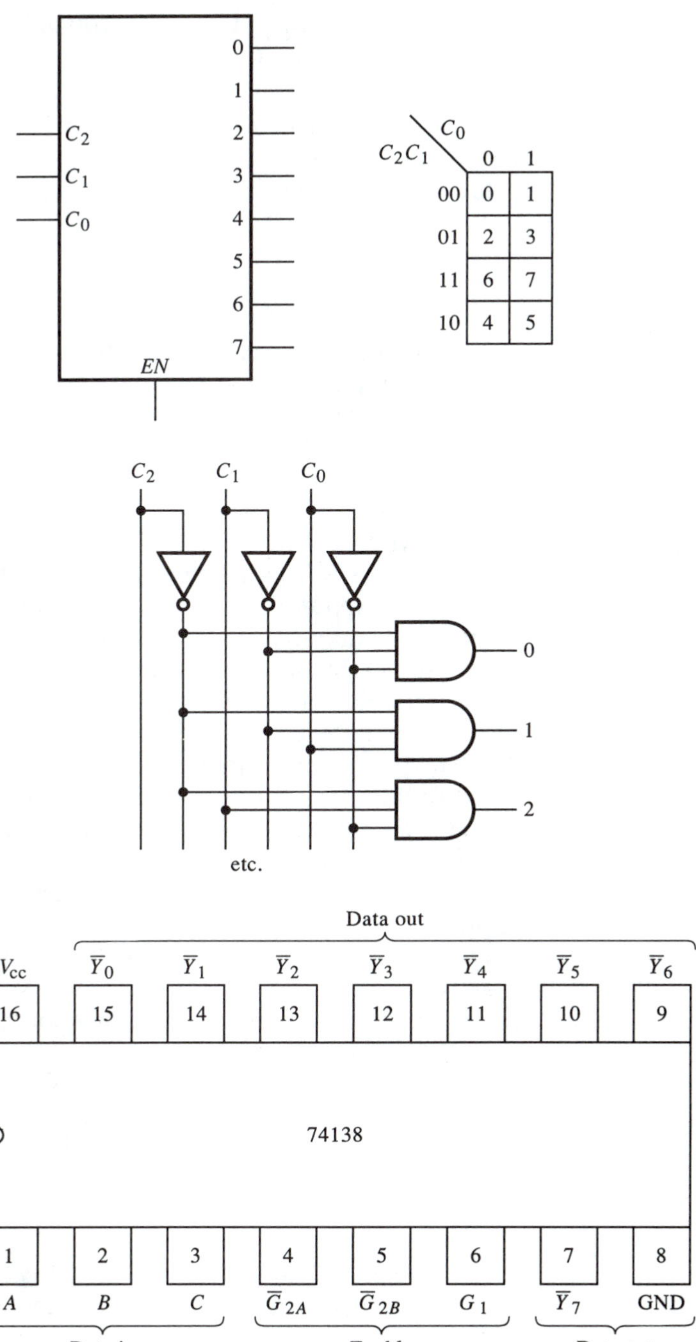


**Figure 3.20.** A three-to-eight decoder, its map, and a part of its internal diagram; pinout of the 74138.

4. Use a three-to-eight decoder to implement a circuit that "recognizes" the codes of 2, 3, 5, and 7, by producing 1 whenever one of them appears on the input.
5. Use a four-to-ten decoder to implement a circuit with the following outputs: $x$ = input code is divisible by 3, $y$ = code represents a number between 3 and 6 (inclusive), $z$ = code is a number greater than 7.

## SUMMARY

This chapter introduced several powerful alternatives to the basic chips presented in Chapter 2. The structures that we described speed up design, reduce the number of chips, save space, power, and money, and increase speed and reliability. They can be divided in two categories: devices that can be used to design general combinational circuits, and special purpose devices that implement frequently needed functions.

The first category includes MUXs, ROMs, and PLDs. Multiplexers are useful for small truth tables, whereas ROMs are advantageous for large truth tables. Combinational PLDs are AND/OR arrays used to implement formulas rather than truth tables. Unlike MUXs, ROMs and PLDs must be customized for each application. Depending on how this is done, one distinguishes mask-programmed devices that can only be programmed by the manufacturer and devices that may be customized by the user with special programming equipment. The former group includes ROMs and HALs; the latter includes PROMs, EPROMs, EEPROMs, PALs, and others. The required number of copies of the circuit, its complexity, and the desired operating parameters determine which variety is best.

Multiplexers, PLDs, and ROMs are also important as internal building blocks of complicated chips.

The second category of MSI and LSI devices covered in this chapter include chips that provide frequently needed functions and thus simplify design. As an example of these devices, we presented decoders and mentioned their use as code recognizers in computer interfaces.

This chapter also introduced the terms SSI, MSI, LSI, and VLSI that refer to the number of gates present on a chip: its level of integration.

## REVIEW QUESTIONS

1. Define the following terms: Active High/Low, SSI, MSI, LSI, VLSI, multiplexer, demultiplexer, multiplexing, serial/parallel communication, multiplexer tree, folding, data selector/distributor, read-only memory, RAM, ROM, RWM, PROM, EPROM, EEPROM, programmable logic device, encoder, decoder, strobe.

2. Describe the following procedures: design with MUXs (with and without folding), design with MUX trees, design with ROMs, design with PLDs.

## REFERENCES

The following titles listed in the references at the end of the book are relevant to this chapter:

Advanced Micro Devices. *Programmable Logic Handbook.*

Monolithic Memories. *Programmable Logic Handbook.*

D. Smith. *Programmable Logic Devices.*

Texas Instruments. *The TTL Data Book.*

# CHAPTER 4

# SEQUENTIAL CIRCUITS—COMPONENTS AND ANALYSIS

## AN OVERVIEW

This chapter deals with the representation and analysis of sequential circuits and their components. It begins with a description of two equivalent representations of the behavior of sequential circuits, the transition graph and the transition table. Both are then used to define flip-flops and latches, the basic storage elements. We will examine the different control mechanisms (level and edge sensitivity) and types (D, T, JK, and RS) of these elements and demonstrate their operation using examples. Discussion of the concepts and idealized behavior of registers and counters, is accompanied by information about physical parameters and their effect on the operation of sequential circuits.

Once we have defined the basic components, we will use them to analyze sequential circuits. Finally, we will consider asynchronous circuits and the problems that they can cause.

## IMPORTANT WORDS

Asynchronous, counter (up/down, synchronous/asynchronous, presettable), cycle edge, equation (characteristic, excitation, transition), excitation circuit, flip-flop (D,T,JK,RS), hold time, internal state and variable, latch, level, master-slave, modulus, output circuit, race (critical/uncritical), sequencer, setup time, stable state, state diagram, state machine, synchronous, transition equation, transition graph, transition table, volatile.

## 4.1 REPRESENTATION OF THE BEHAVIOR OF SEQUENTIAL CIRCUITS

The outputs of a sequential circuit depend on its present and past inputs, and the same input combination can thus produce one result for one sequence of inputs and another result for a different input history. Because the input history determines the operation of the circuit, it must be stored in the circuit's memory as a binary code; this code is called the (internal) state of the circuit. In terms of this new terminology, we can say that the output of a sequential circuit depends on its input and on its internal state, which captures the history of past operation.

Our analysis leads to the following model of a sequential circuit. Let $q$ denote the present state, the state at time $t$; $Q$ the next state, the value of $q$ at time $t + 1$; $x$ the input; and $y$ the output. A sequential circuit can then be described by two equations.

The transition equation

$$Q = f(q,x)$$

yields the next state given the system's present state and input. The output equation

$$y = g(q)$$

yields the system's output in its current state.

The transition equation, also called the next-state equation, describes how the new state depends on the old state and the current input; the output equation defines output in terms of the current state. Note that in our formulation the output does not depend on current inputs. We will see later that this minor restriction simplifies certain considerations while leaving the model sufficiently general for our needs.

Because the transition equation relates the system's next state to its present state and input, it is, in fact, a function of time:

$$Q = q(t + 1) = f(q(t),x)$$

The time-dependent behavior of sequential circuits makes them very different from combinational functions, which are independent of time, and indicates that truth tables will not be sufficient to describe sequential behavior.

One way to represent our mathematical model is by a transition graph, also called a state diagram. These diagrams represent a given state as a circle or a node labeled with the state's codes and outputs and connected to its "*successor*" states (Figure 4.1). Each transition forms a directed edge in the graph, and is labeled with the input that causes it. The term "successor" is defined as

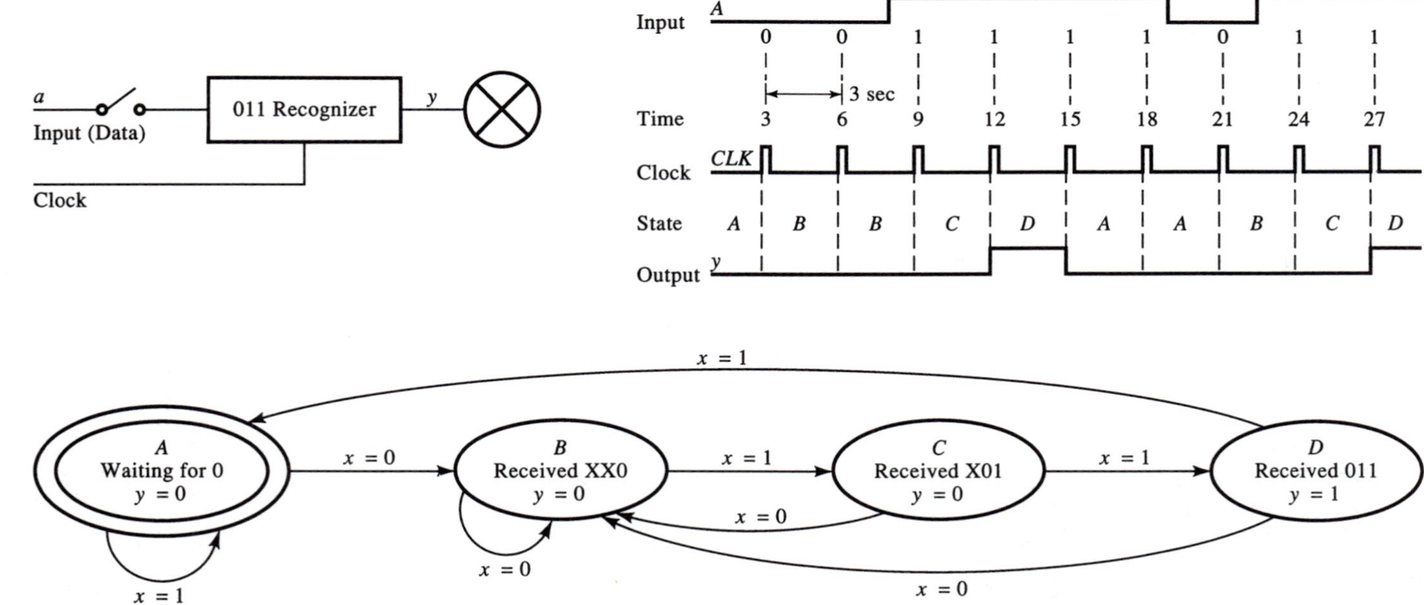


**Figure 4.1.** Sequential circuit, its transition graph, and an example of its operation.

follows: Node $B$ is a successor of node $A$ is there is an input $x$ that causes a transition from $A$ to $B$.

$$B = f(A,x)$$

One could say that $B$ is the state whose history is the history of state $A$ augmented by input $x$. In the transition graph in Figure 4.1, the successor of $D$ are $A$ and $B$, and $B$ is a successor of states $A$, $B$, $C$, and $D$. Obviously, different circuits can have the same transitions but yield different outputs, and states that yield identical outputs can be connected in different order. Consequently, outputs and transitions are independent and can be implemented by separate circuits called the excitation and output circuits. The excitation circuit enforces transitions, while the output circuit produces outputs.

We will now illustrate these concepts using the circuit in Figure 4.1. Its input is connected to a switch and its output to a light. Every 3 seconds, the circuit checks the position of the switch. When it finds that the last three inputs form the sequence (Off, On, On), or (0,1,1), it turns the light On to indicate that the sequence has occurred. The circuit "recognizes" the 011 sequence and this is expressed by the transition graph which we will now explain.

We can interpret the transition graph in the following manner: When the circuit is turned On, it starts in the initial state represented by the doubly circled node $A$. When the circuit is in this state, there are either no previous inputs or else the inputs are irrelevant to the recognition of sequence (0,1,1). The circuit is thus waiting for the first 0 of the sequence.

The input may be 0 or 1 (Off or On), and so two edges exit from state $A$. If the input is 0, the circuit enters a state that represents the possibility that the 0 just received is the beginning of the expected (0,1,1) sequence. To indicate this, we labeled state $B$ "received $xx0$." By $xx$ we mean that previous inputs, if any, are irrelevant.

If the input in state $A$ is 1, no new information relevant to future behavior has been obtained: The circuit still has not received the first Off value that it is waiting for. Because "no relevant information" is the meaning of state $A$, the edge labeled 0 leads back to $A$.

The rest of the graph can be explained similarly and we find that the four indicated states are sufficient to describe the desired behavior.

The history of the circuit (the state information) is stored as binary codes and our circuit has four different states. We therefore need two-bit codes to represent it and two one-bit storage elements to implement it. If we assign internal codes to states as in Figure 4.2, we can express the transition graph with nodes labeled by codes instead of verbal descriptions.

Another way to describe a circuit's behavior is by transition and output tables. While transition graphs are good for illustrating circuit operation, tables are better for analysis and design. A transition table describes the edges

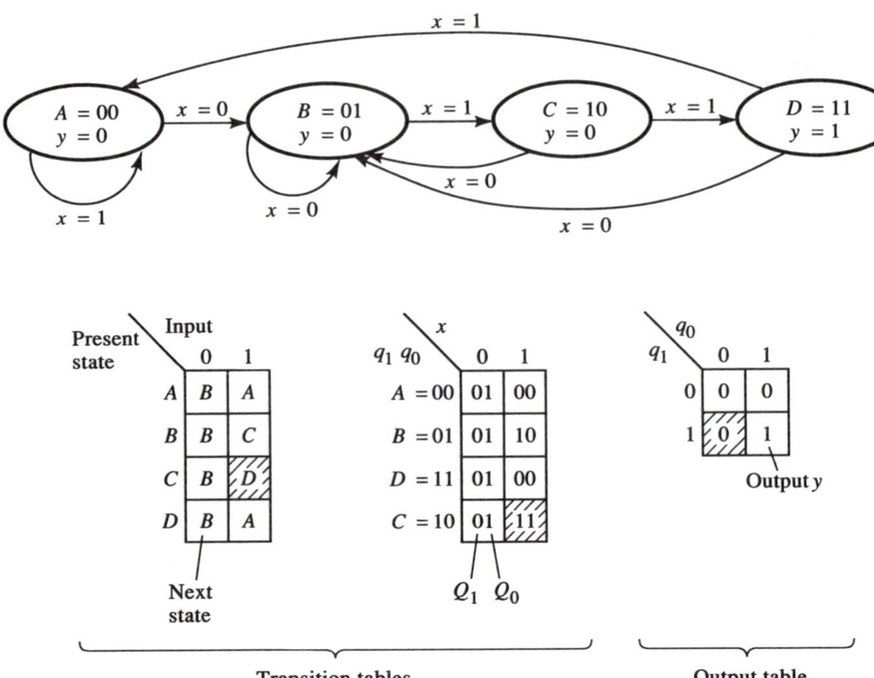


| Present state \ Input | 0 | 1 |
|---|---|---|
| A | B | A |
| B | B | C |
| C | B | D |
| D | B | A |

| $q_1 q_0$ \ x | 0 | 1 |
|---|---|---|
| A = 00 | 01 | 00 |
| B = 01 | 01 | 10 |
| D = 11 | 01 | 00 |
| C = 10 | 01 | 11 |

| $q_1$ \ $q_0$ | 0 | 1 |
|---|---|---|
| 0 | 0 | 0 |
| 1 | 0 | 1 |

**Figure 4.2.** Representation of the transition graph from Figure 4.1 with internal codes; transition and output tables.

of a transition graph, the next state $Q$ as a function of the present state $q$ and input $x$. The output table shows output $y$ as a function of the present state $q$. We will now show how the tables are constructed. For the circuit in Figures 4.1 and 4.2, if the system is in node $C$ and the input is 1, the next state will be $D$. The output in state $C$ is 0. Thus the transition table entry labeled $C$ and $x = 1$ is $D$ and the corresponding output table entry contains 0. This situation is highlighted in the diagram.

Both tables can be easily obtained from the graph, and similarly the graph can be constructed from the tables. Therefore the graph and the tables are equivalent, and both describe the functions $f$ and $g$ in our formal model.

If we have the transition graph or the transition tables for a circuit and know its present state and the sequence of future inputs, we can predict the sequence of successive states and outputs. Note that this can be done without knowing the internal structure of the circuit. In fact, one can design many different circuits to implement the same graph and table.

Although the graph and the tables give a complete description of the circuit's abstract behavior, they do not predict its physical behavior, its timing diagram. To draw the timing diagram we must also know what type of storage elements are being used. Once we have the transition information and have determined the type of storage elements, however, we can draw the circuit's timing diagram without knowing its internal connections.

In closing, let us note that sequential circuits physically implement the formal mathematical model of an important type of computing machine called the finite-state machine, or the "finite-state automaton." Because finite-state automata capture many of the essential properties of computers, they are very important in several areas of computer science.

## Exercises

1. Consider a sequential circuit with input $x$ and states $A$ (the initial state), $B$, and $C$. Outputs in the states are 0, 1, and 1, respectively. The transition from $A$ is always to $B$. From $B$, the transition is to $C$ when $x = 1$ and to $A$ when $x = 0$. The transition from $C$ is to $C$ when $x = 1$ and to $A$ when $x = 0$.

   Draw the transition graph, determine how many bits (internal variables) are needed to encode the states, select an (arbitrary) state assignment, and label the nodes with their codes. Convert the graph to a table and then convert the table back to a graph. The new and the initial graph should be the same. Repeat with a different state assignment.
2. Repeat Exercise 1 for a no-input circuit that outputs the repetitive sequence (00, 01, 10, 11, 00, 01, 10, 11, 00,...). How many different states does this circuit have? Why is it called a modulo-4 (mod-4) up counter? (*Hint*: Convert the sequence of outputs to decimal codes. Mod-4 arithmetic works with remainders of division by 4.)
3. Repeat Exercise 1 for a no-input circuit that outputs sequence (111, 110, 101, 100, 011, 010, 001, 000, 111, 110, 101,...). Why is this circuit called a mod-8 down-counter?
4. Consider the following table:

| State | Input $x$ 0 | 1 | Output $y$ |
|---|---|---|---|
| $A$ | $B$ | $C$ | 00 |
| $B$ | $C$ | $A$ | 01 |
| $C$ | $A$ | $B$ | 10 |

   Draw its transition graph, determine how many bits (internal variables) are needed to encode the states, assign codes to states, and add them to the graph. Convert the graph to a table and convert the table back to a graph. Check that the obtained graph is the same as the initial one. Repeat with a different state assignment.

5. What is the maximum/minimum number of steps required to exhaustively test a sequential machine with $n$ inputs and $m$-bit internal codes?

## 4.2 FLIP-FLOPS AND LATCHES

The storage of binary codes representing internal states is one of the essential functions of sequential circuits. In this section, we will describe the two basic storage elements, flip-flops and latches. Because all other storage devices are either based on them or can be explained with reference to them, the role of flip-flops and latches in sequential circuits is similar to the role of gates in combinational circuits.

A flip-flop or a latch is a "memory cell" that stores one bit of information, a logic 0 or a logic 1. Its inputs allow one to change (write) the stored data and its outputs are windows that allow one to read the stored value.

Reading is nondestructive; it does not change the stored value. Writing is destructive because the new value replaces (overwrites) the old value. Both flip-flops and latches are "volatile," which means that they lose their stored values when the power is turned Off.

Flip-flops and latches differ in the control signals that determine when the data inputs take effect. In addition, the various kinds of flip-flops and latches differ in how their data inputs control what is stored. According to the function of their data inputs, flip-flops and latches are classified as D, T, JK, and RS.

We will now examine the "when" and "how" aspects separately.

### Flip-Flops versus Latches

The most common definition of latches and flip-flops is as follows:

> *Latches* are *level sensitive*; writing to a latch is controlled by the logic level of an input usually called the "enable" or "strobe." When the strobe is active, the latch is open for writing via its data inputs. When the strobe is disabled, the latch does not respond to its data lines. Some latches have active High strobes, others are active Low strobes (Figure 4.3).
>
> Flip-flops are edge sensitive; they are activated by the edge, the transition, the change in level of the control signal. The control signal is usually called the *clock*. An active transition of the clock enables writing; at all other times data inputs have no effect on the contents of the flip-flop (Figure 4.3). Some flip-flops are activated by the Low-to-High transition (the "positive" edge) and others by the Low-to-High (the "negative" edge).

According to this classification, the following types of latches and flip-flops are possible:

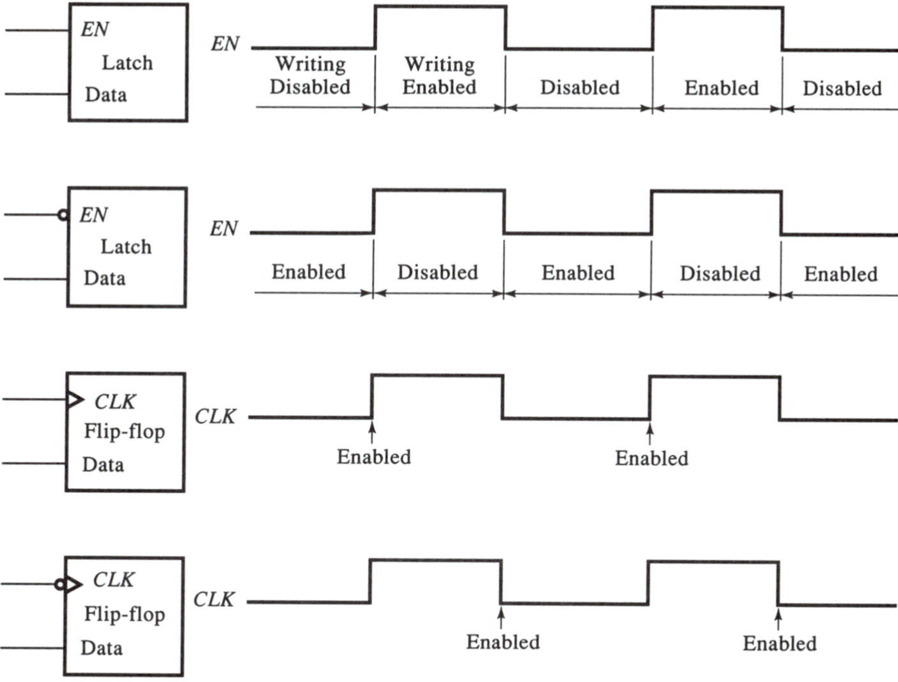


**Figure 4.3.** Four types of memory elements and their operation. The triangle on the clock input *CLK* indicates edge sensitivity.

Active High latch. Data inputs affect the stored value only when $EN = 1$.

Active Low latch. Data inputs are active when $EN = 0$.

Positive-edge triggered flip-flop. Data inputs are active during the change of the clock signal from 0 to 1.

Negative-edge triggered flip-flop. Data inputs are active when the clock signal goes from 1 to 0.

It should be stressed that enable or clock inputs control only writing. Reading of flip-flops and latches is possible at any time.

There exists another type of storage cell called the master–slave flip-flop or latch. It reads the data on one edge or during one level of the control signal, stores it, and outputs it on the following (inverse) edge or during the next level. The storage operation is thus performed in two steps. We will not use master–slave flip-flops because they are not very common.

To understand why we need several types of storage elements we must examine the role of time in sequential circuits.

Our model of a sequential circuit treats time as a discrete quantity, one which advances in indivisible units, rather than a continuous quantity, which is infinitely divisible. Sequential circuits achieve discretization by using well-defined events like clock pulses to control their storage elements. Treating time as a discrete variable is a major conceptual step similar to the conversion of physical signals into logic signals. Just as a logic device imposes a binary interpretation on a continuous signal, the clock imposes discreteness and sequencing on continuous time. Without the discreteness created by the pulses of a clock or by a series of other events even the concept of a sequence is meaningless (Figure 4.4).

Imposing discrete time intervals on sequential circuits means that one observes internal states and outputs at certain instants, leaving the time between them for transitions and for the stabilization of signals. We will see later that without this careful control, signals in transition may interact with one another. To avoid any interactions, the instants at which transitions are initiated must be precisely delimited. The very tight timing control that this implies can best be implemented by activating storage elements only for very short periods of time. Short, well-defined levels are difficult to create but sharp, and therefore brief, clock edges provide such control. This is why flip-flops are the basic building blocks of most sequential circuits.

The fact that sequential circuits use flip-flops controlled by clock signals does not mean that all sequential circuits are fully synchronous. (Events that happen at the same time are said to be "synchronous." Events that happen at different times are "asynchronous." In our context, events are synchronous if they are controlled by a shared clock signal.) In many circuits, some components need not or cannot be synchronized with the circuit clock and their capture thus requires latches. Computer memories and peripheral devices such as keyboards are prime examples. Both flip-flops and latches are thus necessary.

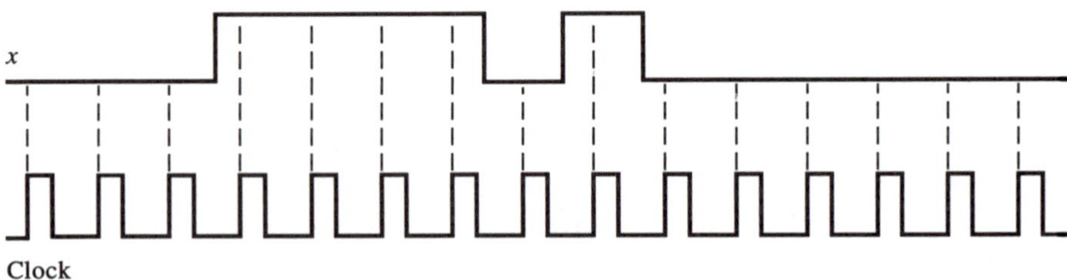


**Figure 4.4.** Discrete time intervals imposed by the clock on a synchronous circuit underlie the concept of a sequence. Without a clock, signal $x$ has no structure and all one can say about it is that it changes between 0 and 1. By adding a clock to mark time, the signal can be described as a sequence, in this case, (0,0,0,1,1,1,1,0,1,0,0,0,0,0,0).

### Exercises

1. Draw an arbitrary input signal and a control signal (enable/clock). Analyze how the circuit in Exercise 1 of Section 4.1 responds to it.
   a. Assume that the circuit uses active High latches. Repeat the analysis for active Low latches using the same input and enable signals.
   b. Assume that positive-edge triggered flip-flops are used. Repeat the exercise assuming that negative-edge triggered flip-flops are used.
2. Repeat the previous exercise with a two-input/two-input circuit described by a transition graph.
3. Repeat Exercise 1 but use the transition table.
4. Repeat Exercise 1 but describe the sequence of states and transitions symbolically rather than by timing diagrams. To what extent are the symbolic description and the timing diagram equivalent? Which provides more information?

### D-, T-, JK-, and RS-Flip-Flops and Latches

According to the number and effect of data inputs we distinguish D-, T-, RS-, and JK-flip-flops.

The *D-flip-flop*, also called the "data" or "delay" flip-flop, has only one data input, which is called $D$. When the flip-flop is activated it simply stores the value that was present on $D$ when the clock edge arrived (Figure 4.5). Note the following:

Because storage elements like latches or flip-flops are elementary sequential circuits, their transition behavior can be described by a transition graph, table, or equation. (A flip-flop's transition equation is called its *characteristic equation.*)

Positive- and negative-edge triggered flip-flops have identical transition graphs and tables. The difference between them is when they respond, not how they respond. This independence of the transition mechanism and the activation method holds for all flip-flops and latches, and for sequential circuits in general.

The output of a flip-flop is denoted by $Q$. In tables and equations, we call this signal $q$ when we mean its present value, and $Q$ when we mean the value after the arrival of the clock edge.

Most commercial flip-flops and latches have both $Q$ and $\overline{Q}$ outputs, which eliminates the need for an inverter if $\overline{Q}$ is needed.

Each node in our transition graph is marked with a single symbol—the stored value—that is also the output of the flip-flop.

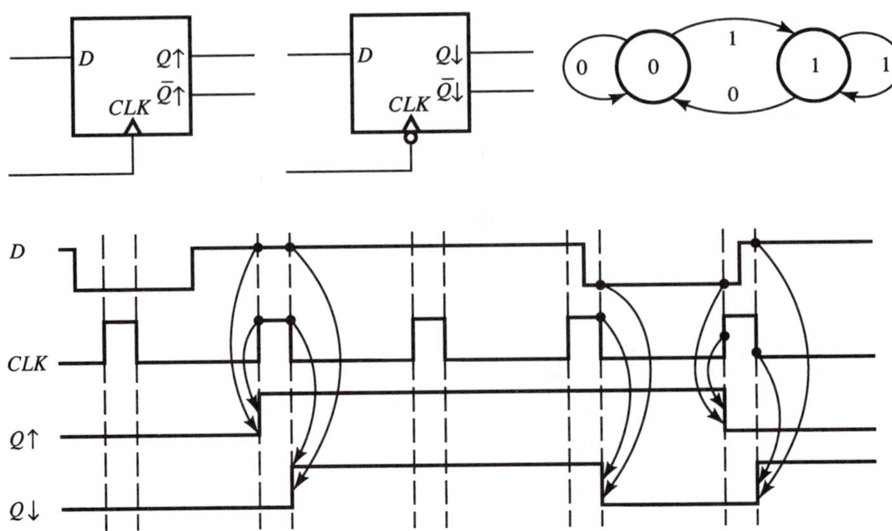


**Figure 4.5.** Positive- and negative-edge triggered D-flip-flops, their transition graph, and an example of operation. Symbols $Q\uparrow$ and $Q\downarrow$ denote the output of positive- and negative-edge triggered flip-flops, respectively.

An example of a commercial D-flip-flop is the 7474 chip whose pinout is shown in Figure 4.6. The 7474 is called a "dual positive-edge-triggered D-flip-flop with preset and clear" because it contains two independent flip-flops with special inputs *PR* and *CLR*. Input *PR* stands for preset, or simply set, and its Activation "sets" the flip-flop to 1. Input *CLR* stands for clear; when activated, it "clears" the flip-flop to 0. Both *CLR* and *PR* are asynchronous, which means that their effect is immediate and independent of the clock signal. When activated, *CLR* clears and *PR* sets the flip-flop regardless of whether the clock is making a transition. They override all other signals because they have a higher priority, and the only restriction on them is that they must not be actived simultaneously. In the 7474, both *PR* and *CLR* are active Low.

Preset and clear are often used to initialize and reset an entire sequential circuit. Initialization places the circuit in the desired starting state when power is first applied. Without it, the circuit would start in an unpredictable state and its behavior would appear random. Resetting can occur at any time, not just at power-up, and its effect is similar to initialization. It puts the circuit into a known state, often the same as the initial one.

The *T-flip-flop* ("toggle" flip-flop) has a single input that is called *T*. When $T = 1$ on the active clock edge, the value stored in the flip-flop is inverted, or toggled. The value $T = 0$ has no effect; in other words, the stored value remains stored as long as $T = 0$. The T-flip-flop (Figure 4.7) is used in counters but is not commercially available by itself. If needed, it can be easily constructed from other flip-flops.

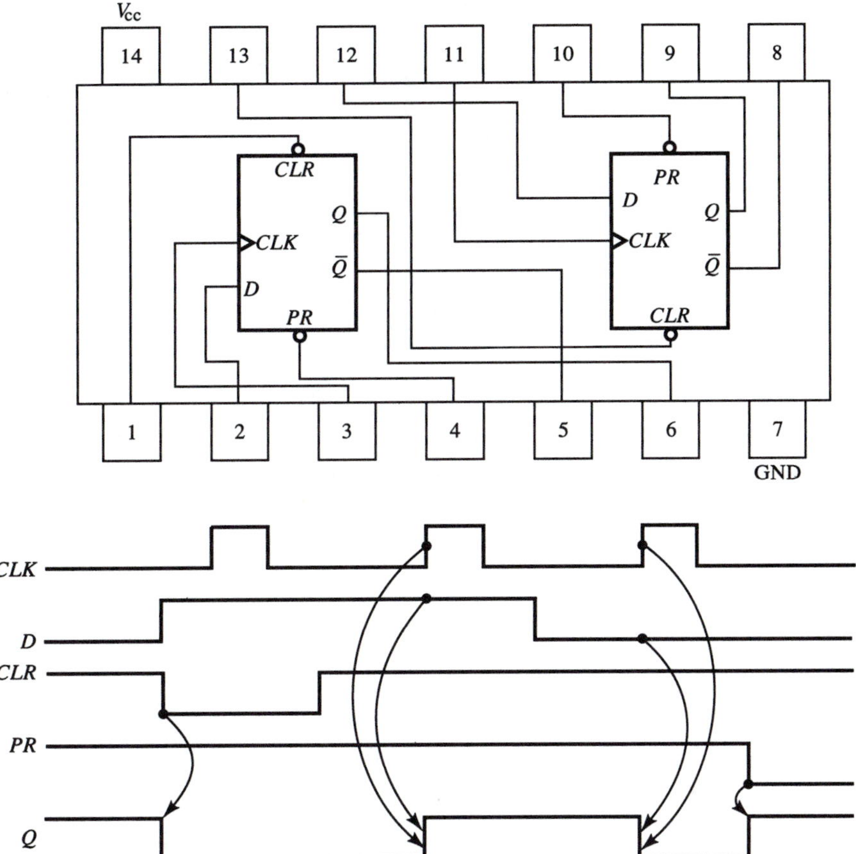


**Figure 4.6.** The 7474 D-flip-flop and an example of its operation with an unknown initial state. Arrows indicate the causes of transitions. Note that the positive- and negative-edge triggered flip-flops produce different outputs even though their inputs are the same.

The *JK-flip-flop* (Figure 4.8) has inputs $J$ and $K$. Active $J$ sets, and active $K$ clears the stored value. (Remember, $K$ "Klears".) Input $J = K = 1$ toggles; input $J = K = 0$ does not change the stored value. Note the operation of the master-slave variation of the flip-flop denoted $Q_{ms}$; its internal master flip-flop on input responds on the positive edge and its slave flip-flop on output follows on the negative edge. Altogether, it behaves as a delayed positive-edge triggered flip-flop.

The *RS-flip-flop* ("reset–set" flip-flop) works just like the JK-flip-flop except that the combination $R = S = 1$ produces unpredictable transitions and is disallowed. Input $R$ resets (clears); input $S$ sets.

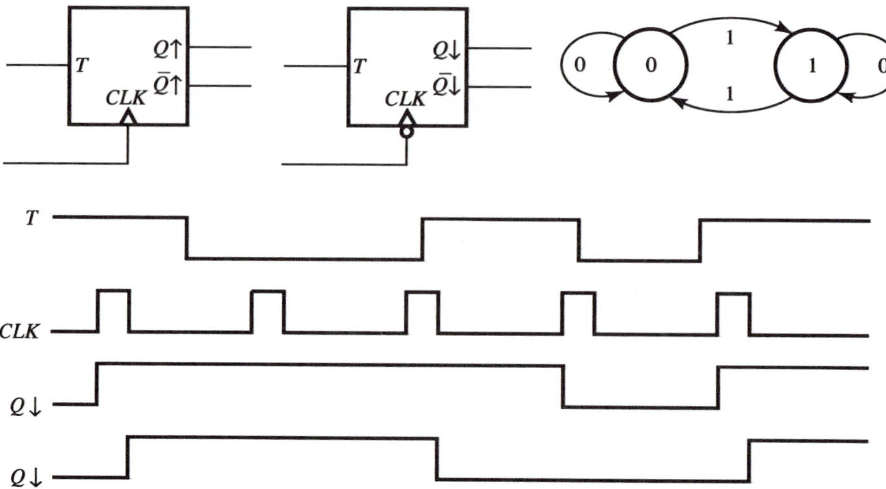


**Figure 4.7.** The T-flip-flop: its symbol, transition graph, and an example of its operation.

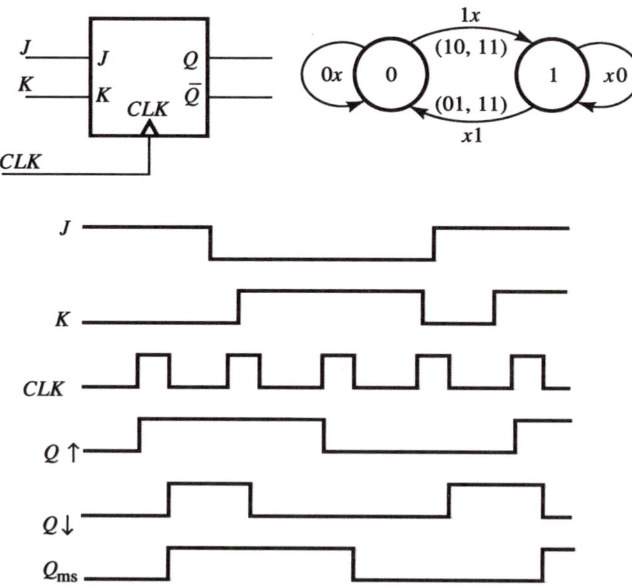


**Figure 4.8.** The JK-flip-flop: its symbol, transition graph, and example of its operation. Element $Q_{ms}$ is the output of a master-slave flip-flop.

Latches are available only in the D and RS varieties. Latches of the $T$ and $JR$ varieties would be useless because toggling without edge control starts a sequence of transitions between 0 and 1 that continues as long as the latch is enabled and in the toggling mode. The frequency of these 0→1→0→1 oscillations would be very high, in the tens of MHz (1 Mega = 1 million, 1 Hertz = 1 cycle per second), but would be unpredictable because it depends on the timing parameters of the chip, its age, load, and temperature. The final state of the latch would thus also be unpredictable.

Note that when a D-latch is enabled, its $Q$ output follows its $D$ input. In other words, an enabled D-latch is "transparent." This state is also known as "write-through."

Although latches and flip-flops are memory elements, they are normally implemented as a gate-based *feedback circuit*. Figure 4.9 shows an example of such a circuit implementing the RS-latch. It is left to the reader to show that the input combinations (00), (01), and (10) produce mutually consistent output, and that transitions to these states are also in agreement with the definition of an RS-latch. Input combination $R = S = 1$, on the other hand, produces contradictory outputs $Q = \overline{Q}$, and transition from this state is unpredictable because it depends on the relative speeds of the two gates. This explains why the combination $R = S$ is disallowed.

To conclude our presentation, the following table summarizes the main concepts introduced in this section

**Flip-Flops and Latches**

| Classification by Control Input: | |
|---|---|
| flip-flop | edge sensitive |
| latch | level sensitive |
| master-slave | stores in two steps |
| **Classification by Data Inputs:** | |
| $D$ | next state = value of $D$ when activated |
| $T$ | toggles when $T = 1$ |
| $JK$ | $J$ sets, $K$ clears, (00) no change, (11) toggles |
| $RS$ | $R$ resets (clears), $S$ sets, (00) no change, (11) disallowed |

**Exercises**

1. Draw arbitrary timing diagrams for the $D$ and clock inputs of a positive-edge triggered D-flip-flop and find its output signal.
2. Repeat Exercise 1 for a negative-edge triggered D-flip-flop using the same input signal.

3. Repeat Exercise 1 for a High- and Low-level sensitive D-latch.
4. Repeat the above exercises for T-, RS-, and JK-flip-flops and for latches, and indicate where this creates problems.
5. Identify the following flip-flops and latches: 7473, 7474, 7475, 7476, 74107, 74174, 74175.
6. "To store 1 in a D-flip-flop, *D* must be equal to 1 at the time of the active clock edge. To store 0, *D* must be equal to 0." Give a similar verbal description of the operation of other flip-flops.
7. Simulate all types of latches and flip-flops.
8. Draw the transition tables of D-, T-, JK-, and RS-flip-flops.
9. Find characteristic equations for all types of flip-flops. (*Hint*: Treat transition tables as Karnaugh maps.)
10. Analyze the operation of the circuit in Figure 4.9.
11. A master–slave flip-flop consists of two flip-flops connected in series. The master responds on the positive edge and the slave follows on the negative edge. Use this information to construct the internal diagram of a master-slave JK-flip-flop using two ordinary positive-edge triggered JK-flip-flops and draw a sample timing diagram of its operation.

## 4.3 PHYSICAL PARAMETERS OF STORAGE ELEMENTS

The output of a flip-flop or a latch cannot change instantaneously. Storage elements, like gates and other logic devices, experience propagation delays. They are also subject to several additional timing constraints (Figure 4.10) that must be considered when designing time-critical circuits.

Some of the timing parameters of flip-flops are related to data inputs; others are related to the clock signal. The setup and hold times determine how long the data signal must be stable during the data inputs to guarantee that it will be properly stored. The remaining parameters describe the clock signal. We will now briefly explain their meaning; for typical values, see the "switching parameters" in data sheets (Appendix 3).

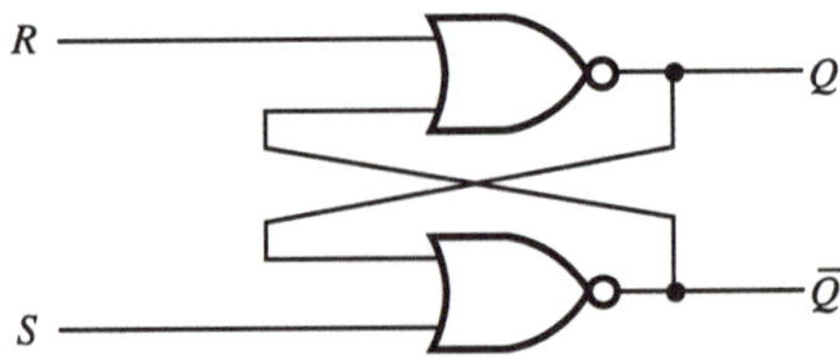


**Figure 4.9.** Implementation of an RS-latch.

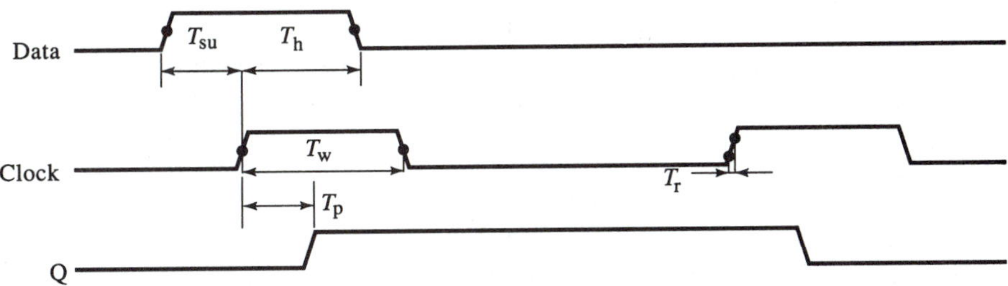


**Figure 4.10.** Timing parameters: setup time $T_{su}$, hold time $T_h$, propagation time $T_p$, rise time, $T_r$, and pulse width $T_w$.

The *setup time* $T_{su}$ is the minimum time for which the data signal must be stable before the active edge of the clock. In other words, the manufacturer guarantees that if data inputs are stable for at least $T_{su}$ before triggering, the flip-flop will operate as expected. If the input is not stable at least $T_{su}$ before the edge, it may not have the anticipated effect and can throw the circuit into a "metastable" state, in which operation becomes unpredictable for several consecutive clock cycles. Fortunately, the setup time is negligibly short under most circumstances. For the flip-flops in the 74 family, for example, the setup time is typically around 20 ns.

The *hold time* $T_h$ is the minimum time for which the data signal must be stable after the clock edge. Its value is usually zero or may even be negative, in which case the data input may be released before the arrival of the edge. Negative hold time is also referred to as release time.

Another timing parameter given in data sheets is the minimum *width of the clock pulse* $T_w$ (in nsec) and the maximum frequency of operation $f$ (in MHz). The maximum frequency is the maximum number of times the flip-flops can be rewritten in one second.

The speed of the clock can also be specified by its period $T$ (nsec), which is the separation of consecutive active edges. The relation between period and frequency is

$$f = 1/T$$

Most flip-flops require sharp clock transitions. Data sheets prescribe that the duration of the clock edge, measured between 10% and 90% of the nominal voltage values, must not exceed the *rise time* $T_r$. In other words, the transition must not take longer than $T_r$ (usually around 10 ns).

For a few storage elements, data sheets prescribe the recovery time. As the name implies, this is the time during which the component must be "left alone" to recover from the previous access.

Timing and frequency restrictions need not be considered in slower circuits but become critical if the system runs at high speed. Although most of the circuits that we will build in the lab do not require such speed, an understanding of timing is essential to comprehend the speed limitations of digital circuits like computers. We will thus give a detailed example of timing analysis in the next chapter.

**Exercises**

1. Find the switching parameters of the 7473, 7474, 7475, 7476, 74107, 74174, and 74175 flip-flops and latches.
2. Examine the parameters of the 54- ("military") counterparts of the 74-version of some of the above chips.

## 4.4 ANALYSIS OF SEQUENTIAL CIRCUITS WITH FLIP-FLOPS

We have already mentioned that sequential circuits can be divided into two large groups—synchronous and asynchronous. Both types of circuits can be analyzed in the same way but asynchronous circuits have certain unpleasant properties and it is thus easier to deal with synchronous circuits first. We will now review the definition of both categories and describe the analysis of synchronous circuits; we will discuss the behavior of asynchronous circuits in Section 4.7.

Synchronous circuits (Figure 4.11) use only flip-flops and share a common clock that controls all of their transitions. The clock simultaneously pulses all

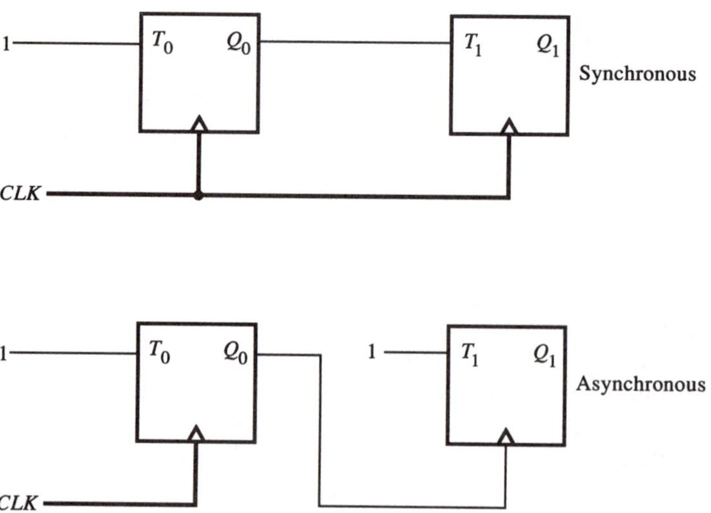


**Figure 4.11.** Synchronous and asynchronous circuit.

storage elements and the time between edges is left for the stabilization of internal signals and inputs. This eliminates interactions between individual transitions as well as the effects of timing differences and propagation delays and makes circuit operation safer.

In asynchronous circuits, some storage functions are not controlled by the clock, and transitions may thus cause chains of further transitions. Properly operating asynchronous circuits are more difficult to design, but asynchronous operation is necessary in at least some parts of most digital systems. As an example, every computer contains interfaces to external signals that are not controlled by the clock, arrive unpredictably, and must be stored asynchronously. Fortunately, nearly all circuits are synchronous with at most a simple asynchronous interface that is easy to understand and design (Figure 4.12).

After this brief introduction, we can now return to our main subject, the analysis of sequential circuits. Informally, circuit analysis is the process of identifying what the circuit does; in this case it entails the construction of a transition graph. Formally, our goal is to use the logic diagram to find the next-state and output equations

$$Q = f(q,x) \qquad \text{Next-state (transition) equation}$$

$$y = g(q) \qquad \text{Output equation}$$

The basis of analysis is the model in Figure 4.13. It contains edge-sensitive storage with a shared clock, an excitation circuit that combines inputs and stored values to force transitions, and an output circuit controlled by internal states. Input changes between transitions have no immediate effect on outputs, and output is thus synchronized with the clock.

We will now derive the procedure for analysis using the example in Figure 4.14.

State transitions (changes in the contents of the flip-flop) are the result of the data inputs of the flip-flop and its internal transition mechanism. The

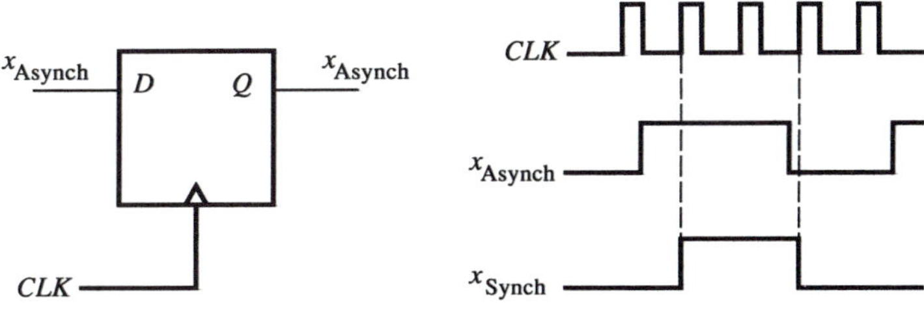


**Figure 4.12.** Synchronizing circuit.

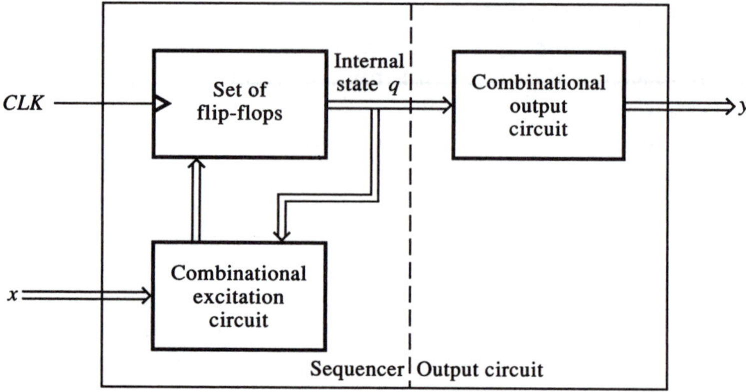


**Figure 4.13.** General diagram of a synchronous circuit.

next-state equation thus combines the description of the excitation circuit that controls the flip-flop's data input and the description of the transition mechanism of the flip-flop (its characteristic equation). In our case,

$T = e(q,x) = q + x$ Excitation equation of our flip-flop

$Q = c(q,T)$ Characteristic equation of the flip-flop

In these equations, $T$ is an internal variable of the circuit and must be eliminated by substituting the excitation equation into the characteristic equation:

$$Q = c(q,T) = c(q,e(q,x)) = c(q,q+x)$$

Finally, we need to derive the characteristic equation $c(q,T)$ to find the transition equation. This is easy as $c(q,T)$ describes the flip-flop's transition mechanism. Using Figure 4.15 we get

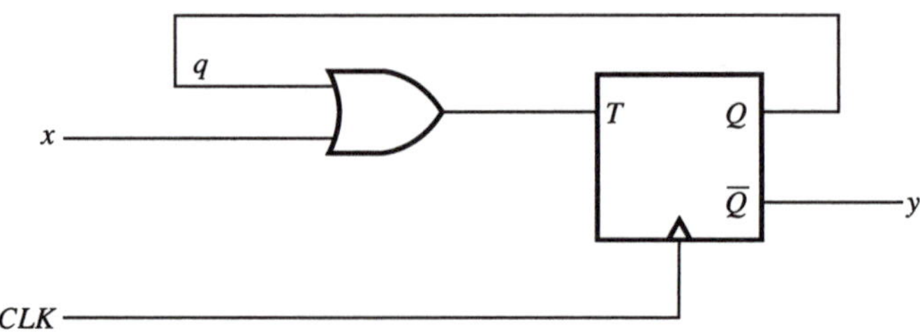


**Figure 4.14.** Sample sequential circuit.

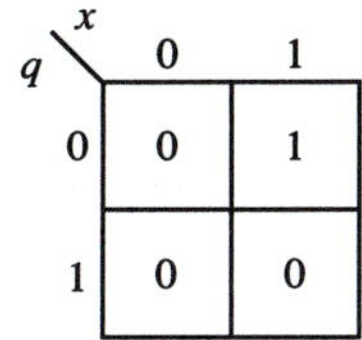


**Figure 4.15.** Transition table of a T-flip-flop.

$$Q = q\overline{T} + \overline{q}T = q \oplus T$$

We substitute for $T$ to obtain the final result,

$$Q = q\cdot(\overline{q + x}) + \overline{q}\cdot(q + x) = \overline{q}x$$

which is the desired transition function of the circuit. The output equation

$$y = \overline{q}$$

is easily obtained from the diagram. The complete description of the circuit is thus

| | |
|---|---|
| $Q = \overline{q}x$ | Transition equation |
| $y = \overline{q}$ | Output equation |

This completes the analysis of our sample circuit. If we wish, we can now convert the two equations into a transition graph or table. Because the circuit has one flip-flop, which can store either 0 or 1, the graph has two states. Outputs associated with these states are given by the $y$ equation, and transitions are derived from the next-state equation. Figure 4.16 shows the resulting graph.

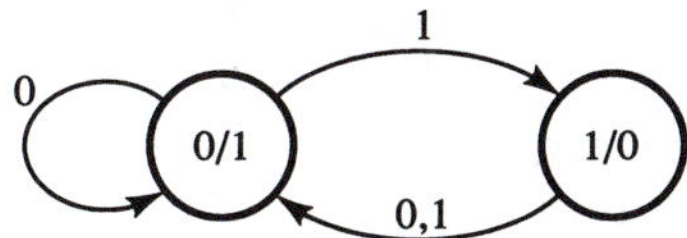


**Figure 4.16.** Transition graph of the circuit in Figure 4.14. The nodes are marked by state and output.

We can summarize the procedure for circuit analysis as follows:

1. Find excitation equations by expressing the data inputs of all flip-flops in terms of the circuits connected to them.
2. Get the next-state equations by substituting excitation equations into characteristic equations. The characteristic equation is obtained from the transition table of the flip-flop.

If the transition graph is desired, one must continue as follows:

3. Draw one node for each possible combination of flip-flop states. (The graph of a circuit with $n$ flip-flops will have $2^n$ states.) Use state codes as node labels.
4. For each combination of state $q$ and input $x$ calculate the next state $Q$ from the next-state equations; draw an arc from $q$ to $Q$; and label it $x$.
5. The last step of analysis is to obtain the output equations relating circuit outputs to flip-flop states and calculate outputs for each node.

Note that the procedure basically consists of two steps: transition analysis and output analysis. Transition analysis constructs a blank transition graph having all transitions but no outputs; output analysis fills in the blank nodes. This division corresponds to dividing a sequential circuit into a sequencer, which enforces transitions, and an output circuit, which produces the desired output (Figure 4.13).

We will now demonstrate the procedure one more time using the circuit in Figure 4.17.

1. The excitation equations are

$$J_0 = x \cdot \overline{q}_1$$
$$K_0 = 0$$
$$J_1 = 1$$
$$K_1 = x + q_1$$

2. The characteristic equation of the JK-flip-flop obtained from the $JK$ transition table in Figure 4.18 is

$$Q_i = J \cdot \overline{q}_i + \overline{K} \cdot q_i$$

Substituting for $J$ and $K$ from step 1 we get

$$Q_0 = (x \cdot \overline{q}_1) \cdot \overline{q_0} + \overline{0} \cdot q_0 = x \cdot \overline{q_0} \cdot \overline{q_1} + q_0$$
$$Q_1 = 1 \cdot \overline{q_1} + (\overline{x + q_1}) \cdot \mathrm{q}_1 = \mathrm{q}_1$$

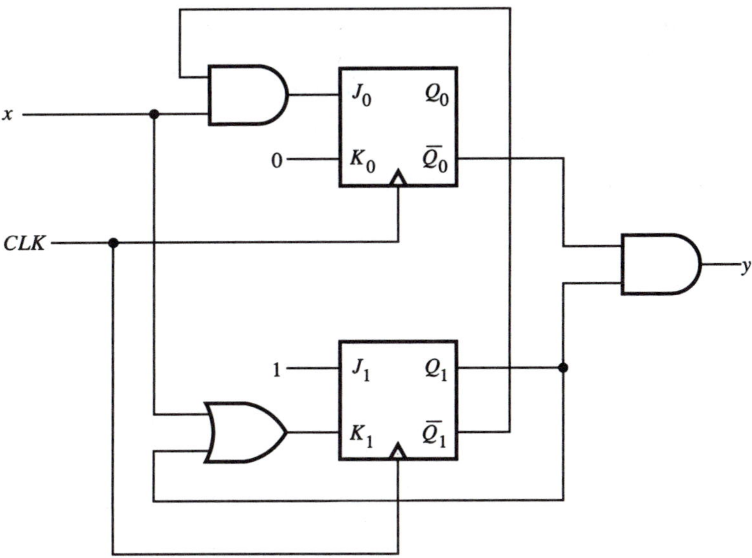


**Figure 4.17.** Sequential circuit.

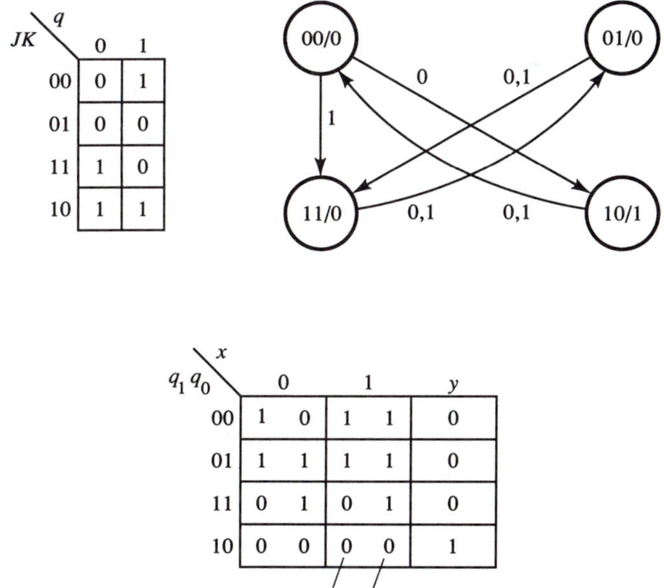


| JK \ q | 0 | 1 |
|---|---|---|
| 00 | 0 | 1 |
| 01 | 0 | 0 |
| 11 | 1 | 0 |
| 10 | 1 | 1 |

| $q_1 q_0$ \ x | 0 | | 1 | | y |
|---|---|---|---|---|---|
| 00 | 1 | 0 | 1 | 1 | 0 |
| 01 | 1 | 1 | 1 | 1 | 0 |
| 11 | 0 | 1 | 0 | 1 | 0 |
| 10 | 0 | 0 | 0 | 0 | 1 |

**Figure 4.18.** Transition table $Q$ of a JK-flip-flop (left) and analysis of the circuit in Figure 4.17.

3. The transition graph resulting from step 2 has four states $(q_1q_0) = (00)$, (01), (10), and (11).
4. The transitions are obtained from equations for $Q_0$ and $Q_1$. As an example, if we are in state (00) and the input is 1, the next state is (11) because

$$Q_0 = x\cdot\overline{q_0}\cdot\overline{q_1} + q_0 = 1\cdot\bar{0}\cdot\bar{0} + 0 = 1$$
$$Q_1 = \overline{q_1} = 1$$

   This means that there is an arc from (00) to (11) labeled 1, the value of $x$ for this transition. Drawing arcs directly from equations is awkward. We recommend constructing the transition table first and drawing the graph from it.
5. The output equation is

$$y = \overline{q_1}\cdot q_2$$

   It can be used to calculate outputs for individual nodes. As an example, the output in state (10) is 0. In Figure 4.18, the transition and output tables are combined into one table.

This completes our presentation of the analysis of circuits with flip-flops. The method applies also to chips that use flip-flops as internal components, such as sequential PLDs. Because the method does not depend on the timing of transitions, it applies to asynchronous circuits using, for example, latches as well. The timing behavior will, of course, be different.

**Exercises**

1. Derive the characteristic equations of D- and RS-flip-flops. Take advantage of don't-care conditions wherever possible.
2. Draw a synchronous circuit with positive-edge triggered D-flip-flops and analyze it. Repeat the exercise for negative-edge triggered flip-flops.
3. Analyze a circuit containing T-flip-flops, RS-flip-flops, and JK-flip-flops. Note that the analysis of circuits with RS-flip-flops requires checking that the disallowed combination $(R,S) = (1,1)$ never occurs. If it does, the circuit's response is unpredictable.
4. Repeat Exercise 3 with a circuit containing two flip-flops of different kinds.
5. Repeat Exercise 3 for a circuit containing a positive-edge triggered and a negative-edge triggered flip-flop.
6. Repeat Exercise 3 for a circuit with two outputs.
7. Repeat Exercise 3 for the circuit in Figure 4.19, whose output has a direct connection to its input. Is it necessary to change our procedure? That is, is it necessary to adopt a new form of description of the circuit's behavior?

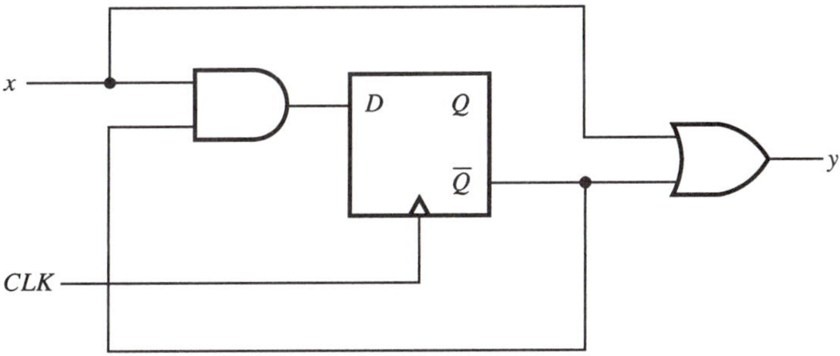


**Figure 4.19.** Circuit that violates our model because its output depends not only on the state but also on the input.

(*Hint*: Is it sufficient to write output values into the nodes?) Draw a timing diagram illustrating the asynchronous behavior of the output.

8. Our model of a sequential circuit does not provide any control over the arrival of the input, which is, in fact, asynchronous. In what way can this interfere with the operation of the abstract model or with the operation of a real circuit? Is it necessary to make some assumptions about the timing of the asynchronous input to guarantee correct operation?
9. Circuits with feedbacks, such as the RS-circuit in Figure 4.9, can be analyzed by inserting imaginary D-latches at appropriate places, in this case at the outputs of the gates. (Remember that D-latches are transparent.) Use this approach to analyze the circuit in Figure 4.9 and relate the result to the definition of an RS-latch.

## 4.5 REGISTERS

A register is a collection of flip-flops used to store a group of related bits such as a code. Because the group of the bits is treated as a single entity, all of the flip-flops in the register share the same clock. In addition to storage, registers can usually perform operations known as "shifting left" or "shifting right." In shifting left, the bit pattern stored in the internally connected flip-flops moves one position to the left and a new value is loaded into the rightmost flip-flop. Shifting right entails the same procedure but in the opposite direction. Several classes of registers are available for different applications. They differ in the way they provide access to their flip-flops (Figure 4.20) and in their shifting capabilities.

Parallel-in parallel-out (PIPO) registers have pins to access the inputs and outputs of all internal flip-flops. They are particularly useful for storing codes in computers.

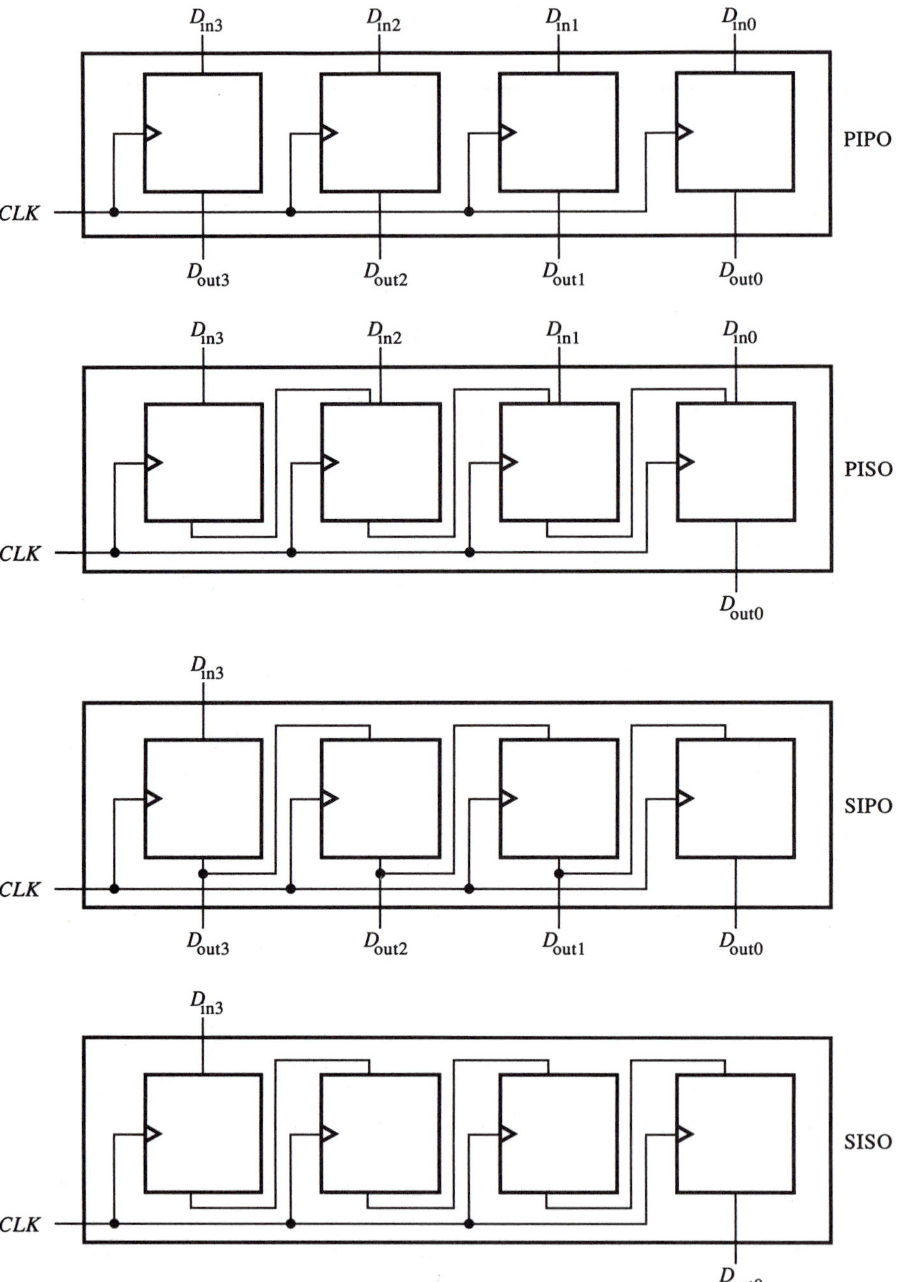


**Figure 4.20.** Four classes of registers: PIPO, PISO, SIPO, and SISO.

Parallel-in serial-out (PISO) registers have pins to access all flip-flop inputs, but only the output of the rightmost flip-flop is accessible.

Serial-in parallel-out (SIPO) registers complement PISO registers: Only the leftmost flip-flop's input is accessible but each output has a pin. Synchronized PISO and SIPO registers are useful for serial communication (Figure 4.21).

Serial-in serial-out (SISO) registers provide access only to the input of the leftmost and the output of the rightmost flip-flop. Their use is based on loading and shifting. Because the first bit that enters is the first bit that exits, these registers are also called first-in first-out (FIFO) registers. They are used to implement queues, a very important concept in many computer applications.

Different types of registers have different pin requirements. An $n$-bit PIPO chips needs $2n$ data pins; PISO and SIPO chips have $n + 1$ data pins; and SISO chips need only two data pins, no matter how many flip-flops they contain. The number of available pins is one of the biggest restrictions on integrated circuit packaging, and consequently all types of registers except SISO registers are limited in the number of internal flip-flops that they can accommodate. Because they can accommodate an unlimited number of in-

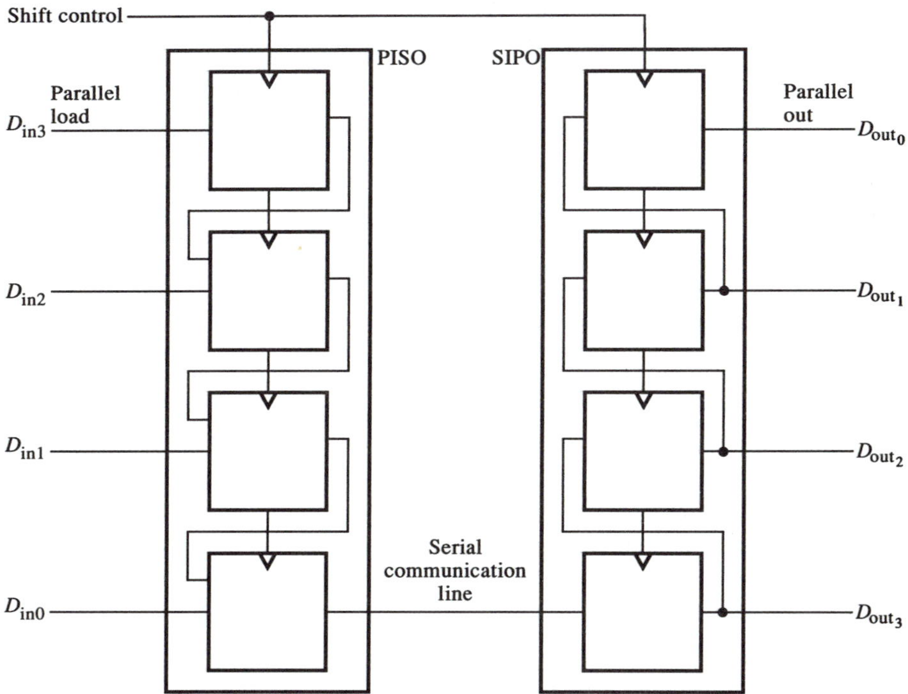


**Figure 4.21.** Use of PISO and SIPO registers in serial communication.

ternal flip-flops SISO registers are very well suited for storage and they are used as sequential memory. (In this context the term "sequential" means that the data is accessed in sequence, by shifting the bits internally around the register and accessing them one after another through the single input or output pin.) Note that the simplicity of access to sequential (FIFO) memories is achieved at a considerable decrease in access speed.

First-in first-out memories are available in several forms. One is a large-capacity semiconductor SISO chip. For example, SISO chips containing 4096 nine-bit registers (rather than individual bits) used in communication. Another variety of FIFO memory is the "magnetic bubble memory," in which storage is based on magnetic rather than semiconductor chip principles. Floppy- and hard-disk drives (Chapter 11) are also FIFO memories.

Magnetic bubble memories are nonvolatile; that is, stored data does not disappear when the power is turned off. They are typically available with 1 Mbit capacities. They are sometimes used as small capacity substitutes for floppy disk, taking advantage of their lack of mechanical parts and the resulting reliability.

To illustrate the internal structure of a register, Figure 4.22 shows the 7491 eight-bit SISO shift-right circuit. The diagram demonstrates the implementation of shifting. The purpose of the inverter on the clock line is to amplify the signal, which must drive the eight internal clock inputs without loading the external clock signal. Note the two serial inputs; one can be used as input enable.

## Exercises

1. Draw a sample timing diagram of the main signals in register-based serial communication.
2. Assume that an eight-bit SISO register has been cleared and the following sequence loaded into it by consecutive clock pulses starting at time $t$:

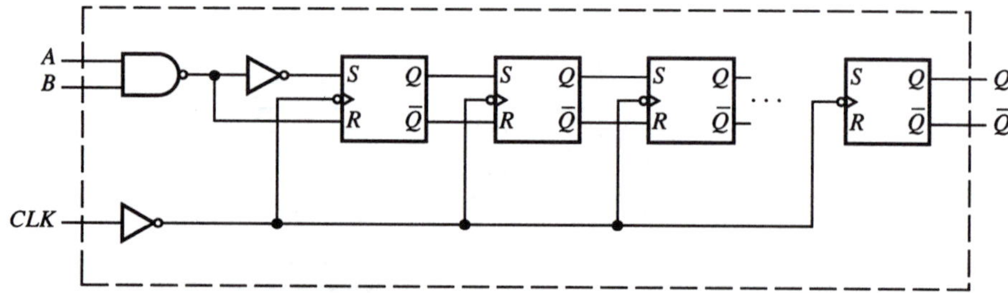


**Figure 4.22.** Internal structure of the 7491 SISO eight-bit shift register.

0111011110101. Show the corresponding output sequence beginning at time $t$.

3. Find the types and switching parameters of the following registers: 7494, 7495, 7496, 74165, 74173, 74299.
4. Explain how the 7491 in Figure 4.22 shifts.
5. Design a shift-right/shift-left (also called shift up/down) register.
6. Design a read/write sequential memory based in a SISO register. The following signals should be available: data in, read/write control, count (to show the current position of "bit 0"), and data out.

## 4.6 COUNTERS

The basic function of counter is to count clock pulses. More elaborate types of counters have additional inputs that make them suitable for the design of sequential circuits.

The simplest possible counter is a T-flip-flop with its $T$ input permanently connected to 1 (Figure 4.23). Each positive clock edge toggles $Q$, and consecutive edges thus produce sequence (0, 1, 0, 1,...). Because this is a repetitive sequence of length two, the circuit is a mod-2 or base-2 counter. Note that the frequency of $Q$ is one-half of the frequency of the clock input, and the counter can thus also be used as a frequency divider.

Counters can be classified by the type of edge on which they increment, the length of their counting sequence (their modulus), whether they count up or down, and by other parameters that will be introduced later. To illustrate these concepts, Figure 4.24 shows the behavior of a mod-4 positive-edge

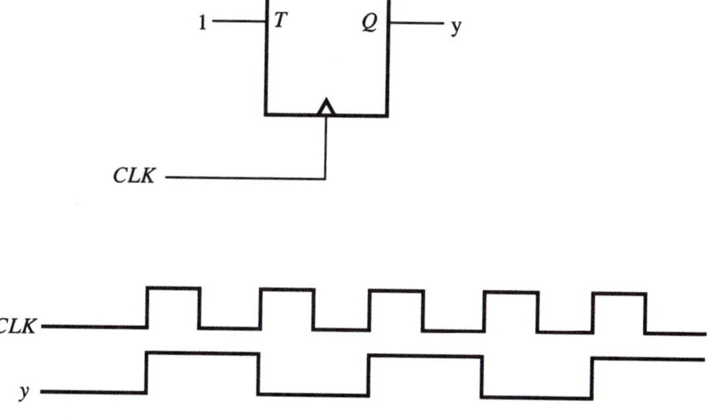


**Figure 4.23.** The T-flip-flop as a modulo-2 counter.

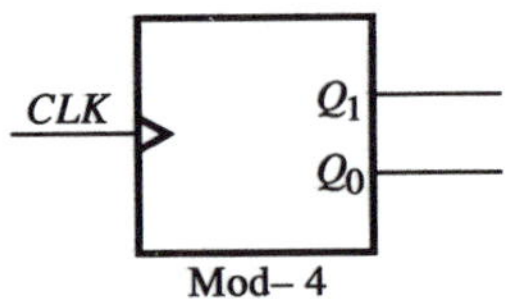


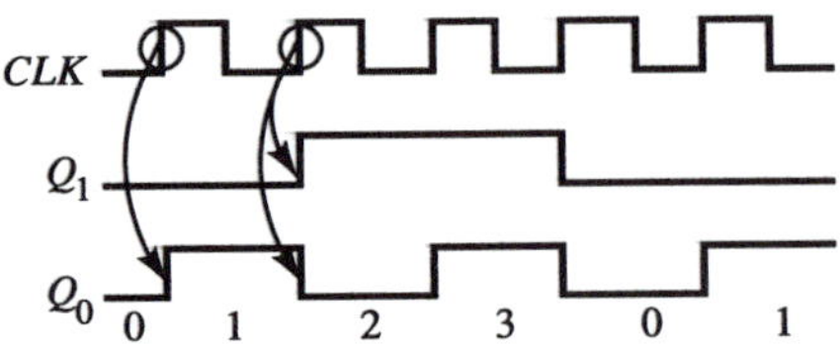


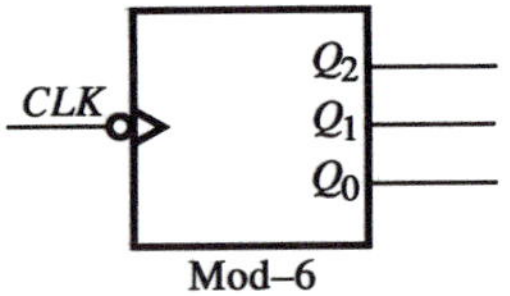


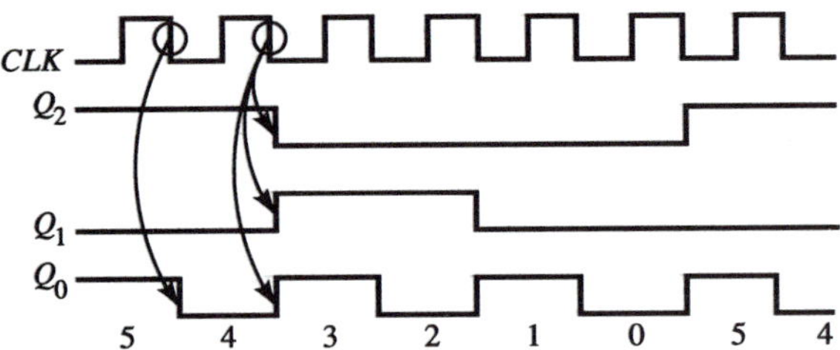


**Figure 4.24.** Symbol and operation of a mod-4 positive-edge triggered up counter and a mod-6 negative-edge triggered down counter.

triggered up counter and mod-6 negative-edge triggered down counter. The first counts (00, 01, 10, 11, 00, 01, 10, and so on), and the second counts (101, 100, 011, 010, 001, 000, 101, 100, and so on). Individual bits of each count are denoted $Q_2$ (the most significant bit, or MSB), $Q_1$, and $Q_0$ (the least significant bit, or LSB). In this notation, the weight of bit $Q_i$ is $2^i$ in positional representation. Another frequently used notation is ($Q_4$, $Q_2$, $Q_1$), where the subscript denotes the weight of the $i$th bit in positional notation.

In addition to the clock input, many counters have a "clear" input that resets the count to 0. Some counters also have "preset" data inputs that can set or clear individual $Q_i$s. We will see that these presettable counters are very useful for sequential design. They are controlled by a load input ($LD$) and work as follows (Figure 4.25):

> When input $LD$ is inactive, the device behaves as an ordinary counter and inputs $D_i$ have no effect.
>
> When input $LD$ is active, the counter does not count and the values of $D_i$ are loaded into $Q_i$. In this mode, the counter behaves as a collection of D-flip-flops loaded from inputs $D_i$.

In short,

> When $LD$ is active, $Q$ becomes $D$.
>
> When $LD$ is inactive, $Q$ becomes $Q + 1$ modulo-$N$ on the next edge.

Depending on when loading takes place, presettable counters are categorized as "fully synchronous" and "asynchronous." A fully synchronous counter loads on the active edge of the clock signal when counting would normally occur. An asynchronous counter loads as soon as input $LD$ is activated, even if there is no clock edge; thus $LD$ overrides the clock. We will concentrate on fully synchronous presettable counters because asynchronous counters present the same problems as all asynchronous circuits.

The operation of a counter can be described by a transition graph (Figure 4.26). Because the basic nonpresettable counter has no data inputs, transitions on its graph are not labeled. (The clock is not an input because it only triggers transitions and has no effect on where they go). Each node contains the code of the internal state, which is also the output of the counter.

One can obtain the transition graph of a presettable counter by extending the graphs of a basic counter but such a diagram would be very cluttered because presetting makes possible transitions between any two nodes. We will not draw this graph because the operation of a presettable counter is obvious and the drawing would only obscure it.

Depending on the triggering of their internal flip-flops, counters are classified as synchronous or asynchronous. The latter are also called "ripple" counters. Note that this classification is independent of the similar division of presettable counters: One convention refers to internal triggering and the other to the operation of preset and clear inputs.

In synchronous counters (Figure 4.26), all of the internal flip-flops are triggered by the same clock signal. In ripple counters (Figure 4.27), only the LSB flip-flop is triggered by the clock signal, and the remaining flip-flops are controlled by the transitions that ripple through the counter from the LSB. If

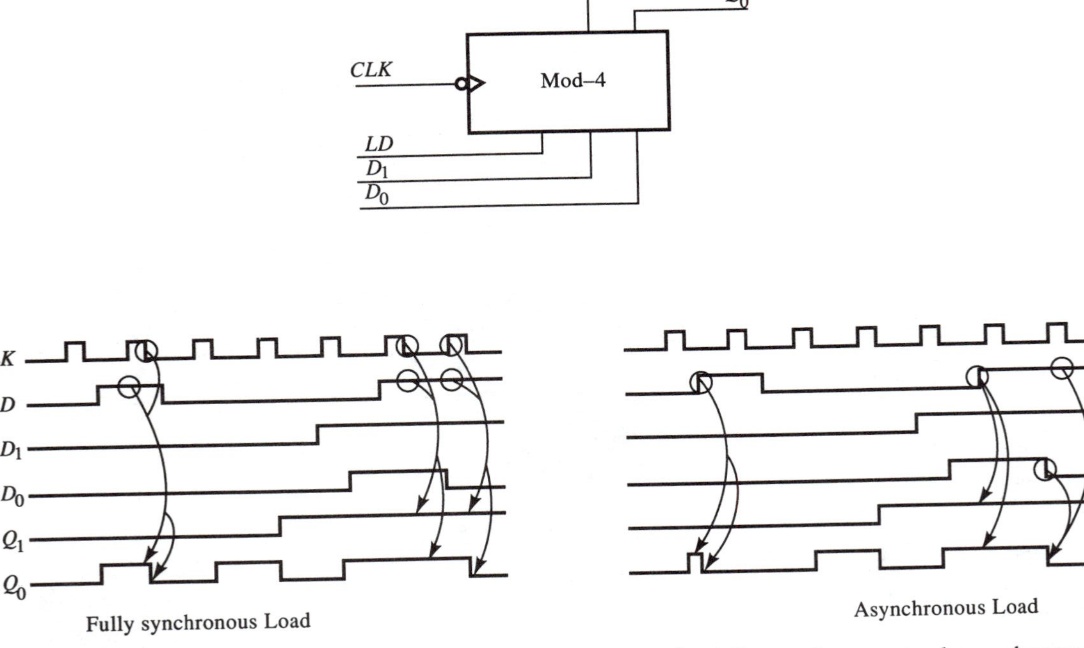


**Figure 4.25.** Presettable counter and an example of its operation for fully synchronous and asynchronous $LD$.

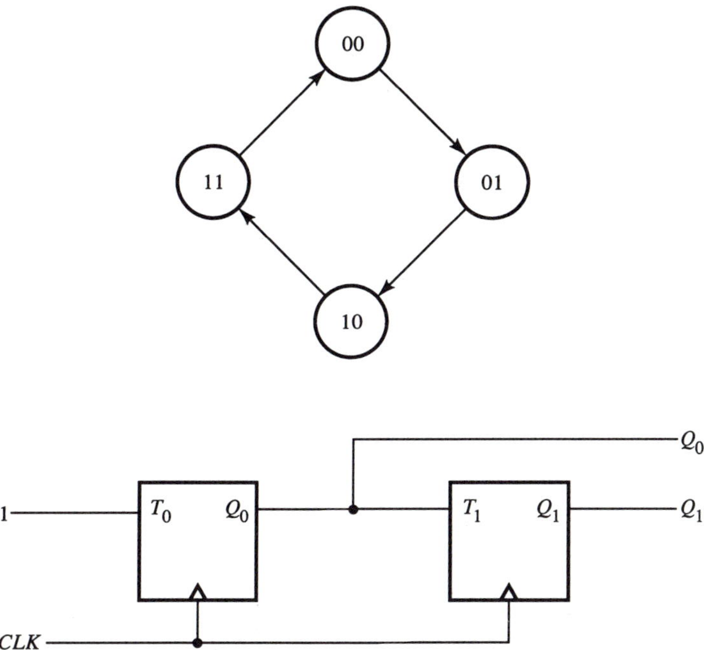


**Figure 4.26.** Transition graph of a synchronous mod-4 counter and its possible implementation.

properly designed, the intermediate transitions die out rapidly and the flip-flops settle into a new steady state.

Although its internal implementation is asynchronous, the ripple counter can be used as a building block in synchronous circuits. Its transition is triggered by the edge of the system clock, and when correctly used its intermediate transitions are no more threatening than the propagation delays of flip-flops. Unfortunately, improperly used asynchronous counters can cause serious problems (Section 4.7).

Why do we need counters triggered in two different ways? The answer is that they both have advantages. Ripple counters are usually simpler but a change in the state of one internal flip-flop can cause a domino-like sequence of transitions. This makes asynchronous counters slower and can cause a potentially dangerous sequence of intermediate outputs before the value reaches a steady state (Figure 4.27). Synchronous counters are faster and somewhat safer to use because all their outputs change simultaneously. Their internal implementation, however, is usually more complicated.

Figure 4.28 shows the 7492 ripple counter. This is a multipurpose chip that can be used as a mod-2 or mod-6 counter, as well as a mod-12 counter when its mod-2 and mod-6 counters are connected together. In the mod-12 mode of operation, the edge of the MSB output of one counter (its slowest changing

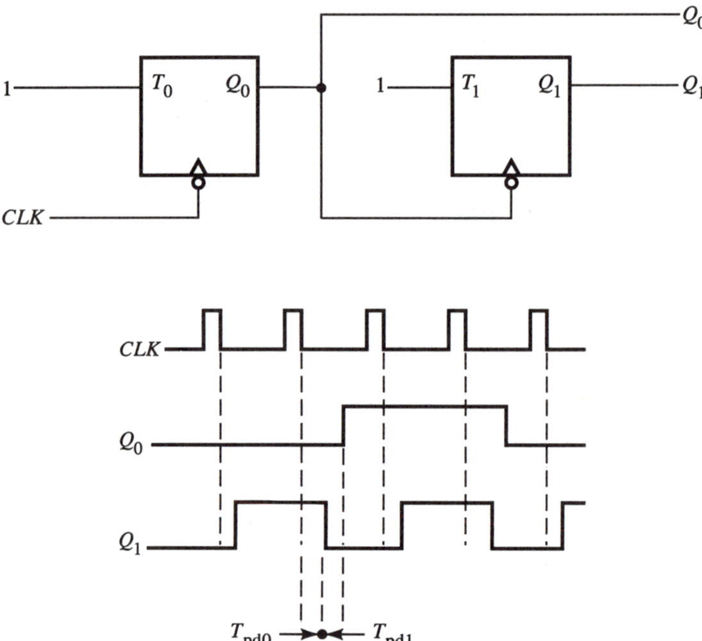


**Figure 4.27.** Diagram and Operation of a mod-4 asynchronous (ripple) counter.

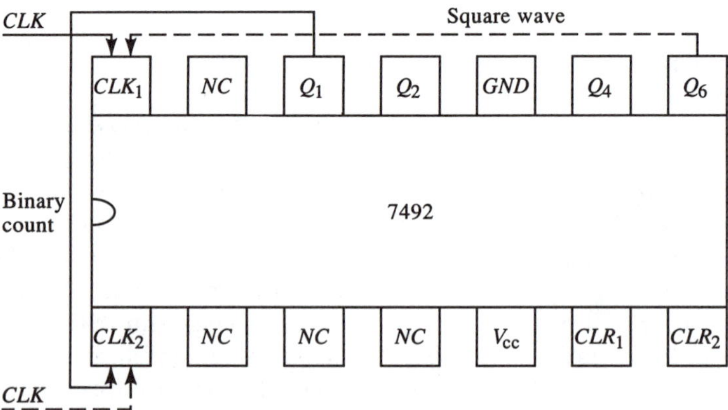


**Figure 4.28.** The 7492 base-12 ripple counter. The label *NC* means that a pin is not connected. Note the unusual marking of *Q* pins.

bit) is used as the clock of the other counter. Because this can be done either by connecting the output of mod-2 to the clock of mod-6 or by connecting the output of mod-6 to the clock of mod-2, two modes of operation can be obtained (Figure 4.29). One produces the sequence (0, 1, 2, 3,..., 10, 11, 0, 1,...) and the other generates a "square wave" symmetric output. The MSB of the square wave is High for six clock pulses and Low for the remaining six. This mode of operation allows us to extend the concept of counting: In a general sense a counter is any circuit that produces a periodically repeating sequence of codes.

**Exercises**

1. Recapitulate the classification of counters according to the following parameters: modulus, presettability, synchronous or asynchronous loading or internal operation, up/down counting, clear.
2. Determine the type (modulus, presettability, active edge, and other parameters) of the following counters: 7490, 7492, 74142, 74160, 74161, 74190, 74191, 74192, 74193.
3. Draw the outputs of a positive-edge triggered base-12 up counter. Repeat with a negative-edge triggered up counter and a down counter.
4. Complete the timing diagram shown in Figure 4.30. Do a similar example with a presettable base-16 down-counter.
5. Analyze the internal transitions made by the ripple counter in Figure 4.28 and use the result to explain why the operation of a ripple counter is slower than that of a synchronous counter. Explain why using a sufficiently slow clock makes the intermediate transitions acceptable.
6. What is the code sequence of the square-wave mode of operation of the mod-12 counter?
7. Outputs of the regular mod-12 counter are weighted 8:4:2:1. What are the weights of the square wave mod-12 counter?
8. Why is a circuit that counts from 0 to $n - 1$ called a mod-$n$ counter?
9. Almost all computers use counters as "frequency dividers." Explain this application by showing that the frequency of the most significant bit of a mod-$n$ counter is $f/n$, where $f$ is the frequency of the clock input.
10. Draw the complete transition graph of a presettable mod-4 counter.
11. Derive the characteristic equation of a mod-4 up counter and a mod-8 down counter.
12. Derive the characteristic equation of a presettable mod-4 up counter.

## 4.7 ANALYSIS OF SEQUENTIAL CIRCUITS WITH PRESETTABLE COUNTERS

Ordinary counters can only count, and no other control of their transitions is possible. This makes them uninteresting for the design of general sequential

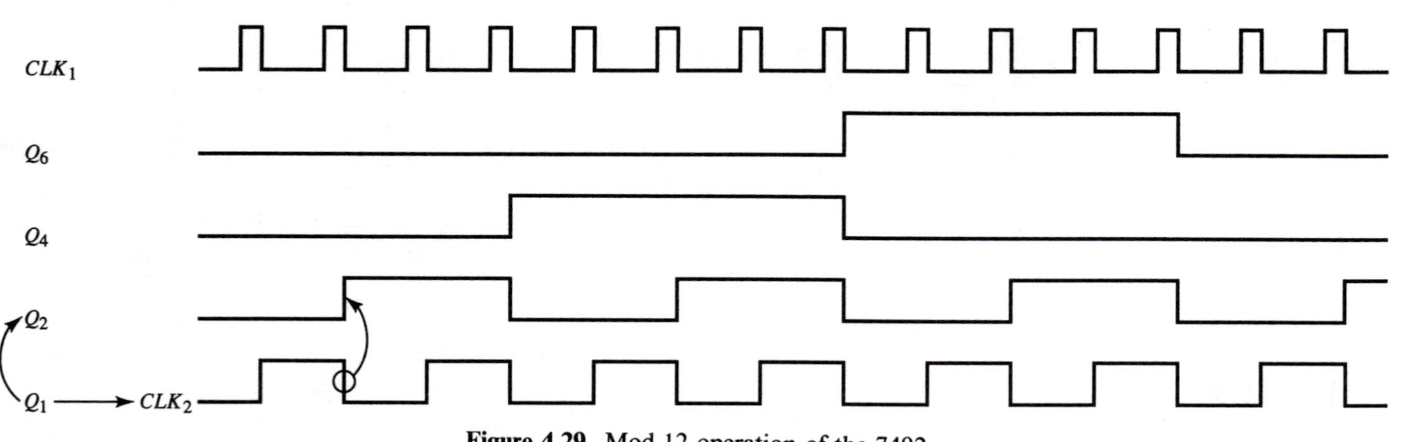


**Figure 4.29.** Mod-12 operation of the 7492.

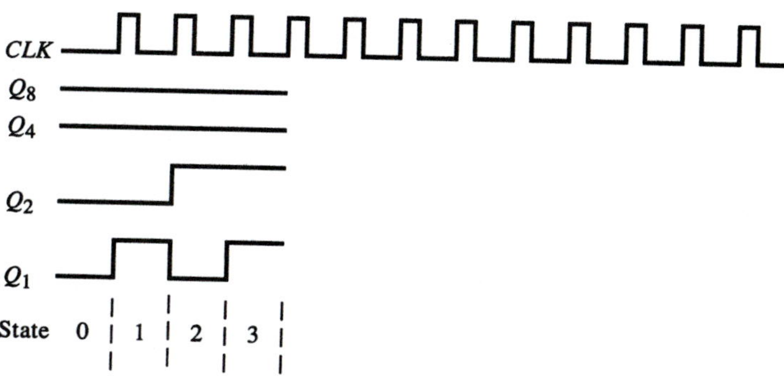


**Figure 4.30.** Incomplete timing diagram of a decade (base-10) positive-edge triggered presettable up counter.

circuits. Presettable counters, on the other hand, can be loaded with any next state and are thus just as flexible as flip-flops. Moreover, the built-in transition mechanism of counting can simplify the required excitation circuits. Presettable counters are thus useful building blocks and we will now show how to analyze circuits that use them. Because of our bias toward synchronous circuits we will consider only fully synchronous presettable counters in which loading is synchronized with the triggering edge of the clock.

As we know, the principle of analysis of sequential circuits is

1. Construct excitation formulas.
2. Combine the transition mechanism of the storage elements and the excitation formulas to get the transition table and graph.
3. Construct the output formulas and complete the graph.

When analyzing circuits with flip-flops we took advantage of characteristic equations. This approach is not attractive for circuits with presettable counters because their characteristic equations are too complicated. To analyze circuits with counters we thus use a tabular method that combines our verbal definition of counters with excitation functions to get circuit transition tables one entry at a time. We will demonstrate this procedure on the circuit in Figure 4.31.

1. Excitation equations are

$$LD = x$$

$$D_1 = 1$$

$$D_0 = q_0$$

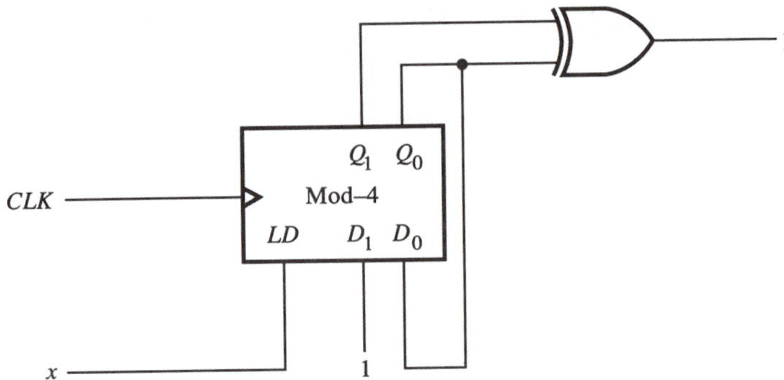


**Figure 4.31.** Sequential circuit using a presettable counter with active High inputs.

Before we proceed to the next step, it is useful to convert these functions into excitation tables of the same shape as the desired transfer table (Figure 4.32). Note that we don't need to calculate the values of $D_1$ and $D_0$ for those entries where $LD = 1$. These values are irrelevant for circuit behavior because they will never be loaded and consequently have no effect on the next state.

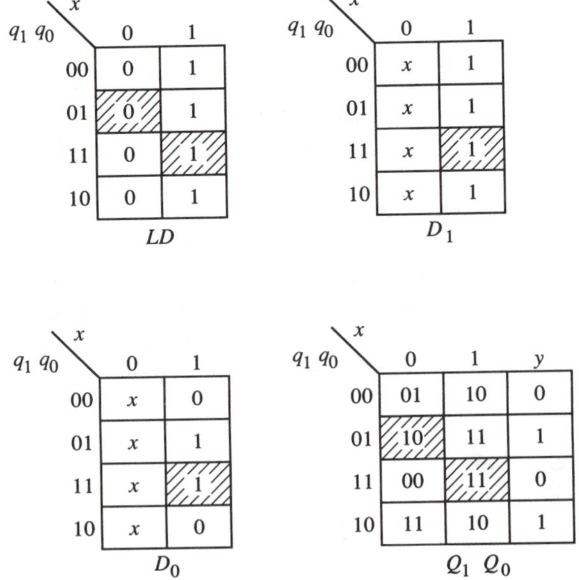

LD

| $q_1 q_0$ \ $x$ | 0 | 1 |
|---|---|---|
| 00 | 0 | 1 |
| 01 | 0 | 1 |
| 11 | 0 | 1 |
| 10 | 0 | 1 |

$D_1$

| $q_1 q_0$ \ $x$ | 0 | 1 |
|---|---|---|
| 00 | $x$ | 1 |
| 01 | $x$ | 1 |
| 11 | $x$ | 1 |
| 10 | $x$ | 1 |

$D_0$

| $q_1 q_0$ \ $x$ | 0 | 1 |
|---|---|---|
| 00 | $x$ | 0 |
| 01 | $x$ | 1 |
| 11 | $x$ | 1 |
| 10 | $x$ | 0 |

$Q_1 Q_0$

| $q_1 q_0$ \ $x$ | 0 | 1 | $y$ |
|---|---|---|---|
| 00 | 01 | 10 | 0 |
| 01 | 10 | 11 | 1 |
| 11 | 00 | 11 | 0 |
| 10 | 11 | 10 | 1 |

**Figure 4.32.** Excitation tables and transition table of the circuit in Figure 4.31. The cells analyzed in the text are highlighted.

2. Obtain individual entries of the next-state table. Because the operation of the presettable counter depends on input *LD*, the calculation is performed as follows:

   If the *LD* entry for the given cell is not active the counter counts and the next state is

$$(Q_1Q_0) = (q_1q_0) + 1 \text{ mod-}N$$

   where $N$ is the modulus of the counter. As an example, $LD = 0$ for $(q_1q_0x) = (010)$, and so $(Q_1Q_0) = (01) + 1 = (10)$ for this cell (highlighted).

   When *LD* is active, the counter loads and

$$(Q_1Q_o) = (D_1D_0)$$

   where $D_1$ and $D_0$ are found in the corresponding entries in the $D_1$ and $D_0$ tables. As an example, $LD = 1$ for $(q_1q_0x) = (111)$ (highlighted) and the corresponding entry in the transition table is thus $(Q_1Q_0) = (D_1D_0) = (11)$.
3. The output equation $y = q_1$ *XOR* $q_0$ is used in the usual way.

This completes the analysis of the circuit and a transition graph can now be drawn if desired. Although the procedure is more cumbersome than the analysis of flip-flop-based circuits, it is still mechanical. Note that one can use a similar table-based approach for flip-flops as well.

**Exercises**

1. Draw several sequential circuits with presettable counters and analyze them.
2. Draw several sequential circuits with ordinary counters and analyze them.
3. Analyze a flip-flop-based circuit using the tabular method.

## 4.8 WHAT CAN GO WRONG

We will now give two examples to illustrate the most common problems with sequential circuits. Both are due to *asynchronous* operation which explains why we avoid asynchronous circuits.

**Example 1** A mod-3 down counter producing sequence (10, 01, 00, 10, 01, 00,...) can be built from a presettable mod-4 down-counter and a circuit that resets it to (10) when the counter attempts to make a transition to (11) (Figure 4.33). Note that this solution assumes that the reset is asynchronous; otherwise resetting would occur on the edge following the transition to (11), and we need a transition that occurs as soon as $q_1$ and $q_0$ reach 1.

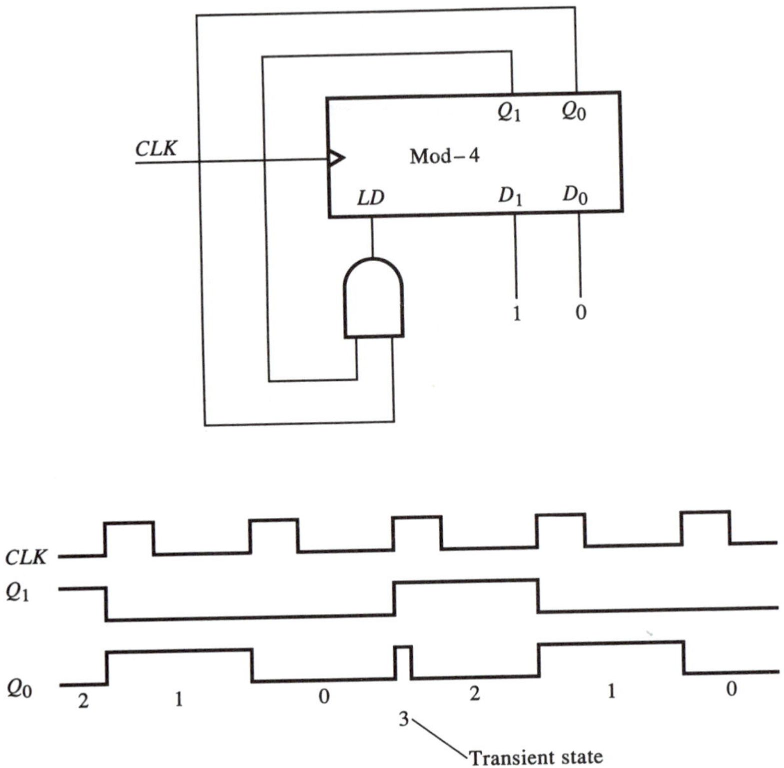


**Figure 4.33.** Asynchronous circuit and its expected operation. The counter used in the circuit has asynchronous reset and its internal operation is asynchronous as well.

If the circuit uses the asynchronous mod-4 ripple counter from Figure 4.34, there is a brief period during the transition between states (10) and (01) when $(q_1q_0) = (11)$. Transition (10)→(01) is thus in reality (10)→(11)→(01). Even though the intermediate state 11 is very brief, it can trigger the AND gate and reset the counter to (10) as shown at the bottom of the figure. Our circuit thus never enters state (01) and its counting sequence becomes (10, (11), 10, (11),...), where the codes in interior parentheses appear only briefly. A circuit that seemed reasonable thus does not perform the desired function due to multiple transitions in a single clock cycle. The problem would not occur with a fully synchronous counter as long as it was given enough time to propagate the delay and setup.

Note that a hazard present in the excitation circuit of an asynchronous sequential circuit might cause similar problems.

**Example 2.** Consider the asynchronous circuit with permanently enabled latches in Figure 4.35. Its transition table is obtained in the same way as that

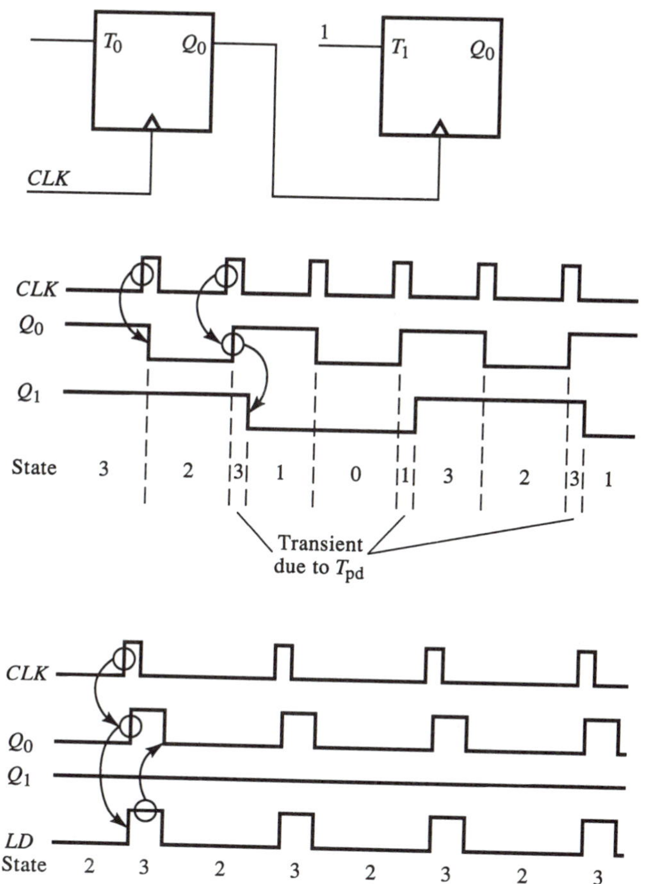


**Figure 4.34.** Mod-4 counter without preset (*top*); its operation (*middle*); and the real behavior of the circuit in Figure 4.33 (*bottom*).

of a synchronous circuit because synchronous and asynchronous circuits having the same structure make the same transitions—only the clock control is missing.

Assume that the circuit is in state (00), and the input changes from 0 to 1. According to the transition table, the next state is (11) and the values stored in the two latches should thus change from 0 to 1. However, because the two latches cannot have exactly the same propagation delays there will be a *race* between their transitions, and one will respond faster than the other. Let us now explore the consequences.

***Case 1.*** If $FF_1$ wins the race and changes first, the state of the circuit becomes (10), the second row and the first column in the transition table. Although all latches are enabled, no further changes occur. The next state for state (10) and

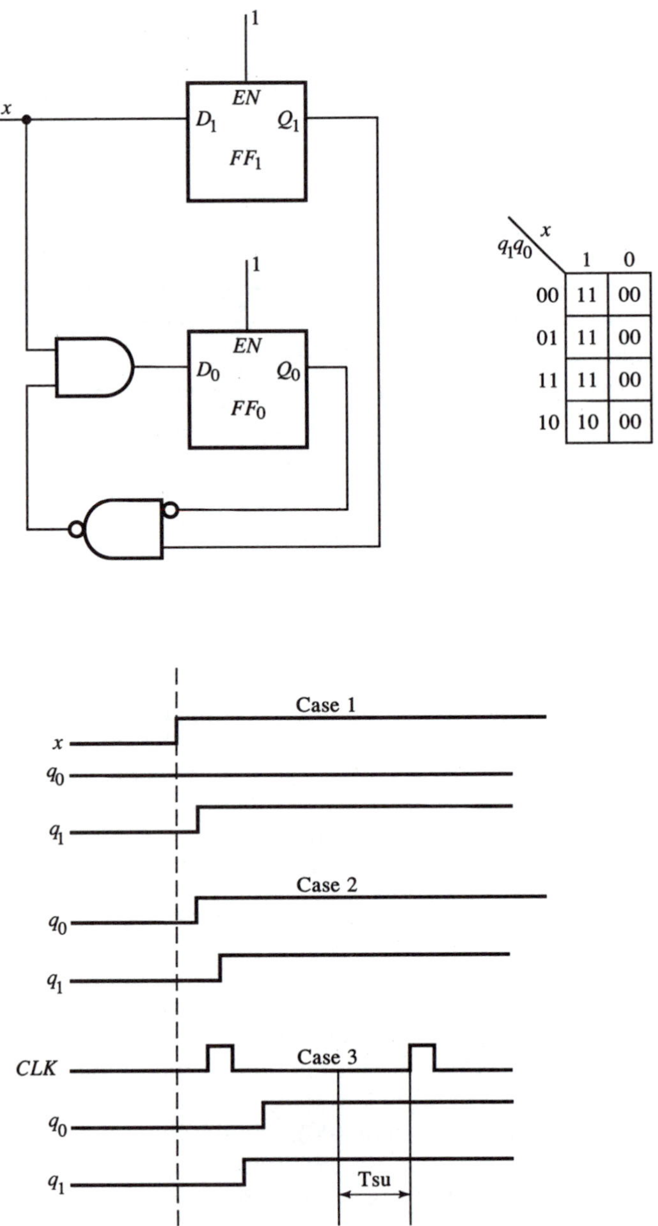


**Figure 4.35.** Asynchronous circuit with a race and its possible behaviors. The bottom diagram shows that even the worst behavior has no effect if the circuit is synchronous and properly timed.

input 1 is again (10). It is thus stable, and no other transition occurs unless the input changes to 0. As a result, instead of going to the anticipated (11) state, the circuit gets stuck in state (10) and its operation is faulty. The outcome of the race is *critical.* Admittedly, this happens only if the combination of timing parameters of the circuit allows it, but the potential for faulty behavior exists.

***Case 2.*** If the output of $FF_0$ changes before $FF_1$, the circuit goes to state (01). This state, however, is not stable with input 1 and the circuit goes to state (11). Because state (11) is stable—its next state with input 1 is again (11)—the circuit remains in it. This behavior is acceptable in spite of the race and the intermediate state. In other words, this outcome of the race is *noncritical.*

We conclude that the circuit is defective because it allows a critical race with a potential for disaster. Note that there is nothing wrong with a circuit containing only noncritical races.

A race occurs when a transition in a circuit with latches requires a simultaneous change of two or more state variables. If we changed our asynchronous circuit into a synchronous one by using flip-flops instead of latches, the race between outputs would still occur but would have no effect on transitions in a properly timed circuit. This is shown as case 3 in Figure 4.35. A flip-flop responds only at the edge of the clock. If the signals are stable for $T_{su}$ before the clock; in other words, if transitions subside before the edge, their transient behavior before the arrival of the clock has no effect. If we did not provide enough time to prevent conflicts of setup with transitions, a fatal race or another malfunction could occur even in a synchronous circuit with flip-flops. In a synchronous circuit the problem can be avoided by proper timing, whereas in an asynchronous circuit such control is not available.

The two examples presented above do not cover all possible problems with sequential circuits but show that asynchronous circuits pose added difficulties, whereas synchronous circuits are safe if their timing is sufficiently conservative. Problems with asynchronous circuits can be eliminated by proper design but the solution is more difficult and its complexity increases with circuit size. This is why complicated circuits such as computers are essentially synchronous.

## Exercises

1. Redesign the circuit in Example 1 using a fully synchronous counter.
2. Analyze the circuit from Exercise 1 to show that it is indeed a mod-4 counter.
3. Explain why the circuit in Figure 4.36 (adapted from Passafiume) should work as a decade (mod-10) down-counter. Perform a detailed timing analysis and show why it is not a decade down counter.
4. Show that Example 1 is, in fact, a critical race.
5. Analyze the tables in Figure 4.37 assuming that they are implemented with asynchronous circuits. Find stable states, infinite cycles (loops of repetitive

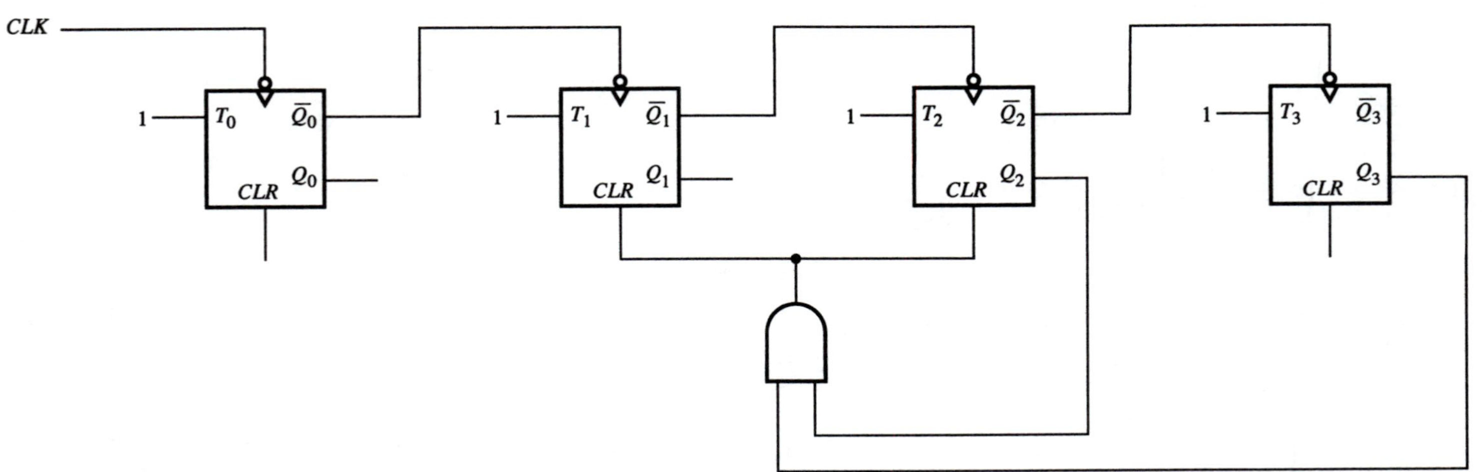


**Figure 4.36.** Decade down counter that does not work.

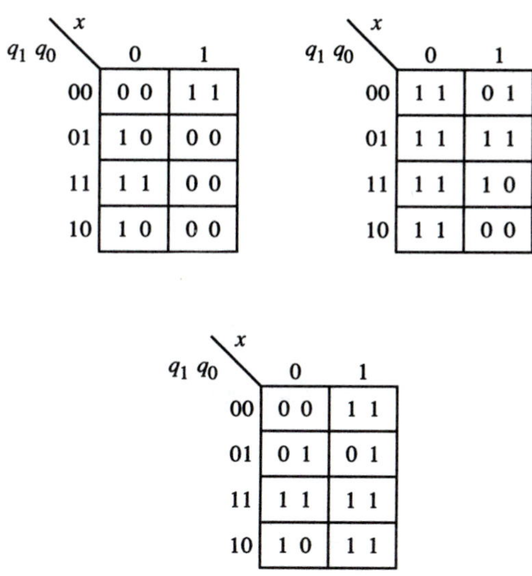

| $q_1 q_0$ \ $x$ | 0 | 1 |
|---|---|---|
| 00 | 0 0 | 1 1 |
| 01 | 1 0 | 0 0 |
| 11 | 1 1 | 0 0 |
| 10 | 1 0 | 0 0 |

| $q_1 q_0$ \ $x$ | 0 | 1 |
|---|---|---|
| 00 | 1 1 | 0 1 |
| 01 | 1 1 | 1 1 |
| 11 | 1 1 | 1 0 |
| 10 | 1 1 | 0 0 |

| $q_1 q_0$ \ $x$ | 0 | 1 |
|---|---|---|
| 00 | 0 0 | 1 1 |
| 01 | 0 1 | 0 1 |
| 11 | 1 1 | 1 1 |
| 10 | 1 0 | 1 1 |

**Figure 4.37.** Transition tables with cycles and races.

transitions), and races. Determine which races are critical and which are not. Would any problems arise if the circuits were synchronous? What is the effect of cycles?

6. If the inverter in the circuit in Figure 4.38 has a nonnegligible delay, the excitation circuit contains a hazard. Analyze its effect. (*Hint*: Treat the delay as an imaginary D-latch and construct the transition table in the usual way. Compare with the transition table of the same circuit without the hazard. Is there a race? If so, is it critical?)
7. Show that one of the following state assignments in the transition graph in Figure 4.39 creates a critical race but the other does not:

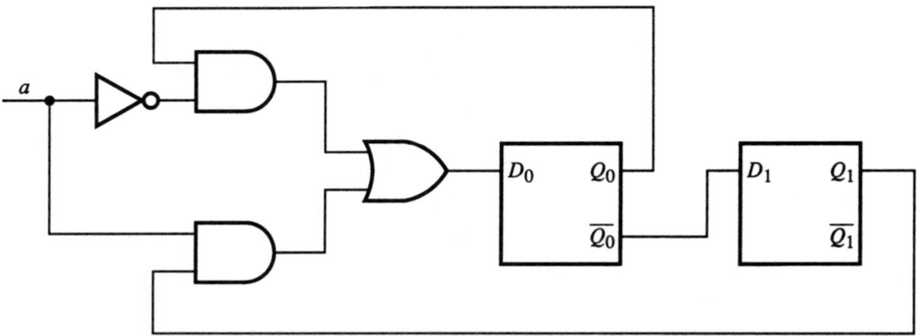


**Figure 4.38.** Circuit with a hazard.

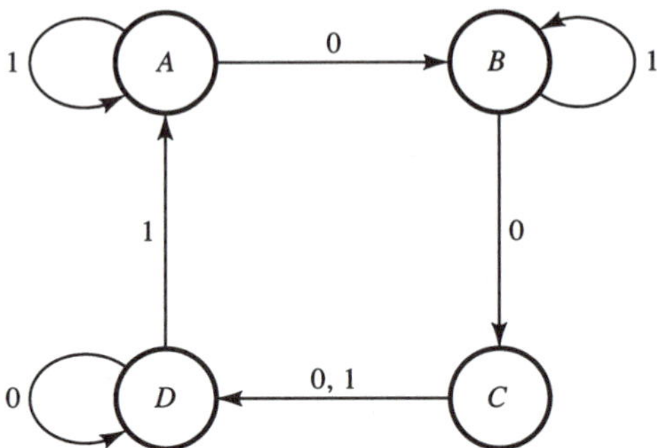


**Figure 4.39.** Transition graph that contains a race with a certain state assignment.

$A = 11 \quad B = 01 \quad C = 10 \quad D = 00$

$A = 01 \quad B = 11 \quad C = 10 \quad D = 00$

This example indicates that a change in state assignment may remove a critical race from an asynchronous circuit.

8. The bottom transition table in Figure 4.37 contains a race. However, the same transitions to the circled stable states could be achieved by redirecting certain transitions through additional intermediate unstable states. Show how.
9. Design an experiment that will demonstrate the race in Example 2 in this section. (*Hint*: We must be able to control the delays in the critical signal paths.)

## SUMMARY

The behavior of sequential circuits cannot be described by truth tables because one input may produce different outputs in different contexts. Thus sequential circuits require a new representation. We introduced three conventions to describe their behavior: functions, transition tables, and graphs.

The basis of sequential circuits is storage, and the fundamental storage elements are edge-sensitive flip-flops and level-sensitive latches. According to the number and operation of their data inputs, flip-flops and latches are classified as D, T, JK, and RS, and can be described by their transition tables or by characteristic (transition) equations.

Analysis of sequential circuits is the process of deriving a behavioral description—transition graph, table, or equation—from the logic diagram.

Circuits with flip-flops can be analyzed as follows: Derive the excitation equations (inputs of storage elements as functions of their outputs and circuit inputs), find the transition equations by substituting the excitation equations into the characteristic equations, and obtain the output equations (outputs as functions of present state).

Collections of flip-flops controlled by a shared clock signal are called registers. Most have a built-in shifting ability. According to their input and output access (serial or parallel), they can be grouped into four categories: PIPO, PISO, SIPO, and SISO.

Some sequential circuits use counters instead of flip-flops. A counter in the general sense is a circuit that produces a repetitive sequence of outputs. In a more restrictive sense, counters count clock pulses and output the code of the count. They are classified as up, down, ripple, synchronous, presettable, and nonpresettable, and according to the maximum length of their counting sequence (the modulus). Presettable fully synchronous counters are useful for sequential design. They can either count or be forced to load the individual flip-flops and their operation is fully synchronized with the edge of the clock signal.

The use of characteristic equations for the analysis of sequential circuits with presettable counters is impractical. The most convenient approach is to calculate individual entries of the transition table from the excitation table.

Sequential circuits can be classified as synchronous (all transitions triggered by a shared clock signal) or asynchronous (some transitions are free-running). Asynchronous circuits are subject to malfunctions such as races and cycles, all related to the intermediate states of internal states and their interaction. Tight control over transitions can be provided by clock edges end eliminates these dangers; most practical sequential circuits are thus synchronous. The design of trouble free asynchronous circuits is possible but more difficult.

## REVIEW QUESTIONS

1. Define the following terms: internal state and variable; transition graph, table, and equation; state machine; edge; level; D-, T-, JK-, and RS-flip-flops and latches; volatile; master–slave; setup time; hold time; frequency; characteristic, excitation, transition, and output equations; excitation and output circuits; sequencer; up-, down-, synchronous, asynchronous, and presettable counters; modulus; synchronous and asynchronous circuits; critical and noncritical races; cycle; stable state.
2. Describe the following procedures: Construction of the characteristic equation, analysis of circuits using flip-flops or latches, analysis of circuits with fully synchronous presettable counters, and recognition of races and cycles.

## REFERENCES

The following titles listed in the references at the end of the book are relevant to this chapter:

A. D. Friedman. *Fundamentals of Logic Design and Switching Theory.*

Z. Kohavi. *Switching and Finite Automata Theory.*

J. F. Passafiume, and M. Douglass. *Digital Logic Design: Tutorials and Lab Exercises.*

# CHAPTER 5

# DESIGN OF SYNCHRONOUS SEQUENTIAL CIRCUITS

## AN OVERVIEW

To design a sequential circuit, we must first construct its transition graph or an equivalent description, select the building blocks, and convert the specification into a circuit. We will discuss all of these tasks in this chapter. We will begin with several examples of the construction of a transition graph from a specification and continue with the design of circuits based on flip-flops. Design, the inverse of analysis, begins with the transition table and ends with excitation and output circuits.

Correct circuit structure does not guarantee proper operation even for synchronous circuits; timing is equally important. We will show how to analyze the timing of a circuit and how to generate a clock signal.

We will then discuss the use of presettable counters in designing circuits. This procedure is very similar to design using flip-flops.

Finally, we will discuss programmable logic devices with storage and their use in sequential design.

## IMPORTANT WORDS

Clock (duty cycle, frequency, period, phase, skew, width of pulse), crystal, HTGT (function, table), timing analysis.

## 5.1 CONSTRUCTING TRANSITION GRAPHS

The first step in the design of a sequential circuit—the construction of its transition graph or table—is an intuitive process. There are no rules for it but one should follow the general guidelines that apply to all problem solving:

Formulate a clear understanding of the problem.

If the problem is large, divide it into subproblems.

Document the solution for later reference.

Verify the solution at least by testing well-selected cases.

We will consider a few examples to illustrate the basic procedure.

**Example 1.** We are to construct the transition graph of a mod-4 up/down counter controlled by a direction input *DIR*. When $DIR = 0$, the counter counts up and outputs the binary codes of (0, 1, 2, 3, 0, 1, ...); when $DIR = 1$, it counts down and produces the sequence (3, 2, 1, 0, 3, 2, ...).

The circuit regularly cycles through four states, and its transition graph thus has four nodes that are traversed in one direction when $DIR = 0$ and in the opposite direction when $DIR = 1$. This completely defines the transition graph (Figure 5.1).

**Example 2.** We are to design a (101) recognizer, a circuit that outputs 1 when the last three inputs received are (101). The problem has three possible interpretations:

1. Only the first (101) sequence is recognized. As an example,

input 000111<u>101</u>0010101

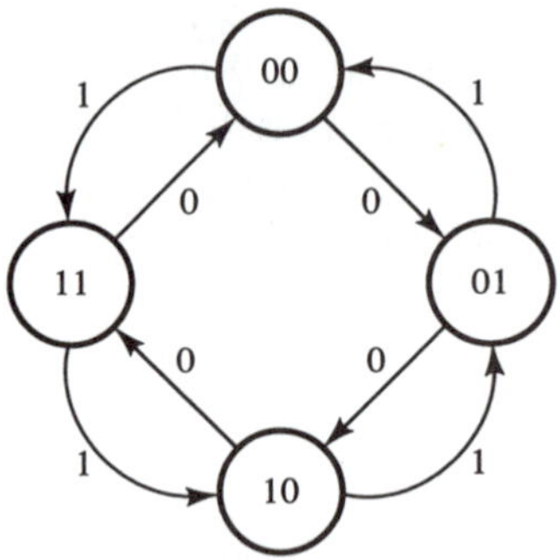


**Figure 5.1.** Transition graph of a mod-4 up/down counter.

produces

output 0000000010000000

2. The circuit recognizes all (101) sequences. In our example,

input 0001111010010101

produces

output 0000000010000101

Note that the last (101) sequence overlaps the one immediately preceeding it.

3. The circuit recognizes only nonoverlapping sequences, and

input 0001111010010101

produces

output 0000000010000100

Note that the last, overlapping (101) sequence is not accepted.

We will now construct the transition graphs for all three variations of the problem.

***Case 1—Single (101) Sequence.*** It is easy to design the "main line" of the graph, the sequence of transitions that recognizes the sequence (sequence $A \to B \to C \to D$ in Figure 5.2). Next, we must complete all the unresolved transitions and check whether any more states are needed.

If the input in state $A$ is 0, we must go to $A$ again because its function is "waiting for the first 1." If the input in state $B$ is 1, we stay in state $B$, whose function is "received a 1 that might be the beginning of the sequence." If we

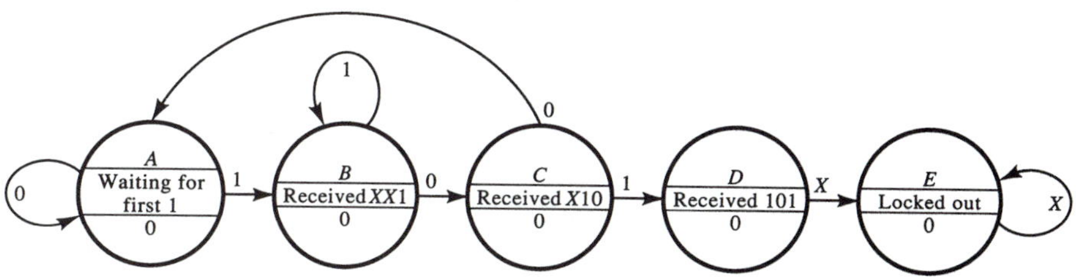


**Figure 5.2.** Recognizer of a single (101) sequence.

receive 0 in state $C$, we must go back to state $A$ because the sequence received up to this point is then useless and we must start looking for a 1.

When the recognizer reaches state $D$, it has fulfilled its purpose and must be disabled by entering a state from which it cannot exit. The transition from $D$ is thus to a new state $E$. Because there must be no escape from this state, all transitions from $E$ are back to itself. State $E$ is sometimes called the "absorbing state."

***Case 2—Overlapping (101) Sequences.*** Because the desired sequence is the same as in Case 1, the recognizing part of the graph is the same. The only difference is that we don't quit after recognizing the string (state $D$), but continue looking for another (101) sequence. Input 1 in state $D$ could be the beginning of a new sequence and requires a transition to state $B$. If the input in $D$ is 0, the 1 that got us to $D$ combined with the current 0 could be the beginning of an overlapping (101) sequence and we must thus proceed to state $C$ (Figure 5.3).

***Case 3—Nonoverlapping (101) Sequences.*** The sequence to be recognized is the same and the behavior is repetitive as in Case 2. The only difference between the two graphs is in the transitions from state $D$ because overlapping sequences are not allowed in Case *3*. An input 0 received in $D$ cannot be part of a nonoverlapping sequence and the transition is to state $A$ (Figure 5.4).

Recognizers are useful in data communications and devices like electronic locks; they also provide simple problems for the design of sequential circuits.

## Exercises

1. Draw the transition graph and table of a one-input circuit that recognizes sequence (1001). Consider all alternatives.
2. Repeat Exercise 1 for a two-input circuit recognizing the sequence (00, 01, 10).
3. Repeat Exercise 1 for a one-input circuit that accepts either (0111) or (100).

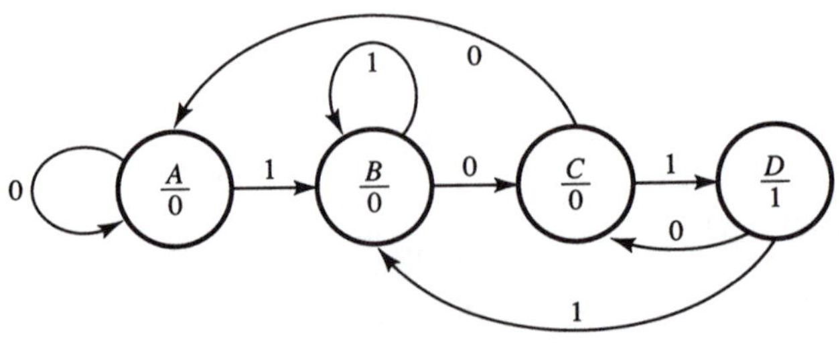


**Figure 5.3.** Recognizer of overlapping (101) sequences.

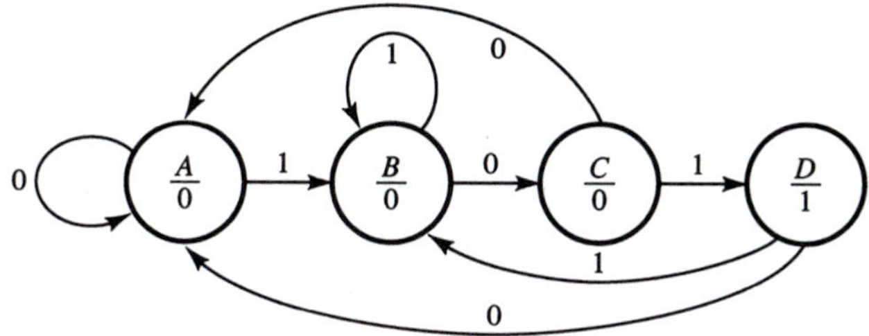


**Figure 5.4.** Recognizer of nonoverlapping (101) sequences.

4. Repeat Exercise 1 for a circuit that accepts sequence (101) if it is preceded by sequence (11).
5. Repeat Exercise 1 for a circuit that accepts sequence (101) if it is preceded by sequence (11) or by sequence (00).
6. Draw the transition graph of a circuit that behaves as a mod-4 counter when its control input $CI = 1$ and as a mod-5 counter when $CI = 0$.
7. Draw the transition graph of a circuit that outputs its input sequence delayed by one unit of clock time. As an example, input (0011101) should produce output ($X$0011101) where $X$ is the irrelevant initial output.
8. Draw the transition graph of a two-output circuit that produces the sum of its two last inputs. The output is repeated for synchronization with the input. As an example, input

$$i \quad \underline{00}\,\underline{01}\,\underline{10}\,\underline{11}$$

should produce outputs

$$s_1 \quad \underline{XX}\,\underline{00}\,\underline{00}\,\underline{00}\,\underline{11}$$

$$s_0 \quad \underline{XX}\,\underline{00}\,\underline{11}\,\underline{11}\,\underline{00}$$

because $0 + 0 = 00$, $0 + 1 = 1 + 0 = 01$, and so on. The circuit is a sequential binary adder.

## 5.2 DESIGN WITH FLIP-FLOPS

We wish to design a synchronous circuit with flip-flops to implement the transition graph in Figure 5.5. Our knowledge of analysis and the fact that design is the inverse of analysis suggest that we must proceed as follows:

1. Determine how many flip-flops are needed.
2. Choose flip-flops.
3. Assign codes to states.

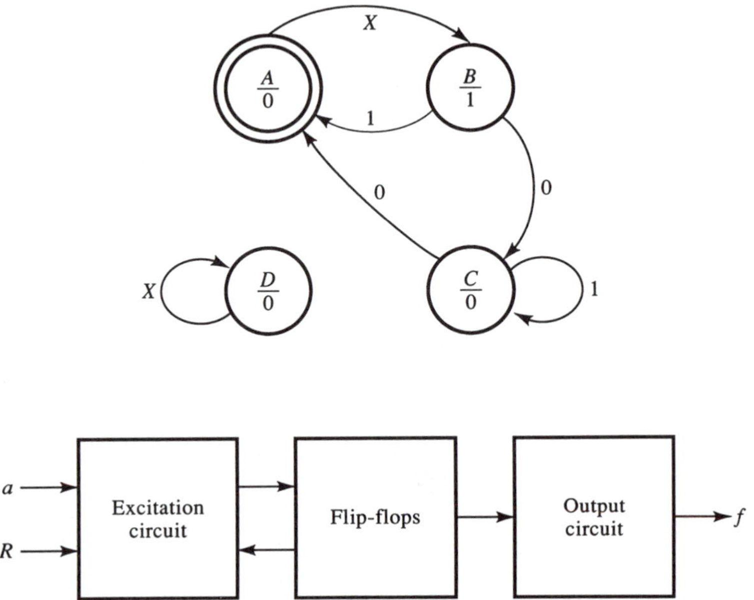


**Figure 5.5.** Transition graph and general structure of a sequential circuit. The initial state is denoted by a double circle. The reset input $R$, which returns the circuit to state $A$, is not shown in the transition graph.

4. Construct excitation equations.
5. Design the initialization circuit.
6. Design the output circuit.

The first five steps constitute the design of the sequencer; Step 6 is the design of the output circuit.

We will now solve our problem using this procedure. In the process, we will introduce systematic solutions for some steps and make arbitrary decisions for questions that depend on economic or engineering considerations or whose formal solutions are too complicated.

Step 1—Number of flip-flops: Our transition graph has four states and we thus need four different codes. This requires two-bit codes and therefore two flip-flops.

Step 2—Selecting flip-flops: Initially we will use T-flip-flops $FF_1$ and $FF_0$ but we will later redesign the circuit using JK-flip-flops. We will discuss the implications later.

Step 3—Assignment of codes: It is intuitively clear that some assignments may result in simpler circuits than others but we will not concern ourselves with this question. Instead we shall assign codes arbitrarily as follows:

| State | Corresponding $FF_1$,$FF_0$ code |
|---|---|
| $A$ | 00 |
| $B$ | 01 |
| $C$ | 10 |
| $D$ | 11 |

Step 4—Excitation equations: The excitation circuit forces the system to make transitions and the best way to design it is to start with the transition tables of the circuit (Figure 5.6) and the flip-flops. (For some flip-flops the characteristic equations can be inverted and the excitation equations derived in an analytical way; this is left as an exercise.)

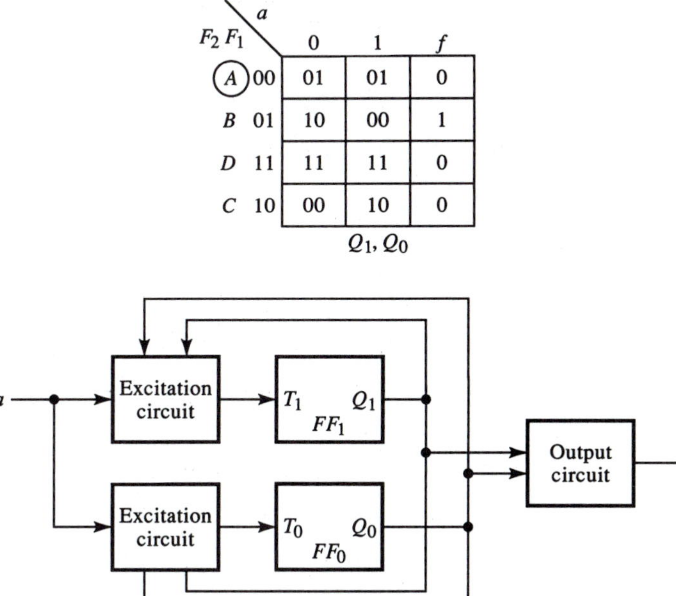


**Figure 5.6.** Transition table and structure of the circuit.

Although we could use the transition table of the T-flip-flop to design the excitation circuit, this approach would be somewhat unnatural. After all, the transition table tells us what happens when we apply a certain input but we want to know which input to apply to get from a given state to the specified next state. In other words, we want to know "how to get there" rather than "what will happen if we do this." To facilitate this process, we will convert the transition table into a *how to get there* (HTGT) table as in Figure 5.7. A more formal name for this table is the "inverted transition table."

An example of how one constructs the entries of the HTGT table is highlighted in the diagram: To change a T-flip-flop's output from $q = 0$ to $Q = 1$ (the entries marked by circles) we must apply $T = 1$ (the entry marked by a square). The HTGT cell labeled $(q,Q) = (0,1)$ thus contains $T = 1$ and means, "To get from 0 to 1, apply $T = 1$." Other entries are obtained similarly.

The construction of excitation tables is now simple. As an example consider the circled entries in Figure 5.8. The value of $T_1$ for $(q_1,q_0,a) = (1,0,1)$ must move flip-flop $FF_1$ from $q_1$ to $Q_1$. The transition table shows that the desired $Q_1$ is 1. We thus need an $FF_1$ transition from $q_1 = 1$ to $Q_1 = 1$ and this, according to the HTGT table in Figure 5.7, requires $T_1 = 0$.

Similarly, the $(q_1,q_0,a) = (0,1,1)$ entry for $T_0$ (marked by rectangles) takes flip-flop $FF_0$ from $q_0 = 1$ to $Q_0 = 0$, and this requires $T_0 = 1$.

After completing the excitation tables in this way, we get

$$T_1 = \overline{a}\,\overline{q_1}q_0 + \overline{a}q_1\overline{q_0} = \overline{a}\cdot(q_1 \oplus q_0)$$

$$T_0 = \overline{q_1}$$

Step 5—Initialization: According to the specification, the circuit is initialized and reset by input $R$. Because we assigned code 00 to the initial state $A$, initialization can be done by clearing the two flip-flops; this is much simpler than including $R$ among the variables of the excitation circuit.

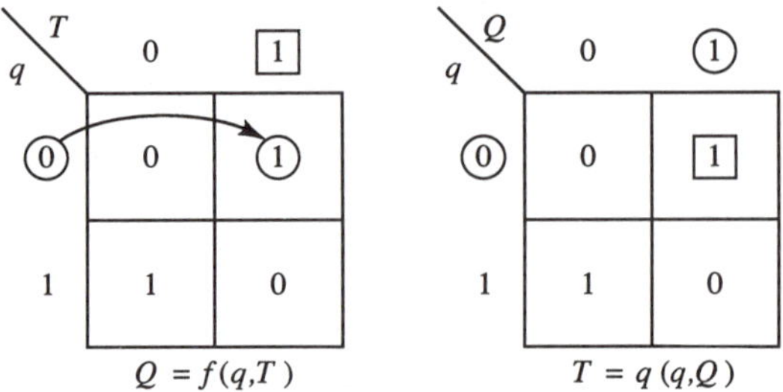


**Figure 5.7.** Transition table (*left*) and HTGT tables of the T-flip-flop.

The sequencer implementing the transition part of the transition graph is now complete. The last step is to design the output circuit.

Step 6—Output: According to the specification (Figure 5.8), the output function is

$$f = \overline{q_1} \cdot q_0$$

The diagram of the whole circuit appears in Figure 5.9.

The use of the HTGT table for a T-flip-flop is unnecessary: We don't need a table to realize, for example, that changing the output of a T-flip-flop from 0 to 1 requires toggling. Similarly, HTGT tables are not needed for D-flip-flops. However, the HTGT table is very helpful for JK- and RS-flip-flops, which we will demonstrate redesigning our circuit using JK-flip-flops.

We will skip the first two steps and use the same state assignment as before. For Step 3 we need the $J$ and $K$ HTGT tables of the JK-flip-flop given in Figure 5.10. The following examples explain their structure:

> The boxed $J$ entry $(q,Q) = (0,0)$ in the $J$ and $K$ tables should contain the value of $J$ and $K$ needed to get from $q = 0$ to $Q = 0$. The $JK$ transition table shows that there are two ways to get from 0 to 0—by $(J,K) = (0,0)$ and by $(J,K) = (0,1)$—and both require that $J = 0$. When $J = 0$, the value of $K$ is irrelevant and the corresponding entry in the $K$ table is thus a don't-care.

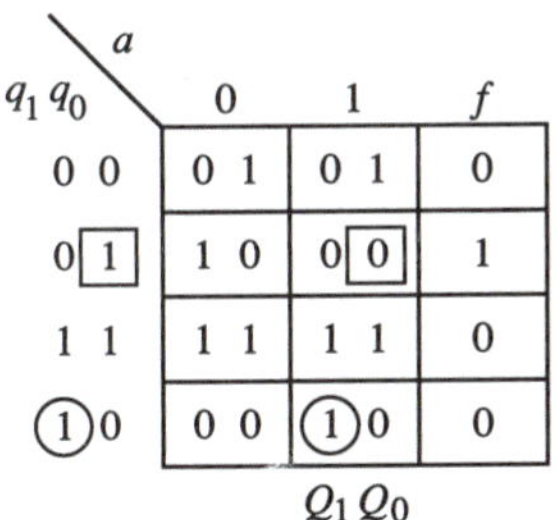

| $q_1 q_0$ \ $a$ | 0 | 1 | $f$ |
|---|---|---|---|
| 0 0 | 0 1 | 0 1 | 0 |
| 0 1 | 1 0 | 0 0 | 1 |
| 1 1 | 1 1 | 1 1 | 0 |
| 1 0 | 0 0 | 1 0 | 0 |

$Q_1 Q_0$

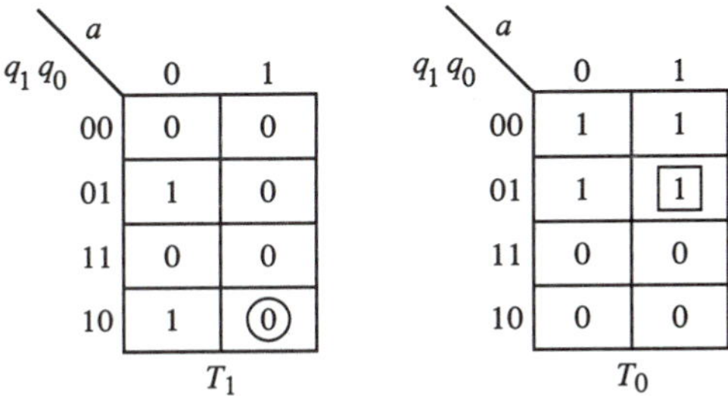

| $q_1 q_0$ \ $a$ | 0 | 1 |
|---|---|---|
| 00 | 0 | 0 |
| 01 | 1 | 0 |
| 11 | 0 | 0 |
| 10 | 1 | 0 |

$T_1$

| $q_1 q_0$ \ $a$ | 0 | 1 |
|---|---|---|
| 00 | 1 | 1 |
| 01 | 1 | 1 |
| 11 | 0 | 0 |
| 10 | 0 | 0 |

$T_0$

**Figure 5.8.** Transition and excitation tables.

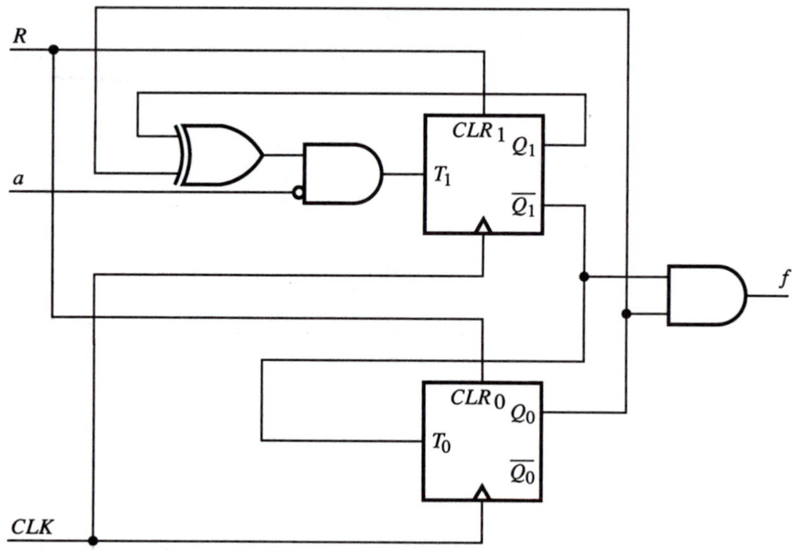


**Figure 5.9.** Circuit implementing the given transition table.

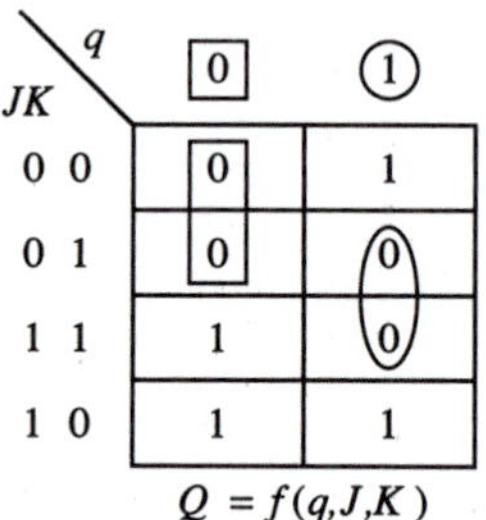

| JK \ q | 0 | 1 |
|---|---|---|
| 0 0 | 0 | 1 |
| 0 1 | 0 | 0 |
| 1 1 | 1 | 0 |
| 1 0 | 1 | 1 |

$Q = f(q,J,K)$

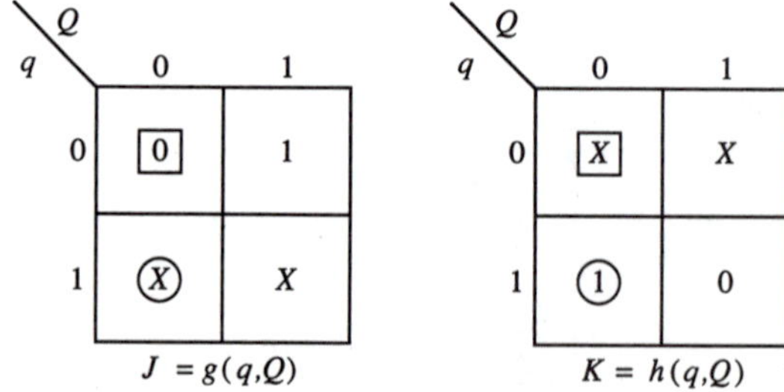

| q \ Q | 0 | 1 |
|---|---|---|
| 0 | 0 | 1 |
| 1 | X | X |

$J = g(q,Q)$

| q \ Q | 0 | 1 |
|---|---|---|
| 0 | X | X |
| 1 | 1 | 0 |

$K = h(q,Q)$

**Figure 5.10** Transition table (*top*) of the JK-flip-flop and HTGT tables fo $J$ and $K$ obtained from it.

The circled entry for $(q,Q) = (1,0)$ in the $J$ and $K$ tables corresponds to the transition from 1 to 0. There are two ways to make this transition, $(J,K) = (0,1)$ and $(J,K) = (1,1)$. As long as $K = 1$, the transition occurs regardless of the value of $J$, and the corresponding entries in the $J$ and $K$ tables are thus $X$ and 1.

We can now return to our problem. If we draw the HTGT and transition tables side by side (Figure 5.11), we can easily obtain the excitation tables for $J_1$, $K_1$, $J_0$, and $K_0$.

As an example, the circled upper left entry in the $J_1$ and $K_1$ tables (excitation of $FF_1$) corresponds to the transition of $q_1$ from 0 to 0 in the transition table. According to the $J$ and $K$ HTGT tables, this calls for $J_1 = 0$ and $K_1 = X$. Similarly, the transition from $q_0 = 1$ to $Q_0 = 1$, which is marked by rectangles, requires $J_0 = X$ and $K_0 = 0$. The remaining entries are obtained similarly. By using Karnaugh map minimization we finally obtain the following excitation equations:

$$J_1 = q_0\overline{a} \qquad K_1 = \overline{q_1}\cdot\overline{a}$$

$$J_0 = \overline{q_1} \qquad K_0 = \overline{q_1}$$

Steps 5 and 6 give the same result as before, and Figure 5.12 shows the completed circuit. Note that the excitation circuits are simpler than in the T-based implementation. This is not surprising because JK-flip-flops are more flexible and one can expect that their control will be simpler.

## Exercises

1. Analyze our solutions to show that they really implement the desired transition graph.
2. Solve the problem again using
   a. different state assignments
   b. D- or RS-flip-flops
   c. one D- and one T-flip-flop.
3. Because flip-flops are sequential devices, they can be constructed from other flip-flops. Design a JK-flip-flop using a D-flip-flop. Build a D-flip-flop from a JK-flip-flop, and a T-flip-flop from a JK-flip-flop.
4. Design a circuit to produce the repetitive output sequence (01, 01,00,10, ...). There is no external input.
5. Design the unit delay function from Section 5.1. Try all types of flip-flops and find the simplest solution.
6. Extend Exercise 5 to an $n$-units-of-time delay function.

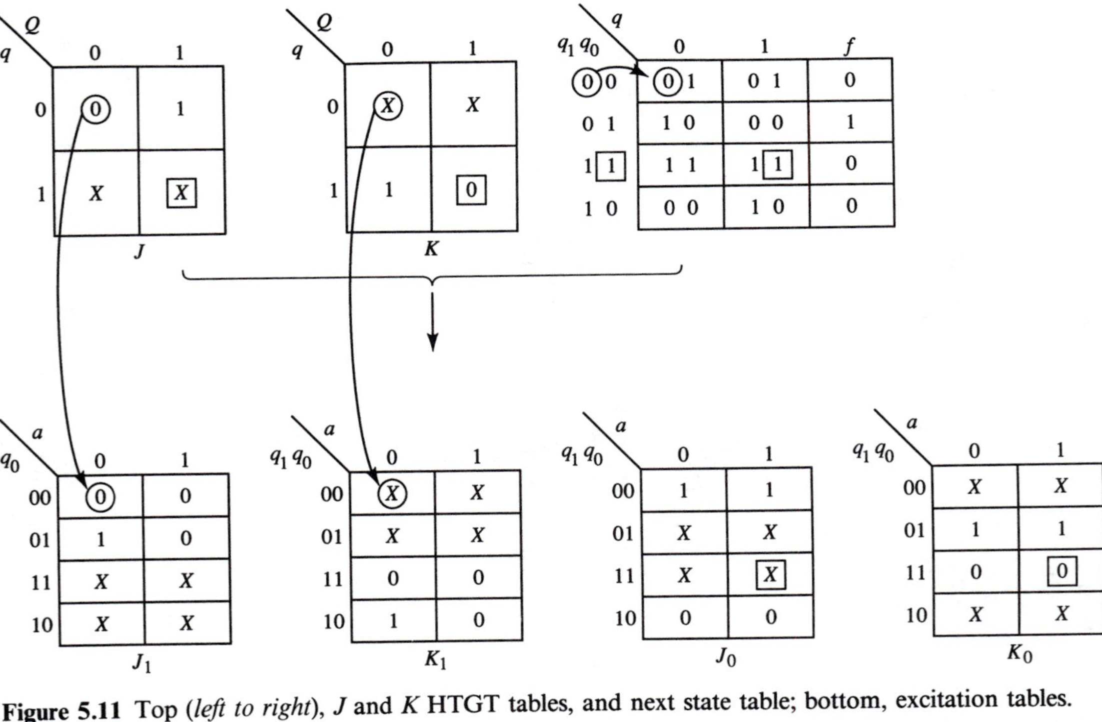


**Figure 5.11** Top (*left to right*), $J$ and $K$ HTGT tables, and next state table; bottom, excitation tables.

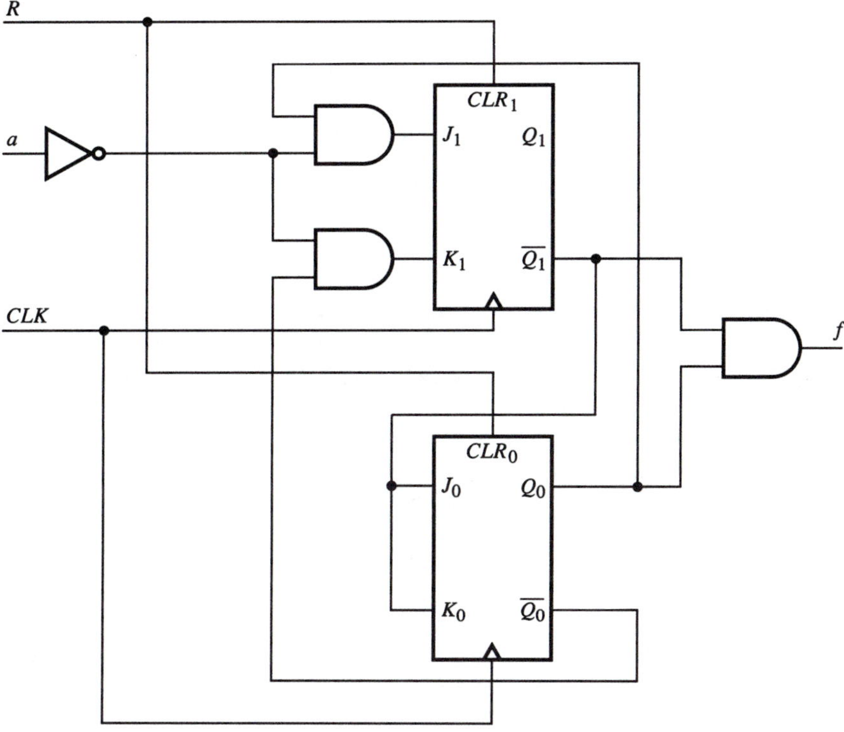


**Figure 5.12.** Implementation with JK-flip-flops.

7. Design circuits for the transition graphs in Section 5.1.
8. Solve the JK-flip-flop example directly using the *JK* transition table instead of the HTGT table.
9. The characteristic equations of D- and T-flip-flops can be inverted as follows:

| | | |
|---|---|---|
| $Q = D$ | becomes | $D = Q$ |
| $Q = T \oplus q$ | becomes | $Q \oplus q = T \oplus q \oplus q = T$ |
| | becomes | $T = Q \oplus q$ |

We can use these equations to design sequential circuits by substituting the transition equation into the inverted characteristic equation or by making certain conclusions about the relation between the transition and excitation tables. Explain the details of this process and use it to design circuits for

Transition equations

$$Q_1 = a + \overline{q_0} \qquad \text{and} \qquad Q_0 = a \cdot q_1 + \overline{q_0}$$

A specification given by a transition graph.

10. The $J$ and $K$ HTGT tables can be treated as Karnaugh maps, converted into HTGT equations, and the result treated as inverted characteristic equations in Exercise 9. Use this approach to design the circuits from Exercise 9 with JK-flip-flops. Repeat for RS-flip-flops.
11. The method proposed in Exercise 10 seems to contradict our previous claim that *JK* and *RS* characteristic equations cannot be inverted. Explain. (*Hint:* Construct several circuits with JK-flip-flops using both the tabular and the analytic method and compare the results. Note that the results are not always the same. Does this mean that one of the methods is incorrect? If not, what does it mean? Does one of the two methods give consistently better results? If so, why?)

## 5.3 TIMING

As we know, all storage elements in a synchronous circuit are controlled by the same signal, usually a sequence of periodic pulses with a fixed period and width as in Figure 5.13. For safe operation, the speed of the clock (the number of pulses per second) must not exceed an upper limit given by the structure of the circuit and the parameters of its components. We will now show how to calculate this value and describe how to generate a clock signal with the desired parameters.

### Timing Analysis

The speed of a clock must allow all circuit components to make transitions to steady values and must leave flip-flop inputs unaltered long enough before the next edge to satisfy setup limits. If the input of device $B$ requires outputs from device $A$, we must assume that $B$ does not have correct inputs until device $A$

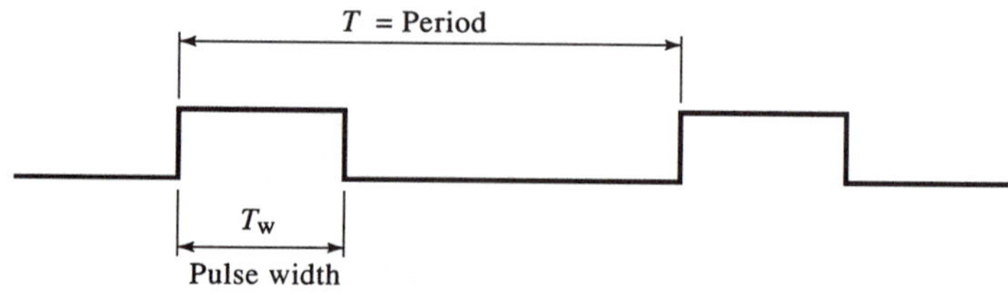


**Figure 5.13.** Clock waveform and its parameters.

has had enough time to produce stable outputs under the worst conditions. Furthermore, if a signal passes through a chain of devices, their delays must be added together. To find the minimum period of the clock $T_{min}$ we must find the signal path that has the largest sum of delays.

What kind of signal paths are we interested in? This is determined by the goal of timing analysis: We want to find the maximum speed of the circuit, in other words, the minimum separation of consecutive active clock edges. Because the purpose of the clock is to pulse data into storage elements, our signal paths begin where the pulse affects the circuit—at the output of storage elements. The active edge following the clocking of data into the "source" storage element at the start of the path saves the result into the "destination" storage elements at its end. The end of a signal path is thus the input of a storage element.

Storage-to-storage paths are not the only ones that must be considered. If some timing constraints are imposed on a circuit's inputs, we must also consider paths starting at external inputs and ending at storage inputs. Similarly, if there are timing requirements on the output signals, we must consider paths beginning at the storage output and ending at circuit outputs. Their delays determine the time required for the output signal to stabilize, and when the output can be used by another circuit.

Complicated circuits contain many signal paths and timing analysis must then be performed by a computer program. The design of such programs is an advanced subject and we shall restrict ourselves to demonstrating the principles of the procedure on the simple circuit shown in Figure 5.14. To minimize calculations, we have selected two paths that seem to represent the worst delays.

Path 1 starts at $Q_0$, passes through the AND and OR gates, and stops at $J_0$. The first event to consider is the delay between the clocking of data into the flip-flop and its stabilization on the $Q_0$ output; this is the flip-flop's propagation delay $T_{pFF}$ (Figure 5.15). The AND gate input coming from the output of the flip-flop must be assumed invalid until $T_{pFF}$ after the edge. (We will neglect delays along the wires between the processing elements because the signal travels about 30 cm in 1 nsec, and gate delays are 10–20 nsec. In circuits using superfast chips, one would have to take into account even such small delays as these.

When the signal safely arrives at the input of the AND gate, we must wait $T_{pAND}$ to be certain that the AND output is stable and valid. Only then can we be certain that the OR gate has a valid input from this AND. The OR gate, of course, operates continuously but we must assume that its output is invalid until all inputs are valid and the result has had time to propagate through the gate. †Timing analysis allows one to calculate the clock signal so that flip-flops will store the result only after all of the intermediate transitions have died down.

†Thus the intermediate results have no effect on the overall operation of the circuit.

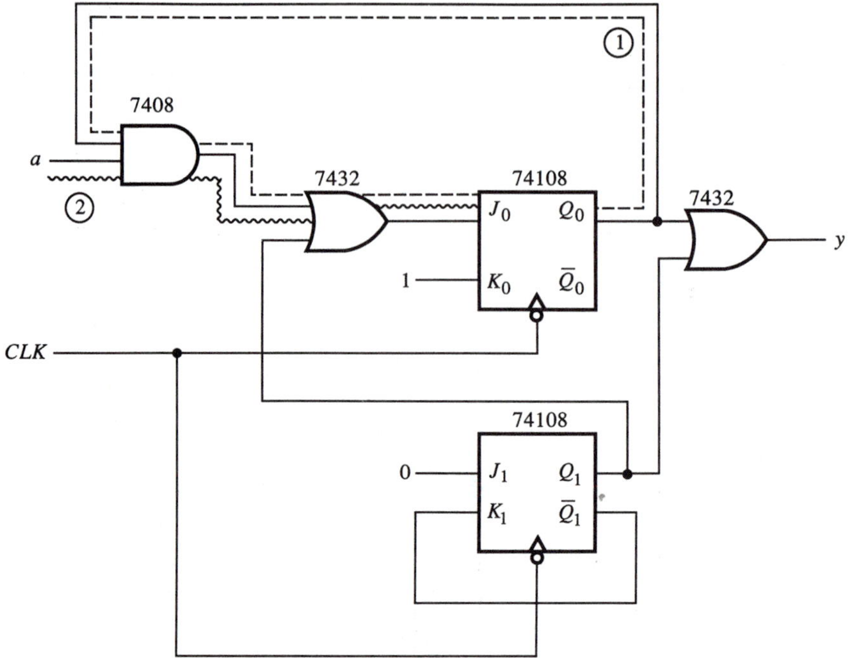


**Figure 5.14.** Sample circuit with highlighted paths.

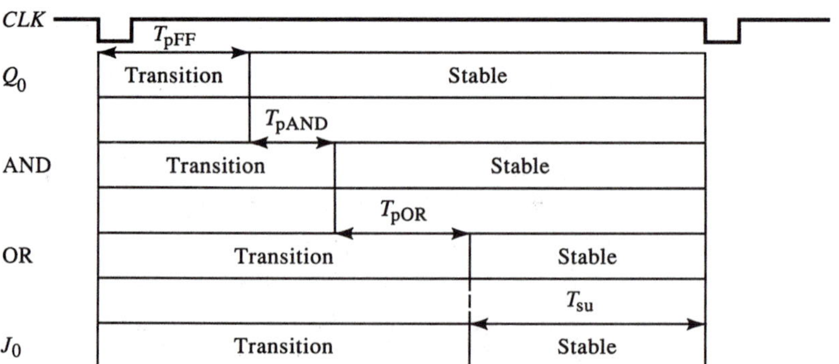


**Figure 5.15.** Illustration of the timing analysis of Path 1.

At time $T_{pFF} + T_{pAND} + T_{pOR}$ the output of the OR gate is stable and can be stored via $J_0$. Because the flip-flop requires setup time $T_{su}$, the active edge that triggers it must not occur until at least $T_{su}$ after the output of the OR gate settles down. Altogether, the minimum delay between two consecutive edges required to satisfy the delay of Path 1 is thus

$$T_1 = T_{pFF} + T_{pAND} + T_{pOR} + T_{su}$$

as indicated in Figure 5.15. Substituting the worst delay and setup times from data books gives

$$T_1 = 82 \text{ nsec}$$

Path 2 starts at input $a$. For the sake of the example, we will assume that signal $a$ has been generated by another circuit synchronized with the same clock and that its value becomes stable at most $T_{pa} = 37$ nsec after the active edge. The delay time $T_2$ through this path is thus

$$T_2 = T_{pa} + T_{pAND} + T_{pOR} + T_{su}$$

which gives

$$T_2 = 99 \text{ nsec}$$

Path 2 is thus the worse of the two; it is the critical path and the minimum clock period that guarantees correct operation by allowing all transients to settle down and the flip-flop to set up is thus

$$T_{min} = \max(T_1, T_2) = T_2 = 99 \text{ nsec}$$

The corresponding frequency $f_{max}$ is $1/T_{min}$, or approximately 10 MHz. According to data sheets, the maximum frequency at which the 74108 flip-flop can operate is 50 MHz, so we are safe.

We have concluded that the circuit can safely operate with clock frequencies up to but not exceeding 10 MHz. Faster operation could cause the flip-flops to store signals that are still in transition or force them to enter an unpredictable metastable state.

What if the calculated maximum speed is not sufficient? We have several alternatives:

Redesign the circuit. As an example, reassigning codes to states or using different types of flip-flops may yield a circuit with fewer gates, or no gates at all, and consequently shorter path delays.

One may be able to reduce the number of states and the number of flip-flops without affecting the operation. There is a simple formal procedure for doing this but it is beyond the scope of this text.

Use different components. As an example, different flip-flop chips have slightly different propagation delays and setup times. One could also use counters or sequential PLDs instead of flip-flops.

Test a batch of chips and select the ones with the shortest propagation delays.

Use a different logic family. The 74S Schottki family is about two times faster than the regular 74 family and even faster families are available.

Redefine the problem. A different transition diagram may yield a faster circuit.

Use an asynchronous circuit in which not all of the flip-flops are bound to the clock signal. This may yield a faster circuit but the extra design complications required to make the circuit safe are usually not worth the effect, particularly if the circuit is nontrivial.

Get another job.

This completes our formal example of timing analysis but one should keep a few other things in mind:

The hold time of flip-flops. For the 74108, $T_h = 0$ and we need not worry about it. Otherwise we would have to make certain that inputs $J$ and $K$ remain unchanged for $T_h$ after the active edge. This is likely to be accomplished by the normal delays of excitation signals; if it is not, extra delays could be added and an analysis of minimum guaranteed delays would then be necessary.

The pulse width $T_w$. The 74108 table indicates that the pulse must stay High for at least 10 nsec and Low for at least 15 nsec. One must consider this parameter in designing the timing of the clock signal.

The propagation delay of the output signal may impose restrictions on the circuits that use it. In our circuit, the path of the output signal starts at the flip-flop and passes through the OR gate. This gives

$$T_{py} = T_{pFF} + T_{pOR} = 20 \text{ ns} + 22 \text{ ns} = 42 \text{ nsec}$$

Any circuit depending on $y$ must thus wait at least 42 nsec after the clock edge before the output is guaranteed to be valid.

To conclude this section let us make the following comments:

1. While maximum delays form the basis of timing analysis, minimum delays may also have to be analyzed. This was already mentioned in the context of the hold time and we will now consider another example. In Figure 5.16, the inverter controls the onset of the active edge of *FF*. If the inverter is faster than assumed, *FF* will be activated sooner and its data input may not satisfy the setup time requirement.
2. Real circuits are usually much more complicated than our example and their analysis may require one to consider the shape of signals as well as delays. Moreover, different parts of complex circuits are often activated by different edges of the same clock or by edges of several synchronized clocks (a multiphase clock). Situations such as these require timing analysis by a computer program.
3. To eliminate all possible sources of problems, timing analysis of fast circuits must consider delays between individual phases of the clock and the arrival of the clock pulse to different points in the circuit; this delay is called the "clock skew."

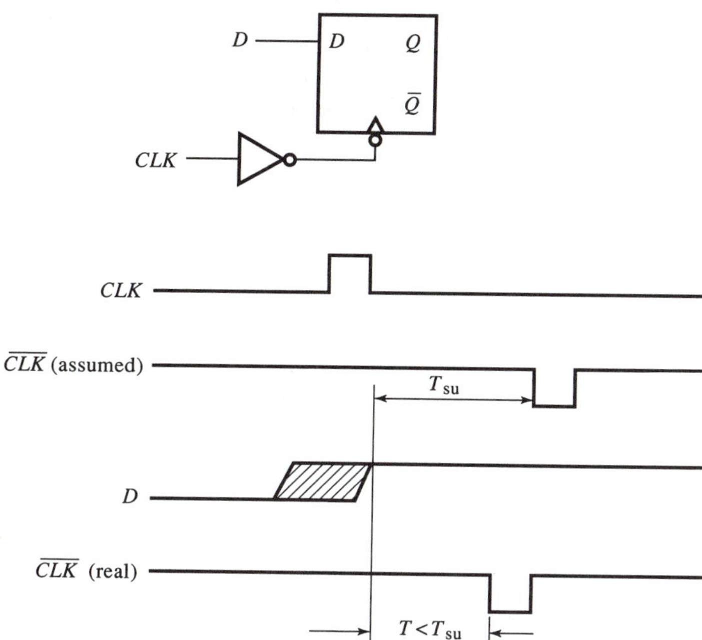


**Figure 5.16.** Potential problem with short delay.

## Exercises

1. Find and analyze the remaining data paths in our problem.
2. Perform timing analysis of the circuits in Section 5.2.
3. Extend our analysis by assuming that the hold time of the flip-flop is not zero.

## Generation of the Clock Signal

Now that we know how to calculate clock parameters, we will show how to produce clock pulses. Most clock circuits have two parts. One part produces a raw high-frequency signal; the other divides the original frequency and modifies the signal's shape to generate the required clock signal (Figure 5.17).

The circuit that generates the original raw signal may be based on special purpose chips such as the 555 timer, or may use a crystal or a gate–resistor–capacitor circuit. The first two solutions are the most common.

Clock signals based on the 555 timer chip (Figure 5.18) or similar integrated circuits are not very stable, because the parameters of resistors and capacitors depend on temperature and age, and are limited to frequencies below 100 kHz. They are not used often in computers.

*Crystal*-based circuits can produce very high, stable frequencies and are used in most computer circuits. Their operation is based on the piezoelectric principle, which relates mechanical vibrations to an oscillating voltage on the faces of a quartz crystal. Figure 5.18 shows a simple circuit that produces a high-frequency clock signal in this way. Note that the output of the crystal

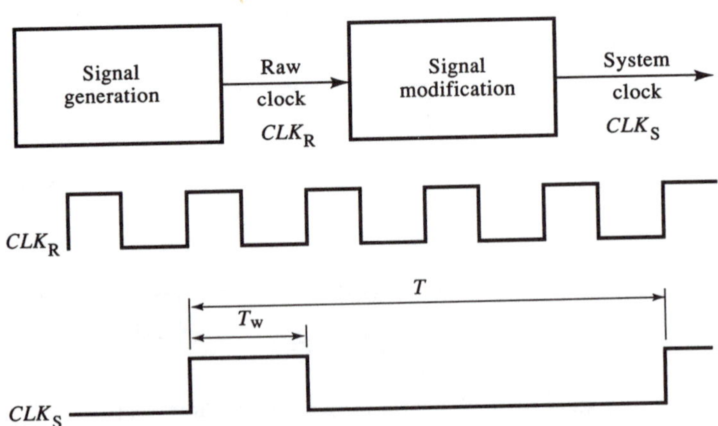


**Figure 5.17.** General structure of a clock generator and clock pulse terminology.

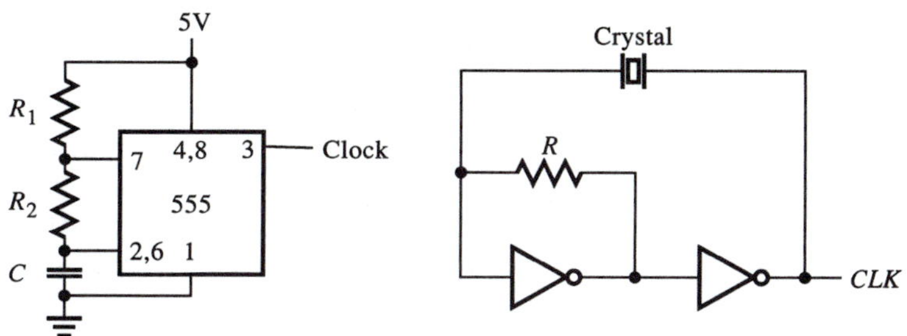


**Figure 5.18.** Using the 555 chip and a crystal to generate a clock signal. The resistors and capacitors in the 555 circuit control the frequency $f$ and the duty factor $d$ according to the formulas $f = 1.44/(c(R_1+2R_2))$ and $d = T_w/(T - T_w) = (R_1+R_2)/R_2$.

must be conditioned to obtain a signal with clean transitions and appropriate voltage levels.

Whatever its source, the raw clock signal must be processed to obtain the desired final shape and frequency. When the specification is simple (such as signal $\Phi_0$ in Figure 5.19), it can be obtained by dividing the high-frequency output $\Phi$ of the crystal by a counter. More complicated signals such as $\Phi_1$ can be generated with more complicated sequential circuits.

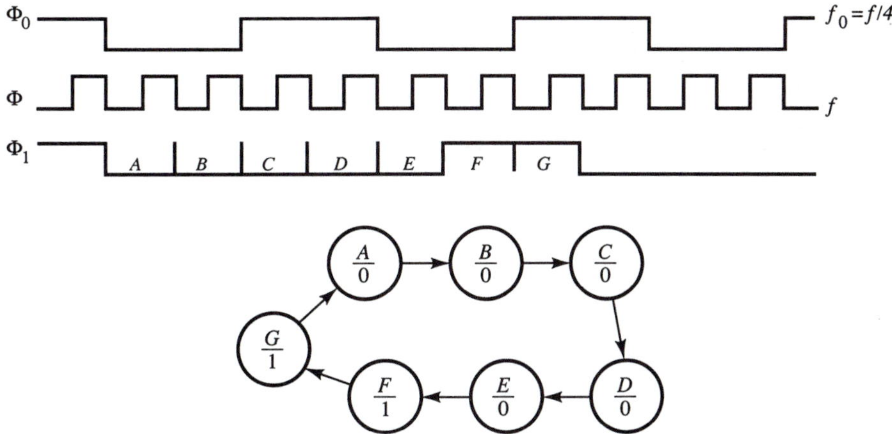


**Figure 5.19.** Simple clock signal $\Phi_0$ on the top can be obtained by dividing the higher frequency signal $\Phi$. The more complex waveform $\Phi_1$ can be represented by a transition graph and can be generated by a sequential circuit.

For mass-produced circuits with critical and complex timing, possibly involving several phases of one clock (a multiphase clock), a special-purpose integrated circuit is usually available to perform the conversion from the raw square wave to the clock signal. As an example, manufacturers of CPU chips for computers fabricate clock-generator integrated circuits that output the clock signals required by their CPUs and that often perform some additional functions as well. Sometimes, clock generation is implemented on the CPU chip itself.

### Exercises

1. Show how to produce a $\frac{4}{5}$ MHz signal with a 200-nsec pulse width using a crystal-generated clock. Assume that crystals with all integer frequencies from 1 MHz to 20 MHz are available.
2. Design a circuit to generate the two related clock signals in Figure 5.20.

## 5.4 DESIGN WITH PRESETTABLE COUNTERS

Design with presettable counters is based on the same principles as design with flip-flops. We will derive and demonstrate the procedure on the example in Figure 5.21.

The circuit has five internal states and we will design it using the readily available fully asynchronous mod-8 counter. We may assign internal states and codes any way we wish but the following reasoning shows that there is an easy way to achieve better (that is, simpler) results than random assignment.

As we know, a presettable counter changes state either by loading or by counting. If it loads, the bits loaded into the data inputs become the next state. If it counts, the next state is calculated from the present state and data inputs are irrelevant because they are not loaded. The corresponding data entries in the excitation tables are don't-cares because they are not used, and this is likely to simplify the solution. Consequently, it is advantageous to use counting transitions as often as possible and to avoid loading. This can be

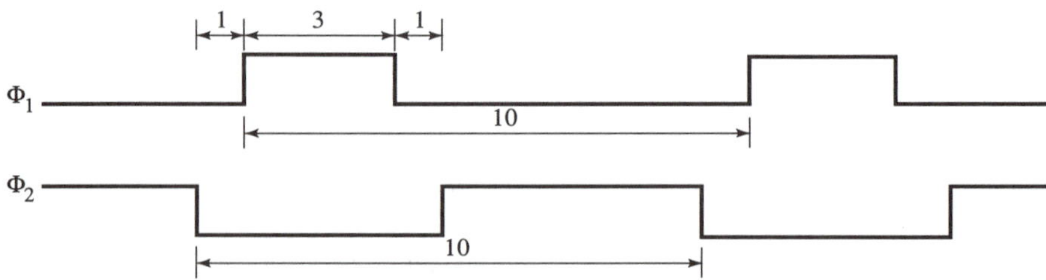


**Figure 5.20.** Two-phase clock signal.

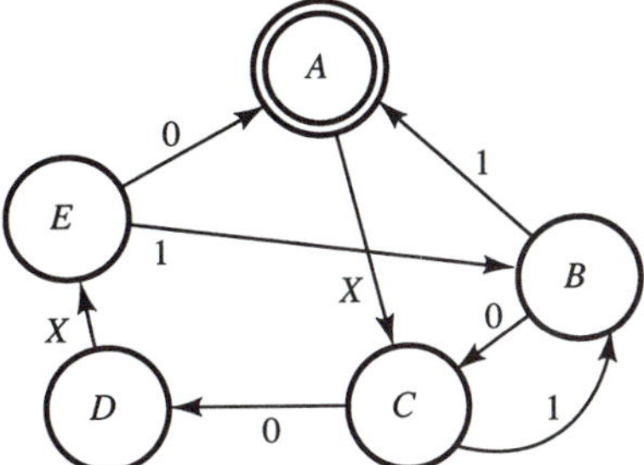


**Figure 5.21.** Transition graph of a circuit to be implemented with counters. Outputs are omitted to simplify the problem.

achieved by finding the longest possible sequence of transitions in the graph and assigning successive codes to them. Transitions along this path are then performed by "counting."

In the example in Figure 5.21, the longest path consists of transitions $A \rightarrow C \rightarrow D \rightarrow E \rightarrow B$ and these states should thus be given consecutive codes. Does the exact assignment make a difference? We will show that there is one assignment that is particularly advantageous: The initial state to which the circuit is reset on initialization is $A$. If we assign $A = (000)$, we can perform initialization via the input *CLR* of the counter and eliminate reset from data input and *LD* equations. The same approach can be used for all other transitions to $A$ with the result of creating additional don't-cares in the excitation tables. On the basis of this reasoning, we will assign codes as follows:

| State | Code |
|---|---|
| *A* | 000 |
| *C* | 001 |
| *D* | 010 |
| *E* | 011 |
| *B* | 100 |

Our transition diagram has only five states and three of the eight codes available to the mod-8 counter are thus left unassigned. Although these states should never be reached if everything works as expected, we will design the circuit so that if an unused state is accidentally reached, the circuit will reset to state $A$.

Having performed this analysis, we can now construct the excitation tables (Figure 5.22) and find the excitation circuits for *CLR*, *LD*, and the data inputs $D_i$.

The cells in the transition table fall into three categories: those that define "counting" transitions, those that are obtained by clearing, and those that must be loaded.

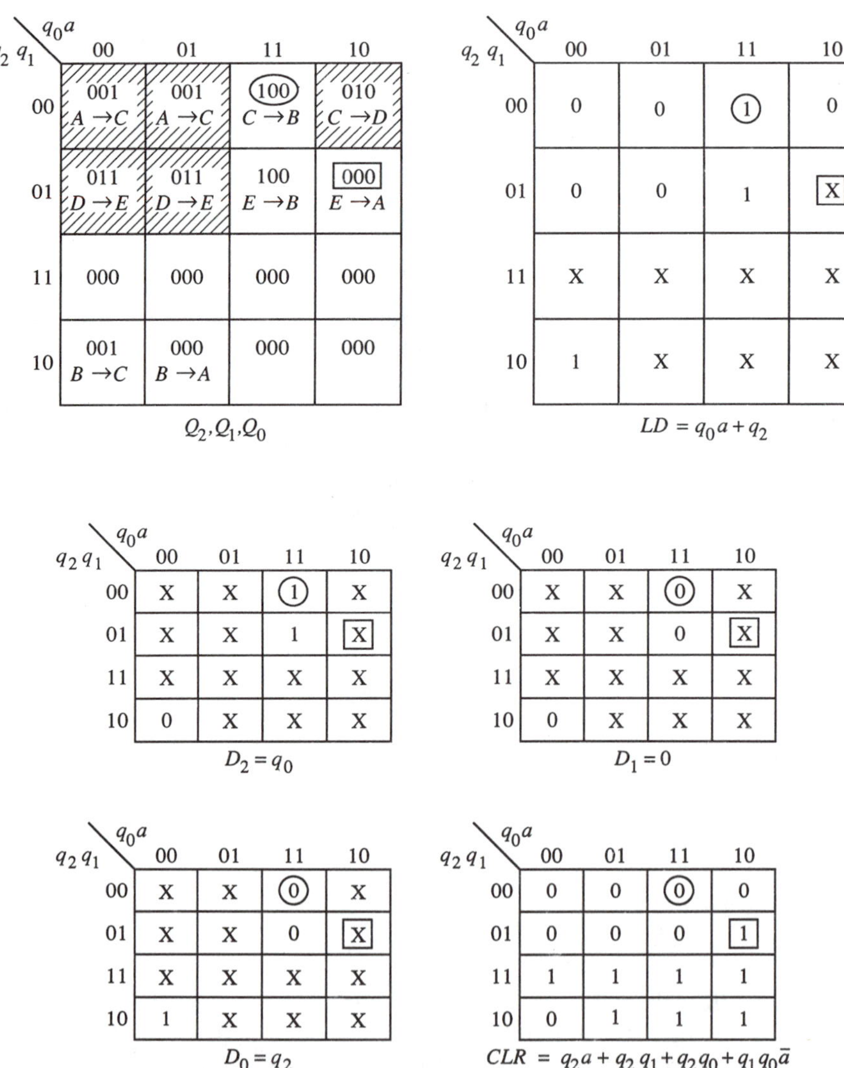

| $q_2 q_1$ \ $q_0 a$ | 00 | 01 | 11 | 10 |
|---|---|---|---|---|
| 00 | 001 $A \to C$ | 001 $A \to C$ | (100) $C \to B$ | 010 $C \to D$ |
| 01 | 011 $D \to E$ | 011 $D \to E$ | 100 $E \to B$ | [000] $E \to A$ |
| 11 | 000 | 000 | 000 | 000 |
| 10 | 001 $B \to C$ | 000 $B \to A$ | 000 | 000 |

$Q_2, Q_1, Q_0$

| $q_2 q_1$ \ $q_0 a$ | 00 | 01 | 11 | 10 |
|---|---|---|---|---|
| 00 | 0 | 0 | (1) | 0 |
| 01 | 0 | 0 | 1 | [X] |
| 11 | X | X | X | X |
| 10 | 1 | X | X | X |

$LD = q_0 a + q_2$

| $q_2 q_1$ \ $q_0 a$ | 00 | 01 | 11 | 10 |
|---|---|---|---|---|
| 00 | X | X | (1) | X |
| 01 | X | X | 1 | [X] |
| 11 | X | X | X | X |
| 10 | 0 | X | X | X |

$D_2 = q_0$

| $q_2 q_1$ \ $q_0 a$ | 00 | 01 | 11 | 10 |
|---|---|---|---|---|
| 00 | X | X | (0) | X |
| 01 | X | X | 0 | [X] |
| 11 | X | X | X | X |
| 10 | 0 | X | X | X |

$D_1 = 0$

| $q_2 q_1$ \ $q_0 a$ | 00 | 01 | 11 | 10 |
|---|---|---|---|---|
| 00 | X | X | (0) | X |
| 01 | X | X | 0 | [X] |
| 11 | X | X | X | X |
| 10 | 1 | X | X | X |

$D_0 = q_2$

| $q_2 q_1$ \ $q_0 a$ | 00 | 01 | 11 | 10 |
|---|---|---|---|---|
| 00 | 0 | 0 | (0) | 0 |
| 01 | 0 | 0 | 0 | [1] |
| 11 | 1 | 1 | 1 | 1 |
| 10 | 0 | 1 | 1 | 1 |

$CLR = q_2 a + q_2 q_1 + q_2 q_0 + q_1 q_0 \bar{a}$

**Figure 5.22.** Next state (*upper left*), *LD*, *CLR*, and data tables to implement the transition graph in Figure 5.21.

The hashed cells in the transition table are "counting" entries because their next state is $9 + 1$ mod-8. These transitions are obtained without loading. Assuming that *LD* is active High for our counter, these entries have 0s in the *LD* table and don't-cares in the data input tables. (No loading implies that data inputs are irrelevant.)

When the next state is (000)—in the boxed cell, for example—the transition is performed by the synchronous *CLR* input of the counter. For these combinations, *LD* and all data inputs are don't-cares.

All of the remaining transitions are achieved by loading, and the combinations to be loaded are the codes of the next states: $(D_2D_1D_0) = (Q_2Q_1Q_0)$. To illustrate how such entries are obtained, we will now explain the circled cells in the next-state, *LD*, and data-input tables: Transition from (001) to (100) on $a = 1$ requires loading because $001 + 1 \neq 100$, and so $LD = 1$. The desired next state is (100), and so $D_2 = 1$, $D_1 = 0$, and $D_0 = 0$. Naturally, $CLR = 0$.

After constructing the excitation tables, and finding the formulas, we finally obtain the complete sequencer shown in Figure 5.23. Design of the output circuit is the same as for flip-flop-based circuits.

**Exercises**

1. Solve the problems in Section 5.1 with presettable counters.
2. How would one design the circuit in this section if the counter had an asynchronous *CLR* input?
3. Perform timing analysis of the circuit in Figure 5.23.
4. Solve the problem from Section 5.4 using other state assignments and compare the results.

## 5.5 ADVANCED INTEGRATED CIRCUITS FOR SEQUENTIAL DESIGN

All sequential circuits depend on the same basic components: a collection of AND/OR gates and memory elements. This suggests that the basic PLD structure augmented with a collection of flip-flops would be a very useful building block. Because sequential circuits form the basis of many digital systems, the idea of fabricating a sufficiently powerful "programmable" chip to implement all required functions or to automate the design of special purpose chips is very appealing. Several manufacturers thus produce a variety of sequential PLDs suitable for the implementation of sequential circuits and we will now give an example of their use.

**Example.** We are to use a PLD to design a circuit described by the transition table in Figure 5.24. Because the circuit has eight states we need a circuit with three flip-flops. We will thus use the PAL 16R6, which contains six D-flip-

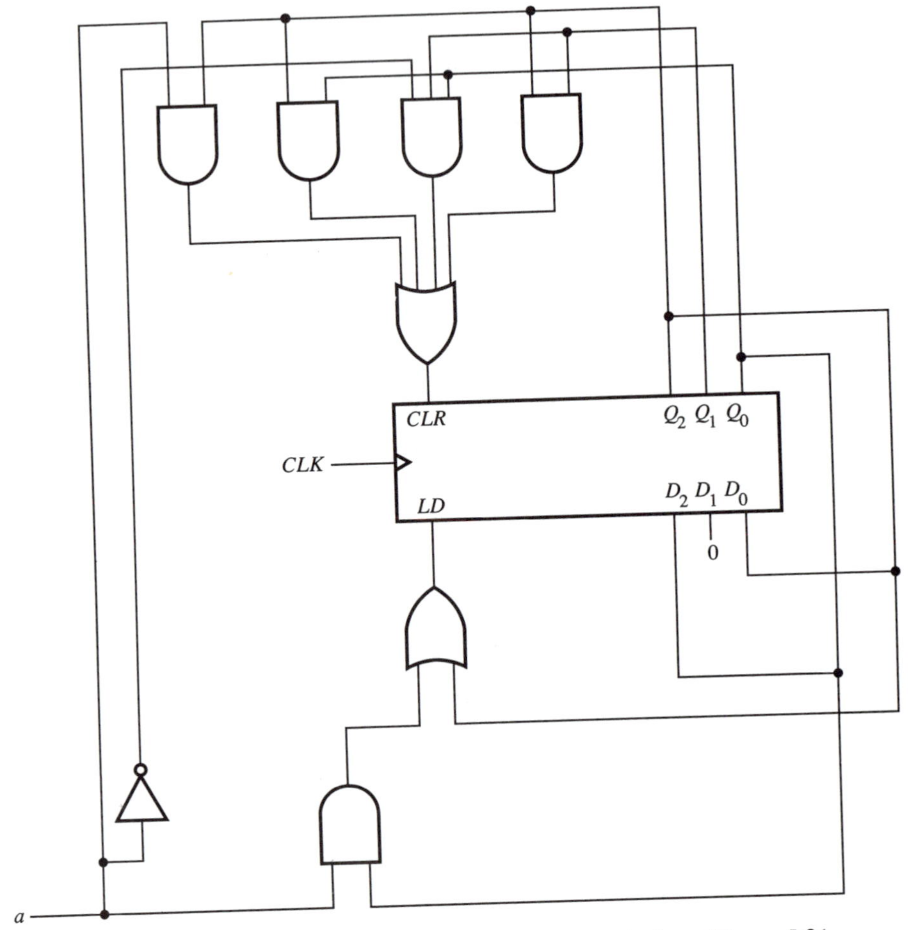


**Figure 5.23.** Implementation of the transition graph from Figure 5.21.

flops. The design of the circuit is identical to the method introduced in Section 5.2. The transition tables are treated as excitation tables and we obtain the following formulas:

$$D_2 = a \cdot q_0 + q_i \cdot \overline{q_2}$$

$$D_1 = \overline{q_1} \cdot q_0 + a$$

$$D_0 = a \cdot q_2 \cdot q_1 \cdot \overline{q_0} + \overline{q_1}$$

$$Y = q_1 + q_2 \cdot \overline{q_0}$$

These equations can be manually converted into the fuse map in Figure 5.25. In practice, computer programs are available that automate the design

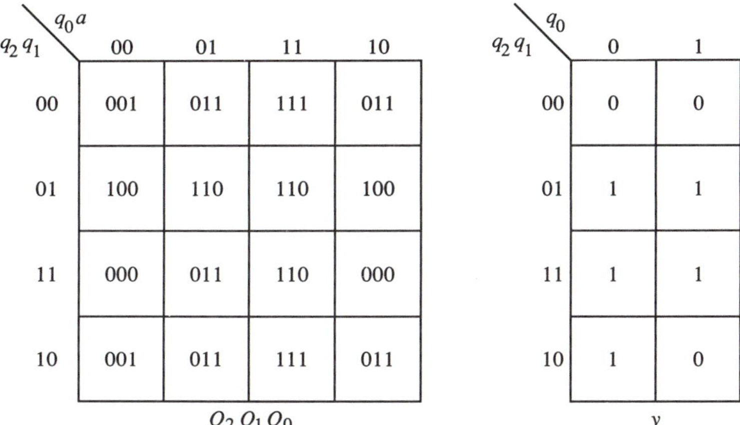


**Figure 5.24.** Transition and output tables for a PAL-based circuit.

of the fuse map from the specification. Note that the circuit requires only one chip; in fact, only a part of the chip is used and the remaining gates and flip-flops could be used for another circuit.

Programmable logic devices are very popular and are available with a wide variety of structures (combinational only, combinational with D-, T-, or JK-flip-flops, programmable output polarity, and so on), speeds, number of gates, and number of inputs. Some are mask programmable, others are fuse programmable, and some are erasable and reprogrammable.

### Exercises

1. Redesign the circuits from the previous sections using PLDs.
2. Redesign the circuit from this section using flip-flops and counters and compare the number of chips required in each approach.

## SUMMARY

The design of synchronous circuits consists of designing the sequencer that implements the transitions in the transition graph and the output circuit that produces the desired outputs. A sequence's design depends on the type of the selected storage elements but the design of the output circuit is always the same.

For circuits using flip-flops or PLDs, excitation equations are obtained by combining the next-state and the HTGT inverted transition tables. For circuits containing counters we try to take advantage of the built-in counting mechanism and assign states to create the longest possible path that can be traversed by incrementing the counter. This creates don't-care entries in the

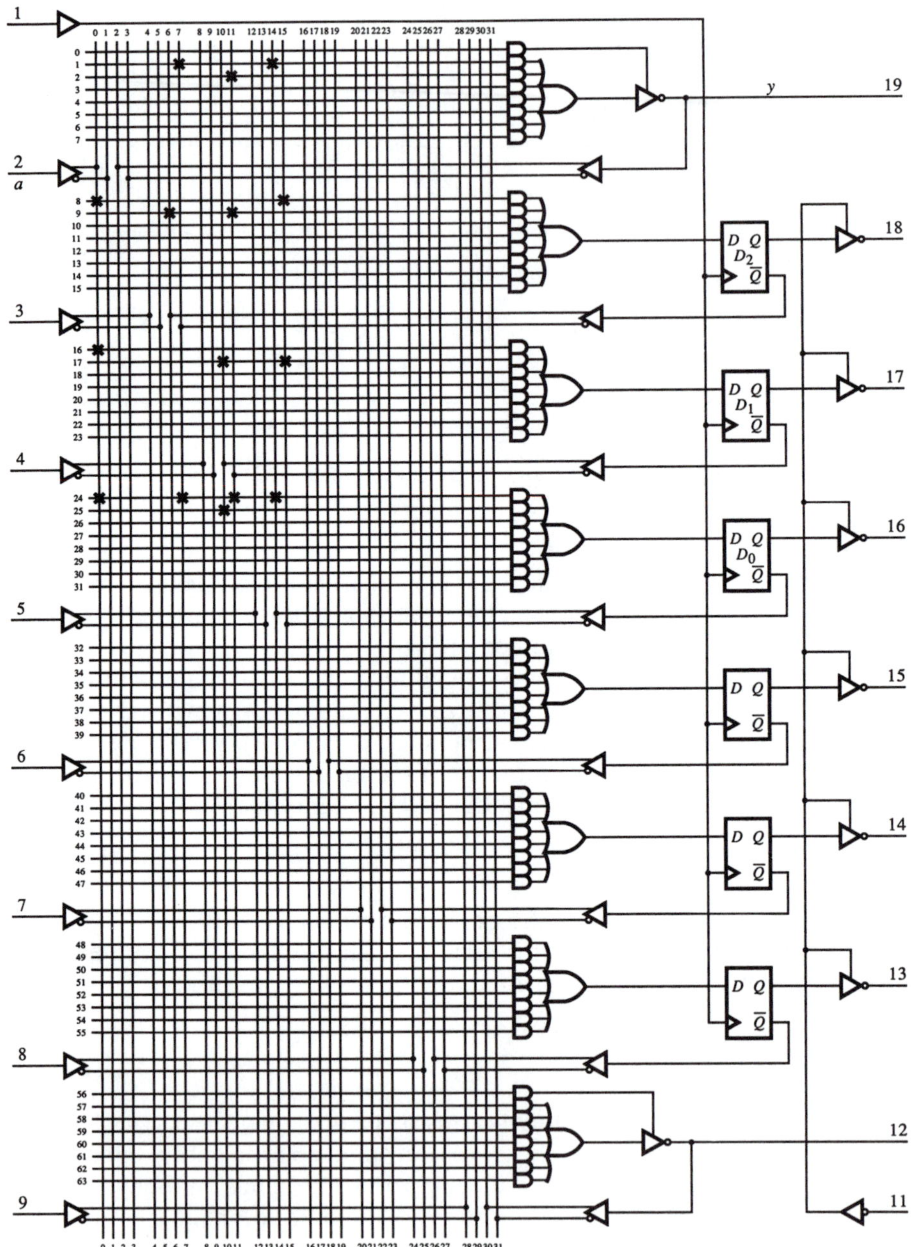


**Figure 5.25.** The PAL 16R6 fuse map for the problem in Figure 5.24. (Marked on original reproduced with the permission of Monolithic Memories.)

excitation tables and simplifies the excitation circuits. We can also take advantage of the *CLR* input.

The methods that we have presented are intuitively clear and easy to use but other approaches and refinements are available. These include algorithms that minimize the number of states in the transition graph, code assignments that minimize the excitation circuits, the use of asynchronous circuits, and so on. These topics are beyond the scope of our book.

The formal procedures that we have developed guarantee that the structure of the circuit matches the transition graph being implemented. To make sure that the circuit will work as expected, we must also consider the timing of the clock signal. This is done by examining all delay paths and using a clock whose period is at least as long as the longest signal-path delay.

To provide a background for the design of sequential circuits, we have shown how one designs clock generators. We saw that clocks usually consist of two parts: a circuit that generates the raw clock signal and a circuit that imposes the desired timing parameters on it. The raw signal is produced by a crystal with a conditioning circuit; the final signal is generated either by counters or by special integrated circuits. The latter are used in circuits that are produced in large quantities and that require complex and accurate timing.

Finally, we considered an example of design using PLDs that again shows that PLDs reduce chip count.

## REVIEW QUESTIONS

1. Define the following terms: HTGT table, clock, duty cycle, frequency, period, phase, skew, width of pulse, crystal, timer, timing analysis, sequential PLD.
2. Describe the following procedures: Construction of the HTGT table, design of sequential circuits with flip-flops, design with counters, timing analysis of sequential circuits.

## REFERENCES

The following titles listed in the references at the end of the book are relevant to this chapter:

Monolithic Memories. *Programmable Logic Handbook.*

A. D. Friedman. *Fundamentals of Logic Design and Switching Theory.*

Monolithic Memories. *Programmable Logic Handbook.*

D. Smith. *Programmable Logic Devices.*

# CHAPTER 6

# CODES, OPERATIONS, AND CIRCUITS

## AN OVERVIEW

Having dealt with individual bits we now change our perspective to deal with information processing at the level of codes. This chapter deals with code conventions, operations, and certain storage and processing components; the next chapter introduces the processing and transfer of codes and the principles of design of digital systems.

Digital systems like computers usually process text and numbers using one of a few common coding conventions. The most popular character convention for encoding text is ASCII. The most common number conventions are unsigned (pure) binary for non-negative integers, signed binary (two's complement) for positive and negative integers, floating-point for "REAL" numbers, and BCD for decimal arithmetic. We will introduce all these systems and explain arithmetic operations in them. We will conclude with a description of hexadecimal notation, a programmer's shorthand for binary codes.

In addition to conventions and operations we will present several logic circuits for arithmetic operations.

## IMPORTANT WORDS

ALU, ANSI, ASCII, BCD, bit-wise logic, byte, characteristic, control character, EBCDIC, fixed-point notation, flag, floating-point, full adder, hexadecimal, hidden bit, least significant bit (LSB), mantissa, most significant bit (MSB), normalization, octal notation, overflow, even/odd parity, radix, real number, ripple-carry adder, rounding, shifting, sign-magnitude, signed notation, truncation, two's complement, underflow, unsigned notation.

## 6.1 CODES

Before starting our presentation of the most common code systems, let us analyze what codes are and why we need them.

Codes are conventions for representing information and without them information cannot be exchanged or processed. Codes can use any physical means that can be recognized by humans or machines; even speech and "body language" are coding conventions. Codes have no inherent meaning and their interpretation depends only on the person or machine that uses them.

The arbitrary character of coding is apparent from the fact that the same words or gestures may mean different things in different languages and cultures. This poses no problem as long as the communicating subjects use the same convention. In digital systems, the "user" is normally a computer program and code interpretation is thus imposed by the person that created the program or the machine.

What do we mean by "interpreting" a code? In the end, the meaning of a code is measured by its use, the way in which the "listener" reacts to the encoded information. In a computer program any interpretation, however unconventional, will produce meaningful results if the program treats the codes consistently, assuming the same meaning in the same context.

It is worth noting that the ultimate user of computer codes, the programmer, does not have much control over the choice of the code used internally by the computer. Most programs are written in Pascal, C, Ada, COBOL, FORTRAN, or other programming languages and are translated into internal binary representation by the compiler program that determines the internal representation. In spite of this limitation, the programmer must understand the principles of coding to be able to take advantage of the choices that are available.

After this general introduction, we are now ready to survey the conventions used for encoding various types of information: instructions that control digital systems, text, and numbers.

*Instruction codes* vary from one computer to another; there are no standards, and we have nothing to say about them for now.

The display of *text* requires symbols that can be printed (letters, digits, punctuation symbols, and other special characters) and commands that control communication and elementary display operations (the line feed, carriage return, backspacing, the "bell," and other functions). Codes in the first group are known as "printable" characters. Those in the second group are "non-printable" or "control" characters.

*Numbers* are numeric values, and we must distinguish between their printed representation (numerals composed of digits) and the internal computer representation used for calculations. When we talk about numbers we have in mind the internal representation used by computers for arithmetic. Numbers can be represented in several conventions, each having its advantages, disadvantages, and specific applications. We will restrict our attention to those most commonly used for computer arithmetic.

Internal number codes are not suitable for display. Because they are used for internal processing and not for display the criteria for their design differ from those for the design of codes of digits. If a computer sends a number code to a display device, it may produce a symbol if it happens to coincide with the code of a text code but it will never represent the internally understood numeric value. A program that alternates between input, output, and internal calculations must therefore convert between the internal binary number codes used for calculations and their external representation by digits, printable character codes.

## 6.2 CHARACTER CODES

Character codes for representing text were invented long before the first computers were built; the Morse code for telegraphy is a well-known example. With the emergence of computers, much research effort has gone into coding and several new conventions have been devised. The two systems that have become most popular are ASCII (American Standard Code for Information Interchange) and EBCDIC (Extended BCD Interchange Code). The latter has been used mainly by IBM and its importance and popularity are directly related to the importance of IBM computers. Lately, EBCDIC has been largely replaced by ASCII, which has certain advantages. An important extension of ASCII is ANSI, a convention approved by the American National Standards Institute.

Although ASCII is now widely accepted, work on coding systems has not stopped, and new developments reflect the evolving needs of programmers, such as the growing use of graphics. It is generally acknowledged that ASCII is not adequate for certain modern applications but no single replacement system has been widely accepted so far. One can safely predict that ASCII will remain the main character code for the near future and its successor will almost certainly contain ASCII as a subset.

The existence of a widely accepted character code is very important for several reasons. One is that a standard makes it possible to design devices such as printers and terminals that can work with any computer and program. Another is that standardization can improve the internal efficiency of computer operation. If, for example, there existed widely used standards to represent graphics information, semiconductor manufacturers could start mass producing powerful and inexpensive chips to automate much of the work that must now be done by specialized hardware or by software. All computers would appear as identical graphics devices to all graphics programs, which could then be developed in single versions, largely independent of the computer. The present lack of a graphics standard means that each computer handles graphics differently. Programs thus require expensive conversions to run on different computers and they often lose efficiency in the process.

What are the criteria that guide the design of a character standard for computer use? Apart from completeness (the standard must be able to represent all currently needed types of information and must allow for future extension), the two main considerations are efficiency of storage and processing.

### Efficiency of Storage

The size of computer memories is always limited and one must be concerned with storing information efficiently. There exists a relatively simple procedure for finding the encoding that minimizes the total number of bits needed to store a given body of information, but its result depends on the text being stored. Thus it must be calculated for each body of text separately. Moreover, optimal coding requires codes of different lengths and this complicates storage, retrieval, and processing. Truly optimal encoding is thus impractical and all popular character conventions use fixed codes of constant length.

The total number of characters needed to display ordinary text (upper- and lower-case letters, digits, punctuation, control characters, and so on) is close to 128 and consequently requires seven-bit codes (Figure 6.1). However, seven-bit codes are not suited for storage because the size of memory cells in modern computers is usually a multiple of eight. Seven-bit ASCII codes are thus normally stored as eight-bit groups or *bytes*, and this leaves one bit available for other uses. Two common uses of the extra bit are described below.

To allow for expansion beyond the predefined 128 characters, ASCII contains an "escape" character (called ESC) whose function is to indicate that the following codes are not to be interpreted in the usual way. ANSI, for example, uses "escape (ESC) sequences" to define a number of special functions, such as control of display on computer terminals. Some examples are:

| ANSI Code | Meaning |
|---|---|
| ESC[P*n*A | Move cursor up by *n* lines |
| ESC[P*n*B | Move cursor down by *n* lines |
| ESC[P*n*C | Move cursor right by *n* positions |
| ESC[P*n*D | Move cursor left by *n* positions |
| ESC[K | Erase from cursor position to end of line |
| ESC[2J | Erase entire screen |
| ESC7 | Save cursor attributes (blinking, shape, etc.) |
| ESC8 | Restore cursor to former attributes |

| | $b_6,b_5,b_4$ | | | | | | | |
|---|---|---|---|---|---|---|---|---|
| $b_3,b_2,b_1,b_0$ | 000 | 001 | 010 | 011 | 100 | 101 | 110 | 111 |
| 0000 | NUL | DLE | space | 0 | @ | P | ` | p |
| 0001 | SOH | DC1 | ! | 1 | A | Q | a | q |
| 0010 | STX | DC2 | " | 2 | B | R | b | r |
| 0011 | ETX | DC3 | # | 3 | C | S | c | s |
| 0100 | EOT | DC4 | $ | 4 | D | T | d | t |
| 0101 | ENQ | NAK | % | 5 | E | U | e | u |
| 0110 | ACK | SYN | & | 6 | F | V | f | v |
| 0111 | BEL | ETB | ' | 7 | G | W | g | w |
| 1000 | BS | CAN | ( | 8 | H | X | h | x |
| 1001 | HT | EM | ) | 9 | I | Y | i | y |
| 1010 | LF | SUB | * | : | J | Z | j | z |
| 1011 | VT | ESC | + | ; | K | [ | k | { |
| 1100 | FF | FS | ' | < | L | \ | l | \| |
| 1101 | CR | GS | - | = | M | ] | m | { |
| 1110 | SO | RS | . | > | N | ^ | n | ~ |
| 1111 | SI | US | / | ? | O | _ | o | DEL |

**Figure 6.1.** Seven-bit ASCII codes of printable symbols and control characters. Code bits are denoted $b_6,b_5,b_4,b_3,b_2,b_1,b_0$. A few symbols have several representations. As an example, the dollar sign "$" may be used to represent currency symbols in different countries.

The cursor is a visual representation of the active position on the screen, usually a blinking rectangular block.

One of the goals of the ANSI convention was to standardize control codes used by computer terminals. Unfortunately, manufacturers often use their own escape sequences rather than ANSI.

## Ease of Processing

In many applications, considerable computer time is spent in alphabetic and numeric searching; sorting; and converting from digits to numeric values, from lower- to upper-case letters. The most efficient way to perform these operations is to design character codes so that they can be treated as numbers; in other words, one tries to preserve useful relations between characters as relations between the numeric values of their codes. Suitable code assignment can also simplify the design of certain types of hardware, such as keyboard encoders, and important software, such as compilers. Some consequences of these points can be seen in the following properties of ASCII:

Consecutive letters have codes with consecutive numeric values. (The numeric value of the code of *A* is 65, the code of *B* is 66, and so on.)

Codes of capital letters are grouped together, as are codes of lower-case letters, digits, and control characters. Unfortunately, some other groups of related characters, such as punctuation and arithmetic symbols, do not have consecutive codes.

Codes of corresponding upper- and lower-case letters differ only in the value of the second bit (*A* is 1000001, *a* is 1100001), and this simplifies conversion.

Codes of upper-case letters precede codes of lower-case letters as in telephone directories and encyclopedias.

The blank space (code 32) precedes all letters. As a consequence, *ab* precedes *abc* as one would expect.

Codes of digits are derived from BCD codes (the last four bits give the numeric value).

### The Eighth Bit

We mentioned that seven-bit ASCII codes are usually stored in eight-bit memory cells. This leaves the leftmost bit (the most significant bit, or MSB) available for other purposes. Its two main uses are as follows:

One-half of the 256 eight-bit codes may be used for ASCII and the other half for special symbols. As an example, all binary codes starting with 0 could be ASCII codes while the remaining 128 codes, which start with 1, might represent Greek letters, graphics symbols, useful patterns of dots in the dot matrix, and so on. This use of the eighth bit ("extended ASCII") is common but not standard.

The eighth bit can be used to generate odd or even parity. A code is said to have odd (even) parity if the total number of ones in it is odd (even). As an example,

0000000, 1111110, 1010101 are even-parity seven-bit codes

1111111, 0000001, 1000000 are odd-parity seven-bit codes

By making the eighth bit 0 or 1 we can control the parity of the whole eight-bit code and use it to monitor the correctness of communication of a stream of codes between two devices. If, for example, a computer sends an even parity code and the printer detects that the parity of the received signal is odd, the code was corrupted during transmission and should be retransmitted. Error detection based on parity is built into many devices, such as computer terminals, but is rarely used. It is, however, frequently used to monitor the correctness of data stored in memory, and memories with an extra parity bit are relatively common. In an odd-parity nine-bit memory, each eight-bit code is accompanied by a ninth parity bit whose value is such that the complete nine-bit code has odd parity.

## Exercises

1. Use the ASCII table in Figure 6.1 to determine what a terminal that does not recognize ANSI will display when it receives the ANSI code to move the cursor up by thirteen lines. Assume that the terminal ignores the ESC character.
2. Explain how to perform alphabetical sorting of ASCII codes using arithmetic operations. Formulate a sorting algorithm for a character convention in which character codes are assigned without regard for their relationship.
3. Non-ASCII conventions may be preferable for certain display devices. As an example, define codes to display digits on a seven-segment display.
4. Design a case-shift circuit that automatically generates correct upper-case letter codes from lower-case letter codes when the *SHIFT* signal is On. Make sure that the circuit only affects letter codes.
5. Explain why six codes are inserted between upper- and lower-case letters in ASCII. (*Hint:* How would one have to modify the *SHIFT* circuit if codes of the lower-case characters immediately followed codes of the upper-case letters?)
6. Design a circuit to convert ASCII codes of digits into their four-bit BCD equivalents preceded by four 0s. As an example, 0110000 should be converted to 00000000, and so on. Make sure that only digit codes are affected.
7. Code C represents a digit if its numeric value is between 49 and 57. This can be expressed as

   code value of C in the range [49..57]

   or, in Pascal

   ord(*C*) IN [49..57]

   Describe similarly the condition that C is

a. an upper-case letter
b. a letter
c. a letter between *D* and *M*
d. an arithmetic operator.

8. Assume that the following codes were sent with even parity: 01101011, 10010100, 10000111, 00000000, 11111111, 10101010. Which of these were corrupted in transmission?
9. Express 0, 1, *a*, and *A* as odd-parity ASCII-based eight-bit codes.
10. Is it possible to detect that two bits of an even-parity code have been distorted by transmission?
11. Design the following combinational circuits:
    a. an even-parity generator: input seven-bit ASCII code, output eight-bit ASCII even-parity code
    b. a parity tester: input eight ASCII bits, output High when the code has even parity, Low otherwise
    c. a parity tester/generator with inputs to control desired parity and mode of operation. (See the 74180 and 74280 chips for comparison.)
12. Show that circuits for parity generation and testing are the worst possible problem for two-level AND/OR implementation because their canonic formulas cannot be simplified.
13. The simplest implementation of parity checking is by cascaded XOR gates. Construct the circuit. (*Hint:* The circuit is based on the following definition of parity: The parity of a one-bit code is off iff the bit is 1. The parity of an *n*-bit code is odd if the parity of its first *n*-1 bits is odd and the *n*th bit is 0 or if the parity of its first *n*-1 bits is even and the *n*th bit is 1.)
14. Explain why odd parity is more popular than even parity. (*Hint:* What happens when a line between two communicating devices is shorted to the ground or loses power?)
15. Explain the statement "Code standards are moving targets."
16. Make a detailed analogy between character and number codes on the one hand and the uses of numbers by humans on the other. Which codes relate to mental calculations and which to written records of such calculations?

## 6.3 AN OVERVIEW OF NUMBER CONVENTIONS

Computers use numbers in various contexts and each has its preferred representation:

Counting requires only positive integers and 0; the best convention for this purpose is *unsigned (pure) binary.*

Calculations with positive and negative integers normally use *signed codes*, also called *two's complement* notation. In some situations, two's complement is replaced by the *sign-magnitude* representation.

Calculations in engineering and science applications require high accuracy and a broad range of magnitudes that can be obtained with *floating point* representation.

Accurate decimal calculations and applications with a great deal of decimal input and output use BCD representation.

Industrial applications, such as the reading of sensors and the control of activators, often use special conventions.

We will now present the principles of all these conventions, with the exception of the last category.

## 6.4 UNSIGNED BINARY

Unsigned binary is used for non-negative numbers (positive numbers and zero). In most applications, the codes represent integers but the representation of fractional values is also possible.

### The Integer Convention

Unsigned or pure binary is simply the positional representation introduced in Chapter 2 and its principle is the same as that of ordinary decimal notation. Each position in the code has a fixed weight that is a power of the base (also called the "radix") and the value of the code is the sum of its weighted digits. The base is 2 in binary, 8 in octal, 10 in decimal, 16 in hexadecimal, and so on. As an example, code 101 represents the following: (The symbol "*" denotes arithmetic multiplication.) In decimal,

$$\begin{aligned}101_{10} &= 1 \times 100 + 0 \times 10 + 1 \times 1 \\ &= 1 \times 10^2 + 0 \times 10^1 + 1 \times 10^0\end{aligned}$$

in binary,

$$\begin{aligned}101_2 &= 1 \times 4 + 0 \times 2 + 1 \times 1 \\ &= 1 \times 2^2 + 0 \times 2^1 + 1 \times 2^0 \\ &= 5_{10}\end{aligned}$$

in octal,

$$\begin{aligned}101_8 &= 1 \times 8^2 + 0 \times 8^1 + 1 \times 8^0 \\ &= 65_{10}\end{aligned}$$

and in hexadecimal,

$$\begin{aligned}101_{16} &= 1 \times 16^2 + 0 \times 16^1 + 1 \times 16^0 \\ &= 257_{10}\end{aligned}$$

Inversely, the binary code of $101_{10}$ is

$$\begin{aligned}1100101_2 &= 1 \times 64 + 1 \times 32 + 1 \times 4 + 1 \times 1 \\ &= 1 \times 2^6 + 1 \times 2^5 + 1 \times 2^2 + 1 \times 2^0\end{aligned}$$

Because we often need to convert between decimal and binary (by hand or by a computer program) we will now demonstrate how to do so efficiently. The procedure is based on Horner's rule, which states that a polynomial such as

$$f(x) = a_3 \times x^3 + a_2 \times x^2 + a_1 \times x^1 + a_0 \times x^0$$

can be expressed as

$$f(x) = a_0 + x \times (a_1 + x \times (a_2 + a_3 \times x))$$

Using this convention, the meaning of the pure binary code $(a_3a_2a_1a_0)$ is obtained by replacing $x$ with 2:

$$\begin{aligned}(a_3a_2a_1a_0)_2 &= a_3 \times 2^3 + a_2 \times 2^2 + a_1 \times 2^1 + a_0 \times 2^0 \\ &= a_0 + 2 \times (a_1 + 2 \times (a_2 + 2 \times a_3))\end{aligned}$$

From this expression, we can see that if we divide a decimal value by 2, the remainder is $a_0$ and the quotient is $(a_1 + 2 \times (a_2 + 2 \times a_3))$. Dividing the new quotient by 2 gives a new quotient with remainder $a_1$; another division produces $a_2$; and so on. The process starts with the least significant bit (LSB) and is repeated until all digits of the binary code are obtained. A formal description of this method of conversion from decimal to binary is as follows:

```
pos := 0;                    {Start with the LSB in the code}
WHILE value>0 DO
  BEGIN
    apos  := value mod 2;    {Remainder of division by 2}
    value:= value div 2;     {Quotient of division by 2}
    pos  := pos+1;           {Next position}
  END
```

Initially, *value* is the value to be converted. The following is an example of the use of this algorithm to calculate the binary code of decimal 212:

| pos | Value (quotient) | Remainder |
|---|---|---|
| 0 | 212 | $0 = a_0$ LSB of the code |
| 1 | 106 | $0 = a_1$ |
| 2 | 53 | $1 = a_2$ |
| 3 | 26 | $0 = a_3$ |
| 4 | 13 | $1 = a_4$ |
| 5 | 6 | $0 = a_5$ |
| 6 | 3 | $1 = a_6$ |
| 7 | 1 | $1 = a_7$ MSB of the code |

The binary code of $212_{10}$ is thus $11010100_2$.

Conversion from binary to decimal is also based on Horner's rule but starts from the inside: To convert binary to decimal, multiply the MSB by 2, add the next bit, multiply the result by 2, and so on:

```
value := a_n;                    {Start with the MSB}
pos   := n;
WHILE pos>0 DO
  BEGIN
    value := 2×value + a_pos;
    pos   := pos−1;
  END;
```

As an example, the decimal value of binary 11010100 is obtained as follows:

| pos | $a_{pos}$ | Value |
|---|---|---|
| 7 | 1 | 1 |
| 6 | 1 | 3 |
| 5 | 0 | 6 |
| 4 | 1 | 13 |
| 3 | 0 | 26 |
| 2 | 1 | 53 |
| 1 | 0 | 106 |
| 0 | 0 | 212 Result |

The two conversions are complementary and the procedures are thus reversed: One starts from the MSB and multiplies while the other starts from the LSB and divides.

**Exercises**

1. Convert the decimal values 152, 31, and 255 to eight-bit binary codes.
2. Convert 10101010, 00110011, 11111111 to decimal.
3. Formulate conversion procedures for other bases and demonstrate them by converting $786_{10}$ to hexadecimal and octal, and $756_{16}$ and $756_8$ to decimal.
4. Printer logic assumes that inputs are ASCII codes. What would be printed if a printer received the unsigned eight-bit binary codes of 21, 54, 127, or 255? Assume no parity checking.

**Representation of Fractions**

The system with weights

$$.., 16, 8, 4, 2, 1$$

that we have used so far is called integer representation because it can represent only integer numbers. One can think of each integer code as having a decimal point behind the rightmost bit.

Integer representation is not the only possible form of positional notation. Any system whose weights are successive powers of the base is positional. If the weights are negative powers of 2 ($\frac{1}{2}$, $\frac{1}{4}$, $\frac{1}{8}$, ...) we obtain another useful positional system, which is called "fractional." In fractional representation, the "decimal" point precedes the MSB. An eight-bit binary code $(a_7,a_6,\ldots,a_1,a_0)$ means

$$a_7 2^7 + a_6 2^6 + \ldots + a_1 2^1 + a_0 2^0$$

in integer representations and

$$a_7 2^{-1} + a_6 2^{-2} + \ldots + a_1 2^{-7} + a_0 2^{-8}$$

in fractional representation. Because the exponents are negative, the code should be written as $(a_{-1},a_{-2},\ldots,a_{-7},a_{-8})$.

As an example of the different interpretations, in integer representation 01100001 means

$$01100001. = 2^6 + 2^5 + 2^0 = 97$$

and in fractional representation it means

$$\begin{aligned} .01100001 &= 2^{-2} + 2^{-3} + 2^{-8} \\ &= \frac{1}{4} + \frac{1}{8} + \frac{1}{256} \\ &= \frac{97}{256} \end{aligned}$$

A simple way to calculate the value of a fractional code is to convert it to integer and divide:

$$\begin{aligned} .01100001 &= 01100001. \times 2^{-8} \\ &= \frac{97}{2^8} \\ &= \frac{97}{256} \end{aligned}$$

Fractional representation is important because it forms the basis of the standard floating-point convention.

It is worth noting that the integer and fractional systems are not the only two possibilities: The decimal point can be located anywhere within the code, any number of bits before the MSB, or any number of bits behind the LSB. The weights of individual positions may thus be assigned arbitrarily as long as they are consecutive powers of two as in

$$\ldots\ 2^3\ 2^2\ 2^1\ 2^0\ 2^{-1}\ 2^{-2}\ \ldots$$

The decimal point is not explicitly included in the code and its proper interpretation is only in the mind of the user or the programmer; that is, the computer is not concerned about it.

### Exercises

1. What is the value of 01100001 in ASCII code, integer binary, fractional binary, binary with the decimal point in the middle of the code, with the decimal point preceding the MSB by three bits, or with the decimal point following the LSB by four bits? What is the code's value when interpreted as a decimal number?
2. Represent the numbers 7.75, 13.125, 8.12, and 86.125 using eight-bit codes with the decimal point between the third and fourth bit from the left. (*Hint:* convert integer and fractional parts separately.)
3. What is the effect of the position of the decimal point on the range of values that can be represented with a fixed number of bits and on the accuracy of representation—the "distance" between two consecutive codes?
4. Formulate conversion algorithms for fractional codes.

## Arithmetic

Unsigned arithmetic is easy to understand because the principles of pure binary, decimal, and all other positional systems are the same. We will now describe the fundamentals of addition, subtraction, multiplication, and division, and we will present several basic arithmetic circuits.

## Addition

The basis of this operation is right-to-left bit-wise addition of aligned codes. Carry-out becomes carry-in for the next position:

| | Symbolic Description | Example |
|---|---|---|
| $c$ | Carry-in from the previous column | 1 |
| $a$ | First operand | 1 |
| $b$ | Second operand | 0 |
| $cs$ | Carry-out and sum | 10 |

We can express one-bit addition by tables (Figure 6.2) that can be used to construct a combined sum-and-carry circuit called the *full adder.*

The following example illustrates multidigit addition of decimal and binary codes:

| Decimal | | Binary | |
|---|---|---|---|
| Carry-in | 10 | Carry-in | 1011000 |
| First operand | 36 | First operand | 0100100 |
| Second operand | 45 | Second operand | 0101101 |
| Result | 81 | | 1010001 |

Because multibit addition is reiterated one-bit addition, the adder for two $n$-bit codes can be obtained as a chain of full adders with interconnected carries (Figure 6.3). The resulting *ripple-carry adder* forms the basis of most multibit adders. It is a simple device, and because it consists of a string of identical circuits its internal structure is regular, which is very desirable for implementation.

Unfortunately, the ripple-carry adder is relatively slow because the rightmost carry may have to propagate through the entire adder before the output stabilizes at its final value. We will now demonstrate carry propagation

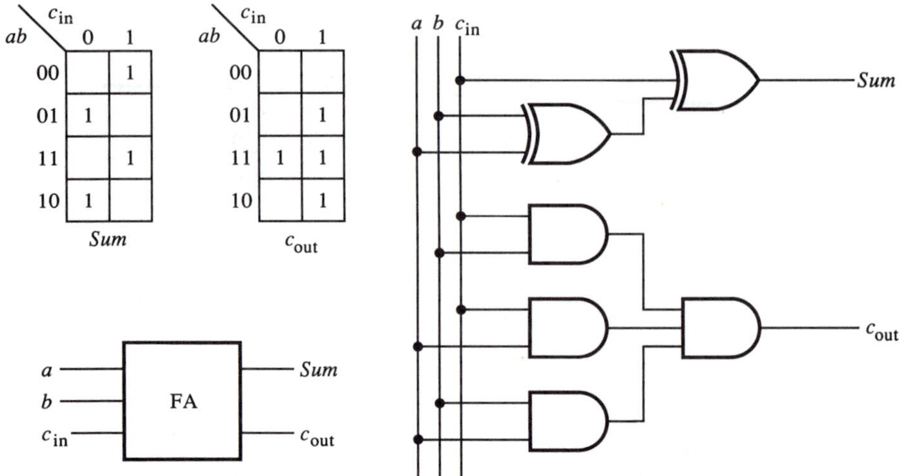


**Figure 6.2.** Sum and carry-out tables and the full adder.

through a circuit using as our example the sequence of steps involved in the ripple-carry addition of (00100100) + (00101101). The outputs are observed at times separated by the propagation delay $T_{pFA}$ of a single full adder. Figure 6.3 gives another perspective of this operation, showing that outputs are in transition between $T_{pFA}$ and $2T_{pFA}$, between $3T_{pFA}$ and $4T_{pFA}$, and so on.

| | | |
|---|---|---|
| 0 0 0 0 0 0 0 0 | $c_{in}$ | Assumed initial value |
| 0 0 1 0 0 1 0 0 | $a$ | |
| 0 0 1 0 1 1 0 1 | $b$ | State at time 0 |
| 0 0 0 0 1 0 0 1 | | Bit-wise sum of $a + b + c_{in}$ |
| 0 0 1 0 0 1 0 0 | | Bit-wise $c_{out}$ |
| ↙ ↙ ↙ ↙ ↙ ↙ ↙ | | Output ($c_{out}$) becomes $c_{in}$ of next *FA* |
| 0 1 0 0 1 0 0 0 | $c_{in}$ | |
| 0 0 1 0 0 1 0 0 | a | |
| 0 0 1 0 1 1 0 1 | b | State at time $T_{pFA}$ |
| 0 1 0 0 0 0 0 1 | | Bit-wise sum of $a + b + c_{in}$ |
| 0 0 1 0 1 1 0 0 | | Bit-wise $c_{out}$ |
| ↙ ↙ ↙ ↙ ↙ ↙ ↙ | | Output ($c_{out}$) becomes $c_{in}$ of next *FA* |
| 0 1 0 1 1 0 0 0 | $c_{in}$ | |

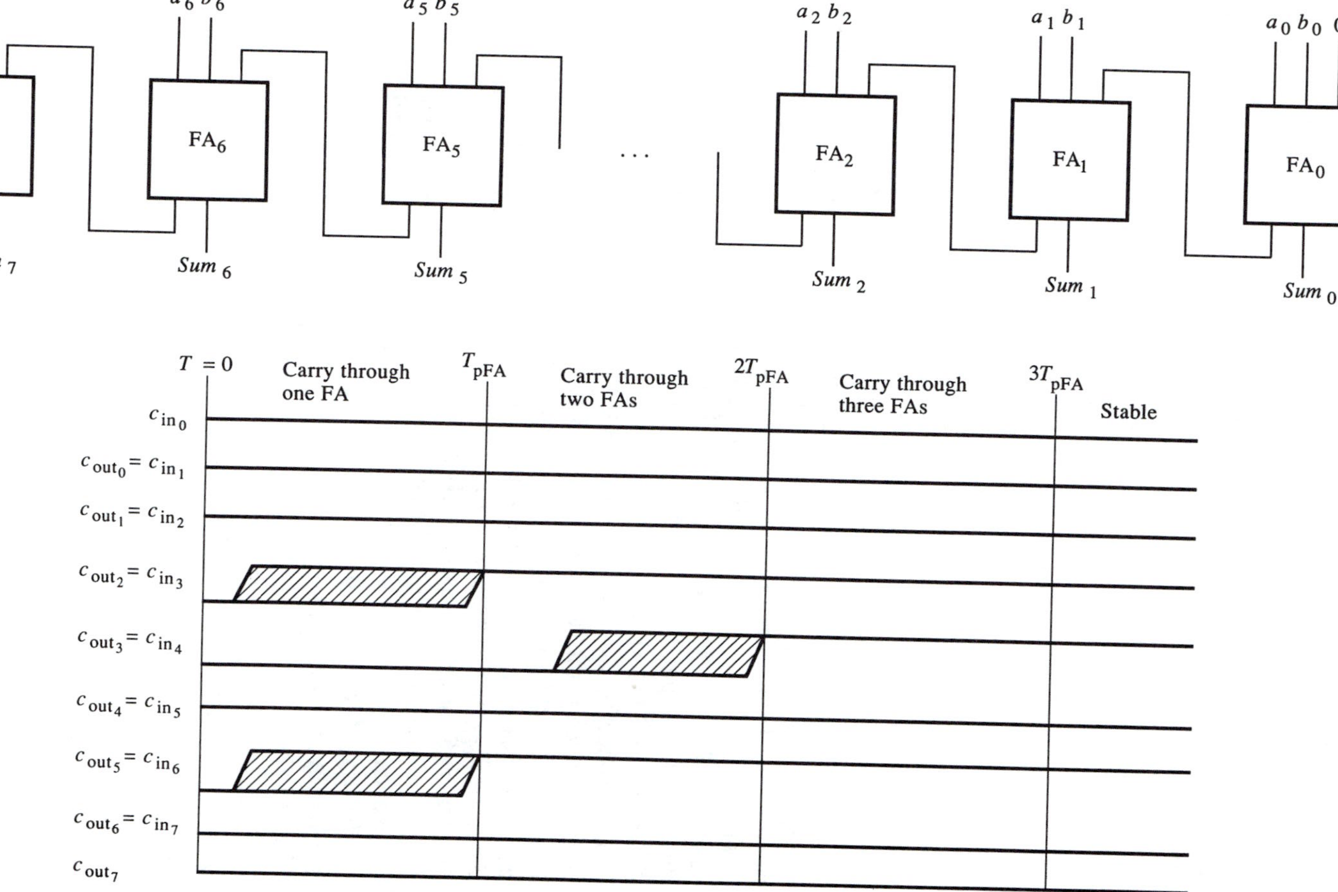


**Figure 6.3.** Eight-bit ripple-carry adder and the sequence of its carry signals for the example in the text.

| | | |
|---|---|---|
| 0 0 1 0 0 1 0 0 | $a$ | |
| 0 0 1 0 1 1 0 1 | $b$ | State at time $2T_{pFA}$ |
| 0 1 0 1 0 0 0 1 | | Bit-wise sum of $a + b + c_{in}$ |
| 0 0 1 0 1 1 0 0 | | Bit-wise $c_{out}$ |
| ↙ ↙ ↙ ↙ ↙ ↙ ↙ | | Output ($c_{out}$) becomes $c_{in}$ of next $FA$ |
| 0 1 0 1 1 0 0 0 | $c_{in}$ | |
| 0 0 1 0 0 1 0 0 | $a$ | |
| 0 0 1 0 1 1 0 1 | $b$ | State at time $3T_{pFA}$ |

Because the carriers generated at $2T_{pFA}$ are the same as those generated at $3T_{pFA}$, all *FA*s have the same inputs beginning at time $3T_{pFA}$ and no further change of outputs will occur as long as the inputs remain unchanged. The calculation of the result thus took $2T_{pFA}$.

The value of $T_{pFA}$, the propagation delay through a single full adder, can be calculated from the logic diagram of the full adder. If we build the adder using the 7400 two-input NAND, 7410 three-input NAND, and 7486 two-input XOR, we find that $T_{pFA} = 60$ nsec.

The propagation delay required by a particular pair of operands would be of importance if the adder worked as a part of an asynchronous circuit. If, however, the adder is a part of a synchronous circuit, only the worst possible add time is relevant. For an eight-bit ripple-carry adder the worst possible delay is $8T_{pFA}$ or 240 nsec, a considerable length of time in the operation of a computer. Standard four-bit TTL adders (7483 and 74283) operate faster than our analysis indicates because they speed up carry propagation by "lookahead" (Exercise 9). Their worst propagation delay is around 25 nsec.

The sum of two $n$-bit codes may be $n + 1$ bits long because it may generate a carry (in programming denoted $C$). If $C = 0$ the $n$-result result is correct but if $C = 1$ the $n$-bit code is incomplete and $n + 1$ bits are needed to represent it:

| | | |
|---|---|---|
| Resulting carry | 100000000 | Carry-out ↓ |
| First operand | 10000000 | |
| Second operand | 10000000 | |
| Incorrect sum | 00000000 | Correct code 1 00000000 |

Because of this, all $n$-bit adders output an $n$-bit sum and the carry-out. The carry-out is also needed to cascade smaller adders together for addition of larger operands.

## Exercises

1. Add the following decimal values in unsigned binary using eight-bit codes: 121 + 52, 89 + 93, and 131 + 152.
2. Explore arithmetic on codes for seven-segment displays and explain the popularity of positional notation.
3. Calculate how many $T_{pFA}$ steps it takes to add 31 + 93 and 56 + 111 using 8-bit codes. Does the delay depend on the number of bits in the code?
4. Give an example of eight-bit addition that requires $8T_{pFA}$ to produce the final sum.
5. Give examples of eight-bit additions that produce nine-bit results.
6. Draw a detailed diagram of an eight-bit adder built from two 74283 four-bit adders.
7. Design a two-bit adder for $(a_1a_0) + (b_1b_0)$ as a two-level AND–OR circuit. Compare its regularity, complexity, and speed with that of a two-bit ripple-carry adder.
8. Design a *half adder.* This device is identical to a full adder but has only two inputs.
9. Almost all modern adders use the procedure known as *lookahead* to speed up calculation by speeding up carry propagation: A binary full adder number $i$ outputs a carry if its operands produce a carry; if adder number $i - 1$ produces a carry and adder $i$ allows it to propagate; or if adder $i - 2$ produces a carry and adder $i - 1$ allows it to propagate; and so on. A binary adder produces a carry if both of its operands are 1. A binary adder propagates a carry if at least one of its operands is 1.

   Use this description to construct a four-bit lookahead adder that calculates overall "generate" and "propagate" functions.
10. Design a sixteen-bit adder using four-bit adders with carry-generate and carry-propagate outputs and inputs. Compare the speed and the complexity of regular and lookahead adders.

### Subtraction

Subtraction can be performed from right to left, much like addition. When subtracting a larger value from a smaller one, we must borrow from the next position. As an example,

$$\begin{array}{r} 101 \\ -011 \\ \hline 010 \end{array}$$

is performed from right to left as follows:

Bit 0: $1 - 1 = 0$

Bit 1: $0 - 1$ requires a borrow and is performed as $10 - 1 = 1$.

Bit 2: The borrow from bit 1 must now be subtracted and the operation is $1 - 1 - 0 = 0$.

If binary subtraction seems more difficult than addition, the reader should initially try doing it using successive table lookups in subtraction and borrow tables (Figure 6.4). The "borrow" table is constructed from the following rules:

If subtraction requires a borrow, a borrow-out is produced. The borrow-out generated in one column becomes the borrow-in in the next column.

The presence of borrow-in means that subtraction in the previous column required a borrow. Subtraction in this column is thus $(a - 1) - b$.

As pure binary does not allow negative numbers, subtraction is used only to decrement positive counts or to compare two numbers. Comparison is very important and we will now present a table that reduces comparison to subtraction, and a simple logic operation on two indicator bits called the *carry flag* and the *zero flag*. (Computer circuits use the same circuit for addition and subtraction; the carry and borrow signals are identical and are usually referred to collectively as "carry.") If $Z$ represents the zero flag ($Z = 1$ if the result is zero, $Z = 0$ otherwise), and $C$ the carry (borrow) we can describe the results of comparisons as follows:

| Relation | Meaning | C/Z Logic Condition | Explanation |
|---|---|---|---|
| $a<b$ | $a-b<0$ | $C$ | Borrow required |
| $a\leq b$ | $a-b\leq 0$ | $C+Z$ | Borrow required OR zero |
| $a>b$ | $a-b>0$ | $\overline{C}\cdot\overline{Z}=\overline{C+Z}$ | Inverse of $a\leq b$ |
| $a\geq b$ | $a-b\geq 0$ | $\overline{C}$ | Inverse of $a<b$ |
| $a=b$ | $a-b=0$ | $Z$ | |
| $a\neq b$ | $a-b\neq 0$ | $\overline{Z}$ | |

To test whether, for example, $a\leq b$, we calculate $a - b$ and check if $C + Z$ is 1. A knowledge of these and similar rules that relate flags to arithmetic conditions is essential for computer arithmetic.

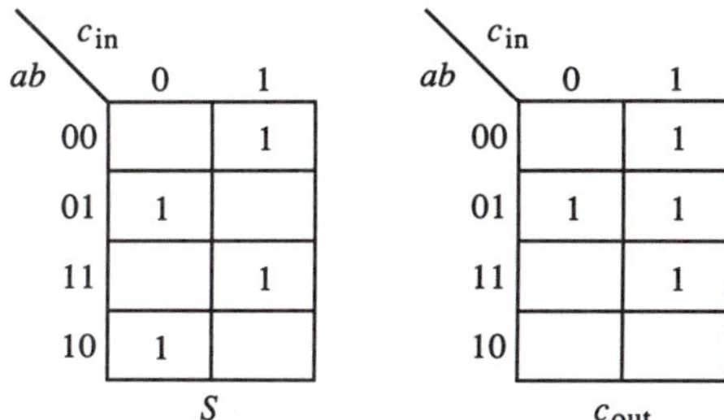


**Figure 6.4.** Difference and borrow-out tables for bit-wise binary subtraction. Borrow-in and borrow-out are denoted $c_{in}$ and $c_{out}$ because adder and subtractor circuits are usually combined and the carry inputs and outputs are used for borrow when subtraction is desired. For the same reason, the "difference" output is usually called "sum."

## Exercises

1. Subtract the following in binary: 36 − 21, 211 − 131, 24 − 51.
2. Prove the correctness of subtraction and comparison tables.
3. Express comparisons of (23,31), (159,135), and (121,121) using $Z$ and $C$ and indicate which relations from the above table hold.
4. Design a "full subtractor" on the basis of subtraction tables and compare it with the full adder.
5. Design a "ripple-carry subtractor" based on the full subtractor.
6. Design a "programmable adder/subtractor" with inputs $a$, $b$, $c_{in}$; and $S$, and outputs $Sum$ and $c_{out}$. The circuit is to perform subtraction when $S = 1$ and addition otherwise.
7. Design a programmable ripple-carry adder/subtractor using programmable adder/subtractors.
8. Design a four-bit comparator.
9. Design a two-bit subtractor for $(a_1a_0) - (b_1b_0)$ as a two-level AND–OR circuit.

## Multiplication

Multiplication is, by definition, repeated addition. For example,

$$7 \times 3 = 3 + 3 + 3 + 3 + 3 + 3 + 3$$

However, multiplication by repeated addition would be extremely inefficient —imagine calculating 99 × 121 by adding 99 a total of 121 times. Fortunately, positional notation makes this unnecessary. In binary, as in decimal, multidigit multiplication can be performed by repeated one-digit multiplication followed by shifting and addition:

```
 Decimal            Binary

    13             00001101
  × 12           × 00001100
    26             00000000
   13             00000000
   156           00001101
                00001101
               00000000
              00000000
             00000000
            00000000
            000000010011100 = 156₁₀
```

This example shows that multiplication in binary is even simpler than in decimal because we only need to multiply by 1 or 0. Multiplication by 0 is unnecessary and can be skipped; and multiplication by 1 amounts to copying the code. The procedure to multiply two $n$-bit numbers $a$ and $b$ is thus as follows:

```
result := 0;
FOR i := 0 TO n−1 DO                 {n is the length of the code}
  BEGIN
    IF bi = 1
      THEN result := result + a;     {Update intermediate result}
    Shift a left by one position;
  END;
```

Note that the number of bits in the result may be as large as the sum of the lengths of the operands. As an example, the product of two eight-bit operands may be sixteen bits long.

Our example can be generalized to form the basis of a fast multiplier. If we restrict ourselves to four-bit operands, the calculation can be expressed as follows:

| | | | | | | |
|---|---|---|---|---|---|---|
| | | | $a_0b_3$ | $a_0b_2$ | $a_0b_1$ | $a_0b_0$ |
| | | $a_1b_3$ | $a_1b_2$ | $a_1b_1$ | $a_1b_0$ | |
| | $a_2b_3$ | $a_2b_2$ | $a_2b_1$ | $a_2b_0$ | | |
| $a_3b_3$ | $a_3b_2$ | $a_3b_1$ | $a_3b_0$ | | | |

All bits in the same column have the same weight, and the carry generated in column $k$ is added to the binary value in column $k + 1$ because a carry-out of position $k$ has weight $2^{k+1}$. The pattern can be implemented by an array of full adders as in Figure 6.5. This structure is very appealing because it consists of identical cells that are interconnected in a regular way.

There are a number of other multiplication circuits differing in complexity and speed of operation and some of them are commercially available. Further discussion is beyond the scope of this book.

### Division

Division is somewhat similar to multiplication and consists of repeated subtraction and addition. The most obvious division algorithm is "restoring division." To divide $a$ by $b$, one proceeds as follows:

```
B := b aligned with a; q := 0;
REPEAT
  a := a − B;              {Trial and error}
  If a<0
    THEN                   {We should not have subtracted}
      BEGIN
        a := a + B;        {Restore a}
        Shift quotient q left with LSB(quotient) := 0;
      END
    ELSE Shift quotient q left with LSB(quotient) := 1;
  Shift B right;
UNTIL a≦B;
{The resulting a is the remainder of division}
```

In the following example, this algorithm is used to divide 37 by 4. Individual passes through the loop are separated by a horizontal line.

| | | |
|---|---|---|
| $a$ | 100101 | {37} |
| $B$ | 100 | {4} |
| $a - B$ | 000101 → $q := 1$; | |
| $a$ | 000101 | |
| $B$ | 100 | |
| $a - B$ is negative → $q := 10$; | restore $a$ | |

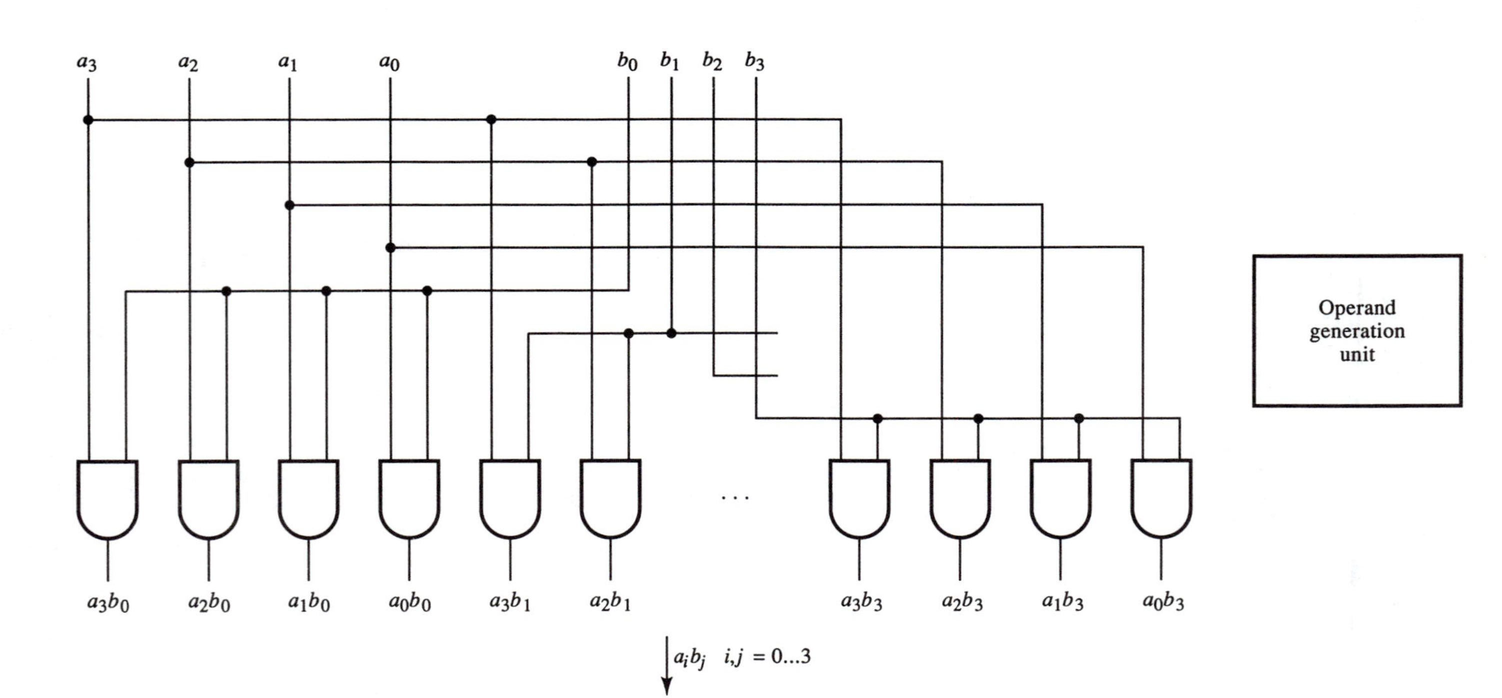

$a_3$
$a_2$
$a_1$
$a_0$
$b_0$
$b_1$
$b_2$
$b_3$
Operand generation unit
$a_3b_0$
$a_2b_0$
$a_1b_0$
$a_0b_0$
$a_3b_1$
$a_2b_1$
. . .
$a_3b_3$
$a_2b_3$
$a_1b_3$
$a_0b_3$
$a_ib_j \quad i,j = 0...3$

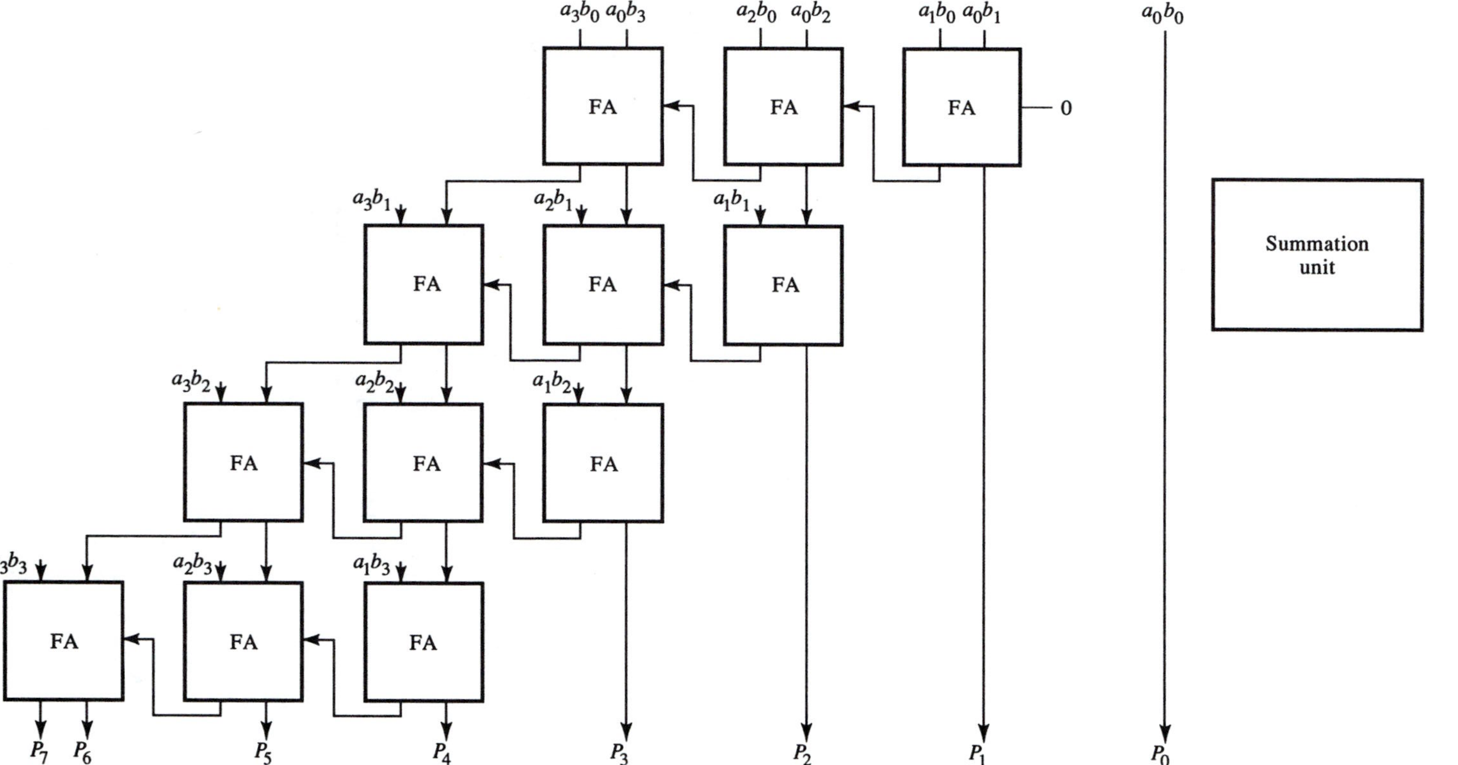


**Figure 6.5.** Unsigned multiplication implemented with a cellular array of full adders. We have taken advantage of the fact that binary AND and multiplication give the same result.

| | |
|---|---|
| $a$ | 000101 |
| $B$ | 100 |
| $a - B$ is negative $\rightarrow q := 100;$ | restore $a$ |
| $a$ | 000101 |
| $B$ | 100 |
| $a - B$ | 000001 $\rightarrow q := 1001;$ |
| $a$ | 1 |
| $a<B$ | End of division, quotient = 1001; remainder = 1; |

Division is a time consuming operation and although there are a number of alternative procedures to speed it up these faster algorithms, as usual, require more complex hardware. The interested reader is referred to specialized texts for further detail.

In closing, note the following properties of the presented methods:

With multiplication we know exactly how many times to add, whereas division must be repeated until the result becomes negative; thus the number of steps is not known beforehand.

Multiplication requires only addition and shifting; restoring division also requires subtraction.

Multiplication is based on shifting left, which is equivalent to multiplying by 2, but division uses shifting right, or division by 2. A single shift right produces the quotient and the remainder of division by 2 as in the following examples:

| **Original code** | **Shifted code** | **Quotient** | **Remainder** |
|---|---|---|---|
| Remainder lost in shifting ↓ | Shift in ↓ | | |
| 1011011$\underline{0}$ | $\rightarrow$ $\underline{0}$1011011 | (182 $\rightarrow$ 91) | 0 |
| 0010000$\underline{1}$ | $\rightarrow$ $\underline{0}$0010000 | (33 $\rightarrow$ 16) | 1 |

Shifting left and right are very important, simple operations. The best place to implement them is where the codes are stored—in registers.

## Exercises

1. Multiply 13 × 14 and 100 × 99 in binary.
2. Use the arithmetic meaning of shifting to determine the value of 00001010. (*Hint:* 1010 is 101 shifted left.) Repeat for 00110000 and 01100110.
3. Consider a fixed-size code; for example, an eight-bit code. When is multiplication by 2 equal to shifting left? (*Hint:* Compare the double of the original code with the shifted code.)
4. When is division by 2 equal to shifting right? (Hint: Compare the original multiplied by 2 with the shifted code.)
5. Calculate the quotient and the remainder of 52÷12 and 113÷48 in binary.
6. Show that the algorithms for binary addition, subtraction, multiplication, and division are independent of the position of the decimal point. In particular, show that the fractional and integer arithmetic algorithms are the same and produce identical codes using different interpretation. Note that this means that the circuits are also position-independent.
7. Prove that the product of two $n$-bit unsigned codes requires up to $2n$ bits. (*Hint:* What is the product of the two largest $n$-bit unsigned numbers?)
8. An important convention closely related to unsigned notation is sign-magnitude representation. It uses the MSB for sign (0 for +, 1 for −) and the remaining bits for the unsigned magnitude. As an example,

   01000001 is 65

   11000001 is −65

   Sign-magnitude is not a pure positional representation because the MSB has no weight. Analyze the following aspects of sign-magnitude representation: The range of values represented by eight-bit codes, negation, addition, and subtraction. Compare with unsigned binary.

   An interesting property of sign-magnitude is that it has two codes for 0. Fractional representation and similar variations on the basic sign-magnitude convention are, of course, also possible. Sign-magnitude is used in floating-point representation and in interfacing to some industrial devices. It is not used for integer arithmetic because its addition is relatively complicated.

## 6.5 SIGNED BINARY (TWO'S COMPLEMENT) NOTATION

Unsigned binary is an efficient system but its inability to represent negative numbers is a major limitation. The sign-magnitude system (one bit for the sign and the rest for unsigned magnitude) can represent positive and negative numbers but its arithmetic is too complex. (See Exercise 8 in Section 6.4.) The system used by most modern computers for positive and negative integers is two's complement representation, which is an interesting and natural variation on unsigned binary. The two's complement system is also called "signed binary" or "integer representation."

If we want to use a positional notation to represent positive and negative values, its positions must have both positive and negative weights. To make the range of positive numbers approximately equal to the range of negative numbers, the MSB weight must have one sign and the remaining weights the opposite sign. As an example, an eight-bit system with weights (−128,64,32,16,8,4,2,1) can represent numbers from

$$10000000 = -128 + 0 + 0 + 0 + 0 + 0 + 0 + 0 = -128$$

to

$$01111111 = 0 + 64 + 32 + 16 + 8 + 4 + 2 + 1 = +127$$

With this weight assignment, all codes starting with 1 have negative values and all codes starting with 0 are either positive or 0:

$$\begin{aligned} x &= (1,a_6,a_5,a_4,a_3,a_2,a_1,a_0) \\ &= -128 + 64 \times a_6 + 32 \times a_5 + 16 \times a_4 + 8 \times a_3 + 4 \times a_2 + 2 \times a_1 + a_0 \end{aligned}$$

and thus $x = <0$.

$$\begin{aligned} y &= (0,a_6,a_5,a_4,a_3,a_2,a_1,a_0) \\ &= 64 \times a_6 + 32 \times a_5 + 16 \times a_4 + 8 \times a_3 + 4 \times a_2 + 2 \times a_1 + a_0 \end{aligned}$$

and thus $y \geq 0$.

The MSB is thus called the "sign bit" because it determines the sign. Note the following:

The sign bit has a weight and is part of the magnitude. This differs from the sign-magnitude representation, in which the sign bit does not have any weight. Because of this, the sign bit cannot be treated separately from the rest of the code. In particular, for negative numbers, the rest of the code does not represent the full magnitude. As an example, the magnitude of 11111111 is not 01111111.

Signed and unsigned codes of non-negative numbers are the same. As an example, 01110101 has the same value in two's complement and in pure binary.

Because two's complement can represent both positive and negative numbers we must know how to negate a code; in other words, we must know how to find the code of the number with the opposite sign. We can derive the algorithm for converting the code of $z$ to the code of $-z$ as follows: Let $\overline{z}$ be the code obtained by inverting each bit of $z$. Because exactly one of $a_i$ and $\overline{a_i}$ is 1, the arithmetic sum of $a_i$ and $\overline{a_i}$ is 1 and

$$\begin{aligned} z + \overline{z} &= -128 \times (a_7 + \overline{a_7}) + 64 \times (a_6 + \overline{a_6}) + \ldots + (a_0 + \overline{a_0}) \\ &= -128 \times 1 + 64 \times 1 + \ldots + 1 \\ &= (11111111) \\ &= -1 \end{aligned}$$

This result holds for any number of bits and therefore

$$-z = z + 1$$

Thus to negate a two's complement code we must invert all bits and add 1. To demonstrate this procedure we will now negate the code of decimal 75 to get the code of $-75$ and then negate it once more to retrieve the code of 75:

$$75 = 01001011 \xrightarrow{\text{Complement bits}} 10110100 \xrightarrow{\text{Add 1}} 10110101 = -75$$

and

$$-75 = 10110101 \xrightarrow{\text{Complement bits}} 01001010 \xrightarrow{\text{Add 1}} 01001011 = 75$$

One can also use this rule to design a hardware negator as the combination of a block of inverters and a ripple-carry adder (Figure 6.6).

How can we convert a two's complement code to decimal? For non-negative numbers, two's complement codes are identical to pure binary and we can thus use the procedure that we derived earlier. For negative numbers (codes starting with 1), we can proceed as follows: Negate the code (invert and add 1) to obtain a new code starting with 0, calculate its decimal value as for unsigned numbers, and negate the result. As an example, if we want to know the value of 10110101 (a negative number), we negate it to get 01001011, which is 75; 10110101 thus represents $-75$. The algorithm can also be used to obtain the two's complement code of a negative decimal number by finding the code of the number's magnitude and negating it. As an example, to find

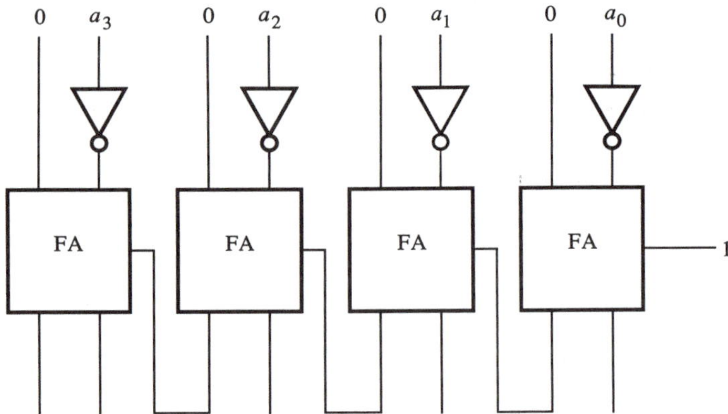


**Figure 6.6.** Four-bit negator.

the code of −75, calculate the code of 75 (01001011) and negate it (10110101).

A more direct method is to treat the first bit separately. As an example,

$$100101 = -32 + 00101_2 = -32 + 5 = -27$$

Conversely, the six-bit two's complement code of −27 is negative and must start with 1. This contributes −32 to the code's value. The remaining five bits must then represent 5 and the whole code is thus 100101.

Note that two's complement notation has more negative codes than positive codes. There are, for example, 256 different eight-bit codes; 128 start with 1 and are negative, 127 are positive and one is 0. The mysterious extra negative code is 10000000 and represents −128. One might think that negating 10000000 would give the code of 128, but it gives again 10000000.

When dealing with numbers, we will use the term "negate" to refer to changing the sign of a number ("obtaining a negative number") and the terms "complement" or "invert" to refer to the bit-by-bit (bit-wise) NOT operation.

## Exercises

1. Develop an algorithm based on Horner's rule for conversions between two's complement and decimal.
2. Convert the following decimal numbers to eight-bit signed codes if possible: −1, 0, 1, 13, −13, 121, −121, 128, and −128. Note that the relation between the codes of −1 and 0 makes sense in terms of $-1 + 1 = 0$.
3. Convert the following two's complement codes to decimal: 00101101, 10010111, 11111111, 01111111, and 10000000.

4. Negate the codes in Exercise 3 and check that they represent the correct values.
5. When one examines two's complement codes and their negated values, such as

$$\underline{0110}11 \rightarrow \underline{1001}01 \qquad \text{and} \qquad \underline{100}100 \rightarrow \underline{011}100$$

   one notices that the negated code starts with a sequence of complemented original bits (underlined) and continues with a sequence identical to the original. Closer examination suggests that one can negate a two's complement code by finding the rightmost 1, complementing all bits to its left, and leaving the rest unchanged. Test this simple method on a few examples and explain why it works.
6. Analyze fractional representation in two's complement notation.
7. The leftmost digit that cannot be deleted without changing the value of a code is called the first significant digit. As an example, the first significant digit of 00253 is 2 because the number can be written 253 with no loss of information. How can one determine the first significant bit in the two's complement code?
8. Should we classify the ordinary decimal representation of positive and negative numbers as "pure," "ten's complement," or as sign-magnitude?
9. Another convention that has occasionally been used to represent positive and negative numbers is *one's complement*. The only difference between this system and two's complement is that for negative numbers, one's complement is simply the bit-wise NOT of the magnitude. For example, one's complement code of 65 is 01000001 (same as pure binary or two's complement) and the code of −65 is thus 10111110. (The two's complement code of −65 is 10111111.)

   Find eight-bit one's complement codes of 127, −127, 64, −64, and 0.

   Find decimal values of the following eight-bit one's complement codes: 00001110, 11110001, 00000000, and 11111111.

   What is the range of numbers that can be represented with eight-bit one's complement codes? How many different values are there? Is there a missing or duplicated code?
10. What is the likely reason for using 0 to indicate positive and 1 to indicate negative in the sign-magnitude representation?

### Arithmetic

The most interesting and useful property of two's complement is that addition is performed as in pure binary and is independent of the sign of the two operands. In other words, the same procedure is used to add two positive numbers, two negative numbers, and a negative and a positive number. Note that this means that the sign bit participates in addition along with all other bits. The reader should prove this property as an exercise. We will limit our discussion to a few examples:

$$\begin{array}{rr}
63 & 00111111 \\
\underline{+55} & \underline{00110111} \\
118 & 01110110
\end{array}
\qquad
\begin{array}{rr}
-63 & 11000001 \\
+\underline{(-55)} & \underline{11001001} \\
-118 & (1)10001010
\end{array}$$

The "carry-out" in the second example can be ignored and the remaining eight bits give the correct result. Similarly,

$$\begin{array}{rr}
63 & 00111111 \\
+\underline{(-55)} & \underline{11001001} \\
8 & (1)00001000
\end{array}
\qquad
\begin{array}{rr}
-63 & 11000001 \\
\underline{+55} & \underline{00110111} \\
-\ 8 & 11111000
\end{array}$$

The carry-out can again be ignored.

Because addition in two's complement is identical to addition in unsigned notation the hardware for addition is the same and produces the same codes in both cases; only the interpretation of the result is different. As an example, the result 11111000 above is valid in both notations but means

$$193 + 55 = 248$$

in unsigned binary and

$$-63 + 55 = -8$$

in signed binary.

In the two preceeding examples we claimed that the carry-out can be ignored. As we know, this would be incorrect in pure binary notation where a carry means that the result overflows the number of bits allocated to it and that if the result is represented only by the allocated number of bits, the code is incorrect. Naturally, an overflow can also occur in two's complement but it has a different form. Two examples of *overflow* are

$$\begin{array}{rcr}
64 & & 01000000 \\
\underline{+65} & & \underline{01000001} \\
129 & \neq & 10000001
\end{array}
\qquad
\begin{array}{rcr}
-64 & & 11000000 \\
+\underline{(-65)} & & \underline{10111111} \\
-129 & \neq & (1)01111111
\end{array}$$

The overflow is immediately noticeable because the two operands have the same sign while the result has the opposite sign: The sum of two positive numbers cannot be negative and the sum of two negative numbers cannot be positive. (Note that the first example does not produce an overflow in pure binary.)

We need to formulate a rule for recognizing the overflow so that we don't confuse it with the harmless lost carry. In our examples, overflow occurred when the two operands had the same sign and the result had the opposite sign. Can the sum of a positive and a negative number also overflow? The answer is no for the following reason: If $a \geq 0$ and $b < 0$ are two signed numbers with valid $n$-bit codes and abs ($x$) denotes the absolute value (magnitude) of $x$, then

$$\text{abs}(a + b) = \text{abs}(\text{abs}(a) - \text{abs}(b)) \leq \max(\text{abs}(a),\text{abs}(b))$$

In words, the magnitude of the sum of a positive and a negative number is smaller than or equal to the larger of the two magnitudes. If $a$ and $b$ have valid codes and the magnitude of $a + b$ cannot exceed the larger of the two magnitudes, then $a + b$ must also have a valid $n$-bit code and overflow is thus impossible.

Our analysis proves the following rule: The sum $a + b$ produces an overflow in two's complement notation iff $a$ and $b$ have the same sign and the result has the opposite sign.

## Exercises

1. Show that if we want to extend a two's complement code from $n$ bits to $n + k$ bits without changing its value, we must add $k$ copies of the sign bit at the start of the code.
2. Use the result of Exercise 1 to prove that if two's complement addition produces a carry-out but there is no overflow, the carry-out can be ignored.
3. Design a circuit to generate an overflow flag $V$ such that $V = 1$ when an overflow occurs.
4. Do the following calculations in eight-bit two's complement notation: $13 + 121$, $13 + (-121)$, $(-13) + 121$, and $(-13) + (-121)$. Check the result in decimal.
5. Could the two's complement sum of two eight-bit codes overflow if we had nine bits to store the results?
6. Prove that the condition for an overflow can also be stated as follows: An overflow occurs iff the carry into the MSB and the carry out of the MSB are different. Show that this formulation simplifies the overflow circuit.
7. Show that $n$-bit two's complement codes can be negated by subtraction from $2^n$. As an example, the code of $-0110$ is $10000 - 0110$. This is why the notation is called two's complement.
8. Two's complement is the radix complement representation for radix 2. Use the previous exercise to define ten's complement representation and

show that in a five-digit ten's complement system, the code of 123 is 00123 and the code of −123 is 99877.

9. Show that ten's complement addition follows rules similar to that of two's complement addition.
10. One's complement addition is performed by adding the codes as in pure binary and then adding the carry from the MSB to the LSB of the result. This is called "end-round addition." And the following in eight-bit one's complement: 13 + 71, −3 + (−4), 5 + (−2), and (−2) + (−4) and check the result.
11. Compare the complexity and speed of negation and addition of $n$-bit two's and one's complement representation.

**Subtraction**

Subtraction can be performed as negation and addition because

$$a - b = a + (-b)$$

For example,

$$3 - 5 = 3 + (-5) = -2$$

and so

| Subtraction | → | Addition | |
|---|---|---|---|
| 00000011 | → | 00000011 | (Same) |
| −00000101 | → | +11111011 | (Negated) |
| | | 11111110 = −2 | |

Similarly, (−5) − (−3) = (−5) + (−(−3)) = −2 and so

| Subtraction | → | Addition | |
|---|---|---|---|
| 11111011 | → | 11111011 | (Same) |
| −11111101 | → | 00000011 | (Negated) |
| | | 11111110 = −2 | |

Subtraction by negation and addition is the basis of the simple subtractor shown in Figure 6.7. The circuit uses the negator from the previous section.

We have already mentioned that an important application of subtraction is comparison and we will now derive comparison rules for two's complement numbers:

The statement $a<b$ means $a - b<0$. The result of subtraction is negative if it is negative and correct, or if it appears non-negative but resulted from

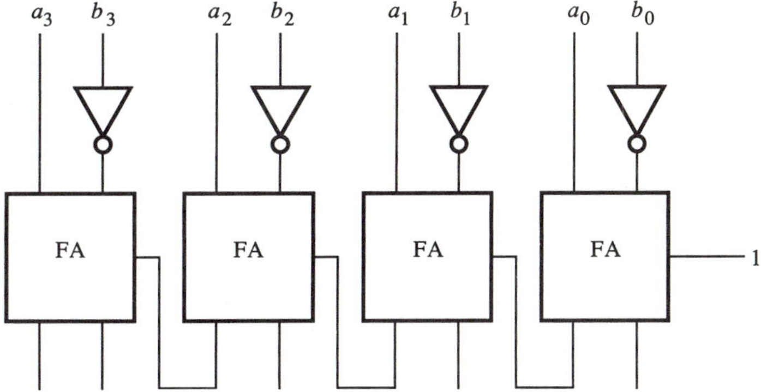


**Figure 6.7.** Four-bit two's complement subtractor.

an overflow. If $S$ and $V$ are the sign and overflow flags, this condition can be represented as $S$ XOR $V$.

The statement $a \leq b$ means $a - b \leq 0$, which holds if $a - b < 0$ or if the result is zero. If $Z$ is the zero flag, this can be represented as ($S$ XOR $V$) + $Z$.

The statement $a = b$ means $a - b = 0$ and can be represented by $Z$.

All other cases can be obtained as the logic inverse of these three situations. As an example, $a \geq b$ is the inverse of $a < b$. Our results can be summarized as follows:

| **Relationship** | **Condition** | |
|---|---|---|
| $a<b$ | $S$ XOR $V$ | Alternatively $S \neq V$ |
| $a \leq$b | ($S$ XOR $V$) + $Z$ | |
| $a>b$ | $\overline{(S \text{ XOR } V) + Z}$ | |
| $a \geq$b | $\overline{S \text{ XOR } V}$ | Alternatively $S = V$ |
| $a = b$ | $Z$ | |
| $a \neq b$ | $\overline{Z}$ | |

### Exercises

1. Explain the subtractor shown in Figure 6.7.
2. Show that signed and unsigned subtraction are identical and can thus use the same hardware. Note this implies that it is not necessary to learn pure binary subtraction.

3. Subtract the following in eight-bit two's complement notation and check the results in decimal: 12 − 45, 45 − (−12), 12 − (−45), (−12) − (−45), and 45 − 12.
4. Modify the ripple-carry adder so that it can be used to add or subtract both signed and unsigned numbers under the control of a special "mode" input.
5. Summarize the rules for overflow in signed and unsigned addition.
6. Justify the conditions for $a > b$ and $a \geq b$ directly instead of negating the inverse conditions as above.
7. State the conditions for overflow in subtraction.
8. Replacing subtraction with addition requires caution because the carry obtained by pure binary addition and the borrow obtained by two's complement subtraction are not always the same. Demonstrate this by calculating (−1) − (−96) and (−1) + (96) using eight-bit codes. Repeat for (−127) − (112) and (−127) + (−112). Analyze the problem.

### Multiplication and Division

The algorithm for pure binary multiplication works with positive two's complement codes but not with negative ones. As an example, if we treated (−3) × 5 as pure binary, we would get

```
        11111101
×       00000101
        --------
        00000000
       00000101
      00000101
     00000101
    00000101
   00000101
  00000101
  ---------------
  000010011111001
```

which is an incorrect two's complement result.

Because positive numbers have the same signed and unsigned codes, multiplication of non-negative numbers is the same in both systems. The most obvious way to multiply two's complement numbers therefore is to convert two's complement codes to their magnitudes, multiply them as unsigned codes, and change the sign of the result if necessary. This procedure is somewhat slow as negation requires addition.

Another approach is to obtain the formula for

$$\begin{aligned} a \cdot b &= (-a_n 2^n + \Sigma a_i 2^i)\,(-b_n 2^n + \Sigma b_i 2^i) \\ &= a_{n-1} b_{n-1} 2^{2n-2} + \Sigma a_i b_j 2^{i+j} \\ &\quad - \Sigma a_i b_{n-1} 2^{n-1+i} - \Sigma a_{n-1} \mathrm{b}_i 2^{n-1+i} \end{aligned}$$

where $i = 0, \ldots, n - 1$, and the sums are over $(i, j = 0, \ldots, n - 2)$. We can restructure this result to obtain an expression that we can convert into a cellular array similar to the cellular multiplier for unsigned binary. The resulting circuit is faster than multiplication by conversion to positive pure binary but is somewhat more complicated.

A very important special case of multiplication is multiplication by 2, which can be performed by shifting left. Let us analyze the conditions under which shifting left and multiplication by 2 are the same. Let

$$x = (a_7 a_6 \ldots a_2 a_1 a_0) \xrightarrow{\text{Shift left}} (a_6 a_5 \ldots a_1 z)$$

where $z$ is the value shifted into the rightmost bit. To determine the correct value of $z$ and the conditions under which the result represents $2x$, we must compare $2x$ to the value of the new code $y$:

$$\begin{aligned} 2x &= 2 \times (-128 \times a_7 + 64 \times a_6 + \ldots + 2 \times a_1 + a_0) \\ &= -256 \times a_7 + 128 \times a_6 + 64 \times a_5 + \ldots + 4 \times a_1 + 2 \times a_0 \\ y &= (a_6 a_5 \ldots a_1 z) \\ &= -128 \times a_6 + 64 \times a_5 + \ldots + 4 \times a_1 + 2 \times a_0 + z \end{aligned}$$

It is clear that for $2x = y$ we must shift 0 into the LSB and must satisfy

$$-256 \times a_7 + 128 \times a_6 + -128 \times a_6$$

which happens when $a_6 = a_7$. In summary, when shifting left to multiply by 2, shift 0 into the LSB; the result is the double of the original code iff both codes have the same sign bit.

Two's complement division algorithms and circuits are related to those for pure binary division. We will not discuss them here but shall restrict our attention to the analysis of shifting right for division by 2 or, more accurately, to the calculation of the quotient $x$ DIV 2. If

$$x = (a_7 a_6 \ldots a_2 a_1 a_0)$$

and $y$ is the code of $x$ shifted right,

$$\begin{aligned} y &= (z a_7 a_6 \ldots a_2 a_1) \\ &= -128 \times z + 64 \times a_7 + \ldots + 2 \times a_2 + a_1 \end{aligned}$$

shifting gives the quotient of $x$ DIV 2 iff $y$ is equal to

$$x \text{ DIV } 2 = (-128 \times a_7 + 64 \times a_6 + \ldots + 2 \times a_1 + a_0) \text{ DIV } 2$$
$$= -64 \times a_7 + 32 \times a_6 + .. + a_1$$

Thus $y = x$ DIV 2 holds iff $z = a_7$. The removed LSB is the remainder of the division.

Consequently, to shift a two's complement right for division by 2, we must shift a copy of the sign bit into the MSB. This is different from shifting right in unsigned notation, where one always shifts 0 into the MSB.

To distinguish the two different kinds of shifts, unsigned shift right is called *logic shift right* and signed shift right is called *arithmetic shift right*. Shift left for multiplication is the same in signed and unsigned arithmetic and is called arithmetic shift left. Some computers distinguish logic and arithmetic shift left but both are usually implemented in the same way. If there is a difference between arithmetic and logic shift it is in their effect on the *S*, *C*, and *V* flags.

All of the shifts introduced above are illustrated in Figure 6.8.

## Exercises

1. Show how to implement arithmetic shifts left and right with an up/down shift register.
2. Extend the circuit in the previous exercise to generate the *C*, *V*, *S*, and *Z* flags. Distinguish logic and arithmetic shifts.
3. Multiply $13 \times 26$, $(-13) \times 26$, $13 \times (-26)$, and $(-13) \times (-26)$ in two's complement.

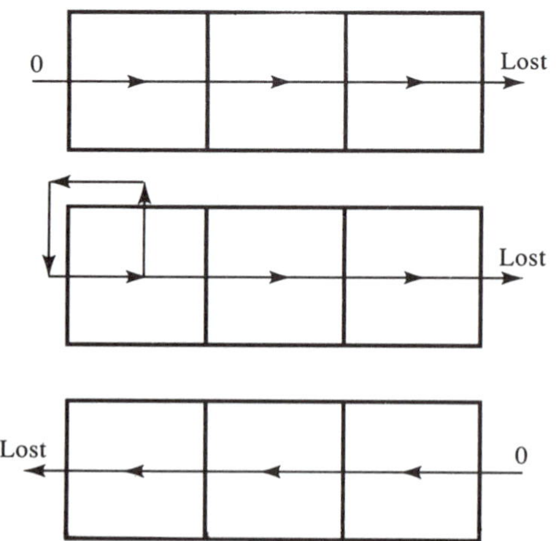


**Figure 6.8.** Arithmetic and logic shift right and left.

4. What would be the effect of arithmetic shift left on flags?
5. Design a cellular two's complement multiplier.
6. Compare two's complement and sign-magnitude multiplication.

## 6.6 THE ARITHMETIC LOGIC UNIT

All computer arithmetic is usually performed by a single circuit called the arithmetic logic unit or simply the ALU (Figure 6.9). As the name implies, the ALU performs not only arithmetic but also various bit-wise logic operations, including the following:

| Operation | | Example |
|---|---|---|
| AND: | | 00110100 |
| | AND | 11110001 |
| | Result | 00110000 |
| OR: | | 00110100 |
| | OR | 11110001 |
| | Result | 11110101 |
| NOT: | NOT | (11100101) = 00011010 |

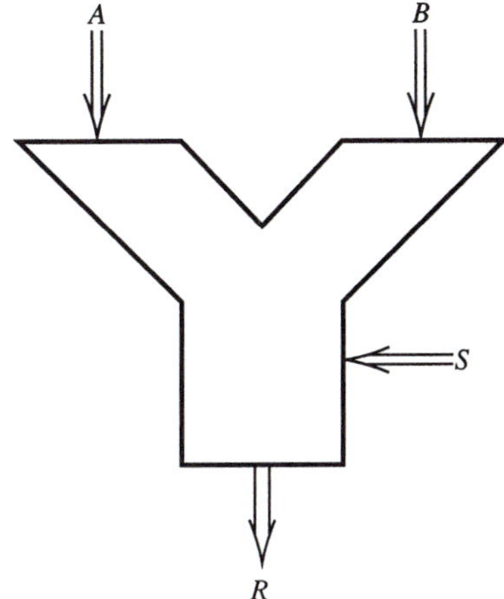


**Figure 6.9.** The standard ALU symbol with its main inputs and outputs: $A$ and $B$ are the two operands, $R$ is the result, and $S$ selects the desired function.

As we noted earlier, the last operation is sometimes referred to as one's complement.

An example of a commercially available ALU is the 74181 chip. It uses four-bit operands and produces a four-bit result, has a carry input and output, and performs a number of arithmetic and logic functions including addition, subtraction, and comparison. One can also generate lookahead outputs that speed up multibit arithmetic by cascading several 74181s and combining them with the 74182 lookahead carry generator. The 74181 has four function-select inputs and a "mode" input to choose logic or arithmetic operation. A table showing all its functions appears in Appendix 2.

Add times for the 74181 four-bit are 24 nsec, and multibit arithmetic in ripple-carry arrangements of several 74181s requires a multiple of this basic time. As an example, sixty-bit ripple-carry addition with fifteen cascaded 74181s takes 360 nsec. If we combine the 74181 with the 74182 lookahead chip, addition proceeds much faster, requiring 36 nsec for two to four 74181s and 60 nsec for up to fifteen 74181s (sixty-bit addition).

Another example of an arithmetic logic integrated circuit is the 74281 four-bit accumulator. This twenty-four pin chip combines the most important arithmetic and logic functions of the 74181 ALU with shift and storage. It can add a four-bit input $A$ to the contents of internal register $B$; compute $A - B$ and $B - A$; complement; and perform the operations AND, OR, NAN, NOR, XOR, and XNOR. The positive-edge triggered internal register can be loaded and shifted left or right. Shifting is arithmetic or logic. The arithmetic circuit uses carry lookahead and may be cascaded for multibit operation. Cascading makes possible multibit shifting, both logic and arithmetic. The chip can also be used with the 74182 lookahead carry generator.

All modern computers, except for the large ones, use *central processing unit* (CPU) chips, which combine the ALU functions with other operations, and do not require separate ALUs. We will consider two such devices in a later chapter. Although CPU chips perform all basic arithmetic operations, most of them do not perform all of the arithmetic operations required by application programs. As an example, many programming languages use sixteen-bit integers but small CPUs provide only eight-bit integers, or a limited range of operations on sixteen-bit codes. Similarly, small eight- and sixteen-bit CPUs do not have floating-point hardware for REAL numbers. On these machines, the built-in hardware must be complemented by software, programs that execute the missing operations as a sequence of more primitive built-in operations. To write this software the programmer must have a good understanding of arithmetic algorithms.

As an alternative to implementing more complicated arithmetic in software, many computers complement their CPUs with an *arithmetic coprocessor* chip, which can perform arithmetic operations much faster than softwear. We will briefly return to arithmetic coprocessors later.

## Exercises

1. Why is the 74181 ALU so fast? A ripple-carry adder with so many levels of logic should be much slower. (*Hint:* Check the diagram of the 74181 to see if it uses ripple-carry addition.)
2. Estimate the speed and complexity of a purely combinational (two-level AND/OR) four-bit adder.
3. Repeat the previous exercise for other arithmetic operations.
4. Show how to connect two 74181s for eight-bit operation.
5. Appendix 1 explains the term "open collector (OC) output." The comparator output of the 74181 is OC and this feature can be used when several 74181s are connected for multibit operation. Explain.
6. Explain the operation of the 74182 lookahead carry generator. Describe how to connect the 74182 to the 74181 ALU.
7. The result of "$a$ AND $b$" can be obtained from the carry-out output of a full adder having inputs $a$, $b$, and $c_{in} = 0$. Prove this and find which other logic functions can also be obtained from the outputs of a full adder. Explain how this could be used to design an ALU.
8. Design a four-bit ADD/AND/OR/NOT ALU using an ADD module, an AND module, an OR module, a NOT module, and a decoder to select the desired function. Designing circuits in this modular fashion is easier than trying to take advantage of special properties of components, such as using full adders to save gates. What is the disadvantage of this approach?
9. How many steps are required to exhaustively test the 74181 ALU? How should a lazy student test the 74181 in a lab experiment?

## 6.7 FLOATING-POINT REPRESENTATION

We have shown that shifting the weights assigned to individual digits in positional codes is equivalent to moving the decimal point. One can use this property to encode very small or very large magnitudes. However, once the position of the decimal point has been decided, the range of values that can be represented is fixed. This is why signed and unsigned notations are also called *fixed point* representations. The disadvantage of fixed-point systems is that while they can represent very small or very large magnitudes in different contexts, they cannot express small and large magnitudes within the same context.

Another disadvantage of signed and unsigned notations is that their accuracy, which is the difference between two consecutive codes, is absolute. As an example, the accuracy of all numbers in an integer system using six significant decimal digits is 1. For full-scale numbers like 123456 this represents six-digit accuracy (one in a million) but for small numbers like 6 the accuracy is only one in ten. In many calculations, we need to perform accurate calculations using very large and very small magnitudes while maintaining a constant relative accuracy. Fixed-point representation is then insufficient, and one must allow the position of the decimal point to "float." This can be accomplished by representing numbers as a pair of numbers (magnitude, scaling factor) as in the following examples:

$$0.000000000000132 = 0.132 \times 10^{-12} \quad \text{or} \quad (0.132,-12)$$

$$-1320000000000.000 = -0.132 \times 10^{13} \quad \text{or} \quad (-0.132,13)$$

This system, which is often used in engineering and science applications, is called "scientific notation." In computer science, a related notation is called floating-point representation. In high-level programming languages such as Pascal, floating-point numbers are usually called "REAL."

Different groupings of bits to describe magnitudes and scaling factors provide different accuracies and ranges, and many floating-point conventions have thus been devised. We will consider two examples in the next section. First, however, we will make a few general comments and formulate several definitions:

To maximize the use of available digits the magnitude—also called the *mantissa* or significand—is usually expressed in a *normalized* form using fractional sign-magnitude notation.

The number of bits used for the mantissa and the exponent determines the accuracy and the dynamic range (scope of magnitudes) of the code. More bits in the mantissa provide greater accuracy (more significant digits), more bits in the exponent give a greater dynamic range. On the other hand, additional code bits also require additional memory, longer processing times, and more complex circuits. To give the user some control over these tradeoffs, some programming languages provide a choice between higher and lower precision arithmetic.

The implied base of the scaling factor is usually 2 or a power of 2, such as 8 or 16.

The exponent is usually represented in *biased representation*, which means that its value has been shifted by some constant and is expressed in unsigned notation. Biased representation is advantageous for comparing exponents and for the representation of 0. A biased exponent is called the *characteristic*. We will give several examples in the next section.

## Exercises

1. Which choice of scaling weights would be suitable to represent the following values in fixed-point unsigned eight-bit notation? Choose one set of

weights for the first set of values and another for the second set. What is the range of values that can be represented and the accuracy of such representations?

134985, 129782, 65901, and 181932

.0000132, .0003214, and .000051.

2. How are the accuracy and range of floating-point representation affected by adding one bit to
   a. the mantissa
   b. the exponent.

   Illustrate the results graphically.

### Floating-Point Notations and Standards

We will now describe the floating-point notation used in a popular Pascal compiler and a recent floating-point standard that is becoming widely used for both hardware and software implementations of floating-point arithmetic.

**Example 1—A Pascal Compiler's Floating-Point System.** One popular Pascal compiler has a six-byte floating-point system that uses five bytes for normalized sign-magnitude fractional mantissa and one byte for the exponent expressed as a characteristic (Figure 6.10). The coding of the mantissa is based on normalization, the fact that the mantissa of all numbers except 0 can be scaled to the form 0.1*xxxx*. As an example, one can write

$$1101.1100 = .11011100 \times 2^4$$

$$.001101 = .1101 \times 2^{-2}$$

and both mantissas begin 0.1; this is what is meant by the term "normalized mantissa." Because the leading 1 appears at the beginning of every mantissa

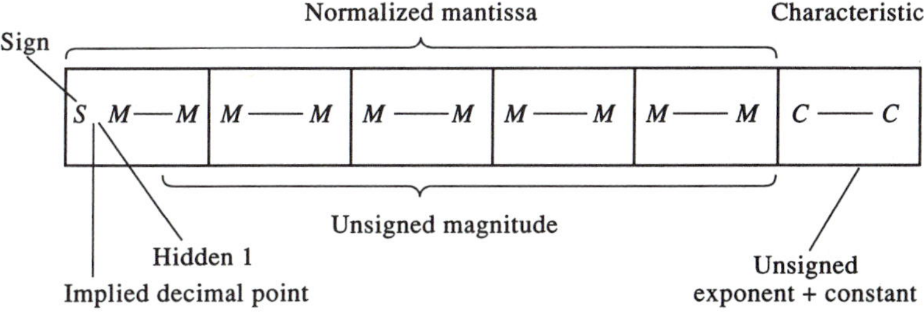


**Figure 6.10.** A floating-point notation. Each group is one byte long.

(except for the code of 0), it need not be stored in memory, and the saved location can be used to extend the accuracy of the rest of the code. The missing, but implied leading 1 is called the hidden 1.

As an example of the hidden-1 convention, the following five-byte mantissa

$$\underline{0}0000001 \quad 00000000 \quad 10001000 \quad 01110100 \quad 00011000$$

represents

$$+0.10000001 \quad 00000000 \quad 10001000 \quad 01110100 \quad 00011000$$

because the underlined 0 is the sign bit, the code is fractional and the leading 1 is implied.

The meaning of the characteristic representing the exponent of the sealing factor is

$$characteristic = exponent + bias$$

where the bias is a constant selected on the basis of the number of bits allocated for the characteristic.

What is a suitable value for the bias? In our case, the characteristic is eight bits long, and ranges from 00000000 to 11111111. The value of the smallest characteristic, corresponding to the smallest exponent *min*, is thus 0 and so

$$min + bias = 0$$

The largest possible characteristic, corresponding to the largest exponent *max*, is 11111111, or 255, and so

$$max + bias = 255$$

The range of the scaling factors $2^{exp}$ is from $2^{min}$ to $2^{max}$. To obtain a symmetric range we thus need

$$min = -max$$

which gives

$$bias = 128$$

and

$$characteristic = exp + 128$$

or

$$exp = characteristic - 128$$

In this system, also called "excess-128 representation," the characteristic 00000000 corresponds to −128 and the characteristic 11111111 to 127. Because characteristic 00000000 has a special use (explained below), the smallest available exponent is −127 and the ranges are thus perfectly symmetric.

The following are several examples of complete six-byte codes in this notation:

Mantissa Characteristic

11001000 00000000 00000000 00000000 00000000 10000110

↑

Sign bit

represents

$$-.1100100000000000000000000000000000000000 \times 2^{10000110 - 128}$$

↑

Hidden bit (not stored in memory and not shown in the code)

which is

$$-\tfrac{25}{32} \times 2^{134 - 128} = -\tfrac{25}{32} \times 2^{6} = 25$$

As another example,

01001000 00000000 00000000 00000000 00000000 00100000

↑

Sign bit

represents

$$+.1100100000000000000000000000000000000000 \times 2^{00100000 - 128}$$

↑

Hidden bit

or

$$+\tfrac{25}{32} \times 2^{32-128} = \tfrac{25}{32} \times 2^{-96}$$

The number with the largest possible magnitude is

$s$1111111 11111111 11111111 11111111 11111111 11111111

which is $\pm(1 - 2^{-40}) \times 2^{127}$, or approximately $10^{38}$; $s$ is the sign.* The number with the smallest magnitude is

$s$0000000 00000000 00000000 00000000 00000000 00000001

which is $\pm 2^{-128}$, or approximately $10^{-38}$.

What about the mysterious code having characteristic 00000000? We need it to represent the number 0: On one hand, we have the hidden-1 convention; on the other, the number 0, cannot have any 1s in its magnitude. The solution is to represent 0 as an all-zero code

00000000 00000000 00000000 00000000 00000000 00000000

and to disallow characteristic 00000000 for any other value.

After this introduction, let us now explain how to convert decimal codes to floating point. For example, to find the code of 262.125 we first note that the number is positive; the sign bit is thus 0. Because

$$\begin{aligned} 262.125 &= 262 + \tfrac{1}{8} \\ &= 100000110.001 \\ &= 0.100000110001 \times 2^8 \end{aligned}$$

the mantissa starts with 00000110001 (the leading 1 is hidden) and the characteristic is

$$\begin{aligned} \mathit{characteristic} &= \mathit{exp} + \mathit{bias} \\ &= 8 + 128 \\ &= 10000 + 10000000 \\ &= 10001000 \end{aligned}$$

*Approximate conversions of powers of 2 to powers of 10 are best performed using logarithms as in $2^{127} = 10^{127 \log_{10} 2}$.

The complete code is

00000110 00100000 00000000 00000000 00000000 10001000

In this example, we were able to express the code accurately with the given number of bits. When accurate representation is impossible, we must either truncate the mantissa by deleting all bits beyond the last position or round it off by finding the nearest forty-bit approximation. This can be done by adding 1 to the LSB and truncating the result.

What is the *relative accuracy* or granularity of this notation? Because two consecutive codes $a$ and $b$ differ only in the value of the last bit of their mantissas, the absolute accuracy is

$$\begin{aligned} a - b &= (0.1xxxxx\ldots xx1 \times scale) - (0.1xxxxx\ldots xx0 \times scale) \\ &= 0.000000\ldots 001 \times scale \\ &= 2^{-40} \times scale \end{aligned}$$

The relative accuracy, the absolute accuracy divided by the scaling factor, is thus forty binary digits, or about twelve decimal digits, because $2^{40} \approx 10^{12}$. As an example, a fourteen-digit decimal number can thus only be represented with the loss of two decimal digits.

While on the topic of accuracy, we must make a note of the relation of decimal and binary systems. The two representations are incompatible in the sense that certain decimal fractions cannot be expressed accurately by any finite number of binary digits. On the other hand, any binary fraction can be expressed by a finite number of decimal digits. This is a familiar phenomenon from decimal notation where $\frac{1}{3}$, which could be written as 0.1 in base 3, requires the infinite decimal expansion 0.333. . . . The same thing happens, for example, when we convert 0.7 from decimal to binary:

$$0.7 = \tfrac{7}{10} = 0.1011\ 0011\ 0011\ \ldots$$

Because binary floating-point representation cannot accurately express all decimal fractions, applications that require exact decimal arithmetic must use another principle. We will discuss this topic later.

**Example 2—The IEEE 754 Floating-Point Standard.** A set of rules becomes a standard when an important manufacturer or customer decides to use it (and others are more or less forced to use it as well) or when a group of manufacturers, users, and scientists decides to convert the accumulated theory and experience into a rigorously defined system. Examples of the former are the "military," IBM, and DEC "de facto" floating-point standard, an example of the latter is the IEEE standard.

The IEEE 754, one of the most recent and widely accepted floating-point standards, was developed in 1982 by the Institute of Electrical and Electronic Engineers (IEEE). It defines code formats, their operations, and the handling of special situations. The formats are divided into two groups—basic and extended—and each is further subdivided into single- and double-sized codes. All groups use 2 as the base of the scaling factor.

In the basic group single-size codes are thirty-two bits long and consist of the sign bit, an eight-bit exponent with bias 127, and a twenty-three bit magnitude in fractional representation. In the double-size basic format, codes are sixty-four bits long with an eleven-bit exponent and a fifty-two bit fraction.

The standard has special codes for $\pm$ infinity to handle overflows and NaN ("Not a Number") codes to indicate results of illegal operations. Zero is represented by an all-zero code; infinite and NaN codes have the characteristic 255. Arithmetic operations on infinite codes are allowed but because certain operations are meaningless, such as infinity divided by infinity or infinity minus infinity, their results are NaN codes. The 754 also allows denormalized numbers: When the magnitude of a result is smaller than the smallest normalized code but is greater than 0, an attempt is made to represent the number using mantissa that has no hidden bit and that has the characteristic 00000000. This makes possible codes for several extra orders of very small magnitudes.

In addition to formats, the IEEE standard defines the following operations: addition, subtraction, division, multiplication, square root, comparison, conversion to and from alternative floating-point formats, BCD, and integer representations. "Exception" and "trap" rules prescribe what should happen when an invalid operation, such as division by 0, is executed or when an overflow occurs. The user has the option to enable or disable the traps. If the traps are enabled, invalid operations performed by the CPU activate a special program written by the user, the trap handler, and supply information about the nature of the trap, the type of operation performed, the operands, and so on. If the traps are disabled, the program that causes an illegal operation is not notified when the violation occurs.

The IEEE 754 standard has been generally accepted by manufacturers of floating-point computer hardware. This not only simplifies computer design but also makes programming easier because it guarantees that programs will produce the same results on different computers.

## Exercises

1. Which of the following decimal numbers can be represented by a finite number of bits?

   0.1, 0.2, 0.3, 0.4, 0.5

2. Convert the following between floating-point and decimal representations assuming a floating-point representation using a one-byte sign-magnitude mantissa with a hidden bit and a one-byte characteristic with bias 128:
   a. −13.45, 256789.12, and −0.000000142
   b. 00000000 1011111, 11111111 10000000, and 10101010 10101010.
3. Give examples of addition, subtraction, multiplication, and division that produce an overflow, a result too large for the size of the code or an underflow, a magnitude too small for the allowed exponent. Use the format from Exercise 2.
4. How many bits would be required to provide the same dynamic range in unsigned notation as in the floating-point notation in Exercise 2? Repeat the calculation for the single-precision IEEE format.
5. What is the accuracy of the IEEE format?
6. Derive a formula for the number of significant decimal digits for given formats of mantissa and exponent.
7. Express range in terms of the number of bits in the exponent and the base of the scaling factor.
8. List the advantages and disadvantages of fixed-point and floating-point notations.
9. Which operations with 0, infinity, and NaN codes produce NaN codes?
10. Compare the results of truncating two's-complement and sign-magnitude mantissas.
11. Design a circuit to perform rounding. Note that its implementation requires that the ALU operate with extra bits beyond the LSB.
12. Compare the complexity of rounding and truncation.
13. Name some advantages of using biased rather than two's complement exponent.

### Arithmetic

We will demonstrate the principles of floating-point arithmetic on addition; the extension to other operations is obvious. To make our example easier to follow, we will use decimal rather than binary codes and assume a four-digit fractional mantissa and a one-digit exponent.

When we want to add

$$\begin{aligned}(3491,4) + (6782,6) &= .3491 \times 10^4 + .6782 \times 10^6 \\ &= 3491 + 678200\end{aligned}$$

we must first align the two mantissas:

3491
678200

Because we can only store four digits of each code and do not want to lose the most significant ones, the alignment is accomplished by shifting the operand with the smaller exponent to the right by a number of positions equal to the difference between the two exponents:

```
                                        The four stored digits
                                        ↓↓↓↓
      3491     must be aligned to       0034(91)
    678200                              6782(00)
                                        --------
                                        6816(00)
```

which is equivalent to (3491,4) + (6782,6) = (6816,6). Note that we lost two significant digits because only four digits can be stored and the correct result requires six. A similar loss of accuracy never occurs with fixed-point representation, where the result is either correct or overflows.

As another example, consider

$$(3491,6) + (6782,6) = .3491 \times 10^6 + .6782 \times 10^6$$
$$= 349100 + 678200$$

In this case, no initial alignment is necessary and the mantissas can be added immediately to give (10273,6). However, the result has one more digit than we can store and must be renormalized by shifting the mantissa and decrementing the exponent. This gives (1027,7), again with a loss of accuracy.

These two examples demonstrate the process of floating-point addition:

1. Align mantissas by shifting the one with the smaller exponent right by a number of positions equal to the difference between the two exponents. Replace the smaller exponent with the larger one.
2. Add aligned mantissas.
3. Renormalize the result if necessary.

As we have seen, floating-point representation provides an almost unlimited range and accuracy and is irreplaceable in some applications. At the same time, it has some disadvantages: It is much more complex, and therefore slower and more expensive, than fixed-point arithmetic; it usually leads to a loss of accuracy; it is inherently inaccurate for decimal data; and it requires more storage bits. Because of these disadvantages, one should use REAL numbers only where necessary.

Because floating-point processing is complex, simple computers do not have the necessary hardware and must use software to perform floating-point operations. However, modern VLSI technology makes it possible to create relatively inexpensive but powerful arithmetic chips to implement floating-point arithmetic and various other useful functions, such as multibyte integers, transcendental functions, and code conversions. These chips, called arithmetic coprocessors, make fast and sophisticated arithmetic possible even on small computers.

The popularity of floating-point arithmetic has been enhanced by the existence of standards like the IEEE 754 and the need for accurate calculations in applications like computer graphics and CAD.

### Exercises

1. High accuracy does not guarantee consistent and correct results. As an example, floating-point arithmetic is not associative because it is not always true that

$$A + (B + C) = (A + B) + C$$

Show this using $A = 10^6$, $B = -10^6$, and $C = 1$ in the decimal floating-point notation with the four-decimal-digit mantissa and one-digit exponent used above.
2. Use the same representation as in Exercise 1 to show what happens when one adds decimal 1000 twenty-thousand times. The result is completely wrong even though the representation can easily express the correct result.
3. What is the effect of using base 16 instead of base 2 on the range, the accuracy, the concept of the normalized mantissa, and the mechanics of alignment? Repeat the calculation for radix 8. Radix 16 has been used by some IBM computers, radix 8 by Burroughs computers.
4. Why is the base of the scaling factor usually a power of the radix of the representation (for example, 2, 8, or 16 for base 2)? (*Hint:* Consider alignment.)
5. Write a series of programs to compare the speed of floating-point and integer arithmetic on a computer such as the IBM PC.
6. Explain why the speed of floating-point arithmetic is often found to depend on the type of operands. Write a program to test whether this is true on an available computer. Does this finding apply to other number representations as well?
7. Explain the advantages of normalized mantissa.
8. Use the decimal representation from this section to analyze floating-point multiplication.

### Arithmetic Coprocessors

We have mentioned that modern integrated circuit technology makes possible arithmetic chips that are much more complicated than the 74181. An example is the 8087 numeric data coprocessor by Intel and its more advanced versions: 80187, 80287, and 80387. The 8087 is a 40-pin chip capable of arithmetic with eight-, sixteen-, thirty-two, and sixty-four bit integers, IEEE floating-point reals, and eighteen-digit BCD operands. It can add, subtract, multiply, divide, and calculate square roots and transcendental functions like tangent and logarithm.

The 8087 is very different from the 74181 ALU and similar chips. While the 74181 is a combinational circuit, the 8087 is a processor, a complex sequential circuit of the kind covered in Chapters 8 through 10 of this book. Whereas the 74181 reads its data and function inputs and immediately outputs the result, the 8087 receives an instruction code and calculates the result in a sequence of steps that use its own and the computer's memory and the system clock.

Chips such as the 8087 are very important for applications that require extensive calculations, but they are not as easy to use as the 74181 because they must be programmed. They are also more expensive, costing up to several hundred dollars rather than a few dollars like the 74181. For many applications, this is a small price to pay for the increase in speed that they offer. In fact, a number of advanced applications can be run on small computers only because of the existence of chips such as the 8087.

## 6.8 BCD REPRESENTATION

The representation covered so far satisfy almost all computing needs. Pure binary is perfect for non-negative numbers, two's complement is ideal for the most common operations on integers, and floating-point is the only way to represent REAL numbers. When used properly, these notations are relatively memory efficient and fast. There are, however, two reasons why none of these systems is satisfactory in certain applications; both are related to the fact that computers use the binary system in their internal operation while humans use the decimal system. The first reason is that neither fixed nor floating-point arithmetic can accurately handle fractional decimals. The second is that most computer programs require decimal input and output (I/O) of data. We have already discussed the loss of accuracy associated with performing binary arithmetic on decimal numbers; we will now illustrate the second problem with an example.

Consider the input of the decimal quantity 154 via a computer keyboard. Typing "1" produces the ASCII code for 1. A computer program strips the code of its non-BCD prefix and remembers its value. Typing "5" generates the code for 5, which must be converted from ASCII, and added to the previous value multiplied by 10. The intermediate result is 15. Typing "4" produces the code for 4, which must be converted to binary 4 and combined with the previous value to obtain 154. The complete sequence is as follows:

| ASCII input | Binary | Intermediate result |
|---|---|---|
| "1" = 00110001 | →00000001 | 00000001 |
| "5" = 00110101 | →00000101 | 00001010 + 00000101 = 00001111 |
| "4" = 00110100 | →00000100 | 10010110 + 00000100 = 10011010 |

This process requires a relatively large number of operations. Similarly, output of the internal results to the screen or printer requires the inverse conversion from binary to ASCII, which is equally time consuming.

Let us now analyze the seriousness of these problems. Computer programs generally fall between two extremes—those that require extensive decimal input and output and relatively few calculations (I/O-bound problems in data processing), and those having relatively little I/O but many calculations (computation-bound problems mainly in engineering and science). To maximize the speed of execution, one should select a representation that gives the best tradeoff between I/O conversion, accuracy, and speed of arithmetic operations. Internal arithmetic can be done much more efficiently in the fixed- and floating-point representations covered so far. If, however, the amount of internal arithmetic required by a given program is small with respect to the amount of I/O conversion, the advantage of fast arithmetic may be outweighed by the delays imposed by converting to and from decimal. In such cases representations that are less efficient for arithmetic but that require less I/O conversion may be preferable.

As we know, the difficulties associated with accuracy and I/O conversion are related to the incompatibility of decimal and binary. Consequently, the best solution is to represent decimal numbers as a sequence of BCD codes of their individual digits—a mixture of binary and decimal. The following example shows that this notation preserves some of the simplicity of positional arithmetic because it is to some extent positional, as the following example of addition shows:

| Decimal | BCD |
|---|---|
| 13.2 | 0001 0011 0010 |
| 24.6 | 0010 0100 0110 |
| 37.8 | 0011 0111 1000 |

The correct result on the right was obtained by treating the four-bit BCD codes as a single twelve-bit unsigned binary code. Unfortunately, the next example shows that this approach does not always work:

| | |
|---|---|
| 2.97 | 0010 1001 0111 |
| 3.84 | 0011 1000 0100 |
| 6.81 | 0110 0001 1011 |

The result is incorrect and the rightmost four bits are not even a BCD code. This is because BCD is not truly positional. However, one can correct the problem by adding 6 whenever the sum of the two BCD digits exceeds 9:

```
0010      1001 0111
0011      1000 0100
0110 (1)0001 1011   ←  Intermediate result
0000      0110 0110   ←  Add 6 where intermediate result exceeds 9
0110      1000 0001   ←  Correct final result
```

Because of its pseudopositional character, BCD addition can be implemented by a ripple-carry BCD adder (Figure 6.11) based on BCD full adders shown in Figure 6.12. With reference to our example and Figure 6.12, the principle of single-digit BCD addition can be expressed as follows:

IF condition
  THEN sum := sum + 6

where

$$\begin{aligned} \textit{condition} &= \text{binary } \textit{sum} > 9 \\ &= (\textit{sum} \text{ IN } [10..15]) \text{ OR } \textit{carry-out} \\ &= c_3 + (\text{Karnaugh map in Figure 6.12}) \end{aligned}$$

and

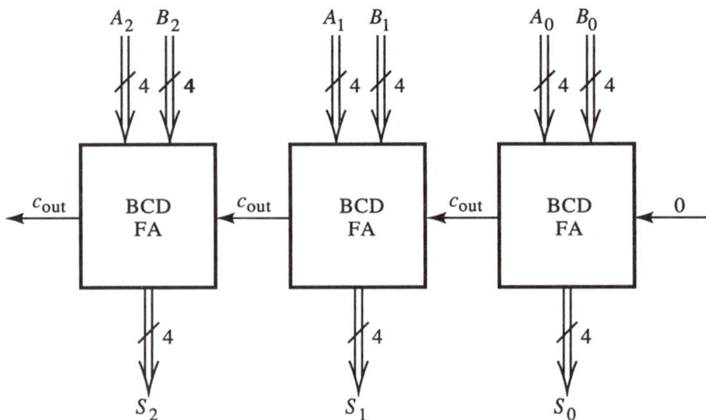


**Figure 6.11.** Multidigit BCD addition by a ripple-carry BCD adder.

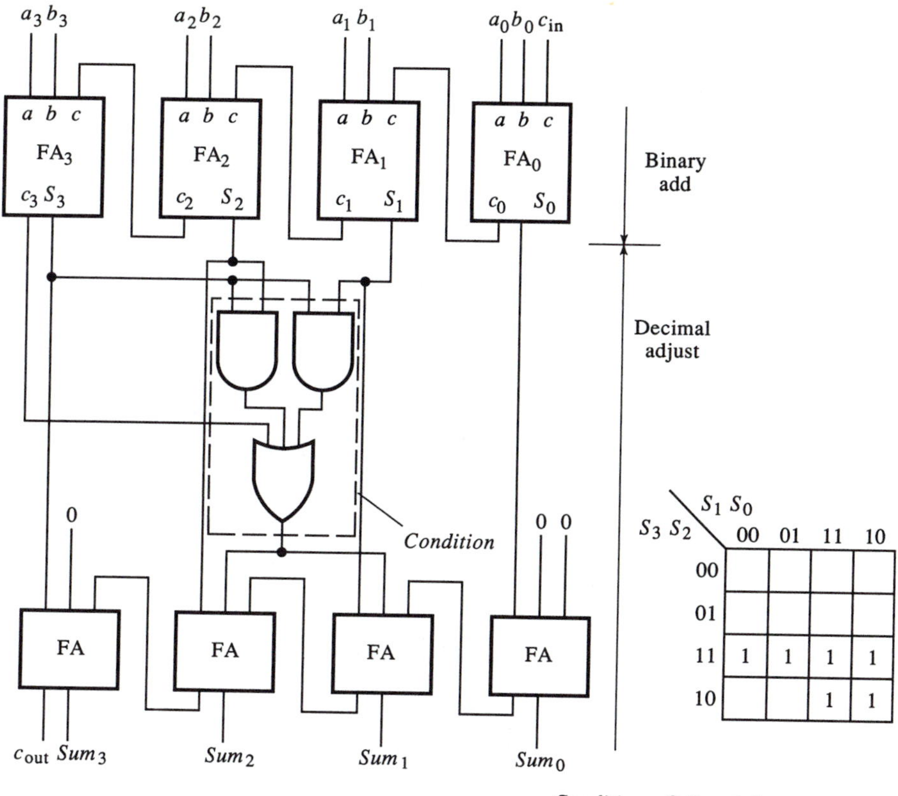


**Figure 6.12.** Karnaugh map of *condition*, and the detailed structure of a BCD full adder.

$$\text{sum} := \text{sum} + 6$$

means

$$\text{sum} := \text{sum} + (0110)$$

or

$$s_3 = s_3 + 0$$
$$s_2 = s_2 + 1$$
$$s_1 = s_1 + 1$$
$$s_0 = s_0 + 0$$

One can implement this formal description using two levels of ordinary full adders in which the middle two adders in the bottom row corresponding to row's $s_2$ and $s_1$ above have an input equal to the imposed condition; a True condition is treated as the numeric value 1:

$$s_2 = s_2 + condition$$

$$s_1 = s_1 + condition$$

This solution reaps a benefit from mixing the logic and arithmetic meaning of the condition bit.

It is clear that BCD representation requires more complicated, thus slower and more expensive, hardware than fixed-point binary arithmetic. It also uses more memory (Exercise 5), and should be used only when necessary.

Many computers do not have BCD arithmetic hardware. Instead, they have circuits that test whether BCD adjustment is needed and provide a special instruction to adjust the code. On such computers, BCD addition is performed as follows:

Add the BCD codes as if they were pure binary

Execute the decimal adjust instruction, which performs BCD adjustment if necessary;

This algorithm parallels the structure of the BCD adder in Figure 6.12. The test of the if-necessary condition is implemented as a "half-carry" flag-similar to the *C*, *S*, *V*, and *Z* flags discussed previously.

## Exercises

1. Show the steps involved in converting 154, entered as a string of ASCII codes, to binary and BCD.
2. Convert the following between decimal and BCD:
   a. 1234.56, 0.012 (the decimal point is, of course, invisible and implied as in fixed-point representation)
   b. 0010100001111001, 1001000101010111.
3. Perform the following operations in BCD: 13.2 + 4.92, 456 + 31, and 45.6 + 3.1.
4. Demonstrate the validity of the principle of decimal adjustment.
5. Analyze BCD subtraction and other arithmetic operations.
6. Calculate the ratio of the number of bits required to store a very large number in pure binary and in BCD.
7. Calculate the speed of a BCD full adder and that of a four-bit binary adder.

8. Show the details of converting $154_{10}$ from internal eight-bit pure binary to ASCII.
9. Make a detailed comparison of I/O conversion between ASCII and binary and between ASCII and BCD.
10. Assume that it takes $I_{BCD}$ microseconds to convert a decimal number to BCD and $I_b$ to convert it to binary. Assume that addition takes $A_{BCD}$ in BCD and $A_b$ in binary. Derive a formula that could be used to decide whether a program with a given amount of arithmetic and I/O should use BCD or binary representation. Note that this approach ignores the question of whether absolute decimal accuracy is required or not.
11. Estimate the values of $I_{BCD}$, $I_b$, $A_{BCD}$, and $A_b$.
12. Show how to modify an eight-bit ripple-carry binary adder to generate an $H$ flag to test for BCD adjustment after binary addition.

## 6.9 HEXADECIMAL AND OCTAL NOTATIONS

All of the representations we have discussed up to this point used by modern computers. We will now present the hexadecimal and octal notations, which are used by programmers as a coding shorthand but not by computer hardware.

The need for a coding shorthand dates back to the first days of computing, when programming was done in binary rather than in languages like Pascal. Even though today's practice is very different, it is still sometimes necessary to write programs in which some information is represented as bits and bytes rather than as text and numbers.

Full binary codes are relatively long, tedious to input and read, and easily mistyped or misread. As an example, imagine entering three bytes in binary described as follows: Bits 5, 3, and 1 in byte 1 are set; only bits 6, 4, 3, and 0 are OFF in byte 2; and the middle four bits of byte 3 are set. Check to see if the following three codes are correct

00101010 10110011 000111000

and then try to type them quickly. Programs written in assembly language, which is discussed in Chapter 10, may contain many such codes and it is easy to see why one would want to replace them with shorter, more readable symbols.

Compactness is not the only property that a suitable shorthand should have. It is equally important that conversion to and from binary be easy. This criterion eliminates decimal notation because conversion between decimal and binary is not straightforward. We will now show that hexadecimal (base 16) representation satisfies both requirements. It reduces the size of binary codes to one-quarter and its conversion does not require any calculations.

A hexadecimal code such as

$$(\ldots b_2 b_1 b_0)$$

where $b_i$ is the symbol of a number between 0 and 15, represents

$$\ldots + 16^2 b_2 + 16^1 b_1 + 16^0 b_0 = \ldots + 256 b_2 + 16 b_1 + b_0$$

Consider now a binary code $(a_7 a_6 a_5 a_4 a_3 a_2 a_1 a_0)$ whose value is

$$\begin{aligned} V &= 128a_7 + 64a_6 + 32a_5 + 16a_4 + 8a_3 + 4a_2 + 2a_1 + a_0 \\ &= 16(8a_7 + 4a_6 + 2a_5 + a_4) + (8a_3 + 4a_2 + 2a_1 + a_0) \\ &= 16(a_7 a_6 a_5 a_4) + (a_3 a_2 a_1 a_0) \end{aligned}$$

The codes in parentheses represent values between 0000 and 1111; in other words numbers between 0 and 15. The binary code $(a_7 a_6 a_5 a_4 a_3 a_2 a_1 a_0)$ is thus equivalent to a hexadecimal code $(b_1, b_0)$ with

$$\begin{aligned} b_0 &= 8a_3 + 4a_2 + 2a_1 + a_0 \\ b_1 &= 8a_7 + 4a_6 + 2a_5 + a_4 \end{aligned}$$

This establishes the following procedure for converting between binary and hexadecimal:

Divide the binary code into groups of four bits starting from the right.

Convert each individual group into hexadecimal.

This procedure requires no calculation except for the conversion of independent four-bit patterns to numbers between 0 and 15. Translation from hexadecimal to binary is equally simple and consists of converting each hexadecimal digit into four binary bits. Compare this to the process of conversion between decimal and binary.

Before we can give an example of the use of these principles, we must choose symbols to represent the numbers from 0 to 15. The standard convention is to use the digits 0 to 9 in their ordinary meaning and the letters A, B, C, D, E, F to represent the numbers 10 through 15.

We can now illustrate both conversions on the following examples:

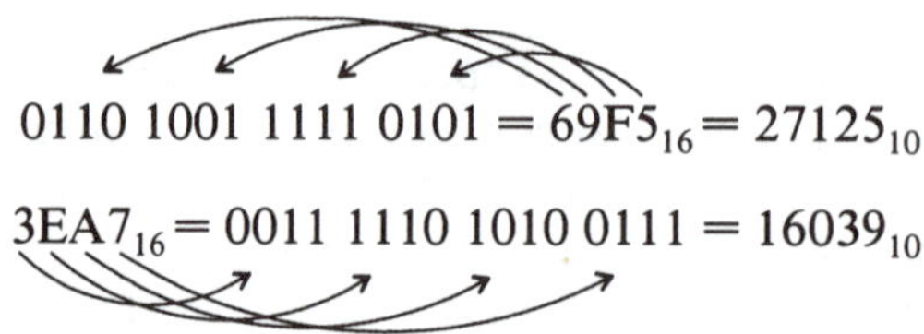

Our analysis shows that hexadecimal is a good shorthand whereas decimal is not. Are there other suitable shorthands? Any system whose base is a power of 2 is easily converted to binary; thus base 4, base 8, and base 32 are the obvious candidates.

If we used base 4, we would reduce every pair of binary symbols to one digit (0...3). The size of each binary code would thus be cut to one-half, which is not a sufficient saving.

Base 8, or octal, codes replace each triplet of binary symbols by one octal symbol (digits 0 to 7). This reduces the length of the code to one-third, which is attractive. However, if we operate with byte-based codes as most modern computers do, the three-bit size of the group is awkward: Octal requires that we divide each eight-bit code into groups of two, three, and three bits. Octal notation was popular when many computers were based on six-bit codes (and used six-bit ASCII without lower-case letters).

Base 32 would be a very efficient shorthand as it would replace each group of five bits with one code ($32 = 2^5$). The resulting division of eight-bit binary codes into groups of three and five is, however, inconvenient and base 32 would require many unfamiliar symbols.

Our analysis shows that base 16 is an excellent compromise: It provides a good saving, cutting the size of the code to one-quarter; fits nicely into one byte (two "hex" digits for one byte); and requires only five extra symbols.

Although hexadecimal can be used to represent any binary codes, not just numbers, it is essentially a number representation. Because it is positional, arithmetic with it is the same as with unsigned binary. As an example, the sum

$$\begin{array}{r} 36 \\ \underline{8A} \\ C0 \end{array}$$

is calculated in the usual way, using the fact that hexadecimal 6 + A is 6 + 10 = 16 in decimal, or 10 in hexadecimal. The hexadecimal result of 6 + A is thus 0 and a carry of 1. Also, 3 + 8 + carry = 12 in decimal, which is C in hexadecimal. No carry is generated.

We have, so far, used hexadecimal only for positive values but it is often necessary to represent negative numbers in hexadecimal as well. We could, of course, do this by converting the negative value to two's complement and expressing the binary code in hexadecimal but this is unnecessary. A little trick allows us to easily obtain hexadecimal codes directly from the hexadecimal code of the magnitude.

Consider, as an example, eight-bit codes of the form $(xxxx)(xxxx)$. As we know, the code of $-(xxxx)(xxxx)$ can be obtained as $1(0000)(0000)-(xxxx)(xxxx)$, or $100-XX$ in hexadecimal. But 100 = FF + 1 thus

$$-XX = 100 - XX = \mathrm{FF} + 1 - XX$$
$$= (\mathrm{FF} - XX) + 1$$

Here, the subtraction FF $- XX$ is very easy because FF is the largest two-digit hexadecimal code and the operation is thus always possible without a borrow.

The following example uses this principle to find the hexadecimal code of $-17_{16}$:

$$\begin{array}{r} \mathrm{FF} \\ \underline{-17} \\ \mathrm{E8} + 1 = \mathrm{E9} \end{array}$$

The hexadecimal code of $-17_{16}$ is thus E9.

While an understanding hexadecimal arithmetic is useful, one does not have to be fluent in it because one rarely needs to perform such calculations by hand. Most of the hexadecimal codes a computer scientist may have to read are hexadecimal "dumps" of computer memory, and these consist mostly of instruction codes with some text and only a few numbers. If one needs to read them, it is not with the purpose of checking that the computer can add but rather to verify that a program works with the correct bit patterns. Little or no arithmetic is thus required.

### Exercises

1. Type the following four lines and have another student check to see if they have been typed correctly. Comment on the experience.

   00101011 01110101 11001011 00100010 10011101 00111100 10001001

   10001011 11000011 00010010 00101011 01100010 10010100 01101011

   10011101 00111100 10001001 11000011 10010010 00101011 01100010

   00101011 01100010 10010100 01101011 11001011 00100010 10011101

2. Convert the following between hexadecimal and binary:

   A12, 3FC2, 1263,

   001010011011,111010110111, 1101010001101010

3. Convert the following between octal and binary:

   351, 258, 470,

   001010011011, 111010110111, 1101010001101010

4. Compare the lengths of the binary, octal, and hexadecimal codes in Exercises 2 and 3.
5. What is the meaning of 345 in decimal, octal, and hexadecimal? Convert the codes to binary.

   Because codes like 345 and 101 are ambiguous if their base is not stated, computer programmers normally use "H" to represent hexadecimal, "Q" for octal, "B" for binary, and no symbol for decimal (decimal is the *default*) as in 101H, 101Q, 101B, and 101. Other symbols, such as "$" for hexadecimal and "%" for binary, are also used.
6. Perform the following hexadecimal arithmetic operations: 12 + 14, 15 + 15, 19 + 14, 1A + 1F, 19 + 19, 16 − 12, 1F − 10, 1F − 1B, 2C − 1F.
7. Construct a hexadecimal addition table.
8. Find the hexadecimal codes of two's complement −01001010, 11010010, −00101111, and 01011010; and of decimal −5, −9, and −13.

## SUMMARY

Information is represented in computers by codes, which are groups of bits. We have described the most common coding conventions for text (characters) and numbers and we have constructed several circuits for binary arithmetic.

The most common character convention is seven-bit ASCII. Its 128 codes represent letters, digits, punctuation symbols, and other printable characters, as well as nonprintable "control" characters. When ASCII codes are stored in eight-bit memory cells, the eighth bit can be used for parity (to improve the reliability of communication) or to extend the basic 128 character set by 128 special characters.

ASCII satisfies the needs of text processing but provides no support for other types of information such as graphics. Although a number of extensions of ASCII have been proposed, none have been widely accepted so far.

The most important number conventions can be divided into four categories:

Fixed-point (used mainly for integers)

Floating-point (reals)

BCD (decimal numbers)

Hexadecimal (shorthand notation)

The first category includes pure (unsigned) binary, two's complement (signed binary), and sign-magnitude representation. All three systems use a fixed assignment of weights to bit positions and this can be interpreted as fixed placement of the decimal point; hence the name fixed-point (FP) notation. The decimal point can be fixed in any position in or out of the code, but integer systems (decimal point behind the last bit) and fractional systems (decimal point in front of the first bit) are most common.

Pure binary is ordinary positional representation and cannot express negative numbers. Two's complement is also positional but allows negative numbers because its leading bit has negative weight. Sign-magnitude notation allows positive and negative numbers but is only partially positional. It is used in floating-point codes.

Pure binary and two's complement arithmetic operations are almost identical, and most of them can be implemented by the same circuits. The differences lie in the nature of shifting, multiplication, division, and in the interpretation of certain conditions.

Because the number of bits used to represent a code in a given computer program is fixed, some operations produce results whose codes are too long to fit into the available bits and a carry or an overflow occurs. We have shown how to recognize these conditions.

An important use of integer arithmetic is the comparison of magnitudes. Its basis is subtraction and logic operations on carry, overflow, sign, and zero indicators (flags).

When we need to work with large and small magnitudes simultaneously and desire constant relative accuracy, fixed-point notation is unsuitable and we must use REAL arithmetic based on floating-point (FLP) representations. A floating-point number is represented by a mantissa, the normalized magnitude, and an exponent, which determines the position of the decimal point. The mantissa is usually in fractional sign-magnitude notation and the exponent is expressed as a characteristic, a biased exponent in unsigned notation. Advantages of the floating-point representation include its large dynamic range and constant relative accuracy. Because of its memory requirements and complex arithmetic, however, floating-point notation should be used only when necessary.

None of these conventions can provide accurate fractional decimal arithmetic and easy conversion between decimal I/O and binary internal representation. This is why we need BCD notation, which is based on binary representation of individual decimal digits. BCD is a semipositional system; its arithmetic is similar to unsigned arithmetic but is more complex and therefore slower. Because BCD also uses memory inefficiently, it should be used only when necessary.

The variety of available number representations seems to offer the programmer many choices in selecting the notation best suited for a given problem. In practice, however, most programs are written in a high-level language, allowing only integer, BCD, and REAL numbers, and are automatically translated by a compiler. This leaves the programmer very little control over internal number representation.

In addition to the above systems, which are used in hardware and software implementations of arithmetic, we explained hexadecimal and octal representations, which are used mainly as a shorthand to make binary codes more readable and easier to write.

Among the hardware discussed in this chapter, the most important are full adders and ripple-carry adders. The full adder operates on two one-bit operands and a carry and produces a sum and a carry-out bit. It is the basis of the multibit ripple-carry adder and a number of other arithmetic and logic circuits. Ripple-carry adders are chains of full adders. They are simple but slow; faster and more complicated circuits are also available. Fast adders normally use the same principle as ripple-carry adders but speed up carry propagation.

We have shown basic circuits for subtraction, multiplication, and BCD addition, and discussed commercially available ALUs capable of a number of arithmetic and logic operations. We outlined an arithmetic processor as an example of a more sophisticated processing component.

## REVIEW QUESTIONS

1. Define the following terms: ASCII, ANSI, EBCDIC, control character, printable character, byte, even/odd parity, fixed-point notation, unsigned (pure binary) notation, carry, borrow, full adder, ripple-carry adder, LSB, MSB, signed (two's complement) notation, overflow, flag (carry, overflow, sign, zero), radix, register, shifting, sign-magnitude notation, ALU, arithmetic processor, bit-wise logic, real number, floating-point, characteristic, mantissa, normalization, hidden bit, rounding, truncation, underflow, floating-point standard, BCD, hexadecimal, and octal notation.
2. Describe the following procedures: Conversion between decimal and pure binary, two's complement, BCD, sign-magnitude, floating-point, hexadecimal; negation of two's complement and hexadecimal codes; multiplication in pure binary and two's complement; division in pure binary; comparison in pure binary and two's complement; detection of overflow; and BCD and floating-point addition.

## REFERENCES

The following titles listed in the references at the end of the book are relevant to this chapter:

C. Ashton, et al. *Designer's Guide to Floating-Point Processing.*

K. Hwang. *Computer Arithmetic: Principles, Architecture, and Design.*

# CHAPTER 7

# PRINCIPLES OF DIGITAL SYSTEMS

## AN OVERVIEW

In this chapter we will study digital systems—code-level sequential circuits.

In the first section, we will introduce the block diagram of a digital system and its main parts: the processing elements, storage, and control. We studied registers and processing elements like the ALU in earlier chapters; here we will introduce memory and the control unit.

Individual parts of digital systems require signal paths for the transfer of codes. The data paths are often realized as buses and we will explain their purpose, components, and implementation.

Finally, we will turn to the control unit that implements sequencing of events in the digital system and activates the desired events. We will demonstrate two alternative design methods, hardwired control and microprogramming.

## IMPORTANT WORDS

Block diagram, bus (uni- and bi-directional), control store, control unit (hardwired, microprogrammed), data path, firmware, microcode (horizontal, vertical), microinstruction, microprogram, open collector, RAM (static, dynamic), RTL, sequencer, transceiver, tristate.

## 7.1 DIGITAL SYSTEMS AND BLOCK DIAGRAMS

For the purpose of our discussion, we will define a digital system as a sequential circuit that operates on codes. Because digital systems are characterized by the transfer of codes between registers, they are best studied at the register transfer level rather than at the bit-oriented gate level at which we introduced combinational and sequential circuits.

The relation between the register transfer level and the gate level is similar to that between electronic and gate-level circuits: Although gates are electronic circuits, the electronic complexity of circuits made from gates is such that higher-level gate perspective greatly simplifies their study and design. The shift from gate to register-transfer perspectives also allows us to concentrate on the main principles of digital systems and hide low-level details.

What are the implications of the functional and structural differences between bit-level sequential circuits and code-level digital systems?

The functional complexity of most digital systems makes it impractical to represent their behavior by transition graphs. The number of states may be in the thousands and the number of controlled signals in the hundreds. Our examples in Sections 7.4 and 7.5 are simple enough so that we can use transition graphs to describe their operation, but more complex systems like computers are better specified with hardware description languages and similar formal or semiformal high level descriptions. Such descriptions can also be used for simulation or even for automated hardware design.

The complex structure of digital systems is both apparent and real. Most of the complexity results from the complexity of the functions involved but much is due to duplication, the fact that operating on codes instead of single bits requires multiple copies of identical components and connections—one for each bit of the code. Complete logic diagrams of digital systems showing all of the signal paths and components would be cluttered and would obscure the structure. To represent digital systems we thus use *block diagrams* whose building blocks are units like ALUs and memory and whose signal paths are control lines and multibit code highways called *buses*.

Figure 7.1 shows a simple digital system containing all major register-transfer level signal paths and parts. Paths include data paths, control points, and control lines:

Data paths carry codes between storage and processing blocks. The term "data" is used here in the sense of code and can refer to ASCII or number codes, instructions, or memory addresses. Each data path is shown by a double line and represents several identical one-bit connections, possibly with devices that amplify and condition the signal.

Control points on data paths act as valves that block or pass the codes. They are shown as circles on the data paths.

Control lines carry individual control signals that select ALU functions, load data into registers, increment counters, open or close control points, and so on. They are shown as single lines.

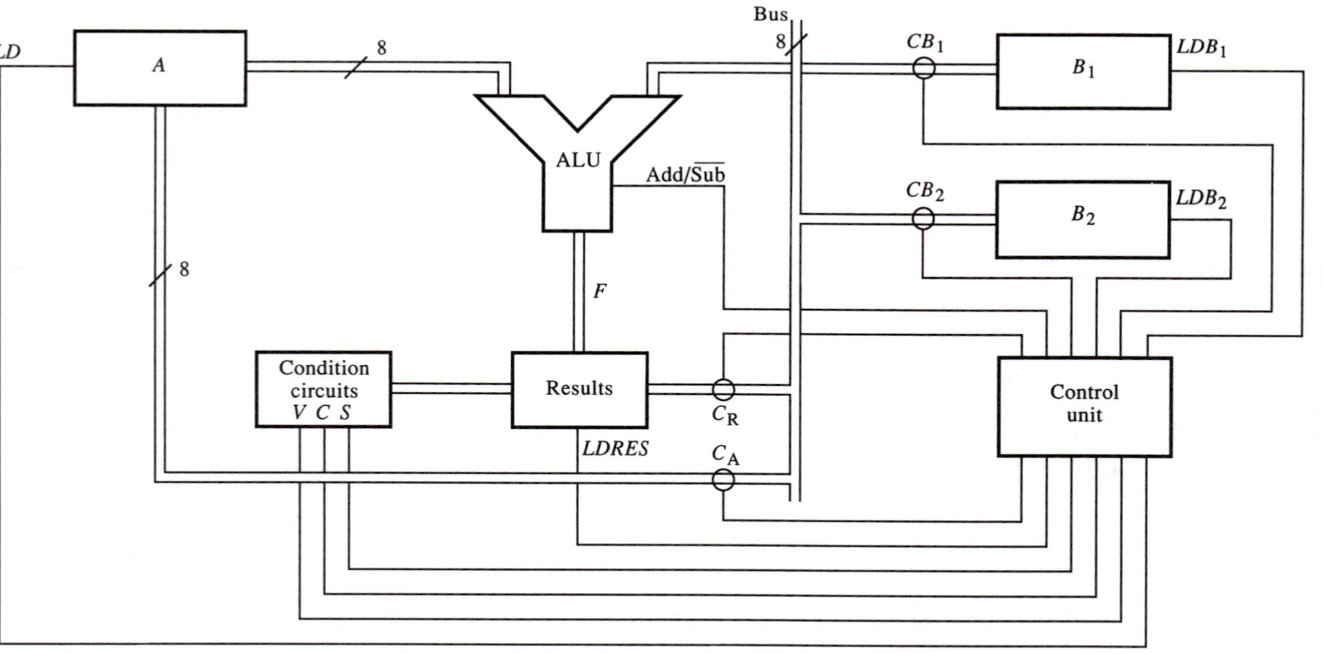


**Figure 7.1.** Block diagram of a digital system.

The major parts of the register-transfer level are the storage and processing components and the control units:

Storage components include registers, counters, and memory. The diagram in Figure 7.1 contains registers $A$, $B_1$, $B_2$, and $RESULT$.

Processing components include devices like Arithmetic Logic Units.

The control unit enforces the required sequence of events by generating control signals that activate control points, memories, ALUs, and so on. The control unit is driven by a clock.

To illustrate the operation of a digital system, we will now consider a sequence of transfers that could take place in the circuit shown in Figure 7.1. Assume that the system is to load $B_1$ from $B_2$, add $A$ and $B_1$, and store the result in $RESULT$. Symbolically, we can describe this as

$$B_2 \rightarrow B_1$$
$$A + B_1 \rightarrow RESULT$$

Figure 7.1 illustrates that the chain of events needed to achieve this is as follows (Figure 7.2):

Clock cycle $N$: The control unit activates $CB_2$ and $LBD_1$ to let the value from $B_2$ enter the bus and to prepare its loading into register $B_1$.

Cycle $N + 1$: The active edge of the clock starts loading data into register $B_1$. Its outputs $QB_1$ begin to change and become stable after $T_{pDB}$, the propagation delay of register $B_1$. The processing delay of the ALU causes output $F$ to assume its final value $T_{pDF}$ after $Q_A$ stabilizes.

Concurrently with data transfer and processing, the control unit generates the control signal $LDRES$ required to load register $RESULT$ from $F$ in cycle $N + 2$.The delay between the clock edge and the transition of $LDRES$ from 0 to 1 is due to the delays of the control unit.

Cycle $N + 2$: Because $LDRES$ is ON when the clock edge arrives, register $RESULT$ starts loading. The operation is completed $T_{pDR}$ later.

The required operations have now been completed.

## 7.2 DATA TRANSFERS AND BUSES

The presence of several registers and an ALU in Figure 7.1 indicates that data in digital systems must often move between multiple sources and destinations. Figure 7.3 shows that if we connected every pair of devices that must

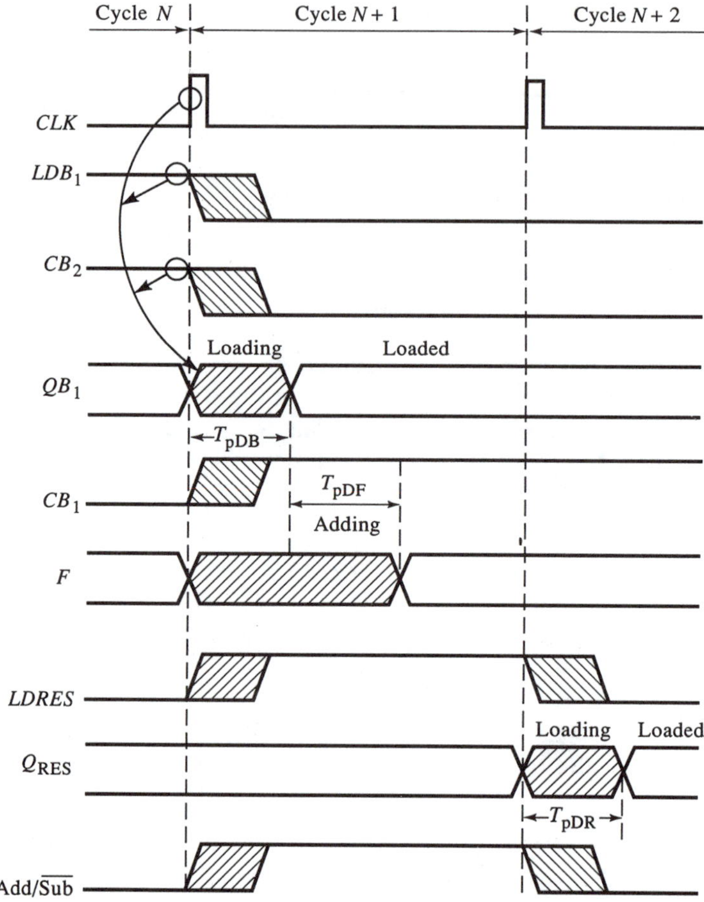


**Figure 7.2.** Timing diagram of a data transfer. Values of multibit signals are represented by two parallel lines. Hatched areas indicate periods in which the signals are undergoing a transition; otherwise, the signals are stable.

communicate there would be many multibit connections, which would consume much space and require many additional circuits.

We could use MUXs to implement the connections as in Figure 7.4 but even with data paths only eight bits wide, each register would need six 4–1 MUXs for input, and the complete system would require a total of twenty-four 4–1 MUXs or twelve chips. The number of wires leaving each register output would be twenty-four (eight bits to each of the three remaining registers) for ninety-six output wires altogether. Additional connections would be necessary for inputs and control signals.

One can find a better solution by considering the analogy of a road map. If we were to connect several scattered villages to one another, we would design

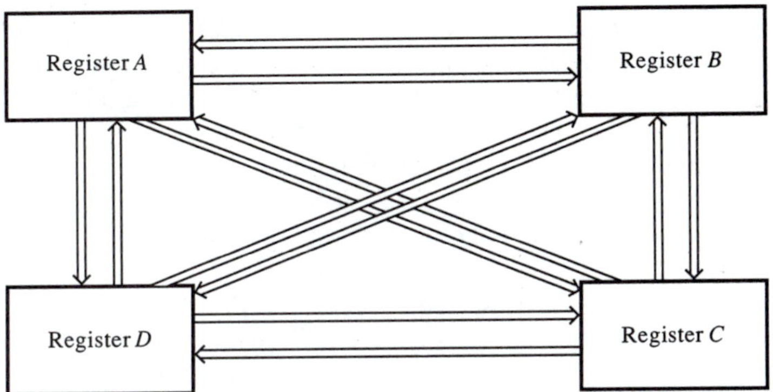


**Figure 7.3.** System in which four registers must communicate with each other. To simplify the example, no processing units are shown.

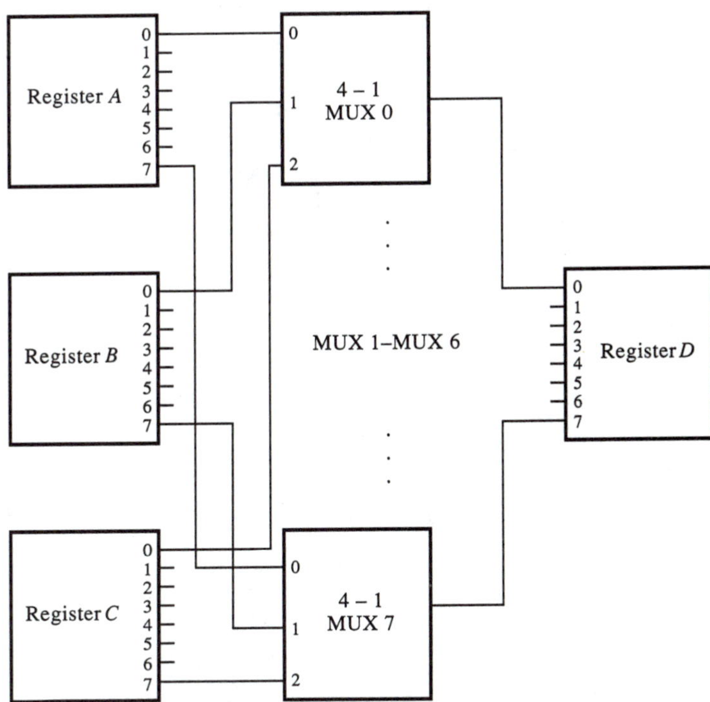


**Figure 7.4.** Part of the circuit needed to connect all registers in Figure 7.3 to each other. Control signals are not shown.

a single highway with controlled exits rather than individual roads connecting all of the villages. The same approach is used in digital systems. The data highway connecting multiple sources and destinations of data is usually called the bus. With a bus, the four-register system can be converted to a neat structure of eight conductors with "exits" to individual registers, as shown in Figure 7.5.

Even a brief look at the diagram raises several questions:

1. Each line of the bus is connected to an output pin of each register, and the outputs of all registers are thus connected together. However, connecting several outputs together creates an undetermined signal that can destroy some of the components. How can this be prevented?
2. The diagram suggests that both inputs and outputs are connected to the same line. Can one wire conduct signals in both directions? If so, what determines the direction?
3. How are the source and destinations for a particular transfer selected?

We will now answer these questions.

1. The connection of multiple logic outputs to a single conductor is possible if the devices are equipped with either OC or tristate outputs.

The open collector circuit was used in older implementations of buses. As it is now much less common than tristate outputs, we leave its presentation for Appendix 1.

One can think of a tristate device as an ordinary logic component with a switch on its output (Figure 7.6). The switch can be opened or closed by an enable signal and the component can thus operate in one of two modes: When enabled, it behaves as an ordinary logic device and produces logic 0 or 1. When disabled, the output is disconnected and devices attached to it are unaware of its existence. The disabled output is said to be "floated" or in the "high impedance state" and its value is denoted by $Z$, the engineering symbol for impedance. The reader should keep in mind that $Z$ is not a new logic value but a symbol indicating "no logic signal." The name "tristate," or

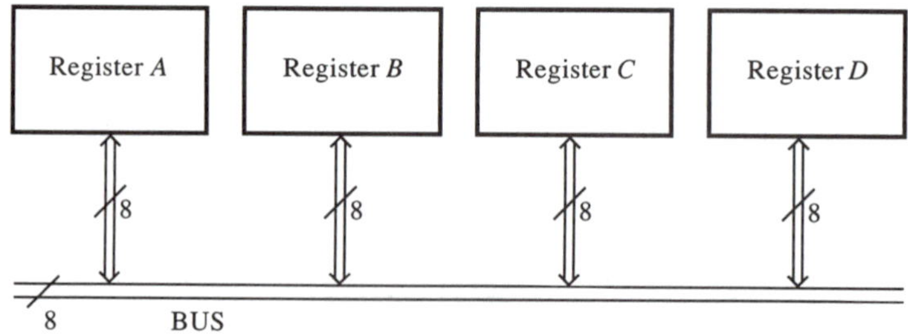


**Figure 7.5.** Solution of the four-register problem using a bus.

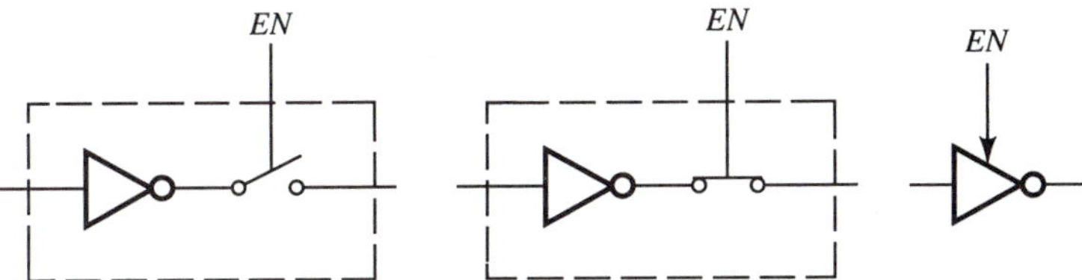


**Figure 7.6.** Principle of an enabled and a disabled tristate inverter and its conventional symbol.

"three-state," thus means that the output can have one of three values: 0, 1 (logic values), or $Z$ (no value).

The behavior of a tristate output can be described as follows:

IF enabled

THEN output is logic 0 or 1 as for an equivalent component without tristate output

ELSE output is $Z$ and does not contribute any logic signal to the rest of the circuit

Naturally, the output switch is not mechanical but electronic, and the speed of switching between enabled and disabled states is comparable to gate propagation delays.

Figure 7.7 shows the connection of several tristate outputs to a single line, the principle of a bus. Each tristate output is a control point, a valve that passes data when enabled and blocks it when disabled. Because a tristate is just a logic output followed by a switch, the basic rule of logic signals holds even for tristate devices: Several tristate outputs connected to the same line must not be enabled simultaneously.

Even though the restriction on active outputs is the same as for ordinary TTL outputs, the "output enable" signal gives us the control that makes it possible to connect several tristate outputs together (Figure 7.7), something that is impossible with ordinary outputs. The reader should note that open collector outputs allow even conflicting logic values to coexist and produce a predictable logic signal. This means that they do not require an extra control signal.

All of the components used in bus applications are available with tristate outputs. They include inverters, multiplexers, flip-flops, registers, memories, line drivers and buffers. Noninverting drivers and buffers have no logic effect on the signal and merely amplify and control it.

2. We now turn to the problem of using a single line for both input and output. A line that conducts signals in both directions is called "bidirectional." Bidirectionality is achieved by using tristate devices arranged as in

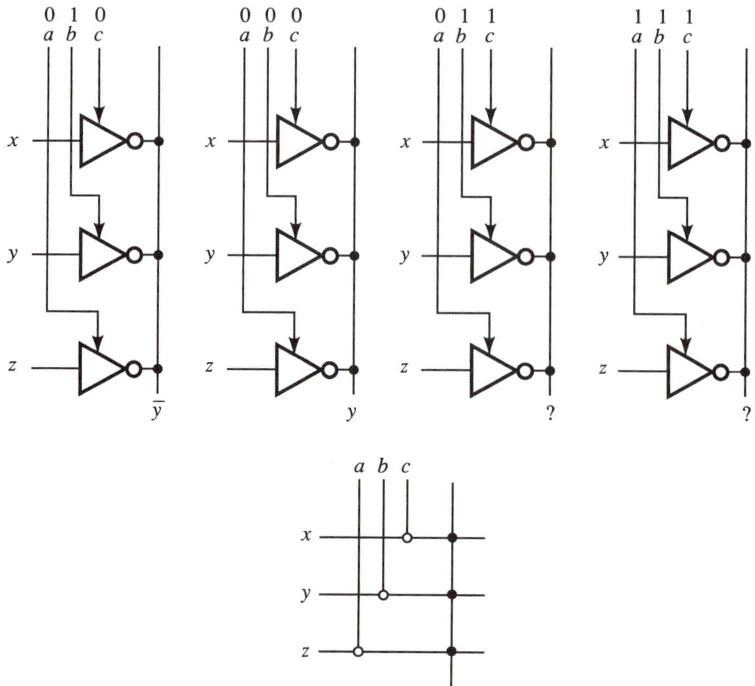


**Figure 7.7.** Allowed and disallowed combinations of tristate outputs: top, (*left to right*) allowed, allowed, disallowed, disallowed; (*bottom*) the equivalent "control point" representation.

Figure 7.8. When the left-to-right control line is High, the left-to-right path is open and the right-to-left path is closed; when the direction control is Low, data flows from right to left. At any particular time, the wire is thus set to conduct the signal in one direction only.

Bidirectional control is available in the form of transceiver chips, such as the 74242 inverting and the 74243 noninverting transceiver, or built into the I/O lines of a more complicated chip. As an example, the 74299 universal shift register (Figure 7.9) has bidirectional data lines. Because its bidirectional pins are used for input and output (multiplexed I/O), the total number of I/O pins required by the chip is cut in half. The price of this simplification is that input and output cannot be performed simultaneously.

The signal controlling a tristate output is usually called output enable (OE), chip enable (CE), or chip select (CS). Note that chips with bidirectional I/O must also have a read/write input that selects the direction of the transfer.

3. Our understanding of tristate devices and bidirectional lines allows us to deal with the third problem, the selection of sources and destinations and the implementation of control points.

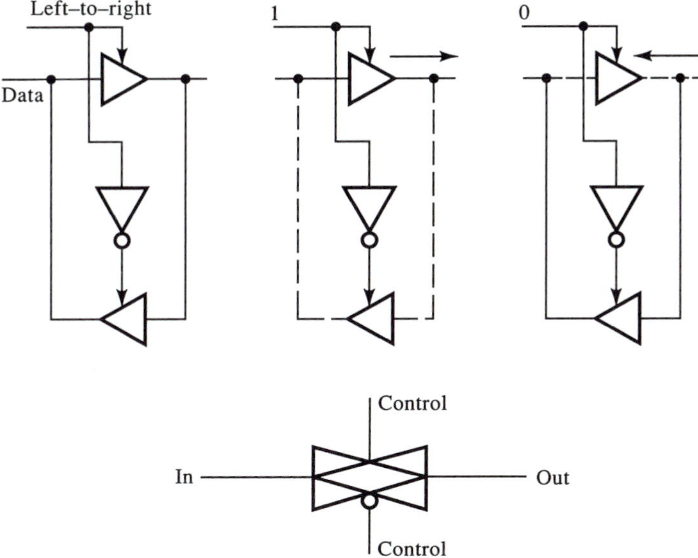


**Figure 7.8.** Bidirectional transceiver, its two modes of operation, and its symbolic representation.

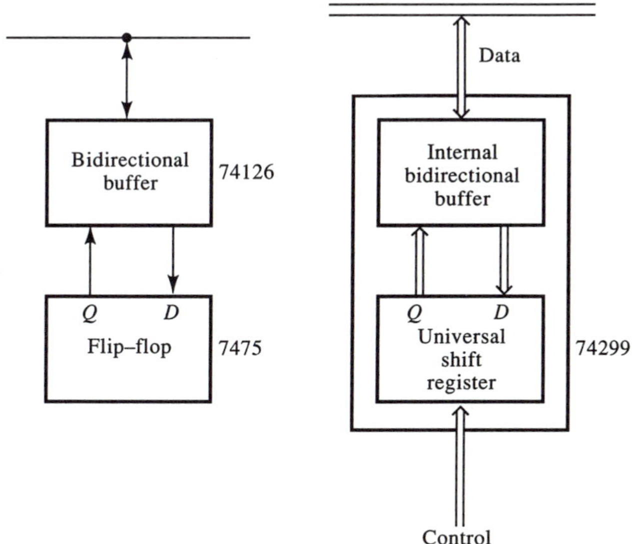


**Figure 7.9.** Bidirectional I/O can be obtained with a special chip or as a part of another function.

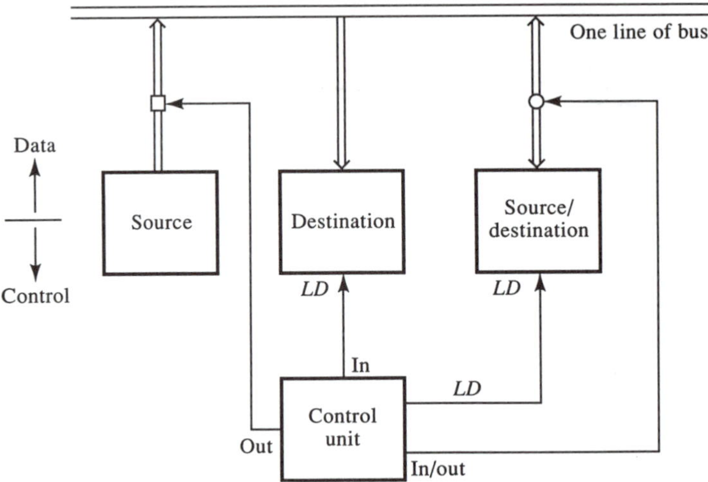


**Figure 7.10.** Connecting storage elements to a bus (*left to right*): cases (1b), (2), and (3) from the text. We use squares for unidirectional and circles for bidirectional control points.

Tristate devices make possible both unidirectional and bidirectional lines (Figure 7.10). The choice of a uni- or bidirectional line and the inclusion of control points depends on the desired function:

1. If the device only outputs data on the bus, there are two possibilities:
   a. If only one device writes to the bus, no control point is necessary because control is needed only to prevent several connected outputs from being activated simultaneously and causing a conflict.
   b. If several devices write to the bus, a control point is needed to prevent logic and electric conflict.The control point is a unidirectional tristate output or a line driver or buffer.
2. If the device only inputs data from the bus, no control point is needed because any number of devices may "listen" to the same signal if it is strong enough. Reading is achieved by the *LD* signal of a register or a similar arrangement.

   To guarantee that the signal received from the bus is not weakened by too many listening devices, inputs of devices connected to buses often pass through drivers or buffers even when the logic of the connection does not require it. This reduces the load on the device that generates the signal, increases electric ruggedness and tolerance to power fluctuations, main-

tains the shape of the signal, and makes it possible to interface devices using different voltages.
3. If the device uses the connection to the bus for both reading and writing, a transceiver is required to create a bidirectional line.

To illustrate these principles, Figure 7.11 shows a complete logic diagram of our four-register example using external tristate transceivers and registers with ordinary ("totem pole") rather than tristate outputs. The indicated control combination activates the simultaneous transfer from $A$ to $B$ and $C$ (single source, two destinations). The data path of register $D$ is set for reading but no reading into $D$ takes place because the $LD$ input of register $D$ is inactive. Note how much less readable this detailed diagram is than the block diagram even though they both contain the same information.

We can summarize the concepts presented in this section as follows: A bus allows multiple sources and destinations to communicate using a minimum number of connections. If several devices output data to the same bus, they must be individually controlled and have tristate or open collector outputs. At any instant, at most one of the tristate sources connected to the bus may be enabled because at most one code may be transferred over the bus at a time; this restriction limits the speed of the system. Although only one device may "speak" at a time, any number of devices may "listen" simultaneously.

A system may have one or more buses depending on the complexity of internal communication and the required speed. Additional buses allow more simultaneous communication, which increases speed but makes the system more complicated and expensive. Simple systems that have very few connections and very fast systems that have connections between all sources and destinations may not have any bus.

## Exercises

1. Assume that the unidirectional outputs and inputs of a register with separate input and output pins are connected to the same bus, each by its own set of connections. What is the result of a simultaneous load and output enable operation? Draw a timing diagram to show what happens.
2. Show how to implement a bus in which any one of registers $A_i$ may be the source of data and any number of registers $B_i$ may be the destination:
   a. Use registers with ordinary outputs and transceiver chips.
   b. Use registers with separate inputs and tristate outputs.
   c. Use registers with multiplexed inputs and tristate outputs.
   d. Do not use tristate devices.
3. Can a bidirectional line be implemented without tristate outputs? Justify.
4. Explain why it is unacceptable to use only the in/$\overline{\text{out}}$ signal to control both the loading of the rightmost register and its control point in Figure 7.10.

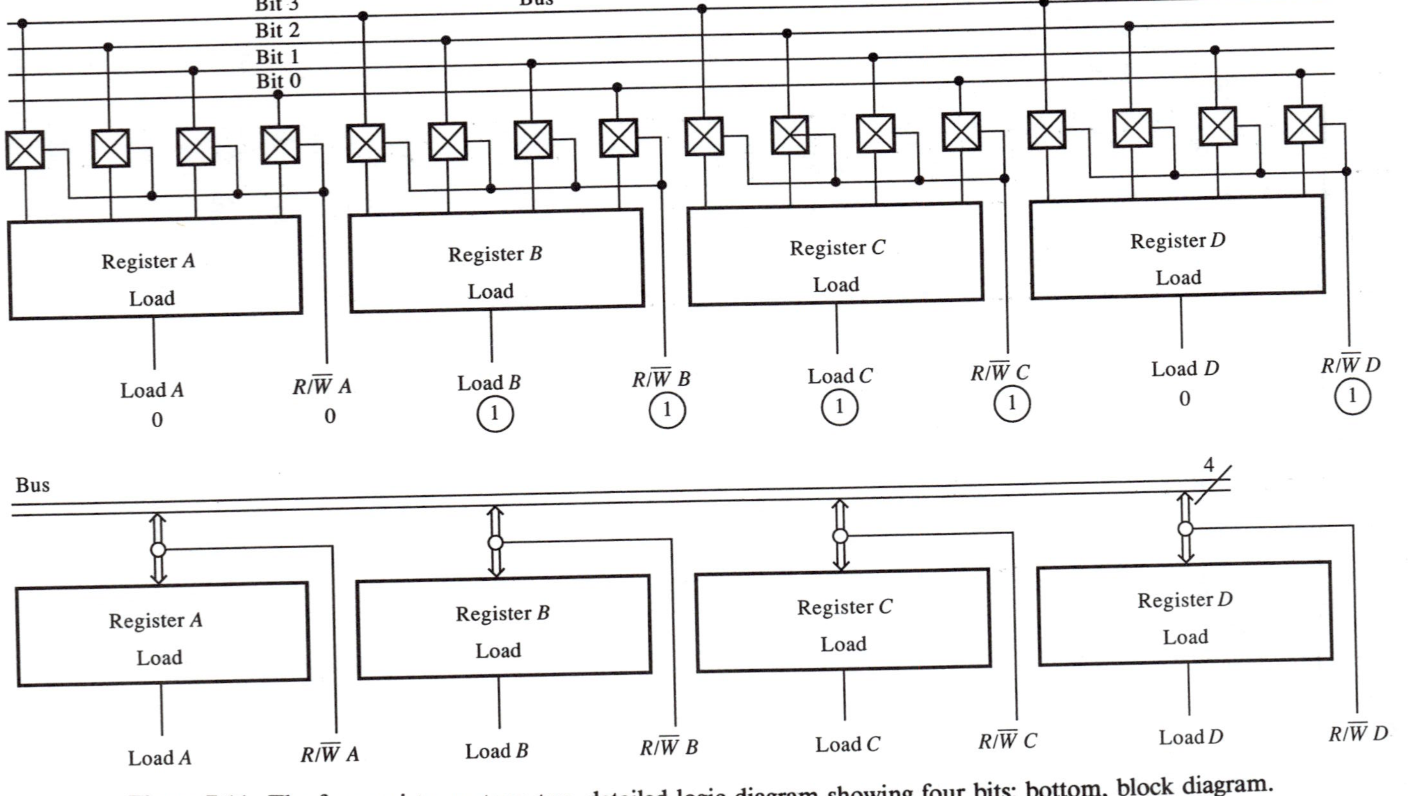


**Figure 7.11.** The four-register system: top, detailed logic diagram showing four bits; bottom, block diagram.

## 7.3 MEMORIES

As we saw in Chapter 3, a memory chip is an array of memory cells (Figure 7.12). Each cell has a unique address—a number between 0 and $2^n - 1$, where $n$ is the number of address pins of the chip—and this address allows us to access each cell independently.

Depending on whether or not the contents of individual cells can be modified, memories are categorized as ROMs and RAMs.

We discussed ROMs in Chapter 3 and we will now concentrate on RAMs. The acronym RAM stands for "random access memory," which means that cells with different addresses can be accessed in any order and that data can be read or written in the same amount of time. The name RAM for read/write memories is somewhat confusing because ROM chips also have the random access property, and some authors thus refer to read/write memories as "RWMs."

Random access memory chips are available in two technologies: TTL and MOS. (N-MOS or C-MOS, both discussed in Appendix 1). TTL RAMs are now used relatively rarely because they can provide only very small memory capacities. However, we will give an example of TTL RAM chip because of our previous concentration on TTL.

The 74189 TTL RAM (Figure 7.13) contains 16 cells with four bits each for a total capacity of sixty four bits. It is thus called a 16 × 4 sixty-four bit RAM.

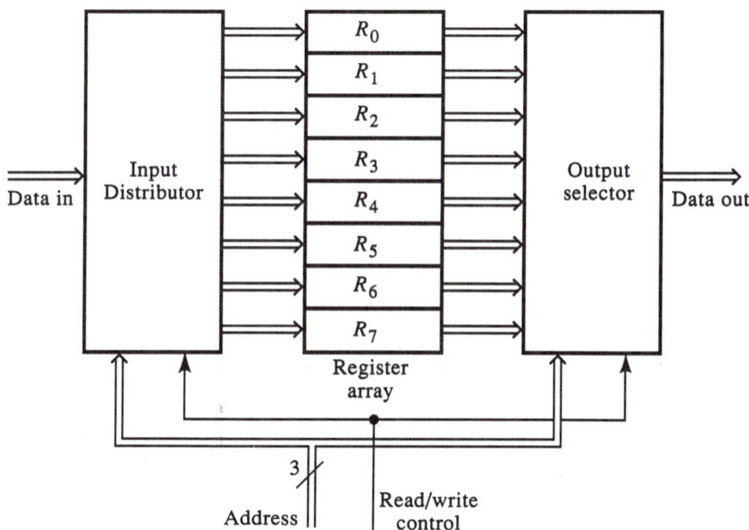


**Figure 7.12.** Principle of a memory chip.

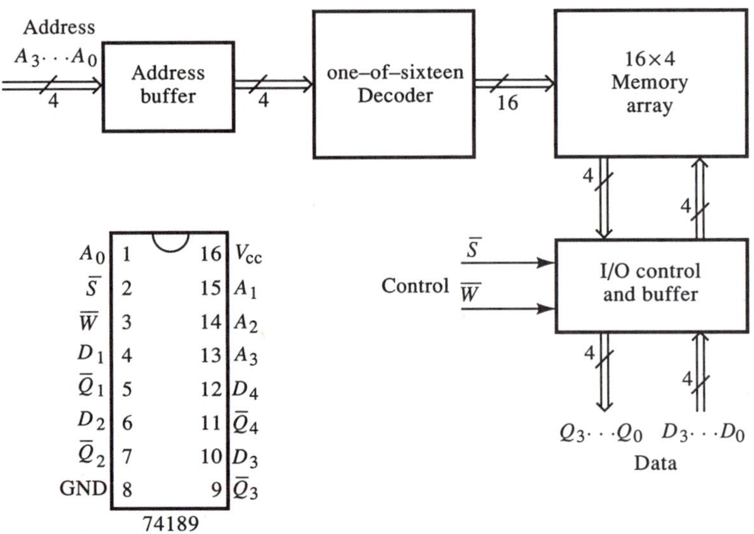


**Figure 7.13.** Pinout and internal block diagram of the 74189.

The 74189 has four address pins to allow access to sixteen memory locations numbered 0 to 15. The data lines are unidirectional, with four $D$ pins for input and four $Q$ pins for inverted output. There are also two control inputs: Input $S$ (active Low) selects or inhibits chip access, and $W$ controls whether the selected chip is read from or written to. The effect of $S$ and $C$ can be summarized as follows:

| $S$ | $W$ | Function |
|---|---|---|
| 0 | 0 | Data stored in location $A_3 \ldots A_0$ can be read from pins $Q_3 \ldots Q_0$ |
| 0 | 1 | Data present on pins $D_3 \ldots D_0$ is written to the memory cell whose address is $A_3 \ldots A_0$ |
| 1 | $X$ | Outputs $Q_3 \ldots Q_0$ tristated; inputs $D_3 \ldots D_0$ have no effect |

The *access time* of the 74189 is 25 nsec; this is the time that must be allowed between activation of the chip enable signal and the completion of a read or write operation.

As we have already mentioned, most memory chips now in use are not TTL but N-MOS or C-MOS. Below we list the main differences between TTL and N-MOS or C-MOS memories:

MOS memories are much denser. Chip capacities of 256k bits are common and capacities up to 4 Mbits are available as well.

MOS chips, especially C-MOS chips, have much smaller power consumption.

MOS chips are slower than TTL chips, with access times usually between 100 nsec and 200 nsec. Faster MOS memories are available but are expensive.

We can divide MOS RAMs into two categories: dynamic RAMs (DRAMs) and static RAMs (SRAMs). Static RAMs are based on latches and keep the stored data as long as the power is ON, just like TTL memories. Dynamic RAMs are based on capacitors formed by transistors. The capacitors represent data as stored charges and lose it in milliseconds even if the power is ON. Consequently, they must be periodically rewritten or "refreshed." Rewriting does not require that the data be read and written back, and it takes very little time. It does, however, require an extra circuit or a memory controller chip. In addition to the need for refresh, DRAMs also have a longer *cycle time*, the minimum time between consecutive memory accesses, because their internal storage cells must be recharged after each access.

As long as the need for a longer cycle time and for extra components is acceptable, these disadvantages of DRAMs are balanced by their internal simplicity and the resulting much larger storage capacity. Dynamic DRAM capacities are normally one generation ahead of SRAMs. For example, at a time when the maximum DRAM capacity is 1M, the maximum SRAM capacity may be only 256k. This means that even with the refresh circuit, the number of chips required to implement memory of a given size is smaller with DRAM chips. In addition, DRAMs are also cheaper than SRAMs. Altogether, DRAMs are generally preferred to SRAMs, sometimes even when their lower speed slows down the system. The use of SRAMs is limited to applications requiring high speed.

An example of an NMOS RAM chip is the TMX4C1024 DRAM made by Texas Instruments. This is a 1Mx1 bit DRAM twenty-six pin chip with an access time between 100 nsec and 200 nsec. It has ten address pins, one bidirectional data pin, and two power supply pins. The remaining pins are used for control (chip select, read/write, and refresh). Note that there are only 10 address pins although 1M addressing requires twenty bits. The twenty-bit address is supplied in two ten-bit parts as a "row" and "column" address, and is stored in a special register on the chip, reflecting the internal two-dimensional organization of the memory array. The identification of the two distinct parts of the address requires its own control pin.

We will now show (Figure 7.14) how to use the 74189 TTL RAM to implement a region of sixty-four consecutive eight-bit memory locations addressed 000000...111111, or 0–63. Although the example uses a TTL chip, the same procedure applies to MOS chips as well.

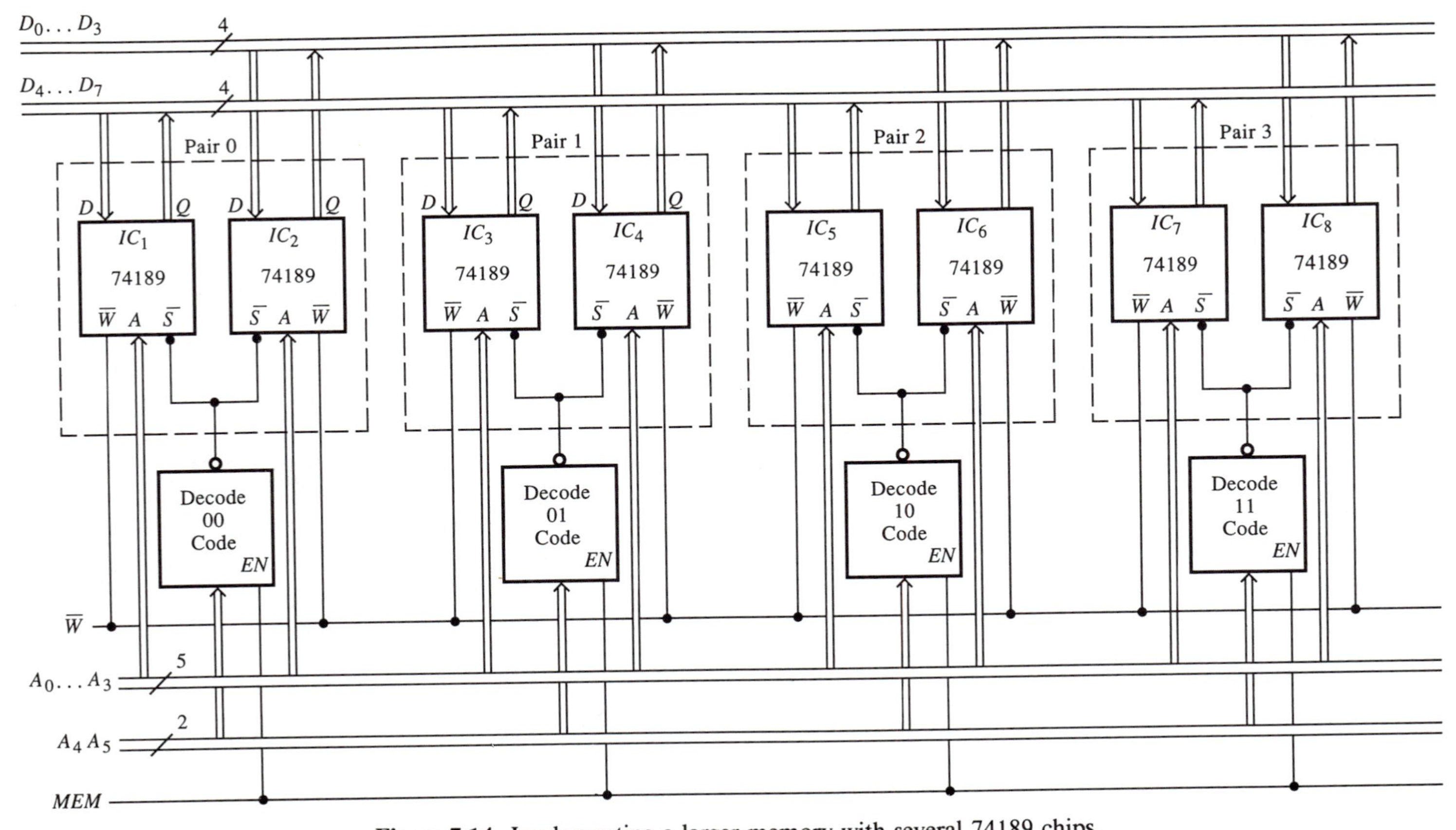


**Figure 7.14.** Implementing a larger memory with several 74189 chips.

As we know, the sixteen-word 74189 has four address lines ($16 = 2^4$) and a pair of four-bit data lines. Our circuit, however, requires six address lines and eight data lines because we desire sixty-four eight-bit "words" ($64 = 2^6$). For each word we must couple two four-bit words, and thus we need two chips to implement each sixteen-word part of the sixty-four word "address space." Four such pairs will implement all sixty-four words. Pair 0 will cover addresses 000000 to 001111; pair 1, addresses 010000 to 011111; and so on. The most significant (leftmost) two bits of the address select and enable the corresponding chip pair in the following way. All addresses referring to pair 0 start with 00, addresses referring to pair 1 start with 01, and so on. The last four bits of the address select a location within the selected pair. As an example, address 010111 selects location 0111 on both chips of pair 1 and address 110111 selects address 0111 on pair 3. Because the four least significant bits of the address determine the on-chip address, they are connected identically to each of the eight chips.

Most digital systems do not access memory in each clock cycle and memories thus require an additional signal to indicate whether access is desired. When this signal, called *MEM* in our diagram, is active, the two most significant bits of the address select a pair of chips, the *W* signal determines the direction of the transfer (read or write), and the selected pair of chips responds in the desired way. All other chips remain tristated. When the *MEM* signal is Off, no memory access is desired, no chip is selected, and all outputs are tristated.

As an example, chips $IC_1$ and $IC_2$ implement addresses 000000...001111 of the memory space. When *MEM* is active, any address of the form 00*xxxx* (that is, any address starting with 00) activates their decoder, which enables $IC_1$ and $IC_2$ through their *S* control input. All other decoders reject the address and no other memory chips are enabled. Depending on the value of *W*, a read or write operation now takes place. If the *W* signal is On, data from lines $D_0 \ldots D_3$ are written into memory location *xxxx* of $IC_1$ and data from lines $D_4 \ldots D_7$ into memory location *xxxx* of $IC_2$. If *W* is Off, data from memory location *xxxx* in $IC_1$ are read onto lines $D_0 \ldots D_3$ and data from memory location *xxxx* in $IC_2$ go on lines $D_4 \ldots D_7$.

Chips $IC_3$ and $IC_4$ similarly implement address space 010000...011111 because they are the only chips activated by addresses starting with 01. Chips $IC_5$ and $IC_6$ implement space 100000...101111, and chips $IC_7$ and $IC_8$ implement addresses 110000...111111. The decoders are usually TTL decoder chips but one can also use a logic circuit having individual gates.

To complete the design of our memory circuit, we must determine the timing constraints on the signals that control it. The basic limitation is that a selected chip may be enabled only when its data, address, and read/write control inputs are stable. Otherwise, an undesirable, catastrophic operation could result. If, for example, the chip was enabled while the *W* signal was making a transition, it could perform a spurious write operation before *W* changes.

Because the ultimate control is by the *MEM* signal, MEM must be activated after the address, data, and *W* signals have had enough time to stabilize. The standard solution is to use a two-phase clock, letting the first phase $\Phi_1$ generate the address, read/write, and data signals, and using the second phase $\Phi_2$ to activate the *MEM* signal. Such a timing diagram is shown in Figure 7.15.

Although our example uses 74189s, the same principles apply to memories using chips of other sizes and types (N-MOS, C-MOS). Dynamic RAM chips would also require a refresh circuit or a memory controller chip; ROM chips have no read/write control.

We now conclude with a few general notes on RAM and ROM chips and alternative memory technologies.

Memory chips can be implemented with different architectures. (The term "architecture" refers to a chip's appearance to the designer who will use it in a digital system.) As an example, a 2048-bit (2k-bit) ROM may be implemented as 256 eight-bit words (the 74370), 512 four-bit words (the 74371), or a 2k $\times$ 1 chip. Each architecture results in a different number of address and data pins and influences the physical size, cost, and usefulness of the chip. There is no single best memory chip architecture. As an example, eight-bit memory cells are useful because most computers are based on eight-bit codes. On the other hand, many computers perform parity checking of memory data and store eight-bit codes with a parity bit in nine-bit memory locations; this requires nine-bit or one- and eight-bit memory chips.

As we already mentioned in Chapter 4, random access memories (RAMs and ROMs) are not the only memories used in digital systems; sequential access memories are equally important. In *sequential memories*, data are stored in consecutive memory locations (Figure 7.16) and are accessed one after another in a fixed order. This results in long and uneven access times.

Sequential memories can be divided into solid state memory devices (semiconductor and magnetic bubble memories) with no moving mechanical parts

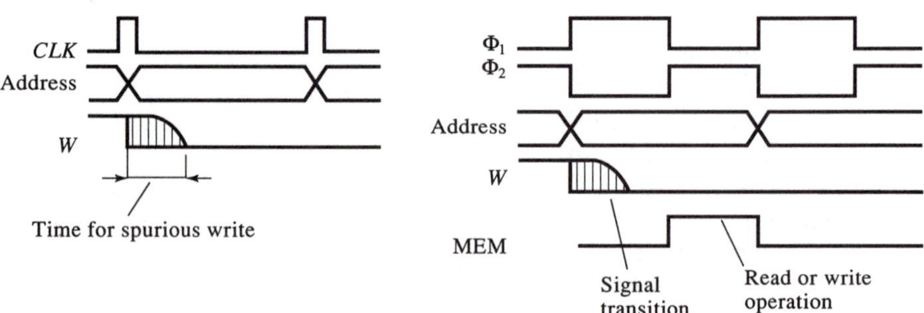


**Figure 7.15.** Spurious write operation (*left*) with incorrect signal timing; timing that eliminates spurious operation (*right*).

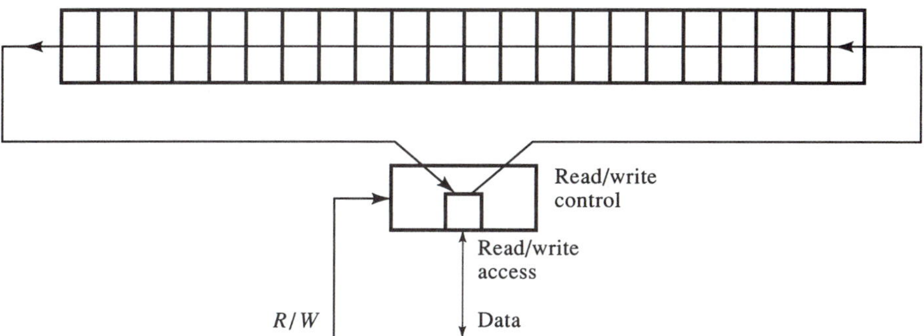


**Figure 7.16.** Principle of sequential memories.

and mechanically based devices with moving parts, such as floppy, hard, and optical disks and magnetic tapes. Whereas solid state sequential devices are relatively expensive, mechanically based devices are relatively inexpensive per stored bit. They are also nonvolatile, which means that they retain information even when power is turned Off. Magnetic bubble memories are also nonvolatile but are more expensive. They are, however, much more rugged because they have no moving parts. We will return to the subject of sequential memory devices in Chapter 11.

## Exercises

1. Explain the internal block diagram of the 74189 RAM. What is the purpose of the internal buffers?
2. The terms DRAM and SRAM are normally used only for MOS memories. If the classification were extended, would TTL RAMs be classified as static or as dynamic?
3. How would the diagram in Figure 7.14 change if the 74189 had bidirectional data pins?
4. Draw block diagrams of the following memory systems using fictitious 64 × 8 memory chips: 256 × 8, 128 × 16, and 64 × 8. Design the decoding circuit and select suitable TTL decoder chips. Assume that the data pins are bidirectional, as is normally the case. Show an alternative implementation of decoding using gates instead of decoder chips.
5. How many data and address pins are required on a 1-Mbit DRAM chip organized as 1M × 1, 512k × 2, 256k × 4, and 128k × 8? Assume that the data pins are bidirectional.
6. Draw the complete wiring diagram of our eight-bit memory circuit using the 74138 three-to-eight decoder and taking advantage of its multiple enable inputs.
7. Design a sequential memory using shift register.

## 7.4 EXAMPLE OF OPERATION OF A DIGITAL SYSTEM

Before we can design digital systems, we must be certain to understand their operation, and we will now examine the detailed operation of a simple digital system, the sequential multiplier in Figure 7.17. The circuit performs four-bit multiplication in a sequence of steps and is, presumably, part of a larger system such as a computer. The computer is controlled by a clock and

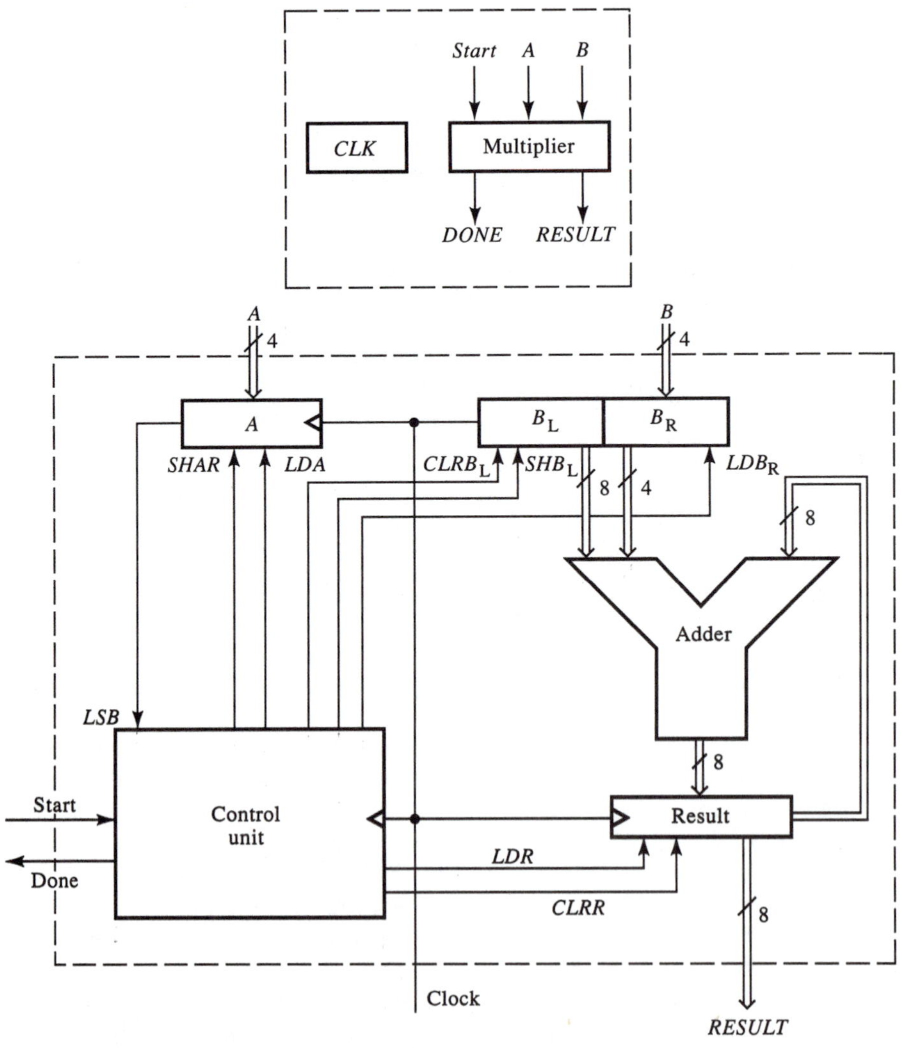


**Figure 7.17.** Block diagram of a system containing a sequential multiplier; block diagram of the multiplier.

communicates with the multiplier by inputs *A*, *B*, and *START*, and outputs *RESULT* and *DONE*.

The multiplier consists of a four-bit shift-right register *A*, eight-bit registers *B* and *RESULT*, an eight-bit adder, and a control unit. The only output of register *A* is the LSB of the code stored in it. Register *B* has two four-bit sections joined for shifting left: The left half $B_L$ can be cleared by the $CLRB_L$ signal; the right half $B_R$ can be loaded by $LDB_R$. Register *RESULT* can be cleared, loaded from the adder, or shifted left. All shifts are logic shifts and 0 is shifted into the vacated position. There is no bus because the circuit does not need it.

The internal structure of the control unit is not shown but its operation—multiplication by repeated addition and shifting—is described by the *control graph*, a transition graph with names of the active signals, in Figure 7.18.

In state (0), the initial state, the multiplier waits for the external signal *START* to make a transition to state (1). When *START* arrives, the multiplier goes through states (1) to (5) and returns to state (0), where it activates *DONE* to indicate that the calculation is finished, the result ready, and the multiplier prepared for another calculation.

Let us now analyze the operation of the multiplier in detail (Figure 7.19).

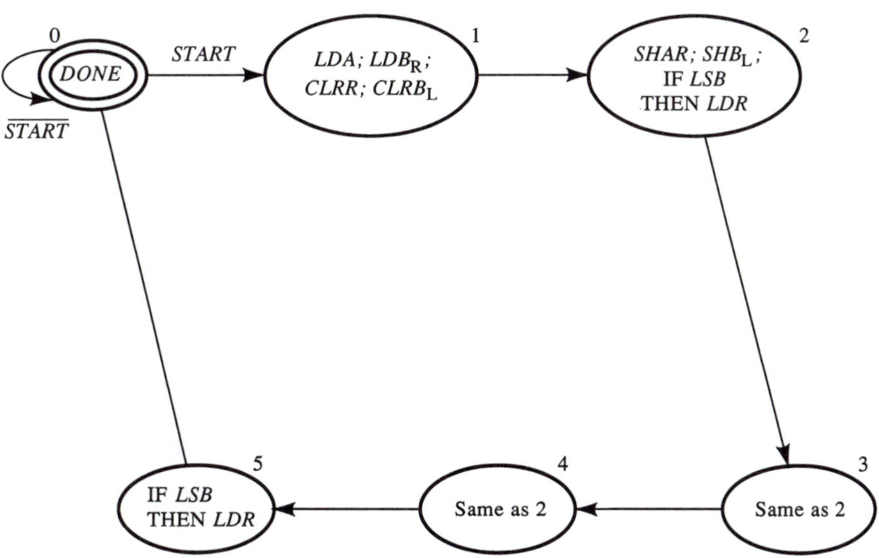


**Figure 7.18.** Control graph of the control unit. Control signals are inactive unless explicitly listed.

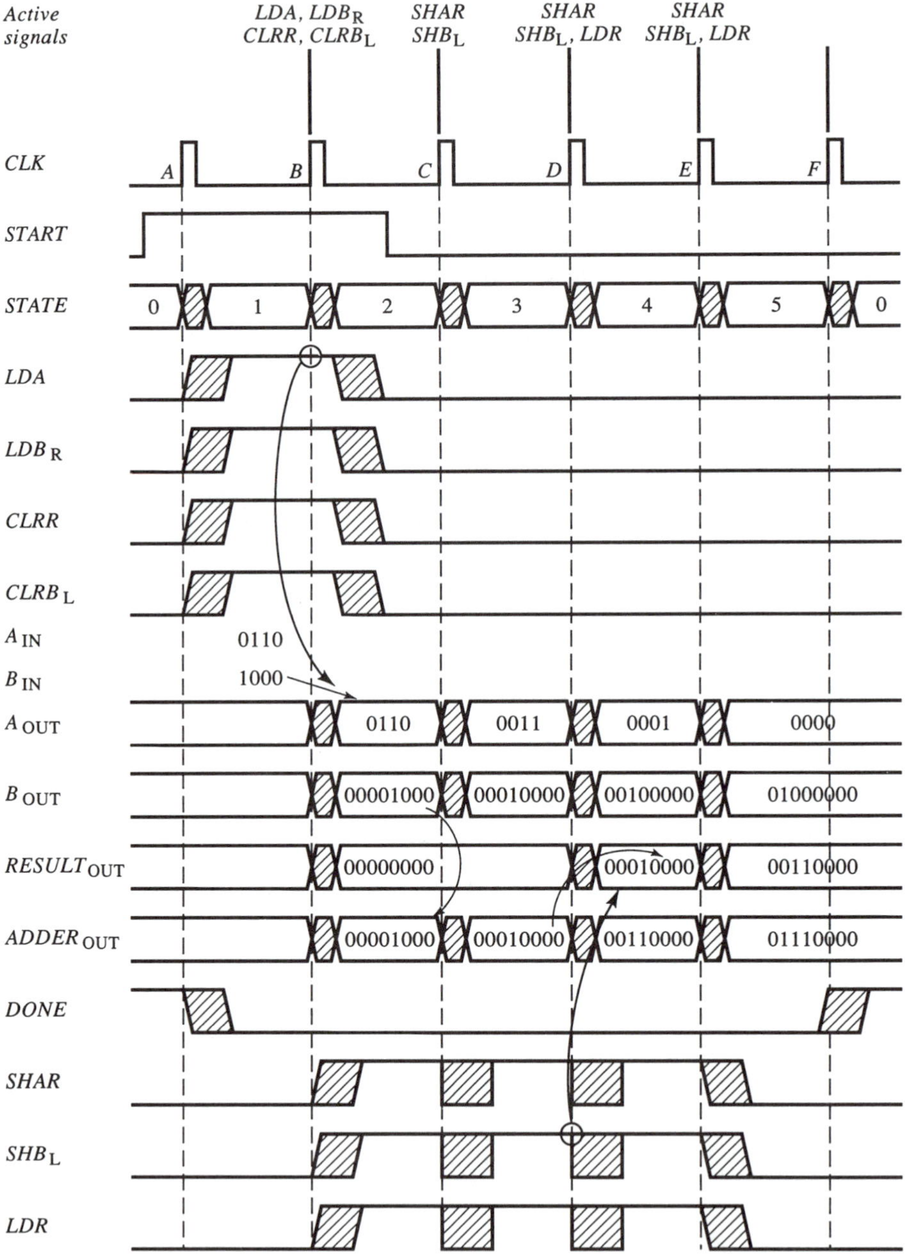


**Figure 7.19.** Example of operation with operands $A = 0110$ and $B = 1000$.

The system idles in the initial state until the external system activates the *START* signal. When this happens, the following sequence of steps takes place:

When clock edge *A* arrives, the control unit starts a transition to the new state; the hashed part of *STATE* indicates that a transition is under way. After the necessary delays, *STATE* reaches state (1) and begins to generate the prescribed control signals. This requires another delay and eventually *LDA*, $LDB_R$, *CLRR*, $CLRB_L$, and *DONE* are activated and stabilize. Nothing else happens because no other control signals were On at the moment of arrival of edge *A*.

When clock edge *B* arrives, the control signals generated in state (1) are active and force register *A* to start loading the values now on its inputs. These values are stored and become available on output $A_{out}$ some time later. Other control signals have similar effects and all registers assume new values that appear on the adder's inputs. (For instance, *A* becomes 0110 $=6_{10}$, *B* becomes 1000 $= 8_{10}$.) The final outputs of the adder stabilize some time after the output of registers.

Starting on the same edge, the control unit begins a transition to state (2). When it reaches state (2), it begins to calculate new control signals. Eventually, *SHAR* and *SHBL* are activated but *LDR* is not because the LSB of the stable value now in *A* is 0.

When clock edge *C* arrives, *SHAR* and *SHBL* are On and stable, and registers *A* and *B* thus start shifting. Some time later, their outputs stabilize and after a few moments, the sum of *B* and *RESULT* appears on the output of the adder. At the same time the control unit makes a transition to state (3) and begins generating control signals *SHAR*, *SHBL*, and *LDR*. Signal *LDR* is produced because the value of the LSB is now 1.

When clock edge *D* arrives, the active control signals are *SHAR*, *SHBL*, and *LDR*. Signals *SHAR* and *SHBL* start shifting *A* and *B*, and *LDR* loads *RESULT* with 00010000, the value on the input of *RESULT* at the moment of edge arrival. After a little while, *A* and *B* stabilize at the value of the shifted codes, and *RESULT* stabilizes at the new sum. The adder starts adding the new *B* and *RESULT*, and the sum stabilizes before the next edge. Edge *D* also activates the control unit to make a transition to state (4), generate control signals, and so on.

The sequence continues in this way until state (0) is reached again and *DONE* is activated. The value 00110000 $= 48_{10}$, the correct product of 6 and 8, is now in *RESULT*. The multiplier activates the *DONE* signal to indicate that the product is available and starts idling in state (0), waiting for *START* to trigger another multiplication with new operands supplied by the system.

The design and construction of a similar multiplier is suggested as a lab project in Appendix 2.

**Exercises**

1. Show the sequence of steps executed by the multiplier for the input combinations below. Check the correctness of the result.

$$A = 1001,\ B = 1011$$

$$A = 0011,\ B = 0110$$

2. Our multiplier requires the same amount of time for each multiplication. This is a waste because some operand pairs require fewer steps: For instance, $A \times B$, with $A = 1XXX$, requires all five register loads; in other words, five steps. However, $A = 01XX$ could be done in four steps; $A = 001X$ could be done in three steps; $A = 0001$ could be done in two steps, and $A = 0000$ could be done in one step. Modify the control graph and the block diagram to take advantage of these findings and to speed up the operation. What is the price of the increase in speed?

## 7.5 DESIGN EXAMPLE

To design a digital system we must

obtain the specification, including the detailed control graph and a block diagram with all major blocks, data paths, and control signals

design the control unit and other parts

select components to implement the logic diagram

perform timing analysis to confirm that the system can operate at the required speed.

We will now demonstrate this procedure on an example. The circuit that we will design does not perform any useful function, and was selected because it is simple and illustrates the main aspects of digital systems and the design process.

We are to design a system whose main parts are registers $A$ and $B$ and a four-bit ALU, and whose desired behavior is as follows:

```
REPEAT
   Add A to B;
   IF the result is zero
```

```
  THEN
    BEGIN
      Copy result to A;
      Subtract B from A;
      Copy A to B
      Copy result of subtraction to A;
    END
  ELSE
    BEGIN
      Copy result to B;
      Add A to B;
      Copy B to A;
      IF the result of addition was 0
        THEN copy it to B;
    END
FOREVER;
```

**Step 1 — Specification**

The specification of the circuit is incomplete: Data paths are not prescribed, control signals remain to be specified, and the functional description must be converted into a sequence of states and events. However, the information is sufficient to let us make the necessary decisions and to derive the complete block and control diagrams. Our first conclusions are as follows:

The description of the behavior shows that the result of an arithmetic operation ($RESULT = 0$) is needed several steps after it was calculated. We will use flip-flop $Z$ to hold it.

To isolate the output of the adder from the registers, we will connect its output to register *RESULT*.

Data is transferred between $A$, $B$, and *RESULT* and we will use a bus with bidirectional and unidirectional connections.

With these extensions of the original specification, all required transfers are possible and the detailed block diagram with all parts and paths can be constructed (Figure 7.20). This lets us convert the behavioral description into a control graph (Figure 7.21). The following notes explain some of the details:

If an arithmetic operation is required, the control signal that initiates it is created at the start of the clock period and the result becomes available

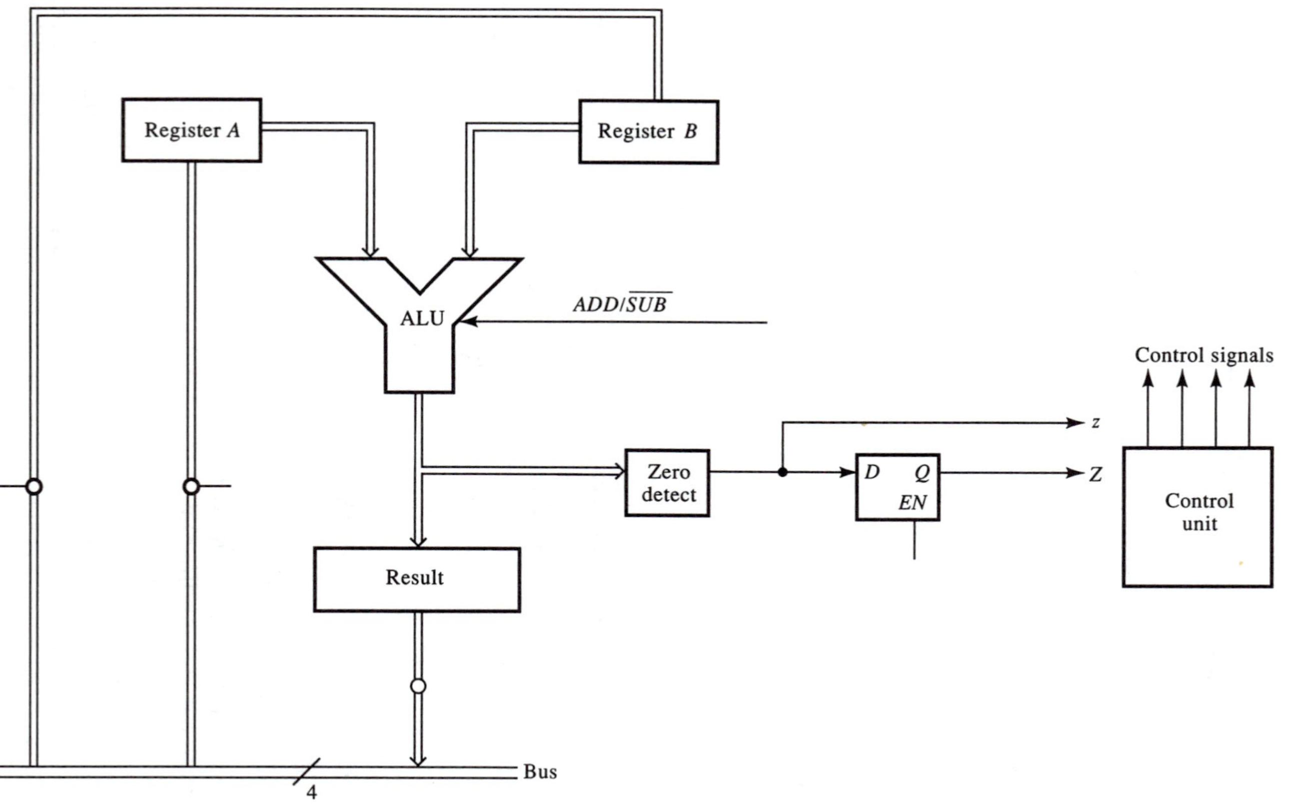


**Figure 7.20.** Block diagram of the system.

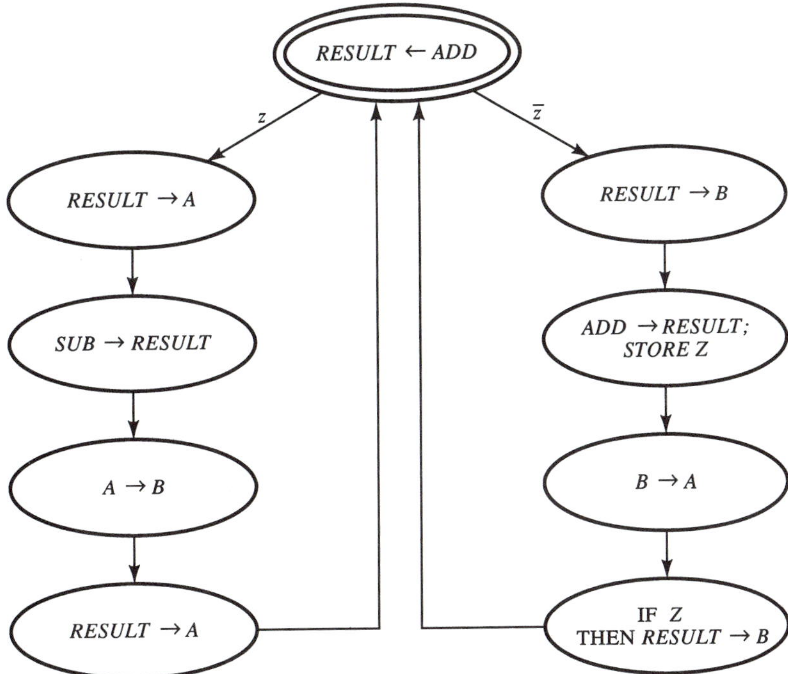


**Figure 7.21.** Control graph of the system. Note that symbols $z$ (current *RESULT*=0) and $Z$ (the value of $z$ stored in flip-flop $Z$) represent different signals.

before the next active clock edge. The ALU operation and the storage of the result can thus be activated in the same state.

The value of $z$ needed to decide between a transition to state (1) or to state (6) is calculated in state (0) and is available before the end of state (0) marked by the next edge. It can thus be used to force the sequencer of the control unit to make the correct transition.

It might appear that events in states (3) and (4) could be executed in a single state with the following effect:

> Transfer *RESULT*→*A* causes the output of *RESULT*, the value in the register before the edge, to be passed to the input of *A* and loaded into *A* at the edge of the next clock pulse.
>
> Transfer *A*→*B* loads the value that is present in *A* in the current cycle into *B* at the edge of the next clock pulse.
>
> Altogether, the value loaded into *B* is the value stored in *A* before it was replaced by the value from *RESULT*.

This analysis is correct except that we have only one bus and only one code can be on the bus during one state. Simultaneous transfers such as *RESULT*→*A* and *A*→*B* are thus impossible.

States (8) and (9) could also be merged into one state if it were not for the bus. As it is, state (8) is wasted when $z = 0$.

The last two notes show how buses reduce the amount of communication possible at one time and slow down the system. The decision to use a bus and how many buses to use is a tradeoff between speed, complexity, and cost.

We now have the control graph and a complete block diagram with all parts and data paths. We can determine the list of necessary control signals from the block diagram and the control sequence as follows:

In state (0) we must load register *RESULT*, and this requires signal *LDRESULT*.

To load register *A* in state (1) we need signal *LDA*.

Register *RESULT* must be copied to *A* in state (1) and this requires the activation of the path from *RESULT* to the bus and to the input of register *A*. We thus need control signals *R*→*BUS* and *A*→*BUS*.

Control signal *B*→*BUS* is needed for the transfer of *RESULT* to *B* in state (6).

Register *B* is loaded in state (6) and we thus need signal *LDB*.

The ALU either adds or subtracts and we thus need $ADD/\overline{SUB}$.

To load the *Z* flip-flop in state (7) we need *LDZ*.

In summary, the control unit must produce control signals *LDA*, *LDB*, *LDRESULT*, *LDZ*, $ADD/\overline{SUB}$, *A*→*BUS*, *B*→*BUS*, and *R*→*BUS*.

Note that the *RESULT*→bus path is unidirectional because only transfers out of *RESULT* to the bus are required, but the *A*→bus and *B*→bus paths are bidirectional because transfers out of *A* and *B*, as well as to *A* and *B*, are required.

This completes the identification of data and control signal paths and we can proceed to the design of the components.

### Step 2—Design of Components

All parts except the zero decoder and the control unit are available as off-the-shelf chips. The zero decoder is to be On iff the result is 0; in other words, if none of the result bits is 1:

$$z = \overline{F_3 + F_2 + F_1 + F_0}$$

Finally, we must design the control unit, the state machine, which produces the transitions between states and generates the control signals that trigger the prescribed events. It is convenient to divide the control unit into two modules that implement these functions separately (Figure 7.22): the *sequencer*, which enforces transitions, and the *signal generator*, which produces control signals activating the required actions. This division is equivalent to the division of a sequential circuit into a sequencer and an output circuit, and the design also follows a similar procedure.

There are nine states and we will thus use the 74162 fully synchronous presettable decade counter as the basis of the sequencer. Following the procedure established in Chapter 5 we will start with a code assignment that takes advantage of counting and then design the *LD* and data tables (Figure 7.23). Because the signal generator will need states and not their codes, the output of the counter is connected to a decoder.

To get a better understanding of the system, it is useful to divide the control signals into three categories:

Register and flip-flop loads *LDA*, *LDB*, *LDRESULT*, and *LDZ*

Control point signals *R→BUS*, *A→BUS*, and *B→BUS*

ALU function select $ADD/\overline{SUB}$

To find the formulas for the individual signals, we must consider all the states in which they are required and the conditions under which they occur.

Signal *LDA* is activated when we need to load data into register *A*; in other words, when *A* is the destination of a transfer:

$$\ldots \rightarrow A$$

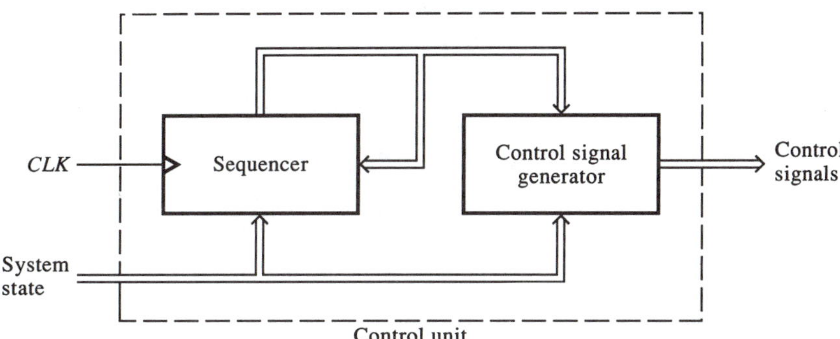


**Figure 7.22.** Sequencer–signal generator block diagram of the control unit.

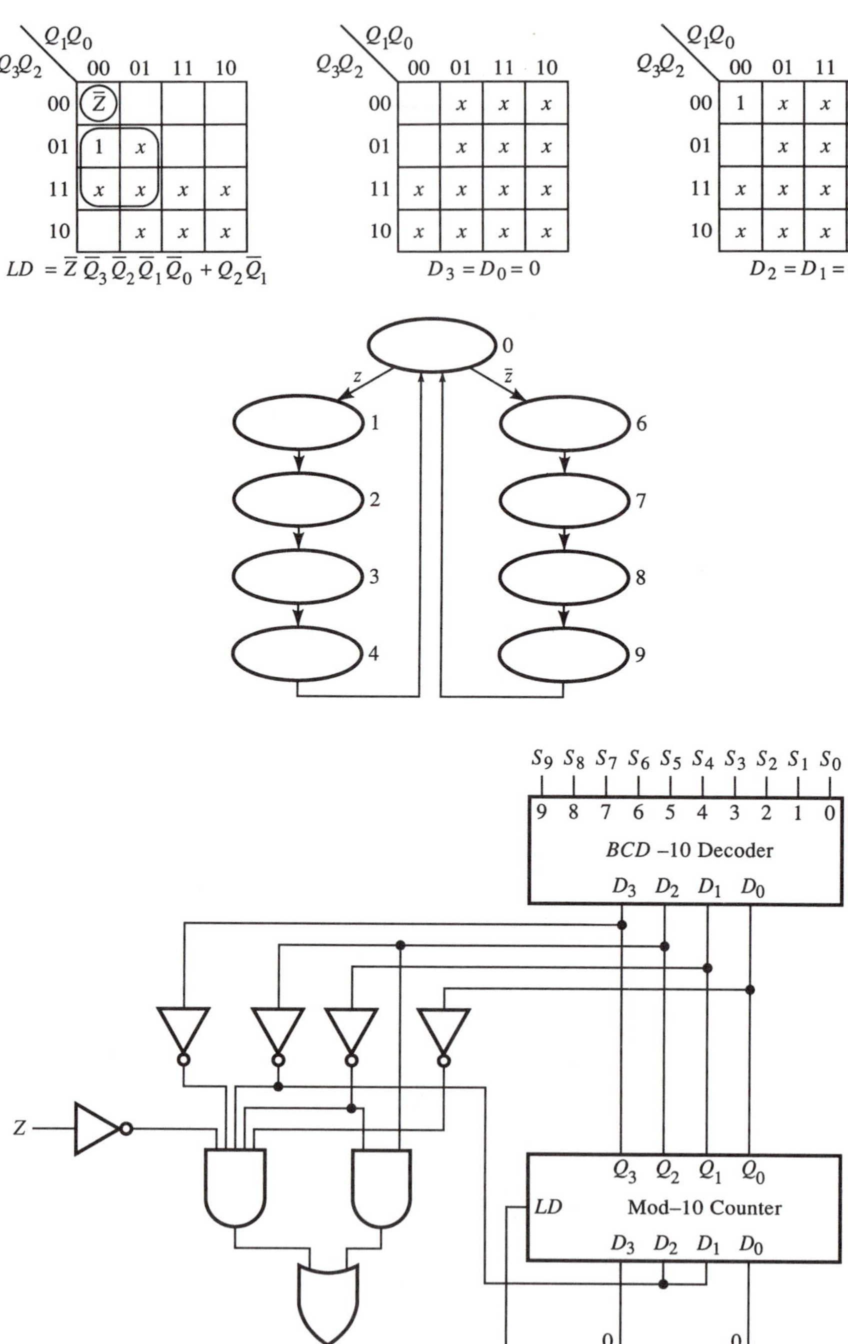


**Figure 7.23.** Transition graph (without control signals), excitation tables, and logic diagram of the sequencer.

The control graph in Figure 7.21 shows that this happens in states (1), (4), and (8). No additional conditions are prescribed and so

$$LDA = S_1 + S_4 + S_8$$

Here $S_1$, $S_4$, and $S_8$ are the outputs of the sequencer's state decoder.
Signal *LDB* is activated in states (3), (6), and if *Z* is set, in state (9):

$$LDB = S_3 + S_6 + Z \cdot S_9$$

Signal *LDRESULT* saves the result of an arithmetic operation. As this happens in states (0), (2), and (7).

$$LDRESULT = S_0 + S_2 + S_7$$

Signal *LDZ* is activated in state (7)

$$LDZ = S_7$$

Signal *R→BUS* is activated when *RESULT* is the source of a data transfer over the bus. Figure 7.20 and the transition graph show that this happens in states (1), (4), (6), and (9) (if *Z* is set):

$$R{\rightarrow}BUS = S_1 + S_4 + S_6 + Z \cdot S_9$$

Note that we have used signal *R→BUS* rather than *BUS→R*. This is because the loading of the register is controlled by *LDRESULT* and the bus-to-register path can thus be open by default.
It is left to the reader to show that

$$A{\rightarrow}BUS = S_3 \qquad \text{for } A{\rightarrow}B$$

$$B{\rightarrow}BUS = S_8 \qquad \text{for } B{\rightarrow}A$$

$$ADD/\overline{SUB} = S_0 + S_7$$

The formula for $ADD/\overline{SUB}$ implies that the ALU subtracts in all states other than (0) and (7). Although we do not want to subtract in all of these states, the extra operations do not create any problems. The rest of the circuit is unaffected by the output of the ALU, except in state (2), because the ALU output is isolated from the bus by register *RESULT*.
The logic design of the control signal generator (Figure 7.24) and the whole control unit is now complete.

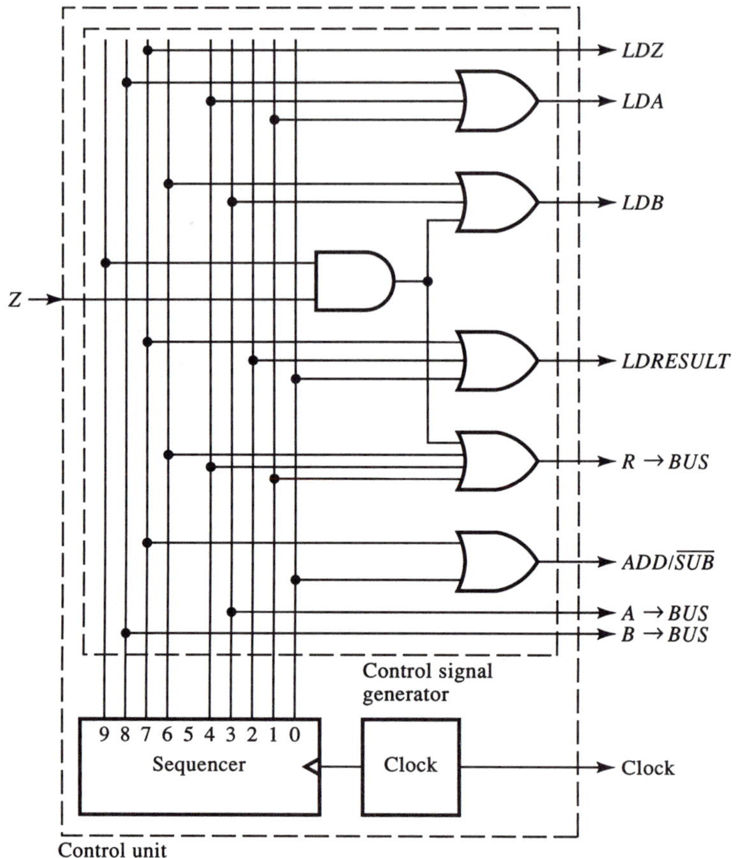


**Figure 7.24.** Control signal generator.

## Step 3—Components

Now that we have the logic diagram of the control unit we must select components to implement it. We will start with the following chips:

7442 BCD-to-decimal decoder, $T_p = 30$ nsec.

74162 Fully synchronous presettable positive-edge triggered decade counter, $T_{su} = 25$ nsec, $T_p = 35$ nsec.

74173 Four-bit D-type positive-edge triggered PIPO register with tristate outputs, $T_{su} = 10$ nsec, $T_p = 43$ nsec.

74181 Four-bit ALU, $T_p = 35$ nsec. Note that ALU function control requires that the $ADD/\overline{SUB}$ signal be encoded to generate the necessary signals. This is left as an exercise.

74243 Noninverting transceiver, $T_e = 30$ nsec (to disable or to enable and transfer).

74244 Noninverting line driver, $T_e = 30$ nsec.

74379 D-flip-flop with enable, $T_{su} = 25$ nsec, $T_p = 27$ nsec, $T_H = 5$ nsec.

All of these registers and counters are positive-edge triggered. Because the outputs of the 7442 decoder are active Low, we must modify our control formulas as follows:

$$\begin{aligned}
LDA &= S_1 + S_4 + S_8 \\
&= \overline{\overline{S_1}\,\overline{S_4}\,\overline{S_8}} \\
LDB &= S_3 + S_6 + z\cdot S_9 \\
&= \overline{\overline{S_3}\,\overline{S_6}\,\overline{(z\cdot S_9)}} \\
\overline{LDRESULT} &= S_0 + S_2 + S_7 \\
&= \overline{\overline{S_0}\,\overline{S_2}\,\overline{S_7}} \\
R{\rightarrow}BUS &= S_1 + S_4 + S_6 + z\cdot S_9 \\
&= \overline{\overline{S_1}\,\overline{S_4}\,\overline{S_6}\,\overline{(z\cdot S_9)}} \\
ADD/\overline{SUB} &= S_0 + S_7 \\
&= \overline{\overline{S_0}\,\overline{S_7}}
\end{aligned}$$

The $LD$ input of the 74162 counter is also active Low and its excitation circuit must thus be modified as well. Figure 7.25 shows how this can be done by "moving the bubbles" to get a circuit realizable with commercial gates. The enable signal of the 74379 flip-flop is active Low and the inverted $S_7$ signal can thus drive it directly. The same applies to the 74243 transceiver.

Finally, we select gates to implement the combinational glue:

7400 Two-input NAND, $T_p = 22$ nsec

7404 Hex inverter, $T_p = 22$ nsec

7410 Three-input NAND, $T_p = 22$ nsec

7420 Four-input NAND, $T_p = 22$ nsec

7408 Two-input AND, $T_p = 20$ nsec

7430 Eight-input NAND, $T_p = 22$ nsec

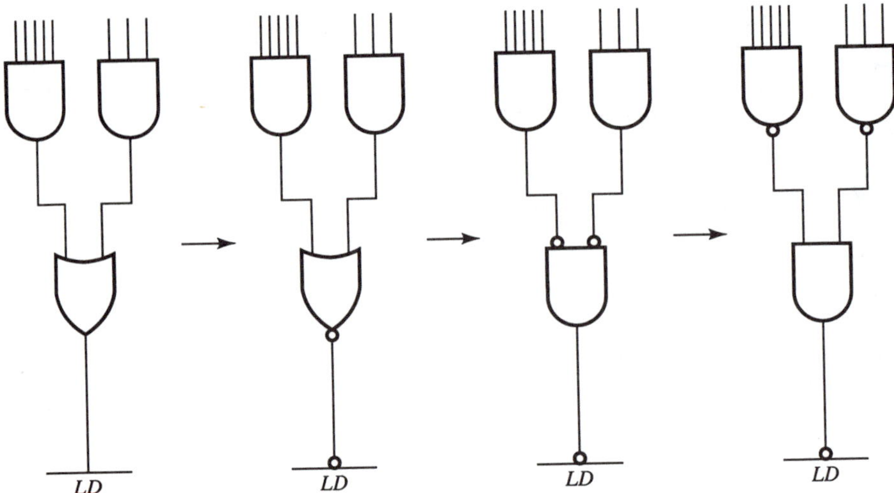


**Figure 7.25.** Transformation of the *LD* excitation circuit.

## Step 4—Timing Analysis

When the clock outputs an active edge, the system executes actions corresponding to the control signals active at the moment of the edge, makes a transition to the new state, and produces control signals. (The principles were demonstrated in Section 7.4.) The following sequence of events thus occurs:

> To enter a new state, the control unit processes the excitation signals established in the previous state. The state counter advances or loads and the stabilized count, the state code, propagates through the state decoder.
>
> State information propagates through the control circuits and creates stable control signals to activate control points, Loads, and ALU operations, if any.
>
> Before the next clock edge arrives, inputs of all storage elements must be stable for a time at least equal to the longest setup time.

Timing analysis must establish conditions under which all these restrictions can be satisfied with the switching parameters of the selected components. The analysis is performed in the usual way: We find the data and signal paths that seem to require the longest propagation time and calculate the total delay by adding the corresponding component delays.

According to Figure 7.26, the following paths are probably the longest ones and should be analyzed. The following analysis is illustrated in Figure 7.27.

Path 1 is Counter→decoder→control circuit→ALU→*RESULT*.

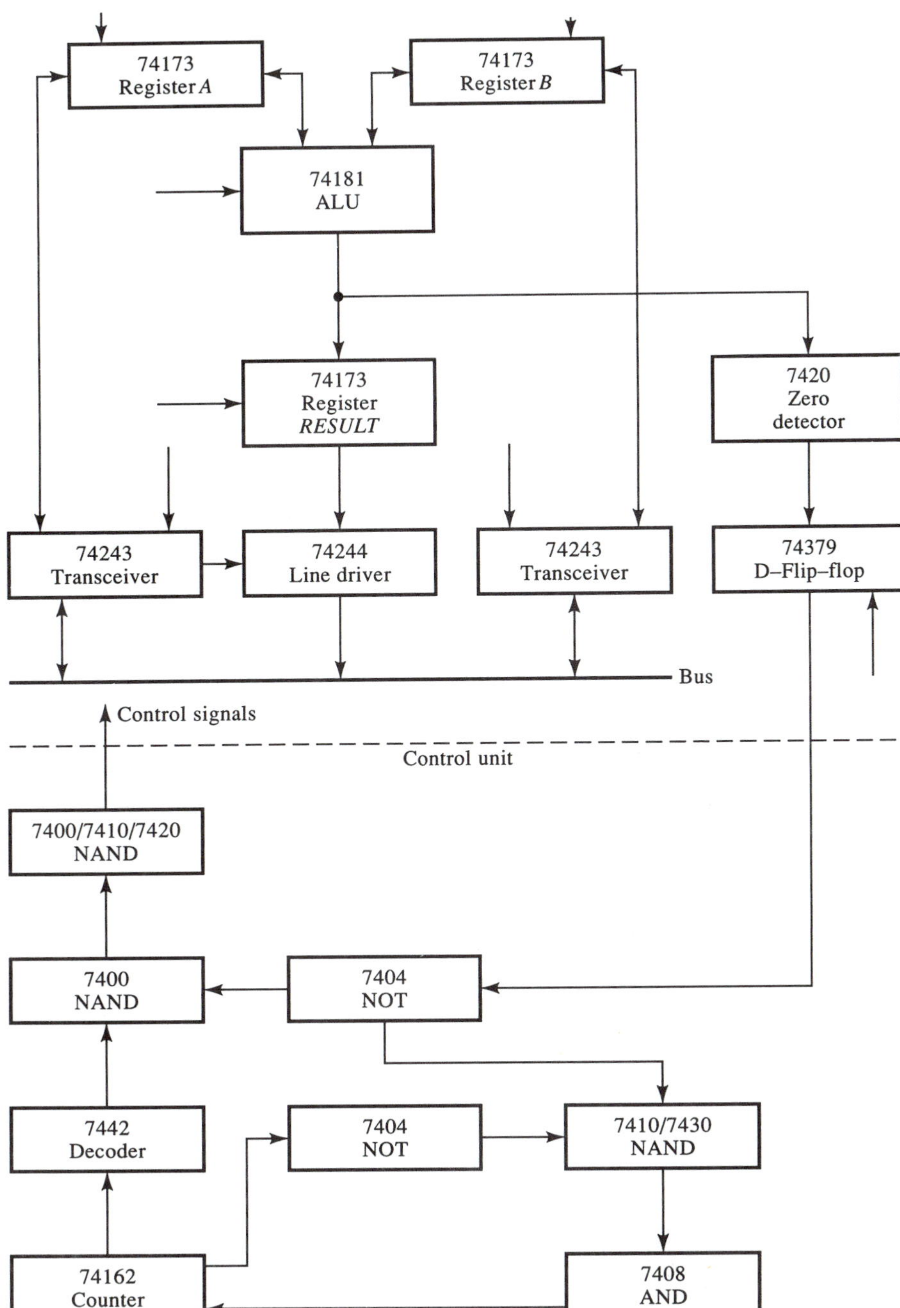


**Figure 7.26.** Schematic diagram of the data paths with the selected TTL chips.

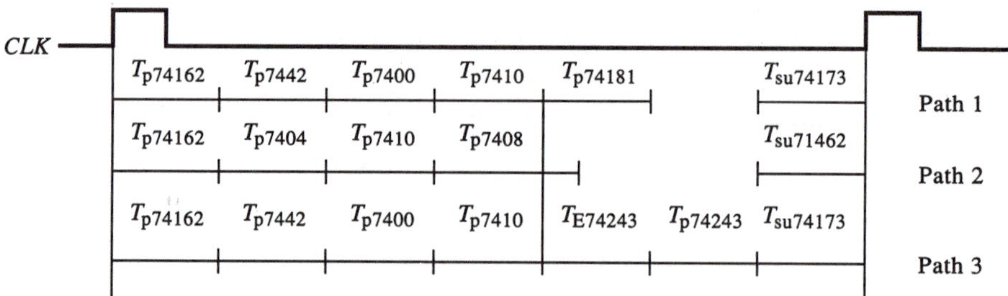


**Figure 7.27.** Delays associated with the three selected signal paths.

This is the

$$\ldots \rightarrow RESULT$$

path. The calculation is as follows:

$$\begin{aligned}
T_1 &= T_c + T_{p74181} + T_{su74173} \\
&= T_{p74162} + T_{p7442} + T_{p7400} + T_{p7410} + T_{p74181} + T_{su74173} \\
&= (35 + 30 + 22 + 22) + (35 + 10) \\
&= 154 \text{ nsec}
\end{aligned}$$

The value of $T_c$, the time needed to produce the control signals, is 109 nsec. Path 2 is Counter→decoder→excitation circuit→counter. This is the sequencer path. The corresponding calculation is

$$\begin{aligned}
T_2 &= T_{p74162} + T_{p7404} + T_{p7410} + T_{p7408} + T_{su74162} \\
&= 35 + 22 + 22 + 27 + 25 \\
&= 131 \text{ nsec}
\end{aligned}$$

Path 3 is Counter→decoder→control circuit→transceiver→destination register. This path sets up and performs the $A \rightarrow B$ data transfer. The corresponding calculation is

$$\begin{aligned}
T_3 &= T_c + T_{e74243} + T_{p74243} + T_{su74173} \\
&= 109 + 30 + 18 + 10 \\
&= 167 \text{ nsec}
\end{aligned}$$

This calculation is based on the fact that to get the signal from $A$ to $B$ we must first enable the transceivers (both are enabled simultaneously) and let the signal that arrived through the first enabled transceiver to propagate through the second transceiver and reach the input of the destination register. Because the enable delay $T_e$ is counted from the activation of the enable signal to the appearance of a stable signal on the output of the transceiver, the delay of both control points is included in $T_e$. As both transceivers are enabled simultaneously, we need only count $T_e$ once and add the propagation delay for the second transceiver to it.

Assuming that the above three paths are indeed critical, we can now calculate the minimum acceptable separation of clock pulses, that is, the duration of one state:

$$\begin{aligned} T_{\text{min}} &= \max(T_1, T_2, T_3) \\ &= 167 \text{ nsec} \end{aligned}$$

The duration of one state in a digital system is usually called the period of the *machine cycle.* The corresponding maximum clock frequency is

$$\begin{aligned} f_{\text{max}} &= 1/T_{\text{min}} \\ &= \frac{1}{0.000000167} \\ &= 6 \text{ MHz} \end{aligned}$$

A maximum of some six million states can thus be executed in one second.

Finally, we must check the hold time of the D-flip-flop. The $D$ input of the zero-flag flip-flop must not change within $T_{h74379}$ $T_h$ after the clock edge. The $D$ input comes from the zero-detect circuit that depends on the output of the ALU. This in turn depends on the outputs of registers $A$ and $B$. The path's minimum delay is the sum of the minimum delays of the individual components, which is certainly longer than the 5-nsec hold time of the 74379. The hold time limit is thus satisfied.

This completes the design and timing analysis of our system. We have again ignored delays along wires connecting individual chips because they are negligible in our circuit.

In closing, we will now recapitulate the design procedure:

1. Obtain the initial specification of the system consisting of a rough block diagram and a description of the desired sequence of operations.
2. Construct the detailed control sequence and the block diagram with main modules and data paths. If the system is simple, the control sequence may be represented by a control graph, otherwise a more formal and compact specification is needed. Make sure that the block diagram and the control graph are consistent and that they allow conflict-free execution of all operations specified within each state. Pay particular attention to the rule that only one data transfer is allowed over a single bus at a time.

3. Define the data paths and control signals needed to implement the prescribed operation.
4. Design the processing modules.
5. Design the control unit:
   a. Construct the sequencer to implement the desired transitions. Use flip-flops or counters and methods from Chapter 5.
   b. Construct the control circuit to generate control signals from formulas containing states in which the signals are to be generated and conditions under which they occur.
6. Select components and obtain their parameters. Make sure that operating conditions like fan-out constraints are satisfied.
7. Perform timing analysis.

In all steps, take advantage of available computer aids to speed up design and obtain more reliable results.

## Exercises

1. Redesign the sequencer and control signal generator using a PAL and compare the number of chips required. Note that the implementation may be impossible if one blindly follows the structure developed above because the PAL chip may not have enough modules to implement the counter and the state decoder separately. This problem can be solved by generating control signals without decoding the state code.
2. We omitted the $ADD/\overline{SUB}$ control of the ALU. Add this circuit and determine how it affects the timing analysis.
3. Check that no suspicious paths were missed in our timing analysis.
4. There are two possible paths through our control graph. Calculate the number of machine cycles required by each.
5. Could we increase the speed of the control unit by using different components, such as flip-flops, MUXs, PALs, or PLAs? What would be the effect of using faster technology, such as the 74S family?
6. In our calculations, we used values from the maximum-delay column in the data book. How would the numbers change if we used typical delays? A typical delay is a delay expected in typical operating conditions; *max* values are those expected at the limit of allowed operating conditions.
7. The time to execute one complete pass through the control sequence depends not only on the length of the machine cycle but also on the number of states that must be executed. To maximize the speed of the system we must therefore primarily optimize the control sequence as well. A detailed study of the control sequence and the circuit may reveal ways in which this can be achieved. Examine our problem and simplify

its control graph if possible. Any changes (including structural) are allowed as long as the overall function is preserved.

8. How much time is needed for three complete cycles through the complete transition sequence assuming that initial conditions are $A = 0000$ and $B = 0010$?
9. Design and analyze the system from Section 7.4.
10. Design and analyze the system from Exercise 1 in Section 7.4.
11. Design a four-bit divider.
12. Design a system that controls the transfer of data from one block of memory to another. When activated by a *START* signal, the control unit loads the start address of the source of data, the start address of the destination of the data, and the number of eight-bit words to be transmitted. These values are supplied from outside. It then uses the system clock to transmit the data and activates the *DONE* signal when the transfer is finished. This system is similar to DMA controllers used by most computers for very fast data transfers (Chapter 12).
13. Add a reset–initialize module to the circuit designed in this section.

## 7.6 MICROPROGRAMMING—ANOTHER METHOD OF CONTROLLER DESIGN

We have seen that a control graph unambiguously describes the behavior of a control unit and can be used to trace its operation quite mechanically. One can even use the control graph to develop a computer program to simulate the control unit at the level of register operations, transfers, and control signals.

If the control unit can be simulated by a computer program, couldn't one generate the control signals themselves by an inexpensive computer and thus implement the control unit?

The idea is valid but impractical in this form because an inexpensive general-purpose computer could not produce control signals fast enough to control most digital systems. The reason is that because of their generality such computers are too slow to implement many specific applications. Consequently, to implement program-generated control, we need a special-purpose computer-like machine dedicated to the specific control problem.

A control unit constructed on this principle is called a *microprogrammed* control unit. Control units designed as in Section 7.5 are called *hardwired.* A microprogrammed control unit thus generates transitions and signals by executing a special program stored in its memory. The program is called a *microprogram* and its instructions are called *microinstructions* or microcodes. (Do not confuse microprogramming with programming microcomputers.)

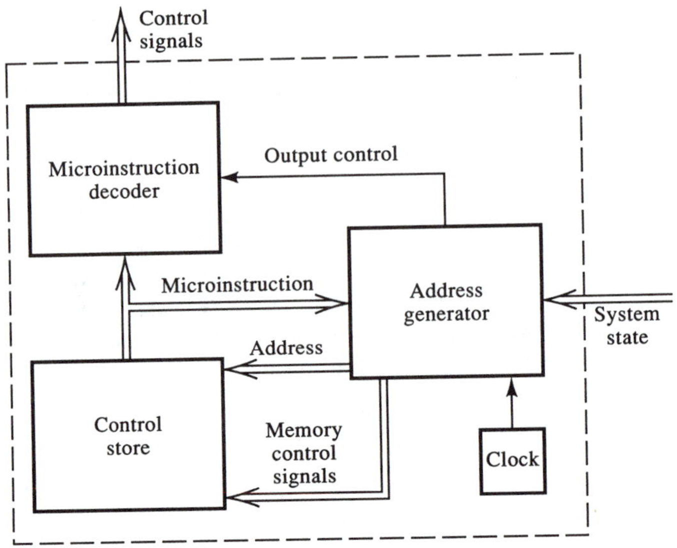


**Figure 7.28.** Block diagram of a microprogrammed control unit.

The control unit of a microprogrammed machine (Figure 7.28) consists of a memory to store the microprogram (the control store), and a controller (control unit). The controller contains a circuit that calculates the address from which the next microinstruction is fetched (the address generator) and a microinstruction decoder to convert the fetched codes into control signals.

How does a microprogrammed control unit work? Assume that the machine has been reset to its initial state (Figure 7.29). The following events then take place:

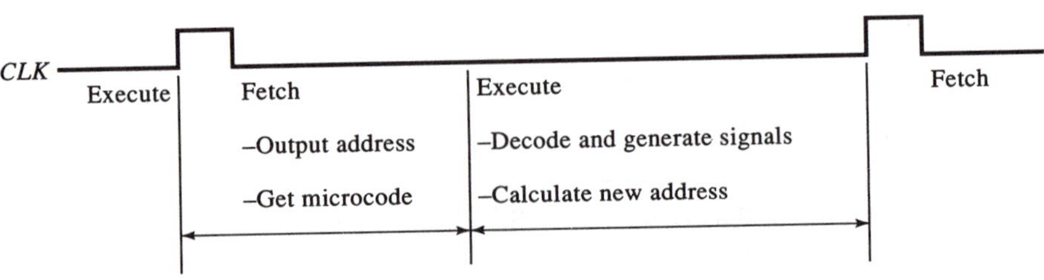


**Figure 7.29.** Operation of a microprogrammed control unit.

1. Fetch microcode

   The address generator sends the address of the next microinstruction to the control store.

   The control store outputs the code.

2. Execute microcode

   The microcode decoder converts the microinstruction into control signals.

   The address generator calculates the address of the next microinstruction.

   After leaving the control signals active for the required length of time, the clock forces the transition to the next state and the fetch–execute sequence is repeated with the next microinstruction.

To demonstrate the principle of microprogrammed control, we will now redesign the hardwired control unit from Section 7.5 as a microprogrammed unit. The rest of the system will remain unchanged. This example is intended only as an introduction to microprogrammed control. We will solve a more substantial problem in Chapter 10.

To design a microprogrammed control unit, we must write the microprogram and construct the address generator and the microinstruction decoder.

The microprogram is a sequence of microcodes, and we must first define the microcode format. That is, we must decide how many bits a microcode should have and what their meaning will be. Because the ultimate purpose of the microcode is to produce control signals, it is natural to assign one bit to each control signal that we want to generate. When the bit is On, the signal is activated; when it is Off, the signal is disabled. In the case of the system in Section 7.5, the control unit must produce eight control signals; we will thus use eight-bit microcodes and assign their bits as in Figure 7.30. With this approach, signal values are equal to the values of the bits in the microcode, there is no encoding and we do not need a microcode decoder.

The strategy that we have adopted—direct representation of signals by bits—is called "horizontal" microprogramming. It eliminates or simplifies the decoder but requires as many bits per microcode as there are signals. For more substantial systems, this could result in a very large (wide) control store. An alternative approach would be to encode the signals into short codes to minimize the length of the microcode, and to use a decoder to convert the microcodes into control signals. Such an approach is called "vertical" microprogramming. In practice, control units do not use pure horizontal or pure vertical microprogramming but a compromise between minimal and maximal encoding that gives a good tradeoff between complexity, cost, and speed.

In our approach, each microinstruction represents one state and microcodes can thus be stored at addresses identical to state numbers: the micro-

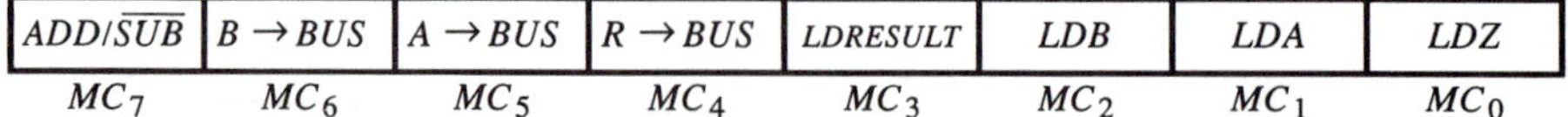


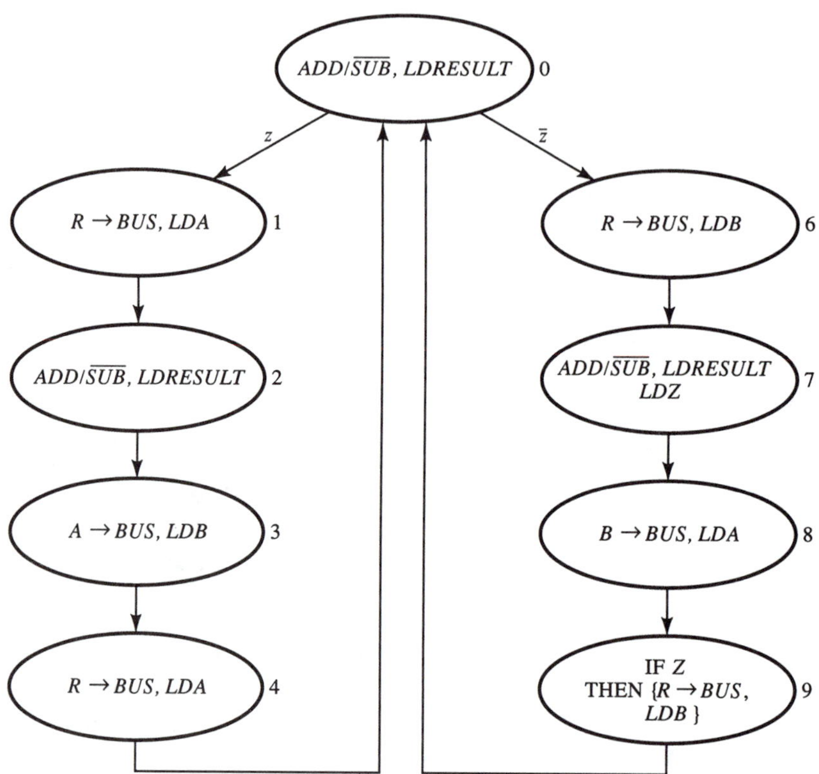


**Figure 7.30.** Microcode format and the control graph.

code of state (0) at address 0, the microcode of state (1) at address 1, and so on. Because the sequencer of our hardwired control unit calculates state numbers, it can be used as the address generator (Figure 7.31). Note that we omitted the state decoder because we are using state codes as addresses.

To complete the microprogrammed control unit, it only remains to write the microprogram by converting each state of the control graph (Figure 7.30) into a microinstruction. We will now show how this is done by analyzing a few microinstructions.

The microcode stored at address 0, the code for state (0), is 10001000 because only signals *ADD/$\overline{SUB}$* and *LDRESULT* are On in state (0). The microcode at address 1 is 00010010 because only signals *R→BUS* and *LDA* are On in state (1). The microcode at address 2 is 00001000 because only

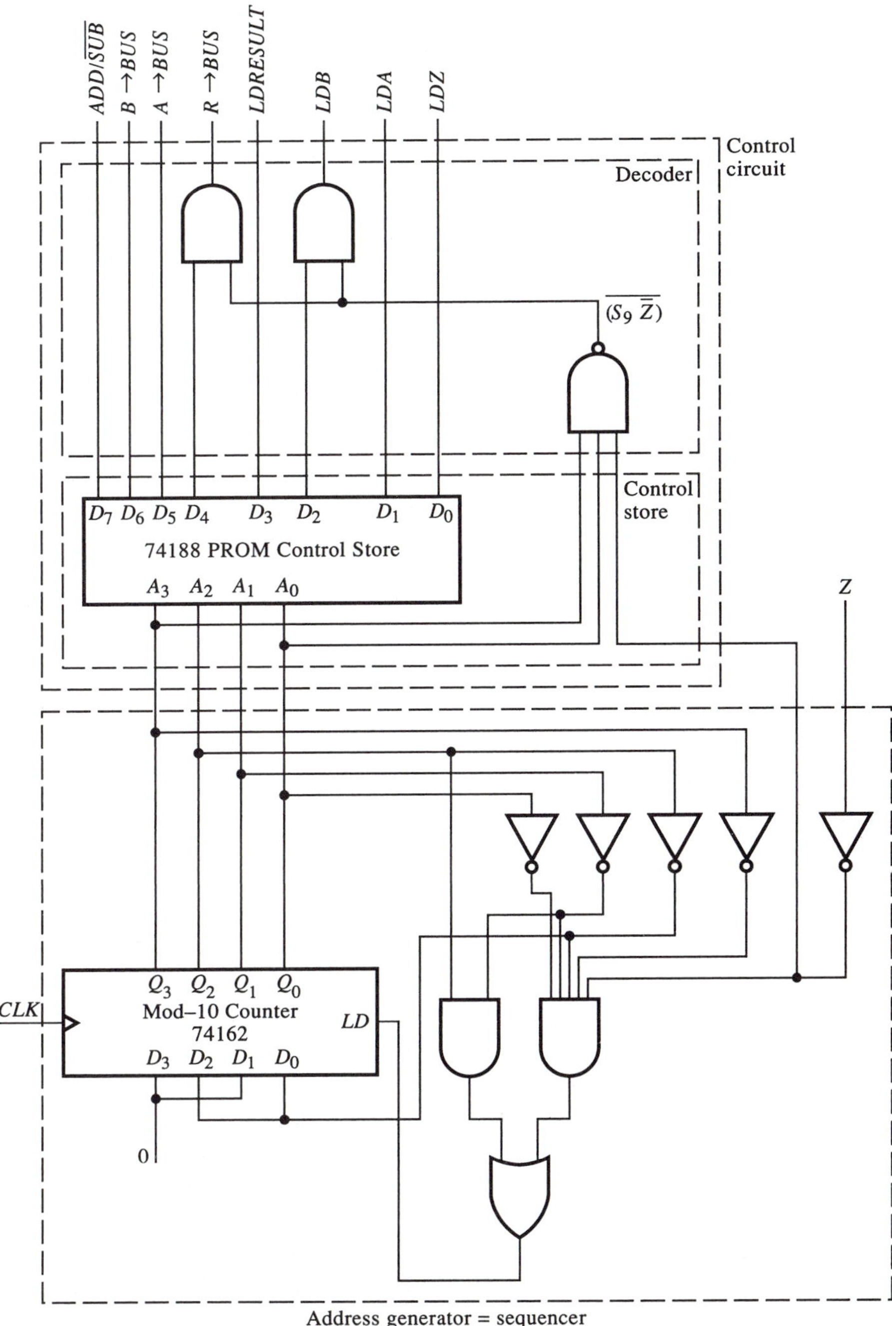


**Figure 7.31.** Detailed diagram of the microprogrammed control unit.

*LDRESULT* is On in state (2). The remaining microinstructions are obtained in the same way and the whole microprogram is as follows:

| Address | Microcode |
|---|---|
| 0 | 10001000 |
| 1 | 00010010 |
| 2 | 00001000 |
| 3 | 00100100 |
| 4 | 00010010 |
| 5 | XXXXXXXX (not used) |
| 6 | 00010100 |
| 7 | 10001001 |
| 8 | 01000010 |
| 9 | 00010100 |

Unfortunately, our approach fails on state (9), whose outcome depends on the value of $Z$. To solve this problem, we must redefine either the microcode or the decoder. (We have not needed a decoder up to this point.) We will use the second approach and leave the microcode as is. The microinstruction in state (9) should produce *LDB* only if $Z$=0. In all other states, the presence of the control bit is the only condition for generating *LDB*. This means that *LDB* is On if $MC_2$ is On, unless we are in state (9) and $Z$ is Off. A similar reasoning applies to signal $R{\rightarrow}BUS$ and we get

$$LDB = MC_2 \cdot \overline{S_9 \cdot \overline{Z}}$$

$$R{\rightarrow}BUS = MC_4 \cdot \overline{S_9 \cdot \overline{Z}}$$

where $MC_i$ refers to the $i$th bit of the microcode. These two equations define the decoder (Figure 7.31); all other signals are obtained directly from the microcode.

Now that we have the logic diagram and the microprogram, we must select components. The sequencer (address generator) is the same as in Section 7.5. The decoder will use TTL gates, and the microprogram will be stored in a PROM; otherwise, it would be erased when power is turned Off. A microprogram stored in a ROM is often referred to as "firmware." We will use the 74188 32 × 8 PROM but we need only ten of the thirty-two words available because the microprogram is only ten microinstructions long.

### Exercises

1. Draw the complete logic diagram of our system including all parts and connections.
2. List and comment on the sequence of microinstructions executed when $z = 0$ and when $z = 1$.

### Timing Analysis

The only difference between microprogrammed and hardwired systems is in the control unit. Thus we only need to recalculate the timing of the control unit. Its delay consists of the generation of a new address by the address generator, the reading of microcode from the PROM, and the processing of signals by the two-input AND gate:

$$\begin{aligned} T_C &= T_{pd74162} + T_{pd74188} + T_{pd7408} \\ &= 35 + 50 + 27 \\ &= 112 \text{ nsec} \end{aligned}$$

Compare this with the 109 ns required by the hardwired control unit in Section 7.5. The hardwired control unit is slightly faster than the microprogrammed one. This is a typical result and is easy to explain: Reading the microcode from a PROM is more time consuming than generating it with a few gates. In most real systems the timing difference is greater because longer microprograms require larger, and thus slower, ROM chips for the control store. Also, typical microprogrammed control units need more complex signal decoding than our very simple example. Other reasons why microprogrammed control units are slower will emerge when we design a more substantial control unit in Chapter 10.

To find the maximum delay of the whole system and the period of the clock of the system, we must add $T_c$ to the duration of the longest operation found in Section 7.5:

$$\begin{aligned} T_{max} &= T_c + T_{pd74181} + T_{su74173} \\ &= 112 + 35 + 10 \\ &= 157 \text{ nsec} \end{aligned}$$

This calculation completes the design of our microprogrammed control unit.

## Final Remarks

Real microprogrammed systems are much more complicated than our example. Microcodes may be hundreds of bits wide and the microprogram may be several hundred microinstructions long. The decoder is also more complicated and the structure of the control unit is more complex. Nevertheless we can draw several conclusions from our example:

> Microprogrammed control units are easier to design. Very often, the design consists mainly of writing the microprogram because chips designed to implement the basic building blocks of microprogrammed control units are commercially available.
>
> Microprogrammed control units are more flexible because the correction of design errors and the modification of specifications usually require changes only in the microprogram. There is normally no need to add or remove chips or connections, or to redesign the circuit board, for example.
>
> Microprograms can be extended using diagnostic routines to check that the circuit works as expected. This simplifies testing during production and in the field. Designing self-testing into a hardwired control unit is more difficult.
>
> Hardwired control units can operate faster because control signals and next states are generated directly from state codes rather than decoded from instructions fetched from the control store.

Our findings show that both hardwired and microprogrammed control have advantages and disadvantages. Both are used extensively in computer design.

To conclude this section, let us note that another approach to control is to complement the ROM control store with a RAM and allow the user to extend the control program by writing additional microinstructions into the RAM. In such a microprogrammable control unit, the user can extend the function of the digital system during operation.

Storing the code in a RAM is, in principle, equivalent to ordinary computer programming. Each computer program effectively converts the computer on which it runs into a special-purpose machine dedicated to the problem solved by the program. The transition from fully hardwired logic to programmed computers is thus gradual and all these alternatives are equivalent in their generality; only their operating and economic parameters are different.

## Exercises

1. Rank the different implementations of control units according to their speed, ease of design, flexibility, modifiability, complexity, and perma-

nence. Consider hardwired and microprogrammed control units as well as programs running on general-purpose computers.

2. Convert the hardwired control units from the exercises in the previous section to microprogrammed control units.

## SUMMARY

The structure of digital systems is best represented by block diagrams showing major functional blocks (storage, ALU, and control unit) and data transfer and control paths.

If we want to process and transfer codes in systems with multiple data sources and destinations, the most economical solution is to use shared data paths called buses. To make it possible to connect many data sources together, buses are devices with open collector or tristate outputs. The more popular tristate devices are essentially electronic switches that can disconnect the signal from the rest of the circuit. Except for this extra level of control, tristates are constrained by the same limitation as ordinary logic outputs: At most one of the tristate outputs connected together may be enabled at a time. This restriction does not apply to OC devices.

Following the discussion of data transfer, we illustrated the operation of a digital system on a serial multiplier. We then designed a complete simple system, proceeding in the following sequence of steps: formulation of a structural and behavioral specification, design of processing modules, design of the control unit, selection of components, and timing analysis.

In this sequence, the design of the control unit is the major new topic. We showed that two approaches are possible: hardwiring and microprogramming. The design of a hardwired control unit follows along the lines of sequential circuit design presented in Chapter 5. A microprogrammed control unit is based on encoding signals into microcodes, organizing them into a microprogram, storing the microprogram in the control store, and executing it by fetching and decoding the microinstructions to generate the desired control signals.

A comparison of hardwired and microprogrammed control units shows that hardwired control units can operate faster but that microprogrammed ones are easier to design and modify. Both approaches are used in computer design.

## REVIEW QUESTIONS

1. Define the following terms: Block diagram, data path, bus unidirectional, bidirectional, tristate, open collector, transceiver, line driver, RAM, control unit (hardwired, microprogrammed), control store, sequencer, microcode (horizontal, vertical), microprogram, microcode decoder, firmware.

2. Describe the following procedures: design of hardwired and microprogrammed control unit.

## REFERENCES

The following titles listed in the references at the end of the book are relevant to this chapter:

J. D. Mosley. *Static RAMs.*

M. Wright. *Dynamic RAMs.*

# CHAPTER 8

# A MODEL COMPUTER

## AN OVERVIEW

After presenting general principles of digital systems in Chapter 7, we are now ready to deal with a special category of digital systems—computers. Computers are digital systems that operate by executing programs. To execute programs, a computer needs both hardware components and software support (programs). In this and the following three chapters we will focus mainly on hardware, but our interest will gradually shift toward software.

One can view the main components of a computer—its CPU, memory, I/O devices, and buses—from two perspectives. The perspective of the user is called *computer architecture* while the view of the computer's designer is called *computer organization*. In this chapter we will develop the specification of the architecture of a simple CPU called "TOY." In Chapter 9 we will consider its design.

To determine the architecture of TOY, we will examine basic programming tasks like input, output, assignment, and control of flow of execution. After selecting instructions that will allow us to execute these tasks on TOY, we will add these logic signals required for communication between TOY and memory and I/O devices.

We present TOY as a vehicle for showing the principles on which a CPU architecture might be designed and implemented. Because of the introductory nature of our presentation, TOY is too primitive to be of any practical use. Detailed discussion of a real CPU, the 6800 by Motorola, thus follows in Chapter 10. To make the transition to the 6800 smoother, the features of TOY resemble those of the 6800.

## IMPORTANT WORDS

Accumulator, address, address space, addressing mode (absolute, extended, immediate), bus (address, control, data), computer architecture, computer organization, condition code register, control signal, CPU, conditional jump, fetch/execute cycle, flag, I/O, instruction (control-of-flow, data manipulation, data transfer), instruction set, instruction register, interface, I/O space, jump instruction (conditional, unconditional), label, machine instruction, memory (primary, secondary), mnemonic, multiprocessor, object code, opcode, peripheral, program counter, software, source code, two-phase clock, uniprocessor, word.

## 8.1 STRUCTURE AND BASIC OPERATION OF A SIMPLE COMPUTER

To manipulate data and communicate with the external world, a computer must have the following parts:

A processor that executes instructions and controls the whole system.

A memory that stores programs and data.

Input and output devices for communicating with the external world.

Communication paths between the individual parts: buses.

The processor fetches data from memory, performs calculations, stores results, and communicates with I/O devices. It is usually called the central processing unit or CPU to distinguish it from other controllers present in the system that may be mainly in charge of I/O devices.

The memory stores data and programs. It should be very large and fast to allow efficient execution of complicated programs. The memory should also be nonvolatile so that programs and data files are not lost when the computer is turned off. Finally, the memory should not be too expensive. A single storage technology cannot satisfy all of these requirements because fast memories are expensive and volatile. To strike a balance between capacity, speed and cost, most computers thus use a fast but relatively small primary RAM and ROM semiconductor memory and a much larger but slower secondary memory, such as a disk drive. The primary memory is also often called the main memory while the secondary memory is called auxiliary memory or mass storage.

To make the best use of the two storage technologies, the CPU treats them differently. Executing programs must be in main memory so that the CPU can access them at its own speed. When a program is not used by the CPU, it resides in a file in secondary memory. Because the secondary memory is relatively slow, the CPU treats it as an I/O device. Computer operation is characterized by constant transitions from one program to another, and frequent transfers of programs and data between main and auxiliary memory are thus required.

Input and output devices are often called "peripherals" because they are on the periphery of the CPU-memory core of the computer. Peripherals include keyboards, printers, displays, disk drives, and other devices connected to the CPU via *interfaces.*

The main purpose of an interface is to allow the CPU to address a device and communicate with it. Sometimes the interface also changes the voltage level or the shape of the signal. An interface is usually a simple decoder chip but in some cases it may contain a processor or a controller almost as complex as the CPU itself.

In addition to computers with a single CPU, multiprocessor systems with several interconnected CPUs are becoming increasingly common. In the following presentation, however, we will deal with the simple, traditional uniprocessor model outlined above and illustrated in Figure 8.1

How does a computer work? To illustrate the basic principles, consider the execution of the Pascal statement.

WRITE(PRINTER,X+Y)

which calculates the sum of $X$ and $Y$ and prints it out. The CPU performs this task by executing a sequence of *machine instructions.* Their codes are stored in the main memory and the CPU must fetch and execute them one after another. A typical sequence on a small computer could be as follows:

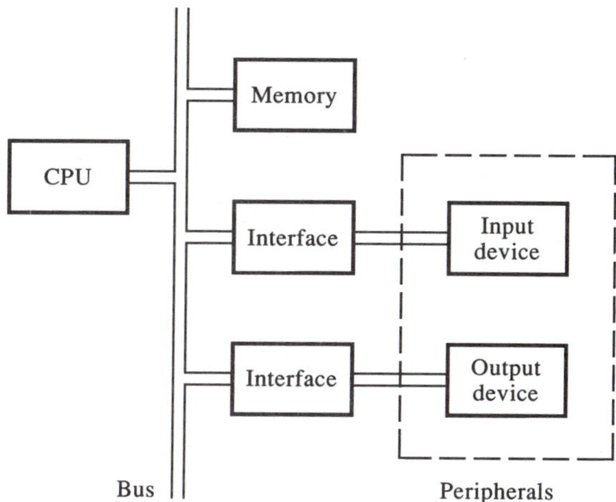


**Figure 8.1.** Structure of a computer.

1. To calculate $X + Y$, the CPU executes instructions that fetch the values of $X$ and $Y$ from memory and add them together. The resulting binary code is converted into a sequence of ASCII characters for the printer by another block of machine instructions.
2. The CPU must then test whether the printer is ready by checking the status of its interface. If the printer is available, the CPU sends the code of the result to the interface; the interface and the printer's logic circuit take care of the rest. If the printer is not ready—because it is disconnected or printing something else or because paper is jammed—the CPU either aborts the execution of the WRITE statement and displays an error message or continues checking the printer's status until the data can be transmitted.

Let us now explain how the CPU handles individual instructions. Each instruction is represented by a code stored in the main memory. To process an instruction, the CPU fetches its operation code (*opcode*), which determines its function, decodes it, and executes it. Because decoding and execution overlap, instruction processing is best thought of as the repeated execution of a fetch and execute cycle (Figure 8.2). Fetching and execution are repeated over and over until a special instruction or signal halts the CPU or until the CPU is turned Off.

### Computer Architecture and Organization

We have noted that computer systems can be viewed in two ways. The user's point of view is usually called computer architecture while the perspective that concentrates on the implementation of computer architecture is called computer organization. In a narrow sense, computer organization is concerned only with the hardware aspects of computer implementation; in a wider sense, it deals with the operation of the complete computer system and thus includes both hardware and software.

Computer architecture has its software and hardware aspects. Software aspects include the number and types of available instructions (the *instruction set*), the types of data processed by instructions (one-byte, two-byte, pure binary, two's complement, or floating point), the size of addressable memory, and so on. Hardware aspects of architecture include the function of the signals

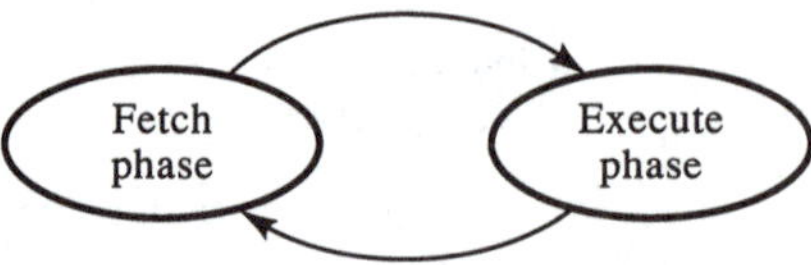


**Figure 8.2.** CPU operation.

exchanged between the CPU, the memory, and the peripherals, and their timing. The software aspects are essential for the programmer; the designer of interfaces must be familiar with the hardware aspects.

The subject of computer organization is the implementation of all aspects of architecture—the decoding and execution of instructions, the generation of signals for communication with memory and I/O devices, and so on.

### Exercises

1. The Motorola 6800 CPU uses one byte to represent the opcode of an instruction. What is the maximum number of instructions that the 6800 could have?
2. The 6800 uses sixteen-bit addresses. How many different memory locations can it access?
3. Repeat Exercise 2 for the Intel 8088 CPU, which uses twenty-bit addresses.

## 8.2 SOFTWARE ASPECTS OF TOY ARCHITECTURE

In the rest of this chapter, we are going to define the architecture of a simple CPU that we will call TOY. To do this, we will examine a sequence of essential programming tasks (including I/O, assignment, and the simple control of program flow) and decide which instructions TOY needs to implement them. Because our goal is to acquire a basic understanding of CPU operation, even the completed TOY will not be able to solve all types of programming problems. Our discussion will show the direction in which TOY could be extended to become a useful CPU. Remember, also, that our intention here is not to demonstrate how to program a computer but rather to determine the type of facilities that a computer must have so that it can solve typical programming tasks.

**Task 1—Input** If *C* is a character variable, the statement

READ(C)

reads a single ASCII code from the keyboard and stores it in the memory location reserved for *C*. Because ASCII characters are normally stored as eight-bit entities, TOY's communication with the keyboard will be in one-byte parcels. One-byte codes are a suitable unit of information for other uses as well and we will thus make eight bits the "word size" of TOY. This means that all data on TOY will be transferred in eight-bit packets, the size of all codes will be one or more bytes, and TOY's internal processing will be based on eight-bit codes.

In principle, the code read from the keyboard could go directly to the memory location allocated to variable *C*. This would be somewhat difficult to implement, however, and most computers thus transmit data through an intermediate register in the CPU. TOY will follow this practice and store data retrieved from memory or an input device in an internal *accumulator* register denoted *AC*. The accumulator will also hold intermediate results of calculations.

Under these conditions, the READ statement requires two steps:

| Operation | Instruction |
|---|---|
| Keyboard → accumulator | Input data from keyboard |
| Accumulator → memory | Store data in memory |

Both the input and the store instruction must include an address: The input instruction must specify that the input device is the keyboard while the "store" instruction must designate the memory address of *C*. The format and function of input and store instructions will thus be as follows:

| Mnemonic | Example | Meaning |
|---|---|---|
| IN | IN $00 | Byte from device 00 → accumulator |
| ST | ST $13 | Accumulator → memory location $13 |

Note that:

A mnemonic is an abbreviated name of an instruction.

We use the dollar sign "$" to denote hexadecimal numbers, which is consistent with the notation used on the 6800 CPU presented in Chapter 10. Some other computers, such as the IBM PC, denote hexadecimal by "H," as in 13H.

Although we often use hexadecimal notation, codes are really stored in binary. Hexadecimal is only a shorthand.

The instruction ST $13 means that a copy of the code now in accumulator is sent to location $13. It does not mean that the stored value is $13. Similarly, IN $00 means "fetch data from the input device whose address is $00" and not "load 00 into the accumulator."

Instruction ST stores a copy of the accumulator; it does not change the value in the accumulator.

The address part of IN identifies an I/O device. A one-byte I/O address is sufficient because there are usually only a few I/O devices; this allows for up to 256 different device addresses. The I/O space of TOY will thus contain 256 addresses. We will assume that the address of the keyboard is 00.

How large should the memory space be? In other words, how many memory locations should ST be allowed to select from? Because TOY is an eight-bit CPU, the address size should be a multiple of one byte. An eight-bit address allows only 256 addresses (from $00 to $FF), which is not enough to store the code and data of even simple programs. Two bytes contain sixteen bits and allow $2^{16}$-64k or 65,536 addresses ($0000 to $FFFF), which is quite sufficient for our needs. TOY will thus use *two-byte memory addresses* giving a memory space of 64k. Instruction ST $13 should thus be written ST $0013.

We can now write a program to solve our problem. If *C* is stored at location $0013, TOY implementation of READ (*C*) is

```
IN    00
ST    $0013
```

To save typing, we will usually write "ST $13" instead of "ST $0013," leaving leading 0s out. This is just a shorthand and we must remember that when the instruction is stored in memory, it must include a full two-byte address.

**Task 2—Output** The reverse of READ(*C*) is

WRITE(C)

This statement fetches a one-byte value from the memory location assigned to *C* and displays it on the screen. It requires loading *C* into the accumulator and then sending the contents of the accumulator to the display. To make this possible, we must add two new instructions: "load data from memory," and "output data to a device":

| Mnemonic | Example | Meaning |
|---|---|---|
| LD | LD $0013 | Contents of location $0013 → accumulator |
| OUT | OUT $3B | Contents of accumulator → device $3B |

Instruction LD (LOAD) copies the code in the specified memory location into the accumulator, leaving the original contents of memory unchanged.

Note that LD $0013 means "load *AC* from location $0013" and not "load $0013 into *AC*."

Because the I/O space has 256 addresses, OUT uses a one-byte address to specify the I/O device. It outputs a copy of *AC* without changing *AC* itself.

Instruction LD accesses the same 64k memory as ST and is followed by a two-byte memory address.

If the address of the display is 01, WRITE(*C*) is implemented as

```
LD      $13
OUT     $01
```

where LD $13 is an abbreviation for LD $0013.

Our treatment of input and output is a simplification of real I/O programs. We will present more details in Chapter 12.

**Task 3—Assignment** Let us now implement the assignment statement

X := Y

If *X* and *Y* are one-byte quantities, this statement can be performed by loading *Y* into the accumulator and storing the accumulator in location *X*. Assuming that *X* is stored in location $3421 and *Y* at $3445, the program is

```
LD    $3445    ;  Get value of Y
ST    $3421    ;  Store it in X
```

No new instructions are needed. The text following the semicolon is not an executable part of the program; it is a comment that we have added for documentation.

**Task 4—Negation** Negation, as in

X := − Y

is the simplest arithmetic operation. Most CPUs perform arithmetic only on data stored in the accumulator and we will do the same with TOY. If *X* and *Y* are one-byte signed numbers stored in locations $3000 and $3001, the above assignment statement will be implemented by

```
LD      $3001    ;  Get Y into the accumulator
NEG              ;  Negate accumulator
ST      $3000    ;  Store accumulator in X
```

Where we have introduced a new instruction, NEG, that performs two's complement of one-byte numbers. Note that it does not have an explicit operand.

**Task 5—Addition** The Statement

X := Y + Z

requires loading *Y* into the accumulator, adding *Z* to it, and storing the result in *X*. If *X*, *Y*, and *Z* are byte-sized numbers stored in locations $1234, $1235, and $1236, the statement can be implemented by

```
LD     $1235   ;  Load Y from $1235 into accumulator AC
ADD    $1236   ;  Add Z from $1236 to the accumulator
ST     $1234   ;  Store result in X at address $1234
```

The ADD instruction adds the accumulator and a copy of the contents of the specified memory location and leaves the result in the accumulator. Note that the instruction requires only one address even though two operands and one result are involved.

**Task 6—Subtraction**

An assignment statement involving subtraction, such as

X := Y − Z

could be implemented with addition and negation. However, subtraction is needed so often that most computers have a special instruction for it and so will TOY.

Subtraction on TOY will be performed on data stored in the accumulator, just like addition. If *X*, *Y*,, and *Z* are stored at $1234, $1235, and $1236, our assignment statement can be implemented as follows:

```
LD     $1235   ;  Load Y
SUB    $1236   ;  Subtract Z
ST     $1234   ;  Save result in X
```

If the original values of *X*, *Y*, and *Z* are $42, $A0, and $17, the new values will be $89, $A0, and $17.

Note that SUB *X* means "subtract the contents of *X* from the accumulator" rather than "subtract accumulator from *X*."

Instructions ADD and SUB can be described symbolically as follows:

| Mnemonic | Example | Description |
|---|---|---|
| ADD | ADD $13 | Accumulator + [$13] → accumulator |
| SUB | SUB $13 | Accumulator − [$13] → accumulator |

Here [$13] denotes the contents of memory location $0013.

### Program Execution

Having introduced a few basic instructions, we will now examine the mechanics of their execution in more detail. After all, we want to eventually design TOY and so we must understand how it works. To this end, we will show how our last program is stored in memory and executed.

As we have already explained, each instruction has a unique binary opcode that specifies its operation. We will select opcodes in Chapter 9; for this discussion, they are irrelevant and we will represent them by mnemonics. The opcode is stored in memory and may be followed by an operand: Instructions IN, LD, OUT, and ST have an operand; NEG does not.

Instructions that are to be executed in sequence are also stored sequentially, and during execution the CPU simply fetches their codes from consecutive addresses and executes them.

Assuming that TOY opcodes are one byte long and that the first instruction is stored at location $0100, our program will be stored in memory as follows:

| Address (hexadecimal) | Contents | Meaning |
|---|---|---|
| 0100 | LD | Binary opcode of LD |
| 0101 | $12 | First half of two-byte address |
| 0102 | $35 | Second half of two-byte address |
| 0103 | SUB | Binary opcode of SUB |
| 0104 | $12 | First half of two-byte address |
| 0105 | $36 | Second half of two-byte address |
| 0106 | ST | Binary opcode of ST |
| 0107 | $12 | First half of two-byte address |
| 0108 | $34 | Second half of two-byte address |

To fetch an instruction, the CPU must know the address at which it is stored, and for this function it has a special register called the *program counter* or *PC*. At the beginning of the execution of our program, *PC* must therefore

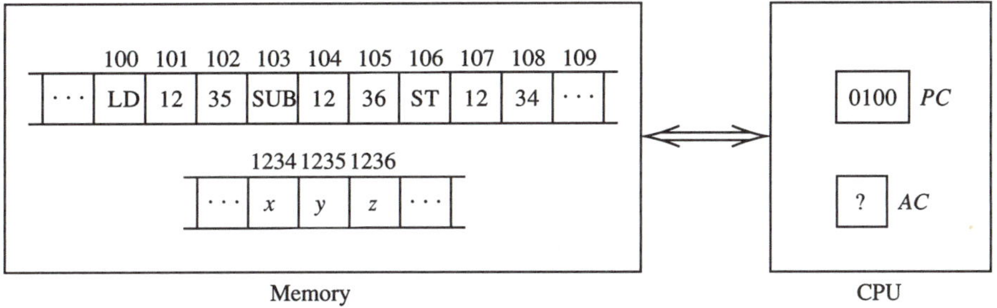


**Figure 8.3.** TOY before the execution of the sample program.

contain address \$0100 (Figure 8.3). The execution of the program then goes as follows:

Fetch the opcode from the address stored in *PC* (\$0100).

Decode the opcode. A two-byte address must follow the instruction LD, to fetch it TOY increments *PC* from \$0100 to \$0101.

Fetch the first byte of data address from the location whose address is stored in *PC* (\$0101) and increment *PC* again (to \$0102) to get ready for the second address byte.

Fetch the next byte of data address from location \$0102 and increment *PC* to \$0103 to prepare for the next instruction. The address of the operand of LD (\$1235) is now in the CPU.

Execute the LD instruction by fetching the contents of location \$1235 into the accumulator. Instruction LD is now completely executed.

Fetch the opcode of the next instruction (SUB) from the address in *PC*. Increment *PC* to get ready for its address part.

Continue in this fashion until the CPU is halted by a special instruction or until the power is turned off.

This sequence is performed under the control of the system clock.

**Task 7—Input, arithmetic, and output** We are to write the TOY version of the following statements assuming that *X*, *Y*, and *Z* are one-byte signed integers stored in locations \$2100, \$2101, and \$2102:

```
READ(X,Y,Z);
WRITE(X+Y−Z)
```

The CPU must first fetch the values of *X, Y*, and *Z* from the input device into memory and this is implemented as follows:

```
IN    $00      ;  Load X from the keyboard into AC
ST    $2100    ;  Store it in memory
IN    $00      ;  Get Y
ST    $2101    ;  Store it in memory
IN    $00      ;  Get Z
ST    $2102    ;  Store it in memory
```

Now we must evaluate the expression and output the result:

```
LD     $2100   ;  Load AC from memory location X
ADD    $2101   ;  Add Y to get X+Y
SUB    $2102   ;  Subtract Z to get X+Y−Z
OUT    $01     ;  Display
```

No new instructions are necessary.

**Task 8—Two-byte arithmetic** One-byte numbers are useful for small counts but most calculations with integers require at least two bytes. After all, one-byte two's complement numbers cover only the range from − 128 to + 127. To perform

X := Y + Z

with two-byte numbers, we must first add the two least significant bytes to get the least significant byte (LSB) of the sum and then add the two most significant bytes and the carry generated by the first addition. As an example,

| | MSB | LSB |
|---|---|---|
| Carry | 1 | |
| *Y* | 00101100 | 10001001 |
| *Z* | 00000010 | 11000010 |
| *X* | 00101111 | 01001011 |

Because the ADD instruction does not add the carry to its two operands, we need a new instruction: "add with carry," or ADC. There will also be a corresponding subtract instruction SBC for "subtract with carry" because computer architects use the terms "carry" and "borrow" interchangeably.

Assume that the two bytes of each operand are stored in the order MSB, LSB. If *X* is stored in locations $1000 and $1001, *Y* in $2000 and $2001, and *Z* in $3000 and 3001$, the program is

```
                ; First the LSB calculation
LD     $2001    ; Load LSB of the first operand
ADD    $3001    ; Add LSB of the second operand
ST     $1001    ; Store LSB of result
                ; Now the MSB calculation
LD     $2000    ; Load MSB of the first operand
ADC    $3000    ; Add MSB of the second operand and the carry
ST     $1000    ; Store MSB of result
```

Where does the carry come from? We mentioned in Chapter 6 that values such as carry, sign, and overflow are stored in special purpose flip-flops called *flags*. Because we will need several more flags to represent various other conditions, the TOY CPU will have a *condition code register CC* and the carry will be one of its flags.

Which instructions should affect the *C* flag? For some instructions, such as ADD or SUB, the effect on *C* is obvious; for others, such as IN and LD, it is not and different computer architects use different solutions. TOY treats *C* and other flags according to the table given at the end of this section.

**Task 9—Constants** In addition to variables, programs often use constants as in

X := Y + 3

It might appear that this could be implemented by storing 3 somewhere in memory and then proceeding as with variables. However, how would the code "number 3" get into the computer in the first place? We could ask the user to type "3" and use IN and ST but this would be very awkward. It is much better to add instructions that contain the value of the operand rather than its address. Instructions of this type are said to use *immediate* addressing. To avoid confusion, instructions that specify an operand by its address are said to use *absolute*, or *direct*, addressing. The following are several examples that illustrate differences between absolute and immediate addressing:

| Instruction | Meaning |
|---|---|
| LD #$13 | Load value $13 into *AC* (immediate); symbolically: $13 → *AC* |
| LD $13 | Load data from address $0013 into *AC* (absolute); symbolically: [$13] → *AC* |
| ADD #$13 | Add value $13 to *AC* (immediate); symbolically: [*AC*] + 13 → *AC* |
| ADD $13 | Add data from address $0013 to *AC* (absolute); symbolically: [*AC*] + [$13] → *AC* |

The symbol "#" denotes immediate addressing.

Note that ADD and ADD # perform the same calculation. The only difference is in their *addressing modes*—how they get the operand. One uses immediate addressing when the value of the operand is known beforehand, in other words, when the operand is a constant. Absolute addressing is used for variables.

If $X$ and $Y$ are stored in locations \$1000 and \$2000, the solution of our problem is

```
LD      $2000
ADD     #3
ST      $1000
```

We could obtain the same result with

```
LD      #3
ADD     $2000
ST      $1000
```

which shows that immediate addressing is useful not only for LD but for other instructions as well. The table at the end of this section shows which addressing modes are allowed for different TOY instructions.

**Notation**

Although the hexadecimal shorthand makes it easier to read and write programs, the process is still tiresome and error-prone. Because we already use symbols for opcodes, we will now start using symbols for operands as well. As an example, if $X$ and $Y$ represent the addresses at which $X$ and $Y$ are stored,

```
LD      #3
ADD     Y     ;  Symbol of operand instead of its address
ST      X     ;  Symbol of operand instead of its address
```

has the same meaning as our previous program. Using symbols for addresses, a first step toward symbolic assembly language programming, makes programs more readable and easier to write. However, before execution, all symbols must be replaced with binary codes because the CPU can only work with binary codes.

**Task 10—Multiplication and division** Like most simple CPUs, TOY will not have "multiply" or "divide" instructions. Under these circumstances, the most natural strategy for multiplication is repeated addition. As an example,

X := 4*Y

can be calculated by adding *Y* to itself three times:

```
LD      Y
ADD     Y
ADD     Y
ADD     Y
```

Although this works very well for multiplication by small numbers, it would be awkward and inefficient for large products, such as 128 × *Y*. A much better approach is to use addition combined with shifting.

As we have seen, binary multiplication by 2 is equivalent to shifting left. Because the shift-accumulator-left instruction is easy to implement in hardware and is useful for other operations as well, we will add it to TOY's instruction set and call it SL. With shift left, multiplication by 128 can be implemented by

```
LD    Y
SL          ;  2*Y
SL          ;  4*Y
SL          ;  8*Y
SL          ;  16*Y
SL          ;  32*Y
SL          ;  64*Y
SL          ;  128*Y
```

We can extend this approach to multiplication by any constant. As an example,

X := 41*Y

can be calculated as

X := Y + 8*Y + 32*Y

and performed by repeated shifting, addition, and storage of intermediate results:

```
LD      Y
SL
SL
```

```
SL              ;  8*Y
ST     TEMP     ;  Save the result for later use.
SL
SL              ;  32*Y
ADD    TEMP     ;  32*Y + 8*Y
ADD    Y        ;  32*Y + 8*Y + Y
ST X
```

Another approach to multiplication (presented in Chapter 6) is to shift one operand, test its rightmost bit, and then perform conditional addition of the second operand. This approach must be used when both operands are variables as in

```
Y := Y*Z
```

Because it requires test instructions that we have not introduced yet, we cannot present it at this point.

The division of signed numbers by a power of 2, as in

```
X := Y DIV 8      {Quotient}
X := Y MOD 16     {Remainder}
```

can be implemented with arithmetic shift right: Shift all bits and copy the sign bit. TOY will thus have an ASR instruction. For completeness, we will include a "logic shift right" (LSR) instruction that does not copy the sign bit. Finally tests, such as the one required for the second method of multiplication, require access to the bit shifted out of the accumulator and this is best achieved by shifting the outermost bit into the carry flag. All our shift operations will work this way. The student is referred to the table at the end of this section for a complete description.

**Task 11—Code conversion** A frequently needed operation is conversion between ASCII and BCD, as in the following problem:

> Read the ASCII code of a decimal digit from the keyboard and convert it to the corresponding BCD code.

Because ASCII codes of decimal digits are BCD codes preceded by binary 0011, conversion from ASCII to binary requires clearing the four leading bits. This can be done by performing the operation *code* and 00001111; the four leading 0s clear the prefix 0011 and the four trailing 1s leave the BCD part intact. The conversion program can thus be implemented as follows:

```
IN      KBD             ; Read ASCII code from the keyboard
AND     #%00001111      ; AND accumulator with immediate binary
                        ; mask
ST      X               ; Store resulting BCD code in memory
```

The symbol KBD represents the address of the keyboard; % indicates a binary code. Note that the resulting BCD code occupies only four of the eight bits and the leading four bits in the code are thus wasted. This representation is called unpacked BCD. For more efficient storage we can put two BCD digits into a single byte; this is called packed BCD.

The inverse conversion from unpacked BCD to ASCII can be done with the OR instruction:

```
LD      X               ; Load BCD code from memory. Presumably,
                        ; the leading four bits are 0000
OR      #%00110000      ; OR accumulator with immediate binary mask
```

This completes the data transfer and processing part of TOY's instruction set, and we will now move on to instructions that allow us to control the flow of execution as in the IF, WHILE, and FOR statements.

**Task 12—Conditional execution** The calculation and output of the absolute value of $x$ can be performed as

```
IF X < 0
  Then X := −X;
WRITE(X)
```

The THEN part can be implemented by

```
LD      X
NEG
```

and must be bypassed if condition $X<0$ fails. There are two ways to do this. One way is to test the condition, jumping to the THEN part if the test succeeds and to the WRITE part otherwise:

```
IF X < 0
  THEN GOTO THEN_PART;
  GOTO NEXT;
THEN_PART: X := − X;
NEXT: WRITE(X)
```

The other solution is to invert the condition, jumping to bypass the THEN part if the inverted condition fails:

```
IF X >= 0      {Inverted condition}
  THEN GOTO NEXT;
X := −X;
NEXT: WRITE(X)
```

The second solution is better because it is shorter and therefore faster. To implement it, we need a new instruction to test whether $X \geq 0$ and to jump if the test succeeds; we will call this instruction "jump if greater or equal," or JGE. Because the jump takes place only when condition $X \geq 0$ holds, JGE is called a *conditional jump*. Its definition is as follows:

| Instruction | Example | Description |
|---|---|---|
| JGE | JGE $0207 | Jump to $0207 if the last result was greater than or equal to 0; otherwise proceed to next instruction |

Because we are dealing with two's complement codes, JGE must have access to the sign bit of the result of the last instruction; its copy will be kept in flag $N$. (Flag $N$ is 1 when the sign bit is set; in other words, when the number is negative.) The rules according to which individual instructions affect the $N$ flag are summarized at the end of this section.

Instruction JGE examines $N$, which has been affected by a previous instruction, and forces a jump if $N = 0$. Because the address of the next instruction is always in the program counter, the jump is implemented by loading $PC$ with the destination address.

The solution of our problem can be written as

```
        LD     X
        JGE    DISP    ; DISP represents the destination address of
                       ; the jump
        NEG            ; We don't need to load X because it is still
                       ; in the accumulator
        ST     X
DISP    OUT    CRT     ; Display the result on the CRT display
```

The entity *DISP* is a *label*, a symbol representing the address at which opcode OUT is stored. Like other symbols, one uses labels to simplify program representation by eliminating the need for binary and other codes.

Naturally, before we execute the program, we must convert labels and all other symbols to numeric values and we will now show how to do this. If the first instruction of the program is stored at address $01FC and if *X* is stored at $373A, the hexadecimal version of the executable code (with the exception of symbolic opcodes) is as follows:

| Address | Contents | Function |
|---|---|---|
| $01FC | LD | Load *X* into *AC* (sign → *N*) |
| $01FD | $37 | First byte of the address of *X* |
| $01FE | $3A | Second byte of the address of *X* |
| $01FF | JGE | Skip THEN if necessary |
| $0200 | $02 | High part of jump destination |
| $0201 | $06 | Low part of jump destination |
| $0202 | NEG | |
| $0203 | ST | Opcode |
| $0204 | $37 | MSB of the address of *X* |
| $0205 | $3A | LSB of the address of *X* |
| $0206 | OUT | Display—this is jump destination |
| $0207 | $01 | Address of display |

This listing was obtained in two passes through the original symbolic representation of the program (the *source code*).

In the first pass, we went through the source code one instruction after another, calculated how many bytes each required, and used this information to determine the address of each instruction. We had not created any codes at this point; in particular, we left the address part of JGE empty (we did not even know its value when we reached this point) and only reserved two bytes for it.

In the second pass, we read the sequence of instructions again and assigned appropriate codes to individual addresses. In particular, when we reached JGE we filled in the jump destination—the address of the opcode of OUT found in the first pass. The result of the second pass was the executable code listed above, which is also referred to as the object code.

**Task 13—IF-THEN with a different condition** The statement

```
IF X≠0
  THEN READY(Y)
```

requires a conditional jump with condition "result is equal to 0." We thus need another conditional jump with condition "jump if equal to 0," or JEQ. The source code of the corresponding program is

```
        LD    X
        JEQ   NEXT
        IN    KBD
        ST    Y
NEXT    . . .
```

If the program starts at location 4321H, the resulting object code is

```
$4321   LD    X       ; Requires three memory locations
$4324   JEQ   $432D   ; Three memory locations
$4327   IN    KBD     ; Two memory locations
$4329   ST    Y       ; Three memory locations
$432D   . . .         ; Next instruction
```

Because condition equals-zero cannot be tested with out existing flags, we will add a new flag called $Z$ (for "zero"). The condition $Z = 1$ means that the result of the last instruction was 0. (Take careful note of this standard convention as beginners sometimes find it confusing.)

**Task 14—IF-THEN-ELSE** The following code fragment

```
IF X >= Y
  THEN MIN := Y
  ELSE MIN := X;
WRITE(MIN)
```

calculates and displays the minimum of $X$ and $Y$.

In this case, our problem is not to bypass a segment of instructions, but rather to select one of two segments. If the condition succeeds, the CPU executes the THEN part and skips the ELSE part. Otherwise, it skips the THEN part and executes the ELSE part.

Although the IF-THEN-ELSE statement is "two-dimensional" in essence (Figure 8.4), its code must be stored "linearly" in consecutive memory locations, for example as follows:

Test the condition and jump to the code of the THEN part if the test succeeds.

Code of the ELSE section.

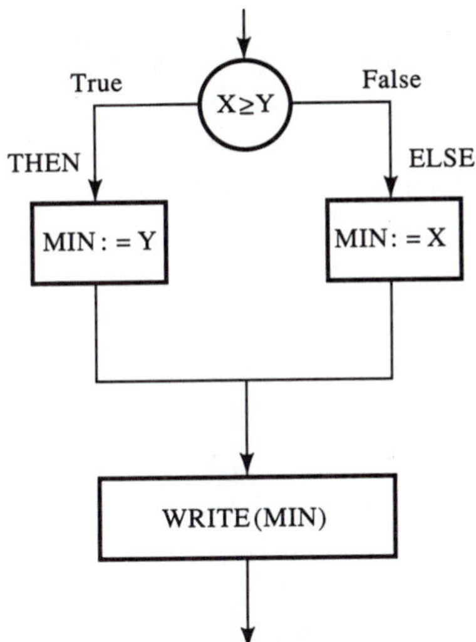


**Figure 8.4.** Flowchart of IF-THEN-ELSE. The circle indicates a condition.

Instruction to skip the THEN section.

Code of the THEN section.

Code following the IF-THEN-ELSE statement.

Let us now examine the individual steps. Condition

IF X >= Y

is equivalent to

IF X−Y >= 0

and the conditional jump can thus be implemented by calculating $X-Y$ and using subtraction followed by JGE. If the operands are two's complement codes, subtraction may produce an overflow, and to perform the proper comparison JGE must examine not only the sign but also the overflow condition of the result (Chapter 6). Thus we must add overflow flag $V$ to the condition code register; it will be set if the last operation produced an overflow.

The third step, "skip the THEN section," is a jump without any condition attached to it. It is an unconditional jump, a new instruction called simply "jump" or JMP. The complete solution of Task 14 is as follows:

| Label | Instruction | | Comment |
|---|---|---|---|
| | LD | $X$ | ; Prepare for the calculation of $X - Y$ |
| | SUB | $Y$ | ; $AC = X - Y$, flags are affected |
| | JGE | THEN | ; If $X{-}Y \geq 0$, jump to the THEN part |
| ELSE | LD | $X$ | ; $X < Y$ |
| | ST | MIN | ; $MIN := X$ |
| | JMP | WRITE | ; Skip ELSE part |
| THEN | LD | $Y$ | ; $Y \leq X$ |
| | ST | MIN | ; $MIN := Y$ |
| WRITE | OUT | CRT | ; Display *MIN* |

Both the THEN and ELSE parts end with ST *MIN*, and we can improve the program by moving the command ST *MIN* to the WRITE label to avoid duplication:

```
        LD    X      ; Prepare to calculate X-Y
        SUB   Y      ; AC = X-Y, flags are affected
        JGE   THEN   ; Conditional jump to the THEN code
ELSE    LD    X      ; X < Y
        JMP   WRITE  ; Skip ELSE part
THEN    LD    Y      ; Y ≤ X
WRITE   ST    MIN    ; Store the minimum form AC in MIN
        OUT   CRT    ; Display MIN
```

This solution is no faster than the original one because the number of executed instructions is the same as before, but it saves three memory locations.

The program again uses labels to represent the addresses of opcodes. Labels ELSE and WRITE are the destination addresses of jumps; THEN is used only for documentation.

Using JGE, JEQ, and JMP we can test all arithmetic conditions on signed numbers: Less-than is the inverse of greater-or-equal; not-equal is the inverse of equal; greater-than is the combination of greater-or-equal and not-equal; and so on. In principle, no other conditional jumps for signed arithmetic are needed. In practice, most computers have a special conditional jump for each arithmetic condition to simplify programs and to speed up execution. Moreover, most conditions require one version for signed and another for unsigned numbers because each representation requires different flag tests. (See Chapter 6 for further detail.)

Pascal provides several other control statements, such as FOR, WHILE, and REPEAT, as well as procedures and functions. Some of these constructs can be easily implemented with existing TOY instructions, others would require awkward solutions, and some cannot be implemented on TOY at all. Because our immediate goal is to design a very simple computer, we will stop adding instructions at this point and return to programming considerations in Chapter 10.

The software architecture of our CPU is now defined: TOY uses one-byte words; that is, it is an eight-bit CPU. It has I/O and memory access instructions. Its I/O space has 256 addresses and the size of its address space is 64k. All data processed by instructions passes through an eight-bit accumulator *AC*, which also stores intermediate results. TOY has a condition code register and four of its eight bits are used for flags: *C* (carry), *N* (negative sign), *V* (overflow), and *Z* (zero).

The instruction set provides two addressing modes, absolute and immediate. We can categorize TOY instructions as those that move data between memory and registers, those that process data via arithmetic or logic operations, and those that control the flow of program execution (jumps). The description of individual instructions is as follows:

| Instruction | Function | Effect on Flags *C* | *N* | *V* | *Z* | Addressing Modes |
|---|---|---|---|---|---|---|
| ADC | $[AC] + OP + C \rightarrow AC$ | ↕ | ↕ | ↕ | ↕ | I,A |
| ADD | $[AC] + OP \rightarrow AC$ | ↕ | ↕ | ↕ | ↕ | I,A |
| AND | $[AC]$ AND $OP \rightarrow AC$ | • | ↕ | R | ↕ | I,A |
| ASR | Arithmetic shift right *AC* | ↕ | ↕ | R | ↕ | IMP |
| IN | Input device $\rightarrow AC$ | • | ↕ | R | ↕ | A |
| JEQ | IF *Z* THEN $OP \rightarrow PC$ | • | • | • | • | A |
| JGE | IF $\overline{N \oplus V}$ THEN $OP \rightarrow PC$ | • | • | • | • | A |
| JMP | $OP \rightarrow PC$ | • | • | • | • | A |
| LD | $OP \rightarrow AC$ | • | ↕ | R | ↕ | I,A |
| LSR | Logic shift right *AC* | ↕ | ↕ | R | ↕ | IMP |
| NEG | $-[AC] \rightarrow$ AC | • | ↕ | R | ↕ | IMP |
| SBC | $[AC] - OP - C \rightarrow AC$ | ↕ | ↕ | ↕ | ↕ | I,A |
| SL | Shift left *AC* | ↕ | R | R | R | IMP |
| ST | $[AC] \rightarrow$ memory | • | • | • | • | A |
| SUB | $[AC] - OP \rightarrow AC$ | ↕ | ↕ | ↕ | ↕ | I,A |
| OR | $[AC]$ OR $OP \rightarrow AC$ | • | ↕ | R | ↕ | I,A |
| OUT | $[AC] \rightarrow$ output device | • | • | • | • | A |

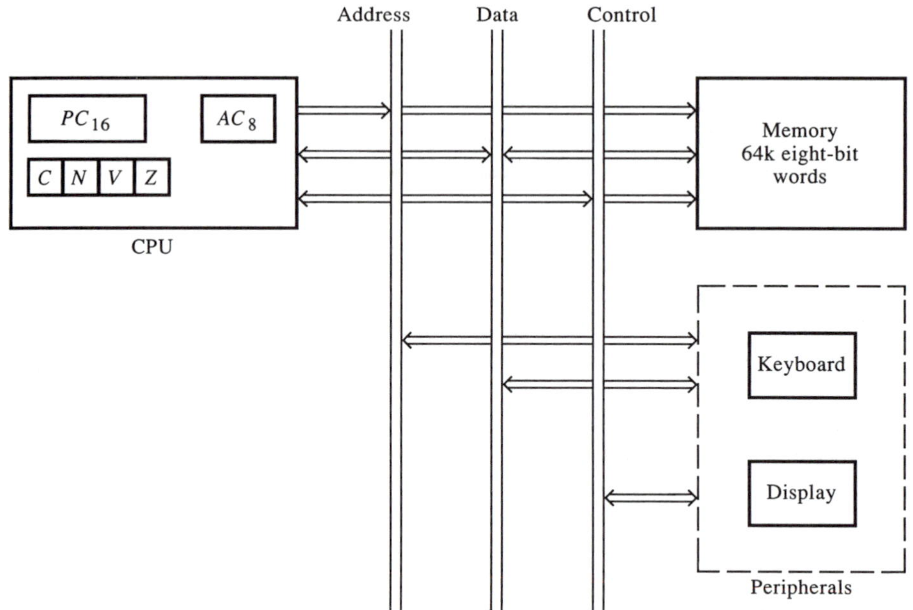


**Figure 8.5.** Block diagram of TOY. Interfaces are not shown.

The symbol "↕" means that the instruction affects the flag; "•" means no effect; "R" means that the instruction always resets the flag; "I" denotes immediate addressing; "A" is absolute addressing; "IMP" is implied addressing (no operand); "OP" is the value of the operand. In general, the effect of instructions on flags follows the 6800 CPU's conventions.

The block diagram of TOY is shown in Figure 8.5.

**Exercises**

Although this chapter is not about programming, most of the following exercises are of a programming nature. This is because a computer architect must have a good understanding of individual instructions, their limitations, and the needs of programmers.

1. Does the CPU stop when it reaches the last instruction in a program? If not, what does it do?
2. What happens when the CPU reaches the last address in the address space? (*Hint*: Register *PC* is a counter.)
3. Write a program to display

   Enter number between 10 and 100

4. Write a program to calculate and display $X - (Y + Z)$ assuming that $X$, $Y$, and $Z$ are one-byte numbers. Repeat for two-byte numbers.

5. Trace the execution of Task 7.
6. Write a program to negate a two-byte number.
7. Write a program to calculate $X + 381 - Z$ assuming that $X$ and $Z$ are two-byte numbers.
8. Write a program to calculate $217X$ assuming that $X$ is a one-byte number and the result is a two-byte number.
9. Describe the machine level implementation of multiplication by shifting and conditional addition. Determine if any new facilities should be added to TOY to implement it and write the corresponding program.
10. Write a program to calculate $X$ DIV 17 (quotient) and $X$ MOD 17 (remainder).
11. Write a program to pack a two-digit unpacked BCD code. Write a program to perform the inverse conversion.
12. Write a program to convert a two-digit packed BCD code stored in location $X$ to ASCII.
13. Write a program to convert a two-digit unpacked BCD code to binary and vice versa.
14. Write a program to calculate $X + Y$ where $X$ and $Y$ are two unpacked BCD numbers.
15. Implement the following conditional statements:

```
IF X ≤ 0
  THEN X:=0;
IF X>Y
  THEN exchange values of X and Y
```

16. Which instructions should be added to TOY's instruction set to make tests of common conditions easier?
17. Implement the following:

```
WRITE('Enter number between 10 and 100');
READ(X);
IF NOT (X IN [10..100])
  THEN WRITE ('Illegal input')
```

18. Implement the following:

```
READ(X);
FOR I := 1 TO 5 DO
  BEGIN
    READ(Y);
    X := X + Y;
  END
```

19. Implement a simple REPEAT loop.
20. Which of the programs developed in this section can be used with unsigned numbers?
21. Which instructions would have to be added to TOY's instruction set to make unsigned arithmetic possible? What about BCD arithmetic?
22. Some of the programs in the above exercises can only be implemented in a very awkward way. Which instructions or facilities would one add to TOY to simplify their implementation?
23. Convert the solution of Task 14 to hexadecimal assuming that $X$ and $Y$ are stored in locations $A54B and $A54C.
24. Explain why it is desirable for LD to change the $N$ flag and clear the $V$ flag. (*Hint*: Refer to Task 12 and consider JGE.)

## 8.3 HARDWARE ASPECTS OF TOY ARCHITECTURE

TOY needs the following data paths and signals to access memory and communicate with I/O devices:

An eight-bit data bus to memory and I/O devices

A sixteen-bit address bus shared between I/O devices and memory. Input and output devices will use only eight bits because TOY's I/O instructions use eight-bit addresses.

Because memory and I/O devices share the same address bus, a signal is needed to distinguish between memory and I/O access. We will call it $IO/\overline{MEM}$. When High, this signal indicates an I/O operation; when Low, the CPU is assessing memory.

Data may travel to the CPU (a READ operation) or from it (a WRITE operation), and TOY must thus have an $R/\overline{W}$ signal to indicate this. As the name suggests, the signal is High for a READ operation and Low for a WRITE operation.

The signals defined so far do not satisfy all our needs. Consider, for example, the NEG instruction, which operates on the accumulator and does not access memory or I/O devices. Whatever values TOY outputs for $R/\overline{W}$ and $IO/\overline{MEM}$ during its execution, the signals will select either an I/O device or a memory for a read or a write operation and this is not desired. We thus need another signal to tell the memory and I/O devices if they should respond to $R/\overline{W}$ and $IO/\overline{MEM}$ signals; in other words, if the CPU is requesting a data transfer. We will call this signal *DTR* for "data transfer." It will be High when the CPU is performing a data transfer involving memory or I/O, and Low during internal TOY operations.

To separate successive internal CPU states and to control memory access, TOY needs a clock signal. To determine the nature of the clock signal, we must analyze the events during memory access.

To read from or write to a memory chip, the CPU must select the chip, output the address, and indicate whether reading or writing is desired. For writing, it must also provide data. All these signals must be supplied at the correct time because a memory chip should be selected only when address, data (in the case of writing), $R/\overline{W}$, $IO/\overline{MEM}$ and $DTR$ signals are stable on its pins. Consequently, all signals except chip select should be output in one step, and the select signal should be produced in the next step. All signals produced in the first step must remain active during the second step as well.

Each READ and WRITE operation thus consists of two separate events and one can achieve this most easily by using two clock signals, or two phases of one signal, as in Figure 8.6. When the first phase signal ($\Phi_1$) is active, the CPU outputs all control, data, and address signals and allows them to stabilize on the pins of memory and I/O interface chips. The control signals then remain active until the next positive edge of $\Phi_1$.

If the DTR signal is active, the second phase of the clock (signal $\Phi_2$) activates the selection of the desired memory chip or I/O device and the CPU performs the transfer. The interval between two consecutive active edges of $\Phi_1$ constitutes one machine cycle.

We can also describe the function of the two phases as follows: During $\Phi_1$, the CPU announces its intention to perform a data transfer and supplies all necessary information. Signal $\Phi_2$ then indicates when to execute the operation.

To illustrate the use of all these signals, Figure 8.7 shows the timing of control signals for several types of bus activities.

Real CPUs, such as the 6800 discussed in Chapter 10, use similar signals and timing to these.

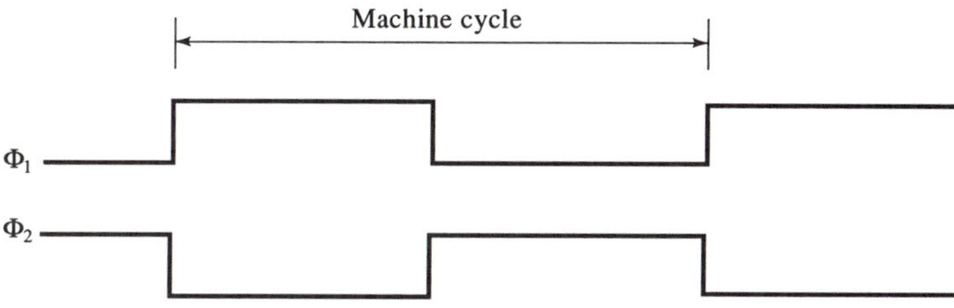


**Figure 8.6.** TOY's two-phase clock.

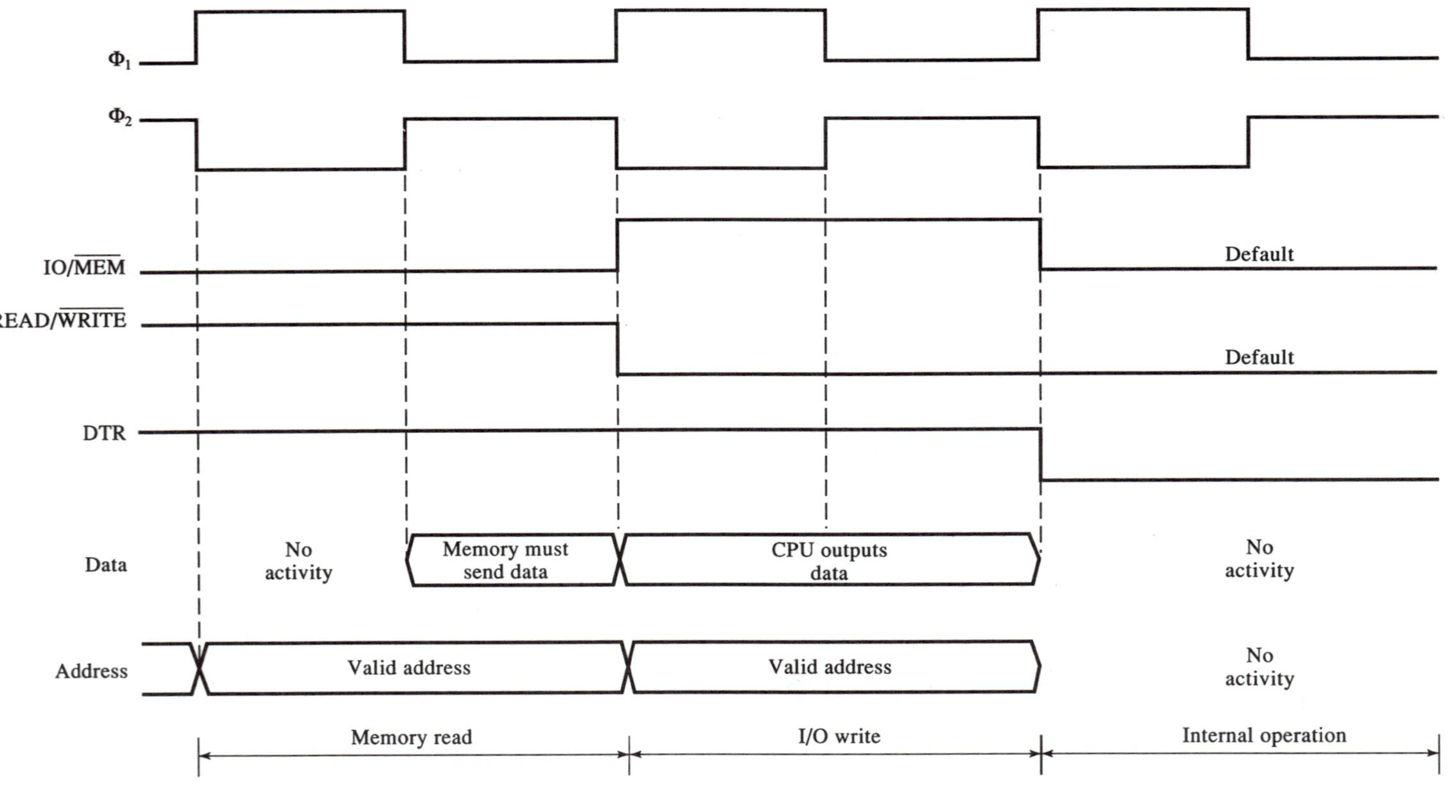


**Figure 8.7.** Left to right: TOY's timing of a memory READ operation, such as opcode or operand fetch; an I/O WRITE operation as in the last part of the execution of OUT *X*; and an internal CPU operation with no data transfer, as during execution of NEG.

## Exercise

1. Draw detailed timing diagrams of the execution of the following instructions: LD $1342, ST $1342, LD #62, ST #93, ADD $1342, NEG, IN 17, ADD #42, and OUT $64.

## SUMMARY

A computer consists of a CPU, memory, and input/output (peripheral) devices. The CPU fetches instructions from memory and executes them; it also sends signals that control the rest of the system.

Memory is usually divided into two levels: the fast, relatively small, and volatile main memory, and the slow, large, and nonvolatile secondary memory. The main memory works at CPU speed and supplies instructions and data for execution. The secondary memory stores files containing data and programs that the CPU is not currently executing. The main memory uses semiconductor chips; the secondary memory uses disk or tape drives.

Devices such as the keyboard, display, printer, and disk drives are outside of the "inner computer" (the CPU and main memory) and are thus called peripherals. The CPU accesses peripherals and main memory differently.

The view of a computer from the perspective of the user is called computer architecture and has software and hardware aspects. The former include the instruction set of the CPU, its word size, the size of the address space, and other parameters. The latter consist of the set of signals that the CPU sends to or receives from memory and peripheral devices. Software aspects of architecture are essential for programmers; hardware aspects are the basis of interfacing between the CPU, memory and peripheral devices.

The alternative perspective, computer organization, concentrates on the logic design of the computer. Its focus is the internal implementation of computer architecture.

In this chapter, we defined the architecture of a very simple CPU called TOY. It has the following parameters: eight-bit word size, a 64k address space, a 256-address I/O space, one internal accumulator, a control register with four flags, and a basic set of data transfer, data manipulation, and control instructions designed for signed arithmetic. Three addressing modes —implied (no operand specified), absolute (operand is address) and immediate (operand is value)—are available.

TOY is a one-address CPU which means that most of its data processing instructions require the specification of one operand; the accumulator is the implicit source of the second operand and the destination of the result. The 6800 CPU by Motorola that we will present in Chapter 10 is another example of a single-address CPU. Many current CPUs use a two-address scheme in which most instructions contain the address of the source and destination data; the "destination" address also identifies the second operand. The 8086 CPU that we will introduce in Chapter 10 is an example of such a machine. We will introduce other addressing schemes and approaches to computer architecture in Chapter 13.

The basis of TOY's operation is the clock signal, whose two phases ensure the proper timing of data transfers, define the machine cycle, and control internal CPU operations. Other TOY control signals are $IO/\overline{MEM}$, which is used to distinguish memory and I/O access; $R/\overline{W}$, which defines the direction of flow in data transfers; and DTR, which distinguishes data transfer states from states in which the CPU performs an internal operation.

We introduced the following concepts: mnemonic (symbolic instruction name), comment (text included in program listing for documentation), and label (symbolic name representing address of instruction). We showed that programs are easier to read and write when their internal binary representation is replaced by hexadecimal or, better still, symbolic names. Before programs are loaded into the computer for execution symbolic names must, of course, be converted from the symbolic source code into executable binary object code.

## REVIEW QUESTIONS

1. Define the following terms: hardware, software, interface, controller, memory (primary, secondary), architecture, organization, bus (address, control, data), machine instruction, address, address space, peripheral, accumulator, addressing mode (absolute, immediate), condition code register, control signal, control bus, CPU, flag, I/O, I/O space, instruction (control of flow, data manipulation, data transfer), instruction set, instruction register, program counter, fetch/execute cycle, jump instruction (conditional, unconditional), label, source code, object code, mnemonic, opcode, two-phase clock, word.
2. Describe the operation of the following TOY instructions: ADC, ADD, AND, ASR, IN, JEQ, JGE, JMP, LD, LSR, NEG, SBC, SL, ST, SUB, OR, OUT.
3. Give an example of the use of each TOY instruction.
4. Explain the use of TOY flags.
5. Explain the use of the following TOY signals: $IO/\overline{MEM}$, $R/\overline{W}$, DTR, $\Phi_1$, $\Phi_2$.
6. Describe TOY's architecture.

## REFERENCES

The following titles listed in the references at the end of the book are relevant to this chapter:

D. L. Dietmeyer. *Logic Design of Digital Systems.*

G. G. Langdon, Jr. *Computer Design.*

D. J. Nesin. *Process Organization and Microprogramming.*

# CHAPTER 9

# DESIGN OF A SIMPLE CPU

## AN OVERVIEW

In this chapter we will implement the TOY CPU whose architecture we defined in Chapter 8. Inasmuch as a CPU is just a special type of a digital circuit, its design follows the procedure explained in Chapter 7. We will start by constructing TOY's block diagram and control graph, identifying control signals, and designing the hardwired and microprogrammed control unit.

The design of a hardwired control unit begins with the sequencer. One must then construct and implement equations for the control signal generator, and perform timing analysis to find the maximum speed at which the CPU can safely operate.

Except for the control unit, a microprogrammed CPU is the same as a hardwired one. The process of designing a microprogrammed control unit consists of selecting the microcode format, writing the microprogram, and designing hardware components like the microinstruction decoder and the controller. Two extreme approaches to the design of the microinstruction format are horizontal microprogramming, which has no encoding of control signals, and vertical microprogramming, which has maximal encoding. Both methods have their advantages and we will use an intermediate approach.

All microprogrammed control units share the same building blocks, and to simplify the design several manufacturers offer "slices" of these components; design based on these slices is called "bit-slice design."

The TOY CPU is very simple and its design is easy. The design of a more realistic CPU would be much more complicated but the principles used in our exposition would remain valid. We will see an indication of the soundness of our results in the next chapter when we discuss the 6800 CPU chip and find that its parameters are similar to those derived for TOY in this chapter.

## IMPORTANT WORDS

Address generator, bit-slice design, control graph, clock phase, control signal generator, control store, control unit (hardwired, microprogrammed), fetch/execute phase, instruction decoder, instruction register, machine cycle, microprogram, microprogramming (horizontal, vertical), sequencer, system bus, timing analysis.

## 9.1 TOY CPU—SPECIFICATION

In Chapter 8, we selected the following parameters for the TOY CPU:

Word size one byte

Operation oriented towards processing of two's complement codes

Address size two bytes for memory access, one byte for I/O

One eight-bit accumulator called *AC*

Condition code register with *C*, *N*, *V*, and *Z* flags

Two-phase clock with nonoverlapping phases $\Phi_1$ and $\Phi_2$

$READ/\overline{WRITE}$, $IO/\overline{MEM}$, and *DTR* signals to indicate, respectively, the direction of data transfer, I/O or memory access, and data transfer or internal CPU operation

Data transfer that takes place during phase $\Phi_2$

Implied, immediate, and absolute addressing.

The instruction set for TOY was presented in Chapter 8; we have duplicated it on the following page for the reader's convenience.

Here the symbol " ⇕ " means that flag is affected; "•" means no effect; "*R*" means flag reset; "I" is immediate addressing; "A" is absolute addressing; and "*OP*" is the operand.

This specification is sufficiently detailed to allow us to design the CPU. We will proceed in the usual sequence: identification of major parts and signal paths, construction of the control graph, logic design of the control unit, selection of components, and timing analysis.

### Major Parts

To determine the parts of the CPU, we must examine the required functions. According to the specification, TOY has an accumulator, a program counter, and a condition code register. These, however, are only the registers "visible"

| Instruction | Function | Effect on Flags C | N | V | Z | Addressing Modes |
|---|---|---|---|---|---|---|
| ADC | $[AC] + OP + C \rightarrow AC$ | ⇕ | ⇕ | ⇕ | ⇕ | I,A |
| ADD | $[AC] + OP \rightarrow AC$ | ⇕ | ⇕ | ⇕ | ⇕ | I,A |
| AND | $[AC]$ AND $OP \rightarrow AC$ | • | ⇕ | R | ⇕ | I,A |
| ASR | Arithmetic shift right | ⇕ | ⇕ | R | ⇕ | |
| IN | Input device $\rightarrow AC$ | • | ⇕ | R | ⇕ | A |
| JEQ | IF $Z$ THEN $OP \rightarrow PC$ | • | • | • | • | A |
| JGE | IF $\overline{N \oplus V}$ THEN $OP \rightarrow PC$ | • | • | • | • | A |
| JMP | $OP \rightarrow PC$ | • | • | • | • | A |
| LD | $OP \rightarrow AC$ | • | ⇕ | R | ⇕ | I,A |
| LSR | Logic shift right | ⇕ | ⇕ | R | ⇕ | |
| NEG | $-[AC] \rightarrow AC$ | • | ⇕ | R | ⇕ | |
| SBC | $[AC] - OP - C \rightarrow AC$ | ⇕ | ⇕ | ⇕ | ⇕ | I,A |
| SL | Shift left | ⇕ | R | R | R | |
| ST | $[AC] \rightarrow$ memory | • | • | • | • | A |
| SUB | $[AC] - OP \rightarrow AC$ | ⇕ | ⇕ | ⇕ | ⇕ | I,A |
| OR | $[AC]$ OR $OP \rightarrow AC$ | • | ⇕ | R | ⇕ | I,A |
| OUT | $[AC] \rightarrow$ output device | • | • | • | • | A |

to the programmer; additional registers and components are necessary to implement the desired behavior.

In the course of processing, each instruction is fetched from memory and executed. To fetch an instruction, the CPU puts its address on the address bus and reads the opcode placed by the memory on the data bus. The control signals needed for memory access are transmitted over control lines that form the external control bus (Figure 9.1). The address, control, and data buses constitute the *system bus*, which provides the means for all communication between the CPU, memory, and I/O devices.

After getting the opcode, the CPU may have to fetch an immediate operand, an address, or an operand specified by an absolute memory or I/O address. Immediate operands and addresses (as in LD #$13) are parts of instructions and are stored in locations immediately following opcodes. Values of operands specified by absolute addressing, such as ADD $31A5, are not included in the instruction code and may be stored anywhere in memory (in this case at address $3115). Because the CPU must not lose track of its

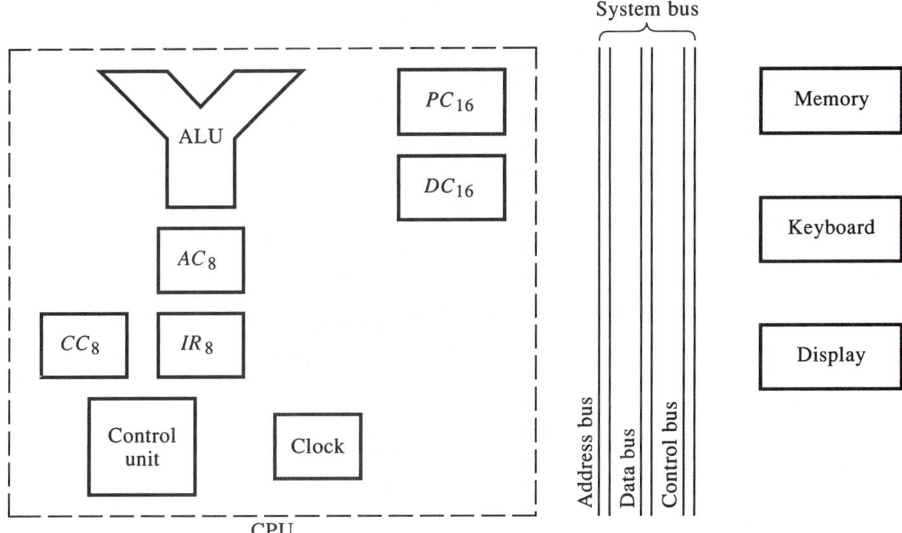


**Figure 9.1.** Main parts of the TOY CPU.

place in the program while fetching data, instruction addresses and data addresses must be kept separate. In addition to the program counter *PC*, which stores instruction address, TOY will thus have a *data counter DC* to hold the data address. Both *PC* and *DC* must be sixteen bits long because they must be able to access any memory location.

An opcode fetched from memory must be held in the CPU until the instruction is completely executed. The holding place is usually called the highlight instruction register *IR*.

Processing required by arithmetic and logic instructions will be performed by an ALU. Finally, to make possible shift instructions, the accumulator will be implemented by a shift register.

### Major Signal Paths

To simplify TOY as much as possible, we will use a single eight-bit internal bus for internal data transfers (Figure 9.2). This bus will accommodate communication between

The external data bus and the accumulator

The data bus and ALU

The address bus and *DC* and *PC* for address manipulation.

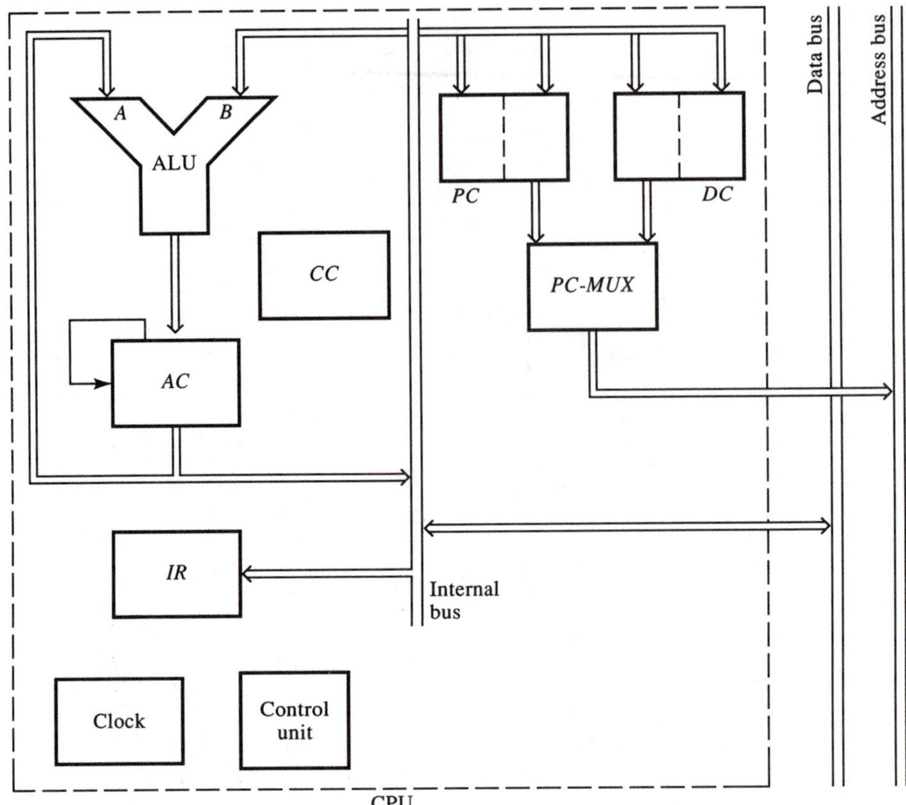


**Figure 9.2.** More detailed diagram showing CPU data paths.

In addition to the internal bus, we also need

A direct connection from the ALU to *AC* because arithmetic results go directly to the accumulator

A direct connection from *AC* to one of the inputs of the ALU because ALU instructions always get one operand from *AC*

A connection from the MSB of *AC* back to itself for arithmetic shifts

A connection from *DC* and *PC* to the address bus: Because the address can come from *DC* or *PC*, the connection will be via a 2 – 1 MUX.

This completes our initial specification. We will use it during the construction of the control graph to check that all necessary transfers are possible and will update it if necessary.

## Control Graph

As we explained in Chapter 8, each instruction is processed in two major steps—the fetch phase and the execute phase—and we will divide the control graph accordingly (Figure 9.3). During the fetch phase, the CPU obtains an opcode from memory and loads it into the instruction register. The fetch phase is the same for every instruction. The sequence of events in the execute phase depends on the opcode but certain parts, such as address or operand fetch, are the same for all instructions that need them.

At the beginning of the fetch phase, the address in *PC* must be sent to memory via the address bus and all control signals necessary to read the opcode must be activated. The enabled memory chip then places the opcode on the data bus during $\Phi_2$ and the CPU stores it in *IR*.

Examination of Figure 9.2 shows that all these events can occur in a single state because they do not create any conflict in the use of buses. The necessary control signals are activated at the start of $\Phi_1$ and left active for the entire machine cycle. The data transfer (in this case opcode fetch) is then activated by $\Phi_2$.

Another operation that must be performed in the fetch phase is the incrementation of *PC* to prepare for fetching the operand or the opcode of the next institution. The following analysis shows that this is always necessary:

The operand of an immediate instruction is stored behind the opcode.

The address part of instructions with absolute addressing (including jumps) is stored behind the opcode.

Opcodes of instructions with inherent addressing are followed by the opcode of the next instruction.

The signal to increment the program counter can be activated during the fetch phase as long as the output of *PC* remains unchanged while it is used to access the opcode. Incrementing therefore must not occur until the start of the next machine cycle: the leading edge of the next $\Phi_1$. If we connect *PC*'s clock input to phase $\Phi_1$, INC *PC* can be activated during phase $\Phi_1$ and incrementing will occur on the following $\Phi_1$ edge as desired. Because the same reasoning applies to all internal load and count operations, we will use $\Phi_1$ to

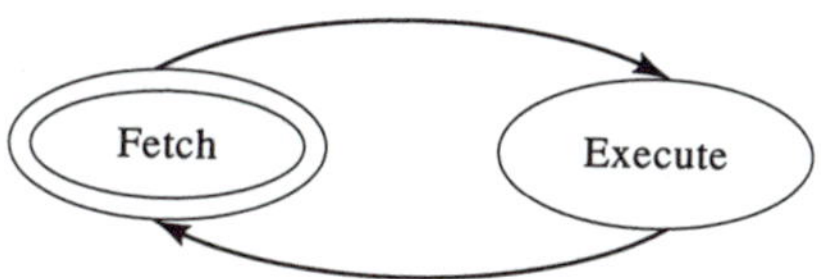


**Figure 9.3.** Processing an instruction.

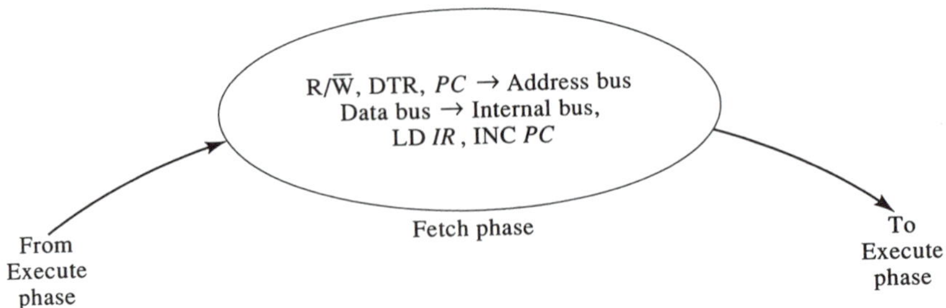


**Figure 9.4.** Control signals and transfers activated during the fetch phase.

clock all CPU registers and counters. With the data paths shown in Figure 9.2, the actions that we enumerated can be implemented as in Figure 9.4.

Figure 9.5 illustrates the timing of the fetch phase:

1. During phase $\Phi_1$ the address bus multiplexer (AB-MUX) outputs $PC$ (opcode address) on the address bus and the CPU produces control signals to activate the data transfer and get ready to increment $PC$ and load $IR$.
2. Phase $\Phi_2$ enables memory via the $\Phi_2$ signal, and the memory places the opcode on the data bus. The code then travels via the internal CPU bus to the input of $IR$. The positive edge of the following $\Phi_1$ phase loads the opcode into $IR$ and increments $PC$.

Naturally, all of these actions require enough time to satisfy chip delays and setup restrictions and we will eventually have to perform a timing analysis to determine the timing limits.

To simplify the analysis of the execute phase, we will divide TOY instructions into several groups according to the actions shared between them:

| Group | Type/addressing | Instructions |
|---|---|---|
| $G_1$ | Immediate | ADC, ADD, AND, LD, OR, SBC, SUB |
| $G_2$ | Absolute with data fetch | ADC, ADD, AND, LD, OR, SBC, SUB |
| $G_3$ | Absolute with data store | ST |
| $G_4$ | Absolute with jump | JEQ, JGE, JMP |
| $G_5$ | Input/output | IN, OUT |
| $G_6$ | Implied | ASR, LSR, NEG, SL |

All groups except $G_6$ require the fetching of one or more bytes after the opcode:

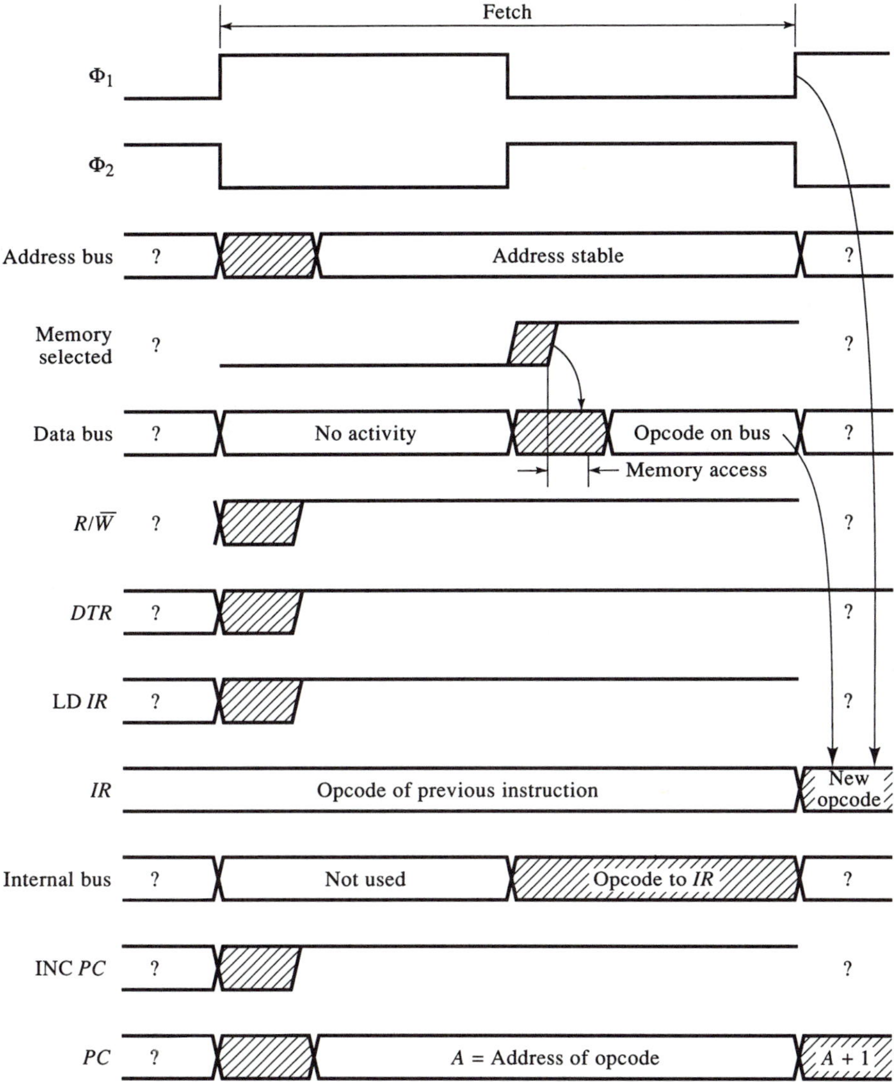


**Figure 9.5.** Timing of the fetch phase. Hatched areas represent transitions.

Group $G_1$ fetches a one-byte operand.

Group $G_2$ fetches two address bytes and then a one-byte operand.

Group $G_3$ fetches two address bytes and stores one byte in memory.

Group $G_4$ fetches a two-byte address.

Group $G_5$ fetches a one-byte address of an I/O device and then fetches or stores an operand.

This classification determines the basic structure of the execution part of the control graph (Figure 9.6) and can be used to construct the more detailed graph in Figure 9.7. The details are left to the reader as we will restrict ourselves to a few notes:

Address fetch in states $S_1$ and $S_2$ is very similar to opcode fetch in state $S_0$. The differences are that

Memory addresses are two bytes long and two consecutive fetches are thus necessary.

The address is loaded into the data counter rather than into *PC*.

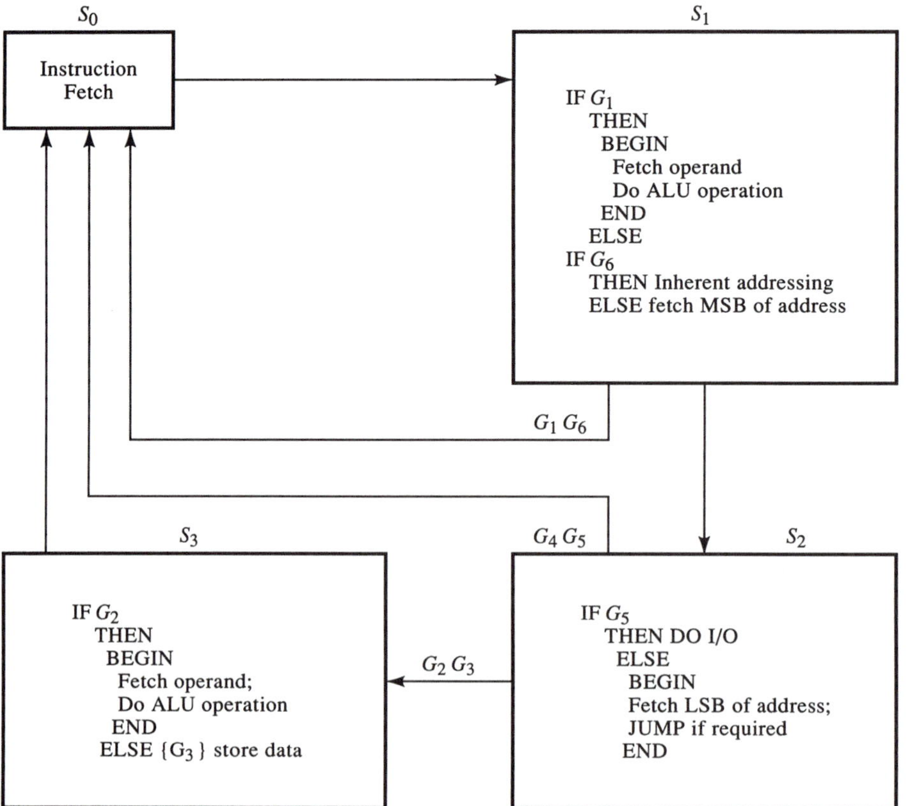


**Figure 9.6.** High-level form of the control graph.

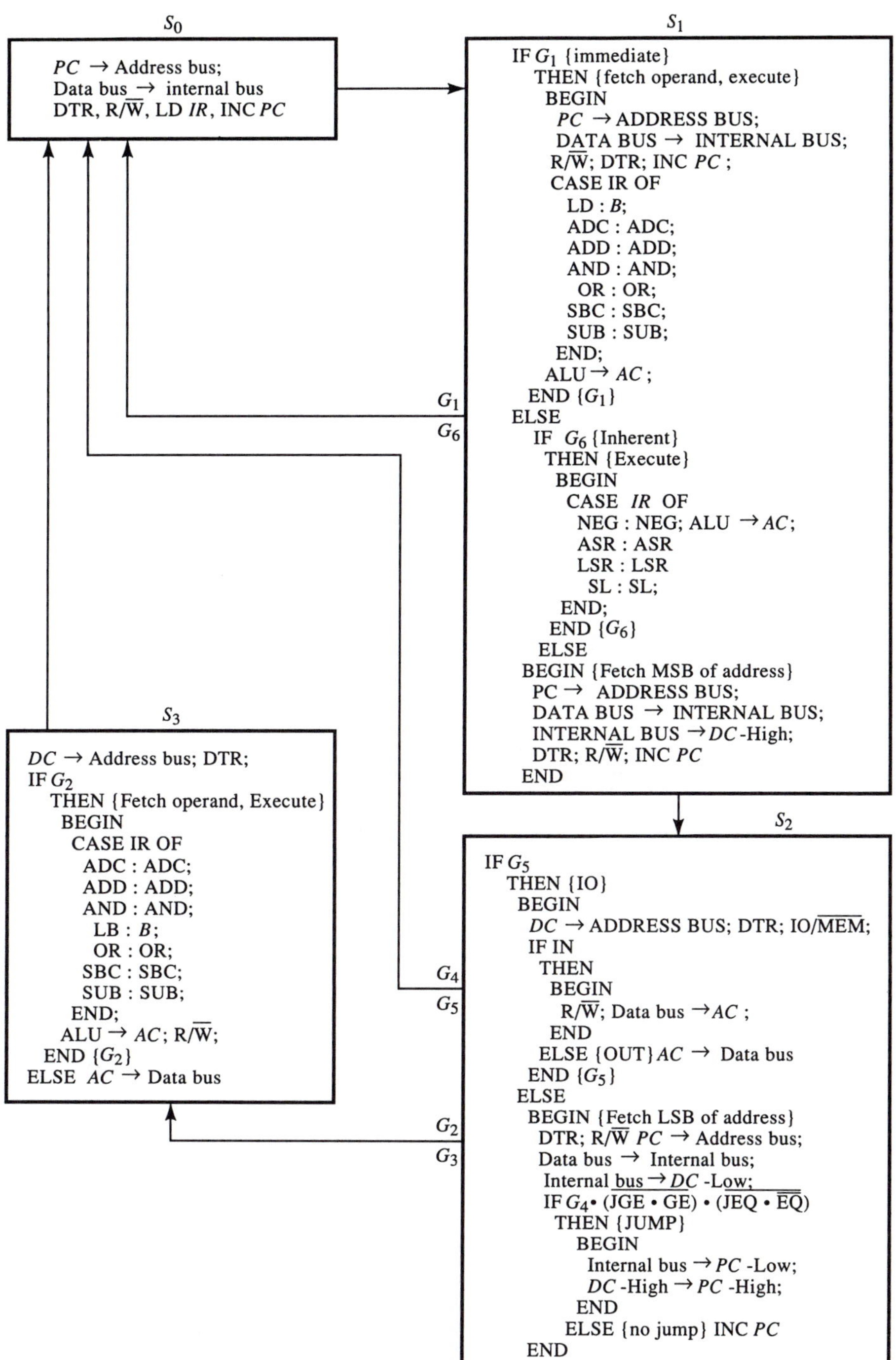


**Figure 9.7.** Complete control graph.

For $G_4$ instructions (jumps), the fetched address is transferred into the *PC* if the instruction is an unconditional jump JMP or a successful conditional jump. The second alternative occurs when the instruction is JGE and condition GE is True, or when the instruction is JEQ and the EQ condition holds:

$$jump = \text{JMP} + \text{JGE}\cdot\text{GE} + \text{JEQ}\cdot\text{EQ}$$

Another way to formulate the equation is as follows: A jump occurs for each instruction in $G_4$ unless it is a failed conditional jump:

$$\begin{aligned} jump &= G_4\cdot\overline{\text{failed conditional jump}} \\ &= G_4\cdot\overline{(\text{failed JGE}) + (\text{failed JEQ})} \\ &= G_4\cdot\overline{\text{failed JGE}}\cdot\overline{\text{failed JEQ}} \\ &= \text{G}_4\cdot\overline{\text{JGE}\cdot\overline{\text{GE}}}\;\overline{\text{JEQ}\cdot\overline{\text{EQ}}} \end{aligned}$$

We will use the second formulation.

If the jump does not occur, the program counter is incremented to prepare for fetching the next instruction.

In instructions that fetch or store data (IN, LD, ALU instructions, ST, and OUT), the memory gets the operand address from the data counter.

In LD, IN, and ALU instructions:

Operand fetch and execution can occur in the same cycle if enough time is allowed for the ALU operation. The timing diagram in Figure 9.8 shows that this does not create any logical conflicts.

The same ALU signals are generated for immediate and absolute addressing.

Instructions LD and IN can load the accumulator through port *B* of the ALU to eliminate the need for another *AC* input.

States that do not access memory do not need phase $\Phi_2$. It is, however, easier to occasionally waste a phase than to try to avoid this irregularity, which occurs only infrequently.

It is worth repeating that all of the signals specified in a given state are activated simultaneously. As an example, when the CPU reaches state $S_2$ during the execution of a jump instruction, the control signals that load both halves of *PC* and the low half of *DC* are activated at the same time; the registers are then loaded simultaneously by the following positive edge of $\Phi_1$. In other words, the actions specified inside a state should not be read as

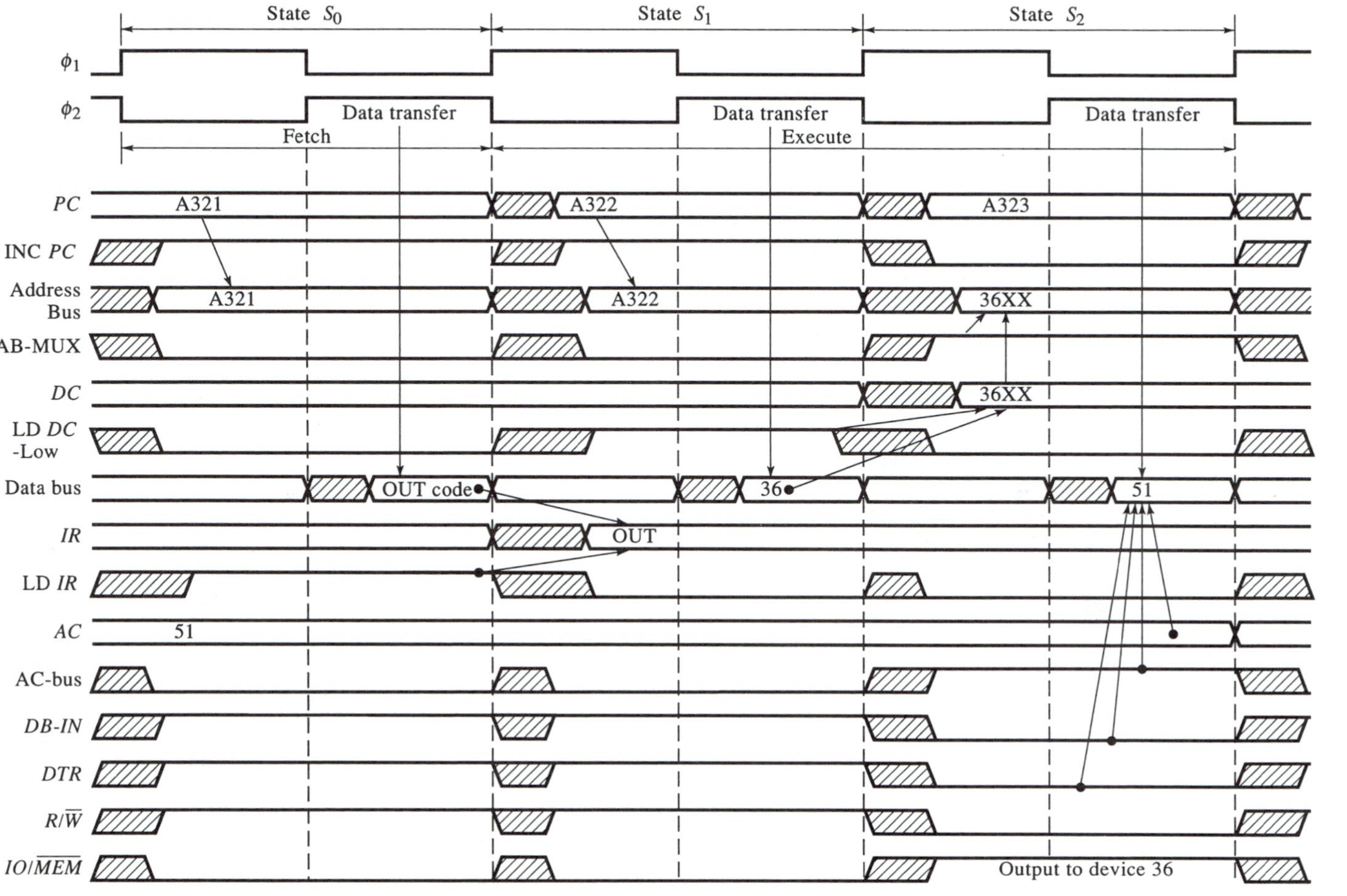


**Figure 9.8.** Timing diagram of instruction OUT \$36 stored at \$A321. Hexadecimal codes are assumed.

a sequential Pascal program with individual "statements" taking place one after another—all events activated within a given state are concurrent.

Control of the condition code register is left as an exercise.

### Exercises

1. Explain the details of the diagram in Figure 9.8.
2. Draw a detailed timing diagram of ADD #51, NEG, and SUB $3128.
3. Draw a state-by-state "trace" of the execution of the sequence LD #$1A, ADD $3214, ST $3220. Show the contents of the memory locations affected by the sequence; registers *AC*, *PC*, *DC*, *IR*, and *CC*; the values on the address and data buses; and signals *DTR*, $IO/\overline{MEM}$, $R/\overline{W}$, $\Phi_1$, and $\Phi_2$. Assume that the program starts at location $0100 and that the contents of $3214 and $3220 are $2F and $31.
4. Add handling of the condition code register to the control graph.
5. Our specification of the control graph has certain implications for the structure of the CPU. Update Figure 9.2 accordingly paying special attention to control points, data paths, and additional components that may be required.
6. Can the second formula for jump be derived from the first one by algebraic manipulation? If not, explain how they can be equivalent.

## 9.2 A HARDWIRED TOY CONTROL UNIT

Now that we have a complete specification of TOY, we can design its control unit: the sequencer, which enforces state transitions, and the signal generator, which produces control signals.

### The Sequencer

The sequencer implements state transitions. Because the control graph (Figure 9.7) has four states, the sequencer can use a mod-4 counter. All forced transitions are back to state $S_0$, which can be achieved with a synchronous clear; the counter thus does not have to be presettable. The table of the *CLR* function is shown in Figure 9.9 and the complete sequencer diagram appears in Figure 9.10. Note that the circuit depends on the identification of individual instruction groups by the instruction decoder. We must leave the design of the instruction decoder for later because we have not yet decided the opcodes.

The sequencer is also responsible for initializing TOY on power-up (when the computer is turned on) and on reset (when the user presses the reset button). The power-up/reset circuit is based on an RC delay (see Appendix 1); it is connected to the *CLR* input of the state counter because the initial state is $S_0$.

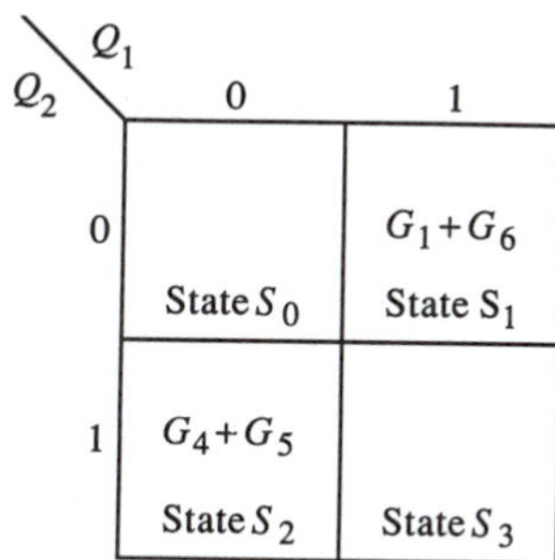


**Figure 9.9.** The *CLR* function of the sequencer of TOY's control unit; $CLR = (G_1 + G_6)\cdot S_1 + (G_4 + G_5)\cdot S_2$.

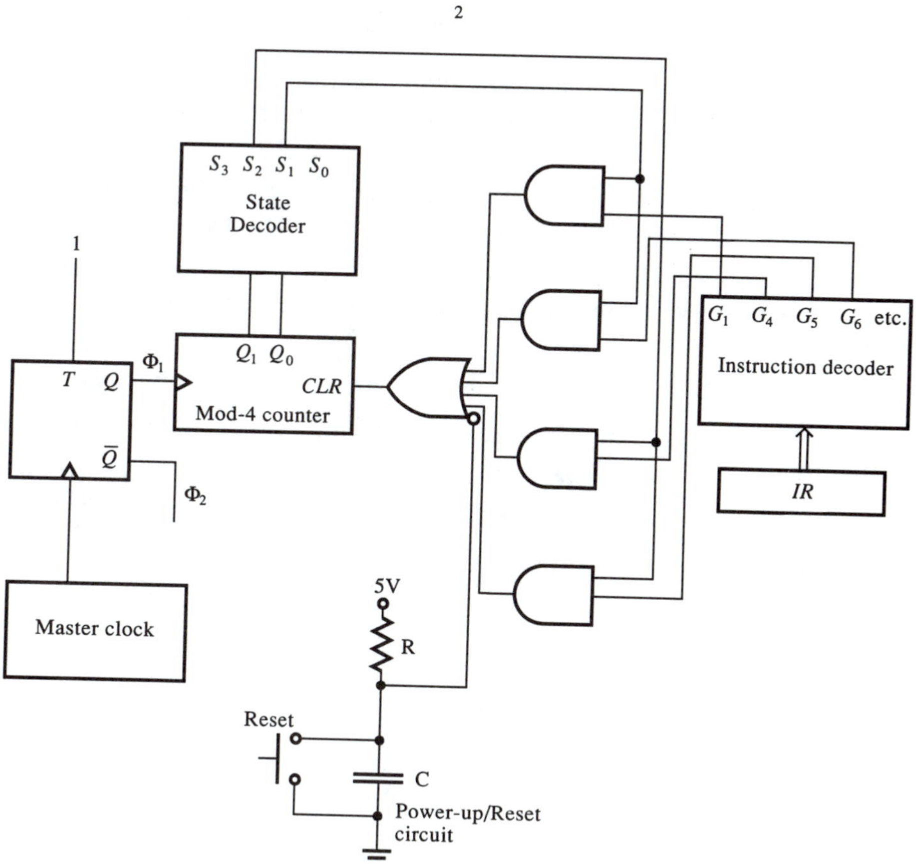

**Figure 9.10.** TOY's sequencer.

We must also define the initial state of TOY's internal registers. The initial contents of *IR* are irrelevant as on reset the sequencer enters the fetch phase and loads *IR* with the first opcode. The contents of *PC* determine the location of the first instruction. Some CPUs load the opcode of the first instruction from a fixed memory location, others obtain the address of the first instruction from a fixed location. We will use the former approach and let TOY read the first instruction from address 0000. This requires that we clear *PC* on power-up reset.

The initial values of flags *C*, *N*, *V*, and Z will be 0 and will be cleared on power up/reset. The initial contents of *DC* and *AC* are irrelevant because they will be loaded by the first instruction that has an operand.

## The Control Signal Generator

To design the control signal generator, we must identify all required control signals from the control graph and the CPU diagram and find their equations. Figure 9.11 shows that the following internal control signals are needed:

$AB - MUX$, to control the *PC*/*DC*→address bus multiplexer. Condition $AB - MUX = 1$ selects *DC* as the source of the bus; $AB - MUX = 0$ selects *PC*.

$AC - BUS$, to control the *AC*→internal bus connection. Condition $AC - BUS = 1$ allows the output from *AC* on the internal bus.

*ADC*, *ADD*, *AND*, *B*, *OR*, *NEG*, *SUB*, and *SBC*, to control the ALU. Signal *B* controls the "write-through" path that allows operand *B* to pass through the ALU unchanged.

*ASR*, *LSR*, and *SL* (encoded together as *SH*), to control the shifting of *AC*.

*DB-IN*, to control the bidirectional transceiver for CPU←→data bus transfers.

*LD AC*, to load *AC* from the ALU.

*LD DC-Low*, and *LD DC-High*, to load the two halves of *DC*.

*LD IR*, and *INC PC*, which are self-explanatory.

*LD PC*, to load *PC* from the internal bus and from *DC*.

*EQ* (equal-to-zero) and *GE* (greater-or-equal-to-zero), status signals that are not produced by the signal generator but that control it.

The control unit must also create the following external control signals:

$IO/\overline{MEM}$, to distinguish I/O from memory access (1 for I/O, 0 for memory).

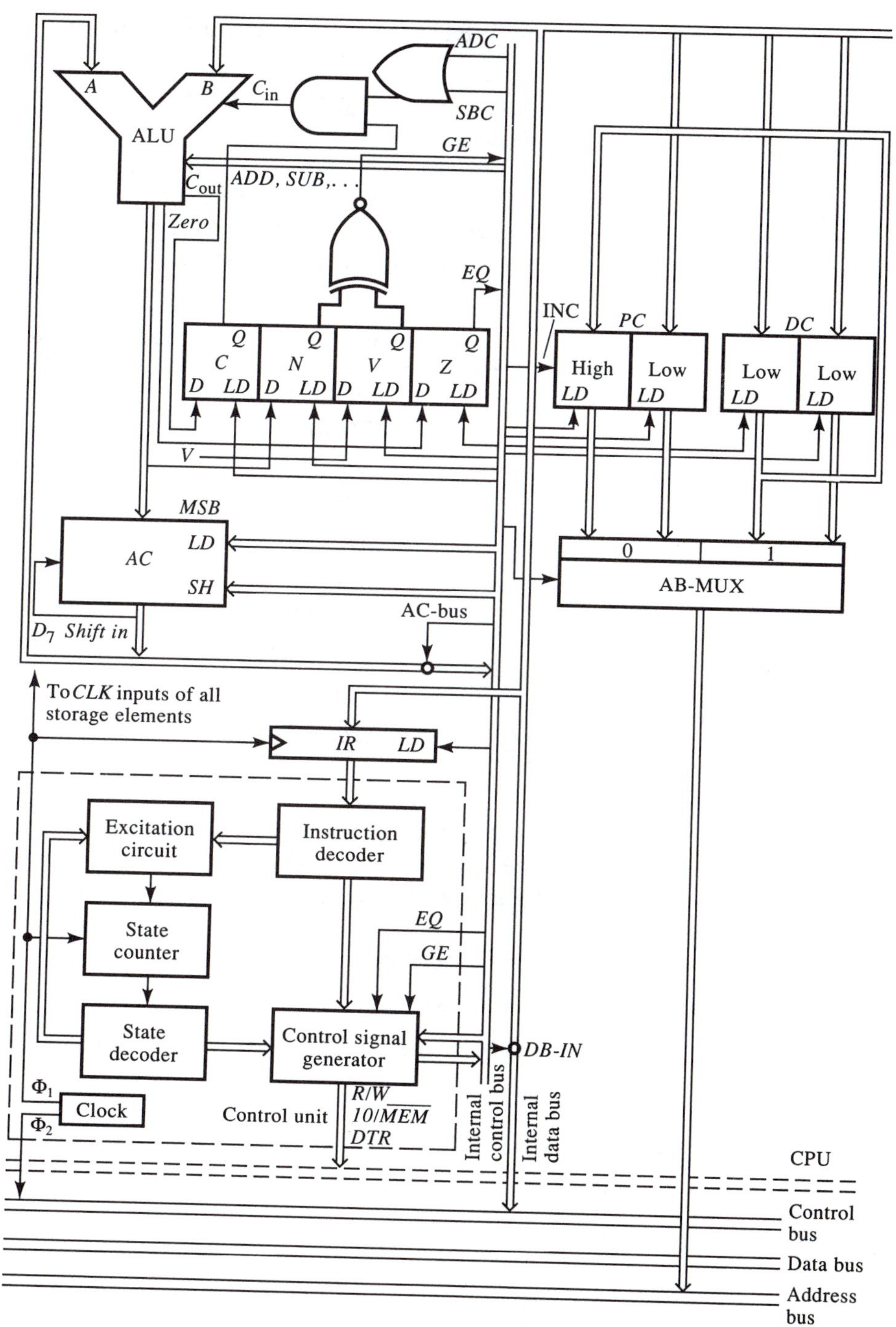


**Figure 9.11.** CPU block diagram showing most control signals.

$R/\overline{W}$, to distinguish READ and WRITE memory access (0 for WRITE, 1 for READ).

*DTR*, to distinguish data transfer and internal CPU states (0 for internal CPU operation, 1 for data transfer).

Our next task is to examine the control graph and collect the conditions under which the above signals are generated. To facilitate this, we will first translate high-level references in the control graph into control signals:

| Description | Performed by Activating Signal |
|---|---|
| $AC \rightarrow$ data bus | $AC - BUS$, $\overline{DB - IN}$ |
| ALU $\rightarrow AC$ | $LD\ AC$ |
| Data bus $\rightarrow AC$ | $DB - IN$, $B$, $LD\ AC$ |
| Data bus $\rightarrow$ internal bus | $DB - IN$ |
| $DC \rightarrow$ address bus | $AB - MUX$ |
| $DC$-High $\rightarrow PC$-High | $LD\ PC$ |
| Internal bus $\rightarrow DC$-High | $LD\ DC\text{-}High$ |
| Internal bus $\rightarrow DC$-Low | $LD\ DC\text{-}Low$ |
| Internal bus $\rightarrow PC$-Low | $LD\ PC$ |
| $PC \rightarrow$ address bus | $\overline{AB - MUX}$ |

Negated signals, such as $\overline{AB - MUX}$ on the last line, can be excluded from further consideration if we make all control signals Low by default. Combining this table and the control graph we obtain the following equations:

$$AB - MUX = S_1 \cdot G_1 + S_2 \cdot G_5 + S_3$$

$$AC - Bus = S_2 \cdot \text{OUT} + S_3 \cdot \text{ST}$$

$$ADC = (S_1 + S_3) \cdot \text{ADC (Activate signal } ADC \text{ if } IR = ADC)$$

$$ADD = (S_1 + S_3) \cdot \text{ADD}$$

$$AND = (S_1 + S_3) \cdot \text{AND}$$

$$ASR = S_1 \cdot \text{ASR}$$

$$B = (S_1 + S_3) \cdot \text{LD}$$

$$DTR = \overline{S_1 \cdot G_6}$$

$$DB - IN = S_0 + S_1 \cdot \overline{G_6} + S_2 \cdot \overline{\text{OUT}} + S_3 \cdot \text{ST}$$

$$EQ = Z$$

$$GE = \overline{N \text{ XOR } V}$$

and so forth.

To simplify our notation, "ADC," "ADD," "AND," and other names denote a signal when used on the left-hand side of these equations, and an instruction name when used on the right-hand side.

Note that when $DB - IN$ is Off, the value on the internal data bus goes to the system data bus (by default) even when this is not required. This is acceptable as all data communication on TOY is via the CPU, and CPU signals thus cannot interfere with other signals on the bus. Most real CPUs allow other devices to control the external data bus and more sophisticated control is then necessary. This also applies to the address and control bus.

Figure 9.12 contains a partial diagram of the control signal generator showing the implementation of some of the equations.

### Instruction Decoder

We have seen that both the sequencer and the control signal generator depend on the instruction decoder, which converts opcodes into signals such as $G_1$, $G_2$, ADD, LSR, and so on. Before we can design it, we must first define the opcodes of individual instructions.

In principle, one can assign opcodes arbitrarily but the instruction decoder will be simpler if we approach this task systematically. TOY has seventeen different instructions and 3 addressing modes. When we count all possible combinations, we find that the decoder must recognize 23 different valid opcodes. Because we have allocated one byte to each opcode, 256 opcodes are possible and we thus have a lot of freedom in code assignment.

The control graph and the drawing of the decoder in Figure 9.12 show that the two major tasks of the instruction decoder are to recognize the group to which the code in *IR* belongs and to recognize individual instructions. To make this easier, we will divide the opcode byte into a group subfield that specifies the group, and an instruction subfield that defines the type of instruction (ADD, ADC, AND, and so on) as in Figure 9.13.

Because we have six groups, the group subfield requires three bits, which leaves five bits for the instruction subfield. This is more than enough, and leaves room for one to expand the instruction set if desired. Real CPUs use similar code assignment schemes but their encoding is much more restrictive because it must usually accommodate many more instructions and addressing modes.

The code in the group subfield will be equal to the number of the group: 001 for $G_1$, 010 for $G_2$, and so on. The instruction subfield will be encoded alphabetically:

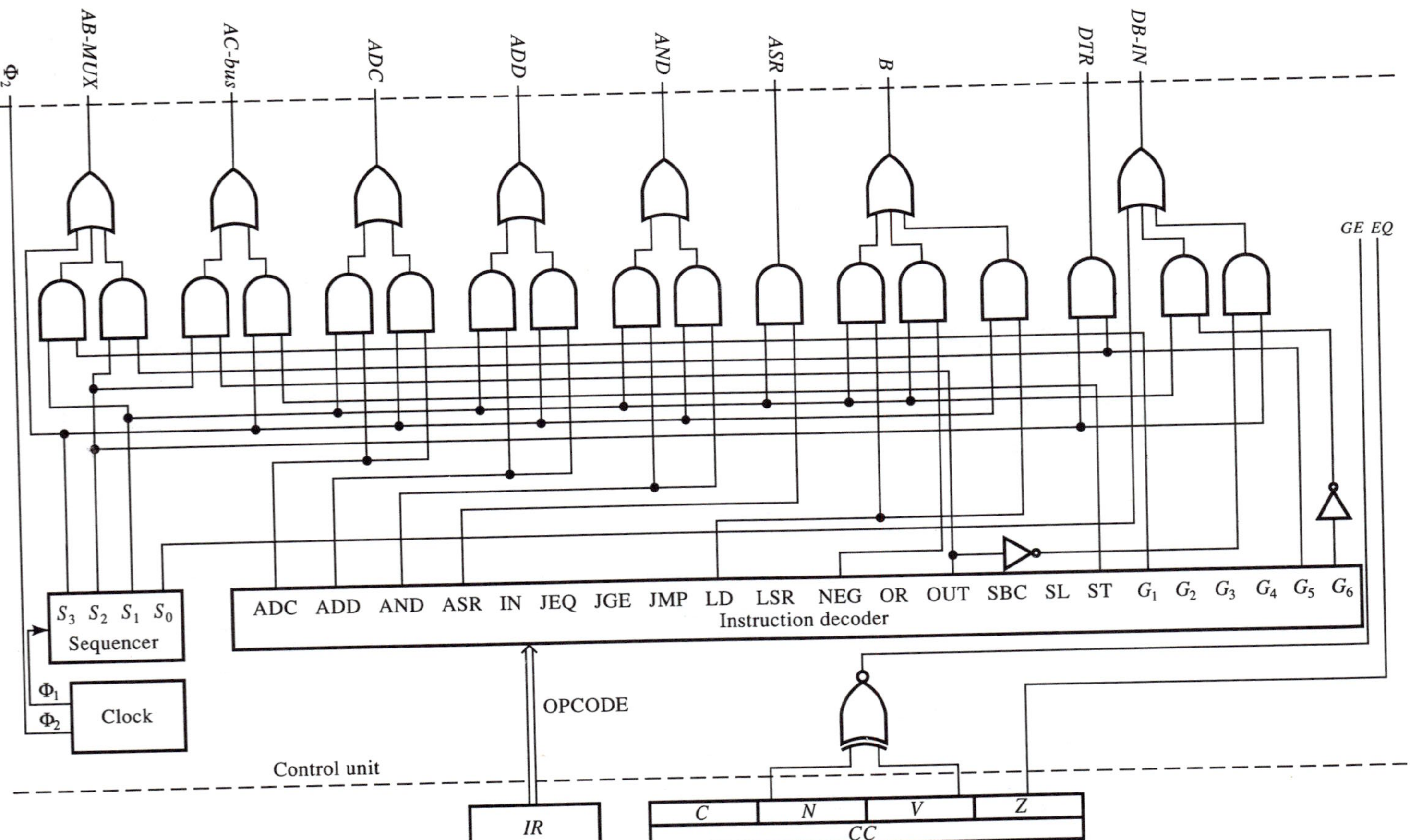


**Figure 9.12.** Detailed logic diagram of a part of the control signal generator.

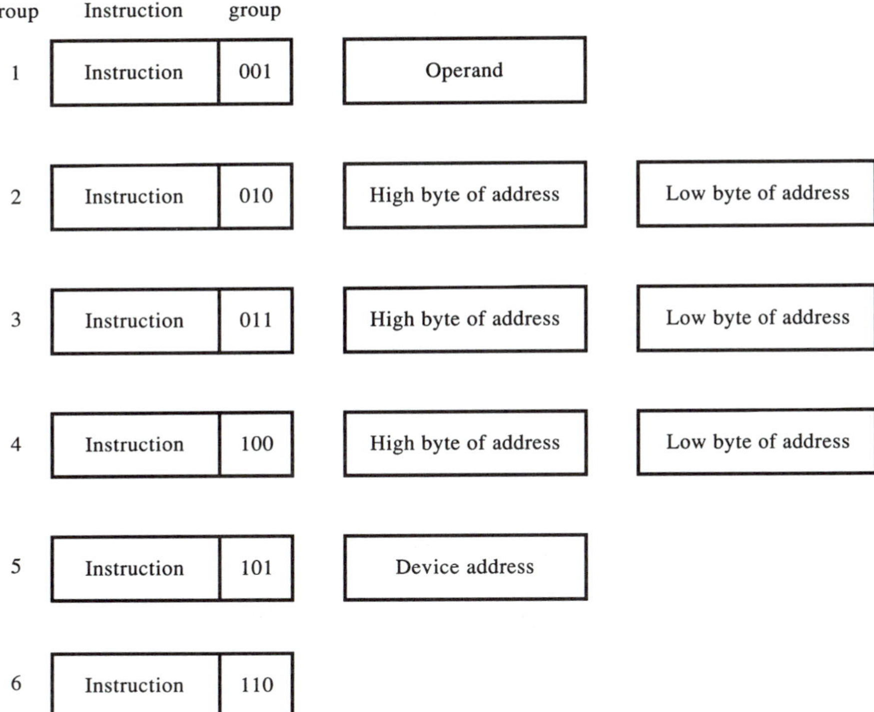


**Figure 9.13.** TOY opcode format.

| Instruction | Instruction Part of Opcode |
|---|---|
| ADC | 00000 |
| ADD | 00001 |
| AND | 00010 |
| ASR | 00011 |
| IN | 00100 |
| JEQ | 00101 |
| JGE | 00110 |
| JMP | 00111 |
| LD | 01000 |
| LSR | 01001 |
| NEG | 01010 |
| OR | 01011 |
| OUT | 01100 |
| SBC | 01101 |
| SL | 01110 |
| ST | 01111 |
| SUB | 10000 |

A few examples of opcodes resulting from this assignment are as follows:

| Opcode | Instruction |
|---|---|
| 10000001 | SUB immediate |
| 10000010 | SUB absolute |
| 01010110 | NEG |
| 00101100 | JEQ |

The first five bits represent the instruction; the last three define the group. Figure 9.14 shows the instruction decoder corresponding to our opcode encoding.

The control unit is now finished. To obtain a measure of its complexity, we can convert its logic and storage elements to two-input gates, counting a flip-flop as 2 such gates, a four-input AND gate as 2 two-input AND gates, the eight-bit ALU (two 74181s) as 150 gates, and so on. This is left as an exercise for the reader. For comparison, the CPU of the VAX 11/780, a popular medium size computer, requires some 100,000 gates.

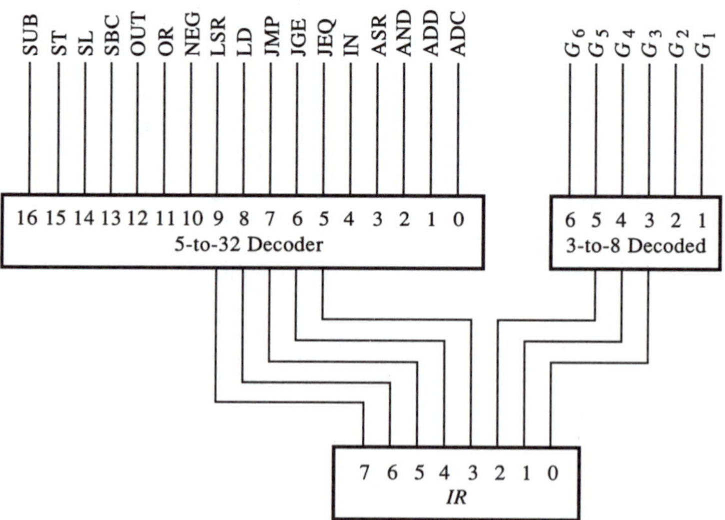


**Figure 9.14.** Instruction decoder.

## Choice of Components and Timing Analysis

The logic design of TOY is now complete. It is left as an exercise for the reader to select chips, adjust the logic diagrams for the selected gates if necessary, and draw the wiring diagram. Although these steps are quite mechanical, intelligent choice of components can simplify the circuit and make it physically smaller, more reliable, and faster.

The final task we will consider is the timing analysis needed to determine how fast the CPU can run without violating the constraints of propagation delays and setup and hold times. An exact analysis requires parameters of the selected chips, but we will estimate their values on the basis of TTL data books:

| Function | Value (nsec) |
|---|---|
| Gate propagation time | 15 |
| Transceiver propagation time | 10 |
| Enable time | 20 |
| MUX propagation time | 30 |
| Decoder propagation time | 40 |
| ALU propagation time | 100 (Eight-bit ripple carry) |
| Flip-flop propagation time | 10 |
| Setup time | 30 |
| Hold time | 0 |
| Counter propagation time | 40 |
| Setup time | 40 |
| Hold time | 0 |
| Register propagation time | 30 |
| Setup time | 30 |
| Hold time | 0 |
| 64k × 1 dynamic RAM (MOS) | 200 (Not part of CPU) |

The proper way to find the maximum operating speed is to calculate the delays of all signal paths and identify the longest one. We will again use the simpler strategy of selecting a few signal paths that appear critical, calculating their delays, and using the maximum value as the upper limit of TOY's speed. We will evaluate the data paths involved in the following events (Figure 9.15):

Getting the address from the program counter on the address bus (Event 1). This event must be finished before the end of phase $\Phi_1$.

Getting the contents of *AC* on the data bus (Event 2). This event must also be finished before the end of phase $\Phi_1$.

Loading data from memory into the accumulator (Event 3). This event must be executed in phase $\Phi_2$.

The detailed analysis of individual events is as follows:

Event 1—*PC*→address bus—consists of the calculation of the new state by the sequencer, followed by the calculation of control signals by the control signal generator, and propagation of the contents of *PC* through the multiplexer. Stabilization of the output of *PC* occurs in parallel with state transition and the generation of control signals. As it represents much shorter delay, we will ignore it.

The time required by the sequencer to enter a new state (Figure 9.9) consists of the time needed to update the counter after activation by $\Phi_1$ and the propagation delay of the state decoder:

$$T_{seq} = 40 \text{ ns} + 40 \text{ ns}$$
$$= 80 \text{ nsec}$$

When the output of the sequencer is stable, the circuit is in a new state and the signal generator (Figure 9.11) can calculate new control signals. Because the signal generator path is two gates long, it requires 30 nsec. Altogether, the generation of control signals takes

$$T_c = 80 \text{ ns} + 30 \text{ ns} = 110 \text{ nsec}$$

When the control signals are stable, they establish a path through the multiplexer and the contents of *PC* propagate to the address bus. The multiplexer delay is 30 nsec and the total delay is thus

$$T_{event1} = 110 \text{ ns} + 30 \text{ ns} = 140 \text{ nsec}$$

Event 2—*AC*→data bus: Because the accumulator may first have to be loaded, *AC*→data bus begins with the propagation delay of the *AC* register to allow *AC* values to stabilize on its output. The data is then transferred through the transceiver. The *AC* delay occurs in parallel with state transitions and the generation of control signals; because it is much shorter than the generation of control signals, it can be ignored.

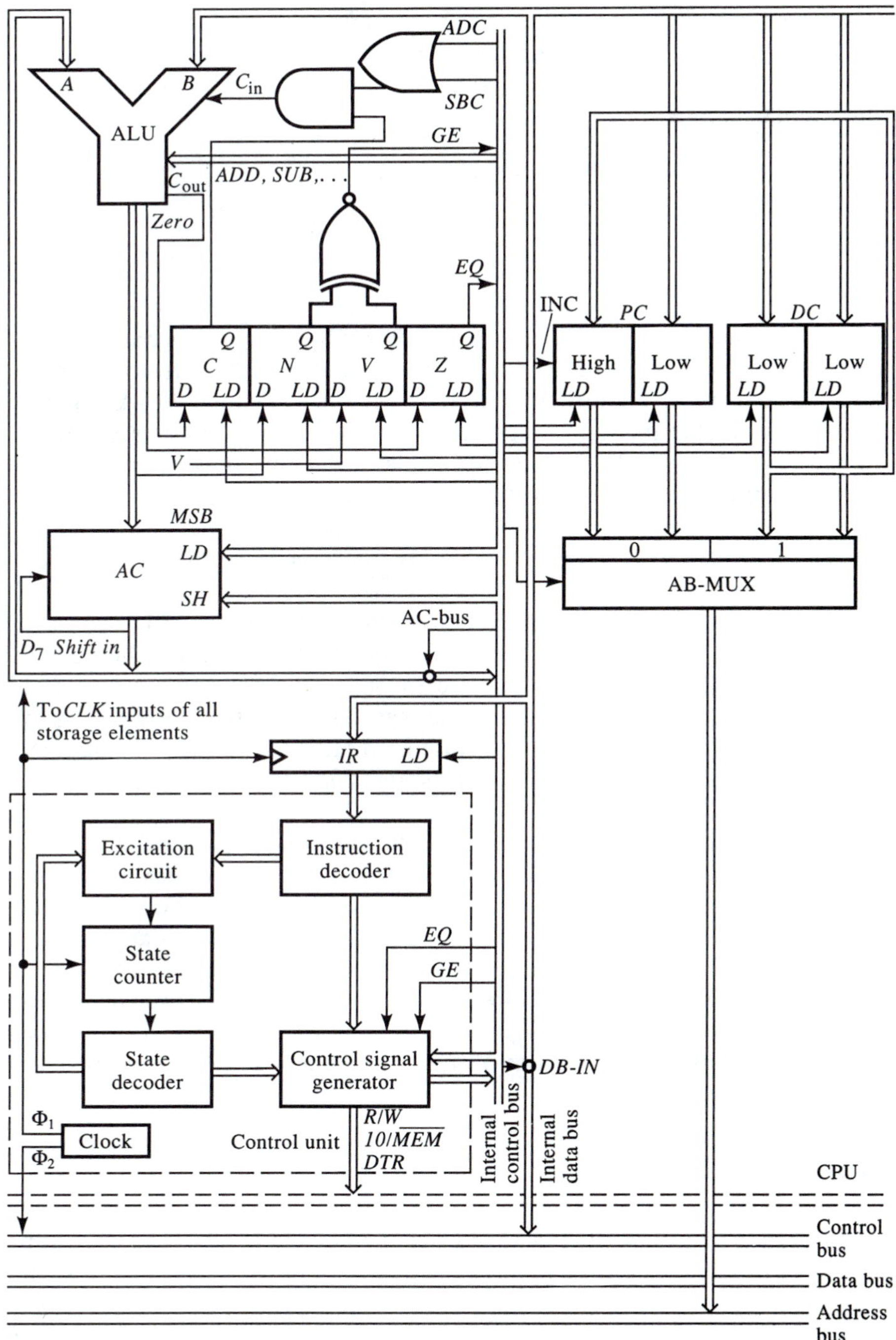


**Figure 9.15.** CPU block diagram.

We have already calculated that the state transition and the generation of control signals require 110 nsec. Enabling and propagation through the transceiver takes 20 nsec (both are included in the enable time) and the total delay for Event 2 is thus

$$T_{event2} = T_c + 20 \text{ ns}$$
$$= 110 \text{ ns} + 20 \text{ ns}$$
$$= 130 \text{ nsec}$$

Event 3—Memory→*AC*—occurs in phase $\Phi_2$. Control signals have already been generated in phase $\Phi_1$. In $\Phi_2$, the memory chip must be selected and this requires activation of its decoder interface (Chapter 11). Data must then be accessed in memory, transmitted through the DB-IN transceiver, and passed through the ALU, and the accumulator must be allowed enough time for its setup before loading on the next $\Phi_1$ edge. This requires

$$T_{event3} = 40 \text{ nsec} + 200 \text{ nsec} + 10 \text{ nsec} + 100 \text{ nsec} + 30 \text{ nsec} = 380 \text{ nsec}$$

Assuming that these three events cover the most critical CPU delays, we find that phase $\Phi_1$ must be at least 140 ns and phase $\Phi_2$ at least 380 nsec. If we make both phases equal, each phase must be at least 380 nsec and the complete machine cycle must then be at least 760 nsec. This corresponds to a 1.6-MHz maximum frequency. Because the limiting factor here is the memory and not the CPU, one could increase TOY's speed by using faster memory chips.

We have calculated the maximum possible speed, but the clock can run at slower speeds as well. The advantage of operating at a slower speed is that it consumes less power because logic gates consume extra power during switching (change of output). Increased power consumption leads to greater dissipated heat, which means that the computer may need a fan. This further increases the unit's power requirements, physical size, and weight. Unlike TOY, some commercial CPUs have also a minimum speed because their internal registers are dynamic and must be regularly refreshed by the clock signal, just like DRAMs.

### Overall Speed

Although the length of the machine cycle is important, the speed of a computer is ultimately measured by the time that it requires to solve a computing problem. Depending on the use of the CPU, the "typical" problem may be a scientific calculation, a data base access, the activation of a value in a nuclear power plant, and so on. When measured in this way, speed depends not only on the frequency of the clock but also on the instruction set of the CPU, the instruction mix needed for the given task, and the number of machine cycles required to execute each instruction.

To calculate TOY's speed in this sense, we would have to find the relative frequency with which each instruction appears in a typical program and calculate a weighted average over the entire instructions set. Because we do not have a "typical problem," we cannot evaluate TOY in such a global sense. We will thus assume that all instructions are executed equally frequently. Consequently, the average instruction speed is the nonweighted average of instruction speeds. Using the table below, we can calculate that TOY's instructions on the average require $69/24 = 2.875$ machine cycles, or 2.185 nsec, for a 760-nsec machine cycle.

| Instruction | Number of Machine Cycles (from control graph) |
|---|---|
| ADC | 2/4 (Immediate/absolute addressing) |
| ADD | 2/4 |
| AND | 2/4 |
| ASR | 2 |
| IN | 3 |
| JEQ | 3 |
| JGE | 3 |
| JMP | 3 |
| LD | 2/4 |
| LSR | 2 |
| NEG | 2 |
| OR | 2/4 |
| OUT | 3 |
| SBC | 2/4 |
| SL | 2 |
| ST | 4 |
| SUB | 2/4 |

### Closing Notes on the Design Procedure

Our presentation of TOY's design might impart the impression that we designed TOY in an hour. In reality, our progress was not as smooth as it might appear. The instruction set was chosen and then changed; opcodes were selected and rejected; diagrams were drawn, found to be incorrect and modified; equations were formulated; more detailed diagrams were drawn; and timing diagrams were constructed only to find that the design contains further errors. Considering the difficulty we have encountered in designing a CPU on paper, it is clear that before spending additional time building the physical circuit, its design should be verified by simulation. How should we approach this task?

Before building the CPU, we will eventually have to verify its detailed logic, but it would be inappropriate to start simulation at gate level. The logic diagram is complex and a lot of work would be required just to enter circuit description into the computer. Also, the results would be difficult to evaluate because we will initially be interested in codes rather than in individual signals. Because time spent on gate-level simulation would be wasted if there were errors in the control graph, the proper approach is to first simulate the CPU at the register-transfer level to confirm the validity of the control sequence, and then to use gate-level simulation to test that the detailed logic actually implements the verified control graph. In the case of designing a CPU chip, this would be followed by even more detailed testing of critical paths at electronic level.

## Exercises

1. Could we speed up execution of conditional jumps by testing the condition as soon as the opcode is recognized and skipping the fetch of the destination address if it is not needed? If yes, would we have to change TOY's design?
2. Trace the execution of the following instructions through the control graph: LD $4A32, JMP $34AB, LD #$28, NEG, JEQ $3214, SUB #12, and JMP $98A1. List the sequence of steps entered during fetch and execution and the activated control signals. Show the data transfers on the CPU block diagram.
3. Derive the missing control signal equations.
4. The term "direct," or "page-zero" addressing is sometimes used to describe the following addressing mode: The address part of the operand is one byte long and specifies the low part of the address; the high part is assumed to be 00. As an example, LD $13 in zero-page addressing means the same as LD $0013 in absolute addressing. Add zero-page addressing to the control graph and modify the CPU accordingly.
5. Assign instruction codes randomly without regard for grouping and compare the complexity of the resulting decoder.
6. Design the sequencer and the signal generator using PLDs and calculate the saving in chips and the difference in speed.
7. Redesign TOY by implementing each group of instructions as a separate sequence of states. Discuss the advantages and disadvantages of this approach.
8. Calculate how long it takes to execute selected programs from Chapter 8 assuming a 760-nsec machine cycle.

9. Find the binary opcode of the following instructions: ADD immediate, JGE, ASR, and LD absolute.
10. Which instructions have the following opcodes: 01000001, 00111010, 00100101, and 01101001?
11. Opcodes 00111110, 00100010, and 01001100 are illegal because they do not represent valid TOY instructions. Because a memory location can contain an illegal opcode, it is interesting to analyze the response of the CPU to such situations. The basis of this analysis is, of course, the control graph.

    Predict what the CPU will do when the illegal opcodes listed above are fetched from memory. Note that illegal opcodes are not a peculiarity of TOY; any CPU that does not utilize all possible opcodes has illegal opcodes in its instruction set.
12. How many tests would be required for the exhaustive testing of TOY?
13. Explain how one would proceed to design a restricted test of TOY's hardwired control unit.
14. What is the maximum speed of the TOY CPU, without regard for the speed of memory? (The memory is a component independent of the CPU).
15. Find the approximate number of two-input gates required to implement TOY's CPU.

## 9.3 A MICROPROGRAMMED TOY CPU

In this section we will design a microprogrammed version of TOY's control unit. The rest of the CPU remains the same as for the hardwired control unit. First, however, we will review the main concepts and terminology presented in Chapter 7.

A microprogrammed control unit consists of a control store, a microaddress generator, a microinstruction register, a microinstruction decoder, and a controller (Figure 9.16).

The control store contains the microprogram, a sequence of microinstructions implementing the control sequence. To distinguish instructions executed by TOY from microinstructions, we will call instructions such as IN, LD, and ADD "macroinstructions." The microaddress generator calculates the address of the next microinstruction to the fetched from the control store. This microinstruction is loaded into the microinstruction register and is converted to control signals by the microinstruction decoder. The controller coordinates the operation of the whole microprogrammed control unit.

The design of a microprogrammed control unit consists of selecting a microinstruction format, writing the microprogram, and designing the hardware components.

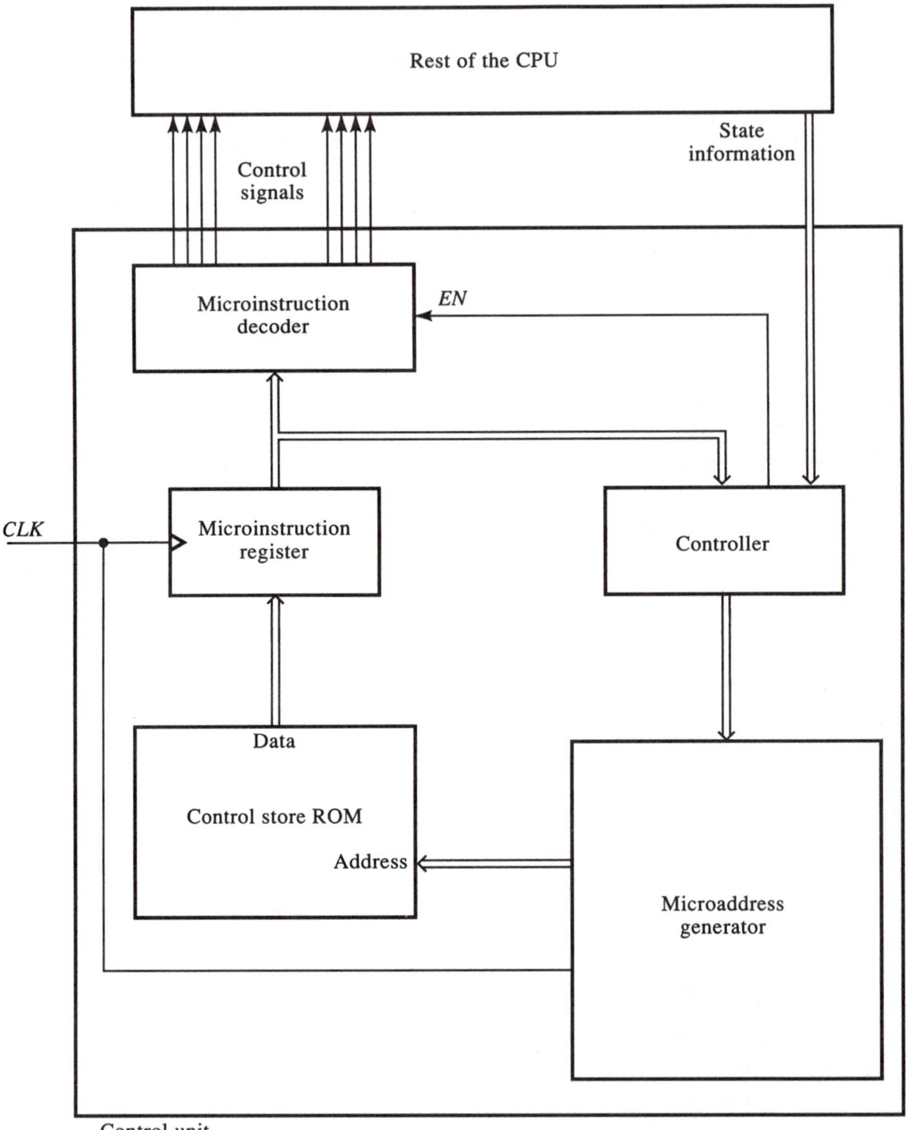


**Figure 9.16.** Preliminary diagram of a microprogrammed control unit.

### The Microinstruction Format

The microinstruction format must satisfy the following requirements:

It must be possible to generate each combination of control signals specified in the control graph.

It must be possible to make all prescribed state transitions.

It must be possible to test all conditions prescribed in the control graph.

In addition, the microprogram should not require a large control store and its function should not be difficult to modify or extend. This requires a compromise between the two extreme approaches presented in Chapter 7— horizontal and vertical microprogramming. In a pure horizontal format, each control signal has its own bit. On TOY, this would require twenty-three bits because our control unit must generate twenty-three different control signals. In a pure vertical format, control signals are encoded into as few bits as possible. Horizontal microprogramming provides complete flexibility because access to individual signals is unlimited. Also, the microinstruction decoder is simpler because control signals are not encoded.

In vertical microprogramming, only signals encoded into different subfields of the code can be accessed simultaneously and this is a limiting factor. On the other hand, vertical microcodes are shorter and the control store thus requires fewer bits.

We will leave an examination of the principles of pure horizontal and pure vertical design as an exercise. We will encode control signals by grouping them intuitively and by representing each group as a subfield of the microcode.

To see how one formulates a strategy for such a mixed approach, consider signals $DTR$ and $R/\overline{W}$. If we decided that $DTR$ and $R/\overline{W}$ will share one bit of the microcode (using, for example, 0 to activate $DTR$, and 1 to activate $R/\overline{W}$), we would run into a problem: In certain states in our control graph, both $DTR$ and $R/\overline{W}$ must be active, which is impossible if the bit assigned to $DTR$ and $R/\overline{W}$ can activate only one of them at a time. The key to grouping and encoding control signals into subfields therefore is to be sure that the grouped signals are never needed simultaneously. If we satisfy this rule, we can reduce the number of bits without limiting access to control signals because every nonconflicting group of control signals can be activated simultaneously.

The obvious candidate for grouping is the set of signals that activate ALU operations because the ALU can only execute one operation at a time. All ALU signals can thus be represented by one subfield. We have eight ALU control signals, which means we need three bits to encode them. This saves five bits over the use of one bit for each signal. The encoding will be as follows:

| ALU Subfield | Signal |
|---|---|
| 000 | *ADC* |
| 001 | *ADD* |
| 010 | *AND* |
| 011 | *B* |
| 100 | *NEG* |
| 101 | *OR* |
| 110 | *SBC* |
| 111 | *SUB* |

Shift operations are also mutually exclusive because the accumulator cannot be shifted left and right at the same time. We can thus assign a single subfield to shifts as well. We need one code for selecting *ASR*, one for *LSR*, one for *SL*, and one for "no shift." Altogether, four two-bit codes are required, a saving of one bit over horizontal microprogramming. We will assign the codes as follows:

| Shift Subfield | Signal |
|---|---|
| 00 | *NO SHIFT* |
| 01 | *ASR* |
| 10 | *LSR* |
| 11 | *SL* |

One could continue the grouping process, but we will assign each of the remaining control signals its own bit as in Figure 9.17.

We have now assigned bits to control signals but this does not complete the design of the microcode format because the microprogram must also reflect the ordering of transitions between states in the control graph. Because most state transitions occur in a linear sequence, microinstructions can usually be

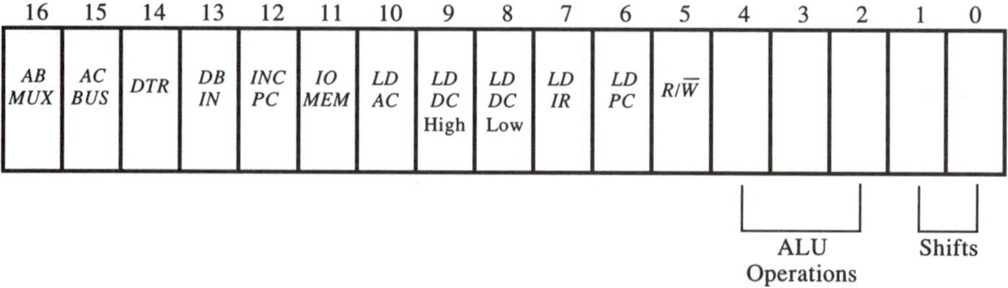


**Figure 9.17.** Assignment of microinstruction bits to control signals.

stored and executed sequentially, as in an ordinary program. Some transitions, however, cannot be achieved in this way. One example is the handling of conditional jumps JGE and JEQ. Both jumps require the evaluation of a formula involving flags and the execution of one sequence of actions when the test succeeds and another when it fails.

Another transition that cannot be executed by proceeding to the next microinstruction is the return to the fetch phase after the execution of an instruction. If the microcode for the fetch phase starts at location 0 of the control store, each instruction sequence must end with a microcode jump to location 0.

Finally, a large group of microcode jumps or one multiway jump will be present at the end of the fetch phase, when the appropriate sequence that executes the fetched opcode must be selected. We will use the multiway jump rather than a sequence of ordinary two-way jumps, as it greatly increases the speed of execution. We will see later how a multiway jump can be implemented.

To distinguish jump microinstructions ("microjumps") from the microinstructions that generate control signals ("control microinstructions"), we will add one bit at the start of the microcode as in Figure 9.18.

For control microinstructions the meaning of the remaining bits will be as in our initial microcode format, but for microjumps the remaining bits must contain information about the nature of the jump. Because we have three types of microjumps (unconditional to the start of the fetch phase, multiway to the start of execution of each opcode, and conditional to the start of an alternative microcode sequence) we will use the next two bits to indicate which type of jump is required. For conditional microjumps, the rest of the code must identify the condition to be tested and the destination address if the condition succeeds. To convey this information, our microinstruction format will be as in Figure 9.19.

At this point, the reader may be wondering what the format of multiway jumps is and how they can be implemented. After all, a single microinstruction cannot specify many different destination addresses at the same time.

The answer is that because the destination address of a multiway jump is the start of a microprogram sequence implementing a specific macroinstruction, it is a function of the opcode of the macroinstruction currently in the instruction register. Consequently, it can either be calculated from the opcode

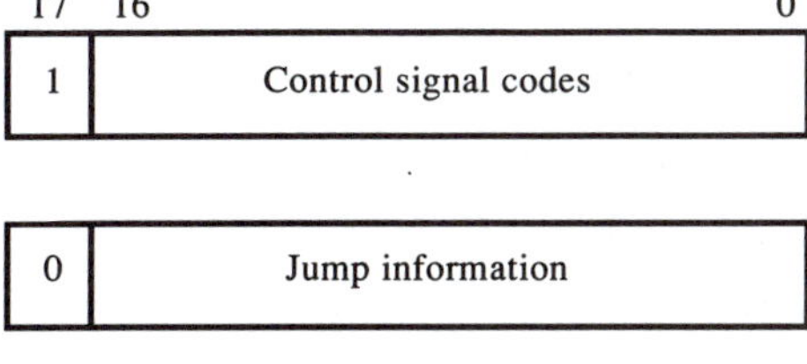


**Figure 9.18.** Updated microinstruction format.

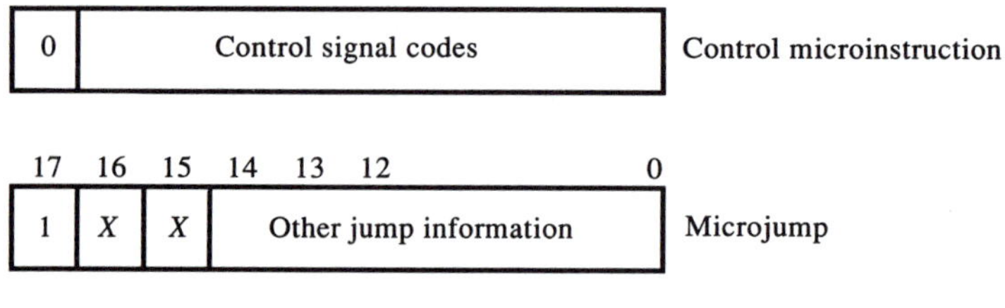


**Figure 9.19.** Microinstruction format further updated.

by a combinational circuit or read from an "address ROM." We will use the ROM approach (Figure 9.20).

After clarifying the implementation of microcode-level addressing modes, we must now return to our microinstruction format because it is still incomplete; the field "other jump information" is still undefined.

In the case of a jump to the start of the fetch phase (where the destination address is 0) and for multiway jumps where the destination address is read from the address ROM, we don't need any further information. For conditional microjumps, however, the microcode must specify which condition is to be tested. Because we have only two conditional jump macroinstructions (JGE and JEQ) and two types of tests (GE and EQ), we only need one bit to specify the condition. To allow for further expansion, however, we will allocate three bits ($M_{14}M_{13}M_{12}$) for this purpose, encoding GE as 100 and EQ as 010. A jump to the microinstruction that loads *PC* from *DC*, and thus completes the execution of JEQ or JGE, is taken when the condition succeeds; otherwise, a microinstruction incrementing *PC* is executed. This resolves all our questions and the final microinstruction format is as in Figure 9.21.

## The Microprogram

The basis of the microprogram is the control graph, which must perform the same function as in the hardwired control unit. However, because each

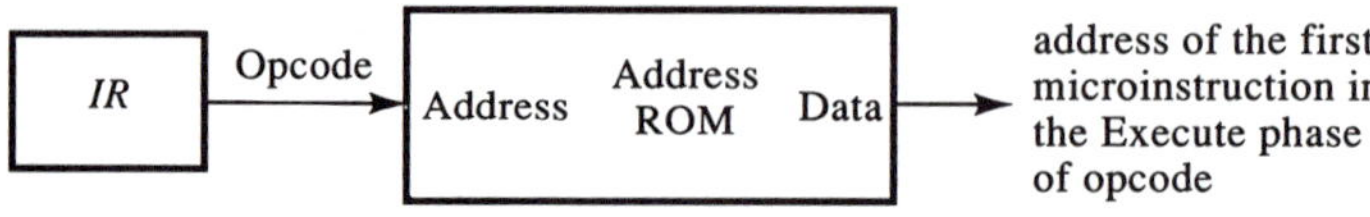


**Figure 9.20.** Implementation of after-fetch multiway jumps with a ROM.

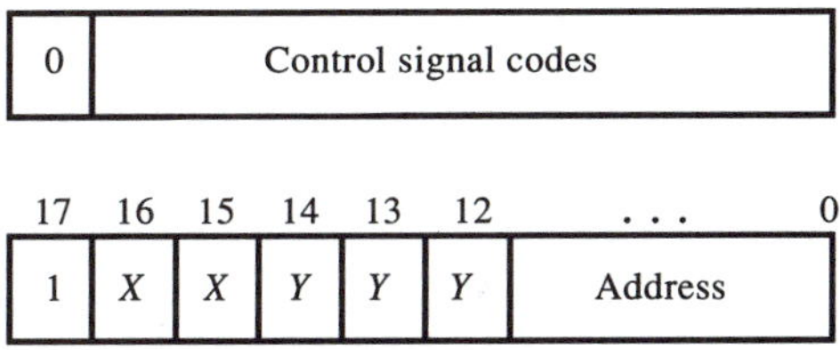


1*XX* = 100 – Microjump to start of Fetch phase
101 – Multiway microjump
110 – Conditional microjump *(YYY = condition)*

**Figure 9.21.** Final microinstruction format; *Address* is present only in conditional jump microinstructions.

instruction will have its own execution sequence, we will convert the graph to the form in Figure 9.22, in which states that were shared by several instructions in the hardware control graph are split into separate states for individual instructions. The graph is organized so that each state corresponds to a single microinstruction.

The modified control graph leads to the following symbolic description of the microprogram:

| State | MA | Microinstruction |
|---|---|---|
| FETCH | 00 | DB-IN, DTR, $R/\overline{W}$, LD *IR*, INC *PC* |
| | 01 | Multiway jump |
| ADCIMM | 02 | DB-IN, DTR, $R/\overline{W}$, INC *PC*, ADC, LD *AC* |
| | 03 | GOTO FETCH |
| ADCABS | 04 | DB-IN, LD DC-HIGH, DTR, $R/\overline{W}$, INC *PC* |
| | 05 | DTR, $R/\overline{W}$, DB IN, LD *DC*-Low, INC *PC* |
| | 06 | DB-IN, DTR, $R/\overline{W}$, INC *PC*, ADC, LD *AC* |
| | 07 | GOTO FETCH |
| ADDIMM | 08 | DB-IN, DTR, $R/\overline{W}$, INC *PC*, ADD, LD *AC* |
| | 09 | GOTO FETCH |
| ADDABS | 0A | DB-IN, LD *DC*-High, DTR, $R/\overline{W}$, INC *PC* |
| | 0B | DTR, $R/\overline{W}$, DB IN, LD *DC*-Low, INC *PC* |
| | 0C | DB-IN, DTR, $R/\overline{W}$, INC *PC*, ADD, LD *AC* |
| | 0D | GOTO FETCH |
| | and so on for the remaining instructions | |

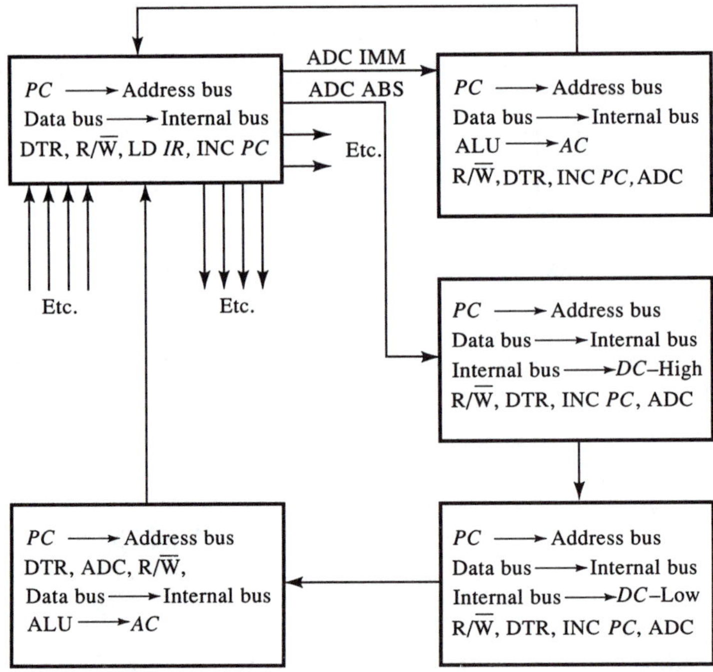


**Figure 9.22.** Part of the control graph modified so that each instruction has its own execution sequence.

We have denoted the hexadecimal microinstruction address in the control store as "MA." Labels ADCIMM, ADCABS, and so on, mark the beginning of the execute phases implementing individual macroinstructions.

Given this symbolic specification, we can now write the binary form of the microprogram. This is simple because each line of the symbolic description corresponds to exactly one microinstruction and the line numbers are microinstruction addresses. Combining the microcode format with the symbolic specification gives the following code:

| Address | Code |
|---|---|
| 00 | 000111000010100000 |
| 01 | 101000000000000000 |
| 02 | 000111010000100000 |
| 03 | 100000000000000000 |
| | and so on |

It is left to the reader to complete the listing. Although laborious and error-prone the process is mechanical, which means that it can be performed by a computer program. If the input of the translator is relatively close to the microprogram format (low level), the translator is called a microcode assembler. If the input is relatively abstract, the program is called a microcode compiler. The distinction is similar to the difference between assemblers for programs written in assembly language and compilers for programs written in Pascal. We will clarify it further in Chapter 15.

What type of memory should we use to store the microprogram? Because the microprogram must be available to the control unit at all times, is must be stored in a ROM. However, the control stores of some microprogrammed control units also contain a RAM area that can be used to extend the ROM-based microprogram. On such "microprogrammable" CPUs, the user can add his own code to the basic ROM microprogram and create new instructions. Microprogrammable CPUs can emulate other CPUs and their instruction sets can be extended.

The term "emulation" refers to the ability to execute another computer's instructions. It can be achieved by adding appropriate microcode sequences to the control store. There must, of course, be some basic similarity between the emulated and emulating machines, such as word length, available CPU registers, and so on.

Emulation can also be performed by adding or substituting ROM. User microprogrammability, however, makes it possible to achieve emulation without touching the hardware.

Microprogrammability can also be used to add instructions that speed up the execution of frequently needed operations. As an example, one might want to extend the TOY instruction set by adding a "multiply" instruction, new addressing modes, or specialized instructions, such as conversion between binary and ASCII or memory search for a specific character. The microprogram to implement these additional instructions would not be difficult to write and would not require any hardware changes if TOY had a RAM control store. Compare how difficult such a modification would be on a hardwired control unit.

### Hardware Components of the Microprogrammed Control Unit

The control unit consists of the control store, the microaddress generator, the microinstruction register, the microinstruction decoder, and the controller (Figure 9.23).

The control store is a ROM containing the microprogram developed in the previous section.

The microinstruction register is a standard register.

The microaddress generator calculates the address of the next instruction and puts it on the address lines of the control store. As we explained before, the next microaddress is obtained in one of four ways:

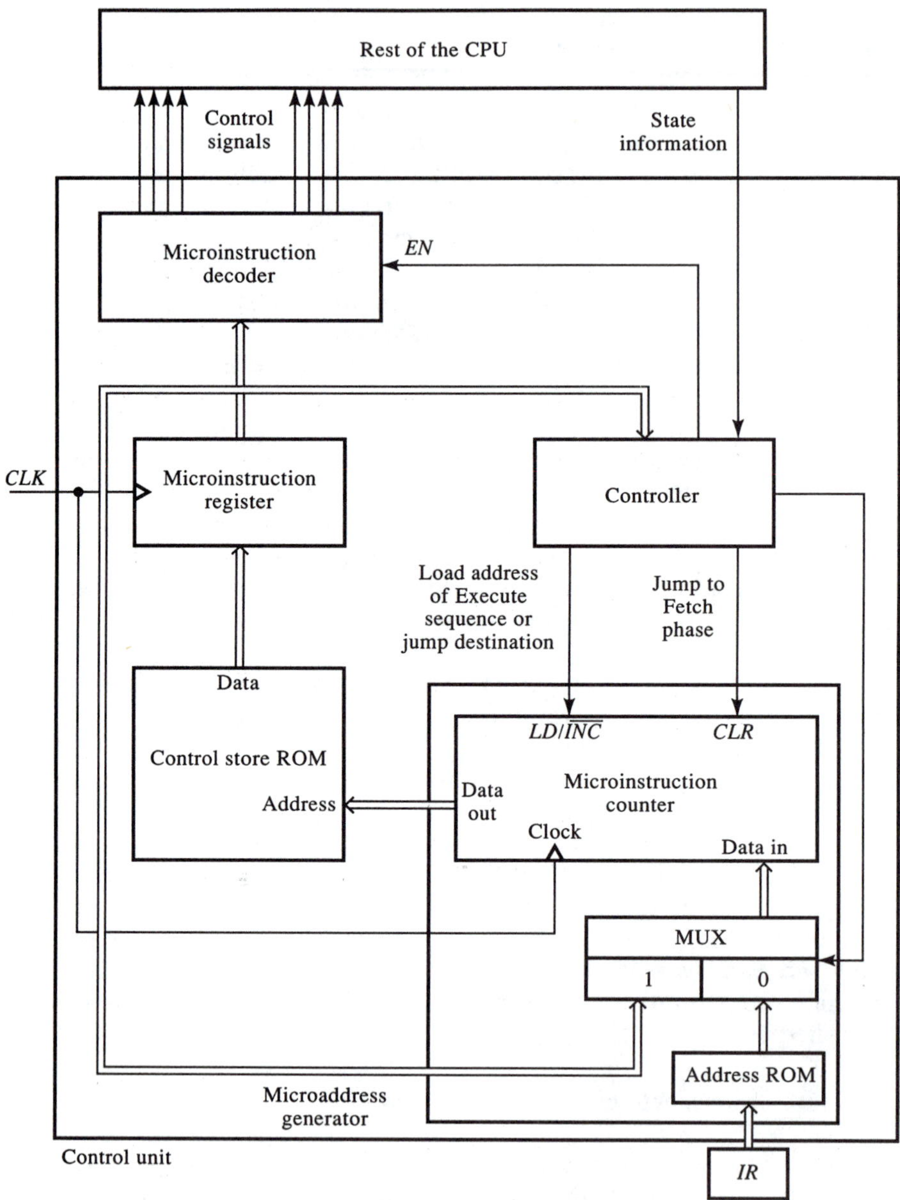


**Figure 9.23.** Microprogrammed control unit.

1. By incrementing the current microaddress (when the current microinstruction is a control microinstruction or a failed microjump)
2. By clearing the microaddress (for return to the fetch phase at the end of the execution of the current instruction)
3. By reading the microaddress from the address ROM (to jump to the start of the execution phase after the fetch of the opcode)
4. By loading the microaddress from the microinstruction in the microinstruction register (for a successful conditional microjump).

All of these functions can be accomplished with a presettable counter, a multiplexer, and an address ROM as shown in the diagram.

Having decided the general structure of the address generator, we will determine the architecture and contents of the address ROM before turning to the remaining hardware components.

Because the address ROM converts the opcode in *IR* into a microjump address, the data stored in the ROM are addresses into the microprogram. How many bits one should allocate to each such address is determined by the desired size of the control store, which in turn depends on the size of the microprogram. Because the TOY microprogram is short, we will restrict the size of the control store to 256 microinstructions and the word size of the address ROM will thus be eight bits ($256 = 2^8$).

TOY opcodes that serve as addresses into the address ROM also happen to be one byte long so that the address ROM space contains 256 locations and the architecture of the address ROM is thus $256 \times 8$, or 256 locations containing eight-bit microprogram addresses. Because TOY has only 23 valid opcodes, there are only 23 microcode sequences and only 23 of the 256 locations in the address ROM will thus be used. This is very wasteful and it would be more economical to implement the ROM with PLD logic. In microprogrammed CPU chips, microaddress address generation is also usually performed by an on-chip PLA array, which occupies less space than an on-chip ROM.

The mapping of addresses into the contents of the address ROM is as follows: If $X$ is a valid opcode, location $X$ (selected by opcode $X$ in *IR*) of the address ROM contains the address of the start of the execution sequence of instruction $X$. As an example, the opcode of "ADC immediate" is 00000001 and the start of its execution sequence is at \$02. (See the microprogram above.) Consequently, the content of location 00000001 is \$02 = 00000010.

Similarly, the code of "ADC absolute" is 00000010 and the start of its execution sequence is at \$04. Consequently, the content of location 00000010 is \$04. The code of "ADD immediate" is 00001001 and the start of its execution sequence in the microprogram is at address \$08. Consequently, the content of location 00001001 in the address ROM is \$08. One may determine the contents of all other locations whose addresses are valid TOY opcodes in the same way.

We must also ask what is stored at addresses that do not correspond to valid opcodes and that will be selected if the CPU fetches an illegal input. We have two options:

Develop a microprogrammed trap sequence that causes the CPU to perform some special operation indicating that an illegal opcode has been encountered. The address of the trap sequence would be stored in all locations of the address ROM that correspond to illegal opcodes. This is the best solution, and also the most complicated one.

Fill locations corresponding to illegal codes with 0s, the address of the start of the fetch phase. Illegal opcodes will thus be ignored and skipped. This simple solution is not quite satisfactory because a program containing illegal opcodes would run and could produce an invalid result that might be mistaken as correct.

The next part of the control unit is the microinstruction decoder, which converts control codes into control signals (Figure 9.24). Because the control signals are not encoded, the only function of the decoder is to disable the control output when the microinstruction is not a control microinstruction. It consists of a block of AND gates.

The last part of control unit hardware is the *controller* whose function is limited to the control of the operation of the microaddress generator.

If the current content of the microinstruction register is a control microinstruction or a failed conditional jump, the controller disables the *LD* and *CLR* inputs of the microaddress counter and the counter increments on the edge of the next clock pulse.

If the microinstruction is a successful microjump, there are three possibilities:

1. If the microjump is an unconditional jump to the fetch phase, the counter must be cleared by activating the *CLR* signal. In our microcode format (Figure 9.21), this can be expressed as follows:

$$\begin{aligned} CLR &= \text{unconditional microjump} \\ &= M_{17} \cdot \overline{M_{16}} \cdot \overline{M_{15}} \end{aligned}$$

2. If the microjump is a successful conditional jump, the counter must be loaded from the address part of the microinstruction code in the microinstruction register (see Case 3) and this means that the multiplexer must be activated:

$$\begin{aligned} MUX &= (\text{conditional jump}) \cdot (\text{successful test}) \\ &= M_{17} \cdot M_{16} \cdot (M_{14} \cdot GE + M_{13} \cdot EQ) \end{aligned}$$

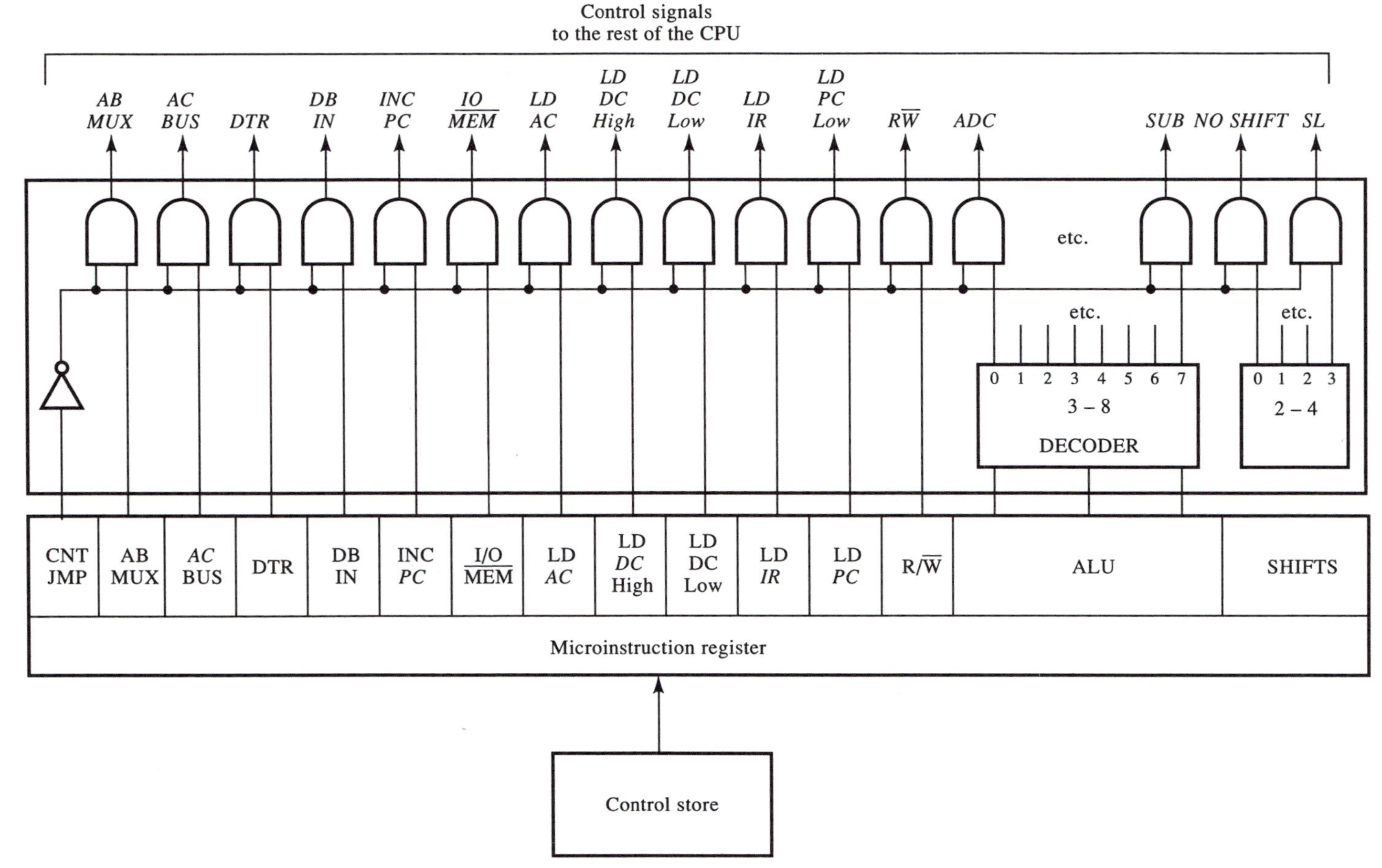


**Figure 9.24.** Microinstruction decoder.

Values $GE$ and $EQ$ are obtained from TOY's flags.

3. If the microjump is ROM-generated, the controller activates the $LD$ input of the counter and the counter loads the address supplied by the address ROM. According to the microcode format, this can be expressed as

$$LD = M_{17} \cdot \overline{M_{16}} \cdot M_{15} + M_{17} \cdot M_{16} \cdot (M_{14} \cdot GE + M_{13} \cdot EQ)$$

The second part of this expression corresponds to a successful conditional microjump as in Case 2. Note that the MUX is not activated in Case 3.

This completes the design of the controller (Figure 9.25) and the microprogrammed control unit. The block diagram and the function of the CPU are the same as for the hardwired control unit.

The next step after completing the design is to select components and perform the circuit's timing analysis. This is very similar to the timing analysis of the hardwired control unit and is left as an exercise. It should be noted that although the timing analysis at the level of signal paths will give similar results for both the hardwired and the microprogrammed control unit, timing analysis at the level of instruction execution will give different results. This is because the microprogrammed control unit wastes machine cycles on unproductive microjumps and the execution of individual instructions thus requires more steps.

**Exercises**

1. Complete the microprogram algorithm.
2. Complete the binary form of the microprogram.
3. Draw a detailed timing diagram of the execution of NOT and IN $31.
4. Add microcode to perform conversion from ASCII to BCD. Describe how the ASCII-to-BCD instruction could be implemented in a hardwired control unit. Finally, compare the difficulty of adding a new instruction to a microprogrammed and a hardwired control unit in terms of design effort and hardware modifications.
5. What changes to TOY would be required to allow microcoded implementation of multiplication?
6. How could be convert our microprogrammed control unit into a microprogrammable one? Remember that there must be a way to load the user-written microcode into the RAM part of the control store and to access the control code of the new opcodes.
7. The microcode could be further compressed by reusing the principle of mutually exclusive operations. As an example, ALU operations and accumulator shifts never occur together and could share one subfield of the microcode. Explore this and other possibilities.
8. Perform detailed timing analysis of the microprogrammed control unit assuming that the microprogram is stored in a ROM such as the 256 × 4

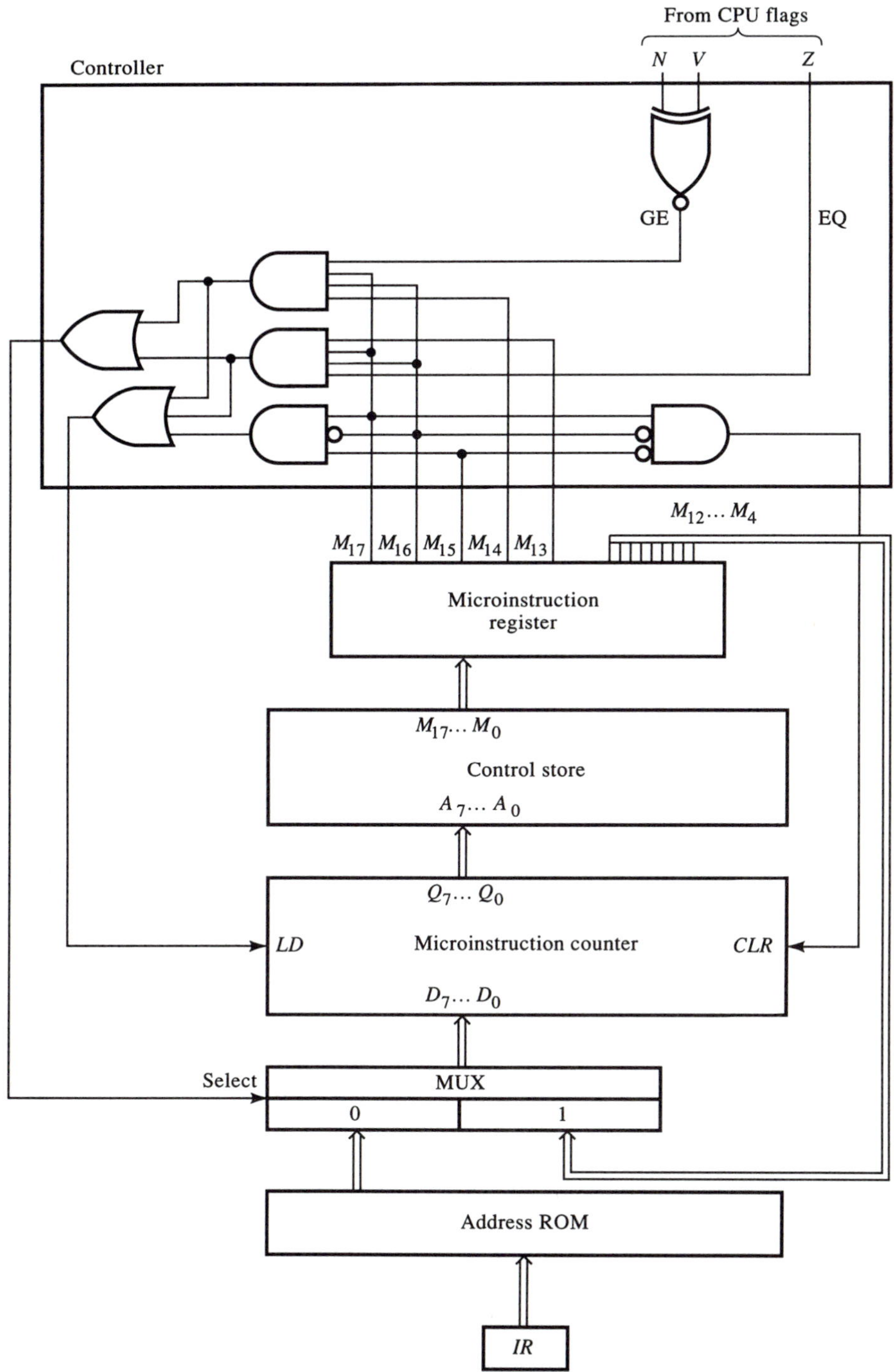


**Figure 9.25.** Controller of the microprogrammed CPU.

TBP24S10 PROM by Texas Instruments, which returns data 20 nsec after the chip is selected.

9. Explain why dedicated microcode sequences are faster than sequences of machine instructions.
10. With our assignment of bits in the microcode, one ALU signal is always active and the ALU is thus always calculating a result. Could this create any problems?
11. Compute the average number of microinstructions/states needed to execute one machine instruction. How many would be required if we implemented the after-fetch jump by conditional microjumps instead of by using the multiway jump?
12. Assume that the control graph of TOY has been modified as shown in Figure 9.26 and write a microprogram for it. Note that although the multiway jump after fetch remains, the unconditional and conditional jumps are generalized and require one to modify the format of jump microinstructions: The destination address must now be explicitly specified.
13. In Figure 9.26, all conditional jumps, with the exception of the after-fetch multiway branch, select only one of two destinations. This can be achieved with individual conditional microjumps without much deterioration in speed. (Evaluate the slowdown.) If, however, the jumps required a selection from several possibilities, they would each have to be implemented with a single multiway jump based on the address ROM. Show how this could be implemented by modifying the format of the multiway jump microconstruction.

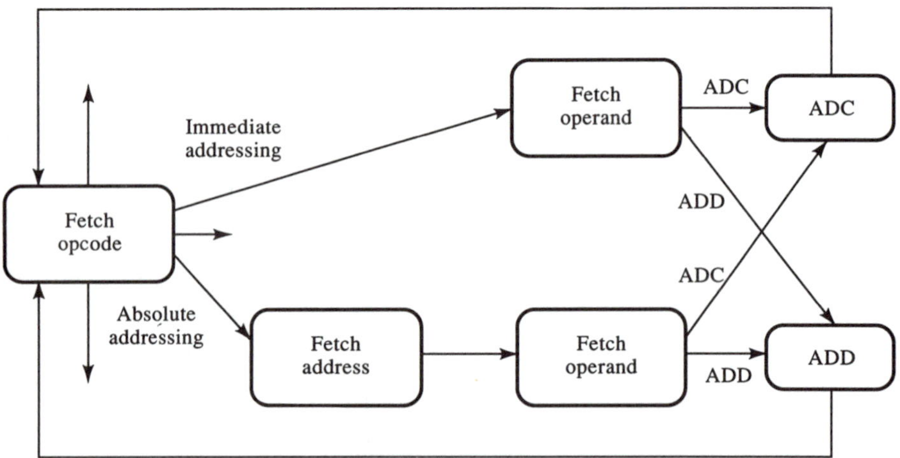


**Figure 9.26.** High-level control graph for Exercise 12.

14. Explain why it is better to implement the execution of each microinstruction as a separate sequence rather than to follow directly the control graph designed for the hardwired control unit. (*Hint:* Write a high-level description of the alternative microprogram and calculate the average number of machine cycles required to execute an instruction.)
15. How many tests would be required for the exhaustive testing of TOY?
16. Explain how one could design a restricted test set for TOY's microprogrammed control unit.
17. Explore what would happen if the control store contained illegal microinstruction codes.
18. Draw the detailed diagram of the instruction register–address ROM–microinstruction counter interface.
19. Suggest how trapping illegal instructions could be implemented and modify the microprogram accordingly.

### Bit-Slice CPU Design

Each microprogrammed CPU consists of a few basic types of units including the controller, the ALU, registers, multiplexers, and the control store. Examination of these components shows that they can all be built from slices. As an example, a thirty-two-bit ALU can be obtained by connecting eight four-bit ALU slices and using the ripple carry principle or lookahead. Similarly, a twenty-four-bit wide control store can be built by connecting three eight-bit ROMs in parallel.

The controller can also be built from slices. Its function is to generate addresses of microinstructions and to send them to the control store. Microaddresses are obtained in one of several ways: by evaluating conditions, by incrementing the current microaddress, by fetching a new microaddress from a microaddress store, or by extracting it from the microinstruction itself. Obviously, this function can be obtained by connecting parallel blocks of logic that perform these functions on, for example, four-bit slices of the microinstruction address.

Because the same reasoning applies to other components of a microprogrammed control unit as well, the design of a microprogrammed CPU could be considerably simplified if slices of the ALU, the controller, registers, multiplexers, and other components were commercially available as signal-compatible high-speed integrated circuits. A number of such parts are indeed manufactured, for example by Advanced Microdevices. They are frequently used to build microprogrammed CPUs and special purpose controllers.

## SUMMARY

Although we have only touched on CPU implementation and have used only the more obvious approaches, we can make the following general conclusions:

The CPU is a special digital system and its design follows the same principles as the design of other digital systems.

The heart of the CPU, its control unit, can be hardwired or microprogrammed.

Microprogrammed and hardwired CPUs compare as follows: The design of microprogrammed control units is easier, faster, and much more flexible. Hardwired control units perform somewhat faster mainly because they implement state transitions in hardware rather than by wasteful microjumps. In most applications, the greater potential speed of hardwired control units is less important than their more difficult and expensive design. Most modern CPUs are thus microprogrammed and are only converted to hardwired versions if they are commercially successful. Very fast CPUs are hardwired too.

One of the essential parameters of a microprogrammed control unit is the microcode format, which can be selected from a wide range between the extremes of pure vertical and pure horizontal coding. Horizontal microprogramming allows easy modification of CPU function whereas a vertically microprogrammed CPU might require recoding to access certain control signals. Horizontal microprograms need little microcode decoding but their control store is larger because microcodes are long. The choice of the microcode format has implications for design, complexity, and operating speed.

A microprogrammed CPU gains extra flexibility when a part of its control store is a RAM and the programmer can create his own microcode. Such microprogrammable CPUs can be used to emulate other CPUs or to create new instructions that speed up execution of frequently needed special operations. In practice, few commercial CPUs are microprogrammable.

Although most CPUs are designed essentially at the level of transistors, microprogrammed control units can also be built from slices of ALU, storage, sequencer, and other functions. Integrated circuits for this purpose are commercially available and are used to build fast bit-slice CPUs and controllers for specialized applications.

## REVIEW QUESTIONS

1. Define the following terms: Address generator, bit-slice design, control graph, control unit, fetch/execute phase, system bus, clock phase, machine cycle, hardwired control unit, instruction register, instruction decoder, control signal generator, microprogrammed control unit, control store, microprogram, microprogramming (horizontal, vertical), sequencer, timing analysis.

2. List the main steps in designing
   a. a hardwired control unit,
   b. a microprogrammed control unit.

## REFERENCES

The following titles listed in the references at the end of the book are relevant to this chapter:

D. L. Dietmeyer. *Logic Design of Digital Systems.*

G. G. Langdon, Jr. *Computer Design.*

D. J. Nesin. *Process Organization and Microprogramming.*

# CHAPTER 10

# A REAL CPU AND ITS PROGRAMMING

## AN OVERVIEW

In this chapter, we will examine the software aspects of the Motorola MC6800 CPU; we will cover its hardware aspects in Chapter 12. Although the 6800 was designed about two decades ago, it is well suited for our needs because it has a simple structure and instruction set and because various teaching aids, such as laboratory kits and software simulators, are available for it. Besides, the 6800 and its more recent relatives are still widely used in various applications.

Because we designed TOY to resemble the 6800, many of its features will be familiar but some instructions and addressing modes will be new. We will explain all major classes of instructions and illustrate their use on programming examples. To make it possible to write and test the programs in symbolic form, we will also introduce the principles of assembly language programming.

To provide a broader picture of computer architecture, we will also outline the basics of the more recent 8086 family of CPUs designed by Intel and used in the IBM PC and related machines. We will consider computer architecture further in Chapter 13.

## IMPORTANT WORDS

Accumulator, address, address space, addressing mode (direct, extended, indexed, indirect, implied, inherent, relative), assembly language programming, flag, index register, I/O port, label, linker, loader, macro, memory segment, nibble, pseudoinstruction, recursion, relocatable code, segment, stack, stack pointer, subroutine.

## 10.1 THE 6800—HISTORY AND BASIC ARCHITECTURE

Until relatively recently, CPUs were large circuits containing many chips. Although such CPUs are still used in large computers, most current CPUs are implemented on a single chip. The MC6800 introduced by Motorola in the early 1970s was one of the first such CPUs. Although the 6800 no longer represents the state of the art, there are several reasons why we will use it to introduce the basics of computer architecture:

The 6800 architecture is simple and intuitively obvious.

Its features are typical for traditional CPUs and understanding them makes it easier to understand more complex CPUs.

The 6800 is the basis of a whole family of CPUs that remain very popular, particularly in industrial applications.

The 6800 family includes a variety of support chips that simplify I/O programming and interfacing and that are used even with other CPUs. Understanding the 6800 helps to understand the support chips as well.

The 6800 is very inexpensive and easy to use.

Microcomputer kits based on the 6800 and its relatives are available from Heathkit and can be used for very interesting experiments. The reader can also program the 6800 using our simulator.

The 6800 is an eight-bit CPU, which means that it communicates with memory over an eight-bit data bus and that most of its instructions work with eight-bit data. The eight-bit orientation is characteristic of early single-chip CPUs; more recent CPU chips are sixteen- or even thirty-two-bit oriented and large computers have up to sixty-four bit words.

For storage of intermediate results and for internal data manipulation, the 6800 has two accumulators called *A* and *B* (Figure 10.1). They are, of course, eight bits wide.

As with most eight-bit CPUs, the 6800 has a sixteen-bit address bus and can access 64k locations, with addresses from $0000 to $FFFF. In other words, its address space is 64k. The program counter and other internal registers used for addressing are sixteen bits wide.

The 6800 has an eight-bit condition code register *CC* and two sixteen-bit registers: the stack pointer *SP* and the index register *X*. Both *SP* and *X* are used mainly for addressing.

The condition code register *CCR* contains six flags: *H* half carry; *I*, interrupt; *N*, negative; *Z*, zero; *V*, overflow; and *C*, carry. The *H* flag stores the intermediate carry for conversion from binary to BCD. Flag *I* is used for interrupts (Chapter 12). The remaining flags are used mainly for arithmetic: Flag *N* contains a copy of the sign bit; *Z* is set when an operation produces

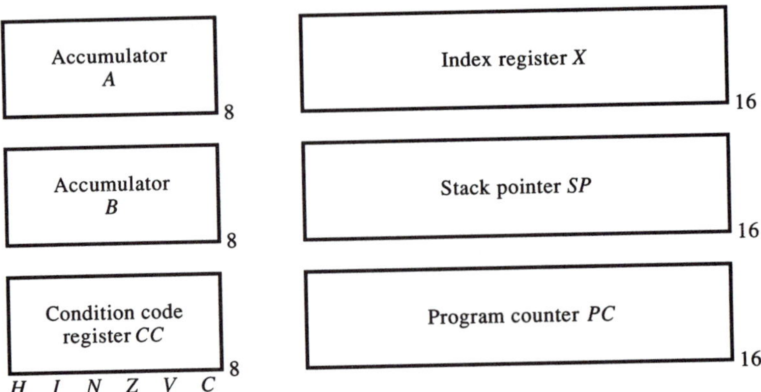


**Figure 10.1.** Internal registers of the MC6800 CPU.

zero; *V* is set when a two's complement overflow occurs; and *C* is carry or borrow.

The 6800 has 107 basic instructions, and because most of them can be used with several addressing modes there are a total of 199 valid opcodes (Figure 10.2). All opcodes are one byte long but some instructions have one- or two-byte operands, and instruction length thus varies from one to three bytes. Because the number of instructions is relatively small, the opcode format is well organized and has been structured into subfields as on TOY.

About two-thirds of the CPU's instructions are dedicated to data manipulation, such as loading, storing, arithmetic and logic. Most of the remaining instructions are various types of jumps used to control a program's flow. A few instructions do not fall into any of these categories and provide functions like controlling the flags and the *X* and *SP* registers.

Unlike TOY, the 6800 has no I/O instruction and treats I/O devices like memory locations. This approach is called *memory-mapped I/O* and we will demonstrate it later.

## 10.2 A PREVIEW OF THE 6800 INSTRUCTION SET

Figure 10.2 shows the complete 6800 instruction set. In this table, instructions are divided into four categories: accumulator and memory, index register and stack, jump and branch, and *CC* register instructions. The table is further divided into columns giving an instruction's symbolic name, its code and timing information (organized by addressing mode), a symbolic description, and its effect on condition flags. We will now present the instruction set using a slightly different classification.

## Instruction Groups

A common way to classify instructions is according to whether they transfer data, change data, control the flow of execution, or perform a function that does not fall into any of these groups.

*Data transfer instructions* move data between memory and internal CPU registers. On the 6800, they include LDAA and LDAB to load accumulators *A* and *B* from memory, STAA and STAB to store their contents in memory, LDX and STX to load and store the sixteen-bit index register, TAB and TBA to transfer the contents of *A* to *B* and vice versa, and others.

*Data processing instructions* perform ALU operations on registers and memory. They include the addition of memory data to an accumulator (ADDA and ADDB), the addition of accumulator data to another accumulator (ABA), addition with carry (ADCA and ADCB), incrementation and decrementation (INC and DEC), subtraction, and the logic (ANDA, ORAA, etc.), shift, and rotate instructions. There is no multiplication or division.

Rotate instructions are similar to shifts but they treat accumulators as circular structures and consequently do not destroy the operand; the operand's original value can be restored by rotating a code enough times or by rotating it in the opposite direction. In contrast, shift instructions treat the accumulator as a linear structure and destroy the original value.

As with all CPUs, one must be careful when using instructions that appear to have similar effects. As an example, both "ADDA #1" and "INCA" add 1 to accumulator *A*. However, whereas ADDA affects all flags except *I*, INCA does not affect *H* and *C*. As a consequence, some instructions that depend on *H* and *C*, such as certain conditional jumps and BCD conversion, may produce different results depending on whether they are performed after ADDA or INCA. We will give an example shortly.

In addition to instructions that perform an ALU operation and store the result in a register or a memory location, the 6800 has instructions that calculate an ALU result but do not save it. These instructions, which include "compare" (CMPA and CMPB), "bit test" (BITA and BITB), and "test" (TSTA and TSTB), modify only flags and are used for tests before conditional jumps.

Instruction CMP performs subtraction and is used to compare two numbers. Bit tests perform AND and are used to check the value of individual bits. Test instructions subtract 0 to determine if a number is zero and whether it is positive or negative.

*Control-of-flow instructions* include conditional and unconditional jumps and jumps to subroutines. Subroutines are machine level equivalents of procedures and functions in high-level languages like Pascal and will be considered later. Conditional jumps test a variety of conditions, resulting mainly from comparisons of signed and unsigned numbers.

Instructions in this category can be subdivided into jumps and branches. Jumps use a sixteen-bit destination address and can thus reach any memory

| Accumulator and memory | | IMMED | | | DIRECT | | | INDEX | | | EXTEND | | | INNER | | | (All rejector labels refer to contents) | 5 | 4 | 3 | 2 | 1 | 0 |
|---|---|---|---|---|---|---|---|---|---|---|---|---|---|---|---|---|---|---|---|---|---|---|---|
| Operations | Mnemonic | OP | ~ | # | OP | ~ | # | OP | ~ | # | OP | ~ | # | OP | ~ | # | | H | I | N | Z | V | C |
| ADD | ADDA | SB | 2 | 2 | S6 | 3 | 2 | A8 | 5 | 2 | B8 | 4 | 3 | | | | $A+M \rightarrow A$ | ↕ | • | ↕ | ↕ | ↕ | ↕ |
| | ADDB | CB | 2 | 2 | D6 | 3 | 2 | E8 | 5 | 2 | F8 | 4 | 3 | | | | $B+M \rightarrow B$ | ↕ | • | ↕ | ↕ | ↕ | ↕ |
| Add acmltrs | ABA | | | | | | | | | | | | | 1B | 2 | 1 | $A+B \rightarrow A$ | ↕ | • | ↕ | ↕ | ↕ | ↕ |
| Add with carry | ADCA | S9 | 2 | 2 | S9 | 3 | 2 | A9 | 5 | 2 | B9 | 4 | 3 | | | | $A+M+C \rightarrow A$ | ↕ | • | ↕ | ↕ | ↕ | ↕ |
| | ADCB | C9 | 2 | 2 | D9 | 3 | 2 | E9 | 5 | 2 | F9 | 4 | 3 | | | | $B+M+C \rightarrow B$ | ↕ | • | ↕ | ↕ | ↕ | ↕ |
| AND | ANDA | B4 | 2 | 2 | S4 | 3 | 2 | A4 | 5 | 2 | B4 | 4 | 3 | | | | $A \cdot M \rightarrow A$ | • | • | ↕ | ↕ | R | • |
| | ANDB | C4 | 2 | 2 | D4 | 3 | 2 | E4 | 5 | 2 | F4 | 4 | 3 | | | | $B \cdot M \rightarrow B$ | • | • | ↕ | ↕ | R | • |
| Bit test | BITA | B5 | 2 | 2 | S5 | 3 | 2 | A5 | 5 | 2 | B5 | 4 | 3 | | | | $A \cdot M$ | • | • | ↕ | ↕ | R | • |
| | BITB | C5 | 2 | 2 | D5 | 3 | 2 | E5 | 5 | 2 | F5 | 4 | 3 | | | | $B \cdot M$ | • | • | ↕ | ↕ | R | • |
| Clear | CLR | | | | | | | 6F | 7 | 2 | 7F | 6 | 3 | | | | $00 \rightarrow M$ | • | • | R | S | R | R |
| | CLRA | | | | | | | | | | | | | 4F | 2 | 1 | $00 \rightarrow A$ | • | • | R | S | R | R |
| | CLRB | | | | | | | | | | | | | 5F | 2 | 1 | $00 \rightarrow B$ | • | • | R | S | R | R |
| Compare | CMPA | S1 | 2 | 2 | S1 | 3 | 2 | A1 | 5 | 2 | B1 | 4 | 3 | | | | $A-M$ | • | • | ↕ | ↕ | ↕ | ↕ |
| | CMPB | C1 | 2 | 2 | D1 | 3 | 2 | E1 | 5 | 2 | F1 | 4 | 3 | | | | $B-M$ | • | • | ↕ | ↕ | ↕ | ↕ |
| Compare acmltrs | CBA | | | | | | | | | | | | | 11 | 2 | 1 | $A-B$ | • | • | ↕ | ↕ | ↕ | ↕ |
| Complement, 1's | COM | | | | | | | 63 | 7 | 2 | 73 | 6 | 3 | | | | $\overline{M} \rightarrow M$ | • | • | ↕ | ↕ | R | S |
| | COMA | | | | | | | | | | | | | 43 | 2 | 1 | $\overline{A} \rightarrow A$ | • | • | ↕ | ↕ | R | S |
| | COME | | | | | | | | | | | | | 53 | 2 | 1 | $\overline{B} \rightarrow B$ | • | • | ↕ | ↕ | R | S |
| Complement, 2's | NEG | | | | | | | 60 | 7 | 2 | 70 | 6 | 3 | | | | $00-M \rightarrow M$ | • | • | ↕ | ↕ | ① | ② |
| (Negate) | NEGA | | | | | | | | | | | | | 40 | 2 | 1 | $00-A \rightarrow A$ | • | • | ↕ | ↕ | ① | ② |
| | NEGB | | | | | | | | | | | | | 50 | 2 | 1 | $00-B \rightarrow B$ | • | • | ↕ | ↕ | ① | ② |
| Decimal adjust, A | DAA | | | | | | | | | | | | | 19 | 2 | 1 | Converts binary Add. of BCO characters into BCO format | • | • | ↕ | ↕ | ↕ | ③ |
| Decrement | DEC | | | | | | | GA | 7 | 2 | 7A | 6 | 3 | | | | $M-1 \rightarrow M$ | • | • | ↕ | ↕ | ④ | • |
| | DECA | | | | | | | | | | | | | 4A | 2 | 1 | $A-1 \rightarrow A$ | • | • | ↕ | ↕ | ④ | • |
| | DECB | | | | | | | | | | | | | 5A | 2 | 1 | $B-1 \rightarrow B$ | • | • | ↕ | ↕ | ④ | • |
| Exclusive, OR | EORA | S8 | 2 | 2 | S8 | 3 | 2 | A8 | 5 | 2 | B8 | 4 | 3 | | | | $A \cdot M \rightarrow A$ | • | • | ↕ | ↕ | R | • |
| | EORB | C8 | 2 | 2 | D8 | 3 | 2 | E8 | 5 | 2 | F8 | 4 | 3 | | | | $B \cdot M \rightarrow B$ | • | • | ↕ | ↕ | R | • |
| Increment | INC | | | | | | | SC | 7 | 2 | 7C | 6 | 3 | | | | $M+1 \rightarrow M$ | • | • | ↕ | ↕ | ⑤ | • |
| | INCA | | | | | | | | | | | | | 4C | 2 | 1 | $A+1 \rightarrow A$ | • | • | ↕ | ↕ | ⑤ | • |
| | INCB | | | | | | | | | | | | | 5C | 2 | 1 | $B+1 \rightarrow B$ | • | • | ↕ | ↕ | ⑤ | • |
| Lead acmltr | LOAA | S6 | 2 | 2 | S6 | 3 | 2 | A6 | 5 | 2 | B6 | 4 | 3 | | | | $M \rightarrow A$ | • | • | ↕ | ↕ | R | • |
| | LOAB | C6 | 2 | 2 | D6 | 3 | 2 | A6 | 5 | 2 | F6 | 4 | 3 | | | | $M \rightarrow B$ | • | • | ↕ | ↕ | R | • |
| Or, inclusive | ORAA | SA | 2 | 2 | SA | 3 | 2 | AA | 5 | 2 | BA | 4 | 3 | | | | $A+M \rightarrow A$ | • | • | ↕ | ↕ | R | • |
| | ORAB | CA | 2 | 2 | DA | 3 | 2 | EA | 5 | 2 | FA | 4 | 3 | | | | $B+M \rightarrow B$ | • | • | ↕ | ↕ | R | • |
| Push Data | PSHA | | | | | | | | | | | | | 36 | 4 | 1 | $A \rightarrow M_{SP}. SP-1 \rightarrow SP$ | • | • | • | • | • | • |
| Pull Data | PSHB | | | | | | | | | | | | | 37 | 4 | 1 | $B \rightarrow M_{SP}. SP-1 \rightarrow SP$ | • | • | • | • | • | • |
| | PULA | | | | | | | | | | | | | 32 | 4 | 1 | $SP+1 \rightarrow SP. M_{SP.} \rightarrow A$ | • | • | • | • | • | • |
| Rotate left | PULB | | | | | | | | | | | | | 33 | 4 | 1 | $SP+1 \rightarrow SP. M_{SP.} \rightarrow B$ | • | • | • | • | • | • |
| | ROL | | | | | | | 69 | 7 | 2 | 79 | 6 | 3 | | | | M | • | • | ↕ | ↕ | ⑥ | ↕ |
| | ROLA | | | | | | | | | | | | | 49 | 2 | 1 | A | • | • | ↕ | ↕ | ⑥ | ↕ |
| Rotate right | ROLB | | | | | | | | | | | | | 59 | 2 | 1 | B C $b_7$ ← $b_0$ | • | • | ↕ | ↕ | ⑥ | ↕ |
| | ROR | | | | | | | 66 | 7 | 2 | 76 | 6 | 3 | | | | M | • | • | ↕ | ↕ | ⑥ | ↕ |
| | RORA | | | | | | | | | | | | | 46 | 2 | 1 | A | • | • | ↕ | ↕ | ⑥ | ↕ |
| Shift left, arithmetic | RORB | | | | | | | | | | | | | 56 | 2 | 1 | B C $b_7$ → $b_0$ | • | • | ↕ | ↕ | ⑥ | ↕ |
| | ASL | | | | | | | 68 | 7 | 2 | 78 | 6 | 3 | | | | M ← | • | • | ↕ | ↕ | ⑥ | ↕ |
| | ASLA | | | | | | | | | | | | | 48 | 2 | 1 | A ← 0 | • | • | ↕ | ↕ | ⑥ | ↕ |
| Shift right, arithmetic | ASLB | | | | | | | | | | | | | 58 | 2 | 1 | B C $b_7$ $b_0$ | • | • | ↕ | ↕ | ⑥ | ↕ |
| | ASR | | | | | | | G7 | 7 | 2 | 77 | 6 | 3 | | | | M → | • | • | ↕ | ↕ | ⑥ | ↕ |
| | ASRA | | | | | | | | | | | | | 47 | 2 | 1 | A → | • | • | ↕ | ↕ | ⑥ | ↕ |
| Shift right, logic | ASRB | | | | | | | | | | | | | 57 | 2 | 1 | B $b_7$ $b_0$ C | • | • | ↕ | ↕ | ⑥ | ↕ |
| | LSR | | | | | | | 64 | 7 | 2 | 74 | 6 | 3 | | | | M → | • | • | R | ↕ | ⑥ | ↕ |
| | LSRA | | | | | | | | | | | | | 44 | 2 | 1 | A 0 → → | • | • | R | ↕ | ⑥ | ↕ |
| Store acmltr | LSRB | | | | | | | | | | | | | 54 | 2 | 1 | B $b_7$ $b_0$ C | • | • | R | ↕ | ⑥ | ↕ |
| | STAA | | | | 97 | 4 | 2 | A7 | 6 | 2 | B7 | 5 | 3 | | | | $A \rightarrow M$ | • | • | ↕ | ↕ | R | • |
| Subtract | STAB | | | | D7 | 4 | 2 | E7 | 6 | 2 | F7 | 5 | 3 | | | | $B \rightarrow M$ | • | • | ↕ | ↕ | R | • |
| | SUBA | S0 | 2 | 2 | 90 | 3 | 2 | A0 | 5 | 2 | BO | 4 | 3 | | | | $A-M \rightarrow A$ | • | • | ↕ | ↕ | ↕ | ↕ |
| Subtract acmltrs | SUBB | C0 | 2 | 2 | D0 | 3 | 2 | E0 | 5 | 2 | F0 | 4 | 3 | | | | $B-M \rightarrow B$ | • | • | ↕ | ↕ | ↕ | ↕ |
| Subtr. with carry | SBA | | | | | | | | | | | | | 10 | 2 | 1 | $A-B \rightarrow A$ | • | • | ↕ | ↕ | ↕ | ↕ |
| | SBCA | S2 | 2 | 2 | 92 | 3 | 2 | A2 | 5 | 2 | B2 | 4 | 3 | | | | $A-M-C \rightarrow A$ | • | • | ↕ | ↕ | ↕ | ↕ |
| Transfer acmltrs | SBCB | C2 | 2 | 2 | D2 | 3 | 2 | E2 | 5 | 2 | F2 | 4 | 3 | | | | $B-M-C \rightarrow B$ | • | • | ↕ | ↕ | ↕ | ↕ |
| | TAB | | | | | | | | | | | | | 16 | 2 | 1 | $A \rightarrow B$ | • | • | ↕ | ↕ | R | • |
| Test, zero or minus | TBA | | | | | | | | | | | | | 17 | 2 | 1 | $B \rightarrow A$ | • | • | ↕ | ↕ | R | • |
| | TST | | | | | | | 60 | 7 | 2 | 70 | 6 | 3 | | | | $M-00$ | • | • | ↕ | ↕ | R | R |
| | TSTA | | | | | | | | | | | | | 40 | 2 | 1 | $A-00$ | • | • | ↕ | ↕ | R | R |
| | TSTB | | | | | | | | | | | | | 50 | 2 | 1 | $B-00$ | • | • | ↕ | ↕ | R | R |

Continued on next page

**Figure 10.2.** Instruction set of the MC6800. The column labeled "~" contains the number of machine cycles required by the instruction; column "#" gives the total number of bytes, including the opcode. More complicated or less obvious effects are documented by footnotes at the end of the table. (Reprinted with modifications with the permission of Motorola.)

| Index register and stack Pointer operations | Mnemonic | IMMED OP | ~ | # | DIRECT OP | ~ | # | INDEX OP | ~ | # | EXTEND OP | ~ | # | INHER OP | ~ | # | Boolean/arithmetic operation | 5 H | 4 I | 3 N | 2 Z | 1 V | 0 C |
|---|---|---|---|---|---|---|---|---|---|---|---|---|---|---|---|---|---|---|---|---|---|---|---|
| Compare index reg | CPX | 8C | 3 | 3 | 9C | 4 | 2 | AC | 6 | 2 | BC | 5 | 3 | | | | $(X_H/X_L) - (M/M+1)$ | • | • | ⑦ | ↕ | ⑧ | • |
| Decrement index reg | DEX | | | | | | | | | | | | | 09 | 4 | 1 | $X - 1 \rightarrow X$ | • | • | • | ↕ | • | • |
| Decrement stack pntr | DES | | | | | | | | | | | | | 34 | 4 | 1 | $SP - 1 \rightarrow SP$ | • | • | • | • | • | • |
| Increment index reg | INX | | | | | | | | | | | | | 08 | 4 | 1 | $X + 1 \rightarrow X$ | • | • | • | ↕ | • | • |
| Increment stack pntr | INS | | | | | | | | | | | | | 31 | 4 | 1 | $SP + 1 \rightarrow SP$ | • | • | • | • | • | • |
| Load index reg | LDX | CE | 3 | 3 | DE | 4 | 2 | EE | 6 | 2 | FE | 5 | 3 | | | | $M \rightarrow X_H (M+1) \rightarrow X_L$ | • | • | ⑨ | ↕ | R | • |
| Load stack pntr | LDS | 8E | 3 | 3 | 9E | 4 | 2 | AE | 6 | 2 | BE | 5 | 3 | | | | $M \rightarrow SP_H (M+1) \rightarrow SP_L$ | • | • | ⑨ | ↕ | R | • |
| Store index reg | STX | | | | DF | 5 | 2 | EF | 7 | 2 | FF | 6 | 3 | | | | $X_H \rightarrow M, X_L \rightarrow (M+1)$ | • | • | ⑨ | ↕ | R | • |
| Store stack pntr | STS | | | | 9F | 5 | 2 | AF | 7 | 2 | BF | 6 | 3 | | | | $SP_H \rightarrow M, SP_L \rightarrow (M+1)$ | • | • | ⑨ | ↕ | R | • |
| Indx reg → Stack pntr | TXS | | | | | | | | | | | | | 35 | 4 | 1 | $X - 1 \rightarrow SP$ | • | • | • | • | • | • |
| Stack pntr → Indx reg | TSX | | | | | | | | | | | | | 30 | 4 | 1 | $SP + 1 \rightarrow X$ | • | • | • | • | • | • |

| Jump and branch Operations | Mnemonic | RELATIVE OP | ~ | # | INDEX OP | ~ | # | EXTEND OP | ~ | # | INHER OP | ~ | # | Branch test | 5 H | 4 I | 3 N | 2 Z | 1 V | 0 C |
|---|---|---|---|---|---|---|---|---|---|---|---|---|---|---|---|---|---|---|---|---|
| Branch always | BRA | 20 | 4 | 2 | | | | | | | | | | None | • | • | • | • | • | • |
| Branch if carry clear | BCC | 24 | 4 | 2 | | | | | | | | | | $C = 0$ | • | • | • | • | • | • |
| Branch if carry set | BCS | 25 | 4 | 2 | | | | | | | | | | $C = 1$ | • | • | • | • | • | • |
| Branch if = 0 | BEQ | 27 | 4 | 2 | | | | | | | | | | $Z = 1$ | • | • | • | • | • | • |
| Branch if ≥ 0 | BGE | 2C | 4 | 2 | | | | | | | | | | $N \cdot V = 0$ | • | • | • | • | • | • |
| Branch if > 0 | BGT | 2E | 4 | 2 | | | | | | | | | | $Z + (N \cdot V) = 0$ | • | • | • | • | • | • |
| Branch if higher | BHI | 22 | 4 | 2 | | | | | | | | | | $C + Z = 0$ | • | • | • | • | • | • |
| Branch if ≤ 0 | BLE | 2F | 4 | 2 | | | | | | | | | | $Z + (N \cdot V) = 1$ | • | • | • | • | • | • |
| Branch if lower or same | BLS | 23 | 4 | 2 | | | | | | | | | | $C + Z = 1$ | • | • | • | • | • | • |
| Branch if < 0 | BLT | 2D | 4 | 2 | | | | | | | | | | $N \cdot V = 1$ | • | • | • | • | • | • |
| Branch if minus | BMI | 2B | 4 | 2 | | | | | | | | | | $N = 1$ | • | • | • | • | • | • |
| Branch if ≠ 0 | BNE | 26 | 4 | 2 | | | | | | | | | | $Z = 0$ | • | • | • | • | • | • |
| Branch if overflow clear | BVC | 28 | 4 | 2 | | | | | | | | | | $V = 0$ | • | • | • | • | • | • |
| Branch if overflow set | BVS | 29 | 4 | 2 | | | | | | | | | | $V = 1$ | • | • | • | • | • | • |
| Branch if plus | BPL | 2A | 4 | 2 | | | | | | | | | | $N = 0$ | • | • | • | • | • | • |
| Branch to subroutine | BSR | 8D | 8 | 2 | | | | | | | | | | See text | • | • | • | • | • | • |
| Jump | JMP | | | | 6E | 4 | 2 | 7E | 3 | 3 | | | | See text | • | • | • | • | • | • |
| Jump to subroutine | JSR | | | | AD | 8 | 2 | 8D | 9 | 3 | | | | See text | • | • | • | • | • | • |
| No operation | NOP | | | | | | | | | | 01 | 2 | 1 | Advances prog. cntr. only | • | • | • | • | • | • |
| Return from interrupt | RTI | | | | | | | | | | 3B | 10 | 1 | See text | ⑩ | | | | | |
| Return from subroutine | RTS | | | | | | | | | | 39 | 5 | 1 | See text | • | • | • | • | • | • |
| Software interrupt | SWI | | | | | | | | | | 3F | 12 | 1 | See text | • | S | • | • | • | • |
| Wait for interrupt | WAI | | | | | | | | | | 3E | 9 | 1 | See text | • | ⑪ | • | • | • | • |

| Conditions code register Operations | Mnemonic | INHER OP | ~ | # | Boolean operation | 5 H | 4 I | 3 N | 2 Z | 1 V | 0 C |
|---|---|---|---|---|---|---|---|---|---|---|---|
| Clear carry | CLC | OC | 2 | 1 | $0 \rightarrow C$ | • | • | • | • | • | R |
| Clear interrupt mask | CLI | OE | 2 | 1 | $0 \rightarrow I$ | • | R | • | • | • | • |
| Clear overflow | CLV | OA | 2 | 1 | $0 \rightarrow V$ | • | • | • | • | R | • |
| Set carry | SEC | OD | 2 | 1 | $1 \rightarrow C$ | • | • | • | • | • | S |
| Set interrupt mask | SEI | OF | 2 | 1 | $1 \rightarrow I$ | • | S | • | • | • | • |
| Set overflow | SEV | OB | 2 | 1 | $1 \rightarrow V$ | • | • | • | • | S | • |
| Acmltr $A$ → $CCR$ | TAP | O6 | 2 | 1 | $A \rightarrow CCR$ | ⑫ | | | | | |
| $CCR$ → acmltr$A$ | TPA | O7 | 2 | 1 | $CCR \rightarrow A$ | • | • | • | • | • | • |

LEGEND:

| | | | |
|---|---|---|---|
| OP | Operation code (hexadecimal) | 00 | Byte = Zero |
| ~ | Number of MPU cycles | $H$ | Half-carry from bit 3 |
| # | Number of program bytes | $I$ | Interrupt mask |
| + | Arithmetic plus | $N$ | Negative (sign bit) |
| – | Arithmetic minus | $Z$ | Zero (byte) |
| • | Boolean AND | $V$ | Overflow, Z's complement |
| $M_{SP}$ | Contents of memory location pointed to be stack pointer | $C$ | Carry from bit 7 |
| | | $R$ | Reset always |
| | | $S$ | Set always |
| | | ↕ | Test and set if true, cleared otherwise |
| + | Boolean inclusive OR | • | Not affected |
| • | Boolean exclusive OR | $CCR$ | Condition code register |
| $\overline{M}$ | Complement of M | LS | Least significant |
| → | Transfer into | MS | Most significant |
| 0 | Bit = zero | | |

Condition code register notes:

(Bit set if test is true and cleared otherwise)

① (Bit V) Test: Result = 10000000?
② (Bit C) Test: Result = 00000000?
③ (Bit V) Test: Decimal value of most significant BCO Character greater than nine? (Not cleared if previously set.)
④ (Bit V) Test: Operand = 10000000 prior to execution?
⑤ (Bit V) Test: Operand = 01111111 prior to execution?
⑥ (Bit V) Test: Set equal to result of $N \cdot C$ after shift has occurred.
⑦ (Bit N) Test: Sign bit of MS byte of result = 1?
⑧ (Bit V) Test: 2's complement overflow from subtraction of LS bytes?
⑨ (Bit N) Test: Result less than zero? (Bit 15 = 1)
⑩ (All) Lead condition code register from Stack. (See special operations)
⑪ (Bit I) Set when interrupt occurs. If previously set, a non-maskable interrupt is required to exit the wait state.
⑫ (ALL) Set according to the contents of accumulator $A$

location within the 64k address space. Branches use *relative addressing* with an eight-bit offset and can reach only a 256-byte window around the instruction. We will explain the details later on programming examples.

As we know, the CPU decides whether a conditional branch is to be taken by evaluating a logic expression involving flags. The expression must be true for the branch to occur. All conditions listed in the table should be familiar as they are identical to the conditions for signed and unsigned comparison explained in Chapter 6. We will now give two examples:

Branch if carry flag set (BCS) causes a jump if the last instruction that affected flag $C$ set its value to 1. It can be used to test the result of addition, subtraction, or comparison of unsigned numbers: Result $C = 1$ after *OP1-OP2* means $op1 < op2$. Another use of BCS is to test the bit shifted out by shift and rotate instructions; this is useful, for example, for multiplication and division.

Branch if less than zero (BLT) causes a jump when

$$N \text{ XOR } V = 1$$

The presence of $V$ in the expression indicates that the instruction is used with signed numbers. The condition is True when the result of subtraction of two signed numbers was less than 0. Instruction BLT is essentially the two's complement equivalent of BCS.

These two examples show that the 6800 has two sets of arithmetic conditions: one for pure binary, and one for two's complement numbers. The choice of the correct instruction may be critical for proper program behavior. As an example, *OP1* = 10000000 is greater than *OP2* = 00111000 if the codes are pure binary but smaller than *OP2* if the codes are two's complement. As a consequence,

```
LDAA  OP1
CMPA  OP2
BGT . . .        ;  Two's complement "greater than zero" test
```

does not cause a jump but

```
LDAA  OP1
CMPA  OP2
BHI . . .        ;  Pure binary "greater than zero" test
```

does. The incorrect use of conditions is one of the most common programming mistakes, but the appropriate branch instructions are easy to recognize: Signed numbers involve $V$ and $N$ flags, unsigned numbers do not.

As another example of the subtleties of flags, the sequence

```
CLC            ; Clear carry
LDAA #$FF
INCA           ; A = FF + 1 = 0
BCS . . .      ; Branch if carry set
```

does not cause a branch because INCA does not affect the carry flag but

```
CLC
LDAA #$FF
ADDA #1
BCS . . .
```

does because the ADD instruction in this case sets the Carry flag. Both instructions have the same effect on accumulator *A*.

Miscellaneous instructions include those that set or clear individual flags, temporarily stop the CPU, and others.

### 6800 Addressing Modes

The 6800 CPU's addressing modes include immediate, extended (Motorola's name for absolute addressing), direct (a short form of absolute addressing), implied (inherent), relative, and indexed. The use of the stack to access data is, in fact, also an addressing mode. We will explain all of these addressing modes and demonstrate them on programming examples in the next section.

It is useful to note that the addressing mode influences the number of machine cycles required by an instruction because instructions with different addressing modes differ in their number of bytes and in the number of fetches they require. Furthermore, relative and indexed addressing and operations involving the stack require time-consuming internal CPU calculations and transfers.

While we are on the subject of speed, note that instructions available on both TOY and the 6800 require the same number of machine cycles. The TOY model also explains the duration of many instructions available only on the 6800 but fails sometimes because the internal architecture of the 6800 is different.

### Accumulators

Accumulators are used for storing intermediate results and for counting in loops. Because access to operands in accumulators is much faster than access to data in memory, data should be kept in accumulators rather than in memory whenever possible.

With a few exceptions, the role of accumulators *A* and *B* is symmetric; what can be done with *A* can usually be done with *B* as well. As an example, ALU operations on data from memory can be performed with *A* and *B* in the same way. This is very useful as differences between registers are confusing and complicate programming.

Asymmetric uses of the accumulators include the instruction ABA, which adds *A* to *B* and leaves the result in *A*; SBA, a similar special instruction for subtraction; and DAA, which converts the binary result of addition in *A* to BCD using the *H* flag. These instructions have no counterparts involving *B*.

## The Lack of Conventions

Motorola calls bit-by-bit negation "one's complement" and denotes it COM. Manufacturers of some other CPUs use a different instruction name for the same operation. Similar inconsistencies exist for other instructions and addressing modes because there is no standard terminology. Although this is annoying, it is not as serious as the fact that an instruction may sometimes have different effects on flags on different CPUs. This applies, for example, to load and store instructions. As a consequence, the rightmost column of Figure 10.2 may be different on different CPUs even though the instructions are otherwise identical. Such inconsistencies can make program logic incompatible between different computers.

## Exercises

1. Execute (manually, on the Heathkit computer, or with our simulator) at least ten 6800 instructions using all addressing modes and note the result, including the effect on flags.
2. Find all instructions that violate the symmetry of the 6800 instruction set with respect to accumulators *A* and *B*.
3. Which conditional branches should be used with unsigned numbers and which with unsigned numbers? Find conditional branches that apply to both representations.
4. List conditional branches that could have a different outcome depending on whether they are preceded by ADDA #1 or INC. Give examples of data that will produce different results.
5. Find all pairs of instructions that produce similar but not identical results.
6. Examine the instruction set table and find the logic of the opcode format. As an example, how does the opcode reflect the addressing mode or the accumulator used, and how are opcodes of similar operations encoded? Organize the results in a table.

## 10.3 PROGRAMMING EXAMPLES

In this section we will introduce the basics of 6800 architecture using a sequence of programming problems. Although we will present several programming techniques and demonstrate the relation between high-level and machine language programs, our aim is to explain the 6800 rather than to cover all aspects of low-level programming.

To make it possible to write programs in symbolic form, we will progressively introduce the basic concepts and terminology of *assembly language programming.* Our format is consistent with Motorola's definition and the assembler program available for the book can be used to convert symbolic programs into a form directly executable on our simulator or on the Heathkit microcomputer.

**Problem 1—I/O and Decimal Arithmetic** We are to implement the following Pascal fragment

```
READ(OP1,OP2);        {Read from keyboard}
WRITE(OP1+OP2)        {Write on display}
```

using the 6800 CPU's instructions and assuming one-byte operands read in BCD form directly from the keyboard.

The 6800 CPU uses memory-mapped I/O, which means that it treats its I/O devices as memory locations. Ignoring the subtleties of I/O programming for now (we will formulate the proper solution later), the principle of the program is as follows:

```
LDAA KBD     ; Read one byte from the keyboard
STAA OP1     ; Store it in memory location OP1
LDAB KBD     ; Read another byte from the keyboard
STAB OP2     ; Store it in memory location OP2
ABA          ; Add the two inputs
DAA          ; Convert the result from binary to BCD
STAA DISP    ; Show the result on the display
WAI          ; Stop execution (assuming ET-3400 computer)
```

The address of the keyboard is symbolically represented as KBD, and the address of the display is DISP.

The "wait" instruction WAI stops the CPU until its reset or interrupt signal are activated. (We will discuss these signals later.) Each program for the Heathkit computer or our simulator should end with WAI.

If the keyboard and display addresses are KBD = \$6000 and DISP = \$6010 and if the first instruction of the program is stored at location \$10, *OP1* at location \$1000 and *OP2* at location \$1001, the instruction table in Figure 10.2 can be used to obtain the following hexadecimal version of the program:

| **Address** | **Code** | **Corresponding Symbolic Code** |
|---|---|---|
| 0010 | B6 60 00 | LDAA KBD |
| 0013 | B7 10 00 | STAA OP1 |
| 0016 | F6 60 00 | LDAB KBD |
| 0019 | F7 10 01 | STAB OP2 |
| 001C | 1B | ABA |
| 001D | 19 | DAA |
| 001E | B7 60 10 | STAA DISP |
| 0021 | 3E | WAI |

Note that if we only want to read the two numbers and output their sum, we do not need to store the operands in memory—STAA and STAB are necessary only if *OP1* and *OP2* are needed later in the program. We only included the two STA instructions to show a literal translation of the Pascal statements. In Pascal a task cannot be programmed without variables, and our program is thus a first demonstration of the fact that some problems can be solved more simply at machine level than in a high-level language.

There is another way to implement this program. If we store *OP1* and *OP2* on *page zero*, the first 256 memory locations with addresses 0000 to 00FF, we can use direct addressing. In direct addressing, only the second byte of the address is specified and the CPU assumes that the first byte is 00. As an example,

```
LDAA $7F
```

in direct addressing is equivalent to LDAA \$007F in "extended" addressing. If *OP1* and *OP2* are stored in locations \$00A0 and \$00A1 and if we use direct addressing, the program becomes:

| **Address** | **Code** | **Corresponding Symbolic Code** | |
|---|---|---|---|
| 0010 | B6 60 00 | LDAA KBD | |
| 0013 | 97 A0 | STAA OP1 | Direct addressing |
| 0015 | F6 60 00 | LDAB KBD | |
| 0018 | D7 A1 | STAB OP2 | Direct addressing |

```
001A    1B          ABA
001B    19          DAA
001C    B7 60 10    STAA DISP
001F    3E          WAI
```

The advantage of direct addressing is that it shortens programs and allows them to run faster because it requires fewer memory fetches.

Because direct addressing saves memory and time, we would prefer to put all data on page zero. Unfortunately, most programs need more than 256 bytes for data and other "pages" must thus be used as well. To make the best use of direct addressing, therefore, one should use page zero for the data that is accessed most often. (A *page* on the 6800 is a 256-byte memory region starting at location $*XX*00. As an example, region $0000 to $00FF is page zero, $0100 to $01FF is page one, and so on. For obvious reasons, bits $A_{15}$ to $A_8$ are sometimes called page bits.)

**Problem 2—Two-Byte Arithmetic** We want to implement the following statement using two-byte integers:

OP1 := (OP2 + 3) − OP3

Because the 6800 is an eight-bit CPU, two-byte arithmetic requires the use of a carry. We will calculate *OP1* by first calculating both bytes of *OP2 + 3,* and then subtracting *OP3* from the result. We will use accumulator *A* for the LSB part of results and *B* for the MSB part. The program is as follows:

```
                    ; Load OP2
LDAA      OP2L      ; Low byte of OP2
LDAB      OP2H      ; High byte of OP2
                    ; Calculate OP2+3
ADDA #3             ; Addition must start from LSB.
ADCB #0             ; Calculation of MSB using the C flag from
                    ; LSB calculation (high type of 3 is 0)
                    ; Subtract OP3.
SUBA      OP3L      ; Start with LSB.
SBCB      OP3H      ; MSB calculation with "carry" (borrow)
                    ; Store result
STAB      OP1H      ; Store MSB of final result
STAA      OP1L      ; Store low byte of final result
WAI
```

To obtain an executable version of this symbolic *source code* program, we must convert all symbols to hexadecimal values. This can be done manually or automatically, using our assembler program.

If we want to translate the program using the assembler, we must add information indicating where the program and the data are stored, whether the memory locations containing the operands are initialized, and so on. We will now show the proper form of the above program ready for assembly, assuming that the data and the program are stored starting at location $100 and that *OP2* and *OP3* are initialized to $1357 and $2A3E, respectively:

```
        ORG $100     ; Store data and program starting at $100
OP1L    DS 1         ; Reserve one byte for OP1L, don't initialize
OP1H    DS 1         ; Reserve one byte for OP1H, don't initialize
OP2L    DB $13       ; Reserve one byte for OP2L, initialize to
                     ; $13
OP2H    DB $57       ; Reserve one byte for OP2H, initialize to
                     ; $57
OP3L    DB $2A       ; Reserve one byte for OP3L, initialize to
                     ; $2A
OP3H    DB $3E       ; Reserve one byte for OP3H, initialize to
                     ; $3E
                     ; Load OP2
START   LDAA OP2L    ; Low byte of OP2
        LDAB OP2H    ; High byte of OP2
                     ; Calculate OP2+3
        ADDA #3      ; Addition must start from LSB
        ADCB #0      ; Calculation of MSB using the C flag from
                     ; LSB calculation (high byte of 3 is 0)
                     ; Subtract OP3
        SUBA OP3L    ; Start with LSB
        SBCB OP3H    ; MSB calculation with carry
                     ; Store result
        STAB OP1H    ; Store MSB of final result
        STAA OP1L    ; Store low byte of final result
        WAI
        END START
```

Codes ORG, DS, DB, and END are not 6800 instructions but assembler *pseudoinstructions* or *directives*. Directive ORG, for "origin," informs the assembler where the code will be stored; DS, for "define space," reserves the indicated number of bytes (in our case one byte) for the specified symbol; DB, for "define byte," reserves space and initializes it to the given value. Directive END marks the end of the program and the START symbol behind it indicates that the first instruction to be executed is stored at location START. Whereas "ORG," "DB," "DS," and "END" are fixed parts of the assembly language, "START," "OP1L," "OP1H," and the other symbols are our own labels, selected specifically for this program. If the labels were replaced consistently with other symbols, the program would still be correct. As an example, we could have used "BEGIN" instead of "START" without changing the resulting executable code.

After storing the program in a file called, for example, PROBLEM2 and assembling it, the assembler produces an *object code* file PROBLEM2.OBJ and a listing file PROBLEM2.LST. File PROBLEM2.OBJ contains the hexadecimal version of the machine code, which can be directly executed on our simulator. File PROBLEM2.LST contains the listing of the source file accompanied by the hexadecimal object code. In our case, the LST file is as follows:

| Line | Address | Code | Source Code | | |
|---|---|---|---|---|---|
| 001 | | | | ORG $100 | ; Store data and<br>; program starting at<br>; $100 |
| 002 | 0100 | 00 | OP1 | LDS 1 | ; Reserve one byte for<br>; OP1L; don't initialize |
| 003 | 0101 | 00 | OP1 | HDS 1 | ; Reserve one byte for<br>; OP1H; don't<br>; initialize |
| 004 | 0102 | 13 | OP2 | LDB $13 | ; Reserve one byte for<br>; OP2L; initialize to<br>; $13 |
| 005 | 0103 | 57 | OP2 | HDB $57 | ; Reserve one byte for<br>; OP2H; initialize to<br>; $57 |
| 006 | 0104 | 2A | OP3 | LDB $2A | ; Reserve one byte for<br>; OP3L; initialize to<br>; $2A |
| 007 | 0105 | 3E | OP3 | HDB $3E | ; Reserve one byte for<br>; OP3H; initialize to<br>; $3E |
| 008 | | | | | ; Load OP2 |
| 009 | 0109 | B6 01 02 | START | LDAA OP2L | ; Low byte of OP2 |
| 010 | 010C | F6 01 03 | | LDAB OP2H | ; High byte of OP2 |
| 011 | | | | | ; Calculate OP2 + 3 |

*(Continued)*

| Address | Code | Source Code | |
|---|---|---|---|
| 010E | 8B 03 | ADDA #3 | ; Addition must start ; from LSB |
| 0110 | C9 00 | ADCB #0 | ; Calculation of MSB ; the C flag from |
| | | | ; LSB calculation ; (high byte of 3 is 0) |
| | | | ; Subtract OP3 |
| 0113 | B0 01 04 | SUBA OP3L | ; Start with LSB |
| 0116 | F2 01 05 | SBCB OP3H | ; MSB calculation ; with carry |
| | | | ; Store result |
| 0119 | F7 01 01 | STAB OP1H | ; Store MSB of final ; result |
| 011C | B7 01 00 | STAA OP1L | ; Store low byte of ; final result |
| 011D | 3E | WAI | |
| | | END START | |

**Problem 3 — Program to Create a 510-$\mu$sec Delay** Accurate timing delays are often required in the control of printers, disk drives, and other devices. They can be generated either by hardware (a timer chip, basically a counter) or by software. In this section, we will show how to create delays using software. Our ultimate goal is to show how to implement loops.

The clock of the computer is usually very accurate, and exact time delays can thus be produced as follows:

```
I := M;
REPEAT
  Do something that takes time while causing
    minimal changes to memory and registers;
  I := I−1;
UNTIL I = 0
```

This algorithm can be converted to the following code:

```
        LDAA #M     ;  I := M
REP     DEC A       ;  I := I−1
        BNE REP     ;  Do it again if I>0
        WAI
```

Instruction BNE stands for "branch if not equal to zero" and uses relative addressing, which we will explain shortly.

The delay is caused by executing the DECA and BNE REP loop. We can calculate the value of $M$ needed to obtain the desired delay as follows:

Instructions LDAA and DECA take two machine cycles each; BNE takes four. Initialization by LDAA is performed only once but the instructions in the loop are executed $M$ times. The whole program thus requires $2 + 6M$ machine cycles. If the clock speed is 1 MHz, the program creates a delay of $2 + 6M$ microseconds ($\mu$s). To obtain a delay of $d$ $\mu$sec, $M$ must satisfy

$$d = 2 + 6M$$

which gives

$$\begin{aligned} M &= \text{ROUND}((d - 2)/6) \\ &= \text{ROUND}((510 - 2)/6) \\ &= 84 \end{aligned}$$

The complete source program ready for assembly is thus as follows:

```
M       EQU 84      ; Delay count
        LDAA #M     ; I := M
LOOP    DEC A       ; I := I−1
        BNE LOOP    ; Do it again if I≥1
        WAI
        END
```

The EQU ("equate") pseudoinstruction is similar to Pascal's CONST: It makes $M$ equivalent to 84; subsequently whenever the assembler encounters $M$, it substitutes 84 for it. Just as with Pascal's CONST, EQU does not reserve any space. Compare this to DB and DS, which reserve space and behave like Pascal's VAR. The advantage to using EQU is that if we decide to change the value of the constant, we only need to change its EQU definition and the assembly process then automatically substitutes the correct new value throughout the program. Because we have omitted the ORG pseudoinstruction the assembler will assume that the first code is to be stored at location 0. Because END is not followed by a label, the program is assumed to begin with the first assembled code.

For a 1-MHz clock, the delay will be accurate to within 3 $\mu$sec, which is probably sufficient. If we need better accuracy, we can add a NOP instruction (no operation, do nothing) behind the loop. The advantage of NOP is that it does not effect memory, registers, or flags.

Because $M$ is a one-byte value, the maximum delay that our program can produce is

$$2 + (6 \times 255) = 1531\ \mu\text{sec}$$

This is obtained with $M = 255$.

For longer delays, we can insert one or more NOP instructions into the loop as follows:

```
        LDAA #M
REP     DEC A
        NOP          ; Waste more time
        BNE REP
        WAI
```

This approach is acceptable for delays that can be counted in milliseconds but very large delays would require too many NOPs and we will have to find a better strategy. Before looking at this problem, however, we must explain relative addressing.

**Relative Addressing**

In jumps with absolute (extended) addressing, such as JMP $1287, the destination address is given in the instruction. In jumps using relative addressing (branches), such as BNE $41, the destination address is obtained by adding the current value of *PC* to the offset given in the instruction, in this case $41. In essence, relative addressing specifies how far to jump rather than where to jump. Because the offset is treated as a signed number, it can be positive or negative.

When calculating the offset, we must realize that when the 6800 CPU reaches the calculation of the destination address, the *PC* already contains the address of the instruction following the branch (Figure 10.3). Consequently,

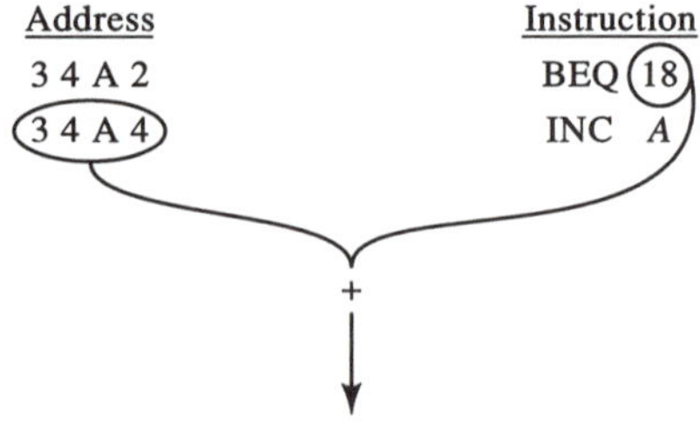


**Figure 10.3.** Example of calculation of the destination address in relative addressing. The offset is treated as a two's complement number.

the *PC* value from which the destination address is calculated is not the address of the branch instruction but the address of the instruction behind it.

Consider, as another example,

```
0000            LDAA #M
0002    LOOP    DEC A
0003            BNE LOOP
0005            WAI
```

To understand how this code is converted to machine code, we must realize that the offset is calculated from the instruction following BNE LOOP, in other words from location 0005. Because the destination is location LOOP at address 0002, the offset is −3, or FD hexadecimal. The hexadecimal version of the program is thus

```
0000    86 53
0002    4A
0003    26 FD
0005    3E
```

Note that although we calculated the offset assuming that the program starts at address 0000, the instruction remains correct even if the program's position in memory changes. If, for example, the program starts in location $6781, the same code still causes a jump to DEC *A* because the offset between the two locations is independent of the program's place in memory. Relative addressing thus makes the code relocatable; that is, insensitive to its location.

Relocatable programs can be placed in one memory region during one execution and in another during the next execution. Also, the same segment of relocatable code can be inserted into one program at one place and into another program at another place. This is important for frequently used code segments like multiplication routines that may be included in many different programs and located at a different address each time. Relocatability is essential on large computers where the same program may be placed into different memory regions at different times or even relocated during execution.

Although relative addressing has its advantages, it is not "better" than extended addressing. For one thing, relative addressing is useless if the location to which we want to jump is fixed. A relocated program using a branch instruction would jump the same distance as before relocation and end up at a different address. For a jump to a fixed address, we must thus use a jump instruction with extended addressing. (In the 6800 terminology, "jumps" use extended addressing while "branches" use relative addressing.) Both addressing modes thus have their uses.

Another limitation of branches on the 6800 is their short range; the one-byte offset allows jumps within at most 127 locations forward and 128 locations back. For longer jumps, 6800 programs must thus use the jump instruction. A minor difficulty with this strategy is that all 6800 jumps are unconditional and long conditional jumps must thus be created by combining branches and jumps. As an example, to obtain the effect of

```
JEQ $549A     ;  Nonexistent 6800 instruction
```

we must use

```
   BNE NEXT    ;  Skip jump if condition EQ fails
   JMP $549A
NEXT . . .
```

It is interesting to note that although 6800 branch instructions are two bytes long and the jumps three bytes long, the CPU requires more machine cycles for branches. It is left to the reader to speculate why this is so.

The 6800 uses relative addressing only for branches but other CPUs may allow it for other instructions as well. One can then extend the benefits of relative addressing to other uses.

**Problem 4—Nested Loops for Longer Delays** If the required delay is too long for a single loop, we can use two loops:

```
I := M;
REPEAT
  J := N;           {Start of inner loop}
  REPEAT
    J := J − 1;
  UNTIL J = 0;      {End of inner loop}
  I := I − 1;
UNTIL I = 0
```

This represents $M \times N$ repetitions and can be converted to the following form, which uses accumulator $A$ for variable $I$ and accumulator $B$ for variable $J$:

```
     LDAA #M    ;  Use A for I
REP1 LDAB #N    ;  Start of external loop on I
REP2 DECB       ;  Inner loop on J
     BNE REP2   ;  Inner loop not finished yet
     DECA       ;  Inner loop done, back to outer loop
     BNE REP1   ;  If not done, repeat
     WAI
```

The student may calculate the longest possible delay that can be obtained with this approach, and may convert the program into a form that can be assembled and that will create a delay of 100 msec.

**Another Approach to Programmed Delays**

The reason why the loop in Problem 3 cannot implement long delays is that the maximum count that can be stored in a one-byte accumulator is too small. The obvious remedy is to use a loop with a two-byte count stored in a sixteen-bit register, such as the stack pointer or the index register. Because the stack pointer cannot be easily incremented and has other important uses, we must use the index register. With this approach, longer delays can be produced as follows:

```
        LDX    #N      ; Load sixteen-bit count
REP     DEX            ; Decrement index register
        BNE    REP     ; until it reaches 0
        WAI
```

This program has the same effect as the nested loops but it is simpler and more elegant. It is left to the student to determine how to calculate the value of $N$ and to show that this approach gives approximately the same maximum delay as the double-loop solution. The student should also convert the program into the proper source code form for a 100-msec delay.

Note that instructions DEX and INX affect only the $Z$ flag and the only conditional branches that can be used to test the end of the loop are thus BEQ and BNE. If we need a more complicated comparison, we must insert a CPX instruction (compare index register) before the branch.

Although the index register is useful for simple two-byte calculations of the kind used in this problem, its main function is indexing; that is, addressing arrays. We will demonstrate this function in Problem 6. First, however, we will consider another example involving loops.

**Problem 5—Multiplication** We are to implement the following statement assuming that the operands and the result are one-byte pure binary numbers:

OP1 := OP2 × OP3

Because the 6800 does not have a "multiply" instruction, the best approach would be to use shifting and addition; it is left as an exercise for the student. We will instead use the easier but much less efficient repeated addition:

```
OP1 := 0; I := 1;
WHILE I ≤ OP2 DO
  BEGIN
```

```
    OP1 := OP1 + OP3;
    I := I + 1;
  END
```

Because *OP1* and *OP2* are one-byte values, counting can be implemented with accumulators:

```
        ORG   $0        ; Data area
OP1     DS    1         ; Reserve space for result
OP2     DB    15        ; Reserve space and initialize
OP3     DB    11
        ORG   $10       ; Code area
                        ; Use accumulators A and B for OP1 and
                        ; I
        CLRA            ; OP1 := 0
        LDAB  #1        ; I := 1
WHILE   CMPB  OP2       ; I>OP2 ? (Comparison of pure binary
                        ; codes)
        BHI   DONE;     ; If so, skip rest of WHILE statement
        ADDA  OP3       ; Body of the WHILE statement
        INCB            ; I := I+ 1
        BRA   WHILE     ; Return to test the WHILE condition
DONE    STAA  OP1
        WAI
        END
```

In this program, we allocated separate memory segments to data and instructions, somewhat like Pascal programs, to achieve a more organized program structure. On some CPUs, such as the 8086 introduced at the end of this chapter, separation of data and code is automatic; built into the CPU architecture.

**Problem 6 — A Memory Block Operation** Manipulations involving blocks of consecutive memory locations (arrays) usually perform the same operation on each element. An example of a block operation is clearing a memory block as in

```
CLR $1000
CLR $1001
CLR $1002
```

.

.

and so on

This explicit element-by-element approach is very efficient for small arrays but clumsy for large arrays and impossible if the size of the array varies. One solution is to use a loop as in

```
FOR I := 0 TO N DO
  OP[I] := 0
```

and have the program modify the address part of the CLR instruction during each pass through the loop.

Unfortunately, if one used the addressing modes presented so far the execution of this program would modify the address part of each instruction that accesses the array, and this is considered unacceptable in modern programming.

Because the essence of our problem is the manipulation of addresses, we need an easy way to modify the address of the operand; that is, we need a new addressing mode. This can be implemented by adding a special CPU register in which we can store the address of an operand and whose contents can be easily incremented, decremented, and tested. This is exactly what the index register does.

In indexed addressing, the effective address, the address at which the operand is stored, is obtained as the sum of the contents of the index register and the offset given in the instruction (Figure 10.4). As an example, if the index register contains \$3241, instruction

```
LDAA $13,X     ;  Indexed addressing with offset $13
```

means "load *A* from location \$3421 + \$13 = \$3434." If the index register contains \$A324, then the same instruction loads *A* from location \$A337.

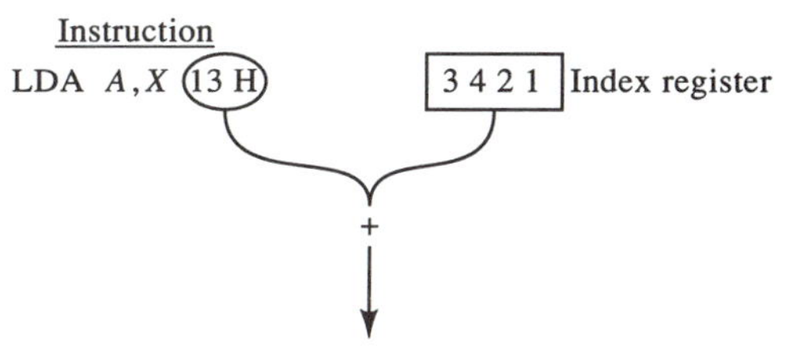


**Figure 10.4.** Indexed addressing. The offset is a pure binary number.

On the 6800, the offset given in the instruction is a one-byte unsigned number and its value is thus between 0 and 255. Note that this is different from relative addressing, where the offset is a signed number between −128 and 127.

With indexed addressing, consecutive memory locations can be accessed by a loop that increments or decrements the index register while leaving the offset part of the instruction (and thus the program) unchanged. For an array of forty elements, our problem can be solved as follows:

```
N       EQU 40         ; Array size
OP      DS  N          ; N memory locations reserved for OP.
START   LDX #OP        ; Load address of OP[0] into index
                       ; register
LOOP    CLR 0,X        ; Clear OP[I] using indexed addressing
                       ; with offset 0
        INX            ; Increment address in index register
        CPX #OP+N+1    ; Are we done (I>N)?
        BNE LOOP       ; Branch if not the last address
        WAI
        END START
```

This program illustrates the typical use of indexed addressing: accessing a block of consecutive memory locations with an unchanging instruction (in this case CLR 0,*X*) and incrementing or decrementing the index register.

By the way, as "*X*" normally refers to the index register, we cannot use it as variable name without creating chaos. Similarly, we must not use "*A*" or "*B*" as identifiers to avoid confusion between variables, constants, labels, and registers.

**Problem 7—Block Operations and Boolean Variables** One of the most common programming tasks is searching a string (a character array) for a specific character. The following algorithm solves one such problem: finding the first occurrence of the ASCII code of letter *A* in an array of characters called *C*:

```
FOUND := False; I := 1;
REPEAT
  IF C[I] = 'A'
    THEN FOUND := True
    ELSE I := I + 1      {Not found, go to next element if any}
UNTIL FOUND OR (I > N)
```

Before writing the program, we must decide how to represent the Boolean variable *FOUND*. In Chapter 1, we mentioned that True is equivalent to logic

1 and False to logic 0; with eight-bit codes, we will thus use 00000000 to represent False, and 11111111 (the inverse of 00000000) to represent True. This is consistent with 6800 logic instructions and the basic laws of logic. As an example, we would expect that the result of

OP AND True

(where *OP* is a Boolean variable) is *OP* because $x \cdot 1 = 1$. Indeed, loading accumulator *A* with 11111111 and using instruction ANDA on the contents of *OP* leaves each bit of *OP* unchanged.

We would similarly expect that

OP AND False

gives False because $x \cdot 0 = 0$. When this is implemented by using the AND instruction on *OP* and 00000000, the result is 00000000 or False. The reader can verify that all other 6800 logic instructions are also consistent with this representation.

With this convention, we can solve our problem as follows:

```
                                ; Use A for FOUND, B for C[I], X for I
N          EQU ...              ; The size of array C
C          DB ...               ; Initial values of C
START      CLRA                 ; FOUND := False
           LDX #C               ; Address of C[1]
LOOP       LDAB 0,X             ; Get C[I] for testing
           CMPB #'A'            ; Is C [I] = 'A'?
           BNE MORE             ; If no, go to next element of array C
           COMA                 ; Code is 'A' — assign True to FOUND
                                ; by complementing accumulator A
           BRA DONE             ; Exit from loop
MORE       INX                  ; It was not 'A' increment index
           CPX #C+N+1           ; Are we finished? C+N+1 is address
                                ; of the last element of C plus 1
           BNE LOOP             ; If not, do another loop
DONE       WAI                  ; End of program
                                ; Either A=FF and X=address of 'A'
                                ; or A=00 and digit not found
           END START
```

Remember that to assemble and run the program, we must fill in values for *N* and *C*.

Close examination of the program reveals that variable *FOUND* is not really needed and the program can be simplified to the following form:

```
                                ; Use B for C[I], X for I
N          EQU ...              ; The size of array C
C          DB ...               ; Initial values of C
START      LDX #C               ; Address of C[1]
LOOP       LDAB 0,X             ; Get C[I] for testing
           CMPB #'A'            ; Is C[I] = 'A'?
           BEQ DONE             ; Yes, quit
  MORE     INX                  ; It was not 'A', increment index
           CPX #C+N+1           ; Are we finished?
           BNE LOOP             ; No, do another loop
  DONE     WAI                  ; Either address in X is within bounds
                                ; and 'A' was found or X is out of
                                ; bounds and 'A' was not found
           END START
```

This version is shorter and faster than the original one, which again demonstrates that programs may be more efficient in machine language than in Pascal.

**Problem 8—More Complicated Search** We are to search string *C* for the ASCII code of a digit between 0 and 9. An algorithm solving this task in the style of the second program in Problem 7 (without Boolean variables) is as follows:

```
I := 1;
REPEAT
  IF C[I] IN ['0' . . '9']     {Assume ASCII codes}
    THEN EXIT
    ELSE I := I + 1
UNTIL (I≠N+1)                  {If I>N on exit, C does not contain any digits}
```

The problem is essentially the same as the previous problem; only the condition is different. Because the 6800 does not have any instructions to test condition

C[I] IN ['0' . . '9']

we must convert it to the following equivalent sequence of two simpler tests that the 6800 can handle:

(C[I] ≧ '0') AND (C[I] ≦ '9')

With this modification, we can implement the algorithm as follows:

```
                              ; B is used for array C, X for index I
N          EQU ...            ; The size of array C
C          DB  ...            ; Initial values of C
START      LDX #C             ; Address of C[I]
REP        LDAB 0,X           ; Get C[I] for testing
           CMPB #'0'          ; Compare C[I] with ASCII code of '0'
           BMI MORE           ; C[I] < '0' cannot be a digit
           CMPB #'9'          ; Compare with ASCII code of '9'
           BHI MORE           ; C[I] > '9', cannot be a digit
           BRA DONE           ; It is a digit, end of program
MORE       INX                ; Increment array index
           CPX #C+N+1         ; Are we finished?
           BNE REP            ; No, do another loop
DONE       WAI                ; Digit is found if X is within bounds
           END START
```

We use unsigned branches BHI and BMI rather than two's complement branches BGT and BLT because it is more natural to treat ASCII codes as non-negative integers.

**Problem 9—Block Move** Another frequently needed string operation is to copy (move) a block of data from one memory region to another as in

```
FOR I := N DOWNTO 1 DO
  OP1[I] := OP2[I]
```

Using the index register for addressing and moving data through accumulator *A*, this can be implemented as follows:

```
                                ; A = intermediate storage, X = I
N        EQU    ...             ; Size of arrays OP1 and OP2
OP1      DS     N               ; Reserve space for destination
                                ; array
OP2      DB     ...             ; Initialize values of source array
OFF      EQU    OP2-OP1         ; Offset between the two arrays
START    LDX    #OP1+N          ; Initialize I to address of OP1[N]
LOOP     CPX    #OP1            ; Is I = address of OP1[1]?
         BEQ    DONE            ; If so, exit from loop
```

```
        LDAA   OFFSET, X    ; Get OP2[I] with offset OFFSET
        STAA   O,X          ; Save it in OP1[I]
        DEX                 ; Decrement index I
        BRA    LOOP         ; Return to check loop condition
DONE    WAI
        END    START
```

The offset *OFFSET* between arrays *OP1* and *OP2* is the distance from *OP1*[*I*] to *OP2*[*I*].

This program uses the offset to access two different arrays with a single value in the index register and shows the full power of indexed addressing. It also indicates the major restriction of its implementation on the 6800: Because the offset is a one-byte unsigned number it is limited to non-negative values smaller than 256 and our solution can only be used for small arrays. On some CPUs, the offset is two bytes long, but on the 6800, moves involving greater offsets must either use the index register in a more complicated way or else use the stack. We will consider both methods.

**Problem 10—Block Moves Over Longer Distance** We can use the following algorithm to implement block moves over large distances with the index register: Load the accumulator using one setting of *X*; increment *X*; save it in memory; reload the index register with a new value; save the accumulator using the new value of *X*; increment and save *X*; reload it; and so on:

```
Initialize array addresses to OP1[1] and OP2[1];
I := 1;
WHILE NOT index <= N DO
  BEGIN
    Load X with the address of OP2[I];
    Load accumulator A from OP2 using the index register;
    Increment index register and save it in memory;
    Load X with address of OP1[I];
    Save accumulator A in OP1 using indexed addressing;
    Increment index register and save it in memory
  END
```

This can be implemented by the following program:

```
                            ; Use A for intermediate storage, X
                            ; for address of element with index I
N       EQU    ...          ; Size of OP1 and OP2
OP2     DB     ...          ; Initial values of OP2
```

```
OP1      DS     N          ;  Space for OP1
ADD1     DS     2          ;  To hold address of element in OP1
ADD2     DS     2          ;  To hold address of element in OP2
                           ;  Store address of OP1[1] in locations
                           ;  ADD1 and ADD1+1
START    LDX    #OP1
         STX    ADD1       ;  This instruction stores two bytes
                           ;  Store address of OP2[1] in locations
                           ;  ADD2 and ADD2+1
         LDX    #OP2
         STX    ADD2
                           ;  Now execute the LOOP
LOOP     CPX    #OP2+N     ;  Last element processed?
         BEQ    DONE       ;  Exit loop if done
         LDAA   O,X        ;  Not done, get the value of OP2[I]
         INX               ;  Update address of OP2[I]
         STX    ADD2       ;  Save updated address of OP2[I]
         LDX    ADD1       ;  Get address of OP1[I]
         STAA   O,X        ;  Store OP2[I] in OP1[I]
         INX               ;  Update address of OP1[I]
         STX    ADD1       ;  Save updated address of OP1[I]
         LDX    ADD2       ;  Get address of OP2[I]
         BRA    LOOP       ;  Return to test condition
DONE     WAI
         END    START
```

**Problem 11—Block Moves Over Longer Distance Using the Stack** A *stack* is a data structure analagous to a pile of cafeteria trays. Items can be added to the stack, an operation called "push," or removed from it, an operation called "pull" or "pop," only from the top. A pushed item covers the item previously on the top of the stack, a popped item uncovers the one underneath. On the 6800, the stack is stored in the same RAM memory as instructions and data (Figure 10.5) but some CPUs distinguish the part of memory allocated to the stack from data and program memory regions.

Because the stack is accessed only at the top, the CPU must know where the top of the stack is. For this purpose, the 6800 has a special sixteen-bit register called the stack pointer or *SP* that "points" to the top of the stack.

Because push and pop change the location of the top of the stack, they change the value of the stack pointer. For reasons we will consider later, the

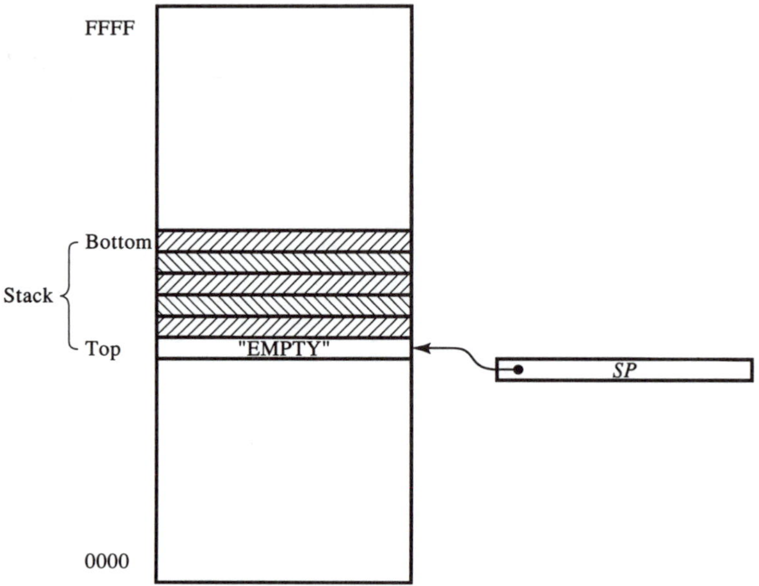


**Figure 10.5.** Stack on the 6800 CPU.

stack "grows" from high to low memory and its "bottom" thus has a higher address than its "top." When we push an item on the stack, the address in *SP* is thus decremented.

*Push instructions* on the 6800 operate only on accumulators and are called PSHA and PSHB. Instruction PSHA copies accumulator *A* to the top of the stack, the location whose address is now in *SP*, and then updates *SP* by subtracting 1 from it:

PSHA: [A] → MEM[SP], SP − 1 → SP

Instruction PSHB is similar but uses register *B*.

*Pop instructions* on the 6800 are called PULA and PULB. Because "PUL" is the inverse of "PSH," it first increments the stack by 1 and then copies the data from the address now in *SP* into the accumulator.

PULA: SP + 1 → SP, MEM[SP] 0A

Instruction PULB is similar. The student is urged to use our simulator to gain a better understanding of stack operations.

Our description of PSH and PUL shows that the 6800 stack pointer points to the next available memory location on the stack. On some CPUs the stack pointer points to the data on the top of the stack rather than to the "vacant" location on the top.

It is important to understand that although we say PUL "removes" data from the stack, it does not actually change the contents of the corresponding memory location; the contents remain the same and only the address in the stack pointer changes. Thus one can access data even after it has been "removed" but this violates the purpose of the stack.

Moreover, although in principle one can obtain the stack data only by popping, there is nothing to prevent us from accessing any bytes inside the stack by instructions other than PUL. After all, the stack is just a segment of ordinary memory space and all instructions, such as ADD, LDA, and STA, apply to it. Generally, one avoids accessing the stack with instructions other than PUL except in a few special situations, such as during the execution of subroutines (Problem 16). The reason for this is that in most of its applications the use of the stack is based on the assumption that its access is only via PSH and PUL. This will become clear later.

Because many computer programs depend on the stack, one of the first things that a computer must do when it is turned on is to initialize the stack pointer. Otherwise, *SP* contains a random value and stack access will have disastrous effects because it will modify data in some unpredictable region of memory.

Among other things, the 6800 can use stacks for long data moves. For example, we can treat the memory block that we want to move as a stack, pop its elements into an accumulator, and use indexed addressing to save the accumulator in the destination array. The algorithm is as follows:

```
Initialize SP to the start of OP2;
Initialize X to the start of OP1;
FOR I := 1 TO N DO
  BEGIN
    Pop OP2 to accumulator A;
    Save accumulator A in OP2 using indexed addressing
  END
```

We can implement this algorithm with the following simple program:

```
                              ; A = intermediate storage
        N       EQU...        ; Size of array
        OP1     DS  N
        OP2     DB  ...
START   LDS     #OP2-1        ; Address of OP2[1]-1 is needed be-
                              ; cause PUL first increments SP and
                              ; then gets the data
        LDX     #OP1          ; Address of OP1[1]
```

```
LOOP    PUL     A          ; Get OP2[I]
        STAA    O,X        ; Save it in OP1[I]
        INX                ; Increment I
        CPX     #OP1+N     ; Check against last address + 1
        BNE     LOOP       ; Repeat if we are not done
        WAI
        END     START
```

Figure 10.6 shows the first two transfers. Note that our only reason for using the stack in this instance is that the 6800 lacks special block instructions or more powerful indexed addressing. The main use of the stack is for subroutines and related concepts, as we will illustrate in the following problems.

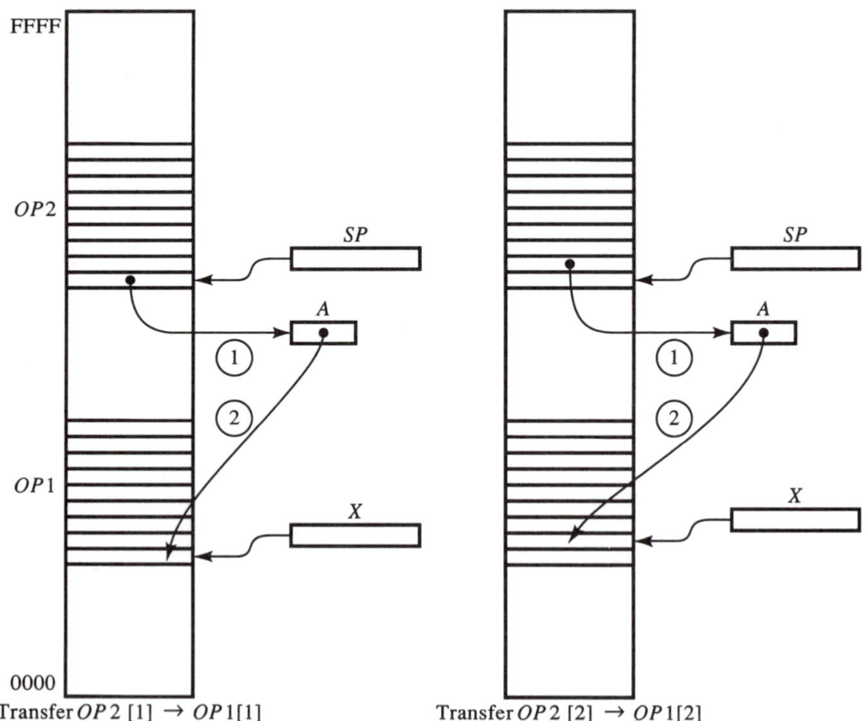


**Figure 10.6.** Transfer of the first two elements of a block using the stack. The state of *SP* indicates its value after the transfer.

**Problem 12—I/O with Subroutine** Let us return to our first problem and implement

```
READ(OP1,OP2);      {Single-digit operands}
WRITE(OP1+OP2)      {Two-digit result}
```

as it should be, using the I/O facilities available in the ROM of the Heathkit ET-3400 computer.

The details of I/O operations require an understanding of peripherals that is outside the interest and competence of most programmers. All computers thus provide I/O functions as a set of prepackaged program segments called *I/O subroutines* that are part of a program called the *operating system.* (On the ET-3400, the operating system is very primitive and is called a monitor.) To perform an I/O operation, the user simply "calls" the I/O subroutine with a jump-to-subroutine or a branch-to-subroutine instruction (JSR or BSR). The segment is then executed, and execution returns to the original program. Conceptually, subroutines are machine-level equivalents of Pascal procedures and functions and are used in the same way.

For our problem, we need the following ET-3400 I/O subroutines:

Subroutine INCH reads the key activated on the keyboard and returns its one-byte code in accumulator *A*. The ET-3400 has only sixteen "hexadecimal" keys.

Subroutine OUTHEX displays the bottom half, or nibble, of accumulator *A* as a hexadecimal digit. The ET-3400 uses 6 seven-segment LEDs for display.

Subroutine REDIS ("reset display") resets ET-3400 display to the leftmost digit.

The names "INCH," "OUTHEX," and "REDIS" are simply labels that represent addresses of the corresponding subroutines in the ET-3400 monitor.

With this background, the problem can be implemented as follows:

```
                                ; Use of registers:
                                ; A = argument of I/O
                                ; subroutines
                                ; B = unpacking of BCD result
INCH      EQU     $FDF4         ; Address of input subroutine
OUTHEX    EQU     $FE28         ; Address of output subroutine
REDIS     EQU     $FCBC         ; Address of display reset
                                ; subroutine
```

```
OP1     DS      1
OP2     DS      1
START   JSR     INCH      ; Jump to input subroutine to
                          ; read key
                          ; Returns key code in A
        STAA    OP1       ; Save byte returned by INCH
                          ; in OP1
        JSR     INCH      ; Jump to input subroutine to
                          ; read key
                          ; Code of pressed key is left in A
        STAA    OP2       ; Save byte returned by INCH
                          ; in OP2
        ADDA    OP1       ; Add OP1 to OP2 now in
                          ; accumulator A
        DAA               ; Convert to BCD
                          ; Result could be two digits long
                          ; and must be split (unpacked)
                          ; into two BCD digits for display
        TAB               ; Copy the result to B
        SRA               ; Shift A right four times to get
                          ; the high
        SRA               ; nibble into the lower half of A
        SRA
        SRA
                          ; Display the most significant
                          ; digit
        JSR     REDIS     ; Initialize display before output
        JSR     OUTHEX    ; Output A via subroutine
        TBA               ; Restore code for output of low
                          ; nibble
        JRS     OUTHEX    ; Output second digit
        WAI
        END     START
```

Note that we do not have to understand the internal operation of INCH, REDIS, and OUTHEX to use them. All we need is to know their starting addresses and the arguments they require or return.

### How Subroutines Work

When the CPU encounters a subroutine call instruction, it jumps to the specified address, the start of the subroutine, and executes the subroutine. It then returns to the instruction following the place from which the call was made. As an example, assume that the first JSR OUTHEX instruction is stored at $0100. Because the address of OUTHEX is $FE28, JSR OUTHEX and the following instruction are encoded as

| Address | Code | Symbolic Form |
|---|---|---|
| 0100 | BD $FE28 | JSR OUTHEX |
| 0103 | 17 | TBA |
| 0104 | etc. | |

When the CPU encounters JSR OUTHEX, it jumps to location $FE28, executes the OUTHEX subroutine, and returns to continue with TBA. (We use JSR with extended addressing because the starting address of OUTHEX is too far to be reached by relative addressing with BSR.)

To return to the calling program, the CPU saves the *return address* before making the jump and reloads it into the *PC* at the end of the subroutine (Figure 10.7).

Because there is no special register to save the return address in the CPU, the return address must be kept in a safe place in memory where it is unlikely to be accidentally destroyed by the subroutine. The stack, if properly used, offers such a safe place and the return address is thus stored on the stack.

The return from a subroutine with its reloading of the *PC* is performed by instruction RTS, "return from subroutine." This instruction does not need an operand; it just pops the return address from the stack into *PC*. Updating the stack pointer, which occurs during pushing and popping, is a part of JSR, BSR, and RTS.

One can summarize the subroutine mechanism as follows:

When the CPU encounters a JSR or BSR instruction, it pushes the return address on the stack and jumps to the start of the subroutine.

When the CPU encounters the RTS instruction, it pops the address from the stack into the program counter and this returns execution to the calling program.

It might appear that the stack is no safer than any other memory location because the value on the top of the stack can be overwritten just like any memory location or the stack pointer changed and the address of the top of

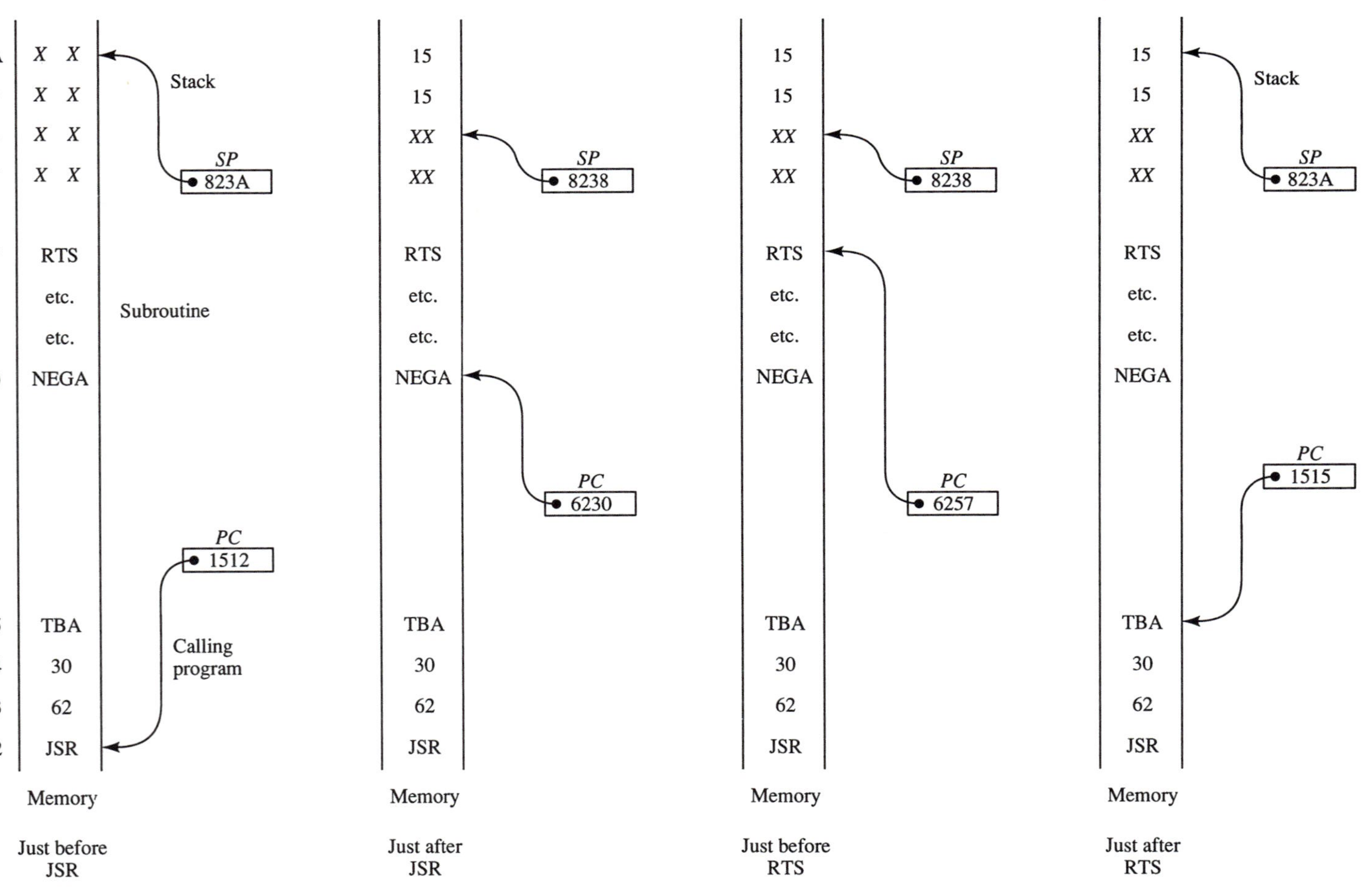


**Figure 10.7.** Subroutine call, execution, and return.

the stack corrupted. In actuality the stack is safe if it is sufficiently large and allocated a memory region that does not interfere with the program code and data, and if every "push" inside each subroutine is matched with a following "pop" before execution returns from the subroutine. When these conditions are satisfied, the contents of the stack in the region bottom-return address cannot be overwritten by other program data, and the stack pointer contains the correct address at the moment of execution of RTS. Making sure that all these conditions are satisfied is, of course, the responsibility of the programmer.

In addition to the security that it provides, the stack automatically guarantees that subroutine calls nested to unlimited and unknown depths execute correctly. We will illustrate this in Problem 14.

**Problem 13—Table Lookup** Many problems require selection of a value from a table. In Pascal, this is usually implemented by the CASE statement or an array. In machine language programming, it can, for example, be done with indexed addressing. We will demonstrate the technique on a program performing output to ET-3400's seven-segment display (Figure 10.8).

We are to write a program to read a key and display its symbol (a hexadecimal digit between 0 and F) on the leftmost digit. The program is to stop when 0 is pressed. A possible algorithm is as follows:

```
REPEAT
  READ(KEY);       {Read a key on the ET-3400}
  Reset Display,
  CASE KEY OF
    0; WRITE('0');
    1; WRITE('1');
    .
    .
    .
```

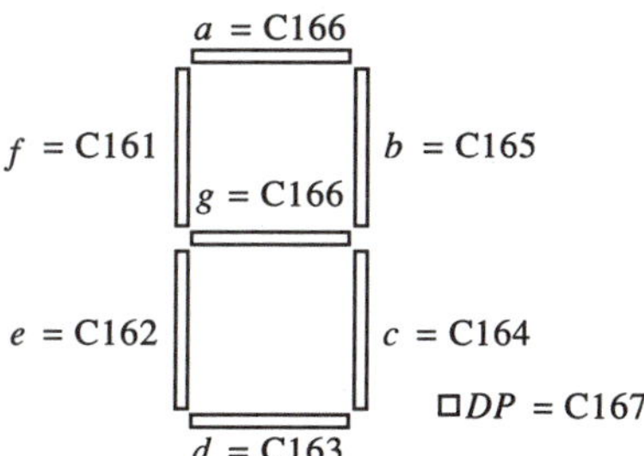


**Figure 10.8.** Leftmost display digit on the ET-3400 and the hexadecimal addresses of its individual segments.

```
    .
    F: WRITE('F');
    END;
UNTIL KEY = 0
```

The CASE statement is used because segment patterns cannot be calculated from any formula. The codes that are to be sent to the display must be extracted from the following table, which was obtained by determining which LEDs are on for individual digits.

| Displayed Character | LED Pattern (*DP,a,b,c,d,e,f,g*) |
|---|---|
| 0 | 0111 0111 = 7E |
| 1 | 0011 0000 = 30 |
| 2 | 0110 1101 = 6D |
| . | . |
| . | . |
| . | . |
| F | 0100 0111 = 47 |

In our solution, we will get the code pattern by using the key code (0 to F) as an index into the table and then calling subroutine OUTCH to display the pattern. Ideally, we would like to be able to convert the table index to the value of the table element by one or two instructions and this is possible on some CPUs, including some successors of the 6800. On the 6800 CPU, however, direct selection of the correct code is impossible. One way to access the correct code is to step through the table as follows:

Assume the code of the hex key is in accumulator $A$.

Initialize $X$ to point to line 0 of the table.

If the code in $A$ is 0, we are done—the address of the code is in $X$.

Otherwise, decrement the value in $A$ and increment $X$ to point to the next line.

If $A$ is 0, $X$ points at the correct line and we are done.

Otherwise, increment $X$ and decrement $A$, and so on.

This is, however, very inefficient, especially for large tables. A much better solution is to replace the loop with the following steps: Load the sum of the offset and the address of the start of the table into the index register and then use indexed addressing. The program becomes particularly simple if the table is stored at the start of a page (address \$*XX*00). In this case, no addition is needed and the code can be loaded into the low part of the index register via an address variable:

```
                                ; A = pattern, X = index of
                                ; pattern
TABLE                           ; Codes of segment patterns
                                ; for symbols 0 to F
        DB      $7E, $30, $6D, $79, $33, $5B, $5F, $70,
        DB      $7F, $7B, $77, $1F, $4E, $3D, $4F, $47
ZERO    EQU     7EA$            ; The pattern representing 0
INCH    EQU     $FDF4           ; Address of input subroutine
OUTCH   EQU     $FE3A           ; Address of pattern-display
                                ; subroutine
REDIS   EQU     $FCBC           ; Start of display-reset subroutine
ADDR    DS      2               ; Two bytes initialized to 0
                                ; Initialize index register
START   LDX     #TABLE          ; Address of element 0 of the table
        STX     ADDR            ; Store address of start of table
REPT    JSR     INCH            ; Get key into accumulator A
                                ; Find the bit pattern for the
                                ; key code
        STAA    ADDR+1          ; Update lower byte of ADDR so
                                ; that it
                                ; points to the desired pattern
        LDX     ADDR            ; X := address of pattern within
                                ; table
        LDAA    0,X             ; A := pattern from table using
                                ; indexed addressing
                                ; now display the code
        JSR     REDIS           ; Reset display
        JSR     OUTHEX          ; Display it (code of pattern is in A)
```

```
UNTIL   CMPA   #ZERO    ; Is the code in A the 0 pattern?
        BNE    REPT     ; If not, repeat the whole procedure
        WAI             ; Last key was 0, stop
        END    START
```

It is left to the student to analyze and execute the program.

**Problem 14—Writing Subroutines** Having explained how subroutines work and having demonstrated their use, we will now write a subroutine. Our subroutine will read two BCD digits from the keyboard, convert them to unsigned binary, and return the result in *A*. As an example, if we press keys "7" and "6" the subroutine should produce 01001100, the binary equivalent of 76.

The algorithm follows:

```
READ(D1);          {MSB}
RES := 10*D1;
READ(D0);          {LSB}
RES := RES + D0
```

Multiplication by ten can be accomplished by shifting

$10 \times x = 8 \times x + 2 \times x$

and the complete subroutine is as follows:

```
TOBIN              ; Subroutine to read two BCD codes and
                   ; convert them to a binary number
                   ; Returns result in A, modifies B
                   ; No check is performed to see if the keys
                   ; represent BCD values
        JSR INCH   ; Reads the first digit into A
                   ; Multiply by 10 by shifting and addition
        ASLA       ; 2*D1
        TAB        ; Save it for addition later
        ASLA       ; 4*D1
        ASLA       ; 8*D1
        ABA        ; 10*D1 = 8*D1 + 2*D1
        TAB        ; Save 10*D1 in B before reading next
                   ; digit
        JSR INCH   ; Read the second digit D0 into A
```

```
ABA          ; A = 10*D1 + D0
RTS          ; Return to the calling program
```

Label TOBIN is equivalent to the address of JSR INCH.

Thus the only feature that distinguishes a subroutine from an ordinary program sequence is that it ends with RTS.

An interesting aspect of TOBIN is that it calls another subroutine, the monitor subroutine INCH. The call on INCH is then nested inside every call on TOBIN. In fact, INCH itself calls another monitor subroutine called ENCODE and the subroutine calls are thus nested three levels deep. Figure 10.9 shows that this does not cause any problems as long as the subroutines do not violate the integrity of the stack.

An unpleasant property of TOBIN is that it destroys the contents of *B*. If INCH behaved like this, it would destroy the intermediate result before we could execute ABA. We can easily eliminate this problem, however, by saving *B* on the stack when we enter TOBIN and restoring it to its original value just before the exit by RTS. This is left as an exercise for the reader.

**Problem 15—Recursive Subroutines** Any procedure, function, or subroutine that calls itself is said to be *recursive*. Although recursion is quite common in advanced Pascal programs it is rare in machine-level programming. However, an understanding of machine-level recursion clarifies high-level language recursion and helps one to understand how stacks and subroutines operate.

As an illustration, we will use recursion to calculate the sum of numbers 1 to *N* with the following algorithm:

```
FUNCTION SUM(N:BYTE):BYTE;
  BEGIN
    IF N IN [0,1]
      THEN SUM(N) = N
      ELSE SUM(N) = SUM(N−1) + N
  END;
```

This solution is, of course, quite artificial as

SUM(N) = N*(N+1) DIV 2

but the problem is simple and serves our purpose.

When the value of *N* is 0 or 1, *SUM* behaves as an ordinary nonrecursive function. If $N = 2$, the first call of *SUM* leads to the ELSE statement, which calls *SUM* again—this time with argument $N - 1 = 1$. This second call uses the THEN part of *SUM* and returns 1. The ELSE statement of the first call of *SUM* now adds 1 to the original value of *N*, $N = 2$ and the function termi-

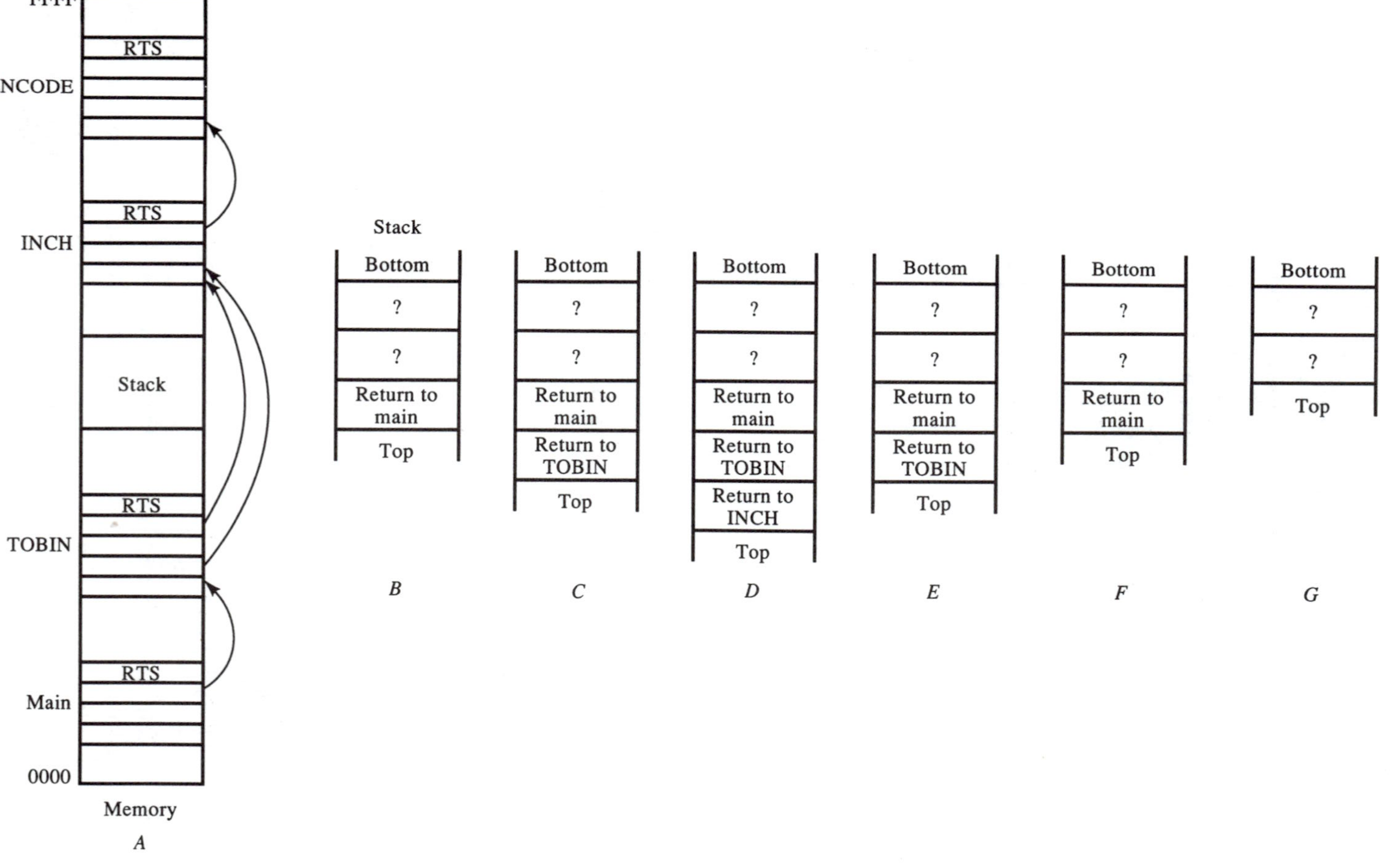


**Figure 10.9.** Execution of BSR TOBIN: a, the layout of the program in memory; b, the stack just after the call of TOBIN; c, just after the call of INCH; d, just after the call of ENCODE; e, just after the return from ENCODE; f, just after the return from INCH; g, just after the return from TOBIN.

nates and returns 3, which is the correct value. A similar, but longer, sequence of steps is executed for larger values of *N* and it is useful to perform a few traces manually. Pay special attention to the correct value of *N* associated with each call of *SUM*.

The implementation of this problem on the 6800 is shown below. The THEN and ELSE labels correspond to the THEN and ELSE statement in the Pascal version of the algorithm.

```
                        ; Input B = N, output A = SUM
SUM                     ; Recursive calculation of the sum of numbers
                        ; from 1 to N using one-byte unsigned codes
                        ; Initial value of N must be in B
                        ; result is returned in A
        CMPB #1         ; Check whether N in accumulator B is >1
        BHI ELSE        ; Jump to a recursive call if N>1
THEN    TBA             ; N is 0 or 1, load result into A
        RTS             ; Done with this call of SUM
ELSE    PSHB            ; Save the current value of N on the stack
        DECB            ; Decrement N
        BSR SUM         ; SUM calls itself to calculate SUM(N−1) and
                        ; returns result in A
        PULB            ; Get previous value of N and
        ABA             ; add it to SUM(N−1) to get SUM(N)
        RTS             ; after pulling B, SP is now as on entry to SUM
```

Note that at the time of each RTS, the stack is as on entry to SUM.

Figure 10.10 shows the operation of SUM for $N = 3$. Note that it uses the stack to preserve *N* for later calculation while passing the value of $N - 1$ as the argument of the recursive call.

We could use subroutine SUM in a program as follows:

```
. . .
JSR INCH        ; Read the value of N
JSR SUM         ; Call the subroutine
JSR OUTHEX      ; Output result
. . .
```

Note that the program and the subroutine will only work for small values of *N*.

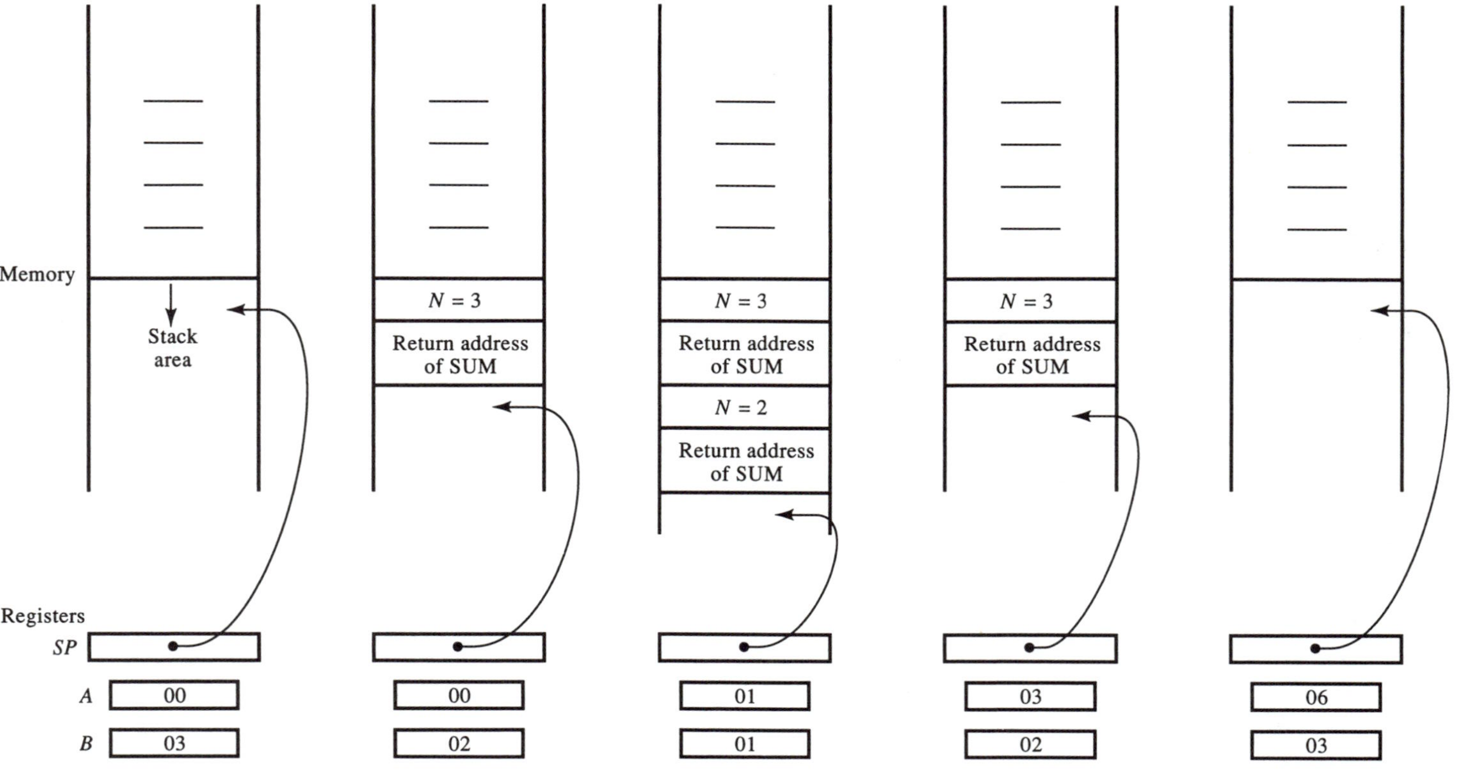


**Figure 10.10.** State of the stack and accumulators $A$ and $B$ during successive calls and exits from recursive subroutine SUM.

**Problem 16—Passing Arguments to and from Subroutines** If a subroutine has one or two one-byte parameters, arguments can be passed to a subroutine in accumulators as in the previous example. A large number of bytes, such as an array, can be passed by supplying the array's memory address in the index register. The most common method of parameter passing used by compilers for languages like Pascal, however, is to use the stack. The following example demonstrates the principle of this approach.

Consider a Pascal procedure such as

```
PROCEDURE Proc(X1,X2,X3,X4:BYTE)
```

and a call such as

```
Proc(13,71,Y,Z)
```

In translating this call, a Pascal compiler would create code to push the values of the arguments on the stack and to call the procedure. On return from the call, the compiled code would remove the arguments from the stack. The code generated by the compiler for the *call* might be as follows:

```
LDAA #13    ; Push value of first argument on stack
PSHA
LDAA #71    ; Push value of second argument on stack
PSHA
LDAA Y      ; Push the value of argument Y
PSHA
LDAA Z      ; Push the value of argument Z
PSHA
JSR PROC    ; Jump to the body of the procedure
INS         ; Clean the stack on return from the call
INS         ; by incrementing SP to its value before the call
INS
INS
```

Note that instruction INS is better here than the more natural PUL because INS does not change the accumulator.

The code implementing the *body* of the procedure could read as follows:

```
TSX         ; Transfer SP+1 (address of top element on stack)
            ; to X
            ; Arguments will be accessed by indexed addressing
            ; Note that top item on stack is
```

```
            ; the two-byte return address, not the value of X1
            ; Now to access, for example, X3
LDAB 4,X    ; X3 is four bytes above the top item on stack
```

In practice, Pascal compilers use the stack not only for passing parameters, but also for storing local variables, calculating arithmetic and logic expressions, and passing information about the current context (that is, the location of nearest higher level variables declared in the previously called procedures or main program). The stack segment containing all this information is called the procedure's *activation record.*

The use of the activation record to store local variables and to evaluate expressions arises from the nature of Pascal: The execution of Pascal programs is "dynamic," which means that the order in which procedures are called may depend on the values of data and may reach any depth. No memory is thus safe to store a procedure's variables and parameters statically, (in fixed locations for the whole execution), and one must use the stack, which is dynamic and keeps only active information nested in the correct order.

The fact that procedure calls in Pascal may be any number of levels deep is due to recursion and makes the amount of required memory unpredictable. Programs in languages that do not allow recursion, such as conventional BASIC, use a predictable amount of memory and one can then assign fixed memory locations to variables and parameters. Such "static" allocation simplifies and speeds up execution but restricts the power of the language.

This concludes our demonstration of basic programming techniques and justification of the main 6800 instructions and addressing modes. We will present further examples in the following chapters.

## Exercises

1. Select ten 6800 instructions and test their execution using the Heathkit computer or our simulator. Record the changes of memory and register values and flags.
2. Convert the first four programs in this section to hexadecimal machine code.
3. Explain how a delay program could be used to calculate the clock speed of a 6800-based computer.
4. Write a program that creates a 5-sec delay.
5. Implement multiplication using the index register.
6. Compare multiplication by shifting and adding with repeated addition.
7. What would happen if one used "signed" branch instructions in Problem 8?
8. Implement a block move over a long distance in the "DOWNTO" rather than the "TO" direction. When are each of these used?

9. The 6800 and its relatives are often used to replace hardwired logic. In such a case, the truth tables of one or more logic functions are stored in a table, and packed to occupy one bit per table entry per function. Write a program that will send the value of function $i$ for a given argument to bit 0 of a device at address *DEV*. (*Hint*: Retrieve the correct table entry, mask out the bits of all functions except function $i$ using a table of masks, and shift bit $i$ into the rightmost position.)
10. Some older CPUs store the return address of subroutine calls in the first location of the called subroutine. Does this practice allow nested and recursive calls?
11. Show the stack position of the arguments and the return address in Problem 16.
12. How deep does the stack in Problem 15 get for $N = 10$?
13. In Problem 16, we used the index register to access subroutine arguments on the stack. Our solution destroys the original value in $X$ and this may be undesirable. Modify the code so that $X$ has the original value upon return from the subroutine.
14. Describe how an activation record could be organized and used. Draw a diagram.
15. Code produced by Pascal compilers deals with VAR parameters by putting their addresses on the stack. Why? (*Hint:* Can the compiler predict where the variables will be stored? Can it predict the order in which procedures are called?)
16. Draw a diagram showing a succession of activation records during the execution of a skeletal Pascal program with procedures.
17. Test the programs in this section with carefully selected data.
18. How many tests would have to be performed to exhaustively test the instruction set of the 6800 if its ALU can be assumed to work correctly? How many tests would be required to test the ALU as well? What else should one test to determine that the CPU works correctly?
19. Write and test programs to solve the following problems:

    a. Addition of absolute values of two signed numbers

    b. $A := B + C$ where $A$, $B$, and $C$ are arrays.

    c. Finding the largest value in an array of unsigned one-byte integers.

    d. Repeat Exercise b using signed numbers.

    e. Binary to ASCII conversion of eight-bit unsigned codes.

    f. Calculation of the first 10 BCD digits of $\frac{1}{7}$.

    g. Incrementation of a four-byte non-negative number.

    h. Comparison of two four-byte integers.

    i. BCD addition for four-digit numbers.

j. Sorting an array of one-byte integers.

k. Inverting the order of elements in a byte array.

l. Inverting the order of elements in a double-byte array.

## 10.4 ASSEMBLY LANGUAGE PROGRAMMING

Assembly language programming was invented soon after the first computers were built; it was a great improvement over programming in binary, octal, or hexadecimal machine code. Some time later, high-level languages like COBOL, FORTRAN, ALGOL, Pascal, and C were introduced and most programs are now written using them.

Because programming in assembly language is much more awkward than programming in high-level languages its use is now restricted mainly to programs or parts of programs that require very efficient implementation: A good assembly language programmer can still produce better code than a high-level language compiler. Although the need for assembly language programming has decreased, the student of computers must still be familiar with its principles. The purpose of this section is to summarize the concepts introduced so far and to present a few new ones. The student is referred to one of the specialized texts for in-depth coverage.

In its most elementary form, an assembly language is a symbolic representation of machine instructions and the data used by a program. It consists of machine instruction mnemonics such as LDAA, pseudoinstruction mnemonics such as DB, labels for names of memory locations, symbolic names for variables and constants, and comments.

The process of writing, assembling, and running an assembly language program with the help of a simple assembler is as follows:

One writes the program in symbolic form following exact assembly language rules and stores the resulting source code in a file. The source code is processed by an *assembler* program that converts it to a binary object code executable by the computer. The assembler translates mnemonics into binary opcodes, pseudoinstructions into actions such as reserving space for variables, and calculates addresses corresponding to labels. It also converts decimal, hexadecimal, and string values to binary, and calculates expressions used as symbolic addresses and operands.

To execute the object code produced by the assembler, the programmer calls the *loader* program, which reads the object code file, loads it into memory and starts its execution. In practice, one usually calls the loader simply by typing the name of the file with the object code.

The conversion of assembly language programs to executable code using more sophisticated assemblers requires a slightly more complicated procedure because such programs frequently consist of several modules written and assembled by different programmers, or extracted from a program library. All these pieces are stored in different files on the disk and must be combined into one module before execution. This involves assigning appropriate address spaces to individual modules, calculating destination addresses of jumps from one module to another, finding addresses of data used in one module and declared in another, and so on. This linking process is performed by a linker program and the resulting executable code can be loaded into memory and executed. Often, the linked file is not directly executable and a final transformation is performed by the loader while the program is copied from a file to memory. Figure 10.11 summarizes the whole process.

## Advanced Assembler Features

The most important of the additional features provided by sophisticated assemblers is the *macro*, a named sequence of instructions used by the

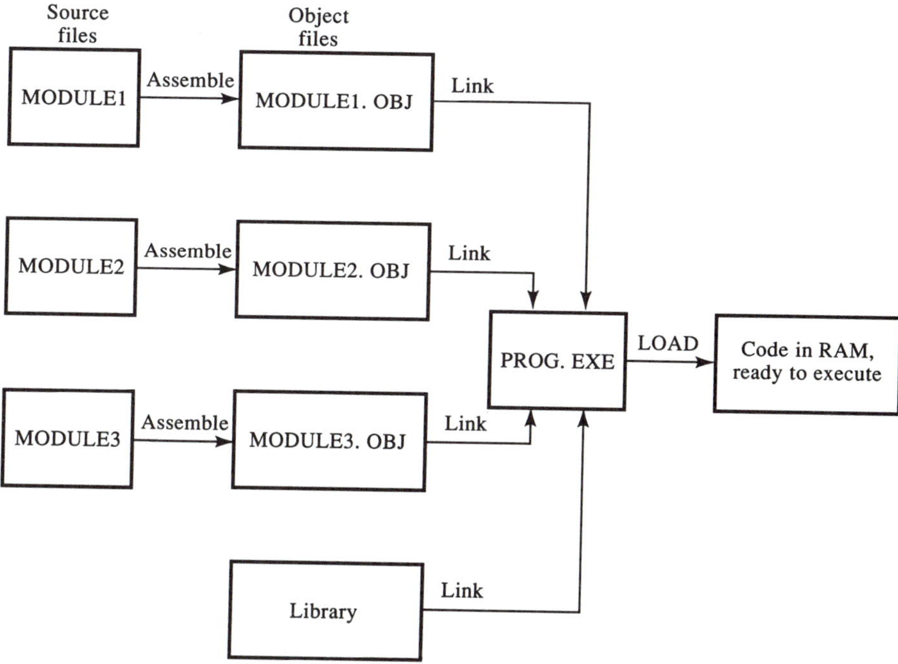


**Figure 10.11.** Converting an assembly language program to executable form and executing it.

programmer as a shorthand convention. A macro must be declared (the declaration defines its meaning), and a macro call inserted in the code wherever the macro is needed.

A macro declaration in its simplest form is a named sequence of instructions such as

```
DELAY   MACRO       ;  Macro heading
        LDX #FF00   ;  Macro body
LOOP    DEX         ;
        BNE LOOP    ;
        ENDMACRO    ;  End
```

When the assembler encounters a macro call in the source code, for example,

```
. . .
STAA CRT
DELAY          ;  Macro call
LDAA CHAR
. . .
```

it "expands" the macro name and replaces it with a copy of the declaration. In our case, the fragment above becomes

```
        . . .
        STAA CRT
        LDX #FF00   ;  Expanded macro
LOOP    DEX         ;  Expanded macro
        BNE LOOP    ;  Expanded macro
        LDAA CHAR
        . . .
```

After expanding the macro, the assembler converts it into machine code, just like the rest of the program.

One uses macros for frequently needed instruction sequences, often to replace instructions not available on a particular computer. As an example, a 6800 programmer would find it useful to have a collection of macros that perform arithmetic operations, such as signed and unsigned multiplication and division, floating-point addition and subtraction, and conversion between binary and BCD. Another important category of macro applications are for I/O functions, such as the conversion of ASCII input into binary, the output of strings of characters, and so on.

Macros resemble procedures, and more advanced macros allow parameters just like procedures. As an example, the parameters of a macro that displays a string on the screen could be the value of the string and its position on the screen. A macro to multiply two-byte numbers could have parameters specifying the address of operands and the result. Our DELAY macro could also be generalized by adding the value of the delay as a parameter. When calling a macro, the programmer replaces the parameter with the actual argument as in Pascal procedure calls.

Although there is some similarity between macros and subroutines—both are used to implement a self-contained segment of code—there are important differences as well.

A macro is a programmer's shorthand, a named segment of code expanded by the assembler whenever it encounters the macro call. Although macros shorten the source code, they do not reduce the size of the object code: Each macro call creates a new copy of the macro and the complete code of the macro body thus appears in the program as many times as the macro is invoked in the program. This duplication of code can consume a great deal of memory space if the macro is long and used often; macros are therefore used mainly for short sequences of instructions.

A subroutine is a machine feature, accessed via the subroutine call instruction and exited by the RTS instruction. Like a macro, one uses a subroutine to encapsulate a segment of instructions implementing a frequently needed function. Unlike a macro, the code of a subroutine appears in the program only once and the use of subroutines thus shortens object code.

Access to a subroutine requires the execution of a BSR or JSR instruction and return to the calling segment requires execution of RTS. This increases the time needed to execute the body of the subroutine itself. Such "overhead" does not arise with a macro because its body is copied into the program at the place it is called and executed without any jumps or returns. The fact that the overhead of subroutine jump and return becomes relatively more prominent when a subroutine is short is another reason why subroutines are used mainly for longer instruction sequences and macros for short ones.

Another important advanced concept of assembly language programming is *conditional assembly*. It can be implemented by one of several special pseudoinstructions that inform the assembler that the following block of source code should be assembled only if a certain condition (such as the value of a certain symbol) is satisfied. If the condition fails, the assembler skips that part of the code as if it were a comment.

Typically, one uses conditional assembly for code added to the program for debugging. The code is used during development, and when the program is finalized its assembly is bypassed by changing the value of the symbol controlling its assembly. Consequently, the debugging segment is not present in the final object code. The segment is, however, left in the source code as it may be needed later for further testing.

Another use of conditional assembly is to integrate different versions of the same program into a single piece of source code. As an example, a program may use different memory regions for different amounts of available RAM or may use different display routines for different terminals.

Conditional assembly is also frequently used with macros. As an example, CPUs like the 8086 outlined in the next section have instructions that work with several different data types. The load instruction, for example, has one form to load one half of a sixteen-bit register and another to load the whole register. To make a macro more general, it is advantageous to design it to work with both one- and two-byte operands. In each case, the assembler must use a different load instruction and this can be implemented by using conditional assembly inside the macro.

We will return to the subject of assembly language programming in Chapter 14 to discuss the operation of the assembler itself.

### Exercises

1. Explain the advantages of assembly language programming over machine language programming.
2. Describe the steps involved in assembling and executing an assembly language program.
3. Explain the concepts of a macro and conditional assembly and give examples of their uses.
4. How do subroutines and macros differ in their principles and applications?

## 10.5 THE 8086 FAMILY OF CPUs

The 6800 CPU by Motorola is well-suited to introducing traditional CPUs but it is too primitive for the needs of modern computers; its current use is restricted to industrial controllers and similar applications. We will thus complement its presentation by outlining the more recent 8086 family of CPUs. In the following chapters, we will similarly complement further discussion of the 6800 with 8086 information, and the description of the 6800-based ET-3400 educational computer with an outline of the IBM PC personal computer, which uses the 8088 member of the 8086 family.

As we already mentioned, at the end of the 1960s integrated circuit technology had advanced to the point that the number of transistors that could be put on a one chip was sufficient to build a complete, although very simple, CPU.

The first CPUs on a chip developed at that time were four-bit CPUs that were used as controllers in circuits previously requiring many TTL chips. The introduction of such CPUs made possible a substantial decrease in chip count—the number of chips needed to implement a logic function. Because chip count is an essential parameter in electronic design, digital designers started converting many of their products from hardwired logic to programmed logic based on software, one-chip CPUs, and interface chips developed especially for them.

The success of four-bit CPUs lead to a flood of new CPU chips by Intel, Motorola, Texas Instruments, National Semiconductor, Mostek, Zilog, and others. Some of these companies were already established semiconductor manufacturers but others were formed just to produce one-chip CPUs and related products.

The first CPU powerful enough for major digital functions and even simple computers was the 8080 by Intel, which was followed by Motorola's 6800. Both appeared very shortly after the first four-bit CPUs. Although they were intended mainly as controllers, they also became the basis of the first personal microcomputers.

After a short period of "garage-built" computers like the Apple and the Commodore (both using the 6502 CPU by Mostek, a relative of the 6800), a host of machines based on the 8080 and Zilog's Z80 emerged and became popular. (The first series of Tandy computers used the Z80.) Although all of these computers used eight-bit CPUs with a 64k address space, few of them actually had 64k memories because memory chip capacities were low and the chips were expensive. Peripherals were also primitive by today's standards.

By the end of the 1970s, a new generation of CPUs using sixteen-bit words had emerged and began to be used as the basis of much more powerful machines that very quickly replaced eight-bit computers. Although a number of manufacturers now produce sixteen-bit CPUs for a variety of applications, the personal computer market settled on the 8086 family by Intel, and the 68000 family by Motorola.

The 8086 family is used in IBM PC computers, their successors, and "clones;" the 6800 family is used in the Apple Macintosh. As we do not have enough room to describe both, we will restrict ourselves to a brief description of the Intel 8086 family. We will see that although these CPUs are quite different from our familiar 6800, there are nevertheless enough similarities to make them easy to understand. The same comparison and conclusion holds for most other CPUs as well.

### Basic 8086 Architecture

The 8086 and 8088 were the first of a family of related Intel CPUs. Among their successors the most prominent members are the 80286, which is used in the IBM PC/AT ("advanced technology") and the 80386, which is used in the most advanced of the current IBM personal computers, the high-level models of the PS/2.* All CPUs in the 8086 family are "upward compatible," which means that the more advanced members can execute instructions of the less advanced CPUs. Thus, users can transport programs developed for one computer to another, more powerful CPU computer without changes, although minor modifications may occasionally be advisable to take advantage of the more advanced CPUs.

The 8086, 8088, and 80286 are sixteen-bit CPUs, which means that their architecture is based on sixteen-bit operands. Internal registers are sixteen bits wide, the ALU operates on sixteen-bit values, and the data buses are sixteen bits wide. The 80386 is a thirty-two-bit CPU. We will concentrate on the 8086 and 8088 CPUs, which form the basis of the family.

The only major difference between the 8086 and the 8088 is that the 8086 has sixteen data pins and the 8088 only eight. The advantage of having only eight data pins is that it makes design somewhat simpler because the system bus is narrower, card connectors are shorter, and established eight-bit support devices are available at low cost and in large quantities. The disadvantage of having eight data pins on a sixteen-bit CPU is that each sixteen-bit data unit must be sent in two eight-bit packets in consecutive machine cycles, which decreases execution speed. The simplicity of 8088-based computers was the reason why this CPU was selected for the IBM PC computer; the advantage of sixteen data pins was the reason why some IBM competitors use the 8086 in their PC clones. We will concentrate on the 8088.

The 8088 uses twenty-bit addresses and can thus access 1 Mbyte memory locations. Its architecture, however, is such that the CPU never "sees" the entire address space and can only use four 64k "segments": one for program code, one for data, one for the stack, and one for "extra" uses, mainly block operations. Special instructions can place each of the four segments anywhere in memory, even in overlapping address ranges.

The placement of each segment in memory and the location of data or instructions within a segment are determined by a pair of registers. One, the segment register, defines where the segment starts while the other specifies an offset within the segment.† Both registers are sixteen bits wide to match the sixteen-bit internal buses and the sixteen-bit ALU, which appears to contradict our statement that addresses are twenty bits long. In reality, the twenty-bit address is obtained by shifting the segment register left four bits, and adding the offset register.

As an example, the address of the current instruction is obtained by combining the contents of the code segment register *CS* and the instruction

*An 80486 CPU has recently been developed and a few computers using it have already been announced.

†The name of the second register depends on the type of the segment.

pointer *IP*. (The combined *CS* and *IP* registers are effectively equivalent to a program counter.) If *CS* contains 6806H (Intel uses "H" for hexadecimal) and *IP* contains 2372H, the address of the instruction is

| | |
|---|---|
| 6806 | Start of segment |
| 2372 | Offset from segment start |
| 6A3D2 | Full address |

In Intel notation, this address is denoted 6806:2372H.

*Registers* in the 8088 CPU can be divided into the following groups: general purpose registers, address registers, data registers, and flag registers (Figure 10.12). All are sixteen bits wide.

General purpose registers (*AX*, *BX*, *CX*, and *DX*) are used to hold operands and results. Each can be accessed as a sixteen-bit entity or by high or low one-byte halves, for example as *AH* and *AL*. Although most instructions can be used with any general purpose register, each register also has its special functions.

Register *AX* is called the "accumulator" and is used as the destination of selected arithmetic instructions, such as multiplication and division. Some of the instructions that work with all registers have shorter codes when used with *AX*. Register *BX* is the "base" register and, in addition to general purpose

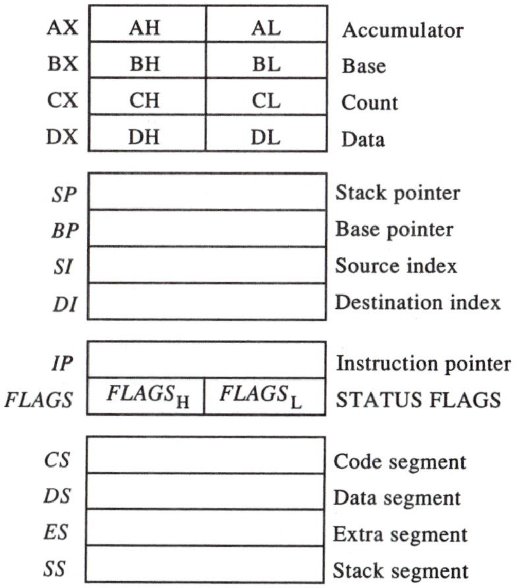

| | | | |
|---|---|---|---|
| AX | AH | AL | Accumulator |
| BX | BH | BL | Base |
| CX | CH | CL | Count |
| DX | DH | DL | Data |
| *SP* | | | Stack pointer |
| *BP* | | | Base pointer |
| *SI* | | | Source index |
| *DI* | | | Destination index |
| *IP* | | | Instruction pointer |
| *FLAGS* | $FLAGS_H$ | $FLAGS_L$ | STATUS FLAGS |
| *CS* | | | Code segment |
| *DS* | | | Data segment |
| *ES* | | | Extra segment |
| *SS* | | | Stack segment |

**Figure 10.12.** The 8088 CPU registers.

uses, is used to address arrays (see addressing modes below). Register *CX* is the "counter"; its special use is in loops and block instructions. Register *DX* is the "data" register and is used in multibyte multiplication and division. The names "accumulator," "base," "counter," and "data" should help one to remember the meaning of *AX*, *BX*, *CX*, and *DX*, however, they have been chosen mainly for convenience and do not fully capture the specialized register functions.

Address registers consist of segment registers *CS*, *DS*, *SS*, and *ES*; the instruction pointer *IP*; and pointer and index registers *BP*, *DI*, *SI*, and *SP*. Register *CS* determines the position of the code segment; *DS* defines the data segment; and *SS* and *SP* define the stack segment and the top of the stack. Register *ES* is the "extra segment" register and is used mainly to identify one block of data in operations involving two blocks.

Register *BP* is the base pointer. It is used with registers *DI* (destination index) and *SI* (source index) mainly to access arrays and similar data structures. In block operations, *SI* points to an element in the source block and *DI* to the corresponding element in the destination block.

The flag register contains status and control flags. Status flags include the usual arithmetic and logic flags; control flags include the interrupt flag, direction flag for controlling the direction of block instructions (see below), and the trap flag for single-step program execution.

The 8088 instruction set has approximately 100 basic instructions, and most are similar to those found on the 6800. Many of the 8088 instructions have eight- and sixteen-bit variations and use additional data types and addressing modes; the total number of valid opcodes is thus very large. Instruction sizes range from one to seven bytes and their execution time from 2 machine cycles for instructions that manipulate flags to 190 for two's complement division.

Instruction execution time is not constant for several reasons. First, the number of cycles required by certain instructions, such as multiplication and division, depends on the operand. As an example, two's complement sixteen-bit multiplication takes between 128 and 154 machine cycles. Furthermore, the 8088 overlaps the fetching of the next instruction with the execution of the current instruction, and this complicates the calculation of program speed.

The overlap of fetch and execution is made possible by several extra CPU registers, which store up to four bytes prefetched from locations following the current opcode. The prefetch occurs when the current instruction does not use the system bus. Because of prefetch, the opcode of the next instruction usually is already in the CPU when the current instruction finishes execution, and this speeds up program execution. Because the number of useful bytes present in the instruction queue varies during execution and because jumps disrupt prefetching, calculation of the exact number of cycles needed to execute a given program depends on data.

Examination of the 8088 instruction set reveals a variety of MOVE instructions, arithmetic and logic instructions (including addition, subtraction, multiplication, and division) with signed and unsigned data as well as using BCD and ASCII codes. Block operations perform block moves and searches using a single instruction, and this can save many instruction fetches and much execution time.* A group of instructions allows one to execute a loop a predetermined number of times, or until an "equal" or "not equal" condition is encountered using only one instruction.

Jumps can use relative or absolute addressing and their various forms can access any location within the current code segment (intrasegment jumps) or anywhere in memory (intersegment jumps).

The 8088 provides two types of routines, subroutines and interrupt routines. They differ in how they are accessed, what happens when they are accessed, and how return from them is executed.

*Subroutines* are accessed by CALL instructions with intrasegment or intersegment addresses. Intrasegment calls access locations within the current segment and use direct or indirect addressing. With direct addressing, a sixteen-bit offset is specified in the instruction; indirect addressing uses offset stored in a register or memory. Return from a subroutine is by "near" (intrasegment) or by "far" (intersegment) RET.

*Interrupt routines* can be accessed either by the interrupt instruction INT or by an interrupt signal produced by an I/O device. We will discuss the concept of interrupt signals fully in Chapter 12 but we should note the advantage of being able to achieve the same effect either by software or by hardware.

Instruction INT is essentially an indirect CALL whose four-byte segment and offset address is stored in a table at the beginning of the address space. Instruction INT has a one-byte operand that is called the "type" of the interrupt. Because there are 256 one-byte codes, there are 256 interrupts and the interrupt table occupies 256 × 4 bytes. To jump to the start of an interrupt routine, the CPU multiplies the interrupt type by 4 and loads the *CS* and *IP* registers from the resulting address. As an example,

```
INT 23
```

causes the CPU to get the new values of *CS* and *IP* from memory locations 92, 93, 94, and 95.

Interrupt instructions are very useful because they allow efficient and flexible access to frequently needed code. They form the basis of the MS-DOS operating system used on the IBM PC, which we will outline in Chapter 14.

---

*The direction of a block operation, up or down is determined by the value of the direction flag.

Another difference between interrupt routines and subroutines is that INT saves not only the return address (*CS* and *IP*) like CALL, but also the flag register. Because of this difference, return from interrupt requires a special instruction IRET.

The 8088 does not use memory-mapped I/O because it has special *I/O instructions*. The address of the I/O "port" (a window for communication with an I/O device) is either given in the I/O instruction or stored in the *DX* register. In the first case, the port address is one byte long; in the second, it is two bytes long.

Addressing modes on the 8088 include immediate addressing, direct addressing, register indirect addressing, and combinations of these modes. Intel's definition of direct addressing is that the instruction contains a sixteen-bit offset from the start of the segment. In register indirect addressing, the offset is stored in a register specified by the opcode.

The following combinations of the basic modes are possible: Register indirect with offset, in which an offset constant is specified in the instruction and added to the offset stored in a register; register indirect with base and index, in which the contents of a base register and an index register are added to obtain the offset; and register indirect with base, index, and offset, in which the offset given in the instruction is added to the offsets stored in the named registers. These modes are used for addressing complex data structures, such as arrays, records, and arrays of records. As an example, record field employee[3].id in a structure like

```
TYPE entry =        RECORD
          name        : STRING[15];
          address     : STRING[10];
          telephone   : INTEGER;
          id          : INTEGER;
          END;
       employees      : ARRAY [1..n_employees] OF entry;
VAR    employee: employees;
```

can be accessed by loading the base pointer *BP* with the address of employee[1], loading the destination register *DI* with the offset of three records, and using an offset to identify the position of field *id* within the record. A single instruction can thus perform a complicated data access. The student should attempt to address employee[3].ID with the 6800 instruction set to see how useful the 8088 addressing modes are.

Addressing modes on the 8088 also include stack addressing with push and pop instructions, and inherent (implied) addressing where the data source, if any, is implied by the instruction.

One special 8088 instruction deserves to be mentioned. The escape instruction ESC tells the CPU that the following code is not intended for the CPU but for a coprocessor. *Coprocessors* are essentially special purpose CPUs designed for functions that are not implemented as 8088 instructions because they are too complex. The most important Intel coprocessor is the 8087 arithmetic, or "math," coprocessor and its successors. It can very efficiently perform a variety of arithmetic operations, such as long integer arithmetic, additional BCD instructions, a variety of floating-point operations, and functions such as exp, log, cos, sin, and others.

The 8087 chip is especially useful in graphics and simulations, applications that require extensive calculations. Where a special calculation such as a trigonometric function is needed, the program contains ESC followed by the appropriate 8087 instruction. When the CPU encounters ESC, it passes control to the 8087, which reads and executes the next code and informs the CPU when it is finished. This symbiosis can considerably speed up "compute-bound" programs.

The concept of cooperating processors can be extended even further to include many CPU chips with shared or local memories that are able to communicate with one another. We will briefly outline this topic, multiprocessor architecture, in Chapter 13.

### Exercises

1. Intrasegment branches on the 8088 use eight- or sixteen-bit offsets. Eight-bit offsets are treated as two's complement numbers as on the 6800. Sixteen-bit offsets are treated as pure binary numbers and the calculation is performed MOD 64k with no effect on the code segment register *CS*. Explain why this always gives a destination within the current segment and why it can be used to access any memory location within the segment. Explain how this helps to preserve the integrity of individual segments.
2. Why is it necessary to distinguish "near" and "far" subroutine returns?
3. Give examples of address calculation of the various 8088 addressing modes.

## SUMMARY

Motorola's MC 6800 is a useful introduction to CPU architecture because of its simple conventional features. It is an eight-bit CPU, which means that its internal registers, ALU, and instructions are oriented towards eight-bit data. Its addresses are sixteen bits wide, giving a 64k address space.

The 6800 has two general purpose eight-bit registers (accumulators) called *A* and *B* whose functions are almost interchangeable. Accumulators *A* and *B* are used as sources of operands and as recipients of results in most arithmetic and logic operations. The 6800 also has two sixteen-bit registers, the index register and the stack pointer, used mainly for address manipulation. The index register $X$ simplifies operations on blocks of data (arrays); the stack pointer $SP$ is used mainly for operations related to subroutines.

The remaining registers "visible" to the user are the program counter and the control code register. The sixteen-bit program counter holds the address of the next instruction, and the control code register is a collection of arithmetic and control flags.

Addressing modes on the 6800 include immediate, extended, direct, relative, indexed, stack, and inherent (implied) addressing. In extended addressing, the instruction contains the full sixteen-bit address of the operand. Direct addressing uses only the low byte of the address, and the high byte is assumed to be zero. Conditional jumps use relative addressing in which the one-byte offset given in the instruction is treated as a two's complement number and added to the address of the next instruction to obtain the effective address. This makes possible forward and backward jumps within a limited range, which is usually sufficient to implement loops and conditional operations.

In indexed addressing, the address is obtained as the sum of the index register and the offset given in the instruction. Indexed addressing allows one to access a sequence of memory locations by incrementing or decrementing the contents of the index register, without changing the address part of the instruction.

Stack addressing uses the stack, a memory region accessed only from its top. The address of the top of the stack is stored in the stack pointer register. Stack manipulations involve the push, pull, subroutine-jump, and return-from-subroutine instructions, which update the value of the pointer to always point to the first available location on the top of the stack.

The stack is a very important programming structure because it enforces a discipline for the orderly execution of nested tasks. If a sequence of nested operations uses the stack, it unwinds in the reverse order in which it was initiated. This is essential for nested procedures and functions and their implementation by subroutines.

The main data types on the 6800 are eight-bit pure binary, two's complement, and BCD numbers. Signed and unsigned data are processed by the same arithmetic instructions; the only difference between them is that they affect different flags and require different conditional instructions. BCD arithmetic is restricted to the decimal adjust instruction, which converts the result of binary addition into a valid BCD code.

The 6800 does not have any I/O instructions and its I/O is memory-mapped, which means that I/O ports are treated as memory locations. This has the disadvantage that a portion of the address space must be dedicated to I/O devices at the expense of space available for program and data. The advantage of memory-mapped I/O is that all instructions addressing memory can be used to address I/O devices, and individual bytes or bits in I/O ports can thus be tested, negated, shifted, and so on, as if the devices were memory locations.

The 6800 has a number of limitations that make it unsuitable for all but very simple computers. The major limitations are its eight-bit orientation, 64k address space, lack of instructions and addressing modes for certain very common problems (multiplication, division, and operations on blocks of data), and relatively slow clock speed. The address space is insufficient for more substantial programs, and the lack of powerful instructions makes programs long, awkward, and slow. Removing restrictions such as these was one of the major incentives for the development of the more powerful members of the 6800 family and sixteen-bit CPUs.

As an example of a sixteen-bit CPU, we outlined the 8086 family of CPUs by Intel. We concentrated on the 8088 because it is used in the popular IBM PC. The main advantages of the 8088 over the 6800 are its sixteen-bit orientation, better facilities for the execution of high-level languages (richer data types and addressing modes, larger and better organized address space, and instructions better suited for high-level tasks), higher speed, and better interfacing facilities. All these features are important criteria of progress in CPU design.

Even though the 8088 is much better suited for computing than the 6800, it still has its limitations. Its data types are restrictive, the address space is not large enough, its ability to cooperate with other processors is limited, and its speed is not sufficient. Elimination of these shortcomings was the main justification of the more advanced 80286, 80386, and 80486 CPUs and specialized support chips, such as the 8087, 80287, and 80387 arithmetic coprocessors.

Naturally, development in CPU architecture and technology has not ended with the 8086 family and new CPUs are constantly being designed. Although the latest one-chip CPUs are extremely powerful, computer manufacturers continue to develop CPUs whose operation requires transistor counts that are well beyond the possibilities of a single chip and common semiconductor technologies. Such CPUs still contain many chips.

In spite of the enormous progress in CPU technology and architecture, the principles of most computer architectures remain essentially unchanged. Thus, understanding a traditional CPU like the 6800 provides a good basis for understanding even the latest developments in CPU design.

## REVIEW QUESTIONS

1. Define the following terms: Accumulator, address, address space, addressing mode (direct, extended, indexed, indirect, implied, inherent, relative), assembly language programming, coprocessor, flag, index register, I/O port, label, linker, loader, macro, memory segment, nibble, pseudoinstruction, recursion, relocatable code, segment, stack, stack pointer, subroutine.

2. Define the main categories of instructions.
3. Explain typical uses of various addressing modes.

## REFERENCES

The following titles listed in the references at the end of the book are relevant to this chapter:

R. Bishop. *Basic Microprocessors and the 6800.*

R. Findlay. *6800 Software Gourmet Guide & Cookbook.*

L. A. Leventhal. *6800 Assembly Language Programming.*

A. Osborne. *An Introduction to Microprocessors.*

M. Sargent III and R. L. Shoemaker. *The IBM PC from the Inside Out.*

# CHAPTER 11

# PERIPHERAL DEVICES AND PRINCIPLES OF COMMUNICATION

## AN OVERVIEW

A computer consists of a CPU, memory, and I/O devices (peripherals) that communicate with the external world. Peripherals include keyboards, mice, displays, printers, terminals, and disk drives, as well as the less frequently used scanners, tablets, plotters, joy-sticks, audio I/O devices, and others.

Programming I/O operations and I/O interfacing require an understanding of the principles of peripherals, which is why we will introduce this subject in this chapter. We will examine hardware interfaces between peripherals and the principles of I/O programming in Chapter 12, although we will consider a few examples in this chapter as well.

Finally, we will introduce the increasingly important subject of digital communication.

## IMPORTANT WORDS

ACIA, burst transfer, character generator, computer terminal, CRT, CRT controller, current loop, cycle stealing, disk drive (controller, floppy, hard), dot-matrix printer, handshake, I/O driver, keyboard (matrix, encoder), modem, modulation, parallel communication, PIA, port, protocol, raster scan display, RS-232-C, scan code, serial communication, synchronous/asynchronous communication, UART.

## 11.1 INTRODUCTION

If one defines the CPU, memory, and buses as the "inner" computer, then I/O devices should be called peripherals (Figure 11.1). Although many peripherals are physically separated from the main computer and have their own power supplies, some, such as disk drives and modems, are often located inside the computer.

The basic peripherals include a keyboard and a display, a disk drive for storing program and data files, and a printer for producing "hard copy" records. The "mouse" is quickly becoming a standard complement of the keyboard as a means of pointing at locations on the screen. Other peripherals that are found more or less frequently on personal computers include the following: Scanners are used to convert graphics or printed text into bits as the user drags the scanner across the image. Graphic tablets are used to convert maps, drawings, and similar graphic information into internal computer representation by tracing the picture on the tablet. Joy-sticks and tracking balls are devices used somewhat like the mouse. The light pen allows one to select items on the screen by touching them. Plotters output graphical information. Audio I/O devices are used mainly for speech output and input (still in its infancy), and for music. A terminal combines a keyboard with a display and is used to access larger computers that do not have a keyboard and a display attached to them.

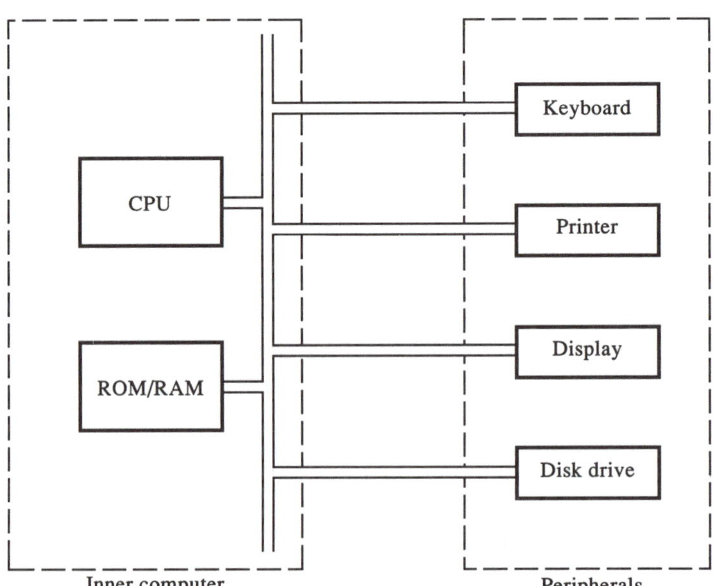


**Figure 11.1.** Inner computer and peripherals.

In addition to these standard peripherals, a number of other devices are used with computers in industrial processes, home appliances, and similar applications. These include cash register wands and similar sensors of various physical and chemical properties, such as position, pressure, temperature, strength of magnetic field, light, and acidity. Whereas sensors are input devices, activators are output devices. They are used to open and close valves, control lights and temperatures, activate motors, and so on.

The computer controls each of its peripheral devices through a program called the *device driver*. In essence, the device driver is a collection of routines that convert high-level commands, such as "turn the disk drive motor on" or "read data from the disk drive," into low-level signals that control the peripheral, report the result, and take care of error conditions.

Writing a device driver requires an intimate knowledge of the computer and the peripheral. Because few programmers have this background, drivers of standard devices are included in the *operating system*, a program that provides the interface between the computer and its user and that is supplied with the computer. Device drivers of less common peripherals are supplied by the supplier of the device and attached to the operating system by the user. Operating systems are the subject of Chapter 14 but we will consider examples of device drivers in this and the following chapters.

### General Structure of Peripheral Devices

Each peripheral has three major parts: an electrical or electromechanical component, a logic circuit that controls it, and an interface between the device and the computer.

While it is obvious that different devices such as printers and displays operate on different physical principles, even devices in the same category may operate differently. For example, there are two distinct types of displays, each with several subcategories; several different keyboard principles; and at least five major groups of printers. In spite of this variety, all of the peripherals in a category use the same basic logic and communicate with the computer in a similar manner.

The function of a peripheral's internal logic is to perform as much control as possible within the device to minimize the involvement of the main CPU. This internal logic may be implemented by custom circuits designed specifically for this task or, more commonly, by a controller chip, a special purpose CPU-like device. Internal logic can also be implemented by a general purpose CPU, for example, the 6800, which is controlled by a program stored in the peripheral's ROM.

The *interface* between the CPU and the peripheral governs communication between the device and the computer. It must recognize when the CPU addresses the peripheral, captures the command, transmits it to the device, and receives or returns data or status information to the CPU. In some cases, the interface must also be able to request the CPU's attention with an interrupt signal.

The essence of an interface is a circuit that recognizes the control signals produced by the CPU and the address assigned to the device's registers that hold data, commands, and status information. All peripheral interfaces are essentially the same and their design depends mainly on the architecture of the CPU; we will address this topic in the next chapter.

As an example illustrating these concepts, consider a typical dot-matrix printer, whose operational principle is the selective activation of tiny hammers that impact an ink ribbon. Its main components are two motors that move the printer head and position the paper, and electromagnets that control the hammers. The printer's internal logic consists of circuits that control individual hammers, move the head in the desired direction, check that the paper is not jammed, and so forth. Communication with the CPU takes the form of data, commands, and status information messages like "printer busy," "paper jammed," or "out of paper." The interface consists of an address decoder, which controls access to two or three registers that hold data, status, and control information. After this general introduction, we will now turn to a more detailed examination of the main peripherals.

## 11.2 KEYBOARDS

The keys of most keyboards are electric switches that make or break an electric path (Figure 11.2). Because switches are essentially springs, a pressed or released key bounces back and forth between its two extreme positions for a while after its activation. Each bounce creates a 0–1 transition, and bouncing thus produces a sequence of apparent key activations that can last up to 10 msec. A single activation of the key for the letter *A* could thus be inter-

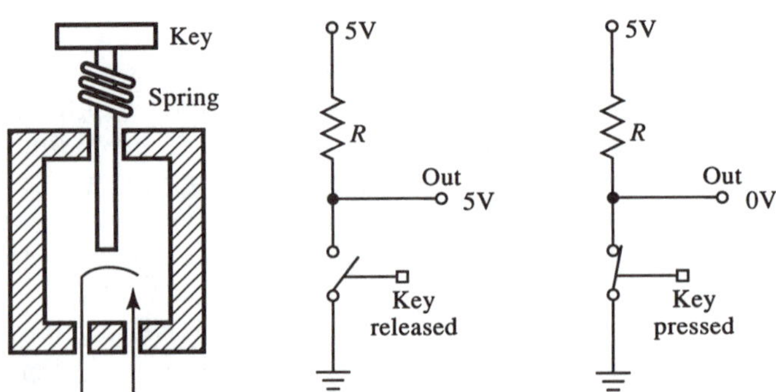


**Figure 11.2.** Principle of a mechanical key.

preted as many successive *A*s and this could create problems. The effects of bouncing must thus be controlled by hardware or software.

Hardware debouncing can be accomplished with latches or similar memory circuits. As this approach requires one circuit per key, it is normally used only for small keyboards. Computer keyboards, which typically have ninety or more keys, are usually debounced by software that is either stored in the keyboard's encoder chip or executed by a CPU. When key activation is detected by the software system, the circuit waits to allow bouncing to die down and then checks to see if the signal is still on. If the key signal is still active, it is reported as a legitimate key depression; otherwise, it is dismissed as a glitch or an accidentally stroked key.

In addition to bouncing, traditional switches have another problem: Their contacts are not protected from the environment and suffer by corrosion due to humidity and dust in the air. Also, as the electrical contact is broken in releasing the key, an electric arc is formed that melts and corrodes the contact surfaces. Conductivity progressively deteriorates and the keys become less reliable. This is why keyboards with traditional keys are falling out of favor and new types of keys are becoming popular. Some designs use sealed and magnetically controlled contacts to eliminate environmental effects; others use capacitors to eliminate physical contact altogether.

Although different key designs operate on different physical principles, the logic principle is common to all. Therefore, although we will assume traditional keys, most of our discussion applies to other types of keys as well.

Figure 11.2 shows that when a switch is activated, it closes a path to the ground, and the voltage on its output drops to a 0V, giving logic 0. An inactive (open) switch produces a 5-V output, or logic 1.

In addition to keyboards, many computer applications use individual switches, for example, to reset the computer, but keyboards remain the most important switch application. A keyboard circuit must detect not only whether a key is active but also which one it is. An obvious approach is to connect the keys in a linear array having consecutive memory or I/O addresses as in Figure 11.3 and to monitor key activation by repeatedly scanning individual lines:

```
{Scan}
ADDRESS := 0;
REPEAT
  ADDRESS := (ADDRESS + 1) MOD 10;
UNTIL DATA[ADDRESS] = 0; {Key active}
{Convert address of active key to key code}
KEY_CODE := Some part of ADDRESS;
```

The disadvantage of such a linear arrangement is that it requires many components and connections and a separate signal test for each key. For

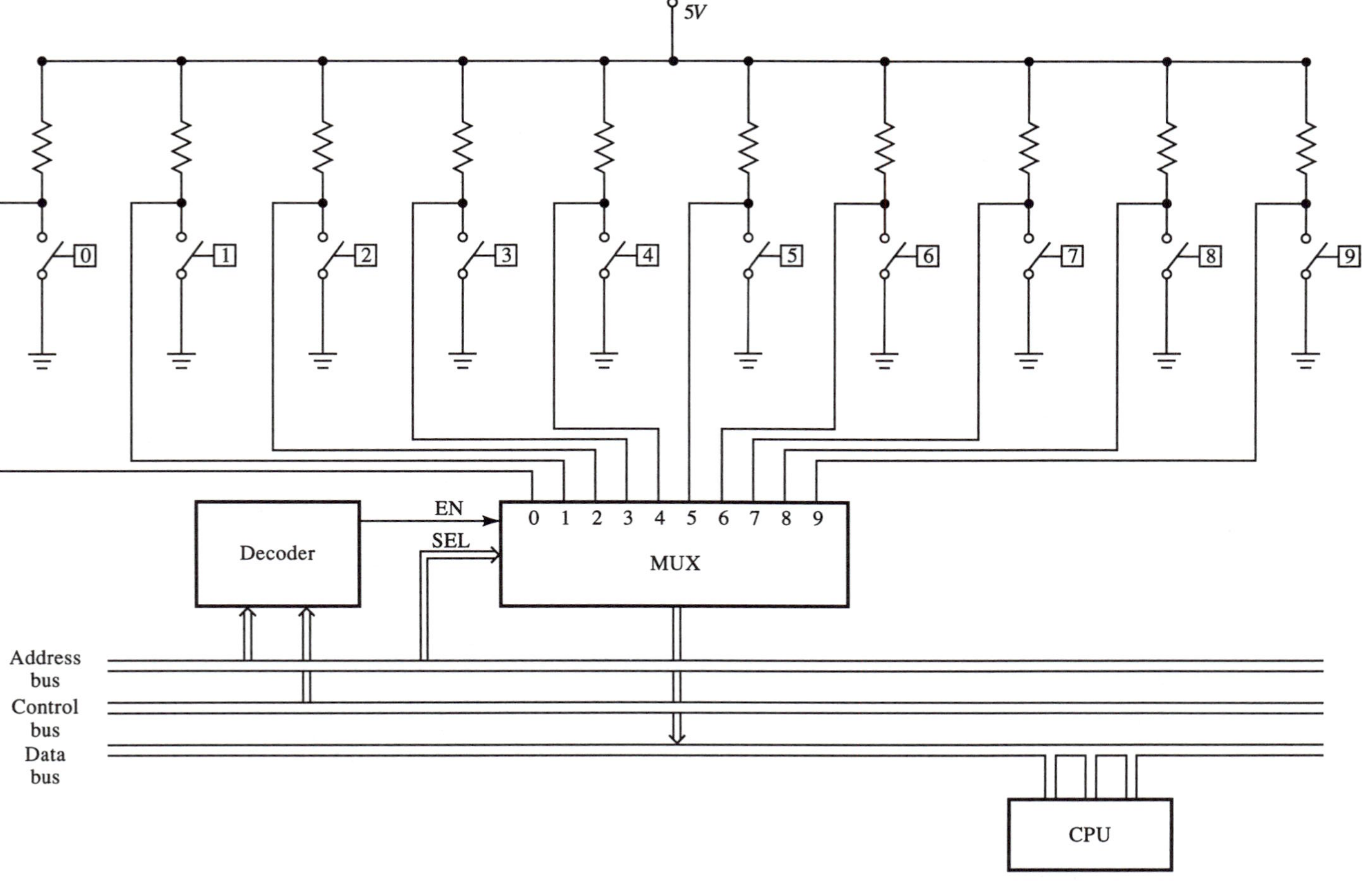


**Figure 11.3.** Linear keyboard arrangement. The MUX must have a tristate output so that its output does not interfere with outputs of other devices connected to the data bus.

keyboards having many keys, the circuit and its associated logic would become too bulky. A much more efficient approach is to arrange the keys in a two-dimensional matrix as in the "hex" keyboard (sixteen-key) in Figure 11.4

In this circuit, each key is at the intersection of a row and a column. The keyboard controller scans individual columns by activating them one by one via decoders with active Low outputs, and reads row values on the data bus. If the activated column contains a pressed key, its row output is 0, otherwise, the output is 1.

Assume, for example, that key *A* is pressed and all other keys are released. When the controller outputs address \$6000, the decoder of the leftmost column outputs 0 while all other columns are connected to the 1 outputs from inactive decoders. Because all of the keys in the column at far left are open, all row voltages are logic 1s and the controller reads *XXXX*1111 from the data bus (Figure 11.5). It concludes that none of the keys in the column

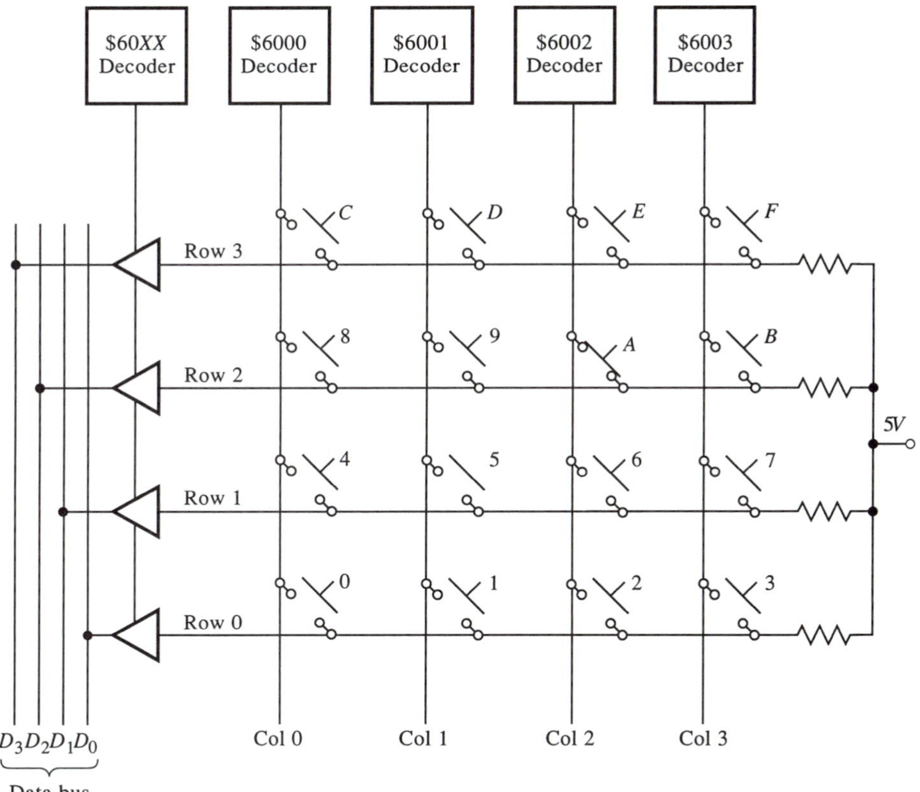


**Figure 11.4.** Two-dimensional arrangement of a sixteen-key keyboard. Key *A* is active. A single decoder chip should be used to simplify the circuit.

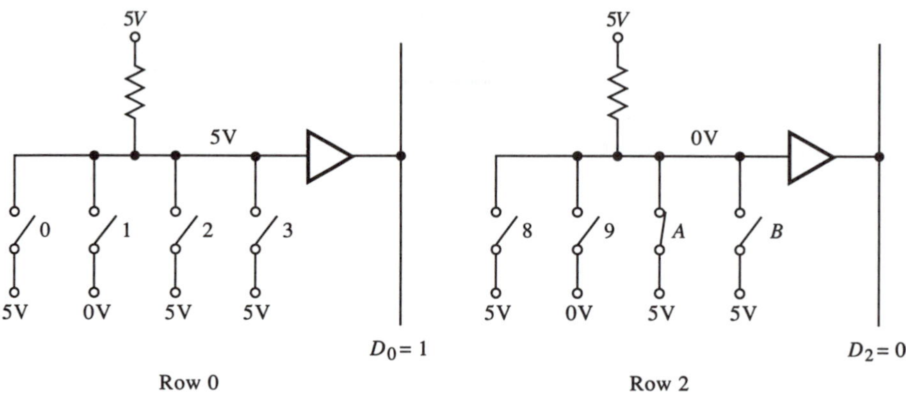


**Figure 11.5.** Electrical equivalent of rows 0 and 2 during LDA *A* \$6002 when key *A* is pressed.

are active and proceeds to the next column by outputting address \$6001. The reading is again *XXXX*1111 and the controller proceeds to the column whose address is \$6002. This time, the voltage path from 5 V through the resistor of row 2 and switch *A* is connected to logic 0. Bit 2 of the data bus thus becomes 0, and the controller reads *XXXX*1011 and concludes that a key is pressed. From the address of the activated column and from the bit pattern it finds that the pressed key is *A*, and sends its code to the computer.

We could implement the keyboard controller with a 6800 CPU using the following key detection routine:

```
INP                             ; Keyboard input routine
                                ; Code of active key returned
                                ; in accumulator A,
                                ; X is used for scanning
KBD     EQU     $6000           ; Address of column 0 of the
                                ; keyboard
TEMP    DS      2
                                ; Scanning
START   LDX     #KBD            ; X := address of column 0
NEXT    LDAB    O,X             ; Read column into
                                ; accumulator B
        COMB                    ; Negate (first step in
                                ; detection)
        BNE     DECODE          ; If one of the negated bits is 1,
                                ; a key is active, stop scanning
        INX                     ; Otherwise, go to next
                                ; column
```

```
        CPX    #KBD+4    ; Was this the last column?
        BNE    NEXT      ; If not, continue
        BRA    START     ; Else start again from
                         ; column 0
DECODE  STX    TEMP      ; Low byte in X is column
                         ; number
ROW                      ; Find row number and calcu-
                         ; late key code using formula
                         ; Key = 4*ActiveRow +
                         ; ActiveColumn
                         ; Left as an exercise
        RTS
```

This routine does not implement the whole controller because it only detects key activation and does not remove bouncing.

Figure 11.6 shows the principle of keyboard scanning by hardware. The detection of a pressed key activates the detection–debouncing circuit and causes the system to stop scanning. If a new check, performed after a debouncing delay, finds that the key is still active, the circuit sends a signal to the computer, which combines the column code from the counter and the row data from the keyboard to find the code of the active key. After processing the code, the computer reactivates the counter and scanning resumes. Because most of the work is done by the hardware, the CPU does not have to waste time by continuously scanning the keyboard.

In practice, keyboard scanning is usually performed by a keyboard encoder chip that operates on the same principle as our circuit, by a dedicated CPU, or by a combination of both. The circuit usually performs the following additional functions:

Encoding of simultaneously pressed keys. Most keyboard keys produce different codes when pressed with *SHIFT* or *CTRL*. Moreover, some computers use special conventions for certain special key combinations. On the IBM PC, for example, the combination *SHIFT* and *PrtSc* prints the screen; *CTRL, ALT*, and *DEL* pressed together reset the computer, and so on. The encoder (whether hardware- or software-based) must recognize these situations and return proper codes to the CPU. Sometimes, the bulk of keyboard interpretation is left to the CPU to make the scheme more flexible. The computer then uses codes produced by the encoder as addresses to a table of the desired codes that is stored in a ROM or a RAM.

*N*-key rollover. Even moderately fast typists press one or more keys before completely releasing a previously pressed one. To prevent the confusion that could result from this, keyboard controllers use one of three techniques: Key lockout, two-key rollover, or *N*-key rollover.

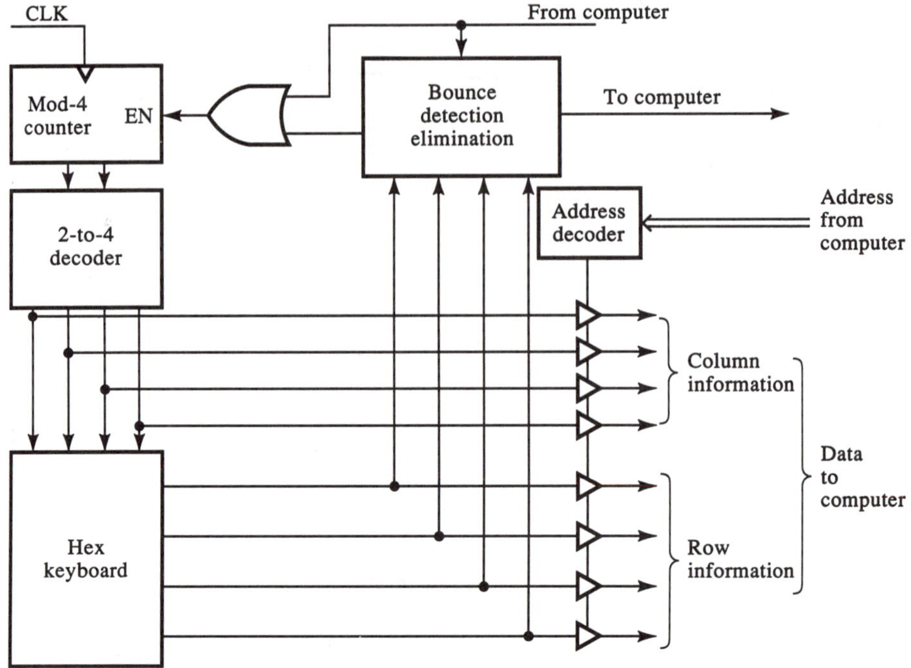


**Figure 11.6.** Simple keyboard scan circuit.

In the first method, the encoder locks up (stops scanning) as soon as it detects an active key and does not produce new codes until the key is released. This approach is used by the circuit in Figure 11.6 and by the software decoder on the Heathkit ET-3400 microcomputer (Chapter 12). The method is simple but unsatisfactory as multiple key activations cause loss of input.

With two-key rollover, a second key may be pressed before the first is released and the encoder recognizes and encodes both. The circuit is more complex but the keyboard is much easier to use.

The third option, *N*-key rollover, is an extension of two-key rollover. Up to *N* keys may be active at the same time and all will be encoded and sent to the computer. This method is, of course, best for the typist because no information is lost even when the typist is very fast; however, it is also the most complicated and expensive scheme to implement.

**Example** The IBM PC keyboard is connected to the computer by a four-wire cable providing 5 V and 0 V and two-bidirectional signal lines. It has eighty-three keys divided into a typewriter pad, a numeric pad, and ten function keys. The keys are not electromechanical switches but use capacitive technology.

Each key has two codes—"make" and "break." The make-code is produced when the key is pressed; the break-code is returned when the key is released. This scheme allows the computer to detect whether a key is still pressed (a feature needed, for example, to handle the *SHIFT* key) and adds an extra dimension to the keyboard. Break-codes are obtained by adding $80 to make-codes.

The codes produced by the IBM keyboard are not ASCII codes; they are "scan codes" assigned to the keyboard matrix in a geometric fashion. The task of converting the scan codes into proper codes is left to the computer, whose keyboard driver program interprets scan codes using a table stored in RAM. Note that the use of scan rather than ASCII codes is necessary because several keys, such as *Home, PgUp*, ↑, ↓, and function keys do not have any equivalents in the ASCII standard.

Because the conversion of scan codes is done by software, all of the keys are reprogrammable by changing the contents of the RAM table. As an example, the left *SHIFT* key could be programmed to produce letter *A*, letter *A* could play the role of *SHIFT*, and so on.

The IBM PC keyboard contains its own CPU that tests the keyboard when the computer is turned on, performs scanning, buffers (remembers) up to twenty key codes not yet consumed by the main CPU, and maintains bidirectional communication with the computer.

## Exercises

1. What would our hex keyboard encoder do if two keys were active simultaneously? Consider the following three possibilities: the keys are in the same column, in the same row, neither of these.
2. We mentioned that the advantage of a matrix keyboard over linear organization is simplicity of circuitry. How many tests for active signals are required for a linear arrangement and a two-dimensional matrix arrangement of a hexadecimal keyboard? How many for a ninety-key keyboard?
3. Does linear keyboard organization have any advantages?
4. Design a circuit to implement two-key rollover.
5. Modify the keyboard program given above to include handling of the *SHIFT* key.
6. Upper- and lower-case letter keys on the IBM PC keyboard have the same scan code. When can this be useful?

7. Write a scanning routine for the linear keyboard in Figure 11.3 scanned by a 6800 CPU.

## 11.3 DISPLAYS

Computer displays can be divided into two categories: cathode-ray tubes and flat panels. *Cathode-ray tube displays* (CRTs) work like television screens. Their main advantages are good readability, resolution, and speed; their disadvantages are their large size and weight, high power consumption, and dangerously high internal voltages. Cathode-ray tube displays are presently much more common than flat panel displays and we will describe them in more detail later in this section.

*Flat panel displays* can be divided into segmented and dot-matrix displays. The former include light emitting displays (LEDs), seven-segment LEDs, and similar devices made of individually controlled light emitting elements. Their use is restricted to instruments and appliances. Dot-matrix displays are grids of individually controlled dots that form patterns such as letters, digits, and graphics. They are becoming increasingly common in computers, particularly the portable ones.

According to their operational principle, dot-matrix displays are classified as liquid crystal displays (LCDs), plasma displays, gas-discharge panels, and others. The liquid crystal displays are most common. In an LCD electric voltage controls a layer of crystals whose orientation determines their reaction to light. When oriented in one direction, the crystals allow light to pass, in the perpendicular orientation they block or reflect it.

The advantages of LCDs and other flat panels include their small size and weight, low power consumption, and low voltage compatible with logic signals. All of these properties are important, especially for portable devices powered by batteries. The disadvantages of LCDs are lower resolution and readability, and slower response times than CRTs. The need for high-quality portable displays is a great research incentive, and the parameters of LCDs and other flat panel displays are quickly improving.

Although the physical principles of flat panel displays and CRTs are different, most of the logic principles are the same.

### CRT Displays

A computer CRT display (Figure 11.7) consists of a logic circuit that converts high-level control signals and ASCII codes into low-level control signals, a video circuit that converts logic signals into continuous analog signals for the CRT tube, and the CRT tube itself.

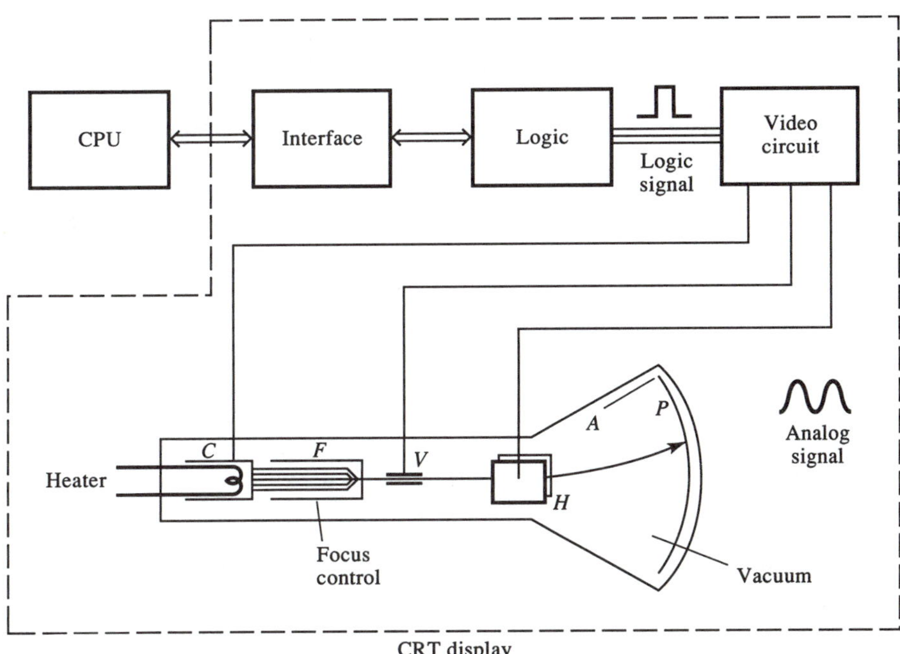


**Figure 11.7.** Block diagram of a CRT display and the main parts of the CRT tube: *A*, anode; *C*, cathode; *F*, focusing electrode; *H*, horizontal deflection plates; *P*, phosphor coating; $V_1$ vertical deflection plates.

The CRT is an evacuated glass tube containing several electrodes—plates, cylinders, and grids—connected to precisely controlled voltages. The electrode on the left of the tube in Figure 11.7 is called the cathode, which means that it is connected to a negative voltage. It is heated by a wire and its high temperature increases the energy of the electrons inside it. Those electrons that reach sufficiently high energies escape from the cathode and form an electron cloud around it.

The electrode at the other end of the tube is called the anode, which means that it is connected to a positive voltage. The electrons that escape from the heated cathode are negative, and are attracted to the anode. The resulting stream of electrons moves through a negatively charged grid, which focuses the stream into a narrow beam that proceeds towards the right end of the tube. (Because the tube is evacuated, the electrons flow unhindered by gas molecules.) On its way through the CRT, the beam passes through deflection plates or coils whose charges or magnetic fields determine where the electrons will strike the right end of the tube.

The inner wall of the screen on the righthand side of the tube is coated with phosphor. When an electron hits the coating, the phosphor changes its kinetic energy to heat and light, producing a lighted spot whose brightness depends on the beam's energy. When the beam is removed, the dot remains visible for a period of time lasting a fraction of a second or more, depending on the persistence of the phosphor and the energy of the beam. Most CRTs use phosphors of relatively short persistence to allow the display to change quickly.

Phosphors differ not only by their persistence but also by the color of produced light. This makes possible monochrome (single color) monitors of various colors as well as multicolor displays. Screens of color displays are coated with groups of tiny cells or strips or red, green, and blue (RGB) phosphor, and other colors are obtained by combining red, green, and blue dots of suitably matched intensities (Figure 11.8). Red, green, and blue dots are usually controlled by three separate beams, but some displays use a single beam.

To produce an image, the beam moves across the screen exciting one phosphor dot after another. Because the dots are only briefly visible, the screen must be continuously refreshed (rewritten) to create the illusion of a stable picture. Depending on the order in which the elements of the picture are written, CRTs are divided into raster scan and vector scan displays (Figure 11.9).

*Vector scan CRTs* produce images by drawing straight lines from one point to another. By making the lines short, even very smooth geometric shapes can be created. When the picture becomes complicated, the number of lines to be drawn and refreshed becomes very large and beam control must be very fast. Alternatively, one can use phosphors of longer persistence to reduce the refresh rate.

Vector scan CRTs are used only for advanced graphics applications because text and simple graphics can be displayed more efficiently using raster scan

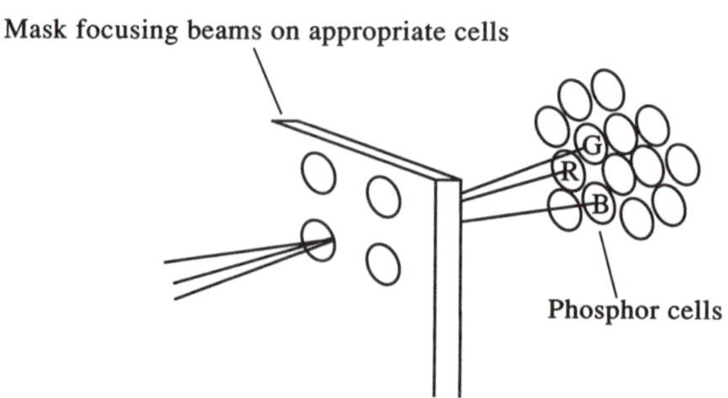


**Figure 11.8.** Principle of color CRT.

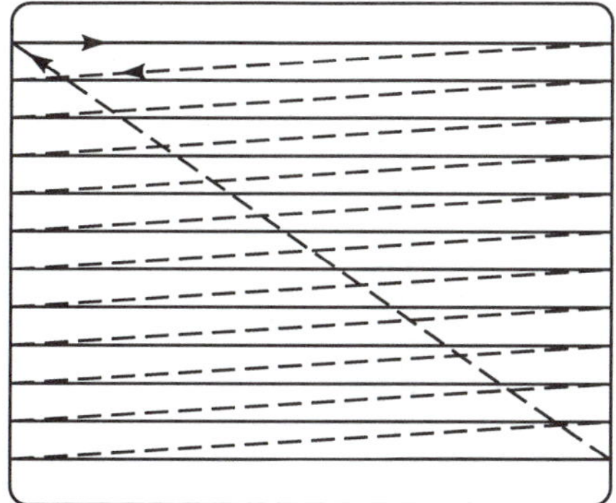

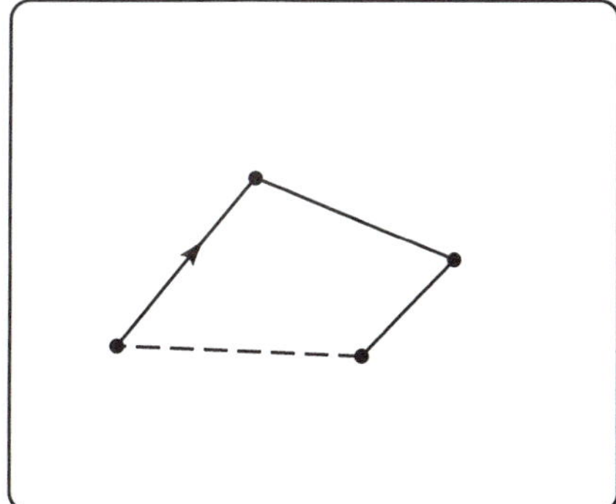

**Figure 11.9.** Raster scan (*left*) and vector scan (*right*) CRTs.

CRTs. In the following, we will restrict our attention to the much more common raster scan CRTs.

*Raster scan CRTs* approximate continuous lines as patterns of dots drawn on a fixed grid, or raster. The dots are refreshed one horizontal row after another from top to bottom (Figure 11.9). Where a visible dot is to be formed, the beam's intensity is turned up; otherwise, its intensity is turned down. The maximum number of dots that can be displayed on one line depends on the CRT and its control circuit, and determines the resolution of the screen. Resolution is measured in "pixels," or "pels" (picture elements, that is, dots). As an example, the IBM display described at the end of this section uses 720 pixels per line.

Computer displays are descendants of television sets and their operating characteristics are similar. On the American continent, the frequency at which the beam of a television set rewrites lines (the horizontal scan frequency) is 15,750 Hz, and the vertical scan frequency is 60 Hz. This can be used to produce either 60 complete screens (frames) per second, each having 262.5 lines ($262.5 \times 60 = 15{,}750$), or 30 pairs of half-frames (fields), consisting of even only and odd only lines. In this "interlaced mode," the CRT displays 525 lines ($525 \times 30 = 15{,}750$) per second and produces a sharper picture, but with more flicker.

Refresh frequencies of computer displays are similar to those of televisions' but vary from one system to another. This is because different CRTs use a different amount of "overscan," which is the extent of extra sweep beyond the grid of displayed dots. Overscan removes picture distortion caused by a decreased linearity of control near the end of the horizontal and vertical scan. It is interesting to note that although overscanning cannot be used to write beyond the last dot, it can be used to control the color of the border of color displays.

These principles are sufficient to understand the signals that must be produced by the video circuit and controlled by CRT logic: A raster scan CRT requires one signal to control horizontal tracing and retracing (horizontal sync), one signal for vertical control (vertical sync), and one signal to control beam intensity (Figure 11.10). Color displays must have signals to control red, green, and blue beam intensities, hence the name "RGB monitor." On "composite video" monitors, R, G, and B intensities are combined into a single signal.

Although television sets and computer displays use the same principle, we must explain one important difference in their operation before we can deal with CRT logic. On a television set, the control of horizontal and vertical scan as well as beam intensity is derived from the signal captured by the antenna or received from a cable. On a computer display, the picture is defined by the computer program that controls the display. Whereas the picture on a television screen changes continuously and follows the antenna signal, a computer display must remain unchanged until it is modified by the program. Because the screen must be refreshed even when the computer is not sending any signals, display information must be stored in a memory attached to the CRT. This memory is called the *screen refresh memory*, or the "refresh" ("display" or "video") RAM (Figure 11.11).

## Modes of Raster Scan CRT Operation

If we want to display an irregular picture on a raster scan CRT, we must store each individual dot in the refresh memory. On the other hand, if we want to display one of a few fixed patterns, such as a row of letters, display information can be encoded and memory space saved. The two uses thus have

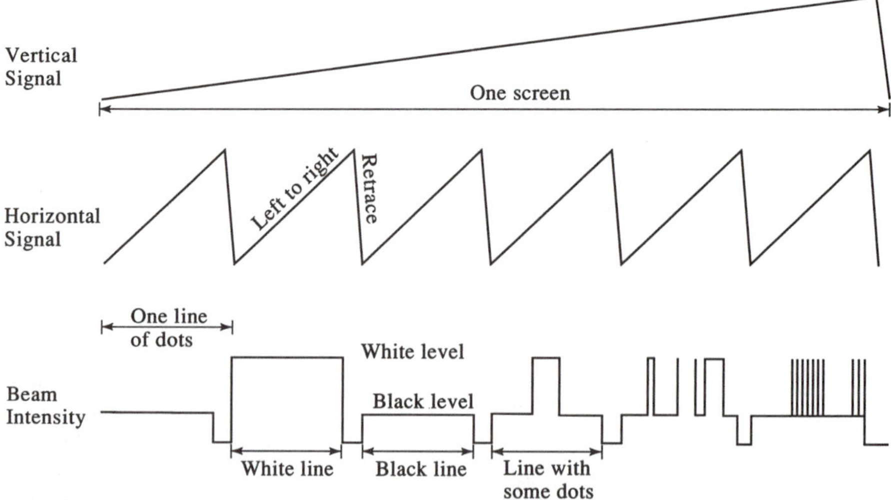


**Figure 11.10.** Signals controlling the beam.

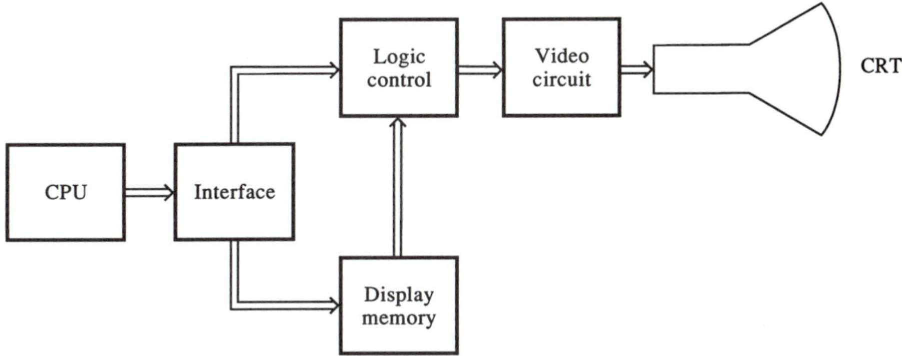


**Figure 11.11.** To refresh the screen, computer displays must have memory.

different requirements and this is why most computer displays operate in either graphics ("bit-mapped") or text (encoded) modes. We will now examine both, starting with the graphics monochrome mode.

In the simplest *graphics monochrome mode*, each dot can assume only On or Off modes, and its intensity can be represented by logic 1 or logic 0. Consequently, the size of the display RAM must be at least equal to the total number of dots on the screen, which is the product of the number of dot rows and the number of dot columns. As an example, a monochrome display with 720 dots per row and 350 dot rows has 250,560 dots and requires 250,560 memory bits, or 31,320 bytes. This can be satisfied with a 32k × 8 RAM.

Even for monochrome displays, one bit per dot is usually insufficient. If the screen can display dots with several intensities, or if the dots can blink or be displayed with reversed foreground (background) colors, additional bits and a larger memory are necessary to describe the dot parameters. For a display RAM of given size, having more dot attributes means displaying fewer dots on the screen and vice versa.

The dot information stored in the display RAM is processed by a logic circuit consisting essentially of a single chip called the *CRT controller* or CRTC. In the simplest single intensity monochrome display with no attributes the CRTC works as follows: It reads one byte from the display RAM, converts it into a sequence of eight On/Off dots and sends them to the video circuit. It then reads the second byte, converts it to the next eight dots, sends them to the video circuit, and so on. After displaying the last eight dots of the current line, the CRTC activates the horizontal sync signal to move the beam to the start of the next row and reads the byte corresponding to the first eight dots of the next row. When it reaches the lower right corner, the CRTC activates the vertical sync signal and returns the beam to the start of the first row of the screen.

We will now illustrate the operation of the graphics mode on an example. We will assume that our programming language allows us to specify a line with end points (*X0*, *Y0*) and (*X1*, *Y1*) by

LINE(X0,Y0,X1,Y1)

The compiler translates this statement into instructions that calculate the position of all intermediate dots approximating this line on the dot grid (Figure 11.12). The code then groups the On/Off dot values into bytes and stores them at appropriate addresses in the display RAM. The computer's only task in this process is to execute this program; all other functions are performed by the *CRT logic* (Figure 11.13), which will be explained next.

To start the display of a new screen, the CRTC sends address (*line* = 0, *column* = 0) to the display RAM, which outputs the first byte. This eight-bit code must be converted into a string of eight bits for the video circuit to control the intensity of the beam and this is achieved by a shift register. To keep pace with the supply of eight-bit codes, the frequency of the video shift register (the dot frequency) must be eight times that of the CRTC (the character or byte frequency). At the same time, the CRTC produces the horizontal and vertical sync signals that move the beam across the screen.

When all eight bits have been sent to the video circuit and displayed, the CRTC requests the contents of RAM display location (*line* = 0, *column* = 1). The display RAM sends the code directly to the video shift register, which converts it into a sequence of bits, and so on until the entire row is displayed. The next row and eventually the whole screen are displayed in the same way. The process then begins again from row 0. When the computer changes the contents of the display RAM, the next scan of the changed code in the display RAM will produce the new picture. The response of the screen to the program that controls it is thus very fast.

Let us now turn to the *text mode* of operation. In this mode, the displayed patterns are limited to the small number of combinations corresponding to ASCII codes and can only be displayed at fixed column and line character positions. In comparison, in the graphics mode any pattern can be displayed at any dot position on the screen. The advantage of the limited number of choices in the text mode is that display information can be encoded rather

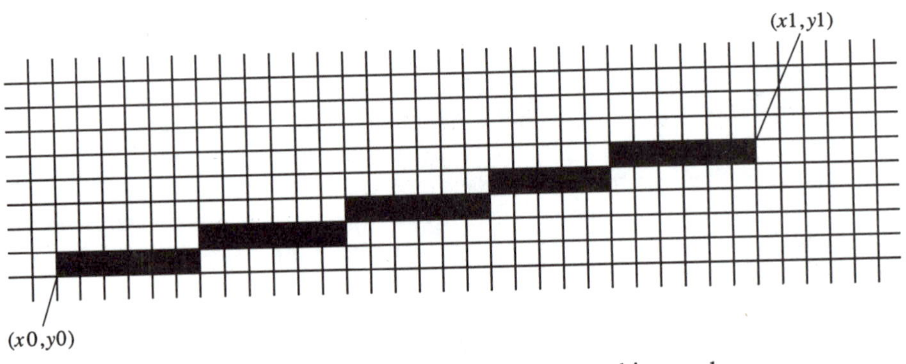


**Figure 11.12.** Drawing a line in the graphics mode.

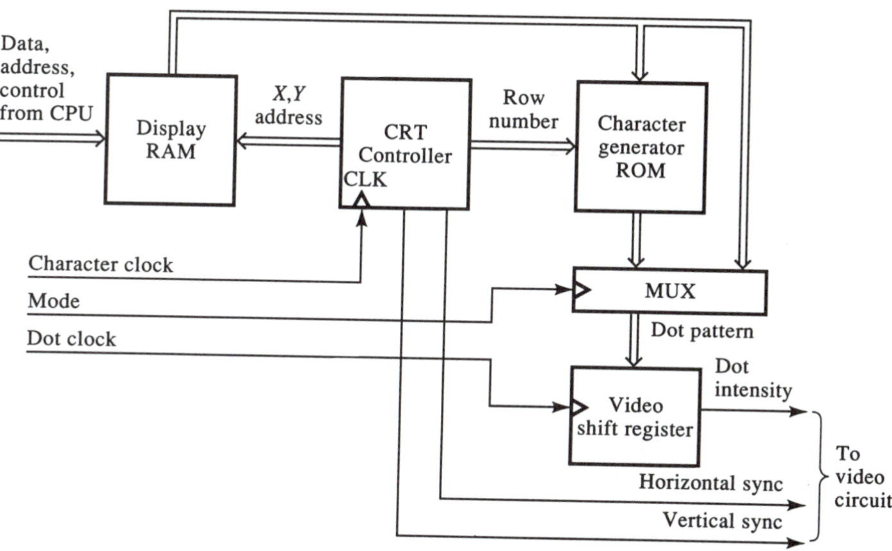


**Figure 11.13.** Cathode-ray tube logic. In the graphics mode, the MUX selects input from the RAM; in the text mode, it selects input from the character generator ROM.

than stored dot by dot, which means that we can use a similar display memory.

The information needed for each character position in the text mode is the value of the ASCII code of the displayed character. Because a typical computer screen has twenty-five lines of eighty characters each, only $25 \times 80 = 2{,}000$ bytes are needed and a 2k display RAM is thus sufficient. Compare this to the amount of memory required in the graphics mode.

As we have already mentioned, the price of saving memory in the text mode is a limited set of patterns that can be displayed. Graphics information cannot be displayed in this mode although a few codes are usually reserved for basic shapes, such as straight vertical or horizontal lines or the corners of a box. These extra shapes, are possible because ASCII uses only 128 combinations, leaving 128 codes to be assigned for other patterns. This nonstandard character set is referred to as "extended ASCII."

In reality, the text mode uses more than 2k bytes because most monochrome displays use *character attributes*, such as blinking, underlining, reverse or normal video, and highlighting. Each character byte is thus accompanied by an attribute byte and this doubles the required size of the display RAM.

Many display circuits are designed to operate in either the graphics mode or the text mode and the large graphics display RAM is thus available for the text mode as well. One way to take advantage of this arrangement is to store several consecutive pages of text in the display RAM at a time. As an example, a 16K graphics display RAM can store four consecutive pages of text with attributes. This makes possible practically instantaneous switching between two pages by sending command to the CRTC to change the display RAM address of the first character on the screen.

Let us now examine how the text mode works. Because each character consists of several rows of dots, the dot matrix in Figure 11.14, the CRT circuit must convert each ASCII code into a sequence of dot patterns, one for each row of the raster, and this is most easily done with a ROM. As an illustration, consider the execution of the following Pascal statement:

```
WRITE('AB')
```

The compiler translates the statement into machine code that stores the ASCII codes for *A* and *B* at appropriate addresses in the display RAM. If, for example, the two letters are to be displayed in the upper left corner, the codes for *A* and *B* will be stored in locations (*line* = 0, *column* = 0) and (*line* = 0, *column* = 1). This is all the CPU has to do; the rest is done by the CRTC.

To display the screen, the CRT controller sends the line and column address of the top left character position (*line* = 0, *column* = 0) to the RAM, and the RAM sends the ASCII code for *A*, to the character ROM. At the same time, the CRTC sends [*dot row* = 0] to the *character generator ROM* (Figure 11.13) to indicate that it desires the pattern for the top row of dots of the character whose ASCII code is coming from the display RAM. The ROM treats the combination (*ASCII code, row number*) as an address, and sends the byte corresponding to the dot pattern of the top row of *A* to the video shift register. From there, the pattern goes, bit by bit, to the video circuit, just as in the graphics mode.

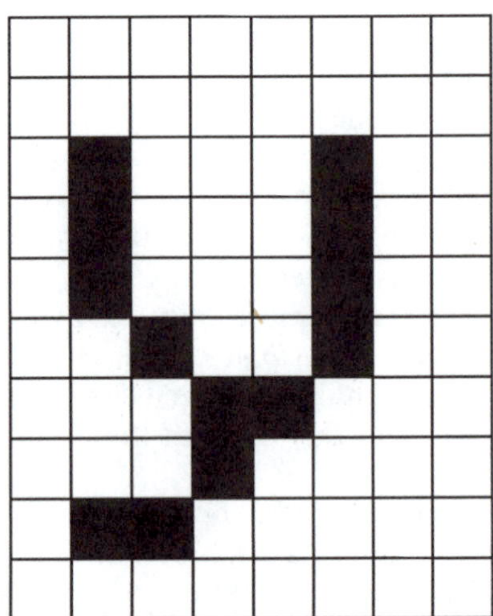

**Figure 11.14.** An 8 $\times$ 10 character matrix.

When the video shift register outputs all the bits of the pattern, the CRTC sends address (*line* = 0, *column* = 1) to the RAM and (*dot row* = 0) to the ROM. The display RAM sends ASCII *B* to the ROM, which outputs the dot pattern for the top row (*row* = 0) of *B*. The pattern goes to the video shift register, and so on. Eventually, dot patterns of the top row of all characters on the top text line are displayed and the CRTC proceeds to the next row of the same line of text.

The CRTC again sends address (*line* = 0, *column* = 0) to the RAM but (*dot row* = 1) to the ROM. The RAM again outputs ASCII *A*; the ROM outputs the dot pattern for the second dot row (*row* = 1) of letter *A*; and the second row of *A* is displayed. The second row of *B* is then displayed in the same way, and so on for the whole second row of the first line of text. The third row is displayed next, and so on, until all rows of the first line of text are displayed. The next line of text and, eventually, the entire screen are then displayed. Writing then begins again from the top. Again, when the CPU changes a value in the display RAM, the new information is displayed almost instantaneously.

In reality, the operation of the CRTC is slightly more complicated because it must control more parameters. First, the display is usually capable of switching between graphics and text modes. In the text mode, it may use one of several different dot matrices, or fonts, selected from different regions in the character ROM under CRTC control. The CRTC must also keep track of character attributes so that characters are underlined, blinked, or displayed with half intensity as desired. On color displays, characters also have foreground and background colors. The CRTC produces additional control signals, such as CURSOR, which determines whether the current character is displayed as a cursor or as an ordinary character. In the graphics mode, the CRTC can be programmed for different resolutions, combinations of colors (pallets), and so on.

To make all these functions possible, the CRTC has several registers that contain information like the current mode of operation, the position of the cursor, and the address of the display RAM to be treated as the upper left corner of the screen. Because its mode of operation can be changed at any time by storing the appropriate code in its control register, the CRTC is said to be programmable. We will see other examples of programmable chips later.

### CPU – Display Interface

Having examined the physical and logic principles of the CRT display, we are now ready to discuss the interface between the CPU and the CRT. To the CPU, the display is just a block of addresses, and the CRT controller is just another block of addresses corresponding to the CRTC's internal registers. Communication between the CPU and the CRT is thus restricted to programming the CRTC by writing to its control registers and writing dot patterns or character codes and their attributes to the display RAM. Note that the CPU can also read the status of the CRTC and the contents of the display RAM. A program can thus read what is displayed on the CRT.

Because the display memory must be accessible simultaneously to the CPU, the CRTC, and the character generator ROM (Figure 11.13), its interface is not as simple as for an ordinary RAM. The CPU must be able to write to the display RAM and this requires access to its address and data pins. The CRTC must be able to select a character from the display RAM and needs access to its address pins. The output from the display RAM goes to the ROM character generator and the data pins of the RAM are thus connected to the address pins of the ROM. Address pins of the display RAM can thus be accessed both by the CPU and the CRTC.

The shared RAM access can be implemented by a 2–1 MUX controlled by the CPU as in Figure 11.15. In this arrangement, CPU access to the display RAM blocks out the CRTC's access to the RAM's address pins and consequently the codes arriving at the address input of the display RAM at this time are unrelated to the row and column coordinates of the beam. The incorrect dot patterns on the display RAM's output cause momentary confusion of the video circuit's input and the display flickers, causing "snow." To avoid this, the CPU should write to the display RAM only during the vertical retrace time when the beam is blanked out as it moves from the bottom right to the upper left corner and the CRTC does not access the RAM during this time. Such access can be achieved under proper program control but the program must be synchronized with the system clock via a logic signal. In Chapter 12 we will see how this can be done.

The blanking interval is approximately one msec, which may be enough to rewrite the entire display RAM, particularly if one uses direct memory access (Chapter 12). Note that the separation of the address lines of the display RAM (the secondary address bus) from the main address bus also insures that the CRTC's access of video address lines does not interfere with the CPU's access to the system bus.

Another way to access display memory is to use a special RAM chip designed to allow simultaneous CPU and CRTC access: a two-port memory with one port for the CPU and one for the CRTC. Special video RAM chips (VRAMs) provide this facility and have other useful features, such as serial display output and single bit writing for bit-mapped displays.

To close this section, we will consider two examples of commercial raster scan CRTs.

**Example 1** The IBM PC monochrome display is attached to the computer by two cables, one for signals and one for power. The display operates only in the text mode, displaying twenty-five lines of eighty characters. The logic circuit is on an adapter card that is plugged into the computer. The card contains a 4k static RAM divided into 2k for character codes and 2k for attribute codes. (DRAM would require memory refresh.) Attributes include intensity, background, underlining, and reverse or normal display.

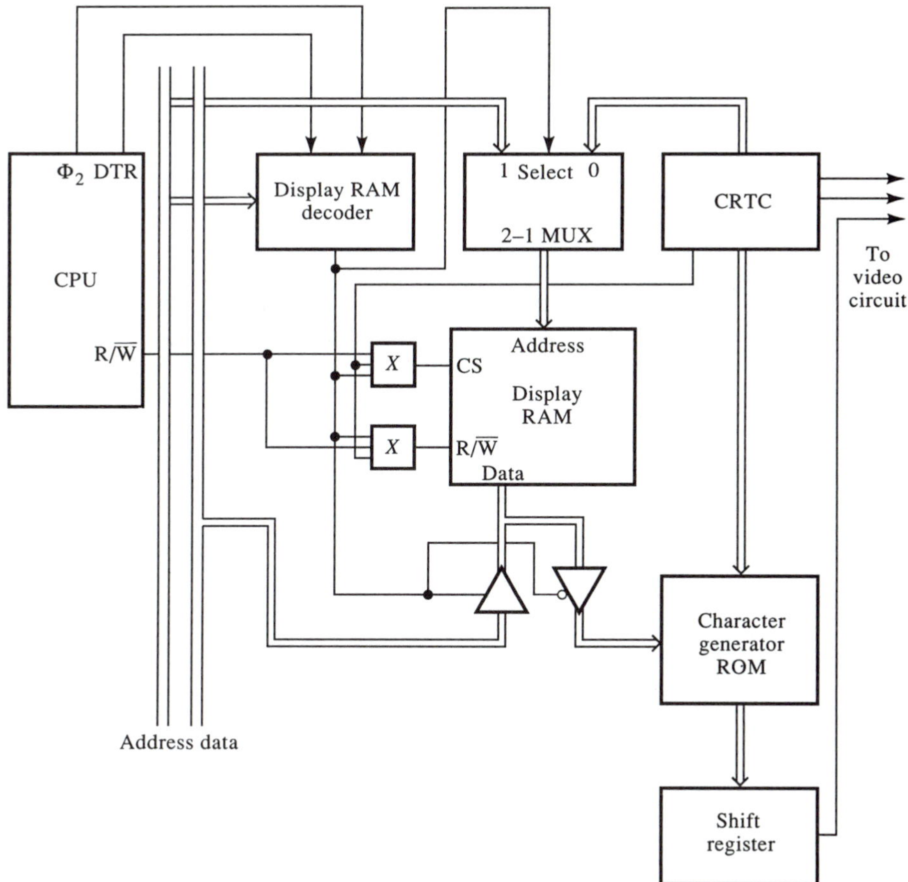


**Figure 11.15.** Block diagram showing how shared access to the display RAM could be achieved. The student should design the R/$\overline{W}$ and CS excitation circuits of the display RAM marked *X*.

The 4k display RAM, the display buffer, is controlled by the programmable Motorola 6845 CRTC chip. In case of conflict with the CPU, the CRTC has priority of access.

Dot patterns are produced by an 8k character generator ROM that recognizes 256 extended ASCII eight-bit codes and produces standard English characters, additional symbols for German, French, Spanish, and other alphabets, and various graphics characters.

Uppercase letters are drawn in $7 \times 9$ dot matrices inside a $9 \times 14$ character box. Because there are twenty-five lines of eighty characters, this requires $9 \times 80 = 720$ dot columns and $14 \times 25 = 350$ rows. The screen is refreshed with a 50-Hz frequency and the horizontal scan frequency is 18,432 Hz because of overscan. The number of dots refreshed per second is 50 × 720 × 350 = 12,600,000 and the dot refresh frequency is thus 12.6 MHz.

**Example 2** The IBM PC color monitor adapter card has the following parameters: It can be used to control a display with composite video signals, such as an ordinary television set, or an RGB monitor with three separate RGB intensity signals. It uses the Motorola 6845 CRTC and has a 16k display memory.

The adapter can operate in either the text or the graphics mode. In the text mode, the RAM stores ASCII codes and character attributes. Codes that would specify underlining, blinking, and other parameters on the monochrome adapter become codes of background and foreground colors.

In the graphics mode, the number of bits assigned to one dot allows a compromise between the number of colors and resolution. Increasing the number of bits per dot increases the number of available RGB intensities and thus the number of colors $N_c$, but decreases the number of pels $N_d$ on the screen.

The adapter can be programmed to produce high-resolution (620 × 200 dots), medium-resolution (320 × 200 dots), and low-resolution display. In high resolution, only two colors are available because each dot is represented by a single bit. In medium resolution, each dot has two bits, which allows four colors. In the low-resolution mode, one pel is a square of 2 × 2 dots, which cuts the number of pels to one-quarter but increases the number of possible colors to sixteen. This mode is intended mainly for ordinary televisions, which are incapable of providing the high-speed response required by the high dot frequency in higher resolution modes.

Both the monochrome and the color adapters use noninterlaced operation.

Graphics capabilities are one of the most valued aspects of modern computer applications and this is reflected in the ever increasing variety of personal computer graphics cards. After the monochrome and color adapters, IBM introduced the higher resolution Enhanced Graphics Adapter (EGA) and the even more advanced video graphics array (VGA) adapter; other types of PC graphics adapters are available as well.

## Exercises

1. How much memory is present on the IBM Enhanced Graphics Adapter (EGA) card if its monochrome mode of operation has 640 × 350 resolution?
2. Describe the operation of the text display mode in the form of an algorithm.
3. Calculate the frequencies of the character clock and the dot clock assuming a horizontal scan frequency of 15,750 Hz, eighty characters per line, and no overscan. Repeat with a ten-character overscan.
4. How many rows could the IBM PC display on the screen with its vertical

and horizontal scan frequencies? Compare this with the 350 rows actually displayed. What happens to the remaining rows?

5. The IBM PC uses 350 rows and 720 columns to display twenty-five lines of eighty characters of text in the monochrome mode. What size of character matrix does this give? This number is larger than the $7 \times 9$ matrix used to display one character. What is the purpose of the remaining dots?
6. Identify the control and data lines required by a character generator ROM to display 256 characters as $7 \times 9$ dot matrices and calculate the size of the ROM.
7. The CRTC chip has a register for the address of the first screen character in the display RAM. Explain how it can be used to scroll the text up and down the screen.
8. How much time is required to rewrite the whole screen of the IBM PC with the color graphics adapter in the text mode assuming that it takes 100 nsec to transfer one byte? Repeat the calculation for the graphics mode.
9. How fast a 6800 CPU would one need to transfer a 2000-byte screen from the system memory to the display memory in one millisecond? (*Hint*: Write the program and count the machine cycles.)
10. On the 8088 CPU, a single instruction can be used to transfer a block of bytes. To transfer one byte, this instruction requires 18 machine cycles. How fast would the CPU have to run to solve the problem in the previous exercise? (*Note*: At the time of this writing the fastest computers, which use the more advanced 80386 chip, have a 33-MHz clock.)
11. Is it important to be able to rewrite the whole screen during a single vertical retrace?
12. What is the advantage of the serial output available on VRAMs?
13. Use Karnaugh maps to design the CS and $R/\overline{W}$ excitation circuits for the display RAM in Figure 11.15.
14. Memory chip manufacturers expect to market a 4-Mbit DRAM with a 80-nsec access time in 1990. Such a memory chip could accommodate a display RAM of dimension $1024 \times 1024 \times 4$ bits per pel. Is this access time sufficient for a display with a 60-Hz refresh rate?
15. Derive a formula relating the size of the display RAM to the number of pels and the number of colors.

## 11.4 COMPUTER TERMINALS

A CRT terminal is the combination of a keyboard and a CRT display. (Hardcopy terminals use printers instead of CRTs.) Terminals are used with computers that do not have a built-in or attached keyboard and display; these are mainly large computers that serve many users at one time. The keyboard and the display of a terminal are implemented as we have explained in previous sections and their internal control is by a built-in CPU dedicated to this purpose.

The connection between the computer and the terminal is usually serial: one bit at a time. The data transfer rate can be selected by switches or can be programmed; typically it is in the range 50–19,200 bits per second. Because the serial transfer of a single code requires at least seven ASCII bits and several additional bits for synchronization (Section 11.7), ten or eleven bits are needed to transfer one character code, and the character transfer rate is thus approximately one-tenth of the bit transfer rate.

All terminals provide some control over the mode of operation either by switches or by special control characters sent to the terminal by the computer. Selectable features include the number of bits transmitted per ASCII code, the transfer rate (bits per second), code parity, and positive or inverted display.

In addition to alphanumeric keys, terminal keyboards often have function keys and keys that perform special operations, such as activating a printer attached to the terminal, switching to local mode, and clearing the screen or its "unprotected" part. (Any position on the screen may be protected from writing under program control.) Function keys can usually be programmed to produce a short sequence of codes when activated, which is useful in word processing and similar applications where certain commands require a sequence of control codes.

Terminals can usually operate in one of two different modes: half or full duplex. In the *half duplex* mode, data is transferred unidirectionally, but the direction of transfer can be changed. When a key is pressed, the terminal displays the character and sends it to the computer. In the *full duplex* mode, the terminal and the computer can send and receive data simultaneously; when a key is activated, the terminal sends the code to the computer but does not display it. If it is desired to "echo" (display) the character on the screen, the computer must be programmed to send it back to the terminal.

Computer terminals range from "dumb" to "intelligent." Most are controlled by built-in CPUs and ROM-based programs and their intelligence depends mainly on the sophistication of the ROM program. One useful feature of intelligent terminals is emulation, the ability to respond to the control commands of other terminals. A terminal with emulation capability can be used with programs written for other terminals.

Although keyboards and displays are relatively simple devices, their control by the computer is quite complex. The terminal driver program running on the main computer (whether it controls a terminal or the keyboard–CRT combination of a personal computer) must respond to interrupt signals from the keyboard and write keyboard input into a keyboard buffer in the memory. The input from the keyboard may be processed one character at a time, which is called the "raw mode" of operation, or one line of text at a time. The raw mode is used by programs like word processors where each character is meaningful and the user may not use the return key for a long time. On the other hand, when the user is not inside an editor he may want to edit the line by various keys before sending it to the CPU by pressing *ENTER*. In this case, the line-at-a-time mode is preferable.

The keyboard part of the terminal driver also handles the *ENTER* key. This key produces the carriage return character *CR* on some keyboards, but *CR* and *LF* (line feed), or *LF* and *CR* on others. The keyboard driver may have to process this raw input.

The display part of the terminal driver is even more complicated than the keyboard driver. Its main function is to keep the display up to date with respect to many operations, including the following:

Echoing keys received from the keyboard on the screen

Handling the *TAB* code

Displaying lines longer than 80 characters

Timing (the response speed of most terminals is limited and artificial delays may have to be inserted between consecutive codes sent by a program to the display)

Interpreting carriage return and other codes that change the position of the cursor

Interpreting special code combinations such as "repeat the previous command," "erase the current line," and so on

Handling the backspace code

Scrolling when the bottom line is finished.

It is not surprising that the terminal driver may be more than a thousand machine instructions long.

The importance of terminals has diminished with the availability of personal computers, which can be used as their "intelligent" replacement.

## Exercises

1. Assume that the ASCII image of the screen is stored in a 2k memory buffer. How long does it take to rewrite the screen of a terminal with a serial interface using a data transfer rate of 9600 bits per second? Compare the result with the time required to rewrite a memory-mapped screen with an access time of 100 nsec.
2. Explain how to program a computer so that a password typed by the user is not shown on the screen. Consider both a memory-mapped terminal (the standard keyboard–CRT combination of a personal computer) and a regular terminal with half and full duplex modes of transmission.

## 11.5 PRINTERS

Printers come in many varieties and differ in speed, cost, the quality of output, and physical size. One way to classify them is as impact and nonimpact printers. The former print by impacting a ribbon and producing an impression on paper; the latter produce output without physical contact with the paper.

*Nonimpact printers* include ink jet printers, laser printers, LED bar printers, and certain dot matrix printers. The relatively expensive ink jet printers form characters or graphics by spraying charged microscopic droplets of ink on the paper.

In laser printers, a high-energy beam of light produced by a laser gun is focused by lenses and directed towards the desired position on paper. The page then passes through a toner, which clings to the activated positions and is baked onto the paper as in office copying machines. Light emitting display bar printers use the same principle but the source of light is a bar of small LEDs rather than a single laser beam; the complicated and sensitive focusing assembly is eliminated.

Nonimpact dot-matrix printers produce characters by burning dot patterns into a heat sensitive layer on special paper.

All of these printers can produce high-quality text or graphic output. At present, laser printers are the most common but they suffer from relative mechanical complexity, sensitivity to precise alignment, and difficulty in producing color output at a reasonable speed.

*Impact printers* are based on mechanical contact between the ribbon and paper. In fully formed character printers the character is formed by the impact of a single font; in dot matrix printers it is a matrix of individually produced dots as in raster scan CRTs.

Fully formed character printers include daisy wheel and rotating head printers that are used mainly with small computers (now rarely used), and various types of line printers used by large computers. Daisy wheel and rotating head printers are relatively slow but produce very good, "letter quality," output. Both are essentially electrically controlled typewriters and differ in the way in which the character is formed. A rotating head printer is practically identical to a conventional typewriter; the daisy wheel printer uses a rotating disk with individual characters on its circumference and prints by striking the desired font with a computer-controlled hammer.

Line printers are large, fast, and expensive machines that print all characters on the line in one step and many lines per minute. In one arrangement, a band carrying one or more copies of all printable characters moves between the ribbon and the paper. In each print position, a hammer is located behind the band. When the desired character moves into position, the hammer strikes the band and the ink ribbon prints the character.

In dot matrix printers, output consists of dots, just as in raster scan CRT displays. We will consider impact dot-matrix printers in more detail because their low cost, good quality of output, and reasonable speed have made them very popular.

### Dot Matrix Impact Printers

The basic component of a dot matrix impact printer is the print head (Figure 11.16), which contains one or more tiny hammers (also called wires or pins) controlled by electromagnets and springs. When a pin is activated, it hits an ink ribbon positioned between the head and the paper and creates a dot on the paper. Most printers have several pins (seven, nine, and twenty-four are common values) arranged in one or two vertical columns and print by activating all desired column dots simultaneously. A motor moves the head along the paper, and each horizontal sweep produces a complete line of text or graphics.

Like raster scan CRTs, dot matrix printers can operate in either the text or the graphics mode. In the text or "font" mode, the printer produces dots from ASCII codes using a character generator ROM. The font ROM often contains several alternative fonts and the controller can select a different style by addressing a different section of the ROM address space.

In the graphics, or dot-addressable mode, all dot values are supplied by the computer program. The ability to print graphics is one of the main advantages of dot matrix printers over printers producing fully formed characters.

The internal logic of a dot matrix printer (Figure 11.17) controls the hammers, the motor of the print head carriage, the motor that moves the

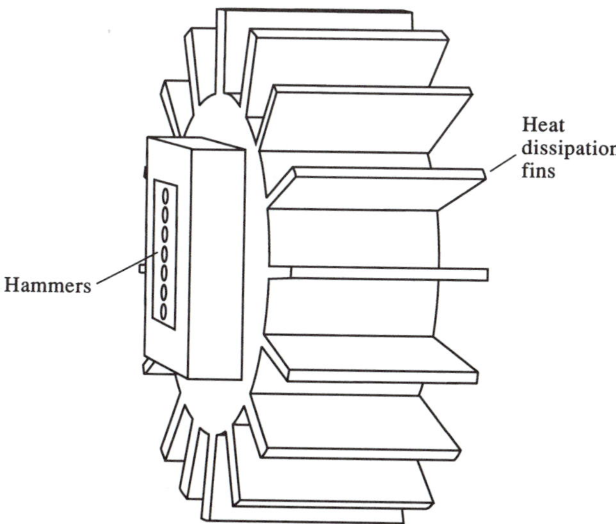


**Figure 11.16.** Print head of a dot matrix printer.

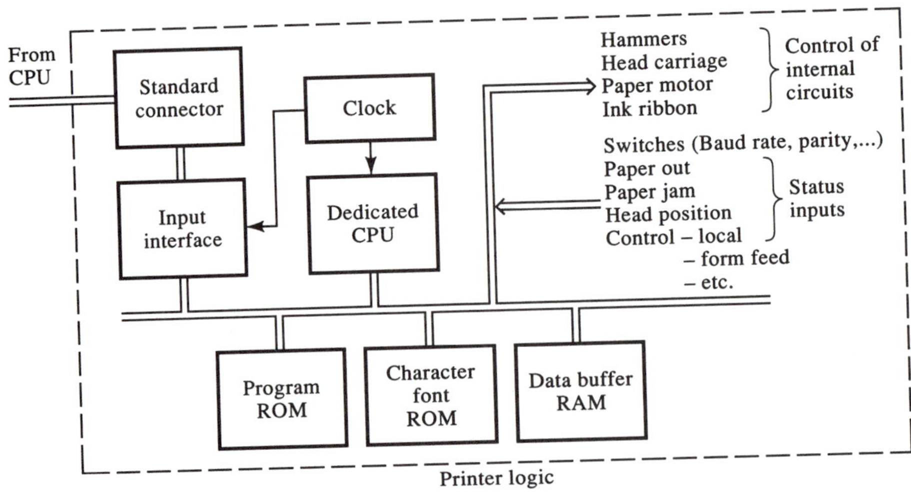


**Figure 11.17.** Block diagram of a dot matrix printer.

paper, and the ribbon motor. It also converts ASCII codes to dot patterns, recognizes the setting of printer switches, detects abnormal conditions like jammed paper or an overheated head, and communicates with the computer. The printer's logic must keep track of the character and the line being printed as well as the currently printing column. If the printer is bidirectional, the controller must also be able to print backwards. Placing the control of all of these functions into the printer greatly simplifies the task of the main CPU.

Communication with the computer includes status information messages ("ready to print," "busy," "jammed," "out of paper,"), the capture of printable data and commands sent by the CPU, and the interpretation of commands received from the computer (initialize, select font, select print density).

Printer logic consists of the character ROM, a RAM buffer to store the data to be printed, and a control circuit. The RAM buffer is usually large enough to hold at least several lines of text but much larger buffer sizes are common.

The control circuit is often based on a built-in CPU fully dedicated to the tasks listed above. The advantages of this approach are that the circuit has fewer components than it would under hardwired control, and that the mode of operation is easier to change because it requires only a change in the control program in the printer's ROM. The control program can also contain test and diagnostic routines.

We will now describe several printer functions and mechanisms beginning with paper fault detection.

The circuit in Figure 11.18, forms the basis of paper fault detection. When the photosensitive transistor receives light from the LED, it closes the path between 5V and ground like a switch and the output is logic 0. When the light

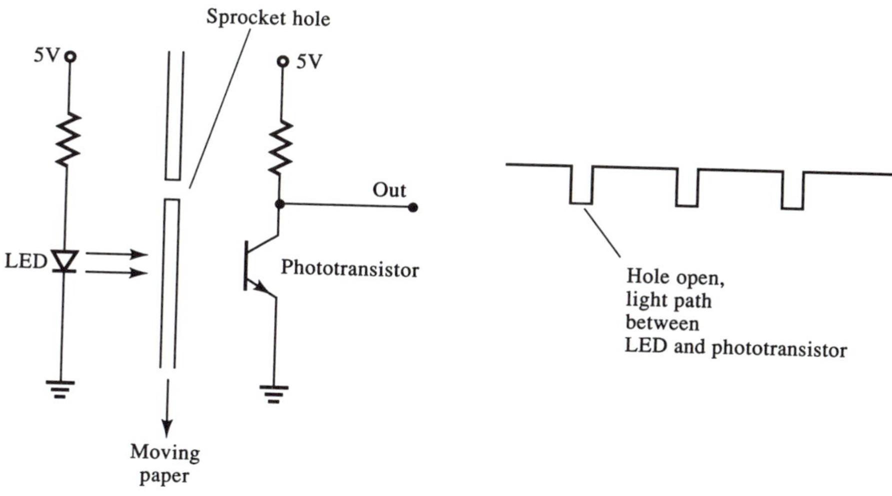


**Figure 11.18.** Paper sensor and its correct output.

path is obscured, the transistor is Off, the path open, and the output is 5V (logic 1). The LED–transistor pair is positioned at the edge of the paper and the light path opened only by the sprocket holes in the paper. In regular operation, the sensor produces a series of pulses as the sprocket holes move between the LED and the transistor. When paper is jammed or missing, the path is permanently closed or open and the circuit produces a constant output 0 or 1. This condition is recognized by printer logic. A similar circuit is used to sense the "home position" of the print head at the start of a line.

Another aspect of dot-matrix printer operation is the control of the position of the print head. To produce high-quality output, the dots must be very accurately positioned and this is achieved by using a *stepper motor*. Because stepper motors are also used in disk drives, we will now briefly outline their operation.

A stepper motor essentially consists of two assemblies of magnets, one moving and the other static (Figure 11.19). The moving magnet is called the "rotor," the stationary one is the "stator." It is well known that two magnets will tend to position themselves so that their North and South poles are aligned. In a stepper motor the magnets in the rotor align themselves with the magnetic field produced by several individually controlled stator magnets and the rotor's position thus depends on the control of stator magnets.

Whereas the rotor is an ordinary permanent magnet, stator magnets are coils, and their fields are produced by electric currents. The field of each coil is controlled by turning the current through them on or off. The fields produced by individual coils combine to create a field oriented in any desired direction and the rotor can thus be moved to precisely defined positions, for example in 15-degree steps.

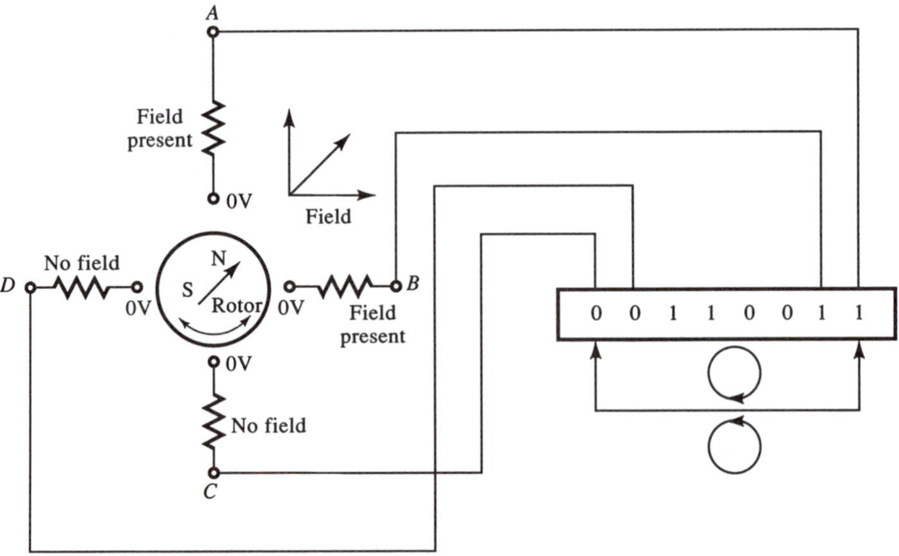


**Figure 11.19.** Stepper motor and its logic control.

The current through individual coils is controlled by logic signals and clockwise or counterclockwise rotation is achieved by feeding the coils a suitable bit pattern and rotating it left or right through a shift register. The reader may show that the arrangement in Figure 11.9 produces clockwise rotation of the rotor when the shift register is rotated right.

Let us now briefly outline the communication between a computer and a printer. When a computer is turned on, it must first initialize all of its peripherals and interfaces. By sending appropriate codes, it programs the CRTC and sets up the disk drive parameters and the parameters of the serial and parallel interfaces to its peripherals.

When the printer interface is initialized to the proper transmission speed and data format, a communication path between the CPU and the printer is established and the printer itself can then be set up. Although the default initialization (font, dot density, and other parameters) occurs when the printer is turned on and is given by the position of its DIP switches, the computer can change the setting by sending command characters at any time.

When all of the interfaces and peripherals are initialized, the computer begins executing user programs. If a program requires printing, the CPU sends data codes or command characters to the printer to initiate printing or to change the setting.

**Example** The FX-85 manufactured by Epson is a typical dot-matrix printer. Its main features are as follows:

Eight international character sets: USA, France, Germany, UK, Denmark I, Sweden, Italy, Spain, Japan, Norway, and Denmark II

User-defined characters that can be stored in the printer's 8k buffer RAM

Emphasized, double strike, and standard printing

Program selection of parameters, including

line width,

text or graphics mode,

line spacing,

underlining,

standard or compressed printing,

superscript and subscript,

position of left margin

Program specification of user-defined characters

Five draft and near-letter quality (NLQ) fonts

Printing speed 160 characters per second (cps)

48–272 characters per line depending on font and mode

Dot density in graphics mode

240 dots per inch horizontally,

72 dots per inch vertically

Paper feed speed 150 msec per line

Mean time between failures (MTBF) 5 million lines

Print head life one hundred thousand characters

Character size (depends on font and mode)

width 1–4 mm,

height 1.6–3.1 mm

Bidirectional printing in text mode, unidirectional in dot mode

Nine-pin print head with pin diameter 0.35 mm

The interface between the Epson printer and the computer follows the very common *Centronics parallel standard*. Its parameters include the number of lines in the connecting cable, their functions, and the timing and logic of printer-computer communication. The connecting cable provides two sets of eight lines to transfer eight-bit ASCII or control codes, three ground connections, and several control lines. Only one of the two sets of data lines is normally used for communication; the other is used for ground connection to improve the quality of signal transmission. Control signals originating in the printer include:

Signal BUSY-High when the printer cannot receive data from the computer because its buffer is full.

Signal PE is High when the printer is out of paper.

Signal SLCT informs the computer that the printer is selected (on-line rather than in-local mode as for off-line testing).

Signal $\overline{\text{ERROR}}$ is Low when the printer is in an error state, such as when it is out of paper.

Signal $\overline{\text{ACKNLG}}$ is an active Low pulse indicating that the printer has consumed the data sent by the computer and is ready for more.

Printer control signals included in the interface but originating in the computer include:

Signals DATA1 through DATA8 are used to transmit the eight-bit codes of printable and nonprintable (control) characters

Signal $\overline{\text{STROBE}}$, which is active Low, indicates that data has been sent to the printer.

Signal $\overline{\text{INIT}}$, which is active Low, resets the printer to its initial mode.

Except for reinitialization, the computer controls the printer by sending data and command sequences synchronized by an exchange of control and status signals, or "handshaking." These control and status signals are required to establish the transfer of each byte from the CPU to the printer. They are transmitted over control lines and are used to get printer's attention and to confirm that it received the code. The exchange between the computer and the printer follows a well-defined *handshake protocol* by which the computer requests an operation and the printer confirms its execution. Figure 11.20 illustrates the principle: When the computer has a code to send, it first checks whether the printer is ready. If it finds that the printer is available (NOT BUSY), it puts data on the data lines, waits 0.5 $\mu$sec, and activates the $\overline{\text{STROBE}}$ signal. The printer then activates its BUSY output and reads the character. If the character is printable, it is printed; otherwise it is decoded and used to change the printer's mode of operation. When the printer digests the input, it activates the $\overline{\text{ACKNLG}}$ line to inform the computer that it is ready for more data and turns BUSY Off. The computer can then send another code.

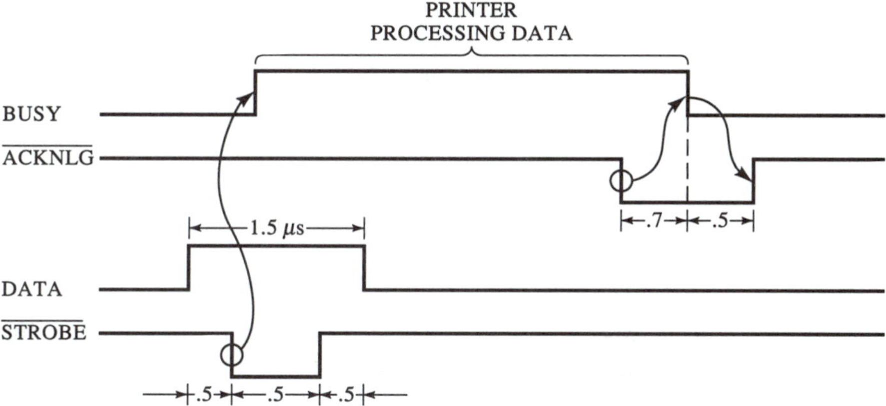


**Figure 11.20.** Timing of the parallel interface of the Epson FX-85 printer. Signals DATA and $\overline{\text{STROBE}}$ come from the computer; signals BUSY and $\overline{\text{ACKNLG}}$ are produced by the printer.

Command sequences are also sent on data lines. They include standard control characters, such as carriage return, line feed, and form feed (advance to the start of the next page); and printer-specific functions, such as select or deselect emphasized printing, or expanded printing (double width). These additional functions are encoded in Escape sequences. On the FX-85, for example, *ESC Y* selects the double-density graphics mode, *ESC @* initializes the printer, and *ESC S1* selects subscript printing. The FX-85 manual contains several pages of other commands.

Instead of, or in addition to the parallel interface described above, many printers use the RS-232-C serial interface, which we will consider in Section 11.7.

## Exercises

1. Assume that a printer's ROM contains four character fonts, each consisting of 256 characters. Describe a circuit that would allow the desired font to be selected by switches. Repeat the exercise for control by codes from the computer.
2. Formulate an algorithm describing basic printer control in the font mode and in the graphics mode.
3. When can the paper jam circuit distinguish between jammed paper and no paper?
4. Illustrate the logic control of a stepper motor by drawing diagrams of several consecutive states of clockwise or counterclockwise motion.

5. Describe how a 6800-controlled printer could implement bidirectional printing.
6. What is the function of individual codes in the dot matrix character generator ROM? Compare with the character generator ROM of a CRT display.

## 11.6 DISK DRIVES

All modern computers use at least two storage technologies: semiconductor RAMs and ROMs, and magnetic disks. RAMs and ROMs are fast but expensive. Disk storage is relatively inexpensive and nonvolatile but is too slow to match CPU speed. As an example, the average data access time on a fast personal computer hard disk is around 20 msec whereas a typical CPU clock speed is around 10MHz. There is no point in combining a fast CPU with a memory that is more than a thousand times slower; thus, the relatively slow disk and tape technologies are used as secondary storage for files, but not for the cycle-to-cycle accessing of instruction and data codes. Semiconductor RAMs and ROMs thus remain necessary as main memory to store executing programs. To illustrate these points, the following table summarizes representative cost and access parameters of several types of memories:

| Technology | Cost per Bit (dollars) | Average Access Time (seconds) |
|---|---|---|
| RAM | 0.0001 | 0.0000001 |
| EPROM | 0.0002 | 0.0000002 |
| Hard Disk (with drive) | 0.000001 | 0.0500000 |
| Floppy disk | 0.0000001 | 0.1000000 |

Because secondary memory is slow, the CPU accesses it as a peripheral device rather than by load and store instructions. When a program or a data file that is stored on a disk is needed for execution, it must first be loaded into the primary RAM memory.

Although three secondary or "mass stored" technologies (magnetic tapes, and magnetic and optical disks) are now widely used, we will concentrate on magnetic disks, which are the most popular—especially on personal computers.

### Principles of Disk Storage

The physical basis of disk storage is the coating of a rigid or a flexible disk with a thin emulsion containing magnetizable iron oxide (Figure 11.21). Before recording, the magnetizable domains are randomly oriented and their mag-

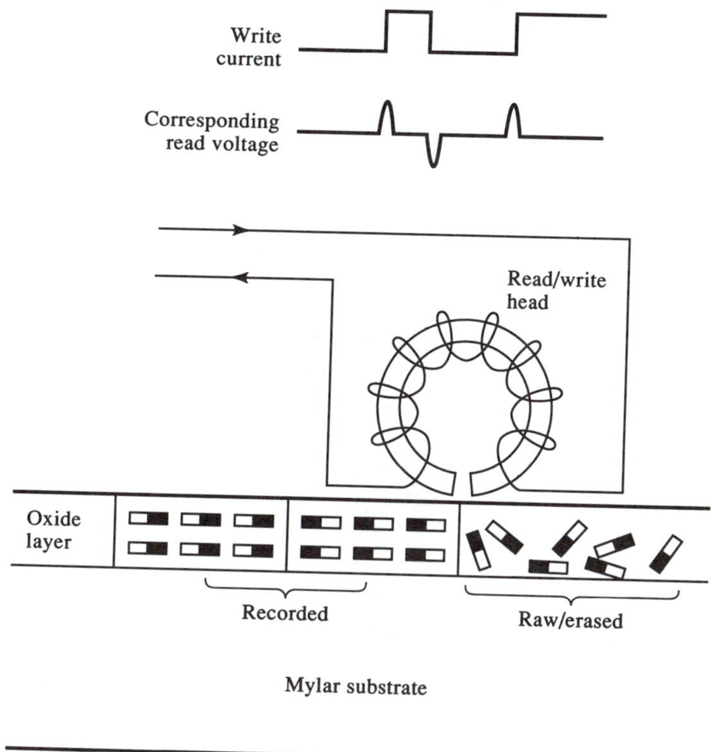


**Figure 11.21.** Principle of magnetic recording: top, the signal; bottom, the device.

netic effects cancel out. Because magnets tend to align themselves along external magnetic fields, exposing a disk's surface to a sufficiently strong magnetic field orients the exposed magnetic domains in the same direction. This imposed magnetism can be subsequently detected; that is, it can be read. The operational principle is similar to that of audio and computer tapes and cassettes.

Reading and writing is performed by a read–write head placed very close to the magnetizable coating. For writing, current is sent through the coil in the head assembly. This creates a magnetic field that is forced into the disk's surface by the gap in the head, because the gap presents greater resistance to the magnetic field, and magnetizes the coating. The orientation of the field depends on the direction of the current.

Reading is based on the fact that a changing magnetic field will induce a voltage in a wire. When the boundary between two domains that are magnetized in opposite directions passes under the read–write head, the voltage generated in its coil is sensed as a pulse and amplified. Changes in the orientation of adjacent regions ("bit cells") on the disk thus produce pulses that can be used to represent binary information. (The bit cells are not physically separated; they are defined by the timing of the read–write operation.)

The way in which the pulses encode the stored information determines the density with which data can be written and the complexity of the encoding and decoding circuit. The most obvious approach is to use a pulse to represent logic 1 and no pulse as logic 0. This has the disadvantage that a long sequence of 0s would generate no signals and reading could lose synchronism with the moving recording surface.

For proper operation, it is thus necessary to record not only data but also clock signals (Figure 11.22). In the simplest method, called *frequency modulation* or FM, each bit cell begins with a clock pulse and data is recorded in the middle of the cell: a pulse for a logic 1 and no pulse for logic 0. If the frequency of clock pulses is $F$, the density of pulses in a sequence of bit cells storing 1s is thus $2F$ whereas pulses in cells storing 0 have frequency $F$. This is why the method is also called F2F encoding.

*Modified FM* (MFM) improves FM recording efficiently by using fewer reversals of the magnetization to store the same amount of data. In principle, a clock pulse is recorded only when necessary; that is, if its absence would cause a loss of synchronization. Because no pulse is represented as logic 0, MFM records a clock pulse if and only if the current bit is 0 and the previous bit was also 0. In this method, each bit cell contains at most one pulse, and two consecutive cells always contain at least one pulse. Synchronization is therefore guaranteed and yet fewer field reversal are required.

This analysis shows that for a given maximum pulse recording density, MFM allows larger storage density than F2F: The maximum frequency of pulses in MFM recording is one-half that of FM recording, which means that it can store twice as much information in the same space. Modified MFM is currently the most common encoding method even though it requires more

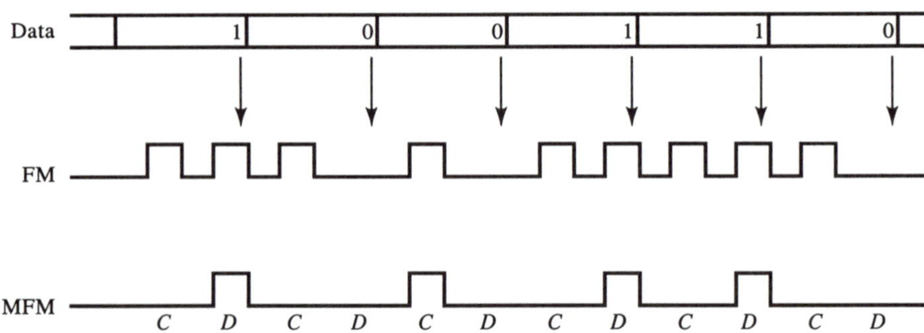


**Figure 11.22.** Frequency modulated and modified FM encoding: $C$, a clock pulse; $D$, a data pulse.

complicated logic. More complicated and more powerful methods are also available and becoming increasingly popular.

Magnetic tapes use the same principle as magnetic disks, the only difference between the two technologies being the manner in which the recorded information is accessed. In tape drives, the recording medium is a tape. Information is thus stored sequentially, one byte after another, and must be read in the same order in which it was written. It may thus take a rather long time before a desired data record is reached.

In disk storage, the record is made on concentric tracks on a rotating disk and the head accesses it by moving linearly in the radial direction (Figure 11.23) and then waiting as the sector rotates underneath. Data access is thus a combination of direct access to the desired track and sequential access (waiting for the block to rotate into position). This is inherently faster than the purely sequential access of tapes.

Let us now turn to the layout of the whole disk. Although different computers organize records on disks in different ways, the basic principle is the same and we will demonstrate it on one of the formats used by the IBM PC and compatible computers.

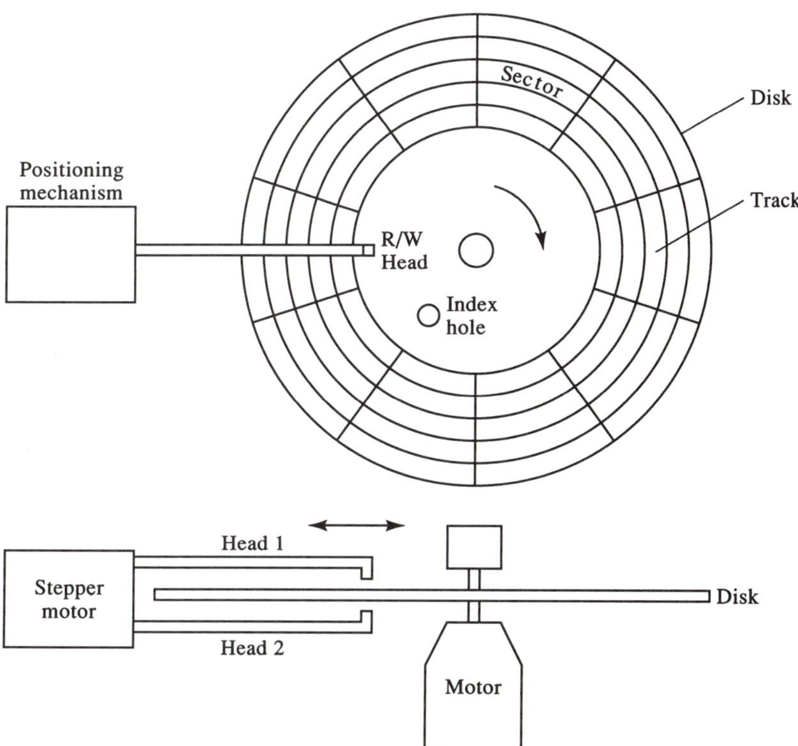


**Figure 11.23.** Disk organization and main parts of a disk drive.

The most common IBM PC format used on floppy disks (see below) is double-sided double density (DSDD). In this format, 40 tracks are recorded on each side of the disk, with 48 tracks per inch (tpi). Each side has its own read–write head.

Each track is divided into ten sectors, one for control information and the rest for data. Each sector contains 512 bytes stored serially, bit by bit. Sectors are numbered and the first sector on the track is identified by an index hole punched into the disk and sensed by the disk drive.* The total capacity of the IBM disk is 360 kbytes.

The information stored in each sector consists of a preamble, data, and a postamble. The preamble contains the number of the sector and other information needed for identification and synchronization. The postamble contains a cyclic redundancy code (CRC), which is a sophisticated error detection code that allows the disk drive to check whether the information was stored and read correctly. Each sector is followed by a gap for if sectors were stored back to back and read and written at slightly different speeds, information from one sector could spill over into the following one. For similar reasons, tracks are separated by guard bands.

Note that the presence of preambles, postambles, and other extra information means that the number of bits that can be stored on a disk (its "unformatted capacity") is not the same as the number of data bits that can be stored ("formatted capacity"). Formatted capacity may be as little as 60% of the unformatted capacity.

Disks can be divided into two major categories: floppy (flexible) and hard (rigid). Floppy disks are removable, hard disks are usually installed permanently in the disk drive. A third category, cartridge disks, is much less common.

*Floppy disks* are available with 8-, 5-¼, and 3-inch diameters, the trend being towards smaller and smaller physical sizes. The 8- and 5-¼ inch disks are enclosed in a flexible jacket but the 3-inch disks have a solid cover. Because floppy disks can be removed from the drive, the user can create a disk library with an unlimited number of diskettes. Floppy disks can also be transported and read on another computer as long as it has a program to process the appropriate disk format. Floppy disks are therefore easily shared.

The disadvantage of floppy disks is that the disk drive mechanism is open and unprotected from environmental humidity and dust. This vulnerability and the flexibility of the disk material limits the density of storage and places an upper limit on safe rates of disk rotation. Two common values are 300 or 360 rpm (revolutions per minute). Because the rate at which bits are transferred to and from the disk is equal the product of the storage density and rotation speed, relatively small values for the rotation speed and density mean

---

*Such a disk is said to be "soft-sectored;" on "hard-sectored disks" each sector is identified by its own hole and an extra hole precedes the first sector. Hard-sectored disks are not used much anymore.

that the data transfer rate is low. The "latency time," the average time between locating a track and finding the desired sector on it, is affected in the same way.

*Hard disks,* also called rigid, fixed, or Winchester disks, are hermetically sealed inside the disk drive assembly. Because they are protected against the environment, they can store information more densely, giving more bits per track and more tracks on the disk surface. Hard disk capacities are thus high, starting with 10 Mbytes, 20 Mbytes, and 30 Mbytes for personal computers and going much higher for large computers. Higher capacities are obtained by increasing the recording density and by packing several disk platters into one assembly.

A typical hard disk has from 300 to 600 tracks with 17 data sectors per track and contains two platters with a total of three or four recording surfaces. Because the supporting material is rigid, hard disks can rotate faster than floppy disks (3600 rpm) and this, in combination with a higher recording density, allows faster access and higher data transfer rates.

*Cartridge disks* combine the advantages of floppy and hard disks. Cartridge disks are rigid and are enclosed in a protective container. Unlike hard disks, cartridge disks can be removed from the drive but their speed and storage capacity approach those of hard disks. In spite of these advantages, cartridge disks are not very popular because the relatively complex structure required to let the disk drive mechanism access the disk makes them expensive.

Another concept related to disk storage is the *RAM disk.* These are not really disks at all but are a part of the computer's RAM memory set aside to be logically accessed as a disk. When a file stored on a permanent disk is needed for processing, it can be moved from the disk to the RAM, where it can be accessed very quickly. If the file is modified in processing it must, of course, be transferred back to a permanent disk before the computer is shut off. This form of storage requires that the computer have adequate RAM memory and the appropriate software to treat it as a disk drive.

### Mechanics, Electronics, and Logic of Disk Drives

A disk drive consists of mechanical parts, electronics, and logic control (Figure 11.24). The essential mechanical parts are the drive motor and the read–write head with its positioning mechanism.

The speed of the drive motor must be maintained very accurately because irregularities can cause incorrect reading or writing. Maintaining a constant speed is not easy because the mechanical load on the drive motor changes—particularly on floppy disks, where the head is "loaded" (brought in contact with disk surface) for access, the disk surface is uneven, and the friction between the rotating disk and the protective jacket of different disks is different. The most common way to maintain a constant speed is to use a servomotor, an electric motor whose speed is continuously measured and compared with the desired value; the amplified difference is used for correction.

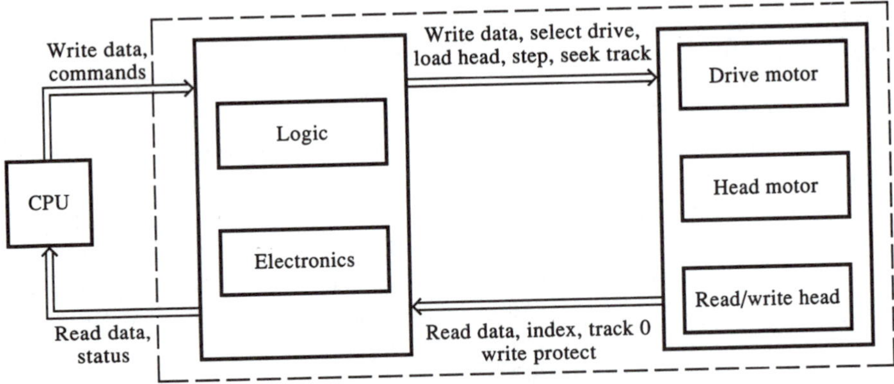


**Figure 11.24.** Block diagram of a disk drive.

Accurate positioning of the read–write head is equally important and is usually achieved with a stepper motor or a similar precise mechanism. The rotation of the motor is converted to linear motion by a lead screw and a nut in a track or another mechanism (Figure 11.25).

The electronics of the disk drive converts voltages used by the read–write head, motors, and sensing circuits into TTL level logic signals and vice versa. The details are complex and beyond the scope of this book.

The logic control of the disk drive has the following functions: It converts high-level commands from the computer into signals that control the drive, senses the drive's status and reports it to the computer. Most of this is done by a single chip called the disk controller. To illustrate its function we will briefly describe the Intel 8272A FDC (for "floppy disk controller") used on the IBM PC.

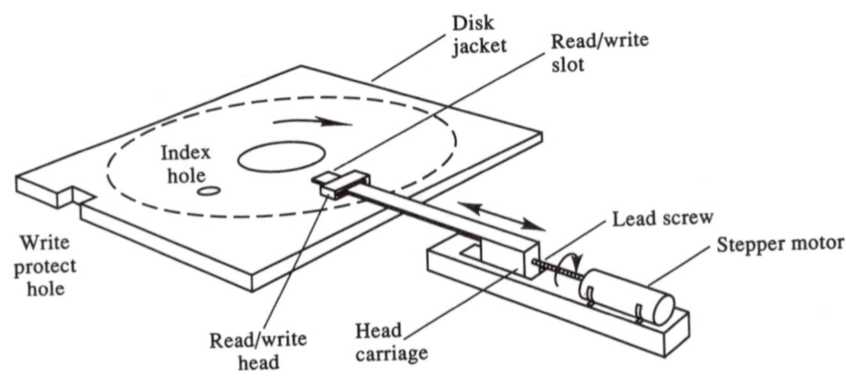


**Figure 11.25.** Disk and head positioning mechanisms.

The 8272A FDC (Figure 11.26) can control up to four disk drives. It provides an interface between the computer and disk drive electronics. Some of the signals that it sends and receives on the disk drive side are as follows:

An 8-MHz clock times data transfers, stepping, and other functions.

The disk drive transfers one bit at a time using one write and one read data pin. Because the data format is parallel on the computer side, the FDC performs serial–parallel conversion.

An index pulse is sent each time the index hole passes through the LED phototransistor detector.

Signal Track0 is active when the head is above the outermost track.

Signal MFM determines whether FM or MFM recording is used.

Signal $\overline{RW}$/SEEK is 0 when the FDC requests a data transfer and 1 for head positioning operation. The value of $\overline{RW}$/SEEK determines the meaning of some other signals.

The head load signal brings the read–write head in contact with the disk.

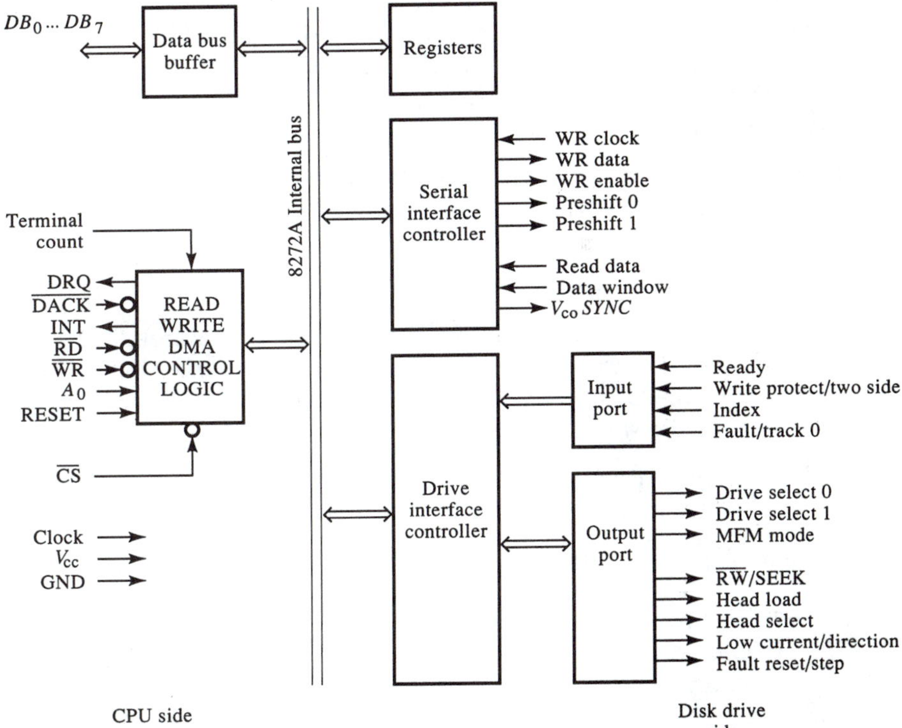


**Figure 11.26.** Block diagram of the 8272A FDC by Intel.

The head select signal selects the top or bottom surface head.

The low current or direction signal requests writing with lower current when $\overline{\text{RW}}$/SEEK = 0. (Writing on the innermost tracks where the storage density is higher requires lower current.) In the SEEK mode ($\overline{\text{RW}}$/SEEK = 1), this signal specifies whether the head should move toward or away from the center of the disk ("in" or "out").

The fault reset and step signal is used to clear fault information in the RW mode, and requests another step of the read–write head in the SEEK mode.

The most important signals on the CPU side are:

Eight data pins to transmit data and commands. The FDC is programmable and can execute fifteen instructions (commands) received from the computer. These commands request that the FDC execute functions such as reading, writing, positioning the head over a track with a specified number, determining the location of track 0, and formatting a raw disk (initialization). Formatting creates track identification, preambles, and so on.

DRQ (DMA request). The term "DMA" stands for "direct memory transfer" and refers to direct communication between the FDC and memory without the involvement of the CPU. To request DMA, which speeds up disk-memory transfers, the FDC sends DRQ to the CPU when it is ready for the transfer.

DACK (DMA acknowledge). This is the computer's response to DRQ. Active DACK means that the CPU has granted the DMA request and the transfer can begin.

INT (interrupt). It is used by the controller to get the CPU's attention.

RD, WR, $A_0$. For each of the four disk drives that it can control, the 8272A has several internal registers that store data and status information. The CPU uses signals RD, WR, and $A_0$ to specify whether it wants to access the data register or the status register.

Signal CS is chip select and performs the same function as on memory chips; it activates the data pins and connects the FDC to the CPU data bus.

Reset puts the FDC into an idling state.

This short outline shows that the FDC performs a lot of low-level work for the CPU. It considerably simplifies the tasks of the CPU but still leaves much difficult programming for the writer of the disk driver routine. The FDC also simplifies the work of the hardware designer by implementing most control logic; however, a good understanding of its operation is still required to design a complete disk drive controller.

Although we have limited our presentation to floppy disk drives, the principles remain the same for hard disks.

### CPU Control of Data Transfers

Every formatted disk contains a *directory*, a table of contents, with an entry for every file stored on the disk. Each entry includes the name of the file, the location of its first sector, and its access information (for example, read/write or read only) (Chapter 14). The sector number is a combination of track and position on the track. When a program needs to read a file stored on the disk, it first finds the directory's entry for the file, determines the sector containing the desired record, and sends a SEEK command to the disk controller to position the head over the track on which the sector is stored. While the controller is moving the head, the CPU can continue with another task.

When the head is positioned, the disk controller notifies the CPU, which then issues a READ command with the position of the sector to be transferred and returns to its original task. When the controller locates the sector, it asks the CPU for an authorization for the transfer and when the request is granted it transfers the data to memory. The process of writing to the disk is similar.

The transfer itself can be performed either by the CPU or by direct memory access. The rate at which the disk drive produces or consumes data is usually so high that DMA must be used. Because DMA is so important for disk operation, we will now briefly outline its principles and return to the subject again in the next chapter.

*Direct memory transfer* can be performed in one of two ways: one sector at a time (burst mode) or one byte at a time (cycle stealing). In both methods a DMA controller temporarily halts the CPU and transfers the data. "Burst transfer" is used when the disk controller has its own memory buffer and works as follows: After the disk controller gets a read request, it reads the data from the disk one byte at a time and stores it in the buffer. (In the meantime, the CPU may be executing another program.) When the whole sector is in the buffer, the disk controller requests a DMA, the CPU halts program execution, and the sector is directly transferred to the main memory without going through the CPU. Because the CPU is halted only during the actual buffer-to-memory transfer, the length of time during which it is inactive is minimal.

If the disk controller does not have a buffer, it must transfer each byte when it arrives from the disk drive before the next byte arrives. Because the time separation of data coming from the disk drive may be in tens of microseconds, halting the CPU for the duration of the transfer of a complete sector would be wasteful. Consequently, the disk controller transfers the bytes one at a time, allowing the CPU to continue executing other programs between the transfers. Because this procedure amounts to stealing individual machine cycles from the CPU, it is called "cycle stealing." When a cycle-stealing DMA request is made, the CPU completes the current instruction, grants the DMA request, halts for two or three machine cycles while a byte is transferred, and resumes control.

Although the transfer of a single sector in the burst mode is straightforward, transfer of several consecutive sectors requires further consideration. While the burst transfer of the first sector is taking place, the disk keeps moving and by the time the transfer is complete the start of the next sector is past the head. If the next sector of the file were stored adjacent to the current sector, the disk controller would now have to wait almost one full revolution before it could read and transmit the information. To eliminate this delay and to minimize the transfer time required by multiple sectors, consecutive sectors of a file are thus often "skewed," or stored in nonconsecutive disk sectors. The number of sectors that should be skipped for optimal recording is called the interleave factor. A 1:1 interleave factor means that consecutive file sectors are stored back-to-back; it indicates a very fast disk controller.

As we already mentioned, communication between the CPU and the disk drive is performed by the disk driver program. Its task is to convert requests from user programs into commands that the FDC can execute and to take care of error conditions and timing. The tasks of the disk driver include converting requests to create or delete files, converting sector numbers into track and sector positions, generating appropriate commands to the FDC, and waiting for the drive motor to come up to speed, or turning it off if it has been inactive for a certain amount of time, and so on.

Some examples of error handling are the following: If the disk driver routine encounters a CRC error, it retries the operation several times. (The problem may be due, for instance, to a speck of dust on the disk) the driver either succeeds finally or reports an error. If the disk driver finds the wrong value for a sector number in the preamble, the cause may be a random error, disk drive misalignment, a disk written on a differently calibrated disk or an incorrect disk format. In response to this problem the driver will probably order the disk controller to send the head to the home position, reset the track count to 0, SEEK the desired track, and try again.

The disk driver is usually the most complicated device drivers in the operating system.

**Example—IBM PC/XT Fixed and Floppy Disk Drives** The 10-Mbyte fixed disk drive on the IBM PC/XT contains two 5-¼ inch double-sided nonremovable disks. Each surface has 306 tracks and is serviced by one head assembly. Track density is 345 tpi and each track contains 17 sectors with 512 bytes each. The technical reference manual also uses the term "cylinder," which refers to all tracks in the disk drive assembly that have the same number; physically, it corresponds to a cylindrical section through the disks. Because the disk drive has four recording surfaces, each cylinder consists of four tracks.

The disk mechanism and the disk platters are sealed in a recirculating environment with a 0.3-micron filter. Thermal insulation assures a stable internal temperature and prevents thermal expansion of the disk that could shift track positions. The track-to-track step time is 3 msec and disk speed is 3600 rpm. Drive motor start and stop times are 250 msec. Data transfer rate is 5 Mbits per second. Power supply voltages are 12 V for the motor and 5 V for the logic circuits.

The IBM PC/XT 5-¼ inch double-sided floppy disk drive rotates at 300 rpm, has 40 tracks recorded at a density of 48 tpi, and provides a storage capacity of 360 Kbytes. The data transfer rate is 250 Kbits per second.

Because fixed and floppy disk drives are critical components of modern computers, the enormous competition in the computer market forces manufacturers to constantly improve disk capacity, speed, and size. Consequently, the devices described above are technically obsolete but are still used quite often. To indicate the progress in disk drive technology, the following are maximal values reached by 3-½ inch hard disk drives in 1989: capacity greater than 200 MByte with data recorded on two or more data surfaces, average access time as low as 15 msec, data transfer rates up to 10 MBytes per second, and mean time between failures of 50,000 hours, or almost six years.

All of these parameters cannot be incorporated in a single disk drive as some of them are in mutual conflict. For example, high speed requires increased power, which shortens the life of the disk. A representative state-of-the-art device is the BP-100 from C.Itoh Electronics, which has a capacity of 133 MBytes on two data surfaces with two read–write heads, an average access time of 29 msec, a data transfer rate of 7.5 MBytes per second, a recording density of 57,000 bits per inch, and a track density of 1,720 tpi.

Another example is the DK31/12C by Hitachi America with a capacity of 251 MBytes on six surfaces with 12 heads, a 20-msec average access time, 38,000 bits per inch, and 1,660 tpi. The data transfer rate is 6 Mbytes per second.

To speed up data access even more, some disk drives are equipped with a RAM "cache memory," which is filled with several consecutive segments from the disk when a read operation is performed even when no more sectors are currently required. Because files on well-organized fast disks are stored in consecutive segments, this approach makes it possible to obtain the next sector later from the sequence of prefetched blocks from the disk drive's RAM cache at microsecond access times rather than access them on the disk at millisecond speeds.

## Exercises

1. Calculate the average time needed to access a sector on a DSDD floppy disk. Assume that it takes 5 msec for the head to move from track to track, 15 msec for the head to settle when it reaches the desired track, and that the disk rotates at 300 rpm. The head starts in the home (outermost) position. The average access to a sector includes the time for the head to move from track 0 to the middle track (track access or seek time), the head

settling time, and the time needed for one-half rotation (latency time). Compare the result with the 100-nsec access time of a RAM.
2. Repeat for the IBM PC/XT hard disk described above.
3. Calculate the data transfer rate (number of bytes transferred per second) of the floppy disk drive and the hard disk drive in the previous exercises. Assume the parameters given for the IBM PC disk drives. Compare the result with the data transfer rate of a RAM. Use this analysis to identify the major bottleneck of disk drives.
4. What percentage of disk surface is used for recording on a 40-track 5-1/4 inch floppy disk with 48 tpi?
5. What is the delay between two consecutive bytes read from the IBM PC floppy disk? Repeat for the hard disk.
6. Compare how long it would take to transfer one sector of an IBM-formatted floppy disk using burst mode transfer to that required by cycle stealing. Assume that system clock frequency is 10 MHz and that the memory access time is 100 nsec. How long is the CPU halted in each case if cycle stealing requires two machine cycles per activation and burst transfer requires one machine cycle per transferred byte?
7. Name some of the parameters that RAM disk software must control to make the RAM appear as a disk.

## 11.7 COMMUNICATION—PRINCIPLES, STANDARDS, AND EQUIPMENT

Communication between computers and their peripherals or other computers can be classified by the distance, the nature of the physical signal, and the form in which it is transmitted. In this section, we will concentrate on the most common types of short distance communication.

Depending on the physical nature of the signal, one distinguishes electrical, optical, radio, and microwave communication. Of these, electrical signals are most common. One may classify electrical communication according to the amplitude of the signal, as TTL level and RS-232 level. Depending on the parameters of the signal, one may distinguish several kinds of modulation. Finally, according to the mode of transmission, one recognizes serial (one bit at a time) and parallel (entire code at a time) transmission.

We will now present the principles of modulation and consider several aspects of parallel and serial communication.

### Modulation

An electric signal is characterized by its amplitude and, if the signal is periodic, by its frequency and timing (phase). All of these parameters, either in combination or individually, can be used to represent information.

The representation of logic 0 and logic 1 by two different amplitudes is called amplitude modulation, or AM. In frequency modulation, or FM, logic 0 and 1 are represented by periodic (usually sinusoidal) waveforms having identical amplitudes but different frequencies. In phase-shift modulation, logic 0 may be represented, for example, by a sine wave 180 degrees out of phase with the sine wave representing logic 1. (In other words, the sine wave representing 0 is the inverse of the sine wave representing 1. The frequency and amplitude of both waveforms are the same.)

Frequency and phase-shift modulations are less susceptible to noise than amplitude modulation and are thus better suited for transmitting digital information. They are, however, more difficult to implement.

Amplitude modulated TTL signals of the kind used in logic circuits offer the most efficient internal representation of logic values but cannot be transmitted over a distance greater than a few feet before becoming distorted and unrecognizable. For communication over longer distances, TTL signals must thus be transformed (modulated) into another form that uses different voltage levels or different representation to limit distortion to acceptable levels. Most often, the modulated signal is an FM signal.

The receiver of the transmitted FM signal is usually another computer or digital system, and the received signal must therefore be demodulated back to AM when it reaches its destination. Because the devices at either end of the line usually communicate in both directions, each end must be able to modulate and demodulate the signal; the device that performs these two conversions is called a *modem* (for modulator/demodulator). Its function is the passive conversion of transmitted signal from one form to another. Although the term "modem" could be applied to any device that converts one representation of information to another, it is commonly understood to refer to a device that converts AM signals on the logic signal end to FM signals transmitted over telephone lines on the other.

The most common medium of long distance communication is the telephone line. Because telephone lines were built long before computers came into existence, their parameters reflect the properties of the human voice rather than the needs of computers. From the point of view of communication, the essential parameter of the line is the maximum frequency of the sine wave that can be transmitted without distortion because its value determines the number of bits that can be transmitted per second. On ordinary telephone lines, this limit is 3 KHz, which is adequate to transmit voice with satisfactory quality. Unfortunately, the following reasoning shows that this limit imposes serious restrictions on digital communication.

In a crude approximation, a sine wave can be thought of as two pulses and the 3-KHz limit of the telephone line thus means that no more than 6,000 pulses can be transmitted in a second. In reality, the limitation is even stricter because a sinusoidal signal undergoes gentle transitions between its extremal values whereas discrete pulses undergo sharp transitions. That is, the slope of a sinusoidal curve changes gradually, at a rate that is related to its frequency and a sharp pulse is thus (from the point of view of transmission) closely related to a high-frequency sine wave. A series of distinguishable sharp pulses would therefore require a much better transmission line than a sine wave with the same frequency.

Because TTL signals are unacceptably distorted by transmission, they must be transformed into a smoother form that is more tolerant of the given restrictions. The modulated signal will still transfer 0s and 1s, but the logic values will not be represented as levels having sharp transitions and their transmission rate will be limited by the 3-KHz cutoff.

From the point of view of communication, each type of modulation transmits a different maximum number of bits per second and requires different transmission facilities. For given line parameters, AM transmits at the lowest speed but is the easiest to implement whereas PM transmits at the fastest speed and is the most complicated. One can improve transmission rates by combining different types of modulation, such as AM and PM, in the same system. In the following we will concentrate on FM because it is the most commonly used form of transmission. Note, however, that PM and combinations of PM and AM are becoming increasingly popular due to growing demands on communication speed.

As we mentioned, frequency modulated signals represent logic values by sinusoidal voltages, using different frequencies for logic 0 and logic 1 (Figure 11.27). Most commonly, the signals for 0 and 1 are obtained by adding or subtracting an offset to the frequency of the basic signal, which is called the "carrier." Because the logic value of the signal is a function of its shift with respect to the carrier frequency, this method is called "frequency-shift keying" or FSK.

Several FSK standards are in use but the most common is Bell-103 (Figure 11.28). Bell-103 uses four different frequencies, making it possible to communicate in both directions at the same time, a mode of operation known as full duplex.

Two of the four Bell-103 frequencies are used by the device that establishes the connection (the "originate" or "caller" device) and the other two by the called device (the "answer" device). The originator carrier frequency is 1170 Hz, the answer carrier frequency is 2125 Hz, and both use a 100-Hz offset to

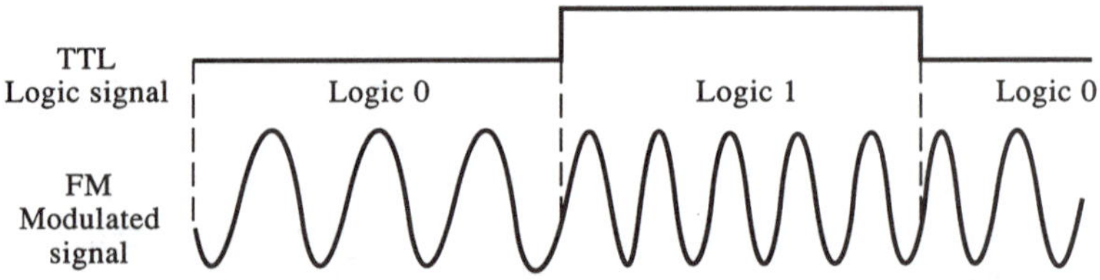


**Figure 11.27.** Frequency-shift keying (FSK) representation of binary information.

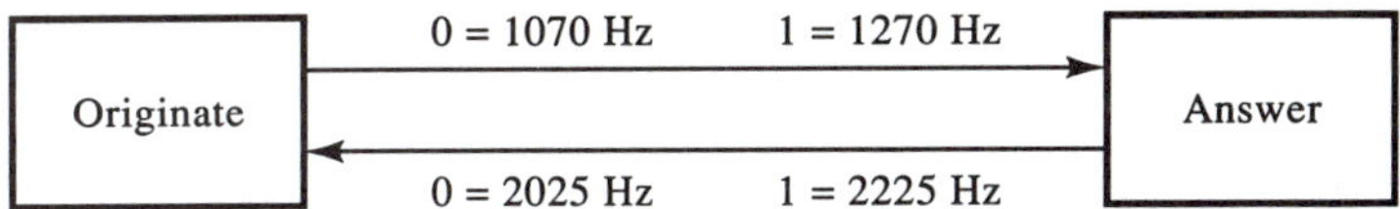


**Figure 11.28.** Transmission over a telephone line.

represent logic 0 and 1. The caller modem thus sends logic 0 as a burst of sine waves with frequency 1070 Hz, and logic 1 as a burst of 1270-Hz sine waves. It receives 0 as 2025 Hz and 1 as 2225 Hz. Interpretation of frequencies by the answer modem is reversed. Each burst is allocated the same amount of time whose duration can be derived as follows.

To recognize the frequency of the signal, the receiver must get at least two complete sine waves. Because the period of a sine wave of frequency 1070 Hz is about 1msec, the signal must be at least 2 msec long for proper recognition. Among the standard transmission speeds 330 bits per second (bps), or $1/330 = 3$ msec per bit, is the nearest lower standard, and the maximum transmission rate possible with Bell-103 is thus 330 bps.

After this brief introduction to modulation, we will now present the most common forms of serial and parallel communication and their typical components.

## Serial and Parallel Communication

In serial communication, a code is transmitted one bit after another; in parallel communication, all bits of a code are transmitted simultaneously. This has implications both for the speed of transmission and its cost.

If we can transmit one event every $t$ seconds, it will take $N \times t$ seconds to send an $N$-bit code serially but only $t$ seconds to transmit it in parallel. Parallel communication is thus considerably faster. For many uses, however, slower speed is acceptable and is offset by the simplicity of serial communication, which uses fewer wires and driver circuits. Moreover, a one-line communication channel, the telephone network, is available around the world.

Because of its cost, parallel communication is restricted mainly to short distances such as internal computer buses and devices in close proximity of the computer, and situations requiring a high transmission speed. In typical computer environments, it is used mainly with disk drives and some keyboards and printers.

We will now describe the most common serial and parallel conventions, the RS-232-C and current loop serial standards, and the Centronics parallel convention.

## Principles of RS-232-C

The standard RS-232-C is a version of the RS-232 serial communication standard designed by EIA, the Electronics Industries Association. It uses AM, and with several auxiliary standards specifies the number and function of wires in a connecting cable, voltage levels, data transfer rates, and the format of transmitted data.

The original purpose of RS-232 was to standardize the connection between a computer and its modem (Figure 11.29), which forms one section of the long path between two computers or between a computer and a terminal. Other sections of the path, such as the telephone line, are controlled by other standards like Bell-103.

However, the communicating devices need not be two computers or a computer and a terminal, and the interface to the telephone line does not have to be a modem. This is why RS-232-C does not use the terms "computer" and "modem" but rather *data terminal equipment* (DTE) and data communication equipment (DCE). Data terminal equipment is the source of information (usually a computer) and DCE is the transmitting device, normally a modem. Standard RS-232-C governs the path between the DTE and its DCE whereas Bell-103 rules the rest of the path. Each section uses its own form of modulation, its own voltage levels, and so on.

Although the original concern of RS-232-C was communication between a computer and a remote terminal, it has become so popular that it is now used even for direct communication where no modem is involved. Most personal computers have a built-in RS-232-C interface (frequently called the serial interface) and use it to communicate directly with printers, mice, and other peripherals or computers.

The main RS-232-C features are as follows:

Standard RS-232-C is an AM system like TTL. Logic 0 and 1 are thus represented by voltage levels but their amplitudes are different from TTL levels: For data, any voltage between −3 V and −25 V is treated as logic 1 and any voltage between +3 V and +25 V is logic 0 (negative logic). Control and timing signals use the same levels but positive logic.

The connector between the cable and the DTE or DCE is not prescribed but it usually has twenty-five pins, each with a specific function, such as

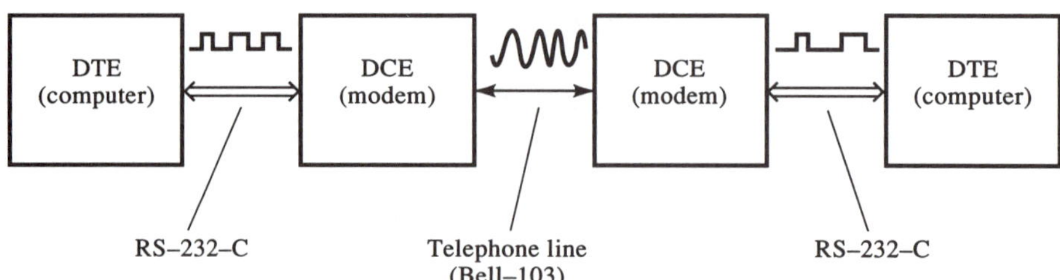


**Figure 11.29.** Long distance communication. The part governed by RS-232-C is highlighted.

data, control, timing, and ground. Although twenty-five signals are defined, the number of wires used in typical computer applications is much smaller, often as few as three and the connections are then also smaller.

On the basis of the prescribed electric parameters for the path, EIA discourages transmission over more than 50 feet. Good cables, however, allow RS-232-C communication over several hundred feet.

Standard RS-232-C transmission may be synchronous or asynchronous. In *synchronous* transmission, whose additional parameters are prescribed by standard RS-334, one of the required signals is the clock, and the code is transmitted in blocks preceded by a preamble and accompanied by the clock signal.

In the much more common *asynchronous* mode (standard RS-404), there is no synchronizing signal and each of the communicating devices has its own clock. Both clocks must have approximately the same frequency but need not be synchronized. Coordination is achieved by surrounding each transmitted code by a frame of one "start" bit and 1, 1-½ or 2 "stop" bits surrounding the data bits (Figure 11.30). One stop bit is used when transmitting at higher speeds, two stop bits are used at low transmission rates. The start bit is Low because it must interrupt the High idling state of the transmission line; stop bits are High.

A series of transmission rates in the range 50–19,200 bps is prescribed. For faster communication and distances up to 4,000 ft, EIA has designed standards RS-422 and RS-423.

In asynchronous communication, data parcels are seven- or eight-bit codes, such as ASCII, and are transmitted one bit at a time with the least significant bit sent first. An additional parity bit is optional. Several possible combinations of the parity bit, code length, and the number of stop bits are allowed. Typically, ten bits are required to transmit an eight-bit code and the character transmission speed is thus usually one-tenth of the bit transmission speed. As an example, a transmission rate of 330 bps uses one start

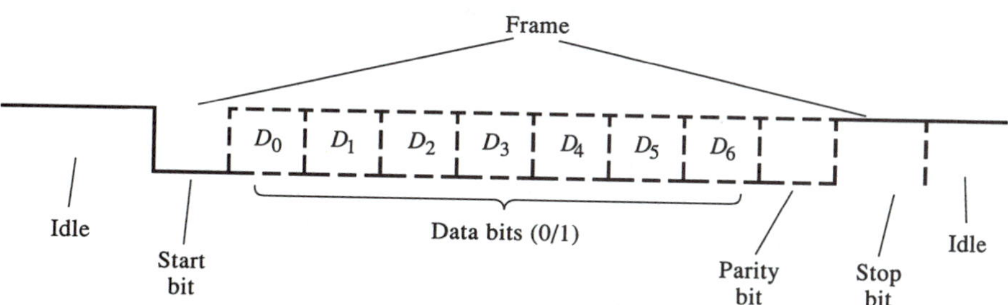


**Figure 11.30.** Example of an RS-232 (RS-404) data format.

bit, eight data bits, and two stop bits (eleven bits per code), resulting in thirty characters transmitted per second.

Signals transmitted in the asynchronous mode are synchronized as follows: The receiving device recognizes an incoming code by the change of level due to the arrival of the start bit. It then finds the start bit's center because it samples the signal at a frequency that is a multiple of the bit frequency, and uses this center point to identify and sample the center of the following data signals. Both the sender and the receiver must, of course, be set for the same transmission rate but because the receiver synchronizes its clock on each start bit, small differences in clock rates do not endanger transmission.

In most computer applications, communication involves the exchange of individual bytes between a peripheral and a computer and no further rules beyond those defining the transmission rates, voltage levels, and data format are needed. In more complicated situations, such as in communication between two remote devices, the RS-232 line is only a part of a chain of connections—often involving several computers, satellite transmission, and individual connections—must be created and confirmed in a sequence of handshaking signals.

For example, the principle of handshaking required for two devices to communicate via modems is similar to that of human communication over a telephone line, where both the caller and the called implicitly follow a communication protocol: The caller picks up the handset, waits for the line tone, and dials the number; the caller picks up the handset at the other end; and so on. For cases such as these, the RS-232-C standard defines several handshaking protocols, such as the one in Figure 11.31. We can understand the procedure better by thinking of the communicating sites as two people, a caller and a call recipient. The diagram shows only one part of the communication (one person talking to the other); a dialog is an extension of the same procedure.

### Modems

As we have seen, one end of an RS-232-C line is often a modem and we will now look at this device in more detail.

Although the main function of a modem is modulation, even the simplest ("dumb") modem performs additional functions we will consider later. More advanced ("smart" or "intelligent") modems can also dial the destination's telephone number, select one of several modes of modulation, automatically adjust to the frequency used by the caller, and so on. A smart modem contains a CPU that interprets signals coming from the originator and recognizes them as data or commands requesting, for example, the dialing of a number.

In addition to categorizing modems as dumb or smart, one may also classify them as acoustic or direct according to how they are connected to the

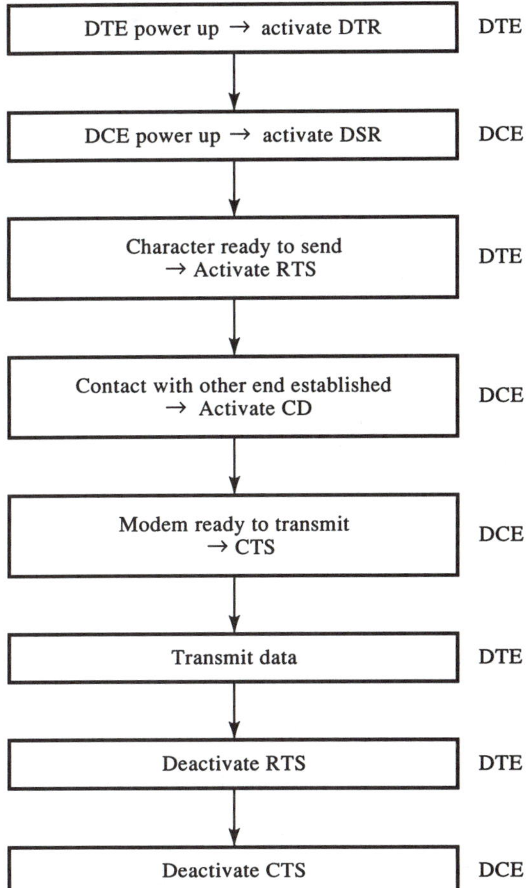


**Figure 11.31.** Main parts of the RS-232 handshaking algorithm: DTE is usually a computer and DCE a modem. Symbols "DTR," "DSR," and others are names of RS-232 signals. See page 490.

telephone line. Acoustic modems convert TTL signals to sound and transmit it via an ordinary telephone handset inserted into an acoustic coupler. Direct modems produce voltages rather than sound and are connected directly to the telephone line. Modems can also be classified as stand-alone devices or as modem cards plugged into the computer.

Modem signals on the side of the telephone line are standard telephone signals (ringing, busy, data), and the basic modem functions are to detect that a connection with the other end is established and to receive or send data. On the computer (DTE) side, the modem (DCE) generates signals for data, control, and handshaking between the caller and the called (Figure 11.32).

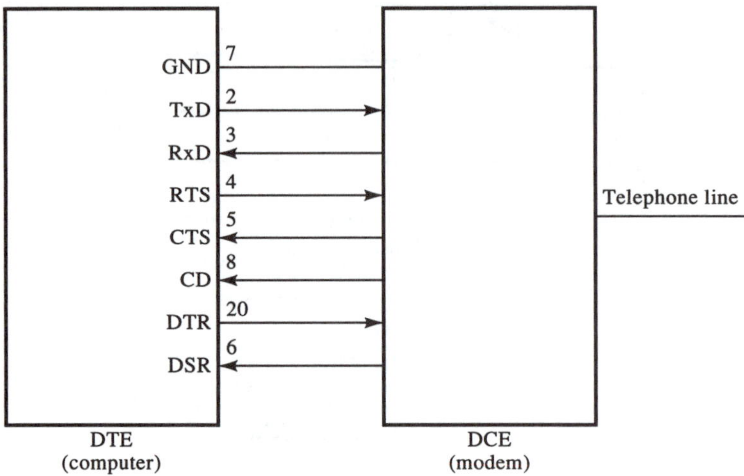


**Figure 11.32.** Main RS-232-C signals.

Signals sent by the modem to the DTE are as follows:

Carrier detect (CD) is activated by the modem when it detects a call over the telephone line. It is deactivated when the transmission from the caller is finished to allow communication in the opposite direction.

Clear to send (CTS) indicates that the modem is ready to send data.

Data set ready (DSR) is activated when the modem is powered up and ready to communicate with its computer.

Signals from the DTE to the modem are as follows:

Data terminal ready (DTR) activated by the DTE when it is ready to communicate with its modem.

Request to send (RTS) is activated by the DTE when it wants to send data via the modem.

Finally, the two lines over which the DTE and the DCE exchange data are called RxD, for "receive data" (the line on which the DTE receives serial data), and TxD, for "transmit data" (the line on which the DTE sends serial data). ("Receive" and "transmit" are thus viewed from the perspective of the DTE, usually a computer.)

Modern modems increase data transmission rates and reliability of communication by using more advanced coding techniques and more complex circuits. One way to achieve better results is to pack more bits into the signal by using multiple rather than binary levels. As an example, the quadratic amplitude modulation (QAM) method combines amplitude and phase modulation using two different amplitudes and four phase shifts to create eight different types of signals. Each signal can thus represent a group of three data bits and for a given signal rate the bit transmission rate is thus increased threefold.

In the context of multilevel signals we can now define the term *Baud rate*. If a communication signal can have several different states (defined by amplitudes, phases, frequencies, or a combination of these), the Baud rate is the maximum number of state changes that can be transmitted per second. On a binary signal, the Baud rate is identical to the number of bits per second but with multilevel transmission, the two concepts are different. As an example, the bit rate of the QAM method with eight signal states is three times the transmission Baud rate because each of the eight states represents three bits.

Another way to achieve a high transmission rate is to transmit data at a speed higher that the maximum allowed for error-free communication and to add extra bits to correct errors if they occur. Even though the extra bits decrease the amount of useful information transmitted in a message, the transmission rate of useful information is higher because the errors that will inevitably occur can be corrected. An example of this approach is trellis coded modulation (TCM).

The subject of data communication is very complex and we have only scratched the surface. As an example, the signal transmitted over a telephone line usually passes through several switching centers where it is routed and possibly encoded, decoded, and checked; and may undergo further modulation as it travels. The line itself does not have to be an ordinary wire and communication over longer distances most likely involves transmission via communication satellites. Further details on communication and related topics, such as networks, are covered in specialized books listed in the references.

### RS-232-C in Situations That Do Not Involve Modems

If we had a computer or a printer (a DTE device) and a modem (DCE), both with RS-232-C interfaces, we could simply connect the corresponding signals and immediately use the system. This is because the DTE interface is internally connected to act as a master but the modem interface is internally connected for the slave mode of operation. As a consequence, the DTE treats line 2, for example, as a line over which to send data for transmission whereas the modem treats the same line as a line on which to receive data and pass it on to the telephone line for transmission.

If, on the other hand, we had two devices whose RS-232-C connections were both designed as masters, we would not get a working interface by simply connecting the corresponding pins together. For example, the master connection of pin 2 is designed to send data out and is thus unidirectional. To obtain matching connections the signals must thus be connected as shown by the solid lines in Figure 11.33. As an example, lines 2 and 3 are swapped so that data sent by one device is treated as received data by the other device. This arrangement tricks each of the two devices into thinking that it is communicating with a modem; because no modem is actually involved, it is called a "null modem." It can be implemented by a special connector or by simply swapping the wires in the connection as indicated.

The situation can be complicated further by an incomplete match of the signals produced and received by the two communicating devices. Such situations arise because manufacturers use different subsets of RS-232 to implement their interfaces. As an example, the IBM PC serial interface adapter implements all signals required for a modem connection and expects a modem-like response from the device connected to it. Unfortunately, many devices, such as printers, generate only a few, possibly only three of these signals.

Because of its design, when the IBM PC wants to send data via its serial adapter, it activates the RTS line and expects that the other device will activate the CTS line. If it does not, the IBM PC will not transmit. If the other device does not produce the CTS signal, the solution is to connect the adapter's RTS back to its CTS pin (one of the dotted lines) and thus trick the IBM PC into thinking that its counterpart is responding: The RTS activated by the PC becomes its own active CTS input and transmission can thus proceed.

This example demonstrates the unfortunate fact that in some cases it is not possible to simply connect two "RS-232 compatible" interfaces; although the interfaces may be compatible with the RS-232 standard in the sense that they

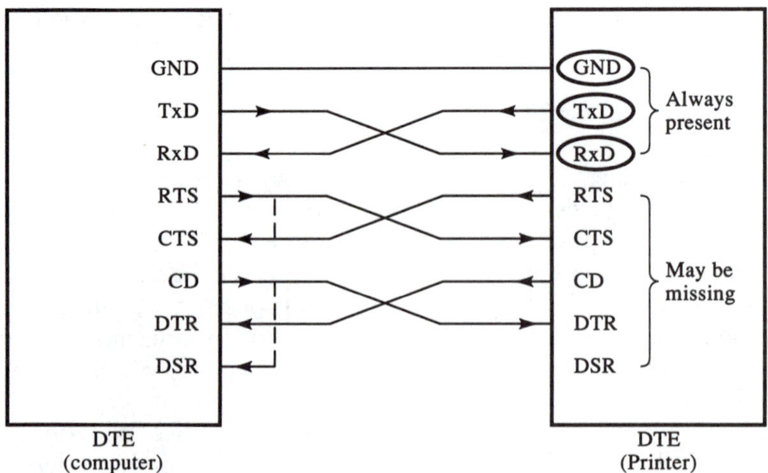


**Figure 11.33.** Signals on the IBM PC serial port and their connection to a device with a DTE interface. Solid lines show the preferred connections; dotted lines show the connections required when the other device has only the basic signals.

each use a subset of its signals, they are not necessarily compatible with one another. Connecting two RTS-232 compatible interfaces thus requires that one examine the signals of both interfaces and check how they are designed.

### Serial-Parallel and Voltage Level Conversion

Having explained the RS-232-C logic, we will now turn to the RS-232 interface, which is needed to convert between the serial RS-232-C level signals and the parallel TTL signals. An RS-232-C interface (Figure 11.34) has two stages:

Conversion between parallel and serial data, combined with recognition of RS-232-C serial formats at TTL levels

Voltage conversion between TTL and RS-232-C levels.

Voltage conversion between TTL and RS-232 levels normally uses the 1488 and 1489 chips and requires no further comment. Serial-parallel conversion and other RS-232-C functions are implemented by one of several TTL level serial-parallel converter chips, collectively known as *universal asynchronous receiver/transmitters*, or UARTs. As an example of a UART, we will describe the 6800 Motorola family chip, the asynchronous communications interface adapter or ACIA.

### MC 6850—The ACIA

The ACIA is one of several "support chips" in the Motorola 6800 family. Others include the parallel interface chip (PIA), which we will cover in the next section, a timer chip that produces timing signals, and CRT and floppy disk controller chips. Although designed mainly for the 6800 family, these components are used with other CPUs as well.

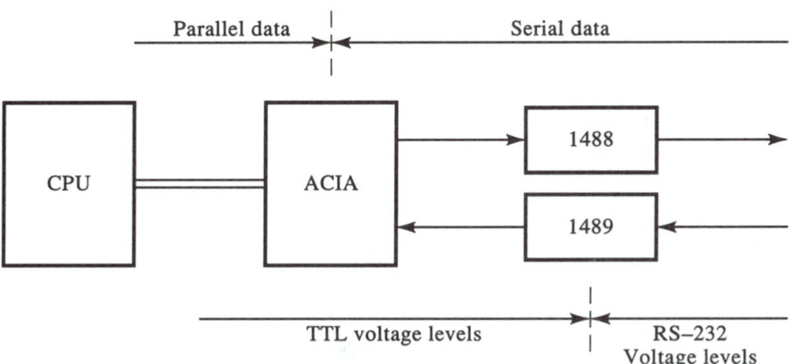


**Figure 11.34.** Block diagram of an RS-232-C interface.

The ACIA translates between parallel data on the CPU side and serial data with RS-232-C format on the other (Figure 11.35). Only TTL levels compatible with standard logic components are involved. In addition to data, address, and control pins, the ACIA also provides signals needed to operate a modem. All signals are compatible with the 6800 CPU in the sense that they correspond in function and logic level to signals expected by the 6800. As an example, IRQ is active Low on both the ACIA and the 6800 pins, and no additional logic gates are thus needed to connect these pins of the two chips together.

The 6850 contains two ports, logic inputs and outputs that act like doors or windows through which the CPU can access peripheral devices. To the 6800 CPU, a port is a memory address associated with a peripheral. One ACIA port contains a data register to hold the code being sent to a peripheral by the CPU; the other contains a register to hold the code sent by a peripheral to the CPU. The two ports share a control register and a status register.

The *control register* makes the ACIA programmable. It acts somewhat like a CPU instruction register in that the value stored in it determines parameters of the ACIA's operation, such as the format of serial data (seven bits, even parity and two stop bits; seven bits, odd parity and two stop bits; and so on for a total of eight possibilities) and the frequency at which serial data is transmitted. (The external clock inputs are internally divided by a number given by the contents of the control register.) The code in the control register also

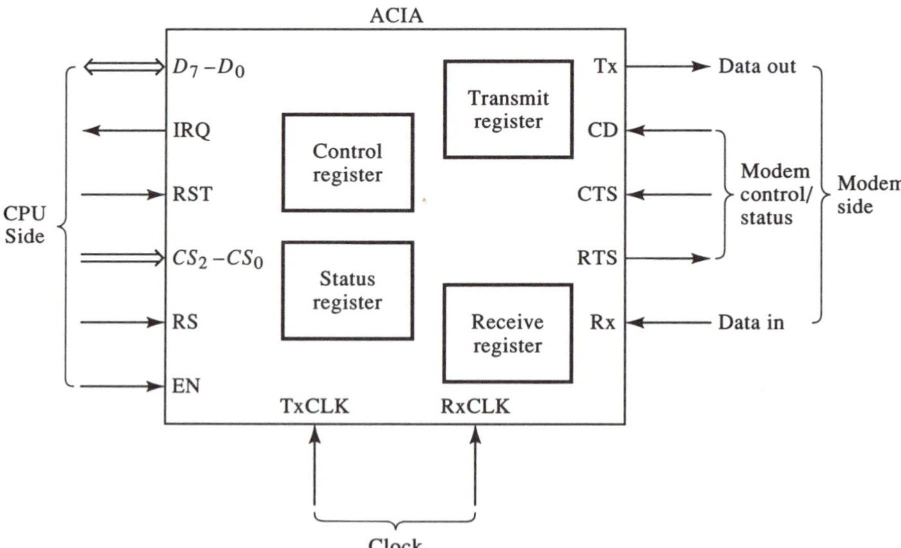


**Figure 11.35.** Block diagram of the 6850 ACIA. Signal IRQ is interrupt request (used to request CPU's attention); EN is chip enable; CS is chip select; RST is reset; and RS (register select) is for the addressing of internal registers.

determines whether the ACIA interrupts the CPU when it receives and assembles a new word or completely transmits one, and so on. The code is, of course, written into the control register by the CPU when it initializes the system or modifies its operating mode.

The *status register* allows the CPU to check whether the ACIA is ready to transmit another code, whether it has received and assembled a new code, whether received data has arrived in the expected format (correct parity and number of stop bits), and whether the modem (if present) can transmit. Appendix 5 gives a detailed specification of the functions of individual pins and other information necessary to program the ACIA, and we will consider an example of its use in Chapter 12.

The ACIA is not difficult to use but detailed coverage of its different modes of operation is beyond the scope of this text. In essence, the ACIA must first be initialized to the desired mode by a proper control word sent by the CPU, and then accessed whenever a transfer is required. To send data out, the CPU waits until the status code of the ACIA indicates that it is ready (finished transmitting the previous code) and then stores the data to be sent in the transmit data register. The ACIA takes care of the rest: sending the start bit, shifting the code out one bit at a time, calculating and sending the parity bit, and generating the desired number of stop bits.

To send a sequence of codes via the ACIA, the CPU can use one of two strategies. One is to execute a loop in which the CPU continues monitoring the ACIA, waiting until it is ready for code, and then loads the data as above. Another strategy is to deposit the first code in the data register, return to another program, and let the ACIA use an interrupt signal to inform the CPU when the current code is transmitted and the ACIA is ready. The ACIA can work in either way and the desired mode of operation is determined by the value in the control register.

Input via the ACIA similarly can be handled in two ways. The CPU either continues checking the status bit, waiting until the ACIA receives and assembles a new code, or else the ACIA is programmed to activate the interrupt signal when a complete code is received and assembled.

The ACIA saves the CPU much time that it would otherwise have to spend creating or testing start and stop bits and shifting the data, all the while making sure that the timing corresponds to the desired Baud rate. The hardware interface to the transmission line is also simplified.

### Current Loop Interfaces

As we mentioned, RS-232-C can be used only for relatively short distances. This result is to be expected because the resistance to current passing through a wire causes signal voltages to drop off, and the longer the wire, the greater the drop in voltage. One way around this problem is to amplify the signal after a certain distance has been traversed. Another solution is to represent logic values as current rather than voltage because most of the current flowing into a wire at one end also flows out from the other end. Pushing current of required intensity through a wire is just a matter of creating a sufficient voltage difference over its length and providing a low resistance path. This is the principle of current loop interfaces, which can be used for distances up to several kilometers without special amplification devices.

In the current loop interface, logic 0 is represented by no current and logic 1 by 20 mA or 60 mA. Like RS-232-C, the current loop interface is used for serial communication. It is, however, more common in industrial applications than in personal computers.

### Centronics Parallel Interfaces

This popular "de facto" standard for parallel printer interfaces was developed by Centronics, a printer manufacturer. It is used by most current printers and we outlined its principles in our description of the Epson FX-85.

The Centronics interface normally uses 36-pin connectors and prescribes the electric, timing, and logic parameters of a collection of data, timing, status, control, and power signals. It has two sets of eight-bit data lines but the second set is normally connected to the ground to minimize noise. All signals use TTL level voltages. Because Centronics is not a formal standard, manufacturers use it in slightly different ways but all are similar to the arrangement described in our outline of the Epson printer.

Most modern computers have a built-in Centronics-like interface. On the IBM PC, for example, it is provided as a "parallel interface adapter card" with a twenty-five pin connector. Sometimes, both Centronics and RS-232-C interfaces are available on a single card.

The following algorithm shows how a CPU could send a sequence of codes to a printer using Centronics signals compatible with the definition in Figure 11.20:

```
REPEAT
   Wait until printer NOT BUSY;
   Output data on data lines;
   Activate STROBE signal;            {Positive edge of STROBE}
   Deactivate STROBE signal;          {Negative edge of STROBE}
   Remove data from the data lines;
UNTIL all data transmitted;
```

Note that the sequence must guarantee that the prescribed timing relations are satisfied.

Because the data must remain active while STROBE is activated and deactivated, the interface between the CPU and the printer must contain a data register port. Another port is required for the BUSY line from the printer and the STROBE line from the CPU. The BUSY port, however, does not have to be a register because BUSY is held active by the printer.

There are other ways to implement the CPU-printer communication. As an example, instead of being locked into a loop, the CPU could send one character, return to another program, and resume transmission when the printer sends the BUSY or the ACKNLG signal to indicate that it is ready.

Because the needs of a Centronics interface (transparent input ports and output ports with registers) are similar to those of many other parallel interfaces, a number of specialized chips providing all the necessary signals and functions are available. One of them is the MC 6821 PIA by Motorola.

## MC 6821—The PIA

The PIA (peripheral interface adapter) is a programmable chip, which provides two parallel ports for 6800-based computers. All of its signals use TTL voltage levels and can thus be used by other CPUs as well. The active levels (Low and High) are, however, matched with the active levels of the 6800 CPU's signals.

The two 6821 parallel ports called *A* and *B* (Figure 11.36) are functionally almost identical. Each contains three internal registers: an output (data) register called *OR* for data output, a control register called *CR* to control

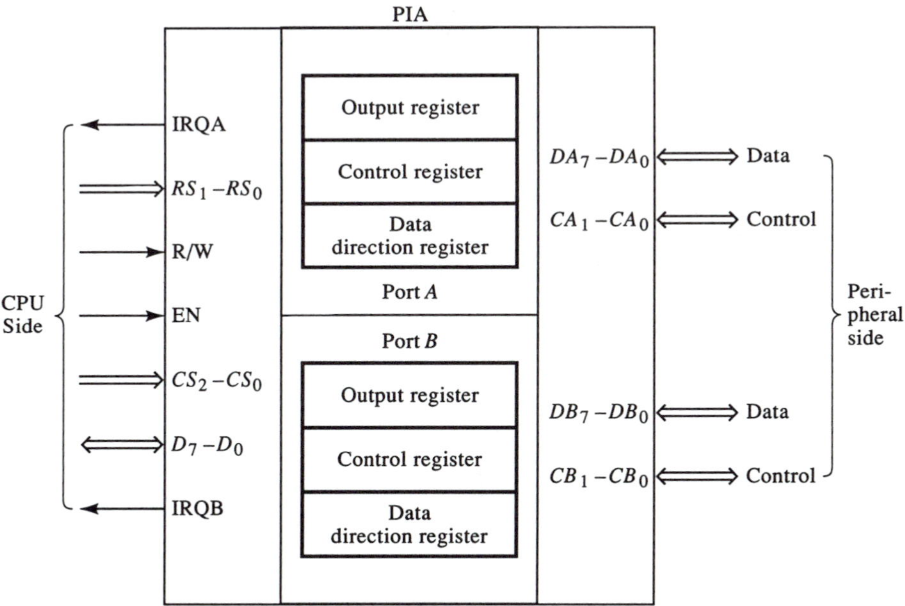


**Figure 11.36.** Block diagram of the 6821 PIA. Signals IRQA and IRQB (interrupt request) are used to request CPU's attention; EN is enable; CS is chip select; RST is reset; and RS (register select) is for the addressing of internal registers.

PIA's mode of operation, and a data direction register called *DDR* to control the direction of data flow through individual data lines.

On the CPU side, the PIA has eight data pins that can be internally channeled to port *A* or port *B* by placing the proper address on PIA's address pins. The PIA data registers latch the data written into them by the CPU until the CPU sends new data. Input, on the other hand, is "transparent," which means that there is no latch between the CPU and the peripheral. When the CPU reads an input port, it thus directly reads the (amplified) values on the data lines of the I/O device. This arrangement is compatible with the needs of the Centronics interface described in the previous section.

The interrupt signal of the PIA can be programmed to inform the CPU about the activity on the peripheral side of the chip.

On the peripheral side of the PIA, each port has eight data pins and two control lines that can be programmed for several different kinds of handshaking between the CPU and the peripheral. As an example, one can program the PIA to produce an interrupt signal when it receives a control signal from the peripheral and send an acknowledgement signal to the peripheral at the same time. The first informs the CPU that new data have arrived, the second tells the peripheral that its data have been received.

Each data line of each port can be programmed as input or output by storing 0 (input) or 1 (output) in the data direction register of the port. (As usual, terms "input" and "output" are defined from the CPU's perspective.)

The CPU treats the PIA like any other programmable chip: First it must be initialized for the desired mode of operation via its control register and then it can be accessed whenever needed. The PIA is not difficult to use but explaining all its modes of operation is beyond the scope of this book and we will restrict ourselves to an example of a simple Centronics interface.

The logical way to handle all Centronics signals would be to use a three-port interface. One port would be used for data, one for control, and one for status signals. Parallel interface chips with three ports are available but if we do not use all signals, we can do with the PIA's two ports, as shown in Figure 11.37.

Our circuit uses port *A* as a combined status and control port, and port *B* for data. One line of port *A*, for example line 0, is programmed as input and is connected to the BUSY line from the printer; another line, for example line 1,

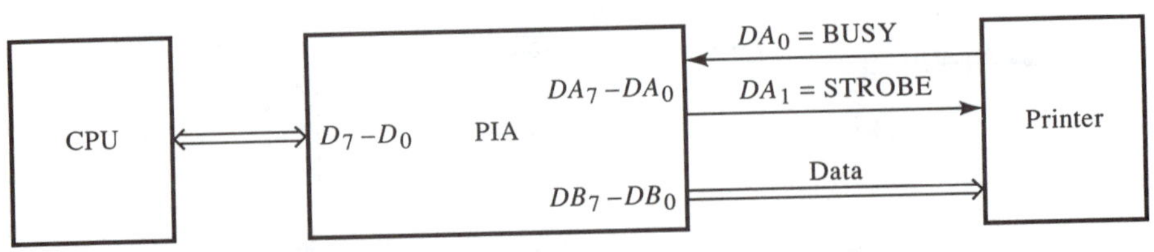


**Figure 11.37.** Implementing a simple Centronics interface with the PIA. Signals needed to address the PIA are not shown.

is programmed as output and is connected to printer's STROBE. We will ignore the other signals, such as printer error conditions, and leave a more complete interface as an exercise. The algorithm to send a sequence of bytes to the printer is as follows:

```
Initialize PIA's mode of operation, including directions of data lines;
When output to printer is required,
  REPEAT
    Wait until BUSY=0 by repeatedly testing line 0 of port A;
    Output data to data register of port B;
    Activate STROBE by turning line 1 of port A On and Off
UNTIL all data transmitted
```

**Exercises**

1. How many sine waves of each of the four frequencies of a Bell-103 signal are transmitted at 330 Baud? (Remember that each bit is allocated the same amount of time.)
2. Compare the voltage levels and waveforms used by TTL, Bell-103, and RS-232-C signals.
3. Explain the structure and the main components of communication between a computer and a distant peripheral.
4. Explain the purpose of the following conventions and standards: Bell-103, RS-232-C, current loop, Centronics.
5. Explain asynchronous serial communication and the purpose and structure of a data frame.
6. When and why must a TTL signal be modulated?
7. Figure 11.38 shows the codes assigned to individual amplitude and phase combinations of a QAM pattern. Draw a timing diagram using this pattern to encode the bit sequence (100101001) assuming that two full

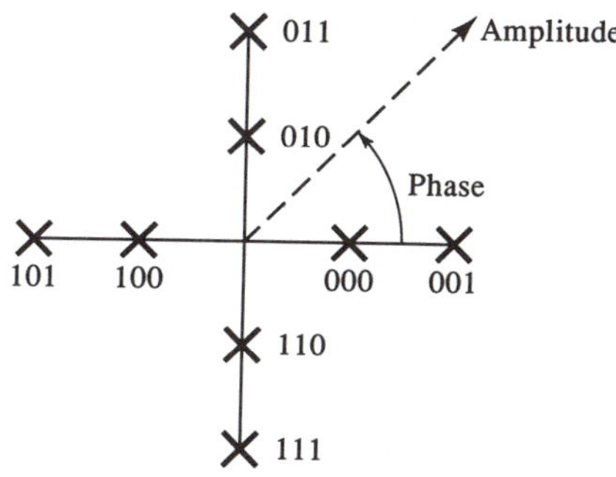


**Figure 11.38.** A QAM pattern.

sine waves are used for each code. Compare the amount of time required to transmit the code with QAM and AM modulation using sine waves of the same frequency.

8. Write a 6800 program to implement serial input and output without the ACIA. The CPU must store the transmitted data in an external latch treated as a memory location. Assume that the address of the output latch is $7000, the CPU frequency is 1 MHz, the desired format is seven data bits followed by an even parity bit and 1-½ stop bits, and the transmission rate is 330 Baud.
9. Convert the program from Exercise 8 into a subroutine whose parameters are the number of data bits, parity, and the number of stop bits.
10. List the functions that the ACIA performs in addition to the functions of the subroutine in Exercise 8.
11. Estimate the saving of CPU time achieved by using an ACIA instead of a program as in Exercise 8. Assume that the transmission rate is 330 bps. Repeat with 9600 bps.
12. Which of the following signal representations are used by the Centronics standard: TTL, Bell-103, RS-232-C?
13. Study the ACIA and PIA descriptions in Appendix 5 and write a program to initialize them for a selected mode of operation.
14. Modify our example of a Centronics interface to allow handling of the error status of the printer.
15. Write a 6800 subroutine implementing Centronics output via a PIA. The character to be printed is assumed to be in accumulator *A* when the subroutine is called. If the subroutine fails to establish contact with the printer after five attempts, it should terminate and return $FF in accumulator *B*. Accumulator *B* returns 0 if the operation succeeds.
16. Why is the idling state in RS-232 High, and the start bit Low, and the stop bit High?

## SUMMARY

Peripherals (I/O devices) are used by the computer to communicate with the external world. They include devices external to the computer, such as the keyboard, display, and printer, as well as devices inside the chasis of the computer such as floppy or hard disk drives.

The logic of internal control of a peripheral is usually complicated and to simplify the task of the main CPU, as much control is built into the device as possible. Although this considerably reduces the involvement of the main CPU, writing programs that perform I/O operations (device drivers) still requires a level of understanding that is beyond the competence of most programmers. As a consequence, device drivers are supplied with the computer or the peripheral and constitute one of the main parts of an operating system.

In preparation for detailed coverage of I/O programming and interfacing in Chapter 12, we presented principles of operation of the main types of peripherals, including keyboards, displays, computer terminals, printers, and disk drives; we concentrated on the most popular implementations of each.

Keyboards are based on switches, usually arranged as two-dimensional arrays to minimize the complexity of the supporting logic. The keyboard controller whose function is to detect key activation and convert it into a key code uses the principle of scanning: It activates one column of the key matrix after another and reads the rows, looking for a logic value that indicates a key has been pressed. When it detects a pressed key, the encoder calculates its code from the column and row number.

Keyboard control can be performed by hardware (a keyboard encoder chip) or by software. Often, a CPU built into the keyboard is dedicated to this task. More sophisticated keyboards perform a variety of other functions in addition to simple detection of key closures. They recognize combinations of keys activated at the same time, produce different codes when a key is pressed or released, and can handle a sequence of keys activated in quick succession. Very often, the codes produced by the controller are not ASCII codes but scan codes assigned to keys in geometric fashion.

Most computer displays use the CRT principle. However, CRTs are bulky and heavy and there is much interest in smaller flat devices like LCD displays.

The operational principle of a CRT is a high-energy electron beam pointed at a phosphor-coated screen where its impact creates a flash of light. Displays of text or graphic patterns are achieved by moving the beam around the screen.

Computers use two kinds of CRT displays, raster scan and vector. In vector CRTs, the beam is moved from one point to another in the order prescribed by the program creating the image. These displays are used only for graphics applications. Ordinary CRT displays use raster scan, in which the electron beam is moved in a regular pattern across the screen and its intensity turned up or down to produce dots of different brightness. Graphics or characters displayed on raster scan CRTs are made of individual dots. Both vector and raster scan CRT displays must be regularly refreshed because the persistence of phosphor coating is short. The display information needed for refresh is stored in a RAM.

Raster scan displays can work either in the text or in the graphics mode. The principle of text mode operation is as follows: The ASCII code of each position displayed on the screen is stored in the display RAM. The display RAM is repeatedly read by the CRT controller, and the codes are converted to dot patterns by a character generator ROM and transmitted to the video circuit one bit at a time by a shift register. The display RAM is also accessible to the main CPU, and the image on the screen can be changed by writing new ASCII codes into it. In the graphics mode, the character generator ROM is bypassed and the display RAM stores the actual dot patterns.

Color display CRTs are coated with three kinds of phosphor producing red, green, and blue dots. Each color is usually accessed by its own beam and colors other than red, green, and blue are obtained by varying the intensity of the beams.

Computer terminals combine keyboards and displays. They are used mostly with large computers that can serve many users at the same time. In addition to the keyboard and CRT circuitry, computer terminals often have a serial printer interface.

Of the many varieties of printers currently available, impact dot-matrix printers are the most common. They produce output by propelling tiny hammers against a ribbon and making dots on the paper. Characters and graphics are formed as combinations of dots as in CRT raster scan displays.

Although the internal logic of dot matrix printers is relatively complex the printer–computer interface is simple. (The logic must control individual hammers, move ribbon and paper, convert ASCII codes to dot patterns, and monitor the status of the printer.) It consists of data lines that transmit command and dot pattern or ASCII codes, status lines through which the computer can determine if the printer is ready, and control lines that activate the printer and alert it when a new code is sent. The programming interface is also relatively simple; it consists of initializing the printer and its interface when the computer is turned on, transmitting codes when an application program requires output, and sending commands that change the printer's mode of operation.

Disk drives are the most complex peripherals. The two major categories are floppy and hard disks. Both use flat disks with a magnetizable coat, but the underlying material is rigid in hard disks and flexible in floppy disks. The advantage of floppies is that they are removable and can thus be transported and used to build an unlimited library of information. Hard disks, on the other hand, have much larger capacities and are faster.

Information recorded on a disk is stored in circular tracks divided into sectors. Usually, both sides of the disk are used. Reading and writing is performed by a read–write head that can move radially to locate the desired track on the rotating disk. Because the information is stored very densely, the rotation and positioning mechanisms must be very accurate. Due to the high rotation speed and dense recording, data transfer rates are very high, reaching 10 Mbytes per second on some hard disk drives.

Most of the complex control required by disk drives is implemented by special purpose chips known as floppy or hard disk controllers. Even though the controller greatly simplifies the computer's task, the disk driver routine is still very complex because there are many parameters that must be considered and controlled with proper timing.

A discussion of peripherals would be incomplete without an outline of the communication between the computer and its peripherals or another computer. Over very short distances, digital information can be transmitted by TTL signals (0 V and 5 V) but voltage levels and transitions become distorted when the distance exceeds a few feet. For longer distances, digital information must be converted to a different representation and voltage. The most important concepts here are modulation, modem, RS-232-C, and current loop.

Apart from the On/Off representation (Am modulation) used by TTL signals, the most common form of modulation is FM where logic 0 and 1 are represented by sine waves of different frequencies. Sine waves have smooth transitions between extremal values, and if their frequency is not too high, they can be transmitted undistorted even over ordinary telephone lines. In this case, information is transmitted in serial form, one bit at a time, usually at a transmission rate of 330 bps or 1200 bps. Both modulation and demodulation are performed by a single device called the modem.

For transmission over distances up to 50 ft, digital information can be sent without modulation but the voltage level must be increased. To lower the cost of the interface circuit and the connecting cable, transmission is usually serial. The most common serial standard is RS-232-C, which defines twenty-five signal lines and prescribes their voltage levels. Two forms of serial communication are possible, synchronous and asynchronous, but asynchronous communication where individual bytes are sent at random times is much more common. To achieve synchronization between the sender and the receiver, a frame of bits with a predefined format surrounds the transmitted code. The RS-232-C convention was originally designed for communication via modems but is now very common even for direct communication between computers and peripherals. Unfortunately, all manufacturers do not follow the same conventions and care is required when connecting "RS-232 compatible" devices.

An alternative to the RS-232-C voltage standard is the current loop standard, which defines logic 0 and 1 in terms of electric current. The current loop standard can be used over longer distances than RS-232-C but is not very popular except in industrial applications.

An alternative to serial communication is parallel communication, where an entire code is transmitted at one time. It is used mostly over very short distances because of the cost of the interconnecting cables. The most common parallel convention is Centronics, developed for communication with printers. It uses TTL levels and prescribes data, control, and status signals as well as a handshaking protocol that establishes the dialog required for communication between the computer and the printer.

Because all computers need a serial or a parallel interface to communicate with their peripherals, a number of chips have been developed that implement the serial and parallel interface functions and reduce the number of required components. We described two of them, the ACIA and the PIA serial and parallel interface chips for the 6800 CPU.

The ACIA is used for serial communication and implements parallel–serial conversion between parallel data on the computer side and serial data on the peripheral side. It can be programmed to produce one of several formats of asynchronous frames and provides signals for communication with a modem.

The PIA is used for parallel communication. It latches data produced by the CPU and holds it until it is rewritten by the CPU. It also recognized and generates signals for handshaking with peripherals and can be programmed to interrupt the CPU when the peripheral requires its attention.

Chips such as the ACIA and PIA form the basis of most serial and parallel interfaces and are examples of support chips that semiconductor manufacturers provide for their CPU chips. All support chips in a CPU family are designed to be compatible with the CPU, producing logic signals and transitions required by that particular CPU's hardware architecture.

## REVIEW QUESTIONS

1. Define the following terms: ACIA, burst transfer, character generator, computer terminal, CRT, CRT controller, current loop, disk drive (controller, floppy, hard), cycle stealing, dot-matrix printer, handshake, I/O driver, keyboard (matrix, encoder), modem, modulation, parallel communication, PIA, port, protocol, raster scan display, RS-232-C, scan code, serial communication, synchronous/asynchronous communication, and UART.
2. Describe briefly the principles of keyboards, CRT raster scan displays, terminals, dot-matrix printers, and disk drives.

## REFERENCES

The following titles listed in the references at the end of the book are relevant to this chapter:

R. Bishop. *Basic Microprocessors and the 6800.*

U. D. Black. *Data Communications and Distributed Networks.*

D. J. Dailey. *Small Computer Theory and Applications.*

D. Hall. *Microprocessors and Interfacing: Programming and Hardware.*

G. J. Lipovski. *Single- and Multiple-Chip Microcomputer Interfacing.*

R. T. Paynter. *Microcomputer Operation, Troubleshooting, and Repair.*

M. Sargent III and R. L. Shoemaker. *The IBM PC from the Inside Out.*

B. Sklar. *Digital Communications.*

# CHAPTER 12

# INPUT AND OUTPUT PROGRAMMING AND INTERFACING

## AN OVERVIEW

The implementation of input and output has both hardware and software aspects. The hardware aspect of I/O is the interface, the physical connection between the device and the CPU. Its logic depends on the hardware architectures of the peripheral and the CPU, in other words, the function and timing of their signals. Although the details differ among CPUs, the differences are small and the principles of interface design are the same on all computers.

The software aspect of I/O is the strategy used to perform the I/O operation. Different approaches are distinguished by data transfer rates, the role of the CPU, and the complexity of the interface. The choice depends on the speed of the I/O device, the urgency of the I/O operation, and the time that the CPU can dedicate to it. One can distinguish the following I/O methods:

Programmed and polled I/O where the CPU is fully in charge, initiating and performing the complete operation

Interrupt-driven I/O, in which the operation is initiated by the I/O device and performed by the CPU

Direct memory access (DMA) where the data transfer is performed by a controller other than the CPU.

In this chapter, we will present both the hardware and software principles of I/O on the basis of the 6800 CPU architecture. To complement the picture, the chapter closes with a brief outline of I/O aspects of the Intel 8088 CPU.

## IMPORTANT WORDS

ACIA, buffer, control signal, decoder, device driver, direct memory access (DMA), DMA controller (DMAC), interrupt (arbitration, maskable, non-maskable, handler, priority, table, vector), interrupt-driven I/O, parallel interface, PIA, polling, programmed I/O, reset, serial interface, timer, UART, USART.

## 12.1 INTRODUCTION TO HARDWARE ARCHITECTURE

A computer consists of the CPU, memory, and peripherals, all connected by the *system bus*: the combination of the address, data, and the control buses (Figure 12.1). Most of the time, the computer is controlled by the CPU that sends control signals and addresses to devices with which it wants to communicate, and exchanges data with them.

Recognizing that a device is being addressed and mediating communication with the CPU is the function of the *interface* between the device and the bus. The details of the interface and the signals required to set up and maintain the data transfer depend on the CPU, the device, and the type of operation being performed.

As we saw in Chapter 11, I/O devices produce and consume data at very different speeds. At the low end, modems usually operate at 330 Baud or 30 characters per second. The fastest typist probably types at most ten characters per second (cps) but a good dot-matrix printer consumes data at 200 cps. The

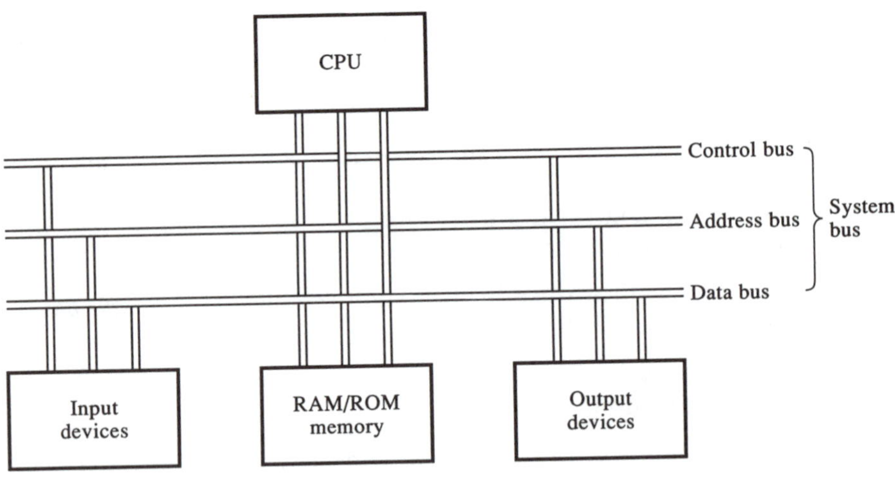


**Figure 12.1.** Block diagram of a small computer.

transfer rate of floppy disk drives is in tens of thousands of bytes per second, and hard disk transfer rates reach one million bytes per second and higher.

When we compare these data transmission rates with the speed of the CPU, we see that a 6800 CPU with a 1-MHz clock can execute at least 2,000 instructions between two consecutive activations of a keyboard and can easily service a printer or a modem, but may have difficulty keeping up with a floppy disk drive. The data transfer rate of a hard disk is beyond its power. The obvious conclusion is that each type of peripheral requires different I/O techniques.

Although computer memories usually work at the speed of the CPU, many CPUs are faster than acceptably priced memory chips and the mismatch between the speed of the CPU and the speed of the accessed device thus extends beyond peripherals.

Another consideration that determines which I/O method should be used is the urgency of CPU response to the request for an I/O operation. If, for example, a signal from a disk drive controller indicates that the disk drive is ready to read to transfer a byte, the CPU must respond immediately or the opportunity will be lost. If, on the other hand, the keyboard signals that a key was pressed, the CPU does not have to consume it immediately because another key will not be pressed for a considerable time.

When selecting an appropriate I/O method, one must also consider how much time the CPU can afford to spend on the operation. A dedicated keyboard CPU can spend all its time scanning the keys because it has nothing else to do. On the other hand, the CPU in charge of the entire computer can only service the keyboard if a keyboard operation is requested. The two situations require different approaches.

An essential requirement shared by all I/O methods is synchronization: Because the CPU and the peripherals work at different speeds, the CPU must be able to determine whether the device is ready for the I/O operation. If the CPU cannot afford to waste its time with repeated tests, the task of initiating the operation when the device is ready must be left to the peripheral. The peripheral must then be able to produce a special signal to notify the CPU.

Although different CPUs use different I/O instructions, control signals, and timing, the underlying principles are always the same. In this sense, the following material based on the 6800 applies to other CPUs as well.

### Exercises

1. Calculate how many extra instructions a 6800 CPU running at 1 MHz can execute during data transfers involving different types of peripherals.
2. Demonstrate that the transfer rate of hard disks is too high for a 1-MHz 6800 CPU. (*Hint:* Write a program to transfer a block of data and calculate its data transfer rate.)

## 12.2 BASIC HARDWARE ARCHITECTURE OF THE 6800 CPU

Before we can start designing an interface, we must understand the CPU signals that the interface will process. The main 6800 control signals and their timing are similar to the signals that we defined on TOY.

TOY's DTR signal, which indicates that a data transfer is underway, is called VMA (valid memory access) on the 6800; it is High when the 6800 performs a data transfer and Low during an internal CPU operation.

Signal $R/\overline{W}$ is the same as on TOY: When VMA is active, $R/\overline{W}$ is High when the CPU reads from a memory address and Low when it writes. Signal $R/\overline{W}$ is meaningless when VMA is Low.

Because the 6800 does not have any I/O instructions and does not distinguish between memory and I/O access, it does not have TOY's $IO/\overline{MEM}$ signal.

Synchronization between the CPU and the accessed device is achieved by a two-phase clock. Phase $\Phi_1$ is used for internal CPU operation and marks the start of a new machine cycle; it activates all control, data, and address signals. Phase $\Phi_2$ activates the desired I/O operation. For a write operation, it signals that data is on the bus; for a read operation, it signals that it expects data on the bus. As on TOY, data transfers thus occur during $\Phi_2$.

A device monitoring the 6800 signals can distinguish only four different states: reading, writing, internal CPU operation, and idling CPU state. In the idling state, CPU's connections to the system bus are tristated and the bus can be controlled by another controller. This controller would have to produce the same bus signals as the CPU because interfaces are designed for CPU signals. In this sense, there are only three bus states: reading or writing controlled by the CPU or another controller, and no bus activity.

For both read and write operations, $VMA = 1$ (Figure 12.2). In a read operation, the CPU expects the data some time before the end of phase $\Phi_2$. During a write operation, the CPU outputs data in phase $\Phi_2$. It is thus convenient to use signal VMA $\cdot$ $\Phi_2$ to control both input and output.

We will now demonstrate the read and write cycles using the example of executing two consecutive instructions: LDAB #$55 followed by STAB $2000.

Assume that the 6800 CPU is about to execute LDAB #$55 stored at address $1234. This instruction requires two machine cycles and the events that occur are as follows (Figure 12.3):

1. Machine cycle 1—Instruction fetch. Phase $\Phi_1$ activates the $R/\overline{W}$ and VMA signals, outputs the address on the address bus, and starts incrementing the program counter.

   Phase $\Phi_2$ informs the memory and I/O devices that a data transfer is underway, and memory must put the code from address $1234 on the data bus before the end of this phase. The CPU then loads the code ($C6) into its instruction register.

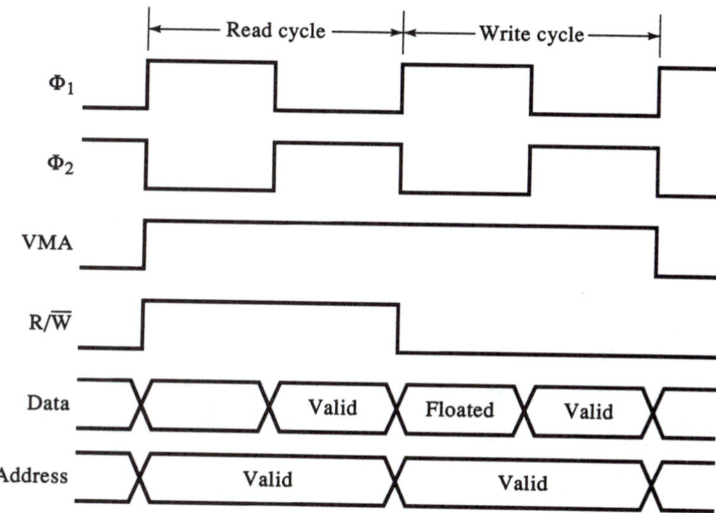


**Figure 12.2.** Timing of 6800 read and write operations.

2. Machine cycle 2—Execution. The opcode is now in the instruction register and has been recognized, and the program counter contains \$1235. The CPU reads the operand just as in machine cycle 1 but the received code (\$55) goes to accumulator *B*. The program counter is again incremented and the CPU is ready to fetch another instruction.

Note that as far as the memory and I/O devices are concerned, the two machine cycles perform exactly the same operation: read. Memory and I/O do not know or care that the first code was an opcode and went to the instruction register, whereas the second was an operand and was loaded into accumulator *B*.

After executing LDAB # the CPU proceeds to instruction STAB \$2000 stored at address \$1236. The program counter has already been updated.

1. Machine cycle 1—Fetch. Signals R/$\overline{W}$ and VMA are On and the transfer occurs in phase $\Phi_2$ as before. The opcode (\$F7) is fetched into the instruction register and the program counter incremented.
2. Machine cycle 2—Start of execution. The CPU decodes the instruction and recognizes that it must get a two-byte address. It fetches the high byte from address \$1237, loads it into the high part of the data counter, and increments *PC*. Signals R/$\overline{W}$ and VMA are On throughout the machine cycle and the transfer occurs in phase $\Phi_2$.
3. Machine cycle 3. The CPU fetches the second byte of the address, saves it in the data counter, and increments *PC* to get ready for the next instruction fetch. Signals R/$\overline{W}$ and VMA are On and the transfer occurs in phase $\Phi_2$. The complete address of the operand (\$2000) is now in *DC*.

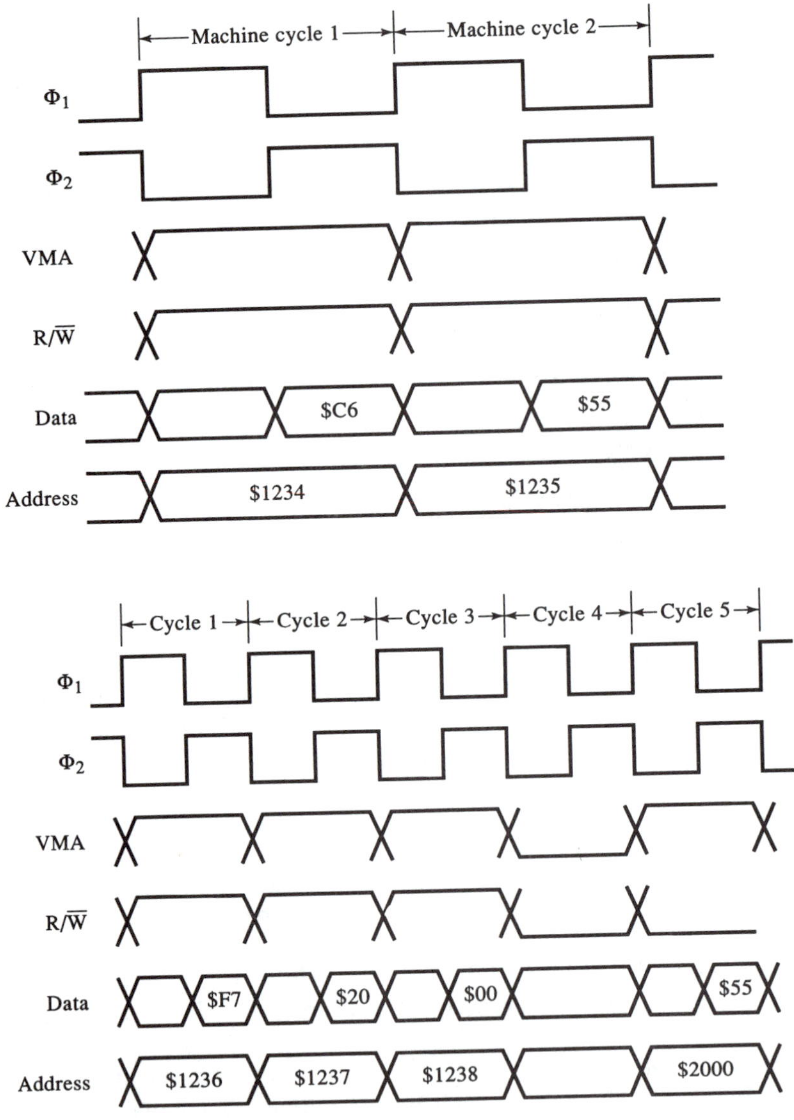


**Figure 12.3.** Execution of LDAB #$55 (*top*) and STAB $2000 (*bottom*).

4. Machine cycle 4. According to the instruction table, STAB requires five machine cycles. Because cycle 5 is used to output *B* on the data bus, cycle 4 is an internal CPU operation. (The timing of control signals is summarized in 6800 data sheets; it cannot be explained with reference to TOY's internal structure because the 6800's internal organization is different.) During this cycle, VMA is Off because this is an internal operation, and memory and I/O devices thus ignore $R/\overline{W}$ and the signals on the address bus.

5. Machine cycle 5. The CPU outputs a copy of $A$ on the data bus and the contents of the address register on the address bus; VMA becomes 1 to indicate a data transfer, and R/$\overline{W}$ becomes 0 to indicate a write operation. Memory is activated by $\Phi_2$ and stores the data ($55), and the CPU is ready to fetch the next instruction.

   Note that our example demonstrates all three types of bus activities and illustrates all situations that an interface must be able to recognize.

### Exercise

1. Draw and explain the timing diagram of the following instructions: NEG, PSH, LDAA 13,$X$.

## 12.3 INTRODUCTION TO MEMORY AND I/O INTERFACING

### Memory Interfacing

The 6800 has sixteen address lines to access a 64k memory space. If we could implement the whole memory space with a single 64k × 8 RAM chip, we would simply connect the sixteen lines of the address bus to the sixteen address pins of the memory chip, the data bus to the data pins, and the R/$\overline{W}$ signal from the CPU to the R/$\overline{W}$ pin of the RAM chip. Because a data transfer takes place in phase $\Phi_2$ if VMA is On, the combination VMA · $\Phi_2$ would be connected to the chip select input of the RAM (Figure 12.4).

Unfortunately, reality is not so simple because one part of the address space must usually be implemented with a ROM, another part with RAM, and some addresses must be reserved for I/O (Figure 12.5). Moreover, available memory chips usually do not have the capacity that we need, and the required

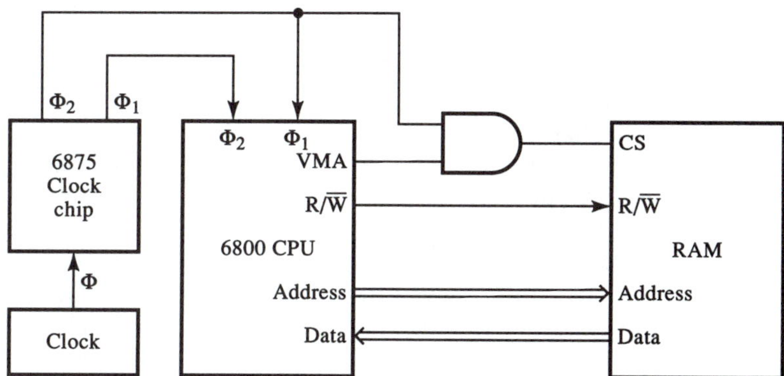


**Figure 12.4.** Principle of 6800 CPU memory interfacing.

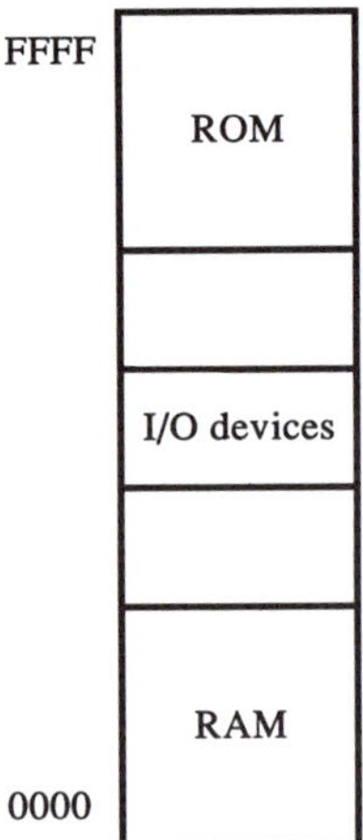


**Figure 12.5.** Typical address map of a 6800-based computer.

memory must be obtained by combining several chips. The most important consequence of this is that chip select inputs require not only recognition of data transfer (VMA) and its proper timing ($\Phi_2$) but also recognition of the address range assigned to the chip. Before we explain how to deal with this, let us explain why memory must be divided between ROM, RAM, and I/O, and how this can best be done.

The reason why a part of the address space must be assigned to I/O is that the 6800 uses memory-mapped addressing. To understand why we need a ROM, we must explain how the CPU behaves when the power is turned on.

To make it possible for the CPU to find the start of the startup program, the 6800 has a special reset pin RST and its activation initializes the program counter, somewhat like the reset circuit in TOY. When RST is activated by a circuit connected to the power line or to a reset switch, the 6800 reads the value in memory locations $FFFE and $FFFF and loads it into the program counter. The two bytes stored in locations $FFFE and $FFFF (the *reset vector*) are thus the address of the first instruction to be executed, the start of the initialization program. If, for example, locations $FFFE and $FFFF contained $0200, the first instruction of the startup program would be fetched from location 0200. On the ET-3400, the contents of $FFFE and $FFFF are $FC00 and the opcode of the first instruction is thus fetched from location $FC00 (Figure 12.6).

Because the address of the first instruction executed after reset comes from $FFFE and $FFFF, the correct value must be available when the power is turned on and thus locations $FFFE and $FFFF cannot be in a RAM. On some computers, these locations are implemented by switches but more commonly they are stored in a ROM and the rest of the ROM chip is used for

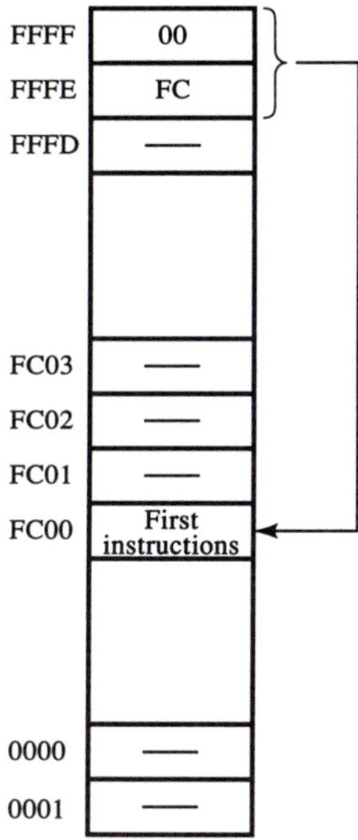


**Figure 12.6.** Power up and reset on the ET-3400.

the initialization program. This is why the top of the 6800 memory space is usually occupied by a ROM.

Let us now take a look at the bottom of the address space. As we know, the 6800 has a special addressing mode called direct addressing, which is used to access page zero (addresses $0000 to $00FF). Because instructions using direct addressing are shorter and execute faster, they are used as much as possible and as much data as possible is stored on page zero. This is why the bottom of the address space in 6800-based computers normally contains a RAM.

After this analysis, we will now design interfaces of a simple system with the following memory map:

| Address Range ($) | Device |
|---|---|
| 0000–00FF | RAM (256 bytes) |
| 6000–6005 | Keyboard matrix |
| 7000–7007 | Display (LEDs) |
| FCOO–FFFF | ROM (1 kbytes) |

Let us start with the *ROM interface* assuming that the ROM is implemented with a 1k × 8 chip with ten address pins (1k = $2^{10}$) and eight data pins. Because a ROM is only read, it does not have a R/$\overline{W}$ pin. Assume that the ROM has one chip select pin CS, which must be active to output ROM data on the data bus. When CS is Off, ROM outputs are tristated to allow other devices to share the data bus with the ROM.

Data pins of the ROM are connected directly to the data bus. Address pins are connected to the ten least significant lines of the address bus (otherwise, the ROM would not implement consecutive memory locations). To determine what is connected to the CS pin, we must formulate the conditions under which the chip is to be selected. Because the ROM must be activated when the CPU is performing a read operation and addressing the memory space allocated to the ROM, the condition for activation of the ROM is

$$CS = (\textit{read operation}) \cdot (\textit{address in ROM's address range})$$

The "read" condition can be expressed as

$$\textit{read} = VMA \cdot R/\overline{W} \cdot \Phi_2$$

but the R/$\overline{W}$ signal can be left out because a ROM does not need it; if a program attempts to write to a ROM, it has no effect.

The "address" condition can be expressed in terms of address bits. Because the ROM is to occupy the top 1k of the address space, its addresses range from \$FC00 to \$FFFF or 11111100 00000000 to 11111111 11111111 in binary. Each address of the form 111111*XX XXXXXXXX* thus selects the ROM. The "address" condition is thus

$$\textit{address} = A_{15} \cdot A_{14} \cdot A_{13} \cdot A_{12} \cdot A_{11} \cdot A_{10}$$

Combining the read and address conditions finally gives

$$CS = VMA \cdot \Phi_2 \cdot A_{15} \cdot A_{14} \cdot A_{13} \cdot A_{12} \cdot A_{11} \cdot A_{10}$$

which can be implemented as in Figure 12.7.

Although this formula is correct, it is, in our case unnecessarily complicated. It can be significantly simplified when we realize that the memory map of our system has large holes. In particular, the ROM is the only device in the upper quarter of the address space (\$C000 to \$FFFF or 1100*XXXX XXXXXXXX* to 1111*XXXX XXXXXXXX*), and no conflict will arise if we let it use all addresses in that area. Because the upper quarter is fully determined by $A_{15} = 1$ and $A_{14} = 1$, we can ignore all address lines except $A_{15}$ and $A_{14}$ and the decoder can thus be reduced to

$$CS = VMA \cdot \Phi_2 \cdot A_{15} \cdot A_{14}$$

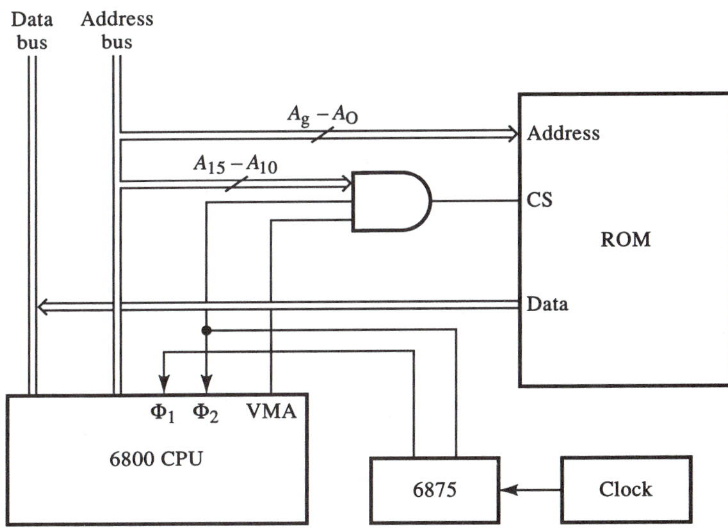


**Figure 12.7.** Interface of a 1k × 8 ROM occupying the top of the address space. The 6875 clock chip converts the row clock signal to properly timed phases $\Phi_1$ and $\Phi_2$.

This formula and the resulting decoder are much simpler then our original solution. Because the decoding formula does not use all address lines, it implements *partial decoding*. Our original approach is called *full decoding*.

Note that if a program tries to access an upper quarter location that is not in the ROM's space, partial decoding will activate the ROM and a data transfer may take place. This is incorrect but because this event occurs only when the program is incorrect (it accesses "unpopulated" addresses), no additional harm is done.

To summarize, full addressing decodes the address bus so that each address has a unique memory location. The size of the recognized address space is thus identical to the size of the implemented ("populated") memory space. In partial addressing, several addresses may refer to the same memory location and the size of the decoded address space is some multiple of the physically implemented space. In our case, the decoder selects the ROM for any address that begins 11. As an example, \$C013, \$D013, \$E013, and \$F013 all select the same memory location whose internal ten-bit ROM address is 0000010011 (the last ten bits of the sixteen-bit address). Partial addressing is possible when the system does not use a block of addresses containing the implemented address space.

It would seem that partial decoding is always superior to full decoding because it simplifies the decoder. In reality, partial decoding does create one problem: It complicates changes in the memory space. As an example, if we decided to increase the size of the ROM in our partially decoded system to 2k, we would have to change the decoder. With full decoding, this would not be necessary.

Let us now design the RAM interface. The principles are the same as for the ROM except that the R/$\overline{W}$ signal from the control bus must now be connected to the R/$\overline{W}$ pin of the RAM chip. The 256 bytes assigned to the RAM cover the address range from 00000000 00000000 to 00000000 11111111, the chip responds to all addresses of the form 00000000 *XXXXXXXX*, and the eight least significant bits of the address bus are thus connected to RAM address pins.

We can again use partial decoding and take advantage of the holes in the address space. As the RAM is the only device in the bottom quarter of the address space (addresses $0000 to 3FFF or 0000*XXXX XXXXXXXX* to 0011*XXXX XXXXXXXX*), the RAM decoder only needs to recognize that the first two bits of the address are 0 and the chip enable signal can thus be simplified to

$$CS = VMA \cdot \Phi_2 \cdot \overline{A_{15}} \cdot \overline{A_{14}}$$

Assume now that the RAM is implemented with two 256 × 4 static RAM chips. Because both chips respond to the same addresses and are activated at the same time (each chip contains one-half of each eight-bit word), address and control lines are connected to them identically. Data pins of the chip that implements the upper half of each word are connected to lines $D_7$ to $D_4$ of the data bus; data pins of the other chip are connected to lines $D_3$ to $D_0$ (Figure 12.8).

This completes the interfacing of the RAM. If we used dynamic RAMs, the interface would also require a refresh circuit.

Finally, we will design interfaces for the two I/O devices. As we know from the previous chapter, I/O interfaces usually have data and status registers or tristateable buffers (possibly embedded in ACIA or PIA chips) whose control is similar to the control of ROM and RAM chips. Decoding I/O interfaces thus consists of finding formulas for chip enable inputs and is, in principle, identical to memory decoding.

Because the 6800 treats I/O as memory, it makes no distinction between addressing I/O, RAM, or ROM. In our memory map, the input device occupies the six consecutive memory locations $6000 to $6005 and the three least significant address bits must thus be connected directly to the interface. For full decoding, we would have to decode all the remaining thirteen address lines but the keyboard is the only device using the address region $6000 to $6FFF (0110111 *XXXXXXXX* to 0110111 *XXXXXXXX*) and its decoder thus only needs to recognize 0110*XXXX XXXXXXXXX*. Only the first four bits of the address must thus be decoded which gives the following formula:

$$CS = VMA \cdot \Phi_2 \cdot \overline{A_{15}} \cdot A_{14} \cdot A_{13} \cdot \overline{A_{12}}$$

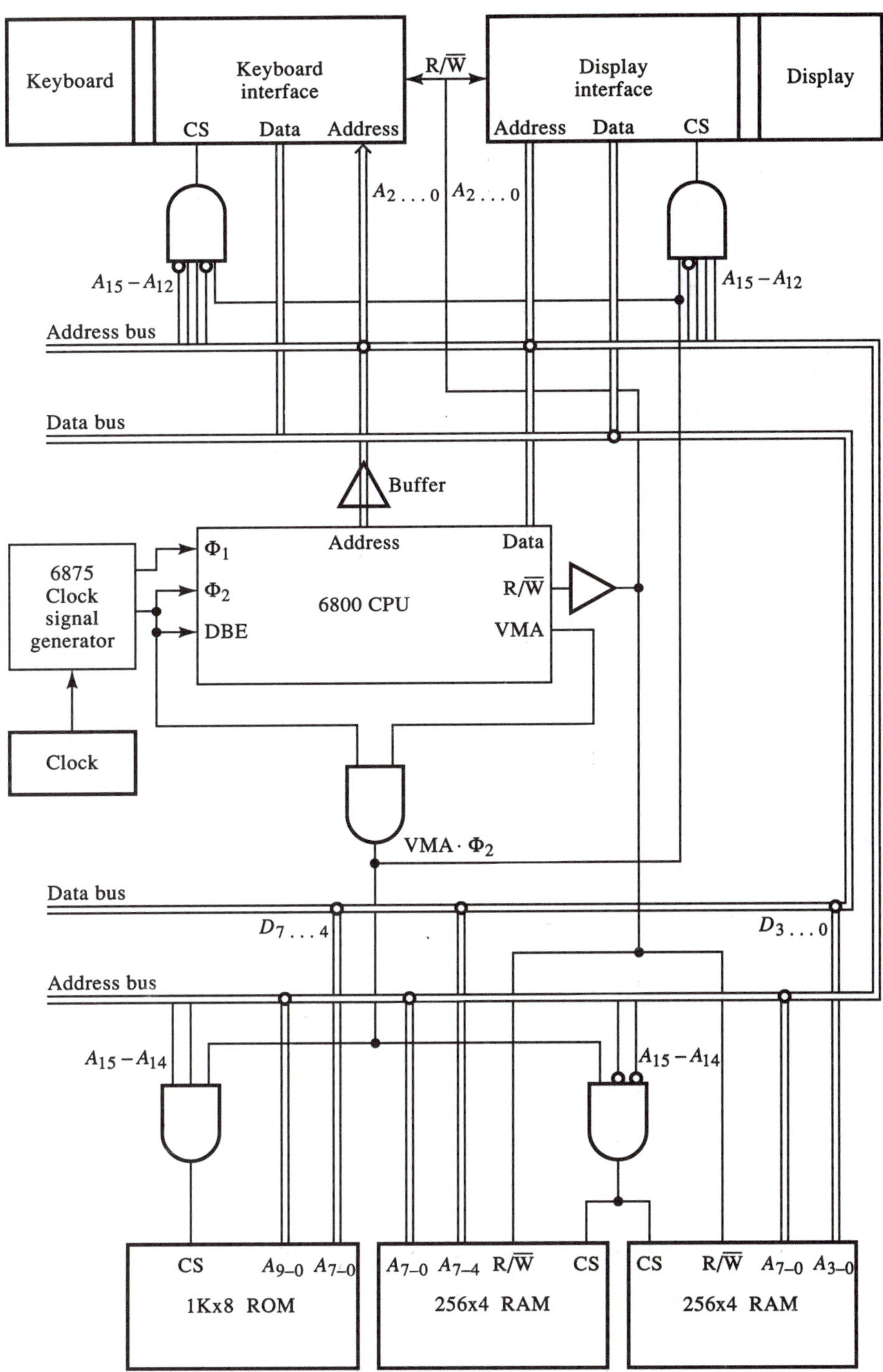


**Figure 12.8.** Complete 6800-based computer.

The display decoder is treated similarly and the corresponding formula is

$$CS = VMA \cdot \Phi_2 \cdot \overline{A_{15}} \cdot A_{14} \cdot A_{13} \cdot A_{12}$$

It is worth noting that the nature of both the keyboard and the display interface is the same and contains data, status, and control registers; in other words, both input and output ports. One should not be led to think that input devices have only input ports or that output devices have only output ports. Consequently, the R/$\overline{\text{W}}$ signal will probably be connected to the interface as well. (Both the ACIA and the PIA chips have R/$\overline{\text{W}}$ inputs.)

The complete system is shown in Figure 12.8. Decoding could also be performed by a decoder chip producing the CS signals for all devices. This would save components over the implementation of individual formulas by individual gates. Note in the diagram that address and R/$\overline{\text{W}}$ lines are buffered because they are used by several devices and 6800 pins have a fan-out of only one TTL load. Data lines are not buffered because the data bus is only used by one device at a time. Buffering of the VMA $\cdot$ $\Phi_2$ signal is performed by the AND gate that calculates the signal. The 6875 clock chip converts a raw clock signal into two accurately timed phases.

This concludes our introduction to interfacing. As we stated at the beginning, the principles apply to any device and to all I/O methods. The only complication that may arise is that peripherals such as relay switches, lights, and motors require more current than logic gates can provide and others, such as RS-232-C lines, work with different voltage levels. In cases like these, CPU signals must be connected to devices that amplify or transform them.

After presenting the principles, we are now ready to examine how they are used in a real computer, the Heathkit ET-3400.

**Exercises**

1. Why are address pins of RAM chips connected to the least significant bits of the address bus?
2. Replace the 1k ROM at the top of memory space in our example with a 2k ROM. Use two 1k × 8 ROMs and compare the changes required in the original design if full and partial addressing are used.
3. How many chips would be saved in our example by using suitable decoders instead of gates?
4. Show that the keyboard and display interfaces in our example do not require $A_{13}$.
5. Formulate a systematic procedure for partial decoding. (*Note:* Consider the result of Exercise 4.)
6. Derive minimal formulas for partial decoding in the following situations:
   a. Output device with address \$B7F1 and empty space \$B000...\$B7FF.
   b. Input device with address \$310 and occupied space 0...\$1FF, \$FC00...\$FFFF.

7. Construct the interface circuits for the previous exercise using only NAND and NOR gates with up to eight inputs. (*Hint*: To obtain large AND functions, remember that DeMorgan's rules imply that a NAND/NOR combination is equivalent to AND, and so on.)
8. Compare the importance of partial decoding when gates or decoders are used.

## 12.4 CASE STUDY—THE HEATHKIT ET-3400 COMPUTER

The ET-3400 Microcomputer Trainer is the first in a series of educational computers produced by Heathkit. Although later models use more recent members of the 6800 family, their structure and software are almost identical.

The ET-3400 is very simple in comparison with computers such as the IBM PC, but it contains most of the elements found in more sophisticated systems. The advantage of its simplicity is that it can be analyzed in detail.

The ET-3400 contains a 6800 CPU, ROM and RAM memory, a seventeen-key keyboard, and six seven-segment displays (Figure 12.9). It also has a breadboard, switches, and LEDs for experiments.

The memory map of the ET-3400 is as follows:

| **Address Range ($)** | **Device** |
|---|---|
| 0000–01FF | Two 256-byte RAM segments |
| C003–C00E | Keyboard |
| C110–C16F | Display |
| FCOO–FFFF | ROM |

The decoder circuit implementing this map (Figure 12.10) uses partial decoding with three 4-to-10 decoder chips connected in series. Formulas for individual decoder outputs in the diagram can be found by proceeding from the address bus towards CS signals or from the end of the decoding chain. Using the first approach, we would first construct formulas describing the outputs of the first decoder, use them to find formulas for outputs of the second decoder, and so on. With the second approach, we start from the enable signals. As an example, the diagram shows that ROM is enabled by

$$\begin{aligned} CS &= CS_0 \cdot \overline{CS_1} \cdot CS_2 \cdot CS_3 \\ &= A_{12} \cdot (\overline{D_1 = 7}) \cdot A_{11} \cdot A_{10} \end{aligned}$$

where $(D_1 = 7)$ denotes active output 7 of decoder $D_1$. Signal $(D_1 = 7)$ is active when the decoder's input signals $(\overline{\text{VMA} \cdot \Phi_2})$, $A_{15}$, $A_{14}$, and $A_{13}$ are 0111 and this can be described by the formula

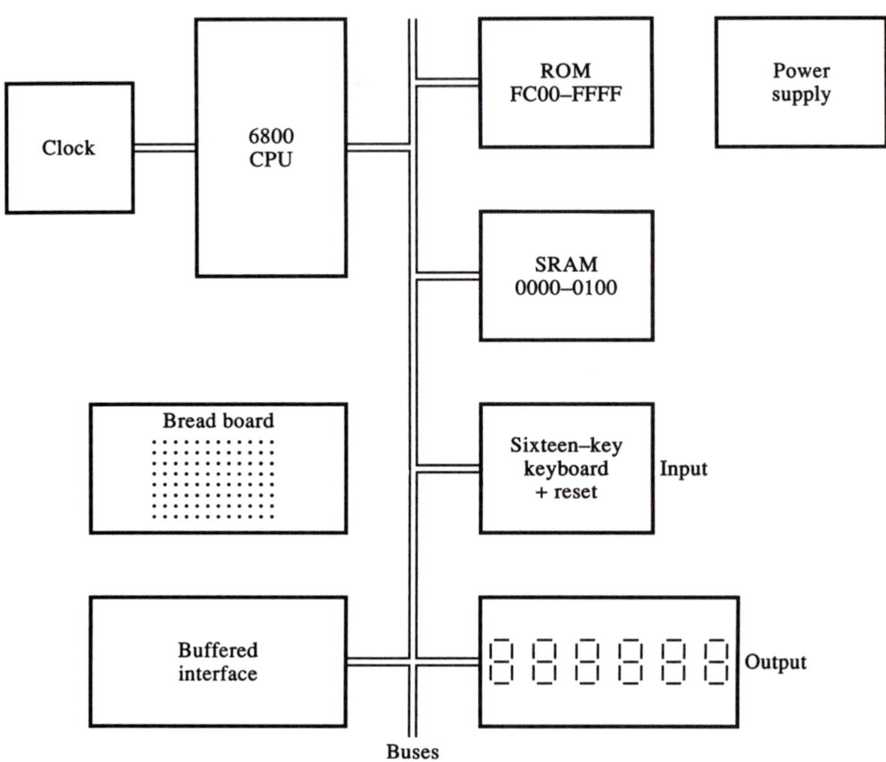


**Figure 12.9.** Block diagram of Heathkit ET-3400.

$$\overline{\overline{VMA \cdot \Phi_2}} \cdot A_{15} \cdot A_{14} \cdot A_{13}$$

or

$$VMA \cdot \Phi_2 \cdot A_{15} \cdot A_{14} \cdot A_{13}$$

Substituting into the original expression gives

$$CS = VMA \cdot \Phi_2 \cdot A_{15} \cdot A_{14} \cdot A_{13} \cdot A_{12} \cdot A_{11} \cdot A_{10}$$

The ROM is thus enabled by all addresses of the form 111111*XX* *XXXXXXXX* which means that it implements address space $FC00 to $FFFF. Because the ROM's ten address pins are connected to address lines $A_9$ to $A_0$, all address lines are used and the decoding is full. This approach is used because the four CS inputs of the ROM provide a built-in logic function and make partial decoding unnecessary.

The *RAM interface* is similar to our example in the previous section and its analysis is left to the reader.

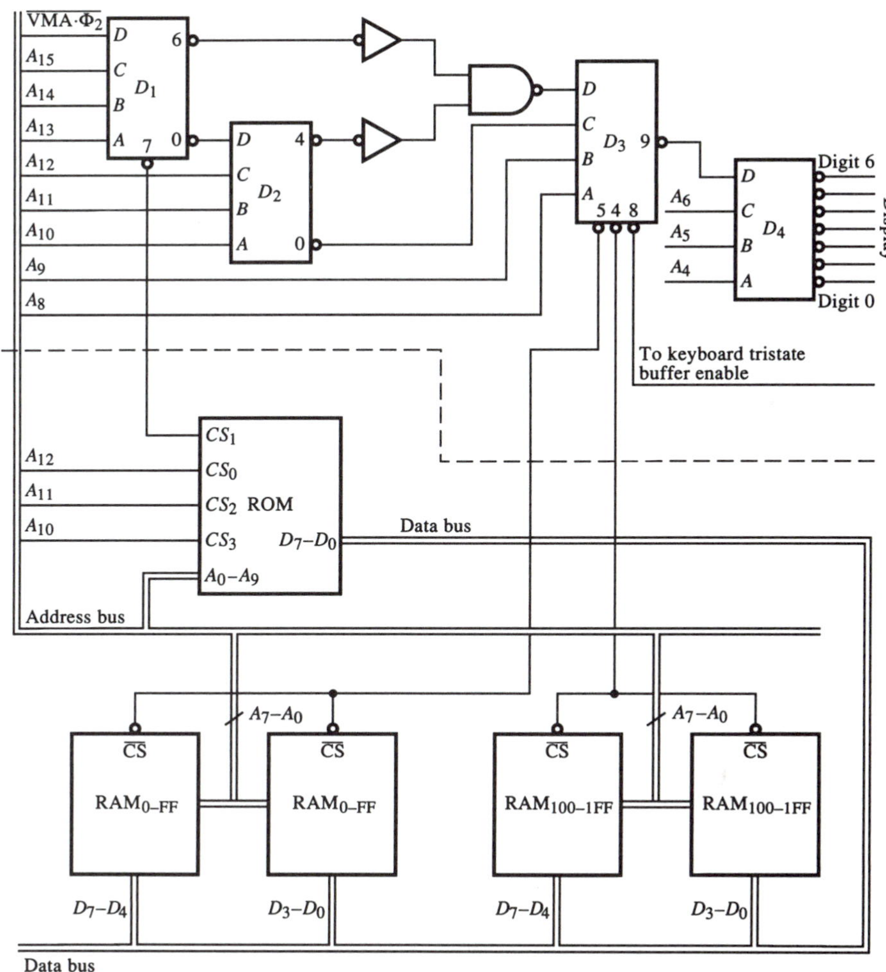


**Figure 12.10.** The ET-3400 decoder (*top*) and memory (*bottom*).

The keyboard of the ET-3400 (Figure 12.11) is a seventeen-key matrix, and the decoding and debouncing of all keys except *RESET* is fully under the control of software stored in the ROM.

The six rows of the keyboard are connected to the data bus by tristate buffers. This is necessary to prevent conflicts between signals from the keyboard and signals from other devices also connected to the bus. The buffer is controlled by output $O_8$ of decoder $D_1$ and is enabled when the CPU issues an LDA instruction whose address begins with C00. The three least significant address bits $A_2$, $A_1$, and $A_0$ select keyboard columns.

As we explained in the section on keyboards, the CPU monitors the keyboard by scanning its columns. It selects a column by placing 0 on its input.

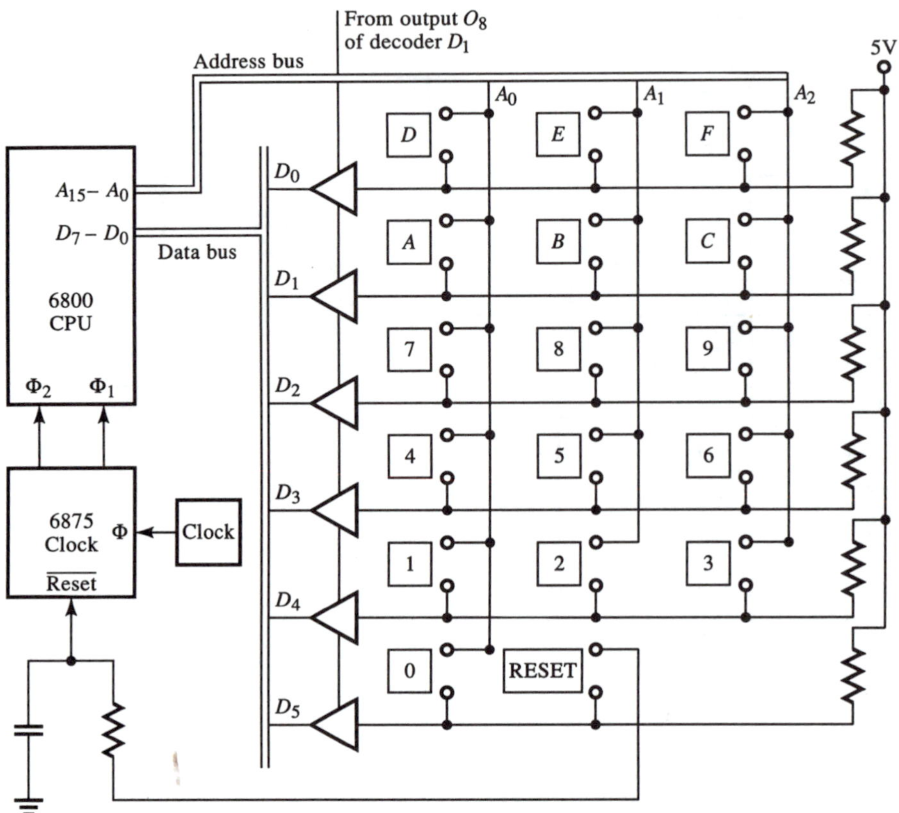


**Figure 12.11.** Hexadecimal keyboard of the ET-3400.

Consequently, addresses that activate individual columns are binary $X110$, $X101$, and $X011$ or hexadecimal 6 or E, 5 or D, and 3 or B. (The first bit is not connected and is thus a don't-care.) When we combine decoding of rows (the tristate buffers) and columns, we find that the three keyboard columns can be read for example by LDAA $C006, LDAB $C005, and LDAA $C003.

As we saw in Chapter 10, the ET-3400 ROM contains subroutines that allow the user to access the keyboard and the display, and to perform other functions. As an example, instead of writing a program to scan the keyboard, the user can call subroutine INCH stored in the ROM. When a program calls INCH, the subroutine waits for a key to be pressed and returns its code in accumulator $A$. This is a simple device driver and we will now explore it in some detail.

The essence of INCH is as follows:

REPEAT
  Scan keyboard {Subroutine ENCODE}

UNTIL key pressed;
Return code of pressed key in accumulator A

Subroutine ENCODE scans the keys using LDAA and LDAB instructions with the column addresses given above. We will not discuss ENCODE but will take a closer look at the rest of INCH.

Although our description captures the essence of keyboard control, the details are slightly more complicated. To see why, consider the following program that reads two keys and displays their codes on the leftmost two digits:

```
JSR REDIS      ; Initialize display
JSR INCH       ; Read first key
JSR OUTHEX     ; Display its value on the first digit
JSR INCH       ; Read second key
JSR OUTHEX     ; Display its value on the second digit
WAI
```

Assume that INCH is implemented according to the algorithm given above. When called the first time, it enters the REPEAT loop and waits until a key is pressed. It then returns to the main program which calls OUTHEX and displays the code. If the CPU clock runs at 1 MHz and if INCH consist of forty instructions taking five machine cycles each, it takes 200 $\mu$sec from the moment the first key is pressed until INCH is called for the second time. Now, the typist probably doesn't release a pressed key within 200 $\mu$sec. The second call of INCH thus finds that the key is still pressed and returns its code again. But this is the same key that was displayed before and the result of the second reading is thus different from what was intended.

To eliminate this problem, the algorithm for INCH must be modified as follows:

```
{First make sure that we do not read a key already processed}
REPEAT
   Scan keyboard
UNTIL key not pressed;
{Now wait for a new key to be pressed}
REPEAT
   Scan keyboard;
UNTIL key pressed;
Return code of pressed key in accumulator A
```

Let us now convert this algorithm to assembly language. To do this, we must know how to communicate with ENCODE. The details of its operation are not important but the basic point is that ENCODE returns 0 in the *C* flag if it finds that no key, or more than one key, is pressed, and 1 if a single key is pressed. The code of the key is returned in accumulator *A*.

With this information, INCH can be formulated as follows:

```
INCH                         ;  First wait for no key
LOOP1       BSR ENCODE
            BCS LOOP1        ;  Repeat if key still pressed
                             ;  Now wait for active key
LOOP2       BSR ENCODE       ;  Check for active key
            BCC LOOP2        ;  Repeat if no key active
            RTS
```

In reality, even this version is not quite correct because it ignores key bounce. As we know, when a key is pressed, the contact closes and opens several times and produces a sequence of Highs and Lows (Figure 12.12). To see why this invalidates our version of INCH, consider again our program that reads two consecutive key closures and displays the digits.

When the program reads the first code and returns to read the second key, INCH waits for the sequence of events: no key pressed, key pressed.

Because it takes only a few microseconds to process the first key activation, the keyboard signal is still oscillating when the program returns to check it for the second key because bouncing can last up to 10 msec. During the bouncing, the program will eventually detect no activity and a pressed key—the same key as before. Thus the CPU will again read the same key. To remove this problem, we can take advantage of the fact that bouncing will not last longer than 10 msec and insert a delay into the INCH subroutine to wait for the bouncing to cease. This is left as an exercise.

More sophisticated keyboards do not require such complicated software because the work is performed by the keyboard controller. Still, typical

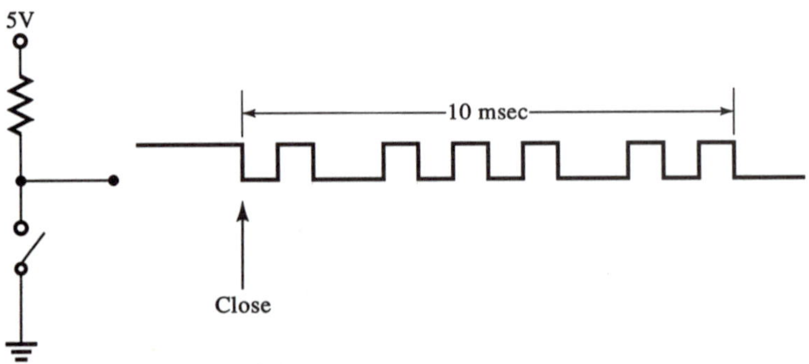


**Figure 12.12.** Key bounce.

keyboard drivers are much more complicated than INCH because they perform many additional functions.

The lesson to be learned is that to write a good device driver, one must understand the intricacies of both the device's operation (in this case, bouncing) and its use (here, the fact that the typist releases the keys slowly).

The display of the ET-3400 (Figure 12.13) consists of six seven-segment digits connected to six 74259 addressable eight-bit latches. Each latch in the 74259 stores the value of one segment of the corresponding digit.

All eight latches of each 74259 share input pin *D* but each internal latch has its own output pin. To turn a segment On or Off, the program selects the appropriate 74259 chip and activates its *EN* pin via the address decoder

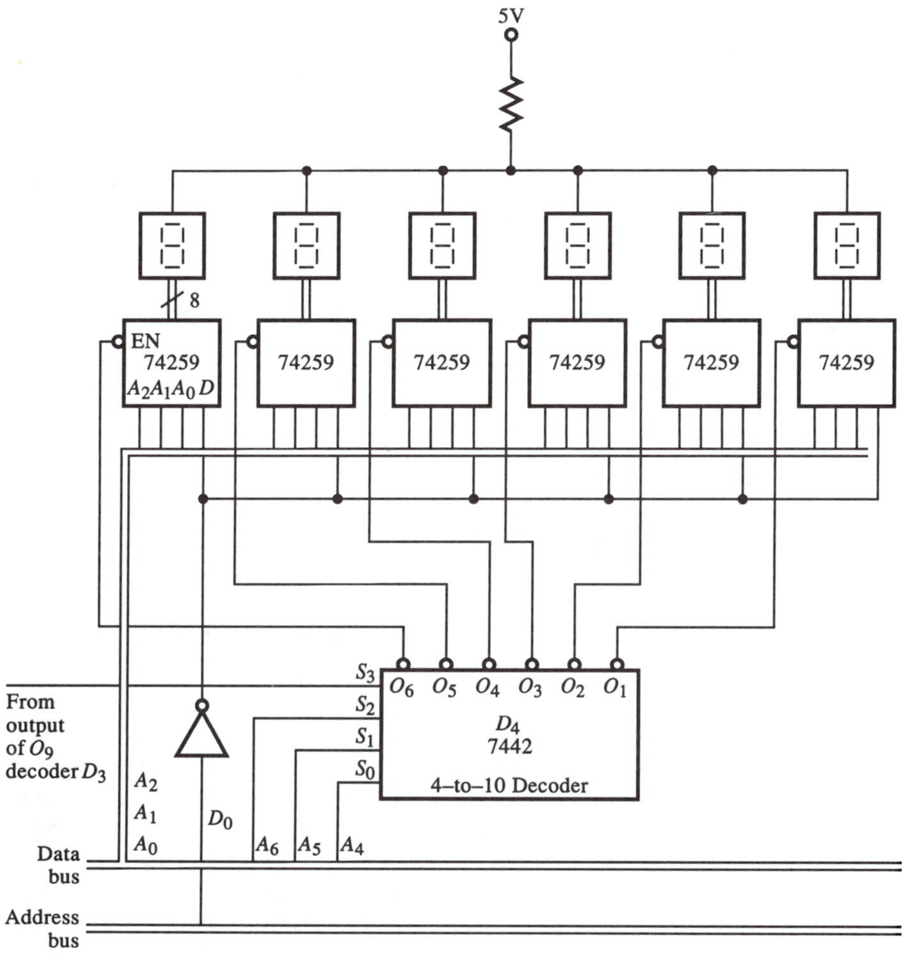


**Figure 12.13.** The ET-3400 display.

(labeled $D_4$ in Figure 12.10), one of the eight latches on the chip via the three 74259 address pins, and places the desired value on the $D$ input via bit $D_0$ of the data bus. The CPU can thus control the patterns stored in the latches and the displayed pattern, by storing 0 or 1 in bit 0 of the accumulator and executing an STA instruction.

Let us now analyze the interface in more detail. Working from a digit back towards the address bus we find that $A_2$, $A_1$, and $A_0$ select a latch corresponding to one of the eight segments on a given digit. The latch—display digit—is selected by decoder $D_4$, which is controlled by bits $A_6$, $A_5$, and $A_4$ of the address bus. Finally, decoder $D_4$ itself is selected by the output of decoder $D_3$ and the enabling address can be traced to \$C1. Combining all this information, we can interpret display address \$C1*XY* as follows: Address \$C1 selects the display decoder, *X* selects digit number *X* (the leftmost digit has number 6, the rightmost digit has number 1), and *Y* selects the segment. Segment numbers are 7 for *DP* (decimal point), 6 for *a*, and so on. As an example, instruction

```
STAA $C140
```

writes bit $D_0$ of accumulator *A* to segment 0 (*g*) of display 4 (third digit from the left). To determine whether a segment is turned On by $D_0 = 0$ or $D_0 = 1$, note that bit $D_0$ of the data bus is inverted before it enters the addressable register so that 1 is stored as 0, and 0 as 1. The seven-segment display uses a common anode arrangement, which means that 0 turns a segment On and 1 turns it Off. The value of $D_0$ is thus essentially inverted twice before it reaches the segment and consequently $D_0 = 1$ turns a segment On and $D_0 = 0$ turns if Off.

Because the interface does not use all address lines, the display decoding is partial, just as for the keyboard. Several different addresses may thus be used to access the same segment.

As an example of display control, the following instructions turn segment *b* of the leftmost digit On:

```
LDAA $01      ;  Rightmost bit D0=1 to turn segment On
STAA $C165    ;  Write to appropriate latch
```

The control of individual segments is the basis of all ET-3400 output. To display a letter or a digit, we must load an accumulator with the desired bit pattern and execute a loop in which the successive latches are addressed one after another and the accumulator rotated to move individual bits into position $D_0$ for display. Subroutine OUTCH in ET-3400's ROM performs just this operation. It displays the pattern stored in accumulator *A* on the digit whose address is in memory location *DIGADD* = \$00F0. Before the call, the value in *DIGADD* must be set to the address of segment *DP* in the selected display.

To conclude our description of the ET-3400, Figure 12.14 shows the diagram of its CPU circuit. (One can obtain the complete diagram of the ET-3400 with the exception of the power supply by combining all our partial diagrams.) Note that although the ET-3400 does not use every 6800 control signal, all are available for experiments via connectors. Some are tied to a suitable voltage level so as not to disturb the CPU when they are not controlled by an external circuit.

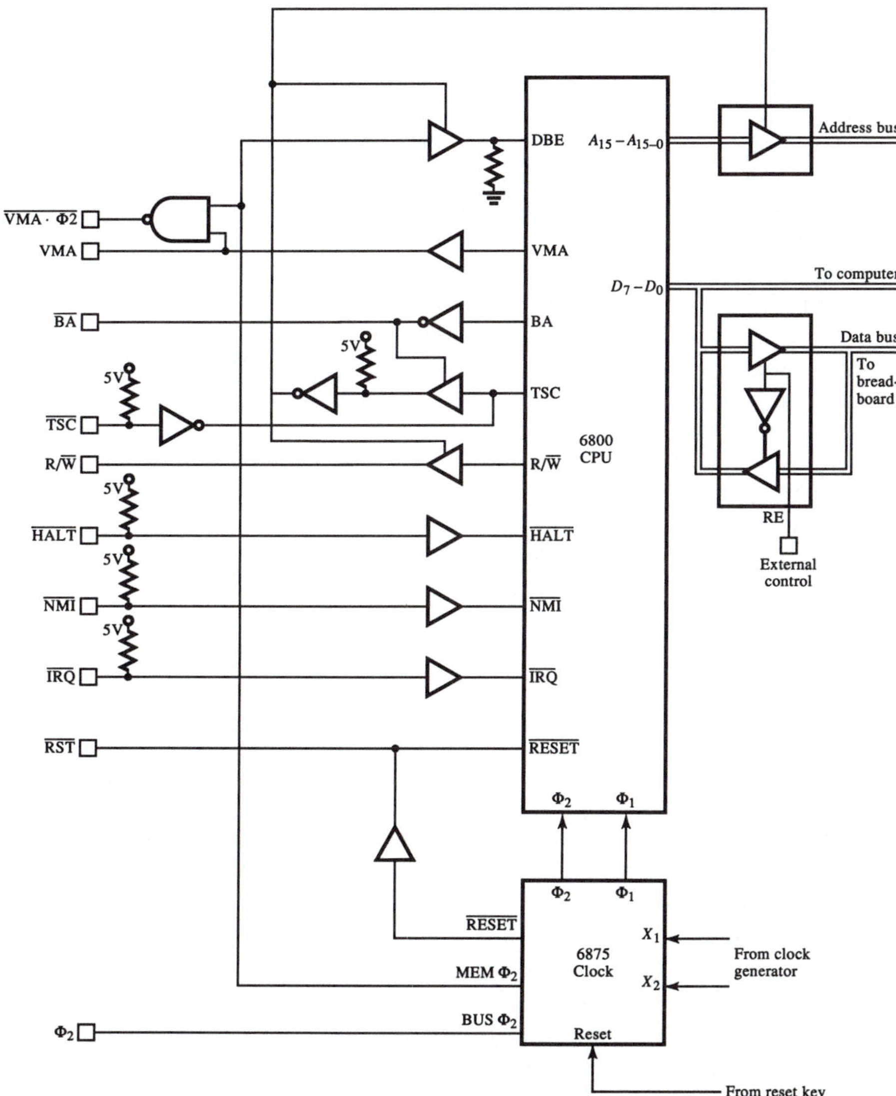


**Figure 12.14.** Control processing unit circuit of the ET-3400.

As an example, the $\overline{\text{TSC}}$ (tristate control) external input that controls the state of the CPU's address and R/$\overline{\text{W}}$ pins is connected to 5 V, or logic 1, through an inverter. If this input is not connected to an external voltage, $\overline{\text{TSC}}$ is High, the logic value of *TSC* is thus logic 0, and as a result the address and R/$\overline{\text{W}}$ pins are not tristated. If an external voltage is connected to the $\overline{\text{TSC}}$ connector, its level controls the state of address and R/$\overline{\text{W}}$ CPU pins. When the external signal is High, the situation is as before and address and R/$\overline{\text{W}}$ pins are not tristated. When the external signal is Low, it pulls $\overline{\text{TSC}}$ to Low voltage level; the TSC input of the CPU is thus High and the address bus and R/$\overline{\text{W}}$ pins of the CPU are tristated.

The address bus, R/$\overline{\text{W}}$, and some other control outputs of the CPU are buffered to increase fan-out. The buffers are controlled by the inverse of the signal controlling the TSC input of the 6800; the external TSC signal also governs DBE (data bus enable). Thus, by controlling the external TSC signal one controls the state of all CPU outputs to the system bus.

Note also the transceiver connected to the data bus to allow the connection of additional devices. Its state is controlled by the read enable signal RE. In an experiment using this interface, RE would be produced by a decoder designed to recognize the device's address and control signals. The decoder would be constructed along the principles explained in the previous section. Our diagram contains some additional signals, such as NMI and IRQ; these will be explained shortly.

## Exercises

1. What are the advantages and disadvantages of implementing the reset vector with a switch rather than storing it in a ROM? Draw a diagram showing the switch connections and decoding.
2. Find expressions for signals that enable the individual outputs of the decoder of the ET-3400.
3. Design a minimal decoder for a 256-byte RAM added to the system in address region $10*XX*.
4. Repeat Exercise 3 for an output device that has been allocated addresses $A000 to $A00F.
5. Show how the decoder and the RAM from Exercise 4 would be connected to the ET-3400. Could one use the existing decoder?
6. Write and test subroutine ENCODE.
7. Write and test subroutine INCH.
8. Most typists do not completely release a key before pressing another one. What effect does this have on INCH?
9. Write a program that measures how long a key is pressed.
10. Draw a timing diagram illustrating the operation of ENCODE.
11. Write and test subroutine OUTCH to display a bit pattern stored in accumulator *A*.
12. Write and test subroutine OUTHEX to display a hexadecimal digit

whose code is stored in accumulator *A*. Use a table with segment patterns and table lookup.

13. Show how a ROM could be used to implement the decoder circuit of the ET-3400. What are the advantages and disadvantages of this approach?

## 12.5 PARALLEL AND SERIAL INTERFACES

Because most peripherals communicate with the CPU using a standard serial or a parallel interface, interfaces similar to the RS-232-C and the Centronics are built into most computers. Adding a new peripheral then becomes a matter of connecting the peripheral and the computer by a cable, and no interface needs to be designed and built. In this section, we will describe how serial and parallel interfaces could be implemented on a 6800-based computer.

### Parallel Interfaces

As we have already indicated, a simple Centronics parallel interface can be implemented with the 6821 PIA. One of the PIA's eight-bit ports would be assigned to data lines, the other to control and status lines. In addition to the PIA, the parallel interface would contain a decoder of the kind described in the previous section and a cable connector. The decoder could either be designed to recognize a specific fixed address range, or its address could be selectable by jumpers (relocatable wired connections) or DIP switches.

One would use the first approach (fixed address range) if the device driver routine was written for a fixed address. The second approach (selectable range) would be necessary if a whole memory region were allocated for I/O devices and the addresses were not fixed. In this case, which is a common arrangement on personal computers, users can select different combinations of peripherals; thus their interfaces cannot have fixed addresses and instead must provide a means for address selection. We will now design such an interface.

Assume that the address region allocated to I/O devices is from \$6000 to \$60FF and the rest of the \$6000 to \$6FFF range is not used. Assume also that the third hexadecimal digit is to be used as the address of the device card, and that the last hexadecimal digit will select a port on the card itself. Add-on devices can thus use any address of the form 0110*XXXX YYYYZZZZ*, where *X* is a don't-care (allowing partial decoding) and the *YYYY* part determines the address of the card. The *ZZZZ* part is the internal address used, for example, to address internal PIA registers on our parallel interface.

The *YYYY* part of the address is to be selectable by switches on the card. As an example, the four switches corresponding to the *Y*s in the address could be positioned to select card addresses in the region \$6000–\$600F, or \$6010–\$601F.

From this specification, we can conclude that the device select signal is

$$DS = VMA \cdot \overline{A_{15}} \cdot A_{14} \cdot A_{13} \cdot \overline{A_{12}} \cdot Y_7 \cdot Y_6 \cdot Y_5 \cdot Y_4$$

where $Y_i$ is either $A_i$ or $\overline{A_i}$, depending on the position of switch $DIP_i$. Phase $\Phi_2$ does not appear in the formula because it is connected directly to the $E$ input of the PIA. When applying the $DS$ formula to select the PIA, we must note that the PIA is selected when $CS_0$, $CS_1$, and $\overline{CS_2} = 1$. This simplifies the decoder because some of the AND operations can be performed inside the PIA.

For each bit in the $YYYY$ part of the address, we need a circuit to select $A_i$ or $\overline{A_i}$ and this can best be done with XOR as

$$A_i \text{ XOR } 0 = A_i \qquad A_i \text{ XOR } 1 = \overline{A_i}$$

One input of the XOR gate can thus be connected to $A_i$ and the other to a switch, producing 0 or 1 (Figure 12.15). The switch is set by the user to assign the desired address to the circuit.

This circuit constitutes the hardware part of the interface. In operation, the desired behavior of the parallel interface is obtained by initializing the PIA before an I/O operation. The PIA can be programmed to work in several operating modes, which makes the interface very flexible.

As an example of a commercial parallel interface, consider the IBM printer adapter card. This card uses a twenty-five pin connector and responds to three input and two output instructions from the computer. These instructions can write or read data via the card, program the adapter, and read the status. One of the programmable features is the option to send an interrupt signal to the CPU when the printer sends an ACKNLG pulse.

## Exercises

1. What is the maximum number of internal addresses available to an add-on device in our example?
2. How many devices such as the one that we designed can be installed in our system?
3. Change the interface assuming that the I/O space is from \$8000H to \$8400, that up to sixteen add-on devices are possible, and that each device can use the last six bits of the address.
4. Show the position of the switches required to address the interface as \$6*X*80–\$6*X*8F.
5. Use Appendix 5 to write a PIA initialization program for an Epson printer assuming that the interface is addressed as in Exercise 3.
6. Write the data transfer part of a simple printer driver under the assumptions given in previous exercises. Ignore printer error conditions.

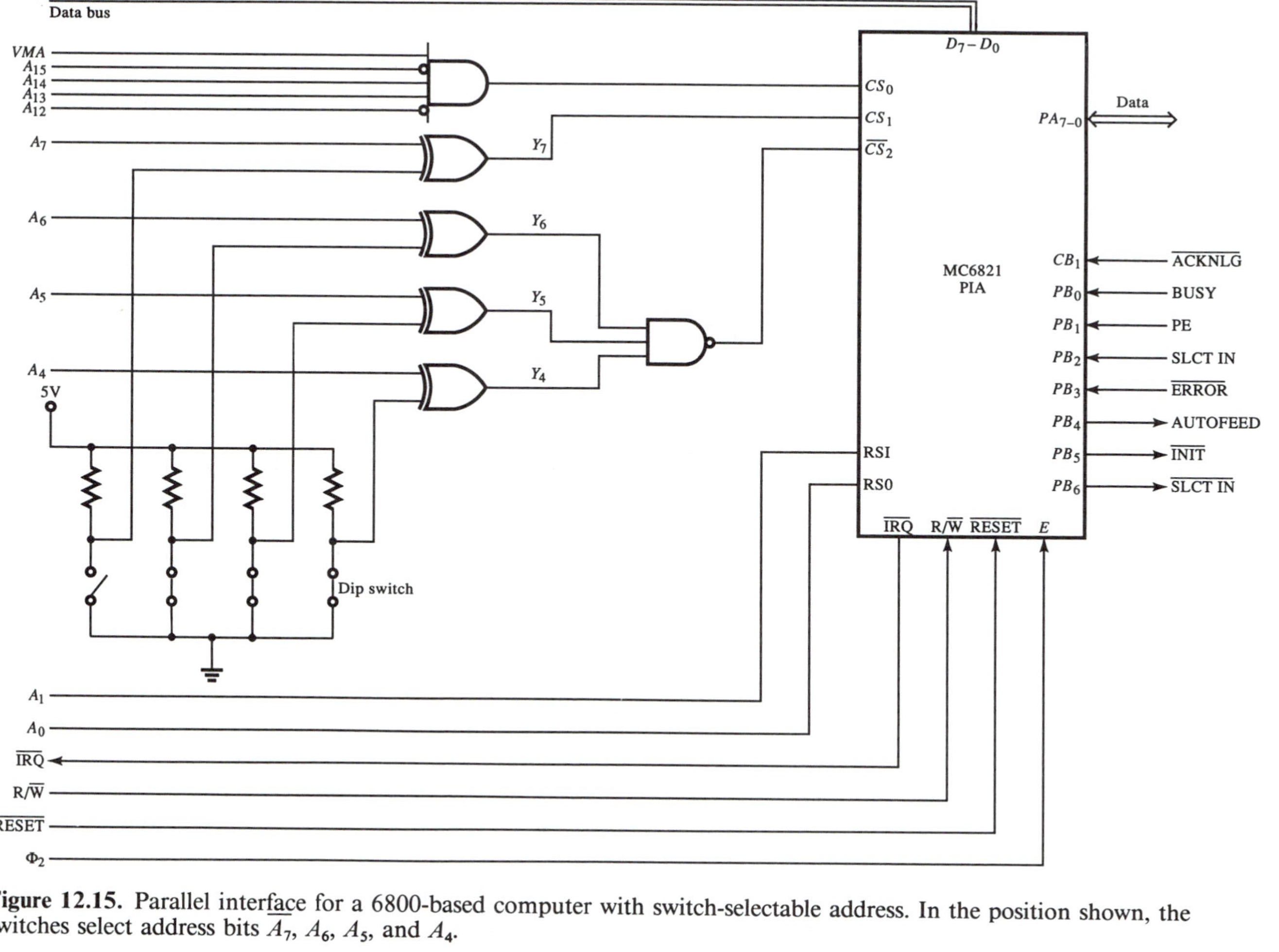


**Figure 12.15.** Parallel interface for a 6800-based computer with switch-selectable address. In the position shown, the switches select address bits $\overline{A_7}$, $A_6$, $A_5$, and $A_4$.

### Serial Interfaces

Most serial interfaces use the RS-232 standard and consist of three parts: a decoder; a TTL-level parallel/serial converter, such as the 6850 ACIA; and a converter between TTL and RS-232 voltage levels. If the I/O address space is allocated as in the previous section, the formula for the decoder is the same as for the parallel interface, and the complete circuit is as in Figure 12.16. (Jumpers are shown instead of switches.) Conversion between 0-V/5-V TTL levels and −12-V/+12-V RS-232 levels is performed by the 1488 and 1489 chips.

As an example of a commercial serial interface, the IBM asynchronous communications adapter has the following features: It uses a twenty-five pin connector and provides a choice between current loop and RS-232-level communication. The operating mode and the address assigned to the card are selectable by jumpers, with two address choices because MS-DOS (the operating system of the IBM PC) allows two "COM" (serial communication) devices.

The heart of the card is the Intel 8250 asynchronous communication element, a chip similar to the ACIA. The card has its own clock and can be programmed for transmission rates 50–9600 Baud and for various code formats. It also provides modem control functions. An IBM synchronous communications adapter card using a USART (universal synchronous/asynchronous receiver/transmitter) chip is also available.

### Exercises

1. What is the device select formula for the circuit in Figure 12.16?
2. (a) Show the jumper setting that will select interface addresses \$6E00–\$6EFF.
   (b) Use Appendix 5 to write a program to initialize the interface for the following parameters: Transfer rate = clock DIV 64, code length eight bits, odd parity, one stop bit, no interrupts.
3. What should be the frequency of the ACIA clock input in Exercise 2 to obtain a transfer rate of 330 bps?
4. Write a device driver for the serial card. The program should consist of two subroutines: one which tests that a word has been received and loads it into accumulator *A*, another which waits until the ACIA is ready to transmit and then outputs the contents of accumulator *A* to the ACIA.

## 12.6 INPUT/OUTPUT STRATEGIES—AN INTRODUCTION

We are now ready to deal with the software aspects of I/O operations. As we have seen, different I/O situations require different I/O strategies because peripherals have a wide range of speeds and urgency of servicing, and require the involvement of the CPU to a varying extent.

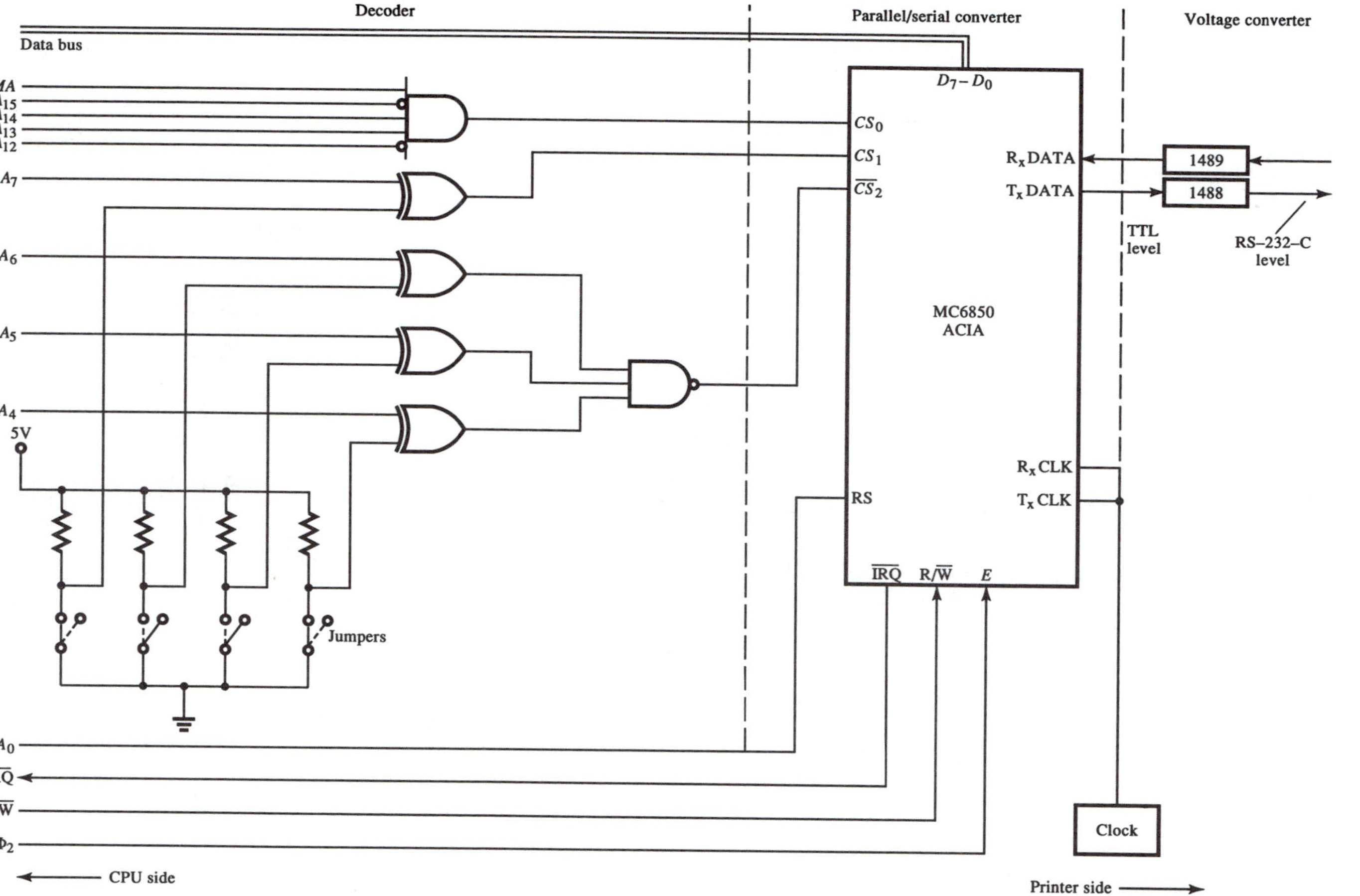


**Figure 12.16.** Serial interface with jumper-selectable address. In the setting shown, jumpers select address bits $A_7$, $\overline{A_6}$, $\overline{A_5}$, and $A_4$.

The most obvious way to perform an I/O operation is to place it under complete CPU control. This method is usually called *programmed I/O*. An example of a situation in which it is appropriate is output to the ET-3400 display as performed by subroutine OUTCH, which simply sends data to the address assigned to the display. The characteristic properties of programmed I/O are that the operation is initiated and performed by the program, and that the program does not test whether the peripheral is ready or not.

Subroutine INCH handles the ET-3400 keyboard in a slightly different fashion. As we have seen, when INCH is called it does not merely read a key and return its code; it enters a loop and waits for the sequence: no active key, active key. When a key is pressed, INCH enters a debouncing loop, tests again, and then translates the received data into a code and returns to the calling program. This is an example of *polling*. In polled I/O, the program tests whether the device is ready for the operation. If it is, the I/O operation is performed; otherwise, the program either enters a loop and waits until the device is ready or returns to report a failure and continues with other tasks.

As an example of a situation that is marginally suitable for polling, consider the problem of sending data to a printer with a large data buffer. When a program requires output, it fills a data buffer in the computer's memory with the data and calls the printer driver. The driver program waits until the printer is ready, sends a block of data to the printer buffer, waits until the printer consumes it, sends another block, and so on, until all data is transmitted:

```
REPEAT
  REPEAT                        {Polling}
    Read printer status signal  {Polling}
  UNTIL printer ready;          {Polling}
  Send data to printer buffer
UNTIL all data transmitted
```

This approach is fine if the CPU has nothing else to do but is unacceptable otherwise because the printer is relatively slow, and waiting for it wastes a good deal of CPU time. Most word processing programs, for example, would allow editing while the printer is printing, and service the printer only when it indicates that it is ready for a new line. This approach, in which the I/O device sends a signal to interrupt CPU operation when it needs its attention, is called *interrupt-driven I/O*.

An interrupt-driven printer interface could be implemented by connecting the printer's BUSY or ACKNLG line to a PIA and programming the PIA to send an interrupt request to a special CPU control pin whenever BUSY or ACKNLG are activated. An interrupt-driven printer driver could be described as follows:

```
REPEAT
  Execute background program until an interrupt arrives
    Then send next line of output;
  Return to interrupted program;
UNTIL no more output available
```

Interrupts form the operational basis of all but the most primitive computers. It is important to realize that interrupt-driven operation does not increase the speed of I/O. The difference between interrupt-driven and program-driven operation is not in how the operation is performed but in how it is triggered. In programmed and polled I/O, the stimulus comes from the program; in interrupt-driven I/O, the stimulus arrives from the device and this improves the utilization of the CPU by removing the need for a polling loop.

Another example of interrupt-driven operation is disk I/O. Because finding the desired location on the disk may take 100 msec or more, the best way to access the disk is for the CPU to issue a SEEK command to the disk controller, continue execution of the current program, and return to the disk when its controller generates an interrupt to indicate that it has positioned the head.

Although a printer interrupt and a disk controller interrupt operate on the same principle, there is a major difference in their servicing. While the CPU can easily transmit the data required by the printer, data transfer between the disk controller and memory is usually faster than the CPU can manage. To illustrate the problem, assume that the CPU is to transfer a 256-byte sector from the disk (address DISK) to memory locations \$1000–\$10FF (addresses *FIRST* and *LAST*), and that a byte is transmitted as soon as it is read from the disk. This can be accomplished as follows:

```
LDX #FIRST
LOOP LDAA DISK     ;  Five machine cycles
STAA 0,X           ;  Six machine cycles
INX                ;  Four machine cycles
CPX #LAST+1        ;  Three machine cycles
BNE LOOP           ;  Four machine cycles
```

One pass through the loop requires twenty-two machine cycles and takes 22 $\mu$sec with a 1-MHz clock. The program can thus transfer at most 45,000 bytes per second, which is too slow for a hard disk drive.

The problem is not that the memory cannot handle the speed; its access time is probably 100 nsec and it can thus accommodate transfer rates up to 10 Mbytes per second. The bottleneck is the CPU's handling of the data transfer.

For one thing, the data must pass through accumulator *A* even though the transfer is between the drive and memory. Also, the processes of updating the address by incrementing *X*, and testing the address in the index register take time. Finally, it is very time consuming to fetch and execute each individual instruction. This analysis suggests that the way to increase the speed of the data transfer is to bypass the CPU and transfer data directly between the I/O device and the memory, and to control the data transfer by a hardware controller rather than a program. This method is called *direct memory access* or DMA.

Direct memory access is the fastest possible I/O method and is used to communicate with disk drives, display RAMs, printers that require a lot of data (bit-mapped graphics), and similar devices. There is, of course, a price to be paid for the increased speed: Unlike the CPU-driven methods, DMA requires a special DMA controller (DMAC) to take over the system bus for the duration of the transfer.

Implementation of I/O by DMA does not exclude the simultaneous use of other I/O methods. In fact, our example shows that the DMA operation is usually triggered by an interrupt from the device that requires the transfer. Moreover, the response to the interrupt may involve polling to determine which device issued the interrupt and which function is requested by the interrupt.

The I/O strategies we have discussed can be summarized as follows:

| I/O Method | Properties |
|---|---|
| Programmed | Slow, requires complete CPU control, assumes that I/O device is available. Only a basic interface is required. |
| Polled | Slow, requires complete CPU control to test whether the device is available. Only a basic interface is required. |
| Interrupt driven | Slightly slower than programmed I/O because of interrupt request overhead, but does not require full CPU involvement. CPU must be able to handle interrupt signals. Interface is usually more complicated. |
| DMA | Very fast. Excludes CPU from control over the system bus. Requires special controller. |

After this brief introduction, we will now show how these I/O strategies can be implemented on the 6800 CPU.

## Exercises

1. Give examples of I/O operations and recommend suitable strategies.
2. Classify the I/O programs given in this and the previous chapter.

## 12.7 PROGRAMMED AND POLLED I/O

Programmed I/O is equivalent to memory access and we have already explained it using the OUTCH subroutine as an example.

We demonstrated the principle of polling on the INCH subroutine, which waits for an active key and returns its code. As another example, let us examine how a 6800-based computer could send data to a terminal using an RS-232 interface. On the CPU side, the send and receive data lines from the terminal are connected to an ACIA chip, which is connected to the data bus of the CPU (Figure 12.17).

Our system will use the convention that when a program needs to display data on the terminal, it stores the text and a "sentinel" code in the computer's display buffer. The sentinel is a special character that indicates the end of the text. (We will use *ETX*, which is ASCII code 03.) The display buffer is a memory area allocated to hold the data before it is sent to the terminal. When the data is in the buffer, the program calls the terminal driver routine, which transfers the buffer to the terminal.

The driver's job is to send the contents of the buffer to the ACIA one byte at a time. The ACIA converts each code to serial form and transmits it to the terminal. Writing to the ACIA requires polling because serial transmission is slow and the CPU must continue testing the ACIA until it is ready for the next code. (An alternative is to use interrupts.) The subroutine could be as follows:

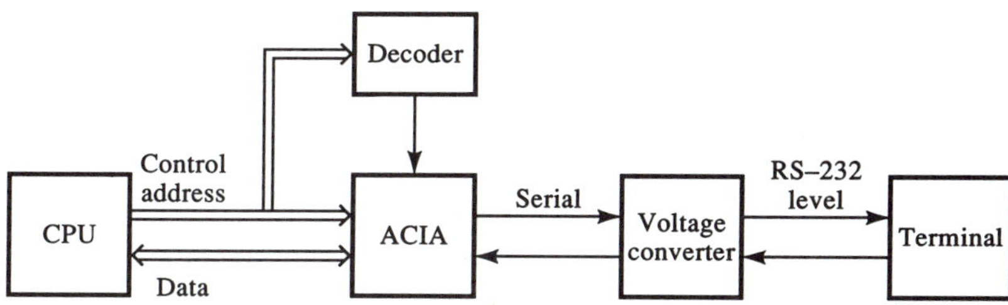


**Figure 12.17.** Block diagram of a terminal-CPU interface.

```
TERM                      ; Send the contents of the text buffer to
                          ; the terminal
                          ; First save registers A and X used by the
                          ; subroutine
                          ; So that they can be restored to original
                          ; values on exit
        PSHA              ; CRT_B is the address of the buffer
                          ; CRT is ACIA's data port
        STX TEMP          ; STATUS is ACIA's status port
                          ; TEMP is an auxiliary location
                          ; Now transfer the text buffer
        LDX #CRT_B        ; Load address of start of text buffer
LOOP    LDAA O,X          ; Load character from buffer
        CMPA #ETX         ; Is it the sentinel?
        BNE NEXT          ; If not, send it
        PULA              ; If yes, end of text,
        LDX TEMP          ; restore registers
        RTS               ; and return from driver
NEXT    LDAB #READY       ; Load "ACIA ready" pattern
                          ; For testing and poll
POLL    CMPB,STATUS       ; Compare "ready" pattern
                          ; With ACIA status
        BNE POLL          ; If the ACIA is not ready,
                          ; repeat test
        STAA CRT          ; ACIA ready, send the code
                          ; to its output port
        INX               ; Get ready for the next character
        BRA LOOP          ; Repeat for the next character
```

## Exercises

1. In a burglar alarm system controlled by a 6800 CPU eight doors are connected to switches. One of the functions of the system is to display the status of the doors on LEDs. Draw a diagram of the system and write a loop that continuously checks door positions and displays them on eight

LEDs. The eight bits of the door status port have address *DOOR*, the eight bits of the LED output port are at address *LED*. Which I/O strategy is used?

2. One of the functions of an industrial controller is to activate a motor if the four rightmost or the four leftmost control switches are On. If all eight switches are On, the controller stops the motor. If none of the switches is On, the controller blinks an LED display by turning on and off odd- and then even-numbered LEDs. Write a program to implement these functions. The switch input is at address *SWITCH*, the LED port at address *LED*, and the motor is controlled by the rightmost bit of output port *MOTOR*.
3. The simplest music generators use a speaker controlled by a series of pulses from the computer. The higher the pulse frequency, the higher the pitch of the tone. Write a music generator that works by reading tone descriptions from a "tune buffer" and converting them into a sequence of pulses of appropriate frequency and duration. Each tone is described by the code of the note and its duration. Use table lookup to generate tones from codes.
4. Write a program to output data in serial form at 330 Baud with one start and two stop bits without using an ACIA. The code to be transmitted is in memory location *DATA*, the output line is connected to bit 0 of port *LINE*. (This and other functions are automatically performed by the ACIA.) What is the maximum Baud rate at which a 6800 CPU with a 1-MHz clock can perform serial transmission?
5. Write a program to initialize the ACIA for the example in the text and find the value of the *READY* code.
6. To move the cursor to a new display line, programs usually insert a carriage return into the output text. Most terminals, however, require carriage return *CR* and linefeed *LF* to go to the start of a new line. Modify the driver program in this section to replace *CR* with (*CR* and *LF*).
7. Modify the ACIA program in the text to halt and jump to an error routine if the ACIA is not ready within 1 sec after the first test of its status.
8. What does the CMP status instruction in our TERM program do? Could the program be simplified if the "ready-to-transmit" bit was stored in a different position of the status register of the ACIA?
9. Design an input interface with status and data registers so that the following functions are automatically performed: When the input device stores data in the data register, the "data-ready" bit of the status register is set. When the CPU reads the data port, the data-ready bit is automatically cleared. Note that this is one of the functions performed by the PIA and the ACIA.
10. Describe how an MUX could be used to handle several slow I/O devices. Does this arrangement have any advantages?

## 12.8 INTERRUPT DRIVEN I/O

Interrupt driven I/O is used when the CPU cannot be dedicated to the I/O task where it would waste time in the polling loop. The steps in interrupt-driven I/O (Figure 12.18) are as follows:

When a peripheral device requires attention, it activates an interrupt signal to the CPU. (On the 6800, IRQ is active Low.)

The CPU

Completes the current instruction

Saves all information necessary for later resumption of the original program

Executes the *interrupt handler* (a program that locates the interrupting device, identifies the requested operation, and performs it)

Restores the saved information

Resumes execution of the interrupted program.

Some of these steps are performed automatically by the CPU hardware and others by software; the part executed by hardware varies from one CPU to another.

In two important aspects, the CPU's response to an interrupt is identical to a subroutine jump: Both break the linear order of execution in order to jump to another code sequence and then return to the original program. The main difference is that a subroutine jump is triggered by software (an instruction) whereas a jump to the code that services the interrupt is triggered by hardware (an interrupt signal).

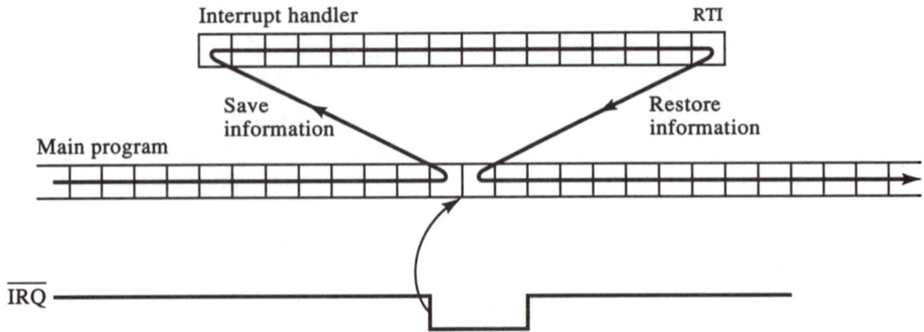


**Figure 12.18.** Interrupt sequence.

In light of their similarity, it is fair to say that an interrupt is essentially a hardware-triggered subroutine jump. In fact, most CPUs have a "jump-to-interrupt" or "software-interrupt" instruction that can access interrupt handlers as if they were subroutines. We will see examples of this later.

Because the transfer to an interrupt routine is triggered by a signal from a device that is not synchronized with the CPU, its arrival is unpredictable. The program from which the jump is made thus cannot prepare for it and the CPU must be able to find the destination address (the start of the interrupt handler) by itself. Central processing units deal with this problem differently and some possibilities are as follows:

The opcode of the first instruction of the interrupt handler is stored in a fixed memory location. This is too restrictive.

The address of the interrupt handler is stored in a fixed memory location. When the CPU is interrupted, it gets the address of the start of the interrupt handler (the *interrupt vector*) from this location and continues execution from there.

This approach is quite flexible as the interrupt routine can be stored anywhere, and is not difficult to implement. It is used on the 6800 and its principle is the same as for the RESET sequence. (Signal RESET is essentially a special kind of interrupt.)

In response to the interrupt, the CPU outputs a special "interrupt-acknowledge" signal and the interrupting device puts the address of the start of its interrupt handler on the data bus. The CPU then loads it into *PC*. This method is known as *vectored interrupt* and it is very practical when there are several possible interrupt sources.

A factor that complicates interrupt handling is that most computers have more than one device capable of producing an interrupt. Because the devices are independent, one can generate an interrupt while the other's interrupt is being serviced. It is even possible that several interrupts arrive simultaneously. Because the CPU can handle only one device at a time, this creates new problems: Which of several interrupting devices should be serviced first? Should an interrupt be allowed to interrupt an interrupt handler? If not, what happens to the new interrupt? If yes, will the nesting of interrupts cause any problems? We will examine each of these questions in turn.

To make it possible to decide the order in which interrupts should be serviced, competing interrupts must be assigned priorities to reflect their relative importance.

When we examine situations under which multiple interrupts can be activated simultaneously, we find that some interrupts should be interruptible but others should not. If, for example, a DMA controller generates an interrupt while a printer interrupt handler is executing, the printer handler should be suspended and the DMA interrupt allowed to proceed because it is more urgent. If, on the other hand, the DMA handler is executing and a printer interrupt arrives, the CPU should ignore the printer until the DMA interrupt handler is finished.

To provide control over the interruptibility of individual handlers, most CPUs have at least two interrupt inputs: maskable and nonmaskable. *Maskable* interrupts may be disabled (masked) by hardware or by special instructions to protect interrupt routines from interruption. *Nonmaskable* interrupts are always enabled. Critical signals, such as power-down warnings, are connected to the nonmaskable line; others are connected to the maskable line. Information about whether maskable interrupts are enabled or not is stored in the interrupt flag of the CPU control code register.

To make sure that the interrupt handler can execute at least its first instruction before it is interrupted, part of the CPU's response to an interrupt is to disable further maskable interrupts. If the interrupt handler wants interrupts enabled, it can execute the "enable-interrupts" instruction.

The use of interrupt-enable and interrupt-disable instructions extends beyond interrupt handlers. In certain applications even the main program contains sections that must not be interrupted. This occurs particularly when several tasks require the same resource, such as memory, or when a task requires exact timing. As an example, a program that reads and then increments a certain memory location should not be interrupted by an interrupt that changes the value of that location. A program executing an exact delay should also be uninterruptible. In situations like these, the critical section of the code starts with an interrupt-disable and ends with an interrupt-enable instruction.

The next issue is how the CPU guarantees that nested interrupts will not destroy the interrupted context. The solution is obvious when one considers the similarity of interrupts and subroutines. As we know, subroutine jumps may be nested to any depth if their private information, such as their return addresses, is stored on the stack. Similarly, if the CPU stores information belonging to interrupts on the stack, interrupt nesting is safe. In fact, nesting a combination of interrupts and subroutines is also safe.

Finally, what happens to interrupts that were not accepted because the interrupt flag was disabled? The answer is that return from interrupt normally re-enables interrupt inputs and if the signal is still active, the CPU will thus respond to it.

### Interrupts on the 6800 CPU

The 6800 maskable and nonmaskable interrupts are called $\overline{IRQ}$ (interrupt request) and *NMI* (nonmaskable interrupt). In addition to these two signals, several other 6800 features are related to interrupts.

Figure 12.19 shows that when $\overline{IRQ}$ is activated (Low), the CPU completes the current instruction and tests the interrupt flag *I* in the condition code

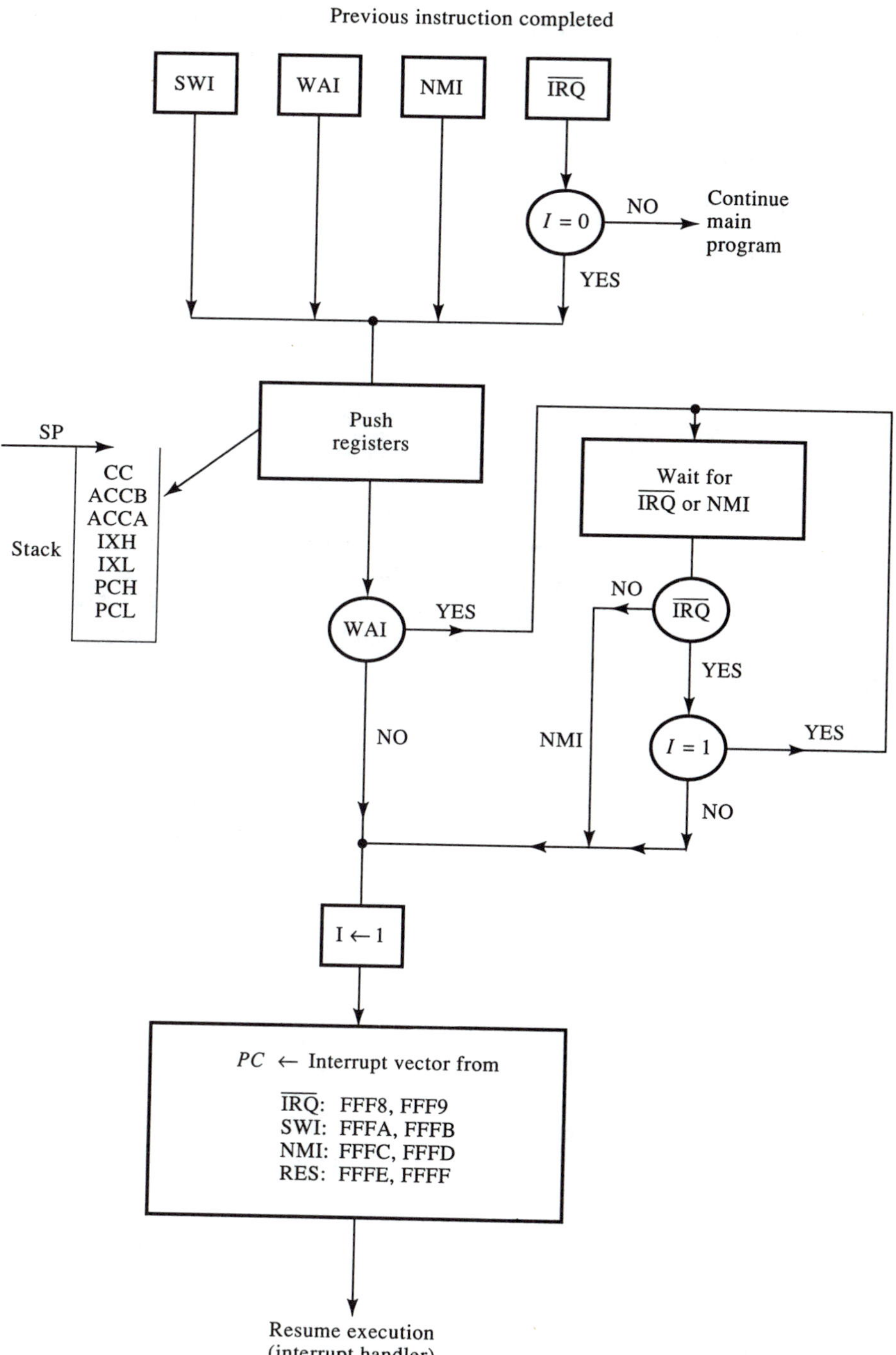


**Figure 12.19.** Interrupt handling on the 6800.

register. If $I = 1$, interrupts are disabled and the 6800 ignores the interrupt and proceeds to the next instruction. No machine cycles are lost. If $I = 0$, interrupts are enabled and the CPU

Saves all registers (*A*, *B*, *X*, *CC*, *PC*) except *SP* on the stack

Disables further interrupts by setting the *I* flag

Fetches the address of the start of the interrupt handler from locations $FFF8 and $FFF9 and loads it into *PC*

Returns control to software; the instruction whose address is now in *PC* is fetched and executed.

Execution continues until the CPU encounters the return-from-interrupt (RTI) instruction. Return-from-interrupt restores all registers, including the program counter, from the stack and execution thus returns to the original program.

Note that if the interrupt handler was activated by IRQ, RTI automatically re-enables interrupts because it restores the condition control register and thus the *I* flag. Obviously the *I* flag must have been originally enabled because IRQ was executed. Interrupts can also be enabled explicitly by executing the clear-interrupt flag (*CLI*).

Disabling or masking interrupts is accomplished by the set interrupt flag instruction (SEI). As we have mentioned, SEI can be executed before a program enters a critical portion of code that uses a shared resource or that is time dependent: An example of the latter situation is software-driven byte-at-a-time data transfer between a disk and memory. The routine could be as follows:

```
SEI     ; Disable interrupt before
        ; Start of critical section
. . .   ; Critical section
```

We will now return to the 6800 interrupt sequence. As a first step in its execution, the 6800 automatically saves all registers because it assumes that they will be used by the interrupt handler and that their original value must be preserved. This work could also be done by the interrupt handler itself, but that would take more time.

Many CPUs do not save all registers but let the interrupt handler save those registers that its uses. (All CPUs store *PC* and the control code register.) This approach assumes that the interrupt handler will not need all registers and that saving and restoring them would be a waste of time. This is sensible, especially when the CPU has many registers. Central processing units that on this principle must, of course have PUSH and PULL instructions that apply to all registers so that the interrupt handler can save and restore them.

**Example 1 — Interrupt Driven Serial Input** Consider a 6800 CPU computer that uses a terminal for input and output. The interface between the CPU and the terminal is an ACIA chip programmed to generate an interrupt when it receives a character from the keyboard. The ACIA interrupt signal is connected to the IRQ pin of the 6800 as in Figure 12.20.

When the CPU receives IRQ, indicating that a key was pressed, the interrupt handler reads the status register of the ACIA and checks whether the code was received without error. If there is an error, the handler jumps to an error routine; otherwise it reads the received character from the ACIA (which then automatically resets the ACIA's status bit) and stores it into a keyboard buffer — a memory area allocated for data received from the terminal and not yet consumed by the program. The character then stays in the buffer until a program consumes it. The interrupt handler is as follows:

```
KBD                              ; Keyboard input handler activated
                                 ; by IRQ
         LDAA #NERR              ; Code of "no error" status
         CMPA STATUS             ; Compare with ACIA status register
         BNE ERROR               ; On error, jump to error handler,
         . . .                   ; otherwise store code in buffer
         RTI                     ; Return from interrupt
ERROR    . . .                   ; Error handler
         RTI                     ; Return to interrupted program
```

**Example 2 — Multiple Interrupt Driven Devices** On most computers, interrupts may arrive from any of several sources. We will now demonstrate how to handle such situations.

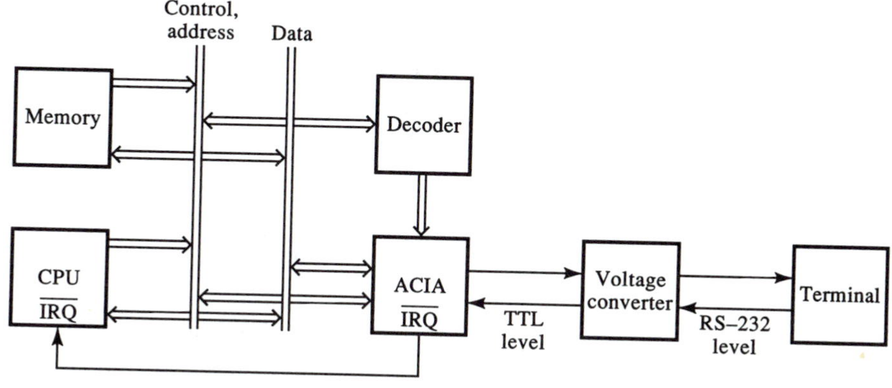


**Figure 12.20.** Block diagram of a terminal-computer interface.

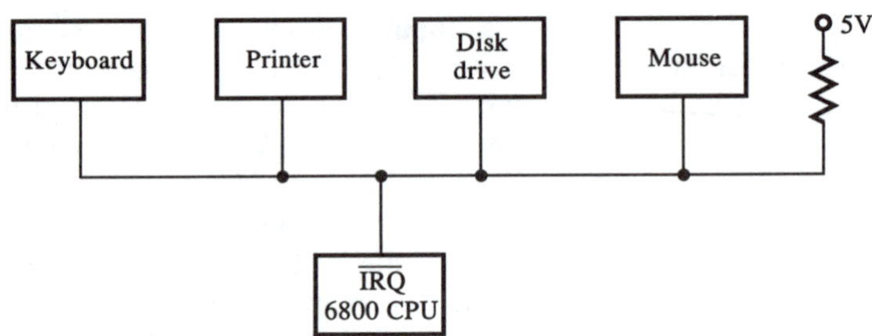


**Figure 12.21.** A computer with four interrupting devices. Note that the circuit implies that all devices use open collector IRQ outputs. A solution with ordinary logic is left as an exercise.

Consider a computer with a keyboard, printer, disk drive, and mouse, all interrupt-driven (Figure 12.21). Any of these devices may interrupt at any time, possibly several of them simultaneously. Their interrupts must thus be prioritized.

To implement prioritization with software, when the interrupt handler is activated it polls the devices one after another until it finds one whose status indicates that it has requested an interrupt. The handler then jumps to the appropriate driver, services the request, and resumes the interrupted program. As the devices are polled in a fixed order, priorities are enforced by the polling sequence: The device that is polled first has the highest priority because it will be serviced before any other device.

To make polling possible, each device's interface must have a status bit indicating whether the device requested an interrupt or not. The ACIA and the PIA provide a status bit in each port but we will assume tailormade individual interfaces with the status bit of each device stored in bit 7 of it ACIA or PIA port. This makes it possible to test the status directly with a TST instruction. The interrupt handler could then be as follows:

```
HANDLER   TST DISK_ST    ; Test status of disk controller
                         ; Is the disk interrupting?
          BMI DISK       ; If yes, service it
          TST MOUSE_ST   ; No. Is it the mouse?
          BMI MOUSE      ; If yes, service it
          TST PRINT_ST   ; No. Is it the printer?
          BMI PRINTER    ; If yes, service it
KBD       . . .          ; None of the above, it must be
                         ; the keyboard
          . . .          ; Code of keyboard driver
```

```
          RTI
MOUSE     . . .         ; Code of mouse driver
          RTI
DISK      . . .         ; Code of disk drive handler
          RTI
PRINTER   . . .         ; Code of printer driver
          RTI
```

In this program, individual driver routines may or may not re-enable the interrupt. If they don't, further interrupts remain unanswered until the interrupt handler executes RTI, which resets *I*. If higher level interrupts than the one being serviced exist and require immediate service, the driver must re-enable interrupts by executing SEI. If another interrupt—either of higher or lower priority—is active or becomes active, the CPU is interrupted and must re-execute the complete polling sequence. If the new interrupt has higher priority than the current one, it will be executed and the final RTI will return execution back to the unfinished interrupt. If the new interrupt has lower priority, its servicing will be delayed, its interrupt signal deactivated (otherwise it would keep interrupting), and its identification saved in memory so that it can be serviced later.

The handling of interrupt priorities by software is obviously rather complicated and slow and this explains why interrupts are often arbitrated by hardware, using one of several priority encoder chips designed for this purpose. The 74348, for example, has eight inputs for interrupts coming from up to eight different sources. When one or more inputs are activated, the decoder sends a STROBE signal to the IRQ pin of the CPU and outputs the code of the highest priority active interrupt (Figure 12.22). The interrupt handler can use the code to find the handler of the highest priority interrupting device. One possible approach is to store addresses of individual handlers in a table and access them using indexed addressing. Because each entry in the table is two bytes long, and because the consecutive entries are offset by 2, the number of the interrupt must be multiplied by 2 to access the correct address. The handler could be as follows:

```
ENCODER   EQU   . . .        ; Address of priority
                             ; encoder output
MOUSE     EQU   . . .        ; Address of
                             ; mouse handler
DISK1     EQU   . . .        ; Address of
                             ; disk 1 handler
DISK2     EQU   . . .        ; Address of
                             ; disk 2 handler
```

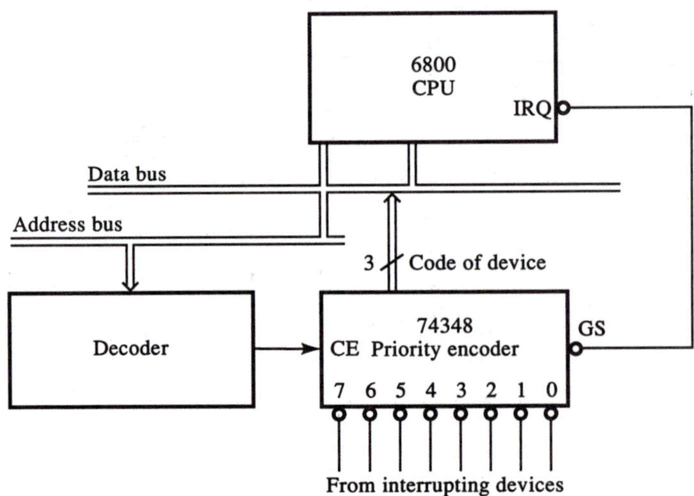


**Figure 12.22.** Interrupt arbitration with the 74348 priority encoder.

```
PRT1      EQU    . . .                        ; Address of
                                              ; printer 1
                                              ; handler
PRT2      EQU    . . .                        ; Address of
                                              ; printer 2
                                              ; handler
          ORG    $00                          ; Store table on
                                              ; page 0
                                              ; First table of
                                              ; handler
                                              ; addresses
TABLE     DB     MOUSE,DISK1,DISK2, PRT1,PRT2
TEMP      DS 2                                ; Will be used
                                              ; for address of
                                              ; handler
                                              ; to be loaded
                                              ; into the index
                                              ; register
          ORG    $100                         ; Code segment.
HANDLER   LDAA   ENCODER                      ; Read the
                                              ; number of the
                                              ; highest priority
```

```
                                        ; interrupt from
                                        ; the priority
                                        ; encoder
          ASLA                          ; Shift to
                                        ; multiply by
                                        ; two
          STAA      TEMP+1              ; Save as low
                                        ; part of table
                                        ; address
          CLR       TEMP                ; Low part of
                                        ; table address
                                        ; is 0
          LDX       TEMP                ; X := address
                                        ; of address of
                                        ; handler
          LDX       O,X                 ; X := address
                                        ; of handler
                                        ; (MOUSE,
                                        ; DISK1, etc.)
          JSR       O,X                 ; Jump to
                                        ; handler via
                                        ; index register
          RTI                           ; End of main
                                        ; part of
                                        ; interrupt
                                        ; handler
MOUSE     . . .                         ; Handler of
                                        ; mouse
          RTS
DISK1     . . .                         ; Handler of
                                        ; disk drive 1
          RTS
          . . .                         ; Etc.
PRT2      . . .                         ; Handler of
                                        ; printer 2
          RTS
```

This program is nontrivial in its use and access of the table; the student should study it carefully.

Another approach to the handling of prioritized interrupts is to use a more powerful chip that not only prioritizes its interrupt inputs but also stores the addresses of their handlers. (Addresses are loaded into the chip by the initialization program.) When one or more devices request an interrupt, the CPU select the chip, which then outputs the address of the beginning of the interrupt handler of the highest priority device. One such chip is Intel's 8259 programmable interrupt control unit (PICU) which outputs not only the address of the interrupt handler but also the opcode of a jump to it. Because the opcode and the timing are designed for the 8080 CPU, the PICU is not suited for use with the 6800 CPU.

### Exercises

1. Explain what is meant when one says that two interrupts arrive "simultaneously."
2. Modify the diagram of the fetch/execute CPU cycle to show handling of maskable and nonmaskable interrupt signals.
3. What is the difference between RTI and RTS instructions?
4. Find the values of the bit patterns of the various PIA and ACIA status tests in the programs in this section.
5. Which device in Example 2 has the highest priority?
6. Write an error subroutine for terminal input. When called it should display the message "keyboard error, please reenter" on the terminal.
7. Write a BUFFER subroutine that stores a new key code in the keyboard buffer. The buffer is to be treated as circular; in other words, its last location is assumed to be followed by the first location. Be sure to deal with buffer overflow: When a character is sent to a full buffer, ignore it and sound a beep.
8. Write an interrupt-driven driver for an Epson-like printer. Assume that data is initially in a data buffer in memory. Before sending the first character, the driver must test whether the printer is ready; the rest of output should be interrupt-driven using the ACKNLG signal from the printer. When all data is out, the printer interrupts one last time but the interrupt handler ignores this.
9. Combine the interrupt-driven keyboard input handler and the printer handler from the previous exercise into a single two-device interrupt handler. The priority of the keyboard interrupt should be higher than that of the printer.
10. Change the terminal I/O scheme so that both input and output are interrupt-driven. Include the printer driver in the interrupt handler.
11. How many memory locations does the 6800 consume when it responds to an interrupt?
12. Design a circuit to convert a pulse from a peripheral to a level IRQ signal. The circuit must have an input to allow the CPU to turn the IRQ signal Off.
13. Why is *SP* not stored on the stack by an interrupt?

14. When the CPU reads from an ACIA data register, the ACIA resets its status bit. Explain how this can be done.
15. Show how ordinary TTL outputs could be used to implement the multiple IRQ signals in Figure 12.21 and compare this with a circuit using OC outputs. How difficult is it to add a new peripheral in each case? Does this help to explain why IRQ is active Low?

### Nonmaskable Interrupt

Nonmaskable interrupt is identical to IRQ except that it cannot be disabled and its interrupt vector is stored at locations $FFFC and $FFFD. Also, NMI is edge-sensitive whereas IRQ is level sensitive. There is no formal difference between interrupt handlers for IRQ and NMI. Because NMI cannot be disabled it is used for interrupts whose importance is critical for the system.

**Example—NMI Used to Keep Time** Most computers use a *timer*: a programmable counter chip that generates a pulse at regular intervals, for example every 10 msec. The frequency of the pulses is derived from the system clock and is obtained by internal division in the timer with a modulus set by an initialization program similar to PIA and ACIA initialization. The output of the timer is usually connected to an interrupt input of the CPU and is used to control various time-dependent functions. Note that the timer does not drive the CPU; this is done by the system clock.

On large computers, the timer is used mainly to switch between "simultaneously" executing programs. In this function, timer interrupts determine slices of time allocated to individual "jobs" and the CPU uses the timer's ticks to switch between several programs that share main memory and that are executed in a round-robin fashion.

On small computers, the timer is used mainly to keep time and date. This information may be displayed on the screen and may be used to "stamp" files so that different versions of the same file may be easily distinguished. The timer can also be used to replace programmed delay loops for time-dependent functions. As an example, the disk drive motor is usually on only during and shortly after disk access. Before a disk operation, the motor must be activated and its speed allowed to stabilize. This takes hundreds of milliseconds and the most efficient way to measure the required time is to program an auxiliary timer to produce an interrupt a specified amount of time after the start command has been issued. Another use of timed interrupts is for the control of pitch and duration of computer generated sounds.

On the IBM PC, the timer generates an interrupt 18.2 times per second and activates an interrupt handler that increments internal time expressed in terms of the number of ticks. We will now show how such a handler could be written for the 6800 CPU.

Assume that the timer is programmed to produce one pulse every second and that its output is connected to the NMI pin of the CPU. We will express time internally in seconds, minutes, hours, days, and years and allocate one byte to each. (Years will be represented by an offset from 1900.)

The principle of the interrupt handler is quite simple:

```
{When NMI arrives, do the following}
{Update seconds}
SECONDS := SECONDS + 1;
IF SECONDS = 60
  THEN
    BEGIN
    {Update minutes}
      SECONDS := 0;
      MINUTES := MINUTES + 1;
      IF MINUTES = 60
        THEN
          BEGIN
          {Update hours}
            MINUTES := 0;
            HOURS := HOURS + 1;
            IF HOURS = 24
              THEN
              . . . {Update days, months, and years}
```

and can be implemented as follows:

```
TIME                          ; Timer interrupt handler
            PSHA              ; Save A, which is used by the handler
            INC TIME          ; Start with seconds
            LDAA #60
            CMPA TIME
            BNE DONE          ; Exit if not 60, else increment
            CLR TIME          ; Time = 60, seconds := 0
            INC TIME+1        ; Increment minutes
            CMPA TIME+1       ; A still contains 60
            BNE DONE
            CLR TIME+1
            INC TIME+2        ; Update hours
```

```
          . . .          ; And so on
DONE      PULA           ; Restore preinterrupt value of A
          RTI            ; Return from interrupt
```

The values of seconds, minutes, and so on are stored at locations *TIME*, *TIME* + 1, etc.

To implement our scheme, the pulse output of the timer must be connected to the NMI input of the 6800 and the address of the handler (the value of label *TIMER*) stored in the NMI vector $FFFC, $FFFD. If, for example, *TIMER* = $9000, the contents of $FFFC, $FFFD must be $9000.

### Other 6800 Interrupt-Related Functions

In addition to IRQ and NMI which are true hardware interrupts, the 6800 has several other related features. One is the reset signal RST, which we have already discussed; another is HALT; and the last two are the software interrupt (SWI) and wait (WAI) instructions.

Reset is, in fact, the highest priority interrupt. When activated, it stops program execution and causes an indirect jump via $FFFE and $FFFF. Unlike IRQ and NMI, it does not save any registers on the stack because it is used to initialize the computer and has no information to preserve.

In order to let the initialization routine start without interruptions, the RESET signal sets *I* and thus disables IRQ. If interrupts are to be enabled, the reset sequence must contain *CLI*.

When the HALT pin of the 6800 chip is activated, the CPU completes the current instruction and then stops until HALT is deactivated. Because the internal CPU registers continue to be refreshed by the clock, the signal can remain active for any length of time. If an interrupt arrives while the CPU is halted, it is latched into the CPU and takes effect when the HALT is deactivated. Signal HALT can be used to execute programs one instruction at a time and for direct memory access. (An example appears in the next section.) For obvious reasons, the HALT signal is also called GO/HALT.

*Software interrupt* (SWI) is an instruction that simulates a hardware interrupt. Its effect is identical to that of NMI and IRQ but its interrupt vector is in locations $FFFA and $FFFB. Software interrupt can be used to test interrupt handler software and as a fast way to save all registers on the stack. It also allows user programs to access the interrupt handler and to take advantage of the device drivers that it may contain. We will use it in Chapter 14 as a basis for communication with our operating system.

When the CPU encounters a wait instruction (WAI), it saves registers just as after an IRQ, NMI, or RST interrupt and stops the CPU until an interrupt arrives. It then responds in the usual way except that it does not save registers because they have already been saved by WAI.

We have already encountered WAI on the ET-3400, where it is used to terminate all programs. (The analysis of its implementation is left as an exercise.) As another example of the use of WAI, the following program shows how one could use it to convert a terminal and a printer into a "typewriter." The program reads a key from the keyboard, writes it on the screen, and prints it. We assume that the terminal runs in the full duplex mode (no echo) and its serial interface uses an ACIA; the printer interface is parallel and uses a PIA. The ACIA is assumed to have been programmed to produce an interrupt when it receives a code from the terminal but the PIA is programmed for polling. Note that although the program uses IRQ internally, it is not an interrupt handler.

```
                                ; Terminal typewriter program
INT         EQU 00F8            ; IRQ interrupt vector on
                                ; ET-3400
                                ; Contents of location $FFF8,
                                ; $FFF9
INITIAL     . . .               ; Code to initialize ACIA and
                                ; PIA
                                ; for desired modes of operation
READ        WAI                 ; Wait for interrupt from ACIA,
                                ; which signals activated key
                                ; The handler is at the end
                                ; of the program listing
RESUME      LDAA ACIA_IN        ; We get here after executing the
                                ; interrupt handler
                                ; Key code ready in ACIA input
                                ; port,
                                ; read it
ACIAPOLL    TST ACIA ST         ; Is the ACIA ready to send echo
                                ; to the terminal?
            BNE ACIAPOLL        ; If not, poll it again
            STAA ACIA_OUT       ; Send character to the screen
                                ; via the ACIA output port
PIAPOLL     LDAB PIA ST         ; Read BUSY status of printer.
            BNE PIAPOLL         ; If busy, poll again
            STAA PIA_DATA       ; Send data to printer
            BRA READ            ; Go and get another key
            ORG INT             ; The interrupt handler
HANDLER     RTI                 ; On interrupt, return to WAI
```

This somewhat unusual program works as follows: After initializing the ACIA and PIA, the CPU executes WAI and halts. When the ACIA activates the IRQ input of the CPU, the CPU jumps to the interrupt handler via the address stored at address *INT* = [$FFF8,$FFF9].

The interrupt handler consists solely of RTI and immediately returns execution to the instruction following the point at which the CPU was interrupted (label *RESUME*). The combined effect of WAI and RTI is thus the same as if we activated and deactivated HALT: Instruction WAI halts the CPU and the interrupt restarts it.

After resuming operation, the program reads the code sent by the terminal, echoes it back to the screen and sends a copy to the printer. It then returns to WAI where it halts and waits for another interrupt from the ACIA.

## Exercises

1. Explain how a large computer could use the timer interrupt to calculate user charges for computer time. Assume that the account number of the currently executing job is stored in some fixed memory location.
2. What is the advantage of using a timer chip rather than software to create accurate delays?
3. What is the separation of IBM PC time ticks in milliseconds?
4. Why can we use WAI but not JSR or BSR to access an interrupt routine?
5. Design a switch-controlled circuit for step-by-step program execution on the 6800.
6. What would the terminal typewriter program do if an ACIA interrupt arrived while the handler was polling the PIA? How likely is this to happen?
7. Complete the timer interrupt handler.
8. Describe what could happen if the timer output was connected to IRQ and if there were other interrupting devices.
9. Explain why ET-3400 programs are terminated by the WAI instruction and how the ET-3400 is restarted after WAI.
10. One disadvantage of saving all registers on interrupt (particularly SWI) and restoring them on interrupt return is that interrupts cannot easily return values in registers. Explain and show how this limitation can be bypassed.
11. The IRQ signal is disabled when the 6800 CPU starts executing the interrupt sequence, but NMI is nonmaskable. Consequently, the NMI input is still active when the NMI handler is entered. Why then does the NMI not interrupt itself?
12. Draw the diagram of the NMI example in the text, complete the interrupt handler, and trace its operation manually.
13. Draw the diagram of the WAI example in the text and trace its operation manually.

## 12.9 DIRECT MEMORY ACCESS

We have shown that some data transfers, such as those involving hard disk drives, are too fast for program control. These transfers must be made directly between the memory and the device rather than through the CPU; hence the name direct memory access or DMA.

In DMA, the CPU temporarily relinquishes control over the system bus and leaves it to the DMAC. Because memory and peripheral interfaces are designed for CPU control, the DMAC's control over the bus must be identical to that of the CPU. Although the memory and peripherals cannot detect any difference between DMAC and CPU control, the DMAC can transfer data much faster than the CPU because it is a specialized device.

Direct memory access is usually performed as follows: When a device is ready for the transfer, it activates the DMAC, which interrupts the CPU and requests control over the system bus. The CPU completes the current instruction or at least the current machine cycle, and informs the DMAC that it can assume control over the bus. The DMAC then transmits the data using the system clock, the address bus, and its own VMA and $R/\overline{W}$ signals in the usual way (Figure 12.23). When the transfer is finished, the DMAC reactivates the CPU and normal operation resumes. Note that although we talk about device–memory transfers, the "device" can also be memory, as when a new

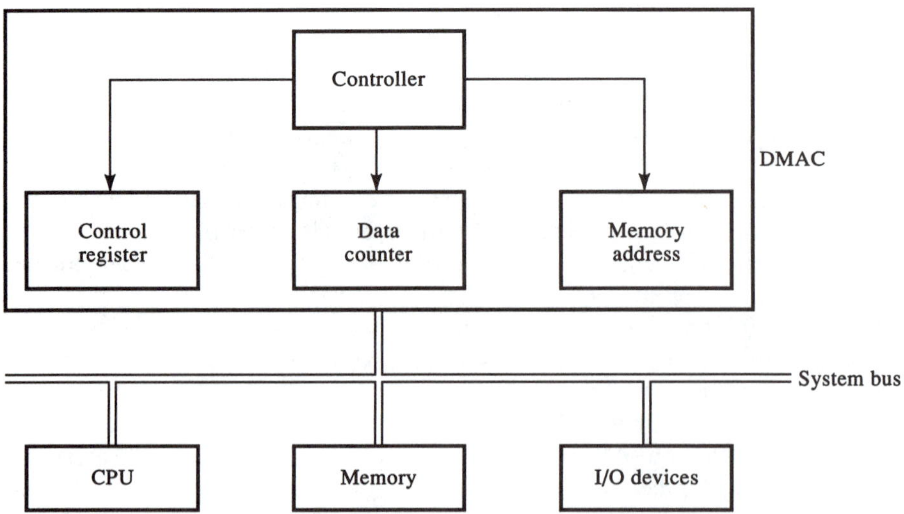


**Figure 12.23.** Block diagram of a system with a DMAC.

screen image is moved from main memory to the display RAM using DMA for greater speed.

Direct memory access can sometimes be performed without halting the CPU by transferring data when the CPU is not using the bus.

**Example—Disk Drive–Memory Transfer** A program needs one 256-byte sector from the disk. It sends a request to the disk controller and informs the DMAC how many bytes are to be transferred and where they are to be stored. When the disk controller gathers the data from the disk into its buffer, it sends a DMA request to the DMAC, which activates the *HALT* signal to the CPU. The CPU halts, and grants control over the system bus to the DMAC. In the burst mode (a whole sector transmitted at a time), the DMAC then executes the following loop using the system clock for synchronization.

```
FOR byte := 1 TO 256 DO
  BEGIN
    Put destination address on address bus and
      Activate VMA, R/W̄;
    {Disk drive controller puts data on the data bus}
    Decrement count of bytes remaining to transfer;
    Increment memory address;
  END
```

The algorithm describes the internal logic of the DMAC; no CPU programming is involved.

If the transfer is byte-by-byte (cycle stealing) rather than via the burst mode, the DMAC returns control to the CPU after each byte and requests it again when the next byte is ready. In all cases, the DMAC informs the CPU when the transfer is complete.

DMA control is usually implemented with a commercial chip, such as the 6800 compatible MC6844 DMAC described in the next section.

## The 6844 DMAC

The 6844 has four DMA channels, which means that it can control up to four different devices. It has several modes of operation and each channel can be programmed for a different mode.

The chip contains three shared registers and an additional set of registers for each channel (Figure 12.24). The three shared registers allow one to set priorities for individual channels, control interrupts, generate status information, and perform similar functions.

Each set of channel registers includes a sixteen-bit count register to store the number of bytes remaining to be transferred, a sixteen-bit address register to

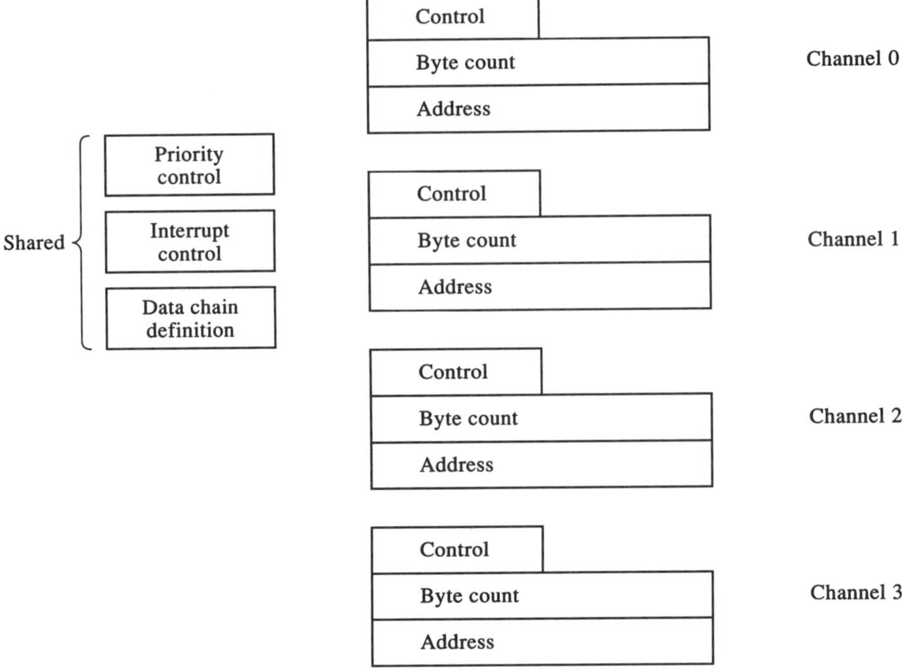


**Figure 12.24.** User programmable registers of the 6844 DMAC.

store the address of the next memory location, and a control register whose contents define the mode of operation of the channel. Some of the available modes are read or write memory-to-device or device-to-memory, cycle stealing or burst, and decrement or increment the address after each byte. The registers are programmed by the CPU during computer initialization or before the start of the transfer.

The following are the most important 6844 pins (Figure 12.25):

Sixteen address pins $A_{15}, \ldots, A_0$ are used as output when the DMAC controls the address bus, and as input when the CPU accesses the DMAC. In the second case, $A_4-A_0$ select one of the twenty-three internal registers.

Eight data pins $D_7, \ldots, D_0$ are used for communication with the CPU. Note that the DMAC never touches the data during the DMA transfer: Data flows directly between the device and memory. Pins $D_7-D_0$ are used either to initialize the DMAC or to read its status.

Signal IRQ/DEND is an interrupt signal used to notify the CPU that all data has been transmitted (DMA end).

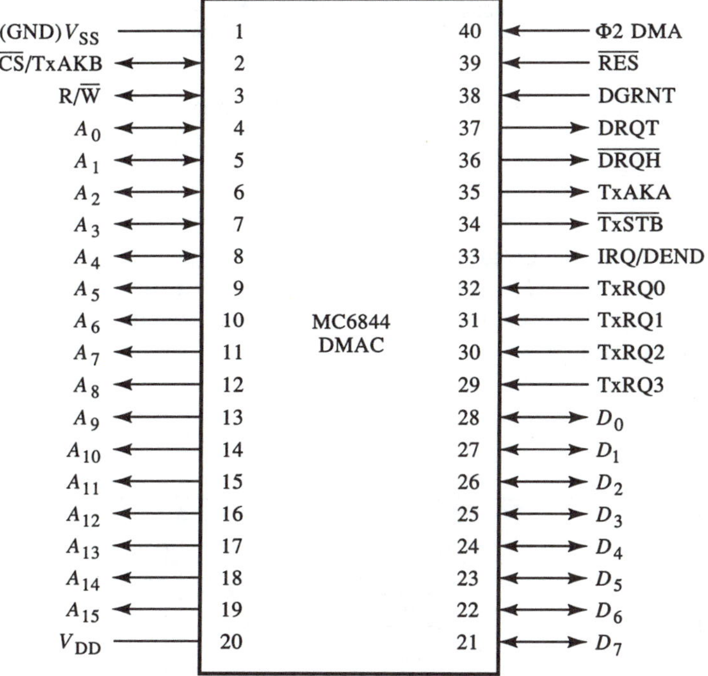


**Figure 12.25.** Pinout of the 6844 DMAC.

Signal TxSTB (transfer strobe) plays the role of VMA. The DMAC uses it to control the system bus when it is in charge.

Signal R/$\overline{W}$ is a bidirectional pin used as input when the CPU communicates with the DMAC, and as output when the DMAC controls a data transfer. In the second case it replaces CPU's R/$\overline{W}$ just as TxSTB replaces VMA.

Signal $\overline{RES}$ resets the DMAC before initialization.

Lines *TxRQ0–TxRQ3* are "transmit request" lines from the four devices that may be connected to the 6844.

Signal CS/TxAKB serves as chip select when the DMAC is accessed by the CPU. Otherwise, it is used with TxAKA to select one of the four DMA channels that can be controlled by the 6844.

Signal DRQT (DMA request) is used by the DMAC to request control over the system bus from the CPU.

Signal DGRNT (DMA grant) is used by the CPU to signal to the DMAC that its DMA request has been granted.

The 6844 can operate in cycle stealing or burst mode.

## Cycle Stealing

When a 6844 channel programmed for cycle stealing is activated by its device (Figures 12.26 and 12.27), it transfers only one byte, using "clock stretching." This mode is used, for example, when a disk controller has only one register to buffer disk data. It works as follows:

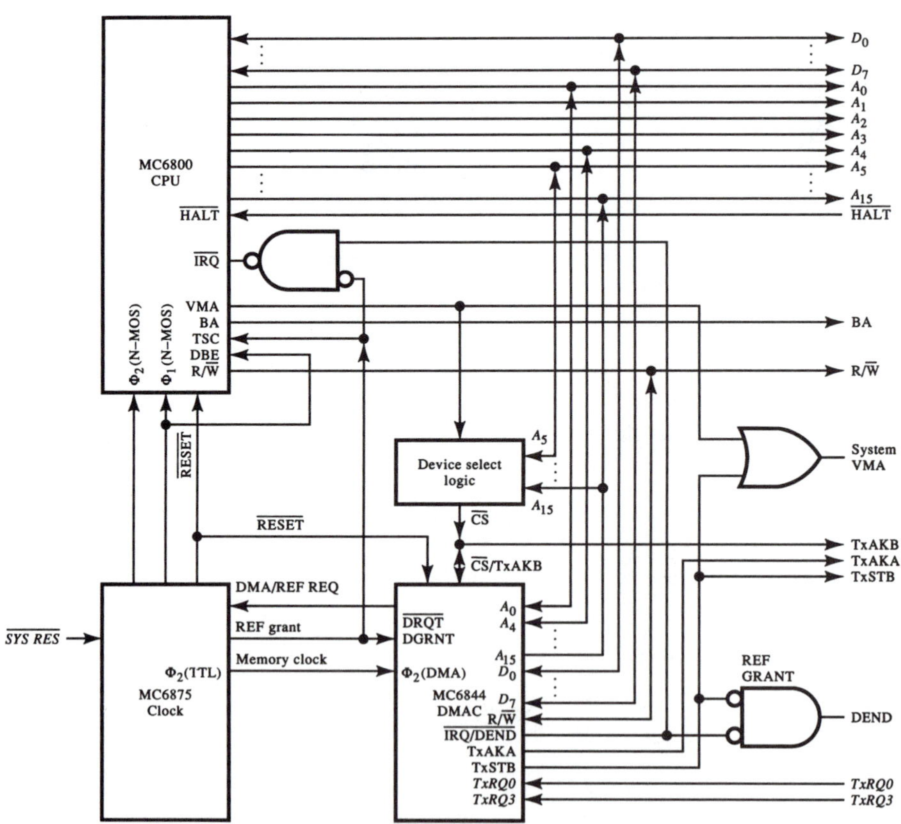


**Figure 12.26.** The 6844 DMAC connected for cycle stealing DMA. Note that the system signal VMA, which is used by device decoders in the system, comes from either the CPU or the DMAC. The clock chip produces one $\Phi_2$ signal for the control of the CPU and another for the DMAC and the rest of the system.

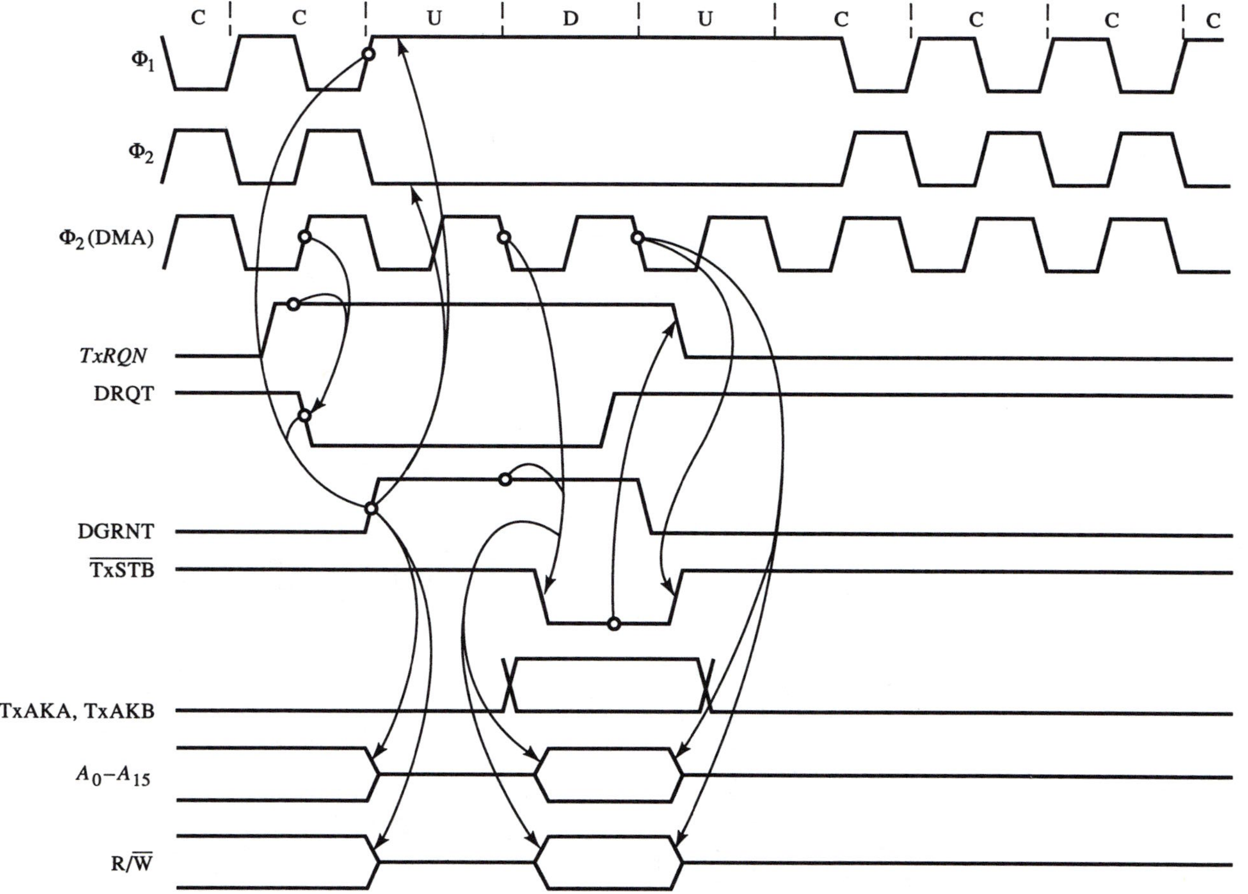


**Figure 12.27.** Timing diagram of DMAC cycle stealing transfer. Symbol "C" indicates a CPU operations machine cycle; "U" indicates an unused machine cycle; "D" indicates a DMA machine cycle.

As soon as the channel device makes a DMA request using its *TxRQ* line, the 6844 activates DRQT. This line is connected to the clock chip, which controls the $\Phi_1$ and $\Phi_2$ inputs of the 6800 CPU. The clock chip lets the CPU finish the current machine cycle and then "stretches" $\Phi_1$ High and $\Phi_2$ Low. This halts the CPU. Because $\Phi_2$ is connected to the DBE pin of the 6800, the data pins of the CPU are tristated, and control over the bus is transferred to the DMAC. By activating *DGRNT*, the clock chip also signals to the DMAC that its DMA request has been granted. It also floats the CPU's address pins, VMA, and $R/\overline{W}$ via *TSC*.

The DMAC now has control over the system bus and transfers a byte between the device and the memory as follows: It places channel code (00,...,11) on TXAKA and TXAKB to ask the requesting device to transfer, and outputs the memory address on the address bus and the equivalent of VMA and $\mathrm{R}/\overline{\mathrm{W}}$ on the control bus. The device transfers a byte and the DMAC updates its internal counter and address register for this channel, and waits until the end of the machine cycle for the completion of the operation. Note that although the CPU's clock is stopped, the system's clock signals keep running and $\Phi_2$ is thus available to control the transfer.

When the byte is transferred, the DMAC deactivates the DRQT line and the clock lets the CPU resume operation. As two cycles are needed to prepare the operation, the transfer of one byte requires three machine cycles. Although this may appear inefficient, it is still much faster than if transferring data using the CPU.

## HALT Burst Mode

This mode is used to transfer blocks of data, for example in memory→display RAM transfers or in disk transfers when the controller has a sufficiently large data buffer. The connections are only slightly different from those in Figure 12.26 and we will now show them.

The operation is again initiated by the device via its *TxR* line. The DMAC responds by activating DRQH (DMA hold request), which is connected to the HALT input of the CPU. We already explained that when this line is activated, the CPU completes the current instruction (which may take up to twelve machine cycles) and then halts. Its data and address pins and $\mathrm{R}/\overline{\mathrm{W}}$ are floated and VMA is Low. The system VMA is thus

$$\begin{aligned} VMA_{\mathrm{sys}} &= VMA + TxSTB \\ &= 0 + TxSTB \\ &= TxSTB \end{aligned}$$

and the DMAC is in control. To indicate that the bus is available, the CPU outputs High on the *BA* (bus available) line.

The DMAC now activates the requesting device and the transfer takes place as in the previous example except that data are sent one byte after another, with address and internal count decremented after each transfer. When the count reaches 0, the DMAC deactivates HALT and activates IRQ/DEND. The CPU then resumes operation.

### Exercises

1. How many machine cycles are needed to transfer one byte under CPU control? How many under DMAC control?
2. Why can the 6844 halt the CPU even before it completes the current instruction in the clock stretching mode but not in the burst mode? (*Hints:* What happens to the clock signal? What is the internal CPU function of the clock signal?)
3. How much time would it take to rewrite the complete display text or graphics memory using DMA at 10 MHz? How fast would the RAM have to be? Which time slot in the CRT's operation should be used for this purpose?

## 12.10 BASIC 8088 HARDWARE ARCHITECTURE

To complement our detailed coverage of the 6800's I/O features, we will now examine the basic aspects of the corresponding facilities of the 8088. Note that although the two CPUs use different instructions and signals, the underlying principles remain the same.

The 8088 has forty pins. Twenty are address pins, but eight of these are also used for data. The shared pins are multiplexed, which means that they transfer data or addresses as needed. Because addresses and data must be on the bus at the same time, multiplexing requires additional circuitry. Figure 12.28 shows that a special external register must be provided to latch the address while the CPU uses the low-order eight address pins for data. The register is controlled by the ALE (address latch enable) signal from the 8288 bus controller which, in turn, depends on status signals from the 8088. Other essential 8088 signals are as follows:

Signals MEMR, MEMW, IOR, and IOW are produced by the 8288 bus controller chip from the 8088's encoded signals. They indicate whether a read or write operation is taking place and whether it is memory or I/O access.

Signal RESET has the same function as on the 6800.

Signals NMI and INTR are maskable and nonmaskable interrupt pins.

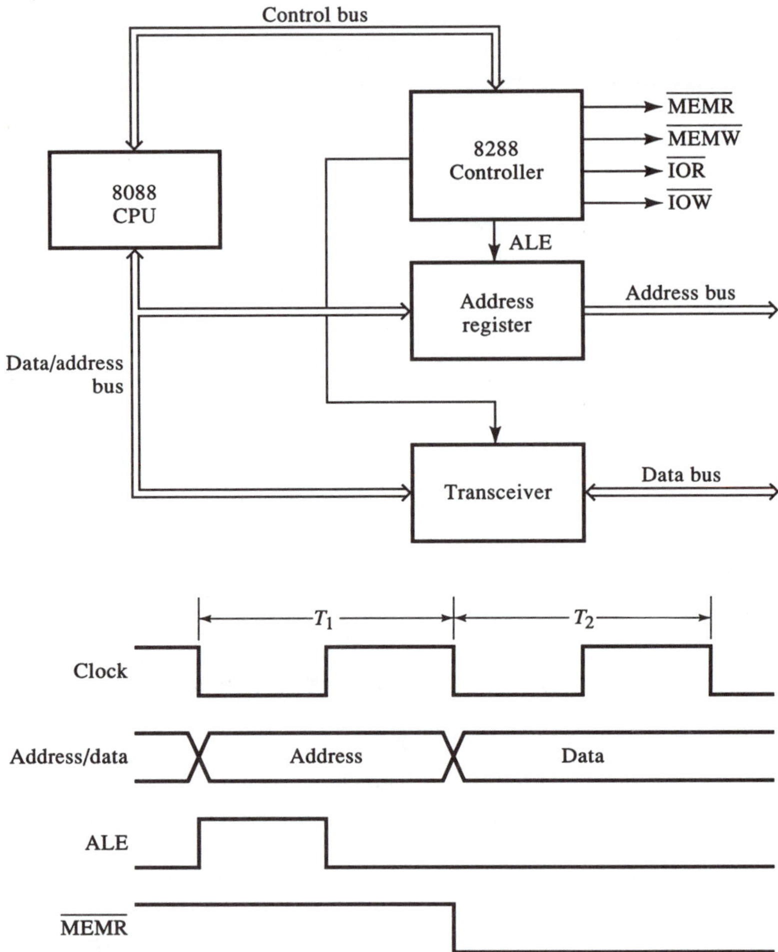


**Figure 12.28.** Block diagram of 8088 address/data multiplexing and the timing diagram of the basic signals of a read cycle.

The timing diagram in Figure 12.28 indicates that the design of address and control signal decoders for the 8088 is similar to that for a 6800-based system.

One major difference between the 8088 and the 6800 is that the 8088 has I/O instructions and does not have to use memory mapping. This saves memory space as the I/O space is separate, but requires an additional control signal to distinguish memory and I/O operations.

One of the most interesting other aspects of 8088 I/O, is the operation of 8088 interrupts. In principle, the function of NMI and INTR is the same as for NMI and IRQ on the 6800. One minor difference is that interrupts only save the flag register and the "program counter": the code segment register *CS* and the instruction pointer *IP*. If the interrupt handler uses other registers, it must push them on the stack by using the appropriate instructions and pop them before executing return from interrupt by PUSH and POP instructions.

A major difference between 6800 and 8088 interrupts is in the way in which the CPU obtains the address of the beginning of the interrupt handler. On the 8088, hardware and software interrupts (instruction INT, explained in Chapter 10) share a table of address vectors, the interrupt table, that is stored in the first $4 \times 256$ bytes of the address space. Hardware and software interrupts are executed in the same way but whereas the "type" of a software interrupt (its one-byte number) is a part of the INT instruction, the type of the maskable hardware interrupt is supplied by the interrupting device or, more commonly, by a priority encoder attached to it. The sequence of a hardware-triggered interrupt is as follows:

When the CPU senses active INTR, it completes the current instruction and the 8288 bus controller activates the INTA (interrupt acknowledge) signal. In response to INTA, the interrupting device or a priority encoder chip puts a one-byte integer (the interrupt type) on the address bus. The CPU saves its *CS* and *IP* registers on the stack, disables interrupts, reads the data bus, and multiplies the type number by 4 to obtain the address of the four-byte address vector in the interrupt table. The four-byte address vector is loaded from this location in the table into *CS* and *IP* and execution continues from there.

The sequence just described applies only to the maskable interrupt. The nonmaskable interrupt is assigned the fixed type number 2. When NMI is activated, the CPU thus does not wait for a type number and obtains the address of the interrupt handler from locations 0008H to 000BH.

The 8088 approach to interrupt handling is very efficient because it eliminates the need for polling.

### Exercises

1. Draw a timing diagram showing how data multiplexing works.
2. The 80286 used in the IBM PC/AT has sixty-eight pins of which twenty-four are used for address and sixteen for data. What sixty-eight implications does this have for speed and the size of the address space?
3. Why does an interrupt vector on the 8088 occupy four memory locations?
4. Explain how the 8088's method of obtaining the interrupt vector speeds up the operation of systems with multiple interrupting sources.

## SUMMARY

The implementation of input and output has both hardware and software aspects. The hardware aspects (how the I/O device is connected to the system bus) depend on the hardware architecture of the CPU and the peripheral (the available control signals and their timing), and the selected I/O method. The software aspects depend on the software architecture of the CPU (its instruction set), the hardware interface, and the selected I/O method.

Central processing units differ in their approach to I/O (memory-mapped or dedicated I/O) and in the facilities that they provide for their implementation. In spite of the differences, I/O is essentially identical for all CPUs, and interfacing techniques learned on one CPU can be easily transferred to another. The main points can be summarized as follows: Each CPU has control signals that inform the system whether the CPU is performing a data transfer or an internal operation. There are always one or more read/write signals, and a timing signal that indicates the start of the actual transfer. The timing signal is delayed with respect to the other signals to allow their logic levels to stabilize. Central processing units with I/O instructions have an additional signal to indicate whether the data transfer involves memory or an I/O device.

In addition to these basic facilities, CPUs provide signals for CPU reset and external control over the CPU's access to the bus. This is necessary to allow an external device to assume bus control for direct memory access.

The variety of I/O strategies is comparable to the variety of CPU architectures. In principle, however, one can distinguish four basic approaches: programmed I/O, polled I/O, interrupt-driven I/O, and direct memory access. All I/O strategies can be reduced to a combination of these.

In programmed I/O, the program that requires the operation simply accesses the device and transfers data. No checking of device status is performed. This approach is used for very simple devices, such as primitive displays.

In polled I/O, the program checks device status and performs the transfer only if it finds that the device is ready. If the device is not ready, the program usually enters a loop and waits until the device becomes available or until the number of unsuccessful tests exceeds some limit that indicates the device is faulty or disconnected. (This condition is called time-out.) Polling is very common and is a part of most I/O operations.

Although polling forms the basis of most I/O, complete reliance on it would make computer operation very inefficient. This is why most computers also use interrupts. In interrupt-driven I/O, the initiative for the I/O operation comes from the device rather than from the program. When the device needs CPU's attention, it activates a special CPU input that forces the CPU to abandon the current program and execute an interrupt handler program that takes care of the situation.

In responding to an interrupt, the CPU completes the current instruction; pushes the program counter, the condition code register, and possibly other registers on the stack; disables further interrupts; and jumps to the first instruction of the interrupt handler. At the end of the interrupt handler, the CPU executes a return-from-interrupt instruction that restores the saved registers and returns to the original program. Interrupt handling is very similar to a subroutine jump, the main difference being that interrupts are hardware-triggered whereas subroutine jumps are software-driven.

One major difference in how CPUs handle interrupts is the manner in which they obtain the address of the interrupt handler (the interrupt vector). On the 6800, the interrupt vector is stored in a fixed memory location. On other CPUs, such as the 8088, the address may be supplied by the interrupting device. This makes interrupt handling more efficient when several interrupt-driven devices are present.

When the required data transfer rate is very high, the CPU must be bypassed and data transferred directly between the device and memory. Direct memory access is controlled by a special circuit or chip called the DMA controller (DMAC). During DMA transfer, the DMAC temporarily assumes control over the system bus and generates all signals normally produced by the CPU. The DMAC must also keep track of memory address and the number of bytes remaining to be transferred. To make DMA possible, DMACs must be able to halt the CPU and tristate its data, address, and control lines.

The design of a peripheral interface usually falls into one of two categories. It either follows the elementary principles explained in this chapter—the circuit must recognize that the CPU is performing a data transfer, identify the address, and wait for a signal indicating the beginning of the transfer—or requires special connections specified by the manufacturer of the device, for example the DMAC. However, few users ever need to design interfaces because most peripherals use a built-in serial or a parallel interface, which is also available on almost all computers. Only standard cables are then necessary and no logic circuits need to be designed or built.

Just as the predominance of serial and parallel standards eliminates the need for custom interfacing, software drivers supplied with the computer or the peripheral make the writing of device driver programs unnecessary in most cases.

## REVIEW QUESTIONS

1. Define the following terms: ACIA, buffer, control signal, decoder, device driver, direct memory access, DMA controller, interrupt (arbitration, maskable, nonmaskable, handler, priority table, vector), interrupt-driven I/O, parallel interface, PIA, polling, programmed I/O, reset, serial interface, timer, and USART.
2. Describe the logic principles of interfacing.
3. Describe a typical interrupt sequence.
4. Describe a DMA sequence.

## REFERENCES

The following titles listed in the references at the end of the book are relevant to this chapter:

R. Bishop. *Basic Microprocessors and the 6800.*

D. Hall. *Microprocessors and Interfacing: Programming and Hardware.*

G. J. Lipovski. *Single- and Multiple-Chip Microcomputer Interfacing.*

M. Sargent III and R. L. Shoemaker. *The IBM PC from the Inside Out.*

A. S. Tanenbaum. *Operating System: Design and Implementation.*

# CHAPTER 13

# FURTHER NOTES ON COMPUTER ARCHITECTURE

## AN OVERVIEW

In the previous chapters, we covered all of the architectural aspects of a simple computer. To broaden our perspective, we will now present a brief overview of some alternative approaches to architecture and some general considerations.

In the first section, we will briefly outline the history of computers. We will then consider the design of instruction sets. We will show how to implement computer memories to achieve a good balance of speed, size, and cost. Next, we will consider the separation of processing and I/O as a means of improving the efficient use of the CPU and increasing the number of programs executed in a unit of time. Finally, we will examine alternative approaches to computer architecture, such as dataflow and neural computing, and we will present the principle of analog computers.

An in-depth study of computer architecture requires a knowledge of advanced topics such as modern programming languages and their implementation, operating systems, and prevailing computer applications. Because the reader is not expected to have this knowledge, our coverage remains at an introductory level.

## IMPORTANT WORDS

Analog computer, array processor, associative memory, cache, CISC architecture, computer generation, data flow computers, hybrid computer, interleaved memory, I/O processor, multiprocessor, orthogonality, parallel processing, pipelining, principle of locality, RISC architecture, SISD/SIMD/MISD/MIMD classification, throughput, virtual addressing.

## 13.1 INTRODUCTION

Until now, we have concentrated on the 6800 CPU because it is easy to understand and contains the main features of a typical CPU. We introduced the 8086 family of CPUs because it is very popular in personal computers and almost everybody involved with computers is likely to use it at one time or another. However, limiting our presentations to these two CPUs and the framework of a personal computer would result in an unrealistic picture of computer architecture; thus we will use this chapter to expand the perspective presented so far. We will start with a brief history of digital computers.

Although the history of computing machines can be traced several centuries back, computers in the sense in which we use the term today emerged in the late 1930s and early 1940s. If we classify the stages mainly on the basis of the underlying technology, the history of computers can be divided into the following four periods, which are usually referred to as generations:

1. First generation (1940–1954). CPUs based on vacuum tube technology, programming initially performed in binary machine language. Development of assembly language programming, minimal built-in support available for programmers. Typical parameters of first computers: forty-bit words, 4k words of memory, 5,000 additions per second.
2. Second generation (1954–1964). CPUs used discrete transistors (no integrated circuits), first high-level programming languages developed (COBOL, FORTRAN, Algol), manufacturer support for the programmer made available (assemblers, compilers). Separation of I/O operations from processing by the main CPU, use of floating-point arithmetic, introduction of the index register, use of magnetic cores for main memory. The introduction of magnetic tape and magnetic drum mass storage made operating systems possible.
3. Third generation (1964–1975). Small- and medium-scale integrated circuits first used, semiconductor memory developed. Widespread use of microprogramming in CPU design, sharing of the CPU, memory, and I/O devices by several programs running concurrently, large multiuser operating systems, emergence of commercial parallel computing.
4. Fourth generation (1975– ). Use of LSI and VLSI technology, CPU on a chip (microprocessor), massive parallelism. Widespread use of personal computers and workstations accompanied by increased emphasis on graphics and user interfaces, networking, and data communications.

As hardware building blocks become more powerful and less expensive, architectures evolve within the scope given by the architect's choice between maximum power at any cost and constant power at minimal cost. The repeated application of choices within these two extremes has led to the development of various classes of machines and we can now distinguish the following categories according to CPU speed, memory capacity, cost, and physical size:

Controllers for industrial applications. A machine in this category consists of a CPU comparable to the 6800 CPU accompanied by a small ROM and RAM (a few kilobytes, possibly on the CPU chip), and peripheral interfaces. The whole computer occupies one circuit board.

Single user personal computers such as the IBM PC and Apple Macintosh families. These use a single-chip CPU from the 8086 Intel family or the 68000 Motorola family, have memory up to 4 Mbytes, floppy and hard disk drives with capacity up to 60 Mbytes, EGA or VGA graphics, and cost up to $10,000.

Single-user workstations such as SUN and Apollo. These were introduced mainly for engineering applications but their use is spreading to other areas. They have fast CPUs (such as the 80386 or 68020) or especially designed CPUs, supported by coprocessors, large memories (4 Mbytes and more); disk storage in hundreds of Mbytes, and powerful graphics, and cost from $10,000 to $50,000.

Multiuser minicomputers and midicomputers, such as the VAX family by DEC. They cost between $20,000 and $500,000 and have correspondingly more powerful hardware and complex software. In many respects, they are scaled-down mainframes.

Mainframes, such as the IBM 370 family. They can accommodate multiple users, and have multichip CPUs, possibly several independent CPUs in one machine, disk storage in Gigabytes ($10^9$), separate I/O and processing. They cost around $1,000,000.

Supercomputers such as the Cray. They feature extra fast technology such as ECL, very careful design in which even the length of signal paths plays a role in CPU speed, and special internal structures, such as pipelining and multiple-unit ALUs, to increase processing speed. They often have multiple processors. Supercomputers cost up to $25,000,000.

Supercomputers, mainframes, and usually even minicomputers are stored in specially designed air-conditioned rooms physically inaccessible to users and serviced by a team of operators.

After this brief introduction, we will now look at several important aspects of computer architectures.

## 13.2 INSTRUCTION SETS

To define an instruction set, the computer architect must choose parameters, such as addressing modes, the kinds of instructions, and their number.

The selection of *addressing modes* depends on the anticipated application. As an example, CPUs for industrial controllers must perform operations such as table lookup to calculate logic functions but do not require the efficient access to deeply nested procedure calls that is needed on general purpose computers for the execution of Pascal-like languages.

An extended discussion of this topic is beyond the scope of this book but it is useful to introduce a classification of instruction sets based on how operands are specified within the instruction.

In "one-address" computers, most instructions specify only a single operand; the other operand (if there is one) and the destination of the result are implied, usually a CPU register. The advantage of this approach is that the instructions are short; the disadvantage is that it cannot provide much variety in the selection of the second operand. The 6800 CPU is an example of such a machine.

In "two-address" computers, instructions requiring two operands explicitly name both; the destination is usually identical to the source of one of the operands. The 8088 CPU is an example of a two-address machine and many other modern CPUs use this approach. Its advantage is that instructions remain relatively short and yet allow selection from a variety of operand sources.

In "three-address" computers, the addresses of both operands and the result are specified. This allows a great variety of combinations of operand and result addresses but the cost is a large instruction size. It is not used much in modern computers.

In "four-address" instruction formats, the instruction contains not only addresses of both operands and the result but also the address of the next instruction. This may be useful at the microprogramming level as it simplifies the design of the control unit.

Finally, there are also "zero-address" (stack oriented) computers and several of them have been designed and successfully commercially implemented.

In zero-address computers, most instructions do not contain any operand address because they get their operands from and leave results on the stack. Note that in addition to zero-address instructions, these CPUs must also have instructions that contain an address; otherwise the stack could not be loaded from or stored in memory. The term "zero-address machine" thus refers to the philosophy of address specification characteristic for the architecture but does not exclude other methods. The same holds for the previously mentioned classes as well. As an example, the 6800 CPU has many instructions using implied addressing with no explicit address and yet it is classified as a one-address CPU.

As for *data types*, the architect must decide how to represent integers, whether to include floating-point numbers, BCD codes, ASCII, and so on. On smaller computers, data types are more primitive because implementation of floating-point arithmetic, for example, is expensive. Large computers have a wider choice of data types and provide longer words for fast calculation with high precision operands.

In selecting the kinds of instructions to be used, the architect is guided by the intended application of the CPU. A CPU designed to control industrial processes, a CPU intended to execute real-time processing of digital signals like digitized speech, a CPU for a personal computer, and a CPU for a supercomputer must satisfy very different expectations. Similarly, a CPU designed for very efficient execution of one programming language, such as Pascal, requires a different instruction set than a general purpose CPU or a CPU designed for a programming language based on a different model of computation, such as LISP, the language used in many applications of artificial intelligence.

An important consideration in instruction set design is its *orthogonality*. By this we mean the extent to which the individual aspects of the instruction set can be combined. As an example, to what extent are general purpose CPU registers interchangeable? Can different addressing modes be used in the same way for all instructions within a given category such as arithmetic? Can different data types be used in the same way within a given instruction category? As an example, if there are instructions for integer multiplication and division and the CPU implements floating-point arithmetic, are there also instructions for floating-point multiplication and division or is floating-point arithmetic limited to addition and subtraction? Similarly, if integer arithmetic is available with four addressing modes, are these available for floating-point arithmetic as well?

An instruction set that is highly symmetrical in this sense is called orthogonal (the term has its origin in mathematics) and is highly desirable. To see why, consider programming a CPU in which register $A$ can be added to register $B$ and the result stored in $A$ but not in $B$; where addition can use indexed addressing but multiplication cannot; where an integer result of addition can be converted to BCD but the result of subtraction cannot; where only BCD adjustment is possible on register $A$, but not on register $B$, and so on. Each deviation from orthogonality is an exception that must be remembered and carefully considered in the planning of a program. As an example, the programmer must anticipate that if, after a chain of operations, results end up in the wrong registers, the contents of registers may have to be reorganized, data stored in memory, and so on, increasing execution time.

As we already know, instruction coding has important consequences for the complexity of the CPU and affects the speed of execution. Non uniform lengths of opcodes also make it difficult or impossible to take advantage of certain arrangements for improving speed, such as instruction pipelining.

The question of the size of the instruction set is also important. Until relatively recently, the prevailing trend in the development of instruction sets was to continue adding new instructions because it was widely believed that specialized instructions speed up program execution by reducing the number of instruction fetches. Unfortunately, careful analysis of performance of various instruction sets indicates that this is often incorrect.

There are two main reasons why CPUs having many instructions are not always faster. The first is rather obvious: Complex instruction set computers (CISC) have more complicated, and therefore slower CPUs. Second, most programs executed by modern CPU are produced by compilation, automatically and with limited user control, and this imposes a certain pattern on the utilization of the instruction set.

Compilers tend to use a small number of instructions because the reasoning that allows a human programmer writing an assembly language program to select the optimal instruction in a particular situation is often too complex for a compiler. As a consequence, compiled code on CISC machines has been found to use only a limited subset of the complete instruction set (for example 60%).

Analyses performed on compiled code also show that there is a mismatch between the needs of modern high-level languages and conventional computer architectures. In essence, many CPUs were designed without enough regard for the development of programming languages and their design was guided by a low-level machine perspective; considerations like "If we want to transfer this code from *A* to *B*, do we have a good instruction to do it?" "If we need to calculate an address, do we have a register to hold it?" "Can we formulate a special instruction that will more efficiently execute an operation that appears in some computer programs?"

Instead architects should have focused on the needs of high level languages, for example: "If we want to execute a program with nested procedures and parameters, do we have facilities to do it efficiently?"

When the analysis was turned in this direction—toward the needs of programming languages rather than the transfer of bits from one place to another—it became clear that although most modern programs are modular and consist of procedures with parameters, conventional CPUs do not have the means to handle this task efficiently. Each procedure call requires the passing of arguments, and the process of passing and of accessing parameters and local variables is the most time consuming operation. Consequently, it is the operation in which the most execution time could be gained by changing the architecture.

As a result of these findings, it was proposed that a modern CPU should have a reduced instruction set (RISC) with a restricted number of addressing modes, and should use the saving in CPU logic to provide many internal registers, most of which would be treated as a stack to minimize the complexity of their access and to match the needs of parameter passing. Preferably, the process of loading procedure parameters on the stack and their access should be performed by hardware and should be transparent (invisible) to the code and the programmer.

The struggle between RISC and CISC architectures is not finished but the RISC philosophy has the upper hand at the moment, and modern CPUs tend to have smaller instruction sets.

## 13.3 MEMORIES

One of the most permanent driving forces in computing has been the need for ever bigger and faster memory. Because fast memory is expensive, modern computers divide storage into several levels to provide a large capacity for the storage of many files, and fast execution at a reasonable cost.

As we have seen, the typical personal computer has two layers of memory: the fast (100-nsec access time) but relatively small (around 1 Mbyte) semiconductor main memory, and the much slower (access time over 30 msec) but much larger (typically 30 Mbytes) secondary storage, usually implemented with floppy and hard disks. As much of the currently executing program and its data as possible are stored in the RAM, while files with data and programs that are not executing, or parts of the current program that do not fit into RAM, are stored on the disk.

Unfortunately, even CPUs used by personal computers are often faster than standard RAM chips and this poses a dilemma: We can either slow down the CPU by introducing "wait states" if the RAM cannot keep up with the CPU, or else reduce the size of the memory but use faster and more expensive RAM chips. Often the best solution is to keep the size of the main memory and the type of RAM chips unchanged and to introduce another memory level between the CPU and the main memory. This new, small-capacity but very fast memory is called the *cache* (Figure 13.1).

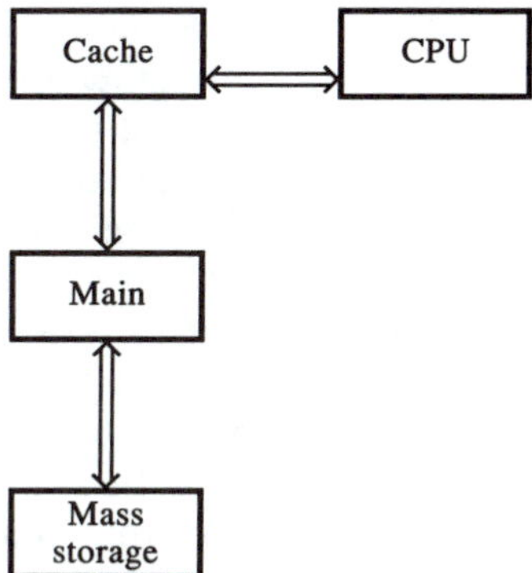


**Figure 13.1.** Multilevel memory with a cache.

How does a computer having a cache, a main memory, and mass storage work? The principle is an extension of the two-level RAM–disk memory model.

When the CPU begins to execute a program, it loads its code and data from a disk file into the main memory. The first block of code and data needed to start execution is also loaded into the cache. As long as program execution stays within the block currently in the cache, the CPU uses the cache, whose very short access time allows the CPU to operate at full speed. When the program generates an address that is not currently in the cache, the code in the cache is swapped with a block of code in the main memory that contains the desired address.

Although this arrangement appears sensible, it is not clear that it will improve the speed of execution. After all, the cache is small and it should not take long before the CPU exhausts the code in the cache and needs a new block. Fortunately, most programs satisfy the "principle of locality," which states that a program spends most of its time executing instructions located in a restricted address region, mainly in short loops executed many times. The same applies to data as well. The consequence is that because the CPU is usually interested in a small part of memory, we do not need to have fast access to a very large memory space, and the cache principle works.

Note that the small size of the cache means that its addresses require only a small number of bits. As an example, a 64k cache requires only sixteen address bits. However, the program in the cache uses the full addressing power of the CPU, for example, thirty-two bits on a 80286-based IBM AT compatible. Consequently, the cache must be supported by "address translation" logic that checks whether the code corresponding to the requested full-size address is in a block now in the cache and converts the full thirty-two bit "virtual" address into a physical address in the cache.

This principle allows programs to reference addresses beyond the limits of the physical memory in which they are stored, and can also be applied to the main memory–mass storage pair. The capacity of the main memory may be, for example, 4 Mbytes requiring twenty-two address bits but programs may use thirty-two bit addresses that are then translated either into a twenty–two bit physical address within the 4 Mbyte main memory, or else into a block of data or code on the disk that must be loaded into memory to replace a block of code that is no longer needed. This arrangement is referred to as *virtual storage.* The division of the memory space into several levels, and virtual addressing provide an almost unlimited address space, allowing the programmer to write programs without concern for the size of memory.

A number of questions arise in connection with virtual addressing regarding the best size of the cache, the best algorithm for selecting which block is to be replaced when a new block is needed, how the algorithm should be implemented (in hardware, software, or a combination of both), and so on. These topics are beyond the range of our book and we will restrict ourselves to only one aspect of cache implementation: the conversion of the virtual address to a physical address.

The cache is usually divided into segments of fixed size and the currently needed blocks are stored in them in a random order. The conversion of the virtual address of an instruction into a physical cache address can thus be accomplished by storing the starting addresses of individual segments in a table and retrieving them using a lookup procedure. Because this lookup must be very fast (otherwise the cache speed would be lost) it cannot use software; in essence, the address must be found in a single step. The most efficient way to do this is to use *associative memory*.

An associative memory consists of a block of memory locations and additional logic that allows it to be treated as a table and to be searched in parallel—all locations at the same time. In many applications, a part of the word stored in each location is a "key" that identifies the code and the rest is data. The key is then used in the parallel search and the rest of the code whose key is found to match the desired key value is returned as the result of the search. In our application, the *n*th element of the table need only store the most significant bits of the virtual address of the segment in the *n*th block of the physical memory, the cache. To find the physical address, the leading bits of the virtual address are treated as a key and placed on the input of the associative memory and the number of the cache segment containing this block is read from it. If the segment is in the cache, the obtained physical address is combined with the remaining part of the instruction (Figure 13.2) to obtain the physical cache address. If the address is not in the table, the required block must be moved into the cache from the main memory or from the disk and replace an existing block. The contents of the associative memory must be changed accordingly.

To conclude this section, let us describe an alternative way to speed up memory access, the method called *interleaving*. If a particular memory chip can be accessed at most once every 100 nsec, then two RAM chips can be alternatively accessed twice every 100 nsec, four chips four times every 100 nsec, and so on. Interleaving memory accesses between two different memory banks can thus double the apparent speed of the memory. This, of course, holds only if the CPU will always find consecutive words in alternative banks, and this is satisfied more easily in some applications than in others. Interleaving is well suited, for example, in display RAMs where memory access is very regular, but it is not so well suited for the main program and data memory.

In the main memory, most code is also accessed in a linear fashion and thus interleaving works most of the time. Jumps and similar nonlinear sequences in program execution, however, break the regular pattern and this means that memory access is not always interleaved. Occasionally, the same memory bank will be accessed two or more times in a row and because a single memory bank is not capable of such speed, the CPU will have to insert one or

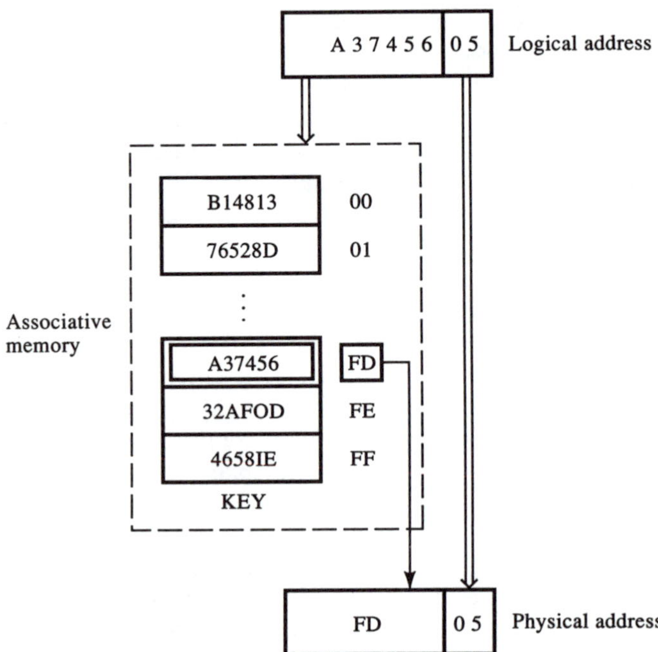


**Figure 13.2.** Conversation between virtual and physical address using associative memory.

more wait states and skip one or more clock cycles to allow the RAM to recover from the previous access. This slows down the operation and requires additional logic.

Both cache memory and interleaving are extensively used at all levels of computers beginning with the more sophisticated types of personal computers.

## Exercises

1. When is it necessary to store the contents of the old block in the main memory during cache reloading, and when can the old block be simply overwritten with the new one?
2. If the address that must be accessed is not in the top-level memory (for example, the cache), the block containing it must be loaded from the lower level memory. There is no single best strategy to determine which of the currently resident blocks should be swapped but two or three intuitively obvious methods give very good performance. Suggest such an algorithm and indicate how it could be physically implemented. Explain how one could evaluate its performance.
3. Show how a small associative memory could be implemented and comment on the complexity of the circuit in comparison with that of an

ordinary RAM. What does the result suggest about the cost of associative memories?

4. Draw a logic diagram of the interface of an interleaved memory in which odd addresses are stored in one bank and even addresses in another. Analyze a typical program to determine what percentage of wait states may have to be generated.
5. List all situations in which a wait state might be required on a 6800- or an 8086-based CPU.

## 13.4 INPUT AND OUTPUT PROCESSING

We have already seen that the CPU and I/O run at very different speeds. On single-user personal computers, where an I/O task may have to be completed before the program can do anything else, it may be acceptable for the CPU to wait until the I/O operation is finished. On a large, powerful, and expensive computer servicing multiple users, however, halting the CPU until a program prints several pages of output is intolerable. In this case, separation of processing and I/O is necessary to achieve high "throughput" (number of programs processed per unit of time) and efficient use of the CPU.

Another situation in which a CPU cannot wait until an I/O operation is completed arises in computer networks, where individual computers or workstations may not even have their own I/O devices and usually share printers and large hard disk drives.

The separation of processing from I/O has a long history. It goes back to second-generation computers, when CPUs became so powerful and expensive that full utilization of the CPU became imperative. These computers were designed so that the CPU was dedicated to processing and overall control, and one or more specialized *I/O processors* (also called IOPs, "channels," or peripheral processing units) inserted between the CPU and the slow peripherals were put in charge of all I/O operations. This arrangement has been used ever since, especially on larger computers. At present, even CPU families such as the 8086 offer I/O coprocessors and the principle of separating processing and I/O is spreading even to smaller computers.

An I/O processor is essentially a CPU with a specialized architecture (particularly the instruction set) designed to control I/O operations. When the main CPU encounters an instruction requesting I/O, it notifies the I/O processor, for example, by sending it an appropriate control signal and the address of the first instruction of an I/O program that must be executed to implement the desired task. Alternatively, the CPU may leave a "message" in a memory segment regularly assessed by the IOP. Because the program running on the main CPU cannot proceed until the I/O operation is completed, the CPU puts the current program on hold and switches to another program. The I/O processor, in the meantime, starts executing the specified I/O program using one of the methods described in Chapter 12. In doing this, it may assign some parts of the I/O operation to another controller, such as a

DMAC, and the process may thus be divided into several levels. When the I/O processor is finished, it notifies the main CPU by an interrupt signal.

### Exercises

1. Draw the block diagram of a computer using a single CPU, a single I/O processor, a cache, a main memory, four disk drives, two magnetic tape drives, and two printers.
2. Define throughput and CPU utilization. Explain their importance in terms of user satisfaction and economy of operation.
3. Outline how one could estimate the increase in throughput achieved by separating I/O from processing. Test the procedure on a typical program for a 6800-based computer.
4. Discuss the main architectural features of an I/O processor, including the instruction set (the instructions, addressing modes, and data types that are needed), and I/O signals.

## 13.5 ALTERNATIVE ARCHITECTURES AND COMPUTATIONAL MODELS

One of the main goals in computer architecture is to design the fastest machine for the given category of problems. Higher speed can be achieved most easily by using faster components but this approach is not really in the domain of a computer architect and has its limits as physical laws make it impossible to overcome barriers like the maximum speed of signal propagation. For the computer architect, the most interesting approach to achieving higher speed is finding more efficient CPU architecture.

Many approaches to CPU architecture have been explored and implemented in the past but their analysis is the subject of more specialized courses. In the rest of this section, we will concentrate on a few approaches that are fundamentally different from the principles presented so far. Most of the ideas we will discuss have been explored in the past but until recently, have had limited commercial impact. With the rapidly decreasing cost and increasing power and ease of design of hardware components, alternative architectures have now finally become viable. This is especially true for the exploitation of parallelism in computer operation; therefore parallelism in computer operation will be our first subject.

### Classification of Computers by Parallelism

We mentioned one form of parallelism in the previous section, where we showed that computers can process more programs by performing processing and I/O in parallel. Parallelism can, however, run deeper as the processing of a single task can often be speeded up by using several processors in parallel.

To put this subject into perspective, we will start by classifying computers according to their degree of parallelism.

We have assumed that a computer consists of a single CPU, a single (possibly hierarchical) memory, and peripherals. This arrangement is referred to as "single instruction stream-single data stream" (SISD) architecture because instructions and operands are fetched sequentially from memory.

If we treat the processing of the instruction stream and the processing of the data stream as independent parameters, we obtain the following additional categories of parallelism:

Single instruction stream-multiple data streams (SIMD)

Multiple instruction streams-single data stream (MISD)

Multiple instruction streams-multiple data streams (MIMD).

Problems involving identical operations applied to a set of elements, as in

```
FOR i := 1 TO n DO
  A[i] := B[i] + C[i1]
```

are best implemented by *SIMD machines*.

This calculation involves *n* independent pairs of elements with the same operation performed on each pair (Figure 13.3). If we send the sequence of instructions (fetch operands, add them, store the result in memory) to *n* separate processors, and if all processors can access the memory simultaneously and independently, the loop can be executed in one *n*th the time required by a single processor.

Many important algorithms, especially in engineering and scientific calculations, contain sections similar to our example and special computers called

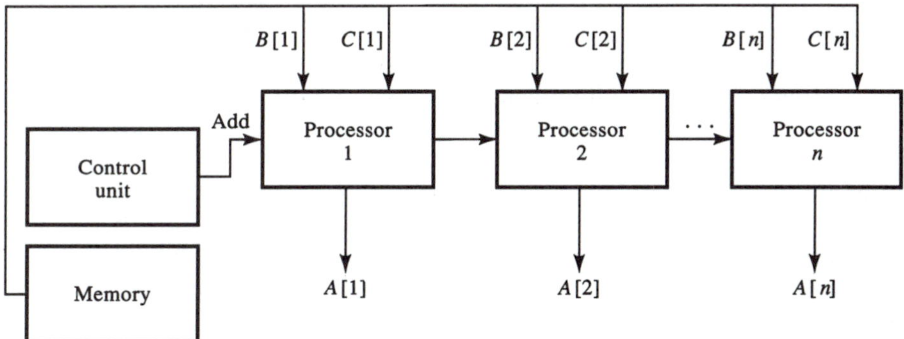


**Figure 13.3.** Processing of an array operation on a SIMD machine.

"array processors" are available to execute them in the style suggested above. According to our classification, array processors are SIMD machines.

Because an array processor has a single source of instructions and multiple processing elements, it consists of a single centralized control unit distributing identical instructions to multiple processors. The processors apply the sequence of instructions to data stored in their private memories and obtained from a central store. The results are returned to the central store as well. Two of the many possible architectures of an array processor are shown in Figure 13.4. Obviously, they provide different amounts of communication between processors, and differ in complexity and the types of tasks for which are they are suited.

Unfortunately, the nature of real problems is such that the theoretical speedup by a factor of $n$ when $n$ processors are used is never achieved in practice for several reasons. First, few algorithms, if any, can be expressed in a purely parallel form. In most cases, sections that can be parallelized alternate with sections that are sequential and the sequential sections do not allow any speedup by using $n$ processors. Also, execution always involves overhead, such as moving data between the memory and the processors or exchanging intermediate results among individual processors, and to some extent sequential operations. The degree of parallelism that can be actually achieved depends on the nature of the problem, the formulation of the algorithm, and the architecture of the machine.

A number of questions arise in connection with SIMD machines such as: Should each processor have its own local memory or should there be only one global memory accessible to all processors at the same time? How is data transmitted from the global memory to the local one? How powerful are the individual processing elements? Can the processing elements communicate directly with one another? If not, how can they communicate? As always, the most powerful solutions are also the most expensive and the problem is how to achieve an efficient solution at an acceptable cost.

In spite of the difficulties and cost, SIMD machines are very popular because many important problems cannot be solved in a reasonable time by any other method and because the cost and power of hardware is decreasing.

*Multiple-instruction single-data machines*, where multiple instruction streams (multiple programs) operate on a single stream of data, are not very interesting computationally except, perhaps, in industrial and similar signal processing applications where one set of measurements may be processed simultaneously in several different ways for several different uses.

*Multiprocessors (MIMD machines)* provide the ultimate form of parallelism. In these machines, several processors capable of independently fetching and executing instructions are connected together to join in the execution of a single program or to execute their programs individually. The individual processors may be traditional machines or may be designed specifically for multiprocessing.

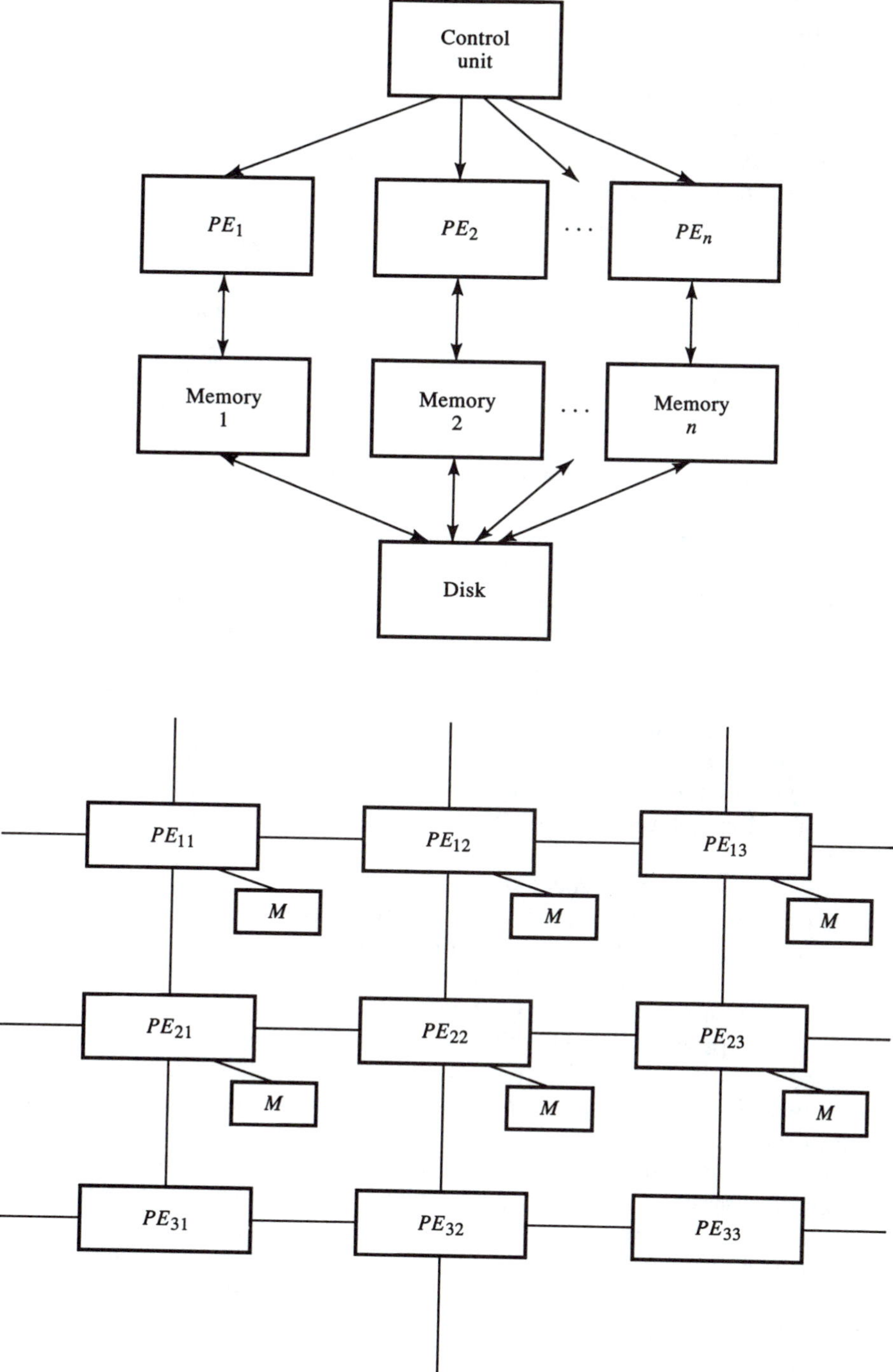


**Figure 13.4.** Two possible array processor architectures: Symbol "PE" stands for "processing element," "M" represents local memory.

When all the processors work on the same problem together, multiprocessors can operate in the SIMD mode and provide the increased processing speed of array processors, or they can each work on a different segment of the same program and provide a different form of speed up.

Because designing a multiprocessor is much more difficult than simply using *n* individual processors, one must ask what advantages an *n*-processor multiprocessor has over *n* independent uniprocessors. One advantage is that its individual processors can be programmed to work together, share their I/O resources (disk drives, printers, and graphics stations), and use them more economically. Also, an *n*-unit multiprocessor is more reliable than *n* independent processors: If one of the processors fails, its task can be automatically transferred to another processor and processing can continue with only a small degradation of performance. This is referred to as "graceful performance degradation."

The questions of multiprocessor architecture are similar to those of SIMD processors but their solution is more difficult. The basic problems are how powerful the individual processors should be, how they should be connected together, and how memory should be implemented. Many arrangements are possible and two of them are shown in Figure 13.5. One approach is to separate the processors from their memories and allow them to communicate via a multidimensional switch. Another approach is to implement processors as CPU/memory units and design a bus system for communication between them. (This method is simpler and cheaper but also slower. It requires some form of addressing and arbitration of the priority of communication over the bus.)

If the processors are connected in a grid where each node is connected only to its neighbors, the architect must decide what constitutes a neighborhood, and its geometric structure. An *n*-dimensional cube and a torus are two possible choices. Other considerations include the number of neighbors, whether there is a fixed master processor that assigns tasks to processors, how powerful the processors are (similar to uniprocessor CPUs or specialized and adapted to the overall architecture), what happens when a processor fails, and how messages and data are communicated between two distant processors within the system.

An equally difficult problem is the programming of a multiprocessor. The design of programming languages that allow the programmer to describe the desired parallelism, the formulation of efficient algorithms to solve various classes of problems, and the design of compilers to convert programs into code that takes maximal advantage of a given architecture are problems that are the subject of intensive research.

Multiprocessor architecture has so many parameters that there is no single optimal design. An architecture that works best for one type of problem may not work well for another and each category of problems requires its own solution.

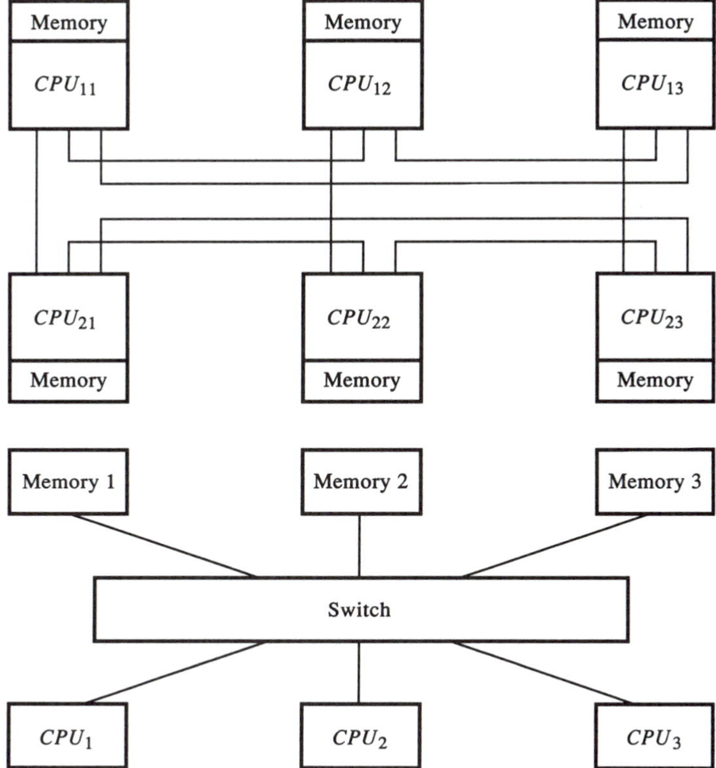


**Figure 13.5.** Two possible multiprocessor architectures.

## Uses of Parallelism Inside Processors

In the previous section, we concentrated on the use of parallelism at the interprocessor level. This, however, is not its only or most common use: Parallelism can also be employed inside a single processor or even at the gate level as in the use of ripple-carry adders rather than lookahead adders.

Because the two basic tasks of a processor are the execution of instructions and the processing of data, parallelism inside a processor can be directed toward the processing of instruction codes and toward the processing of operands.

One way to use parallelism to speed up calculation is to subdivide the ALU into several subunits, each dedicated to a different arithmetic operation and data type (Figure 13.6). Furthermore, those operations that are performed most frequently can be allocated several identical units. On an ALU with several independent units simultaneously performing different types of operations on different data types, a sequence of arithmetic and logic instructions

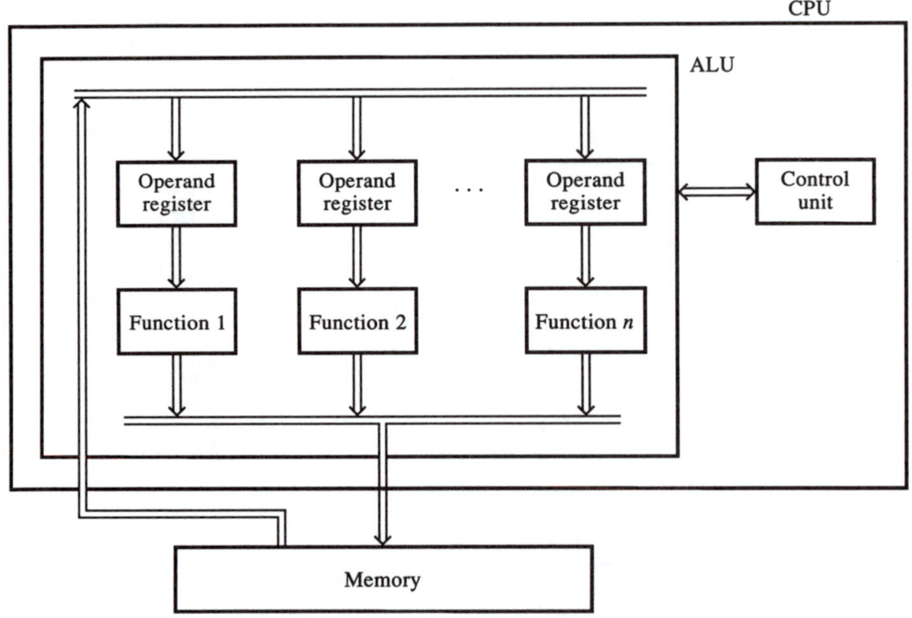


**Figure 13.6.** Parallelism in an ALU with multiple function units.

may be executed in a staggered way, with individual operand pairs passing through stages of processing in a stepwise fashion. Although the individual operations and operands are fed into the ALU sequentially, the effect is similar to parallel execution.

In addition to subdividing the ALU into specialized units, some of the ALU units may themselves be divided into segments and the whole operation treated as an *arithmetic pipeline.*

The principle of pipelining is the division of an operation into several suboperations, with a function unit allocated to each of them, and the individual segments connected by registers so that they can pass intermediate results and yet remain isolated to prevent interference.

As an example, floating-point addition consists of three steps: alignment, addition, and realignment. A floating-point adder may thus be divided into an alignment unit, an adder, and a realignment unit, all separated by registers (Figure 13.7). This arrangement forms a pipeline that can process up to three different pairs of operands simultaneously.

When the first pair of operands enters the pipeline, the two codes are aligned and the results stored in two registers at the next clock pulse. The output of these registers then goes into the adder while another pair of operands enters the alignment unit. On the next clock edge, the result from the adder is stored in the third register and the alignment unit begins to operate on it. At the same time, the pair aligned in the first stage is stored in

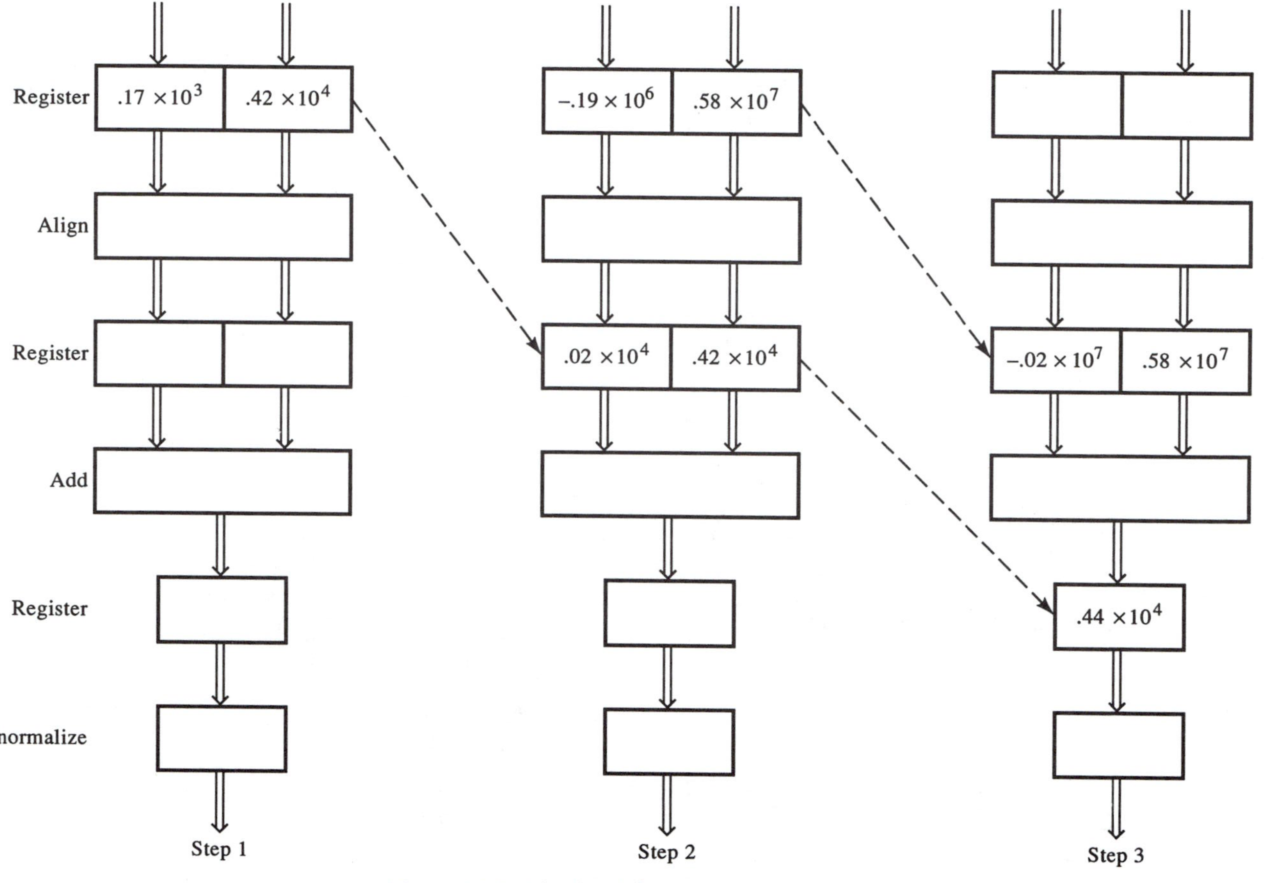


**Figure 13.7.** Pipelined floating-point adder.

the register separating the first two stages and the adder begins to operate on it, and a third pair of operands enters the first stage. In a full utilized pipelined unit operation can thus be up to three times faster than in a single-segment floating-point unit.

As with all forms of parallelism, a parallelized ALU can never achieve the maximum theoretical speedup. One reason for this is that not all of the instructions in a program are ALU operations. Another reason is that sequences of ALU operations do not necessarily consist only of identical operations such as floating-point additions or two's complement divisions. For both reasons, there are gaps in the supply of operands to the ALU and its subunits. A third reason why execution is not always parallel is that instructions in a sequence may be mutually dependent; one operation may have to be completed before another one can be started. Sometimes, reordering the instructions can make pipelining possible and speed up program execution. Effective use of the built-in parallelism thus requires careful scheduling.

Another form of pipelining is the *instruction pipeline.* In this arrangement, the execution of an instruction is divided into self-contained steps, such as the fetch phase, decoding phase, operand fetch, operation phase, and result store phase. While a new instruction is being fetched, the previous instruction may be decoded; and the one fetched before it may be fetching its operands. Our segmentation has five phases, and as many as five instructions could thus be in the pipeline simultaneously, yielding a five-fold speedup of execution (Figure 13.8).

To be beneficial, instruction pipelining does not have to be active in the sense that every segment of the pipeline performs some processing. Even passive pipelining can significantly improve CPU performance and is commonly used on relatively simple CPUs, such as the 8086. In passive pipelining instruction opcodes are fetched from memory during machine cycles when the CPU is not using the bus for data transfers and are stored in a set of internal pipeline registers where they wait for their turn in execution. Although the subsequent processing may be purely sequential, a speedup is achieved because the execution of an instruction can begin as soon as the previous instruction is completed, eliminating waiting for instruction fetch.

The full speedup theoretically offered by pipelining materializes under certain conditions. One is that execution of each phase of the pipeline must require approximately the same amount of time so that each segment cycle can shift its result into the next segment without waiting. This can often be achieved with proper design of the instruction set, suitable segmentation of the operation, and careful design of the circuit's segments.

A second condition is that the pipeline always be full. This condition is satisfied in the case of an instruction pipeline because the CPU can always fetch one instruction after another. In the ALU pipeline, this can only be achieved if the program contains chains of arithmetic operations.

Even a full pipeline is not sufficient to speed up execution. A third condition is that none of the work performed in the pipeline be wasted. This is not

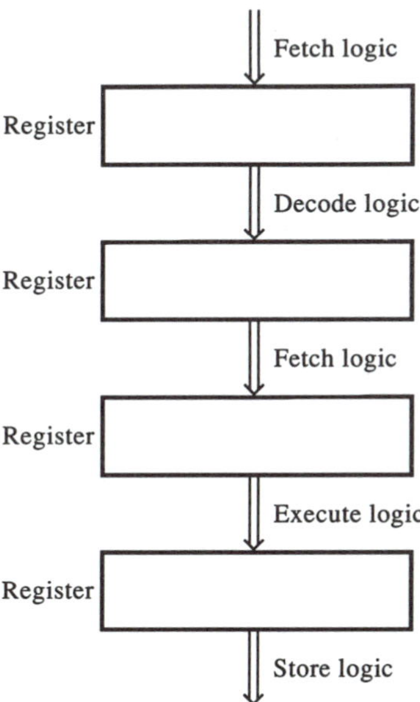


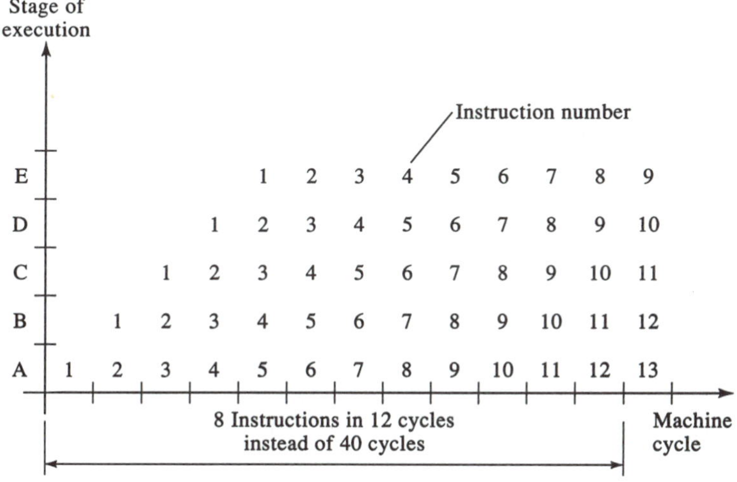


**Figure 13.8.** Instruction pipeline and its operation.

always the case in the instruction pipeline. The execution flow of a sequence of instructions containing a conditional jump depends on the evaluation of a condition, and the condition usually cannot be evaluated until the instruction preceding the jump is executed. Consequently, instructions following the jump are in the pipeline before the condition can be evaluated, and if the condition is satisfied and the jump taken, the pipeline must be emptied and refilled.

Our brief analysis shows that parallelism increases processing speed but the effective speedup is always below the theoretical limit. At present, even CPUs used in personal computers contain some form of parallelism, such as instruction prefetch. However, whereas the amount of pipelining available to designers of inexpensive CPUs is restricted by the limits on the cost of the CPU, designers of supercomputers do not have to worry about such restrictions. As their goal is to maximize the speed at almost any cost, they do not need to be concerned how much a particular pipeline is used: If a problem can be solved more quickly with a pipeline, the pipeline is worth having.

### Nonconventional CPU Architectures and Computational Models

We have implicitly assumed a model of computation that uses binary circuits and is driven by instructions fetching operands and storing results. In this section, we will briefly outline two alternative digital approaches—data flow and neural computing—and a nondigital (analog) computational model.

The *dataflow computing* model is the "opposite" of our model, which assumes that a program written in, for example, Pascal produces a sequence of instructions that fetch data and operate on them. Instructions, in fact, flow through the processor and their arrival to the CPU triggers data transfer and operations.

In a dataflow computer, the model is reversed: Data are loaded into a network of simple processors and flow through it, being processed by individual nodes. As an example, to evaluate an expression, data are fed into the input of the network, individual nodes wait until they receive all their operands and then "fire," producing a result and passing it to the next node.

When we analyze the basic operations required in a computing task, we find that a dataflow computer needs the following types of processors:

Arithmetic processors performing addition, subtraction, and so on.

Gates that pass or block data according to the value of a condition. These elements are called T-gates and F-gates because they pass data if a condition evaluated by another element is True or False.

Logic operators ("deciders") that evaluate logic expressions.

Data links that duplicate data tokens and release multiple copies to other processors for further processing.

Instead of discussing the general properties of data flow computing, we will conclude with the example in Figure 13.9, which shows a dataflow structure to calculate the arithmetic expression $(a + 3) - 2 \times (b + a + 3)$ and a block

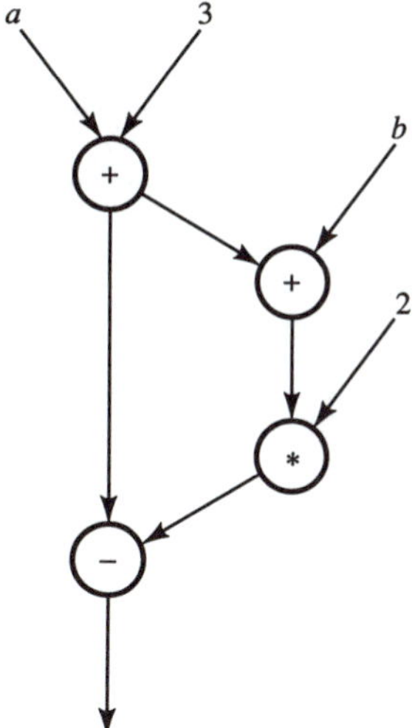


**Figure 13.9.** Dataflow structure to calculate $(a + 3) - 2 \times (b + a + 3)$.

diagram of the possible architectural implementation of a dataflow computer (Figure 13.10).

The dataflow computer in Figure 13.10 works as follows: The memory consists of cells containing complete instructions with room for addresses and data values. Originally, some of the instructions may be incomplete. When an instruction contains all its operands, it is activated and sent to an appropriate functional or control processing unit that produces the result and sends it, along with the address of its destination cell, to the distribution network. From here, the operand goes into the appropriate location in the memory.

At present, data flow computing is used mainly as a theoretical model and in experimental hardware.

Another unconventional model of computing, called *neural computing*, is based on emulation of the most powerful computing machine, a biological organism.

Just like all forms of digital computing presented so far, neural computing is binary and is based on combinational elements. The differences between the conventional and the neural model are that the building elements are described in terms of adjustable "threshold functions" and that the machines consist of regularly structured networks of threshold elements using various types of potentially modifiable architectures.

The computing element of a neural computer is the threshold element, a formalized implementation of the basic building block of all biological control systems, the neuron. A neuron is a component having multiple binary inputs and a binary output that becomes active when the sum of its weighted

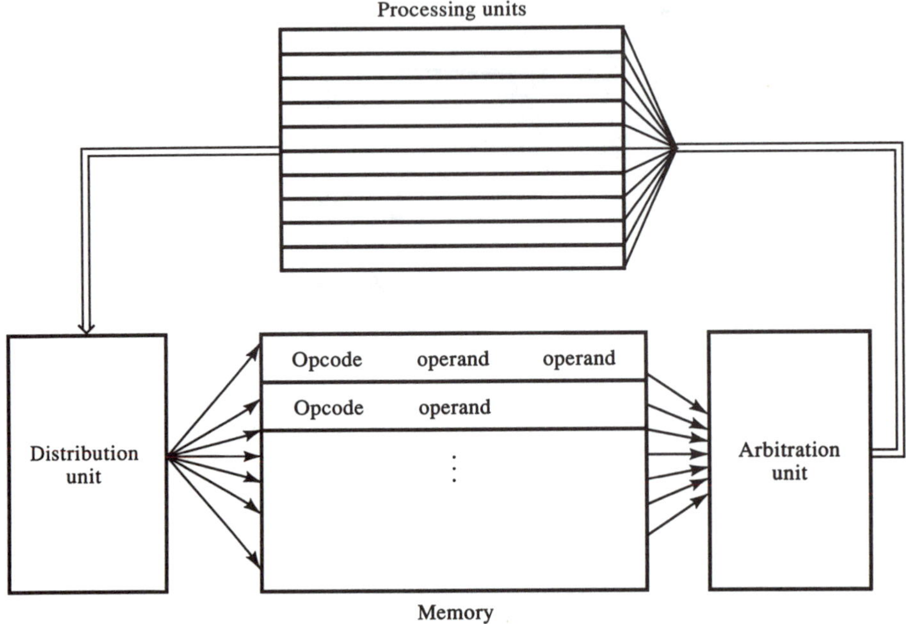


**Figure 13.10.** Block diagram of a possible dataflow architecture.

inputs exceeds the threshold (Figure 13.11): $\Sigma W_i a_i > T$. The threshold element is, in effect, a generalized majority voter.

Although there are Boolean functions that cannot be realized by a single threshold element, threshold functions can implement all basic gates and thus all logic functions. A two-input AND gate, for example, can be implemented as a two-input threshold device with weights 1 and 1, and threshold 1. The device produces a 1 iff

$$a \times 1 + b \times 1 > 1$$

A two-input OR gate can be attained as a threshold device with inputs weights 1 and 1, and threshold 0. An inverter is a single-input threshold device with a negative input weight (−1) and threshold −1.

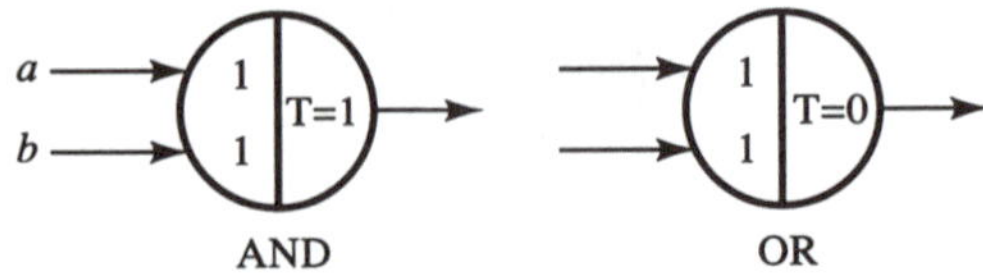


**Figure 13.11.** Implementation of AND and OR gates using threshold components.

Because threshold elements can realize any logic function, they can replace gates in the design of conventional digital computers. However, this is not their major application; neural computers emulating the properties of biological systems are more interesting.

Just like biological systems, neural computers are networks of interconnected neurons (threshold elements). The challenge in designing a neural computer for a given application is to find an effective architecture of interconnections and appropriate weights for the inputs of individual elements.

It is clear that for a network resembling even a fraction of a system like the human visual system, the number of weights and connections that would have to be calculated and set is enormous and unachievable in a realistic amount of time. However, one of the most interesting aspects of natural neural systems is that they are adaptable and adjust to the requirements of a task. The second challenge in the design of neural computers is thus to find efficient algorithms to guide the adaptation of weights, thresholds, and possibly even architectures to a given task.

Neural computing is a relatively old research area of computer science and its current popularity is due to recent developments in technology that have made it possible to build chips implementing complex neural modules, and to progress in the design of efficient algorithms for neural net adaptation. "Programming" of neural computers consists mainly of the selection of a suitable network architecture and an appropriate adaptation algorithm.

Just like biological neural systems, artificial neural systems seem to be best suited for specialized tasks that require many parallel computations, such as the recognition of visual patterns. Obviously, neural computing is based on completely different principles than the digital systems we have covered. The nature of the main problems in this discipline is more mathematical and further coverage is beyond the scope of this book. We will thus proceed to the last topic of this chapter, analog computing.

Although we have presented several different approaches to computing, all were discrete and, in fact, binary. Although discrete models based on bases different from 2 have also been explored (mostly theoretically), they are not commonly used, at least not in CPU design. There exists, however, a very different approach to computing based on analog rather than discrete (digital) calculations.

In *analog computing*, signals are continuous and interpreted as continuous rather than as representing discrete ranges. Similarly, the basic functions in analog computations are not binary (AND, OR, and so on) but are continuous functions like straight lines, parabolas, exponentials and nonlinear continuous functions.

Analog components are based on the properties of circuits having resistors, capacitors and feedback connections. Their basic building blocks are amplifiers, which allow multiplication of a signal's magnitude by a constant, weighted summation, integration, and differentiation (Figure 13.12). In addi-

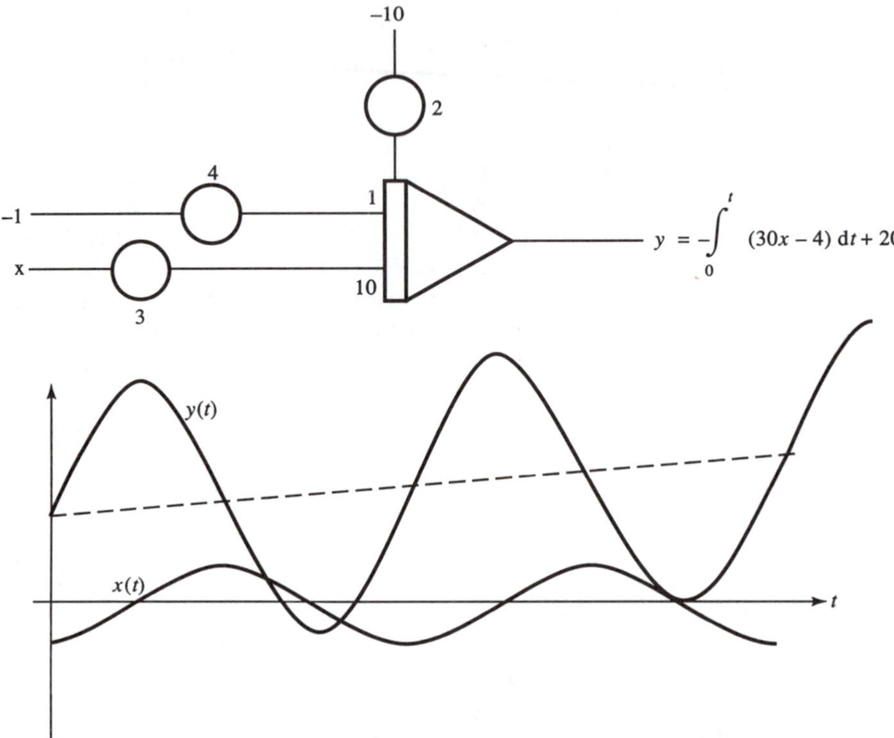


**Figure 13.12.** Symbolic representation of an analog circuit performing integration and an example of its operation. The triangular symbol represents an integrator; the circles are potentiometers (adjustable resistors); and lines are connecting wires. Input signal $x$ may be generated by another circuit or by the analog computer itself. Several circuits of this kind can be connected together to solve a set of differential equations.

tion, components that produce nonlinear signal transformations, such as step functions, are also present.

Analog computers are used to obtain the time-dependent behavior of signals that can be described by differential equations, rather than to calculate exact numeric values like digital computers. Their inputs are electrical signals with constant, linear, sinusoidal, and similar behavior, and their outputs are continuous voltages, usually displayed on screens and plotted on plotters. Programming of analog computers resembles the design of a logic circuit more than computer programming. It consists of formulating a set of equations (mostly differential) that describe the problem, and drawing a wiring diagram showing how to connect the building blocks that implement the desired equations.

Analog computing used to be very popular in engineering and scientific applications, and in the 1940s and 1950s it was much more widespread than digital computing. It was used to model physical phenomena and to design industrial processes and their control. Later, it was overshadowed by the inexpensive and much more accurate digital computing. (Analog computations always produce only approximate results.) However, recent renewed interest in neural computing and the fact that many difficult problems can be expressed in terms of differential equations that can be solved very conveniently with analog computers (possibly based on physical principles other than electric signals, such as the behavior of light) has led to a resurrection of interest in analog computing as well.

One can expect that analog computing will regain some of its popularity, possibly in areas completely different from its origin, for example, in an extension of neural computing to analog signals. One of its most likely future forms is "hybrid computing," a symbiosis of digital and analog computing.

## Exercises

1. What are the advantages and disadvantages of the two array processor architectures shown in Figure 13.4?
2. A typical application of array processors is for operations on one-dimensional or multidimensional arrays, such as the calculation of a product of two matrices

$$A[k,l] = \sum B[k,j] \times C[j,l]$$

   where $k$, $l$, and $j$ range from 1 to $n$. Outline how this calculation could be done in the two architectures in Figure 13.4 and estimate the ratio of the time required for arithmetic processing to the "routing time" needed to transfer the intermediate results between the individual processors.
3. Draw a diagram showing the connections between processors in
   a. a two-dimensional cube arrangement
   b. a three-dimensional cube arrangement
   c. a toroidal arrangement

   For each, name one physical problem for which the architecture is suited.
4. Outline how active instruction pipelining could be implemented on a microprogrammed CPU. Draw a block diagram.
5. Show how eight-bit sequential add-shift multiplication could be implemented by a pipeline. What is the maximum speedup achievable over an ordinary sequential multiplier? How does the speed and the complexity of the circuit compare with that of the cellular multiplier introduced in Chapter 6?
6. Analyze a program involving many calculations (a "compute-bound" problem) and estimate how much the multiplication pipeline would speed up its execution.
7. Draw a diagram showing how a passive instruction pipeline could be implemented.

8. Draw a block diagram showing how jumps could be handled by a passive pipeline.
9. How could the disruption caused by a jump instruction in an instruction pipeline be minimized? Consider conditional and unconditional jumps separately.
10. Draw a diagram showing dataflow implementation of

```
IF (x+3) < (y−6)
   THEN z := x+7
   ELSE z := 2*y+4
```

11. Explain how the "program" in Figure 13.9 could be executed by the dataflow architecture in Figure 13.1. Repeat for the problem in Exercise 9.
12. How could two-input XOR and NOR gates and a three-input AND gate be implemented with threshold functions?
13. Formulate an algorithm for the calculation of weights and the threshold to find a threshold element implementing a given truth table. Does the algorithm always give a solution?
14. Show that the Boolean function $f = ab + cd$ cannot be realized with a single threshold element.
15. Formulate an algorithm for finding the logic function implemented by a given threshold element. Use the algorithm to find the function implemented by a three-input element with weights 1, −2, 3 and threshold 1.
16. Show how to implement $(ab + c) \cdot (a + b)$ using threshold devices. (*Hint*: Use NOT, AND, and OR building blocks.)
17. Draw a diagram showing how the following set of equations could be solved on an analog computer:

$$x(t) = -2 \times t + \int (3 \times x(t) + 2 \times y(t))dt$$
$$y(t) = 3 + 2 \times x(t) - \int (x(t) + y(t))dt$$

The symbol for an adder is a triangle; the symbol for an integrater is shown in Figure 13.12.

## SUMMARY

The purpose of this chapter was to put computer architecture into a broader context by presenting some general questions and unconventional approaches to computing.

After presenting a brief history of computing, our first topic was the design of instruction sets. We saw that a computer architect must decide what type of addressing to use, which and how many instructions to include in the instruction set, which data types to process, and similar questions. Decisions are guided by questions of available technology, cost, and the intended application of the CPU. We noted that careful analysis of typical modern programs suggests that it may be preferable to design CPUs with restricted rather than large instruction sets and to include a large stack of internal registers to speed up the processing of the very common nested procedures.

In the next section we dealt with memory architectures. To obtain a good combination of speed and cost, memories of modern computers are hierarchical, using as many as three levels of memory from disk-based mass storage, through main semiconductor memories, to very fast cache memories. Although the increased number of levels greatly improves performance at an acceptable cost, it poses difficult questions, such as the distribution and swapping of code among the various memories. We also mentioned that memory access times are always slower than the speed of the fastest CPUs and that this problem can be solved by interleaving.

In the next section we dealt with I/O, particularly on large computers, and showed that its separation from processing by the main CPU introduces a form of parallelism that increases the throughput of the computer. Where this approach is used, the operation of the computer is under the control of the main CPU, and I/O is performed by specialized computers called I/O processors.

The idea of parallelism was extended in the next section. We began with a classification of computers according to the degree of parallelism in the processing of instruction and data streams and defined array processors and multiprocessors. Although all forms of parallelism lead to increased performance, the actual speedup is always far below the theoretical maximum.

Parallelism does not have to be limited to the processor level. We showed that many computers use other forms of parallelism to speed up the processing of arithmetic and logic operations and execution of instructions. A powerful approach is pipelining, where execution is divided into well-defined independent stages.

In the last section, we introduced several less common forms of computing: dataflow computing, neural computing, and analog computing. In dataflow computing, data flows through a network of processors that wait for data and pass results as soon as an operation can be executed. Neural computers are adaptable networks of binary threshold elements whose outputs fire when the weighted sum of their inputs exceeds a threshold. In analog computers, signals are analog rather than discrete. Analog computers are used mainly for problems that can be described by differential equations and in many cases produce sufficiently accurate results much faster than their digital counterparts.

## REVIEW QUESTION

1. Explain the following terms: Analog computer, associative memory, cache, CISC architecture, computer generation, dataflow computers, hybrid computer, interleaved memory, I/O processor, multiprocessor, orthogonality, parallel processing, pipelining, principle of locality, RISC architecture, SISD/SIMD/MISD/MIMD classification, throughput, and virtual addressing.

## REFERENCES

The following titles listed in the references at the end of the book are relevant to this chapter:

J.-L. Baer. *Computer Systems Architecture.*

J. P. Hayes. *Computer Architecture and Organization.*

K. Huang and F. L. Briggs. *Computer Architecture and Parallel Processing.*

Z. Kohavi. *Switching and Finite Automata Theory.*

J. A. Sharp. *An Introduction to Distributed and Parallel Processing.*

# CHAPTER 14

# OPERATING SYSTEMS

## AN OVERVIEW

An operating system is a collection of programs providing an interface between the user and the computer, and between user programs and hardware. For computer operation, the operating system is just as important as the hardware and is usually supplied with the computer.

The more visible function of an operating system is that it allows the user to type commands requesting various system functions, such as the display of a file directory, disk formatting, and the execution of application programs like word processors, spread sheets, or computer games. When the user types a command, the command interpreter of the operating system decodes it and initiates its execution. When the task is completed, the operating system regains control and the user can enter another command.

The less visible but equally important function of an operating system is to provide tools allowing programs to control I/O devices, access files, and so on, without having to concern themselves with the details of I/O operations and similar intricate but routine tasks. The major components of this part of the operating system are the file system, which is responsible for the creation, deletion, and access to files stored on the disk; the command interpreter; and device drivers (subroutines mediating access to I/O operations).

Operating systems of large computers are much more complicated. They allow the sharing of main memory between several programs (multiprogramming), let several users use the computer simultaneously (time-sharing), and make secondary storage available to many users while preventing conflicts between them.

Whether the operating system is small or large, its role is to ensure that the system's resources are used as efficiently and safely as possible and with the least discomfort for the user.

In this chapter, we will restrict ourselves to operating systems of small computers. After a brief introduction, we will describe an embryonic operating system, the "monitor" of the Heathkit ET-3400, and then give an outline of MS-DOS, the widely used operating system of the IBM PC family of computers.

In the last section we will present OS68, a simple operating system designed for this text and patterned after MS-DOS. Our purpose is to demonstrate how operating system facilities can be used in the familiar 6800 programming environment and to provide a tool for experimentation with the basic programming concepts. We will also use OS68 as the basis of a simple compiler in the next chapter.

## IMPORTANT WORDS

Application program, BIOS, booting, command interpreter, device driver, DOS, logic service, monitor, multiprogramming, multitasking, system program, time sharing.

## 14.1 OPERATING SYSTEMS—AN INTRODUCTION

Most modern personal computers operate as follows: When the computer is turned on, its displays a message about the installed operating system and available resources, such as the amount of memory, and then enters a loop where it accepts and executes the user's commands. From the material presented in previous chapters, it is clear that this behavior requires some rather complicated programs. The collection of these programs is called the operating system (OS).

When we analyze the operation of a computer, we see that the operating system must contain a program that initializes the computer when it is turned on (the booting program), a program that interprets commands (the command interpreter), and routines that allow user programs to access and control computer resources, such as the memory, keyboard, display, printer, and secondary storage. Whereas the function of the command interpreter is visible to the user, the software that provides an interface to computer resources is hidden; it serves both the command interpreter and the programs that the user loads into memory for execution. This part of the operating system is a collection of tools, a toolbox accessible to all programs running on the computer. To help understand the functions and structure of operating systems, we will now briefly outline their evolution.

On the first computers, users initially wrote not only their application programs but also routines for I/O. Eventually, routines controlling peripherals and other generally useful programs became a part of the computing environment and the nucleus of the operating system. Communication between the user and the computer then assumed the form of commands entered via the available input devices (initially punched paper cards) and decoded by the command interpreter routine.

In the 1950s and 1960s, CPU speed, the size of memory, and the speed and capacity of secondary storage made it possible and economically desirable to let several programs share memory at one time and take turns in their use of the CPU (*multiprogramming*).

Some time later, another feature called *time-sharing* was added. With time-sharing, several users can access one computer simultaneously, using their own terminals. In reality, the simultaneous servicing of several users is only an illusion: The speed with which large computers can switch from one user to another makes it appear that several processes are taking place at the same time. Although this is achieved mainly by powerful hardware, the coordination of the overlapping demands of individual processes competing for the available hardware requires complicated software that forms a major part of the operating system.

The functions that an operating system of a time-shared and multiprogrammed computer must provide include the following:

Control of many computer terminals

Management of several programs sharing the CPU

Prevention of conflicts between user programs and the operating system

Protection of files from programs that are not authorized to use them

Protection of the operating system from user programs

Allocation of shared peripherals.

Modern computer hardware ranges from controllers dedicated to the control of simple devices such as keyboards; through personal computers, minicomputers, and mainframes; to ultrafast supercomputers and multiprocessor systems using many cooperating CPUs with private and shared memories. Furthermore, all these types of devices may be joined together in computer networks. This broad range of hardware is matched by a corresponding spectrum of operating systems. The simplest operating systems may require less than 1k of memory and reside in a ROM. They are often called monitors and can be found on simple computers designed for instrument control or education. The Heathkit ET-3400 microcomputer has such a monitor and we will describe it in the next section.

More advanced operating systems such as those used by personal computers (for example the MS-DOS system designed by Microsoft for the IBM PC) contain functions allowing the control of color and monochrome displays, printers, tape drives, and floppy and hard disk drives. These systems include programs that format disks, create, copy, and erase files, list directories, and test the computer's resources (memory, disk drive, keyboard, display, and others). Although a part of such an operating system resides in ROM and RAM memory, the programs are so large that most modules must be stored on disk and loaded into memory only when required. To give an example of such an operating system, we will later describe the structure and functions of MS-DOS. Operating systems of large computers are outside the scope of our coverage.

## 14.2 THE HEATHKIT ET-3400 MONITOR

The basis of an operating system is the architecture of the computer on which it runs. The architecture of the ET-3400 consists of the following:

A 6800 or 6808 Motorola CPU

256 or 512 bytes of memory starting at address 0

A 1k ROM at the top of the 64k address space

A seventeen-key keyboard

Six seven-segment LEDs

A breadboard, switches, LED lights, and connectors for experiments.

The organization of the memory space is as follows:

| Address Range ($) | Device |
|---|---|
| 0000–01FF | Two 256-byte RAM segments for user programs |
| C003–C00E | Keyboard |
| C110–C16F | Display |
| FC00–FFFF | 1k ROM for the monitor |

The ET-3400's monitor is small and is stored entirely in a ROM because it must be available when power is turned on. Because power-up activates the CPU *RESET* function, which performs an indirect jump via locations [$FFFE,$FFFF], these locations must be in a ROM and the whole 1k ROM chip is thus located at the top of the address space. Some of the data used by the monitor, such as the address of the digit used for display or the monitor stack, are variable, and the monitor thus also uses several RAM locations.

Data and commands are entered via the keyboard. To minimize the complexity of command interpretation, each of the seventeen keys has a special function that is executed when the key is pressed in the command mode of operation. Pressing a command key on the ET-3400 is thus equivalent to typing a command on a more sophisticated computer and no decoding beyond recognition of the active key is necessary. When the ET-3400 is not in the command mode, the keys can be read in the usual way.

The seventeen available keys/commands allow computer reset, display of the contents of internal registers on the seven-segment LEDs, display and editing of the contents of memory, initiation of program execution (one-instruction-at-a-time or whole program), and setting of breakpoints for debugging. (A breakpoint is an address marked by the user. When a breakpoint is reached during program execution the program stops and the user can examine and modify the contents of accumulators and memory.)

The operation of the monitor can be described as follows:

```
Initialize; {Power-up initialization of memory and display}
REPEAT
  Wait for command;
  Recognize and execute the command
FOREVER
```

Pressing the *RESET* key activates the *RESET* interrupt of the CPU and activates a program that reinitializes the monitor exactly like the power up.

The REPEAT statement can be expanded as follows:

```
REPEAT
  Wait for a key to be pressed and decode it;
  CASE key OF {Execute a command}
    0: Reset;
    1: Display accumulator A;
    2: Display accumulator B;
    . . .
    8: Execute the opcode whose address is in the program counter; {Single-
    step execution}
    9: Set breakpoint;
    . . .
    D: Execute program starting at the specified address;
    E: Display contents of specified memory location;
    F: Increment PC and display data at this address;
  END;
FOREVER
```

Most commands invoke built-in monitor functions but keys 8 and *D* activate execution of user commands. Command interpretation is performed by treating the address of the key as a pointer into a table containing the starting addresses of individual functions, and by jumping to the appropriate routine using indexed addressing. The principle is similar to table lookup introduced in Chapter 10.

Different monitor functions share certain operations, such as reading the keyboard and displaying one or more bytes on the LEDs. These operations are also useful for user programs and are implemented as subroutines stored in the monitor ROM. They include INCH, OUTHEX, and other subroutines, some of them introduced in previous chapters. Their operation is based on two or three low-level routines that scan the keyboard and activate seven-segment displays, and these simple routines (explained in Chapters 11 and 12) are the basic ET-3400 device drivers.

Because the higher level functions, such as the display of a string of characters, are relatively complicated they are broken down into more elementary functions. As an example, reading a key is divided into the detection of key activation, software debouncing, another detection, and key encoding. Most monitor functions thus depend on lower level functions, and the monitor is hierarchical, consisting of several layers of code from the most primitive device drivers to the most powerful and general routines. This is typical of all operating systems.

Altogether, the ET-3400 monitor consists of about thirty subroutines. As in larger operating systems, some routines perform function that have only internal uses and that are worthless for user programs. Others are helpful in user programs as well. Subroutine STEP, which displays the code of the next instruction and executes it, is an example of a subroutine of the first kind—it is difficult to imagine any use for it in a typical program. Subroutine INCH, which inputs a character from the keyboard, is a subroutine of the second kind as many user programs and several monitor routines need to read the keyboard and will use it.

In larger operating systems, subroutines that provide services for other programs are often divided into low-level device drivers and higher level functions sometimes called "logic services." Logic services perform more complicated operations, usually by calling device drivers. On the ET-3400, the basic ENCODE and OUTCH functions that detect key activity and output a character to the display could be considered simple device drivers. Function OUTSTR, which displays one byte as two hexadecimal digits by calling OUTCH twice, could be classified as a logic service.

The division of subroutines into device drivers, logic services, and auxiliary routines has several advantages. One is that it makes the monitor program easier to write because individual routines have more limited tasks: A device driver performs only an elementary device operation and logic service can call it without having to know how the elementary function is performed. Structuring also makes the operating system more flexible because the internal modification of a logic service or a device driver should not affect its use.

We have seen examples of device drivers in the previous chapters. Monitor routine INCH listed below is an example of what we might call a simple logic service:

```
INCH                        ; Waits for new key activation,
                            ; performs debouncing,
                            ; and returns code of active key in
                            ; accumulator A
                            ; Uses and modifies accumulator A,
                            ; the C flag, and
                            ; auxiliary memory locations aux and
                            ; aux+1
        PSHB                ; Save current value of B because B
                            ; will be sued by INCH
                            ; Wait until all keys are released to
                            ; avoid accepting
                            ; a key that has already been encoded
                            ; by a previous call on INCH
                            ; To make sure that the lack
                            ; of active signal
                            ; is not just an Off bounce of a
                            ; recently closed key,
                            ; check the "keyboard clear"
                            ; condition TIME times
INC1    LDAB    #COUNT      ; Loop count for number of key tests
INC2    BSR     ENCODE      ; Device driver ENCODE scans the
                            ; keyboard and returns key code in
                            ; accumulator A; C=0 if no key is
                            ; active
                            ; or for multiple key activation
        BCS     INC1        ; If key pressed, start again
        DECB                ; Update count of tests
        BNE     INC2        ; Repeat test enough times
                            ; Now we know that all keys are
                            ; released; wait for
                            ; active key and then confirm
                            ; activation by checking
                            ; several times
```

```
INC3    LDAB    #COUNT    ; Loop count for number of key tests
INC4    BSR     ENCODE    ; Start of loop
        BCC     INC3      ; No key pressed, restart loop
        DECB              ; Key pressed, update loop count
        BNE     INC4      ; Repeat loop if not finished
        PULB              ; Finished, restore B
        RTS
```

Although the ET-3400 monitor is so simple that it does not even qualify as an operating system, our analysis shows that it is not a trivial program, at least not by our standards. The simplicity of function of the ET-3400 and its monitor on the one hand, and the relative complexity of the monitor program on the other indicate how complex more substantial operating systems must be.

**Exercise**

1. If we could increase the size of the ET-3400 monitor ROM from 1k to 2k, what additional functions would be desirable?

## 14.3 THE MS-DOS OPERATING SYSTEM

The Microsoft Disk Operating System (MS-DOS) is an operating system designed by Microsoft and used on IBM PC, IBM PC/XT, and IBM computers and their "clones." Before starting our presentation of MS-DOS, we will outline the architecture of the IBM PC.

The IBM PC and IBM PC/XT use the Intel 8088 CPU; the IBM PC/AT uses the 80286, a more advanced member of the 8086 family. The most advanced IBM personal computer at the time of writing is the PS/2, and its most powerful types use the 80386 CPU. Although the successive models of IBM personal computers are progressively more and more powerful, they remain sufficiently similar to be upward compatible. In other words, the upper end models can execute programs written for the lower end models as well.

The basic configuration of an IBM PC is 256k–640k ROM and RAM memory, two floppy disk drives or one floppy and one hard disk, a keyboard, and a monochrome or color monitor. Among the hardware options available from IBM and other manufacturers are various peripherals and adapters (interface cards) for serial and parallel communication, music, clock and calendar functions, and so on. For monitors, there is a choice of interfaces ranging from the lower resolution color graphics adapter (CGA) to the higher resolution enhanced graphics adapter (EGA) and video graphics array (VGA) cards.

In addition to the personal computers available from IBM, a variety of more or less compatible personal computers are produced by other manufacturers. Although most of them can execute almost all programs written for the IBM PC, they are not identical component-by-component or instruction-by-instruction because copyright and patent laws forbid exact copies. All clone makers must therefore redesign some of the software and hardware while trying to preserve compatibility. This is not as difficult as it might appear because most application programs communicate with the computer via operating system functions or well-defined parameters such as entry addresses in the memory map. Compatibility of system functions and memory maps can be implemented without violating any laws and incompatibility below the level of operating system calls is thus tolerable.

It is useful to mention that when it comes to the code of the operating system, even IBM PCs are not identical because the code of any operating system undergoes changes as users discover bugs and as enhancements are made. Again, this does not create problems for the programs developed for the computer by users and software developers if compatibility at the level of MS-DOS services is maintained.

After this brief introduction, let us now turn to MS-DOS itself. MS-DOS is one of several operating systems developed for IBM PC computers in 1981. It quickly became very popular and overshadowed its competitors. Its first version was strongly influenced by the popular CP/M operating system used on eight-bit microcomputers until the early 1980s and one of its major goals was to make the conversion of existing CP/M software into MS-DOS as easy as possible. Later versions of MS-DOS abandoned the CP/M model but preserved the original functions as well, for compatibility with existing programs.

In 1983, after several minor revisions of the original version, Microsoft released a new version, MS-DOS 2. The major improvements included the hierarchical structure of the file system and support for hard disk drives. After several revisions of version 2, Microsoft introduced version 3 in 1984. It provides support for larger capacity hard and floppy disks and other new features. The latest, but not yet widely used, is version 4. A major force underlying these changes of MS-DOS is its evolution towards the philosophy of operating systems of larger computers, particularly UNIX. This reflects the development of CPUs from eight-bit CPUs to sixteen- and thirty-two bit CPUs. As the market keeps moving toward thirty-two bit CPUs, the IBM PC, PC/XT, and PC/AT evolved into the PS/2, where MS-DOS was replaced by the OS/2 operating system. Although much more powerful than MS-DOS, OS/2 remains upward compatible with MS-DOS and provides facilities to execute programs written for MS-DOS.

We will now examine the structure and operation of MS-DOS. Because MS-DOS is much too complicated for a detailed discussion in our limited space, our presentation will be greatly simplified; for more details the student should refer to one of the many books dedicated to MS-DOS and the PC family.

### Structure and Basic Operation of MS-DOS

As we have seen, the 8088 uses twenty-bit addresses and has a 1-Mbyte address space; MS-DOS uses this address space as follows:

| Address Range (H) | Device |
|---|---|
| F0000 – FFFFF ( 64k) | MS-DOS: ROM BIOS and ROM BASIC |
| C0000 – EFFFF (216k) | ROM expansion and other uses |
| A0000 – BFFFF (128k) | Display memory |
| 00000 – 9FFFF (640k) | User RAM |

Unlike the ET-3400 monitor, MS-DOS is so large that it cannot fully reside in the available 1-Mbyte memory space. Most of it stays on the disk and is loaded into memory only when required. We will now examine the major parts of MS-DOS and their roles by describing what happens when a PC is turned on and starts executing programs. Note that although our description assumes an IBM PC with a floppy disk drive, an almost identical sequence is executed when the computer has a hard disk drive. The main difference is that the files are then read from the hard disk.

A part of MS-DOS is permanently stored in ROM to initialize the computer when it is turned on. This part is called the "ROM-resident basic I/O system" or ROM BIOS. When the PC is turned on or reset, ROM BIOS is activated, reads the setting of the DIP switches on the computer's board to determine how much memory the computer has and tests the RAM and other devices. This is referred to as "power-on self-test," or POST. After POST, the ROM BIOS checks if the "working disk" on the disk automatically selected by the program contains the "boot record." If the boot record is present, ROM BIOS reads it into RAM, otherwise it displays a message requesting a bootable disk.

The boot record is a short program that first checks whether the disk contains the remaining essential MS-DOS files. If it does, these programs are loaded into the RAM; otherwise an error message is displayed. (The terms "boot record" and "bootstrapping" are derived from the fact that the operating system loads itself into memory as if pulling itself up by the straps of its boots.)

The bootstrap record is stored in a fixed location on the disk in fixed format. This, and the separation of the boot program from the BIOS makes the operating system more flexible. For example, should a manufacturer adopt a disk with a different storage format, only the contents of the boot program need be modified to initialize the disk drive to properly read the remaining files.

When the bootstrap program is loaded, it reads MS-DOS files IO.SYS, MSDOS.SYS, and the command interpreter.

File IO.SYS has two parts: an extension of ROM BIOS written by the maker of the computer, and an initialization program called SYSINIT written by Microsoft. The first part allows MS-DOS to interface with the hardware of this particular computer. This makes it possible to add new devices at new addresses in the I/O space or to change the addresses of standard devices while preserving high-level access to them via MS-DOS services.

The function of SYSINIT is to complete the startup procedure by reading the MSDOS.SYS file into a memory region whose exact location depends on available memory, creating internal tables, reading device drivers, initializing all peripheral controllers, and finally loading the command interpreter.

The first action of SYSINIT is to check whether the disk contains the optional CONFIG.SYS configuration file. This file is used to add devices not anticipated by MS-DOS designers or devices whose drivers are included in MS-DOS but must be modified for one reason or another. It may also contain information about required changes of certain default system parameters and direct SYSINIT to replace the default command interpreter with another one stored on the disk. Program SYSINIT reads the specified driver files and uses them to initialize the corresponding peripherals. It then loads the standard or the new command interpreter. After fulfilling its purpose, SYSINIT is no longer needed and its memory space is made available to user programs.

After describing the initialization procedure, we will now outline the *command interpreter*. Unlike MSDOS.SYS and BIOS functions and services that must reside in memory during program execution, most of the command interpreter is needed only when a program terminates and the user types the next command. This is reflected in its structure and its placement in memory.

The command interpreter has three parts: an initialization section, a resident part, and a transient portion. The initialization part is used only during system initialization and its memory space can be used later by user programs. The resident part provides essential code to allow the display of an error message when the complete command interpreter is not available when needed. It stays in memory at all times. The transient part is responsible for most of the communication with the user. It is located so that executing programs can use its memory space (hence the name "transient"). A special end-program-execution DOS function executed at the end of all regular program checks whether the transient part is in memory and reloads it from the disk if it is not.

When the user enters a command, the command interpreter assembles its individual characters into words and checks whether the command is internal or external. *Internal commands* invoke those MS-DOS routines that reside permanently in the RAM; they include the most common tasks, such as the display of a file on the screen (TYPE) and listing disk directory (DIR). If the command is internal, the interpreter transfers control to it, the CPU executes it, and control returns to the command interpreter.

If the command is not internal, it should be external, which means that its code should be on the disk in a file with extension COM, EXE or BAT. Files with extension COM and EXE contain programs (the difference between them is not important for our purpose), files with extension BAT ("batch") files contain a list of commands to be executed. After finding that a command is not internal, the command interpreter checks the directory of the working disk for a file with the given name and extension COM EXE or BAT. If the file is found, it is loaded into RAM and executed; otherwise an error message is displayed.

External commands are either system or application programs. *System programs* are mainly programs supplied with MS-DOS. They typically provide relatively complex services essential or useful to operate the computer but not used as often as internal commands. Some of them are FORMAT for floppy disk initialization, DSKCOPY for copying one disk to another, and PRINT for printing a file. Programs, such as LINK and DEBUG for linking and testing assembly language programs, also belong to this category.

In addition to programs supplied with MS-DOS, a variety of system packages are available from other sources. They perform functions such as testing the hard disk, performing CPU checks, and providing alternative displays of file directories.

*Application programs* include word processors, spread sheets, games, compilers, and similar programs. The boundary between system programs and application programs is not always clear but the execution of both under MS-DOS follows the same rules.

## More on BIOS and MS-DOS Functions and Services

The basis of MS-DOS tools for user and system programs is that they are implemented as interrupt routines and are accessed by the INT instruction (software interrupt). As we saw in Chapter 10, INT is essentially an indirect subroutine jump and to execute it, the CPU retrieves its starting address from an interrupt table located in the first 1k bytes of the memory space and jumps to the corresponding code.

As an example, to execute instruction INT 8, the CPU saves the current program counter (the combined *CS* and *IP* registers) and the condition code register on the stack and reloads *CS:IP* with the contents of the four bytes starting at address 32. (Each interrupt vector is four bytes long because it contains new values for *CS* and *IP*, and $8 \times 4 = 32$). If these locations contain 8000H and 1200H, *CS* and *IP* are loaded with 800H and 1200H and the first instruction of the interrupt handler will thus be obtained from address $CS:TP = 8000:1200$. Execution continues until the CPU reaches

IRET (return-from-interrupt) where it restores *CS:IP* and the condition code register from the stack and resumes execution of the original program.

A copy of the MS-DOS interrupt table with addresses of individual functions is stored in the ROM BIOS chip and is loaded into RAM during initialization. By placing new versions of individual functions in the RAM and by changing addresses in the interrupt table, any program can direct execution of MS-DOS functions away from the original code and toward the new code.

Whereas the BIOS part of MS-DOS is written by the manufacturer and contains low-level device drivers, MSDOS.SYS contains higher level services and was written by Microsoft. All PC compatibles use the same copy of this part of MS-DOS and this makes them compatible with the IBM PC at the level of MS-DOS functions. In spite of the different origin of the MSDOS module and the BIOS, the two can communicate because MSDOS accesses BIOS via the interrupt table and its code does not contain any information about the absolute location of the code that implements the individual functions. The same applies to all other programs accessing BIOS.

MS-DOS designers suggest that all programs communicate with the computer via high-level MS-DOS functions to preserve their executability on different machines. In reality, many programs do not follow this recommendation because some MS-DOS functions are relatively inefficient and the speed of many programs can be significantly increased by bypassing not only the higher level but sometimes even low-level functions. As an example, display on the screen can be most efficiently performed by writing directly to the screen memory rather than by calling DOS or BIOS functions. The possible incompatibility of PC clones below the DOS level, however, means that this shortcut may result in some difficulties. As an example, if the location of the display RAM in memory is nonstandard (which is rare), programs that write screen directly to memory may fail.

The MSDOS.SYS routines, functions used by user programs to access peripherals and to perform other system tasks, are divided into DOS services and DOS functions. All are accessed by the INT instruction, but whereas each function has its own INT number, all services share the same number and are distinguished by parameters supplied in registers when the INT instruction is executed. (The distinction between services and functions must be mentioned but is not important for our purposes.)

Services and functions include operations such as reading a single character from the keyboard, checking whether a key has been pressed, sending a character to the screen, and a variety of disk operations such as opening, closing, searching, erasing, reading, and writing files. Disk-related operations constitute the major difference between a disk operating system and a simple monitor, and file organization and management are two of the most important tasks facing the designer of an operating system of this type.

Our outline shows that one of the notable features of MS-DOS is its modularity (Figure 14.1). The basis of MS-DOS is the BIOS that forms the

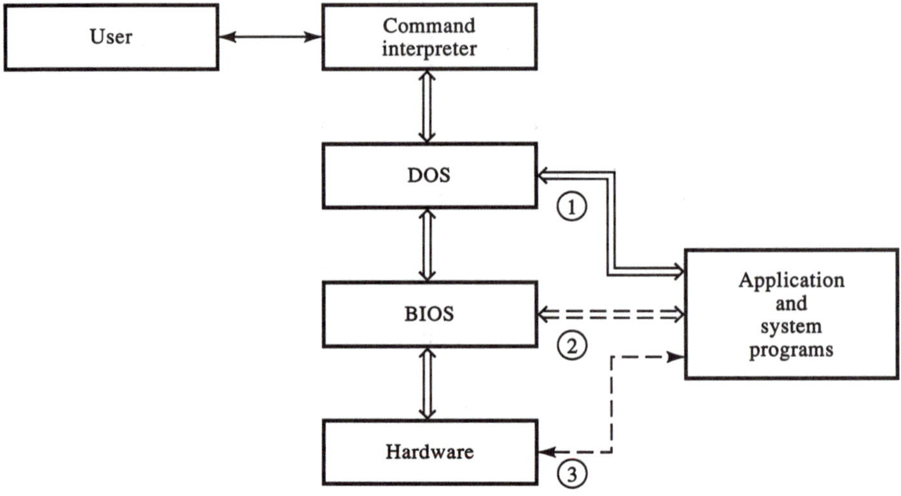


**Figure 14.1.** Hierarchy of an MS-DOS based personal computer. Access labeled "1" is preferred; that labeled "2" is not recommended by Microsoft, and access "3" is to be avoided.

interface between the PC and the DOS supplied by Microsoft. The next layer is the DOS, which provides a standard software interface making possible programs that will run on any PC independently of its hardware and internal BIOS structure. Finally, on top of everything is the command interpreter, the interface between the user and the inner computer: the hardware and the BIOS and DOS software.

### Overview and Examples of MS-DOS Facilities

As we have already explained, operating systems provide tools for users and tools for programs. We will now give examples of both.

Tools provided by MS-DOS for the user include the command interpreter and system programs invoked by commands. The most popular commands are internal (residing permanently in the RAM) to eliminate loading from the disk each time they are needed. The less frequently used programs are external (stored on the disk) to save memory space; they must be loaded into memory each time they are invoked. We will now give several examples of both internal and external commands.

*Internal commands* DATE and TIME allow the user to obtain and set the current date and time. While the computer is running, MS-DOS automatically updates time via hardware interrupts generated by the built-in timer chip, and if the computer has a battery time is maintained even when the computer is off. The internally kept time allows MS-DOS to stamp each file with the time of the file's last modification, giving the user a basis for identifying different versions of the same file.

Internal command DIR displays the directory of the most recently selected working disk. MS-DOS directories have a tree structure (Figure 14.2) and MKDIR and RMDIR commands allow the user to create and remove subdirectories. With CHDIR ("change directory"), one can switch from the current directory to any other directory on the same disk.

Command COPY copies one or more files from the current disk to the same or a different disk. Command REN is used to change the name of a file, DEL to delete a file; TYPE displays a file on the screen.

*External commands* are MS-DOS and user-supplied programs residing on the disk. They are identified by file extensions COM and EXE. Some of the MS-DOS external commands are:

CHKDSK to display the capacity of the disk.

TREE to display a list of all directories and subdirectories on the disk.

FORMAT to format a raw disk.

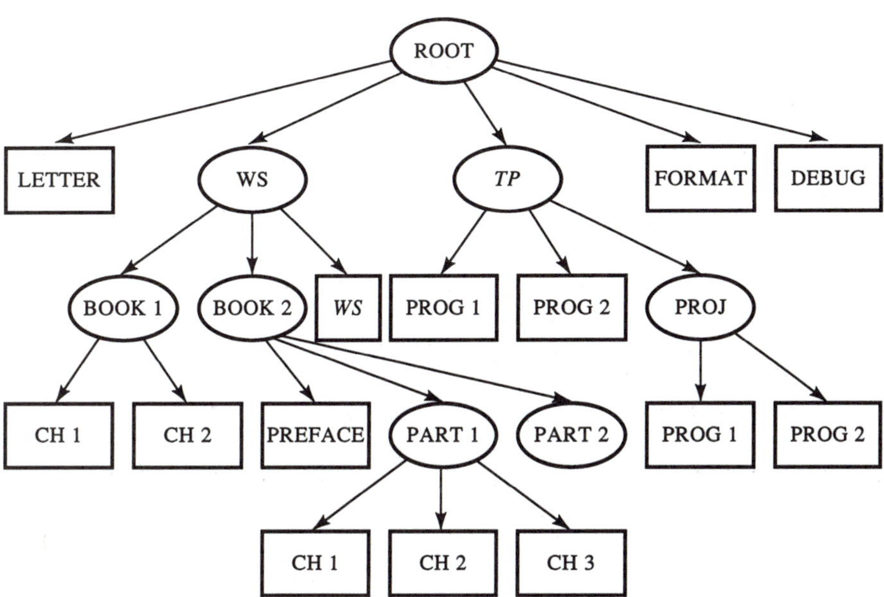


**Figure 14.2.** Hierarchy of MS-DOS directories. Each directory may contain files and subdirectories, and the duplication of file or directory names does not create any confusion as long as the duplicated names are in different directories. Directories may also be empty. In our drawing, directory names are enclosed in ovals and file names are in rectangles.

SYSCOPY copies the system files including the boot track and the command interpreter to the disk.

DSKCOPY copies a disk to another disk preserving the layout of sectors.

PRINT prints a file on the printer. It works in the "background," sending data out when the printer is not busy and allowing the computer to execute other programs otherwise.

RECOVER can retrieve some information from disks with damaged sectors.

There are a number of other external commands but these examples should suffice to give the student an idea of their nature. In addition to the relatively simple commands described above, MS-DOS contains several major programs, including EDLIN, LINK, and DEBUG.

Program EDLIN is a text editor to create and edit files. Because it is line oriented and rather primitive by today's standards it is rarely used. Program LINK is a linker that converts code generated by an assembler into executable code; it can link several separately assembled files into one program. Program DEBUG is a debugger for testing programs at the assembly- or machine-language level. MS-DOS does not include an assembler.

Most programs executed on a PC are not MS-DOS programs. They include word processors such as Wordstar, data base programs such as DBASE, compilers such as Turbo Pascal, assemblers such as MASM, and programs written and complied by the user. Although these programs are not part of MS-DOS they rely on its functions and services for most of their I/O and other operations.

We have already explained that although internal and external commands are the only MS-DOS tools visible to the user, all executing programs rely on MS-DOS for their internal operation. Little I/O can be done without them and even the initialization and termination of program execution require them. To complete our picture of MS-DOS, we will outline the tools that MS-DOS provides to programs (rather than to users) via BIOS and DOS services. As we already explained, all of them are accessed by the INT instruction.

*BIOS services* provide mainly low-level access to I/O devices. By calling these routines, programs can avoid having to deal with obscure details such as port addresses, the programming of peripheral controllers, timing of delays required to access devices such as disk drives and printers, handling of I/O errors, and other tasks that require a deep understanding of hardware details. Access to I/O operations via MS-DOS services also makes all PCs compatible even if the underlying hardware implementation details are different.

The following are some of the BIOS services included in MS-DOS:

| INT Type | Service Group |
|---|---|
| 5 | Print screen on printer |
| 16 | Video services |
| 17 | List of available equipment |
| 18 | Memory size |
| 19 | Disk services |
| 20 | Serial port services |
| 22 | Keyboard services |
| 23 | Parallel port services |
| 25 | Bootstrap |
| 26 | Time set/read |

Most of these interrupts provide several services and the desired one is selected by the value loaded into the *AH* register (the high part of register *AX*) before the call. Individual services in the INT 16 group, for example, return information on the current video mode, allow redefinition of cursor shape and position, reading and writing at cursor position, scrolling, and graphics services. Group 20 allows initialization of the serial port (transmission rate, and so forth), reading, writing, and testing of port status. Group 22 includes testing whether a key is pressed, reading its code, and sensing special keys like *Shift*, *Esc*, and *Alt*. Group 26 interrupts allow a program to obtain or change system time.

As an example of how a BIOS service is used, the following sequence shows how to test whether a key is pressed (function 1, group 22):

```
MOV AH,1      ;  AH := 1 to prepare for function 1 of INT 22
INT 22        ;  Execute group 22 of ROM BIOS keyboard services
```

Upon the completion of this sequence, the computer executes the corresponding BIOS code and returns the result as follows: If a key is pressed, the zero flag *Z* is 0, *AH* contains the key scan code, and *AL* the corresponding ASCII code. If no key is pressed, the *Z* flag is set.

DOS services and functions perform higher level tasks than BIOS functions. Just as BIOS services, they are accessed by loading registers with parameters and executing INT.

There are over twenty DOS services, all accessed by INT 33 and distinguished by the value loaded into *AH* before INT 33 is executed. They include console I/O for reading the keyboard and writing to the display, control of the *COM* port (serial communication) and the printer, a variety of disk services, memory services, country-dependent information such as currency symbol and the style of display of multidigit numbers, and program termination. Each program must call the program termination function when it is finished to allow, among other things, MS-DOS to check that the command interpreter is present when the user enters the next command.

As an example of the use of a DOS service, the following sequence returns system time in registers *C* and *D*:

```
MOV AH,44     ;  Move 44 to AH, time is DOS service 44
INT 33        ;  DOS service
```

Upon return, *CH* (the high part of register *C*) contains the hour (0 to 23), *CL* contains the minutes (0 to 59), *DH* contains the seconds (0 to 59), and *DL* contains the hundreths of seconds (0 to 99).

In addition to DOS services, there are approximately 100 DOS functions that handle directory operations (make, remove, and change), file operations (create, open, rename, close, and delete), I/O device control, the execution and termination of programs, and getting and setting time and date in file directory. As an example of a DOS function, the following sequence sets the video mode to 640 × 350 monochrome EGA graphics:

```
MOV AH,0      ;  Move 0 to AH, function 0 of INT 16
MOV AL,15     ;  Move 15 to AL, parameter of video mode,
              ;  code of 640*350 monochrome EGA graphics
INT 16        ;  Execute interrupt 16
```

### MS-DOS Disks, Files, and Their Management

The information stored on an MS-DOS disk contains files and MS-DOS internal information (Figure 14.3). The disk may or may not contain a boot record and the system files needed to boot up MS-DOS. If these files are present, the disk may be used to boot the computer up. The disk also may or may not contain the command interpreter file. If the command interpreter is missing, MS-DOS will not be able to respond to commands after executing a program that overwrites some of the command interpreter's memory space.

Internal information for the MS-DOS that is stored on the disk consists of a directory and a file allocation table (FAT). These two structures contain the names and locations of all files on the disk (Figure 14.4). The boot record, the directory, and the file allocation table are stored in fixed sectors; files with data and programs use the remaining space. We will now give a simplified explanation of MS-DOS directory and FAT conventions.

The number of sectors occupied by the *directory* depends on the type of disk (double or quadruple density, floppy or hard) and determines how many files can be stored on the disk. The directory is divided into entries describing

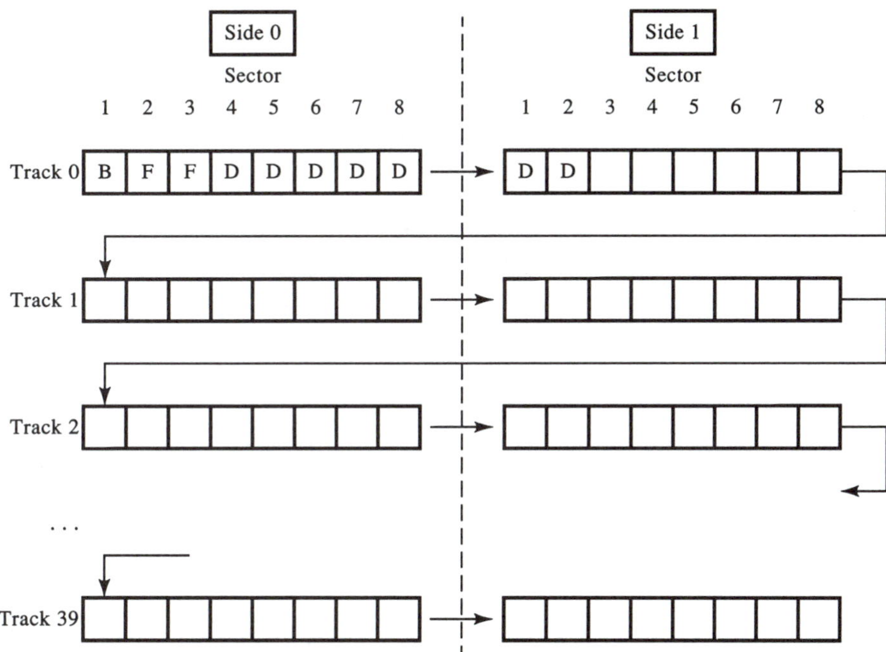


**Figure 14.3.** Organization of a double-sided MS-DOS disk: Sectors *B*, *F*, and *D* are reserved for the boot, FAT, and directory files; all other sectors can be used for files. Lines with arrows indicate the ordering of sectors.

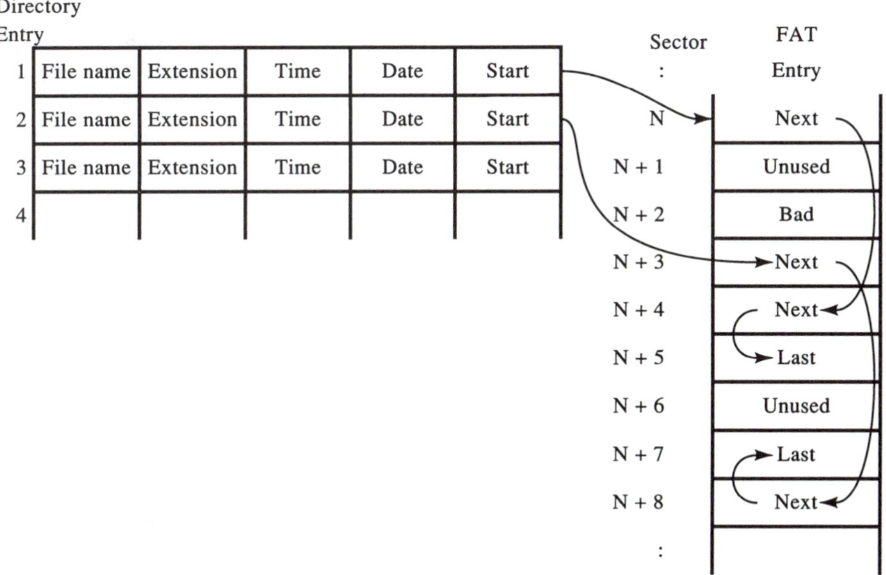


**Figure 14.4.** Example of the layout of directory and FAT contents (simplified).

individual files by their names and extensions, attributes (ordinary file, system file not displayed by the DIR command, etc.), the time and date when the file was last modified, its size (in sectors), and the address of the file's first sector.

The *file allocation table* (FAT) contains a map of all sectors on the disk, marking each sector as available, bad (unusable), or used. When a sector is in use, its FAT entry contains the number of the next sector from the same file or a special code if this is the last sector of the file. This arrangement allows files of arbitrary size within the capacity of the disk. Directory information about the location of the first sector, and the FAT map make it possible to access any sector of the file.

When MS-DOS accesses a disk for the first time, it copies its directory and FAT to the RAM and keeps it there to speed up file operations. All file changes are recorded in the RAM directory and FAT, and copied back to the disk.

### Exercises

Most of the following exercises are intended to indicate how much difficult code the MS-DOS services and functions implement for the user and how much they simplify programming.

1. We stated that when MS-DOS executes the terminate-program function, it checks whether the transient part of the command interpreter is present. How can this be done?
2. Describe how an MS-DOS service or function with a single interrupt number but multiple internal options defined by the contents of *AH* could be implemented.
3. Give a high-level algorithm describing sequential access to a file for reading (define functions if necessary). Extend the description to show how the MS-DOS functions communicate with the disk controller.
4. Repeat Exercise 3 for writing. Include consideration of the handling of the directory and the FAT table when new sectors are needed.
5. Describe how the delete-file function might be implemented.
6. Explain how the set-display-mode function might be implemented.

## 14.4 THE OS68 OPERATING SYSTEM

Our overview of MS-DOS has provided an introduction to the principles of a small operating system, but nontrivial examples of the use of MS-DOS functions would require knowledge of the 8088 assembly language and are beyond the scope of this book. To provide a working environment based on the techniques learned in previous chapters, we will now describe a 6800 CPU-based operating system called OS68 that is similar to a stripped-down MS-DOS and will illustrate its use on several programming examples. The OS68 is not a real operating system but a simulation available from the publisher.

Because the purpose of OS68 is to provide a hands-on introduction to the use of operating system tools, it includes only a few basic functions. Still, our examples give a realistic picture of the dependence of user programs on the operating system.

### Overview of OS68

The OS68 consists of a command interpreter and a set of functions collectively referred to as disk operating system function or DOS functions. While both the command interpreter and the DOS functions are available to the user, their internal implementation is invisible.

The OS68 occupies the top 32k of the address space ($8000 to $FFFF) of a simulated 6800 CPU and user programs must not attempt to modify it. In fact, the OS68 simulator produces a "system crash" if a program attempts to access system memory. The remainder of memory (locations $0000 to $7FFF) is available to user programs. While loading a user program, OS68 initializes the stack pointer to the top of user memory, location $7FFF.

When the user enters OS68, he can use the following commands recognized by command interpreter:

AS to run the 6800 assembler.

DEBUG to debug OS68 programs using on-screen display of internal memory and registers.

DIR to display files in the current directory.

EDIT to create new or edit existing files.

Commands that are names of files assembled by the assembler, compiled by the SIMPLE compiler (Chapter 15), or produced by the user's own translator. The filenames must have extension EX and their format must satisfy the rules explained in Section 15.2.

QUIT to exit from OS68.

As in MS-DOS, OS68 filenames consist of a main part and an optional extension. The main part must be one to eight characters long, the filename extension is at most three characters long. The set of allowed characters is restricted to letters and digits:

| Legal OS68 Filenames | Illegal OS68 Filenames | |
|---|---|---|
| name | name123456789 | (Main part too long) |
| Name1 | name—1 | (Illegal symbol) |
| NAME. | NAME. . . | (Illegal symbol) |
| name.123 | name.1234 | (Extension too long) |

### The OS68 DOS Functions

The DOS functions of the OS68 can be accessed from programs assembled by the assembler described in Chapter 10. They can be divided into the following categories:

0. Keyboard input
1. Screen output
2. Printer output
3. File functions
4. Date and time
5. Program termination

All OS68 DOS functions follow the same basic rules. All are activated by loading accumulator *A* with the number of the function and executing SWI. If other information is required, it is passed via accumulator *B* or the index register. Upon return from a function call, OS68 returns a "success/failure" code in accumulator *A*: On success, *A* returns 0, and a nonzero value means an error. If the operation produces a result, it is returned in memory or in a register. No other registers or memory locations are modified.

Each function passing a variable-length block of characters, such as a filename or a block of bytes read from a file, uses a buffer, a memory area assigned for this purpose by the user program and identified by its starting address passed in the index register. If the length of the string is variable (which is the case for all buffers except for the date and time strings in functions $41 and $42), the first byte is a pure binary number representing the actual length of the string. The buffer must be entirely in the user memory; otherwise, a simulated crash occurs.

We will now give detailed definitions of individual DOS functions and then several examples of their use:

| Number | Name and Description |
|---|---|
| \$01 | Read keyboard without echo. Waits until a key is pressed and returns its ASCII code in accumulator *B* without echoing it on the screen. |
| \$02 | Read keyboard with echo. Same as function \$01 but echoes the key on the screen. |
| \$11 | Position cursor. Places the cursor at the position specified in the index register The MSB contains the column number (1...80); LSB contains the row number (1...24). Return code $A = 1$ indicates illegal coordinates. |
| \$12 | Output a single character on the screen. Displays the character whose ASCII code is stored in accumulator *B* at the current cursor position. The carriage return code CR is treated as a combination of CR and line feed LF. |
| \$13 | Output string from a buffer on the screen. Displays the ASCII string stored in the screen buffer and preceded by its one-byte length. The address of the buffer is selected by the user and supplied in the index register. The carriage return code is treated as a combination of CR and LF. |
| \$21 | Print string from buffer. Displays the ASCII string stored in a buffer in user's memory. The address of the start of the buffer must be supplied in the index register and the string must start with a one-byte number specifying the string's length. Result $A = 1$ is returned if the printer is not ready. |
| \$31 | Create file. Creates a new file and gives it the name supplied in the filename area located in user's memory. The filename area consists of a length byte and the name itself; its address must be supplied in the index register. The function returns $A = 1$ if the file already exists, $A = 2$ for an illegal filename, and $A = 3$ for other errors. |
| \$32 | Delete file. Deletes the file specified by its filename as in function \$31. Returns $A = 1$ if the file does not exist, $A = 2$ for an illegal filename, and $A = 3$ for other errors. |
| \$33 | Reset file. Opens an existing file specified by its name for reading. The length of the filename and the filename itself must be supplied in the filename area located in the user's memory. Its address must be supplied in the index register. Accumulator *B* returns the *handle* assigned for the file by OS68. If the function succeeds, it returns 0 in accumulator |

*(continued)*

| Number | Name and Description |
|---|---|
| | $A$. Result $A = 1$ means file does not exist, $A = 2$ indicates an illegal filename, $A = 3$ indicates that no more handles are available. (The maximum number of handles active at one time is four). Result $A = 4$ indicates another error. |
| \$34 | Rewrite file. Opens an existing file for writing. Error codes and conventions for the specification of the filename are the same as for function \$33. The handle is returned in accumulator $B$. |
| \$35 | Close file. Closes the file whose handle is supplied by the calling program in accumulator $B$ and releases the handle for new use. If the file was open for writing, all data remaining in the buffer and not yet transferred are "flushed" (sent to the file). Returns $A = 1$ for illegal or unassigned handle, and $A = 2$ for other errors. |
| \$36 | Read string from file into buffer. Reads a string of bytes from a file open for reading and identified by its handle in accumulator $B$, and stores it in a buffer whose starting address is supplied in $X$. The number of bytes to be read must be supplied in the first byte of the buffer. On return, the buffer contains the count of bytes actually read (possibly 0), followed by the data. Result $A = 1$ is returned for illegal or unassigned handle, $A = 2$ is returned if the file is not open for reading, $A = 3$ is returned for other errors. |
| \$37 | Write a string from buffer to file. Copies a string from the buffer specified by its starting address in $X$ to the file specified by its handle in accumulator $B$. The number of bytes to be written must be supplied in the first byte of the buffer. Returns $A = 1$ for illegal or unassigned handle, $A = 2$ if the file is not open for writing, and $A = 3$ for other errors. This function does not send data directly to the disk but stores it in an invisible 256-byte system buffer in system memory assigned to the file by the reset function. Because the system waits until the buffer is full before transmitting it, executing function \$37 does not guarantee that the data is actually written to the file. The final transfer of data remaining in the OS68 buffer at the end of a sequence of write operations requires execution of function \$35. |
| \$38 | Get the first filename from the directory. Positions a pointer to the start of the directory and returns the length of the name of the first file and the name itself in the filename area |

*(continued)*

whose address must be supplied in the index register. Result $A = 1$ is returned if the directory is empty.

$39 Get the next filename from the directory. Same as get-first-filename but is used after the first file was obtained by function $38. Result $A = 1$ is returned when there are no more files in the directory, and $A = 2$ is returned if function $38 has not been called first.

$41 Get the current date. Returns the current date in a buffer whose address is given by the user in the index register. On return, the buffer contains a two-byte code for the year, month, and date, and a one-byte code for the day of the week (0...6, with 0 for Sunday). Because the length of the buffer is fixed, there is no length byte. All codes use BCD representation.

$42 Get the current time. Returns the current time in a buffer whose address is given by the user in the index register. On return, the buffer contains two-byte codes of the hour, minute, second, and hundredth of second. Because the length of the returned string is fixed, the buffer does not start with a length byte. All codes use BCD representation.

$51 Terminate program. Returns execution to the command interpreter. This must be the last instruction executed by the program; otherwise, a simulated crash will occur.

---

**Programming Examples**

The following examples show hoe to use OS68 functions to perform various I/O related tasks. To simplify the programs, we leave error checking as an exercise.

**Example 1—Keyboard and Screen I/O** The following program reads keys until *ESC* is pressed. It displays only symbols corresponding to standard printable ASCII codes and ignores all other codes except the carriage return.

```
CR      EQU   $0D    ; ASCII code of carriage return
ESC     EQU   $1B    ; ASCII code of ESC
SPACE   EQU   ' '    ; First printable ASCII code
TILDE   EQU   ' '    ; Last printable ASCII code
INCH    EQU   $01    ; OS68 function 1, get key
                     ; without echo
OUTCH   EQU   $12    ; Function $12, output character
                     ; from B
```

```
STOP    EQU   $51       ; Function $51, return to OS68
LOOP    LDAA  #INCH     ; A : = function number
        SWI             ; Execute get-key function
        CMPB  #ESC      ; Is it the ESC character?
        BEQ   DONE      ; If found quit; else continue
                        ; testing
        CMPB  #CR       ; Is it the carriage return?
        BEQ   SHOW      ; If so, display it
        CMPB  #SPACE    ; Compare with first printable
                        ; symbol
        BMI   LOOP      ; If below, get next character
        CMPB  #TILDE    ; Compare with last printable
                        ; symbol
        BPL   LOOP      ; Not printable, repeat loop
SHOW    LDAA  #OUTCH    ; Code is printable, display
        SWI             ; Execute output-char function
        BRA   LOOP      ; Repeat the loop
DONE    LDAA  #STOP     ; Last character was ESC, exit
        SWI             ; Terminate program execution
        END   LOOP      ; First instruction is at address
                          LOOP
```

To run the program, proceed as follows:

Enter OS68.

Use the EDIT editor to enter the source code into a file called, for example EXAMPLE1, and assemble it. This produces a file with extension EX, in this case the complete filename is EXAMPLE1.EX.

To test the program with the debugger, type DEBUG, load program EXAMPLE1.EX, and execute it in the usual way.

To execute the assembled program, type its full name (EXAMPLE1.EX) or the main part of its name (EXAMPLE1).

To exit from OS68, type QUIT.

**Example 2—Clear Screen's Center and Display a Message** The following program clears five lines in the center of the screen and writes the message

EXAMPLE OF OUTPUT

in the middle:

```
OUTST     EQU    $13                        ; OS68: Output string
STOP      EQU    $51                        ; OS68: Return to
                                            ; OS68
TOXY      EQU    $11                        ; OS68: Position
                                            ; cursor
BLANKS    DB     80,'                                          '
BLANKS1   DB       '                                           '
TEXT      DB     17,'EXAMPLE OF OUTPUT'
                                            ; 17 is the length of
                                            ; the message
TEMP      DS     2                          ; Temporary storage
                                            ; for index register
START                                       ; First clear the five
                                            ; lines in the center
          LDAB   #5                         ; Line counter - to
                                            ; clear five lines
          LDX    #$010A                     ; x = 01 and y = 0A
                                            ; are coordinates
                                            ; of the first line to
                                            ; clear
CLEAR     LDAA   #TOXY
          SWI                               ; Position cursor on
                                            ; start of next line
          STX    TEMP                       ; Preserve X, it will
                                            ; now be used with
                                            ; OUTST
          LDX    #BLANKS                    ; Address of 80 blanks
                                            ; to clear the line
          LDAA   #OUTST
          SWI                               ; Display blanks to
                                            ; clear to end of line
          LDX    TEMP                       ; Reload old value of
                                            ; X and
          INX                               ; increment it to
                                            ; point to next line
```

```
        DECB                        ; Decrement line
                                    ; count
        BNE     CLEAR               ; Repeat loop if not
                                    ; done
                                    ; Now display the
                                    ; message
        LDX     #$200C              ; Position of text on
                                    ; the screen
        LDAA    #TOXY
        SWI                         ; Position cursor
        LDX     #TEXT
        LDAA    #OUTST
        SWI                         ; Display text
        LDAA    #STOP
        SWI
        END     START
```

**Example 3—Display the Number of Files in the Directory** The following program reads the directory, counts the files, and displays the count on the screen:

```
FIRST   EQU     $38         ; Get-first-filename function
NEXT    EQU     $39         ; Get-next-filename function
OUTCH   EQU     $12         ; Display-character function
OUTST   EQU     $13         ; Display-string function
STOP    EQU     $51         ; Return-to-OS68 function
MASK    EQU     %00110000   ; Mask for conversion to
                            ; ASCII digits

MSSG1   DB      23,'The directory contains'
MSSG2   DB      7,' files '
NAME    DS      13          ; Filename area
                            ; (length+filename)
TEMP    DS      1

START                       ; First count the files
        CLRB                ; B will be used for counting
        LDX     #NAME
        LDAA    #FIRST      ; Get the first filename
        SWI
```

```
        CMPA    #1          ; Did function return a file
                            ; name?
        BEQ     SHOW        ; If not, display the count
LOOP    INCB                ; Increment count
        LDAA    #NEXT
        SWI                 ; Get next filename, if any
        CMPA    #1          ; Was a filename returned?
        BEQ     SHOW        ; If no, quit counting
        BRA     LOOP        ; Else get another name
SHOW    LDX     #MSSG1      ; Display first part of message
        LDAA    #OUTST
        SWI
        BSR     DISP        ; Display the count in ASCII
        LDX     #MSSG2      ; Display second part of message
        LDAA    #OUTST
        SWI
        LDAA    #STOP       ; Terminate
        SWI                 ; program execution
DISP                        ; Display value in B as two
                            ; decimal digits. This part of
                            ; the program is left for the
                            ; student to complete.
        END     START
```

Subroutine DISP is used to make the program more readable.

**Example 4—Store Keyboard Input in a File** We wish to write a program to read text from the keyboard and save it in an existing file called 'KBD'. Each line will be up to eighty characters long and will be terminated with a carriage return; the text is terminated by *ESC*. Individual lines are to be stored preceded by their length bytes.

To demonstrate all of the steps in developing the program, we will show the solution in detail. First, the high-level pseudocode algorithm:

```
Open file 'KDB' for writing;
REPEAT
   Initialize variables {Length of line} count and position {Of character, in file
   buffer};
   REPEAT
      Read keyboard;
```

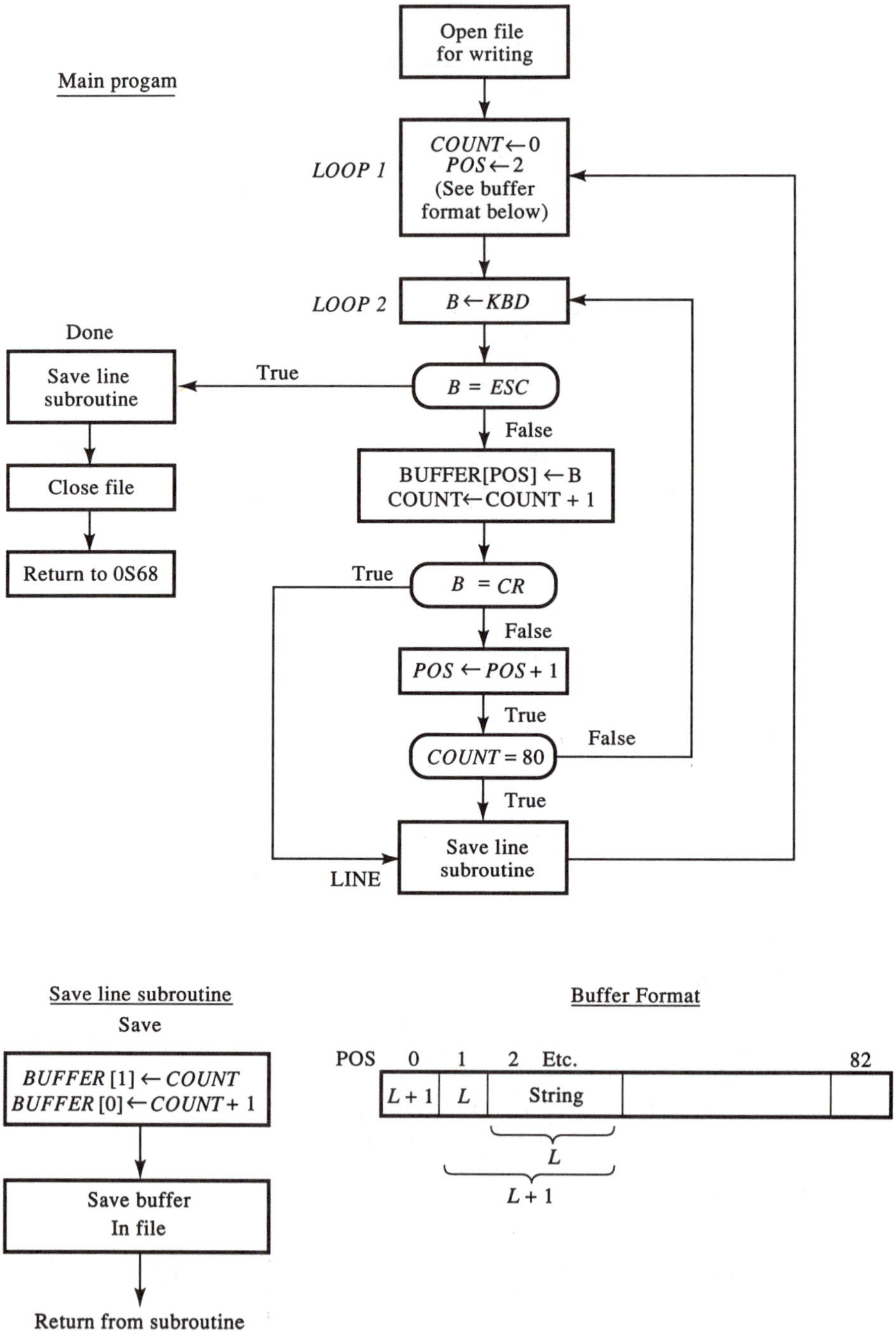

Main progam
Open file for writing
LOOP 1
COUNT←0
POS←2
(See buffer format below)
LOOP 2
B←KBD
Done
Save line subroutine
True
B = ESC
False
BUFFER[POS] ←B
COUNT←COUNT + 1
Close file
Return to 0S68
True
B = CR
False
POS ←POS + 1
True
False
COUNT = 80
True
Save line subroutine
LINE
Save line subroutine
Save
BUFFER [1] ←COUNT
BUFFER [0]←COUNT + 1
Save buffer In file
Return from subroutine
Buffer Format
POS 0 1 2 Etc. 82
L + 1
L
String
L
L + 1

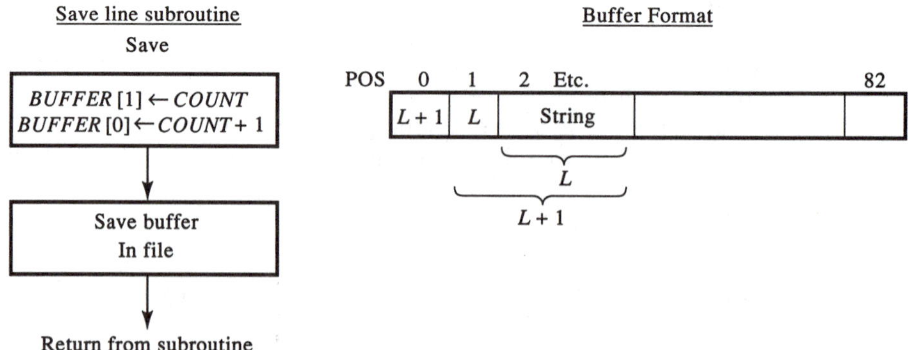

**Figure 14.5.** Flowchart for Example 4 and the structure of the file buffer. All variables will be held in memory, while the position within the buffer (the character's index) will be held in the index register. The strange form of the buffer is required by the "save line" function of 0S68 and the desired line format.

```
    IF NOT character IN [CR,ESC]
      THEN
        BEGIN
          Save character in buffer using value of variable position;
          Update count and position;
        END;
    UNTIL (character IN [CR,ESC]) OR (count=80);
    Store count at the start of the file buffer;
    Save the line and its length in the file;
  UNTIL character=ESC;
  Close file
```

This formulation is useful as the first step in designing the program but is not suitable for the immediate development of the assembly-language code. We will thus convert it into the flowchart in Figure 14.5. The following program can be easily derived from the flowchart:

```
        CLOSE   EQU     $35       ; Close file function
        KBD     EQU     $02       ; Read keyboard with echo
        OPENW   EQU     $34       ; Open file for writing
        STOP    EQU     $51       ; Return to OS68
        WRITE   EQU     $37       ; Write to file
        CR      EQU     $0D       ; Carriage return
        ESC     EQU     $1B
        MAX     EQU     80        ; Maximum length of input line
        BUFFER  DS      82        ; Line with the length byte
        COUNT   DS      1         ; Length of line count
        HANDLE  DS      1         ; File handle
        FNAME   DB      3,'KBD'   ; Filename preceded by its length
START   LDX     #FNAME            ; Prepare the open-file function
        LDAA    #OPENW
        SWI                       ; Open file
        STAB    HANDLE
LOOP1   CLR     COUNT             ; Count: =0
        LDX     #BUFFER+2         ; Leading byte of string
LOOP2   LDAA    #KBD              ; Read keyboard with echo
        SWI
        CMPB    #ESC              ; Test for end of input
        BEQ     DONE              ; Save and exit if character =ESC
        STAB    0,X               ; Else store character in buffer
```

```
        INC     COUNT          ; Increment character count
        CMPB    #CR            ; Test for end of line
        BEQ     LINE           ; If CR, save line and go to next line
        INX                    ; Else increment index
        LDAB    COUNT          ; Load length of line for test
        CMPB    #MAX           ; Is line full?
        BNE     LOOP2          ; If not, go to get next character
LINE    BSR     SAVE           ; Otherwise, save the line
        BRA     LOOP1          ; and go to read next line
DONE    BSR     SAVE           ; Save this line
        LDAA    #CLOSE         ; Close the file
        SWI
        LDAA    #STOP          ; Exit to OS68
        SWI
                               ; Output subroutine
SAVE    LDAB    COUNT
        STAB    BUFFER+1       ; Store count in file buffer
        INCB                   ; The whole string consists of the
        STAB    BUFFER         ; length byte and the line itself
        LDX     #BUFFER
        LDAB    HANDLE
        LDAA    #WRITE         ; Store buffer in file
        SWI
        RTS
        END     START
```

**Example 5—Read and Display an ASCII File** The following program reads file 'KBD' created in Example 4 and displays it on the screen:

```
        CLOSE   EQU     $35        ; Close file
        CRT     EQU     $13        ; Display string on display
        OPENR   EQU     $33        ; Open file for reading
        READ    EQU     $36        ; Read from file
        STOP    EQU     $51        ; Return to OS68
        FNAME   DB      3,'KDB'
        BUFFER  DS      81         ; Shared by file and display
START   LDAA    #OPENR             ; Open file for reading
        SWI                        ; We don't have to store the handle
                                   ; as B will remain unchanged
```

```
LOOP    LDAA    #1              ; Prepare to read the length byte
        STAA    BUFFER          ; from the file
        LDX     #BUFFER         ; Now read it
        LDAA    #READ
        SWI
        TST     BUFFER          ; Is this the last line (BUFFER [1]=0)
        BEQ     DONE            ; If yes, exit
        LDAA    BUFFER+1        ; Length byte is in BUFFER[1]
        STAA    BUFFER          ; Put it in BUFFER [0] to read line
        LDAA    #READ
        SWI                     ; Read the whole line starting with
                                  count
        LDAA    #CRT            ; Display buffer
        SWI                     ;
        BRA     LOOP            ; Go to process next record
DONE    LDAA    #CLOSE          ; Close the file
        SWI                     ; (handle is still in B)
        LDAA    #STOP           ; and quit
        SWI
        END     START
```

**Example 6—Display the Day of the Week** The following program gets the current date from OS68, converts it to the day of the week, and displays it on the screen:

```
OUTST   EQU     $13             ; Display string
DATE    EQU     $41             ; Get date (day is the fourth byte)
STOP    EQU     $51             ; Return to OS68
TODAY   DS      7               ; Reserved for current date
DAY0    DB      6,'SUNDAY'      ; Length of string, string
DAY1    DB      6,'MONDAY'
DAY2    DB      7,'TUESDAY'
DAY3    DB      9,'WEDNESDAY'
DAY4    DB      8,'THURSDAY'
DAY5    DB      6,'FRIDAY'
DAY6    DB      8,'SATURDAY'
                                ; The following are addresses of day
                                ; names
```

```
ADDRESS  DB      DAY0,DAY1,DAY2,
                 DAY3,DAY4,DAY5,
                 DAY6
START    LDX     #TODAY        ; Address of date buffer area
         LDAA    #DATE
         SWI                   ; Read date bytes into TODAY
         LDX     #ADDRESS      ; Start of ADDRESS table
         LDAA    TODAY+6       ; A:=day code
                               ; Now step through ADDRESS table
                               ; to get X to point to name address
LOOP     BEQ     DONE          ; IF A=0, X = correct address
         INX                   ; Each address consists
         INX                   ; of two bytes
         DECA                  ; Update count
         BRA     LOOP
DONE     LDX     0,X           ; X:=address of name of day
         LDAA    #OUTST        ; Get address of name string
         SWI                   ; for display
         LDAA    #STOP         ; Prepare to terminate
         SWI                   ; Terminate program execution
         END     START
```

Note how the index register first gets the address of the addresses of the name and then the address of the name itself.

These examples should suffice to illustrate the use of OS68 DOS functions and the purpose and importance of the operating system for the programmer. Imagine how difficult it would be to write the programs without them by controlling I/O devices and the various data structures directly.

### Exercises

In developing the programs for the following exercises, show all of the following steps: High-level formulation, flowchart, data structures (the assignment of variables to registers and memory), and the assembly-language program. Trace the programs by hand or test them on the simulator.

1. Execute all examples in this section on the simulator.
2. Modify Example 1 to display only printable codes and replace nonprintable codes by periods.
3. Modify all examples in this section to monitor and respond to error conditions reported by the OS68 function calls.

4. Write a program that displays

THE TIME IS *XX* hours, *XX* minutes, *XX* seconds

where *XX* represents a two-digit decimal value.
5. Write a program to prompt the user for an account name and a password and to read them. The username is echoed on the screen, the password is not. Assume that both the username and the password are entered as four letters followed by a carriage return.
6. Modify the previous program to let the user edit input with the backspace key (ASCII $08) to erase the previous character.
7. Modify the previous program to accept up to four-character input and pad shorter entries with trailing blanks.
8. Modify Example 5 to send output to the printer.
9. Read a file, convert lowercase letters to uppercase, and store the result in another file. (*Note*: One can use the same buffer area for both files.)
10. Repeat the previous exercise but store the codes in the original file, overwriting the old values.
11. Repeat the previous exercise but append the new code to the original one. Which functions should be added to OS68 to simplify this task?
12. Write a subroutine to read an integer in the range 0–255 from the keyboard and convert it to binary.
13. Write a subroutine to display a one-byte pure binary number on the screen.
14. Write a program to check whether a file whose name is typed by the user is in the directory.
15. Write the algorithms and draw the flowcharts for all examples in this section.
16. Modify the program in Exercise 8 to time and display the length of its execution.
17. Describe how OS68 might internally use a file handle.
18. Why is it necessary to close a file that is open for writing? Why is it necessary to close a file open for reading?
19. Which additional BIOS functions would be desirable on the OS68?
20. As we know, when the 6800 CPU executes SWI, it pushes all registers on the stack. When it then executes RTI, all registers are restored from the stack. Consequently, the internal implementation of OS68 calls that are activated by SWI cannot merely put results into accumulators and execute RTI because it would destroy the results. How can this problem be solved?
21. Write macros to implement five selected OS68 calls using the format given in Chapter 8. (Our assembler does not handle macros.)
22. Rewrite the examples in this section using the macros from Exercise 20 and compare the new version to the original.

## SUMMARY

To introduce the purpose and structure of operating systems, we described the ET-3400 monitor, MS-DOS, and our simulated OS68. The ET-3400 monitor is so simple that it cannot properly be called an operating system but its study illustrates the essence of operating systems on a very small scale.

The MS-DOS is much more complicated than the ET-3400 monitor, but although the details are complex its philosophy can be understood once a few basic principles are understood.

In essence, MS-DOS is a set of tools that gives the user control over the computer via commands and that allows programs to access peripherals and other MS-DOS resources by calling predefined functions. In this sense, MS-DOS closely resembles the simple ET-3400 monitor as well as the much more complex operating systems of larger computers. The differences are due to the complexity of the hardware that operating systems manage and the facilities that they provide for the user: While the ET-3400 consists of a simple CPU, a small memory, a primitive keyboard, and an elementary display, MS-DOS uses a powerful CPU and manages a large memory, a sophisticated keyboard and display, as well as a disk system and a potentially unlimited variety of other peripherals. The MS-DOS gives the user relatively simple control over all these resources and provides a well-organized file system.

In the last section, we described OS68, a simulated operating system for a 6800 CPU-based computer. The OS68 is not implemented on any commercially available computer but is included in our 6800 simulator. It is suitable to test the use of operating system principles in a familiar environment and provides a basis for the following chapter on translators.

This chapter, like most of this book, is dedicated to concepts applicable mainly to small and personal computers. The tasks of operating systems on large computers are much more complicated. They include multiprogramming, time sharing, and efficient and secure simultaneous service to many users. These operating systems can manage many different peripherals at the same time and the constant competition for resources by individual programs.

## REVIEW QUESTIONS

1. Define the following terms: Application program, BIOS, command interpreter, device driver, DOS, logic service, monitor, multiprogramming, multitasking, system program, and time sharing.
2. Explain what a command on the ET-3400 is and how it is interpreted by the monitor.
3. Outline what happens when an MS-DOS computer is turned on.
4. Explain how the directory and FAT describe the contents of a disk.

5. Describe what happens when a user of an MS-DOS computer types a command.

## REFERENCES

The following titles listed in the references at the end of the book are relevant to this chapter:

D. Comer. *Operating Systems: The XINU Approach.*

R. Duncan. *Advanced MS-DOS.*

Heath Company. *Heathkit Manual for the Microprocessor Trainer Model ET-3400A.*

P. Norton. *Inside the IBM PC.*

# CHAPTER 15

# PROGRAM TRANSLATION

## AN OVERVIEW

We have now reached the point in our coverage of computer operation at which the computer satisfies all of our expectations except for the implementation of programming languages. This last aspect requires an additional layer of software: translation. With translation, we can write programs and implement tasks ranging from computer games through spreadsheets and word processors to new compilers.

According to the type of the programming language being processed, translators are either assemblers, for the translation of assembly-language programs, or compilers (interpreters), for the translation of high-level languages like Pascal or BASIC.

Assembly-language programs consist of machine instructions, pseudoinstructions, and symbolic names for labels, variables, and constants. The translation of machine instructions amounts to table lookup. The translation of pseudoinstructions mostly requires simple operations like reserving memory space. The translation of symbolic names requires the calculation of symbol values and may involve forward references to symbols that are used before they are defined in the program. This problem is usually resolved by processing the source code twice: In the first pass, symbols are gathered in a symbol table and their values calculated; in the second pass, the final code is generated using the symbol table from pass 1. Assemblers of this type are called two-pass assemblers.

Most assembly language programs are small and are used in combination with other modules. Thus assembly is usually only the first step toward creating an executable program. The next task—the creation of a single program from separately assembled modules—is performed by another program called the linker.

The translation of high-level languages is substantially more complicated than assembly and it is useful to divide it into three tasks: scanning, parsing, and code generation.

During scanning, the source code is converted into units such as BEGIN, END, *variable name*, and so on, and these are replaced with codes called tokens. Tokens are passed to the parser, which combines them into more abstract units like declarations and assignment statements, and checks that they conform to the rules of the language. On the basis of the uncovered grammatical structure, the code generator produces code that can be executed.

Although the operating system provides the basic I/O functions needed in the execution of code produced by the compiler, it does not provide operations like integer I/O or the calculation of trigonometric functions. The translator adds the code implementing these and other functions as the so called run-time system.

To illustrate the concepts of translation, we will present a detailed algorithm for an assembler and develop a complete compiler for a simple language. We will also describe some aspects of a commercial Pascal compiler.

## IMPORTANT WORDS

Activation record, code generator, dynamic data, error recovery, forward reference, grammar, heap, lexical analyzer, linker, location counter, nonterminal symbol, optimization, parser, pass, recursive definition, recursive descent parsing, run-time system, scanner, semantics, static data, symbol table, syntax, table driven parser, table generator, terminal symbol, token.

## 15.1 INTRODUCTION

Computers can execute only programs expressed in binary machine code, and the first computer programs were indeed written in binary. This laborious programming style was soon replaced by more abstract symbolic programming methods.

The first improvement was the use of *octal* rather than binary code. Although this did not make the highly encoded character of the program more meaningful, it reduced the size of the code, making it visually more manageable and thus less error prone. The mechanical task of converting octal to binary was performed by a program executed on the computer itself and this converter was the first automatic translator.

Before writing the octal code for translation to binary, many programmers expressed their programs in *symbolic form* resembling assembly language, and translated them to octal by hand. Because the conversion was quite mechanical, it was soon automated too and performed by *assembler* programs. The first assemblers performed only simple conversion from the mnemonic representation of machine instructions into binary code but other features, such as pseudoinstructions, macros, and conditional assembly (Chapter 10), were soon added.

As the size of computer programs increased and as packages of routines such as device drivers and arithmetic routines were developed, it became obvious that the best way to produce large programs was to build them from smaller modules. Individual modules could be written and assembled by different programmers, stored in separate files, and combined into a single executable program by a *linker* program. For execution, the code produced by the linker would be loaded into computer memory by another program called the *loader*, which might perform some additional processing before starting program execution.

Assembly language programming is a significant improvement over binary machine language coding but it is still awkward. It requires a thorough knowledge of the CPU and a great deal of attention to detail. Although still used, mainly to produce very efficient code, assembly language programming has now been largely replaced by programming in high-level languages (HLLs).

The basic HLL concept is that an algorithm can be expressed in a symbolic form governed by strict rules independent of the machine on which it will be implemented, and then mechanically translated into machine code. This makes it possible to write readable and unambiguous algorithms and to do so much more efficiently than with an assembly language.

Another important advantage of HLLs over assembly languages is their portability. The desirability of transporting programs from one computer to another instead of rewriting them is obvious. It is also clear that programs written in one assembly language cannot be executed by a CPU with a different architecture because most assembly language instructions are one-to-one symbolic representations of machine instructions. The existence of high-level programming languages reduces the problem of CPU incompatibility because a program written, for example, in Pascal can be transported from one computer to another, if both have equivalent Pascal translators.

Unfortunately, different HLL translators usually do not produce fully equivalent code. There are several reasons for this: Compilers are written by different programmers and if the definition of the language is not totally unambiguous, the resulting compiler reflects its author's interpretations. Also, differences in CPU architectures and resources, such as word sizes and peripherals, make full portability impossible. Yet, the existence of HLLs makes programs much easier to transport and greatly simplifies program development.

Translators of HLLs can be categorized as *compilers* and *interpreters*. The division is somewhat fuzzy because compilers often have features of interpreters and vice versa, but the following definitions capture the essence of this classification: Interpreters translate the source code and execute it immediately. To a greater or lesser degree, every statement is retranslated each time when it is encountered. Compilers translate the source code into object code only once and do not execute it. The generated object code is stored in a file and can then be executed as many times as desired without any further compiler intervention. To use an analogy, an interpreter program is similar to a human interpreter at the United Nations, who translates a live speech from Russian into English, while a compiler program is like somebody who translates a Russian novel into English.

In the following two sections we will outline the principles of assemblers and compilers. Although assemblers are conceptually simple, writing an assembler that is fast and does not require much memory is an art. Most methods of compilation, on the other hand, rely on advanced concepts, some of them rather difficult to understand. Fortunately, one very popular method of compilation is quite straightforward in principle, and we will thus be able to present a realistic introduction to compilation as well.

### Exercise

1. Write a program that translates octal codes stored in a file to their binary equivalent.

## 15.2 ASSEMBLERS

Assemblers convert symbolic assembly language code into machine code that can be executed directly or after linking with other assembled modules. We will now demonstrate the principle of assembly by manually translating a short program in the 6800 assembly language and then develop a formal assembly algorithm.

Consider the following program for the OS68 operating system:

```
                                ; Two's complement negation of
                                ; an L-byte number N
                                ; N and L≤5 are stored in memory
STOP     EQU            $51     ; "Terminate" function
         ORG $5                 ; Location of data segment
L        DS 1                   ; Reserved for the number of bytes
N        DS 5                   ; Space for number to complement
         ORG            $10     ; Location of code segment
                                ; First negate all bytes
START    LDAB L                 ; B is used for counting
         LDX #N                 ; Address of MSB
LOOP1    COM 0,X                ; Negate
```

```
         INX
         DEC B
         BNE LOOP1       ; Repeat
                         ; Now increment LSB by 1 and
                         ; then propagate Carry
         DEX             ; Back to LSB
         INC 0,X
LOOP2    DEX             ; Point X to next byte
         CPX #N-1        ; Done?
         BEQ DONE        ; If yes, exit
         ADC 0,X         ; Propagate Carry
         BRA LOOP2
DONE     LDAA STOP       ; Return
         SWI             ; to operating system
         END START
```

For reasons that will soon become clear, we will perform the translation in two phases, each time reading the source code from start to end. In the first pass, we will check that all symbols used in the program are acceptable and have been combined in legal ways and we will calculate their values.

In the second pass we will read the source code again, converting instruction codes into opcodes and user symbols into values obtained in pass 1.

**Pass 1**

Our source program starts with comments and blank lines that do not contain any information relevant to code generation. The assembler reads them but does not take any action.

The first meaningful line is

```
STOP     EQU     $51
```

which defines label *STOP*. Because the label may be used later in the program, we must save it in a symbol table. Label *STOP* is followed by the EQU pseudoinstruction and $51 which means that the value of *STOP* is $51. The symbol table becomes

| Symbol | Hexadecimal Value |
|---|---|
| STOP | 0051 |

The next line,

ORG $5

instructs the assembler to start allocating memory from address $0005. To keep track of the continuously changing address of the next location to be used for the assembled code, the assembler stores its value in variable *LocationCounter.* The ORG line thus sets *LocationCounter* to $5. Note that the location counter is an internal assembly variable and has nothing to do with the CPU program counter register, which is a hardware feature of the CPU.

The next line is

L DS 1

It contains another new symbol *L*, which must be added to the symbol table, and the DS (Define Space) pseudoinstruction, which reserves one byte. Symbol *L* represents the address assigned to the reserved byte. The address to be allocated to *L* is copied from variable *LocationCounter* to the symbol table and the location counter is incremented from 5 to 6 as *L* consumes one memory location.

The next line,

N DS 5 ; Number to complement

reserves two bytes for *N*. Symbol *N* is entered into the symbol table and gets its value from the *LocationCounter*, which is then incremented by 5 because the pseudoinstruction reserves five bytes. The value of *LocationCounter* is now $B and the symbol table is

| Symbol | Hexadecimal Value |
|---|---|
| L | 0005 |
| N | 0006 |
| STOP | 0051 |

The next line is another ORG instruction and it changes the value of *LocationCounter* to $10. Line

START LDAB 1

begins with label *START*, a new symbol that must be entered into the symbol table. Because it represents the address of the opcode produced from this line, its value is obtained from *LocationCounter*. Symbol *START* thus gets value $10.

The rest of the line contains LDAB with operand *L*. According to the symbol table, *L* is on page zero, and LDAB can thus use direct addressing. Its code requires two bytes; consequently, *LocationCounter* is incremented by 2 and becomes \$12.

The next instruction is processed similarly and changes the value of *LocationCounter* to \$15. Line

```
LOOP1     COM 0,X     ; Negate
```

starts with label *LOOP1*, a new symbol that will be entered into the symbol table with the current value of *LocationCounter*. (*LOOP1* represents the address of COM 0,X). Because COM 0,X requires two bytes, *LocationCounter* is then incremented by 2. The symbol table is now as follows:

| Symbol | Hexadecimal Value |
|---|---|
| L | 0005 |
| LOOP1 | 0015 |
| N | 0006 |
| START | 0010 |
| STOP | 0051 |

Processing continues in the same way until we reach line

```
CPX #N−1
```

with expression $N - 1$. Because *N* is already in the symbol table, no change to the symbol table is required. The next line

```
BEQ DONE
```

contains symbol *DONE*, which is not in the symbol table. Because BEQ uses *DONE* as an operand (*DONE* is the address of an instruction not yet encountered), this line does not help us determine its value and *DONE* is thus entered into the symbol table undefined. Technically speaking, *DONE* is a *forward reference* to a symbol whose value will, presumably, be established later in the program. If it were not for forward references, we could produce code in a single pass through the source code. The presence of forward references such as *DONE* means that certain values are unknown when their values are needed and a complete code cannot be generated at that point.

The symbol table is now

| Symbol | Hexadecimal Value |
|---|---|
| DONE | ???? |
| L | 0005 |
| LOOP1 | 0015 |
| LOOP2 | 001E |
| N | 0006 |
| START | 0010 |
| STOP | 0051 |

Processing continues until we reach line

DONE    LDAA #STOP

As usual, label *DONE* gets the current value of *LocationCounter*, which is $28. The symbol table becomes

| Symbol | Hexadecimal Value |
|---|---|
| DONE | 0028 |
| L | 0005 |
| LOOP1 | 0015 |
| LOOP2 | 001E |
| N | 0006 |
| START | 0010 |
| STOP | 0051 |

Processing of the rest of the source program follows the same pattern and stops when the END pseudoinstruction is reached.

The first pass through the source code is now complete. Inasmuch as there were no illegal, undefined, or multiply defined symbols, the program is valid and we can proceed to the second pass. The symbol table is complete as it appears above. We can now describe the principle of pass 1 as follows:

```
Initialize symbol table;
LocationCounter := 0; {Default setting}
done := FALSE;
```

```
REPEAT
  READ(line);
  IF label present AND NOT (label IN symbol table)
    THEN enter label into table;
  IF machine instruction
    THEN
      BEGIN
        IF label present
          THEN label := LocationCounter;
        Look up number of bytes N requried by instruction;
        LocationCounter := LocationCounter + N;
      END
    ELSE
      IF pseudoinstruction
        THEN
          CASE pseudoinstruction OF
            DS:  BEGIN
                   IF label present
                     THEN label := LocationCounter;
                   LocationCounter :=
                     LocationCounter + value of argument;
                 END;
            DB : ....      {Left as an exercise}
            END: done := TRUE;
            EQU: label := value of argument;
            ORG: LocationCounter := value of argument;
          END      {CASE}
UNTIL done;
IF errors
  THEN
    BEGIN
      Output error messages;
      HALT;
    END;
```

Further details, the DB pseudoinstruction, and handling of errors are left as an exercise.

## Pass 2

In this pass, we will read the source code again and use the values calculated in pass 1 and stored in the symbol table to produce executable object code.

Pseudoinstruction ORG again initializes *LocationCounter* to $5. Theoretically, the following DS pseudoinstructions only reserve space for variables, but we will initialize the reserved space to 0 to simplify the code. The ORG pseudoinstruction following the DB sequence resets the location counter to $10. The first machine instruction is

```
LDAB    L
```

After locating the code of "LDAB direct" in the table of 6800 instructions and the value of *L* in the symbol table, the assembler finds that the code for LDAB L is D6 05. The remaining instructions are processed in the same way.

When we reach the end of the program, and before we store the object code in a file, we must add some extra information so that OS68 can load the file and execute it. To determine what other information is needed, we must consider what happens when we execute the object code.

To execute the assembled code with OS68, we must type a command that loads the code from the file and initiates its execution. Because the OS68 does not place any restrictions on the location of the code, the object code file must tell OS68 where to locate the code in memory and the address of the first executable instruction.

In our case, the program has two segments—data and machine code—and each is to be loaded into a different memory area. This information must also be included in the object code. Considering all these points, we will use the following structure for the object file:

Address of the first instruction to be executed

Number of segments

Address at which the first code of the first segment will be stored

Length of the first segment in bytes

Address at which the first code of the second segment will be stored

Length of the second segment in bytes

Similar information about all other segments

Code of the first segment

Code of the second segment

Code of all other segments

We assume that the program does not require any additional modules, which eliminates the need for a linker.

We are now ready to list the contents of the object code file. Our sample program has two segments: The first executable instruction is at location $10, the data segment starts at $05, and its length is six bytes. The code segment starts at $10 and its length is twenty-seven ($1B) bytes. The object code file is thus as follows:

| Hexadecimal Code | Comment |
|---|---|
| 00<br>10 | Two-byte address of the first executable instruction |
| 02 | Number of segments |
| 00<br>06 | Two-byte address of the first code of the first segment |
| 00<br>06 | Length of the first segment |
| 00<br>10 | Two-byte address of the first code of the second segment |
| 00<br>1B | Length of the second segment |
| 00<br>00<br>00<br>00<br>00<br>00 | Data segment (six data bytes, all initialized to zero) |
| D6<br>06<br>CE<br>00<br>06<br>63<br>00<br>⋮ | First code of the second segment |
| 3F | Opcode of SWI—the last instruction in the program |

We have now completely analyzed pass 2 and we can describe its operation as follows:

LocationCounter := 0; done := FALSE;

```
REPEAT
  READ(line);
  IF machine instruction
    THEN
      BEGIN
        Look up machine code and symbol values;
        Calculate number of bytes N necessary;
        LocationCounter := LocationCounter  + N;
      END
    ELSE
      IF pseudoinstruction
        THEN
          CASE pseudoinstruction OF
            DB:   LocationCounter := LocationCounter + N;
            DS:   . . .
            END: done := TRUE;
            ORG: BEGIN
                   LocationCounter := value of argument;
                 END;
            And so forth
            END:
UNTIL done;
```

We have left all actions associated with producing the object code file as an exercise.

### Summary of Assembler Operation

In pass 1 the assembler checks that all of the instructions and symbols are legal and builds the symbol table. If it finds errors, such as illegal instruction names or operands, missing or multiply defined symbols, or incorrect pseudoinstructions, it outputs appropriate error messages and stops.

If the first pass succeeded, the assembler enters pass 2, in which it replaces the mnemonics of all machine instructions with their binary codes and converts symbols into values using the symbol table. The code and some housekeeping information are written to the object code file.

### Exercises

1. Complete the missing parts of the assembler algorithm.
2. Write an assembler for TOY.

3. Give five examples of the types of errors that could occur in assembly language programs.
4. Write an ET-3400 loader that loads programs assembled into the format described in this section from a file sent via an RS-232-C interface. Assume the existence of an RS-232 input subroutine called SIN, which returns the next character from the file.
5. Modify the loader from the previous exercise to bootstrap itself. Explain the advantage of bootstrapping in this example. (*Hint*: Describe the exact procedure for both a bootstrapping and a nonbootstrapping loader for the ET-3400 starting from the moment the ET-3400 is turned on.)

## 15.3 COMPILERS AND INTERPRETERS

We already explained that there are two types of translators for high-level language programs: compilers and interpreters. Compilers translate the source code into object code that can then be executed without further compiler intervention. Interpreters translate and execute the source code; they do not produce any object code files. Conceptually, the most complicated function of an interpreter is translation, which is performed in essentially the same way in interpreters and in compilers; we will thus restrict our attention in the rest of this section to compilers only.

Translation produces code whose execution represents the meaning of the source program. In this sense, translation finds the meaning of the source program, and resembles human processing of speech. Exploring this parallel helps one to understand the structure of compilation.

Speech arrives at the ear as a continuous stream of sounds. The auditory system captures the sounds, removes the irrelevant noise, and converts the rest into elementary speech sounds called phonemes. Phonemes are gathered into words. Words are classified as nouns, verbs, and so on, and are gathered into grammatical units like the noun phrase, the verb phrase, and sentence. Finally, the uncovered grammatical structure is used to find the meaning.

In compilation, the listing of the source program (a stream of ASCII codes) is first read from a file. Comments, spaces, and other irrelevant "noise" are removed, and *tokens*—basic units of the given programming language like BEGIN, END, := and WRITE—are recognized and grouped into *syntactic units* like assignment statements and declarations. The uncovered structure is then used to create executable code, which represents the "meaning" of the program.

We can use this analysis to divide the compiler program into the following components: the *reader*, which reads the stream of program characters from a file; the *scanner* (also called the lexical analyzer), which removes irrelevant information like comments, and finds tokens, the *parser*, which recognizes syntactic units; and the *code generator*, which converts the resulting information to machine code. (The scanner module usually subsumes the reader.)

By dividing compilation into several tasks, the problem of compilation is simplified because each task deals with only one aspect of translation: The reader does not need to be concerned about the meaning of the characters that it reads. The scanner only assembles the tokens but does not care how they are obtained or whether they form a meaningful sequence. The parser does not have to deal with individual characters because it works with compact token codes. The code generator does not concern itself with the structure of the program and mechanically outputs sections of code implementing operations like assignment, and calls of the write function of the operating system.

One way to implement a compiler is to separate the scanner, parser, and code generator into separate passes, each processing the completed product of the previous pass. Alternatively, the scanner, parser, and code generator may be more or less closely coupled, the reader performing only one pass over the source code and all modules communicating their results as soon as a suitable unit of information is obtained (Figure 15.1). Both models are used in practice but we will use the second approach because it more closely resembles our speech processing model and because it is more common in compilers for smaller computers.

The driving force of translation is parsing, the recognition of the grammatical structure of the program, because the structure of the source program is the basis of its meaning just as for the spoken or written language. For this reason, and because it can be described more neatly than other parts of compilation, parsing usually receives the most attention in books on translation. Our discussion will also center around the parser.

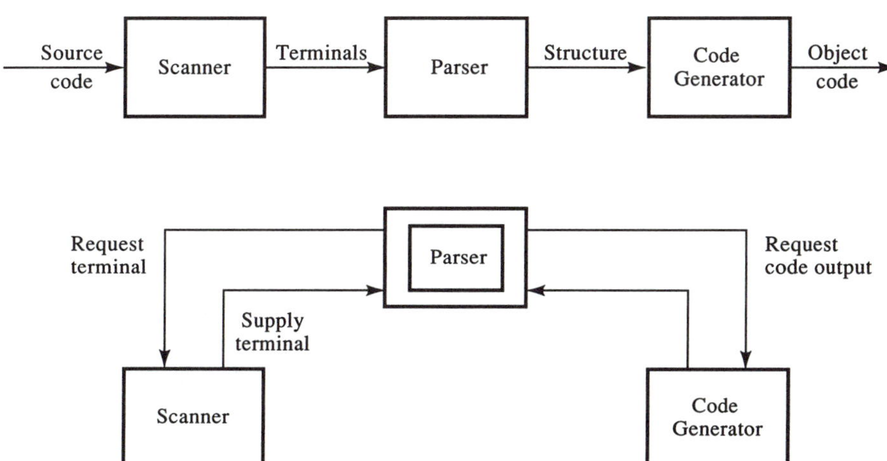


**Figure 15.1.** Compiler as a sequence of passes (*top*) and as a single program consisting of communicating modules (*bottom*).

Several parsing algorithms are available and two or three are commonly used. Most of them have relatively advanced theoretical foundations and are beyond the scope of this book but one, *recursive descent parsing*, is not difficult to understand and we will use it in this section. As recursive descent parsing is very popular, our presentation gives a realistic, although greatly simplified, picture of compilation.

To write a compiler, we must first have a formal definition of the language that we want to compile. Thus we will start by defining a very simple language called SIMPLE and will then develop a compiler to translate SIMPLE programs into 6800 code executable with the OS68.

### Grammar of SIMPLE

Parsing requires a rigorous definition of the parsed language and the most natural way to obtain such a definition is to write one or more representative programs in the language and derive the rules from them. We will derive the rules of SIMPLE from the following sample program:

```
PROGRAM AB;     {Program heading}
  VAR x,y,z;    {Declaration}
  BEGIN {Body}
    WRITE('Enter two numbers ');
    READ(x);
    READ(y);
    z := x + 2 + y - 3;
    WRITE('Result is ');
    WRITE(z);
  END.
```

SIMPLE resembles Pascal, and each SIMPLE program consists of a heading, declarations, and body. Pascal-like comments are also allowed.

The parts of *heading* are the word PROGRAM, an identifier, and a semicolon. The heading has no effect on the execution of the program but must be included.

The heading is followed by *declarations*. All variables used in the program must be declared. SIMPLE has only one data type, the one-byte integer, and there is thus no need to name it.

Declarations are followed by the *body* of the program, which starts with the word "BEGIN" and ends with "END." It consists of a sequence of *statements* separated by semicolons. Only two types of statements are allowed: I/O and assignment. The structure of statements is simple and conventional. As an example, the WRITE statement consists of the word "WRITE" followed by an argument in parentheses. The argument may be a string constant (text surrounded by apostrophes) or a variable name.

By analyzing the program in this way, we can obtain a set of formal rules, the *grammar* of SIMPLE. For a given language, there are always a number of alternative equivalent grammars and one of the possible grammars for SIMPLE is as follows:

*program* ::= heading . declarations . body

*heading* ::= PROGRAM . identifier . ;

*identifier* ::= letter . rest_of_id

*rest_of_id* ::= identifier | ϵ

*letter* ::= A|B|C|..|Z|a|b|c|...|z|

*declarations* ::= VAR . identifiers . ; | ϵ

*identifiers* ::= identifier . rest_of_ids

*rest_of_ids* ::= , . identifiers | ϵ

*body* ::= BEGIN . statements . END

*statements* ::= statement . ; . other_statements

*other_statements* ::= statements | ϵ

*statement* ::= assignment | input | output

*assignment* ::= identifier . := . expression

*expression* ::= [sign] . term . rest_of_exp

*term* ::= identifier | integer

*integer* ::= digit . rest_of_integer

*digit* ::= 0|1|2|3|4|5|6|7|8|9

*rest_of_integer* ::= integer | ϵ

*rest_of_exp* ::= plus_expression | minus_expression | ϵ

*plus_expression* ::= + . term . rest_of_expression

*minus_expression* ::= − . term . rest_of_expression

*input* ::= READ . ( . identifier . )

*output* ::= WRITE . ( . argument . )

*argument* ::= identifier | string_constant

*string_constant* ::= ' . text . '

*text* ::= character . text | ϵ

*character* ::= any_printable_character_other_than_'

*comment* ::= { . string_of_characters_other_than_ } . }

Each rule defines a *syntactic unit* of the language. (Syntactic units are also called *nonterminals*. In the above definitions, *program, heading, declarations,* and *identifier* are nonterminals.)

Our specification of SIMPLE grammar is written using the Backus-Naur Formalism (BNF), which is common in specifications of high-level languages. Each rule has two parts separated by the symbol "::=" (read as "is defined as") and defines the term on the left by the terms on the right. A dot between consecutive elements on the right hand side of a rule indicates concatenation, serial ordering. As an example, the first line means that the syntactic unit program consists of a heading followed by declarations followed by a body.

The right hand side is usually a sequence of nonterminals and words of the language (*terminals*) such as BEGIN and END. (The terms "syntactic unit," "nonterminal," and "terminal" are taken from linguistics. Nonterminals correspond to concepts such as nouns, verbs, adjectives, noun phrases, and verb phrases while terminals correspond to words such as "DOG," "CAT," "RUN," and "SMALL.")

To make our definitions easier to read, we will use lowercase letters for nonterminals and upper case letters for terminals. This does not mean that SIMPLE programs must use capitals for terminals. In fact, SIMPLE is "case insensitive" and does not distinguish between uppercase and lowercase letters, except in string constants.

Symbol "|" indicates choice among several alternative definitions. As an example, a letter can be *A* or *B* or *C*, and so on. (We have not listed all possible values because the meaning is obvious: A "letter" is any lowercase or uppercase letter.)

A sequence of symbols enclosed between "[" and "]" is optional. As an example, an expression in SIMPLE may begin with a plus or minus sign, as in " + 14" or " − x + 3," but does not have to, as in "x + 12."

Symbol "ϵ" (Greek letter epsilon) represents the *empty* (or null) production, a rule that replaces the lefthand side nonterminal with nothing. We use it to allow termination of a sequence of syntactic units that may be repeated any number of times.

Note that some nonterminals are defined partially in terms of themselves. As an example, the nonterminal *statements* is defined as an empty production, or as *statement* followed by a semicolon and *statements*. This essentially means that the number of statements is not fixed. Definitions that describe a nonterminal in terms of itself are called *recursive*. They are very common because they simplify the grammar and consequently the parser. The presence of recursive rules in most languages and their direct use by the parsing method that we are going to use is the reason why our method of parsing is called recursive descent parsing.

Although our definitions do not show it, blank spaces, line feeds, and carriage returns may be inserted between words just as in Pascal. These details could be described by rules but we will omit them to simplify the specification.

SIMPLE has several other rules that are not captured by our definitions:

The length of a string constant may not exceed eighty characters to fit on one line.

The maximum magnitude of an integer is 99.

Identifiers must not be longer than seven letters.

Built-in words PROGRAM, VAR, BEGIN, READ, WRITE, and END are reserved and must not be used as identifiers.

A comment may be inserted between any two terminals and has no effect on the execution of the program.

All identifiers used in a program must be declared.

Identifiers may be declared only once.

Some of these rules can be expressed in the BNF style used for our grammar. As an example, *integer* could be defined by listing all legal integers in the same way as *digit* is defined. Similarly the rules forbidding the use of reserved words for identifiers and limiting their length to at most eight characters could be expressed by listing all legal identifiers. The list would be rather long but finite as the identifier length is limited to at most seven characters.

We have not included the rules for integers and reserved words among the production rules because they are too cumbersome. However, the rules specifying that identifiers used in the program must be declared and that they must not be declared twice cannot be expressed in BNF notation. This is because BNF rules have a single nonterminal on the left hand side and this nonterminal is thus defined free of context. (The nonterminal appears on the left hand side all by itself.) On the other hand, the rule "identifiers must be declared" puts identifiers in the context "declaration – use," and a new form of rule with more elements on the lefthand side, a context-sensitive nrule, is required to express this property. It turns out that parsers of context-sensitive rules are much more complicated than parsers of context-free rules and the use of a more complicated type of grammar is thus not attractive. The fact that we do not use context-sensitive rules naturally does not change the fact that SIMPLE is context-sensitive. It means that this aspect of SIMPLE is not handled by the parser in the same way as all other rules.

This note shows that certain fine points are hidden under the rather obvious language rules. Because the rules and their form determine the design of the parser, subtle theoretical questions must be considered to make sure that the language is properly defined and can be parsed. Problems such as these are beyond the scope of this text but fortunately are not essential for an understanding of the principles of compilation.

## Exercises

1. What is the likely origin of the terms "terminal" and "nonterminal?"
2. List all nonterminals of SIMPLE. List all terminals.
3. Our grammar is only one of many possible grammars for SIMPLE. As an example, *io* could be defined as a nonterminal input statement and OR as a nonterminal output statement. Write a version of SIMPLE grammar and list its nonterminals. Make sure that the grammar describes the same language!
4. Find all recursive definitions in SIMPLE grammar.
5. How many legal integers and identifiers are there in SIMPLE?
6. Extend SIMPLE to allow several arguments for WRITE, include expressions as WRITE arguments, and add WRITELN and other constructs.
7. Express the definition of an identifier as a transition graph. Explain why this suggests that grammatical rules of a certain type are in some sense equivalent to sequential machines.
8. Explain what is meant by "context" and show how BNF notation could be extended to allow context-sensitive rules.
9. Which of the following constructs is illegal in SIMPLE? Explain.
   a. program without declaration
   b. program without body
   c. x1 := − 3
   d. −y := z + 345
   e. abcdefghxyz := 3
   f. READ(x,y)
   g. WRITE(x + 2).
10. Which properties of SIMPLE cannot be described without recursion? Why?

## The Compiler — A Hands-on Analysis

As we have already mentioned, the basis of compilation is parsing, the recognition of the grammatical structure of the source program. There are several efficient parsing strategies and we will use the most obvious one, *top-down* (*recursive descent parsing*). In this section we will show how a compiler based on recursive-descent parsing works by tracing its operation on our sample program. We will then define a formal parsing algorithm in the next section.

All top-down parsers start with the first rule of the grammar and attempt to expand it to match the given source code. According to the top rule of SIMPLE, the first task of our parser is the recognition of a heading. Because headings begin with the word PROGRAM, the parser requests the first terminal from the scanner.

The scanner processes the source program one symbol at a time until it finds a complete terminal. In our program, the first symbols are letters 'P', 'R', 'O', 'G', 'R', 'A', 'M', and a space. The space indicates the end of a word—it is a terminator. The scanner stops reading and informs the parser that the terminal is PROGRAM.

The parser finds that this terminal matches the rule of headings and calls the scanner again, expecting an identifier. To simplify parsing, we will leave the handling of identifiers to the scanner. This is typical for most compilers and constitutes, in fact, a departure from the original grammar: Most compilers do not directly use the "language grammar" and are based on a "compiler grammar." The two grammars, of course, must be equivalent.

When asked for the next word, the scanner gets letters 'A' and 'B' and a semicolon. Because the semicolon is a word by itself, the current word is "AB," which is not a built-in word. It is also not an integer because it begins with a letter. After comparing the structure of "AB" with the rules for various types of SIMPLE words the scanner concludes that it has an identifier and sends it to the parser.

The parser finds that the next item in the rule for the heading is matched, and calls the scanner again, expecting a semicolon. The next word is indeed a semicolon and when the parser receives it, it finds that the definition of the heading is now complete. Because the heading does not have any effect on the execution of the program, the compiler throws this information away.

After completing the parse of the heading, the parser returns to the rule for the program, which has not been completely processed yet, and finds that the next syntactic unit is *declarations*. The first item in the declarations is the terminal VAR and the parser calls the scanner.

The scanner assembles VAR, returns it to the parser, and a match is found. (Before assembling VAR, the scanner recognizes and throws away the comment on the first line. It does not even inform the parser because comments are not a part of the parser's notion of SIMPLE grammar.)

Next, the parser recognizes variables $x$, $y$, and $z$. This information is meaningful because in the generated code the compiler must allocate one byte of memory to each variable. Following the technique used by the assembler, information about user-defined symbols will be kept in the symbol table:

| Variable Number | Variable Name |
|---|---|
| 1 | x |
| 2 | y |
| 3 | z |

Having processed the declarations, the parser returns to the definition of the program, which still has not been completely processed, and finds that the next syntactic unit is *body*. A body starts with the terminal BEGIN; the parser calls the scanner and after finding a match proceeds to the statements.

The nonterminal *statements* has two definitions. One is recursive and begins with *statement*, the other is an empty rule. What should the parser do? One possibility is to try one rule and if it fails, try the other one. This strategy is called backtracking, and can cause the compiler to waste a lot of time. A better approach is to take note of the fact that if we used the empty rule, the next terminal would have to be END (statements are followed by END), whereas the nonempty definition implies that the next terminal is READ or WRITE or an identifier. Thus all we need do to select the proper rule is to look ahead at the next token. Lookahead forms the basis of all parsers because it eliminates false guesses and increases parser efficiency enormously.

To use lookahead, the parser calls the scanner, gets the word "WRITE," and selects the recursive definition (the word is not "END"), which begins with "statement." There are several kinds of statements and each starts with a different terminal. Because the current terminal is WRITE, the proper choice is "io" (input statement). Of the two possible rules for "io," the parser selects the one that begins with "WRITE," matches "WRITE," calls the scanner again, and finds and matches the opening parenthesis. The parser is now faced with a choice between two rules for the argument and so it again uses lookahead. It calls the scanner, which returns

< string constant > with value < Enter two numbers >

The argument is thus a string constant and the proper rule thus is "string constant."

Note that up to this point, the compiler has not generated any executable code but the WRITE operation must be converted to object code that outputs the string constant on the screen by using the I/O functions of the operating system. This will be implemented by jumping to a subroutine that takes the ASCII characters of the string constant, stores them in an output buffer, and calls the OS68 display function. This subroutine, called WRITESTRING, and several others implementing various I/O functions will be gathered in SIMPLE's *run-time system*, a collection of routines whose purpose is essentially to augment the capabilities of the operating system for the needs of the SIMPLE programmer. The compiler will write the code of the run-time system into each object code file produced by compiling a SIMPLE program so that it is available during the execution of the compiled code.

After generating the code for the WRITE statement, the parser analyzes the rest of the line and returns to the definition of "statements," which calls for more statements. After calling the scanner and getting READ, the parser selects the recursive definition and processes the rule for a READ statement.

Its argument $x$ is legal because $x$ is in the symbol table. The parser then calls the code generator to produce a jump to the READNUMBER subroutine of the run-time system, and to generate code to store the keyboard input in the memory location reserved for $x$. (As far as the execution of the program is concerned, the name of the variable is irrelevant and $x$ is simply the first byte in the block of storage allocated to variables.) The next READ statement is processed similarly.

The parser then recognizes that the following statement is an assignment because it starts with an identifier. It remembers that the left hand side is $z$ (the third identifier) and proceeds through the assignment symbol and the expression on the right hand side. It calls the code generator to output a "load extended" instruction to load the value of $x$, then an "add immediate" with value 2, an "add extended" with operand $y$, and a "subtract immediate" with value 3. Finally, a "store extended" instruction is generated to save the result in $z$. This completes the assignment statement. The processing of the rest of the program is left as an exercise.

When the compiler reaches "END," it must produce code to return to the operating system when the execution of the compiled program is complete, and the last generated instruction is therefore the terminate OS68 function. Compilation is now complete. Because the object code is intended for execution by OS68, it must have the form that we defined for code produced by the assembler; this is also left as an exercise.

Let us now summarize our analysis. Compilation consists of interleaved scanning (to recognize terminals), parsing (to recognize syntactic units), and code generation. Some housekeeping, such as generation of the symbol table, is also required. Control resides in the parser, which calls the scanner, selects appropriate language rules, matches them against the terminals supplied by the scanner, calls the code generator, and so on.

Our compiler is a one-pass recursive-descent compiler because it reads the source file only once and uses a recursive descent parser that processes the grammar by calling recursive procedures. (The parser is also called "predictive" because it does not use backtracking and always knows what the next item should be.

To complete this section, we note that the compiler must also be able to deal with illegal SIMPLE programs. This may be very difficult—if the source code contains an error, the parser loses track of its place in the grammar because it cannot find a match. Faced with this situation, many compilers simply produce an error message and abort compilation. Other compilers attempt to recover their position in the grammar and complete the processing of the source code displaying further error messages if necessary.

*Error recovery* is a complex topic beyond the scope of our presentation. Fortunately, most compilers for personal computers do not use it and prefer to display an error message and return the programmer to the source code for correction of the error.

### Exercises

1. The grammatical rules activated during parsing can be pictured as being stacked on top of one another, and removed from the stack when all their components are matched. Show the consecutive states of the stack of active rules for the parsing of the first few lines of our sample program.
2. Finish our description of the processing of the sample program and produce the complete object code in the proper format.
3. Develop an alternative version of SIMPLE grammar and use it to parse the sample program.
4. Write a short SIMPLE program and trace its compilation by hand.

### Implementation of the Compiler

We are now ready to demonstrate selected fragments of the implementation of a SIMPLE compiler. Its full listing and a version that displays the compiler's internal operation are included in the software package mentioned in the preface.

Our compiler consists of four logical modules: initialization, scanner, parser, and code generator. Because the scanner and the code generator are called by the parser, the main program is as follows:

```
BEGIN
  Initialization;
  Parser;          {Calls scanner and code generator}
  OutputCode;      {Writes the object code into a file}
END.
```

*The initialization module* opens the source file, assigns initial values to various variables, creates a table of reserved words, and performs other housekeeping functions.

*The scanner* has three parts: the procedures SkipBlanks, GetWord, and GetToken. Procedure SkipBlanks reads the source code from the file when called, passes over all irrelevant characters and comments, and returns the first meaningful character to GetWord. GetWord assembles the rest of the word from the source file. GetToken recognizes the assembled word and converts it to a predefined code recognizable by the parser. The code of the scanner is as follows:

```
PROCEDURE Scanner;
  BEGIN
    SkipBlanks;
    GetWord;
    GetToken;
  END;
```

When the SkipBlanks or GetWord need a character from the source code, they call procedure NextChar (the "reader"), which checks for the end of the file and returns the next character if there is one:

```
PROCEDURE NextChar(convert:BOOLEAN);
  BEGIN
  IF EOF(source)
    THEN ch := ETX {ETX is end of text: ASCII character 03}
    ELSE
      BEGIN
        READ(source,ch);
        IF convert
          THEN ch := UPCASE(ch);
      END;
  END;
```

To simplify processing by Getword, NextChar converts characters to uppercase unless they are inside a string constant. Conversion is controlled by the Boolean variable *Convert.*

Procedure GetToken recognizes the type of word supplied by GetWord and passes this information to the parser. It converts the word into a code called a token to save the parser the need to re-examine the word (possibly several times) a character at a time to recognize it. For words such as BEGIN, the parser only needs to know the type of the word. In other cases—for example, for an integer—the parser needs to know the token's value and the scanner thus sends both the kind and the value. If the word is illegal, GetToken calls an Error Procedure that displays an error message and aborts compilation. A partial listing of GetToken is as follows:

```
PROCEDURE GetToken; {Converts item to token}
  VAR i, value : INTEGER;
  BEGIN
  {Check if item is reserved by comparing it with elements of a table of
  reserved words}
    i := 0;
    REPEAT
      i := i + 1;
    UNTIL (i > nreserved) OR (item = reserved[i]);
    IF i<= nreserved
      THEN {It is a reserved word}
        BEGIN
```

```
          {Kinds are user-defined and numbered from 0}
          token.kind := kinds (i-1);
          IF token.kind = apostword {Apostrophy}
            THEN {Process string constant: see listing}
        END
    ELSE {Should be id or number}
        BEGIN
          IF item[1] IN letters
            THEN {Should be an id}
              BEGIN
                i := 2;
                IF LENGTH(item) > MaxId
                    THEN Error('Word too long');
                    {Procedure Error displays a message and aborts}
                WHILE i <= LENGTH(item) DO
                  IF item[i] IN letters
                    THEN i := i+1 {Go to next character}
                    ELSE Error('identifier contains an illegal character');
                {Identifier is OK}
                token.kind := idword;
                token.name := item;
              END {Of processing of id}
            ELSE {It must be a number}
              BEGIN {Check that all characters are digits}
                FOR i := 1 TO LENGTH(item) DO
                  IF NOT (item[i] IN ('0'..'9'])
                    THEN ERROR('Illegal word');
                {Check that value is within limits}
                  IF (LENGTH(item) > 2)
                  THEN Error ('Number too large (2 digits max)'),
                token.value := value;
                token.kind := numberword;
              END; {Of processing of a number}
          END {Else id or number}]
        ELSE Error('illegal word');
    END;
```

Note again, that the scanner aborts in the case of error and returns control to the parser only if the word is legal.

The parser is based on SIMPLE grammar although there are a few exceptions; for example, integers, ids, and string constants are processed by the scanner. Its top level implements the definition of the nonterminal *program*:

*program* ::= heading . declarations . body

and reads as follows:

```
PROCEDURE Parser;
  BEGIN
    Scanner; {Get first token}
    Heading;
    IF token.kind = varword
      THEN Declarations; {SIMPLE does not require declarations}
  Body;
END;
```

Again, an error at any stage aborts compilation. Procedure Heading similarly follows the definition

*heading* ::= PROGRAM . identifier . ;

It calls the scanner and checks that the word "PROGRAM" is present, calls the scanner again expecting an identifier, and again, expecting a semicolon. An error at any stage causes execution of the Error procedure, which displays a message and aborts compilation.

```
PROCEDURE Heading;
  BEGIN
    IF token.kind <> programword
      THEN Error('Expected word PROGRAM');
    Scanner; { Get next token }
    IF token.kind <> idword
      THEN Error('Program name is missing');
    Scanner;
    IF token.kind <> semicolonword
      THEN Error('Expected semicolon')
    Scanner; {Lookahead, should return Declarations or Body}
    IF NOT(token.kind IN [varword,beginword])
      THEN Error('Expected VAR or BEGIN');
  END;
```

Note that when procedure Heading starts, it assumes that the first token has already been obtained. The assumption that the next token is available when parsing procedure is entered is a convention used by all parser procedures of our compiler.

Procedure Declarations, which is called after procedure Heading, is entered only if procedure Heading finds the VAR word. It is obtained directly from the rule for declarations:

*declarations* ::= VAR . identifiers . ;

Because the compiler has already recognized VAR when it enters declarations, procedure Declarations looks for a list of identifiers separated by commas, and then a semicolon.

```
PROCEDURE Declarations;
  VAR i : INTEGER;
  BEGIN
    REPEAT {Process list of identifiers}
      Scanner;
      IF token.kind <> idword
      THEN Error('Expected variable name');
      {We have an id. Is this id already declared?}
      i := Idnumber; {Function Idnumber checks if the item is already in the
      symbol table and returns its position if it is.}
      IF i <= nvars {The current length of the symbol tables is contained in
      nvars}
        THEN Error('Already declared');
      {Insert into table if there is still room}
      nvars := nvars + 1;
      IF nvars > maxvars
        THEN Error('Too many variables declared');
      {Tables not full, insert new id}
      varname[nvars] := item;
      {Now expecting a comma or a semicolon}
      Scanner;
      {Now either a comma and another id, or a semicolon}
      IF NOT (token.kind IN [commaword, semicolonword])
        THEN Error('Expected comma or semicolon');
    UNTIL token.kind = semicolonword; {End of declarations}
  Scanner; {Get token following the semicolon for procedure body}
END;
```

The student should match the logic of this procedure with the rule for declarations.

This completes our discussion of parser procedures. The remaining ones are based on the same principles.

The *run-time code* consists of subroutines that read an integer, write an integer, and write a string. Jumps to these subroutines are produced by the compiler during the processing of READ and WRITE statements. The subroutines prepare arguments for OS68 functions and call them. They are similar to the programs developed in Chapter 14.

The *code generator*, consists of procedures Produce1, Produce2, and Produce3, which are called when one-, two-, or three-byte code needs to be generated, as in Produce3(JSR,1234), which generates machine code for JSR 1234. These procedures also check whether the length of the generated object code is within limits:

```
PROCEDURE Produce1(value:BYTE);
BEGIN
  IF location > maxlocation
    THEN Error('Program too long');
  {Otherwise store code and update location counter}
  code[location] := value;
  location := location + 1;
END;
```

It is worth mentioning that some procedures of our compiler do not produce code in the order in which the source program is written. As an example, in an assignment statement, the destination variable is read first because it is on the left, but the code produced by the compiler must first evaluate the expression and then store the result in the variable on the left handside. The compiler must therefore delay saving the result until it has produced code to calculate the value.

Because code generation and other actions performed during compilation occur at well-defined points during parsing, a convenient description of the operation of the compiler could be obtained by inserting action descriptions into the grammar as in the following augmented version of the program rule:

*program* ::= heading . declarations . <action1> . body . <action2>

where action1 reserves space for variables and inserts run-time code, and action2 generates code to return to the operating system.

The *housekeeping functions* of the compiler include initialization, an error procedure which displays a message and aborts execution, and code to save the object code in a file. As an example, the error procedure is as follows:

```
PROCEDURE Error(message:errorstring);
BEGIN
    WRITELN('ERROR; ',message' ');
    WRITELN('Line ',line_num); (Line where error was found)
    HALT: {Abort compiler operation}
END;
```

One of the functions of the housekeeping module is to output the object code into an ".OBJ" object file in the format described above.

**Exercises**

1. Give examples of errors that could be detected by the scanner, the parser, and the code generator, respectively.
2. Which errors in the source code could a compiler correct and how? Why don't most compilers do this?
3. Compilers sometimes do not produce very efficient code. As an example, compile (manually or with our program) for the sequence

   ```
   b := a + 4;
   c := a + 7;
   d := b + c;
   ```

   and then show that much better assembly language code can be produced manually.
4. Add WRITELN and similar features to SIMPLE and its compiler.
5. If we changed the definition of identifiers to

   *identifiers* ::= identifiers . identifier

   *identifiers* ::= identifier

   we could not parse them using a recursive descent parser. Explain.
6. Write a procedure to parse one of the SIMPLE nonterminals, for example *assignment*.
7. Write the run-time subroutines for the SIMPLE compiler. Subroutine WRITENUMBER converts the binary number in accumulator *A* to ASCII and calls OS68 to display the codes on the screen. Subroutine READNUMBER repeatedly calls OS68 to obtain a sequence of ASCII codes terminated by carriage return, converts them to binary and checks that the value is within limits; it aborts program execution and returns to OS68 if the value is not within the range 0–99.
8. Modify the SIMPLE compiler to produce object code to check the result of each arithmetic operation and return control to the operating system if

the result exceeds SIMPLE's limits. This involves a change of code generation and an addition to the run-time system.

9. Write a "test suite" of programs for the SIMPLE compiler. It should test that legal programs are accepted and correctly compiled and that illegal programs are rejected. (*Hint*: Use the grammar definition and the listing of the compiler.)
10. Add actions to the SIMPLE grammar.
11. Give a systematic procedure for writing and testing a compiler based on recursive descent parsing.
12. The following is a typical grammar used by high-level languages for arithmetic expressions:

    *expression* ::= [−] . term . restexpression

    *restexpression* ::= addop. term | ϵ

    *addop* ::= + | −

    *term* ::= factor . restfactor

    *restfactor* ::= multop . factor | ϵ

    *multop* ::= * | /

    *factor* ::= integer | ( . expression )

    Give several examples of expressions and determine whether they are legal under this grammar.
13. Write a parser for the *expression* grammar.
14. Extend the rules for expressions with actions. (*Hint*: Use the stack to store operands and intermediate results.)
15. Write an interpreter for the *expression* language described by the grammar from Exercise 15. The input is from the keyboard, the output is produced upon pressing *ENTER* and goes to the screen. No object code is to be generated.
16. Describe TOY's assembly language in BNF form and use this to write the skeleton of the assembler.
17. Identify the context-sensitive aspects of SIMPLE grammar and explain how they are handled by our compiler.

### General Remarks on Compilation

Although our compiler is very elementary, it contains all the essential features of a real compiler. Compilers for more realistic languages are, however, much more complicated because their syntax is complex, the computing environment richer, and user expectations higher. The following is a list of some of the differences and a few additional notes on compiler writing:

Many compilers optimize the output code in one way or another. The usual goal of optimization is to maximize the speed of execution, but minimization of the space required by the object code is another possibility. Another possible criterion is optimization of the operation of the compiler itself—fitting it into the smallest memory space or maximizing compilation speed.

Recent developments in programming make compilers only a part of a larger *program development environment* designed for team programming. These environments provide functions like program editing, automatic recompilation of modules modified since the last compilation, date and time stamping of successive program versions, and archiving.

It might appear that to produce a compiler, one only needs to write a set of syntax rules and convert them mechanically into a recursive descent-based compiler. This is not entirely true because recursive descent parsing only works if the grammar obeys certain restrictions that guarantee that the parser always knows which procedure to call next. (We have seen an example of a faulty rule in Exercise 5 above). SIMPLE satisfies this requirement because whenever there is a choice between several rules, the next word in the source program determines unequivocally which rule should be used. As an example, statements can be parsed unambigously because the first terminal in a statement (READ, WRITE, or identifier) determines which of the three types of statement is present.

Checking that a grammar satisfies conditions such as these is relatively easy, and most violations that appear in the rules can be corrected. More difficult programs can often be solved by using a more powerful parsing method. When this fails, the grammar must be redesigned.

Exercise 1 in the previous section and Exercise 14 in this section suggest that the stack plays a prominent role in operation of the parser and in the execution of the generated code. Yet, our description of the compiler does not contain any explicit mention of it. This is because our parser uses the stack implicitly: Its presence is hidden in the operation of the Pascal language that we used to implement the compiler. We will now briefly explain how this happens.

Languages like Pascal, which allow recursive procedures and functions, are implemented as follows: When a Pascal program calls a procedure, it stores its parameters, local variables, the return address of the calling program, and other information on the stack and uses the top of this area to evaluate expressions. (We have already mentioned in Chapter 10 that this block of information is called the activation record of the procedure.) Execution of the procedure then begins.

If the active procedure calls another procedure, a new activation record is pushed on the stack and the new procedure begins execution. This can be repeated many times and procedure calls can be nested to any depth as long as their combined activation records do not exceed the amount of memory available for the stack. When a procedure terminates, it removes its activation record from the stack and execution returns to the calling procedure via the return address stored in the activation record. The space occupied by the deactivated record is freed in the usual stack fashion.

Because our parser is written in Pascal or another language that allows recursion (it is a recursive descent parser), the stack mechanism based on activation records is used by the compiler because it is written in Pascal. The stack of the parser that we conceptually described is thus implemented by the stack built into the implementation language. As an example, when a procedure recognizing "statements" calls the procedure recognizing "statement," the mechanism involved in this call at the level of the Pascal code of the compiler adds a new activation record on the stack. On exit from the procedure, the activation record is popped from the stack.

As the concept of activation records created by the code produced by a Pascal compiler indicates, the allocation of space for variables is more complicated than our compiler suggests. We will have a few words to add to this topic in the section on the Turbo Pascal compiler.

It is interesting to comment on the size and CPU time requirements of individual parts of the compiler. For a multipass compiler much larger than ours, Brinch Hansen (see references) has reported that the scanner occupied about 14%, the parser about 67%, the code generator (performing some code optimization) 14%, and housekeeping functions about 5% of the code.

Although the size of the compiler is important, a much more critical parameter is usually its speed. It is thus useful to know what percentage of time the individual components take during compilation. Brinch Hansen found, that the scanner consumed about 45% of the total compilation time, the parser about 34%, and the code generator 21%. To optimize the speed of the compiler, one should thus concentrate on the scanner.

Different compilers have different properties but the finding that lexical analysis takes most of the compilation time applies to the majority of other compilers as well.

### Automatic Compiler Generation

Our construction of the parser from the grammar of SIMPLE was almost mechanical and it is thus not surprising that a parser can be automatically obtained from a grammar by a program called the parser generator.

A parser generator reads the grammar of the language and outputs a table describing it. During compilation, the table can be used to decide when the parser should call the scanner, which word to expect, and which of several alternative rules to use when there is a choice. The parser itself can be implemented by a *driver* program that uses the table to parse the given language. The combination of the prewritten driver and the automatically constructed table constitute a *table-driven parser* for that grammar. To parse a different grammar, the driver can remain unchanged but must use a new table. (Instead of producing a table, the generator can also produce the source code of the parser itself.)

Scanner operation can also be described by a grammar that is, in fact, simpler in a formal sense than the grammar for the parser. Programs that automatically generate table driven scanners are also available.

Finally, even the code generator can be produced almost automatically if the grammar is complemented by a description of the *semantics* of individual constructs of the language. ("Semantics" refers to the "meaning" of a programming construct; that is, what the construct does when it is executed.)

Although a complete compiler can be generated automatically, there are reasons why commercial compilers are still produced manually. One is that compiler generation tools are not available for all computers and all programmers who write compilers are not familiar with them. Also, their use is neither easy nor effortless. Finally, the form of the compiler produced by a compiler generator may be different from the desired form. Compiler generators are thus used mainly for prototyping; for example, to test new langauges. There is, however, no doubt that the importance of automatic compiler generation will increase in the future.

### Turbo Pascal Compiler

To complete this section, we will now present some aspects of a well known commercial product, the Turbo Pascal compiler produced by Borland International. Turbo Pascal is one of the most popular compilers for MS-DOS computers. Its success is due to its high speed of compilation, high quality of compiled code, richness of language features, friendliness of the user interface, and relatively low cost.

Turbo Pascal uses recursive descent parsing, and in this respect it is similar to our own compiler. Consequently, we will limit ourselves to one aspect of compilation that we have not covered so far: how the compiler allocates memory for the execution of object code, in other words, where it puts the code and where it reserves space for data (Figure 15.2). Note that although this aspect of Turbo Pascal is enforced by the compiler, it has to do with the run-time behavior of the generated code rather than the process of compilation itself.

As we know, MS-DOS computers are based on the 8086 family of CPUs, which store code, data, and the stack in separate 64k segments. The code, data, and stack segments are not limited to fixed 64k areas because the location of individual segments in memory can be controlled by the program. Turbo Pascal takes advantage of this and allows the user to divide Pascal programs into units, each of which can occupy up to 64k of memory.

Apart from the concept of a unit, data used by an executing Pascal program can be divided in two groups: static and dynamic. *Static data* consists mainly of global variables. The name "static" is derived from the fact that this data

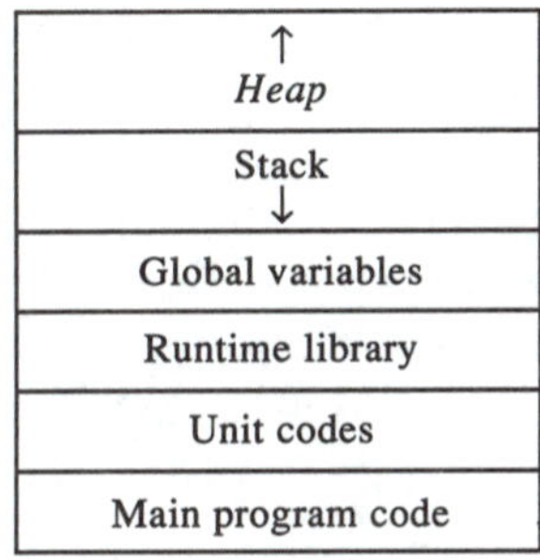


**Figure 15.2.** Memory allocation in Turbo Pascal programs.

must be available in memory from the start of execution of the program until its termination and can thus stay in fixed locations throughout execution.

*Dynamic data* in a general sense consists of all memory locations that are allocated and deallocated at unpredictable instants during the execution of the compiled programs. This category can be divided into two subcategories: activation records (created automatically without the programmer's intervention when a procedure or a function is called and freed when it terminates) and dynamic data in a narrow sense. The latter category includes items generated explicitly by the program during execution, such as records created by the NEW statement and pointers to them.

*Activation records* are created and removed in an orderly fashion by successive procedure calls and exits, and follow the stack discipline. They can thus use the stack in the usual way.

*Dynamic records*, unlike activation records, are created in an order that may be different from the order in which they may be released when they are no longer needed. Consequently, dynamic records use memory in a disorganized way and cannot use the stack. They are stored in a separate area called the *heap* because of the somewhat undisciplined way in which it is managed. Because the organization of the heap lacks discipline, the only way to access it is by pointers, which are simply memory addresses.

Program execution creates and destroys dynamic data in an unpredictable way and the heap quickly becomes disorganized unless the run-time system occasionally or regularly intervenes. Keeping track of the use of this space and allocating and freeing it when records are created and destroyed during program execution is the task of the heap manager.

Another question concerning memory allocation is how to arrange code, static data, the heap, the run-time system, and the stack in memory. If the executable code starts at a fixed location in "low memory" to satisfy the expectations of the operating system, data space must be allocated behind code space. Because of the nature of CPU handling of the stack, the stack grows towards lower addresses. Consequently, the available memory is best used if the heap grows in the opposite direction, away from the stack. This results in the arrangement shown in Figure 15.2.

Note that our reasoning concerning the stack applies not only to compiled but also to assembled programs and in fact explains why CPUs handle the stack the way they do—growing towards low memory so as to restrict program code and dynamic data as little as possible.

## SUMMARY

Because computers can execute only machine instructions, programs written in symbolic form must be translated from the original source code into executable object code.

Depending on how close the programming language is to the architecture of the CPU, we distinguish assembly and high-level programming languages. Whereas translators for assembly language programs (assemblers) are conceptually simple, translators for HLLs (interpreters and compilers) are based on sophisticated theoretical foundations.

The tasks of an assembler are to translate machine instructions from symbolic form to machine code, implement pseudoinstructions, and convert symbolic names to binary code. The fact that symbolic names may appear in the program before their value can be calculated (as in jumps with positive offsets) is the reason why most assemblers produce object code in two passes over the source code. In the first pass, the assembler checks the legality of the source code and calculates the values of the identifiers; in the second pass, it produces the code.

Translators of HLLS can be divided into interpreters and compilers. Interpreters translate the source code and execute it immediately; they do not create any object file. Compilers only translate the source code into object code, which can then be executed separately as many times as desired without further processing. Because most HLL translators are compilers and because translation follows the same principles in interpreters as in compilers, we restricted our presentation to compilers.

Compilation is a complex process and it is useful to divide it into modules performing well-defined logical tasks. The natural division is into scanning, parsing, and code generation.

Scanning is done by the scanner module of the compiler; it is also called the lexical analyzer. Its purpose is to assemble the individual characters of the program into language units such as reserved words, identifiers, integers, and so on, and send them to the parser in the form of tokens, codes expressing the nature of the item. While looking for words, the scanner removes information that has no effect on execution such as blanks and comments.

Parsing is performed by the parser, whose tasks are to check that the source program satisfies the syntax rules of the language and to determine its grammatical structure. As the grammatical structure forms the basis of the meaning of all HLL programs, the parser is the driving force of the compiler. During its operation, it calls the scanner when it needs more input from the source code, and the code generator when it needs to output object code.

Parsers are based on rigorous theoretical principles and several different approaches to their design are available. We demonstrated recursive descent parsing, which is one of the top-down parsing methods. Although this method is intuitively obvious, the proper design of a recursive descent parser requires a certain theoretical background to avoid problems caused by anomalies in the syntax rules of the parsed language.

In its simplest form, the code generator is a procedure that outputs machine code under the control of the parser. In more sophisticated compilers, the code generator improves the quality of the generated code (optimizes it) by determining the best use of CPU registers, restructuring the code to eliminate unnecessary repetition of machine instructions, and so on. A sophisticated compiler may have many parts and require more than ten passes to translate a source program.

An important part of the code produced by the compiler is the run-time system, a collection of subroutines included by the compiler in the object file. The purpose of run-time system subroutines is to complement the facilities available from the operating system and the CPU's instruction set and to provide a complete environment in which all aspects of the given programming language can be implemented.

Because the design of a parser mechanically follows the syntax rules of the language, parsers can be produced automatically. However, the design of a commercial compiler still requires a programming team to guarantee that the product works correctly and generates code that does not require too much memory and executes efficiently.

In the last section, we described how one popular commercial compiler uses memory space. We saw that the unpredictable behavior of dynamic variables and unlimited nesting of procedure calls requires careful planning of memory space allocation. The complexities of memory allocation can be simplified by proper CPU architecture.

## REVIEW QUESTIONS

1. Define the following terms: Activation record, code generator, dynamic data, error recovery, forward reference, grammar, heap, lexical analyzer, linker, location counter, nonterminal symbol, optimization, parser, pass, recursive definition, recursive descent parsing, run-time system, scanner, semantics, static data, symbol table, syntax, table driven parser, table generator, terminal symbol, and token.
2. Explain the operation of a two-pass assembler.
3. Explain the nature of production rules and their limitations.

4. Explain the function of the scanner, parser, and code generator.
5. Explain the operation of a one-pass recursive descent parser.

## REFERENCES

The following titles listed in the references at the end of the book are relevant to this chapter:

P. Brinch Hansen. *Brinch Hansen on Pascal Compilers.*

A. V. Aho, R. Sethi, and J. D. Ullman. *Compilers. Principles, Techniques, and Tools.*

# APPENDIX 1

# ELEMENTS OF ELECTRICITY AND SEMICONDUCTORS, AND OTHER TECHNOLOGIES

## AN OVERVIEW

Although computer architecture and organization can be studied without knowledge of electricity and semiconductors, even an elementary background helps one to understand its hardware aspects better. This appendix presents an introduction to the main concepts of electronics starting with electric charge and proceeding through electric current and voltage, resistance and capacitance, to resistance-capacitance (RC) circuits, the time constant, semiconductors, diodes, transistors, logic families, and the design methods and fabrication of integrated circuits.

## A1.1 ELECTRICITY

The basic concept of electricity is *charge*. Charges, denoted $Q$ and measured in Coulombs, can be positive or negative; like charges repel one another whereas unlike charges attract one another. The mutual effect of charges is expressed in the concept of the *electric field*, the active space around a charge that interacts with other charges and their electric fields. The difference of intensity between two points of an electric field is called *voltage*, denoted V and measured in Volts.

When charges placed in an electric field can move, their flow creates *electric current*. Current is denoted $I$ and is measured in Amperes. Its magnitude is defined as the amount of charge that moves through a given area in a unit of time. More formally,

$$I = \mathrm{d}Q/\mathrm{d}t$$

which represents the amount of charge passing through the area in an infinitesimally small time interval, divided by the length of the interval.

Obstacles in the path of the current slow down the moving charges and the path exhibits *resistance*. Resistance $R$ between two points of an electric path is defined as the ratio of the voltage $V$ between those two points and the flowing current $I$:

$$R = V/I$$

This relation is called the *Ohm's law*; $R$ is measured in Ohms.

To better understand the concepts of voltage, current, and resistance, it is useful to note the similarity between electric current and the flow of water, between voltage and water pressure, and between the resistance of a wire and the resistance of a pipe. When we add water reservoirs to this model, the analogy can be extended to include *capacitors*. A capacitor is a two-terminal (two-wire) device that can hold electric charges. Its operation can be described by formula:

$$Q = CV$$

where $Q$ is charge, and $C$ is capacitance in Farads and $V$ is the voltage between the two terminals of the capacitor.

Because a capacitor normally consists of two plates separated by an insulating material (a dielectric), current cannot flow through it. However, the equation shows that when the voltage between the plates changes, the amount of accumulated charges must also change and this requires that current flow onto one plate and away from the other even though no charges pass through. The phenomenon can be described by the following expression, which is obtained by differentiating the previous equation:

$$I = C\, \mathrm{d}V/\mathrm{d}t$$

In words, the current flowing onto and away from the plates of a capacitor is proportional to the rate at which the voltage across the capacitor changes.

Resistance and capacitance are present in all electric circuits, both in parasitic (unwanted) form and as intentionally inserted resistors and capacitors. In digital circuits, capacitors are placed between the power supply and ground lines (0 V) to eliminate fluctuations (spikes) in the supply voltage that would result from logic transitions. The physical principle of the operation of this arrangement is as follows:

Each $0 \rightarrow 1$ and $1 \rightarrow 0$ logic transition creates a momentary low resistance path between the power line and the ground inside the switching gate. This path causes a brief surge of current through the gate, which leads to an extra load on the power supply that briefly decreases the voltage supplied to other components. Because all components require a certain minimal voltage level for proper operation, an excessive voltage drop could produce a malfunction.

A despiking (shunting) capacitor between the power line and the ground reduces the surge in the following way: When the voltage starts to drop, the capacitor loses some of its accumulated charge, supplying additional current and briefly acting as an additional power supply. When the voltage increases, charge flows onto the capacitor to bring its voltage up to the new level and thus slows down the current surge in the opposite direction. The capacitor's behavior is analogous to a balancing reservoir inserted into a water line with fluctuating consumption.

Another important application for capacitors and resistors is to create delays in reset and power up circuits in computers. Here, a resistor and a capacitor are connected in series to form an *RC circuit* (Figure A1.1). The circuit is connected to the power supply and a control signal such as the *RESET* pin of a CPU chip, and causes the voltage on the *RESET* pin to be delayed with respect to the voltage transition on the input of the CPU when power is turned on. This delay gives the internal circuits of the CPU time to become operational before the *RESET* input activates them. Otherwise, some internal circuits might not properly respond to the *RESET* signal and the *RESET* sequence could fail.

The delay circuit behaves as follows: When the power supply is turned on and the voltage starts growing, current flows through the resistor and the capacitor begins to charge. Our previous analysis shows that the rate at which the voltage across the capacitor changes depends on the capacitance and the charging current. The current, in turn, depends on the voltage across the resistance and the resistance itself. As a consequence, the larger the $R$ and $C$ values, the slower the rate at which charge builds up. In fact, by combining the previous equations and solving the differential equation, we can show that the rate of change depends on the product $RC$ which is thus called the *time constant*. (At time $t = RC$ after the transition from 0V to the full power supply voltage, the voltage across the capacitor reaches approximately 63% of its final value.)

As the voltage across the capacitor grows, the voltage difference across the resistance decreases and with it the current through the resistor and onto the capacitor. Charge thus builds up very rapidly at the beginning and more

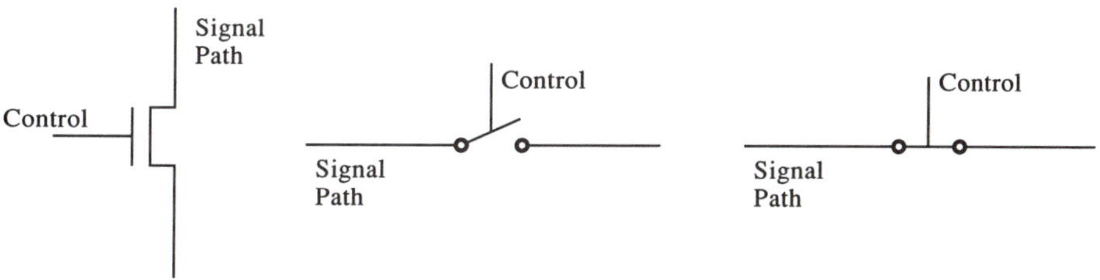


**Figure A1.1.** Resistor–capacitor circuit in a reset circuit; timing diagram of the power and the RESET voltage.

slowly as the capacitor's voltage approaches that of the power line. It can be shown that if the change in the input voltage is a jump, the rate of charge build-up follows an exponential curve. In reality, the voltage on the power line also traces an exponential and the voltage on the capacitor follows a similar but delayed curve.

Other aspects of current and voltage are power and energy. Because electric current is associated with the force acting on a moving charge, it can only be produced by supplying energy. When current flows through a resistor, some of its energy is lost in collisions and is converted to heat (dissipated) at a rate corresponding to the following formula:

$$P = I^2R$$

where $P$ is the power measured in Watts. (This equation can be derived from the fact that voltage corresponds to the work needed to move a unit charge from one point to another, and from Ohm's law.) Unlike resistors, pure capacitors do not heat up or dissipate power. Damage that they may suffer in operation is due to a voltage surge that pierces a conductive hole through the dielectric.

As a consequence of heat dissipation in digital systems, the current flowing through electronic components heats up integrated circuits and resistors. If the heat is not conducted away efficiently, some components soon reach a temperature at which their parameters change, the circuit parameters exceed expected limits, and resistors and integrated circuits may be permanently damaged and the power supply destroyed. Proper cooling of electric circuits is thus essential for their operation. If the chips and circuitboards are not placed too close together, the natural conduction of circulating air may be sufficient to conduct the heat away. In compact circuits, a fan or even a fluid flowing around or through the boards may be required.

Heat dissipation due to current flowing through a resistor also has a useful application as protection against excessive current, that is, fuses. A fuse is essentially a wire produced from an alloy with non-negligible resistance and a low melting point. When the current through the fuse exceeds the value for which it is designed, the generated heat melts the wire and the electric path from the power supply to the device is destroyed and the device disconnected. Excessive current is thus prevented from reaching and damaging the device.

Unwanted (parasitic) resistance and capacitance have the following effects on digital circuits: Resistance, present in any conductor, causes the voltage to drop, along the path of the flowing current and leads to signal attenuation. Eventually, voltage levels may drop below the value prescribed for proper recognition of logic values and cause incorrect interpretation of the signal. A similar effect can also be caused by excessive loading of integrated circuits (exceeding their fan-out specification). When voltage levels drop below the prescribed levels, the entire circuit behaves incorrectly even if it has been designed properly from the logic point of view.

As we have already indicated, capacitance present between any two adjacent but electrically insulated conductors, slows down signal transitions and causes additional electrical loading. This is because a charging capacitor absorbs the charge flowing through the signal path. This can cause logic malfunction and increase propagation delay, leading to a violation of design assumptions and a breakdown of logic operation. The combination of resistance and capacitance is the main cause of even the normal signal delays that occur in logic currents.

Another electrical parameter that must be considered in the design of important signal paths is *inductance*. Its result is spurious voltage generated in a wire under certain conditions that depend on the rate of change of the current through the conductor. (Note that the relationship between current and voltage is different for inductors and capacitors: The current flowing into a capacitor depends on the rate of change of voltage.) Inductance occurs because current flowing through a wire creates a magnetic field and changes in current produce changes in the magnetic field. The changing magnetic field then generates voltage in all conductors within its reach. Inductance can be described as follows:

$$V = L\ \mathrm{d}I/\mathrm{d}t$$

where $L$ is inductance measured in Henrys.

The voltage induced, for example, by sharp transitions in logic signals, creates fluctuations (noise) in adjacent wires and may be improperly interpreted as logic signals or may interfere with the signal transmitted on the path.

Fortunately, the effects of resistance, capacitance, and inductance need not be considered in the design of simple circuits such as those dealt with in this book. The only principle that cannot be neglected is the use of shunting capacitors; some authors suggest that circuits using TTL chips (which create particularly strong spikes) should have one 0.01 – 0.001 $\mu$F capacitor for every four SSI chips, every two MSI chips, and for all packages separated by more than 10 cm.

In closing, it is worth noting, that when certain materials reach a characteristic low temperature dependent on their composition, their resistance suddenly drops to almost zero. This is known as *superconductivity* and is currently the subject of very intensive research. Because resistance is a major limiting factor in many uses of electricity, mastery of superconductivity on an economically attractive scale would lead to dramatic progress in many applications, including digital circuits.

## A1.2 PRINCIPLES OF SEMICONDUCTOR DEVICES

Semiconductors are materials exhibiting high resistance in a very pure state but relatively low resistance when contaminated (doped) with certain other materials. Silicon and gallium arsenide (GaAs) are the two most popular semiconductors in digital components.

Depending on the type of dopant added to the pure material, the charge carriers (free charges) in the semiconductor are either negative (electrons) or positive (holes). When adjacent positively and negatively doped regions (*P* and *N* regions) are formed inside a piece of material, the junction acts as a valve that can open or close a current path under the control of an external voltage. A component consisting of two adjacent *N* and *P* regions is called a *diode*, a combination of several junctions formed within a single piece of material and arranged in a certain geometric pattern forms a *transistor*. Diodes and transistors are the basis of all modern digital components.

A *PN* junction works as follows: Where the *N* and *P* regions meet, some negative carriers from the *N* region escape into the *P* region and vice versa. Electric forces attract the carriers back into their original regions, and these carriers gather around the junction forming a barrier that prevents further charge migration.

When a positive voltage greater than the voltage due to the barrier is connected to the *P* region and a negative voltage to the *N* region, the negative carriers in the barrier are attracted into the *P* region and move towards the positive pole of the power supply and new negative carriers can take their place. A similar action occurs for positive carries in the opposite direction, and an electric current is thus established.

When the power supply is connected in the opposite direction, the barrier is strengthened and current cannot flow. Altogether, the *PN* junction acts as a one-way value that allows current when power is connected in one direction (positive to *P* and negative to *N*) but not in the other.

Diodes play an important auxiliary role inside integrated circuits but their most visible use in digital circuits is as light emitting diodes (LEDs) that emit light when current flows through them. Because the current flows only if the polarity of the voltage across the diode turns the diode on, an LED can be used to detect the polarity of an electric signal. Because logic signals are voltages, logic 0 and 1 can thus be detected with an LED. Note that an LED should always be connected in series with a resistance to make sure that the current does not become large enough to destroy the diode.

Although some of the first logic circuits predominantly used diodes, modern logic components are based on transistors. Depending on the way in which the transistor is formed, one can distinguish two different families: *bipolar*, and unipolar or *field effect* transistors (better known as several varieties of MOS transistors, N-MOS, P-MOS, and C-MOS).

Whether a transistor belongs to the bipolar or MOS family, its basic structure and operation can be described as follows: A transistor is a three-terminal component. Two of the three terminals constitute a path for the current and the third controls the extent to which the current path is open (Figure A1.2). In digital circuits, transistors essentially work either in the fully open or the

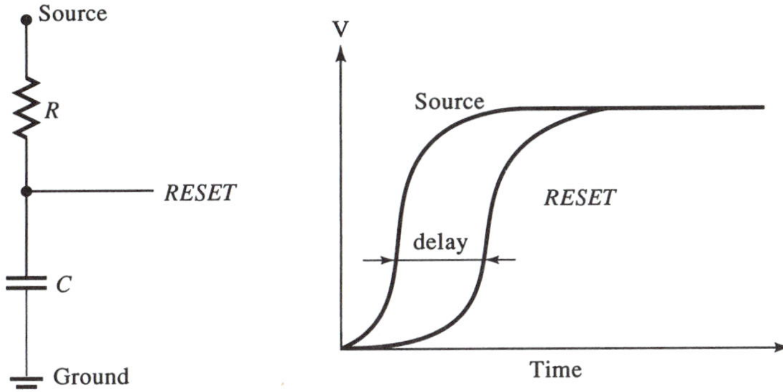


**Figure A1.2.** Model of a digital transistor.

fully closed mode, either conducting or shutting off electric current. That is, they act as two-state On/Off binary devices.

Although transistors are binary devices, all logic circuits, with the exception of some very simple memory cells and certain internal logic circuits in complex chips, contain two or more transistors and some resistors and diodes. Because these circuits can be rather complex, we will not present their internal structure but will limit ourselves to a brief analysis of their operational parameters, which are very important for their use in digital circuits.

Modern bipolar logic comes in two main varieties: TTL (transistor–transistor logic) and ECL (emitter-coupled logic). Both varieties use the same transistors and the same technology but the structure of the circuits implementing individual gates is different. This has implications for speed, complexity of fabrication, required voltages, and power consumption. Emitter-coupled logic circuits are more complicated, require more power, and are more expensive but faster. They are used only in the fastest digital systems, such as supercomputers. Transistor–transistor logic is much more common because it is easier to use and cheaper.

All bipolar devices have relatively large power consumption but are faster than MOS logic. Their main drawback is that the control input of a bipolar transistor has small resistance and this makes basic bipolar logic circuits complex and large. Bipolar technology thus cannot compete with MOS in the number of gates or storage cells that can be placed on a single chip. The small input resistance (properly called "impedance" as it is the result of the combined effect of resistance, capacitance, and inductance) also means that bipolar cells cannot act as capacitors, and this makes them unsuitable for memories—which are most easily fabricated on the principle of capacitance.

Metal-oxide semiconductor (MOS) circuits use transistors that operate on a principle different from the bipolar transistor. Their main advantages are that they consume a fraction of the power of bipolar technologies, can store charge, and allow much greater logic densities due to the simplicity of their basic logic circuits. Negative and complementary MOS circuits (the two most common MOS families) are thus used to make all complex chips, such as advanced CPUs and dynamic and static memories. (Dynamic memories are based on the ability of MOS transistors to hold charge and must be refreshed every 3–4 msec because the charge quickly leaks out. Their storage cells are, however, very simple, and physically small chips with large memory capacity are thus possible. Static memories store information in flip-flop-like circuits based on feedback, which inherently refreshes the memory cell.) The disadvantage of MOS technology is its somewhat lower speed.

Within the MOS family, NMOS has the simplest circuit and thus provides the greatest density. Consequently, it is used for the most complex chips. Complementary MOS circuits use pairs of complementary $P$ and $N$ transistors and have minimal power consumption and greater noise immunity. Because of these advantages, CMOS is used in all applications where their somewhat lower density can be tolerated.

Recently, a technology known as Bi-MOS, which uses a combination of bipolar and MOS transistors to take advantage of both, has become available.

In addition to standard bipolar and MOS components, we should mention two subcategories of semiconductor logic: open collector and tristate devices.

*Open collector* (OC) devices are bipolar components in which the output stage of the logic circuit is incomplete. For proper operation, an OC device requires an additional "pullup" resistor connected between the output pin and the voltage supply.

Because every OC device lacks the same piece of the output circuit, many OC gates can have their outputs connected together (at the lower end of the pullup resistor), something that is not allowed with ordinary gates (Figure A1.3). Outputs tied together in this way, provide an additional logic function

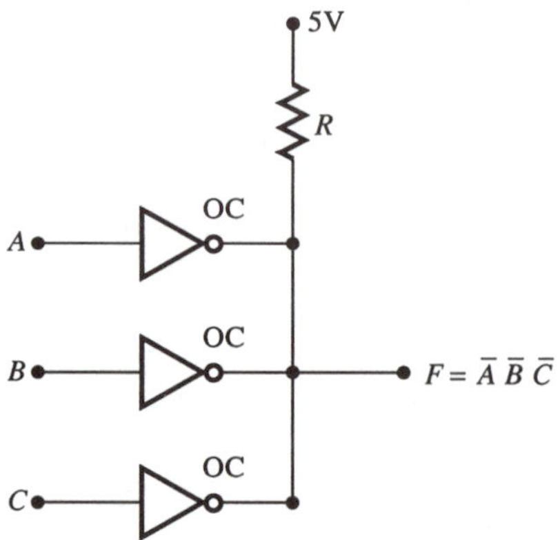


**Figure A1.3.** Several OC devices can be connected together.

and are particularly useful in bus applications where several control signals coming from different sources may have to be connected to a single pin, such as the interrupt input of a CPU.

The extra ("wired") logic provided by the tied OC outputs works as follows: When all the tied outputs produce logic High, the pullup resistors does not have any effect and the combined output is High. If at least one of the OC outputs is Low, the current flowing from the power supply through the pullup causes a voltage drop across the resistor and the tie point assumes logic Low value. Altogether, the connection thus behaves as an AND gate and is thus called wired AND.

Tristate devices are functionally identical to ordinary logic circuits except that they have an additional input that allows the output to be disabled. In this disabled state, the output behaves as a disconnected ("floating" or "high impedance") wire and has no effect on other components connected to it.

Open collector and tristate devices are used in similar applications but tristate devices are more common, mainly because they are easier to use and troubleshoot. Still, certain special needs are better served with OC devices.

Much of the recent interest in semiconductor logic concentrates on the use of GaAs instead of silicon because it provides higher operating speeds and better compatibility with optical signals, which are becoming important in the communication of digital data. Optical computing, the use of light instead or in combination with electricity, is another major research area that also has close relations to GaAs materials.

## A1.3 INTEGRATED CIRCUITS

Although the introduction of diodes and transistors into digital circuits resulted in faster, physically smaller, and more reliable computers, the real revolution in digital hardware started with integrated circuits.

An integrated circuit is a device in which an entire electronic circuit consisting of many transistors, diodes, and their interconnections is implemented on a single piece of material. Depending on the complexity of the circuit, from twenty to a million of transistors can be present on a single integrated circuit.

Although the various families and subfamilies of logic ICs use manufacturing processes that involve slightly different materials and fabrication parameters, the basic procedure is the same for all integrated circuits. All steps require extreme purity of environment and materials and very exact control over temperatures and timing. The skeleton of the manufacturing sequence is as follows:

A cylinder of extremely pure crystalline semiconductor is made.

The cylinder (about 100 mm in diameter) is cut into 0.4-mm thick wafers, and exposed to a dopant that penetrates into the material, creating the substrate on which the circuits will be formed.

Each wafer is coated with a thin layer of silicon dioxide $SiO_2$ whose repeated application at various stages of fabrication insulates the successive layers created on the chip.

The wafer is coated with a photosensitive material (photoresist) and exposed to light filtered through a mask containing the layout of a pattern that is to be copied to the wafer and a photographic image of the mask is thus created on the wafer's surface. (In fact, many copies of the mask and consequently many identical chips are normally created on the surface of the wafer in a single step.)

The photochemical reaction changes the properties of the exposed photoresist, which can now be washed (etched) away. This creates windows in the photoresist on the chip's surface.

A chemical that dissolves $SiO_2$ but not the photoresist is applied and holes are created in the oxide. The photoresist is then washed away and a pattern of $SiO_2$ corresponding to the mask appears on the surface of each wafer.

The wafers are exposed to another dopant that penetrates into the exposed areas on the wafer but not through the oxide mask.

Another coat of photoresist is formed and a new mask is copied on it. (Extreme accuracy in the alignment of the two patterns is required.) The wafers are exposed to light, etched, and the pattern exposed to new coating material or dopant to form conductors or doped regions, and so on. Eventually, a multilayer structure is formed and the superposed layers create a grid of transistors and connections between them.

The circuits formed on the wafer are tested and the working chips marked.

The wafer is cut into individual chips and the working chips coated with insulating oxide ("glass") and mounted on a plastic base. Connections are made between the contact pads of the chip and the pins, and the package is sealed and tested again.

The fabrication process is extremely delicate and the perfection achieved in individual steps determines how many transistors can be put on a single chip and the complexity of devices that can be fabricated. Steady progress in the procedure is the basis of the steadily growing IC density, complexity, speed, and reliability.

Even though there is still room for improvement in fabrication technology, there is a physical limit to the miniaturization that can be achieved. This is because when the thickness of the physical lines reproduced on the wafer drops below approximately 0.1 $\mu$, the physical behavior of the semiconductor changes. (One micron, denoted M, equals 0.000001 m.) At present, the minimum line thickness used in commercial products is around 1 $\mu$ and it will take another ten years or so before the submicron physical limit is reached. Even now, however, further progress requires expensive equipment, in particular, new lithographic devices for copying masks.

The path to further progress lies in extending traditional integrated circuit technology to the use of

Three-dimensional circuits. (Although the current ICs are multilayered, the circuits are essentially two-dimensional.)

Faster materials

New modes of operation and new principles (GaAs, superconductivity, and ballistic transistors with very short obstruction-free paths)

Larger chip areas,

Use of whole wafer circuits with interconnections between individual chips.

The use of different types of signals, such as light instead of electricity, is also being explored. All of these approaches will lead to more complex, faster, and more reliable chips that consume less power and fit into smaller spaces.

Beyond improvements in technology, further progress in computing depends on higher level—architectural—improvements. As an example, greater speed and reliability can be achieved by designing computers with better instruction sets or by connecting many computers together. Similarly, for certain types of problems, approaches based on completely different principles, such as neural computing (Chapter 13), may be advantageous.

More exotic and even closer to nature is biological computing, where components operate on biological principles and the building blocks are organic molecules or artificial biological elements. However, this field is in the earliest stages of development and no practical uses are in sight.

Our discussion of the manufacturing process and the physical parameters of the circuits (the number of transistors per chip, line thickness, and so on) show that manual design of complex chips is impossible. Correct multilayer masks for a chip having a million transistors can only be designed and tested with the help of very sophisticated computer tools. Complex chips require complex computer programs to perform automatically as many design tasks as possible and very fast computers to execute these programs in reasonable time are essential. The use of these computer tools extends from system to logic design and the simulation and generation of test patterns, the construction of masks and checks of their electrical parameters, control of the manufacturing process, and testing of the finished product. In short, the use of computers in integrated circuit technologies encompasses computer-aided design, (CAD), computer-aided manufacturing (CAM), and computer aided-testing (CAT).

Although much work has been done to develop CAD, CAM, and CAT tools, the present state of the art is such that complex designs still require much human intervention. Partly as a result of this, several different design styles are now in use. Integrated circuits intended for mass production and requiring the highest operating parameters are designed from elementary building blocks such as individual gates and memory cells. This method (full custom design) is time consuming and expensive, and its cost can only be justified when it is spread over a very large number of components. Full custom design is used for circuits such as memory chips, CPUs, and large volume controller chips.

In full custom design, computer tools are used extensively to draw and simulate logic diagrams, convert them to chip layouts, test that design rules are satisfied, test signal behavior at transistor level, and so on, but they remain tools, and the chip is largely designed manually. In contrast, programs known as silicon compilers design the complete chip (a complete set of masks) from a formal specification resembling a computer program. At present, silicon compilers are inferior to human designers, particularly in terms of the efficient use of the space on the chip, but they produce the design much faster. Undoubtedly, the use of programs like silicon compilers in IC design will grow with the increasing complexity of chips, experience with existing tools, and the enormous market for truly efficient automation.

Integrated circuits whose specialized use (hence "application specific integrated circuits" of ASICs) limits the required number to smaller quantities, and circuits that must be designed and produced quickly are designed from libraries of higher level building blocks such as ALU circuits or ROMs at chip level. The blocks are combined and "glued" together with interface components added manually. This approach is called semicustom design and is less expensive and faster but the chips are not as efficient in terms of speed, power consumption, and space use, as those obtained with full custom design. Much of the design and production of ASIC chips can be automated.

## REFERENCES

The following titles listed in the references at the end of the book are relevant to this chapter:

H. J. Caulfield, J. Neff, and W. T. Rhodes. *Optical Computing: The Coming Revolution in Optical Signal Processing.*

S. Chou and C. Simonsen. *Chip Voltage: Why Less Is Better.*

E. Connolly. *BiMOS Devices Give Designers the Best of Two Worlds.*

M. Conrad. *The Lure of Molecular Computing.*

L. F. Eastman. *Ballistic Electrons in Compound Semiconductors.*

B. Grob. *Basic Electronics.*

P. J. Hicks. *Semiconductor IC Design and VLSI.*

L. D. Hutcheson and P. Haugen. *Optical Interconnects Replace Hardwire.*

M. I. Nathan and M. Heiblum. *A Gallium Arsenide Ballistic Transistor*?

C. Mead and L. Conway. *Introduction to VLSI Design.*

# APPENDIX 2

# LABORATORY EXPERIMENTS AND SIMULATIONS

## AN OVERVIEW

This appendix contains some general notes on experiments, a detailed description of a sequence of laboratory problems covering the main concepts of the sections on hardware, a description of a lab project, a section on suitable lab equipment, and a sample report.

We consider Laboratory experiments very useful because they give students hands-on experience that clarifies the material covered and makes it more real. If the student does not have enough time for the labs presented here, he may prefer to select only a few from the recommended experiments. In the extreme case, one can even replace experiments with simulations.

## A2.1 SETTING UP AND RUNNING EXPERIMENTS

In our simple experiments, we can treat chips as ideal logic modules and construct circuits without any knowledge of electronics. We also don't have to worry about "live" 5-V wires because the 5-V logic signal is not dangerous.

To prepare and perform an experiment, one should proceed as follows:

Study the problem carefully.

If the problem is complicated, draw the block diagram of the solution showing the major functional blocks and data paths.

Draw a logic diagram of the circuit.

List the anticipated values of outputs for testing the circuit.

Simulate the circuit to check its logic correctness.

Find suitable chips and draw the layout diagram showing the placement of all components. (One can use the life-sized template in Figure A2.1.)

Draw a wiring diagram and make a connection list: For each chip, list the pins that are connected to the power and ground, the input pins that are connected to external inputs such as switches, and the location of all the output pins. (Input connections from other chips are implied; do not list them.) Make sure to connect even those pins that are not used in the current circuit. These pins should be connected to 0V or 5V (preferably via small resistors) in such a way that the overall logic function is preserved.

Insert chips into a "breadboard" (Section A2.4), place them according to the layout diagram and connect them according to the connection list. Check completed connections off the list.

Handle chips carefully because pins are somewhat fragile and bend or break easily. To insert a chip, align its pins with the contact holes in the breadboard (press the two rows of pins closer together against a hard surface if necessary) and push the chip in. To remove a chip, use an IC remover tool or slide a screwdriver underneath and gently lift, alternating the sides. Do not remove or reinsert chips often.

> Be very careful when making connections: Chips can be destroyed when power is connected incorrectly, input and output pins are confused, or several outputs are connected together.
>
> Connect unused pins to ground or to 5 V (logic 0 and logic 1) depending on their function, preferably through a protective 2k–10k resistor. Although unconnected pins normally behave as logic 1, stray voltages may cause malfunctions.
>
> Wiring should be as neat as the wiring diagram and the wires should be cut short, possibly by using measurements on the wiring diagram. Make connections at right angles (no "rat's nests") and do not cross over chips. Use wires of different color to distinguish 5 V, ground, and logic signals. Neater circuits not only look nicer but are also easier to test and correct.

Compare the circuit to the wiring diagram and mark the inspected connections on the diagram. Ask the instructor to check the circuit.

Turn the power on and examine the circuit. The maximum operating temperature of 74 family chips is 70°C and must not be exceeded. If a component is getting too hot to touch, turn the power off and recheck the circuit. The most likely cause of overheating is an incorrect connection, but a faulty or overloaded chip is also a possibility.

Perform the experiment.

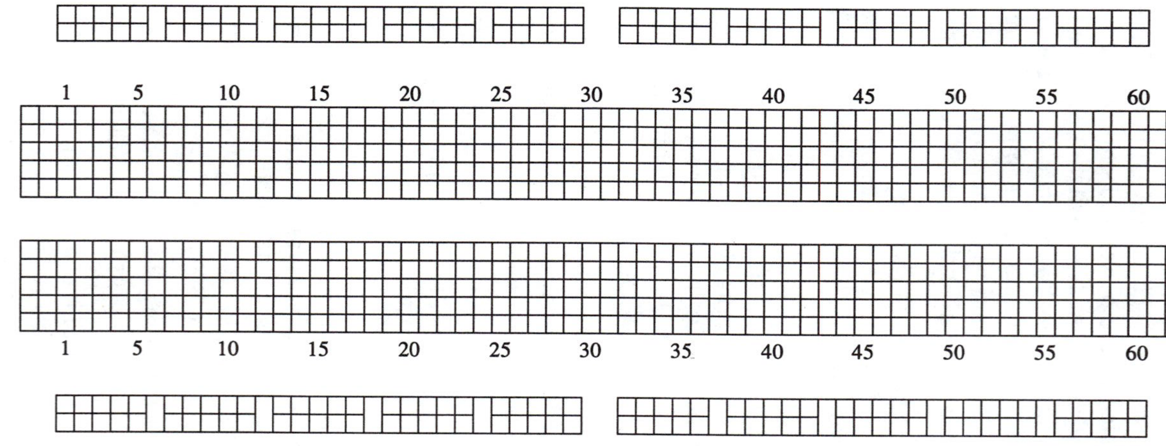


**Figure A2.1.** Breadboard template for use in wiring diagrams.

If the circuit does not work, find the error using the following suggestions. Usually only the first few obvious steps will be necessary.

Examine the logic solution. As an example, if Karnaugh maps are used, check that the specification has been correctly converted to a map, that the labels and prime implicants are correct and that the final formula covers all 1s.

Check that the logic diagram matches the formulas.

If the circuit is not trivial ("trivial" depends on the student's experience) simulate it one more time. Make sure that the simulated and real circuits are the same.

Check that the wiring and logic diagrams and the connection list match and that the function of all pins is clear. This includes not only polarity (active Low/High) but also timing (edge/level sensitivity, synchronous/asynchronous operation).

Check that the physical circuit corresponds to the wiring diagram. Tick off verified connections in the wiring diagram.

Is the circuit properly built? Are all chips properly inserted in the breadboard? (Push them in, look for bent pins.) Are there any loose wires?

Check that the power supply voltage is within 5% of 5 V.

If the circuit still does not work, the student must find the fault—the place up to which the signal is correct and beyond which it is not. This will not be difficult if the circuit has been designed and built according to the following guidelines:

If the circuit is complex, it should be designed, built, and tested in a modular style using subsystems that perform well defined subfunctions. Modules should be tested as soon as they are finished rather than when the whole circuit is completed. If one knows that the modules work, one need only check their interfaces to locate the problem. (Be careful, while working on the circuit, not to pull some of the previously tested connections loose.)

Wiring should be neat and easy to follow and one should be able to disconnect wires without pulling on other wires.

To find the fault, proceed as follows:

Test signals that have an easily tested function.

Test module interfaces if any.

If the circuit cannot be subdivided further into functional blocks, use binary search: Halve the distance between input and output signals and test. If the values are correct, the fault is closer to the output; otherwise it is closer to the input. Repeat this procedure on the faulty part, dividing the circuit into smaller and smaller sections until the problem is located.

Note that testing does not always require finding logic 0 or logic 1. It is often enough to test that a signal keeps changing (as on the address bus of a computer), exhibits a regular pattern (outputs of a counter with a regular clock input), and so on.

After finding the fault, determine its cause. Consider the following possibilities:

The solution is correct but the physical circuit is not. Wires may be misplaced, loose, or broken under insulation (check that the signal is the same on both ends of the wire); contacts may be damaged inside the breadboard; and poorly made soldered connections can cause discontinuities or shorts.

A chip is faulty. Components bought from reputable sources are rarely defective but when many students use the same equipment, damaged chips are not uncommon.

If an input signal does not have the proper voltage level (0–0.8 V for TTL logic 0 and 2.0–5 V for logic 1), the chip interprets it incorrectly. Signals that change rarely or that can be controlled may be measured with a voltmeter; regularly changing signals may be measured with an oscilloscope. Incorrect signal levels may be caused by excessive fan-out (too many chips connected to one output) or an incorrect voltage from the power supply. Excessive fan-out can be corrected by using several gates producing the same output or by using driver chips.

Slow $0 \rightarrow 1$ or $1 \rightarrow 0$ transitions may also cause problems. This can be corrected by using gates with Schmitt trigger inputs to speed up transitions. Minimum transition speeds are listed in databooks and signal shape can be displayed on an oscilloscope.

Inputs may be noisy and can contain "glitches" (brief undesired pulses) or fluctuations of signal levels. This problem can usually be traced to one of the following causes:

Fluctuation of incorrect level of power supply voltage.

Spikes caused by logic transitions in TTL chips. (Use despiking capacitors.)

Glitches or signal distortions induced by signals on adjacent wires. This problem can be removed by rerouting the connections.

Distortions caused by excessively long connections.

Improper timing (hazards, skew).

If it is necessary to remove a chip from the circuit to make a correction, always turn the power off first.

## A2.2 EXPERIMENTS

The following experiments illustrate the main concepts presented in the text. Some are longer than others but if they are prepared and tested before the lab session, one experiment can be completed per week in 90-minute lab slots.

Although the computer experiments are formulated for the 6800 CPU and the Heathkit ET-3400, they can be performed with similar CPUs from the 6800 family and similar experimental boards. Likewise, the suggested TTL and other chips can be replaced by integrated circuits with similar function.

Finally, most of the experiments can also be simulated using our simulator.

Depending on available equipment and his experience, the instructor may want to skip some parts of the suggested experiments or have lab supervisors connect parts of the circuits beforehand. The instructor may change the exact specification of individual experiments, but it is suggested that the general themes be kept.

### Experiment 1—Familiarization with Gates

#### *Purpose*

To gain experience with basic logic functions and integrated circuits.

#### *Outline*

1. Perform a computer simulation.
2. Perform the experiment.
3. Observe a lab demonstration.
4. Write a report.

#### *The Experiment*

Two integrated circuits containing some logic gates will be inserted into the breadboard by the supervisor. Find their type form the 74 . . number printed on them and determine the function of the chip and its pins from the pinout diagrams in Appendix 4.

Check that the power switch is in the off position and connect the power and ground pins of both chips using colored wires. Connect input pins of the first gate on the chip to switches using wires of another color. Connect the output pin of the gate to an LED light. (The LED path should be protected by a 330 Ω resistor.) Ask the instructor to check the connections.

Turn the power on and check the circuit. If everything appears to be normal, perform the tests. Use all the combinations of input switch settings necessary to obtain the truth table of the gate. Repeat for all gates on the chip and for both chips. No further inspection by the lab supervisor is required. If a gate does not work as expected, notify the instructor.

### *Demonstration*

The instructor will demonstrate how to measure logic values using a logic probe, voltages using a voltmeter, and current using an ammeter. The oscilloscope and a logic analyzer will also be demonstrated.

### *Simulation*

Simulate a three-input gate using a simulation program. Try all combinations of inputs needed to construct the truth table.

### *Report*

In this and the following reports, describe the experiment and the demonstration, and include a printout of the simulation. A sample report is given in Section A2.4.

## Experiment 2—Building a Logic Circuit

### *Purpose*

To design a circuit directly from its description and by using canonic formulas.

### *Outline*

1. Perform computer simulation.
2. Perform the experiment.
3. Observe a lab demonstration.
4. Write a report.

### *The Experiment*

The student will design and build a circuit with input switches $S_0$, $S_1$, $S_2$, and $S_3$, and one output connected to an LED. The light should go on if

$S_0$ and $S_3$ are On

OR

$S_0$ is Off but $S_2$ is On

The light should also go on if exactly one of $S_0$ or $S_1$ is On.

Design the circuit from the word description. Show also the canonic sum-of-products and canonic product-of-sums solutions obtained from the truth table.

### *Demonstration*

The student will see the input and output signals of an inverter on an oscilloscope. Observe the shapes, magnitudes, and the difference between the two signals. Estimate the delay between them as the distance between the 50% values on transitions. Are the delays of the up- and down-going transitions different?

### *Simulation*

Simulate all three problems.

## Experiment 3—Design with Karnaugh Maps

### *Purpose*

To gain experience with Karnaugh maps and don't-care conditions.

### *Outline*

1. Perform computer simulation.
2. Perform the experiment.
3. Observe a lab demonstration.
4. Write a report.

### *The Experiment*

The student will design and build a circuit to drive segment *b* of a seven-segment display. Use the Karnaugh map and take advantage of don't-care conditions. You can connect the circuit to a seven-segment display and drive the remaining elements with a seven-segment decoder/driver chip. Test the circuit by connecting its inputs to switches and generating all possible BCD combinations.

*Demonstration*

The student will see an oscilloscope display of a glitch in a simple circuit. Explain its cause.

*Simulation*

Simulate the solutions of the experimental problem and the glitch in

$$f = ac + b\bar{c}$$

assuming that only the inverter has a delay. Suggest a remedy, and show that it indeed removes the problem.

## Experiment 4—Design with NAND Gates

*Purpose*

To design a minimal NAND circuit.

*Outline*

1. Perform computer simulation.
2. Perform the experiment.
3. Observe a lab demonstration.
4. Write a report.

*The Experiment*

The student will design and build a "threshold" circuit that outputs 1 when two or more of its four inputs are 1. For example, inputs 0111 and 0110 should produce 1; and 0100 and 000 should produce 0.

Design the circuit by deriving its minimal AND/OR form and converting it to NAND gates. Connect inputs to switches and outputs to LED lights and test the circuit with all possible binary combinations.

*Demonstration*

The student will see an oscilloscope display of the effect of propagation of a signal through several gates.

*Simulation*

Simulate the experimental problem.

## Experiment 5—Multiplexers and Demultiplexers

### *Purpose*

To become acquainted with multiplexers and demultiplexers and their use in combinational circuits and in the serial communication of parallel data.

### *Outline*

1. Perform the computer simulation.
2. Perform the experiment.
3. Write a report.

### *The Experiment*

***Part 1.*** Design, build, and test a circuit for the problem in Experiment 4 using an 8–1 multiplexer and folding. Compare the solution with the circuit in Experiment 4, with a circuit using a 16–1 multiplexer, with a multiplexer tree using 4–1 and 2–1 multiplexers, and with a multiplexer tree using 2–1 multiplexers and folding. (Do not build these alternative circuits.) Which circuit requires the least number of chips, wires, and space? Connect inputs to switches, outputs to LED lights, and test the circuit with at least five different combinations of operands.

***Part 2.*** Use two 4–1 multiplexers to select two-bit data from one of two sources, and two 1–4 demultiplexers to send it to one of two destinations. Test the circuit with data inputs 00, 01, 10, and 11, sending these values first to one destination and then to the other.

### *Simulation*

Simulate both problems.

## Experiment 6—Familiarization with Flip-flops

### *Purpose*

To observe the differences between latches and flip-flops, triggering modes, and types of storage cells.

### *Outline*

1. Perform the computer simulation.
2. Perform the experiment.
3. Write a report.

**The Experiment** The student will explore the operation of the following storage elements:

7474: Positive-edge triggered D-flip-flop

7475: D-latch (level-sensitive),

7478: Negative-edge triggered JK-flip-flop.

***Part 1.*** Connect the D-input of one element of both the 7474 and the 7475 to the same switch, and their clock/enable pin to a clock signal. Connect $Q$ outputs to LEDs. Set the clock speed to very slow for comfortable observation and compare the operation of the two chips by applying a sequence of $D$ inputs. Note that the output of the 7475 follows its input when enabled by the level input but the 7474 does not; it is activated by the edge. Draw a diagram showing the operation of both components and explain it.

***Part 2.*** Test the *SET* and *CLR* inputs of the 7474 and note that they override the clock. (They are "asynchronous.")

a. Connect the $J$ and $K$ inputs of the 7478 to switches and the clock input to the clock signal. Test all transitions and note when they occur in the clock cycle. Test the operation of *SET* and *CLR* inputs.

b. Show that a JK-flip-flop can be used as a T-flip-flop.

***Simulation***

Simulate all parts of the experiment.

**Experiment 7—Counters and Analysis of a Sequential Circuit**

***Purpose***

To observe the operation of counters and their use in sequential circuits; to verify formal analysis experimentally.

***Outline***

1. Perform computer simulation.
2. Perform the experiment.
3. Write a report.

***The Experiment***

***Part 1.*** Disable the *LOAD* input of a 74163 counter and pulse the clock input to observe its operation.

***Part 2.*** Connect the *DATA* and *LOAD* inputs of the 74160 so that the counter resets to 0 after reaching the count of 8. Initialize the counter to 0 and test circuit operation.

Change the circuit to count from 4 up.

***Part 3.*** Build and analyze a simple circuit with one NAND gate connected to *LD* and one to a data input, and verify the analysis experimentally.

***Simulation***

Simulate all parts of the experiment.

**Experiment 8—Design of a Sequential Circuit**

***Purpose***

To apply the theory of design with flip-flops and counters.

***Outline***

1. Perform computer simulation.
2. Perform the experiment.
3. Write a report.

***The Experiment***

Use a fully synchronous presettable counter to build a sequential circuit with switches $S_1$ and $S_2$ and lights $LED_1$ and $LED_2$. Switch $S_1$ is used to control transitions and $S_2$ for *RESET*. The first LED if Off in the initial state and its further operation is as follows:

> If switch $S_1$ is On in the initial state, $LED_1$ goes On in the second and third state, Off in the fourth state, and then returns to the initial state.
>
> If switch $S_1$ is Off in the initial state, $LED_1$ goes Off for the next state and the circuit then returns to the initial state.

The second LED goes On in the initial state and remains Off at all other times. It is an "initial state indicator."

Connect the circuit to a slow clock signal or to a pulser switch and test it.

***Simulation***

Simulate the problem.

## Experiment 9—Storage and Shifting in Registers

### *Purpose*

Familiarization with PIPO shift registers.

### *Outline*

1. Perform computer simulation.
2. Perform the experiment.
3. Write a report.

### *The Experiment*

***Part 1.*** Test the shift right and load functions of the 7495 PIPO register.

***Part 2.*** Connect the 7495 for shifting left and demonstrate its operation with serial loading.

***Part 3.*** Connect the LSB output to the MSB input and demonstrate loading and "rotation" of the contents of the register.

### *Simulation*

Simulate the experiment.

## Experiment 10—The 74181 ALU

### *Purpose*

To explore some of the functions of the 74181 ALU and verify your understanding of arithmetic.

### *Outline*

1. Perform computer simulation.
2. Perform the experiment.
3. Write a report.

### *The Experiment*

The student will connect and partially test the 74181 4-bit ALU chip. Its 24 pins have the following functions:

The eight pins labelled $A$ and $B$ are for two four-bit operands, pins $F$ are for the result (function), $S$ (Select) and $M$ (Mode) determine the function. Pins

$C_{in}$ and $C_{out}$ are carry-in and carry-out. Pin $A = B$ is the output of the comparator; $P$ and $G$ produce "generate" and "propagate" signals for fast arithmetic. The function table of the chip is as follows:

| **Selection Pins** | | | | **Function Selected** | **Function Selected** |
|---|---|---|---|---|---|
| $S_3$ | $S_2$ | $S_1$ | $S_0$ | $M = 1$ (Logic Mode) | $M = 0$ (Arithmetic Mode) |
| 0 | 0 | 0 | 0 | $\overline{a}$ | $a$ |
| 0 | 0 | 0 | 1 | $\overline{a + b}$ | $a + b$ |
| 0 | 0 | 1 | 0 | $\overline{a + b}$ | $a + \overline{b}$ |
| 0 | 0 | 1 | 1 | 0 | minus 1 |
| 0 | 1 | 0 | 0 | $\overline{ab}$ | $a$ plus $a\overline{b}$ |
| 0 | 1 | 0 | 1 | $\overline{b}$ | $a + b$ plus $a\overline{b}$ |
| 0 | 1 | 1 | 0 | $a$ XOR $b$ | $a$ minus $b$ minus 1 |
| 0 | 1 | 1 | 1 | $a\overline{b}$ | $a\overline{b}$ minus 1 |
| 1 | 0 | 0 | 0 | $\overline{a} + b$ | $a$ plus $ab$ |
| 1 | 0 | 0 | 1 | $\overline{a \text{ XOR b}}$ | a plus $b$ |
| 1 | 0 | 1 | 0 | $b$ | $a + \overline{b}$ plus $ab$ |
| 1 | 0 | 1 | 1 | $ab$ | $ab$ minus 1 |
| 1 | 1 | 0 | 0 | 1 | $a$ plus $a$ |
| 1 | 1 | 0 | 1 | $a + \overline{b}$ | $a + b$ plus $a$ |
| 1 | 1 | 1 | 0 | $a + b$ | $a + \overline{b}$ plus $a$ |
| 1 | 1 | 1 | 1 | $a$ | $a$ minus 1 |

Carry $C_{in}$ has no effect in the logic mode; in the arithmetic mode, it is added to the result to produce $F + \overline{C}_{in}$. Note that $C_{in}$ is active Low.

Connect $A$, $B$, and control inputs $S$ and $M$ to switches (connect wires to 0 or 1 manually if an adequate set of switches is not available), $F$ and $A = B$ to LED lights, and test AND, OR, XOR, $A = B$, NOT $A$, two's complement negation, addition, and subtraction. Use the following pairs of operands:

| | | |
|---|---|---|
| 0111, 0101 | 1000, 0111 | 1111, 1111 |
| 0010, 0111 | 1111, 0111 | 1110, 1101 |

### *Simulation*

Simulate all parts of the problem.

### *Report*

Comment on the obtained results and on overflow and carry. Use both pure binary and two's complement interpretation.

## Experiment 11—Tristate outputs and the 2114 RAM

### *Purpose*

To explore the operation of tristate outputs and their use in random access memory chips.

### *Outline*

1. Perform computer simulation.
2. Perform the experiment.
3. Write a report.

### *The Experiment*

***Part 1.*** Connect switches to the inputs of four tristate buffers individually controlled by a 2-to-4 decoder. All tristate outputs are connected to a single line (simulating one line of a bus) connected to an LED light. The decoder, whose function is to insure that at most one output is connected to the bus at a time, is controlled by two switches.

Test the circuit by sending selected values to the LED. Compare ordinary and tristate outputs and explain the principles of a bus, a control point, a bidirectional line, and reading from and writing to a register connected to the bus.

***Part 2.*** Test the 1k × 4 2114A static RAM with tristate output. The 2114 is a N-MOS rather than TTL chip but its voltage levels are TTL compatible.

The control signals $\overline{CS}$ (chip select) and $\overline{WE}$ (write enable) have the following effect:

| *CS* | *WE* | **Function** |
|---|---|---|
| 0 | 0 | Writing to RAM enabled, output tristated |
| 0 | 1 | Writing disabled, output enabled for reading |
| 1 | 0 | No writing, output tristated |
| 1 | 1 | No writing, output tristated |

Connect control and address signals to switches or wires. Note that in this experiment, only the four least significant bits of the address need to be controlled. Data pins will be connected directly to LED lights for output, and to switches or wires via tristate buffers. The buffers are controlled by the same signal that controls the *CS* input of the RAM. Perform the following steps:

1. Turn the power on and read and record the contents of memory locations 6, 7, 8, 9, and 10.
2. Store binary codes of 0, 3, 6, 9, and 12 in locations 6–10.
3. Check that the values were properly stored.
4. Turn the power off.
5. Repeat steps 1, 2, and 3.

Note the following:

1. To store (write) data in the RAM proceed as follows:

   Deactivate the *CS* signal.

   Set input data and addresses to the desired values.

   Set control signal *WE* for a write operation.

   Activate *CS* to store the data.

   Deactivate *CS* to protect the stored data.
2. Define a similar procedure to read stored data and to display the data on LEDs.

### *Simulation*

Simulate both problems.

### *Report*

List and explain the results. Determine if the read and write steps must be performed in the specified order. Why are the data inputs connected through tristate buffers while the outputs are connected to LEDs directly?

## Experiment 12—Design of a Simple Controller

### *Purpose*

To test the student's understanding of control unit design.

### *Outline*

1. Perform computer simulation.
2. Perform the experiment.
3. Write a report.

### *The Experiment*

The student will design, build, and test a circuit that inputs parallel data and outputs serial data under the control of a clock-driven control unit.

The circuit has a four-bit data input connected to switches, and a control input called *GO*. When activated by *GO* in the idling initial state, the circuit loads data from switches into a four-bit shift register and begins sending the contents of the rightmost bit and shifting right. ("Sending" means that data become available on the output of the register.) When all bits are transmitted, the circuit returns to the initial state and waits for another *GO* signal. Control signal *INIT* resets the circuit to the initial state.

### *Simulation*

Simulate the problem. Include delays.

### *Report*

Draw the circuit's control graph, the block diagram showing its major parts, the logic diagram showing the modules of the block diagram, and a set of waveforms demonstrating the operation. Show the clock signal, input, data in the register, and output.

## Experiment 13—Design of a Simple Microprogrammed Controller

### *Purpose*

To test the student's understanding of microprogrammed control on the problem from Experiment 12.

### *Outline*

1. Repeat Experiment 12 using a microprogrammed rather than hardwired control unit. Store the microprogram manually in an SRAM, such as the 2114A.
2. Write a report.

### *The Experiment*

Build and test the circuit as in Experiment 12.

### *Report*

Show how the circuit from Experiment 12 should be modified to shift only twice and to add a control signal to determine whether to shift left or right. Explain how this would affect the design in Experiment 13 and compare the ease of modification of the hardwired and microprogrammed solution.

## Experiment 14—The Heathkit ET-3400 Microcomputer Trainer

### *Purpose*

To learn how to use the ET-3400 Heathkit microcomputer, explore the basic 6800 instructions and addressing modes, and write a simple program.

### *Outline*

1. Translate, enter and execute the program listed below.
2. Write and execute a program to solve a given problem.
3. Write a report.

### *The Experiment*

***Part 1.*** The following program demonstrates certain basic instructions. Convert it to hexadecimal and store the codes in the ET-3400 starting at location $10. Execute the program step by step and describe the effect of each instruction on condition flags and the relevant registers and memory.

```
LDAB    #$13     ;  Immediate addressing
LDAA    $FFFF    ;  Extended addressing
ABA              ;  Inherent addressing
LDAA    $41      ;  Direct addressing
LDX     $0015
LDAA    $20,X    ;  Indexed addressing
ADDB    22       ;  This value is decimal
ANDA    #98      ;  This value is also decimal
LSRA
LSRA
ASLB
ASLB
```

```
ROL     $0005
ROL     $0005
LDS     $00FF
INCA
DECB
CBA
SBA
NOP
WAI                 ; Always used to end program on the ET-3400
```

*Part 2.* Write, enter, and execute a program that copies the contents of locations FF00...FF09 to locations 0000...0009.

### Experiment 15—Basic 6800 Programming

#### *Purpose*

To practice 6800 programming and to learn the relation between Pascal programs and machine language code.

#### *Outline*

1. Convert several simple Pascal programs to 6800 machine code and execute them on the ET-3400 and the simulator.
2. Write a report.

#### *The Experiment*

Write, test, and demonstrate programs to implement the following programs. Store the code starting at memory location 0.

```
PROGRAM P1;
  VAR X,Y,Z: BYTE;
{X,Y,Z are one-byte pure binary values stored at $88, $89, $8A, respectively}
  BEGIN
  IF X+Y<13
    THEN Z:=X+Y
  END.
PROGRAM P2;
  VAR X,Y,Z: BYTE;
{X,Y, and Z are 2's complement values stored at $88, $89, $8A, respectively}
  BEGIN
```

```
  IF (X>3) AND (X+Y<=7)
    THEN Z:=1
    ELSE
      BEGIN X:=0; Y:=1, Z:=-1;
      END
END.
PROGRAM P3;
  VAR X,Y: ARRAY [0..$10] OF BYTE;
{Use indexed addressing, X is stored at $80,..., Y at $A0,..., X and Y are pure
binary}
  BEGIN
    FOR I:=0 TO $10 DO
      X[I] := Y[I] DIV 4
  END.
PROGRAM P4;     {X and Y are 2's complement stored at $80 and $81,
                respectively}
  VAR X,Y: BYTE;
  BEGIN
    CASE X OF
      1: Y:=0;
      2,3,4: Y:=10;
      0,5: Y:=-1;
      ELSE Y:=-10     {Decimal}
  END.
```

### Experiment 16—Programming the 6800 Using I/O Routines

***Purpose***

To convert high-level I/O operations to machine code and use I/O subroutines from the ET-3400 monitor.

***Outline***

1. Convert several Pascal programs to machine code and execute them on the ET-3400 and the simulator.
2. Write a report.

***The Experiment***

Write, test, and demonstrate the programs listed below. The READ statement reads from the hexadecimal keyboard; output is on the seven-segment display. Use the following I/O subroutines from the ET-3400 monitor:

INCH: Stored at $FDF4, waits for pressed key and stores it code in register *B*.

OUTBYT: Stored at $FE20, displays the contents of accumulator *A* as two hexadecimal digits on the seven-segment display. When OUTBYT is called for the first time, the leftmost two displays are used, then the next two, and so on. The display location can be reset to the leftmost digit by calling subroutine REDIS (reset display) stored at $FCBC.

```
PROGRAM P1;
{Input and output are in hexadecimal}
  VAR X,Y: BYTE;
  BEGIN
    READ(X); READ (Y); WRITE(X+Y)      {Ignore carry out}
  END.
PROGRAM P2;
{X1,X2,X3 are stored as ASCII codes starting at $88}
  VAR X1,X2,X3: INTEGER;
  BEGIN
    WRITE(X1,X2,−X3);      {Ignore minus sign if the result is negative}
  END.
```

## Experiment 17—Interfacing

### *Purpose*

To design interfaces for the 6800 CPU.

### *Outline*

1. Interface a RAM or DIP switches.
2. Write, enter, and test an I/O program.
3. Write a report.

### *The Experiment*

Choose one of the following:

1. Use a 256 × 4 SRAM such as the 2112 to implement 256 bytes starting at address $1000. The rest of the $1000...$1FFF block is unused. (If you use the 2114A 1k × 4 SRAM, enlarge the memory range to $1000...$13FF.)

Test the memory by a program that writes 0s to all locations, reads the data back, and repeats the procedure with 1s. The program displays "OK" if the test succeeds, "FAIL" if it fails.

The program starts by reading the starting address from the keyboard so that it can be used to test any 256-byte memory space. Test the program by running it on the built-in RAM, the monitor ROM (this test should fail), and on some "unpopulated" memory region.

2. Interface ET-3400 DIP switches and LED lights assigning address $1000 to the DIPs and $2000 to the LEDs.

   Write a program to read switch positions every 3 sec, copy their value to the LEDs, and display them in hexadecimal on the display. Note that the LEDs do not have any registers and must be constantly refreshed. The algorithm is as follows:

```
REPEAT
  Read DIPs;
  Display value on the seven-segment display;
  FOR I := 1 TO N DO
    write DIP value to LEDs
FOREVER
```

**Experiment 18—Polled I/O on the ET-3400**

***Purpose***

To gain further experience with interfacing and to write a simple I/O program using polling.

***Outline***

1. Interface DIP switches.
2. Write, enter, and test an I/O program.
3. Write a report.

***The Experiment***

Connect ET-3400 DIP switches to implement an eight-bit input device with address $8000. The MSB is the status bit, the remaining switches represent two hexadecimal digits. Use partial decoding.

Write a program that keeps checking the status of the switches and displays the value of the seven-bit code when the status bit is On; monitor subroutine OUTBYT is used for output. The program runs in a loop that ends when all data switches are turned Off.

## Experiment 19—Interrupt Driven I/O on the ET-3400

### *Purpose*

To gain further experience with interfacing and to practice interrupt driven I/O.

### *Outline*

1. Interface DIP switches and LED lights.
2. Write, enter, and test an I/O program.
3. Write a report.

### *The Experiment*

Choose one of the following two experiments:

1. Interface DIPs as in the previous experiment. Interface LEDs at address $8000 with a register between the data bus and the LEDs. The register will hold the value displayed on the LEDs, eliminating the need for refresh.

   Write a continuously running "background" program that turns on one LED after another, moving the light from right to left with a 1-sec pause on each LED.

   The switches are to be treated as two four-bit devices and their MSBs are connected to the *IRQ* input of the 6800 CPU. When one or both switches are activated, the interrupted program finds which of the two "devices" produced the interrupt, and services it by displaying *L* or *R* on the seven-segment display. The program then waits for the status switch to be turned Off (until then, further interrupts are disabled), erases the message, and returns to the background program. The left "device" has higher priority.
2. A background program alternatively turns all segments of all seven-segment digits of the ET-3400 display On for 1 sec and then Off for 1 sec. The 1-Hz clock from the ET-3400 is connected to the *NMI* interrupt signal and is used as a source of signals for a simulated traffic light controller. The "traffic lights" consist of the three leftmost and the three rightmost LEDs on the board, representing the North–South and the West–East directions respectively. Each group of three LEDs represents the red, amber, and green lights. The lights operate in the usual way, with the green light staying On for 9 sec, the orange light 3 sec, and the red light 6 sec.

The following two experiments are more advanced and may be skipped.

## Experiment 20 — An ACIA–RS-232-C Serial Terminal Interface

### *Purpose*

To experiment with asynchronous communication, RS-232-C interfacing, and to examine the operation of a terminal.

### *Outline*

1. Design and build an ACIA/RS-232-C interface.
2. Write, enter, and test an I/O program to echo keys from a terminal keyboard on the CRT display of the terminal.
3. Write a report.

### *Experiment*

1. Interface the MC6850 ACIA chip (Appendix 5), to addresses $1000 and $1001. The serial lines of the chip will be connected to an RS-232-C voltage converter, which in turn is connected to the send and receive lines from a computer terminal. Connect the ground lines as well. Set the terminal for the full duplex mode and 110 Baud rate. Construct a clock circuit to drive the ACIA at 110 Hz so that it can communicate with the terminal. The clock may be derived from the ET-3400 or using the 555 timer chip.
2. Write a program that initializes the ACIA to produce an interrupt when it receives a code from the terminal, and write an interrupt handler that echoes the input back to the terminal for display and displays the hexadecimal value of the code on the leftmost digit of the ET-3400.

   The algorithm is as follows: The ACIA is initialized (select clock rate, proper frame, and enable interrupt), and *WAI* executed to wait for an interrupt when the ACIA receives a character from the terminal keyboard. When an interrupt is received, the interrupt handler reads the character from the ACIA, sends it to the terminal via the ACIA, displays it on the LED, and returns to the *WAI* instruction.

   Test that the terminal automatically echos keys in the half-duplex mode but not in the full duplex mode.

### *Demonstration*

The student will see an oscilloscope display of the digital input and analog output of a modem. Draw and explain the signals.

## Experiment 21—Serial and Parallel Printer Interface.

### *Purpose*

To learn the operation of a parallel printer interface.

### *Outline*

1. Build an RS-232-C terminal interface and a parallel printer interface.
2. Write, enter, and test a program to read one line from a terminal and send it back to the terminal and to a printer.
3. Write a report.

### *The Experiment*

This experiment is an extension of Experiment 20.

1. Interfaces: The RS-232-C serial interface is the same as in the previous experiment. The parallel interface is implemented by the MC6821 PIA chip (Appendix 5), in the address range $2000...$2FFF. Its device ports are connected to the parallel interface of a printer as follows: On port *A*, line 7 is programmed for input and connected to the printer's *BUSY* line; line 0 is programmed for output and connected to the printer's *STROBE* input. Port *B* is programmed for output and connected to the *DATA* lines of the printer.
2. The program: When a character is received from the terminal, it is echoed and displayed as in the previous experiment, the printer's *BUSY* line is polled and when the printer is ready, the character is sent to it by activating the $\overline{STROBE}$ line and placing the code on the *DATA* lines. The $\overline{STROBE}$ signal on a parallel printer interface is an active Low pulse. The pulse can be produced by turning $\overline{STROBE}$ Off and On.

   Note that when *ENTER* is pressed on a keyboard, only the carriage return character is usually sent. However, for the proper display of a new line the printer requires a carriage return and a line feed.
3. Determine how the PIA can be programmed to generate the strobe signal automatically and modify the interface and the program accordingly.

## Components Needed for the Experiments

The following components or their equivalents are required: 2114A, MC6821, MC6850, 7400, 7402, 7404, 7408, 7410, 7420, 7421, 7432, 7474, 7475, 7478, 7486, 7495, 74125, 74138, 74153, 74155, 74163, 74181, 74248. Their pinouts appear in Appendix 4 or are available from the publisher.

## A2.3 A LAB PROJECT

The following is a description of a project that can be assigned after covering Chapter 7. Its first part is to design a very simple "arithmetic coprocessor" and the second part is to interface it to the 6800 CPU. For a second project, replace multiplication with division. Another possible project is the design, interfacing, and use of a very simple DMA controller.

### Part 1

Design, build, and test a circuit to multiply two four-bit pure binary numbers using the shift add sequential approach. Circuit inputs are a control signal *GO* and two four-bit binary operands. The output is an eight-bit result. The circuit starts in the idling state and waits for the activation of the *GO* signal; it then executes the multiplication sequence. (*Hints*: The circuit is similar to the circuit discussed in Chapter 7 but can be built with only three four-bit registers: one to hold the operand, which is added at each step; one to hold the intermediate sum; and one for the second operand whose LSB is used to determine whether addition takes place. This operand is shifted right in each step, making room for the result, which is progressively loaded from the left.)

In addition to building the circuit, perform its timing analysis and compare its speed with that of the cellular combinational multiplier presented in Chapter 6. Compare also the number of chips required by the two circuits.

### Part 2

Interface the circuit from Part 1 to the 6800 CPU at address $8000. This address is to be used both to load the two operands via an STA instruction and to read the result with an LDA instruction.

Write a program that reads two one-byte operands from the keyboard, stores them in operand registers, reads the result, displays it, waits for a key to be pressed, reads the keyboard again and repeats the loop until the input is 0. Perform timing analysis to determine whether the circuit can complete multiplication within a simple LDA and STA sequence or whether additional idling instructions are necessary.

Compare the speed of this "coprocessor" with the speed of multiplication performed by software on a 6800-based computer.

Write a program that performs 10,000 multiplications by executing 100 loops on 100 operands stored in memory using first multiplication by software, and then the coprocessor. No results are to be displayed. Use the program to confirm the timing analysis performed in Part 1.

### Suggestions for the Instructor

This project encompasses most of the concepts presented in this book and is considerably more complicated than the experiments. Students should be given a sequence in which to implement the project and deadlines for the completion of each step. This will help to complete the project on time and will teach the students a systematic approach to design. The natural steps are as follows:

Draw the logic diagram for Part 1.

Draw the layout diagram and make a connection list.

Build the circuit using the layout diagram and connection list, and test it. (Observe the power voltage on the oscilloscope, add bypass capacitors between the power and ground for every three chips, observe again, and measure the required current.)

Write a report for Part 1.

Draw the logic diagram for Part 2.

Draw the wiring diagram.

Write the program.

Build the interface, check if the power supply of the computer can handle the whole circuit or if a separate power supply is needed for the circuit. (If yes, connect the grounds of both power supplies together.)

Test the program and the operation of the whole circuit.

Complete the report.

At Acadia University we allocate one term for the project and give students the solutions after each step that requires correction. Students thus find their own solutions but a uniform approach is enforced, which makes it possible to use one set of components, simplifies implementation and testing, and demonstrates a well formulated solution. In our course, students borrow the breadboards and chips from the lab and make the connections at home.

## A2.4 LAB ORGANIZATION AND EQUIPMENT

Experiments are usually performed on equipment permanently located in the lab. We suggest leaving the room open and supervised outside scheduled laboratory hours to give students more access to equipment and help. An interesting alternative is to provide students with individual kits to prepare and test experiments at home.

Doing experiments in pairs makes the students and the instructor feel more secure. It also fosters cooperation, and students learn more. If time is short, instructors can set up the more complicated experiments and have students perform only the measurement and discuss the design in their reports.

Each experiment must be demonstrated to the supervisor and a report describing the problem, experimental results, and evaluation handed in by the group. A possible format is shown in Section A2.5. Where simulation is required, the report should contain printouts and their evaluation. We assign 50% of the lab mark for demonstration of the solution in the lab and 50% for the report. In the report, we mark correctness, neatness, and good writing style.

### Lab Equipment

Experiments can be done on breadboards with built-in or separate power supplies. Breadboards, power supplies, chips, wires, and tools can be bought from the Heathkit company, in stores such as Radio Shack or from mail order companies advertising in *Byte* magazine and similar publications.

Breadboards usually contain two types of contact (tie point) strips: two-column "bus strips" for connections to the power supply, and five-column "quick-set" strips for logic signals. Chips, DIP switches, LED lights, resistors, capacitors, and gauge #22 wires can be inserted directly into the tie points. Wires should be stripped just enough to allow insertion. Tie points are internally connected to allow power distribution around the board via bus strips, and to provide four contacts for each pin of a chip inserted in the quick-set strip.

Breadboards usually do not have built in switches or LEDs. One can use an additional commercially available or home-made board with switches and lights and a source of clock signals based, for example, on the 555 chip. These facilities can also be built on the breadboard itself.

To be able to perform experiments at home, students can use a tieboard to set up the logic circuit, a set of chips, and an auxiliary board with I/O and clock facilities, a flat cable connector, and an AC adaptor for a power supply. For some experiments, the student will need access to a computer from the Heathkit ET-3400 microcomputer trainer family.

Some demonstrations and experiments require the following additional equipment:

An oscilloscope, dual trace, at least 10-MHz frequency response

A digital voltmeter

An analog voltmeter

A logic analyzer.

Useful but not necessary equipment includes the following:

EPROM programmer

EPROM eraser

Chip tester.

Some of these instruments are also available as special purpose boards for personal computers. As example is a logic analyzer for the IBM personal computer from Heathkit. Cards such as these usually cost much less than dedicated instruments; can implement many functions and provide unusual data processing capabilities, such as the comparison of consecutive measurements and various forms of display and printouts. They also allow new types of experiments and provide an interesting example of a computer application normally not encountered in computer science courses.

## A2.5 A SAMPLE LAB REPORT

Reports must be typed and conform to a prescribed format; a copy of lab notes signed by the instructor after the demonstration must be included as a proof of completion of the experiment. The report is marked for correctness, neatness, clarity, completeness, style, and spelling.

The report must demonstrate that the student understands the material and knows how to follow the proper design and construction methods. It must include the following information: appropriate background, answers to questions that the reader might ask about the results and the conditions under which the measurements were conducted, and information useful for a reconstruction of the experiment. Positive results are just as important as a record of encountered problems and their explanations.

A typical report contains the following parts:

Student name(s)

Title of experiment

Statement of purpose

Short statement of problem

For each part of the experiment

  Diagrams (block, logic, layout, wiring) and their derivation

  List of components and connections

  Experimental procedure and results (timing diagrams, tables, graphs)

Evaluation (difficulties encountered, lessons learned, notes that may be useful for a person repeating the experiment)

Answers to questions stated in the description

Simulation results

Computer printouts, if any.

In the following example, the illustrations (R.1 – R.4) and simulation printouts are not shown because the report is provided only as a sample.

**Experiment 1 — Familiarization with Gates**

***Purpose***

To gain experience with gates and truth tables.

***Short Description***

In this lab we were to perform a simulation and an experiment on gates and observe a demonstration of basic measuring devices.

***Experiment***

The first part of this lab was a simulation of a multi-input gate. Commented printouts of the simulation are attached. The following is a description of the experiment and the demonstration.

***Part 1.*** The instructor inserted two unconnected chips into the breadboard. Our task was to find their types and function, make the necessary connections, and test whether all gates work.

From the numbers printed on the packages, we determined that our chips were the 7400 quad two-input NAND and the quad two-input AND 7408. After identifying their pinouts (Figure R.1) we:

Checked that the power switch on the breadboard was off

Connected 5 V to $V_{cc}$ and 0 V to the *GND* pins

Connected the inputs of the first gate to DIP switches and its output to an LED light

Asked the supervisor to verify the connections

Turned the power on and checked that the chips didn't overheat

Tested all input combinations and recorded the observed values (logic 1 = LED is On).

The last step was repeated for all remaining gates on the chip.

The wiring diagram in Figure R.1 shows the connections used for testing of the first gate on each chip.

We obtained the following results:

| 7400 2-in NAND | | 7408 2-in AND | |
|---|---|---|---|
| *a b* | *f1 f2 f3 f4* | *a b* | *f1 f2 f3 f4* |
| 0 0 | 1 1 1 1 | 0 0 | 0 0 0 0 |
| 0 1 | 1 1 1 1 | 0 1 | 0 0 0 0 |
| 1 0 | 1 1 1 1 | 1 0 | 0 0 1 0 |
| 1 1 | 0 0 0 0 | 1 1 | 1 1 1 1 |

We notified the instructor that the third AND gate on the 7408 appears to be faulty.

***Part 2.*** We examined the instruments described below and used them to measure logic values, voltages, and currents on a circuit set up by the instructor (Figure R.2).

A logic probe used LED lights to display On, Off, and "pulse train" (fast sequence of 0s and 1s) values. Our logic probe also emits a tone of different pitch for different values.

We used both an analog and a digital voltmeter to measure voltages on the output of an inverter and obtained the following values: Logic 0 = 0.4 V; logic 1 = 3.2 V. This agrees with the expected value ranges.

An ammeter measures current. We used it to measure the current supplied to the whole chip (instrument inserted between the power supply and the $V_{cc}$ pin of the chip), and the current into the input and output of the inverter. We observed that when all inverters are in use, the whole chip consumed 6 mA (0.006 A) with all outputs High and 18 mA with all outputs Low. The output of one inverter was $-400\ \mu$A ($-0.4$ A) when High and 16 mA when Low. The negative sign indicates that the current flows out of the chip. The input receives 40 $\mu$A when High and produces 1.6 mA when Low. The fan-out of the chip (the number of inputs that can be connected to its output) is thus $400/40 = 16/1.6 = 10$. This is typical for TTL chips.

We then used an oscilloscope and a logic analyzer to observe the signal at the point indicated in Figure R.3. The oscilloscope shows a continuous analog signal whereas the logic analyzer displays its two-value logic equivalent, a square wave. The oscilloscope makes it possible to measure voltage magnitudes and timing, such as the rise and fall times of a signal or delay between two signals.

A sketch of our observations in Figure R.4 shows that the rise and fall times of the output signal measured between 10% and 90% of steady values were too short for our scope. The delay between the input and output of the inverter was 12 nsec for the $0 \rightarrow 1$ transition and 9 nsec for the $1 \rightarrow 0$ transition. This agrees with values given in data sheets.

### *Conclusion*

Simulation allowed us to examine the behavior of gates for different inputs. Even phenomena that require specialized equipment, such as logic analyzers, can be easily simulated and understood.

We learned how to determine the function of a chip and its pins from its type number and pinout and how to connect a circuit. We also obtained several truth tables and compared them with the expected ones; one chip was found to be defective.

Several instruments were used to observe important physical parameters of chips and electric signals and their logic counterparts.

In summary, we practiced the principles of abstract and applied logic, observed relations between abstract (gate level) and physical (electronic level) signals, and obtained a feeling for the physical parameters of commercial chips.

## REFERENCES

The following titles listed in the references at the end of the book are relevant to this chapter:

R. E. Gasperini. *Digital Experiments.*

Heathkit books.

P. Kantrowitz and G. Kousourou. *Electronic Measurements.*

D. Lancaster. *TTL Cookbook.*

J. F. Passafiume and M. Douglas. *Digital Logic Design: Tutorials and Lab Exercises.*

Texas Instruments. *The TTL Data Book.*

J. F. Wakerly. *Logic Design Projects Using Standard Integrated Circuits.*

# APPENDIX 3

# SAMPLE DATA SHEETS EXPLAINED

## A3.1 THE 7404 HEX INVERTER

The 7404 Hex Inverter contains six inverters. Its pinout appears in Appendix 4 and we present its parameters below. We have not shown the values for the 5404 (the "military" version of the same chip) because they are almost identical. The main differences are that the operating temperature range for the 54 is −55 – 120°C and the power supply voltage tolerance is 10%, instead of 5% as for the 74 family. We show all of the 74 families (regular 74, high-speed 74H, low-power 74L, low-power Schottky 74LS, and Schottky 74S) although only the 74, 74LS, and the 74S are now used.

**Recommended Operating Conditions**

| | 7404 | | | 74H04 | | | 74L04 | | | 74LS04 | | | 74S04 | | |
|---|---|---|---|---|---|---|---|---|---|---|---|---|---|---|---|
| | min | nom | max | min | nom | max | min | nom | max | min | nom | max | min | nom | max |
| $V_{cc}$ [V] | 4.75 | 5 | 5.25 | 4.75 | 5 | 5.25 | 4.75 | 5 | 5.25 | 4.75 | 5 | 5.25 | 4.75 | 5 | 5.2 |
| $I_{oH}$ [$\mu$A] | | | −400 | | | −500 | | | −200 | | | −400 | | | −100 |
| $I_{oL}$ [mA] | | | 16 | | | 20 | | | 3.6 | | | 8 | | | 2 |
| $T_a$ [°C] | 0 | | 70 | 0 | | 70 | 0 | | 70 | 0 | | 70 | 0 | | 7 |

Note the following:

1. Meaning of symbols:

   nom: Nominal

$I_{oH}$: Steady state High level output current of one gate. The minus sign indicates that it flows out of the gate.

$I_{oL}$: Steady state Low level output current of one gate. It flows into the gate.

$T_a$: Operating free-air temperature.

2. Supply voltage must be within 5% of $V_{cc}$ for the 74 family and within 10% for the 54 family.
3. The minimum and maximum values of $V_{cc}$ and $T_a$ define the range within which the chip will work as described in the following tables.

**Electrical Characteristics Over Recommended Operating Range**

| | 7404 | | | 74H04 | | | 74L04 | | | 74LS04 | | | 74S04 | | |
|---|---|---|---|---|---|---|---|---|---|---|---|---|---|---|---|
| | min | typ | max | min | typ | max | min | typ | max | min | typ | max | min | typ | max |
| $V_{iH}$ [V] | 2 | | | 2 | | | 2 | | | 2 | | | 2 | | |
| $V_{iL}$ [V] | | | 0.8 | | | 0.8 | | | 0.7 | | | 0.7 | | | 0.7 |
| $V_{oH}$ [V] | 2.4 | 3.4 | | 2.4 | 3.5 | | 2.4 | 3.2 | | 2.7 | 3.4 | | 2.7 | 3.4 | |
| $V_{oL}$ [V] | | 0.2 | 0.4 | | 0.2 | 0.4 | | 0.2 | 0.4 | | 0.25 | 0.5 | | | 0.5 |
| $I_L$ [mA] | | | 1 | | | 1 | | | 0.1 | | | 0.1 | | | 1 |
| $I_{iH}$ [$\mu$A] | | | 40 | | | 50 | | | 10 | | | 20 | | | 50 |
| $I_{iL}$ [mA] | | | −1.6 | | | −2 | | | −0.18 | | | −0.4 | | | −2 |
| $I_{os}$ [mA] | −20 | | −55 | −40 | | −100 | −3 | | −15 | −20 | | −100 | −40 | | −100 |

Note the following:

1. Meaning of symbols:

$V_{iH}$: High level input voltage.

$V_{iL}$: Low level input voltage.

$V_{oH}$: High output voltage established at minimum $V_{cc}$ and maximum $V_{iL}$ and $I_{oH}$.

$V_{oL}$: Low level output voltage established at minimum $V_{cc}$, $V_{iH} = 2V$, $I_{oL} = 4mA$.

$I_L$: Input current at maximum $V_{cc}$, $V_i = 5.5V$.

$I_{iH}$: High level input current at maximum $V_{cc}$, $V_{iH} = 2.4V$ (logic 1).

$I_{iL}$: Low level input current at maximum $V_{cc}$, $V_{iL} = 0.4V$ (logic 0).

$I_{os}$: Short-circuit output current (output short circuited to ground and input conditions to establish output level farthest from ground) at maximum $V_{cc}$. Not more than one output may be shorted at a time and the short should not exceed one second.

2. Currents are steady state values. Values during transitions between Low and High are higher and cause intermittent "spikes" (surges) on the power line. When the number of gates in the circuit is large, the surges must be controlled by despiking capacitors (Appendix 1) or the supply voltage will fluctuate more than is allowed by the voltage tolerances given above and the chip will not work correctly.
3. All values are measured under conditions described in the databook.
4. The input of the 7404 inverter represents a standard TTL load and its fan-in is thus 1. This means that it consumes ("sinks") up to $I_{iL} = 40\ \mu A$ in its Low state and produces ("sources") up to $I_{iH} = 1.6$ mA in its High state. Its output can be connected to a maximum of ten standard loads without signal deterioration because

$$\begin{aligned} I_{oH} &= 16 \\ &= 10 \times I_{iH}\ [\text{mA}] \end{aligned}$$

and

$$\begin{aligned} I_{oL} &= 400 \\ &= 10 \times I_{iL}\ [\mu\text{A}] \end{aligned}$$

This means that the fan-out of the 7404 is 10, which is typical for TTL components. Some integrated circuits, such as the 74S04, have different logic High and Low fan-outs. The fan-out is then the smaller of the two values.

5. The min and max values are measured under extreme conditions within the recommended operating range. The typical values are measured at typical operating conditions: $V_{cc} = 5$V and $T_a = 25°$C.

**Supply Current**

| | 7404 | | 74H04 | | 74L04 | | 74LS04 | | 74S04 | |
|---|---|---|---|---|---|---|---|---|---|---|
| | typ | max | typ | max | typ | max | typ | max | typ | max |
| $I_{ccH}$ [mA] | 6 | 12 | 16 | 26 | 0.66 | 1.2 | 1.2 | 2.4 | 15 | 24 |
| $I_{ccL}$ [mA] | 18 | 33 | 40 | 58 | 1.74 | 3.06 | 3.6 | 6.6 | 30 | 54 |
| $I_{cc}$ [mA] | 2 | | 4.5 | | 0.20 | | 0.4 | | 3.75 | |

Note the following:

1. Meaning of symbols:

   $I_{ccH}$: Total supply current into the $V_{cc}$ pin of the chip with outputs High.

   $I_{ccL}$: Total supply current into the $V_{cc}$ pin of the chip with outputs Low.

   $I_{cc}$: Average current into the $V_{cc}$ pin of the chip per gate with 50% duty cycle. It can be used to evaluate the power consumption of a chip whose inverters are not all connected. A "50% duty cycle" means that the measurement is performed with the gate output High half of the time. Note that $I_{cc}$ is one-sixth of the average of $I_{ccH}$ and $I_{ccL}$.

**Switching Characteristics at $V_{cc} = 5V$, $T_a = 25°C$**

| | 7404 | | 74H04 | | 74L04 | | 74LS04 | | 74S04 | |
|---|---|---|---|---|---|---|---|---|---|---|
| | typ | max | typ | max | typ | max | typ | max | typ | max |
| $T_{pLH}$ [nsec] | 12 | 22 | 6 | 10 | 35 | 60 | 9 | 15 | 3 | 4.5 |
| $T_{pHL}$ [nsec] | 8 | 15 | 6.5 | 10 | 31 | 60 | 10 | 15 | 3 | 5 |

Note the following:

1. Meaning of symbols:

   $T_{pLH}$: Low → High propagation delay for a load with a standard input capacitance and resistance: In most cases $C = 15$ pF, $R = 400$ Ohms. It is measured between the 1.5-V points on the transition curve.

   $T_{pHL}$: High → Low propagation delay under the same load conditions.

2. Note the difference in propagation times for different directions of transition.

## A3.2 THE 74165 PARALLEL-LOAD EIGHT-BIT SHIFT REGISTER

The 74165, like many other recent TTL chips, is manufactured only in the most popular families. The Texas Instruments databook lists only the 74165 and the 74LS165.

**Recommended Operating Conditions**

| | 74165 min | 74165 nom | 74165 max | 74LS165 min | 74LS165 nom | 74LS165 max |
|---|---|---|---|---|---|---|
| $V_{cc}$ [V] | 4.75 | 5 | 5.25 | 4.75 | 5 | 5.25 |
| $I_{oH}$ [$\mu$A] | | | −800 | | | −400 |
| $I_{oL}$ [mA] | | | 16 | | | 8 |
| $T_a$ [°C] | 0 | | 70 | 0 | | 70 |
| $F_{cl}$ [MHz] | 0 | | 20 | 0 | | 25 |
| $T_{wcl}$ [nsec] | 25 | | | 25 | | |
| $T_{wld}$ [nsec] | 15 | | | 15 | | |
| $T_{sucl}$ [nsec] | 30 | | | 30 | | |
| $T_{sup}$ [nsec] | 10 | | | 10 | | |
| $T_{sus}$ [nsec] | 20 | | | 20 | | |
| $T_{sush}$ [nsec] | 45 | | | 45 | | |
| $T_h$ [nsec] | 0 | | | 0 | | |

Supply voltage and temperature ranges are the same as for the 7404 and other chips in the 74 family. The speed of the 74LS is approximately the same as that of the regular 74 chip but its power consumption (the product of $V_{cc}$ and $I_{cc}$) is about one-half. The meaning of the new symbols is as follows:

$T_{wcl}$: Minimum width of clock input

$T_{wld}$: Minimum width of load input

$T_{sucl}$: Minimum clock setup time

$T_{sup}$: Minimum parallel input setup time

$T_{sus}$: Minimum serial input setup time

$T_{sush}$: Minimum shift input setup time

$T_h$: Minimum hold time at any input.

**Electrical Characteristics Over Recommended Operating Range**

| | 74165 min | 74165 typ | 74165 max | 74LS165 min | 74LS165 typ | 74LS165 max |
|---|---|---|---|---|---|---|
| $V_{iH}$ [V] | 2 | | | 2 | | |
| $V_{iL}$ [V] | | 0.8 | | | 0.7 | |
| $V_{oH}$ [V] | 2.4 | 3.4 | | 2.4 | 3.4 | |
| $V_{oL}$ [V] | | 0.2 | 0.4 | | 0.2 | 0.4 |

**Electrical Characteristics Over Recommended Operating Range *(continued)***

| | 74165 min | 74165 typ | 74165 max | 74LS165 min | 74LS165 typ | 74LS165 max |
|---|---|---|---|---|---|---|
| $I_L$ [mA] | | | 1 | | | 0.3 |
| $I_{iH}$ sh/ld [$\mu$A] | | | 80 | | | 60 |
| $I_{iH}$ other [$\mu$A] | | | 40 | | | 20 |
| $I_{iL}$ sh/ld [mA] | | | −3.2 | | | −1.2 |
| $I_{iL}$ other [mA] | | | −1.6 | | | −0.4 |
| $I_{os}$ [mA] | −18 | | −55 | −20 | | −100 |
| $I_{cc}$ [mA] | | 42 | 63 | | 21 | 36 |

Most of the symbols are explained in Section A3.1; the term "*sh/ld*" refers to shift and load inputs while "other" refers to other input pins.

**Switching Characteristics at $V_{cc}$ = 5V, $T_a$ = 25°C**

| | | 7404 typ | 7404 max | 74LS04 typ | 74LS04 max |
|---|---|---|---|---|---|
| $F_{max}$ | [MHz] | 20 | 26 | 25 | 35 |
| $T_{pLH}$ ld/x | [nsec] | 21 | 31 | 22 | 35 |
| $T_{pHL}$ ld/x | [nsec] | 27 | 40 | 22 | 35 |
| $T_{pLH}$ cl/x | [nsec] | 16 | 24 | 27 | 40 |
| $T_{pHL}$ cl/x | [nsec] | 21 | 31 | 28 | 40 |
| $T_{pLH}$ H/QH | [nsec] | 11 | 17 | 14 | 25 |
| $T_{pHL}$ H/QH | [nsec] | 24 | 36 | 21 | 30 |
| $T_{pLH}$ H/$\overline{QH}$ | [nsec] | 18 | 27 | 21 | 30 |
| $T_{pHL}$ H/$\overline{QH}$ | [nsec] | 18 | 27 | 16 | 25 |

Propagation times are measured between the load input and any output (*1d/x*), clock input and any output (*cl/x*), *H* data input (the MSB) and *Q* (*H/QH*), and *H* and $\overline{Q}$ (*H/*$\overline{QH}$).

## REFERENCE

The following source listed in the references at the end of the book is relevant to this appendix:

Texas Instruments. *The TTL Data Book.*

# APPENDIX 4

# SOME IMPORTANT CHIPS

## AN OVERVIEW

This appendix contains two lists of the most important 74 series integrated circuits and the pinout diagrams of those that are used in the lab experiments given in Appendix 2. The first list is arranged by function, the second by type number.

## A4.1 INTEGRATED CIRCUIT LIST BY FUNCTION

**Arithmetic and Related Functions**

| | |
|---|---|
| Four-bit accumulator | 74281 |
| One-bit adder | 7480 |
| Two-bit adder | 7482 |
| Four-bit adder | 7483 |
| Four-bit ALU | 74181 |
| Four-bit comparator | 7485 |
| Four-bit multiplier | 74284, 74294 |

**Buffers, Drivers, Interfaces**

| | |
|---|---|
| Inverting | 7404 |
| Two-input NAND | 7437 |
| Four-input NAND | 7440 |
| Noninverting Schmitt trigger | 7414 |
| Tristate | 74125 |
| Tristate | 74126 |

**Counters**

| | |
|---|---|
| Decade, ripple up | 74142 |
| Decade, synchronous up | 74160 |
| Decade | 74176 |
| Decade, synchronous up/down | 74190 |
| Decade, synchronous up/down, carry | 74192 |
| Base-12, ripple up | 7492 |
| Base-16, ripple up | 7493 |
| Base-16, synchronous up | 74161 |
| Base-16, synchronous up/down | 74191 |

**Decoders and Encoders**

| | |
|---|---|
| BCD to 1-of-10 | 7442 |
| BCD to 7-segment | 7447 |

**Flip-flops and Latches (See also the table for memories)**

| | |
|---|---|
| D-flip-flop with clear/preset | 7474 |
| JK-flip-flop with clear, special pinout | 7473 |
| JK-flip-flop with clear/preset | 7476 |
| JK-flip-flop with clear | 74107 |

| Gates | |
|---|---|
| Two-input NAND | 7400 |
| Two-input NOR | 7402 |
| Inverter | 7404 |
| Two-input AND | 7408 |
| Three-input NAND | 7410 |
| Four-input NAND | 7420 |
| Eight-input NAND | 7430 |
| Two-input OR | 7432 |
| Two-input XOR | 7486 |

| Memories | |
|---|---|
| Four-bit D-latch | 7475 |
| Six-bit D-flip-flop | 74174 |
| Four-bit D-flip-flop | 74175 |
| 64 × 4 RAM | 74189 |

| Miscellaneous | |
|---|---|
| Parity generator/checker | 74180 |
| Priority encoder | 74148 |

| Multiplexers and Demultiplexers | |
|---|---|
| Demultiplexer, 1–16 | 74154 |
| Demultiplexer, 1–4 | 74155 |
| Multiplexer, 1–16 | 74150 |
| Multiplexer, 1–8 | 74151 |
| Multiplexer, 1–4 | 74153 |
| Multiplexer, 1–2 | 74157 |

| Registers | |
|---|---|
| Four-bit, right/left, PIPO | 7495 |
| Five-bit, PIPO | 7496 |
| Eight-bit, SIPO | 74164 |
| Eight-bit, PISO | 74165 |
| Four-bit, SISO | 7494 |
| Eight-bit, SISO | 7491 |

## A4.2 INTEGRATED CIRCUIT LIST BY TYPE NUMBER

| Type | Function | Typical 1989 Mail-Order Price (cents) |
|---|---|---|
| 7400 | Two-input NAND | .20 |
| 7402 | Two-input NOR | .20 |
| 7404 | Inverter | .25 |
| 7408 | Two-input AND | .25 |
| 7410 | Three-input NAND | .20 |
| 7414 | Noninverting Schmitt trigger | .45 |
| 7420 | Four-input NAND | .20 |
| 7430 | Eight-input NAND | .20 |
| 7432 | Two-input OR | .30 |
| 7437 | Two-input NAND | .25 |
| 7440 | Four-input NAND | .20 |
| 7442 | BCD to 1-of-10 | .45 |
| 7447 | BCD to 7-segment | .80 |
| 7473 | JK with clear, special pinout | .35 |
| 7474 | D-flip-flop with clear/preset | .35 |
| 7475 | Four-bit D-latch | .40 |
| 7476 | JK with clear/preset | .35 |
| 7480 | Gated Two-bit adder | .70 |
| 7482 | Two-bit adder | .95 |
| 7483 | Four-bit adder | .45 |
| 7485 | Four-bit comparator | .55 |
| 7486 | Two-input XOR | .35 |
| 7489 | 64 × 4 RAM | 1.95 |
| 7491 | Eight-bit SISO register | .65 |
| 7492 | Base-12, ripple up | .45 |
| 7493 | Base-16, ripple up | .35 |
| 7494 | Four-bit PISO | .85 |
| 7495 | Four-bit, right/left, parallel in/out | .50 |
| 7496 | Five-bit, parallel in/out | .70 |
| 74107 | JK with clear | .25 |
| 74125 | Tristate | .45 |
| 74126 | Tristate | .50 |
| 74142 | Decade, ripple up | 2.95 |

(Continued)

## A4.2 INTEGRATED CIRCUIT LIST BY TYPE NUMBER

| Type | Function | Typical 1989 Mail-Order Price (cents) |
|---|---|---|
| 74148 | Priority encoder | 1.20 |
| 74150 | Multiplexer, 1–16 | 1.30 |
| 74151 | Multiplexer, 1–8 | .55 |
| 74153 | Multiplexer, 1–4 | .50 |
| 74154 | Demultiplexer, 1–16 | .60 |
| 74155 | Demultiplexer, 1–4 | .70 |
| 74157 | Multiplexer, 1–2 | .60 |
| 74160 | Decade, synchronous up | .80 |
| 74161 | Base-16, synchronous up | .70 |
| 74164 | Eight-bit, serial in, parallel out | .70 |
| 74165 | Eight-bit, parallel in, serial out | .50 |
| 74174 | Six-bit D-flip-flop | .60 |
| 74175 | Four-bit D-flip-flop | .60 |
| 74176 | Decade | .90 |
| 74180 | Parity generator/checker | .75 |
| 74181 | Four-bit ALU | 1.95 |
| 74189 | 64 × 4 RAM | 4.60 |
| 74190 | Decade, synchronous up/down | .70 |
| 74191 | Base-16, synchronous up/down | .50 |
| 74192 | Decade, synchronous up/down, carry | .80 |
| 74281 | Four-bit accumulator | |
| 74284 | 4 × 4 multiplier | 2.90 |
| 74294 | Four-bit PIPO register | |

### A4.3 PINOUT DIAGRAMS

Pinout diagrams of the 18L4 PAL and other useful chips follow. Most are needed in the experiments described in Appendix 2.

### REFERENCE

A more complete list of TTL chips is available from the following source listed in the references:

Texas Instruments. *The TTL Data Book.*

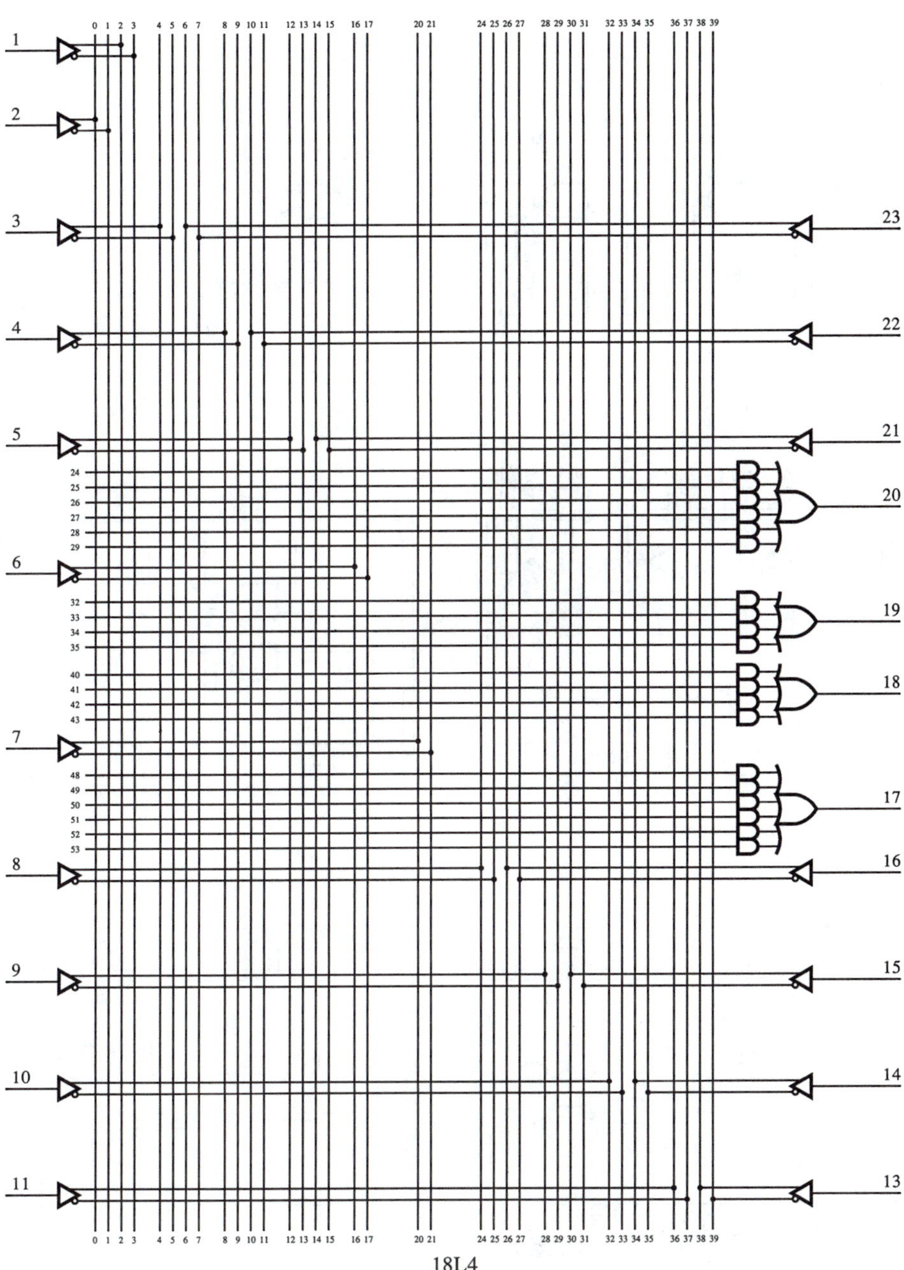

18L4

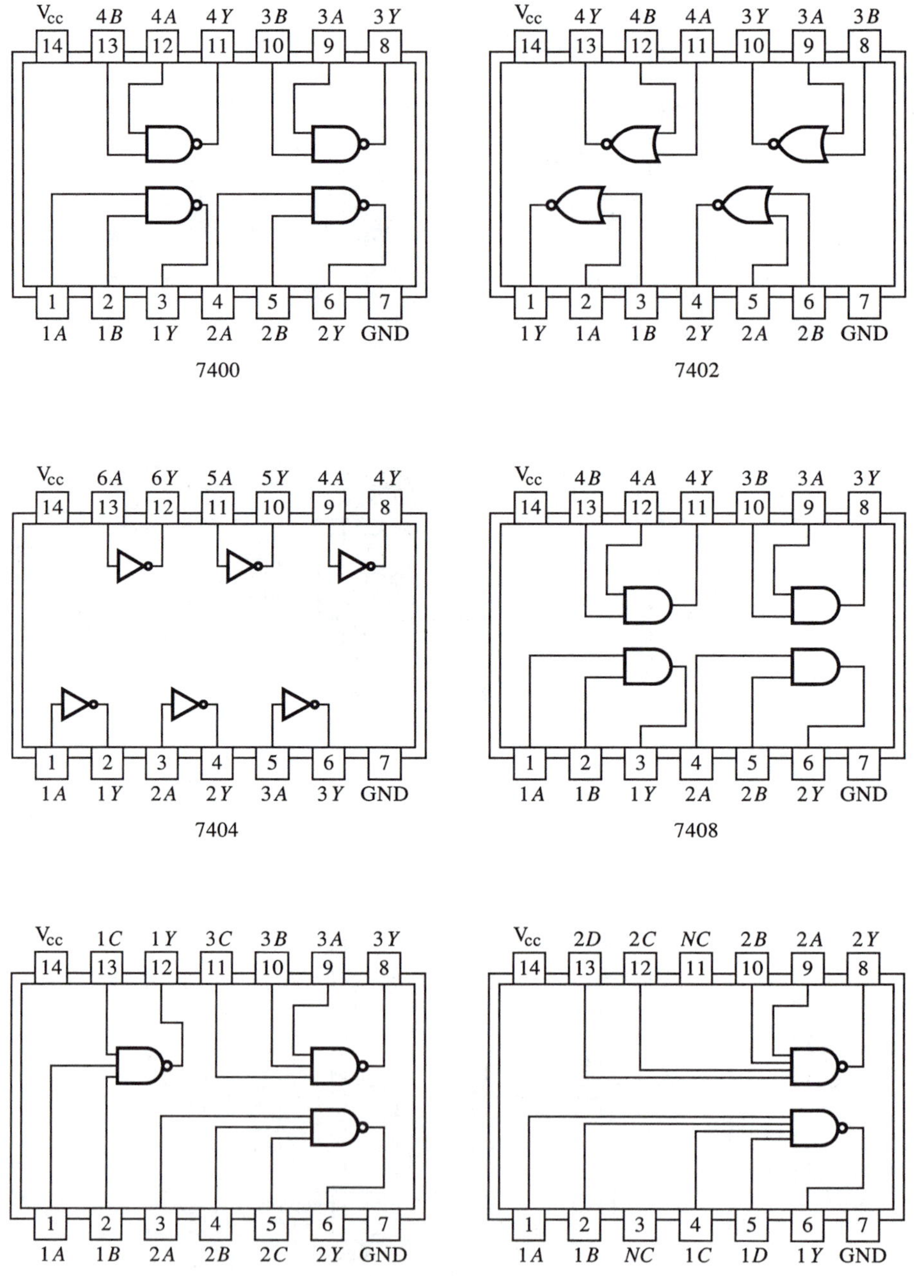


7400

7402

7404

7408

7410

7420

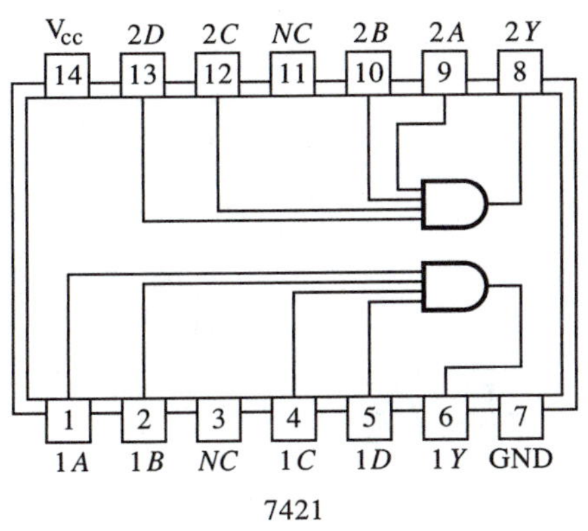


7421

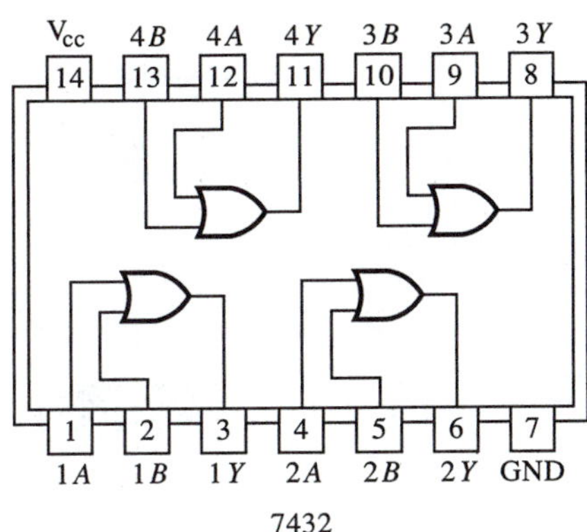


7432

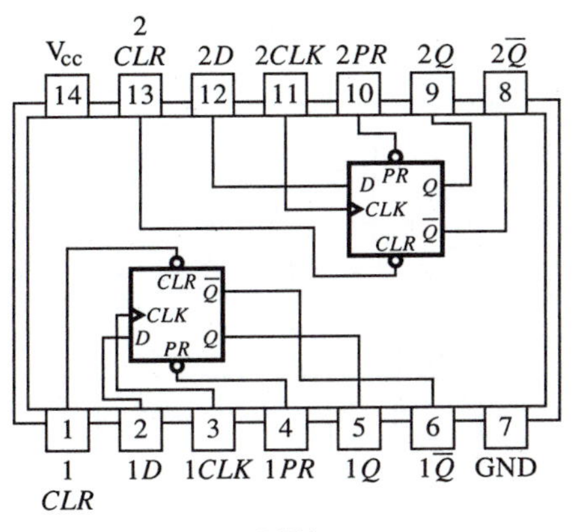


7474

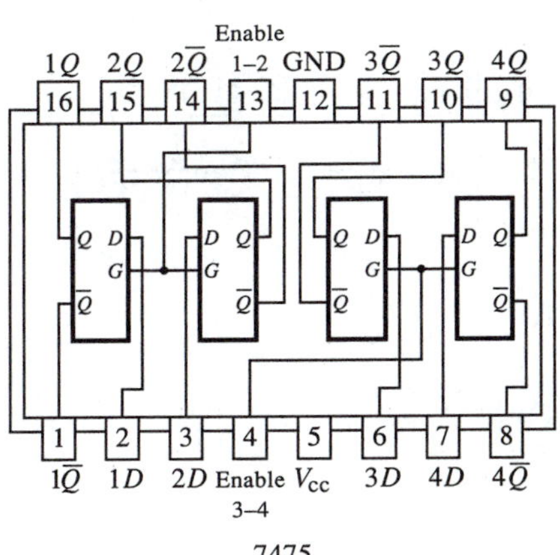


7475

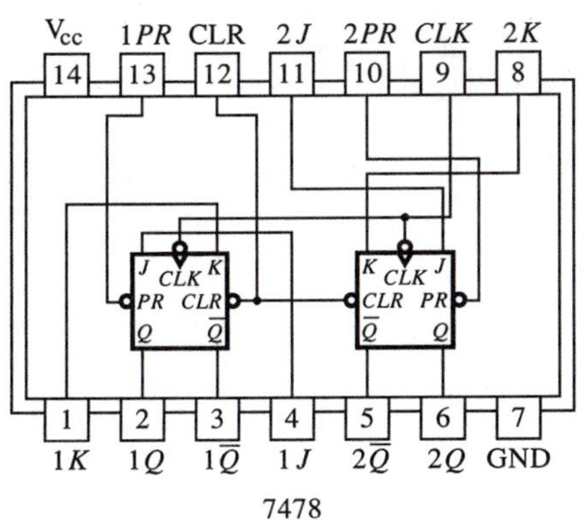


7478

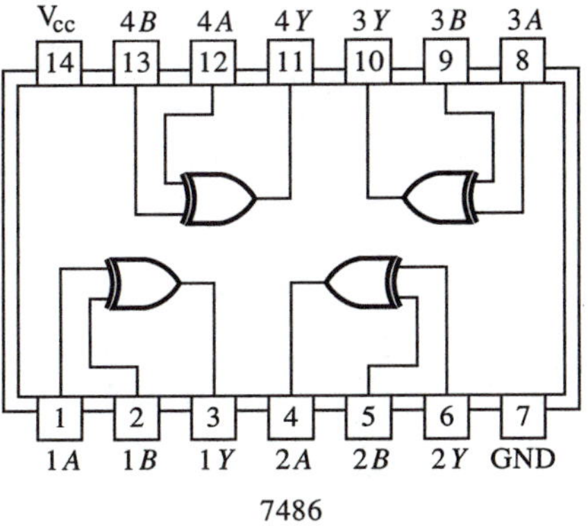


7486

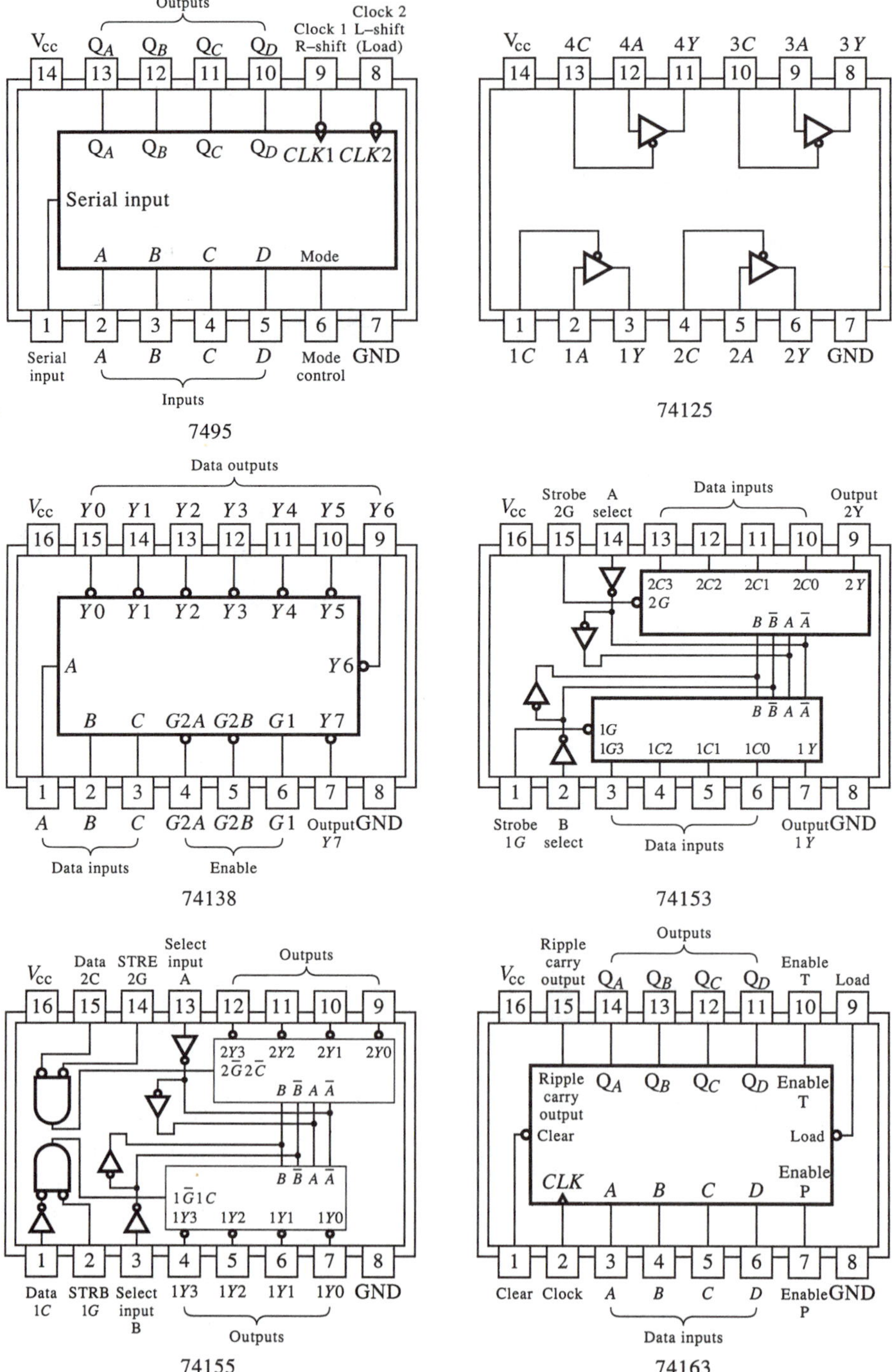

Outputs
Clock 2
Clock 1 L–shift
R–shift (Load)
Vcc QA QB QC QD
Serial input
Mode
Serial input A B C D Mode control GND
Inputs
7495
Vcc 4C 4A 4Y 3C 3A 3Y
1C 1A 1Y 2C 2A 2Y GND
74125
Data outputs
Vcc Y0 Y1 Y2 Y3 Y4 Y5 Y6
A B C G2A G2B G1 Output Y7 GND
Data inputs
Enable
74138
Strobe 2G
A select
Data inputs
Output 2Y
Strobe 1G
B select
Data inputs
Output 1Y
GND
74153
Data 2C
STRE 2G
Select input A
Outputs
Data 1C STRB 1G Select input B 1Y3 1Y2 1Y1 1Y0 GND
Outputs
74155
Ripple carry output
Outputs
Enable T
Load
Clear
CLK
Enable P
Clear Clock A B C D Enable P GND
Data inputs
74163

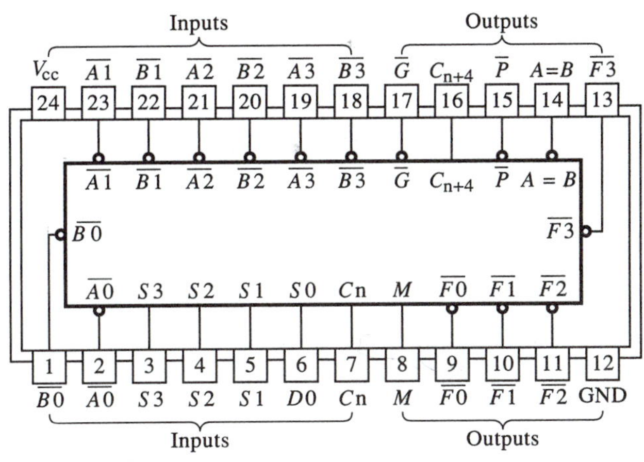
Inputs
Outputs
$V_{cc}$ $\overline{A1}$ $\overline{B1}$ $\overline{A2}$ $\overline{B2}$ $\overline{A3}$ $\overline{B3}$ $\overline{G}$ $C_{n+4}$ $\overline{P}$ $A=B$ $\overline{F3}$
24 23 22 21 20 19 18 17 16 15 14 13
$\overline{B0}$ $\overline{F3}$
$\overline{A0}$ $S3$ $S2$ $S1$ $S0$ $Cn$ $M$ $\overline{F0}$ $\overline{F1}$ $\overline{F2}$
1 2 3 4 5 6 7 8 9 10 11 12
$\overline{B0}$ $\overline{A0}$ $S3$ $S2$ $S1$ $D0$ $Cn$ $M$ $\overline{F0}$ $\overline{F1}$ $\overline{F2}$ GND
Inputs
Outputs
74181

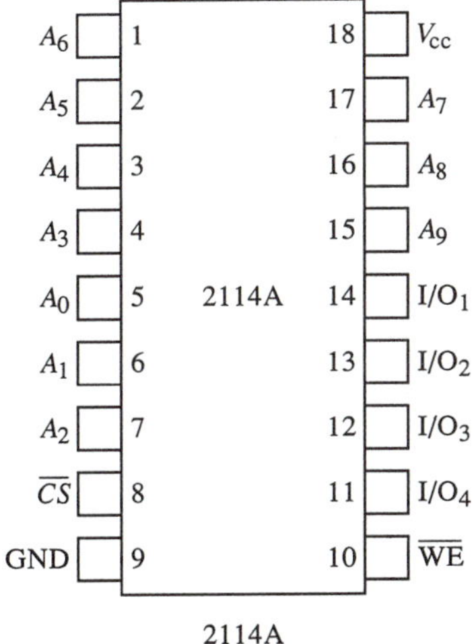
$A_6$ 1 18 $V_{cc}$
$A_5$ 2 17 $A_7$
$A_4$ 3 16 $A_8$
$A_3$ 4 15 $A_9$
$A_0$ 5 2114A 14 $I/O_1$
$A_1$ 6 13 $I/O_2$
$A_2$ 7 12 $I/O_3$
$\overline{CS}$ 8 11 $I/O_4$
GND 9 10 $\overline{WE}$
2114A

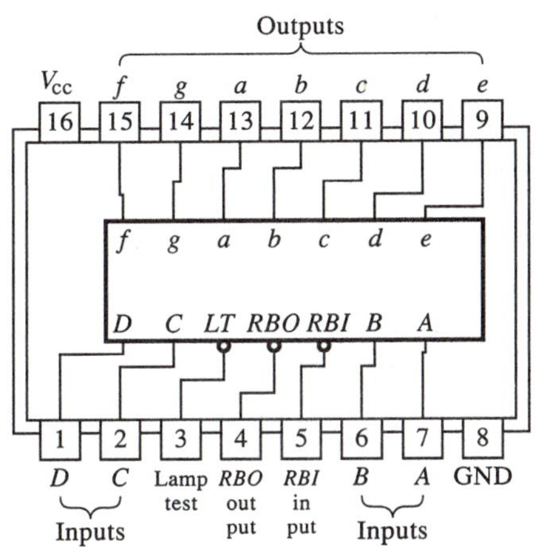
Outputs
$V_{cc}$ $f$ $g$ $a$ $b$ $c$ $d$ $e$
16 15 14 13 12 11 10 9
$f$ $g$ $a$ $b$ $c$ $d$ $e$
$D$ $C$ $LT$ $RBO$ $RBI$ $B$ $A$
1 2 3 4 5 6 7 8
$D$ $C$ Lamp test $RBO$ out put $RBI$ in put $B$ $A$ GND
Inputs
Inputs
74248

# APPENDIX 5

# THE MC6800, PIA, AND ACIA CHIPS

## AN OVERVIEW

This appendix summarizes the MC6800 CPU signals and the programming and interfacing aspects of the parallel peripheral interface adaptor (PIA) and the asynchronous communication interface adaptor (ACIA) chips. The PIA and ACIA are support chips for the Motorola 6800 family of CPUs and their signals are compatible with those of the 6800.

All three chips are NMOS devices whose signal levels are compatible with TTL. Their fan-out parameters are, however, smaller than for typical TTL devices.

We have examined the functions of the PIA and ACIA in the main text; this appendix contains only the pertinent technical information.

## A5.1 THE MC6800 CPU

Figure A5.1 shows the pinout of the 6800.

We have explained most of the signals in detail in the main text and the following is only a brief summary:

$\overline{HALT}$ Lets the CPU finish the current instruction, halts it, activates $BA$ and $VMA$, and floats $R/\overline{W}$ and the address and data bus

$\Phi_1$ Phase 1 of CPU clock

$\overline{IRQ}$ Maskable interrupt

$VMA$ Valid memory address: activated when the CPU puts a valid address on the address bus

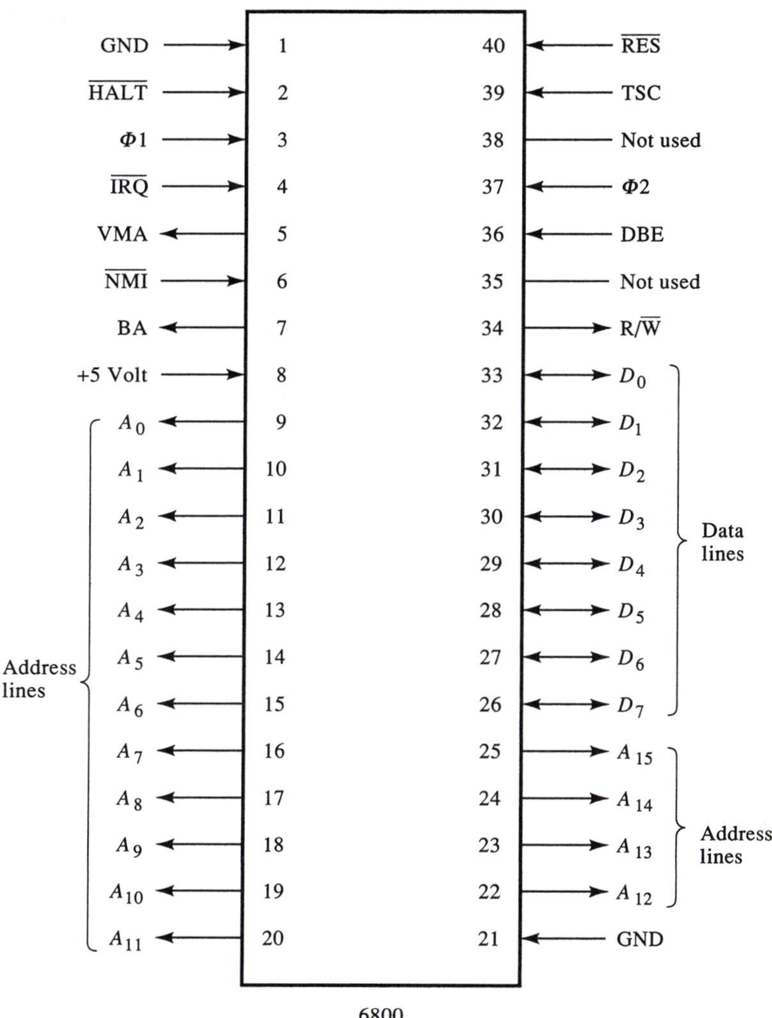


**Figure A5.1.** Pinout of the 6800.

$\overline{NMI}$ Nonmaskable interrupt

$BA$ Bus available; active when data and address pins are floated

$A_{15} \ldots A_0$ Address bus

$D_7 \ldots D_o$ Data bus

$R/W$ Read/write: active for reading

$DBE$ Data bus enable; enables or disables (tristates) CPU data pins

$\Phi_2$ Phase 2 of CPU clock

*TSC* Tristate control: floats address and $R/W$ pins, and deactivates *VMA* and *BA* when active; must not stay active longer than 9.5 $\mu$sec, pin $\Phi_1$ must be held High, $\Phi_2$ Low when *TSC* is active

$\overline{RES}$ Starts the CPU from power down or after reset.

## A5.2 THE MC6821 PIA

The PIA is Motorola's parallel interface chip whose signals are compatible with 6800 CPU family devices (Figure A5.2). Functions of the individual pins follow on the facing page.

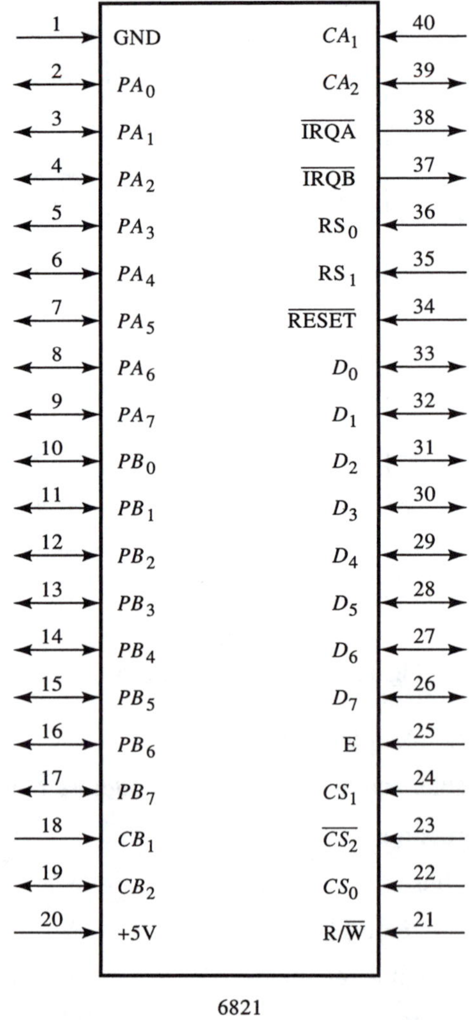


**Figure A5.2.** Pinout of the PIA.

$PA_7 \ldots PA_0$ Port $A$ data lines on device side

$PB_7 \ldots PB_0$ Port $B$ data lines on device side

$CB_1$ Input control line 1 for port $B$: See below.

$CB_2$ Input/output control line 2 for port $B$: See below.

$R/W$ Read/write: connected to the 6800 $R/W$ line.

$CS0$, $CS1$, $\overline{CS2}$ Chip select input for $CS = CS0 \cdot CS1 \cdot \overline{CS2}$.

$E$ Timing signal used for loading internal registers and other internal operations. It is normally connected to the $\Phi_2$ clock signal of the CPU.

$D_7 \ldots D_0$ Data pins on the CPU side.

$\overline{\text{RESET}}$ Resets all internal PIA registers to 0.

$RS_1$, $RS_0$ Register select: addressing of internal registers.

$\overline{IRQA}$, $\overline{IRQB}$ Interrupt requests from ports $A$ and $B$. Both are "open collector" circuits and can be tied together to the $IRQ$ input of the CPU.

$CA_1$ Input control line 1 for port $A$: See below.

$CA_2$ Input/output control line 2 for port $A$: See below.

The functions of the PIA include latching of data on output, automatic generation of handshaking sequences, and automatic activation and deactivation of an interrupt signal.

The PIA consists of two nearly identical ports called $A$ and $B$. Each has an eight-bit control register, an eight-bit data direction register, and an eight bit data register. The operation of each port of the PIA is determined by the code stored in its control register by the CPU, and the direction of individual data lines (input or output) is given by the values stored in the data direction registers.

The functions of individual bits of the control register are almost identical for the $A$ and $B$ ports and the following description is formulated in terms of the $A$ port. Differences are noted where appropriate. Bits 7 and 6 are PIA outputs for the CPU. The remaining bits are PIA inputs written by the CPU and determine the PIA's mode of operation.

Bit 7—*CAL* status flag. Set High by the PIA when signal *CA1* makes an active transition. It is automatically cleared when the PIA reads the data register of port $A$ or when the hardware reset signal is activated. This function is used for polling so that if there are several interrupting devices, the CPU can determine which one activated the *IRQ* signal.

Bit 6—*CA2* status flag/control output. Similar to Bit 7 but goes High on active transitions of *CA2* when *CA2* is programmed as input (bit 5 = 0). This bit has no function when *CA2* is established as output (bit 5 = 1).

Bit 5—*CA2* operation. Storing 0 (1) in this bit establishes *CA2* as input (output).

Bits 4 and 3—*CA2* control. Function of these bits depends on bit 5.

When *CA2* is programmed as input (bit 5 = 0), bit 4 determines what constitutes an active *CA2* transition: When bit 4 = 0, the active transition is High → Low; when it is 1, the active transition is Low → High. Bit 3 controls interrupt; a value 0/(1) disables/(enables) *IRQA* on *CA2* active transition.

When *CA2* is programmed as output (bit 5 = 1), bit 4 = 0 is used to establish the handshaking mode; bit 4 = 1 is used to write to *CA2* through the control register. The details are as follows:

When bit 4 = 0, then bit 3 = 0 establishes "complete handshake." (*CA2* goes High when *CA1* is activated and turns Low following a CPU *READ* of the data register.) Bit 3 = 1 establishes "partial handshake," (*CA2* goes Low for one cycle following a CPU *READ* of data register.) On port *B*, replace the words "CPU *READ*" with "CPU *WRITE*."

When bit 4 = 1, then *CA2* assumes the value of bit 3. In this way, the CPU can directly set or clear *CA2*.

Bit 2—Access to data/direction register. Direction register is selected when bit 2 = 0; bit 2 = 1 selects the data register. This selection bit is necessary because the PIA does not have enough register select pins to address any of its six registers. The addressing scheme is summarized below.

Bit 1—Active CA1 transition. When bit 1 = 0 then bit 7 is set by a High → Low *CA1* transition from the device. When bit 1 = 1, active *CA1* transition is Low → High.

Bit 0—Interrupt request enable. When bit 0 = 1, activation of *CA1* generates *IRQA*. (*CB1* similarly controls *IRQB*.)

### Addressing of PIA Registers

Pin *RS1* = 0 selects port *A*; *RS1* = 1 selects port *B*. Pin *RS0* = 1 selects the control register and *RS0* = 0 selects either the data register or the data direction register. When *RS0* = 0, the data register is selected if bit 2 of the control register of the selected port is 1; the data direction register is selected otherwise.

### The Data Direction Register

For each data line, the corresponding bit of the data direction register determines whether it is an input or an output. Value $DDR_i = 0$ establishes data line $i$ of this port as input to the PIA (and hence to the CPU), $DDR_i = 1$ configures line $i$ as output from the PIA (CPU).

## PIA Initialization

Before a PIA can be used to transmit data, its mode of operation must be initialized by storing the proper codes in its control registers. This is usually done by resetting the PIA with the reset signal (connected to the 6800's reset) and executing an initialization program. Software initialization of the PIA usually consists of three steps:

1. Clear bit 2 of the control register so that the data direction register can be accessed.
2. Store desired values in data direction registers to establish the required direction of individual PIA data lines.
3. Program individual bits of the control register for the desired mode of operation. Because future access will be to the data register (to perform I/O operations), set bit 2.

If the desired mode operation of the PIA is identical with its default reset mode (all bits in all registers cleared) the first two steps are not necessary. Similarly, if the desired direction of data transfer is the same as the default on (all lines used for input because all *DDR* bits are 0), no software initialization of *DDR* is necessary. Naturally, the PIA may be reprogrammed at any time during program execution as well.

If address decoding is implemented so that the two control registers are assigned consecutive addresses, initialization can be performed simultaneously for both ports as follows:

1a. Load index register for step 1.
 b. Store index register at the address of the first control register. (This programs both control registers.)
2a. Load index register for step 2.
 b. Store index register at the address of the first data direction register. (This programs both direction registers.)
3a. Load index register for step 3.
 b. Store index register at the address of the first control register. (This again programs both control registers.)

Note that this method of PIA addressing also makes the data registers adjacent, which is advantageous when the intended use is for sixteen-bit I/O.

### Differences Between Ports A and B

Our description shows that port *A* is best used for input and port *B* for output. The only other difference between the two is that port *A* lines have open collector outputs while port *B* lines have tristate outputs. Both are TTL compatible with a fan-out of two. In some cases, such as the control of LED lights, PIA output thus requires additional buffering.

An important property of both ports is that while their data output is buffered (the data written by the CPU into a PIA data register remains unchanged until it is rewritten by another CPU instruction), the data input is not. This means that when the CPU reads a PIA data port, it is reading directly from the output of the device connected to the corresponding data lines.

## A5.3 THE MC6850 ACIA

Figure A5.3 shows the ACIA pinout.

The functions of individual pins are as follows:

*RX DATA* Receive data from the serial line.

*RX CLOCK* Clock for the "receive" port.

*TX CLOCK* Clock for the "transmit" port.

$\overline{RTS}$ Request to send, a modem control signal.

*TX DATA* Transmit data to the serial line.

$\overline{IRQ}$ Interrupt request from the ACIA to the $\overline{IRQ}$ pin of the 6800 CPU.

*CS0*, *CS1*, $\overline{CS2}$ Chip select input forming the function CS= $CS0 \cdot CS1 \cdot \overline{CS2}$

*RS* Register select: addressing of internal registers.

$R/\overline{W}$ Read/write: connected to CPU $R/\overline{W}$ line.

*E* Enable: used for communication with the CPU, normally connected to $\Phi_2$.

$D_7 \ldots D_0$ Parallel data pins on the CPU side.

$\overline{DCD}$ Data carrier detect: connected to modem's *DCD* output.

*CTS* Clear to send: connected to modem's *CTS* output.

The ACIA has a receive port and a transmit port. Each has its own data register but both share a control register that is used to program the ACIA mode of operation and a status register. All registers are eight bits wide.

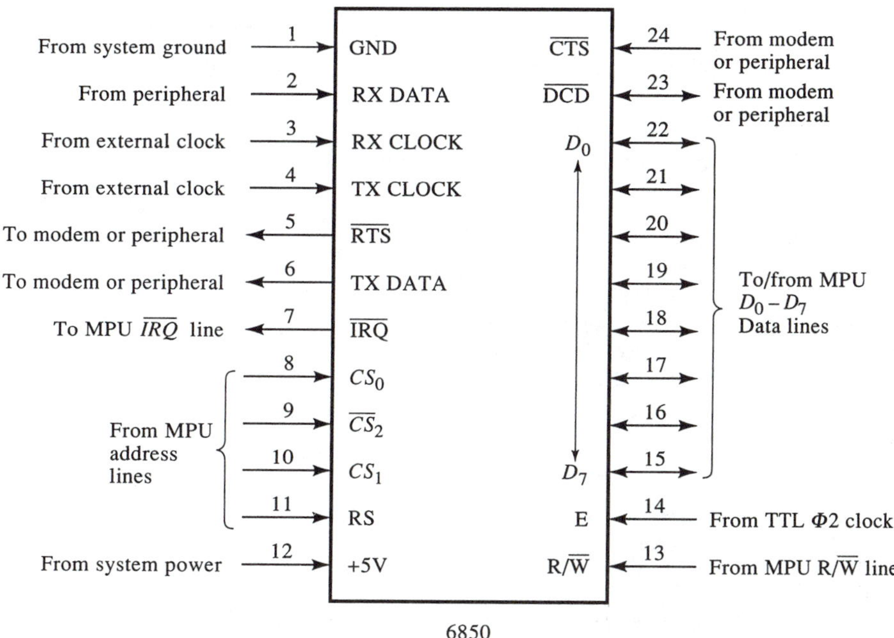


**Figure A5.3.** Pinout of the ACIA.

To send data, the CPU writes data to the transmit data register; to read data received from the serial line, the CPU reads the contents of the data register of the receive port. The selection of the desired register by proper addressing is explained below.

The function of the two ports is to receive the data and convert it from parallel to serial or vice versa, to generate or check the format (start and stop bits and parity), and to exchange control signals with a modem if one is used.

## Control Register

This is a write-only register controlled by the CPU. Its individual bits have the following functions:

Bit 7—Receive interrupt enable. When this bit is set by the CPU, the PIA activates the $IRQ$ signal each time it receives a complete word on its $RX$ data line. When the bit is 0, the PIA does not generate any $\overline{IRQ}$ signals ($IRQ$ is disabled).

Bits 6 and 5—Transmit control.

00 $RTS = 0$, transmit interrupt disabled

01 $RTS = 0$, transmit interrupt enabled

10 $RTS = 1$, transmit interrupt disabled

11 $RTS = 0$, transmit break, transmit interrupt disabled

Signal *RTS* (ready to send) is used to communicate with a modem. When transmit interrupt is enabled, *IRQ* is activated after the word written by the CPU into the transmit register and its frame are completely transmitted. The term "transmit break" means "send logic 0."

Bits 4, 3, and 2—format select. These bits select the format of transmitted or received word as follows:

| Combination | Word Length | Parity | Stop Bits |
|---|---|---|---|
| 000 | 7 | Even | 2 |
| 001 | 7 | Odd | 2 |
| 010 | 7 | Even | 1 |
| 011 | 7 | Odd | 1 |
| 100 | 8 | Even | 2 |
| 101 | 8 | Odd | 1 |
| 110 | 8 | Even | 1 |
| 111 | 8 | Odd | 1 |

Bits 1, 0—Clock divide. Divide the frequency of the transmit and receive clock input or reset (clear) all ACIA registers.

00 Divide clock by 1

01 Divide clock by 16

10 Divide clock by 64

11 Reset ACIA

Note that although "transmit" and "receive" functions share the same division factor, they have separate clock inputs and could operate at different frequencies.

### Status Register

This is a read-only register whose function is to report on various error conditions and on the status of the modem (if one is used). The status register is used for polling so that the CPU can determine which of several interrupting devices activated *IRQ*.

Bit 7—*IRQ*. Set when the ACIA activates *IRQ*. If the ACIA is programmed to generate *IRQ* for both transmit and receive, bits 0 and 1 must be checked to determine the cause of the interrupt. It is automatically cleared when the CPU reads the receive register, writes to the transmit register, or resets the ACIA.

Bit 6—Parity error. Set when the received word's parity disagrees with the programmed parity and cleared when a new word is received or by reset.

Bit 5—Overrun error. Set when a new character is received before the old character was read by the CPU. It is cleared by reading the receive register or master reset.

Bit 4—Framing error. Value 1 indicates the absence of the first bit, which could be due to improper synchronization or transmission.

Bit 3, 2—Modem status. Bit 2 = 0 implies that no data carrier has been detected (*DCD*). Bit 3 = 0 means clear to send (*CTS*).

Bit 1—Transmit register empty. Set when transmit register is empty, indicating that the ACIA is ready for another code. It is cleared when the CPU writes a new word or by master reset.

Bit 0—Receive register full. Set when a new word is ready for the CPU. It is cleared by reading the word or by master reset.

### ACIA Addressing

The ACIA has a single register select signal and four registers, but two of the registers are read-only and two are write-only. Consequently, the following combinations of RS and R/$\overline{\text{W}}$ are used to access the four registers:

| | |
|---|---|
| R/$\overline{\text{W}}$ = 0, RS = 0 | Write to control register |
| R/$\overline{\text{W}}$ = 0, RS = 1 | Write to transmit register |
| R/$\overline{\text{W}}$ = 1, RS = 0 | Read from status register |
| R/$\overline{\text{W}}$ = 1, RS = 1 | Read from receive register. |

### Initialization of the ACIA

On power up, the ACIA should be reset with the signal used to reset the 6800 CPU. Software initialization or resetting of an ACIA consists of two steps:

1. Perform software master reset by writing 1 to bits 0 and 1 of the control register.
2. Program the control register for the desired mode of operation (clock division rate, frame format, and interrupt options).

The sequence is performed by loading the desired bit combinations in a CPU accumulator and storing the accumulator at the address assigned to the ACIA.

## REFERENCE

The following book listed in the references at the end of the book is relevant to this chapter:

R. Bishop. *Basic Microprocessors and the 6800.*

# APPENDIX 6

# A SET OF ALTERNATIVE LOGIC SYMBOLS

Although the symbols that we have introduced for logic gates and other components are widely used, a new set of symbols recommended for use by professional engineers is also available. Unlike the old convention, this is a formal standard adopted by IEEE in 1984 under the name IEEE 91-1984. The new symbols are rectangular and thus easier to draw, stress the placement of inputs on the left and outputs on the right; define a set of basic blocks from which composite symbols can be derived; and allow the designer to indicate components packaged together in a single chip.

Most textbooks and trade magazines still use the old symbols, which are, in fact, also permitted by the new standard. Some publications (databooks), however, use the new standard. We will explain several examples below.

Figure A6.1 shows the new symbol for a NAND gate, used here to describe the 7400 quad two-input NAND consisting of four identical gates. Note the

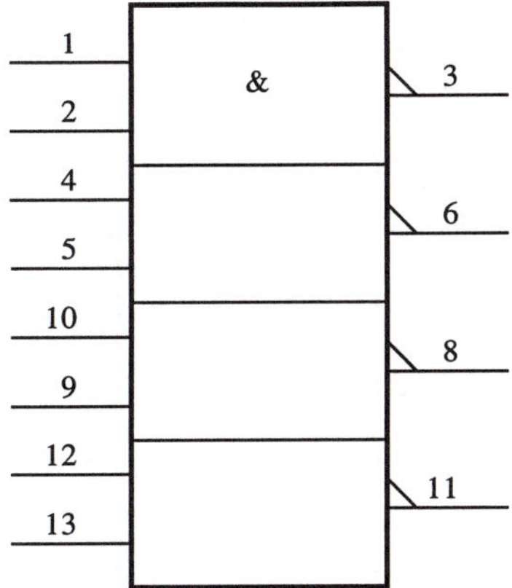


**Figure A6.1.** Equivalent of the 7400 quad two-input NAND.

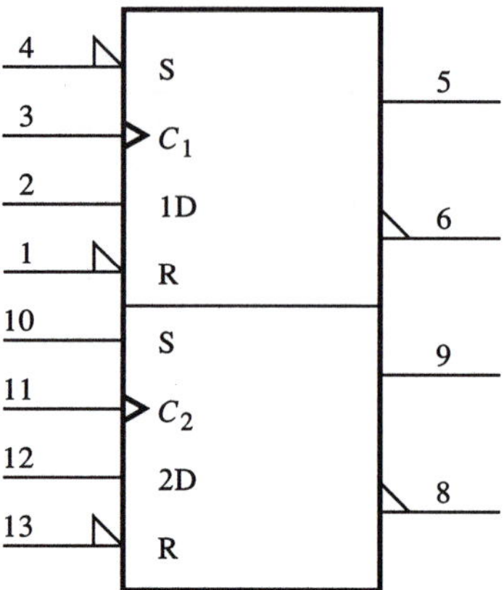


**Figure A6.2.** Representation of the 7474 dual positive-edge triggered D-flip-flop.

symbol "&" that indicates the AND function, the pin numbers (with inputs on the left and outputs on the right), and the triangle, which indicates negation.

Figure A6.2 shows the representation of the 7474 dual D-flip-flop. Note the triangle inside the rectangle indicating that the clock input is edge sensitive, and the triangles outside the rectangle indicating negated (active Low) inputs and outputs.

Our last example in Figure A6.3 shows how a 74138 3-to-8 decoder would be represented by combining simpler symbols. Note that the code inputs are

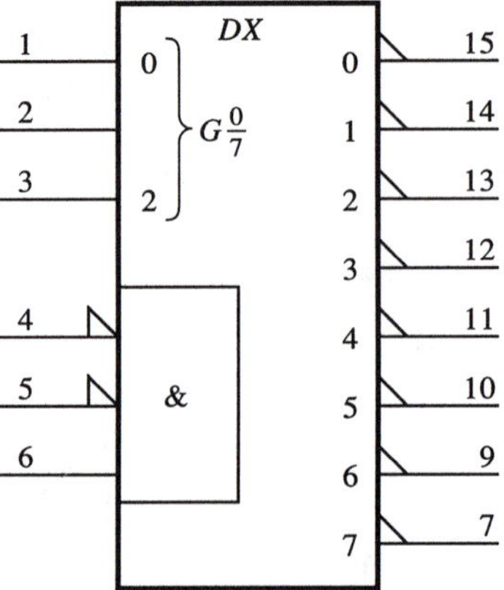


**Figure A6.3.** Representation of the 74138 3-to-8 decoder.

marked with a *G* and indicate that three inputs are decoded into eight lines. The enable inputs are shown as a three-input AND gate with two of its inputs active Low. All outputs are active Low. The symbol "DX" indicates that the component can be used as demultiplexer.

All information about individual symbols and the rules for their combinations can be found in the IEEE standard whose full name is given in the references.

# GLOSSARY

**Absolute Addressing** Form of addressing in which the full code of data or destination addresses is included in the instruction.

**Access Time** The time needed to read data from memory.

**Accumulator** Internal CPU register for intermediate results.

**ACIA (Asynchronous Communication Interface Adaptor)** An integrated circuit performing serial–parallel code conversion and related functions; Motorola's name for UART.

**Activation Record** A data structure containing all information about the currently active procedure or function. It is used in the execution of high-level language programs.

**Active** The logic state in which a signal executes its nominal function. Active Low (High) signals are operative when the signal value is logic 0 (logic 1).

**Address** Code identifying a memory location.

**Address Space** All of the memory addresses theoretically accessible to a CPU.

**Addressing Mode** Procedure used to calculate memory addresses from the code of the instruction.

**Alphanumeric Character** Letter, digit, or punctuation symbol.

**ALU (Arithmetic Logic Unit)** A combinational circuit that performs a variety of arithmetic and logic operations.

**Analog Computer** A computer based on analog (continuous) rather than discrete interpretation of signals.

**Analog Signal** A signal whose value anywhere in a given range is a valid continuous signal.

**AND** Logic product; yields logic 1 iff all inputs are 1.

**ANSI (American National Standards Institute)** Also used to refer to the character code standard approved by ANSI.

**Application Program** A program written for a specific application, such as a word processor, spread sheet, or a game.

**Arithmetic Shift** Shift in which the sign bit is treated separately and whose effect on flags is different than that of Logic Shift.

**Array Processor** A parallel architecture in which each in a group of processors executes the same instruction on its allocated data.

**ASCII (American Standard Code for Information Interchange)** The most common coding convention for the representation of printable and control characters.

**ASIC (Application Specific Integrated Circuit)** A chip developed for a special application using a highly automated design method.

**Assembler** Translator from assembly language to machine code.

**Assembly Language** A programming language based on the symbolic representation of machine instructions.

**Associative Memory** Memory in which locations are addressed by their contents rather than address; also called "content addressable."

**Asynchronous Circuit** A sequential circuit in which at least one storage element is not controlled by the master clock.

**Asynchronous Communication** Communication in which transmitted messages may arrive at random times. It requires transmission of synchronizing information known as the frame.

**Asynchronous Event** An event that may occur at any time without any relation to the circuit clock.

**Baud** Unit of data transfer equal to the number of state changes per second. Usually synonymous with bit per second (bps).

**BCD** Binary coded decimal number representation.

**Biased Representation** Shifted representation of exponent in floating-point numbers.

**Bidirectional** Referring to a path on which signals can travel in both directions; the opposite of unidirectional.

**Bi-MOS** Combination of bipolar and MOS technologies on one chip.

**Binary** A digital signal that can assume one of two values.

**Binary Logic** Set of rules for operations based on 0/1 values.

**BIOS (Basic Input/Output System)** A part of the operating system that is concerned with low-level functions, mainly access to peripherals.

**Bipolar** Semiconductor technology using carriers of both polarities.

**Bistable** An element with two stable states.

**Bit (Binary digit)** A single binary value.

**Bits Per Second (BPS)** Unit of information transfer rate.

**Black Box** A device with controllable inputs and observable outputs, but unknown internal structure.

**Block Diagram** High-level graphical representation of the structure of a circuit that shows the main connections and modules.

**Boolean** Synonym for Binary Logic.

**Bootstrapping** The process by which a small memory resident part of a large program initiates loading of the whole program.

**Branch Instruction** Usually refers to a jump instruction with relative addressing.

**Breadboard** A board used for experiments and prototypes. It is usually equipped with special contacts to allow easy wire connections.

**Breakpoint** An instruction in a program used during debugging. When reached, the program halts and the user can examine and modify memory and registers.

**Bubble Memory** Nonvolatile read–write sequential memory based on solid state magnetic principles.

**Buffer** In the hardware sense, a component that amplifies a signal without changing its logic value or a component holding data until it is transmitted to another device; in the software sense, a memory area used to hold data sent from one process to another, particularly in input/output operations.

**Burn-in** Period of increased stress during component testing.

**Burst Transfer** Transfer of a whole block of data at a time.

**Bus** A collection of wires that carries related signals such as address or data.

**Byte** Group of eight bits.

**Cache Memory** A small, fast memory inserted between the CPU and the main memory or disk controller to speed up memory access.

**CAD** Computer-aided design. Design based on computer tools.

**CAE** Computer-aided engineering.

**CAM** Computer-aided manufacturing.

**Canonic Form** In our context, a sum-of-products, or product-of-sums, representation in which each term contains all variables.

**Carry Flag** A CPU flag containing the carry or borrow resulting from the last arithmetic operation.

**CAT** Computer-aided testing.

**Character** Letter, digit, punctuation, or control symbol.

**Character Generator** Integrated circuit converting ASCII codes to dot patterns for display on a cathode-ray tube terminal or on a dot matrix printer.

**Chip** A small piece of semiconductor material containing a multitransistor electronic circuit; also used for a packaged integrated circuit.

**Chip Enable/Select** A signal that activates a chip.

**Circuit Board** A collection of interconnected devices mounted on a baseboard.

**Clear** An input that clears the stored value to 0.

**Clock** A source of regular pulses.

**Clock Skew** Delay between clock edges.

**C-MOS (Complementary MOS)** Logic family using complementary pairs of N-MOS and P-MOS transistors; features very low power consumption and high noise immunity.

**Code** Group of bits representing information; often used as synonym for program.

**Code Generator** The part of compiler that outputs object code and performs related functions.

**Collating sequence** The order in which symbols are assigned consecutive codes.

**Combinational** Memoryless, producing output by combining current inputs.

**Combinational Circuit** Consisting of gates or gate-based devices without feedback.

**Command Interpreter** The part of operating system that reads user commands and initiates appropriate functions.

**Compiler** A program translating source code to object code, for example, a Pascal program to instructions of the 6800 CPU.

**Complement** Representing the negated value of a number or signal.

**Computer Architecture** Programmer's and system designer's view of a computer including parameters such as the instruction set, size and use of programmable registers, and interfacing signals.

**Computer Organization** Designer's view of a computer including internal buses, control unit design, and so on.

**Computer Terminal** Combination of a keyboard and display or printer.

**Condition Code Register** CPU register whose individual bits (flags) contain the status of the CPU and information on results of CPU operation: These include the interrupt flag, carry flag, zero flag, etc.

**Conditional Jump** Program jump whose execution depends on the validity of a condition, such as the presence of overflow or carry.

**Control Graph** A graphical representation of the sequencing of internal states and its dependence on input.

**Control Memory** Control store.

**Control Signal** A signal that controls an internal operation or data transfer.

**Control Signal Generator** Circuit producing control signals.

**Control Store** The memory holding the microprogram.

**Control Unit** Circuit controlling the operation of a larger sequential circuit, such as a CPU.

**Coprocessor** A processor attached to the CPU to speed up the execution of a function, such as floating-point arithmetic.

**Counter** A circuit counting clock pulses and producing the code of the count; also a circuit generating any regular sequence of codes in step with a clock signal.

**CPU (Central Processing Unit)** Sequential circuit that decodes and executes binary instructions.

**Critical Race** A race that results in incorrect transition.

**Crossassembler** An assembler running on one CPU but producing code for another.

**CRT (Cathode Ray Tube)** The most common form of computer display. Its operation is based on the fact that an electron beam creates a visible spot when it strikes a layer of phosphorus.

**CRT Controller (CRTC)** Circuit controlling all the parameters of a CRT display, such as the intensity of displayed dots and their position on the screen.

**Current Loop** A method of transferring digital data in which 0s and 1s are represented by the presence or absence of an electric current.

**Custom Chip** A chip designed from level building blocks for a specialized application.

**Cycle Stealing** A direct memory access method in which the controller disables the CPU and uses its clock and the system bus to transfer data.

**Cycle Time** The time between successive accesses to a memory device.

**D-Element** Memory element (latch or flip-flop) that copies its input when enabled.

**Dataflow Computer** A computer in which instructions are not executed in the order in which they are stored but in the order in which they receive operands.

**Data Selector** Multiplexer.

**Data Transfer Rate** The number of bits transferred in one second.

**Decoder** A combinational circuit that recognizes one of several possible input codes and activates a corresponding output line.

**DeMorgan's Laws** Rules relating logic sums; products; and negations.

**Demultiplexer (DEMUX)** A circuit that sends an input data signal to one of many output lines. The line is selected by a select code.

**Deterministic Behavior** Behavior that can be accurately predicted.

**Device Driver** A program controlling access to an input/output device.

**Dielectric** Material insulating the plates of a capacitor.

**Digital Signal** A signal that can assume only one of a finite number of values. Opposite of analog signal.

**Digital System** A larger circuit in which a control unit determines the order of operations.

**Diode** A two-terminal electronic component that conducts in one direction only.

**Direct Addressing** On the 6800 CPU, an addressing mode in which the first half of the address is implied to be zero; also known as "page-zero addressing."

**Direct Memory Access (DMA)** The fastest method of data transfer in which a DMA controller disables the CPU and assumes control over the system bus.

**Discrete Signal** Signal that can have only one of a fixed number of values. Opposite of an analog signal.

**Disk Drive** Electromechanical assembly whose purpose is to rotate a magnetic disk and position read/write heads.

**Disk Drive Controller** The interface circuit mediating between high-level commands and data transfers on the CPU side and low-level operations on the disk drive side.

**DMA Controller (DMAC)** Circuit controlling direct memory access transfers.

**Don't Care** A signal value that has no effect on the correct operation of a circuit.

**Dopant** Material introduced into a pure semiconductor to modify its resistance.

**DOS** Disk Operating System. Common name for operating systems of small computers equipped with floppy or hard disk drives.

**Dot matrix Printer** Printer whose output is formed by dot patterns.

**Double Rail** Logic circuit in which both the true and inverted inputs are available.

**DRAM (Dynamic Random Access Memory)** A semiconductor RAM whose contents must be periodically refreshed. *See also* static RAM.

**Driving Capability** Ability to supply signals of sufficient power to other components.

**Driver** A component that generates a strong output signal to drive more than the usual number of devices, a long line, or a power hungry component such as a light or a relay.

**Dual In-Line Package (DIL)** Integrated Circuit package with two parallel rows of pins.

**Duty Cycle** Normally, the ratio of the length of the active part of a clock cycle to the full cycle length; sometimes defined as the ratio of active to nonactive part.

**Dynamic Data** Data created and destroyed during program execution.

**Dynamic Hazard** The occurrence of more than one transition when a single one was expected.

**EBCDIC** Extended Binary Coded Decimal Interchange Code. An eight-bit IBM precursor of ASCII.

**ECC** Error correcting code.

**ECL (Emitter-coupled logic)** The fastest logic family; based on bipolar transistors.

**EDC** Error detecting code.

**Edge** Either of the transitions 0 → or 1 → 0.

**Edge-triggered** Responding to a change in signal level rather than to the level itself.

**EEPROM** Electrically erasable programmable read-only memory.

**EIA** Electronic Industries Association, an institution known for its electronic standards (such as RS-232-C).

**Effective Address** The actual address as opposed to a code from which the address must be calculated.

**Electron Beam Lithography** A controlled beam of electrons used to reproduce mask patterns. Can produce lines less than 1 $\mu$ thick.

**Encoder** Circuit converting one code to another.

**EPROM (Erasable programmable read-only memory)** Some can be erased by ultraviolet light or electric current and reprogrammed.

**Error Recovery** The process of recovering from an error state or illegal input without crashing, for example, in compilers.

**Essential Prime Implicant** A prime implicant that must be included in the final formula to implement the given logic function.

**Excitation Function or Table** Functional or tabular representation of the input of memory elements of a sequential circuit.

**Exclusive OR** Logic operation that yields 1 iff an odd number of inputs are 1.

**Extended addressing** Motorola's name for absolute addressing on the 6800 family of CPUs.

**Fail-safe** System that can shut down safely and possibly maintain limited operation in case of failure.

**Fall time** Duration of the transition from logic 1 to logic 0.

**Family** A collection of integrated circuits using a single basic circuit pattern, physical principle, and set of basic parameters. Examples: C-MOS, MOS, TTL.

**Fan-in** Number of unit loads represented by one input pin. Also used to refer to the collection of inputs of a device.

**Fan-out** Number of unit loads that a given output pin can drive. Also used to refer to the collection of outputs of a device.

**Fault** Permanent or intermittent circuit failure.

**Feedback** Connection from an output of a component that leads (directly or indirectly) to its own input.

**Fetch/Execute Phase** The two major parts of the execution of computer instruction consisting of the fetch of the code and its decoding and execution.

**Field Effect** An electronics principle where the flow through the signal path of a transistor is controlled by an electric field produced by the control signal. Used by the field-effect transistor (FET).

**FIFO** First-in first-out.

**Firmware** Program or microprogram stored in a read-only memory.

**Fixed-point (FP) Representation** Number representation with a fixed position of the imaginary decimal point.

**Flag** A flip-flop used to record the CPU state or the result of executing an instruction. Examples: carry flag, interrupt flag.

**Flip-flop** Basic storage component normally controlled by the edge of a clock signal.

**Floated** Electrically disconnected or equivalent signal.

**Floating-point (FLP) Representation** Number representation allowing a wide range of values. It is based on a signed normalized magnitude and a scaling factor.

**Floppy Disk** A secondary memory storage medium.

**Formatting** Initializing the internal structure of a secondary storage medium such as a tape or disk.

**Forward Reference** The use of an identifier, such as variable or a procedure name, before it is declared in the program.

**Frame** In asynchronous communication, bits added to transmitted data for synchronization.

**GaAs (Gallium arsenide)** Semiconductor material that allows faster switching but is more expensive and not as well mastered as silicon.

**Gate** The physical implementation of one of the basic combinational functions. When used as verb, the control of a signal path by a gate.

**Gate Equivalent** A circuit treated as a standard circuit in a given logic family. Example: A two-input NAND gate in TTL.

**Gate Level** The study of a digital system at the level of logic 0/1 signals.

**Glitch** An unwanted brief transition on a signal line.

**Grammar** A set of formal rules defining a programming language.

**Ground** 0 volts.

**Handshaking** A sequence of logically interlocking signals exchanged by two communicating systems to guarantee faultless communication.

**Hard Failure** Permanent failure.

**Hardwired** Fixed in hardware rather than controlled by a program.

**Hardwired Control Unit** A control unit that is implemented fully by combinational and memory components.

**Hazard** A circuit structure that may cause one or more spurious transitions because of unbalanced delays of interacting logic signals; also, the malfunction itself.

**Heap** A data structure used to store dynamic data, such as records accessed by pointers.

**Heap Manager** Program that manages the heap during execution.

**Hexadecimal** Base-16 number representation using letters A to F to represent values 10 to 15.

**Hidden Bit** Implied leading 1 in a floating-point mantissa.

**High** The higher of two voltage levels used by the logic circuit. Its exact value depends on the logic family used.

**High Impedance** In tristate devices, a synonym of "floated."

**High-Level Language** A symbolic programming language in which algorithms are specified in a form resembling natural language.

**Hold Time** Length of time specified by the manufacturer for which an input signal must remain stable after the occurence of an event (typically a clock edge).

**Horizontal Microprogramming** Microprogram format where individual instruction bits represent individual control signals.

**Hybrid** An integrated circuit obtained by interconnecting several chips in one package.

**Hz (Hertz)** One cycle or event per second.
**IEEE (Institute of Electrical and Electronics Engineers)** An institution that among other activities defines standards.
**Immediate Addressing** Addressing method in which the value of the operand is included in the instruction code.
**Implied Addressing** Addressing method in which the operand is not specified by an address but is implied by the instruction code.
**Implied Logic** The logic function obtained by connecting outputs of open collector gates together; also, "wired logic."
**Index Register** A CPU register used to hold an offset for calculating addresses in Indexed Addressing.
**Indexed Addressing** An addressing method in which the effective address is the sum of the current contents of the index register and an offset given in the instruction.
**Indirect Addressing** An addressing method in which the effective address is found in the memory location whose address is given in the instruction code.
**Inherent Addressing** Synonym of "Implied addressing."
**Instruction** The lowest level computer command accessible to a programmer. According to its type, an instruction can control the flow of program execution, process data, transfer data, or perform other functions.
**Instruction Decoder** The part of the CPU's control unit that recognizes the desired operation from an instruction code.
**Instruction Register** A register used by the CPU to hold the instruction code during its decoding and execution.
**Instruction Set** The collection of all instructions available on a given CPU.
**Integrated Circuit (IC)** A circuit of interconnected transistors and resistors fabricated on a single chip; Synonym of "chip." The term refers both to the electronic circuit and to the sealed package with pins.
**Interface** The physical or logical boundary between two hardware systems or programs.
**Interleaved Memory** Memory in which consecutive addresses are interleaved between different chips to speed up access.
**Interpreter** A program that translates and immediately executes programs written in a high-level language.
**Interrupt** A signal generated by a device external to the CPU that indicates the device requires attention. If the CPU is ready to accept it, it completes the current instruction, executes the interrupt handler, and returns. On many CPUs, a hardware interrupt can be simulated by a special instruction.
**Interrupt Arbitration** THe process of deciding which of several active interrupts should be serviced first.
**Interrupt-Driven I/O** Input/output operation that is activated by an interrupt signal from the I/O device.
**Interrupt Handler** A program executed when an interrupt is activated.
**Interrupt Latency** The time elapsed between the activation of the interrupt signal and the start of execution of the interrupt handler.
**Interrupt Table** A table of the starting addresses of all interrupt handlers available on a given computer. The CPU automatically selects the correct entry on the basis of the parameters of the interrupt signal or instruction.
**Interrupt Vector** The starting address of an interrupt routine.

**I/O** Input/Output.
**I/O Driver** See Device driver.
**I/O Port** An address reserved for an I/O device, possibly including the interface as well.
**I/O Processor** A specialized computer that performs I/O operations under the control of the main CPU.
**I/O Space** On computers with I/O instructions, the range of addresses available for access to I/O devices.
**JEDEC (Joint Electronic Devices Engineering Council)** An organization that formulates standards for integrated circuits.
**JK-Flip-Flop** A flip-flop whose two inputs can set, store, or toggle the internal state.
**Jump Instruction** An instruction that forces the CPU to continue execution from a specified address rather than the address following the instruction as normally happens.
**k** Normally 1000, but in computing context $1024 = 2^{10}$.
**Karnaugh Map** A representation of a truth table that allows visual minimization of combinational circuits.
**Keyboard Encoder** A circuit used to detect key closure, perform key debouncing, and calculate key code.
**Keyboard Matrix** A two-dimensional arrangement of keys that simplifies the necessary electronic and decoding circuitry.
**Label** An identifier representing a place (address) in a program.
**Latch** Basic storage component controlled by the level of an enable signal.
**LCD (Liquid-Crystal Display)** Used as an alternative to LEDs and CRT displays.
**LED (Light Emitting Diode)** A diode that produces light in the conducting state.
**Lexical Analyzer** The part of a high-level language translator that is responsible for reading the stream of source code characters, removing irrelevant information, and assembling terminals; also called the "scanner."
**Linker** A program that combines assembled or compiled program modules into a single executable program.
**Lithography** Method of transferring a circuit pattern (mask) to a chip.
**Loader** A program that loads executable code from a file into memory for execution.
**Location Counter** A variable used by the assembler to keep track of the address of the next object code.
**Logic Diagram** Graphical representation of the structure of a circuit at the level of signal connections, gates, flip-flops, and similar low level components; intermediate between block diagrams and wiring diagrams.
**Logic Family** See Family.
**Logic Shift** Left or right shift in which a 0 is shifted in at one end of the code and the bit at the other end is lost.
**Low** The lower of the two voltage levels used by a logic circuit. Its value depends on the logic family used.
**LSB (Least Significant Bit)** The rightmost of a group of bits.
**LSI (Large-Scale Integration)** Level of circuit integration corresponding approximately to 100–1000 gate equivalents per chip.
**Machine Cycle** Time segment determined by the system clock; elementary unit of time in the execution of an instruction.

**Machine Instruction** See Instruction.
**Macro** A named sequence of instructions that can be executed as a single command or used as a programming shorthand in a program. The term is most often used in the context of assembly language programming.
**Magnetic Bubble Memory** See Bubble Memory.
**Main Memory** Memory accessed by the CPU during instruction and data fetches.
**Mantissa** The value part (value, scaling factor) of the code of a floating-point number.
**Mask** In programming, a bit pattern used to modify the value of certain bits in a code; In the fabrication of integrated circuits, the template of a geometric pattern formed on the surface of a chip.
**Maskable Interrupt** An interrupt that is disabled when invoked. It can also be masked by software.
**Master Slave** Flip-flop whose organization does not allow a change to propagate from input to output on a single clock edge.
**Memory** Collection of memory locations used to hold binary codes. See also RAM, ROM, Main, and Secondary Memory.
**Memory Cycle Time** Time in which a new access to the same memory device is permissible.
**Microinstruction** A code whose execution produces a set of control signals or a jump in the microprogram.
**Microprogram** Sequence of microinstructions implementing control of a digital system such as a CPU.
**Microprogrammable** A CPU whose microprogram can be modified by the user.
**Microprogrammed Control Unit** A control unit whose sequencing and control information is embedded in a microprogram.
**Microprogramming** The process of writing a microprogram; also refers to the format of microprogram instructions.
**MIL STD** Military standard for integrated circuit parameters.
**Mnemonic** Symbolic name for an instruction or data item. Mnemonics are used mainly in the context of assembly language programming.
**Modem** A data communication device used to modulate (demodulate) communication signals before (after) transmission.
**Modulation** Transformation of the physical nature of the signal to optimize the efficiency and reliability of its transmission.
**Monitor** Used to refer to the video display unit of a computer; also used to refer to a small operating system.
**Monolithic** A device formed from a single chip.
**MOS** Metal-oxide silicon (field effect) transistor technology.
**MSB (Most Significant Bit)** The leftmost bit in a code.
**MSI (Medium-Scale Integration)** Level of circuit integration corresponding approximately to 10–100 gate equivalents per chip.
**MTBF (Mean Time Between Failures)** Measure of reliability.
**Multiple-valued Logic** A logic system using more than two logic values.
**Multiplexer (MUX)** A circuit that selects one of several input signals and steers it to a single output; also called "data selector."
**Multiprocessor** A computer containing several cooperating processors, each executing its own program.
**Multiprogramming** The use of a single computer for the "simultaneous" execu-

tion of several programs. In reality, the CPU quickly switches from one program to another, often leaving several of them in main memory at the same time.

**Multitasking** Simultaneous execution of several tasks such as program execution and printing.

**NAND** The logic operation NOT AND.

**NAPLPS (North American Presentation-Level Protocol Syntax)** A recent code standard allowing representation of text and graphics elements.

**Negative Logic** Logic interpretation in which Low(High) is treated as logic 1 (0).

**Neural Computing** Computing based on networks of threshold elements with adaptable behavior.

**Nibble** Four bits; one-half of a byte.

**N-MOS (Negative MOS technology)** The densest semiconductor technology now available. It uses negative charge carriers.

**Noise** Undesirable fluctuations of a physical signal caused by external interference or by varying the input or load of the power supply. Noise can lead to the misinterpretation of logic levels.

**Noise Immunity** The ability of a logic component to correctly interpret signals even when affected by noise.

**Noise Margin** The difference between the output and input limits on voltage level for logic 0 or 1. A quantitative measure of noise immunity.

**Noncritical Race** A race that does not produce an incorrect transition.

**Nonmaskable Interrupt** An interrupt that cannot be disabled.

**Nonterminal** An auxiliary grammatical concept like *delcaration* that is replaced by one or more terminals in the program.

**NOR** The logic operation NOT OR.

**Object code** Code produced by the translation of assembly or high-level language source code.

**Octal** Base-8 number representation.

**OEM** Original equipment manufacturer.

**One's Complement** Number representation in which negative numbers are obtained by negating the codes of positive numbers.

**Opcode** Part of an instruction specifying the operation performed by the instruction.

**Open Collector (OC)** A form of TTL logic in which the output stage of the circuit is incomplete. Outputs of several OC devices can be connected together via a pullup resistor. They are used to connect devices to a bus and to supply additional power.

**Operating System** A collection of programs providing the interface between the computer hardware, higher level programs, and the user. Contains the command interpreter and a collection of routines that simplify access to I/O devices and files. On large computers the operating system performs additional functions needed to efficiently use available resources and to share them between several users.

**OR** Logic sum, yields 0 iff all inputs are 0.

**Orthogonal Instruction Set** An instruction set in which parameters like the addressing mode, data type, and instruction type can be combined uniformly, without exceptions.

**Optical Lithography** A lithographic method used in the fabrication of integrated circuits that is based on the use of ordinary light. It is limited to chips with linewidths greater than 1 $\mu$.

**Oscilloscope** An electronic measuring instrument used to display waveforms on a television-like screen.

**Overflow** Situation arising when the magnitude of the result of an arithmetic operation exceeds the maximum value that can be represented with the given number of bits in the code.

**Page** Used to refer to a block of addresses that have a fixed size and start at a certain address pattern, for example, an address ending with eight zeros.

**Page Zero** Page starting at address 0.

**PAL (Programmable Array Logic)** A sum-of-product chip whose second stage connections can be altered.

**Parallel Communication** Communication of complete codes as opposed to bit-by-bit (serial) communication.

**Parallel Interface** An interface that makes possible parallel communication.

**Parity** Odd(even) parity refers to an odd(even) number of 1s in a binary code.

**Parser** Part of a high-level language translator responsible for recognizing grammatic units, such as statements, declarations, and expressions.

**Pass** A single reading and processing pass over a source program.

**PC** Personal computer (usually an IBM PC compatible); used to refer to a personal computer in general. Also, printed circuit.

**Perfect Induction** A method for proving the equivalence of logic expressions.

**Peripheral** Any device outside the CPU main memory core of a computer; synonymous with "I/O device."

**Phase** The timing shift between two clock signals.

**PIA** Peripheral interface adapter. Motorola's integrated circuit for the implementation of parallel interfaces.

**Pinout** The function of individual pins of a chip.

**PLA (Programmable Logic Array)** A sum-of-products chip whose internal connections can all be altered.

**PLD (Programmable Logic Device)** Any combinational or sequential chip that can be tailored for a specific function. Some of the available varieties are PAL, PLA, ROM, PROM.

**P-MOS (Positive MOS technology)** The first successful MOS technology. Now used as part of C-MOS circuits. It is based on positive charge carriers.

**Poll** To test the status of a series of I/O devices to determine which of them requires attention.

**Pop** To remove an item from the top of the stack.

**Port** See I/O Port.

**Positional Representation** Number representation in which each bit position has a fixed numeric weight.

**Positive Logic** Logic interpretation based on treating Low (High) as logic 0 (1).

**Preset** Flip-flop or latch input that sets the stored value to 1.

**Prime Implicant (PI)** In a sum of products or product of sums, a term that cannot be further simplified.

**Printed Circuit Board** A board whose interchip connections and other basic structures are fabricated from a photographically transferred mask.

**Product of Sums** Logic expression consisting of a product of sum terms containing true or negated inputs; an OR/AND formula.

**Program Counter (PC)** A CPU register used to store the address of the next instruction code to be fetched.

**Programmable Integrated Circuit** A chip whose internal configuration can be permanently or semipermanently changed by a special instrument. Also, a chip whose mode of operation can be controlled by external logic signals.

**Programmed I/O** An I/O method in which the CPU is fully in charge of the operation and no initiative or control is left to the I/O device.

**PROM (Programmable Read-Only Memory)** Its contents can be permanently modified by burning internal fuses.

**Propagation Delay** Time needed before the effect of a change in inputs can be observed on the output.

**Protocol** A convention, usually used to control communication between two devices.

**Pseudoinstruction** A command to the assembler requesting, for example, the allocation of space for data or modification of the value in the location counter.

**Pullup Resistor** A resistor connected between a device and the power supply. Used with OC devices, switches, and unused input pins or pins connected permanently to 1.

**Pure Binary** Positional representation of non-negative numbers with no provision for sign.

**Push** To insert an item on the top of a stack.

**Qualifier** A signal that activates an operation when certain conditions are satisfied.

**Quine-McCluskey Method** A classical tabular method for logic minimization. It is formally equivalent to Karnaugh maps but unlimited with respect to the number of variables.

**Race** A situation occurring when several logic signals are to change their logic values at the same time.

**Radix** The base of a decimal system: 2 in binary, 10 in decimal.

**Random Access Memory (RAM)** An array of memory cells that can be read or written in any order.

**Raster Scan Display** Display in which graphics, letters, and other patterns are formed by writing small dots by scanning the beam horizontally and vertically across the screen and controlling its intensity.

**Read Only Memory (ROM)** An array of memory cells that can be read but not written.

**Read-Write Memory** An alternative name for RAM.

**Recursion** A method of defining a concept or specifying an algorithm by reference to itself.

**Recursive Descent Parser** A parser based on procedures derived from Nonterminal definitions (frequently recursive), and starting from the highest level nonterminal of the grammar.

**Redundancy** Circuit duplication in a logic system, usually employed to increase reliability.

**Refresh** Periodic rewriting of dynamic memory or CRT screen to keep the information up to date.

**Register** A group of latches or flip-flops with shared clock signal. Registers usually allow left and/or right internal shifting of bits.

**Register Transfer Level** The view of digital systems as working with codes stored in registers.

**Relative Addressing** A method of specifying addresses in which the effective address is obtained as the sum of the address in the program counter and an offset given in the instruction. The offset is usually in two's complement form.

**Reliability** The ability to perform the desired function over a long period of time.

**Relocatable Code** A block of instructions whose execution is independent of its location in memory.

**Reset** A restart procedure involving the initialization of internal registers and possibly memory locations and I/O devices.

**Ripple-Carry Adder** An adder in which carries propagate from LSB to MSB.

**Rise Time** Duration of a $0 \rightarrow 1$ transition.

**ROM** Read-only memory.

**Rotation** Equivalent to shifting in a circular register. Bits leaving at one end enter at the other end, possibly passing through an additional flip-flop such as the carry flag.

**RS-232-C** A popular standard for serial communication.

**RS-Element** Memory element (or flip-flop) whose two inputs allow setting or clearing of the internal state. One input combination is disallowed.

**Run-Time System** A collection of routines, such as the heap manager, that are required to execute a translated high-level language program.

**Scan Code** Code produced by a keyboard encoder when a key is pressed. The code is usually assigned in geometric fashion; it must be converted to ASCII or another internal code by a program or a ROM.

**Scanner** Synonym for "lexical analyzer;" also used for a device that reads and digitizes an image.

**Secondary Memory** Memory accessed by the CPU as an I/O device, not for instruction and data fetches. It is usually implemented as floppy or hard disk drive or magnetic tape and is used for files containing data or programs.

**Segment** On some CPUs, such as the 8086 family, refers to a fixed-size block of consecutive memory addresses.

**Semantics** Meaning as opposed to form (syntax).

**Semiconductor** A material that forms the basis of integrated circuits, usually silicon. Semiconductors exhibit high resistance in the pure state but relatively low resistance when mixed with dopants.

**Semicustom IC** Integrated circuit fabricated by using predesigned building blocks.

**Sequence Generator** Circuit generating a repetitive pattern of 0s and 1s.

**Sequencer** Circuit enforcing correct state transitions. In combination with signal generator the sequencer forms a control unit.

**Sequential Circuit** Circuit whose operation depends on present and past inputs.

**Serial Communication** Bit-by-bit communication.

**Serial Interface** Interface between a computer and a transmission line that is required for serial communication. The serial interface performs conversion between the parallel form used by computers and the serial form used for communication; voltage conversion may also be included.

**Set** Synonym of "preset."

**Setup Time** Time before the occurrence of an event (usually a clock edge) during which an input signal must remain stable.

**Seven-Segment Digit** A display consisting of seven individually controlled LED segments arranged to allow the display of any digit.

**Shift Register** Register with control inputs for automatic internal shifting.

**Sign-Magnitude Representation** Number representation using a sign bit and a positional value code.

**Signature Analysis** A testing method.

**Signed Representation** Synonym of "two's complement."

**Silicon Compiler** Computer program for automatic chip design.

**Single In-line Package (SIP)** An integrated circuit packaging technique that uses a single row of pins.

**Single Rail** Circuit with true inputs only.

**Skew** The misalignment of edges of two signals (usually clock signals).

**SMD (Surface Mounted Device)** Integrated circuit packaging technology that does not use pins protruding through the board.

**Soft Failure** Intermittent failure.

**Software Interrupt** An instruction producing the same effect as a hardware interrupt signal.

**Source Code** The original form of an assembly or high-level language program as written by the programmer. It is converted to object code by translation.

**SRAM** Static RAM

**SSI (Small-Scale Integration)** Level of circuit integration with up to 10 gate equivalents per chip.

**Stack** A data structure in which new data is pushed on or popped (pulled) from the top with the help of the stack pointer. The stack is essential for nested operations, such as subroutine calls and interrupts at machine level, the execution of certain languages and for the evaluation of arithmetic expressions in compiled code.

**Stack Machine** A CPU in which the most important instructions get their operands and store results on the stack.

**Stack Pointer (SP)** A CPU register whose contents is the address of the top of the stack.

**State** A collection of values characterizing the present condition of a sequential system.

**State Machine** Sequential circuit.

**Static Data** Data that remains active during the entire execution of a program. Example: global variables in a Pascal program.

**Static Hazard** Back and forth transition of a signal that should remain unchanged due to gate delays.

**Static RAM** Type of RAM in which information need not be continuously refreshed.

**Strobe** A signal used to enable a circuit when all other inputs have stabilized.

**Subroutine** Segment of code accessed by a jump-to-subroutine instruction; allows automatic return to the calling code by a return-from-subroutine instruction. A subroutine allows a single copy of a sequence of instructions to be used from an arbitrary location in the program, thus reducing program size.

**Sum of Products** Logic expression consisting of a sum of product terms containing true or negated inputs; an AND/OR formula.

**Symbol Table** A table containing all the names defined in a program and their values. The symbol table is used by assemblers, compilers, and interpreters.

**Synchronous Communication** Communication in which transmission is synchronized by a clock signal shared by the source and the destination. Messages are transmitted in blocks with additional information about their size and structure.

**Synchronous System** System in which successive events are triggered by a clock signal.

**Syntax** Used to refer to the rules of structure of a programming language as opposed to its meaning (semantics).

**Synthesis** Design.

**System Bus** The collection of address, data, and control signals exchanged between the CPU, memory, and peripheral devices.

**System Program** Program facilitating the interface between application programs and peripheral devices and other computer resources or performing other system-related functions. It includes the operating system, compilers, diagnostic programs, and so on.

**T-Flip-Flop** Flip-flop whose one input toggles the internal state.

**Table-Driven Parser** A parser consisting of a language-independent driver program and a language-dependent table. The table is usually generated automatically from a suitable formal description of the grammar of the language.

**Table Generator** A program that produces a parser table from a formal description of the language. It is used by table-driven parsers.

**Terminal** A synonym for a computer terminal; terminal symbol of a language grammar.

**Terminal Symbol** Predefined word of a programming language, such as "BEGIN," "WHILE," ":=" (assignment symbol).

**Test Set** A set of input combinations used to test a logic circuit.

**Testability** The degree to which a logic circuit's operation can be tested.

**Three State Device** Tristate device.

**Threshold Element** A binary computing element producing logic 1 when the weighted sum of its inputs exceeds a threshold.

**Time-Sharing** The use of a single CPU to accommodate several computer terminals by polling and servicing them one at a time.

**Timing Analysis** Analysis of signal delays in a logic circuit to determine the maximum speed of circuit operation.

**Timing Diagram** A diagram showing the dependence of a signal on time.

**Token** In the context of compilation, code representing a language terminal. It is generated by the scanner and processed by the parser.

**Transceiver** A device based on tristate devices that allows controlled bidirectional transfer of data.

**Transfer Rate** Data transfer rate.

**Transient** Intermediate behavior of a signal between stable states.

**Transistor** A three-terminal electronic component that is the basic building block of integrated circuits. Two wires form a signal path; the third determines whether the path is open or closed.

**Transition Diagram** Diagram representing a transition table.

**Transition Table** Table showing state transitions in a sequential circuit as a function of the input combinations that control them.

**Translator** A program that translates from one programming language to another.

**Tristate Device** A device whose output can be floated (deactivated) by an enable signal. It is used wherever several outputs must be connected together.

**TTL (Transistor–Transistor Logic)** A bipolar logic family characterized by its ease of use, relatively high speed, low power consumption and high driving capability, and small density.

**Twisted Pair** A pair of twisted wires, one of which carries the signal and the other its complement or ground voltage. Twisted pairs are used to reduce signal distortion during long-distance transmissions.

**Two-pass Assembler** An assembler that evaluates all symbols in the source code in its first pass over the source code and produces an object code in a second pass.

**Two-Phase Clock** A clock producing two complementary signals. They are frequently used in CPU control to prevent timing conflicts.

**Two's Complement** The most common representation of signed integers.

**UART (Universal Asynchronous Receiver/Transmitter)** An integrated circuit used to convert between parallel format on the device side and serial data on the transmission line side, and to calculate and decode the frame needed in asynchronous communication.

**Unconditional Jump** A jump instruction whose operation does not depend on any conditions.

**Underflow** Situation that arises when the magnitude of the result of an arithmetic operation is smaller than the smallest code allowed in the given representation.

**Unidirectional** Referring to a path on which signal can travel in one direction only.

**Uniprocessor** A computer based on a single CPU.

**Universal gate** Used to refer to NAND and NOR gates because they can each be used to obtain any logic function.

**Unsigned Representation** Pure binary representation.

**USART** Universal Synchronous/Asynchronous Receiver/Transmitter. Similar to UART but can also handle synchronous communication.

**UVPROM** A PROM that is erasable by ultraviolet light.

**VDU (Video Display Unit)** Usually synonymous with "computer terminal."

**Vertical Microprogramming** Microprogram format in which control signals are highly encoded to shorten microinstruction length.

**VHSIC** Very-high-speed integrated circuit.

**VLSI (Very Large-Scale Integration)** Level of chip integration with more than 1000 gate equivalents per chip. (The limit is not firmly established.)

**Volatile Memory** Memory that loses stored data when the power voltage drops below a prescribed value.

**Wafer** A slice of silicon on which an array of chips is fabricated.

**Wire Wrap** A method of connecting devices by wrapping wire around their pins instead of soldering.

**Wired Logic** Implied logic.

**Wiring Diagram** Diagram showing physical components such as integrated circuits and resistors, wires and connections.

**Word** Formerly used to refer to the basic code size of a computer, often the size of the code transmitted between CPU and memory at one time, or to the size of internal CPU data registers; increasingly used to mean two bytes.

**Wrap-around** Transition from one end of the range of a numeric code to its other end: In pure eight-bit binary $255 + 1 = 0$, and $0 - 1 = 255$.

**WSI (Wafer-scale integration)** The use of several chips on a wafer to produce a single device.

**X-Ray Lithography** Use of x-rays to reproduce mask patterns. The method is capable of producing lines less than 1 $\mu$ thick.

**ZIF (Zero insertion force socket)** A socket that requires minimal insertion force and minimizes integrated circuit pin wear. The socket is based on a clamp and used in testers, PROM programmers, and similar instruments.

# REFERENCES

The following is an annotated list of articles, books, databooks, and periodicals.

## ARTICLES


Ashton, Ch., et al. "Designer's Guide to Floating-Point Processing." A three-part sequence in *EDN* starting January 9, 1986. It is an interesting presentation of floating-point standards and hardware.

Caulfield, H. J., J. Neff, and W. T. Rhodes. "Optical Computing: The Coming Revolution in Optical Signal Processing." *IEEE Spectrum* (November 1986). A survey of the present state of development in optical computing.

Chou, S., and C. Simonsen. "Chip Voltage: Why Less Is Better." *IEEE Spectrum* (February 1987). Discussion of the effort to define a new voltage standard for logic chips and the difficulties involved.

Connolly, E. "BiMOS devices give designers the Best of Two Worlds." *Computer Design* (June 1, 1987). State of technology in chips combining bipolar and MOS.

Conrad, M. "The Lure of Molecular Computing." *IEEE Spectrum* (October 1986). An introduction to current research in molecular and biologic computing.

Eastman, L. F. "Ballistic Electrons in Compound Semiconductors." *IEEE Spectrum* (February 1986). An introduction to current research in superfast transistors.

Harold, P. "Memory-Based CMOS FIFO Buffers Sport Large Capacities, Rival the Speed of Bipolars." *EDN* (March 18, 1987). A survey of several recent FIFO chips.

Hutcheson, L. D., and P. Haugen. "Optical Interconnects Replace Hardwire."

*IEEE Spectrum* (March 1987). An overview of the present use of optics in digital communication.

Mosley, J. D. "Static RAMs." *EDN* (January 8, 1987). A survey of the current state of the art with illustrations and descriptions of current approaches.

Smith, D. "Programmable Logic Devices." *EDN* (May 15, 1986). Describes the trends in devices like PLAs and their more complex versions with memory elements and other enhancements. The article contains a directory of recent products and their parameters.

Wright, M. "Dynamic RAMs." *EDN* (February 20, 1986). A survey of the current state of the art with illustrations and descriptions of current approaches.

## BOOKS

Aho, A. V., R. Sethi, and J. D. Ullman. *Compilers: Principles, Techniques, and Tools*. New York: Addison-Wesley, 1986. An advanced book dealing with all aspects of compilation.

Baer, J.-L. *Computer Systems Architecture*. Rockville, Md.: Computer Science Press, 1980. Extensive coverage of theoretical and practical aspects of computer architecture.

Bishop, R. *Basic Microprocessors and the 6800*. Indianapolis, Ind.: Hayden Book Company, Inc., 1979. Explains software and hardware aspects of the 6800 and the ACIA and PIA support chips.

Black, U. D. *Data Communications and Distributed Networks*. Englewood Cliffs, N.J.: Reston, 1987. An introductory book on data communication.

Comer, D. *Operating System Design: The XINU Approach*. Englewood Cliffs, N.J.: Prentice-Hall, 1984. An advanced book dealing with concrete aspects of operating system design. It presents a complete operating system patterned after the increasingly popular UNIX.

Dailey, D. J. *Small Computer Theory and Applications*. New York: McGraw-Hill, 1988. Operation of the 8088 CPU, memory devices, interfacing, keyboard and display devices, and disk drive operation; contains a chapter on troubleshooting.

Dietmeyer, D. L. *Logic Design of Digital Systems*. Needham Heights, Mass.: Allyn and Bacon, Inc., 1988. Introduction to the logic design of combinational and sequential circuits, design of a hardwired and a microprogrammed version of a toy computer.

Duncan, P. *Advanced MS-DOS*. Redmond, Wash.: Microsoft Press, 1986. An indepth coverage of the internal operation of the MS-DOS operating system.

Findley, R. *6800 Software Gourmet Guide & Cookbook*. Indianapolis, Ind.: Hayden Book Company, Inc., 1976. Contains a discussion of the software aspects of the 6800 CPU and a collection of sample programs.

Friedman, A. D. *Fundamentals of Logic Design and Switching Theory*. Rockville, Md.: Computer Science Press, 1986. A readable presentation of the most important algorithms of logic design.

Gasperini, R. E. *Digital Troubleshooting*. Indianapolis, Ind.: Hayden Book Company, Inc., 1976. Practical information, logic families and their comparison, chip numbering systems.

Gasperini, R. E. *Digital Experiments.* Indianapolis, Ind.: Hayden Book Company, Inc., 1978. Twenty-five commented experiments and integrated circuit diagrams.

Grob, B. *Basic Electronics.* New York: McGraw-Hill, 1984. An introductory text covering topics from Ohm's law to integrated circuits.

Hall, V. D. *Microprocessors and Digital Systems.* New York: McGraw-Hill, 1983, second edition. Written for technicians and oriented toward the practical aspects of digital design.

Hall, D. *Microprocessors and Interfacing: Programming and Hardware.* New York: McGraw-Hill, 1986. Hardware aspects of computers, including interfaces, memory and peripheral devices, and data communication, are demonstrated on the basis of the 8086 CPU.

Per Brinch Hansen. *Brinch Hansen on Pascal Compilers.* Englewood Cliffs, N.J.: Prentice-Hall, 1985. A very readable discussion of a Pascal-like recursive descent compiler. A complete listing of the compiler is included.

Haugn, K., and F. L. Briggs. *Computer Architecture and Parallel Processing.* New York: McGraw-Hill, 1984. An often quoted book on parallel processing.

Hayes, J. P. *Computer Architecture and Organization.* New York: McGraw-Hill, 1988. Coverage of computer design at the architectural level for advanced undergraduate students.

*Heathkit Manual for the Microprocessor Trainer Model ET-3400.* Lexington, Mass.: D.C. Heath & Company, 1981. Assembly manual for the ET-3400 with source code for the monitor, memory map, and other useful information. The Heathkit catalog contains the names of numerous courses covering basic electricity, semiconductors, digital circuits, 6800 CPU programming and interfacing and others. All are very well documented and clearly written.

Hicks, P. J., ed. *Semiconductor IC Design and VLSI.* Peregrinus, 1983. An introductory treatment covering topics from integrated circuit fabrication through logic design methodologies to logic simulation and silicon compilers.

Hwang, K. *Computer Arithmetic: Principles, Architecture, and Design.* New York: John Wiley & Sons, Inc., 1979. A detailed but readable coverage of arithmetic hardware.

Kantrowitz, P., G. Kousourou, and L. Zucker. *Electronic Measurement.* Englewood Cliffs, N.J.: Prentice-Hall, 1979. Deals with the theory and instruments for DC, AC, power and integrated circuit measurements, scopes, and other topics at an introductory level.

Kasten, S. D. *Electronic Prototype Construction.* Indianapolis, Ind.: Howard W. Sams & Co., 1983. Practical aspects of electronic design, such as wirewrapping, printed circuit board design, and packaging.

Kohavi, Z. *Switching and Finite Automata Theory.* New York: McGraw-Hill, 1985. Good coverage of the formal aspects of logic design.

Lancaster, D. *TTL Cookbook.* Indianapolis, Ind.: Howard W. Sams & Co., 1982. An introduction to TTL logic with examples of practical circuits.

Lancaster, D. *CMOS Cookbook.* Indianapolis, Ind.: Howard W. Sams & Co., 1982. An introduction to CMOS logic with examples of practical circuits.

Langdon, G. G., Jr. *Computer Design.* San Jose, Ca.: Computeach Press Inc., 1982. Hardwired and microprogrammed design of a simple CPU. Concentrates on practical aspects and contains appendices on combinational and sequential circuits.

Leventhal, L. A. *6800 Assembly Language Programming.* Berkeley, Ca.: Osborne/McGraw, 1978. Contains a discussion of assembly language programming, 6800 instructions, and a collection of sample programs.

Lipovski, G. J. *Single- and Multiple-Chip Microcomputer Interfacing.* Englewood Cliffs, N.J.: Prentice-Hall and Motorola, 1988. Written for a senior level course on microcomputer design. Uses the 6811 CPU, a recent member of the 6800 family.

Lister, A. M. *Fundamentals of Operating Systems.* New York: Springer-Verlag, Inc., 1979. Introductory presentation of classical aspects of larger operating systems.

MacKenzie, Ch. E. *Coded Character Sets: History and Development.* New York: Addison-Wesley, 1980. Detailed coverage of coding conventions.

Mead, C., and L. Conway. *Introduction to VLSI Design.* New York: Addison Wesley, 1980. The classic text on VLSI design.

Middleton, R. G. *Know Your Oscilloscope.* Indianapolis, Ind.: Howard W. Sams, 1980. The principles, use, and adjustment of oscilloscopes.

Muherjee, A. *Introduction to N-MOS and C-MOS VLSI Systems Design.* Englewood Cliffs, N.J.: Prentice-Hall, 1986. A very readable book that concentrates on design rather than electronic aspects of VLSI design.

Nesin, D. J. *Processor Organization and Microprogramming: A Project Case Study.* Chicago: SRA, 1985. Description of a student project to design a microprogrammed CPU.

Norton, P. *Inside the IBM PC.* New York: Brady Books, 1986. An introduction to the internal aspects of MSDOS.

Osborne, A. *An Introduction to Microcomputers.* Vol. 2. Berkeley, Ca.: Osborne/ McGraw, 1976. Detailed information on popular four- and eight-bit CPUs.

Osborne A., and G. Kane. *Osborne 16-bit Microprocessor Handbook.* Berkeley, Ca.: Osborne/McGraw, 1981. Similar to the eight-bit book, covers eight sixteen-bit CPUs.

Passafiume, J. F., and M. Douglas. *Digital Logic Design: Tutorials and Lab Exercises.* New York: Harper & Row, 1985. Introductory presentation organized by component types.

Paynter, R. T. *Microcomputer Operation, Troubleshooting, and Repair.* Englewood Cliffs, N.J.: Prentice-Hall, 1986. Hardware aspects of computer operation for technicians. Explains the operation of the 6800 CPU and selected peripherals, such as keyboards, printers, and the CRT. Explains how to troubleshoot faculty devices.

Sargent, M. III, and R. L. Shoemaker. *The IBM PC from the Inside Out.* New York: Addison-Wesley, 1986. Covers assembly language programming, hardware aspects, and interfacing of IBM personal computers.

Schweber, W. S. *Integrated Circuits for Computers.* New York: McGraw-Hill, 1986. An introductory coverage that concentrates on practical and troubleshooting aspects. Includes devices ranging from gates to microprocessors.

Sharp, J. A. *An Introduction to Distributed and Parallel Processing.* Cambridge, Mass.: Blackwell Scientific Publications, 1987. A brief introduction to the history, concepts, and implementations.

Sklar, B. *Digital Communications—Fundamentals and Applications.* Englewood Cliffs, N.J.: Prentice-Hall, 1988. Extensive coverage of theoretical and practical aspects of communication.

Smith, R. J. *Electronics—Circuits and Devices.* New York: John Wiley & Sons, 1987. A textbook for engineering students assuming a basic knowledge of electricity. Covers circuit and device principles, digital circuits and analog circuits.

Tanenbaum, A. S. *Operating Systems: Design and Implementation.* Englewood Cliffs, N.J.: Prentice-Hall, 1987. An advanced book on operating systems, it contains detailed discussion and complete C listing of Minix, a UNIX-like operating system implemented on the IBM personal computer. Discussions of general topics and device drivers for selected peripherals are included.

Wakerly, J. F. *Logic Design Projects Using Standard Integrated Circuits.* New York: John Wiley & Sons, 1976. A large number of exercises ranging in difficulty from easy to advanced.

## DATABOOKS AND STANDARDS

In the following references, publication dates are omitted because databooks are frequently reprinted.

*Advanced Micro Devices: Programmable Array Logic Handbook.* Contains technical specifications and examples of use of PALs and other devices.

Institute of Electrical and Electronic Engineers. *IEEE Standard Graphics Symbols for Logic Functions.* ANSI/IEEE Standard 91-1984.

*Monolithic Memories: Programmable Logic Handbook.* Contains technical specifications and examples of use of PALs and PLE devices.

Texas Instruments. *The TTL Data Book.* 4 vols. One of the most popular sources of information on commercial TTL chips.

## MAGAZINES AND JOURNALS

*Byte*

*Computer* (IEEE Publications)

*Computer Design*

*Dr Dobb's Journal*

*EDN*

*ESD* (Electronic System Design)

*PC Magazine*

*Popular Electronics*

*Spectrum* (IEEE Publications)

# INDEX

Page numbers in *italics* indicate illustrations